Harcourt
Language

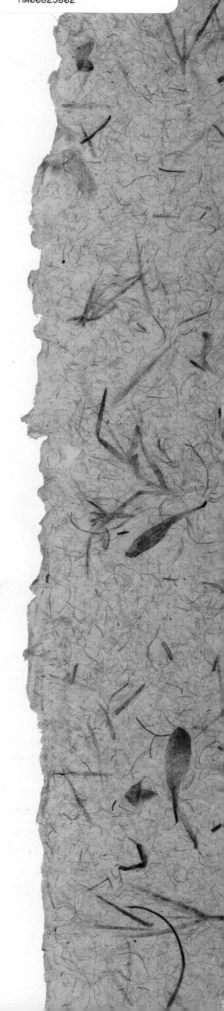

Harcourt

Orlando   Boston   Dallas   Chicago   San Diego

Harcourt Language

Teacher's Edition

SENIOR AUTHORS
Roger C. Farr ◆ Dorothy S. Strickland

AUTHORS
Helen Brown ◆ Karen S. Kutiper ◆ Hallie Kay Yopp

SENIOR CONSULTANT
Asa G. Hilliard III

CONSULTANT
Diane L. Lowe

Harcourt

Orlando   Boston   Dallas   Chicago   San Diego

Visit *The Learning Site!*
www.harcourtschool.com

Harcourt Language

AUTHORS

Senior Authors

DR. ROGER C. FARR

Chancellor's Professor and Director of the Center for Innovation in Assessment, Indiana University

RESEARCH CONTRIBUTIONS:
Assessment, Portfolios,
Reading-Writing Strategies,
Staff Development

DR. DOROTHY S. STRICKLAND

The State of New Jersey Professor of Reading, Rutgers University

RESEARCH CONTRIBUTIONS:
Emergent Literacy,
Linguistic and Cultural Diversity,
Intervention,
Integrated Language Arts,
Writing

Authors

DR. HELEN BROWN

Assistant Superintendent for Metropolitan Nashville Schools, Tennessee

RESEARCH CONTRIBUTIONS: Classroom Management, Listening and Speaking, Staff Development, Curriculum Design

DR. KAREN KUTIPER

English/Language Arts Consultant, Harris County Department of Education, Texas

RESEARCH CONTRIBUTIONS: Classroom Management, Listening and Speaking, Staff Development, Early Literacy

DR. HALLIE KAY YOPP

Professor, Department of Elementary Bilingual and Reading Education, California State University, Fullerton

RESEARCH CONTRIBUTIONS: Emergent Literacy, Word/Vocabulary Development, Kindergarten Assessment

Senior Consultant

DR. ASA G. HILLIARD III

Fuller E. Callaway Professor of Urban Education, Department of Educational Foundations, Georgia State University, Atlanta

RESEARCH CONTRIBUTIONS: Multicultural Literature and Education

Consultant

DR. DIANE L. LOWE

Professor, Education Department, and Advisor to the Master of Education in Literacy and Language Program, Framingham State College, Massachusetts

RESEARCH CONTRIBUTIONS: Literature-based Instruction, Reading Comprehension, Reading and Writing Connections, Reader Response

Contents

Unit 1

Art/Creativity

Grammar: Sentences
Writing: Expressive Writing

CHAPTER 1   Sentences

CHAPTER 2   Subjects/Nouns

CHAPTER 3   Writer's Craft: Personal Voice

Unit 2

Health

Grammar: More About Nouns and Verbs
Writing: Informative/Expository Writing (Explanation)

CHAPTER 7 More About Nouns

CHAPTER 8 Singular and Plural Nouns

CHAPTER 9 Writer's Craft: Paragraphing

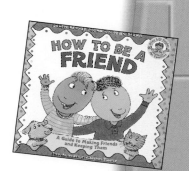

Unit 3

Social Studies

Grammar: More About Verbs
Writing: Persuasive Writing

CHAPTER 13 Main Verbs and Helping Verbs

CHAPTER 14 Present-Tense Verbs

CHAPTER 15 Writer's Craft: Word Choice

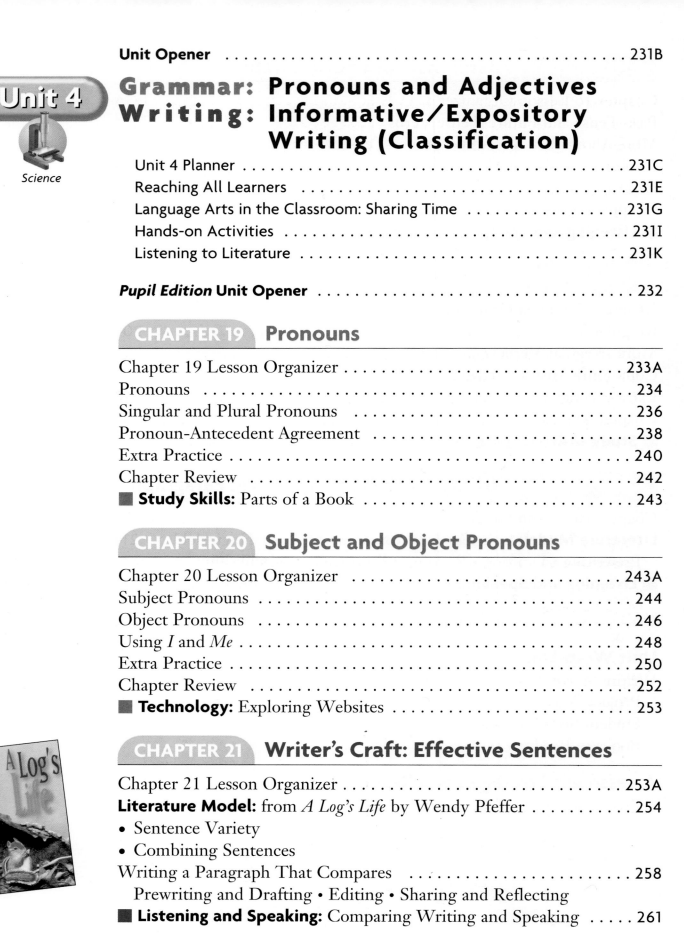

Unit 4

Science

Grammar: Pronouns and Adjectives
Writing: Informative/Expository Writing (Classification)

CHAPTER 19 Pronouns

CHAPTER 20 Subject and Object Pronouns

CHAPTER 21 Writer's Craft: Effective Sentences

CHAPTER 22 More About Pronouns

CHAPTER 23 Adjectives

CHAPTER 24 Writing Workshop: Advantages and Disadvantages Essay

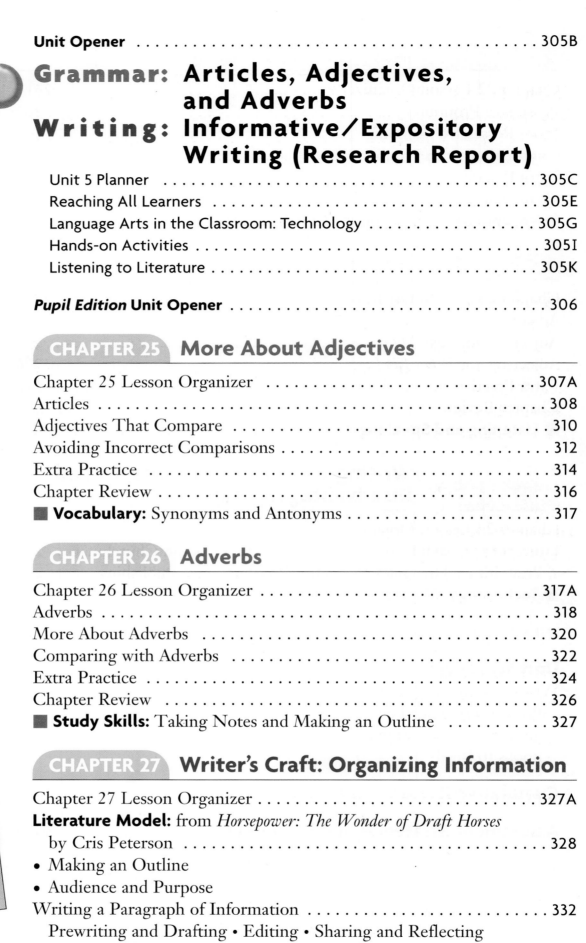

Unit 5
Social Studies

Grammar: Articles, Adjectives, and Adverbs
Writing: Informative/Expository Writing (Research Report)

CHAPTER 25 More About Adjectives

CHAPTER 26 Adverbs

CHAPTER 27 Writer's Craft: Organizing Information

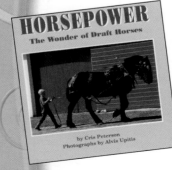

CHAPTER 28 — More About Adverbs and Adjectives

CHAPTER 29 — Easily Confused Words

CHAPTER 30 — Writing Workshop: Research Report

Unit Wrap-Up:

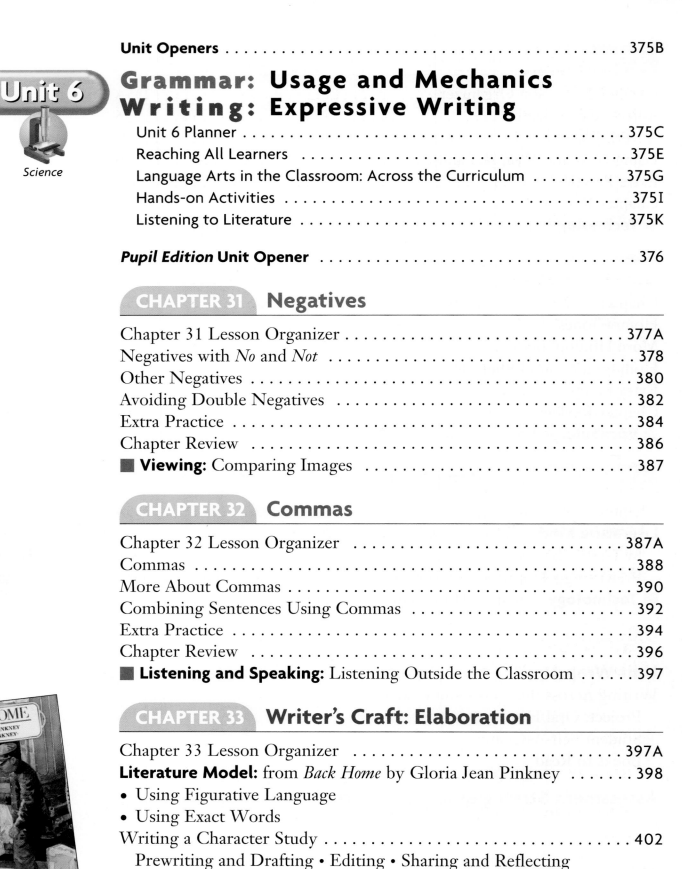

Unit 6

Science

Grammar: Usage and Mechanics
Writing: Expressive Writing

CHAPTER 31   Negatives

CHAPTER 32   Commas

CHAPTER 33   Writer's Craft: Elaboration

Resources

Customizing Instruction

DETERMINING YOUR INSTRUCTIONAL FOCUS

You can use your students' writing to help plan your instruction. First, administer a prompt such as the one at right to determine students' strengths and weaknesses as writers.

INITIAL WRITING PROMPT What is your favorite season? Write a composition for your teacher. Explain which season is your favorite, and tell why. Be sure to support your ideas with facts and details.

Assess whether students:

- ☑ focus on their purpose and audience for writing
- ☑ use an organization that makes sense
- ☑ express their ideas freely and confidently
- ☑ choose effective words and sentence types
- ☑ support their ideas with facts and details
- ☑ use conventions of standard English, including subject-verb agreement, pronoun agreement, and appropriate verb tenses
- ☑ use capitalization and end punctuation appropriately

Use the At a Glance section of the *Pupil Edition* table of contents to identify chapters that cover the skills students need.

UNIT-LEVEL PROMPTS A more specific prompt for each unit is provided in the Reaching All Learners section of this *Teacher's Edition.* You can use these prompts to tailor your instruction for individuals or groups. The Reaching All Learners section also provides classroom management suggestions.

Assessment Resources

- Student Record Forms — R74–R77
- How to Score Writing and The Traits of Good Writing — R78–R79
- Reproducible Rubrics for Writing — R80–R85
- Student Self-Assessment Checklists — R86–R88
- Formal and Informal Assessment Tools — end of unit
- *Language Skills and Writing Assessment* including model papers

To adapt rubrics to a 5- or 6-point scoring system, see How to Score Writing, pages R78–R79 in this *Teacher's Edition.*

Harcourt Language makes it easy to fit thorough, student-centered language arts instruction into your day. You can follow the sequence of the program as it is, or you can use these strategies to suit your individual teaching style.

xx   HARCOURT LANGUAGE

TEACHING WRITING WITH *HARCOURT LANGUAGE*

Harcourt Language gives you the instructional tools you need to develop fluent, confident writers.

Build Fluency and Apply Grammar Skills

SPIRAL REVIEW — DAILY LANGUAGE PRACTICE

BRIDGE TO WRITING
Language instruction should build standard usage to help students become effective communicators. In every grammar chapter, Bridge to Writing applies previously learned grammar skills in a sentence- or paragraph-completion activity.

Writing Connection
Harcourt Language provides a wide variety of brief activities that build creativity, confidence, and fluency. The Writing Connections in every grammar chapter apply grammar skills in Real-Life Writing, Technology, Writer's Craft, Writer's Journal, and cross-curricular activities.

Learn the Strategies Good Writers Use

Writer's Craft
In every unit, this chapter teaches the strategies that help students achieve their highest possible scores—the strategies that make "competent" papers into "outstanding" papers:

• Personal Voice	• Organizing Information
• Effective Sentences	• Elaboration
• Paragraphing	• Word Choice

Students apply writer's craft strategies in fluency-building activities as well as in the context of writing a composition. This experience prepares students for the Writing Workshop chapter.

STANDARDIZED TEST PREP

Harcourt Language makes preparing students for high-stakes tests a top priority. In addition to a Standardized Test Prep page in every grammar chapter, *Harcourt Language* prepares students for writing tests with instruction in Writer's Craft as well as the most commonly tested writing forms.

Apply Writer's Craft to Longer Writing Forms

Writing Workshop
In every unit, this chapter develops proficiency in the writing forms that students encounter most frequently on state and standardized tests:

- Expressive Writing (personal narrative, story)
- Informative/Expository Writing (how-to essay, classification, report)
- Persuasive Writing (persuasive essay)

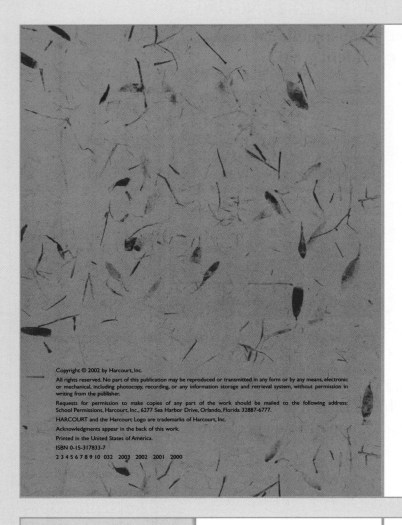

Harcourt Language

SENIOR AUTHORS
Roger C. Farr • Dorothy S. Strickland

AUTHORS
Helen Brown • Karen S. Kutiper • Hallie Kay Yopp

SENIOR CONSULTANT
Asa G. Hilliard III

CONSULTANT
Diane L. Lowe

Harcourt

Orlando   Boston   Dallas   Chicago   San Diego

Visit *The Learning Site!*
www.harcourtschool.com

Contents

Unit 2

Health

Grammar: More About Nouns and Verbs
Writing: Informative Writing:
Explanation 90

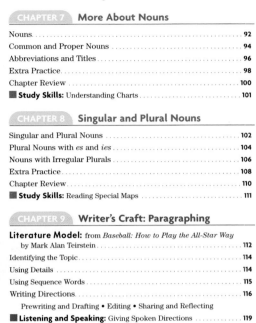

4

5

Unit 3

Social Studies

Grammar: More About Verbs
Writing: Persuasive Writing 164

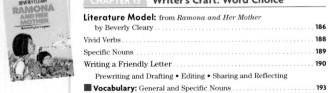
6

7

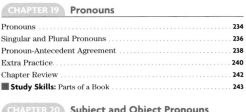

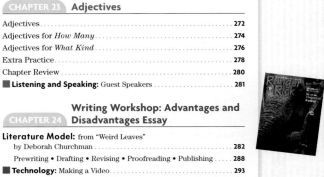

Unit 6

Science

Grammar: Usage and Mechanics
Writing: Expressive Writing   376

Handbook 478

At a Glance

16

17

Introducing the Book

Preview the Book

Before students read pages 18-21, invite them to comment on the cover and then to preview the book by looking through the table of contents. Point out that a table of contents shows everything in a book in order. This book has six units plus a Handbook at the back. Explain that the Handbook is a reference source that will help students in their research and writing. The At a Glance section of the table of contents provides a quick way to find specific grammar, writing, and listening and speaking skills.

Grammar

HOW LANGUAGE WORKS

Have students read page 18, including the definitions of the parts of speech. Then ask volunteers to give an example sentence for each part of speech. Students can model their examples on the ones in the Glossary. You might want to create a bulletin board with examples and illustrations.

Writing

UNDERSTANDING THE WRITING PROCESS

Read aloud the introduction to the writing process, and have students read the information about each step silently. Call on students to retell the information in their own words.

Using Writing Strategies

Strategies Good Writers Use Read page 20 with students and have them tell how and when they use the strategies. Explain that using writing strategies will help students become better writers and will also help them do their best on writing tests. You may want to have volunteers copy the strategy list onto chart paper to display in the classroom.

Keeping a Journal and a Portfolio

Have students read each section of the page and then discuss it. If students do not have notebooks, they can make journals using cardboard, a hole punch, yarn, and paper. Explain that they should write in their journals frequently to record their ideas and reflections. They can also use their journals as a source of ideas that they can discover, develop and refine for longer pieces. Have them reserve a section in the back of their journals for a word bank of interesting words to use in their writing.

You may want to use expandable file folders for portfolios. Keep the portfolios in a special area of the classroom where students can access them easily. In your own records, keep a copy of the Student Record Form for Writing Conferences (page R74) for each student. Annotate the form during portfolio conferences to monitor individual students' growth as writers.

Grammar: How Language Works

We all learn to speak without thinking about how words work. For example, children who grow up speaking English learn to say *the big dog* instead of *the dog big* before they learn about adjectives and nouns. Later, we study grammar to learn about how words work. Learning about grammar helps us become better writers.

The Building Blocks of Language

Words in English can be grouped into different parts of speech. These are the building blocks of language.

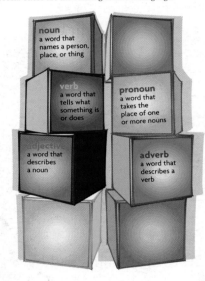

noun
a word that names a person, place, or thing

verb
a word that tells what something is or does

pronoun
a word that takes the place of one or more nouns

adjective
a word that describes a noun

adverb
a word that describes a verb

Writing: Understanding the Writing Process

When you read a book, you do not see the steps the writer took to write it. What you see in a book might be different from the writer's first idea. The writer might have written parts of the book over and over many times.

The writing process can be divided into five steps. Most writers go back and forth through these steps. There is no one correct way to write.

Prewriting
In this step, you plan what you will write. You choose a topic, decide on your audience and purpose, brainstorm ideas, and organize information.

Drafting
In this step, you write out your ideas in sentences and paragraphs. Follow your prewriting plan to write a first draft.

Revising
This step is the first part of editing your writing. You may work by yourself or with a partner or a group. Make changes to make your writing better.

Proofreading
In this step, you finish your editing. Check for errors in grammar, spelling, capitalization, and punctuation. Make a final copy of your writing.

Publishing
Finally, you choose a way to share your work. You may want to add pictures or read your writing aloud to others.

Using Writing Strategies

A **strategy** is a plan for doing something well. Using strategies can help you become a better writer. Read the list of strategies below. You will learn about these and other strategies in this book. As you write, look back at this list to remind yourself of the **strategies good writers use**.

Strategies Good Writers Use

- Set a purpose for your writing.
- Focus on your audience.
- List or draw your main ideas.
- Use an organization that makes sense.
- Use your own personal voice.
- Choose exact, vivid words.
- Use a variety of effective sentences.
- Elaborate with facts and details.
- Group your ideas in paragraphs.
- Proofread to check for errors.

Keeping a Writer's Journal

Many writers keep journals. You can use a journal to make notes and try out new ideas. It is not a place to keep final work. A journal is a place to practice and have fun with writing.

You can keep your own writer's journal. Choose a notebook that you like. Draw pictures on the cover. Then start filling the pages with your notes and ideas.

Vocabulary Power

You can also keep a "word bank" of different kinds of words to use in your writing. Look for the Vocabulary Power word in each chapter. You can also list other new words that you find interesting.

Keeping a Portfolio

A portfolio is a place to keep your writing. You can also use it to show your work.

Student writers often keep two types of portfolios. **Working portfolios** include writings on which you are still working. **Show portfolios** have writings that you are finished with and want to show to others. You can move writings from your working portfolio into your show portfolio.

You can use your portfolios in meetings with your teacher. In meetings, talk about your work. Tell what you are doing and what you like doing. Set goals for yourself as a writer.

Unit 1

Grammar Sentences

Writing Expressive Writing

Dear Uncle Andy,
Today I saw a very large sculpture outdoors. It was taller than the trees!

Mr. Andrew Jones
75 Oak Street
Lincoln, TX
77107

Unit 1

Grammar • Sentences
Writing • Expressive Writing

Introducing the Unit, pp. 22–23

Chapters	Grammar	Writing	Listening/Speaking/Viewing
1 **Sentences** pp. 24–33	**Sentences** **Kinds of Sentences** **Usage and Mechanics:** **Punctuating Sentences** Extra Practice, Chapter Review, Daily Language Practice, Additional Practice: p. 454	**Writing Connections** Greeting Card Kinds of Sentences Social Studies Technology	**Activities** Challenge: Design a Quilt ESL: Question and Answer Building Oral Grammar Summarize **Viewing:** Being a Good Viewer
2 **Subjects and Nouns** pp. 34–43	**Complete and Simple Subjects** **Nouns in Subjects** **Grammar-Writing Connection:** **Combining Sentences:** **Compound Subjects** Extra Practice, Chapter Review, Daily Language Practice, Additional Practice: p. 455	**Writing Connections** Music Conversation Recording Ideas Rhyming Words	**Activities** Oral Warm-Up Making a Poster Building Oral Grammar Summarize **Listening and Speaking:** Being a Good Listener and Speaker
3 **Writer's Craft: Personal Voice** pp. 44–51	**Daily Language Practice** **Hands-on Activities**	**Descriptive Paragraph** Prewriting and Drafting Editing Sharing and Reflecting Self-Initiated Writing	**Activities** Analyze Descriptive Writing Read and Respond to the Model Picture This **Listening and Speaking:** Listen to the Color Summarize
4 **Predicates** pp. 52–61	**Complete and Simple Predicates** **Verbs in Predicates** **Grammar—Writing Connection:** **Combining Sentences:** **Compound Predicates** Extra Practice, Chapter Review, Daily Language Practice, Additional Practice: p. 456	**Writing Connections** Technology Vivid Verbs Describe a Room Technology	**Activities** Challenge: Design a School Study a Building Building Oral Grammar Challenge: Learn a Greeting Summarize
5 **Simple and Compound Sentences** pp. 62–71	**Complete Sentences** **Simple and Compound Sentences** **Grammar-Writing Connection:** **Combining Sentences** Extra Practice, Chapter Review, Daily Language Practice, Additional Practice: p. 457	**Writing Connections** Evaluating Writing Personal Voice News Report Write a Summary	**Activities** **Listening and Speaking:** Oral Book Report Building Oral Grammar Summarize
6 **Writing Workshop: Personal Narrative** pp. 72–83	**Unit 1 Grammar Review** **Daily Language Practice**	**Personal Narrative** Prewriting Drafting Revising Proofreading Publishing Writer's Craft: Personal Voice	**Activities** Reading Like a Writer Read and Respond to the Model Describe a Personal Experience Summarize **Listening and Speaking:** Acting Out a Story

Unit Wrap-Up Writing Across the Curriculum: Social Studies pp. 88–89

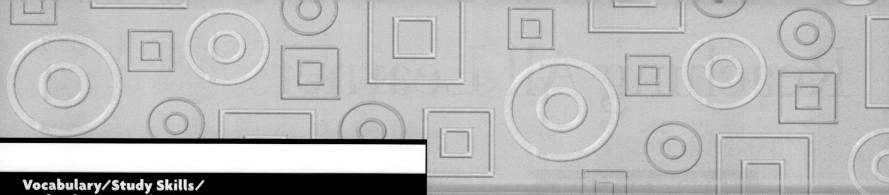

Vocabulary Power

Words of the Week: animated film, cartoon, cinema, motion picture, movie
ESL: Word Order

Vocabulary Power

Words of the Week: device, **instrument,** percussion, utensil, woodwind

Vocabulary Power

Words of the Week: glimmering, glistening, **shimmering,** sparkling, twinkling
Synonym Study
Vocabulary: Colorful Words

Vocabulary Power

Words of the Week: carpenter, electrician, machinist, mason, plumber
Vocabulary: Words from Many Places
Technology: Drawing by Computer
        Our House

Vocabulary Power

Words of the Week: fantasy, imaginary, pretend, tale, yarn
ESL: Compound Subjects, Predicates, and Sentences
E-mail an Author
Study Skills: Being a Good Reader

Vocabulary Power

Words of the Week: episode, event, **experience,** incident, situation

- **Look** at a picture with a friend. Take turns **asking** and **answering** questions about what you **see** and how it makes you feel. Use complete sentences. VIEWING/SPEAKING/LISTENING

- **Listen** and **talk** about favorite songs with some friends. Together make a list of **nouns** used in the lyrics as subjects of sentences. SPEAKING/ LISTENING/WRITING

- **Write** sentences about people, places, and things that you **see** on your way to school. **Describe** how they look, sound, smell, or feel. VIEWING/ WRITING

- **Play** a game of "I Spy" with a friend. Take turns **stating** sentences that tell what you **see.** **Together** try to combine your statements to form compound sentences. VIEWING/SPEAKING

Technology ▬ Resources

Grammar Jingles™ **CD**
Grammar Practice and Assessment **CD-ROM**
Visit *The Learning Site!*
   www.harcourtschool.com
Media Literacy and Communication Skills **Package**
Writing Express **CD-ROM**

Reaching All Learners

Intervention

INTERACTIVE WRITING Interactive writing is a collaborative event in which you work with a group of students in constructing a written message for an authentic purpose, such as retelling or extending a story or writing a how-to essay about a classroom procedure. Throughout the process, your goal is to support students in constructing increasingly complex texts.

- Group students according to instructional needs that you have identified.

- Share with students the physical act of writing words and sentences, as well as deciding what words and sentences to write.

- Carry on a running conversation during which you and your students think aloud about the structure and meaning of the text you are composing.

- Use explicit prompts to help students use their prior knowledge to solve words they want to write. Ask, for example, "Does this word sound right here?"

- Reread frequently with students during the writing process to monitor the message and plan what to write next.

- Use standard spelling and punctuation so that the text can later be reread independently by students.

Challenge

LITERATURE CIRCLES In Literature Circles, small groups of students may read either independently or together, discussing their reactions during and after reading. Grouping more proficient readers together may enable these students to read at a more challenging level or at a faster pace. They may also be encouraged to think of innovative ways to read cooperatively or to share their reactions. If you prefer to group heterogeneously, you may want to designate a student as Discussion Leader.

English as a Second Language

USING REALIA Using more than one sense in the learning process helps students forge multiple connections and thus make sense of new material. You can use a collection of realia not only to teach the names of the items, but also to give students opportunities to practice grammar skills in a meaningful and enjoyable way. The following suggestions apply to lessons in this unit. You can expand and adapt them to fit students' level of proficiency and to teach other skills.

- Choose two items. Have students make up sentences that include the names of these items. Depending on students' level of proficiency, you might specify the type of sentence. For example, a student might be asked to make up a question that includes the words *story* and *pencil*.

- Choose one item. Have students make up a sentence about the item and then identify the simple subject and complete subject of the sentence.

Teaching Grammar from Writing

PRETEST
If you wish to use students' writing to diagnose their needs, use the following prompt.

WRITING PROMPT
Do you remember the very first day you ever went to school? What happened that day? Write about your first day of school. Tell about what happened and how you felt.

EVALUATE AND PLAN
Analyze students' writing to determine how you can best meet their individual needs for instruction. Use the following chart to identify and remedy problems.

COMMON PROBLEMS	CHAPTERS TO USE
Not using correct end punctuation for sentences	Chapter 1: Sentences
Not using compound subjects where appropriate	Chapter 2: Subjects/Nouns
Not using compound predicates where appropriate	Chapter 4: Predicates/Verbs
Not using compound sentences where appropriate	Chapter 5: Simple and Compound Sentences
Not punctuating compound sentences correctly	Chapter 5: Simple and Compound Sentences
Not understanding personal voice	Chapter 3: Writer's Craft: Personal Voice
Having difficulty writing a personal narrative	Chapter 6: Writing a Personal Narrative

Classroom Management

DURING...	SOME STUDENTS CAN...
Grammar Reteaching	Work on the Writing Across the Curriculum project. Use the Challenge Activity Cards.
Independent Practice	Begin the Writing Connection. Work at the activities and stations described in Language Arts in the Classroom.
Portfolio Conferences	Complete Student Self-Assessment forms. (See pages R86–R88 in this *Teacher's Edition.*) Participate in peer conferences.

Approaches to Writing Instruction

LANGUAGE ARTS IN THE CLASSROOM

A variety of approaches to writing instruction may happen in the classroom at any given time. Transitional and self-extending writers will learn using the shared writing and interactive writing approaches, and sometimes a combination of both, to lead them to independent writing. Each of these approaches may be used with the writing process.

The following presents information about each kind of writing approach that you may use with your students.

SHARED WRITING The teacher works with a small group of students, placing the emphasis on the composing process. The teacher and students work together to plan the text, and then the teacher acts as facilitator to help students develop and organize ideas.

INTERACTIVE WRITING Shared writing and interactive writing are similar processes except that in interactive writing the teacher and the students "share the pen." The teacher determines when to involve students in the writing based on the focus of instruction. The teacher models the writing form and shapes students' development of more complex texts. Graphic organizers may be used.

GUIDED WRITING The teacher offers assistance by guiding students' writing, responding to it, and extending students' thinking in the composing process. Guided writing may happen during whole class, small group, or one-to-one instruction as part of Writing Workshop. The teacher's role is one of facilitator, helping students discover what they want to say and how to express it in writing with clarity.

Night Owl

Years ago Hawk organized a grand party invited everyone. Owl decided not to go. He embarrassed because he had no feathers.
Hawk and his friends lent feathers to Owl. Owl made a tiful coat and wore it to th Owl loved t. He left the party early be did nt to take off the coat.
birds still look for Owl during the t their feathers. However, Owl only at night.

Interactive Writing

Interactive writing is a form of assisted writing or scaffolded instruction. The teacher acts as a model, demonstrating how to compose and construct complex texts while both the teacher and students scribe. Self-extending writers use the end product as a reference for their own writing.

The following information presents ways that interactive writing can be effective with self-extending writers and older students.

FOCUS ON NEW GENRES By using a combination of shared writing techniques (in which the teacher models and writes) and interactive writing strategies, self-extending writers can learn how to write new genres. The teacher models the thinking and helps students focus on a particular aspect of the writing form. For example, if the assignment is to write a personal narrative, the teacher draws students' attention to the use of personal voice, sensory details, and imagery.

USE A VARIETY OF STRATEGIES Through teacher coaching, students can learn how to state conclusions, make comparisons, summarize events, and elaborate with supporting details in lengthier and more complex compositions. For example, if the group is writing a persuasive essay, the teacher will give prompts such as:

- **What details can you use to support your argument?**
- **Where should you position those details to be effective?**

REVISE FOR CLARITY Interactive writing is a good way to show students how to revise written texts for clarity. During writing, students can consider two versions of a sentence. Prompt students with questions such as:

- **Which sentence summarizes what happened?**
- **Which sentence gives clearer supporting details?**

Hands-on Activities

Two by Two

MATERIALS: sentence strips with pairs of sentences that have different subjects but the same predicate

DIRECTIONS:

1. Pass out sentence strips. Students move about, reading each other's sentences.

2. Pairs of students whose sentences have the same predicate become partners. They then write one sentence with a **compound subject** to combine both of their sentences.

   Variation: Use sentence pairs with the same subject and different predicates.

The cows are in the barn.

The horses are in the barn.

The boys played tag.

The girls played tag.

Spin It

MATERIALS: simple cardboard spinner, as shown

DIRECTIONS:

1. Two to four players take turns spinning the spinner.

2. The player reads aloud the word on which the spinner stops. He or she then uses that word as the **simple subject** of an original sentence.

   Variation: Write verbs on the spinner to use as simple predicates.

Cut and Paste

MATERIALS: blank sentence strips, pencils or markers, scissors

DIRECTIONS:

1. Have students work in small groups. Give each group three blank sentence strips. Have them write three sentences with different subjects and different predicates on the strips.

2. Students identify the **complete subject** and **complete predicate** of each sentence. Then have them cut the strips apart to separate the subjects and predicates.

3. Have groups exchange their subject and predicate strips and reassemble them so that the sentences make sense.

Our team   won the game.

Lights, Action, Color!

MATERIALS: slips of paper or index cards; box or other container

DIRECTIONS:

1. Write examples of **colorful** words on slips of paper or index cards. You may want to have students brainstorm colorful words.

2. Mix up the slips of paper or cards and place them in a box or other container.

3. Players take turns drawing a word at random from the box and pantomiming or illustrating the word for other players to guess.

4. After players guess the word, that slip of paper or card is put aside, and the next player picks one from those remaining in the box.

What's the Story?

MATERIALS: a list of familiar occupations

DIRECTIONS:

1. Have students work in pairs. Assign each pair an occupation from your list.

2. Students think of and role-play an event that a person in that occupation might include in a **personal narrative.**

3. Classmates must guess the occupation.

truck driver	astronaut
nurse	firefighter
baseball player	chef (or cook)
photographer	dentist
mountain climber	third grade teacher

Musical Sentences

MATERIALS: one card for each player, all blank except for three cards with the words *question, command,* and *exclamation;* audiotape player; taped music

DIRECTIONS:

1. Have students sit in a circle. Give each student a card, face down.

2. Play a tape. When the music begins, players pass the cards around the circle to their left.

3. Players continue passing cards until you stop the tape. Then they turn over their cards.

4. Players holding the question, command, and exclamation cards must make up original sentences of the appropriate type. You may want to suggest topics for each set of sentences, such as sentences about a cat.

5. Repeat the game as many times as you wish.

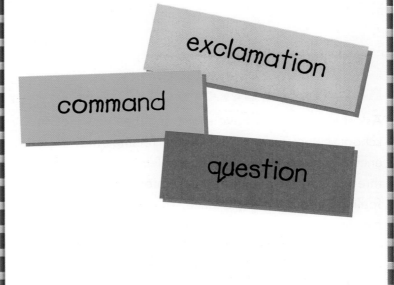

The New Boy

BY JOHN WALSH

THE DOOR SWUNG INWARD. I stood and breathed
The new-school atmosphere:
The smell of polish and disinfectant,
And the flavor of my own fear.

I followed into the cloakroom; the walls
Rang to the shattering noise
Of boys who barged and boys who banged;
Boys and still more boys!

A boot flew by me. Its angry owner
Pursued with force and yell;
Somewhere a man snapped orders; somewhere
There clanged a warning bell.

And there I hung with my new schoolmates;
They pushing and shoving me; I
Unknown, unwanted, pinned to the wall;
On the verge of ready-to-cry.

Then, from the doorway, a boy called out:
"Hey, you over there! You're new!
Don't just stand there propping the wall up!
I'll look after you!"

I turned; I timidly raised my eyes;
He stood and grinned meanwhile;
And my fear died, and my lips answered
Smile for his smile.

He showed me the basins, the rows of pegs;
He hung my cap at the end;
He led me away to my new classroom . . .
And now that boy's my friend.

Building Background

Ask students if they have ever been the "new kid" in school. Have students recall what feelings they experienced, such as fear and anxiety. Tell students that the three poems they will listen to express thoughts and feelings about this experience. Then have students listen for similarities and differences in the poems.

Determine a Purpose for Listening

Tell students that these selections present poetry about making new friends. Ask students to determine whether their purpose for listening is

- to be persuaded to do something.
- to solve problems.
- to see the writer's viewpoint. (to see the writer's viewpoint)

Making Friends

FROM *Nathaniel Talking*
BY ELOISE GREENFIELD

WHEN I WAS IN KINDERGARTEN
this new girl came in our class one day
and the teacher told her to sit beside me
and I didn't know what to say
so I wiggled my nose and made my bunny face
and she laughed
then she puffed out her cheeks
and she made a funny face
and I laughed
so then
we were friends

The New Kid

BY MIKE MAKLEY

OUR BASEBALL TEAM never did very much,
we had me and PeeWee and Earl and Dutch.
And the Oak Street Tigers always got beat
until the new kid moved in on our street.

The kid moved in with a mitt and a bat
and an official New York Yankee hat.
The new kid plays shortstop or second base
and can outrun us all in any place.

The kid never muffs a grounder or fly
no matter how hard it's hit or how high.
And the new kid always acts quite polite,
never yelling or spitting or starting a fight.

We were playing the league champs just last week;
they were trying to break our winning streak.
In the last inning the score was one-one,
when the new kid swung and hit a home run.

A few of the kids and their parents say
they don't believe that the new kid should play.
But she's good as me, Dutch, PeeWee, or Earl,
so we don't care that the new kid's a girl.

Listening Comprehension

LISTEN FOR VIEWPOINT AND COLORFUL WORDS
Explain to students that in these poems, the authors use colorful words to make the experience come alive. Listening for colorful words and the writer's voice will help students see things from the writer's perspective, helping them understand what it's like to be the "new kid."

Have students listen for the words *I, me,* and *we* that show the poems are written from the first-person viewpoint. Explain that this viewpoint makes the subject matter more personal because it is not written as an outsider "looking in," but as a participant in the experience.

PERSONAL RESPONSE *Which poem do you like best? Why?* (Possible responses: I like "Making Friends" best because I think making funny faces is a cute way of showing you are friendly. "The New Boy" is the best because the poet really tells what it is like to be afraid at a new school. I like the last poem because it has a surprise ending and it shows that kids can accept each other despite differences.) INFERENTIAL: MAKE COMPARISONS

Unit 1

Grammar Sentences

Writing Expressive Writing

Introducing the Unit

ORAL LANGUAGE/VIEWING

DISCUSS THE IMAGES Have students look at the sculpture in the photograph. Discuss with them what the artist might be expressing and how the sculpture's color and shapes make them feel. Then direct students' attention to the postcard. Ask them how they can tell that the writer is excited about the sculpture. (He or she uses an exclamatory sentence.) Tell students that written narratives, oral descriptions, and visual art are all ways to express thoughts and feelings. Then ask these questions:

1. **How can a story tell something about its writer?** (Possible response: by describing the writer's thoughts and feelings)

2. **What can speakers use besides words to express themselves?** (Possible responses: gestures and tone of voice)

3. **What kind of art do you think is most expressive? Why?** (Responses will vary.)

ENCOURAGE STUDENTS' QUESTIONS Have students reflect on the different forms people use to express themselves through writing, speaking, and art. Encourage students to develop questions for discussion. Have them write their questions and selected responses in their journals.

Unit 1

Grammar Sentences

Writing Expressive Writing

22

Viewing and Representing

COMPARE/CONTRAST PRINT AND VISUAL MEDIA Show students only the illustrations from an illustrated personal narrative, such as a published diary or autobiography. Then have them read the narrative without the accompanying illustrations. Ask students to write a paragraph comparing and contrasting how the two forms of media tell stories and express ideas. Encourage them to explore how the illustrations reflect what students read or how they differ from the written work.

For evaluation criteria for viewing, see the Viewing Checklist, page R88.

MEDIA LITERACY AND COMMUNICATION SKILLS PACKAGE Use the video to extend students' oral and visual literacy. See *Teacher's Guide* pages 6–7.

Dear Uncle Andy,
 Today I saw a very large sculpture outdoors. It was taller than the trees!

Mr. Andrew Jones
75 Oak Street
Lincoln, TX

USA H
First-Class Rate

23

Have students look over the list of unit contents. Ask volunteers to give examples of the different kinds of sentences. Encourage students to ask questions about sentences, subjects, and predicates. Then point out the two writing chapters and their topics. Ask volunteers to explain what they know about a description and a personal narrative. Tell students that they will learn about expressive writing in this unit.

ART/CREATIVITY CONNECTION Students will explore a variety of art topics in this unit:

- Visual Arts
- Music
- Architecture
- Literature

School-Home Connection

You may want to use School-Home Connection 1, page R92.

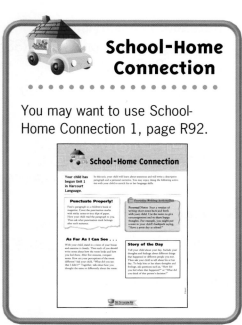

CHAPTER 1

Sentences and Statements

LESSON ORGANIZER	DAY 1	DAY 2
DAILY LANGUAGE PRACTICE ▱ TRANSPARENCIES 1, 2	**1.** The art fair will be in jun. (June) **2.** We can get reddy for it in april. (ready; April) **Bridge to Writing** The show starts on __(day of week)__ .	**1.** the picture has many lovely colors (The; colors.) **2.** some artists use oil paints (Some; paints.) **Bridge to Writing** __(Who word)__ loves that painting.
ORAL WARM-UP Listening/Speaking	Say More 24	Ask Questions 26 Grammar Jingles™ CD Track 1
TEACH/MODEL GRAMMAR KEY ✔ = tested skill	✔ **SENTENCES** 24-25 • To understand and identify complete sentences • To create a greeting card and write descriptive sentences	✔ **KINDS OF SENTENCES** 26-27 • To understand and identify types of sentences • To use sentence types appropriately
Reaching All Learners	**Modified Instruction** Below-Level: Model the Thinking Above-Level: Form Sentences **Reteach:** *Reteach Activities Copying Masters* pp. 1 and R38 **Challenge:** Activity Card 1, R62 *ESL Manual* pp. 8, 9 *Practice Book* p. 1	**Modified Instruction** Below-Level: Read Aloud Above-Level: Rewrite Sentences **Challenge:** Twenty Questions 27 **ESL:** Word Order 26 *ESL Manual* pp. 8, 10 **Reteach:** *Reteach Activities Copying Masters* pp. 2 and R38 *Practice Book* p. 2
WRITING	Writing Connection 25 Real-Life Writing: Greeting Card	Writing Connection 27 Writer's Craft: Kinds of Sentences
CROSS-CURRICULAR/ ENRICHMENT	*Vocabulary Power* Explore Word Meaning 24 **animated film,** cartoon, cinema, motion picture, movie See *Vocabulary Power* book.	*Vocabulary Power* Content-Area Words 24 *Vocabulary Power* p. 1 💻 **Vocabulary activity**

DAY 3

1. may I go to the mooseum? (May; museum)

2. open the dore (Open; door.)

Bridge to Writing (Question word) will we go?

Give Example Sentences 28

Grammar Jingles™ CD Track 1

✔ **PUNCTUATING SENTENCES** 28-29
- To correctly punctuate sentences
- To conduct research and to write sentences

Modified Instruction
Below-Level: Work in Pairs
Above-Level: Write Sentences
ESL: Question and Answer 28
ESL Manual pp. 8, 11
Reteach: *Reteach Activities Copying Masters* pp. 3 and R38
Challenge: Punctuate Sentences 29
Practice Book p. 3

Writing Connection 29
Social Studies

Vocabulary Power

Compare and Contrast 24
Vocabulary Power p. 2

Vocabulary activity

DAY 4

1. how do I get to the museum (How; museum?)

2. take this bus to the last stop (Take; stop.)

Bridge to Writing What a long ride (end mark)

Tell About Yesterday 30

EXTRA PRACTICE 30-31
- To identify sentence types and recognize correct capitalization and punctuation
- To write a review

Practice and assessment

Building Oral Grammar
Sounds of Sentences 31
Challenge: Write an Announcement 31
ESL Manual pp. 8, 12
Practice Book p. 4

Writing Connection 31
Technology

Science: Science Questions 30

Vocabulary Power

Synonyms 24
Vocabulary Power p. 3

Vocabulary activity

DAY 5

1. Whut a beautiful picture (What; picture!)

2. is this my painting (Is; painting?)

Bridge to Writing (Question word) is the museum located? I do not see it (end mark)

TEST PREP **CHAPTER REVIEW** 32-33
- To review sentences and end marks
- To use good viewing strategies

Test preparation

Challenge: Interview the Artist 33
Practice Book p. 5
ESL Manual pp. 8, 13

Writing Application 33
Describe Artwork

Viewing: Being a Good Viewer 33

Vocabulary Power

Multiple-Meaning Words 24

Sentences

OBJECTIVES
- To understand and identify complete sentences
- To create a greeting card and write descriptive sentences

SPIRAL REVIEW

DAILY LANGUAGE PRACTICE

TRANSPARENCY 1

1. The art fair will be in jun. (June)
2. We can get reddy for it in april. (ready; April)

BRIDGE TO WRITING The show starts on __(day of the week)__ .

ORAL WARM-UP

USE PRIOR KNOWLEDGE Write the words *The famous singer* on the board. Ask students to suggest words that say more about the famous artist.

TEACH/MODEL

Read aloud the explanations and examples. Explain that students should look for words that tell *who* or *what* and words that tell what someone or something *is* or *does* to decide whether a group of words is a sentence. They should also make sure the words are in an order that makes sense. Model the thinking, using the Guided Practice examples:

MODEL I know that the words *We went to a folk art museum* are a sentence. *We* tells *who* the sentence is about, and *went to a folk art museum* tells what *We* did. I know the words *Many kinds of art* are not a sentence. The words tell *what*, but there are no words that tell what *Many kinds of art* is or does.

Complete the Guided Practice orally with students.

Vocabulary Power

an·i·ma·ted film [an′ə·mā·təd film] *n.* A series of drawings shown as a motion picture with moving figures. Each picture is slightly changed from the one before to make the drawing seem to move.

24

Sentences

A **sentence** is a group of words that tells a complete thought.

One part of a sentence tells who or what. This part is called the **subject**. The other part of the sentence tells what the subject is or does. This part is called the **predicate**.

Example:

┌subject┐ ┌────── predicate ──────┐
An artist carves the horse from wood.

The words in a sentence are in an order that makes sense. Begin every sentence with a capital letter, and end it with an end mark.

Guided Practice

A. Tell whether each group of words is or is not a sentence. Be able to tell how you know.

Example: We went to a folk art museum. *sentence*
Many kinds of art. *not a sentence*

1. Beautiful quilts with many colors. not a sentence
2. We saw toys from long ago. sentence
3. Made from wood. not a sentence
4. Liked the spinning top best. not a sentence
5. They could spin very fast. sentence

Vocabulary Power

DAY 1 EXPLORE WORD MEANING Introduce and define *animated film*. Give an example of an animated film. Ask: **What are your favorite animated films?**

DAY 2 RELATED WORDS **What are some words that tell about movies?** (See also *Vocabulary Power*, page 1.)

DAY 3 COMPARE AND CONTRAST Ask students to complete the statement: **A movie is like a television show except _____.** Discuss responses. (See also *Vocabulary Power*, page 2.)

DAY 4 SYNONYMS **What are some words that mean almost the same thing as *movie*?** (See also *Vocabulary Power*, page 3.)

DAY 5 MULTIPLE-MEANING WORDS An animated film is a kind of movie. **What are some other meanings of the word *film*?**

Independent Practice

B. For each group of words, write *sentence* if the words make a sentence. Write *not a sentence* if the words do not make a sentence.

Example: Some quilts are folk art.   *sentence*

  6. Made designs on their quilts. not a sentence
  7. Some quilt designs tell stories. sentence
  8. Pictures of people, animals, and plants. not a sentence
  9. Many quilters use well-known patterns. sentence
  10. Other quilters make up their own patterns. sentence

C. Make a sentence using each group of words. Put the words in an order that makes sense.

Example: scraps of cloth quilters use
        Quilters use scraps of cloth.

  11. the scraps different are colors The scraps are different colors.
  12. pieces cut and sew quilters Quilters cut and sew pieces.
  13. together can quilters work Quilters can work together.
  14. stories quilts tell Quilts tell stories.
  15. quilt this animal has designs This quilt has animal designs.

Writing Connection

Real-Life Connection: Greeting Card Fold paper to make a greeting card. Draw a picture of a favorite place on the front. Inside, write a message. On the back, write at least three sentences to tell about the place you drew on the front. Remember that a sentence must tell a complete thought. Start your sentences with capital letters and end them with end marks.

Remember

that a sentence tells a complete thought. The words are in an order that makes sense. Begin every sentence with a capital letter, and end it with an end mark.

25

Independent Practice

Have students complete the Independent Practice, or modify it using these suggestions:

MODIFIED INSTRUCTION

BELOW-LEVEL STUDENTS Work through the Independent Practice with students, modeling the thinking.

ABOVE-LEVEL STUDENTS For the items in Part B that are not sentences, have students add words to form sentences.

Writing Connection

Real-Life Writing: Greeting Card To prepare for making cards, have students contribute to a class discussion about their favorite places. Ask students to describe how these places look and what they would like to tell others about these places.

WRAP-UP/ASSESS

SUMMARIZE How do you decide whether a group of words is a sentence?

RETEACH

INTERVENTION Lessons in **visual, auditory,** and **kinesthetic** modalities: p. R38 and *Reteach Activities Copying Masters*, p. 1.

PRACTICE page 1

Name _____

Sentences

A. If the group of words is a sentence, write *Sentence*. If the group of words is not a sentence, write *Not a sentence*.

  1. The cartoons of Charles Schulz. Not a sentence
  2. Schulz wanted to be a cartoonist when he was very young. Sentence
  3. Was born in 1922 in Minnesota. Not a sentence
  4. Studied art by mail. Not a sentence
  5. He started a comic strip. Sentence

B. Use each group of words to create a sentence. Begin each statement with a capital letter, and end it with a period.

  6. worked Schulz in Saint Paul, Minnesota
    Schulz worked in St. Paul, Minnesota.

  7. taught at an art school he
    He taught at an art school.

  8. began he cartoons drawing
    He began drawing cartoons.

  9. some cartoons bought a magazine
    A magazine bought some cartoons.

TRY THIS! Describe your favorite cartoon or comic strip. Write complete sentences to explain why you like it.

Practice • Sentences   Unit 1 • Chapter 1 **1**

CHALLENGE

DESIGN A QUILT Have students use **Challenge Activity Card 1** (page R62) to create a design for a quilt.

Challenge Activity Card 1
Design a Quilt

Some quilts have pretty patterns and colors, and some tell a story. Think about a quilt you might create. Answer each question below about the quilt you would like to design.
- What shapes or objects will you show or what story will you tell?
- What kind of border will you use?
- What colors will you use?

After you have answered the questions, sketch a design. Color your sketch. Write three sentences to tell about your design.

Sentences

Read these groups of words. Circle each sentence. Put a check mark after each word group that is not a sentence.

A merry-go-round. ✓
(This is fun)
These old wooden horses. ✓
(I will ride that tiger.)

Sentences

Think about a message you want to send.

Form a line with other group members. Take turns starting a whispered message. When it is your turn, whisper a group of words to the person on your left. Be sure your word group is a complete sentence. Each person whispers the message to the next person. The person at the end says the message out loud. Did the right message go down the line? Is it a sentence or not?

Sentences

Think about a message you want to send.

On a strip of paper, write a statement. Begin your statement with a capital letter. End your statement with a period. Then cut the strip into pieces, with one word on each piece. Mix up the pieces, and have the other members of your group put them back together to make a sentence that tells something.

Teacher: Cut apart the activities and distribute to students based on the modalities that are their strengths.
[Visual] You may want to write the word groups on the board. Let volunteers add to the non-sentence word groups to make complete sentences.
[Auditory] Have students meet in groups of five or more for this activity.
[Kinesthetic] If materials are available, have students use strips of construction paper and markers for this activity.

Reteach Activities • Sentences   Unit 1 • Chapter 1 **1**

Kinds of Sentences

OBJECTIVES

- To understand and identify statements, questions, commands, and exclamations
- To use each kind of sentence appropriately in a written announcement

DAILY LANGUAGE PRACTICE

TRANSPARENCY 1

1 the picture has many lovely colors (The; colors.)

2 some artists use oil paints (Some; paints.)

BRIDGE TO WRITING (*Who* word) loves that painting.

ORAL WARM-UP

USE PRIOR KNOWLEDGE Ask students to think of things they could tell about creating a painting. Then have them think of things they would like to ask about painting.

Grammar Jingles™ **CD** Use Track 1 to reinforce students' understanding of sentences.

TEACH/MODEL

Read aloud the explanations and examples. Explain that students can tell whether a sentence is a statement, a question, a command, or an exclamation by thinking about the meaning of the sentence. Model the thinking using the Guided Practice example:

MODEL **The sentence gives a direction. I know that a command gives an order or a direction, so I know the sentence is a command.**

Work through the Guided Practice with students.

CHAPTER 1

Sentences

26

Kinds of Sentences

Statements, questions, commands, and exclamations are different kinds of sentences.

A statement is a sentence that tells something.

A question is a sentence that asks something.

A command is a sentence that gives an order or a direction.

An exclamation is a sentence that shows strong feeling.

Examples:

Statement: We are going to the art museum.

Question: Do you like this picture?

Command: Look at the bright colors.

Exclamation: Wow, this picture is outstanding!

Guided Practice

A. Tell if each sentence is a statement, a question, a command, or an exclamation. Be sure you can explain your answers.

Example: Bring your crayons again tomorrow. *command*

1. I saw your picture. statement
2. Oh, it looks great! exclamation
3. Will you show me how to do it? question
4. Rub over the paper with many colors. command
5. What do I do next? question

Vocabulary Power page 1

Name _____

RELATED WORDS

▶ There are many words that have to do with movies. Look at each category and write the words from the Word Box that best fit each group. Then add your own word to each group.
Additional words will vary. Accept reasonable responses.

| actors | cartoons | photographers |
| comedies | animated films | directors |

WORKERS	KINDS OF MOTION PICTURES
actors	comedies
directors	animated films
photographers	cartoons

▶ Now try these.

| lights | theater | on TV |
| film | cinema | camera |

PLACES TO SEE MOVIES	MOVIE EQUIPMENT
cinema	camera
theater	film
on TV	lights

Vocabulary Power   Unit 1 • Chapter 1   1

ESL

REACHING ALL LEARNERS

WORD ORDER Make sets of cards with the following sentences, writing each word or a period on each card:

Marta walks.

Oscar plays.

Kim reads.

Have students arrange the cards into sentences. Allow them to mix and match words from different sets of cards to make new sentences.

Independent Practice

B. Write whether each sentence is a statement, a question, a command, or an exclamation.

Example: Do you know that a mural is a big painting?
question

6. Shall we paint a mural? *question*
7. That's such a great idea! *exclamation*
8. What do you want me to do? *question*
9. Help me think of an idea. *command*
10. I like to draw people. *statement*
11. How well can you draw plants? *question*
12. We will do a good job together. *statement*
13. I just can't wait to get started! *exclamation*
14. Buy several different colors of paint. *command*
15. I will buy the brushes. *statement*
16. Where shall we paint our mural? *question*
17. Listen to this idea. *command*
18. Can we paint it on the wall over there? *question*
19. We should ask if it is okay to paint the wall. *statement*
20. Hooray, we can do it! *exclamation*

Remember
that a statement is a sentence that tells something. A question is a sentence that asks something. A command gives an order or a direction. An exclamation shows strong feeling.

27

Writing Connection

Writer's Craft: Kinds of Sentences Suppose that you and your friends are planning an art fair at your school. When will the fair be held? What kinds of art will you show? Write an announcement for the fair. Be sure to use each kind of sentence at least once in your announcement.

Independent Practice

Have students complete the Independent Practice, or modify it using these suggestions:

MODIFIED INSTRUCTION

BELOW-LEVEL STUDENTS Have students softly read aloud each sentence to decide whether the words tell something, ask something, give a direction, or express strong feeling.

ABOVE-LEVEL STUDENTS Have students rewrite five of the sentences in Part B, adding or removing words to make a different type of sentence.

Writing Connection

Writer's Craft: Kinds of Sentences Create four columns on the board, labeled *Statements, Questions, Commands,* and *Exclamations.* Have students write one of their sentences in the appropriate column. Students should capitalize their sentences correctly to make their meaning clear.

WRAP-UP/ASSESS

SUMMARIZE Ask students how to tell whether a sentence is a statement, a question, a command, or an exclamation.

RETEACH

REACHING ALL LEARNERS

INTERVENTION Lessons in **visual, auditory,** and **kinesthetic** modalities: p. R38 and *Reteach Activities Copying Masters,* p. 2.

REACHING ALL LEARNERS

PRACTICE page 2

Name _____

Kinds of Sentences

A. Tell whether each sentence is a question, a command, or an exclamation. Be sure you can explain your answers.

1. Tell me about Charles Schulz. _command_
2. Boy, he is the greatest! _exclamation_
3. What was he most famous for? _question_
4. Look at this comic strip. _command_
5. What do you want me to see? _question_

B. Write each sentence correctly. Begin each sentence with a capital letter and use the correct end mark.

6. look at the name of this famous cartoon strip
   Look at the name of this famous cartoon strip.
7. read the name of the cartoonist
   Read the name of the cartoonist.
8. do you see why Charles Schulz is famous
   Do you see why Charles Schulz was famous?
9. what do you think of "Peanuts"
   What do you think of "Peanuts"?
10. wow, it is the best comic strip I ever saw
    Wow, it is the best comic strip I ever saw!

TRY THIS! Draw a comic strip. Have your characters use questions, commands, and exclamations.

2 Unit 1 • Chapter 1   Practice • Sentences

REACHING ALL LEARNERS

CHALLENGE

TWENTY QUESTIONS Have students work in pairs. One student thinks of a mystery person, and the other asks questions to guess who it is. The student who is guessing writes his or her questions, and the other partner writes the answers.

After one student guesses the mystery person, partners switch roles and play again.

Kinds of Sentences

Read each sentence. Circle the sentence if it is a question. Underline the sentence if it gives a command. Put a check mark next to the sentence if it is an exclamation.

Do you have the blue paint?
Hand it to me, please.
Wow, your painting is beautiful! ✓
Do you really think so?

Visual

Kinds of Sentences

Choose a picture in a book or magazine. Show the picture to the group, and say three sentences about it. Make one sentence a question, one a command, and one an exclamation. Let the other members of your group tell what kind of sentence each one is.

Auditory

Kinds of Sentences

On a card, draw a small, colorful picture. Then, with the rest of your group, make three word cards: question, command, and exclamation. Put everyone's picture card and the word cards facedown in separate piles. When it is your turn, choose a picture card and a word card. Your sentence should be the kind named on your word card—question, command, or exclamation. Then put both cards back at the bottom of their piles.

Kinesthetic

Teacher: Cut apart the activities and distribute to students based on the modalities that are their strengths.
(Visual) Write the sentences on the board. Ask students to explain how they identified each kind of sentence.
(Auditory) Make old magazines available, or let students choose photos or artwork from their textbooks.
(Kinesthetic) Have students work in groups of five or more. If possible, have them use index cards and colored markers to prepare their picture cards and word cards.

2 Unit 1 • Chapter 1   Reteach Activities • Sentences

Punctuating Sentences

OBJECTIVES
- To correctly punctuate sentences
- To conduct research and to write and correctly punctuate sentences in a written dialogue

DAILY LANGUAGE PRACTICE

TRANSPARENCY 1

1 may I go to the mooseum? (May; museum)

2 open the dore (Open; door.)

BRIDGE TO WRITING (Question word)
will we go?

ORAL WARM-UP

USE PRIOR KNOWLEDGE Give each of four volunteers a card on which you have written *statement*, *question*, *command*, or *exclamation*. Then have students give an example of the kind of sentence on their card.

Grammar Jingles™ **CD** Use Track 1 to reinforce students' understanding of sentences.

TEACH/MODEL

Tell students that when they ask a question, they say a sentence differently than when they give a command or make an exclamation. End punctuation is one way to show in writing how sentences are different.

Work through the explanation and examples with students. Explain that using correct end marks allows writers to express the words they think and say.

Have students work in pairs to complete the Guided Practice items. Make sure they explain their answers to each other.

Kind of Sentence	End Mark
Statement	.
Question	?
Command	.
Exclamation	!

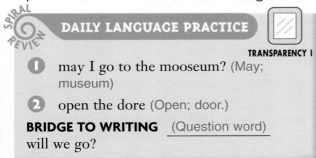

28

Punctuating Sentences

Using punctuation is one way for a writer to make his or her meaning clear.

You know that a sentence tells a complete thought. Every sentence begins with a capital letter. Each kind of sentence must also end with the correct end mark. A statement and a command end with a period. A question ends with a question mark. An exclamation ends with an exclamation point.

Notice the end mark in each kind of sentence below.

Examples:
Statement: Diego Rivera's art shows history**.**

Question: How does art show history**?**

Command: Find out more about Rivera**.**

Exclamation: Wow, that is amazing**!**

Guided Practice

A. Tell what mark you would use at the end of each sentence. Be ready to explain how you know.

Example: Do you like murals ?

1. The ancient Mayans painted murals .
2. Aren't they very old murals ?
3. Study to learn more about them .
4. Some were painted 1,200 years ago .
5. Wow, that's really old !

Vocabulary Power   page 2

Name _____

COMPARE AND CONTRAST

▶ Look at each item. Then put a check in the box of each category that fits the item. Responses may vary slightly.

	watched	heard	watched at a cinema	watched at home	characters can only be heard
1. motion picture	✓	✓	✓	✓	
2. television show	✓	✓		✓	
3. radio show		✓			✓

▶ Read and answer each question. Use complete sentences.

4. What are some differences between a motion picture and a radio show?

_____

_____

5. How are television shows and motion pictures alike?

_____

_____

2   Unit 1 • Chapter 1   Vocabulary Power

ESL

QUESTION AND ANSWER
Engage students in creating brief dialogues. Have one student ask a question and another answer it with a sentence. Tell students they may answer with statements, commands, or exclamations.

Write the sentences on the board, and have students explain the type of end punctuation required.

Independent Practice

B. Write each sentence. Add the correct end mark.

Example: How does animation work
How does animation work?

6. You can try animation for yourself .
7. Choose a character to draw .
8. What do you want your character to do ?
9. Draw ten slightly different pictures of your character .
10. What a great cartoon you drew !

C. Look at the end mark for each sentence. If it is correct, write *correct*. If it is not, rewrite the sentence with the correct end mark.

Examples: You can change the character's face?
You can change the character's face.

11. Staple your pages together. correct
12. What happens when you flip the pages. ?
13. Does the character seem to move. ?
14. Can we do more! ?
15. Animation is fun? ! or .

Writing Connection

Art Think about a piece of art that interests you. Do some research to find out about the person who created it. Then imagine that you are going to meet this person. Write the conversation you might have with him or her. Be sure you use different types of sentences and punctuate them correctly.

Remember
that a statement and a command end with a period. A question ends with a question mark. An exclamation ends with an exclamation point.

29

Independent Practice

Have students complete the Independent Practice, or modify it using these suggestions:

MODIFIED INSTRUCTION

BELOW-LEVEL STUDENTS Have students work in pairs to complete the items.

ABOVE-LEVEL STUDENTS After students complete the items, have them write and correctly punctuate a statement, a command, a question, and an exclamation that a cartoon character might say.

Writing Connection

Social Studies Ask students to choose a partner to play the part of their artist. Then have students act out their written conversation with their partner, asking and answering relevant questions as the class observes.

WRAP-UP/ASSESS

Writer's Journal

SUMMARIZE As a journal activity, have students reflect on how using the correct end marks makes their writing easier for readers to understand. **REFLECTION**

REACHING ALL LEARNERS

RETEACH

INTERVENTION Lessons in **visual, auditory,** and **kinesthetic** modalities, p. R38 and *Reteach Activities Copying Master,* p. 3.

Extra Practice

OBJECTIVES
- To identify sentence types and recognize correct capitalization and punctuation
- To write a review, using different types of sentences and the correct punctuation

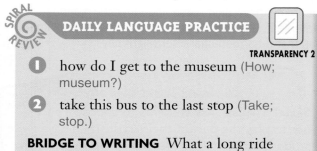

DAILY LANGUAGE PRACTICE

SPIRAL REVIEW

TRANSPARENCY 2

1 how do I get to the museum (How; museum?)

2 take this bus to the last stop (Take; stop.)

BRIDGE TO WRITING What a long ride (end mark)

ORAL WARM-UP

USE PRIOR KNOWLEDGE Write the words *statement*, *question*, *command*, and *exclamation* on the board. Ask students to give examples of each type of sentence about something that happened the day before, and to tell which end mark to use with each sentence.

TEACH/MODEL

Use the Remember box to review sentences and end punctuation. Then model the thinking for the example in Part A:

MODEL The example sentence asks a question and ends with a question mark, so I know that it is a question.

Have students work independently to complete the Extra Practice items.

ADDITIONAL PRACTICE An additional page of Extra Practice is provided on page 454 of the *Pupil Edition*.

Remember

that a sentence tells a complete thought. Every sentence begins with a capital letter. A statement and a command end with a period. A question ends with a question mark, and an exclamation ends with an exclamation point.

For more activities with sentences, visit *The Learning Site:* www.harcourtschool.com

30

Extra Practice

A. Write whether each sentence is a statement, a question, a command, or an exclamation. *pages 26–27*

Example: What is your favorite tool for drawing?
question

1. Jeremy always uses colored markers. statement
2. Why does he like them? question
3. He likes the bright colors. statement
4. He says they help him draw better. statement
5. Does Jeremy draw a lot? question
6. He always has a marker in his pocket. statement
7. Once he forgot to put the cap back on. statement
8. Guess what happened. command
9. Oops, the marker made a stain! exclamation
10. What do you think he did then? question

B. Write each sentence. Add the correct end mark. *pages 28–29*

Example: Does anyone still use crayons
Does anyone still use crayons?

11. Carrie uses crayons to do rubbings .
12. What a great idea she had !
13. How do you do it ?
14. Place a piece of paper on something rough .
15. Rub over the paper with the side of a crayon .

Vocabulary Power page 3

Name _____

SYNONYMS

▶ Write each word from the Word Box next to its synonym. Then write an example for each pair of synonyms. The first one is done for you. Examples will vary. Accept reasonable responses.

tune	motion picture	gem	theater	performer	cartoon

	Synonym	Example
1. movie	motion picture	*Black Beauty*
2. animated film	cartoon	
3. cinema	theater	
4. actor	performer	
5. song	tune	
6. jewel	gem	

▶ Now try these.

stream	town	car	creature	sea	street

7. automobile	car	
8. road	street	
9. river	stream	
10. ocean	sea	
11. city	town	
12. animal	creature	

Vocabulary Power   Unit 1 • Chapter 1   3

Science

SCIENCE QUESTIONS Point out that science experiments are based on questions. Tell students to write one question each on an experiment performed in science class. Then tell them to write a few sentences about the experiment they did and its results. Remind them to use the correct end marks for their questions and their sentences about the experiment.

C. Read each group of words. Put the words in an order that makes sense. Make the kind of sentence shown. Use correct end marks.

pages 24–29

Example: Question – is a planning puppet Peter show
Is Peter planning a puppet show?

16. Statement – puppets have show will the
The show will have puppets.
17. Command – puppets the help make
Help make the puppets.
18. Exclamation – from a puppet that sock made is
That puppet is made from a sock!
19. Statement – television saw I on puppets
I saw puppets on television.
20. Question – is a that finger puppet
Is that a finger puppet?
21. Statement – puppet it finger looks a like
It looks like a finger puppet.
22. Question – you can puppets where buy
Where can you buy puppets?
23. Statement – rather them make would I
I would rather make them.
24. Statement – already you what have you need
You already have what you need.
25. Exclamation – puppets making fun is such
Making puppets is such fun!

31

Writing Connection

Technology Using a computer, write a review of a music concert you heard at your school. What type of music was played? What did you enjoy about the concert? Include each of the four kinds of sentences in your review. Then choose a different font and type size for each kind of sentence. Print your review and share it with your class.

Building Oral Grammar

Remind students that people often change the way they speak to emphasize the different kinds of sentences. Have students say aloud different sentences from the Extra Practice exercises. They should listen for the differences in the way the sentences sound. Tell students that listening carefully will help them understand meaning.

Writing Connection

Technology Students' finished reviews can be displayed on a bulletin board or wall with the title "Our Concert Reviews." Have students compare the fonts and type sizes they chose with those of their classmates.

WRAP-UP/ASSESS

SUMMARIZE Ask students to tell what makes a complete sentence. Then ask them to name the four kinds of sentences and the end marks used with each.

PRACTICE page 4

Name _____

Extra Practice

A. For each group of words, write *Sentence* if the words make a sentence. Write *Not a sentence* if the words do not make a sentence.

1. Most famous for one comic strip. — Not a sentence
2. It is called "Peanuts." — Sentence
3. Started under a different name. — Not a sentence
4. The comic strip's name was changed. — Sentence
5. Schulz has spent his life on "Peanuts." — Sentence

B. Write each sentence and add the correct end mark. Write whether each sentence is a question, a statement, a command, or an exclamation.

6. Tell me about the "Peanuts" cartoon strip
Tell me about the "Peanuts" cartoon strip. command
7. Who are the characters
Who are the characters? question
8. Charlie Brown is the main character
Charlie Brown is the main character. statement

TRY THIS! Write a few sentences about your favorite cartoon character. Be sure to use complete sentences, capitalization, and end marks.

4   Unit 1 • Chapter 1   Practice • Sentences

CHALLENGE

WRITE AN ANNOUNCEMENT

Have students write an announcement telling about an art show at school. Tell students to invite their families to see the artwork. Have them describe the kinds of artwork that viewers will see. Students should include different types of sentences in their announcements. Remind them to capitalize and punctuate correctly.

TECHNOLOGY *Grammar Practice and Assessment* CD-ROM; *Writing Express* CD-ROM

INTERNET Visit *The Learning Site:*
www.harcourtschool.com

Chapter Review

OBJECTIVES

- To review complete sentences, types of sentences, and correct end marks
- To use good viewing strategies to better understand an artwork, and to discuss a visual image

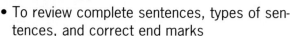

DAILY LANGUAGE PRACTICE

TRANSPARENCY 2

1 Whut a beautiful picture (What; picture!)

2 is this my painting (Is; painting?)

BRIDGE TO WRITING (Question word) is the museum located? I do not see it (end mark)

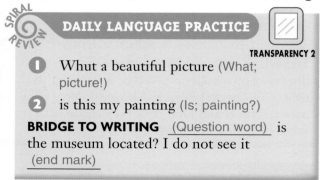

STANDARDIZED TEST PREP

MODEL TEST-TAKING STRATEGIES Have students read the directions on page 32. Tell them that if they cannot answer a question easily, they should eliminate answers they know to be wrong. Remind them that a sentence must have a subject and a predicate, and it must have the correct end mark.

Write this example on the board. Model the thinking:

Did Adam this picture

   1 **A** Did Adam paint this picture.

      B Did Adam paint this picture?

      C Did this picture?

      D Correct as is

MODEL The words in the sample do not have an end mark, and they do not express a complete thought. The words begin with *Did*, which is a question word. Answer B has a question mark and is a complete thought. I know that B is the correct answer.

Have students complete the Chapter Review independently.

STANDARDIZED TEST PREP

For additional test preparation, visit *The Learning Site:* www.harcourtschool.com

Chapter Review

Some of the sentences in this paragraph are underlined. Choose the best way to correct each numbered sentence. Mark the letter for your answer.

> (1) Alexander Calder an artist. (2) Have you ever seen his work. (3) Hanging parts that move he made mobiles with. *Mobile* means "able to move." (4) Can you guess why he called these pieces *mobiles* (5) Also made pieces with no moving parts He called those *stabiles*. Most of Calder's artwork is huge and brightly colored. (6) The work is such fun to look at!

1 A Alexander Calder was an artist. A

   B Alexander Calder was an artist?

   C An artist Alexander was Calder.

   D Correct as is

2 F Seen his work.

   G Work his have you ever?

   H Have you ever seen his work? H

   J Correct as is

3 A He made mobiles with hanging parts that move?

   B He made mobiles with hanging parts that move. B

   C Made mobiles with hanging parts that move.

   D Correct as is

4 F Why he called these pieces *mobiles*.

   G Why he called these pieces *mobiles* can you guess.

   H Can you guess why he called these pieces *mobiles?* H

   J Correct as is

5 A Also made pieces with no moving parts?

   B He also made pieces with no moving parts. B

   C Pieces with no moving parts!

   D Correct as is

6 F The work is fun to look at?

   G Fun to look at.

   H The work fun to look at is.

   J Correct as is J

32

Assessment

· ·

PORTFOLIO ASSESSMENT Have students select their best work from the Writing Connections on pages 25, 27, 29, and 31.

ONGOING ASSESSMENT Evaluate the performance of 4–6 students using appropriate checklists and record forms from pages R74–R77.

INTERNET Activities and exercises to help students prepare for state and standardized assessments appear on *The Learning Site:*

www.harcourtschool.com

Being a Good Viewer

Looking at something carefully will help you understand it better. Here are some strategies for being a good viewer.

A good viewer:

- looks closely at the art.
- takes time to describe it.
- looks at what is happening in the art.
- thinks about what the artist is trying to say.
- forms personal opinions about the artwork.
- discusses thoughts with others.

YOUR TURN

Find a picture, an illustration, or another artwork to discuss with a partner. Use some of the tips above to view the artwork carefully.

1. **Decide on the work of art.**
2. **Tell each other what you see.**
3. **Pay attention to details. Notice colors and the material from which the artwork is made. What do you see first?**
4. **Talk with each other about the meaning or message of the artwork.**
5. **After thinking about the piece, present your ideas to the class.**

TIP Imagine what questions your classmates might ask about the artwork you chose. Be sure you are ready to answer these questions.

33

PRACTICE page 5

REACHING ALL LEARNERS

Name _____

Chapter Review

Choose the best way to correct each numbered sentence. Fill in the oval next to your choice. If a sentence is correct, choose *Correct as is*.

(1) Come to the art show my class is having? (2) It's going to be great fun? (3) Do you have any plans! (4) I hope you are free, (5) Would you like to show some of your artwork. We would be glad to put it up for you. (6) One of Peg's pictures on the wall. (7) Won't believe how beautiful it is?

1
- ⬤ Come to the art show my class is having.
- ○ Come to the art show my class is having!
- ○ The art show my class is having.
- ○ Correct as is

2
- ○ It's going to be great fun.
- ○ It's be great fun?
- ⬤ It's going to be great fun!
- ○ Correct as is

3
- ○ Do you have any plans.
- ⬤ Do you have any plans?
- ○ Do have any plans?
- ○ Correct as is

4
- ○ Hope you free!
- ○ I hope you are free?
- ⬤ I hope you are free.
- ○ Correct as is

5
- ○ Like to show some of your artwork.
- ⬤ Would you like to show some of your artwork?
- ○ Would you like to show some of your artwork!
- ○ Correct as is

6
- ○ One of Peg's pictures on the wall?
- ○ One of Peg's pictures on the wall!
- ⬤ One of Peg's pictures is on the wall.
- ○ Correct as is

7
- ○ Won't believe how beautiful it is!
- ○ Won't believe how beautiful it is.
- ⬤ You won't believe how beautiful it is!
- ○ Correct as is

Practice • Sentences   Unit 1 • Chapter 1 5

CHALLENGE

REACHING ALL LEARNERS

INTERVIEW THE ARTIST Tell students to imagine that they will be interviewing the artist who created the work they examined as a whole group. Have students write questions to ask the artist. They may want to ask about the artist's life or how the artwork was created. Have students edit their sentences for correct capitalization and punctuation.

VIEWING

Being a Good Viewer

TEACH/MODEL

Read through the explanation and viewing strategies with the students.

Select a work of art for students to view as a whole group. Make three columns on the board: *What Is Happening*, *How the Artist Feels*, and *Your Thoughts*. Have students copy these columns onto a sheet of paper. Students should work in small groups to record responses for each column. Help them identify what is happening in the artwork, how the artist may have felt about the subject of the painting, and how the work of art makes them feel. Have students give reasons for their responses.

Provide students with examples of works of art from books, magazines, encyclopedias, or the Internet. Then have students complete the Your Turn activity. Students should use their artworks to clarify and support their spoken messages.

Writer's Journal — **WRITING APPLICATION** Have students describe the artwork they viewed with the whole group and explain their opinion of it in their journals.

WRAP-UP/ASSESS

SUMMARIZE Ask students to name three pieces of advice they would give someone about viewing works of art.

TECHNOLOGY Additional writing activities are provided on the *Writing Express* CD-ROM

LESSON ORGANIZER	DAY 1	DAY 2
DAILY LANGUAGE PRACTICE TRANSPARENCIES 3, 4	1. do you like music (Do; music?) 2. I'm excited about going to the concert (concert!) **Bridge to Writing** (Question word) are we leaving?	1. How long have you played the violin (violin?) 2. i just started oboe lessons (I; lessons.) **Bridge to Writing** (Simple subject) listens to classical music.
ORAL WARM-UP Listening/Speaking	Tell Whom 34	Name the Subject 36 *Grammar Jingles™* CD Track 2
TEACH/MODEL GRAMMAR KEY ✔ = tested skill	✔ **COMPLETE AND SIMPLE SUBJECTS** 34-35 • To understand and identify complete and simple subjects • To write an invitation and identify simple subjects	✔ **NOUNS IN SUBJECTS** 36-37 • To understand and to identify nouns in subjects • To identify complete subjects in original descriptive sentences
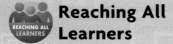 **Reaching All Learners**	**Modified Instruction** Below-Level: Model the Thinking Above-Level: Change Predicate **Reteach:** *Reteach Activities Copying Masters* pp. 4 and R39 **Challenge:** Activity Card 2, R62 *ESL Manual* pp. 14, 15 *Practice Book* p. 6	**Modified Instruction** Below-Level: Determine Subjects Above-Level: Change Noun **ESL:** Building Subjects 36 *ESL Manual* pp. 14, 16 **Reteach:** *Reteach Activities Copying Masters* pp. 5 and R39 **Challenge:** Music Review 37 *Practice Book* p.7
WRITING	Writing Connection 35 Music	Writing Connection 37 Real-Life Writing: Conversation
CROSS-CURRICULAR/ ENRICHMENT	*Vocabulary Power* Explore Word Meaning 34 device, **instrument,** percussion, utensil, woodwind See *Vocabulary Power* book.	*Vocabulary Power* Related Words 34 *Vocabulary Power* p. 4 **Vocabulary activity**

DAY 3

1. All the band instruments are piled in the hallway (hallway.)

2. watch out for that tuba (Watch; tuba!)

Bridge to Writing <u>(Noun)</u> is going to a concert tonight.

Identify the Subject 38
Grammar Jingles™ CD Track 2

✔ **COMBINING SENTENCES: COMPOUND SUBJECTS** 38-39
- To identify and form compound subjects
- To make a list and write sentences with compound subjects

Modified Instruction
Below-Level: Find the Predicate
Above-Level: Rewrite Sentences
Reteach: *Reteach Activities Copying Masters* pp. 6 and R39
Challenge: Write a Description 39
ESL Manual pp. 14, 17
Practice Book p. 8

 Writing Connection 39
Writer's Journal: Recording Ideas

Art : Making a Poster 38

Vocabulary Power

Onomatopoeia 34
Vocabulary Power p. 5
💻 **Vocabulary activity**

DAY 4

1. Our skool's marching band is very good (school's; good.)

2. do you think it will win the prize (Do; prize?)

Bridge to Writing
<u>(Compound subject)</u> play in the band.

Describe Music 40

EXTRA PRACTICE 40-41
- To identify subjects and form compound subjects
- To make a list of rhyming words and create a song
💻 **Practice and assessment**

Building Oral Grammar
Compare Sentences 41
ESL: Tell About Music 40
ESL Manual pp. 14, 18
Challenge: Check the Literature 41
Practice Book p. 9

Writing Connection 41
Writer's Craft: Rhyming Words

Vocabulary Power

Synonyms 34
Vocabulary Power p. 6
💻 **Vocabulary activity**

DAY 5

1. Tryouts for the school band start this afternoon (afternoon.)

2. will Jeanie get to play in the band (Will; band?)

Bridge to Writing The <u>(simple subject)</u> said she could play. <u>(Compound subject)</u> practiced hard for the tryouts.

TEST PREP **CHAPTER REVIEW** 42-43
- To review subjects
- To improve and practice listening and speaking skills
💻 **Test preparation**

Challenge: Prepare for Questions 43
Practice Book p. 10
ESL Manual pp. 14, 19

Writing Application 43
Listening and Speaking

Listening and Speaking: Being a Good Listener and Speaker 43

Vocabulary Power

Exemplification 34

Complete and Simple Subjects

OBJECTIVES
- To understand and identify complete and simple subjects
- To write an invitation and identify the simple subjects in the sentences

DAILY LANGUAGE PRACTICE

TRANSPARENCY 3

1 do you like music (Do; music?)

2 I'm excited about going to the concert (concert!)

BRIDGE TO WRITING　(Question word) are we leaving?

ORAL WARM-UP

USE PRIOR KNOWLEDGE Read aloud this sentence: *My aunt Cara plays the violin.* Ask students to tell whom the sentence is about.

TEACH/MODEL

Remind students that a sentence names someone or something. A sentence tells what someone or something is or does. Read aloud the explanation and examples of complete and simple subjects. Then model the Guided Practice example:

MODEL **I read the sentence and ask myself, Whom or what is it about? The sentence is about *Your friend. Your friend* is the complete subject. The simple subject is the word *friend.***

Complete the Guided Practice sentences orally with students.

Vocabulary Power

in·stru·ment [in′strə·mənt] *n.* A tool for making music.

34

Complete and Simple Subjects

Every complete sentence has a subject and a predicate.

The person, place, or thing the sentence is about is called the simple subject. The complete subject of a sentence includes the simple subject and all the other words in the subject that describe it. Ask yourself whom or what the sentence is about, and this will tell you the subject.

In the examples below, the simple subject is circled and the complete subject is underlined.

Examples:
My friend (Jared) loves music.
The (family) next door to us plays many instruments.

Guided Practice

A. Find the simple and complete subjects in each sentence. Complete subjects are underlined once; simple subjects are underlined twice.

Example: Your friend can play with us.
　　　　friend|simple, Your friend|complete

1. Jared's family makes music together.
2. Each member of the family plays an instrument.
3. His brother plays the banjo.
4. That flute belongs to his sister.
5. His mom is a drummer.

Vocabulary Power

DAY 1 EXPLORE WORD MEANING Introduce and define *instrument.* **What are some different kinds of instruments?**

DAY 2 RELATED WORDS Write on the board: *piano, guitar, violin.* **How are these words related? What other words would fit into this group?** (See also *Vocabulary Power,* page 4.)

DAY 3 ONOMATOPOEIA An onomatopoetic word is a word whose name sounds like the sound it makes. The words *buzz* and *hum* are examples of onomatopoeia. **What are some other examples?** (See also *Vocabulary Power,* page 5.)

DAY 4 SYNONYMS Synonyms are words that mean almost the same thing. **Which of these words are synonyms: *instrument, car, tool?*** (See also *Vocabulary Power,* page 6.)

DAY 5 EXEMPLIFICATION **Draw a picture of a musical instrument you like. Underneath your drawing, make a list of reasons you like that instrument.**

Independent Practice

B. Read each sentence. Write the simple subject in each sentence.

Example: People all over the world have their own music.
People

6. African <u>music</u> uses many drums.
7. Some <u>drums</u> are made from hollow logs.
8. Animal <u>skins</u> are used in some instruments.
9. Some African <u>instruments</u> have strings.
10. <u>Musicians</u> in Africa play flutes, too.

C. Write the complete subject in each sentence.

Example: The silver flute sounds very pretty.
The silver flute

11. <u>People from other countries</u> play flutes as well.
12. <u>Some people</u> found a 9,000-year-old flute in China.
13. <u>The very old flute</u> was made from a bone.
14. <u>The musician next door</u> plays a flute.
15. <u>The old Chinese flute</u> can still make pretty music.

> **Remember**
> that the complete subject is made up of the simple subject and any words that help describe it.

Writing Connection

Music Imagine you have been asked to plan a musical show. Make an invitation. Draw the musicians and their instruments on the stage. Write a few sentences that describe your show. Underline the simple subjects in your sentences.

35

Independent Practice

Have students complete the Independent Practice, or modify it using these suggestions:

MODIFIED INSTRUCTION

BELOW-LEVEL STUDENTS Work through the items with students, modeling the thinking.

ABOVE-LEVEL STUDENTS Have students think of a new predicate for the subject of each sentence.

Writing Connection

Music To begin, students should contribute to a class discussion about musical performances. Ask students to describe clearly their experiences or to describe how different types of music are often performed.

WRAP-UP/ASSESS

SUMMARIZE What is a simple subject? What is a complete subject?

RETEACH

INTERVENTION Lessons in **visual, auditory,** and **kinesthetic** modalities: p. R39 and *Reteach Activities Copying Masters,* p. 4.

CHALLENGE

MAKE A FACT SHEET Have students use **Challenge Activity Card 2** (page R62) to create a fact sheet about a musical instrument.

Nouns in Subjects

OBJECTIVES
- To understand and to identify nouns in subjects
- To identify complete subjects in original descriptive sentences

1 How long have you played the violin (violin?)

2 i just started oboe lessons (I; lessons.)

BRIDGE TO WRITING   (Simple subject)
listens to classical music.

ORAL WARM-UP

USE PRIOR KNOWLEDGE Say this sentence: *People enjoy music.* Ask students to name the subject of the sentence. Have them suggest other words that could go before the subject in the sentence.

***Grammar Jingles*™ CD, Intermediate** Use Track 2 for review and reinforcement of subjects.

TEACH/MODEL

Read aloud the explanation and examples of nouns in subjects. Emphasize that simple subjects are often nouns.

Then model the thinking, using the Guided Practice example sentence:

MODEL **The words in the sentence that name something are *Some music*. These words must be the complete subject. *Music* is a thing. It is also the main word in the subject, so I know that *Music* is a noun that is also the simple subject.**

Have students work through the Guided Practice items in small groups, and then review the items orally with the class.

Nouns in Subjects

The **subject** of a sentence names someone or something. A **noun** can be the most important word in the subject. A noun is a word that names a person, place, or thing.

You know that the subject of a sentence may be more than one word. The simple subject is often a noun. Words that can name whom or what the sentence is about are nouns.

In the sentences below, the complete subject is underlined. Notice that the main word in the complete subject is a noun.

Examples:
Many **people** play music in their homes.

The entire **school** could hear someone singing.

Some **students** knew the song.

DID YOU KNOW?
The oldest instrument ever found is a flute made 33,000 years ago.

36

Guided Practice

A. Identify the complete subject in each sentence. Then tell the noun that is the simple subject.

Example: Some music is very important to people.
Some music|complete subject, music|noun

1. Most people enjoy music. people/noun
2. The children hear music everywhere. children/noun
3. My family enjoys listening to the radio. family/noun
4. The television plays a lot of music too. television/noun
5. Many stores play music on speakers. stores/noun

Vocabulary Power page 4

Name _____

RELATED WORDS

Read each list of words. Think of how they are related. Circle the letter next to the correct topic. Then add a word of your own to each group of words. Additional words will vary. Possible responses are given.

1. flute, clarinet, oboe, _____recorder_____
   A percussion instruments
   B tools
   C colors
   (D) woodwinds

2. fork, spoon, spatula, _____whisk_____
   F music
   (G) utensils
   H foods
   J songs

3. drum, cymbal, tambourine, _____xylophone_____
   (A) percussion instruments
   B woodwinds
   C string instruments
   D horns

4. hammer, wrench, chisel, _____screwdriver_____
   F shapes
   G percussion instruments
   H workers
   (J) devices

5. drummer, pianist, violinist, _____guitarist_____
   A woodwinds
   B percussion instruments
   (C) musicians
   D horns

4 **Unit 1 • Chapter 2**   Vocabulary Power

ESL
REACHING ALL LEARNERS

BUILDING SUBJECTS Write these sentences on the board:

Alba plays the flute.

Music is played in a concert hall.

People dance to music.

Read the sentences with students. Then have each student write the subject of each sentence. Help students find the subject, if necessary, by asking them who or what each sentence is about.

Independent Practice

B. Write each sentence. Underline the complete subject and circle the noun that is the simple subject.

Example: That (song) has a fast beat.

6. That (music) has a pretty sound.
7. The (drummer) in the band beats his drum with drumsticks.
8. Our whole (class) listened to the marching band.
9. The flute (player) plays very well.
10. Our (parents) dance to this music.
11. Your (neighbor) likes to write songs.
12. The (boys) next door practice their music every day.
13. The (audience) claps while you sing.
14. Luisa's (brother) listens to music on the radio.
15. Our (teacher) plays the guitar for us.

Remember that who or what every sentence tells about is the subject. A noun is often the simple subject.

Writing Connection

Real-Life Writing: Conversation Talk with a partner about an instrument you play or would like to play. Would you like to play alone or in a group? How much time would you spend practicing? Write four sentences that describe your instrument. Then underline the complete subject in each sentence.

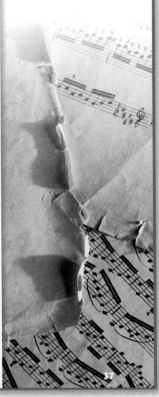

Independent Practice

Have students complete the Independent Practice, or modify it using these suggestions:

MODIFIED INSTRUCTION

BELOW-LEVEL STUDENTS Remind students to ask themselves whom or what the sentence is about before deciding on the complete and simple subjects.

ABOVE-LEVEL STUDENTS Have students rewrite five of the sentences, using a different noun in the subject.

Writing Connection

Real-Life Writing: Conversation Ask students to discuss why knowing how to play an instrument might be a good skill to have. After students record their ideas about a musical instrument, have them go back and check their sentences for correct capitalization and punctuation.

WRAP-UP/ASSESS

SUMMARIZE What do nouns name? When a noun is the main word in the complete subject, what is it also known as?

RETEACH

INTERVENTION Lessons in **visual, auditory,** and **kinesthetic** modalities: p. R39 and *Reteach Activities Copying Masters,* p. 5.

CHALLENGE

MUSIC REVIEW Ask students to write a review of a favorite song. Remind them to give the name of the song and describe what it is about. They should also tell why they like the song. Then have students underline the complete subjects in their reviews.

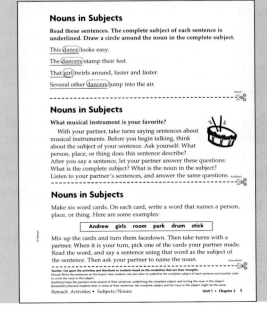

Combining Sentences: Compound Subjects

OBJECTIVES
- To identify and form compound subjects
- To make a list and write sentences with compound subjects

DAILY LANGUAGE PRACTICE

TRANSPARENCY 3

1 All the band instruments are piled in the hallway (hallway.)

2 watch out for that tuba (Watch; tuba!)

BRIDGE TO WRITING __(Noun)__ is going to a concert tonight.

ORAL WARM-UP

USE PRIOR KNOWLEDGE Say the following sentence: *Paula and Elise take piano lessons.* Ask students to name the subject of the sentence.

Grammar Jingles™ **CD, Intermediate** Use Track 2 for review and reinforcement of subjects.

TEACH/MODEL

Tell students that using only sentences with simple subjects can make writing sound choppy. Point out that writers sometimes combine sentences to avoid this problem. Work through the explanation and examples of compound subjects with students. Model the thinking using the second set of example sentences:

MODEL The complete subject in the first sentence is *A banjo.* The complete subject in the second sentence is *A cello.* The predicates in the two sentences are the same, so I can make one sentence by combining the subjects, using *and.*

Work through the Guided Practice with students, or have them complete the exercises in small groups.

38

GRAMMAR-WRITING CONNECTION

Combining Sentences: Compound Subjects

Sentences with compound subjects have two or more subjects.

The subjects in a compound subject share the same predicate. The words *and* and *or* are usually used to join the subjects. Use commas to separate three or more subjects.

Examples:
Guitars and violins are stringed instruments.

Ali, Lupe, and Paul play the guitar.

You can combine two sentences that have the same predicate by joining the two simple subjects with *and.*

Examples:
A banjo has strings. **A cello** has strings.

A banjo and a cello have strings.

Guided Practice

A. Find the compound subject in each sentence.

Example: Diego and Eli play the banjo.
Diego and Eli

1. Yuki, Reta, and Sam play in the band.
2. The boys and the girls enjoy the music.
3. Brianna and Max play the trumpet.
4. Fred or Reta sits next to the drummer.
5. My violin case and your violin case are black.

Vocabulary Power page 5

Name _____

ONOMATOPOEIA

Onomatopoeia words are words that imitate sounds.

Example: *clank, buzz*

▶ **Read each question and illustrate your answer.** Illustrations may vary. Accept reasonable responses.
1. What kind of percussion instrument might make sounds like *boom* and *wham?*

2. In what kind of weather do you hear sounds like *crackle* and *crash?*

3. What kind of animal makes sounds like *chirp, tweet,* and *twitter?*

▶ Pretend you are at a music concert. Make a list of all the sounds you hear. Responses may vary. Accept reasonable responses.

Vocabulary Power   Unit 1 • Chapter 2   5

Art

MAKING A POSTER Have students work in small groups to create posters advertising concerts by musical groups that they like and know something about. Tell them to make their writing interesting by including on the posters at least one sentence that has a compound subject.

Independent Practice

B. Write the sentence. Underline the compound subject in the sentence.

Example: <u>Our band and their band</u> play.

6. <u>Kim and Ray</u> are members of the band.
7. <u>Kim, Ray, and José</u> wear red uniforms.
8. <u>Kim's dad or Ray's mom</u> helps the band.
9. <u>Kim's tuba and Ray's trumpet</u> are new.
10. <u>Two vans or the school bus</u> will take the band.

C. Combine each group of sentences into one sentence that has a compound subject.

Example: The team waits. The band waits.
The team and the band wait.

11. The Alamo School band plays well. Our band plays well. *The Alamo School band and our band play well.*
12. Our school band is in the contest. Her school band is in the contest. *Our school band and her school band are in the contest.*
13. The fans cheer for the teams. The band members cheer for the teams. *The fans and the band members cheer for the teams.*
14. The teams have fun. The bands have fun. The fans have fun. *The teams, the bands, and the fans have fun.*
15. Gina will play in the band next year. Yoko will play in the band next year. *Gina and Yoko will play in the band next year.*

Remember

that compound subjects combine two or more subjects into one sentence using *and* or *or*.

39

Writing Connection

Writer's Journal: Recording Ideas
List as many kinds of music as you can. Choose one kind of music, and write six sentences describing this kind of music. Combine at least two sentences that share a predicate into one sentence.

Independent Practice

Have students complete the Independent Practice, or modify it using these suggestions:

MODIFIED INSTRUCTION

BELOW-LEVEL STUDENTS Tell students to find the predicate in each sentence before they underline the compound subject or combine the sentences.

ABOVE-LEVEL STUDENTS For Part B sentences 6, 8, and 10, ask students to rewrite the sentences, adding a third subject.

Writing Connection

Writer's Journal: Recording Ideas
Before students begin to record their ideas, discuss with them some things that may contribute to the sound of different types of music. These may include beat, words, rhythm, instruments, and mood. Then have students compose sentences with interesting, elaborated subjects.

WRAP-UP/ASSESS

SUMMARIZE Ask students how using compound subjects can improve their writing. **REFLECTION**

RETEACH

INTERVENTION Lessons in **visual**, **auditory**, and **kinesthetic** modalities: p. R39 and *Reteach Activities Copying Masters*, p. 6.

PRACTICE page 8

Name _____

Combining Sentences: Compound Subjects

A. Underline the complete compound subject in each sentence.

1. Judy and Lara are folksingers.
2. Larry and Ron sing folk songs, too.
3. The girls and boys also like folk dancing.
4. Folk songs and folk dances are their favorite ways to enjoy music.
5. Their fathers and mothers like to watch them.

B. Combine each of the following groups of sentences to form one sentence with a compound subject. Remember that you may need to change the verb in the predicate.

6. Men created folk songs. Women created folk songs.
   Men and women created folk songs.

7. The words were passed from singer to singer. The music was passed from singer to singer. The words and music were passed from singer to singer.

8. Pens were not usually used to write down the songs. Paper was not usually used to write down the songs. Pens and paper were not usually used to write down the songs.

▶ **TRY THIS!** Choose two of your favorite music groups. Write about the kind of music they sing or play and what you like about them. Try to use a compound subject in at least one sentence.

8 Unit 1 • Chapter 2   Practice • Subjects/Nouns

CHALLENGE

WRITE A DESCRIPTION Ask students to write a paragraph describing the way they feel when they listen to different kinds of music. Prompt students to add descriptive words to some of their subjects to make their writing more lively and interesting.

Combining Sentences: Compound Subjects

Read each sentence. Circle the subject. Combine the sentences to make a sentence with a compound subject. Write the sentence on the line.

Tonio played the drums. I played the drums.
Tonio and I played the drums.

Jason sang. Mika sang. Darla sang.
Jason, Mika, and Darla sang.

Visual

Combining Sentences: Compound Subjects

Tell a group about games you like to play with your friends and family. Use compound subjects in some of the sentences you say.

When the other members of your group talk, listen carefully. Stand up when you hear a sentence with a compound subject. Be ready to repeat the compound subject of that sentence.

Auditory

Combining Sentences: Compound Subjects

With two other students, act out an action for the rest of your group. Have other group members say sentences about what the three of you are doing.

When others show an action, watch them carefully. Then say a sentence about them. Use a compound subject in your sentence.

Kinesthetic

Teacher: Cut apart the activities and distribute to students based on the modalities that are their strengths.
(Visual) Students can use different colors to mark each compound subject that can be combined.
(Auditory) Allow time for students to prepare the sentences they will say, so they can listen carefully when other group members speak.
(Kinesthetic) After a threesome has mimed an action, have other group members say an original sentence with a compound subject.

6 Unit 1 • Chapter 2   Reteach Activities • Subjects/Nouns

Extra Practice

OBJECTIVES
- To identify complete and simple subjects in sentences and to form compound subjects
- To make a list of rhyming words and create a song, using some of the rhyming words as subjects

SPIRAL REVIEW

DAILY LANGUAGE PRACTICE

TRANSPARENCY 4

1 Our skool's marching band is very good (school's; good.)

2 do you think it will win the prize (Do; prize?)

BRIDGE TO WRITING (Compound subject) _____ play in the band.

ORAL WARM-UP

USE PRIOR KNOWLEDGE Ask students to describe the music they listen to with their friends and family. Point out examples of simple subjects and compound subjects in the sentences they say.

TEACH/MODEL

Use the Remember boxes to review subjects.

Remind students that the simple subject is the word that names the person, place, or thing the sentence is about and is often a noun.

Tell students to work in pairs to complete the Extra Practice items.

Remember

that every sentence has a subject and a predicate. The complete subject is made up of the simple subject and all the other words that help describe it.

For more activities with subjects and nouns, visit *The Learning Site:* www.harcourtschool.com

40

Extra Practice

A. Write each sentence. Underline the complete subject in each one. Then circle the noun that is the simple subject. *pages 34–37*

Example: (Mozart) was a famous composer.

1. (Mozart) was born more than 200 years ago.
2. His (parents) named him Wolfgang.
3. (Wolfgang Mozart) learned to play music at age four.
4. The young (composer) started writing his own music at age five.
5. The (boy) played music in many cities.

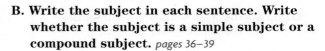

Mozart

B. Write the subject in each sentence. Write whether the subject is a simple subject or a compound subject. *pages 36–39*

Example: June is a famous singer.
June|simple

6. Liberty Elementary School has a chorus that performs. simple
7. Students and teachers are members. compound
8. Some boys and girls in my class are in chorus. compound
9. Hannah and her sisters like singing. compound
10. The girl with red hair and the boy next to her sing in a group. compound
11. Richard practices on Wednesdays. simple
12. Sissy gave a concert at the mall. simple
13. The youngest singer and the oldest singer in the group are best friends. compound
14. Hannah, Madison, and Liah sing a song together. compound
15. Everybody should be quiet when they play. simple

Vocabulary Power page 6

Name _____

SYNONYMS

▶ Read each sentence. Find a word in the Word Box that is a synonym for the underlined word or words in the sentence. Write the word on the line. The first one is done for you.

famous	instrument	hear	concert	drums	flute

1. I love to listen to piano music. _____ hear
2. What kind of tool do you play? _____ instrument
3. Rosa plays a woodwind. _____ flute
4. Carlos prefers to play percussion instruments. _____ drums
5. Do you know any well-known musicians? _____ famous
6. I enjoyed attending the performance. _____ concert

▶ Now try these.

glad	practices	left	bother	tools	utensils

7. It's not polite to disturb people while they are listening to music. _____ bother
8. James put forks and spoons on the table. _____ utensils
9. Ellen used the devices to fix her car. _____ tools
10. We departed when the concert was over. _____ left
11. She was pleased when she got her new horn. _____ glad
12. The musician rehearses every day. _____ practices

6 Unit 1 • Chapter 2   Vocabulary Power

REACHING ALL LEARNERS **ESL**

TELL ABOUT MUSIC Have students share what they know about music from their cultures of origin. Have students dictate sentences to an English-fluent partner, describing the instruments that are used. Then have them read the sentences and underline the subjects once and the predicates twice. They may wish to share song lyrics or bring samples of recorded music to play for the class.

C. Combine each group of sentences into one sentence that has a compound subject. Write the new sentence. *pages 38–39*

Example: John picked the wedding music.
Ana picked the wedding music.
John and Ana picked the wedding music.

16. The bride danced to the music.
The groom danced to the music.
The bride and the groom danced to the music.

17. Her cousin played in the band.
His brother played in the band.
Her cousin and his brother played in the band.

18. The bride wanted louder music.
The guests wanted louder music.
The bride and the guests wanted louder music.

19. Family members asked for a special song.
Friends asked for a special song.
Family members and friends asked for a special song.

20. The families sang along.
The couple sang along.
All their friends sang along.
The families, the couple, and all their friends sang along.

> **Remember**
> that compound subjects combine two or more subjects into one sentence using *and* or *or*.

Writing Connection

Writer's Craft: Rhyming Words Work with a partner to write a song about something you love to do. List some rhyming words about your topic. Use some of the words as subjects in the sentences of your song. Perform the song for the class.

41

Building Oral Grammar

Tell students that combining sentences makes speaking sound smoother. Ask them to work in pairs to read aloud the separate sentences in Part C. Then they should read aloud their combined sentences and compare how they sound.

Writing Connection

Writer's Craft: Rhyming Words Ask students to generate ideas for their list by using a prewriting technique such as brainstorming and listing key thoughts. Tell those who are having trouble thinking of a melody for their song to use a familiar melody.

WRAP-UP/ASSESS

SUMMARIZE Ask students to create a journal entry telling one thing they learned about subjects that will help them as writers. **REFLECTION**

ADDITIONAL PRACTICE An additional page of Extra Practice is provided on page 455 of the *Pupil Edition*.

PRACTICE page 9

Name _____

Extra Practice

A. Read each sentence. Underline the complete subject once. Underline the simple subject twice.

1. My whole family will go to the opera this week.
2. An opera is a story told through music and song.
3. The characters sing words to each other.
4. A whole conversation takes place in a song.
5. The singers in an opera sometimes sing in a different language.

B. Write the complete subject in each sentence. Write whether the subject is *compound* or *not compound*.

6. Folk music and popular music are alike in some ways.
Folk music and popular music; compound

7. Many children and adults know the words to popular songs.
Many children and adults; compound

8. Some folk songs are also widely known.
Some folk songs; not compound

9. People have listened to folk music for hundreds of years.
People; not compound

10. Many popular songs are new.
Many popular songs; not compound

> **TRY THIS!** Work with a partner. Think about a song you both like. Use it as a model to write a song about yourselves and your friends. Use compound subjects in some of the lines of your song.

Practice • Subjects/Nouns   Unit 1 • Chapter 2   9

CHALLENGE

CHECK THE LITERATURE Have students work in small groups to review books or magazines to find examples of compound subjects. Ask students to discuss how these sentences improve the writing.

TECHNOLOGY *Grammar Practice and Assessment* CD-ROM; *Writing Express* CD-ROM

INTERNET Visit *The Learning Site:* www.harcourtschool.com

Chapter Review

OBJECTIVES
• To review subjects
• To improve listening and speaking skills and to practice these skills in a group activity

STANDARDIZED TEST PREP

SPIRAL REVIEW

DAILY LANGUAGE PRACTICE

TRANSPARENCY 4

1 Tryouts for the school band start this afternoon (afternoon.)

2 will Jeanie get to play in the band (Will; band?)

BRIDGE TO WRITING The ___(simple subject)___ said she could play. ___(compound subject)___ practiced hard for the tryouts.

STANDARDIZED TEST PREP

MODEL TEST-TAKING STRATEGIES Have students read the directions on page 42 silently. Remind them to read each possible answer before making a choice. Model the thinking. Write this example on the board:

My friend Anna is trying for a place in the band.

   1 **A** Anna
       B is trying
       C place in the band
       D My friend Anna

MODEL I know that the complete subject is the simple subject and all the other words that describe it. *Anna* is the simple subject. The words *My friend* tell more about the simple subject *Anna, so* the complete subject must be *My friend Anna.*

Have students complete the Chapter Review individually.

STANDARDIZED TEST PREP

Chapter Review

Read the paragraph. Choose the complete subject for each numbered sentence.

> (1) My friend Michael likes to make music. (2) Michael can make music with almost anything. (3) Boxes, jars, and even rocks can be drums. (4) Flutes can be made from straws and plastic pipes. (5) Michael's friend made maracas from oatmeal boxes filled with dried beans. (6) My favorite instrument is a guitar made from rubber bands stretched over a box.

TIP Be sure to read all the answers for a multiple-choice question. Then choose the best answer.

1 **A** My friend Michael A
   B Michael
   C Michael likes
   D music

2 **F** Michael says
   G you can make music
   H Michael H
   J almost anything

3 **A** Boxes
   B Boxes, jars, and even rocks B
   C rocks can be
   D drums

4 **F** Flutes can be made
   G straws
   H straws and plastic pipes
   J Flutes J

5 **A** Michael's friend made
   B Michael's friend B
   C oatmeal boxes
   D filled with dried beans

6 **F** My favorite instrument F
   G My
   H a guitar made from rubber bands
   J a box

For more activities with subjects and nouns, visit *The Learning Site:* www.harcourtschool.com

---

Assessment

PORTFOLIO ASSESSMENT Have students select their best work from the Writing Connections on pages 35, 37, and 41.

ONGOING ASSESSMENT Evaluate the performance of 4–6 students using appropriate checklists and record forms from pages R74–R77.

INTERNET Activities and exercises to help students prepare for state and standardized assessments appear on *The Learning Site:*
www.harcourtschool.com

Being a Good Listener and Speaker

Listening is one of the best ways to learn things. Speaking is a way of sharing ideas and feelings with others. Here are some tips. They will help you become a better listener and speaker.

If you are listening …

- Pay attention to the speaker.
- Don't disturb the listeners.
- Ask questions when the speaker is finished.
- Take notes about what the speaker said.

If you are speaking …

- Speak clearly and correctly.
- Take your time and don't talk too fast.
- Look at your audience.
- Use hand and body movements to illustrate your point.
- Ask your audience for questions.

YOUR TURN

Form small groups and play a guessing game. Pretend that you are a certain type of artist. Introduce yourself to the group, but don't say what you do. The group should ask you questions and guess what you are. Practice the speaking and listening skills you have learned as you play the game.

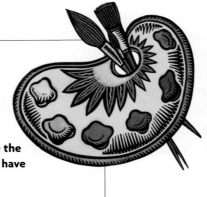

LISTENING AND SPEAKING

Being a Good Listener and Speaker

TEACH/MODEL

Explain that listening and speaking are a part of everyday life. Good listening and speaking skills are important both in and out of school.

Have students read the explanation and tips for listening and speaking. Then read aloud a brief excerpt from a book, magazine, or encyclopedia, and have students practice their listening skills. Have them write down a few questions to ask about what you have read. Then encourage them to ask their questions and take notes from your answers. Students should then work in groups to complete the Your Turn activity.

WRITING APPLICATION Have students use the notes they took to write a brief paragraph telling what they learned.

WRAP-UP/ASSESS

SUMMARIZE Ask students to suggest one piece of advice they would give someone about listening or speaking.

PRACTICE page 10

Name _____

Chapter Review

Choose the complete subject in each sentence. Fill in the oval next to your choice.

(1) My cousin Lupe plays almost every instrument. **(2)** Lupe likes them all. **(3)** Drums, horns, and string instruments are my favorites. **(4)** The cello, the French horn, and the drums are the ones I play. **(5)** Ralph and Eve like to hear us play. **(6)** Some of our other friends play music too. **(7)** Lupe's sister and brother sometimes sing with us. **(8)** Our family enjoys sharing music.

1. ○ My cousin Lupe
   ○ cousin
   ○ My cousin
   ○ Lupe

2. ○ Lupe likes
   ○ Lupe likes them
   ● Lupe
   ○ them all

3. ○ Drums, horns
   ● Drums, horns, and string instruments
   ○ Drums, horns, and string
   ○ drums

4. ○ The cello,
   ○ the French horn
   ○ The cello, the French horn,
   ● The cello, the French horn, and the drums

5. ○ Ralph
   ● Ralph and Eve
   ○ Eve
   ○ Ralph and Eve like

6. ● Some of our other friends
   ○ friends
   ○ our other friends
   ○ Some of our other

7. ○ Lupe's
   ○ Lupe's sister
   ● Lupe's sister and brother
   ○ sister and brother

8. ○ family
   ○ Our
   ○ Our family enjoys
   ● Our family

10 Unit 1 • Chapter 2   Practice • Subjects/Nouns

CHALLENGE

PREPARE FOR QUESTIONS

Tell students that they should be ready to answer questions others may ask after they have spoken to a group. Have students think of a topic they could speak to the class about. Then have them list at least five questions their classmates might ask about that topic. Have students write their answers to these questions.

TECHNOLOGY Additional writing activities are provided on the *Writing Express* CD-ROM

CHAPTER 3

Writer's Craft

Personal Voice
pages 44-51

LESSON ORGANIZER	DAY **1**	DAY **2**
DAILY LANGUAGE PRACTICE ⬜ **TRANSPARENCIES 5, 6**	1. my dog's coat is glossy and black (My; black.) 2. how soft and silky it is (How; is!)	1. my dog has a feathery tail (My; tail.) 2. he waves it like a plume? (He; plume.)
ORAL WARM-UP **Listening/Speaking**	Discuss Prior Descriptions 44	Compare Descriptions 46
TEACH/MODEL **WRITING** 	✔ **PERSONAL VOICE** • To understand descriptive language and analyze its use in a passage • To understand and analyze the use of personal voice and colorful words in descriptive writing **Literature Model:** "Dancing with the Indians" 44 **Analyze the Model** 44 **Analyze Descriptive Writing** 45	**GUIDED WRITING** Writing and Thinking: Write to Record Reflections 47 • To identify a writer's viewpoint and to use colorful words • To record reflections about colorful words **Using Colorful Words** 46 **Writer's Viewpoint** 47
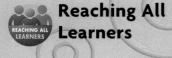 **Reaching All Learners**	**Challenge:** How I See It 45 *ESL Manual* pp. 20, 21	**Challenge:** Color Check 47 *ESL Manual* p. 20
GRAMMAR	**HANDS-ON ACTIVITIES** 21I–21J	**HANDS-ON ACTIVITIES** 21I–21J
CROSS-CURRICULAR/ ENRICHMENT	*Vocabulary Power* Explore Word Meaning 44 glimmering, glistening, **shimmering**, sparkling, twinkling See *Vocabulary Power* book. **Art:** Picture This 45	*Vocabulary Power* Colorful Words 44 *Vocabulary Power* p. 7 **Vocabulary activity** **Vocabulary:** Synonym Study 47

KEY
 ✔ = tested skill

43A **UNIT 1**

DAY 3

1. sometimes my dog is much too friendly (Sometimes; friendly.)
2. he jumps on people and licks their faces (He; faces.)

Describe an Object 48

GUIDED WRITING
- To recognize and analyze the parts of a descriptive paragraph
- To choose a topic and generate ideas for a descriptive paragraph

Descriptive Paragraph 48
Analyze the Model 49
Prewriting and Drafting 49

ESL: Prewriting 49
ESL Manual p. 20

HANDS-ON ACTIVITIES
21I–21J

Vocabulary Power

Word Endings 44
Vocabulary Power p. 8

Listening and Speaking: Listen to the Color 48

Evaluation Criteria: 49

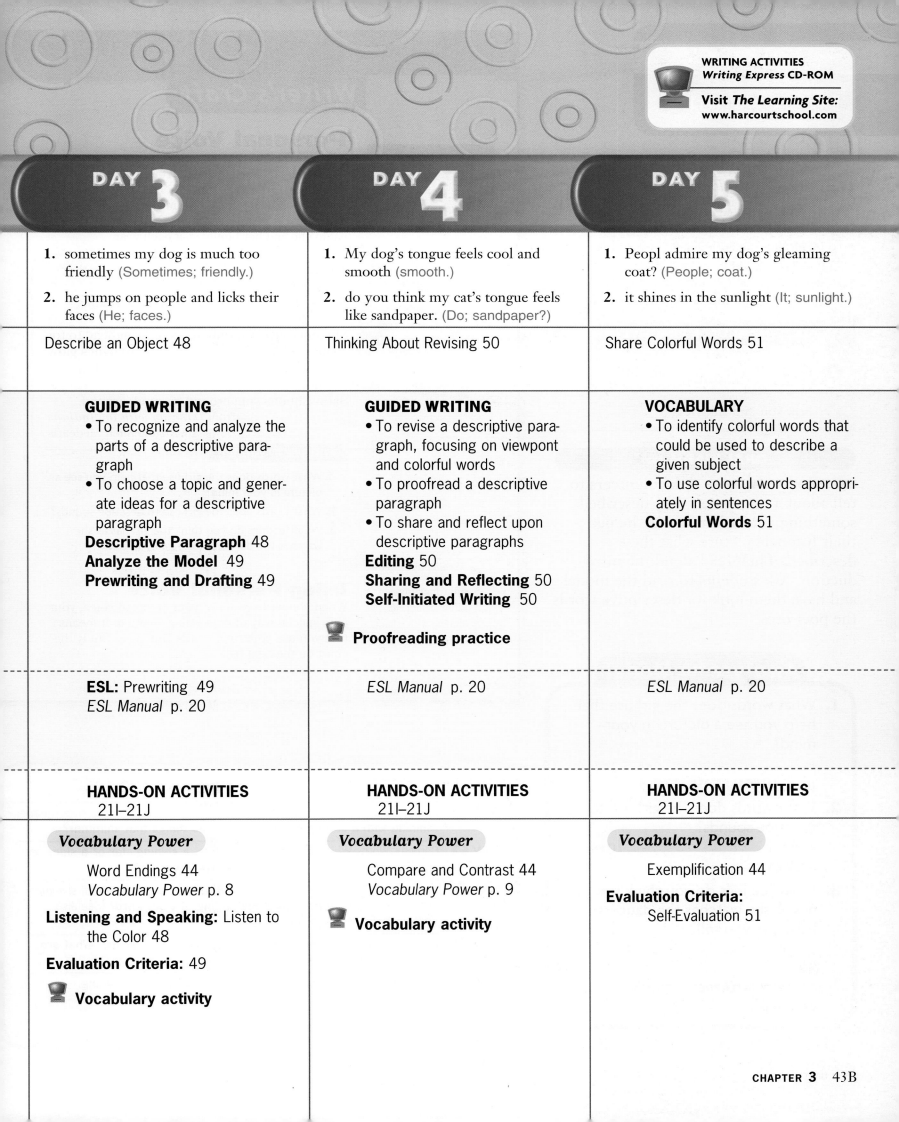 **Vocabulary activity**

DAY 4

1. My dog's tongue feels cool and smooth (smooth.)
2. do you think my cat's tongue feels like sandpaper. (Do; sandpaper?)

Thinking About Revising 50

GUIDED WRITING
- To revise a descriptive paragraph, focusing on viewpont and colorful words
- To proofread a descriptive paragraph
- To share and reflect upon descriptive paragraphs

Editing 50
Sharing and Reflecting 50
Self-Initiated Writing 50

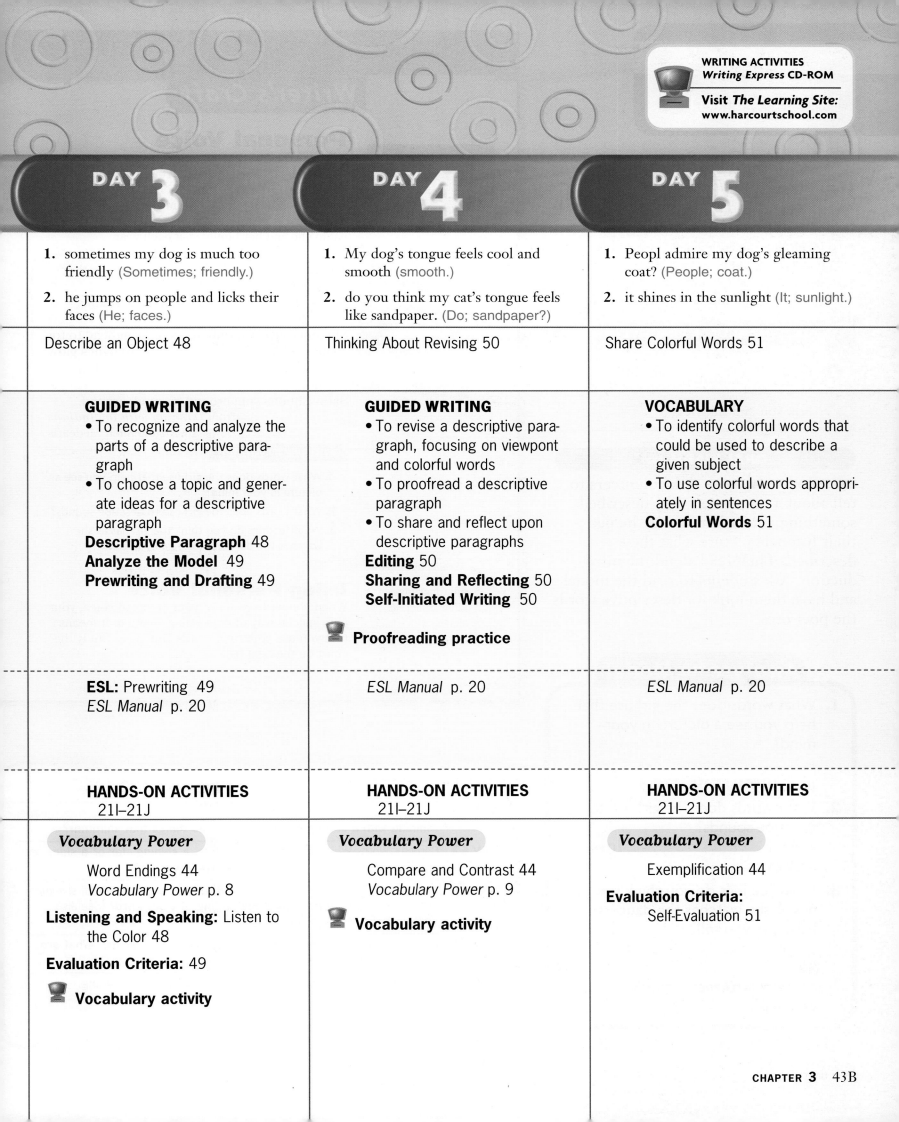 **Proofreading practice**

ESL Manual p. 20

HANDS-ON ACTIVITIES
21I–21J

Vocabulary Power

Compare and Contrast 44
Vocabulary Power p. 9

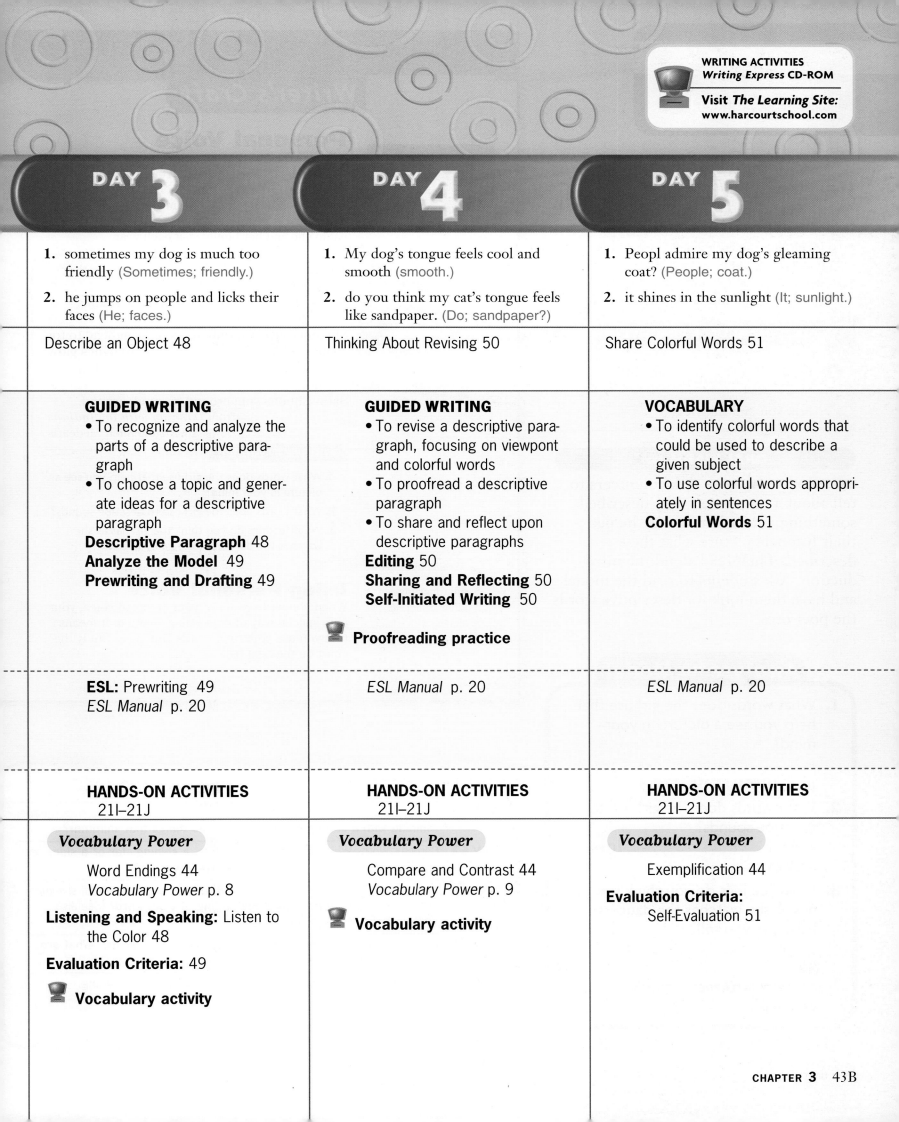 **Vocabulary activity**

DAY 5

1. Peopl admire my dog's gleaming coat? (People; coat.)
2. it shines in the sunlight (It; sunlight.)

Share Colorful Words 51

VOCABULARY
- To identify colorful words that could be used to describe a given subject
- To use colorful words appropriately in sentences

Colorful Words 51

ESL Manual p. 20

HANDS-ON ACTIVITIES
21I–21J

Vocabulary Power

Exemplification 44

Evaluation Criteria:
Self-Evaluation 51

Expressive Writing

Writer's Craft: Personal Voice

OBJECTIVES

- To understand descriptive writing and analyze its use in a passage
- To understand and analyze the use of personal voice and colorful words in descriptive writing

DAILY LANGUAGE PRACTICE

TRANSPARENCY 5

1. my dog's coat is glossy and black (My; black.)

2. how soft and silky it is (How; is!)

ORAL WARM-UP

USE PRIOR KNOWLEDGE Ask volunteers to tell about a time when they described something, and ask how they helped their listeners picture what they described. Then read aloud the introduction. Ask students to read the model, and have them look for descriptive words the poet uses.

Analyze THE Model

1. **What words does the girl use that help you see a picture in your mind?** (Possible responses: *shimmering, float, shining human rainbows, firelight's glow.*) **LITERAL: NOTE DETAILS**

2. **What words does the girl use to describe sounds?** (Possible responses: *tinkling, gentle raindrop sounds*) **LITERAL: NOTE DETAILS**

3. **What feelings do you think the girl has as she watches the dancers? How can you tell?** (Possible responses: She admires the performance. She describes it in a very poetic way.) **CRITICAL: INTERPRET AUTHOR'S VIEWPOINT**

Expressive Writing

Personal Voice

When you describe something, you might tell what you see, hear, smell, or taste. You might tell how something feels when you touch it.

In the following lines, a young girl describes a dance that is performed at the Seminole Indian camp she and her family visit each year.

LITERATURE MODEL

The Ribbon Dance is first. The women gather
around.
Shells on wrists and ankles make a tinkling
sound.
Shimmering satin ribbons float from head to toe,
shining human rainbows in the firelight's glow.
Moccasins of dancers make gentle raindrop
sounds.
Satin ribbons spin around, around, around.

—from *Dancing with the Indians*
by Angela Shelf Medearis

Analyze THE Model

1. What words does the girl use that help you see a picture in your mind?

2. What words does the girl use to describe sounds?

3. What feelings do you think the girl has as she watches the dancers? How can you tell?

Vocabulary Power

shim•mer•ing
[shim′ər•ing] *adj.*
Shining with a faint, unsteady light.

Using Personal Voice

When you write, you use your personal voice, your own special way of expressing yourself. It means that you use your own words and ideas. Study the chart on the next page.

Vocabulary Power

DAY 1 EXPLORE WORD MEANING Introduce and define *shimmering*. **Shimmering means "shining with a soft light." What are some things that shimmer?**

DAY 2 COLORFUL WORDS **Which is more descriptive, a *shining* star or a *shimmering* star? Why?** (See also *Vocabulary Power*, page 7.)

DAY 3 WORD ENDINGS Write on the board: *shimmer, shimmers, shimmered, shimmering*. **What do you notice about the ending of each word?** (See also *Vocabulary Power*, page 8.)

DAY 4 COMPARE AND CONTRAST Have students name things that shimmer. **What are some things that glare?** (See also *Vocabulary Power*, page 9.)

DAY 5 EXEMPLIFICATION **Write *shimmer* in a way that shows its meaning.**

Strategies for Using Personal Voice	How to Use Strategies	Examples
Use colorful words.	• Use interesting words that help your reader picture the thing you are describing.	• Use words like *skipped* or *tiptoed* instead of *went*. Use words like *huge* or *giant* instead of *big*.
Express your own viewpoint.	• Let your reader know how you feel about the subject.	• Suppose you are describing a lizard. If you think it is ugly and scary, say so. If you think it is beautiful and fascinating, say so.

YOUR TURN

THINK ABOUT DESCRIPTIVE WRITING Work with one or two classmates. Look back at stories or poems that you have read. In each one, find parts in which the writer has described something. Take turns reading these parts aloud.

Answer these questions:

1. What is the writer describing?
2. What colorful words does the writer use?
3. How do these words help you see a picture in your mind?
4. How does the writer feel about the subject? How can you tell?

45

USING PERSONAL VOICE Display a picture of a snake, a spider, or another animal that will elicit various responses from students. Ask students to suggest words to describe the creature, and write their responses on the board. Point out any colorful words. Ask: **Which words seem positive, as if the person likes the animal? Which words seem negative, as if the person doesn't like the animal?** Point out that word choice is one way of revealing a writer's "voice" and that students' word choices in this activity reflect how they feel about the animal in the picture.

Discuss the chart on page 45. Then have students read the directions for the Your Turn activity. As students work together to locate and read descriptive passages and poems, offer guidance as needed.

WRAP-UP/ASSESS

SUMMARIZE What are some ways to create an effective description? What is a writer's personal voice?

CHALLENGE

Art

PICTURE THIS Have students work with partners. One student should read a descriptive passage from a story or poem to a partner. The partner tries to picture the thing in his or her mind and then makes a drawing based on this mental picture. Have students take turns choosing a passage and drawing a picture.

Encourage students to share their pictures and descriptions.

HOW I SEE IT Have students explore the effect of viewpoint by following these steps:

- Select a familiar subject.
- Describe the subject the way you think someone who likes or admires it might describe it.
- Write about the subject again. Describe it the way you think someone who doesn't like it or who fears it might describe it.

Ask students to read the descriptions and to comment upon the differences.

TECHNOLOGY Additional writing activities are provided on the *Writing Express* CD-ROM

Writer's Craft: Personal Voice

OBJECTIVES
- To identify a writer's viewpoint and to use colorful words
- To record reflections about personal viewpoints

DAILY LANGUAGE PRACTICE

TRANSPARENCY 5

1 my dog has a feathery tail (My; tail.)

2 he waves it like a plume? (He; plume.)

ORAL WARM-UP

USE PRIOR KNOWLEDGE Read aloud these two sentences: *The dog went up the stairs. The dog bounded up the stairs.* Ask: **Which description is more effective? Why?**

GUIDED WRITING

USING COLORFUL WORDS Explain that colorful words can be nouns or interesting words that tell more about nouns. For example, saying *the hilarious movie* is more interesting and more colorful than saying *the funny movie*. The action word *paraded* is more interesting and colorful than *walked*. Have students choose a colorful word to complete each sentence in Part A, using each word only once.
(1. wrinkled, 2. muddy, 3. huge, 4. yelled, 5. scurried)

As students read the directions for Part B, point out that there are many correct answers. In fact, a variety of answers is a sign of personal voice at work. When students have completed Part B, have volunteers share their revised sentences.
(Possible responses: 6. Look at that awesome bike! 7. She gobbled the apple. 8. Sara heard a scratching sound. 9. Hector scooped up the box. 10. Did you see that hawk? 11. What a glorious sunset! 12. Henry has a German shepherd. 13. We played hopscotch outside. 14. Do you like these sneakers? 15. I will wear a sundress to the social.)

Using Colorful Words

A. Choose a colorful word from the box to complete each sentence. Write the sentence on your paper.

yelled	wrinkled	huge	muddy	scurried

1. The elephant had _____ gray skin.
2. It was drinking some _____ water.
3. It lifted its _____ trunk.
4. "Oh, it's going to spray us!" Timmy _____.
5. Everyone _____ out of the way.

B. Read the sentences. Think of colorful words you can add to create a clear picture for the reader. Write the revised sentences on your paper.

6. Look at that bike.
7. She ate the apple.
8. Sara heard a sound.
9. Hector picked up the box.
10. Did you see that bird?
11. What a beautiful sunset!
12. Henry has a dog.
13. We played outside.
14. Do you like these shoes?
15. I will wear a dress to the party.

Vocabulary Power page 7

Name _____

COLORFUL WORDS

Colorful words make writing more interesting. Read each sentence part and its word choices. Write the most colorful word to complete each sentence part.

1. the _____ sparkling _____ necklace
   pretty sparkling

2. the _____ fluffy _____ bunny
   fluffy soft

3. the _____ twinkling _____ star
   twinkling bright

4. the _____ enormous _____ elephant
   big enormous

5. the _____ glimmering _____ candle
   glimmering nice

6. the _____ sluggish _____ snail
   slow sluggish

7. the _____ shimmering _____ water
   shimmering pretty

8. the _____ glistening _____ jewel
   glistening shiny

9. the _____ fierce _____ bear
   mean fierce

10. the _____ delicious _____ ice-cream cone
    good delicious

Vocabulary Power   Unit 1 • Chapter 3   7

Writer's Viewpoint

C. **Read each description and the questions that follow it. Write the answer to each question on your paper.**

Description 1: There were three plump peaches in the bowl. I could imagine how sweet and juicy they would taste.

16. Does the writer like or dislike peaches?
17. How do you know the writer's viewpoint?

Description 2: The old house was a terrible mess. Everything was dusty and dirty.

18. What is the writer's viewpoint about the house?
19. How do you know how the writer feels?

Description 3: The little bug darted across the floor. It had pretty yellow stripes that seemed to glow in the sunshine.

20. How does the writer feel about the bug?
21. How do you know the writer's viewpoint?

Writing AND Thinking

Writer's Journal

Write to Record Reflections Many writers have favorite subjects that they write about often. In your Writer's Journal, list two or three of your favorite subjects. Then explain your viewpoint on each of these subjects, and tell why you like to write about them.

47

Writer's Viewpoint

Remind students that the words a writer chooses to describe something often suggest how the writer feels about it. Complete Part C orally with students.

(Possible responses: 16. The writer likes peaches. 17. The words *plump, sweet,* and *juicy* tell that the writer likes peaches. 18. The writer has a negative attitude toward the house. 19. Descriptions like *terrible mess* and *dusty and dirty* tell that the writer is unhappy about the house. 20. The writer seems to like the bug. 21. The writer calls the bug *pretty* and says that its yellow stripes *seemed to glow in the sunshine.*

Writing and Thinking

Writer's Journal

Write to Record Reflections Tell students that a subject can be a "favorite subject" for different reasons. Students might like to write about a subject because it is something that they like and know a lot about. Emphasize that what students record in their Writer's Journals is private—that is, students will share this work only if they wish to do so. Give students ample time to record their reflections.

WRAP-UP/ASSESS

SUMMARIZE What are some ways to show personal voice in writing?

CHALLENGE

REACHING ALL LEARNERS

Vocabulary

SYNONYM STUDY Explain to students that colorful words are synonyms for more ordinary words. Use the words *looked at, saw,* and *stared at* as examples. Explain that *stared at* is the most colorful synonym. Then have students brainstorm synonyms for *ran, walked, sat,* and *said.* Ask students to think about when it might be appropriate to use each synonym that they list.

COLOR CHECK Have students choose one of the favorite topics that they listed in their Writer's Journal and write a paragraph about it. Have partners trade paragraphs and analyze each other's writing by doing the following:

- Underline the colorful words that the writer used.
- Name the feelings that these words suggest.
- Explain the viewpoint that is expressed in the paragraph.

Writer's Craft: Personal Voice

OBJECTIVES
- To recognize and analyze the parts of a descriptive paragraph
- To choose a topic and generate ideas for a descriptive paragraph

DAILY LANGUAGE PRACTICE

TRANSPARENCY 5

1 sometimes my dog is much too friendly (Sometimes; friendly.)

2 he jumps on people and licks their faces (He; faces.)

ORAL WARM-UP

USE PRIOR KNOWLEDGE Hold up a common classroom object. Ask students to describe it. Point out that the different words reflect the students' personal voices.

GUIDED WRITING

Descriptive Paragraph

READ AND RESPOND TO THE MODEL Tell students that you will read aloud Darryl's descriptive paragraph, and have them determine a purpose for listening. (to find colorful words; to figure out the writer's viewpoint) When you have finished reading, ask students to discuss Darryl's choice of details and his viewpoint.

FOCUS ON ORGANIZATION Have students reread Darryl's paragraph silently, using the side notes to find the main parts. Point out that Darryl doesn't tell what he's describing until the second sentence.

FOCUS ON WRITER'S CRAFT Ask: **How did Darryl's thoughts about the swans change?** Have students compare the words that Darryl uses at the beginning of the description with those at the end. (at the beginning: skim, skaters, curved; at the end: huge splash, beating, enormous)

Writing a Descriptive Paragraph

In the lines from *Dancing with the Indians*, a girl describes a beautiful dance she saw on a trip with her family. When Darryl went to the park with his family, he saw swans swimming on a pond. Read this descriptive paragraph that Darryl wrote about the swans. Look for colorful words.

MODEL

colorful words

writer's viewpoint

> Some large white birds were swimming on the pond. My dad said they were swans. I watched them skim silently across the water like skaters on ice. Their long necks curved gently from side to side. Suddenly there was a huge splash! The biggest swan rose up, beating the water with its enormous wings. I jumped, and then I laughed. Those swans weren't so gentle and quiet after all!

Analyze THE Model

1. What colorful words does Darryl use to tell what he saw and heard?
2. What words in Darryl's paragraph do you like? Why do you like them?
3. What is Darryl's viewpoint about the swans? How do you know?
4. Does the paragraph give you a clear picture of what Darryl saw and heard? Why or why not?

48

Vocabulary Power page 8

Name _____

WORD ENDINGS

Complete the word puzzles. Add the endings *-s*, *-ed*, and *-ing* to each word.

1. sparkle

   s p a r k l e s
   s p a r k l e d
   s p a r k l i n g

2. twinkle

   t w i n k l e s
   t w i n k l e d
   t w i n k l i n g

3. glimmer

   g l i m m e r s
   g l i m m e r e d
   g l i m m e r i n g

4. glisten

   g l i s t e n s
   g l i s t e n e d
   g l i s t e n i n g

5. shimmer

   s h i m m e r s
   s h i m m e r e d
   s h i m m e r i n g

8 Unit 1 • Chapter 3   Vocabulary Power

Listening and Speaking

LISTEN TO THE COLOR Have students work in pairs to describe an event that occurred during the summer. It may be something they saw or something they did. Students should take turns describing and listening.

Ask students to use colorful words and vocabulary to describe their feelings, ideas, and experiences.

WRITING PROMPT Look around your classroom. Find an interesting object that you would like to describe. You might choose something that you especially like or dislike. Write a paragraph to tell about the object. Use colorful words to help your reader picture the object you are describing. Express your feelings and viewpoint in your writing.

STUDY THE PROMPT Ask yourself these questions:

1. How will you choose a subject to write about?
2. What is your purpose for writing?
3. What will you include in your paragraph?

Prewriting and Drafting

Plan Your Descriptive Paragraph Make a web like this one to help you get started. Write the name of the object in the center of your web.

- colorful words that tell what the object looks like
- colorful words that tell what sound the object might make
- what the object does or what you do with it
- Name of Object
- colorful words that tell how the object feels when you touch it
- your viewpoint about the object
- colorful words that tell about any smell or taste the object might have

USING YOUR Handbook

- Use the Writer's Thesaurus to find colorful words that will help you describe your object.

49

Analyze THE Model

1. **What colorful words does Darryl use to tell what he saw and heard?** (Possible responses: *skim, skaters, curved, huge splash, beating, enormous.*) **LITERAL: NOTE DETAILS**

2. **What words in Darryl's paragraph do you like? Why do you like them?** (Responses will vary.) **CRITICAL: APPRECIATE LANGUAGE**

3. **What is Darryl's viewpoint about the swans? How do you know?** (Possible responses: Darryl thinks that swans are not as gentle and quiet as they seem. He tells us that in the conclusion.) **CRITICAL: INTERPRET AUTHOR'S VIEWPOINT**

4. **Does the paragraph give you a clear picture of what Darryl saw and heard? Why or why not?** (Possible response: The details he uses create a clear picture and capture Darryl's surprise.) **CRITICAL: MAKE JUDGMENTS**

Read the directions for the Your Turn activity with students, emphasizing that students should have a clear opinion about the subject they choose.

Prewriting and Drafting

Have students brainstorm subjects and think about what they might say about each one. Have students create a web to identify colorful words for their description and to clarify their viewpoint. Students may want to number the parts of their webs and present the elements of their descriptions in that order.

WRAP-UP/ASSESS

SUMMARIZE Why are colorful words important in descriptive writing?

Evaluation Criteria

Review the criteria that students should apply:

- Use colorful words
- Express your own writer's viewpoint
- Use proper form for a descriptive paragraph

Work with students to add additional criteria.

ESL

PREWRITING Allow students to brainstorm possible subjects and create their webs with an English-fluent partner. Have students work together to use their Writer's Thesaurus.

Writer's Craft: Personal Voice

OBJECTIVES

- To revise a descriptive paragraph, focusing on viewpoint and colorful words
- To proofread a descriptive paragraph
- To share and reflect upon descriptive paragraphs

1. My dog's tongue feels cool and smooth (smooth.)
2. do you think my cat's tongue feels like sandpaper. (Do; sandpaper?)

ORAL WARM-UP

USE PRIOR KNOWLEDGE What will you think about as you revise the draft of your paragraph?

GUIDED WRITING

Editing

Thoroughly explain the editing marks and model the use of each one.

To help students evaluate their writing, have them trade paragraphs with a partner and study each other's writing. Ask students to respond constructively to each other's writing. After they revise and proofread their paragraphs, have students trade papers again to proofread their partner's work.

Sharing and Reflecting

Encourage students to try to picture the subject as they listen to their classmates' writing. Point out that this will help them recognize the colorful words that make the descriptions effective.

WRAP-UP/ASSESS

SUMMARIZE Why is it important to revise and proofread writing?

Editor's Marks

- ℐ take out text
- ∧ add text
- ◠ move text
- ¶ new paragraph
- ≡ capitalize
- / lowercase
- ◯ correct spelling

Editing

Read over the draft of your paragraph. Do you want to change or add anything? Use this checklist to help you revise your paragraph:

- ☑ Do you think your reader will be able to picture the object?
- ☑ Can you use more colorful words to describe the object?
- ☑ Did you express your viewpoint?
- ☑ How did you use your personal voice in your paragraph?

Use this checklist as you proofread your paragraph:

- ☑ I have begun my sentences with capital letters.
- ☑ I have used the correct end marks for my sentences.
- ☑ I have checked to see that each sentence has a subject and a predicate.
- ☑ I have used a dictionary to check spelling.

Sharing and Reflecting

Writer's Journal

Make a final copy of your paragraph. Then read it to two of your classmates. Listen as they read their paragraphs. Tell what you like best about their descriptions. Share ideas about how you can improve your writing by using colorful words and by expressing your viewpoint. Write your reflections in your Writer's Journal.

50

Vocabulary Power page 9

Name _____

COMPARE AND CONTRAST

The words *glare* and *shimmer* are alike in some ways and different in others. Look at the diagram below. In the center circle, write the word from the Word Box that tells about both words. In the circle with *glare*, write the five words that tell only about *glare*. In the circle with *shimmer*, write the six words that tell only about *shimmer*.

harsh	gentle	soft	fierce
burn	glistening	sparkling	shine
bright	twinkling	uncomfortable	glimmering

glare
harsh
uncomfortable
bright
fierce
burn

both
shine

shimmer
gentle
soft
twinkling
glistening
sparkling
glimmering

Vocabulary Power   Unit 1 • Chapter 3   9

Self-Initiated Writing

Provide students with the opportunity for self-initiated writing by allowing them to use free time in the classroom to write descriptive paragraphs on the topic of their choice.

Colorful Words

A group of third graders thought of colorful words they could use to describe something that shines. Look at the words in the web they made.

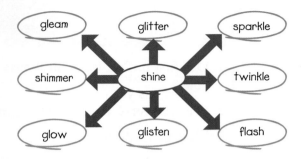

YOUR TURN

Play a game with colorful words. Follow these steps:

STEP 1 Sit in a circle with two or three classmates.

STEP 2 Take turns picking a word from the web.

STEP 3 Challenge the person on your left to use your word in a sentence.

STEP 4 Then that person has a turn to choose a word and challenge the next person. When you make up a sentence, think about the exact meaning of the word. For example, you might say that a star shines, but you probably wouldn't say it flashes.

STEP 5 Continue until you have used all the words.

After you play the game, your group can try making a web of your own. You might brainstorm words that you can use to describe something cold or to describe a sound the wind makes.

51

Evaluation Criteria

• • • • • • • • • • • • • • • • • • • •

SELF-EVALUATION Revisit the Evaluation Criteria to have students informally rate their own writing on a scale of 1 to 4. You might have them use stick-on notes to label their papers.

VOCABULARY
Colorful Words

OBJECTIVES
- To identify colorful words that could be used to describe a given subject
- To use colorful words appropriately in sentences

 DAILY LANGUAGE PRACTICE

TRANSPARENCY 6

1 Peopl admire my dog's gleaming coat? (People; coat.)

2 it shines in the sunlight (It; sunlight.)

ORAL WARM-UP

USE PRIOR KNOWLEDGE Ask volunteers to share words from their descriptions that they think are well chosen and colorful.

TEACH/MODEL

Point out that all the words in the web on page 51 describe something that shines but that not all of them could be used to describe the same thing. For example, stars *twinkle*, but planets *glow*. Have students suggest other things that twinkle.

To prepare for the Your Turn activity, select words at random from the web. Have volunteers name items that might be described by the word.

WRAP-UP/ASSESS

SUMMARIZE Why is it important to know the meanings of colorful words you use in your writing?

Predicates

LESSON ORGANIZER	DAY 1	DAY 2
DAILY LANGUAGE PRACTICE 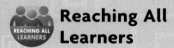 TRANSPARENCIES 7, 8	**1.** my father likes to build things. (My) **2.** He wirks in his shop (works; shop.) **Bridge to Writing** <u>(Subject)</u> has a new house.	**1.** Our first project was a birdhouse (bird-house.) **2.** We used verry tiny nails? (very; nails.) **Bridge to Writing** The birds <u>(predicate)</u> .
ORAL WARM-UP **Listening/Speaking**	Describe What Workers Do 52	Complete the Sentence 54 *Grammar Jingles*™ CD Track 3
TEACH/MODEL **GRAMMAR** **KEY** ✔ = tested skill	✔ **COMPLETE AND SIMPLE PREDICATES** 52-53 • To identify complete and simple predicates in sentences • To identify complete and simple predicates in writing	✔ **VERBS IN PREDICATES** 54-55 • To identify the verb in a predicate • To write descriptive sentences using vivid verbs
Reaching All Learners	**Modified Instruction** Below-Level: Circle the Subject Above-Level: Write New Sentences **Reteach:** *Reteach Activities Copying Masters* pp. 7 and R40 **Challenge:** Activity Card 3, R63 *ESL Manual* pp. 22, 23 *Practice Book* p. 11	**Modified Instruction** Below-Level: Circle the Subject Above-Level: Rewrite Sentences **ESL:** Add Predicates 54 *ESL Manual* pp. 22, 24 **Reteach:** *Reteach Activities Copying Masters* pp. 8 and R40 **Challenge:** Story Setting 55 *Practice Book* p. 12
WRITING	Writing Connection 53 Technology	Writing Connection 55 Writer's Craft: Vivid Verbs
CROSS-CURRICULAR/ ENRICHMENT	*Vocabulary Power* Explore Word Meaning 52 **carpenter,** electrician, machinist, mason, plumber See *Vocabulary Power* book.	*Vocabulary Power* Classify/Categorize 52 *Vocabulary Power* p. 10 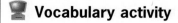 **Vocabulary activity**

DAY 3

1. can we learn to hammer and saw (Can; saw?)

2. My father uses a tape measure (measure.)

Bridge to Writing I (simple predicate) it myself!

Identify Subject and Predicate 56
Grammar Jingles™ CD Track 3

✔ **COMBINING SENTENCES: COMPOUND PREDICATES** 56-57
- To combine sentences to make compound predicates
- To draw a picture and write descriptive sentences

Modified Instruction
Below-Level: Model the Thinking
Above-Level: Rewrite Sentences
ESL: Combine Sentences 56
ESL Manual pp. 22, 25
Reteach: *Reteach Activities Copying Masters* pp. 9 and R40
Challenge: Invention 57
Practice Book p. 13

 Writing Connection 57
Writer's Journal: Describe a Room

Vocabulary Power

Analogies 52
Vocabulary Power p. 11

💻 **Vocabulary activity**

DAY 4

1. A carpenter buildds a house. (builds)

2. the house is so big! (The)

Bridge to Writing I will paint the kitchen (combining word) rake leaves.

Name the Predicate 58

EXTRA PRACTICE 58-59
- To identify predicates and verbs
- To combine sentences by using compound predicates
- To write sentences that compare

💻 **Practice and assessment**

Building Oral Grammar
Read Aloud and Combine Sentences 59
Challenge: Write Sentences 59
ESL Manual pp. 22, 26
Practice Book p. 14

 Writing Connection 59
Technology

Art: Study a Building 58

Vocabulary Power

Compare and Contrast 52
Vocabulary Power p. 12

💻 **Vocabulary activity**

DAY 5

1. Have you learned to cut straight (straight?)

2. carpenters measure boards. (Carpenters)

Bridge to Writing Carpenters (simple predicate) furniture for homes. Architects (compound predicate) new buildings.

TEST PREP **CHAPTER REVIEW** 60-61
- To review verbs and simple, complete, and compound predicates
- To learn and practice greetings in languages other than English

💻 **Test preparation**

Challenge: Learn a Greeting 61
Practice Book p. 15
ESL Manual pp. 22, 27

Writing Application 61
Write a Short Story

Vocabulary: Words from Many Places 61

Vocabulary Power

Explore Word Meaning 52

Complete and Simple Predicates

OBJECTIVES
- To identify complete and simple predicates in sentences
- To identify simple and complete predicates in writing

DAILY LANGUAGE PRACTICE

TRANSPARENCY 7

1 my father likes to build things. (My)

2 He wirks in his shop (works; shop.)

BRIDGE TO WRITING (Subject) has a new house.

ORAL WARM-UP

USE PRIOR KNOWLEDGE Ask students to describe what workers do at a construction site. Ask: **Which words tell what the workers do?**

TEACH/MODEL

Have students read the explanation of simple and complete predicates on page 52. Tell students that to identify the predicate, they should first identify the subject of the sentence. Then they can find the predicate by asking what the subject does or is. Model the thinking, using the Guided Practice example:

MODEL The subject of the sentence is *The builder*. I ask myself what the builder does or is. The words that tell what the builder does are *makes a plan for a new building*. This is the complete predicate. To decide which word is the simple predicate, I look for the main word in the complete predicate. *Makes* must be the simple predicate.

Complete the Guided Practice exercises orally with students.

Vocabulary Power

car·pen·ter
[kär′pən·tər] *n.*
A person who makes, builds, or repairs things, often using wood.

52

Complete and Simple Predicates

Every sentence has a subject and a predicate.

The complete predicate is all the words that tell what the subject of the sentence is or does. The predicate usually follows the subject of a sentence.

The simple predicate is the main word in the complete predicate.

The bold words in the sentences below are the complete predicates. The underlined words are the simple predicates.

Examples:

Houses, schools, and stores <u>are</u> **buildings**.

A building <u>has</u> **many parts**.

The roof <u>covers</u> **the building**.

Guided Practice

A. Read each sentence. Name the complete predicate. Then tell which word is the simple predicate.

Example: The builder makes a plan for a new building.
makes a plan for a new building|makes

Complete predicates are underlined once; simple predicates are underlined twice

1. Mr. Thompson <u>built</u> our new house.
2. He <u>drew</u> a plan for the house.
3. The plan <u>is</u> a blueprint.
4. The blueprint <u>shows</u> all the floors and rooms.
5. My bedroom <u>is</u> the big room upstairs.

Vocabulary Power

DAY 1 EXPLORE WORD MEANING Introduce and define *carpenter*. Ask students if a carpenter ever came to their home. **What are some things a carpenter does?**

DAY 2 CLASSIFY/CATEGORIZE Remind students that a carpenter is one kind of worker. Write on the board: *carpenter, house, photographer, pilot.* **Which word does not belong in this group?** (See also *Vocabulary Power*, page 10.)

DAY 3 ANALOGIES **What word completes this sentence: *Carpenters work with wood. Painters work with _____.*** (See also *Vocabulary Power*, page 11.)

DAY 4 COMPARE AND CONTRAST Ask students to compare and contrast a carpenter and a mason. **How are they alike? How are they different?** (See also *Vocabulary Power*, page 12.)

DAY 5 EXPLORE WORD MEANING Discuss: **What skills might a carpenter need? A plumber?**

Independent Practice

B. Write each sentence. Underline the complete predicate.

Example: The carpenter told us about building a house.
The carpenter told us about building a house.

6. Carpenters follow a blueprint.
7. The frame is wood or steel.
8. The floors in our house have carpets.
9. The walls of my room are blue.
10. This wall has a big picture window.

C. Write each sentence. Underline the simple predicate.

11. The new front door squeaks sometimes.
12. The carpenter planned the house well.
13. This house looks beautiful.
14. Someone built Sasha's home 100 years ago.
15. Our house is new.

Remember that the complete predicate tells what the subject is or does.

Writing Connection

Technology When do you think the place you live in was built? How do you think it was built? Talk to your family members or neighbors about the place you live. Then use a computer or books from the library to find out more about building homes. Write some sentences about what you learn. Then underline the complete predicate in each sentence. Circle the simple predicate.

Independent Practice

Have students complete the Independent Practice, or modify it using these suggestions:

MODIFIED INSTRUCTION

BELOW-LEVEL STUDENTS Have students circle the subject of each sentence before deciding on the complete and simple predicate.

ABOVE-LEVEL STUDENTS Have students write one new sentence for each activity and underline the appropriate part of the sentence.

Writing Connection

Technology Have students contribute to a class discussion of different types of homes and building materials. Students should then write questions for researching their own homes. If possible, have students investigate different ways to build homes by using the Internet.

WRAP-UP/ASSESS

SUMMARIZE Ask students to tell how to find the predicate of a sentence. Ask them to describe the difference between a simple predicate and a complete predicate.

RETEACH

INTERVENTION Lessons in **visual, auditory,** and **kinesthetic** modalities: p. R40 and *Reteach Activities Copying Masters,* p. 7.

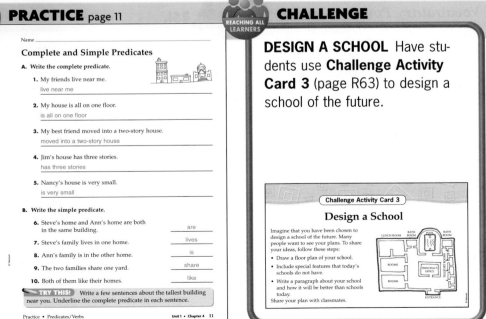

PRACTICE page 11

Name _____

Complete and Simple Predicates

A. Write the complete predicate.

1. My friends live near me.
   live near me
2. My house is all on one floor.
   is all on one floor
3. My best friend moved into a two-story house.
   moved into a two-story house
4. Jim's house has three stories.
   has three stories
5. Nancy's house is very small.
   is very small

B. Write the simple predicate.

6. Steve's home and Ann's home are both in the same building. — are
7. Steve's family lives in one home. — lives
8. Ann's family is in the other home. — is
9. The two families share one yard. — share
10. Both of them like their homes. — like

TRY THIS! Write a few sentences about the tallest building near you. Underline the complete predicate in each sentence.

Practice • Predicates/Verbs   Unit 1 • Chapter 4 **11**

CHALLENGE

DESIGN A SCHOOL Have students use **Challenge Activity Card 3** (page R63) to design a school of the future.

Challenge Activity Card 3

Design a School

Imagine that you have been chosen to design a school of the future. Many people want to see your plans. To share your ideas, follow these steps:
• Draw a floor plan of your school.
• Include special features that today's schools do not have.
• Write a paragraph about your school and how it will be better than schools today.
Share your plan with classmates.

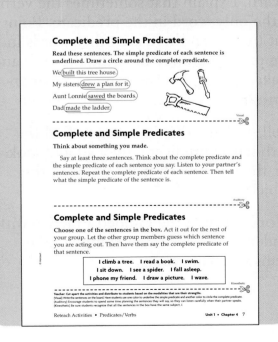

Complete and Simple Predicates

Read these sentences. The simple predicate of each sentence is underlined. Draw a circle around the complete predicate.

We built this tree house.
My sisters drew a plan for it.
Aunt Lonnie sawed the boards.
Dad made the ladder.

Complete and Simple Predicates

Think about something you made.

Say at least three sentences. Think about the complete predicate and the simple predicate of each sentence you say. Listen to your partner's sentences. Repeat the complete predicate of each sentence. Then tell what the simple predicate of the sentence is.

Complete and Simple Predicates

Choose one of the sentences in the box. Act it out for the rest of your group. Let the other group members guess which sentence you are acting out. Then have them say the complete predicate of that sentence.

I climb a tree.   I read a book.   I swim.
I sit down.   I see a spider.   I fall asleep.
I phone my friend.   I draw a picture.   I wave.

Reteach Activities • Predicates/Verbs   Unit 1 • Chapter 4 **7**

Verbs in Predicates

OBJECTIVES
- To identify the verb in a predicate
- To write descriptive sentences, using vivid verbs

DAILY LANGUAGE PRACTICE

TRANSPARENCY 7

1 Our first project was a birdhouse
(birdhouse.)

2 We used verry tiny nails? (very; nails.)

BRIDGE TO WRITING The birds
(predicate) .

ORAL WARM-UP

USE PRIOR KNOWLEDGE Write this sentence on the board: *People _____ in many types of buildings.* Have students suggest words that complete the sentence.

 Grammar Jingles™ **CD, Intermediate** Use Track 3 for review and reinforcement of predicates.

TEACH/MODEL

Read aloud the explanation and examples on page 54. Remind students that the complete predicate is all the words in the predicate. The simple predicate is always a verb. Explain that sometimes the verb is the only word in the predicate. Point out that when there are other words in the predicate, they describe the verb and make writing and speaking more interesting.

Tell students that in order to find the verb in the predicate, they should look for the main word that tells what the subject is or does.

Work through the Guided Practice with students, or have them complete the items in small groups.

 Remember

that every
predicate has a
verb that tells
what the subject
is or does.

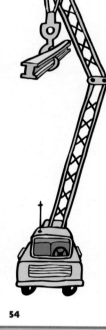

54

Verbs in Predicates

The verb is the main word in the predicate of a sentence.

Every predicate has a verb that tells what the subject is or does. The verb is the same word as the simple predicate. The other words in the predicate tell more about the verb.

The bold words in the sentences below are the complete predicates. The underlined words are the verbs.

Examples:
Jack's father **builds tall buildings in New York**.

The Empire State Building **is steel**.

We **run up the stairs**.

Guided Practice

A. Read each sentence. Find the verb in the underlined predicate.

Example: Some tall buildings *rise more than 100 stories*. rise

1. Construction of these tall buildings takes a year or more. takes
2. The carpenters build the lower floors first. build
3. Cranes lift large pieces of steel. lift
4. The workers construct the stairs. construct
5. Some office buildings have glass walls. have
6. The workers connect the pipes. connect
7. José starts the electric power. starts
8. Large buildings have rooms of many sizes. have
9. Tommy's mom has a new desk. has
10. Tommy sees a pattern in the wallpaper. sees

Vocabulary Power page 10

Name _____

CLASSIFY AND CATEGORIZE

Read each group of words below. Circle the letter of the word that does not belong in each group. Then add a category name for each group. The first one has been done for you.

1	A carpenter	6	F chair
	B mason		G toast
	(C) doctor		H cereal
	D builder		J pancakes
	people who build things		things you eat for breakfast
2	F hammer	7	A electrician
	G nails		B plumber
	H screwdriver		(C) wood
	(J) house		D machinist
	tools		people who fix things
3	A brick	8	F fruit punch
	(B) candle		(G) window
	C wood		H soda
	D steel		J milk
	building materials		things you drink
4	F apple	9	A crayon
	G banana		B pen
	H green bean		C pencil
	(J) grape		(D) tree
	fruits		things you write with
5	A jungle gym	10	F quarter
	B seesaw		G dollar
	C swings		(H) fan
	(D) tomato		J nickel
	playground equipment		coins

10 Unit 1 • Chapter 4   Vocabulary Power

ESL
REACHING ALL LEARNERS

ADD PREDICATES Write the following subjects on the board:

My house

Some apartment buildings

The office building

Our school

Ask students to complete the sentences by adding predicates. Then have them underline the verb in each predicate.

Independent Practice

B. Write each sentence. Underline the complete predicate once. Underline the verb twice.

Example: Mrs. Venegas draws plans for many kinds of buildings.
Mrs. Venegas draws plans for many kinds of buildings.

11. She designs schools, hospitals, and hotels.
12. Mrs. Venegas studies pictures of old buildings.
13. She gets ideas from the pictures.
14. The Venegas Company built the new mall near my house.
15. They made the mall a good shopping place.
16. We shop at the department stores.
17. I like stores with bright lights and soft carpets.
18. The newspaper printed ads for the new mall.
19. Food stands fill the center of the mall.
20. Mrs. Venegas won an award for her design.

Writing Connection

Writer's Craft: Vivid Verbs Think of a place where you like to go. What can you do there? Write about that place, using interesting verbs in your predicates. Then underline the verbs you use.

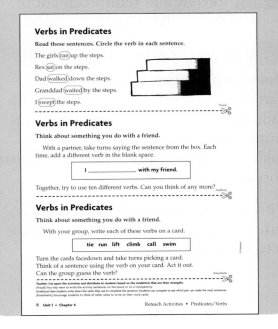

55

Independent Practice

Have students complete the Independent Practice, or modify it using these suggestions:

MODIFIED INSTRUCTION

BELOW-LEVEL STUDENTS For each sentence, ask students to circle the subject and then ask themselves what this subject is or does.

ABOVE-LEVEL STUDENTS Have students select five of the sentences to rewrite with new verbs. Tell them to be sure that the verbs they use make sense in the sentence.

Writing Connection

Writer's Craft: Vivid Verbs As a prewriting technique, show students how to arrange their ideas in a word web with the name of their place in the center circle and the activities they do there in connecting circles. Tell students to use their webs to write their paragraph.

WRAP-UP/ASSESS

SUMMARIZE Ask students how to find the verb in a sentence.

RETEACH

INTERVENTION Lessons in **visual, auditory,** and **kinesthetic** modalities: p. R40 and *Reteach Activities Copying Masters,* p. 8.

PRACTICE page 12

Name _____

Verbs in Predicates

A. Write the verb in the predicate.

1. Builders sometimes build large apartment buildings. — build
2. An apartment building is a building with several homes. — is
3. We call each home an apartment. — call
4. An apartment usually has its own kitchen, living room, bathrooms, and bedrooms. — has
5. Many people live in apartment buildings. — live

B. Write the sentence. Circle the verb.

6. Mr. Vargas owns an apartment building.
   Mr. Vargas (owns) an apartment building.
7. People rent apartments from him.
   People (rent) apartments from him.
8. They pay him money every month for their apartments.
   They (pay) him money every month for their apartments.
9. This money is their rent.
   This money (is) their rent.

TRY THIS! Suppose you lived in an apartment building. What might be good about living there? Circle all the verbs in your predicates.

12 Unit 1 • Chapter 4   Practice • Predicates/Verbs

CHALLENGE

STORY SETTING Have students research different types of houses by using an encyclopedia or the Internet. Then ask students to write a short story featuring one type of house as the setting. After writing, students should underline the verbs in each sentence.

Verbs in Predicates

Read these sentences. Circle the verb in each sentence.

The girls (ran) up the steps.
Rex (sat) on the steps.
Dad (walked) down the steps.
Granddad (waited) by the steps.
I (swept) the steps.

Verbs in Predicates

Think about something you do with a friend.

With a partner, take turns saying the sentence from the box. Each time, add a different verb in the blank space.

I _____ with my friend.

Together, try to use ten different verbs. Can you think of any more?

Verbs in Predicates

Think about something you do with a friend.

With your group, write each of these verbs on a card.

tie   run   lift   climb   call   swim

Turn the cards facedown and take turns picking a card. Think of a sentence using the verb on your card. Act it out. Can the group guess the verb?

8 Unit 1 • Chapter 4   Reteach Activities • Predicates/Verbs

Combining Sentences: Compound Predicates

OBJECTIVES

- To combine sentences to make compound predicates
- To record ideas by drawing a picture and writing descriptive sentences with compound predicates

DAILY LANGUAGE PRACTICE

TRANSPARENCY 7

1 can we learn to hammer and saw (Can; saw?)

2 My father uses a tape measure (measure.)

BRIDGE TO WRITING I _(simple predicate)_ it myself!

ORAL WARM-UP

USE PRIOR KNOWLEDGE Write this sentence on the board: *Sheila paints the walls and hangs curtains.* Ask students to identify the subject and the predicate. Point out that the predicate tells two things that the subject does.

Grammar Jingles™ **CD, Intermediate** Use Track 3 for review and reinforcement of predicates.

TEACH/MODEL

Work through the explanation and examples of compound predicates with students. Remind them that, like compound subjects, compound predicates make writing and speaking smoother and more interesting.

Work through the Guided Practice items with students or have them complete the items in pairs.

Combining Sentences: Compound Predicates

A **compound predicate** is two or more predicates that have the same subject. Each predicate has its own verb. The predicates in a compound predicate are joined by *and* or *or*.

Use commas to separate three or more predicates in a compound predicate.

> **Example:**
> Sarita **draws** pictures *and* **reads** books.
> Every afternoon, Sarita **sleeps, studies,** *or* **plays.**

Combine two or more sentences with the same subject into one with a compound predicate.

> **Example:**
> Mrs. Liang **picked flowers.**
> Mrs. Liang **painted.**
> *Mrs. Liang* **picked flowers and painted.**

Guided Practice

A. Read each sentence. Name the simple predicates in each compound predicate.

Example: We eat dinner inside and relax on the porch.   *eat, relax*

1. Tim <u>plants</u> seeds and <u>waters</u> the garden.
2. We <u>painted</u> the walls and hung drapes.
3. They <u>study</u> books and <u>read</u> magazines.
4. In our yard, we <u>jump</u> rope and <u>play</u> ball.
5. In the kitchen, they <u>cook</u> food and <u>eat</u> lunch.

Vocabulary Power page 11

Name _____

ANALOGIES

In an analogy, two pairs of words go together in the same way.

Examples:
The sun shines in the day. The moon shines at night.
Sun is to *day* as *moon* is to *night*.

▶ Choose a word from the Word Box to complete each analogy.

flowers	watch	wood	pipes	trees

1. A mason works with stone. A carpenter works with ___wood___
2. Apples are fruit. Roses are ___flowers___
3. A beach has sand. A forest has ___trees___
4. An electrician fixes your electrical wiring. A plumber fixes your water ___pipes___
5. A book is something you read. A television set is something you ___watch___

▶ Now try these.

wear	machines	sour	short	kitten

6. *Electricians* are to *electricity* as *machinists* are to ___machines___
7. *Hot* is to *cold* as *tall* is to ___short___
8. *Food* is to *eat* as *clothes* are to ___wear___
9. *Sugar* is to *sweet* as *lemon* is to ___sour___
10. *Dog* is to *puppy* as *cat* is to ___kitten___

Vocabulary Power   Unit 1 • Chapter 4   11

REACHING ALL LEARNERS

ESL

COMBINE SENTENCES Write these sentences on the board:

Luisa plays outside.

Alan cleans his bedroom.

Tina reads magazines.

Luisa watches television.

Tina makes a snack.

Alan walks the dog.

Have students match the sentences that have the same subjects. Then have them combine the sentences to form compound predicates.

Independent Practice

B. Read the sentence pairs. Then write one sentence with a compound predicate.

Example: Painting can be easy. Painting is fun.
Painting can be easy and is fun.

6. Some people buy old furniture. Some people save lots of money. Some people buy old furniture and save lots of money.

7. People paint the furniture. People fix broken parts. People paint the furniture and fix broken parts.

8. This lamp is broken. This lamp needs a new shade. This lamp is broken and needs a new shade.

9. These floors look dirty. These floors need carpet. These floors look dirty and need carpet.

10. The yellow room seems bigger. The yellow room makes people feel happy. The yellow room seems bigger and makes people feel happy.

11. Bright colors are fun to use. Bright colors look good in children's rooms. Bright colors are fun to use and look good in children's rooms.

12. Pictures hang on walls. Pictures make a room more interesting. Pictures hang on walls and make a room more interesting.

13. Mark likes to paint rooms. Mark is good at it. Mark likes to paint rooms and is good at it.

14. Alma picks out paint. Alma buys furniture. Alma picks out paint and buys furniture.

15. Mrs. Young decorates homes. Mrs. Young chooses furniture. Mrs. Young decorates homes and chooses furniture.

Remember that a compound predicate is two or more predicates with the same subject.

Writing Connection

Writer's Journal: Describe a Room
Draw a picture of a room that you would like to have. Write eight sentences about it. Then combine some of your sentences by using compound predicates.

57

Independent Practice

Have students complete the Independent Practice, or modify it using these suggestions:

MODIFIED INSTRUCTION

BELOW-LEVEL STUDENTS Work through the Independent Practice items with students, modeling the thinking.

ABOVE-LEVEL STUDENTS Have students rewrite their combined sentences by adding another predicate to each. Tell students to add commas as needed.

Writing Connection

Writer's Journal: Describe a Room
To begin, have students suggest some special features a room might have. Then have students record their ideas about a room they would like to have by drawing pictures and writing sentences. Remind students to use commas to separate three or more predicates.

WRAP-UP/ASSESS

SUMMARIZE Ask students how they know when to combine two sentences to make a compound predicate.

RETEACH

INTERVENTION Lessons in **visual, auditory,** and **kinesthetic** modalities: p. R40 and *Reteach Activities Copying Masters,* p. 9.

PRACTICE page 13

Name _____

Combining Sentences: Compound Predicates

A. Circle each simple predicate in the compound predicate.

1. Ms. Chung (bought) some land and (drew) plans for two houses.
2. She (ordered) materials, (built) the two homes, and (painted) them.
3. She (chose) furniture and (put) it in one house.
4. She (moved) into one house and (rented) the other to her son.
5. Her son (paid) rent and (helped) in the yard.

B. Each group of sentences below has the same subject. Make one sentence with a compound predicate. Write the new sentence.

6. Ms. Chung went downtown. Ms. Chung shopped for furniture.
   Ms. Chung went downtown and shopped for furniture.

7. She invited her son. She asked for his opinion.
   She invited her son and asked for his opinion.

8. They looked at one chair. They sat down in it.
   They looked at one chair and sat down in it.

9. Ms. Chung tried another chair. Ms. Chung liked it better.
   Ms. Chung tried another chair and liked it better.

10. She chose a chair. She paid for it. She took it home.
    She chose a chair, paid for it, and took it home.

TRY THIS! Write what someone might do to make a home a better place to live. Use some compound predicates. Circle the verbs in each predicate.

Practice • Predicates/Verbs   Unit 1 • **Chapter 4** 13

CHALLENGE

INVENTION Ask students to invent a new furniture item for use in their houses. Students should draw a picture and write a short description of the piece. The description should tell

- the name of the furniture item.
- the purpose the item serves.
- what the item looks like.

Then have students combine some of their sentences using compound predicates.

Combining Sentences: Compound Predicates

Read each sentence. Circle the predicates. Combine the sentences to make a compound predicate.

We (cook.) We (talk.) We (work in the kitchen.)
We cook, talk, and work in the kitchen.

Bitsy (watches him.) Bitsy (waits for a treat.)
Bitsy watches him and waits for a treat.

Visual

Combining Sentences: Compound Predicates

Form a line with other members of your group. Take turns starting a sentence. Use the sentence subject *We* and a short predicate to tell about something students do at school.

Listen carefully to your neighbor. Then say exactly the same sentence, and add another predicate. If you are the fourth person in the line, your sentence will have four predicates. For example, your sentence might be: *We read books, write stories, paint pictures, and go on field trips.*

Auditory

Combining Sentences: Compound Predicates

Think about activities you do with your friends.

Each group member writes four sentences on strips of paper. Use *We* as the subject of each sentence. Put the group's sentences on a table. Take turns picking two sentences. Look for two sentences that could go together. Combine the two sentences with a compound predicate, and say the new sentence.

Kinesthetic

Teacher: Cut apart the activities and distribute to students based on the modalities that are their strengths.
[Visual] Suggest that students first underline the subject in each sentence.
[Auditory] Have students form groups of four or five for this activity.
[Kinesthetic] Students may use construction paper and colored markers to make their sentence strips.

Reteach Activities • Predicates/Verbs   Unit 1 • **Chapter 4** 9

Extra Practice

OBJECTIVES
- To identify simple and complete predicates and verbs
- To combine sentences by using compound predicates
- To write sentences that compare and to identify predicates in writing

DAILY LANGUAGE PRACTICE

TRANSPARENCY 8

1 A carpenter buildds a house. (builds)

2 the house is so big! (The)

BRIDGE TO WRITING I will paint the kitchen ___(combining word)___ rake leaves.

ORAL WARM-UP

USE PRIOR KNOWLEDGE Invite individuals to list some steps involved in building a house. After each statement, have students name the predicate.

TEACH/MODEL

Use the Remember boxes to review simple, complete, and compound predicates. Model the thinking, using the example sentence for Independent Practice A.

MODEL I ask myself, "Which part of the sentence tells what the subject, *Most cities*, does or is?" The answer is *have several government buildings. Have several government buildings* must be the complete predicate. The main word in the predicate is *have*, so *have* must be the simple predicate.

Have students complete the rest of the Extra Practice items independently.

CHAPTER 4
Predicates/Verbs

Remember

that the predicate of a sentence tells what the subject of the sentence is or does. A simple predicate is the main word in the complete predicate.

For additional activities using predicates, visit *The Learning Site:* www.harcourtschool.com

---

Extra Practice

A. Write each sentence. Underline the complete predicate once. Underline the simple predicate twice. *pages 52–53*

Example: Most cities have several government buildings.
Most cities <u>have</u> several government buildings.

1. These buildings <u>are</u> a city hall, a post office, and a firehouse.
2. Carpenters <u>used</u> wood on many of these buildings.
3. Some people <u>plan</u> parks.
4. Some parks <u>have</u> playgrounds and ball fields.
5. People <u>use</u> a park for many purposes.

B. Read each sentence. Write the verb in each sentence. *pages 54–55*

Example: The park planner studies the needs of the people in our town. *studies*

6. People in a small town <u>travel</u> to the park by car or on foot.
7. People in a city sometimes <u>ride</u> a bus to the park.
8. The town park <u>has</u> a parking lot.
9. The city park <u>is</u> near bus and train stops.
10. Young children <u>play</u> on the playground.
11. People <u>water-ski</u> on the lake.
12. The baseball fields <u>need</u> seats.
13. A designer <u>chooses</u> plants for the park.
14. Trees and bushes <u>offer</u> shelter for birds and animals.
15. Ducks and swans <u>swim</u> in the pond.

Vocabulary Power page 12

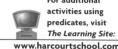

Name _____

COMPARE AND CONTRAST

Complete the following statements. Responses will vary. Possible responses are given.

1. A *carpenter* is like a *mason* except <u>that a carpenter works with wood instead of stone</u>
2. *Wood* is like *brick* because <u>they are both building materials</u>
3. A *plumber* is like an *electrician* except <u>that a plumber fixes water pipes instead of electrical equipment</u>
4. A *hammer* is like a *wrench* because <u>they are both tools</u>
5. A *fork* is like a *spoon* because <u>they are both eating utensils</u>
6. A *cabin* is like a *mansion* except <u>that a cabin is smaller and more roughly built than a mansion</u>
7. A *piano* is like a *flute* because <u>they are both musical instruments</u>
8. A *lake* is like an *ocean* except <u>that it is smaller and has fresh water instead of salt water</u>
9. A *quarter* is like a *dime* except <u>that a quarter is worth more than a dime</u>

12 Unit 1 • Chapter 4   Vocabulary Power

Art

STUDY A BUILDING Have students look through library books, brochures from historic places, or computer encyclopedias to learn more about historic buildings. Tell them to draw one building that interests them. Ask students to create one- or two-sentence captions with compound predicates that tell something interesting or special about their buildings. The captions can be placed at the bottom of their drawings.

C. Read the sentences in each group. Then write one sentence with a compound predicate.

pages 56–57

Example: Sun Lee designs schools.
Sun Lee plans libraries.
Sun Lee designs schools and plans libraries.

16. Decorators pick bright colors for classrooms.
Decorators choose soft colors for the school library. Decorators pick bright colors for classrooms and choose soft colors for the school library.

17. Our school cafeteria looks cheerful.
Our school cafeteria has sturdy tables. Our school cafeteria looks cheerful and has sturdy tables.

18. Gyms and cafeterias hold many students.
Gyms and cafeterias are noisy places. Gyms and cafeterias hold many students and are noisy places.

19. Students often work in groups in classrooms.
Students need lots of space. Students often work in groups in classrooms and need lots of space.

20. Sun Lee gave the computer area good lighting.
Sun Lee chose comfortable chairs.
Sun Lee showed the workers where to put electrical outlets. Sun Lee gave the computer area good lighting, chose comfortable chairs, and showed the workers where to put electrical outlets.

Remember
that a compound predicate is two or more predicates that share the same subject.

Writing Connection
Technology Work with a partner to plan a park, school, or store. First, draw your plan by hand. Then use a computer to draw your plan. How is drawing by hand different from drawing by computer? Write five sentences about the differences. Trade sentences with your partner. Circle the complete predicates in the sentences.

Building Oral Grammar
After students have completed Part C, give them a chance to hear how combined sentences make writing flow more smoothly. Invite pairs to read each item aloud. Have one partner read the pair of sentences as they appear in the exercise. Have the other partner read the combined version. Tell students to listen for the improvement in the flow of the ideas.

Writing Connection
Technology Allow students to use various classroom items to trace shapes for their hand-drawn plans. Remind them that they can use color to enhance their drawings. When students are writing their sentences, tell them to focus on how both the actions taken to create their drawings and the final pictures are different for each method.

WRAP-UP/ASSESS

SUMMARIZE How can you recognize the complete and simple predicates of a sentence? How do you know when to combine predicates?

ADDITIONAL PRACTICE An additional page of Extra Practice is provided on page 456 of the *Pupil Edition*.

PRACTICE page 14

Name _____

Extra Practice

A. Underline the complete predicate once. Underline the verb twice.
1. Mr. Vernon owned a house.
2. He wanted an apartment building.
3. He looked for some land.
4. The land near the lake seemed just right.
5. Mr. Vernon paid for the land.

B. Combine each group of sentences to make one sentence with a compound predicate. Write the new sentence.
6. Mr. Vernon called a builder. Mr. Vernon hired him.
Mr. Vernon called a builder and hired him.

7. They talked. They made some decisions.
They talked and made some decisions.

8. The builder read the plans. The builder followed the plans.
The builder read and followed the plans.

9. He dug a hole. He put in pipes.
He dug a hole and put in pipes.

10. He picked up some nails. He lifted a hammer. He pounded the nails into some boards. He picked up some nails, lifted a hammer, and pounded the nails into some boards.

TRY THIS! Write a short paragraph describing a dream home. Underline each complete predicate. Combine sentences if you can.

14 Unit 1 • Chapter 4   Practice • Predicates/Verbs

CHALLENGE

WRITE SENTENCES Have students select four different verbs from the Extra Practice exercise sentences. Tell them to write two new sentences with compound predicates, using the verbs they selected. When students have finished, ask them to trade papers and underline the verbs in their partner's sentences.

TECHNOLOGY *Grammar Practice and Assessment* CD-ROM; *Writing Express* CD-ROM

INTERNET Visit *The Learning Site:* www.harcourtschool.com

Chapter Review

OBJECTIVES
- To review verbs and complete, simple, and compound predicates
- To learn and practice greetings in languages other than English

STANDARDIZED TEST PREP

SPIRAL REVIEW

DAILY LANGUAGE PRACTICE

TRANSPARENCY 8

1 Have you learned to cut straight (straight?)

2 carpenters measure boards. (Carpenters)

BRIDGE TO WRITING Carpenters __(simple predicate)__ furniture for homes. Architects __(compound predicate)__ new buildings.

STANDARDIZED TEST PREP

MODEL TEST-TAKING STRATEGIES Have students read the first set of directions on page 60 silently.

Point out that there are three types of exercises in this Chapter Review. Remind students that they must read each set of directions carefully so they know what they must do to complete each item. Model the thinking, using the direction line for items 1–4.

MODEL These directions tell me to find the simple predicate in each sentence. I know that the simple predicate is the main word that tells what the subject is or does, so I will read each sentence and find the subject first. Then I will decide which underlined word is the main word in the predicate.

Students should complete the Chapter Review items silently.

STANDARDIZED TEST PREP

TIP Remember to read all the answer choices carefully. Then make your decision.

Chapter Review

Follow the directions for each question. Write the letter of your answer.

For Numbers 1–4, find the simple predicate, or verb, in each sentence.

1 Our class learned about castles.
   A   B   C c   D

2 Castles were beautiful and sturdy.
   A   B B   C   D

3 People made castles from stone.
   A   B B   C   D

4 An army of soldiers lived in the castle.
     A   B   C c   D

5 Find the sentence that is complete and is written correctly.
A Many castles by high walls.
B Surrounded many castles high walls.
C Many castles were surrounded by high walls. c
D Surrounded by high walls.

6 Find the sentence that best combines these two sentences into one.

> *Our class took a trip to a castle.*
> *Our class visited all its rooms.*

A Our class and our teacher took a trip.
B Took a trip to a castle and visited.
C Our class took a trip to a castle and its rooms.
D Our class took a trip to a castle and visited all its rooms. D

For additional test preparation, visit *The Learning Site:* www.harcourtschool.com

---

Assessment

PORTFOLIO ASSESSMENT Have students select their best work from the Writing Connections on pages 53, 55, and 59.

ONGOING ASSESSMENT Evaluate the performance of 4–6 students using appropriate checklists and record forms from pages R74–R77.

INTERNET Activities and exercises to help students prepare for state and standardized assessments appear on *The Learning Site:*
www.harcourtschool.com

Words from Many Places

Suppose you are traveling to Mexico, Japan, and Hawaii. When you get there, you want to be able to say hello to people you meet. Here are some ways to say hello in each place.

In Mexico and most other countries in Central and South America, people speak Spanish. This is how they say hello:

Ho′la [ō′lä]

Say hello in Spanish to a partner. Shake your partner's hand.

In Japan, people speak Japanese. This is one way to say hello:

Ko•ni•chi•wa [kō•nē•chē•wä]

Say hello in Japanese to a partner.

In the state of Hawaii, people speak English most of the time. However, they still use many Hawaiian words. The Hawaiian language uses the same word for *hello* and *good-bye*. This is how to greet someone in Hawaiian:

A•lo•ha [ə•lō′hä]

A person may welcome a visitor to Hawaii by putting a necklace of flowers around the visitor's neck. The necklace is called a lei [lā]. Try greeting a partner in Hawaiian. Pretend to place a lei on your partner.

YOUR TURN

Find France and China on a map. With a partner, use a computer or the school library to learn about these countries. What languages do people in France and in China speak? Find out how to say hello in these languages.

61

VOCABULARY

Words from Many Places

TEACH/MODEL

Ask students to read the first paragraph of the lesson. Ask them in what other ways the ability to speak more than one language can be useful.

This lesson may be a good opportunity for English language learners to share their first languages. Invite students to write "hello" on the board in their first languages.

Have students choose partners and work through the rest of the lesson. Then have students complete the Your Turn activity with their partners.

WRITING APPLICATION Have students use some of the greeting words they have learned in this lesson in a short story about two friends meeting and greeting each other.

WRAP-UP/ASSESS

SUMMARIZE Ask students to explain in their journals why learning a greeting in different languages is important.

 PRACTICE page 15

Name _____

Chapter Review

Read each sentence. The underlined sections may have a mistake. Choose the best way to write the underlined section. Fill in the oval next to your choice. If the underlined section is correct, choose *No mistake.*

(1) I in apartments most of my life. **(2)** I wanted a house with a yard. **(3)** My family also. Father **(4)** went to the country, looked at some land. He **(5)** showed us, the land, and asked our opinion. The whole family **(6)** thought about it discussed it and made a decision.

1 ☐ I lived in apartments most of my life.
☐ I in apartments more of my life.
☐ I in apartments, most of my life.
☐ No mistake

2 ☐ I wanted a house and with a yard.
☐ I wanted a house, wanted a yard.
☐ I wanted, a house with a yard.
☐ No mistake

3 ☐ My family, also.
☐ My family did also.
☐ My family and also.
☐ No mistake

4 ☐ went to the country, looked at, and some land.
☐ went to the country, we looked at some land.
☐ went to the country and looked at some land.
☐ No mistake

5 ☐ showed us the land, asked our opinion.
☐ showed us the land and asked our opinion.
☐ showed us the land and asked our opinion.
☐ No mistake

6 ☐ thought about it discussed it, and made a decision.
☐ thought about it, discussed it, and made a decision.
☐ thought about it and discussed it and made a decision.
☐ No mistake

Practice • Predicates/Verbs

Unit 1 • Chapter 4 15

 CHALLENGE

LEARN A GREETING Have students research ways to say "goodbye" in different languages. Then have students tape record these words. Remind them to speak clearly and slowly when they record. Make the tape available at a listening station so that other students may use it to listen and learn. Suggest that students visit the station in pairs and practice saying the words together.

 TECHNOLOGY Additional writing activities are provided on the *Writing Express* CD-ROM

CHAPTER 5

Simple and Compound Sentences

LESSON ORGANIZER	DAY 1	DAY 2
DAILY LANGUAGE PRACTICE 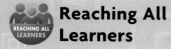 TRANSPARENCIES 9, 10	1. My favorite books are mysteries (mysteries.) 2. have you read the new book by Peggy Parish (Have; Parish?) **Bridge to Writing** (Subject) love her books!	1. i read the greatest book last week! (I) 2. A gurl found a lost dog (girl; dog.) **Bridge to Writing** The dog (predicate) .
ORAL WARM-UP Listening/Speaking	Complete the Sentence 62	Identify Subjects and Predicates 64 *Grammar Jingles*™ CD Track 4
TEACH/MODEL GRAMMAR **KEY** ✔ = tested skill	✔ **COMPLETE SENTENCES** 62-63 • To recognize and write complete sentences • To write a poem and respond constructively in complete sentences to another's writing	✔ **SIMPLE AND COMPOUND SENTENCES** 64-65 • To recognize simple and compound sentences • To use simple and compound sentences in writing
Reaching All Learners	**Modified Instruction** Below-Level: Find Subjects and Predicates Above-Level: Combine Sentences **Reteach:** *Reteach Activities Copying Masters* pp. 10 and R41 **Challenge:** Activity Card 4, R63 *ESL Manual* pp. 28, 29 *Practice Book* p. 16	**Modified Instruction** Below-Level: Look for Two Above-Level: Join Sentences **ESL:** Analyzing Sentences 64 *ESL Manual* pp. 28, 30 **Reteach:** *Reteach Activities Copying Masters* pp. 11 and R41 **Challenge:** A Real Setting 65 *Practice Book* p. 17
WRITING	Writing Connection 63 Writer's Journal: Evaluating Writing	Writing Connection 65 Writer's Craft: Personal Voice
CROSS-CURRICULAR/ ENRICHMENT	*Vocabulary Power* Synonyms 62 **fantasy**, imaginary, pretend, tale, yarn See *Vocabulary Power* book.	*Vocabulary Power* Explore Word Meaning 62 *Vocabulary Power* p. 13 🖥 **Vocabulary activity**

WRITING ACTIVITIES
Writing Express CD-ROM
Visit *The Learning Site:*
www.harcourtschool.com

DAY **3**	DAY **4**	DAY **5**
1. Did you see the movie about aliens that came to Earth (Earth?) 2. the movie was based on a science fiction storie. (The; story.) **Bridge to Writing** The (simple subject) rode in spaceships.	1. Do you know what my favorite magazine is (is?) 2. *national Geographic World* is a wonderful magazine. *(National)* **Bridge to Writing** I look at magazines at the store, (combining word) I borrow them from the library.	1. Libby goes to the library every Thursday (Thursday.) 2. What kind of books does she like (?) **Bridge to Writing** Libby reads books about real people, (combining word) she wants to write books when she grows up.
Combine Two Sentences 66 *Grammar Jingles*™ CD Track 4	Recall a Story 68	
✔ **COMBINING SENTENCES** 66-67 • To combine simple sentences to make compound sentences • To write a news report and revise it by combining sentences	**EXTRA PRACTICE** 68-69 • To recognize complete, simple, and compound sentences • To combine sentences • To write a summary and revise it by combining sentences 🖳 **Practice and assessment**	**TEST PREP CHAPTER REVIEW** 70-71 • To review complete, simple, and compound sentences • To use word processing program features for writing 🖳 **Test preparation**
Modified Instruction Below-Level: Model the Thinking Above-Level: Write Sentences **Reteach:** *Reteach Activities Copying Masters* pp. 12 and R41 **Challenge:** A Historical Era 67 *ESL Manual* pp. 28, 31 *Practice Book* p. 18	**Building Oral Grammar** Noticing Pauses in Sentences 69 **Challenge:** Letter to the Editor 69 *ESL Manual* pp. 28, 31 *Practice Book* p. 19	**Challenge:** Read with Purpose 71 *Practice Book* p. 20 *ESL Manual* pp. 28, 32
Writing Connection 67 Real-Life Writing: News Report	Writing Connection 69 Writer's Craft: Write a Summary	Writing Application 71 Use Notes to Write a Paragraph
Technology: E-mail an Author 66 *Vocabulary Power* Dictionary 62 *Vocabulary Power* p. 14 🖳 **Vocabulary activity**	**Listening and Speaking:** Oral Book Report 68 *Vocabulary Power* Homophones 62 *Vocabulary Power* p. 15 🖳 **Vocabulary activity**	**Study Skills:** Being a Good Reader 71 *Vocabulary Power* Exemplification 62

Complete Sentences

OBJECTIVES
- To recognize and write complete sentences
- To write a poem and respond constructively in complete sentences to another's writing

DAILY LANGUAGE PRACTICE

TRANSPARENCY 9

1 My favorite books are mysteries (mysteries.)

2 have you read the new book by Peggy Parish (Have; Parish?)

BRIDGE TO WRITING <u>(Subject)</u> love her books!

ORAL WARM-UP

USE PRIOR KNOWLEDGE Write these words on the board: *Angela a book*. Ask students to suggest a word that will complete the sentence.

TEACH/MODEL

Have students read the definition of a complete sentence on page 62. Then ask them to compare the left column of the chart with the right. Have volunteers point out the differences between the complete sentences and the incomplete sentences.

Model the thinking, using the Guided Practice examples:

MODEL **The first group of words has a subject and a predicate and tells a complete thought. The second group of words does not express a complete thought. It does not have both a subject and a predicate, so it cannot be a complete sentence.**

Work through the remaining Guided Practice items with students.

Vocabulary Power
fan·ta·sy
[fan′tə·sē] *n.* A story about things and people that could not be real.

62

Complete Sentences

A **complete sentence** is a group of words that has a subject and a predicate. It expresses a complete thought.

A group of words that does not express a complete thought and does not have a subject and a predicate is not a complete sentence.

Examples:

Complete Sentence	Not a Complete Sentence
I like to read stories.	To read stories.
What kind of stories do you like to read?	What kind of stories?
Mary enjoys reading adventure stories.	Reading adventure stories.

Guided Practice

A. Tell whether each group of words is a complete sentence. Explain how you know.

Examples: Children's literature includes many imaginary stories.
complete sentence

Some imaginary stories are.
not a complete sentence

1. About animals who talk. not a sentence
2. The animals talk like people. complete sentence
3. Literature can make children laugh. complete sentence
4. Speaking English very well. not a sentence
5. Characters in some very popular stories. not a sentence

Vocabulary Power

DAY 1 SYNONYMS Introduce and define *fantasy*. Write the following on the board and have students complete it. **Imaginary is/is not a synonym for *fantasy* because** _____. Discuss responses.

DAY 2 EXPLORE WORD MEANING Ask: **What are some differences between fantasy stories and true stories?** (See also *Vocabulary Power*, page 13.)

DAY 3 DICTIONARY **Is *fantasy* a noun or a verb? How could you find out?** (See also *Vocabulary Power*, page 14.)

DAY 4 HOMOPHONES ***Tale* and *tail* are homophones. What are some other examples of homophones?** (See also *Vocabulary Power*, page 15.)

DAY 5 EXEMPLIFICATION **Make up an imaginary character for a fantasy movie. Write a paragraph to describe this character.**

Independent Practice

**B. Read each sentence. Write *complete sentence*
if the group of words is a complete sentence.
If it is not a complete sentence, rewrite the
group of words to make it a complete
sentence.** Responses will vary; possible responses are given.

Example: Writes short poems.
She writes short poems.

6. Sometimes funny and simple. They are sometimes funny and simple.
7. Children's literature may rhyme. complete sentence
8. Mother Goose poems are very old. complete sentence
9. "Little Jack Horner" a nursery rhyme. "Little Jack Horner" is a nursery rhyme.
10. The word *Horner* rhymes with *corner*. complete sentence
11. Some poems are fun to read many times. complete sentence
12. Poems can tell stories. complete sentence
13. Do not have to rhyme. Poems do not have to rhyme.
14. Good poems a long time to write. Good poems can take a long time to write.
15. Some poets very long poems. Some poets write very long poems.

> **Remember**
> that a complete
> sentence is a
> group of words
> that expresses
> a complete
> thought. It has
> a subject and a
> predicate.

Writing Connection

Writer's Journal: Evaluating Writing
Think of an animal character in a story you
have read. Write a poem that describes
this character. Then trade your poem with
a partner, and write two complete sentences in your
journals about each other's poems. Tell something
you liked about your partner's poem. Share your
sentences with each other.

Independent Practice

Have students complete the Independent Practice, or
modify it using these suggestions:

MODIFIED INSTRUCTION

BELOW-LEVEL STUDENTS Tell students to try to
find both a subject and a predicate before deciding
whether each group of words is a complete sentence.

ABOVE-LEVEL STUDENTS Ask students to combine several of the complete sentences into a paragraph. They may need to make changes in some of
the sentences in order to make the paragraph flow
smoothly.

Writing Connection

Writer's Journal: Evaluating Writing
Before students begin to write, have
them brainstorm descriptive words
about their character. Have students
respond constructively to each other's poems.
Remind them to write in complete sentences.

WRAP-UP/ASSESS

SUMMARIZE Ask students how they can
tell that a sentence is complete.

RETEACH

INTERVENTION Lessons in **visual,
auditory,** and **kinesthetic** modalities: p. R41 and *Reteach Activities
Copying Masters,* p. 10.

CHALLENGE

SENTENCES IN POETRY Have
students use **Challenge Activity
Card 4** (page R63) to identify
sentences in a nursery rhyme.

Simple and Compound Sentences

OBJECTIVES
- To recognize simple and compound sentences
- To use simple and compound sentences in writing

DAILY LANGUAGE PRACTICE

TRANSPARENCY 9

1 i read the greatest book last week! (I)

2 A gurl found a lost dog (girl; dog.)

BRIDGE TO WRITING The dog ___(predicate)___ .

ORAL WARM-UP

USE PRIOR KNOWLEDGE Write this sentence on the board: *Authors write, and authors revise.* Have students identify the subjects and predicates in the sentence.

***Grammar Jingles*™ CD, Intermediate** Use Track 4 for review and reinforcement of simple and compound sentences.

TEACH/MODEL

Read aloud the explanation of simple and compound sentences on page 64. Explain that *and* can be used to combine sentences that have similar ideas. *But* is often used when ideas are different. *Or* shows a choice. Tell students that if there is more than one simple sentence in the Guided Practice items, then the sentence is compound. If there is not, then the sentence is simple. Model the thinking for the Guided Practice example:

MODEL The sentence has one subject, and one predicate, and it expresses one complete thought, so I know that it is a simple sentence.

Have students work in groups to complete the rest of the Guided Practice.

Simple and Compound Sentences

A sentence that expresses one complete thought is a **simple sentence**. Two or more simple sentences can be combined to make a **compound sentence**.

The words *and*, *but*, and *or* are usually used to combine the sentences. A comma (,) goes before the combining word.

> **Examples:**
> **Simple Sentences** A fable tells a story. It teaches a lesson.
> **Compound Sentence** A fable tells a story, and it teaches a lesson.

DID YOU KNOW?
April is National Poetry Month in the United States.

Guided Practice

A. Tell whether each sentence is a simple sentence or a compound sentence.

Example: Aesop's Fables are classic literature.
simple sentence

1. Fables are imaginary stories about animals. simple
2. Animal fables can teach the difference between right and wrong. simple
3. Today fables are written down, and adults read them to children. compound
4. Long ago, people told fables aloud. simple
5. "Little Red Riding Hood" is an old fable, but children still like to read it. compound

64

Vocabulary Power   page 13

Name _____

EXPLORE WORD MEANING

Read and respond to the following questions or statements.
Responses may vary. Accept reasonable responses.
1. What books or stories have you read that are fantasies?

_____

2. Would you rather read a story about real people or imaginary people?

_____

3. What are some things that could happen in a yarn that couldn't happen in a true story?

_____

4. What other characters might you read about in a tale about a princess? Possible responses: Kings, queens, princes

5. Pretend you are writing a fantasy story. Draw a picture of the main character in your story. Then name your character.

Vocabulary Power   Unit 1 • Chapter 5   **13**

ESL
REACHING ALL LEARNERS

ANALYZING SENTENCES Have students decide whether each sentence below has a compound subject or a compound predicate, or if it is a compound sentence.

Kate and Jeremy decided to write a book.

They wrote and illustrated it.

They made copies of the book, and they gave a copy to each of their parents.

Independent Practice

B. Read each sentence. Write whether it is a simple sentence or a compound sentence.

> **Example:** She writes books, and she draws pictures.
> *compound sentence*

6. Children's books often have pictures. simple
7. An artist reads the children's story, and then the artist imagines the characters in the book. compound
8. An artist's imagination makes the characters come to life. simple
9. Pictures can be in black and white, or they may be in color. compound
10. Some writers draw their own pictures, but it takes a long time to draw pictures for a book. compound
11. Sometimes authors write about things that have happened. simple
12. A real-life story might include characters that seem real. simple
13. Some real-life stories are happy, but some are sad. compound
14. I enjoy reading these stories. simple
15. I tell my friends about books, and they share books with me. compound

Remember that a simple sentence expresses one complete thought. A compound sentence is two or more simple sentences combined with a comma (,) and a joining word.

Writing Connection

Writer's Craft: Personal Voice Think about something funny that has happened to you. Using simple and compound sentences, tell about the funny thing that happened to you.

65

Independent Practice

Have students complete the Independent Practice, or modify it using these suggestions:

MODIFIED INSTRUCTION

BELOW-LEVEL STUDENTS Remind students to look for two subjects and two predicates before deciding whether a sentence is simple or compound.

ABOVE-LEVEL STUDENTS Ask students to write a sentence that goes with each simple sentence. Then have them join the sentences together to form compound sentences.

Writing Connection

Writer's Craft: Personal Voice Before students begin, explain that one way to develop personal voice in a narrative is to tell the story in the first person. When students finish writing, have them check their stories to be sure they have used compound sentences as well as simple sentences. Tell them to use different combining words in their compound sentences.

WRAP-UP/ASSESS

SUMMARIZE Ask students to tell what the difference is between a simple sentence and a compound sentence.

REACHING ALL LEARNERS

RETEACH

INTERVENTION Lessons in **visual, auditory,** and **kinesthetic** modalities: p. R41 and *Reteach Activities Copying Masters*, p. 11.

REACHING ALL LEARNERS

PRACTICE page 17

Name _____

Simple and Compound Sentences

A. Write whether each sentence is *simple* or *compound*.

1. The author created many characters. _simple_
2. One character was a little girl, and she liked birds. _compound_
3. The little girl lived in a big city with many parks. _simple_
4. The author wrote about the girl's life. _simple_
5. The girl's family was part of the story, but they were not mentioned much. _compound_

B. Use a joining word to combine the simple sentences to make a compound sentence.

6. "Jack and the Beanstalk" is a fable. It is very famous.
   "Jack and the Beanstalk" is a fable and it is very famous.
7. The beanstalk grew into the sky. Jack climbed it anyway.
   The beanstalk grew into the sky, but Jack climbed it anyway.
8. Jack climbed the beanstalk. He found a pot of gold.
   Jack climbed the beanstalk, and he found a pot of gold.
9. An angry giant came after Jack. Jack escaped.
   An angry giant came after Jack, but Jack escaped.

TRY THIS! What is your favorite fable? Write four sentences about it. Use simple and compound sentences in your writing.

Practice • Simple and Compound Sentences   Unit 1 • Chapter 5   17

REACHING ALL LEARNERS

CHALLENGE

A REAL SETTING Have students think of a real-life place they know that might be a good setting for a story. Ask them to write a description of the place, using simple and compound sentences.

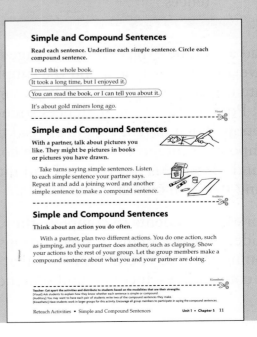

Simple and Compound Sentences

Read each sentence. Underline each simple sentence. Circle each compound sentence.

I read this whole book.
It took a long time, but I enjoyed it.
You can read the book, or I can tell you about it.
It's about gold miners long ago.

Visual

Simple and Compound Sentences

With a partner, talk about pictures you like. They might be pictures in books or pictures you have drawn.

Take turns saying simple sentences. Listen to each simple sentence your partner says. Repeat it and add a joining word and another simple sentence to make a compound sentence.

Auditory

Simple and Compound Sentences

Think about an action you do often.

With a partner, plan two different actions. You do one action, such as jumping, and your partner does another, such as clapping. Show your actions to the rest of your group. Let the group members make a compound sentence about what you and your partner are doing.

Kinesthetic

Teacher: Cut apart the activities and distribute to students based on the modalities that are their strengths.
[Visual] Ask students to explain how they know whether each sentence is simple or compound.
[Auditory] You may want to have each pair of students write two of the compound sentences they make.
[Kinesthetic] Have students work in larger groups for this activity. Encourage all group members to participate in saying the compound sentences.

Reteach Activities • Simple and Compound Sentences   Unit 1 • Chapter 5   11

GRAMMAR—WRITING CONNECTION

Combining Sentences

OBJECTIVES

- To combine simple sentences to make compound sentences
- To write a news report and revise it by combining sentences

DAILY LANGUAGE PRACTICE

TRANSPARENCY 9

1 Did you see the movie about aliens that came to Earth (Earth?)

2 the movie was based on a science fiction storie. (The; story)

BRIDGE TO WRITING The ___(simple subject)___ rode in spaceships.

ORAL WARM-UP

USE PRIOR KNOWLEDGE Write these sentences on the board: *He likes to read stories about the future. He likes stories about history, too.* Ask students to suggest how to make these two sentences into one sentence.

***Grammar Jingles*™ CD, Intermediate** Use Track 4 for review and reinforcement of simple and compound sentences.

TEACH/MODEL

Read aloud the explanations on page 66. Have a volunteer read aloud the simple sentences in the instructional box example. Point out that the sentences sound choppy. Then have a volunteer read the compound sentence. Note that the compound sentence is more varied and interesting than the two short sentences.

Work with students to complete the Guided Practice items in small groups. Remind them to check the placement of the comma in each compound sentence.

GRAMMAR—WRITING CONNECTION

Combining Sentences

When you write, it is a good idea to combine sentences.

Too many short sentences can make your writing seem choppy. Combining sentences can make your writing more lively and interesting.

> **Example:**
> **Simple Sentences** Yolanda might write a mystery story. She might write a science fiction story.
>
> **Compound Sentence** Yolanda might write a mystery story, or she might write a science fiction story.

Guided Practice

A. Use the combining word shown to combine each pair of sentences.

Example: Science fiction stories are about science. They are imaginary. *and*
Science fiction stories are about science, and they are imaginary.

1. Science fiction is one kind of literature. It is not the only kind. *but*
Science fiction is one kind of literature, but it is not the only kind.

2. Some science fiction stories are about outer space. Others take place on Earth. *and*
Some science fiction stories are about outer space, and others take place on Earth.

3. One famous story is about the sea. It is set at the bottom of the ocean. *and*
One famous story is about the sea, and it is set at the bottom of the ocean.

4. A science fiction story may be about computers. It may be about spaceships. *or*
A science fiction story may be about computers, or it may be about spaceships.

5. I like science fiction stories. My brother does not like them. *but*
I like science fiction stories, but my brother does not like them.

66

Vocabulary Power page 14

Name _____

DICTIONARY

Entry words in a dictionary are listed in alphabetical order. An entry word in a dictionary is followed by its pronunciation. Its part of speech is next. If there are two meanings, they are each numbered. Dictionaries sometimes include an example sentence to explain the meaning of the word.

Read the entries below. Then answer the questions.

   imaginary [i•maj′ə•ner•ē] *adj.* Existing only in the imagination, unreal.
   pretend [pri•tend′] *v.* To make believe: *Let's pretend we're movie stars.*
   yarn [yärn] *n.* 1. Any spun strand. 2. A made-up story.

1. How many syllables are in *imaginary*?
   five

2. Is a *yarn* a true story? How do you know?
   No. The dictionary says a *yarn* is made up.

3. Why are there numerals in the meaning of *yarn*?
   Yarn has two meanings; each one is numbered.

4. Make up a new example sentence for *pretend*.
   Possible response: My friend likes to pretend she's my sister.

5. Which word is pronounced this way? [i•maj′ə•ner•ē]
   imaginary

6. Why is *yarn* the last word listed here?
   It comes after the other two words in the alphabet.

14   Unit 1 • Chapter 5   Vocabulary Power

Technology

E-MAIL AN AUTHOR Have students find a website for an author they like or admire. Have them write a brief e-mail to the author explaining why they like his or her work. Tell them to use compound sentences in their e-mail. If students do not have access to the Internet, they can compose a letter to send by regular mail.

Independent Practice

B. Rewrite the following sentences. Use the combining word shown to combine them.

Example: I like to read. She likes to read. *and*
I like to read, and she likes to read.

6. Some of the characters in historical stories are real. Some are made up. *but*
Some of the characters in historical stories are real, but some are made up.

7. A story might tell how people dressed long ago. It might tell what they ate. *or*
A story might tell how people dressed long ago, or it might tell what they ate.

8. Some historical stories include maps. They also may have pictures. *and*
Some historical stories include maps, and they also may have pictures.

9. The maps show where people lived. Sometimes they show where people traveled. *or*
The maps show where people lived, or sometimes they show where people traveled.

10. Some people do not like to read about the past. I enjoy historical stories. *but*
Some people do not like to read about the past, but I enjoy historical stories.

11. *Little House on the Prairie* is set in the late 1800s. It tells about pioneer life. *and*
Little House on the Prairie is set in the late 1800s, and it tells about pioneer life.

12. Laura Ingalls Wilder is the author. There are nine books in the series. *and*
Laura Ingalls Wilder is the author, and there are nine books in the series.

13. The books tell about real events. The story is told by one of the characters. *but*
The books tell about real events, but the story is told by one of the characters.

14. The facts in a historical story should be true. The story should be fun to read. *but*
The facts in a historical story should be true, but the story should be fun to read.

15. Students may learn to write stories like this. They may read them in social studies. *or*
Students may learn to write stories like this, or they may read them in social studies.

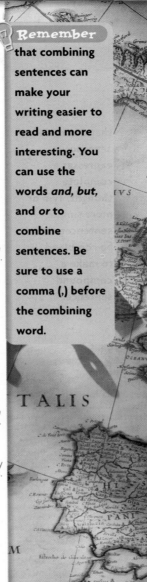

Remember that combining sentences can make your writing easier to read and more interesting. You can use the words *and, but,* and *or* to combine sentences. Be sure to use a comma (,) before the combining word.

Writing Connection

Real-Life Writing: News Report With a partner, write a news report about an upcoming event at your school. Then revise your report by combining sentences that go together.

Independent Practice

Have students complete the Independent Practice, or modify it using these suggestions:

MODIFIED INSTRUCTION

BELOW-LEVEL STUDENTS Work through the Independent Practice with students, modeling the thinking.

ABOVE-LEVEL STUDENTS Ask students to write three more compound sentences about a story they have read about a historical event.

Writing Connection

Real-Life Writing: News Report Point out to students that most news stories answer the six reporter's questions: *Who? What? Why? When? Where?* and *How?* Have students check their completed work to determine that their writing achieves its purposes. Make sure students revise their drafts to include precise words that answer the six questions.

WRAP-UP/ASSESS

SUMMARIZE Ask students: **How do you combine simple sentences? What kind of sentence do you make when you combine two simple sentences?**

RETEACH

INTERVENTION Lessons in **visual, auditory,** and **kinesthetic** modalities: p. R41 and *Reteach Activities Copying Masters,* p. 12.

PRACTICE page 18

Name _____

Combining Sentences

A. Use the combining word in parentheses to combine the sentences. Place a comma before the combining word.

1. "The Boy Who Cried Wolf" is a folktale. It is a very old story.
(and) The Boy Who Cried Wolf" is a folktale, and it is a very old story.

2. The boy cried "Wolf" to warn the people. There was no wolf.
(but) The boy cried "Wolf" to warn the people, but there was no wolf.

3. The people were upset. They asked the boy why he had cried out. (and) The people were upset, and they asked the boy why he had cried out.

B. Read each sentence. Add a comma in the correct place in the compound sentence. If a sentence does not need a comma, leave it as it is.

4. "Little Bo Peep" is a nursery rhyme about a little girl.

5. Little Bo Peep took care of sheep but she lost a few of them.

6. Little Bo Peep found her sheep and then she was happy.

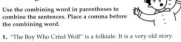 **TRY THIS!** Write a nursery rhyme about people or animals. It can be funny or serious. Join your simple sentences, where you can.

18 Unit 1 • Chapter 5   Practice • Simple and Compound Sentences

---

CHALLENGE

A HISTORICAL ERA Have students choose a time in history that they think might be interesting as the setting for a story. Using at least three compound sentences, they can express why they consider that time an interesting one.

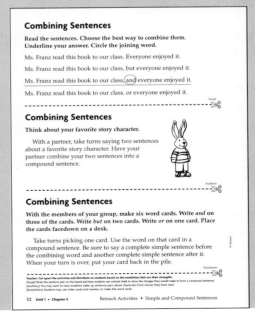

Combining Sentences

Read the sentences. Choose the best way to combine them. Underline your answer. Circle the joining word.

Ms. Franz read this book to our class. Everyone enjoyed it.

Ms. Franz read this book to our class, but everyone enjoyed it.

Ms. Franz read this book to our class, and everyone enjoyed it.

Ms. Franz read this book to our class, or everyone enjoyed it.

Combining Sentences

Think about your favorite story character.

With a partner, take turns saying two sentences about a favorite story character. Have your partner combine your two sentences into a compound sentence.

Combining Sentences

With the members of your group, make six word cards. Write *and* on three of the cards. Write *but* on two cards. Write *or* on one card. Place the cards facedown on a desk.

Take turns picking one card. Use the word on that card in a compound sentence. Be sure to say a complete simple sentence before the combining word and another complete simple sentence after it. When your turn is over, put your card back in the pile.

12 Unit 1 • Chapter 5   Reteach Activities • Simple and Compound Sentences

Extra Practice

OBJECTIVES
- To recognize complete, simple, and compound sentences
- To combine sentences to make compound sentences
- To write a summary and revise it by combining sentences

DAILY LANGUAGE PRACTICE

TRANSPARENCY 10

1. Do you know what my favorite magazine is (is?)
2. *national Geographic World* is a wonderful magazine. (National)

BRIDGE TO WRITING I look at magazines at the store, (combining word) I borrow them from the library.

ORAL WARM-UP

USE PRIOR KNOWLEDGE Ask students to recall a story they have read in class. Ask volunteers to explain what they liked about the story. Encourage students to use simple and compound sentences.

TEACH/MODEL

Use the Remember box to review complete, simple, and compound sentences. Remind students to place a comma before the combining word in compound sentences.

Have students complete the remaining Extra Practice items independently.

 Remember

that a complete sentence expresses a complete thought. Two or more simple sentences can be combined to make a compound sentence.

For more activities with complete sentences, visit *The Learning Site:* www.harcourtschool.com

68

Extra Practice

A. Write *complete sentence* if the group of words is a complete sentence. If it is not a complete sentence, rewrite the group of words to make a complete sentence.

pages 62–63 Responses will vary; possible responses are given.

1. Some magazines about science. Some magazines are about science.
2. Other children's magazines are about history. complete sentence
3. Not have to read every story in the magazine. You do not have to read every story in the magazine.
4. You can learn a lot from magazines. complete sentence
5. Magazines for computer users. There are magazines for computer users.

B. Write whether each sentence is a simple sentence or a compound sentence. *pages 64–65*

Examples: Now and then I read an adventure story. *simple sentence*

The story was about a dangerous trip, and it scared me. *compound sentence*

6. Usually, children love adventure stories. simple
7. The children in the story are brave, and they have many adventures. compound
8. Some adventure stories are set in faraway places, but others take place near home. compound
9. A child in the story was in danger, but his dog saved him. compound
10. Characters in adventure stories hike up mountains, sail boats, and explore caves. simple

---

Vocabulary Power page 15

Name _____

HOMOPHONES

▶ The words in each homophone pair below are pronounced the same but have different spellings and different meanings. Write the word from the Word Box that matches each clue below.

pear–pair	stare–stair	our–hour

Which word means . . .
1. "belongs to us"? ____ our
2. "sixty minutes"? ____ hour
3. "a fruit"? ____ pear
4. "two of something"? ____ pair
5. "something you climb"? ____ stair
6. "to look at"? ____ stare

▶ Now try these.

tale–tail	mail–male	whole–hole

Which word means . . .
7. "what you dig"? ____ hole
8. "all of something"? ____ whole
9. "what a dog wags"? ____ tail
10. "a story"? ____ tale
11. "a letter"? ____ mail
12. "a boy"? ____ male

Vocabulary Power   Unit 1 • Chapter 5   15

Listening and Speaking

ORAL BOOK REPORT Ask students to give an oral book report. On note cards they can write the book title, the author, a summary of the plot, their opinion of the book, and reasons that support their opinion. Students can refer to their note cards as they give their reports. Remind students to choose an appropriate volume and rate for their audience.

C. Use the word shown to combine each pair of sentences. *pages 66–67*

Example: Writers of children's stories work hard. They enjoy what they do. *and*
Writers of children's stories work hard, and they enjoy what they do.

11. Some children like to read aloud. They like to listen to stories. *or* Some children like to read aloud, or they like to listen to stories.

12. Many people write children's books. They must understand children. *and* Many people write children's books, and they must understand children.

13. Some writers know what children like to read. They know how to make children laugh. *and* Some writers know what children like to read, and they know how to make children laugh.

14. Writers must have good ideas. They need good imaginations, too. *and* Writers must have good ideas, and they need good imaginations, too.

15. Pictures can help children understand a story. Words are important, too. *but* Pictures can help children understand a story, but words are important, too.

16–20. Think about a book or story you have enjoyed. Write five compound sentences that tell about the setting, the characters, and the events of the story. *pages 64–65*

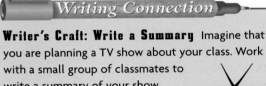

Writing Connection

Writer's Craft: Write a Summary Imagine that you are planning a TV show about your class. Work with a small group of classmates to write a summary of your show. Write at least ten sentences. Then revise your summary. Look for ways you can join sentences.

69

Building Oral Grammar

Students may find it helpful to remember that a comma indicates a pause in a sentence. Noticing where pauses occur naturally as they read aloud can help them place commas correctly. Have students work in pairs to read aloud the compound sentences from Part C. Tell them to notice where they pause naturally as they read. Then ask them to explain a reason or a rule for using a comma in that place in the sentence.

Writing Connection

Writer's Craft: Write a Summary Before students begin to write, have them create a story chart for their TV show. The chart can show characters, setting, and plot. Students can use the chart as the basis for their summary. Students should compose elaborated sentences in their written summaries.

WRAP-UP/ASSESS

SUMMARIZE Ask students how they can tell that a sentence is complete. Ask them to explain how to make a compound sentence. **REFLECTION**

ADDITIONAL PRACTICE An additional page of Extra Practice is provided on page 457 of the *Pupil Edition.*

PRACTICE page 19

Name _____

Extra Practice

A. Write *Complete sentence* if the statement is a complete sentence. Write *Not a sentence* if the statement is not a complete sentence.

1. Humpty Dumpty sat on. _____ Not a sentence

2. Humpty Dumpty fell off the wall. _____ Complete sentence

3. People tried to put him. _____ Not a sentence

4. Even the king's horses tried to help. _____ Complete sentence

5. Nobody could put him together again. _____ Complete sentence

B. Write *simple* or *compound* for each sentence.

6. "Old Mother Hubbard" is a tale about a woman and her dog. _____ simple

7. Her dog was hungry, and she looked for food for him. _____ compound

8. She wanted to give her dog a bone, but she could not find one. _____ compound

9. Her poor dog was very hungry. _____ simple

TRY THIS! Write four sentences describing how Old Mother Hubbard felt when she could not feed her dog. Join your simple sentences.

Practice • Simple and Compound Sentences   Unit 1 • Chapter 5   19

CHALLENGE

LETTER TO THE EDITOR Have students write a letter to the editor of their favorite magazine telling why they like the magazine. Tell them to use both simple and compound sentences in their letter.

TECHNOLOGY *Grammar Practice and Assessment* CD-ROM; *Writing Express* CD-ROM

INTERNET Visit *The Learning Site:*
www.harcourtschool.com

Chapter Review

OBJECTIVES

- To review complete, simple, and compound sentences
- To use word processing program features for writing

 SPIRAL REVIEW

DAILY LANGUAGE PRACTICE

TRANSPARENCY 10

1 Libby goes to the library every Thursday (Thursday.)

2 What kind of books does she like (?)

BRIDGE TO WRITING Libby reads books about real people, (combining word) she wants to write books when she grows up.

STANDARDIZED TEST PREP

MODEL TEST-TAKING STRATEGIES Have students read the directions on page 70 silently.

Remind them to eliminate the answers they know are wrong before deciding which choice is the right answer.

Model the thinking. Write this example on the board:

Mr. White the school librarian.

1 A Mr. White, and the school librarian.

   B Mr. White is the school librarian.

   C The school librarian.

   D Correct as is

MODEL The group of words does not express a complete thought, so it cannot be a sentence. So, D is wrong. The first answer does not include a predicate. Answer C also does not have a predicate. Answer B has a subject and a predicate, and it expresses a complete thought. It must be the correct answer.

Have students complete the Chapter Review independently.

Chapter Review

Choose the best way to write the underlined section of each sentence. Write the letter of your answer. If there is no mistake, choose "Correct as is."

STANDARDIZED TEST PREP

TIP Read the directions first. Try to put them into your own words to be sure you understand what you are supposed to do.

1 Most libraries have a <u>children's room or they have special</u> places for children's books.

   A children's room they have special

   B children's room. Have special

   C children's room, or they have special ᴄ

   D Correct as is

2 <u>Workers in a children's library.</u>

   F The workers in a children's library.

   G Workers in a children's library know children. ɢ

   H In a children's library know children.

   J Correct as is

3 Librarians know what children <u>like to read they buy books</u> that children love.

   A like to read, and they buy books ᴀ

   B like to read buying books

   C like to read, never buy books

   D Correct as is

4 <u>They may read a picture book.</u>

   F Reading a picture book.

   G They may picture book.

   H They may read book.

   J Correct as is ᴊ

For additional test preparations, visit *The Learning Site:* www.harcourtschool.com

70

Assessment

PORTFOLIO ASSESSMENT Have students select their best work from the Writing Connections on pages 65, 67, and 69.

ONGOING ASSESSMENT Evaluate the performance of 4–6 students using appropriate checklists and record forms from pages R74–R77.

INTERNET Activities and exercises to help students prepare for state and standardized assessments appear on *The Learning Site:* www.harcourtschool.com

Being a Good Reader

Good readers read for a purpose. They make sure they understand what they are reading. Being a good reader takes practice. Here are some strategies you can use as you read:

Preview the selection to get an idea of the subject.

Set a Purpose for reading the selection. Are you reading to get information or to be entertained?

Make and Confirm Predictions as you read. Make predictions about what you will learn or what will happen next. Were your predictions correct? You can change your predictions as you read more details about the subject or story.

Use Graphic Organizers to help you focus on your reading purpose. You can use Story Maps for fiction selections. K-W-L Charts are useful when you read nonfiction selections.

Summarize what you have learned as you read parts of the selection. If you are unsure about what you just read, go back and **reread** that part.

YOUR TURN

Choose a short article or story you would like to read. Read the selection once and then summarize what you read. Read the selection again using the strategies you learned above. Write a few sentences comparing how the second reading was different from the first.

71

STUDY SKILLS
Being a Good Reader

TEACH/MODEL

Explain that good readers often decide what information they are looking for before they begin to read. While they read, they keep their questions in mind.

Show students a book or an encyclopedia article about pianos. Ask volunteers to suggest questions about pianos. Explain that to find the information they want, they can skim the book or article and write down the important facts that answer their questions. Then have students write their own questions for investigating.

WRITING APPLICATION Have students use the notes they took to write a brief paragraph telling what they learned.

WRAP-UP/ASSESS

Writer's Journal

SUMMARIZE Ask students to suggest one piece of advice they would give someone about reading to find information.

PRACTICE page 20

REACHING ALL LEARNERS

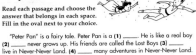

Name _____

Chapter Review

Read each passage and choose the answer that belongs in each space. Fill in the oval next to your choice.

"Peter Pan" is a fairy tale. Peter Pan is a **(1)** _____. He is like a real boy **(2)** _____ never grows up. His friends are called the Lost Boys **(3)** _____ live in Never-Never Land. **(4)** _____ many adventures in Never-Never Land.

Peter Pan took Wendy to Never-Never Land. Wendy took care of Peter **(5)** _____ Lost Boys. After some time, Wendy wanted to go home **(6)** _____ made Peter sad. Wendy went home and grew up **(7)** _____ never forgot Peter Pan.

1 ○ who
  ● boy
  ○ not
  ○ was

2 ○ and
  ○ , and
  ○ , can he
  ● , but he

3 ○ never and
  ○ , sometimes
  ● , and they
  ○ , but

4 ● They have
  ○ Who are
  ○ And, so
  ○ But,

5 ○ , and she
  ○ , but who
  ● and the
  ○ and, the

6 ○ but,
  ● , and this
  ○ and, this
  ○ but, who

7 ○ who was
  ○ tall she
  ● , but she
  ○ but, not

20 **Unit 1 • Chapter 5**   Practice • Simple and Compound Sentences

---

CHALLENGE

REACHING ALL LEARNERS

READ WITH PURPOSE Tell students that they can read for different purposes. Explain that reading can be for being entertained or for getting information.

Pair students and challenge them to read with purpose. Have one student read a short article for entertainment and have another student read the same article for the purpose of getting information. Have each student summarize what he or she read. Discuss how they met each purpose.

TECHNOLOGY Additional writing activities are provided on the *Writing Express* CD-ROM

Writing Workshop

Personal Narrative
pages 72–83

LESSON ORGANIZER	DAY 1	DAY 2
DAILY LANGUAGE PRACTICE TRANSPARENCY 11	1. your personal narrative will tell a story from your past (Your; past.) 2. will you include family, friends, and pets in your story. (Will; story?)	1. i will write about teaching my dog new tricks (I; tricks.) 2. I taught her to sit and shake hands? (hands.)
ORAL WARM-UP **Listening/Speaking**	Discuss Friendship 72 Suggest Reasons for Sharing Personal Experiences 78	Describe Daily Routines 79
TEACH/MODEL **WRITING**	**Literature Model:** "My First American Friend" 73-75 **GUIDED WRITING** ✔ **Prewriting** 78 • To learn strategies for prewriting a personal narrative • To choose a topic and generate ideas for a personal narrative Interactive Writing 78	**GUIDED WRITING** ✔ **Drafting** 79 • To learn strategies for drafting a personal narrative • To draft a personal narrative **Transparency** 12
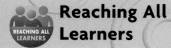 **Reaching All Learners**	**Modified Instruction** 84 Below-Level: Check Punctuation Above-Level: Complete Sentences *ESL Manual* pp. 34, 35	**Modified Instruction** 85 Below-Level: Discuss Unfamiliar Words Above-Level: Create Compound Subjects *ESL Manual* p. 34
GRAMMAR	**Unit 1 Review:** ✔ **Sentences** 84	**Unit 1 Review:** ✔ **Subjects/Nouns** 85
CROSS-CURRICULAR/ ENRICHMENT	**LISTENING AND SPEAKING:** 76 **EVALUATION CRITERIA:** Establish Criteria for Writing 77 **HANDS-ON ACTIVITY:** End Mark Matchup 84 *Vocabulary Power* Explore Word Meaning 74	**HANDS-ON ACTIVITY:** Find a Subject 85 *Vocabulary Power* Context Clues 74 *Vocabulary Power book* p. 16  **Vocabulary activity**

KEY
✔ = tested writing form/skill

episode, event, **experience,** incident, situation
See *Vocabulary Power* book.

DAY 3

1. patience and understanding are needed to teach a dog tricks (Patience; tricks.)

2. Do you know how to teach an old dog new tricks (tricks?)

Add Details 80

GUIDED WRITING
✔ **Revising** 80
- To learn strategies for revising a personal narrative
- To revise a personal narrative

 Transparencies 13a and 13b

Modified Instruction 86
  Below-Level: Find Complete Predicates
  Above-Level: Combine Sentences
ESL Manual p. 34

Unit 1 Review:
✔ **Predicates/Verbs** 86

PEER CONFERENCES: Make Essays Stronger 80

TEST PREP **TEST PREP:** Combining Sentences 86

Vocabulary Power

Multiple-Meaning Words 74
Vocabulary Power book p. 17

 Vocabulary activity

DAY 4

1. My dog can't sit but he knows how to shake hands. (sit,)

2. would you like to teach your dog tricks! (Would; tricks?)

Review Capitalization and Punctuation 81

GUIDED WRITING
✔ **Proofreading** 81
- To learn strategies for proofreading a personal narrative
- To proofread a personal narrative

Transparencies 14a and 14b

Proofreading practice

Modified Instruction 87
  Below-Level: Sentence Clues
  Above-Level: Combine Sentences
ESL: Spelling Aids 81
ESL Manual p. 34

Unit 1 Review:
✔ **Simple and Compound Sentences** 87

TEST PREP **TEST PREP:** Extra Practice 87

Vocabulary Power

Synonyms 74
Vocabulary Power book p. 18

Vocabulary activity

DAY 5

1. My classmates my family, and other dog owners may also train their dogs (classmates,; dogs.)

2. I think Keiko, and Rod want to teach tricks to their dogs? (Keiko and; dogs.)

Compare Publishing Preferences 82

GUIDED WRITING
✔ **Publishing** 82
- To learn strategies for publishing a personal narrative
- To publish a personal narrative by acting it out

Practice and assessment

ESL: Pronunciation Practice 82
ESL Manual p. 34

HANDS-ON ACTIVITIES
21I–21J

LISTENING AND SPEAKING:
  Acting Out a Story 83

Vocabulary Power

Compare and Contrast 74

Using the Literature Model

OBJECTIVE
• To read and analyze a personal narrative

DAILY LANGUAGE PRACTICE

TRANSPARENCY 11

1 your personal narrative will tell a story from your past (Your; past.)

2 will you include family, friends, and pets in your story. (Will; story?)

ORAL WARM-UP

USE PRIOR KNOWLEDGE Read aloud the boldfaced introduction to the personal narrative, and discuss questions such as the following:

1. **What kinds of things might a child moving to America from another country have trouble doing?** (Possible responses: Making friends, speaking the language, getting used to a new school)

2. **In what ways is making new friends difficult?** (Possible responses: You may not know what to talk about at first; you may think people don't like you.)

PREREADING STRATEGIES

PREVIEW/SET PURPOSE Have students read the title, the selection introduction, and the first paragraph of the selection. Ask: **How do you think Sarunna Jin made her first American friend?** Students should give reasons for their predictions. Then have students set their own purpose for reading, or have them read to find out why Jin wrote about her first American friend.

72

School-Home Connection

Family members can help students recall important events in their lives and fill in details that students may have forgotten. Families may want to look at old photographs or letters to help them remember past events.

In Chapter 3, you learned about personal voice. In this chapter, you will use what you learned as you write a personal narrative, a story about yourself. Before you begin, you will read a personal narrative written by a Chinese girl after she came to the United States. As you read, think about the writer's viewpoint and what this story tells about her.

My First American Friend

story by Sarunna Jin
illustrated by Stacey Schuett

Sarunna Jin left her home in China when she was just six years old. As a third-grader, she wrote this narrative about her experience with a special friend when she first came to the United States.

Soon after I got to America, I started first grade. I didn't know any English. That made it difficult for me to do everything. I tried to talk with the other children, but we could not understand each other.

73

OPTIONS FOR READING

READ-ALOUD OPTION Read the personal narrative aloud, and have students listen to determine Jin's audience, purpose, and main reasons for writing.

INDEPENDENT OPTION As students read, have them stop periodically to summarize what they think the narrator's feelings are to that point.

Ask students what problems they think the narrator will encounter in first grade. Use questions like the following to help students monitor their comprehension:

3. **Why couldn't Sarunna Jin and the other first graders understand each other?** (Jin didn't know any English and the other first graders didn't know Chinese.) **LITERAL: NOTE DETAILS**

4. **What purpose might Sarunna Jin have had for telling this narrative?** (Possible response: She might have wanted to share her experience of starting school in a new country.) **INFERENTIAL: DETERMINE AUTHOR'S PURPOSE**

SELECTION SUMMARY

GENRE: PERSONAL NARRATIVE In this personal narrative, Sarunna Jin recalls starting first grade soon after arriving in the United States from China. She did not speak English, so making friends was a difficult task. Finally, a classmate named Ali befriended her despite the language barrier. The next year Ali moved away, but Sarunna's English had improved, and she was able to make many new friends.

ABOUT THE AUTHOR

The young author **Sarunna Jin** came to America from China when she was six years old. When she was in the third grade, she wrote *My First American Friend*. After Ali moved away, she and Sarunna met again two years later at the Young-Publish-a-Book award ceremony. Sarunna wants to be a medical doctor when she grows up.

5. **How do you think the narrator felt when Ali first approached her? Give reasons for your answer.** (Possible response: She probably felt nervous because she didn't speak English but excited at the idea of becoming friends with Ali.) **METACOGNITIVE: DETERMINE CHARACTERS' EMOTIONS**

6. **How did the narrator feel when she found out that Ali was moving? How would you feel in the same situation?** (Possible response: She felt sad. I would be sad, too. I also would feel scared that I might not be able to make more friends.) **CRITICAL: IDENTIFY WITH CHARACTERS**

7. **Do you think Sarunna Jin tells her story well? Why or why not?** (Responses will vary) **CRITICAL: MAKE JUDGMENTS**

8. **How does Sarunna Jin use descriptions and details to help the reader "see" the events in the story?** (Possible responses: She describes Ali's eyes, smile, and hair; she tells how they played together; and she tells how she felt.) **INFERENTIAL: AUTHOR'S CRAFT/APPRECIATE LANGUAGE**

No one played with me. Oh, how sad and lonely I was for my friends that I had left behind! I felt especially sad when my mom read a letter from my grandmother. It said that one of my friends in China had knocked on my grandmother's door and asked, "Is Sarunna back yet?" That made me sadder. Then something happened to make me feel better.

I was sitting at my desk during playtime when a girl named Ali came over to play with me. Ali had blue eyes, a pretty smile, and beautiful blonde hair. I had never seen such pretty hair before. Even though I could only speak a little bit of English, Ali and I had lots of fun together. She let me touch her pretty hair.

From that day on, we always played together at school. Sometimes we played on the swings. Sometimes we played on the slide.

74

Vocabulary Power

DAY 1 EXPLORE WORD MEANING Introduce and define *experience*. Ask: **What are some of your most memorable experiences?**

DAY 2 CONTEXT CLUES Say: *I hope I never have that experience again.* Ask students whether they think this sentence refers to a good experience or an unpleasant one. What clues in the sentence tell them? (See also *Vocabulary Power*, page 16.)

DAY 3 MULTIPLE-MEANING WORDS Explain that *experience* can mean "something one has gone through" or "knowledge gained by doing something." **What are some other words that have more than one meaning?** (See also *Vocabulary Power*, page 17.)

DAY 4 SYNONYMS Many words have similar meanings. What are some synonyms for *experience*? (See also *Vocabulary Power*, page 18.)

DAY 5 COMPARE AND CONTRAST **Do we all have the same experiences? Why or why not?**

In the classroom, we built blocks and painted together. Ali and I became best friends and were very happy.

At the end of the school year, Ali told me that she was moving to another school. I was sad again because my very best friend was leaving. On the last day of school, we hugged and said good-bye.

In second grade, my English improved a lot. I still had some problems with the language, but I made many new friends.

This year, I am in the third grade, and my English is perfect! I have many friends now. I'm very happy, but I'll always remember Ali, my first American friend.

Vocabulary Power

ex•pe•ri•ence
[ik•spir´ē•əns] *n.*
Something one has gone through; knowledge or skill gained by doing something.

Analyze THE *Model*

1. Name some colorful words Sarunna uses to help you imagine the events in her personal narrative.

2. What do the beginning, middle, and ending of a personal narrative do?

3. Think about what Sarunna learned. What would you say if a friend said, "I'm scared about making friends at my new school"?

75

RESPONSE TO LITERATURE

WRITING PROMPT To have students respond in writing to the narrative, use the following prompt:

Why do you think Sarunna Jin chose this event as the topic of a personal narrative? Explain your response in a short paragraph.

Analyze THE *Model*

1. Name some colorful words Sarunna uses to help you imagine the events in her personal narrative. (Possible responses: *sad, lonely, beautiful blonde hair,* and *happy*)
LITERAL: NOTE DETAILS

2. What do the beginning, middle, and ending of a personal narrative do? (Possible response: The beginning tells where and when something happens and introduces the writer. The middle tells what happens and what the writer thinks and feels. The ending tells how things work out.)
INFERENTIAL: TEXT STRUCTURE

3. Think about what Sarunna learned. What would you say if a friend said, "I'm scared about making friends at my new school"? (Possible response: Find a nice person in your class, and ask him or her to do something with you that you both enjoy.) **INFERENTIAL: SYNTHESIZE**

SUMMARIZE THE MODEL

ONE-SENTENCE SUMMARY Ask: **If you were to tell a classmate what this personal narrative is about, what would you say?** Have students write one sentence to summarize the personal narrative. (Possible response: A girl from China meets her first American friend at school.)

TECHNOLOGY Additional writing activities are provided on the *Writing Express* CD-ROM

Parts of a Personal Narrative

OBJECTIVES
- To recognize and understand the parts of a personal narrative
- To analyze and summarize a personal narrative
- To establish criteria for evaluating personal narratives
- To listen critically to a personal narrative

READING LIKE A WRITER

READ AND RESPOND TO THE MODEL Tell students that you will read aloud Marty's personal narrative, and ask them to listen to find out what happened to Marty and what he learned from the event. Then read the personal narrative aloud, and discuss whether Marty's first paragraph introduces the topic of his personal narrative. Discuss whether his last paragraph tells what he learned.

FOCUS ON ORGANIZATION Have students reread the personal narrative independently, stopping after every two paragraphs to summarize the story. Ask: **Why do you think Marty describes his personality before he explains what happened at the school concert?** (Possible response: He wants his audience to understand why he didn't practice for the concert.)

FOCUS ON WRITER'S CRAFT Have students point out examples of Marty's personal voice in the narrative. (Possible responses: "I have always loved to play trumpet"; "'I can play it with my eyes closed!'") Ask: **How does Marty's use of personal voice help you understand his personality?** (Possible response: It lets me know how he thinks and feels about things.)

READING — WRITING CONNECTION

Parts of a Personal Narrative

In her personal narrative, Sarunna Jin described an important event in her life. Study this personal narrative, written by a student named Marty. Pay attention to the parts of a personal narrative.

MODEL

writer's viewpoint

beginning

dialogue/ using *I*

using *my*

middle

Practice Makes Perfect

I have always loved to play the trumpet. When I was in first grade, everyone told me how talented I was, and I believed them. I practiced only the music I liked.

I was in the school band. One day my director said, "Marty, here's a solo. I want you to play it at the fall concert. It's not easy, so make sure you practice it."

"I can play it with my eyes closed!" I said.

The final rehearsal came. I hadn't practiced my solo one bit. The director raised his baton, and we began to play. Everything went fine until my solo. My tone was clear, but the notes and rhythm were all wrong. By the end of the solo, I was almost in tears.

Luckily, I still had one week before our performance. I spent every night that

Listening and Speaking

Working in groups of three, students can each tell about an event that happened to him or her in the past. Prompt them to include information and details to show personal voice. Tell students to use the appropriate vocabulary to describe their ideas, feelings, and experience. Have the two listeners in the group take simple notes and ask questions about the event.

Have students take turns so that each student has a chance to tell about an event.

week practicing my solo. I stayed up as late as my parents would let me, trying to play the solo as well as I could.

    The night of the concert, I played my solo okay, but I did not play my best. My experience taught me that practice is very important. I knew I would certainly be better prepared for our next concert!

details / using *me*

end / writer's viewpoint

Analyze THE Model

1. **Why does Marty begin by writing about his love for playing the trumpet?**

2. **What details does Marty use to help you picture the events of his personal narrative?**

3. **What can you learn from Marty's story?**

Summarize THE Model

Use a flowchart like the one shown here to help you identify the main events in Marty's personal narrative. Then use your flowchart to write a summary of his personal narrative. Be sure to include all the important points. Leave out the details.

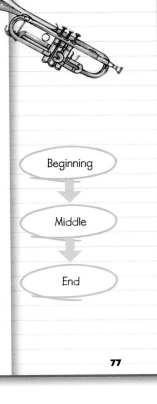

Beginning

↓

Middle

↓

End

Writer's Craft

Personal Voice Find words and sentences in Marty's personal narrative that express his thoughts and feelings. Then tell why Marty includes these words and sentences in his personal narrative.

77

Evaluation Criteria

. . . .

ESTABLISH CRITERIA FOR WRITING Tell students that they will help to evaluate their own personal narratives. Have them turn to the rubric on page 496 in their Handbooks. Explain that if students meet the criteria in the "4" column plus the criteria that you and the class add, they will have produced their best work. Discuss the criteria, and add additional criteria based on your students' needs and interests. Remind students to refer to the rubric as they write their narratives. (A teacher version of the rubric is available on page R80. For more information about evaluating writing, see pages R78–R79 in this *Teacher's Edition.*)

1. **Why does Marty begin by writing about his love for playing the trumpet?** (Possible response: It tells something important about him and introduces the topic of his personal narrative.) **CRITICAL: INTERPRET TEXT STRUCTURE**

2. **What details does Marty use to help you picture the events of his personal narrative?** (Responses may include: He tells the exact words he and his director said to each other; he says that he made mistakes with the notes and rhythm of his solo and that he was almost in tears at the end of it; he explains that he stayed up late practicing.) **LITERAL: NOTE DETAILS**

3. **What can you learn from Marty's story?** (Possible response: Practice makes perfect.) **INFERENTIAL: MAIN IDEA**

SUMMARIZE THE MODEL

Have students work in groups to compare their flowcharts. Ask each group to provide a summary of the personal narrative, based on the completed charts. Evaluate whether students have included all important points while omitting unnecessary details.

WRITER'S CRAFT

PERSONAL VOICE Explain to students that in this selection Marty uses his personal voice when he expresses his own viewpoint. Ask students to recall another way to show personal voice.

TAKE-HOME BOOK 1 provides an additional model of expressive writing and home activities. See *Practice Book* pages 121–124.

Prewriting

OBJECTIVES
• To learn strategies for prewriting a personal narrative
• To choose a topic and generate ideas for a personal narrative

ORAL WARM-UP

USE PRIOR KNOWLEDGE Ask students to tell some reasons authors share their personal experiences.

GUIDED WRITING

Have a volunteer read the writing prompt. Have students identify their purpose and audience. (purpose—to share a personal narrative about doing an activity they love; audience—classmates) Then model finding an appropriate topic.

MODEL **I like playing baseball and watching movies, but the thing I like best is playing with my dog. Teaching her to do tricks was hard, but I learned to be more patient because of that experience.**

Then have students read Marty's model and make their own story maps, using the given prompt or a prompt you assign.

SELF-INITIATED WRITING Have students choose their own topics for personal narratives.

WRAP-UP/ASSESS

SUMMARIZE **How might a story map be helpful for planning a personal narrative?**

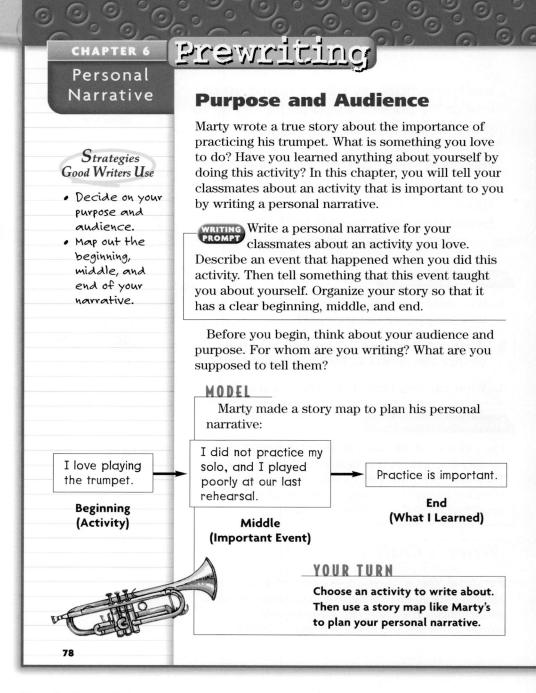

Prewriting

Purpose and Audience

Marty wrote a true story about the importance of practicing his trumpet. What is something you love to do? Have you learned anything about yourself by doing this activity? In this chapter, you will tell your classmates about an activity that is important to you by writing a personal narrative.

WRITING PROMPT Write a personal narrative for your classmates about an activity you love. Describe an event that happened when you did this activity. Then tell something that this event taught you about yourself. Organize your story so that it has a clear beginning, middle, and end.

Before you begin, think about your audience and purpose. For whom are you writing? What are you supposed to tell them?

MODEL

Marty made a story map to plan his personal narrative:

Strategies Good Writers Use
• Decide on your purpose and audience.
• Map out the beginning, middle, and end of your narrative.

I love playing the trumpet.
Beginning (Activity)

I did not practice my solo, and I played poorly at our last rehearsal.
Middle (Important Event)

Practice is important.
End (What I Learned)

YOUR TURN

Choose an activity to write about. Then use a story map like Marty's to plan your personal narrative.

78

Vocabulary Power page 16

Name _____

CONTEXT CLUES

Read each sentence, paying attention to the underlined words. Then answer the questions about each word.

1. We got tickets for the big event.
   What are three events you would need tickets for? Responses will vary. Accept reasonable responses.

2. I can't wait to experience the circus.
   What are some words you could use in place of experience?
   Responses will vary. Accept reasonable responses.

3. We had an incident in our class when our hamster got out.
   What are some other incidents that happen during the school day?
   Responses will vary. Accept reasonable responses.

4. Sue was just in a fun situation. She got to meet a movie star!
   What are some fun situations you have been in?
   Responses will vary. Accept reasonable responses.

5. I can't wait to see the next episode of the show.
   Tell about an episode of your favorite show.

16 Unit 1 • Chapter 6   Vocabulary Power

Interactive Writing

You may want to prewrite and write a first draft as a group. Draw students' attention to the Strategies Good Writers Use. Have students help you complete a story map, including a beginning, a middle, and an end. Then use the Drafting Transparency with students, coaching them to use effective organization and elaboration.

Drafting

Organization and Elaboration

Before you begin your draft, read through these steps:

STEP 1 Begin by describing the activity. Tell readers why you like this activity.

STEP 2 Use details to describe something that happened when you did this activity.

STEP 3 Use the strategies for personal voice you learned in Chapter 3.

STEP 4 End by telling readers what you have learned about yourself as a result of doing this activity.

MODEL

Here is the beginning of Marty's personal narrative. What activity will he describe? How do you know? What clues does Marty give about the lesson he will learn?

> I have always loved to play the trumpet. When I was in first grade, everyone told me how talented I was, and I believed them. I practiced only the music I liked.

YOUR TURN

Write a draft of your personal narrative. Use your story map as a guide. Tell about the event and explain what you learned about yourself. Remember to use your personal voice.

Strategies Good Writers Use

- Use vivid descriptive words.
- Use personal voice to describe your thoughts and feelings.

Use a computer to draft your essay. You can use the Spell-check feature to double-check your spelling.

79

Vocabulary Power page 17

Name _____

MULTIPLE-MEANING WORDS

▶ Many words have more than one meaning. Clues from the sentence will tell you which meaning is being used. Read each sentence below. Circle the letter of the meaning of the underlined word.

1. I had an interesting <u>experience</u> this morning.
   (A) something one has gone through
   B knowledge or skill gained by doing something

2. My uncle has two years of <u>experience</u> as a carpenter.
   A something one has gone through
   (B) knowledge or skill gained by doing something

3. He read the final <u>episode</u> of the play.
   A an event in history
   (B) one of a series of connected stories

4. I went to the <u>event</u> with my sister.
   (A) an important occasion
   B final outcome; result

5. When I get nervous, my hands <u>quiver</u>.
   (A) to make a trembling motion
   B a case for carrying arrows

6. Tammy made a <u>bolt</u> for the exit.
   A a rod for holding something in place
   (B) a sudden start

▶ Write a sentence using one of the meanings of the word *experience*. Then have a partner read your sentence and write on a separate sheet of paper a definition for the meaning of *experience* you used.

_____

Vocabulary Power   Unit 1 • Chapter 6 17

TRANSPARENCY 12

DRAFTING
Personal Narrative

Describe the activity. Tell why you like it.

Use details to describe something that happened when you did this activity. Use personal voice to express your feelings and viewpoint.

Tell readers what you learned about yourself as a result of doing this activity.

Harcourt Language
Level 3   12   Chapter 6
                                    Writing a Personal Narrative

---

Drafting

OBJECTIVES
- To learn strategies for drafting a personal narrative
- To draft a personal narrative

TRANSPARENCY 11

1 i will write about teaching my dog new tricks (I; tricks.)

2 I taught her to sit and shake hands? (hands.)

ORAL WARM-UP

USE PRIOR KNOWLEDGE Ask volunteers to describe their daily routine at school, beginning with the morning and working through the afternoon. Point out that the events are organized in time order. Explain that students may organize the events in their personal narratives in time order, as well.

GUIDED WRITING

Discuss the Organization and Elaboration steps and the model. Ask volunteers to answer the questions that precede the model. (Possible responses: Marty's narrative will describe trumpet playing. He begins by telling that he loves to play the trumpet. His statement "I practiced only the music I liked" suggests that he will learn to practice other kinds of music.)

As students draft their stories, remind them to keep their purpose and audience in mind. Have students use the personal narratives by Sarunna Jin and Marty as models.

WRAP-UP/ASSESS

SUMMARIZE Did you use all your prewriting ideas in your draft? Why or why not?

Revising

OBJECTIVES
- To learn strategies for revising a personal narrative
- To revise a personal narrative

DAILY LANGUAGE PRACTICE

TRANSPARENCY 11

1 patience and understanding are needed to teach a dog tricks
(Patience; tricks.)

2 Do you know how to teach an old dog new tricks (tricks?)

ORAL WARM-UP

USE PRIOR KNOWLEDGE On the board, write: *I taught my dog to do tricks.* Ask students to suggest information or details they could add to make this sentence more specific.

GUIDED WRITING

Review with students the questions listed under Organization and Elaboration. Discuss the model and point out the differences between showing and telling. Explain that Marty's new last sentence shows that he was a bragger, instead of just telling this information, because the new sentence quotes something he said when he was bragging to his director.

Use **Transparencies 13a and 13b** to further model the thinking. Then have students revise their drafts to achieve precise word choices. They can keep their revisions in their working portfolios.

PEER CONFERENCES Have pairs of students use the **Evaluation Criteria** to evaluate their own and each other's writing, responding constructively by identifying strengths and suggesting improvements.

WRAP-UP/ASSESS

SUMMARIZE Which revision improved your personal narrative the most?

Strategies Good Writers Use

- Add information the reader will need to understand the events.
- Take out unnecessary information.
- Join sentences that go together.

Organization and Elaboration

Read your draft carefully. Think about these questions:

- How can I make my beginning, middle, and end stronger?
- Where should I add information or details?
- Is there any information I don't need?
- How can I explain what I learned more clearly?

MODEL

See how Marty revised his personal narrative. What information did he add? Find a sentence that he cut. Look at the last sentence. See how he changed the sentence to "show" instead of "tell" about himself.

> I was in the school band.
> One day my director said, "That's all for today, everyone. Marty, here's a solo. I want you to play it at the fall concert. It's not easy, so make sure you practice it."
> "I can play it with my eyes closed!" I said.
> But I was a bragger, and I thought I never needed to practice.

YOUR TURN

Revise your personal narrative. Add more details to help your reader clearly understand the events. Remove details you do not need. If you would like, you and a partner can trade essays and give each other suggestions.

80

TRANSPARENCIES 13a and 13b

REVISING

> I was in the school band.
> One day my director said, "That's all for today, everyone. Marty, here's a solo. I want you to play it at the fall concert. It's not easy, so make sure you practice it."
> "I can play it with my eyes closed!" I said.
> But I was a bragger, and I thought I never needed to practice.

Harcourt Language
Level 3
13
Chapter 6
Writing a Personal Narrative

Vocabulary Power page 18

Name _____

SYNONYMS

▶ Read each word. Then write a word that means almost the same thing.

tale	incident	kids
exam	intelligent	shine

1. shimmer	_____	shine
2. test	_____	exam
3. smart	_____	intelligent
4. event	_____	incident
5. children	_____	kids
6. story	_____	tale

▶ Now try these.

creature	happy	motion picture
event	kind	angry

7. experience	_____	event
8. glad	_____	happy
9. upset	_____	angry
10. animal	_____	creature
11. friendly	_____	kind
12. movie	_____	motion picture

18   Unit 1 • Chapter 6

Vocabulary Power

Proofreading

Checking Your Language

When you proofread, you look for mistakes in grammar, spelling, punctuation, and capitalization. If you do not fix these mistakes, your writing may not be clear for your readers.

MODEL

Here's how Marty's work continued. After he revised it, he proofread his story. Look at the punctuation he added. What other errors did he fix?

The final rehearsal. I hadn't practiced my ^came^
solo one bit. The director raised his baton. We ^and^
began to play. Everything went fine until
my solo. my tone was clere but the notes and ^clear^
rhythm were all wrong. By the end of the
solo, was almost in taers.

YOUR TURN

Proofread your story. Make sure that you:
- **use complete sentences.**
- **start each sentence with a capital letter.**
- **end each sentence with a punctuation mark.**
- **use correct spelling.**

Strategies Good Writers Use

- Use complete sentences.
- Put a punctuation mark at the end of each sentence.
- Make sure all words are spelled correctly.

Editor's Marks
- ✗ take out text
- ^ add text
- ↷ move text
- ¶ new paragraph
- ☰ capitalize
- / lowercase
- ○ correct spelling

81

TRANSPARENCIES 14a and 14b

PROOFREADING

The final rehearsal. I hadn't ^came^
practiced my solo one bit. The
director raised his baton. We ^and^
began to play. Everything went fine
until my solo. my tone was clere ^clear^
but the notes and rhythm were all
wrong. By the end of the solo,
was almost in taers.

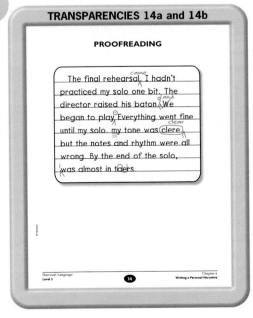

Harcourt Language
Level 1   14   Chapter 6
Writing a Personal Narrative

Proofreading

OBJECTIVES
- To learn strategies for proofreading a personal narrative
- To proofread a personal narrative

SPIRAL REVIEW

DAILY LANGUAGE PRACTICE

TRANSPARENCY 11

1. My dog can't sit but he knows how to shake hands. (sit,)
2. would you like to teach your dog tricks! (Would; tricks?)

ORAL WARM-UP

USE PRIOR KNOWLEDGE Review what students have learned about capitalization and punctuation of simple and compound sentences. Tell them to check those things as they proofread their personal narratives.

GUIDED WRITING

Have students explain how Marty corrected the errors in his work. Use **Transparencies 14a and 14b** to help students practice proofreading. Then have students proofread their personal narratives. Tell them to look for words with the CVC and CVC*e* spelling patterns in their personal narratives. Students should demonstrate increased proficiency in spelling these words correctly.

WRAP-UP/ASSESS

SUMMARIZE Why is it important to proofread your writing?

Visit The Learning Site!
www.harcourtschool.com

Publishing

OBJECTIVES
- To learn strategies for publishing a personal narrative
- To publish a personal narrative by acting it out

DAILY LANGUAGE PRACTICE

TRANSPARENCY 11

1 My classmates my family, and other dog owners may also train their dogs (classmates,; dogs.)

2 I think Keiko, and Rod want to teach tricks to their dogs? (Keiko and; dogs.)

ORAL WARM-UP

USE PRIOR KNOWLEDGE Ask: **Which do you like best: to read a story, to hear it told, or to watch it acted out?** Ask volunteers to explain their answers.

GUIDED WRITING

SHARING YOUR WORK Read and discuss the questions with students. Help them decide where and how to publish their personal narratives.

If computers are available, have students input their personal narratives. Explain that using a computer allows them the opportunity to do a final spell check. Remind them that a spell check does not always find incorrect words, so they should check their work for spelling mistakes using a dictionary, too.

REFLECTING ON YOUR WRITING Use the Portfolio Conferences suggestions at the right.

INTERNET Activities and exercises to help students prepare for state and standardized assessments appear on *The Learning Site:*

www.harcourtschool.com

Sharing Your Work

Now you will publish your personal narrative. Answer these questions to help you decide on the best way to share your work:

1. Who is your audience? How can you publish your personal narrative so that your audience can read and enjoy it?

2. Should you include pictures with your personal narrative to help your readers better imagine the events you're describing?

3. Should you present your personal narrative aloud? To act out your story, use the information on page 83.

USING YOUR
Handbook

Use the rubric on page 496 to evaluate your personal narrative.

Reflecting on Your Writing

Using Your Portfolio What did you learn about your writing in this chapter? Write your answer to each question below.

1. Did your writing meet its purpose?

2. Using the rubric from your Handbook, how would you score your own writing?

Add your answers to your portfolio. Then review your personal narrative. Make a checklist of ways to improve your writing. Add your checklist and your personal narrative to your portfolio.

82

Assessment

. . . .

PORTFOLIO CONFERENCES
Discuss the questions in the *Pupil Edition,* and direct students to write their answers and add them to their portfolios. Tell students you will meet with them individually to discuss their growth as writers. Use the Student Record Form on page R74 to record and monitor students' progress.

ESL

PRONUNCIATION PRACTICE
Have students work with English-fluent partners to read their narratives aloud as their partner listens for any problems with pronunciation. Then have students practice the correct pronunciation for difficult words.

Acting Out a Story

Marty decided to act out his personal narrative. He played his trumpet to act out some parts of it. If you want to act out your personal narrative, follow these steps:

STEP 1 Plan how the people in your personal narrative should look and sound to the audience. Do they use certain hand motions? What are their voices like?

STEP 2 Find props for your narrative. Since your narrative is about something you like doing, find a prop related to that activity. You can use different kinds of clothing, pictures, and other items.

STEP 3 Decide how you want to present your personal narrative. Do you want to read it just as it is written, or do you want to set aside your writing and present it more dramatically? You could even ask your friends in class to help you present your personal narrative as a play.

Oral Presentations

Here are some ways you can improve your oral presentation:

- Find the voice that is right for each person in your narrative. Experiment with your voice. Try using loud voices, soft voices, slow-speaking voices, and so on.
- Imitate the actions and hand motions of people in your narrative.
- Practice presenting your narrative so you do not have to look at the words all the time.

83

LISTENING AND SPEAKING
Acting Out a Story

Discuss ways to make a personal narrative interesting for the audience. Suggest that students present their stories in dialogue instead of narrative form. Discuss nonverbal communication, and have volunteers act out some gestures and facial expressions that might indicate happiness, concern, fear, relief, and so on.

As students prepare their oral presentations, tell them to choose vocabulary that clearly expresses their ideas, feelings, and experiences.

Before students act out their narratives, review and discuss audience manners and listening strategies with the class. Use the Student Record Form on page R76 to assess students' listening and speaking skills.

WRAP-UP/ASSESS

Writer's Journal

SUMMARIZE Ask students to write in their journals to reflect on what they liked about acting out their personal narratives.
REFLECTION

SCORING RUBRIC

4 ADVANCED
Purpose and Audience
- appropriate for audience
- stays focused on purpose

Organization and Elaboration
- clear beginning, middle with events in order, and clear ending
- description and details
- interesting words and phrases
- sentence variety

Language
- uses correct grammar
- uses correct spelling, usage, and mechanics

3 PROFICIENT
Purpose and Audience
- mostly appropriate for audience
- few deviations from purpose

Organization and Elaboration
- has beginning and ending with solution, but order of events in middle is unclear
- some description and details
- some interesting words and phrases
- some sentence variety

Language
- mostly uses correct grammar
- mostly uses correct spelling, usage, and mechanics

2 BASIC
Purpose and Audience
- not appropriate for audience
- often strays from purpose

Organization and Elaboration
- does not have a clear beginning, middle, or ending
- little description and few details
- few interesting words and phrases
- little sentence variety

Language
- incorrect grammar, spelling, usage, or mechanics sometimes makes writing unclear

1 LIMITED
Purpose and Audience
- not appropriate for audience
- purpose is unclear

Organization and Elaboration
- does not have a beginning, middle, or ending
- no description or details
- no interesting words or phrases
- most sentences written incorrectly

Language
- incorrect grammar, spelling, usage, or mechanics often makes writing unclear

For information on adapting this rubric to 5- or 6-point scales, see pages R78–R79.

Unit 1
Grammar Review
CHAPTER 1

Sentences

OBJECTIVES
• To recognize complete sentences
• To identify sentence types
• To use appropriate capitalization and punctuation

Unit Review
MODIFIED INSTRUCTION

BELOW-LEVEL STUDENTS Suggest that as students complete each item in Part B, they use the end mark to check their answer. Point out that the names of two end marks identify the sentence type—that is, a *question mark* is used at the end of a question, and an *exclamation point* is used at the end of an exclamation.

ABOVE-LEVEL STUDENT After students have completed Part A, suggest that they add words to complete the word groups that are not sentences (items 2, 3, and 5). Have students compare and discuss the new, complete sentences.

Unit 1
Grammar Review
CHAPTER 1

Sentences
pages 24–33

84

Sentences   *pages 24–25*

A. Write *sentence* if the group of words is a complete sentence. Write *not a sentence* if the group of words is not a complete sentence.

1. I love folk art. sentence
2. Made drawings on clay pots. not a sentence
3. Pots of many different colors. not a sentence
4. Some artists drew animals on the pots. sentence
5. Want to make some folk art. not a sentence

Kinds of Sentences   *pages 26–27*

B. Write whether each sentence is a statement, a question, a command, or an exclamation.

6. Look at my quilt. command
7. It's so beautiful! exclamation
8. Was it made by a folk artist? question
9. My father bought it at an art show. statement
10. Do you like it? question

Punctuating Sentences   *pages 28–29*

C. Write each sentence correctly. Make a capital letter at the beginning. Use the correct end mark.

11. did you see the quilts at the county fair Did you see the quilts at the county fair?
12. tell me how the quilts were made Tell me how the quilts were made.
13. many scraps of cloth were sewn together Many scraps of clot were sewn togethe
14. how beautiful that quilt is How beautiful that quilt is!
15. it has a very colorful pattern It has a very colorful pattern.

HANDS ON Activity

END MARK MATCHUP Write sentences without end marks on sentence strips, making sure that there are at least two examples of each of the four kinds of sentences. For each sentence, write the correct end mark on another strip. Place all cards in a box in a learning center. Encourage students to visit the center alone or in pairs. Have them match up sentences with the correct end marks until all cards are matched.

Complete and Simple
Subjects *pages 34–35*

A. Write each sentence. Draw one line under the complete subject. Draw two lines under the simple subject.

1. My sister Neela sang my favorite song.
2. Our mother taught it to us years ago.
3. The beautiful song has many high notes.
4. Our music teacher taught Neela how to sing well.
5. Our dog likes to sing along, too.

Nouns in Subjects *pages 36–37*

B. Write the complete subject in each sentence. Then write the noun that is the simple subject.

6. The students in my class brought music to school.
   The students in my class; students
7. My best friend brought a book of folk songs.
   My best friend; friend
8. Carla's favorite music is jazz. *Carla's favorite music; music*
9. The boy next to me brought an old record.
   The boy next to me; boy
10. The teacher shared some of his favorite songs.
    The teacher; teacher

Combining Sentences:
Compound Subjects *pages 38–39*

C. Combine each pair of sentences into one sentence that has a compound subject.
Karen and Jamal studied the piano.
11. Karen studied the piano. Jamal studied the piano.
12. Their parents were very pleased. Their *Their parents*
    grandparents were very pleased. *and grandparents were very pleased.*
13. Their grandmother bought them a piano. Their
    grandfather bought them a piano.
    Their grandmother and grandfather bought them a piano.
14. Their friends came to hear them play. Their
    neighbors came to hear them play.
    Their friends and neighbors came to hear them play.
15. The music rang through the house. The laughter
    rang through the house. *The music and laughter rang through the house.*

Unit 1
Grammar Review
CHAPTER 2
Subjects/
Nouns
pages 34–43

85

Unit 1
Grammar Review
CHAPTER 2

Subjects/Nouns

OBJECTIVES
- To identify complete subjects and simple subjects in sentences
- To identify nouns in subjects
- To combine sentences by creating compound subjects

Unit Review
MODIFIED INSTRUCTION

BELOW-LEVEL STUDENTS Before students begin Part B, read the sentences aloud and offer students the chance to ask about unfamiliar words (such as *jazz* or *record*). Remind students that the simple subject is usually a noun that names a person, place, animal or thing.

ABOVE-LEVEL STUDENTS After students have completed Part C, suggest that they create a second subject for sentences in Part A or B. Have them combine the new subjects with the existing subjects to create sentences with a compound subjects.

HANDS ON Activity

FIND A SUBJECT Have students gather objects from the classroom. Ask a few students to sit beside the objects. Tell students to write complete subjects (not complete sentences) using the students or the objects. You may model a few examples: *the boy with the blue jacket, that green book.* To extend the activity, you might have students add words to the complete subjects to form complete sentences.

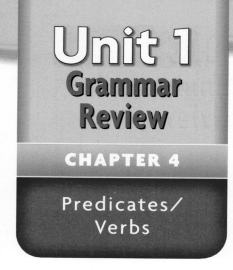

Unit 1
Grammar Review

CHAPTER 4

Predicates/ Verbs

OBJECTIVES

- To identify complete predicates and simple predicates in sentences
- To identify verbs in predicates
- To combine sentences by creating compound predicates

Unit Review

MODIFIED INSTRUCTION

BELOW-LEVEL STUDENTS If students have trouble identifying complete predicates in Part A, have them identify the complete subject in the first part of the sentence. The part of the sentence that remains is the complete predicate.

ABOVE-LEVEL STUDENTS Challenge students to write additional sentences with compound predicates by combining sentences 6 and 7 and sentences 9 and 10 in Part B.

Complete and Simple Predicates *pages 52–53*

A. Write each sentence. Draw one line under the complete predicate. Draw two lines under the simple predicate.

1. Some families buy new houses.
2. Other families build new houses.
3. Some build houses themselves.
4. Others hire a builder.
5. A builder made this house for us.

Verbs in Predicates *pages 54–55*

B. Write each sentence. Underline the verb that is the simple predicate.

6. Larry is a good builder.
7. He knows about building.
8. He hires good workers.
9. He and his builders work as a team.
10. They all do their jobs well.

Combining Sentences: Compound Predicates *pages 56–57*

C. Combine each pair of sentences into one sentence with a compound predicate.

11. Tamika bought an old house. Tamika fixed it up.
    Tamika bought an old house and fixed it up.
12. She chose colors for the kitchen. She bought the paint. *She chose colors for the kitchen and bought the paint.*
13. She painted the kitchen. She let the paint dry. *She painted the kitchen and let the paint dry.*
14. The sink was old. The sink needed new pipes. *The sink was old and needed new pipes.*
15. Tamika took out the old pipes. Tamika put in new ones. *Tamika took out the old pipes and put in new ones.*

TEST PREP

TIP

If a grammar test asks students to combine sentences, make sure the students understand what they are combining. (On this page, for example, each new sentence should combine one subject with two predicates.) Remind students that these combined sentences should not repeat any words. (These sentences should not repeat the subject.)

Complete Sentences   *pages 62–63*

A. Write *sentence* if the group of words is a complete sentence. Write *not a sentence* if the group of words is not a complete sentence.

1. Folktale like this one. not a sentence
2. What are folktales? sentence
3. They are very old stories. sentence
4. Around for thousands of years. not a sentence
5. One person told a tale to another. sentence

Simple and Compound Sentences   *pages 64–65*

B. Write whether each sentence is a simple sentence or a compound sentence.

6. Often the good characters win in folktales. simple
7. Bad characters do mean things, and they are punished. compound
8. Good deeds are often rewarded. simple
9. Some people did not know why something happened, and they made up a story to explain it. compound
10. Some people did not understand thunder, and they told stories to explain what causes it. compound

Combining Sentences   *pages 66–67*

C. Use the combining word in parentheses ( ) to combine each pair of sentences. Be sure to use a comma.

11. This story is a little sad. I like it anyway. (but)
    This story is a little sad, but I like it anyway.
12. I wrote it myself. I drew a picture. (and)
    I wrote it myself, and I drew a picture.
13. A son grows up. He moves far away from his family. (and)
    A son grows up, and he moves far away from his family.
14. He marries the girl he loves. She lives far away. (but)
    He marries the girl he loves, but she lives far away.
15. I may change the ending. I may leave it as it is. (or)
    I may change the ending, or I may leave it as it is.

87

OBJECTIVES
- To recognize complete sentences
- To identify and distinguish between simple sentences and compound sentences
- To create compound sentences by combining sentences

Unit Review
MODIFIED INSTRUCTION

BELOW-LEVEL STUDENTS As students begin Part B, you might point out that in these sentences a comma that is followed by the word *and* may signal a compound sentence.

ABOVE-LEVEL STUDENTS After students have completed Part C, refer them to Part B. Challenge them to combine sentences 6 and 8 to make a compound sentence.

TEST PREP

Activities and exercises to help students prepare for state and standardized assessments appear on our website.

Visit
The Learning Site!
www.harcourtschool.com

Assessment

SKILLS ASSESSMENT Use the **Language Skills and Writing Assessment** to assess the grammar and writing skills taught in this unit. Model papers are included.

PORTFOLIO ASSESSMENT
Schedule portfolio conferences with individual students while others are completing the Unit Review exercises. Have students complete the Self-Assessment Checklist on page R87 and place it in their Show Portfolios. Use the Student Record Form on page R77 to monitor student progress. TEKS 3.19E

Once Upon a Time . . .

OBJECTIVES

- To read a story, and then retell it through pictures, song, and movement

- To write an essay comparing the different ways a story can be told

INTRODUCE THE PROJECT

USE PRIOR KNOWLEDGE Read the introduction aloud to students. As a class, perform "The Itsy Bitsy Spider" or another song that uses gestures. Ask students to think of other stories they know that are told through songs, movement, or pictures.

GENERATE QUESTIONS Have students work in pairs to consider how pictures, songs, and movements can be used to tell stories. Have them write their questions and possible responses in their journals.

Pick a Story

Have small groups choose stories from the books in your classroom. Tell them to reread the story together and answer the questions in this section.

Tell the Story in New Ways

Provide the following items:
- markers, construction paper, glue, and poster board
- an audiocassette and cassettes of children's music

As students tell their stories in movement, remind them to exaggerate their gestures and facial expressions.

Once Upon a Time . . .

Stories can be told in many ways. Sometimes stories are written, but they can also be told through pictures, songs, and movement. Pick a story that you know well. Then tell it in different ways. Here are some steps to help you do this.

Pick a Story

With a group of classmates, pick a story that all of you know. Read the story again, and answer the following questions:

- Who are the characters? Describe them.

- What are the story's main events? List them.

- Where does the story take place? Describe the setting.

- How does the story make you feel? Explain your answer.

Tell the Story in New Ways

- Tell the story through pictures. Plan scenes from the story to illustrate and have each group member draw a scene. Put the pictures on a poster in sequence. Add to or revise the pictures if the story is hard to understand. Display your poster.

- Write a song that tells your story. Assign different parts of the song to each group member. Perform the song for classmates.

- Assign roles to group members, and act out the actions of the story with movement only.

88

Activity

MAKE MASKS Have students make masks to use as they tell their stories. Have them draw their characters' facial expressions. Tell them to color the faces and mount them on poster board. They can use yarn or string to make ties for the masks. Allow them to change masks between scenes or as their characters change moods.

Compare Your Stories

- With your group, discuss the new ways you told the story. What was easy to tell and difficult to tell through pictures, singing, and movement?

- Write a short essay comparing the different ways you told the story. Share your essay with classmates.

Click! A Book About Cameras and Taking Pictures
by Gail Gibbons
NONFICTION
Discover fun facts and helpful hints, as well as how photographs are made and other historical information about the camera.
Award-Winning Author

Arthur Writes a Story
by Marc Brown
FICTION
While trying to outdo the other students in his class, Arthur learns that the best stories come from real life.
Children's Choice

89

Compare Your Stories

Help students organize their essays. Have students contribute to an outline you put on the board showing the processes used in the different methods of telling a story. For example, use *Singing* as a main head with subheads such as **one voice, several voices,** or **animal's voice**. Tell students to focus on the questions listed under "Compare Your Stories." Encourage students to use colorful words and personal voice.

STUDENT SELF-ASSESSMENT

Have students evaluate their own work and raise new questions for further investigation.

Books to Read Students who enjoyed this project might be interested in reading one or more of these books. Have them record reflections on the book or books in their journals. Then ask students to recommend to the class the book from this list that they enjoyed most.

School-Home Connection

Students can work with their families to tell a story using two different storytelling methods. Have them choose a story from their families' experiences. They should decide how to tell the various parts of the story. Encourage students to involve family members in the storytelling.

CHALLENGE

ORGANIZING THE ARCHIVES
Have students create a card file about the storytelling project. Students should provide information such as the title, the method of storytelling, important music or props, a plot summary, and the names of the group members. Students may also reduce illustrations from the stories and include them. Students may return to this card file for ideas throughout the year.

Assessment Strategies and Resources

FORMAL ASSESSMENT

If you want to know more about a student's mastery of the language and writing skills taught in Unit 1, **then** administer the first *Language Skills and Writing Assessment* for Unit 1. The test consists of two parts:

Language Skills: **sentences, subjects/nouns, predicates/verbs, simple and compound sentences,** and **personal voice.**

Writing Task: write a **personal narrative.** Scoring guidelines and model student papers are included.

INFORMAL ASSESSMENT TOOLS

 Using Portfolios

If you want to provide opportunities for ongoing informal assessment throughout the school year, **then** establish the practice of keeping students' work in portfolios. The actual portfolio may be a folder, large envelope, or other container where papers can be stored neatly.

Items that students will accumulate in portfolios include Writing Connection activities, prewriting notes or graphic organizers, and drafts of their writing. When final copies of writing are completed, they can also be added.

You will want to schedule individual portfolio conferences with students to discuss their writing on a regular basis. Use the Student Record Form on page R74 to monitor students' progress and record your notes about their portfolios.

Informal Assessment Reminder

If you used the preinstruction writing prompt suggested in Teaching Grammar from Writing, **then** remember to compare the results with the writing done by students after the grammar and writing instruction.

Unit 2

Grammar More About Nouns and Verbs

Writing Informative/Expository Writing

Nancy's Fruit Salad
apple
orange   melons
strawberries   kiwi
                grapes
• Cut up fruit into bite-size pieces.
• Mix together in a large bowl.

Introducing the Unit, pp. 90–91

Chapters	Grammar	Writing	Listening/ Speaking/Viewing

7
More About Nouns
pp. 92–101
	Nouns
	Common and Proper Nouns
	Usage and Mechanics:
	  Abbreviations and Titles
	Extra Practice, Chapter Review, Daily Language Practice, Additional Practice: p. 458
		Writing Connections
		Word Bank
		Technology
		Safety Poster
		Giving Reasons
			Viewing: Understanding Charts
			Activities
			  Challenge: Fire Safety Poster
			  ESL: Language Sharing
			  Building Oral Grammar
			  Summarize

8
Singular and Plural Nouns
pp. 102–111
	Singular and Plural Nouns
	Plural Nouns with -es and -ies
	Usage and Mechanics: Irregular
	  Plural Nouns
	Extra Practice, Chapter Review, Daily Language Practice, Additional Practice: p. 459
		Writing Connections
		Science
		Writer's Journal: Listing Nouns
		Advertisement
		Clear Explanations
			Viewing: Reading Special Maps
			Activities
			  Challenge: Design a Menu
			  Building Oral Grammar
			  Challenge: Make a Map
			  Summarize

9
Writer's Craft:
Paragraphing
pp. 112–119
	Daily Language Practice
	Hands-on Activities
		Set of Directions
		Prewriting and Drafting
		Editing
		Sharing and Reflecting
		Self-Initiated Writing
			Listening and Speaking: Giving
			  Spoken Directions
			Activities
			  Oral Directions
			  Art Direction
			  Summarize

10
Possessive Nouns
pp. 120–129
	Singular Possessive Nouns
	Plural Possessive Nouns
	Usage and Mechanics: Revising
	  Sentences Using Possessive
	  Nouns
	Extra Practice, Chapter Review, Daily Language Practice, Additional Practice: p. 460
		Writing Connections
		Topic Sentence and Details
		Science
		Recording Ideas
		Letter
			Activities
			  Challenge: Healthy Smiles
			  Building Oral Grammar
			  Summarize

11
Action Verbs and
The Verb *Be*
pp. 130–139
	Verbs
	Action Verbs
	Usage and Mechanics:
	  The Verb *Be*
	Extra Practice, Chapter Review, Daily Language Practice, Additional Practice: p. 461
		Writing Connections
		Reminder List
		Strong Verbs
		Art
		Reflections on Health
			Activities
			  Public Service Announcement
			  Building Oral Grammar
			  Summarize

12
Writing Workshop:
How-To
Essay
pp. 140–153
	Unit 2 Grammar Review
	Daily Language Practice
		How-to Essay
		Prewriting
		Drafting
		Revising
		Proofreading
		Publishing
		Writer's Craft: Paragraphing
			Listening and Speaking: Making an
			  Oral Presentation
			Activities
			  Explaining "How to"
			  Summarize

Unit Wrap-Up   Writing Across the Curriculum: Health, pp. 158–159

Vocabulary/Study Skills/ Technology/ Handwriting

Vocabulary Power

Words of the Week: ***precaution***, *preheat, prehistoric, prejudge, prepay*
Challenge: Compare Charts

Vocabulary Power

Words of the Week: *carbohydrate,* ***nutrient,*** *nutritionist, nutritious, protein*
ESL: Noun Chart
ESL: Irregular Plural Nouns

Vocabulary Power

Words of the Week: *brighten, clarify, explain,* ***illuminate,*** *lighten*
Health: Exercise Web

Vocabulary Power

Words of the Week: ***cavity,*** *chasm, crater, gorge, hollow*
Social Studies: Possessive Web
Challenge: Correct Mistakes
Technology: Writing on the Computer

Vocabulary Power

Words of the Week: *injection, medicine, remedy, treatment,* ***vaccine***
Vocabulary: Categorizing Words

Vocabulary Power

Words of the Week: *assist, collaborate,* ***cooperate,*** *partner, teamwork*
ESL: Make a Checklist

Language Minutes

- **Choose** one letter from the alphabet. **Write** nouns that begin with that letter. **Discuss** your list with a group of friends. Add more nouns to one another's lists. WRITING/LISTENING/SPEAKING

- **Look** at pictures in magazines with a friend. Take turns naming people, places, and things that you see. Use **singular** and **plural** forms to tell how many of each item are in a picture. VIEWING/LISTENING/SPEAKING

- **Write** a short paragraph about your favorite fruit or vegetable. Tell why you like it. WRITING

- **Change** seats with someone across the room. **Tell** the person next to you what you see. Use possessive nouns to make your descriptions clearer. VIEWING/SPEAKING

- **Write** sentences that describe friends and relatives. Use different forms of the **verb** *be* in your descriptions. WRITING

Technology — Resources

Grammar Jingles™ **CD**

Grammar Practice and Assessment **CD-ROM**

Writing Express **CD-ROM**

Media Literacy and Communication Skills **Package**

Visit *The Learning Site!*
  www.harcourtschool.com

Reaching All Learners

Intervention

MINIPERFORMANCES Involve at-risk students in exploring a story over a period of six days.

1. Meet with six to eight students. Read the story aloud. Help students choose roles.

2. Reread the story while students perform the actions of their characters.

3. Reread the story again, pausing when you come to dialogue. Write down characters' speeches in students' own words. Encourage students to add songs, chants, and movements that tap spatial, kinesthetic, and musical learning styles.

4. Give students miniperformance scripts that include their original words. Encourage them to practice at school and at home.

5. Rehearse the performance and help students practice appropriate speaking skills. Create simple costumes.

6. Present the miniperformance to classmates and family members.

English as a Second Language

BOOK CLUBS A Book Club is a small group of students who are reading the same book. Because grouping is based on interest, Book Clubs provide an excellent means of engaging second-language learners with other students in a meaningful way. Members meet daily to read, discuss the book with each other, and write in their reading logs. Students may read aloud with partners and collaborate on writing, providing excellent opportunities for peers to serve as resources for each other's learning.

Challenge

NOUN SEARCHES Give students a variety of opportunities to expand their understanding of nouns. For example, students can use an unabridged dictionary, baby name books, or the Internet to discover the origin and meaning of their own first or last names. Some students might like to delve further into the origin and significance of names in different cultures. Encourage students to use a variety of media to share what they learn.

Multi-age Classrooms

FLEXIBLE GROUPING In addition to meeting the varying needs of their students, teachers in multi-age classrooms also have the task of integrating more than one curriculum into their teaching. However, students' language, reading, and writing needs often overlap. Some will have mastered specific language skills at a particular grade level and others will not, regardless of whether or not the skills have been formally introduced. For this reason, flexible grouping according to instructional goals is a key tool in the multi-age or combination classroom.

For example, you may organize an interactive writing group with a focus on punctuating sentences. You would place students in this group not by grade level but according to your assessment of their individual needs. On another occasion, you may work with another group on a different skill. The new group may include some of the same students plus some others, or perhaps a completely different group of students, depending on the needs you have identified.

Teaching Grammar from Writing

PRETEST
If you wish to use students' writing to diagnose their needs, use the following prompt.

WRITING PROMPT
When you play outdoors with friends or classmates, what games do you enjoy? Write several paragraphs to explain how to play your favorite outdoor game.

EVALUATE AND PLAN
Analyze students' writing to determine how you can best meet their individual needs for instruction. Use the following chart to identify and remedy problems.

COMMON PROBLEMS	CHAPTERS TO USE
Not capitalizing proper nouns	Chapter 7: More About Nouns
Not writing abbreviations correctly	Chapter 7: More About Nouns
Not writing titles correctly	Chapter 7: More About Nouns
Forming plural nouns incorrectly	Chapter 8: Singular and Plural Nouns
Not placing apostrophes correctly in possessive nouns	Chapter 10: Possessive Nouns
Not using the correct forms of the verb *Be*	Chapter 11: Action Verbs and the Verb *Be*
Not understanding paragraphing	Chapter 9: Writer's Craft: Paragraphing
Difficulty writing an explanation of how to do something	Chapter 12: Writing a How-To Essay

Classroom Management

DURING...	SOME STUDENTS CAN...
Grammar Reteaching	Locate and begin reading the books in the Books to Read section of the Writing Across the Curriculum project.
Independent Practice	Work on the Writing Connection. Complete Student Self-Assessment forms. (See pages R86–R88 in this *Teacher's Edition*.)
Portfolio Conferences	Work on *Vocabulary Power* pages. Practice keyboarding and editing skills on the classroom computer or in the computer lab.

Writing Workshop

LANGUAGE ARTS IN THE CLASSROOM

In the Writing Workshop, students learn that writing is an enjoyable, interactive process that helps them grow as writers and thinkers. Establishing the atmosphere of a writing community in the classroom can help your Writing Workshop be a success.

CHARTS Display helpful charts on the writing process. Post Vocabulary Power words. Display reproductions of prewriting graphic organizers and a list of proofreading marks. Have students participate in creating classroom displays.

COMPUTER STATION Set up a typewriter and a computer with appropriate word processing software, manuals, and supplies. Post a sign-up sheet and time limits.

REFERENCE BOOKS Keep dictionaries, spelling lists, a simple thesaurus, and other books that aid and motivate writing, including collections of student writing. An excellent resource is a file box of writing suggestions. Allow students to add their own writing ideas to the "Idea Box."

PORTFOLIOS Students can keep their portfolios in special boxes or crates. Organize portfolios alphabetically by students' first names. Portfolios should be expandable. Use accordion folders, pocket folders, or manila folders with yarn extenders attached to each side. Set up times for students to review their portfolios for revising, presenting, and taking items home.

SUPPLY SHELVES Provide a variety of writing materials including lined and unlined paper in various colors, file cards, construction paper, an inviting assortment of pencils, erasers, crayons, pens, markers, brushes and paint, rubber stamps, and colored stamp pads.

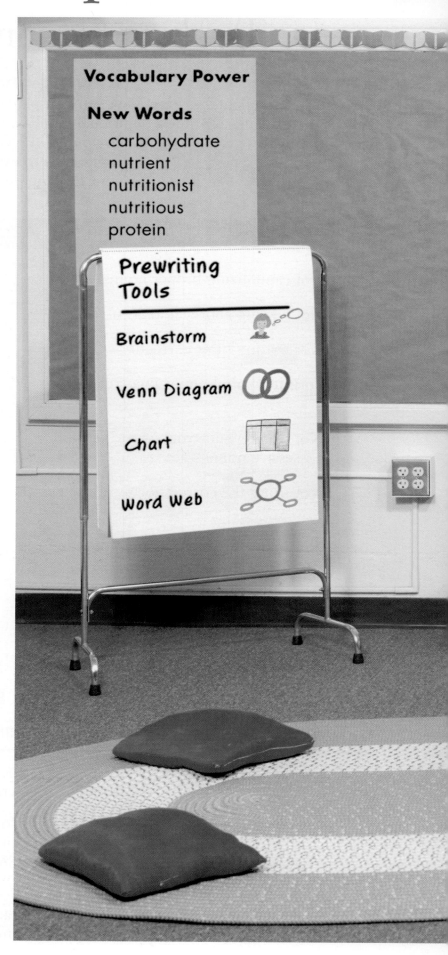

Writing Process

1. Prewrite
2. Draft
3. Revise
4. Proofread
5. Publish

Our Writing Station!

Writing Purposes

- to inform
- to persuade
- to express

Publisher's Corner

white | cards
colors | labels

Picture Box

Idea Box

Portfolios M-Z

Hands-on Activities

What's My Name?

MATERIALS: sets of cards on which you have written common nouns such as *boy, girl, man, woman, teacher, school, street, city, state, country*

DIRECTIONS:

1. Have students work in groups of three or four.

2. Give each group a set of noun cards.

3. Students read the common noun and think of a proper noun that matches it, such as your name for the noun *teacher.*

4. Students write the proper noun on the back of the card, using correct capitalization.

Abbreviation Concentration

MATERIALS: pairs of cards with common abbreviations and the words they stand for

DIRECTIONS:

1. Mix up the abbreviation and word cards and place them face down in rows.

2. Players take turns choosing any two cards and turning them face up.

3. If a player turns over two cards that match, in this case a word and its abbreviation, the player picks up those cards and takes another turn. If the cards do not match, they are turned face down again, and the next player takes a turn.

4. The game continues until no cards remain.

Captions

MATERIALS: old magazines, advertising flyers, catalogs; scissors; construction paper; glue; markers

DIRECTIONS:

1. Have students work in pairs.

2. Students use old magazines or other sources to find and cut out pictures that show different numbers of items.

3. Have students glue their pictures on sheets of construction paper and write captions. If students are not sure how to form the plural of a particular noun, they can look it up in a dictionary.

Picture This

MATERIALS: chalk, chalkboard

DIRECTIONS:

1. Invite students to take turns making simple drawings or stick figures on the board according to your directions.

2. Give directions such as *Draw a boy and his bike. Now draw two boys and their bikes.*

3. Have students write a label for each picture, using possessive nouns.

Time for Action

MATERIALS: slips of paper, box or other container

DIRECTIONS:

1. Have students brainstorm a list of action verbs that can be demonstrated in the classroom. Write the action verbs on slips of paper.

2. Mix up the slips of paper and place them in a box.

3. Students take turns picking a slip of paper from the box and demonstrating the action. Classmates must guess the action verb.

Busy "Be"

MATERIALS: sentences written on chart paper, stick-on notes, markers

DIRECTIONS:

1. Have students work in small groups.

2. Give students a sheet of chart paper on which you have written sentences with blanks.

3. Students read each sentence, write the missing form of the word *be* on a stick-on note, and place the stick-on note in the blank.

4. Students might then write similar sentences to exchange with other groups.

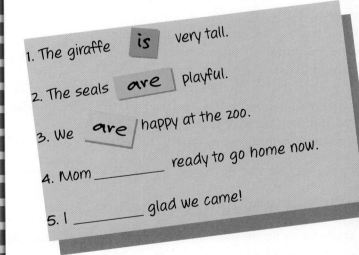

Through Grandpa's Eyes

BY PATRICIA MACLACHLAN

LATER, NANA BRINGS OUT HER CLAY to sculpt my Grandpa's head.

"Sit still," she grumbles.

"I won't," he says, imitating her grumbly voice, making us laugh.

While she works, Grandpa takes out his piece of wood. He holds it when he's thinking. His fingers move back and forth across the wood, making smooth paths like the ones on the stair banister.

"Can I have a piece of thinking wood, too?" I ask.

Grandpa reaches in his shirt pocket and tosses a small bit of wood in my direction. I catch it. It is smooth with no splinters.

"The river is up," says Nana.

Grandpa nods a short nod. "It rained again last night. Did you hear the gurgling in the rain gutter?"

As they talk, my fingers begin a river on my thinking wood. The wood will winter in my pocket so when I am not at Grandpa's house I can still think about Nana, Grandpa, and the river.

When Nana is finished working, Grandpa runs his hand over the sculpture, his fingers soft and quick like butterflies.

"It looks like me," he says, surprised.

My eyes have already told me that it looks like Grandpa. But he shows me how to feel his face with my three middle fingers, and then the clay face.

"Pretend your fingers are water," he tells me.

My waterfall fingers flow down his clay head, filling in the spaces beneath the eyes like little pools before they flow down over the cheeks. It does feel like Grandpa. This time my fingers tell me.

Grandpa and I walk outside, through the front yard and across the field to the river. Grandpa has not been blind forever. He remembers in his mind the gleam of the sun on the river, the Queen Anne's lace in the meadow, and every dahlia in his garden. But he gently takes my elbow as we walk so that I can help show him the path.

"I feel a south wind," says Grandpa.

I can tell which way the wind is blowing because I see the way the tops of the trees lean. Grandpa tells by the feel of the meadow grasses and by the way his hair blows against his face.

When we come to the riverbank, I see that Nana was right. The water is high and has cut in by the willow tree. It flows around and among the roots of the tree, making paths. Paths like Grandpa's on the stair banister and on the thinking wood. I see a blackbird with a red patch on its wing sitting on a cattail. Without thinking, I point my finger.

"What is that bird, Grandpa?" I ask excitedly.

"*Conk-a-ree*," the bird calls to us.

"A red-winged blackbird," says Grandpa promptly.

He can't see my finger pointing. But he hears the song of the bird.

"And somewhere behind the blackbird," he says, listening, "a song sparrow."

Building Background

Ask students to name the five senses and to give examples of how they might use each one. If students can't give specific examples, ask: **What sense do you use when you describe bread baking in the oven?** (sense of smell) **What sense do you use do describe a bird's song?** (sense of hearing)

Then explain that when John spends the day with his grandfather, who is blind, he learns a whole new way of "seeing" the world around him.

Determine a Purpose for Listening

Tell students that this selection is about a young boy's love for his grandfather. Ask students to determine whether their purpose for listening is

• to identify with the characters. (to identify with the characters)

• to solve problems.

• to be persuaded to do something.

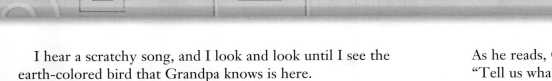

I hear a scratchy song, and I look and look until I see the earth-colored bird that Grandpa knows is here.

Nana calls from the front porch of the house.

"Nana's made hot bread for lunch," he tells me happily. "And spice tea." Spice tea is his favorite.

I close my eyes, but all I can smell is the wet earth by the river.

As we walk back to the house, Grandpa stops suddenly. He bends his head to one side, listening. He points his finger upward.

"Honkers," he whispers.

I look up and see a flock of geese, high in the clouds, flying in a V.

"Canada geese," I tell him.

"Honkers," he insists. And we both laugh.

We walk up the path again and to the yard where Nana is painting the porch chairs. Grandpa smells the paint.

"What color, Nana?" he asks. "I cannot smell the color."

"Blue," I tell him, smiling. "Blue like the sky."

"Blue like the color of Grandpa's eyes," Nana says.

When he was younger, before I can remember, before he was blind, Grandpa did things the way I do. Now, when we drink tea and eat lunch on the porch, Grandpa pours his own cup of tea by putting his finger just inside the rim of the cup to tell him when it is full. He never burns his finger. Afterward, when I wash the dishes, he feels them as he dries them. He even sends some back for me to wash again.

"Next time," says Grandpa, pretending to be cross, "I wash, you dry."

In the afternoon, Grandpa, Nana, and I take our books outside to read under the apple tree. Grandpa reads his book with his fingers, feeling the raised Braille dots that tell him the words.

As he reads, Grandpa laughs out loud.

"Tell us what's funny," says Nana. "Read to us, Papa."

And he does.

Nana and I put down our books to listen. A gray squirrel comes down the trunk of the apple tree, tail high, and seems to listen, too. But Grandpa doesn't see him.

After supper, Grandpa turns on the television. I watch, but Grandpa listens, and the music and the words tell him when something is dangerous or funny, happy or sad.

Somehow, Grandpa knows when it is dark, and he takes me upstairs and tucks me into bed. He bends down to kiss me, his hands feeling my head.

"You need a haircut, John," he says.

Before Grandpa leaves, he pulls the light chain above my bed to turn out the light. But, by mistake, he's turned it on instead. I lie for a moment after he's gone, smiling, before I get up to turn off the light.

Then, when it is dark for me the way it is dark for Grandpa, I hear the night noises that Grandpa hears. The house creaking, the birds singing their last songs of the day, the wind rustling the tree outside my window.

Then, all of a sudden, I hear the sounds of geese overhead. They fly low over the house.

"Grandpa," I call softly, hoping he's heard them too.

"Honkers," he calls back.

"Go to sleep, John," says Nana.

Grandpa says her voice smiles to him. I test it.

"What?" I call to her.

"I said go to sleep," she answers.

She says it sternly. But Grandpa is right. Her voice smiles to me. I know. Because I'm looking through Grandpa's eyes.

Listening Comprehension

LISTEN FOR TOPIC SENTENCES AND DETAILS

After you read the narrative aloud once, reread it to students, pausing periodically to ask them to point out the topic sentences and the details the narrator uses to describe his thoughts. Explain that listening for these elements will help them focus on the main idea to learn what it is like to live with someone who does not see, but "senses," the world around him.

PERSONAL RESPONSE *What type of person is Grandpa? How do you know?* (Responses may vary. Students may say he is funny, wise, loving, and smart. They may also discuss his self-reliance, use of other senses, and love of nature. Grandpa shows his sense of humor when he mimics Nana; he shows he is loving when he says that her voice smiles at him.) INFERENTIAL: DETERMINE CHARACTERS' TRAITS

Unit 2

Unit 2

| Grammar | More About Nouns and Verbs |
| Writing | Informative Writing |

| Grammar | More About Nouns and Verbs |
| Writing | Informative Writing: Explanation |

Introducing the Unit

ORAL LANGUAGE/VIEWING

DISCUSS THE IMAGES Have students look at the photograph. Then direct their attention to the recipe card. Point out that a recipe is a piece of informative writing that tells how to prepare food. Ask students if they have ever followed a recipe, and have volunteers share their experiences. Explain to students that they can find written instructions in many different sources. Ask these questions.

1. **Where might you look if you wanted to find a recipe?** (Possible responses: in a cookbook, in a magazine)

2. **Have you learned any new skills lately? If so, did you learn from a person or another source?** (Responses may vary.)

3. **How might a diagram or illustration make instructions easier to understand?** (Possible response: by showing a process or an action that the words describe)

Writer's Journal

ENCOURAGE STUDENTS' QUESTIONS Have students reflect on sources they could consult to learn how to do something new. Encourage students to develop questions for discussion. Have them write their questions and selected responses in their journals.

90

Viewing and Representing

COMPARE/CONTRAST PRINT AND VISUAL MEDIA Have students look at a set of instructions and a diagram that tell and show how to put something together. Ask them to look at each form of media separately and consider which shows more clearly how to assemble the item. Then have them look at the instructions and diagram together and discuss how the two forms of explanation complement each other.

For evaluation criteria for viewing, see the Viewing Checklist, page R88.

MEDIA LITERACY AND COMMUNICATION SKILLS PACKAGE Use the video to extend students' oral and visual literacy. See *Teacher's Guide* pages 6–7.

Nancy's Fruit Salad

apple
orange   melons
strawberries   kiwi
                  grapes

• Cut up fruit into bite-size pieces.
• Mix together in a large bowl.

91

Read the unit contents with students, and ask them which grammar concepts are already familiar to them. Encourage them to discuss which concepts they would like to learn more about. Explain that they will be learning more about nouns and verbs in this unit. Then ask students to brainstorm aloud different kinds of writing that inform. Write their suggestions on the board. Point out that they will write to inform in this unit by giving directions and by writing a how-to essay.

HEALTH CONNECTION Students will explore a variety of health topics in this unit:

• Health and Safety
• Healthful Foods
• Keeping the Body Fit
• Preventing Disease

School-Home Connection

You may want to use School-Home Connection 2, page R93.

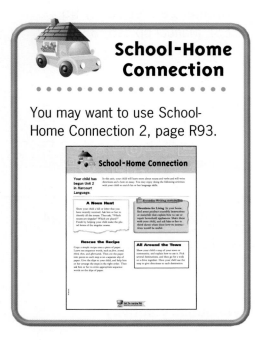

More About Nouns

LESSON ORGANIZER	DAY 1	DAY 2
DAILY LANGUAGE PRACTICE TRANSPARENCIES 15, 16	1. Nina and Fred crossing guards (are crossing guards.) 2. where does Sofia stand (Where; stand?) **Bridge to Writing** I want to be a crossing guard, (combining word) I am not old enough.	1. cleaning products and matches are not toys (Cleaning; toys.) 2. Children should not use them and adults should be careful with them. (them,) **Bridge to Writing** What are some rules for using (noun) safely?
ORAL WARM-UP Listening/Speaking	Answer Questions Using Nouns 92	Identify Nouns 94 *Grammar Jingles*™ CD Track 5
TEACH/MODEL GRAMMAR **KEY** ✔ = tested skill	✔ **NOUNS** 92-93 • To identify and classify nouns • To make lists of nouns	✔ **COMMON AND PROPER NOUNS** 94-95 • To identify common and proper nouns • To search the Internet and to share information
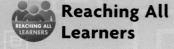 **Reaching All Learners**	**Modified Instruction** Below-Level: Identify Nouns Above-Level: Explain Answers **Reteach:** *Reteach Activities Copying Masters,* pp. 13 and R42 **Challenge:** Activity Card 5, p. R64 *Practice Book* p. 21 *ESL Manual* pp. 36, 37	**Modified Instruction** Below-Level: Make a List Above-Level: Change Nouns **Reteach:** *Reteach Activities Copying Masters,* pp. 14 and R42 **Challenge:** Pet Safety 95 *ESL Manual* pp. 36, 38 *Practice Book* p. 22
WRITING	Writing Connection 93 Writer's Journal: Word Bank	Writing Connection 95 Technology
CROSS-CURRICULAR/ ENRICHMENT	*Vocabulary Power* Explore Word Meaning 92 **precaution,** preheat, prehistoric, prejudge, prepay See *Vocabulary Power* book.	**Health:** Health Pamphlets 94 *Vocabulary Power* Prefixes 92 *Vocabulary Power* p. 19 **Vocabulary activity**

Visit *The Learning Site!*
www.harcourtschool.com
WRITING ACTIVITIES
Writing Express CD-ROM

DAY 3

1. My friend lucy skis and skats in the winter (Lucy; skates; winter.)

2. Ramon skis but he does not sledding. (skis; Possible response: does not go sledding)

Bridge to Writing We go to the skating rink in (proper noun) .

Using Proper Titles 96
Grammar Jingles™ CD Track 5

✔ **ABBREVIATIONS AND TITLES** 96-97
• To identify and use abbreviations and titles
• To make a safety poster using abbreviations

Modified Instruction
Below-Level: Using the Chart
Above-Level: Find Abbreviations
ESL: Language Sharing 96
ESL Manual pp. 36, 39
Reteach: *Reteach Activities Copying Masters* pp. 15 and R42
Challenge: Kitchen Safety 97
Practice Book p. 23

Writing Connection 97
Real-Life Writing: Safety Poster

Vocabulary Power
Word Families 92
Vocabulary Power p. 20
Vocabulary activity

DAY 4

1. why do accidents happen (Why; happen?)

2. Accidents can happen qwickly. (quickly.)

Bridge to Writing My sister went to see (abbreviation) Ortiz, our family doctor, when she got hurt.

Naming Nouns, Titles, and Abbreviations 98

EXTRA PRACTICE 98-99
• To identify and use common and proper nouns, abbreviations, and titles
• To write a paragraph
Practice and assessment

Building Oral Grammar
Give Safety Talk 99
ESL: Work with a Partner 98
ESL Manual pp. 36, 40
Challenge: Travel Tips 99
Practice Book p. 24

Writing Connection 99
Writer's Craft: Giving Reasons

Vocabulary Power
Context Clues 92
Vocabulary Power p. 21
Vocabulary activity

DAY 5

1. John smith hurt his ankle on our hike. (Smith)

2. He tried to stand up but his ankle was twisted (up,; twisted.)

Bridge to Writing We helped him get back to the (common noun) . This happened on (proper noun) .

TEST PREP **CHAPTER REVIEW** 100-101
• To review common and proper nouns, abbreviations, and titles
• To interpret and create charts
Test preparation

Challenge: Compare Charts 101
Practice Book p. 25
ESL Manual pp. 36, 41

Writing Application 101
Explain Survey

Viewing:
Understanding Charts 101
Exemplification 92
Vocabulary Power

More About Nouns

Nouns

OBJECTIVES
- To identify and classify nouns
- To make lists of nouns

 SPIRAL REVIEW

DAILY LANGUAGE PRACTICE

TRANSPARENCY 15

1. Nina and Fred crossing guards (are crossing guards.)
2. where does Sofia stand (Where; stand?)

BRIDGE TO WRITING I want to be a crossing guard, __(combining word)__ I am not old enough.

ORAL WARM-UP

USE PRIOR KNOWLEDGE Ask questions to elicit nouns from students: **What kind of pet do you have? Where are we? What is this thing? Who is this?** Write students' responses on the board.

TEACH/MODEL

Read aloud the explanation and examples of nouns on page 92. For each boldface example, have students tell whether the noun names a person, an animal, a place, or a thing. Model the thinking for the Guided Practice example:

MODEL I know that I do science experiments in a lab. Since a lab is a place, *lab* is a noun. Spills are things I clean up. Things are nouns, so *spills* is also a noun.

Work through the Guided Practice with students, asking them to tell whether each noun names a person, an animal, a place, or a thing.

 CHAPTER **7**

More About Nouns

Vocabulary Power

pre•cau•tion
[pri•kô′ shən] *n.*
Care taken ahead of time; a measure taken to avoid possible harm or danger.

92

Nouns

A noun is a word that names a person, an animal, a place, or a thing.

You can make your writing clearer and more interesting to read by carefully choosing the nouns you use.

Examples:
person: Stay safe by getting an **adult** to help you with cooking.

animal: I keep my **dog** on a leash.

place: Don't run in the **hallways**.

thing: Sometimes we wear **goggles** in science class.

Guided Practice

A. Identify each noun in the sentence.

Example: Keep safe in the lab by cleaning up spills.
lab, spills

1. Check with an adult before eating strange foods. adult, foods
2. Put away your toys. toys
3. Don't leave toys on the stairs. toys, stairs
4. Use a mat in the tub. mat, tub
5. Make sure the water is not too hot. water
6. Never touch a hot stove. stove
7. Ask adults to help you with tools. adults, tools
8. Using electricity near water is unsafe. electricity, water
9. Be careful around a dog you don't know. dog
10. Let adults clean up broken glass. adults, glass

Vocabulary Power

DAY 1 EXPLORE WORD MEANING Introduce and define *precaution*. **If you know it's going to rain, what precautions do you take?**

DAY 2 PREFIXES *Pre-* means "before." *Caution* is a warning. Put them together and you get _____. (See also *Vocabulary Power*, page 19.)

DAY 3 WORD FAMILIES *Caution* and *precaution* are in the same word family. **What are some other words in this word family?** (See also *Vocabulary Power*, page 20.)

DAY 4 CONTEXT CLUES Say: **As a precaution, we boarded up our windows before the big storm.** Ask students to identify the words that help them understand the meaning of precaution. (See also *Vocabulary Power*, page 21.)

DAY 5 EXEMPLIFICATION Traffic signs and warning labels are used as precautions. Ask students to give examples of these kinds of precautions and discuss their uses.

Independent Practice

B. Write the sentence. Underline each noun.

Example: Never run in the hallways at school.
Never run in the <u>hallways</u> at <u>school</u>.

11. Listen to directions from your teacher. directions, teacher
12. Stay seated in your chair. chair
13. Handle scissors carefully. scissors
14. Take turns on the playground. turns, playground
15. Keep the floor clean so you don't trip or slip. floor

C. For each underlined noun, write *person*, *place*, or *thing*.

Example: Sit down on the school <u>bus</u>. *thing*

16. Keep your <u>arms</u> inside the bus. thing
17. Pay attention to the <u>driver</u>. person
18. Talk softly with a <u>friend</u>. person
19. Be careful when you get to your <u>stop</u>. place
20. Look both ways for <u>cars</u>. thing

Remember
that a noun names a person, an animal, a place, or a thing.

Writing Connection

Writer's Journal: Word Bank Writers must be able to choose the right nouns to explain their ideas. Good writers are always adding words to their personal word banks. On a sheet of paper, make three lists labeled *People/Animals*, *Places*, and *Things*. Write as many safety-related words as you can think of in each list. Choose ten words that you might use in your writing. Copy them into your word bank.

People/Animals	Places	Things
firefighter guide dog	police station	fire alarm traffic light

93

Independent Practice

Have students complete the Independent Practice, or modify it using these suggestions:

MODIFIED INSTRUCTION

BELOW-LEVEL STUDENTS As students look for nouns, prompt students to ask themselves, whether the word *the* names a person, an animal, a place, or a thing.

ABOVE-LEVEL STUDENTS For Part B, have students tell how they know that the words they selected are nouns.

Writing Connection

Writer's Journal: Word Bank To help students generate a list of safety-related nouns, have them think about different places where they should pay attention to safety, such as at home, at school, and in areas where they play. Students can then work in pairs to write their lists.

WRAP-UP/ASSESS

SUMMARIZE What is a noun? What are some nouns that name people, animals, places, and things?

REACHING ALL LEARNERS
RETEACH

INTERVENTION Lessons in **visual, auditory,** and **kinesthetic** modalities: p. R42 and *Reteach Activities Copying Masters,* p. 13.

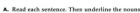

PRACTICE page 21

Name _____

Nouns

A. Read each sentence. Then underline the nouns.

1. We just bought a <u>puppy</u>.
2. My <u>brother</u> and I are careful to keep the <u>puppy</u> safe.
3. We always close the <u>gate</u> so that he cannot get out.
4. If he left the <u>yard</u>, he might get hurt or lost.
5. He tries to sneak out the <u>door</u> when we are not looking.
6. Sometimes he runs to the <u>house</u> of our neighbor.
7. He puts a <u>leash</u> on him and takes him for a <u>walk</u>.

B. For each underlined noun, tell whether it is a person, a place, an animal, or a thing.

8. Some <u>squirrels</u> were playing nearby. — animal
9. The <u>boy</u> picked up a <u>bag</u>. — person, thing
10. He dropped <u>nuts</u> on the <u>ground</u>. — thing, thing
11. He did not hold the <u>food</u> in his <u>fingers</u>. — thing, thing
12. He did not want to get a <u>bite</u> on his <u>hand</u>. — thing, thing

TRY THIS! Write a paragraph about your pet or a friend's pet. In what way is the pet special? Underline the nouns you have used.

Practice • More About Nouns   Unit 2 • Chapter 7 21

REACHING ALL LEARNERS
CHALLENGE

FIRE SAFETY Have students use **Challenge Activity Card 5** (page R64) to create a fire-safety poster for their home.

Challenge Activity Card 5

Fire Safety

Create a fire safety poster for your home. List things that family members should do in case of a fire. Draw a picture of your house like this one, showing doors and windows. Use arrows to show how to exit the house in an emergency.
Underline the nouns in your poster.
Take your poster home and discuss it with your family.

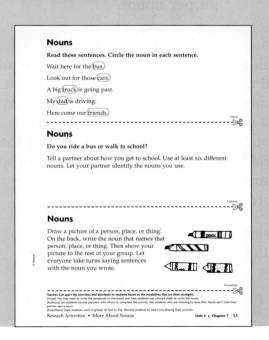

Nouns

Read these sentences. Circle the noun in each sentence.

Wait here for the (bus.)

Look out for those (cars.)

A big (truck) is going past.

My (dad) is driving.

Here come our (friends.)

Visual ✂

Nouns

Do you ride a bus or walk to school?

Tell a partner about how you get to school. Use at least six different nouns. Let your partner identify the nouns you use.

Auditory ✂

Nouns

Draw a picture of a person, place, or thing. On the back, write the noun that names that person, place, or thing. Then show your picture to the rest of your group. Let everyone take turns saying sentences with the noun you wrote.

Kinesthetic

Teacher: Cut apart the activities and distribute to students based on the modalities that are their strengths.
[Visual] You may want to write the sentences on the board and have students use colored chalk to circle the nouns.
[Auditory] Let students choose partners with whom to complete the activity. Ask students who are listening to raise their hands each time their partner says a noun.
[Kinesthetic] Have students work in groups of four or five. Remind students to take turns sharing their pictures.
Reteach Activities • More About Nouns   Unit 2 • Chapter 7 13

Common and Proper Nouns

OBJECTIVES
- To identify common and proper nouns
- To search the Internet and to share information in small groups

DAILY LANGUAGE PRACTICE

TRANSPARENCY 15

1 cleaning products and matches are not toys (Cleaning; toys.)

2 Children should not use them and adults should be careful with them. (them,)

BRIDGE TO WRITING What are some rules for using __(noun)__ safely?

ORAL WARM-UP

USE PRIOR KNOWLEDGE On the board, write: *Jared, Rachel, and Takira are students at my school.* Have students identify each noun and tell whether it names a person or a thing. Then ask students whether they noticed the difference between writing nouns that are names and nouns that aren't.

Grammar Jingles™ **CD, Intermediate** Use Track 5 for review and reinforcement of proper nouns.

TEACH/MODEL

Guide students through the explanation and examples on page 94. Explain that names, titles, days of the week, holidays, and months are all proper nouns and should be capitalized. Tell students that good writers choose common and proper nouns carefully to make their writing more interesting.

Work with students to complete the Guided Practice.

Common and Proper Nouns

A common noun names any person, place, or thing. **A proper noun** is the name of a particular person, place, or thing.

A common noun begins with a lowercase letter. People's titles, names of holidays, days of the week, and months are proper nouns. Begin each important word of a proper noun with a capital letter.

> **Example:**
> **Common nouns**
> For safety, **children** must look before crossing a **street**.
>
> **Proper nouns**
> **Carmen** and **Maria** looked both ways before crossing **East First Street**.
>
> The **Fourth of July** is my favorite holiday.

Guided Practice

A. Tell whether each underlined noun is a common noun or a proper noun.

Example: "Don't run across Main Street," reminded Maria.   *proper, proper*

1. The girls stopped at the curb. common, common
2. Maria looked both ways. proper, common
3. The children waited for the bus in front of Rike's Department Store. common, common, proper
4. Use your eyes and ears to look for cars. common, comm comm
5. We taught our dog Mandy to sit at the curb. proper, common

94

Vocabulary Power page 19

Name _____

PREFIXES

A prefix comes at the beginning of a word and changes the meaning of the word. For example, *pre-* in *precaution* makes the word mean "care taken before something happens." Below are some prefixes and their meanings.

| pre- | before | un- | not |
| re- | again | over- | too much |

Read each group of words below. Write the meaning for each word. The first one is done for you.

1. preheat: _____ heat before
2. overdo: _____ do too much
3. untold: _____ not told
4. prepay: _____ pay before
5. uncut: _____ not cut
6. prejudge: _____ judge before
7. rewrap: _____ wrap again
8. prehistoric: _____ before history
9. overuse: _____ use too much
10. refilled: _____ filled again
11. unwashed: _____ not washed
12. overheat: _____ heat too much
13. retell: _____ tell again
14. unsaid: _____ not said

Vocabulary Power   Unit 2 • Chapter 7   19

Health

HEALTH PAMPHLETS Have students work in small groups to write and illustrate pamphlets on a topic from the list below. Students may use encyclopedias, the Internet, or their health textbooks to find information.

- First Aid
- Reporting Danger
- Safety in a Storm
- Bicycle Safety
- Water Safety

Independent Practice

B. Write each sentence. Capitalize each proper noun.

Example: carmen puts on her seat belt when she rides in the car with grandma.

Carmen puts on her seat belt when she rides in the car with Grandma.

6. Her cat elsa will ride safely in a cat carrier.
   Her cat Elsa will ride safely in a cat carrier.

7. The people in the garcia family use seat belts on long trips to see uncle alan.
   The people in the Garcia family use seat belts on long trips to see Uncle Alan.

8. They also wear seat belts on short trips to los angeles.
   They also wear seat belts on short trips to Los Angeles.

9. mom tells maria not to wave her hands out the window.
   Mom tells Maria not to wave her hands out the window.

10. The children behave so dad can drive safely on their trip to texas.
    The children behave so Dad can drive safely on their trip to Texas.

11. mr. clancy taught us to ride our bikes on safe roads.
    Mr. Clancy taught us to ride our bikes on safe roads.

12. Ask aunt mary to help you check your brakes.
    Ask Aunt Mary to help you check your brakes.

13. Get your bike fixed at main street fix-it shop.
    Get your bike fixed at Main Street Fix-It Shop.

14. I always bicycle with jamie. I always bicycle with Jamie.

15. It is the law in maryland to wear a helmet.
    It is the law in Maryland to wear a helmet.

Remember
that a **common noun** names any person, animal, place, or thing and begins with a lowercase letter. A **proper noun** names a particular person, animal, place, or thing and begins with a capital letter.

Writing Connection

Technology Search the World Wide Web for information about safety topics. Print out the information you find. Work with a group to make a list of safety topics from your searches. Organize the topics by listing them under the labels *People*, *Places*, and *Things*. When you list proper nouns, be sure to use capital letters.

95

Independent Practice

Have students complete the Independent Practice, or modify it using these suggestions:

MODIFIED INSTRUCTION

BELOW-LEVEL STUDENTS Have students write a list of names of family members or friends. Then instruct them to check that they capitalized each name.

ABOVE-LEVEL STUDENTS After they have completed the Independent Practice, ask students to identify the subject of each sentence in Part B. If the subject is a common noun, have them change it to a proper noun and rewrite the sentence. If the subject is a proper noun, have them change it to a common noun and rewrite the sentence.

Writing Connection

Technology Have students work in small groups to take simple notes from the Internet. Then have them share the safety information they found.

WRAP-UP/ASSESS

SUMMARIZE Ask students to explain the differences between common and proper nouns and to give examples.

RETACH
REACHING ALL LEARNERS

INTERVENTION Lessons in **visual, auditory,** and **kinesthetic** modalities: p. R42 and *Reteach Activities Copying Masters,* p. 14.

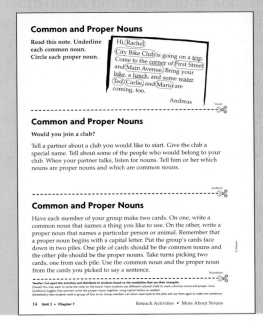

REACHING ALL LEARNERS

PRACTICE page 22

Name _____

Common and Proper Nouns

A. Underline each common noun once and each proper noun twice.

1. This morning Dot and her sister are excited.
2. Their Uncle lives in San Antonio, Texas.
3. Today Uncle George is bringing his family for a visit.
4. Dot and Janice made the house safe for their young cousin.
5. The girls and their friend Amanda fixed the cupboards.

B. Replace the underlined word or words with proper nouns. You may use the names of people, places, and things.
Responses may vary.
6. The girl put all the toys up high except the safe ones.
   Janice put all the toys up high except the safe ones.

7. The visitors will arrive soon.
   The Buchanans will arrive soon.

8. Her aunt will keep the baby away from the stairs.
   Aunt Emma will keep the baby away from the stairs.

9. When she is not around, their uncle will watch the baby.
   When she is not around, their Uncle George will watch the baby.

▶ TRY THIS! Make a list of things you can do to make your home safe for a young visitor. Be sure to capitalize any proper nouns you use.

22 Unit 2 • Chapter 7   Practice • More About Nouns

REACHING ALL LEARNERS

CHALLENGE

PET SAFETY Have students work in groups to make fact sheets on pet safety. Have students find tips for a specific type of animal. Ask students to find information about young, adult, and older animals. Students may organize their findings into categories, such as *General Information, Young Animals, Adult Animals,* and *Older Animals.* Compile the fact sheets in a class book on pet safety.

Common and Proper Nouns

Read this note. Underline each common noun. Circle each proper noun.

Hi, Rachel,
City Bike Club is going on a trip. Come to the corner of First Street and Main Avenue. Bring your bike, a lunch, and some water. Ted, Carlie, and Mario are coming, too.
Andreas

Visual

Common and Proper Nouns

Would you join a club?

Tell a partner about a club you would like to start. Give the club a special name. Tell about some of the people who would belong to your club. When your partner talks, listen for nouns. Tell him or her which nouns are proper nouns and which are common nouns.

Auditory

Common and Proper Nouns

Have each member of your group make two cards. On one, write a common noun that names a thing you like to use. On the other, write a proper noun that names a particular person or animal. Remember that a proper noun begins with a capital letter. Put the group's cards face down in two piles. One pile of cards should be the common nouns and the other pile should be the proper nouns. Take turns picking two cards, one from each pile. Use the common noun and the proper noun from the cards you picked to say a sentence.

Kinesthetic

Teacher: Cut apart the activities and distribute to students based on the modalities that are their strengths.
(Visual) You may want to write the note on the board. Have students use different-colored chalk to mark common nouns and proper nouns.
(Auditory) Suggest that partners write the proper nouns together, using capital letters as needed.
(Kinesthetic) Have students work in groups of four to do this activity. Group members can return used cards to the piles and use them again to make new sentences.

14 Unit 2 • Chapter 7   Reteach Activities • More About Nouns

Abbreviations and Titles

OBJECTIVES
- To identify and use abbreviations and titles
- To make a safety poster using abbreviations

DAILY LANGUAGE PRACTICE

TRANSPARENCY 15

1 My friend lucy skis and skats in the winter (Lucy; skates; winter.)

2 Ramón skis but he does not sled-ding. (skis; Possible response: does not go sledding)

BRIDGE TO WRITING We go to the skat-ing rink in ___(proper noun)___.

ORAL WARM-UP

USE PRIOR KNOWLEDGE Ask students to list the names of school personnel on the board. Point out the titles *Mr.*, *Mrs.*, and *Ms.*

Grammar Jingles™ **CD, Intermediate** Use Track 5 for review and reinforcement of proper nouns.

TEACH/MODEL

Read aloud the explanation of abbrevia-tions and titles on page 96. Have stu-dents look at the chart and name other abbreviations. Explain that abbreviations for common nouns, such as customary measurements and time sequences, are not capitalized and that abbreviations for proper nouns are capitalized. Ask stu-dents to tell where they might see abbre-viations. Point out that only A.M., P.M., and titles should be written as abbrevia-tions in a sentence.

Work with students to complete the Guided Practice.

More Abbreviations	
before noon	A.M.
after noon	P.M.
Street	St.
Avenue	Ave.
Road	Rd.
minutes	min.
seconds	sec.
inches	in.
feet	ft.
yards	yd.
a man	Mr.
a woman	Ms.
a married woman	Mrs.

Abbreviations and Titles

An abbreviation is a short way to write a word.

Use a period after most abbreviations. An abbreviation for a proper noun begins with a capital letter. The **title** of a person, such as *Mr.*, *Mrs.*, *Ms.*, and *Dr.*, begins with a capital letter.

Example:

Ms. Ram told us to take swimming lessons.

The names of days and months may be abbreviated.

Some Common Abbreviations			
Days		**Months**	
Sunday	Sun.	January	Jan.
Monday	Mon.	February	Feb.
Tuesday	Tues.	August	Aug.
Wednesday	Wed.	September	Sept.
Thursday	Thurs.	October	Oct.
Friday	Fri.	November	Nov.
Saturday	Sat.	December	Dec.

Guided Practice

A. Tell the abbreviation for the underlined word or words.

Example: (a man) Marks teaches swimming.   *Mr.*

1. In January, take a class at an indoor pool. Jan.
2. Can you swim in several feet of water? ft.
3. My class is at 10:00 (before noon). A.M.
4. (a woman) Wong is the lifeguard. Ms.
5. The pool is 50 yards long. yd.

Vocabulary Power page 20

REACHING ALL LEARNERS

ESL

LANGUAGE SHARING Have stu-dents share with classmates how names and titles in their first lan-guage are similar to and different from names and titles in English.

Independent Practice

B. Write each sentence. Write out the word for each underlined abbreviation.

Example: I use the equipment carefully on Park <u>St.</u> Playground.   *Street*

6. A precaution I take is to talk only to people I know when I go to the <u>Ave.</u> Mall.   Avenue
7. I keep safe by dressing warmly when I play outside in <u>Feb.</u>   February
8. I skate on ice only if it is many <u>in.</u> thick.   inches
9. I skate at 11:00 <u>A.M.</u>   before noon
10. If I stay outside ten <u>min.</u> without sunscreen, I might get burned.   minutes
11. Do not ride in <u>Dec.</u> if it is icy.   December
12. Use a light and go with an adult if you have to ride after 8:00 <u>P.M.</u>   after noon
13. <u>Mr.</u> Naito said to check your tires.   Mister
14. It may take many <u>sec.</u> to stop your bike.   seconds
15. Do not ride on High <u>Rd.</u>   Road

> **Remember** that an abbreviation is a short way to write a word. Many abbreviations end with a period. Abbreviations for proper nouns begin with a capital letter.

Writing Connection

Real-Life Writing: Safety Poster Use books or the World Wide Web to make a safety poster. Put a safety tip for each day of the week on your poster. Start by writing the abbreviations for the days of the week on your poster paper. Then write a tip after each one. Use colorful drawings to make your poster interesting.

> **This Week's Tips**
> Mon. Don't run in the halls.
> Tues. Wear a helmet when you ride a bike.
> Wed. Take stairs one at a time.
> Thurs. Clean up messes.
> Fri. Cross the street carefully.
> Sat. Take turns on the playground.
> Sun. Wear a seat belt in the car.

97

Independent Practice

Have students complete the Independent Practice, or modify it using these suggestions:

MODIFIED INSTRUCTION

BELOW-LEVEL STUDENTS Tell students to refer to the chart on page 96 to complete Part B.

ABOVE-LEVEL STUDENTS Have students look in their science or social studies textbook to find other abbreviations, such as those using metric measurements. Students can share their findings with classmates.

Writing Connection

Real-Life Writing: Safety Poster Remind students that the purpose of their poster is to provide information and suggestions. Some students may want their poster to have one general topic, but others may decide to have a different topic for each weekday. Students should gain more proficient control of penmanship when they write their safety tips. Display students' posters in the classroom or hallway.

WRAP-UP/ASSESS

SUMMARIZE Ask: **How do you know when to capitalize an abbreviation?**

RETEACH

INTERVENTION Lessons in **visual, auditory,** and **kinesthetic** modalities: p. R42 and *Reteach Activities Copying Masters*, p. 15.

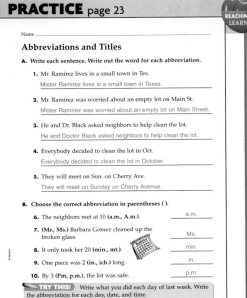

PRACTICE page 23

Name _____

Abbreviations and Titles

A. Write each sentence. Write out the word for each abbreviation.

1. Mr. Ramirez lives in a small town in Tex.
   Mister Ramirez lives in a small town in Texas.
2. Mr. Ramirez was worried about an empty lot on Main St.
   Mister Ramirez was worried about an empty lot on Main Street.
3. He and Dr. Black asked neighbors to help clean the lot.
   He and Doctor Black asked neighbors to help clean the lot.
4. Everybody decided to clean the lot in Oct.
   Everybody decided to clean the lot in October.
5. They will meet on Sun. on Cherry Ave.
   They will meet on Sunday on Cherry Avenue.

B. Choose the correct abbreviation in parentheses ( ).

6. The neighbors met at 10 (a.m., A.m.)   a.m.
7. (Mr., Ms.) Barbara Gomez cleaned up the broken glass.   Ms.
8. It only took her 20 (min., mt.).   min.
9. One piece was 2 (in., ich.) long.   in.
10. By 3 (Pm, p.m.), the lot was safe.   p.m.

> **TRY THIS!** Write what you did each day of last week. Write the abbreviation for each day, date, and time.

Practice • More About Nouns   Unit 2 • Chapter 7   23

CHALLENGE

KITCHEN SAFETY Have students find a recipe that interests them, and have them copy it using the correct abbreviations. Students should think about the utensils and appliances they might use to make the recipe.

Then have students make a flier promoting safety in the kitchen. They should decorate the flier with a border and include several kitchen-safety tips.

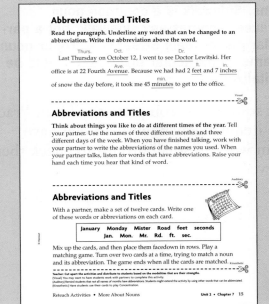

Abbreviations and Titles

Read the paragraph. Underline any word that can be changed to an abbreviation. Write the abbreviation above the word.

Last <u>Thursday</u> on October 12, I went to see <u>Doctor</u> Lewitski. Her office is at 22 Fourth <u>Avenue</u>. Because we had 2 <u>feet</u> and 7 <u>inches</u> of snow the day before, it took me 45 <u>minutes</u> to get to the office.

Abbreviations and Titles

Think about things you like to do at different times of the year. Tell your partner. Use the names of three different months and three different days of the week. When you have finished talking, work with your partner to say the abbreviations of the names you used. When your partner talks, listen for words that have abbreviations. Raise your hand each time you hear that kind of word.

Abbreviations and Titles

With a partner, make a set of twelve cards. Write one of these words or abbreviations on each card.

| January | Monday | Mister | Road | feet | seconds |
| Jan. | Mon. | Mr. | Rd. | ft. | sec. |

Mix up the cards, and then place them facedown in rows. Play a matching game. Turn over two cards at a time, trying to match a noun and its abbreviation. The game ends when all the cards are matched.

Reteach Activities • More About Nouns   Unit 2 • Chapter 7   15

Extra Practice

OBJECTIVES
- To identify and use common and proper nouns, abbreviations, and titles
- To write a paragraph that provides reasons for following a safety rule

DAILY LANGUAGE PRACTICE

TRANSPARENCY 16

1 why do accidents happen (Why; happen?)

2 Accidents can happen qwickly. (quickly.)

BRIDGE TO WRITING My sister went to see (abbreviation) Ortiz, our family doctor, when she got hurt.

ORAL WARM-UP

USE PRIOR KNOWLEDGE Write on the board: *Dr. Kim tells people to keep life jackets in their boats and not to go boating after 6:00 P.M.* Ask students to name the common nouns, proper nouns, titles, and abbreviations.

TEACH/MODEL

Use the Remember box to review common nouns, proper nouns, abbreviations, and titles. Model the thinking for the example in Part B:

MODEL *Sidewalk* and *Main Street* are the nouns. *Sidewalk* is a common noun because it names any sidewalk, not a particular place. *Main Street* is a proper noun. It names a particular place and should be capitalized.

Ask students to complete the Extra Practice items independently. Then have them work in small groups to check their answers.

Remember
that a common noun begins with a lowercase letter. A proper noun begins with a capital letter. An abbreviation ends with a period. Abbreviations for proper nouns and titles for people begin with capital letters.

For more activities with nouns and abbreviations, visit *The Learning Site:* www.harcourtschool.com

98

Extra Practice

A. Write each noun in the sentence.
pages 92–93

Example: Never play with matches or candles.
matches, candles

1. Keep paper away from heaters. paper, heaters
2. Only adults should start fires in fireplaces. adults, fires, fireplaces
3. Your family should get the chimney cleaned. family, chimney
4. Never use the stove without an adult present. stove, adult
5. Have a plan for getting out if there is a fire. plan, fire

B. Write each sentence. Capitalize each proper noun. *pages 94–95*

Example: Skate on the sidewalk, not on main street.
Skate on the sidewalk, not on Main Street.

6. Mr. diaz says we should always wear a helmet and guards when we skate. Diaz
7. Dr. rahim says to warm up your body before skating. Doctor Rahim
8. Skate in lakewood park, where it is safe. Lakewood Park
9. jan stays to the right and felix to the left. Jan, Felix
10. You can buy safety equipment at tommy's super skateland. Tommy's Super Skateland

C. Write the abbreviation for each underlined word. *pages 96–97*

Example: Skate fifty <u>feet</u>, and then stop. *ft.*

11. It is safe to skate at 9:00 (<u>before noon</u>). A.M.
12. At 9:00 (<u>after noon</u>) it is too dark to skate. P.M.
13. Wear a wool cap in <u>January</u>. Jan.
14. Do not let your attention wander for even one <u>minute</u>. min.
15. You may have only one <u>second</u> to get out of the way of another skater. sec.

Vocabulary Power page 21

Name _____

CONTEXT CLUES

Read each sentence. Then write a definition for each underlined word. Possible responses are given.

1. That fossil is so old that it's <u>prehistoric</u>.
   before history

2. We will <u>prepay</u> for our tickets so we won't have to buy them when we get there.
   pay before

3. Sue <u>preheated</u> the oven before she baked the cookies.
   heat before

4. It isn't nice to <u>prejudge</u> people before you get to know them.
   judge before

5. We brought an umbrella as a <u>precaution</u> in case it rains.
   care taken before

6. If you don't do it right, you will need to <u>redo</u> it.
   do again

7. Studying is one way to <u>prepare</u> for a test.
   get ready

8. When my glass was empty, the waiter <u>refilled</u> it.
   fill again

Vocabulary Power   Unit 2 • Chapter 7   21

WORK WITH A PARTNER Have students work with an English-fluent partner to complete the Extra Practice items.

D. If a sentence is capitalized correctly, write
correct. **If there is a mistake, write the**
sentence correctly. *pages 94–97*

Example: "Wear guards whenever you skate,"
said mr. Bell. *Mr.*

16. Wear tape that will shine in the dark if you
skate at 9:00 P.M. correct

17. I need to buy a bandage for my sore foot at
max's super value drugs. Max's Super Value Drugs

18. mr. Day says it's best to point your skates to
the side when you go down stairs. Mr.

19. Do not skate in chung park or anywhere there
is a sign that says not to skate. Chung Park

20. Watch out for twigs or pebbles in your path.
correct

21. Take a trip on our boat, the lucky duck.
Lucky Duck

22. Please remember these safety tips from our
teacher, ms. ashley. Ms. Ashley

23. Do not sail without Mom or dad. Dad

24. Wear the waterworld Boat Company life jacket.
Waterworld

25. Mr. yoon and I look forward to our boat trip.
Mr. Yoon

Writing Connection

Writer's Craft: Giving Reasons Ask several
people to tell their reasons for following a certain
safety tip. Use the list of ideas to write a paragraph
telling why the tip is important for everyone to
follow. Then trade papers with a partner. Underline
each common noun. Then circle each proper noun.

99

Building Oral Grammar

Have students give safety talks to younger students.
Prompt them to think of what younger students need
to know about safety in various places. Have students work in small groups to choose a place for the
talks, plan a presentation for younger students, and
present their work to the class.

Remind students that when they make their presentations, they should choose the appropriate volume and
rate of speaking. They should also clarify and support
their messages by using a prop, such as a chart, of
their safety tips. Prompt students to use vocabulary
from their word banks to describe their ideas clearly.
Classmates can offer suggestions for improving each
presentation. Have volunteers present their work for
other classes.

Writing Connection

Writer's Craft: Giving Reasons Remind students
to capitalize proper nouns as they record their
reflections. Have students write reasons it is
important to follow a particular safety tip.

WRAP-UP/ASSESS

Writer's Journal

SUMMARIZE Have students write
in their journals to reflect on
what they learned about common and proper nouns, abbreviations, and titles. **REFLECTION**

ADDITIONAL PRACTICE An additional page
of Extra Practice is provided on page
458 of the *Pupil Edition*.

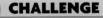

CHALLENGE

REACHING ALL LEARNERS

TRAVEL TIPS Have each student
write a paragraph explaining how
to travel safely by car, on foot, by
bicycle, or on in-line skates. Have
students work with a partner to
revise their paragraphs, replacing
some common nouns with proper
nouns.

TECHNOLOGY *Grammar Practice
and Assessment* CD-ROM;
Writing Express CD-ROM

INTERNET Visit *The Learning Site:*
w w w . h a r c o u r t s c h o o l . c o m

Chapter Review

OBJECTIVES
- To review common and proper nouns, abbreviations, and titles
- To interpret and create charts

SPIRAL REVIEW

DAILY LANGUAGE PRACTICE

TRANSPARENCY 16

1 John smith hurt his ankle on our hike. (Smith)

2 He tried to stand up but his ankle was twisted (up,; twisted.)

BRIDGE TO WRITING We helped him get back to the (common noun). This happened on (proper noun).

STANDARDIZED TEST PREP

MODEL TEST-TAKING STRATEGIES Have students read the directions on page 100 silently.

Tell students that if they are not sure of the answer to a question, they should eliminate choices that are obviously wrong.

Model the thinking. Write this example on the board:

Our coach, ms thompson, tells us to warm up before we play.

1   **A**   Ms Thompson
     B   ms Thompson
     C   Ms. Thompson
     D   No mistake

MODEL   **Ms. Thompson is a particular person, and so I know her name is a proper noun. Proper nouns and titles are capitalized. Answers B and D are not correct because the *ms* in B is not capitalized. I know that A is not correct because *Ms.* is an abbreviation, and so it should be followed by a period. The correct answer is C.**

Have students complete the Chapter Review independently.

STANDARDIZED TEST PREP

Chapter Review

Read the passage. Some sections are underlined. Choose the best way to write each underlined section and mark the letter for your answer. If the underlined section needs no change, mark the choice "No mistake."

> (1) Wonder park has a sign to help you be a safe hiker. (2) The sign says "Beginner Trail 500 yds" (3) The ranger, Kendra Monty, says to be sure you know the weather before you hike. (4) It is not safe to leave in a Jan snowstorm. (5) It also would not be smart to start a long hike at 7:00 P.M. (6) Ms Rivera says you should always hike with an adult.

TIP Read the entire passage first to be sure you understand it. Then reread it to decide on answers.

1   **A**   wonder park
    B   Wonder Park   B
    C   Wonder Pk
    D   No mistake

4   **F**   january
    G   Janry.
    H   January   H
    J   No mistake

2   **F**   yds."   F
    G   yrd"
    H   yrd."
    J   No mistake

5   **A**   7:00.
    B   7:00 A.M.
    C   7 A.M.
    D   No mistake   D

3   **A**   Kendra monty
    B   Ms. Kendra monty
    C   kendra Monty
    D   No mistake   D

6   **F**   Ms. Rivera   F
    G   Ms. rivera
    H   ms. Rivera
    J   No mistake

For additional test preparation, visit *The Learning Site:* www.harcourtschool.com

---

Assessment

PORTFOLIO ASSESSMENT Have students select their best work from the Writing Connections on pages 95, 97, and 99.

ONGOING ASSESSMENT Evaluate the performance of 4–6 students using appropriate checklists and record forms from pages R74–R77.

INTERNET Activities and exercises to help students prepare for state and standardized assessments appear on *The Learning Site:*
www.harcourtschool.com

Understanding Charts

This chart helps you stay safe while swimming. It is important to know how to read charts.

Safe Swimming Conditions				
Number of Swimmers	1–10	11–25	26–35	36–50
Number of Lifeguards	1	1	2	2
Number of Watchers	1	2	3	4

Use the chart to answer these questions.

1. What does the middle row of numbers tell you? *the number of lifeguards needed*
2. How many lifeguards are needed if ten people are swimming? *one*
3. How many watchers are needed if thirty people are swimming? *three*
4. How many people are needed altogether if forty people are swimming? *six*

YOUR TURN

Work with a partner to make your own chart that shows how many people follow safety tips. Here are the steps you should follow:

1. **Decide on three tips you will use. Ask children and adults whether they use each tip. Keep track of their answers.**
2. **Along the top of your chart write the kinds of people you asked : Adults, Children.**
3. **Write the tips along the left side of your chart.**
4. **Fill in the information you collected to show how many children and how many adults use each of the tips.**

101

STUDY SKILLS

Understanding Charts

TEACH/MODEL

Explain that a chart is one way to organize information. Charts are set up so that information can be understood quickly and easily.

Have students turn to page 96 to review the chart on abbreviations. Point out that by using a chart a lot of space was saved and it made the material easy to read and understand.

Point out that most charts contain columns and rows.

WRITING APPLICATION Have students explain in their journals what they discovered in their survey, such as which tip the most or the fewest people followed and so on. **REFLECTION**

WRAP-UP/ASSESS

SUMMARIZE Why are charts useful for presenting information?

PRACTICE page 25

Name _____

Chapter Review

Read the passage. Choose the best way to write each underlined section, and fill in the oval next to your choice. If the underlined section needs no change, fill in the choice *No mistake*.

Safety Committee

(1) The students at Lomita street School formed a committee to study safety. (2) My friend katie was on the committee. (3) The committee met in the room where Mr. Robinson taught. (4) They met on wed. afternoon. (5) The meeting at 3:30 p.m. (6) It lasted for 45 mins. (7) They decided to meet again in Febru.

1. ○ Lomita street school
   ━ Lomita Street School
   ○ Lomita Street school
   ○ No mistake

2. ━ My friend Katie was on the committee.
   ○ My Friend Katie was on the Committee.
   ○ My Friend katie was on the committee.
   ○ No mistake

3. ○ mr. Robinson
   ○ Mtr. Robinson
   ○ Mst. Robinson
   ━ No mistake

4. ○ wedn.
   ○ Wednes.
   ━ Wed.
   ○ No mistake

5. ○ 3:30 P.m.
   ○ 3:30 p.M
   ━ 3:30 P.M.
   ○ No mistake

6. ━ 45 min.
   ○ 45 mn.
   ○ 45 mint.
   ○ No mistake

7. ━ Feb.
   ○ Feb
   ○ Febr.
   ○ No mistake

Practice • More About Nouns

Unit 2 • Chapter 7   25

CHALLENGE

COMPARE CHARTS Have students work in small groups to select a chart from their science or social studies textbook. Have students answer the following questions:

What information is presented in the chart?

Is the chart easy to understand?

Write three facts you learned from looking at the chart.

TECHNOLOGY Additional writing activities are provided on the *Writing Express* CD-ROM

Singular and Plural Nouns
pages 102-111

LESSON ORGANIZER	DAY 1	DAY 2
DAILY LANGUAGE PRACTICE TRANSPARENCIES 17, 18	1. dr. ortiz said my sisters should eat oranges (Dr. Ortiz; oranges.) 2. ms leonard is a cook who makes the best Spaghetti. (Ms. Leonard; spaghetti) **Bridge to Writing** (Compound subject) are very healthful.	1. i had two orange for breakfast (I; oranges; breakfast.) 2. mrs. wilson made a vegetable soups for her family (Mrs. Wilson; soup; family.) **Bridge to Writing** I eat three (plural noun) a day.
ORAL WARM-UP **Listening/Speaking**	Identify Shapes 102	Identify Singular and Plural Nouns 104 *Grammar Jingles*™ CD Track 6
TEACH/MODEL **GRAMMAR** KEY ✔ = tested skill	✔ **SINGULAR AND PLURAL NOUNS** 102-103 • To recognize and correctly form singular and plural nouns • To make lists using singular and plural nouns	✔ **PLURAL NOUNS WITH *ES* AND *IES*** 104-105 • To correctly identify and form the plurals of nouns ending in *s, x, ch, sh,* and *y* • To make lists using singular and plural nouns
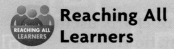 **Reaching All Learners**	**Modified Instruction** Below Level: Model the Thinking Above-Level: Write Original Sentences **Reteach:** *Reteach Activities Copying Masters* pp. 16 and R43 **Challenge:** Activity Card 6, p. R64 *ESL Manual,* pp. 42, 43 *Practice Book* p. 26	**Modified Instruction** Below-Level: Write Nouns Above-Level: List Plural Nouns **ESL:** Noun Chart 104 *ESL Manual* pp. 42, 44 **Reteach:** *Reteach Activities Copying Masters* pp. 17 and R43 **Challenge:** Design a Menu 105 *Practice Book* p. 27
WRITING	Writing Connection 103 Science	Writing Connection 105 Writer's Journal: Listing Nouns
CROSS-CURRICULAR/ ENRICHMENT	*Vocabulary Power* Word Families 102 carbohydrate, **nutrient,** nutritionist, nutritious, protein See *Vocabulary Power* book.	*Vocabulary Power* Explore Word Meaning 102 *Vocabulary Power* p. 22 🖥 **Vocabulary activity**

DAY 3

1. The ladys gave the babys two glasss of milk. (ladies; babies; glasses)
2. The older children ate peachs and berrys (peaches; berries.)

Bridge to Writing <u>(Plural noun)</u> grow on trees.

Identify Irregular Plural Nouns 106
Grammar Jingles™ CD Track 6

✔ **IRREGULAR PLURAL NOUNS** 106-107
- To identify and correctly form irregular plural nouns
- To create a menu using irregular plural nouns

Modified Instruction
Below-Level: Use the Chart
Above-Level: Rewrite Sentences
ESL: Irregular Plural Nouns 106
ESL Manual pp. 42, 45
Reteach: *Reteach Activities Copying Masters* pp. 18 and R43
Challenge: Animal Pairs 107
Practice Book p. 28

Writing Connection 107
    Real-Life Writing: Advertisement

Vocabulary Power
    Content-Area Words 102
    Vocabulary Power p. 23
💻 **Vocabulary activity**

DAY 4

1. The mans ate bowls of spinach salad for lunch (men; lunch.)
2. the spinach was fresh and green (The; green.)

Bridge to Writing As you grow, you will need new <u>(plural noun)</u> to wear.

Say the Plural 108

EXTRA PRACTICE 108-109
- To identify and correctly form singular and plural nouns
- To write a paragraph, using correct plural forms

💻 **Practice and assessment**

Building Oral Grammar
Read Sentences Aloud 109
Challenge: Food Advertisement 109
ESL Manual pp. 42, 46
Practice Book p. 29

Writing Connection 109
    Writer's Craft: Clear Explanations

Health: Alphabet Vitamins 108

Vocabulary Power
    Classify/Categorize 102
    Vocabulary Power p. 24
💻 **Vocabulary activity**

DAY 5

1. We filled boxs of cherrys from the cherry tree (boxes; cherries; tree.)
2. Drinking three glasss of milk gives you strong tooths. (glasses; teeth)

Bridge to Writing My favorite food is <u>(singular noun)</u> . <u>(Proper noun)</u> likes it, too!

TEST PREP **CHAPTER REVIEW** 110
- To review singular and plural nouns
- To understand and interpret special maps

💻 **Test preparation**

Challenge: Make a Map 111
Practice Book p. 30
ESL Manual pp. 42, 47

Writing Application 111
    Write a Paragraph

Viewing: Reading Special Maps 111

Vocabulary Power
    Context Clues 102

CHAPTER 8 101B

Singular and Plural Nouns

OBJECTIVES

- To recognize and correctly form singular and plural nouns
- To make lists, using singular and plural nouns

DAILY LANGUAGE PRACTICE

TRANSPARENCY 17

1 dr. ortiz said my sisters should eat oranges (Dr. Ortiz; oranges.)

2 ms leonard is a cook who makes the best Spaghetti. (Ms. Leonard; spaghetti)

BRIDGE TO WRITING

(Compound subject) are very healthful.

ORAL WARM-UP

USE PRIOR KNOWLEDGE On the board, draw a triangle. Beside the triangle, draw several circles. Ask volunteers to identify the shapes, and write their responses on the board.

TEACH/MODEL

Have a volunteer read aloud the explanation at the top of page 102. Guide students through the chart. Model the thinking for the Guided Practice example:

MODEL The underlined noun is *plants*. I know that most plural nouns end in *s*, so *plants* must be a plural noun.

Work through the Guided Practice with students.

Singular and Plural Nouns

A **singular noun** names one person, animal, place, or thing. A **plural noun** names more than one person, animal, place, or thing.

Nouns can be singular or plural. Add *s* to most singular nouns to form the plural.

Singular Nouns	Plural Nouns
apple	apples
food	foods
plant	plants

Vocabulary Power

nu·tri·ent
[n(y)oo′trē·ənt] *n.*
Something in food that helps people, animals, and plants stay healthy.

102

Guided Practice

A. Tell whether the underlined word in each sentence is a singular noun or a plural noun.

Example: Our food comes from <u>plants</u> and animals.
plural noun

1. People eat different kinds of <u>foods</u>. plural noun
2. Some foods come from <u>plants</u>. plural noun
3. Some foods come from <u>animals</u>. plural noun
4. Think about a <u>lasagna</u>. singular noun
5. The <u>noodle</u> is made of flour. singular noun
6. <u>Grains</u> come from plants. plural noun
7. The tomato <u>sauce</u> comes from plants, too. singular noun
8. The <u>cheese</u> is made of milk from cows. singular noun
9. <u>Spices</u> come from many plants. plural noun
10. Foods from both plants and <u>animals</u> are in lasagna. plural noun

---

Vocabulary Power

DAY 1 WORD FAMILIES Introduce and define *nutrient*. *Nutrient* comes from a word meaning "to feed." **What are some other words related to *nutrient*?**

DAY 2 EXPLORE WORD MEANING **What have you eaten so far today that contains nutrients?** (See also *Vocabulary Power*, page 22.)

DAY 3 CONTENT-AREA WORDS Ask: **What are some nutrients we need to stay healthy?** (See also *Vocabulary Power*, page 23.)

DAY 4 CLASSIFY AND CATEGORIZE **What are some examples of carbohydrates? What are some examples of proteins?** (See also *Vocabulary Power*, page 24.)

DAY 5 CONTEXT CLUES Challenge pairs of students to write at least two sentences that help explain the meaning of *nutrient*. Invite pairs to read their sentences aloud. Ask the class to point out specific words in the sentences that help explain the meaning of *nutrient*.

Independent Practice

B. Write whether the underlined word in each sentence is a singular noun or a plural noun.

Example: A <u>food</u> can come from a plant.
singular noun

11. Think about the <u>meals</u> you eat. plural noun
12. It is easy to recognize each <u>type</u> of food. singular noun
13. Broccoli and <u>cabbages</u> are plants. plural noun
14. <u>Carrots</u> and parsnips are roots. plural noun
15. A <u>peach</u> grows on a tree. singular noun

C. Write the plural noun or nouns in each sentence. Then write the singular form of the noun.

Example: Grains come from plants.
Grains, Grain; plants, plant

16. We eat these plants in different ways. plants, plant; ways, way
17. Breakfast cereals are made from grain. cereals, cereal
18. Noodles, dinner rolls, and crackers are also made from grain. Noodles, Noodle; rolls, roll; crackers, cracker
19. Eggs, steaks, and cheeses come from animals. eggs, egg; steaks, steak; cheeses, cheese; animals, animal
20. Nuts are covered with shells. nuts, nut; shells, shell

Writing Connection

Science Make a list of foods that come from plants. Then make a list of foods that come from animals. Review your two lists with a partner. Point out the singular and plural nouns in your lists.

Remember
that a singular noun names one person, animal, place, or thing, and a plural noun names more than one.

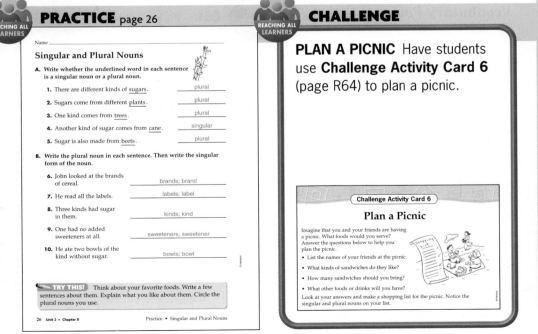
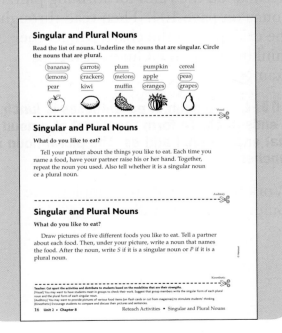

Plural Nouns with *es* and *ies*

OBJECTIVES

- To correctly identify and form the plurals of nouns ending in the letters *s, x, ch, sh,* and *y*
- To make lists, using singular and plural nouns

DAILY LANGUAGE PRACTICE

TRANSPARENCY 17

① i had two orange for breakfast (I; oranges; breakfast.)

② mrs. wilson made a vegetable soups for her family (Mrs. Wilson; soup; family.)

BRIDGE TO WRITING I eat three _____ (plural noun) a day.

ORAL WARM-UP

USE PRIOR KNOWLEDGE Write these words on the board: *classes, families.* Ask: **Are these nouns singular or plural?** Have volunteers spell the singular form of each noun.

Grammar Jingles™ **CD, Intermediate** Use Track 6 for review and reinforcement of singular and plural nouns.

TEACH/MODEL

Read aloud the rules for forming plural nouns on page 104. Then read through the examples in the chart. Model the thinking using the Guided Practice example:

MODEL The noun in parentheses is *lunch.* It ends in *ch.* To form the plural of a noun that ends in *ch,* I add *es.* The plural noun is *lunches.*

Work with students to complete the Guided Practice orally.

Plural Nouns with *es* and *ies*

Some nouns end with *es* or *ies* in the plural form.

Remember that you can make most singular nouns plural by adding *s.* Some nouns end with *s, x, ch,* or *sh.* Add *es* to form the plural of these nouns. To form the plural of a noun that ends with a consonant and *y,* change the *y* to *i* and add *es.* Look at the examples in the chart below.

Singular Nouns	Plural Nouns
glass	glasses
box	boxes
peach	peaches
radish	radishes
baby	babies
berry	berries
puppy	puppies

Guided Practice

A. Give the plural form of the nouns in parentheses ().

Example: Estelle eats healthful (lunch).
lunches

1. Estelle likes to eat vegetable (sandwich). sandwiches
2. She makes one with lettuce and (radish). radishes
3. She eats little (box) of raisins with her lunch. boxes
4. Estelle enjoys fresh (strawberry). strawberries
5. She mixes them with (blueberry). blueberries

Vocabulary Power page 22

Name _____

EXPLORE WORD MEANINGS

Read and answer each question. Use complete sentences.
Responses may vary. Accept reasonable responses.
1. Why is it important to get all of your nutrients?

2. Pretend you are a nutritionist. What are some things you would tell people to eat for breakfast?

3. Apples are an example of a carbohydrate. What are some other examples?

4. Chicken is an example of a protein. What are some other examples?

5. Is candy a nutritious food? Explain your answer.

6. What are some of your favorite nutritious foods?

22   Unit 2 • Chapter 8   Vocabulary Power

ESL

NOUN CHART On the board, create a two-column chart for students to copy. In the left-hand column, list several singular nouns ending in *s, ch, sh, x,* or *y.* In the right-hand column, list the plural form for each. Have students think of other nouns to add to their charts. Remind students to keep the chart for study and future reference.

Independent Practice

B. Write each sentence. Correct the spelling of the underlined plural noun.

Example: Our <u>bodys</u> need vitamins.
Our bodies need vitamins.

6. <u>Studys</u> show that people should eat vegetables. Studies
7. There are different vegetable <u>familyes</u>. families
8. Cabbage can help prevent many <u>illnessies</u>. illnesses
9. <u>Carrotes</u> are rich in vitamin A. Carrots
10. <u>Radishs</u> are fat-free and tasty in salads. Radishes

C. Write the plural form of the nouns in parentheses ( ).

Example: Leafy green vegetables have large (quantity) of nutrients. *quantities*

11. Drink at least three (glass) of milk each day. glasses
12. Some (berry) have vitamin C. berries
13. Vitamin C also comes from fruits like oranges and (peach). peaches
14. Our (body) make vitamin D from sunlight. bodies
15. Fish such as salmon and (anchovy) are good sources of protein. anchovies

Remember that you add *es* to form the plural of a noun that ends with *s*, *x*, *ch*, or *sh*. To form the plural of a noun that ends with a consonant and *y*, change the *y* to *i* and add *es*.

Writing Connection

Writer's Journal: Listing Nouns Do you think you are eating a balanced diet? Make a list of foods you need to add to your diet. Then make a list of unhealthful foods you are eating. Use the correct plural forms for these foods.

105

Independent Practice

Have students complete the Independent Practice, or modify it using these suggestions:

MODIFIED INSTRUCTION

BELOW-LEVEL STUDENTS Have students write the correct spelling of the underlined noun. Remind them to refer to the Remember box to find out how to form the plural correctly.

ABOVE-LEVEL STUDENTS Have students make a list of other plural nouns in the sentences in Part B.

Writing Connection

Writer's Journal: Listing Nouns Have students discuss healthful foods and balanced diets. Have them reflect on how they can make healthful food choices.

WRAP-UP/ASSESS

SUMMARIZE Ask students how to form the plural for a noun that ends in *s*, *x*, *ch*, or *sh*. Ask students how to form the plural for a noun that ends with a consonant and *y*.

RETEACH

INTERVENTION Lessons in **visual, auditory,** and **kinesthetic** modalities: p. R43 and *Reteach Activities Copying Masters*, p. 17.

PRACTICE page 27

Name _____

Plural Nouns with *-es* and *-ies*

A. Write the plural form of the noun in parentheses ( ).

1. The Olsons like their (beet) very fresh. beets
2. They buy (box) of fresh fruits. boxes
3. Parents take their (baby) shopping with them. babies
4. Sometimes a woman gives away (daisy). daisies
5. They have (dish) of fruit for people to taste. dishes

B. Write each sentence, using the plural form of the noun in parentheses ( ).

6. These (peach) are really juicy.
   These peaches are really juicy.
7. We went to an orchard to pick (cherry).
   We went to an orchard to pick cherries.
8. Pete Olson looked at the (berry).
   Pete Olson looked at the berries.
9. My sisters enjoy fresh fruit in their (lunch).
   My sisters enjoy fresh fruit in their lunches.
10. They ate several (bunch) of grapes.
    They ate several bunches of grapes.

TRY THIS! Using plural nouns, list some fruits that you eat. Then write a sentence, telling which fruits are your favorites.

Practice • Singular and Plural Nouns   Unit 2 • Chapter 8   27

CHALLENGE

DESIGN A MENU Tell students to imagine they own a restaurant. Have them work in small groups to design a menu listing healthful foods they serve. Remind students that the menus should include the ingredients in a dish as well as its name (for example, what is in a salad, not just the word *salad*). Groups can display their menus in the classroom.

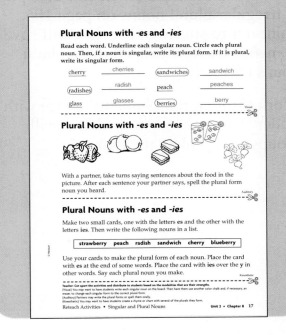

Plural Nouns with *-es* and *-ies*

Read each word. Underline each singular noun. Circle each plural noun. Then, if a noun is singular, write its plural form. If it is plural, write its singular form.

cherry	cherries	(sandwiches)	sandwich
(radishes)	radish	peach	peaches
glass	glasses	(berries)	berry

Plural Nouns with *-es* and *-ies*

With a partner, take turns saying sentences about the food in the picture. After each sentence your partner says, spell the plural form noun you heard.

Plural Nouns with *-es* and *-ies*

Make two small cards, one with the letters *es* and the other with the letters *ies*. Then write the following nouns in a list.

| strawberry | peach | radish | sandwich | cherry | blueberry |

Use your cards to make the plural form of each noun. Place the card with **es** at the end of some words. Place the card with **ies** over the y in other words. Say each plural noun you make.

Reteach Activities • Singular and Plural Nouns   Unit 2 • Chapter 8   17

Irregular Plural Nouns

OBJECTIVES

- To identify and correctly form irregular plural nouns
- To create a menu, using irregular plural nouns

DAILY LANGUAGE PRACTICE

TRANSPARENCY 17

1 The ladys gave the babys two glasss of milk. (ladies; babies; glasses)

2 The older children ate peachs and berrys (peaches; berries.)

BRIDGE TO WRITING (Plural noun) grow on trees.

ORAL WARM-UP

USE PRIOR KNOWLEDGE Tell students: *Everyone wearing blue should tap one foot on the floor.* Then tell students: *Everyone with brown eyes should tap both feet on the floor.* Ask students to tell what the difference is between the words *foot* and *feet*.

Grammar Jingles™ **CD, Intermediate** Use Track 6 for review and reinforcement of singular and plural nouns.

TEACH/MODEL

Read aloud the explanation and examples of irregular plural nouns on page 106. Point out to students that they will have to memorize how to spell these plural nouns correctly.

Work through the Guided Practice with students, or have them work in small groups to complete the items.

Nouns with Irregular Plurals: Spelling Changes	
Singular	**Plural**
child	children
foot	feet
goose	geese
man	men
mouse	mice
tooth	teeth
woman	women

Nouns with Irregular Plurals: No Spelling Changes	
Singular	**Plural**
deer	deer
fish	fish
salmon	salmon
sheep	sheep
trout	trout

106

Nouns with Irregular Plurals

Some nouns change their spelling in the plural form. Other nouns have the same spelling in the singular and the plural forms.

Not all nouns are made plural by adding *s* or *es*. Some nouns change their spelling. Some do not change at all. These nouns have irregular plurals. Look at the examples of nouns with irregular plurals in the charts.

Guided Practice

A. Give the plural form of each noun in parentheses ().

Example: (Trout) are a type of fish.
Trout

1. Adults and (child) need protein in their diets. children
2. Chickens, turkeys, and (goose) are good sources of protein. geese
3. (Fish) are also rich in protein. Fish
4. (Salmon) have special fatty acids. Salmon
5. These fatty acids are found in sardines and (trout), too. trout
6. They can help (man) have healthy hearts. men
7. Cheese has calcium that builds strong bones and (tooth). teeth
8. Cheese is made from the milk of cows, goats, or (sheep). sheep
9. (Child) need calcium to build strong bones. Children
10. (Woman) also need calcium for their bones. Women

Vocabulary Power page 23

Name _____

CONTENT-AREA WORDS

► Read the information below. Then answer each question with the name of a nutrient.

Nutrients help us stay healthy. There are six kinds of nutrients:
- **Proteins** are in meat, eggs, beans, and other foods.
- **Vitamins** help our bodies use other nutrients.
- **Minerals** are in milk, cheese, and other foods.
- **Fats** give us energy. However, too many fats are not good for us.
- **Carbohydrates** are in fruits, vegetables, and grains.
- **Water** helps nutrients move around our bodies and cools us off.

1. Which nutrient helps our body use other nutrients? vitamins
2. Which nutrient should we not eat a lot of? fats
3. Which nutrient cools us off on a hot day? water
4. Which nutrient is found in fruits and vegetables? carbohydrates
5. Which nutrient is found in meat, eggs, and beans? proteins

► Draw a healthy meal. Make sure it includes all the nutrients.

Vocabulary Power   Unit 2 • Chapter 8   23

 ESL

IRREGULAR PLURAL NOUNS
Write each of these words on a separate card: *child, foot, goose, man, mouse, tooth,* and *woman.* Have a student select a card, read it aloud, and say the plural form of the noun. Then have the student write the plural form on the other side of the card. Use these flash cards to provide extra practice for students.

Independent Practice

B. Write each sentence. Use the correct plural form of the noun in parentheses ( ).

Example: Growing (child) need to eat the right foods.
Growing children need to eat the right foods.

11. Marta's skirt is made out of wool from (sheep). sheep
12. Her shoes do not fit her (foot). feet
13. Marta is growing as fast as other healthy (child) do. children
14. Marta is almost four (foot) tall. feet
15. She drinks milk for strong bones and (tooth). teeth
16. Marta and her family eat lots of different (fish). fish
17. They ate three (trout) last night. trout
18. Tonight, they will eat four (salmon). salmon
19. Marta and her sisters will need the proper nutrients to be healthy (woman). women
20. Her brothers will be strong and healthy (man). men

Remember
that some nouns change their spelling in the plural form. Some nouns have the same spelling in the singular and the plural forms.

Writing Connection

Real-Life Writing: Advertisement Pretend that a new seafood restaurant is coming to your community. Write an advertisement for the restaurant. Include the restaurant's name and some of its special dishes. Use at least three irregular plural nouns in your advertisement.

107

Independent Practice

Have students complete the Independent Practice, or modify it using these suggestions:

MODIFIED INSTRUCTION

BELOW-LEVEL STUDENTS Remind students to refer to the chart on page 106 for the correct spelling of each irregular plural noun.

ABOVE-LEVEL STUDENTS Have students rewrite the sentences in Part B, using singular nouns.

Writing Connection

Real-Life Writing: Advertisement If possible, bring in some menus from a local seafood restaurant. Have students use the menus as a model for writing their own menus.

WRAP-UP/ASSESS

SUMMARIZE Ask students to give examples of irregular plural nouns that are different from the singular form and those that are the same as the singular form.

RETEACH

INTERVENTION Lessons in **visual, auditory,** and **kinesthetic** modalities: p. R43 and *Reteach Activities Copying Masters,* p. 18.

CHALLENGE

ANIMAL PAIRS Have students work in pairs to create a collage showing pairs of animals whose names form an irregular plural noun such as *mice*. Students may draw the two animals or find pictures in magazines. Remind students to label the pictures with the irregular plural noun. Suggest that students include mice, sheep, geese, trout, salmon, deer, and moose.

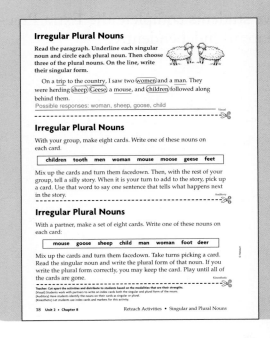

Extra Practice

OBJECTIVES

- To identify and correctly form singular and plural nouns
- To write a paragraph, using correct plural forms

DAILY LANGUAGE PRACTICE

TRANSPARENCY 18

1. The mans ate bowls of spinach salad for lunch (men; lunch.)

2. the spinach was fresh and green (The; green.)

BRIDGE TO WRITING As you grow, you will need new _(plural noun)_ to wear.

ORAL WARM-UP

USE PRIOR KNOWLEDGE Say each of the following singular nouns and ask students to say its plural form: _child, class, sandwich, beach, foot, tooth._

TEACH/MODEL

Use the Remember box to review singular and plural nouns. Then model the thinking for the example in Extra Practice B.

MODEL The word _glass_ ends in _s_, so I know that I must add _es_ to make it plural. The plural form of _glass_ is _glasses._

Have students complete the Extra Practice items independently.

CHAPTER 8

Singular and Plural Nouns

Remember

that singular nouns name one person, animal, place, or thing, and plural nouns name more than one. Form the plural of most nouns by adding _s_ or _es_.

For more activities with singular and plural nouns, visit _The Learning Site:_ www.harcourtschool.com

108

Extra Practice

A. Write the plural noun or nouns in each sentence. _pages 102–103_

Example: The Food Guide Pyramid helps you plan balanced meals.
meals

1. At the bottom of the pyramid are <u>foods</u> made with <u>grains</u>.
2. These <u>foods</u> are full of <u>nutrients</u>.
3. Next come <u>vegetables</u> and <u>fruits</u>, which have <u>vitamins</u> and <u>minerals</u>.
4. Protein comes from <u>meats</u> and dairy <u>products</u>.
5. <u>Nuts</u> and dried <u>peas</u> and <u>beans</u> are also rich in protein.

B. Form a plural noun from the underlined singular noun. _pages 102–105_

Example: Alicia poured two <u>glass</u> of orange juice.
glasses

6. Then she put cereal in two <u>bowl</u>. bowls
7. The cereal came from two different <u>box</u>. boxes
8. She put <u>strawberry</u> on the cereal in one bowl. strawberries
9. She put sliced <u>peach</u> on the cereal in the other bowl. peaches
10. Then she toasted <u>slice</u> of whole-grain bread. slices

---

Vocabulary Power page 24

Name _____

CLASSIFY/CATEGORIZE

Put the words from the Word Box into the correct category. Then add two words of your own to each category.
Order may vary. Additional words may vary.

| peach | bread | eggs | beans |
| fish | potato | meat | cereal |

carbohydrates	proteins
1. peach	fish
2. bread	eggs
3. potato	meat
4. cereal	beans
5.	
6.	

| oranges | soda | chips | chicken |
| candy | peas | bread | gum |

foods that are nutritious	foods that aren't nutritious
7. oranges	candy
8. peas	soda
9. bread	chips
10. chicken	gum
11.	
12.	

24 Unit 2 • Chapter 8   Vocabulary Power

Health

ALPHABET VITAMINS Healthful foods contain various kinds of vitamins. Tell students that vitamins have letter names; write on the board _vitamin A, vitamin B, vitamin C, vitamin D,_ and _vitamin E._ Tell students that to be healthy, a body must have all the vitamins. Have students work in groups to research one kind of vitamin and then create a poster showing the foods rich in that vitamin.

C. Write the plural noun or nouns in each sentence. Then write the singular form of each. *pages 106–107*

Example: Mom called the children to breakfast.
children, child

11. Tim came to the kitchen with bare feet. feet, foot
12. He saw two deer outside the window. deer, deer
13. He heard a flock of geese fly overhead. geese, goose
14. Mom reminded Tom to brush his teeth. teeth, tooth
15. She also reminded him to feed his three fish. fish, fish

D. Write each sentence. Change each underlined singular noun to a plural noun. *pages 102–107*

Example: The two <u>boy</u> were in a hurry.
The two boys were in a hurry.

16. They left their <u>lunch</u> on the table. lunches
17. They would be hungry without their <u>sandwich</u>. sandwiches
18. They would not have <u>vitamin</u> from the fruit. vitamins
19. They also forgot their <u>boot</u>. boots
20. Their <u>foot</u> would get cold and wet. feet
21. Dad ran after the <u>child</u>. children
22. He gave them their <u>shoe</u>. shoes
23. He also gave them <u>hug</u>. hugs
24. The <u>boy</u> ran to catch the school bus. boys
25. They left their <u>book</u> on the table. books

Writing Connection

Writer's Craft: Clear Explanations Write a paragraph that explains how to have a balanced diet. Mention at least six healthful foods in your paragraph. Use the correct plural forms for these foods.

Remember

that some irregular nouns change their spelling in the plural form. Other irregular nouns keep the same spelling in the plural form.

DID YOU KNOW?
In general, fruits and vegetables with dark colors are more nutritious than light-colored ones.

109

Building Oral Grammar

Have students work in pairs to check their Extra Practice items. To provide practice in using regular and irregular plural nouns, have students take turns reading the sentences aloud.

Writing Connection

Writer's Craft: Clear Explanations Have students discuss what they know about good nutrition and healthful foods. Ask volunteers to suggest ways in which a young child's diet might not be healthful and ways they might convince the child to eat more healthful foods. Write their suggestions on the board, and invite students to use the list to help them write their paragraphs.

WRAP-UP/ASSESS

Writer's Journal

SUMMARIZE Have students write in their journals to summarize what they have learned about singular and plural nouns.

ADDITIONAL PRACTICE An additional page of Extra Practice is provided on page 459 of the *Pupil Edition*.

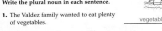
CHALLENGE

REACHING ALL LEARNERS

FOOD ADVERTISEMENT Have students create advertisements for a healthful food item. Each student should write a slogan for the food item as well as a few sentences telling why people should eat that food. Prompt students to underline the plural nouns they use. Have students illustrate their advertisements and display them in the classroom.

TECHNOLOGY *Grammar Practice and Assessment* CD-ROM; *Writing Express* CD-ROM

INTERNET Visit *The Learning Site:* www.harcourtschool.com

Chapter Review

OBJECTIVES
- To review singular and plural nouns
- To understand and interpret special maps

 STANDARDIZED TEST PREP

DAILY LANGUAGE PRACTICE

TRANSPARENCY 18

1. We filled boxs of cherrys from the cherry tree (boxes; cherries; tree.)

2. Drinking three glasss of milk gives you strong tooths. (glasses; teeth)

BRIDGE TO WRITING My favorite food is __(singular noun)__ . __(Proper noun)__ likes it, too!

STANDARDIZED TEST PREP

MODEL TEST-TAKING STRATEGIES Have students read the directions on page 110 silently. Remind them to answer each question by first eliminating answers they know are wrong.

Model the thinking. Write this example on the board:

1. You should eat four servings of _____ every day.

   A berry
   B fruites
   C vegetable
   D vegetables

MODEL The sentence says *four servings,* so I know the answer must be a plural noun. Choices A and C are singular nouns, so I know they are not correct. Choice B is a plural noun, but it is spelled incorrectly, so it can't be the right answer. Choice D is a plural noun, and it is spelled correctly. The answer is D.

Have students complete the test items on their own.

Chapter Review

 STANDARDIZED TEST PREP

Look for mistakes in noun usage in the sentences below. Write the letter of your answer.

TIP Read each answer choice before you decide on your answer.

1 A Fruits and
  B vegetables are grown
  C in many stateses. C
  D (No mistakes)

2 J Oranges and
  K lemons are grown
  L in Florida.
  M (No mistakes) M

3 A Fruits like
  B apples and cherrys grow B
  C on trees in Michigan.
  D (No mistakes)

4 J Wherever childs live, J
  K they can grow fruits
  L and vegetables.
  M (No mistakes)

5 A Carrots and
  B radishies are also good B
  C plants to grow.
  D (No mistakes)

6 J My favorite
  K vegetables are corn
  L and peases. L
  M (No mistakes)

 For additional test preparation, visit *The Learning Site:* www.harcourtschool.com

110

Assessment

PORTFOLIO ASSESSMENT Have students select their best work from the Writing Connections on pages 103, 105, 107, and 109.

ONGOING ASSESSMENT Evaluate the performance of 4–6 students using appropriate checklists and record forms from pages R74–R77.

 INTERNET Activities and exercises to help students prepare for state and standardized assessments appear on *The Learning Site:*
www.harcourtschool.com

Reading Special Maps

Average Dates of Last Spring Frost

- June 1-June 30
- May 1-May 31
- April 1-April 30
- March 1-March 31
- February 1-February 28
- January 1-January 31

Average Dates of First Fall Frost

- July 1-July 31
- August 1-August 31
- September 1-September 30
- October 1-October 31
- November 1-November 30
- December 1-December 31

Most parts of the country have frost. The map on the left shows when the last frost happens in those places. It helps you figure out when the growing season for fruits and vegetables begins. The map on the right shows when the first frost happens. It helps you figure out when the growing season ends.

Choose a state on each map. Then check the dates. You can grow a garden after the last frost happens and before the first frost happens.

YOUR TURN

Map Reading Choose a partner. Look at the two maps together. Talk about what you see on the maps. Then use the maps to answer the questions below.

1. **In what parts of the country does the growing season last almost all year?** southern Florida and southern Texas

2. **Which New England state has the shortest growing season?** Maine

3. **If you lived in Minnesota, what would be the best month for planting a vegetable garden?** June

4. **When might you plant a garden if you lived in central Florida?** March

TIP Make sure that you understand all the words and symbols or pictures on a map. The key is the box that explains the pictures.

111

STUDY SKILLS

Reading Special Maps

TEACH/MODEL

Have volunteers read aloud the captions for the special maps on page 111. Ask: **What kinds of information does the map key give you?** Use examples from different regions of the United States to help students correlate map colors and the map key colors. Point out that every color on the map corresponds to the same color in the map key. Have students interpret the information given about their state in the fall frost map. Then help them interpret the map and key for other states or regions of the country.

Ask students to review their social studies and science texts for other examples of special maps.

WRITING APPLICATION Have each student write a paragraph telling the best time in his or her area to begin a garden and explaining how he or she knows this.

WRAP-UP/ASSESS

Writer's Journal

SUMMARIZE Have students explain in their journals why it is important to be able to read special maps.

TECHNOLOGY Additional writing activities are provided on the *Writing Express* CD-ROM

PRACTICE page 30

Name _____

Chapter Review

Find the correct form of the plural noun that best completes each sentence. Fill in the oval next to your answer.

1 You buy bananas in ____ and peel them.
- bunches
- fruites
- fruits
- bunchs

2 Fruits and vegetables come in many ____.
- form
- forms
- formes
- ferm

3 Oranges and ____ have thick peels.
- lemons
- lemon
- lemones
- lemen

4 ____ are small with thin skin.
- Cherrys
- Cherryes
- Cherry
- Cherries

5 ____ have a pit inside and fuzzy skin outside.
- Peaches
- Peachies
- Peachs
- Peach

6 Most ____ have seeds inside.
- berryes
- berries
- berry
- berrys

7 You find the seeds of ____ on the outside.
- strawberryes
- strawberries
- strawberry
- strawberrys

8 Seeing a red berry reminds me of the eggs laid by ____.
- salmon
- salmones
- salmons
- salmen

30 Unit 2 • Chapter 8   Practice • Singular and Plural Nouns

CHALLENGE

MAKE A MAP Have students work in groups to create a map of the area around their school. Provide these instructions:

- Show streets, bodies of water, parks, and buildings.

- Create a map key. The key may include letters or symbols to designate buildings, such as *L* for library. Students may also use colors or patterns to indicate different areas such as parks or residential areas.

Writer's Craft
Paragraphing
pages 112-119

LESSON ORGANIZER	DAY 1	DAY 2
DAILY LANGUAGE PRACTICE TRANSPARENCIES 19, 20	1. what kinds of things would you like to learn (What; learn?) 2. we are hoping to see butterflys in the garden. (We; butterflies)	1. for this project we measured cut and glued (For; measured, cut,; glued.) 2. Will marcus anna, and Jake help us follow the directions (Marcus, Anna,; directions?)
ORAL WARM-UP Listening/Speaking	Discuss Need for Directions 112	Discuss Paragraphs 114
TEACH/MODEL WRITING 	✔ **PARAGRAPHING** **Literature Model:** from *Baseball: How to Play the All-Star Way* 112 **Analyze the Model** 112 **Analyze Informative Writing** 113	**GUIDED WRITING** **Identifying the Topic** 114 **Using Details** 114 **Using Sequence Words** 115 Writing and Thinking: Write to Record Reflections 115
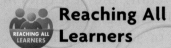 **Reaching All Learners**	**ESL:** Understanding Paragraphs 113 *ESL Manual* pp. 48, 49	**Challenge:** How-To Manual 115 *ESL Manual* p. 48
GRAMMAR	**HANDS-ON ACTIVITIES** 89I–89J	**HANDS-ON ACTIVITIES** 89I–89J
CROSS-CURRICULAR/ ENRICHMENT	*Vocabulary Power* Explore Word Meaning 112 brighten, clarify, explain, **illuminate**, lighten See *Vocabulary Power* book. **Listening and Speaking:** Oral Directions 113	*Vocabulary Power* Analogies 112 *Vocabulary Power* p. 25 **Health Connection:** Exercise Web 115 🏆 **Vocabulary activity**

KEY
✔ = tested skill

WRITING ACTIVITIES
Writing Express CD-ROM

Visit *The Learning Site:*
www.harcourtschool.com

DAY 3

1. Will you reed the directions aloud to the class (read; class?)

2. Choos your supplys carefully. (Choose; supplies)

Discuss the Importance of Sequence 116

GUIDED WRITING
Writing Directions 116
Analyze the Model 117
Prewriting and Drafting 117

ESL: Sharing Culture 117
ESL Manual p. 48

HANDS-ON ACTIVITIES
89I–89J

Vocabulary Power

Antonyms and Synonyms 112
Vocabulary Power p. 26

Listening and Speaking: Art Direction 116

Evaluation Criteria 117

💻 **Vocabulary activity**

DAY 4

1. if you check your watchs, you will see that we are almost out of time. (If; watches,)

2. Please put your projectes into these boxs. (projects; boxes.)

Suggest Strategies for Revising and Proofreading 118

GUIDED WRITING
Editing 118
Sharing and Reflecting 118
Self-Initiated Writing 118
💻 **Proofreading practice**

ESL Manual p. 48

HANDS-ON ACTIVITIES
89I–89J

Vocabulary Power

Multiple-Meaning Words 112
Vocabulary Power p. 27

💻 **Vocabulary activity**

DAY 5

1. i finished my project checked it over, and showed it to my family (I; project,; family.)

2. i'm so happy that everyone liked it (I'm; it!)

Discuss Spoken Directions 119

LISTENING AND SPEAKING:
Giving Spoken Directions 119

ESL Manual p. 48

HANDS-ON ACTIVITIES
89I–89J

Vocabulary Power

Explore Word Meaning 112

Evaluation Criteria: Self-Evaluation 119

Writer's Craft: Paragraphing

OBJECTIVES
- To understand informative writing and to analyze a paragraph that gives directions
- To analyze the use of paragraphing in informative writing

DAILY LANGUAGE PRACTICE

TRANSPARENCY 19

1 what kinds of things would you like to learn (What; learn?)

2 we are hoping to see butterflys in the garden. (We; butterflies)

ORAL WARM-UP

USE PRIOR KNOWLEDGE Ask volunteers to suggest times when they might need to read directions.

Read aloud the introduction and model on page 112. As students listen, ask them to imagine themselves following Don Mattingly's directions. Have students think about whether the directions make sense and would be easy to follow.

Analyze THE *Model*

1. What do these directions tell you how to do? (Possible response: The directions tell how to bat.) **LITERAL: NOTE DETAILS**

2. What words tell you the order of the steps? (Possible responses: *First, Next*) **LITERAL: SEQUENCE**

3. How are the first and second paragraphs different? (Possible response: The second paragraph tells rules for batting, rather than giving step-by-step instructions.) **INFERENTIAL: COMPARE AND CONTRAST**

Writer's Craft

Paragraphing

Informative writing is writing that gives information, or explains something.

Read the following batting directions from *Baseball: How to Play the All-Star Way*. As you read, notice the order of the steps.

LITERATURE MODEL

> "First, you should pick up a bat you can handle, one that's not too heavy," says Mattingly. "… Next, take a shoulder-width stance. Your feet should be a comfortable distance apart, not too wide and not too close together."
>
> Raise the bat. Your hands should be even with your back shoulder. You must always swing level or down on the ball. Never swing up.
>
> —from *Baseball: How to Play the All-Star Way* by Mark Alan Teirstein

Analyze THE *Model*

1. What do these directions tell you how to do?

2. What words tell you the order of the steps?

3. How are the first and second paragraphs different?

Forming Paragraphs

Vocabulary Power

il•lu•mi•nate
[i•lōō′mə•nāt′] *v.*
To light up.

Each sentence in a paragraph tells about one main idea. Putting information into paragraphs is called paragraphing. Look at the chart on the next page to learn more about paragraphing.

Vocabulary Power

DAY 1 EXPLORE WORD MEANING Introduce and define *illuminate*. Write it on the board. **Is this classroom illuminated? How can you tell?**

DAY 2 ANALOGIES **Finish this analogy: *song* is the same as *tune*. *Illuminate* is the same as _____.** (See also *Vocabulary Power*, page 25.)

DAY 3 ANTONYMS AND SYNONYMS Have students complete the following statement: *Darkness* (is/is not) an antonym for *illuminate*. Discuss students' responses. (See also *Vocabulary Power*, page 26.)

DAY 4 MULTIPLE-MEANING WORDS ***Illuminate* means "to explain." What are some other meanings of *illuminate*?** (See also *Vocabulary Power*, page 27.)

DAY 5 EXPLORE WORD MEANING Have students draw pictures to illustrate one of the meanings of *illuminate*. Have volunteers share their drawings with the class.

Strategies for Paragraphing	Applying the Strategies	Examples
Identify your topic.	• Begin each paragraph with a **topic sentence** that states the main idea.	• Fruit is a good snack.
Include details.	• Give **details** about the main idea in other sentences.	• Most fruits taste sweet. Fruit is nutritious.
Use sequence words.	• Use words that show sequence, such as **first**, **next**, and **last**.	• First, you pick a ripe banana. Next, you peel the banana.

YOUR TURN

THINK ABOUT INFORMATIVE WRITING
Work with two classmates. Find magazine articles that give information or explain something. Talk about how the writers used paragraphing.

Answer these questions:

1. What information does the writer give you?

2. What is the main idea of the first paragraph?

3. What details does the writer include?

113

ESL

Listening and Speaking

ORAL DIRECTIONS Have students work in pairs to give directions for a simple activity such as putting on a coat, opening a door, or washing hands. Remind students to use sequence words to tell the order of the steps. Students should listen to their partners' directions and then summarize them. Have students take turns giving directions.

UNDERSTANDING PARA-GRAPHS Give students a copy of an informative paragraph with which they are already familiar, such as a page from their social studies textbook. Have a volunteer underline the topic sentence and then tell the paragraph's main idea. Write the main idea on the board. Ask volunteers to reread the paragraph and list the details included. Write those details on the board under the main idea.

GUIDED WRITING

USING PARAGRAPHING Ask students to think about their social studies or science textbooks. Explain that these are examples of informative writing. Point out that textbooks are often organized into sections: units, chapters, paragraphs, and sentences. Writers use paragraphs to organize information into smaller sections to help readers understand, learn, and remember what they read. Tell students that paragraphs are used in most types of writing, not just informative.

Explain that sequence words tell readers the order of the steps in a process. Point out that it is important to use these words when giving directions so that readers can follow the steps in the correct order. Emphasize the sequence words listed in the chart.

Then ask volunteers to give you simple directions that tell you how to get from your desk to their desk or how to draw a simple shape on the board.

Prepare for the Your Turn activity by bringing in children's science or social studies magazines. Give each group a magazine or a page that contains several paragraphs. Have groups discuss the activity questions and come to an agreement about the answers.

WRAP-UP/ASSESS

SUMMARIZE **Why should a topic sentence be at the beginning of a paragraph? Why are signal words useful?**

TECHNOLOGY Additional writing activities are provided on the *Writing Express* CD-ROM

Writer's Craft: Paragraphing

OBJECTIVES
- To identify effective topic sentences, details, and signal/sequence words
- To record reflections about written directions

1 for this project we measured cut and glued (For; measured, cut,; glued.)

2 Will marcus anna, and Jake help us follow the directions (Marcus, Anna,; directions?)

ORAL WARM-UP

USE PRIOR KNOWLEDGE Ask volunteers to explain how paragraphs make writing clearer and easier to understand.

GUIDED WRITING

IDENTIFYING THE TOPIC Remind students that a topic sentence states the main idea. All the details in the paragraph should give more information about that idea.

Ask students to explain which topic sentence goes with the details and why. (Possible response: *Dogs need people to take care of them* is the topic sentence because the details are about how to take care of a dog.)

USING DETAILS Ask students to decide which sentences give more information about the topic sentence. (*Try to brush your teeth after every meal. Use a small, soft toothbrush and toothpaste. Brush both the front and back of your teeth.*)

Explain to students that when they are writing their own paragraphs, they may notice that unrelated details are included. Tell them that although these details may be interesting and important, they may need to be moved to another paragraph.

Identifying the Topic

A. Read the three topic sentences. Choose the best one for the passage that follows. Write the complete paragraph on your paper. Remember to indent the first line.

TOPIC SENTENCES:

- Dogs and cats are good pets.
- Dogs need people to take care of them.
- Pets are not a lot of work.
- Someone has to feed the dog every day.

Someone has to be sure the dog has enough water to drink. Dogs need to be walked, bathed, and brushed. Some long-haired dogs even get haircuts! All dogs, especially puppies, need someone to play with them.

Using Details

B. Read the topic sentence. Choose three details that fit that topic sentence. Write the complete paragraph on your paper. Remember to indent the first line.

TOPIC SENTENCE:

It is important to keep your teeth clean.

DETAILS:

- Try to brush your teeth after every meal.
- Keep your hands clean by washing them often.
- Use a small, soft toothbrush and toothpaste.
- Brush both the front and back of your teeth.
- Most animals also use their teeth to chew.

Vocabulary Power page 25

Name _____

ANALOGIES

An analogy shows how pairs of words go together.

Examples:
A leaf is part of a tree; a petal is part of a flower.
Leaf is to *tree* as *petal* is to *flower.*

▶ Read each analogy below. Then choose a word from the Word Box to complete the analogy.

Tuesday	instrument	giggle	darken	clarify

1. *Excited* is the opposite of *bored;*
   lighten is the opposite of ____darken____
2. *Tired* is the same as *sleepy;*
   laugh is the same as ____giggle____
3. *Cautious* is the same as *careful;*
   explain is the same as ____clarify____
4. February and March are months;
   Monday and ____Tuesday____ are weekdays.
5. *Assistant* is the same as *helper;*
   tool is the same as ____instrument____

▶ Now try these.

night	happy	plane

6. *Engineer* is to *train* as *pilot* is to ____plane____
7. *Glare* is to *angry* as *smile* is to ____happy____
8. *Forward* is to *backward* as *day* is to ____night____

Vocabulary Power   Unit 2 • Chapter 9   25

Using Sequence Words

C. Write the paragraph on your paper. Choose the best sequence word from the box to fill each blank so that the paragraph makes sense.

Next	Last	After	First

Here is how I made a leaf print. _____ I put the leaf on a sheet of newspaper. _____ I used a small roller to roll paint all over the leaf. _____ that, I placed the leaf on white paper, with the paint side down. I covered the leaf with clean newspaper. _____, I rubbed the newspaper gently to make the print.

Writing AND Thinking

Writer's Journal

Write to Record Reflections Sometimes you have to read directions. Maybe you are playing a new game, making a craft, or taking a test in school. Some directions are easy to follow, but others are not. What makes directions easy or hard to understand? Write your reflections in your Writer's Journal.

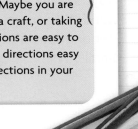

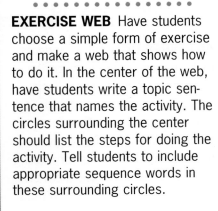

Health

• • • • • • • • • • • • • • •

EXERCISE WEB Have students choose a simple form of exercise and make a web that shows how to do it. In the center of the web, have students write a topic sentence that names the activity. The circles surrounding the center should list the steps for doing the activity. Tell students to include appropriate sequence words in these surrounding circles.

CHALLENGE

HOW-TO MANUAL Have students work in small groups to write a how-to manual for a student who might be new to the classroom or school. Have each group select a different topic, such as how to play favorite classroom games, how to act in the cafeteria, or how to find the restrooms. As they write their instructions, remind students to use sequence words.

USING SEQUENCE WORDS Tell students to begin by reading the entire paragraph silently and thinking about where each sequence word might fit. Then have students copy and complete the paragraph. (Sequence words should be inserted in this order: *First, Next, After, Last.*)

Writing and Thinking

Writer's Journal

Write to Record Reflections Tell students that they may want to think about a time when they were confused by written directions, and to remember what made those directions hard to understand. Tell students to practice paragraphing as they write. Prompt them to write strong topic sentences and to include details in each paragraph. Tell students to make sure they use singular and plural forms of regular nouns correctly while writing their reflections.

WRAP-UP/ASSESS

SUMMARIZE How can using signal words make directions easier to follow?

Writer's Craft: Paragraphing

OBJECTIVES
- To recognize the parts of a paragraph
- To analyze a set of directions
- To choose a topic, generate ideas, and write a set of directions for a recipe

DAILY LANGUAGE PRACTICE

TRANSPARENCY 19

1 Will you reed the directions aloud to the class (read, class?)

2 Choos your supplys carefully. (Choose; supplies)

ORAL WARM-UP

USE PRIOR KNOWLEDGE Ask volunteers to share what might happen if someone were to give directions with the steps out of order.

GUIDED WRITING

Writing Directions

READ AND RESPOND TO THE MODEL Before reading aloud Tina's instructions, ask students to listen for the topic sentences, details, and signal words. Then discuss what students think about Tina's directions. Ask: **Are the directions clear? Are they in an order that makes sense?** Remind students to support their evaluations with examples from the directions.

FOCUS ON ORGANIZATION Have students reread the directions silently, using the sidenotes to identify the main parts of the paragraph. Point out that Tina divides her directions into two paragraphs.

FOCUS ON WRITER'S CRAFT Have students read aloud the two topic sentences in the directions. Ask: **Why does Tina use two paragraphs in her directions?**

Writing Directions

The passage you read explained how to hit a baseball. Tina wanted to tell her classmates how to make a garden sculpture. Read the directions that Tina wrote. Look at the topic sentence and the details in each paragraph. Notice how Tina used signal words to help you understand the sequence.

MODEL

topic sentence

signal words/details

topic sentence

signal words/ details

> Making a garden sculpture is fun and easy. First you take a clay saucer, the kind used under flowerpots. Use crayons to decorate the outside of the saucer. Then fill it about 3/4 of the way with potting soil. Spray the soil with water to make it moist. Next, sprinkle on a layer of grass seed. Cover the seeds with a thin layer of soil and spray again with water.
>
> Now you are ready to enjoy your garden! Place the saucer in a sunny window. Once a day, spray the soil with water. After your garden sprouts, you can add other decorations like twigs, pebbles, shells, or small toys.

116

Vocabulary Power page 26

Name _____

ANTONYMS AND SYNONYMS

▶ Read each word. Find its antonym in the Word Box and write it on the line. Then think of a synonym for the word and write it on the line. Synonyms will vary. Possible responses are given.

quiet	slowly	wrap	confuse	darken

	Antonym	Synonym
1. brighten	darken	lighten
2. clarify	confuse	explain
3. noisy	quiet	loud
4. swiftly	slowly	quickly
5. unwrap	wrap	open

▶ Now try these.

huge	frown	real	lose	sunny

	Antonym	Synonym
6. smile	frown	grin
7. find	lose	discover
8. rainy	sunny	stormy
9. imaginary	real	make-believe
10. tiny	huge	small

26 Unit 2 • Chapter 9   Vocabulary Power

Listening and Speaking

ART DIRECTION Have students make paper decorations for the classroom. Provide paper, scissors, tape, and other art supplies students may need. Then have students work in pairs to give their partner directions for making their decorations. Have them clarify and support their spoken messages using the appropriate objects.

1. What do these directions tell you how to do?

2. What is the main idea of the first paragraph? How do you know?

3. What sequence words does Tina use? Why are they important?

YOUR TURN

WRITING PROMPT Do you know how to make a sandwich, tacos, or other dish? Write at least two paragraphs describing the directions. Share them with your classmates. Each paragraph should have a topic sentence, details, and sequence words.

STUDY THE PROMPT Ask yourself these questions:

1. Who is your audience?

2. What is your purpose for writing?

3. What information will you give your readers?

4. What writing form will you use?

Prewriting and Drafting

Organize Your Ideas Write down the steps for your directions. Then use a chart like this one to plan your paragraphs.

> **FIRST PARAGRAPH**
> Begin with a topic sentence that tells what the reader will learn to do. Give details.

> **OTHER PARAGRAPHS**
> Explain the steps in order. Write a topic sentence for each paragraph. Use sequence words.

117

USING YOUR
Handbook

- Use the Writer's Thesaurus to find signal words to show the order of the steps.

Analyze THE Model

1. **What do these directions tell you how to do?** (Possible response: They tell how to make and enjoy a garden sculpture.) **LITERAL: NOTE DETAILS**

2. **What is the main idea of the first paragraph? How do you know?** (Possible responses: The main idea is that making a garden sculpture is fun and easy. The topic sentence tells this idea, and the other sentences give details about how to make a garden sculpture.) **METACOGNITIVE: MAIN IDEA**

3. **What sequence words does Tina use? Why are they important?** (Possible responses: The sequence words *First, Then, Next, Now, Once a day*, and *After* tell when to do each step.) **INFERENTIAL: IMPORTANT DETAILS**

Have students read the directions for the Your Turn activity. Remind them to think of several topics that interest them and then to choose the one that is also likely to interest their classmates. If students have trouble thinking of ideas, suggest that they write directions for pouring a bowl of cereal or making chocolate milk.

Prewriting and Drafting

As students draft their paragraphs, have them underline their topic sentences and circle any sequence words they use.

WRAP-UP/ASSESS

SUMMARIZE How are your directions similar to Tina's? How are they different?

Evaluation Criteria

Review the criteria that students should apply:

- Use topic sentences and details
- Use sequence words
- Use the correct form for a paragraph that gives directions

Work with students to add other criteria.

REACHING ALL LEARNERS   **ESL**

SHARING CULTURE Suggest that students choose traditional dishes from their own culture. They may enlist the help of family members to check the directions. Prompt students to tell whether the dish they are writing about is usually served on holidays or special occasions or whether it is a dish that is eaten often.

Writer's Craft: Paragraphing

OBJECTIVES
- To revise written directions
- To proofread written directions
- To share and reflect upon directions

ORAL WARM-UP

USE PRIOR KNOWLEDGE Ask students to suggest strategies for revising and proof-reading their directions.

GUIDED WRITING

Editing

As students revise, suggest that they underline each topic sentence and then read each detail to make sure that it is related to the topic. Students may also read their paragraphs aloud to a partner. Students should listen for steps out of order, details that are not about the topic sentence, and missing steps.

Sharing and Reflecting

Ask students to write reflections in their Writer's Journals about their partners' work and their own work. Point out that one way to improve writing skills is to pay attention to another writer's strengths.

WRAP-UP/ASSESS

SUMMARIZE Ask students to briefly tell what they have learned about paragraphing, topic sentences and details, and sequence words.

Editor's Marks

- ℐ take out text
- ∧ add text
- ◯ move text
- ¶ new paragraph
- ≡ capitalize
- / lowercase
- ◯ correct spelling

118

Editing

Read over the draft of your directions. Can you make them easier for your reader to understand? Use this checklist to help you revise the directions.

- ☑ Will your reader be able to follow the directions easily?
- ☑ Are the steps in the right order?
- ☑ Have you used sequence words to help your reader understand the order?
- ☑ Will your reader understand what each paragraph is about?

Use this checklist as you proofread your paragraph.

- ☑ I have begun my sentences with capital letters.
- ☑ I have used the correct end marks for sentences.
- ☑ I have capitalized proper nouns.
- ☑ I have used plural nouns correctly.
- ☑ I have indented the first line of each paragraph.
- ☑ I have used a dictionary to check spelling.

Sharing and Reflecting

Writer's Journal

Make a final copy of your directions. Share them by trading with a partner. Read each other's work and role-play following the directions. Talk about what you liked best and what you might do better next time. Write your reflections in your Writer's Journal.

Vocabulary Power page 27

Name _____

MULTIPLE-MEANING WORDS

▶ Many words have more than one meaning. Clues from the sentence will help you figure out which meaning is being used. Read each sentence below. Circle the letter of the meaning of the underlined word.

1. Turn on the light to illuminate the room.
   A explain; clarify
   Ⓑ light up

2. I had to take some clothes out to lighten my suitcase.
   A make bright
   Ⓑ make less heavy

3. Grandpa told a yarn about his fishing trip.
   Ⓐ made-up adventure story
   B thread used for knitting

4. We play in the park after school.
   Ⓐ piece of land with trees and grass
   B to leave something standing somewhere for a time

5. Al looked at his watch to see what time it was.
   A to look at
   Ⓑ something that shows the time

6. When my sister hears her favorite jingle, she sings along.
   A ringing sound
   Ⓑ catchy song

▶ Write a sentence using the meaning of illuminate that you didn't use above. Sentences will vary. Accept reasonable responses.

_____

_____

Vocabulary Power   Unit 2 • Chapter 9   27

Self-Initiated Writing

Provide students with the opportunity for self-initiated writing by allowing them to use free time in the classroom to write directions on the topics of their choice.

Giving Spoken Directions

You don't always write down the directions you give. Many times you just tell the directions to someone. When you give directions by speaking instead of in writing, you are giving spoken directions.

In some ways, spoken directions and written directions are the same. In other ways, they are different. Look at the Venn diagram to find out how.

Written Directions
reader can go back and read them over
divided into paragraphs

Both
give steps in time order; use signal words for time order

Spoken Directions
listener needs to remember them or ask speaker to repeat them

YOUR TURN

Practice giving spoken directions with one or two classmates. Follow these steps:

STEP 1 Decide what the directions will be about. You might give directions for doing a job on your classroom job chart.

STEP 2 Give the directions out loud. Don't write them down. Each member of your group should take a turn giving directions.

STEP 3 As each person speaks, the others should listen carefully. Then role-play carrying out the directions.

STEP 4 Afterward, discuss what you have learned about giving good spoken directions and why it is important.

Strategies for Listening and Speaking

Use these strategies to give, as well as understand and follow, spoken directions:

• Speakers should use a rate, volume, pitch, and tone that fit their audience and purpose.
• Listeners should listen carefully and remember the order of the steps.

119

LISTENING AND SPEAKING

LISTENING AND SPEAKING
Giving Spoken Directions

OBJECTIVES
• To compare and contrast written and spoken directions
• To practice giving and following spoken directions

SPIRAL REVIEW

DAILY LANGUAGE PRACTICE

TRANSPARENCY 20

1 i finished my project checked it over, and showed it to my family (I; project,; family.)

2 i'm so happy that everyone liked it (I'm; it!)

ORAL WARM-UP

USE PRIOR KNOWLEDGE What are some times when you need to follow spoken directions?

TEACH/MODEL

Explain that sequence words are helpful for spoken directions as well as for written directions.

Ask students to suggest times when written directions might work best and times when spoken directions might work best.

Remind students that it is important to ask questions if they don't understand spoken directions.

WRAP-UP/ASSESS

SUMMARIZE How did telling directions to your classmates differ from writing directions?

Evaluation Criteria

. . . .

SELF-EVALUATION Revisit the Evaluation Criteria to have students informally rate their own writing on a scale of 1 to 4. You might have them use stick-on notes to label their papers.

CHAPTER 10

Possessive Nouns
pages 120-129

LESSON ORGANIZER	DAY 1	DAY 2

 DAILY LANGUAGE PRACTICE

TRANSPARENCIES 21, 22

DAY 1

1. The dentist visited the childs in their classroom today. (children)
2. dr. brady has two office. (Dr. Brady; offices.)

Bridge to Writing He showed the classes how to use a ___(noun)___ .

DAY 2

1. Hollys eyes need to be checked. (Holly's)
2. she stumbled over Jacks books (She; Jack's; books.)

Bridge to Writing ___(Possessive noun)___ glasses are new.

ORAL WARM-UP
Listening/Speaking

DAY 1

Naming Objects 120

DAY 2

Name Necessary Things 122
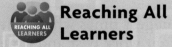 *Grammar Jingles*™ CD Track 7

TEACH/MODEL
GRAMMAR

KEY
✔ = tested skill

DAY 1

✔ **SINGULAR POSSESSIVE NOUNS** 120-121
- To correctly form singular possessive nouns
- To use prewriting techniques to write a paragraph, using singular possessive nouns

DAY 2

✔ **PLURAL POSSESSIVE NOUNS** 122-123
- To correctly form plural possessive nouns
- To write sentences that contain possessive nouns

Reaching All Learners

DAY 1

Modified Instruction
Below-Level: Model the Thinking
Above-Level: Add Sentences
Reteach: *Reteach Activities Copying Masters* pp. 19 and R44
Challenge: Activity Card 7, R65
ESL Manual pp. 50, 51
Practice Book p. 31

DAY 2

Modified Instruction
Below-Level: Write Nouns
Above-Level: Write Sentences
ESL: Compare Possessives 122
ESL Manual pp. 50, 52
Reteach: *Reteach Activities Copying Masters* pp. 20 and R44
Challenge: Comic Strip 123
Practice Book p. 32

WRITING

DAY 1

Writing Connection 121
 Writer's Craft: Topic Sentence and Details

DAY 2

Writing Connection 123
 Science

CROSS-CURRICULAR/ ENRICHMENT

DAY 1

Vocabulary Power
 Explore Word Meaning 120

cavity, chasm, crater, gorge, hollow
See *Vocabulary Power* book.

DAY 2

Vocabulary Power
 Synonyms 120
 Vocabulary Power p. 28
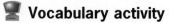 **Vocabulary activity**

DAY 3

1. takiras hard work helped her team win a prize. (Takira's)
2. Three teams prizes are on display. (teams')

Bridge to Writing The soccer team __(predicate)__ .

Identify Errors 124
Grammar Jingles™ CD Track 7

✔ **REVISING SENTENCES USING POSSESSIVE NOUNS** 124-125
 • To revise sentences by using possessive nouns
 • To write a journal, using possessive nouns

Modified Instruction
Below-Level: Model Revising
Above-Level: Rewrite Sentences
Reteach: *Reteach Activities Copying Masters* pp. 21 and R44
Challenge: Advertisement 125
ESL Manual pp. 50, 53
Practice Book p. 33

Writing Connection 125
 Writer's Journal: Recording Ideas

Social Studies: Possessive Web 124

Vocabulary Power
 Classify/Categorize 120
 Vocabulary Power p. 29
 Vocabulary activity

DAY 4

1. Helmets Protect bike riders heads. (protect; riders')
2. Our towns helmet daye was on november 25. (town's; day; November)

Bridge to Writing The __(possessive noun)__ helmets were brightly colored.

Use Possessive Nouns 126

EXTRA PRACTICE 126-127
 • To identify and use singular and plural possessive nouns
 • To write a letter, using sequence words and possessive nouns
 Practice and assessment

Building Oral Grammar
Using Sentence Clues 127
ESL: Work with Possessives 126
ESL Manual pp. 50, 54
Challenge: Write a Description 127
Practice Book p. 34

Writing Connection 127
 Real-Life Writing: Letter

Vocabulary Power
 Multiple-Meaning Words 120
 Vocabulary Power p. 30
 Vocabulary activity

DAY 5

1. Carla went to Dr. Novatos office (Novato's; office.)
2. The dentist found some cavitys in Carlas' teeth. (cavities; Carla's)

Bridge to Writing The dentist gave Carla a new __(noun)__ . Now __(possessive noun)__ brother will go to the dentist.

TEST PREP **CHAPTER REVIEW** 128
 • To review possessive nouns
 • To use a word processing program to revise sentences
 Test preparation

Challenge: Correct Mistakes 129
Practice Book p. 35
ESL Manual pp. 50, 55

Writing Application 129
 Combine Sentences

Technology: Writing on the Computer 129

Vocabulary Power
 Exemplification 120

Singular Possessive Nouns

OBJECTIVES
- To correctly form singular possessive nouns
- To use prewriting techniques to write a paragraph, using singular possessive nouns

DAILY LANGUAGE PRACTICE

TRANSPARENCY 21

1 The dentist visited the childs in their classrooms today. (children)

2 dr brady has two office. (Dr. Brady; offices.)

BRIDGE TO WRITING He showed the classes how to use a (noun) .

ORAL WARM-UP

USE PRIOR KNOWLEDGE Pick up various objects belonging to students while asking: **Whose (object) is this?**

TEACH/MODEL

Discuss the concept of possession or ownership. Guide students through the explanation and example sentences on page 120. Ask students which words in the first sentence are replaced by *dentist's* in the second sentence.

Complete the Guided Practice items orally with students, or have them work in pairs to complete the items.

Vocabulary Power

cav•i•ty [kav′ə•tē] *n.* A small hole in a tooth, caused by decay.

120

Singular Possessive Nouns

A **possessive noun** shows that a person or thing owns or has something.

You have learned that a singular noun names one person, place, animal, or thing. A singular possessive noun shows ownership by one person or thing. Add an apostrophe (') and an *s* to most singular nouns to form a possessive noun. You can use possessive nouns to make sentences shorter and easier to understand.

> **Example:**
> Rita went into the office <u>belonging to the dentist</u>.
> Rita went into the <u>dentist's</u> office.

Guided Practice

A. Tell another way to say each word group, using a singular possessive noun.

> **Example**: the office of Dr. Reno
> *Dr. Reno's office*

1. the dentist of Kerry Kerry's dentist
2. the toothbrush belonging to her sister her sister's toothbrush
3. the bristles of the toothbrush the toothbrush's bristles
4. the health of a tooth a tooth's health
5. the teeth of a person a person's teeth
6. the mouthwash belonging to Kerry Kerry's mouthwash
7. the dental floss belonging to Dad Dad's dental floss
8. the class of Yoko Yoko's class
9. the mouth of a student a student's mouth
10. the tooth of a child a child's tooth

Vocabulary Power

DAY 1 EXPLORE WORD MEANING Introduce and define *cavity*. **Have you ever had a cavity in your tooth? How did the dentist fix it?**

DAY 2 SYNONYMS Write on the board: *cavity, hill, hollow.* **Which two words have a similar meaning?** (See also *Vocabulary Power,* page 28.)

DAY 3 CLASSIFY/CATEGORIZE **Name some words that tell how you feel when you are healthy? When you are sick?** (See also *Vocabulary Power,* page 29.)

DAY 4 MULTIPLE-MEANING WORDS *Cavity* has two meanings: "a small hole in a tooth caused by decay" and "a hollow spot." Name other words that have two meanings. (See also *Vocabulary Power,* page 30.)

DAY 5 EXEMPLIFICATION **Make a list of ways you can prevent cavities. Draw a picture of one of the items on your list.**

Independent Practice

B. Write each group of words in a different way, using a singular possessive noun.

Example: the father of Jamal
Jamal's father

11. the dental floss belonging to the boy   the boy's dental floss
12. the health of a mouth   a mouth's health
13. the store belonging to Mr. Lee   Mr. Lee's store
14. the owner of the store   the store's owner
15. the medicine chest of the bathroom   the bathroom's medicine chest

C. Write the possessive form of each underlined singular noun.

Example: My <u>friend</u> dentist gives each patient a new toothbrush.
friend's

16. My <u>dentist</u> office has a chart on the wall.   dentist's
17. It tells about a <u>food</u> effect on dental health.   food's
18. <u>Candy</u> sugar can cause a cavity in a tooth.   Candy's
19. The <u>chart</u> pictures show foods that are good for your teeth.   chart's
20. I will put the foods on my <u>family</u> shopping list.   family's

Writing Connection

Writer's Craft: Topic Sentence and Details
Write a paragraph about a person who takes good care of his or her teeth and gums. Include at least three possessive nouns in your paragraph, as in "Lia's brother visits the dentist twice a year."

Remember
that a possessive noun shows ownership. Add an apostrophe (') and an *s* to a singular noun to form a singular possessive noun.

121

Independent Practice

Have students complete the Independent Practice, or modify it using these suggestions:

MODIFIED INSTRUCTION

BELOW-LEVEL STUDENTS Work through the Independent Practice with students, modeling the thinking.

ABOVE-LEVEL STUDENTS Have students add to Part C three sentences that include correct forms of singular possessive nouns.

Writing Connection

Writer's Craft: Topic Sentence and Details
Before students write, have them use prewriting techniques such as brainstorming or creating a web to generate ideas about how a person may take care of his or her teeth and gums. Students should use their ideas in their paragraph.

WRAP-UP/ASSESS

SUMMARIZE Ask students how to form singular possessive nouns. Have volunteers give examples of singular possessive nouns.

REACHING ALL LEARNERS

RETEACH

INTERVENTION Lessons in **visual**, **auditory**, and **kinesthetic** modalities: p. R44 and *Reteach Activities Copying Masters*, p. 19.

PRACTICE page 31

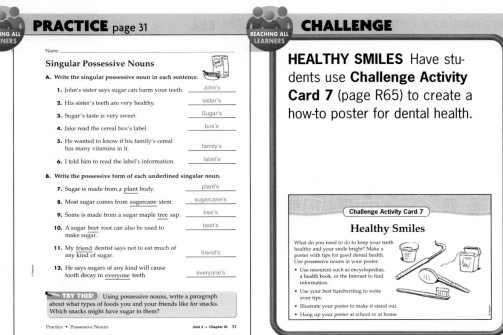

CHALLENGE

HEALTHY SMILES Have students use **Challenge Activity Card 7** (page R65) to create a how-to poster for dental health.

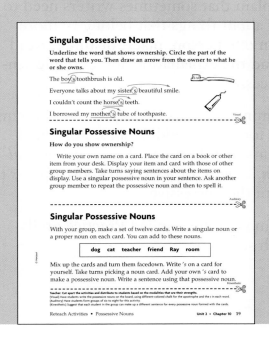

Plural Possessive Nouns

OBJECTIVES
- To correctly form plural possessive nouns
- To write sentences that contain possessive nouns

DAILY LANGUAGE PRACTICE

TRANSPARENCY 21

1 Hollys eyes need to be checked.
(Holly's)

2 she stumbled over Jacks books (She;
Jack's; books.)

BRIDGE TO WRITING (Possessive noun)
glasses are new.

ORAL WARM-UP

USE PRIOR KNOWLEDGE Write these words
on the board: *teachers*, *doctors*, and *students*. Ask students to name some things
needed by teachers, doctors, and students. Write their suggestions on the
board.

Grammar Jingles™ **CD,
Intermediate** Use Track 7 for
review and reinforcement of
possessive nouns.

TEACH/MODEL

Explain that sometimes writers need to
tell about things that belong to more
than one person, place, or thing. Read
aloud the explanation and example sentences.

Remind students that most plural nouns
are formed by adding an *s*. For plural
nouns that do not end in *s*, such as *children*, *women*, or *men*, add apostrophe-*s* to
form the possessive.

Complete the Guided Practice orally
with students.

Plural Possessive Nouns

A possessive noun can be plural.

Remember that a plural noun names more than
one person, place, or thing. A plural possessive
noun shows ownership by more than one person, place,
or thing. To form a plural possessive noun, add only
an apostrophe (') to a plural noun that ends with *s*.

Examples:

All the <u>students'</u> eyes were closed.

Your <u>eyelids'</u> job is to protect your eyes.

A plural possessive noun and a plural noun
ending with *s* are pronounced exactly the same way.

Guided Practice

**A. Tell how to write the possessive form of
each plural noun.**

Example: eyes *eyes'*

1. books books'
2. teachers teachers'
3. friends friends'
4. neighbors neighbors'
5. doctors doctors'
6. parents parents'
7. lenses lenses'
8. irises irises'
9. days days'
10. eyes eyes'

122

Vocabulary Power page 28

Name _____

SYNONYMS

▸ Look in the Word Box for pairs of words that are synonyms.
Write a pair of synonyms on each line. The first one is done
for you.

| cavity | scowl | hollow | sprint | hill | run |
| slope | glossiest | crater | hole | frown | shiniest |

1. _____ cavity/hole
2. _____ slope/hill
3. _____ hollow/crater
4. _____ frown/scowl
5. _____ run/sprint
6. _____ glossiest/shiniest

▸ Now try these.

| glimmering | alike | shimmering | clarify | pile | gorge |
| connected | explain | similar | mound | chasm | fastened |

7. _____ glimmering/shimmering
8. _____ pile/mound
9. _____ similar/alike
10. _____ gorge/chasm
11. _____ clarify/explain
12. _____ connected/fastened

28 Unit 2 • Chapter 10   Vocabulary Power

ESL

COMPARE POSSESSIVES Help
students remember how to form
singular and plural possessives
by comparing the way they are
formed in English to the way they
are formed in students' first languages. Guide them in making
reminder charts like the one
below on cards.

	English	First Language
Singular		
Plural		

Tell students to refer to these
charts as they work through the
chapter's exercises.

Independent Practice

B. Write the possessive form of each underlined plural noun.

Example: two <u>boys</u> eyes
boys'

11. two <u>builders</u> strong hands   *builders'*
12. six <u>nurses</u> office   *nurses'*
13. three <u>teachers</u> eyesight   *teachers'*
14. the <u>babies</u> eyebrows   *babies'*
15. two <u>girls</u> cavities   *girls'*

C. Write each sentence, using the possessive form of the plural noun in parentheses.

Example: The (eyes) health should be protected.
The eyes' health should be protected.

16. Nico and Karen are (builders) helpers.   *builders'*
17. They don't use the (workers) saws.   *workers'*
18. The (saws) edges are very sharp.   *saws'*
19. Dust flies from the (builders) work.   *builders'*
20. The (helpers) eyes are covered by special glasses.   *helpers'*

Remember that a plural possessive noun is formed by adding an apostrophe (') to the end of a plural noun that ends with s.

Writing Connection

Science Think about items your friends or family members use to care for their eyes. Then write several sentences about how these items are helpful. Use at least three plural possessive nouns, as in "My two sisters' desk lights help them not to strain their eyes." Make sure each possessive noun is written correctly.

Independent Practice

Have students complete the Independent Practice, or modify it using these suggestions:

MODIFIED INSTRUCTION

BELOW-LEVEL STUDENTS For Part B, have students write each underlined noun and circle the final *s* before they add the apostrophe. Remind students that the apostrophe must come after the final *s* of plural nouns.

ABOVE-LEVEL STUDENTS Ask students to write complete sentences, using the items in Part B.

Writing Connection

Science Have students participate in a large group discussion about some items that can help and protect one's eyes. Invite students who wear glasses to share their expertise on the topic. Before they write, have students think of friends and family members who use some of these items.

WRAP-UP/ASSESS

SUMMARIZE Have students explain how to form a plural possessive noun.

RETEACH

INTERVENTION Lessons in **visual, auditory,** and **kinesthetic** modalities: p. R44 and *Reteach Activities Copying Masters,* p. 20.

PRACTICE page 32

Name _____

Plural Possessive Nouns

A. Write the possessive form of each underlined plural noun.

1. The teachers had their <u>students</u> attention.   *students'*
2. The students listened to their <u>teachers</u> instructions.   *teachers'*
3. The teachers told them to visit their <u>dentists</u> offices every six months.   *dentists'*
4. They should mark the appointments on their <u>calendars</u> pages.   *calendars'*
5. The students would need their <u>parents</u> help.   *parents'*

B. Write the plural possessive form of the plural noun in parentheses ( ).

6. (Babies) teeth begin to form before they are born.   *Babies'*
7. They form in the (gums) inner parts.   *gums'*
8. The babies depend on their (mothers) food.   *mothers'*
9. Mothers follow their (doctors) advice.   *doctors'*
10. The teeth do not break through the (gums) surfaces until later.   *gums'*

TRY THIS! What might dentists do to take care of their patients' teeth? Write three things a dentist might do for patients. Make sure all the possessive nouns are written correctly.

32   Unit 2 • Chapter 10   Practice • Possessive Nouns

CHALLENGE

COMIC STRIP Have students work in pairs to write and illustrate a comic strip. Students may choose one of the following topics:

- going to the dentist
- exercising
- getting enough sleep

Tell students that their comic strips should present a positive message about the topic. Remind students to use possessive nouns in their comic strips.

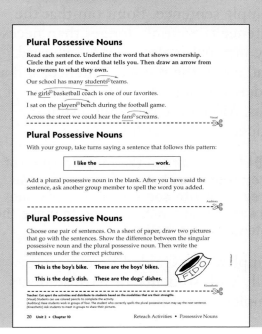

Plural Possessive Nouns

Read each sentence. Underline the word that shows ownership. Circle the part of the word that tells you. Then draw an arrow from the owners to what they own.

Our school has many students' teams.

The girls' basketball coach is one of our favorites.

I sat on the players' bench during the football game.

Across the street we could hear the fans' screams.

Plural Possessive Nouns

With your group, take turns saying a sentence that follows this pattern:

I like the _____ work.

Add a plural possessive noun in the blank. After you have said the sentence, ask another group member to spell the word you added.

Plural Possessive Nouns

Choose one pair of sentences. On a sheet of paper, draw two pictures that go with the sentences. Show the difference between the singular possessive noun and the plural possessive noun. Then write the sentences under the correct pictures.

| This is the boy's bike. | These are the boys' bikes. |
| This is the dog's dish. | These are the dogs' dishes. |

20   Unit 2 • Chapter 10   Reteach Activities • Possessive Nouns

Revising Sentences Using Possessive Nouns

OBJECTIVES
- To revise sentences by using possessive nouns
- To write a journal entry, using possessive nouns

DAILY LANGUAGE PRACTICE

TRANSPARENCY 21

1 takiras hard work helped her team win a prize. (Takira's)

2 Three teams prizes are on display. (teams')

BRIDGE TO WRITING The soccer team _____ (predicate) .

ORAL WARM-UP

USE PRIOR KNOWLEDGE Read aloud the following sentence, and ask students to identify a problem with it: *The children went to the house belonging to the Garcias and played with the toys owned by Irma.*

***Grammar Jingles*™ CD, Intermediate** Use Track 7 for review and reinforcement of possessive nouns.

TEACH/MODEL

Read aloud the instruction and the first example sentence. Point out that the sentence is not only longer than necessary but that it also sounds awkward. Read aloud the revised sentence, and ask students to note the improved flow of ideas. Model the thinking, using the Guided Practice example:

MODEL The phrase *the favorite sport of Corey* sounds awkward. I can also write *Corey's favorite sport*. I can replace the awkward phrase with this one to make the sentence sound better.

Complete the Guided Practice items orally with students, or have students complete the items in small groups.

Revising Sentences Using Possessive Nouns

You learned that you can sometimes shorten a sentence by using a **possessive noun**.

A noun and the phrase *belonging to* or the word *of* can be replaced by a possessive noun.

Example:

The shirts of the players were blue.

The players' shirts were blue.

Be careful to form the possessive forms of singular and plural nouns correctly. An apostrophe in the wrong place can change a word's meaning.

Guided Practice

A. Tell how you could write each sentence, using a possessive noun.

Example: Running is the favorite sport of Corey.
Running is Corey's favorite sport.

1. Exercise is good for the health of your body. Exercise is good for your body's health.
2. It improves the strength of your muscles. It improves your muscles' strength
3. It can also make blood belonging to a person flow better. It can also make a person's blood flow better.
4. Bicycling is the favorite exercise of one child. Bicycling is one child's favorite exercise.
5. Baseball is the favorite sport of many girls. Baseball is many girls' favorite sport.

Vocabulary Power page 29

Name _____

CLASSIFY/CATEGORIZE

▶ Read the headings below and the words in the Word Box. Write each word under the correct heading. Then add a word of your own to each category. Additional words will vary.

weakness	pain	energy
strength	smiles	fever

Signs of Good Health	Signs of Sickness
strength	weakness
smiles	pain
energy	fever

▶ Now try these.

hill	chasm	crater
gorge	mound	bump

Kinds of Holes	Kinds of Raised Land
gorge	hill
chasm	mound
crater	bump

Vocabulary Power   Unit 3 • Chapter 10   29

Social Studies

POSSESSIVE WEB Tell students to select a country or region that they have visited or studied. Have them create a web showing things that the place has. For example, a web about the rainforest could include the words *trees, animals, rivers,* etc. Then have students write one sentence in which they use their place name as a possessive noun. Post students' webs in the classroom.

Independent Practice

B. Write each sentence, using a possessive noun.

Example: The team of my brother practices hard.
My brother's team practices hard.

6. The practice time of the swimmers is in the morning. *The swimmers' practice time is in the morning.*

7. The parents of the athletes make sure they get enough rest. *The athletes' parents make sure they get enough rest.*

8. The bedtime of Davon is early. *Davon's bedtime is early.*

9. He arrives at the swimming pool belonging to the town at 7:00 A.M. *He arrives at the town's swimming pool at 7 A.M.*

10. The coach of the boys makes sure they swim safely. *The boys' coach makes sure they swim safely.*

11. The children of my neighbor exercise together. *My neighbor's children exercise together.*

12. The parents of Brittany enjoy walking. *Brittany's parents enjoy walking.*

13. The first walk of her parents was only a few blocks. *Her parents' first walk was only a few blocks.*

14. The Hermans walk on the streets of their neighborhood. *The Hermans walk on their neighborhood's streets.*

15. The sneakers of the Hermans are bright red. *The Hermans' sneakers are bright red.*

Remember
that you can sometimes shorten a sentence by using a possessive noun to replace the words *belonging to* or *of* and a noun.

125

Writing Connection

Writer's Journal: Recording Ideas
Think about the kinds of exercise you have gotten this week. List them in your journal. Write how each kind of exercise helps the different parts of your body. For example, you might write, "Bicycling strengthens my legs' muscles." Write all possessive nouns correctly.

Independent Practice

Have students complete the Independent Practice, or modify it using these suggestions:

MODIFIED INSTRUCTION

BELOW-LEVEL STUDENTS Write the Part B example on the board. Underline the phrase: *team of my brother.* Model crossing out the original phrase and replacing it with the new one. Have students copy items 6–10 and revise them by using your model.

ABOVE-LEVEL STUDENTS Have students rewrite five of the sentences in Exercise B, using a different possessive noun in each.

Writing Connection

Writer's Journal: Recording Ideas
Before they write in their journals, have students brainstorm with a partner some activities they enjoy that are also good ways to exercise. Have students use some of their key thoughts in their journal entries.

WRAP-UP/ASSESS

SUMMARIZE Ask students how they can revise sentences by using possessive nouns. Ask them to explain how these revisions can improve their writing. **REFLECTION**

RETEACH

INTERVENTION Lessons in **visual, auditory,** and **kinesthetic** modalities: p. R44 and *Reteach Activities Copying Masters,* p. 21.

PRACTICE page 33

Name _____

Revising Sentences Using Possessive Nouns

A. Rewrite each sentence, using a possessive noun.

1. Mr. Perez takes care of the eyesight of his family.
   Mr. Perez takes care of his family's eyesight.

2. He put a good light over the desk of his son.
   He put a good light over his son's desk.

3. He checked the light in the room of his daughter.
   He checked the light in his daughter's room.

4. The eyesight of his wife is getting weaker.
   His wife's eyesight is getting weaker.

5. He suggested that she take the advice of her doctor.
   He suggested that she take her doctor's advice.

B. Write the possessive form of each underlined noun.

6. Ms. Perez plans the day meals carefully. — day's

7. She buys vegetables from the farmer stand. — farmer's

8. The vegetables vitamins will keep the Perez family healthy. — vegetables'

TRY THIS! Write a paragraph about special duties you and your classmates might carry out at school. Circle the possessive nouns in your paragraph.

Practice • Possessive Nouns   Unit 2 • Chapter 10   33

CHALLENGE

ADVERTISEMENT Have students work with a partner to write and illustrate an advertisement for bicycle helmets. The advertisement should tell which stores sell helmets. Remind students to use possessive nouns. Students should also tell why bicycle helmets are important for safety.

Revising Sentences Using Possessive Nouns

On the line, write the owner of each object. Above your answer, write an *S* if the word is a singular possessive noun and *P* if it is a plural possessive noun.

skates belonging to my friends — *P* friends' skates

skateboard belonging to my brother — *S* brother's skateboard

kneepads belonging to Angie — *S* Angie's kneepads

Revising Sentences Using Possessive Nouns

With a partner, take turns saying sentences that follow one of these patterns.

I'm wearing skates belonging to my _____
I'm wearing skates belonging to _____

Add a common noun or a proper noun to complete the sentence. Then have your partner use a possessive noun to revise your sentence.

Revising Sentences Using Possessive Nouns

With a partner, walk around the classroom. Point to objects and use the pattern below to name them. Then turn the phrase into a sentence, using a possessive noun. Use common and proper nouns in your sentences.

skates belonging to my _____
skates belonging to _____

Teacher: Cut apart the activities and distribute to students based on the modalities that are their strength.
(Visual) Have students work cooperatively to write the revised phrases on the board.
(Auditory) Ask students to spell the possessive nouns they use to revise their partners' sentences.
(Kinesthetic) Remind students to use their friends' names in their sentences.

Reteach Activities • Possessive Nouns   Unit 2 • Chapter 10   21

Extra Practice

OBJECTIVES

- To identify and use singular and plural possessive nouns
- To write a letter, using sequence words and possessive nouns

DAILY LANGUAGE PRACTICE

TRANSPARENCY 22

1 Helmets Protect bike riders heads.
(protect; riders')

2 Our towns helmet daye was on november 25. (town's; day; November)

BRIDGE TO WRITING The ___(possessive noun)___ helmets were brightly colored.

ORAL WARM-UP

USE PRIOR KNOWLEDGE Call on volunteers to give sentences about items that belong to other students in the class, using possessive nouns. Have them identify the possessive noun or nouns in their sentences.

TEACH/MODEL

Use the Remember box to review possessive nouns. Model the thinking for the example in Part A:

MODEL *Teacher* is a singular noun. I know that I need to add an apostrophe and *s* to most singular nouns to form the possessive. The possessive form of *teacher* must be *teacher's.*

Have students work individually to complete the Extra Practice items.

Remember

that a possessive noun shows that a person or thing owns or has something. Add an apostrophe (') and an *s* to most singular nouns to form the possessive. Add only an apostrophe to form the possessive of a plural noun that ends with *s.*

For more activities with possessive nouns, visit *The Learning Site:* www.harcourtschool.com

126

Extra Practice

A. Write the possessive form of each singular or plural noun. *pages 120–123*

Example: teacher   *teacher's*

1. Elena   Elena's
2. minutes   minutes'
3. school   school's
4. friend   friend's
5. workouts   workouts'

B. Write whether the underlined possessive noun is singular or plural. *pages 120–123*

Example: Summer is <u>Elena's</u> favorite season.
singular

6. The <u>summer's</u> weather is hot. singular
7. The <u>sun's</u> rays can cause sunburn. singular
8. Sunblock protects skin from the <u>rays'</u> power. plural
9. It stops the sun from burning a <u>person's</u> skin. singular
10. The <u>friends'</u> sunblock prevented sunburn. plural

C. Complete each sentence, using the correct word in parentheses ( ). *pages 120–123*

Example: Bobby went to a (doctors, doctor's) office.
Bobby went to a doctor's office.

11. The family took Bobby to (<u>Dr. Sindy's</u>, Dr. Sindys) office.
12. (Bobbys', <u>Bobby's</u>) doctor gave him a checkup.
13. The doctor looked in the (childs', <u>child's</u>) ears.
14. She took the (boys, <u>boy's</u>) temperature.
15. The doctor answered his (<u>parents'</u>, parents) questions.

Vocabulary Power   page 30

Name _____

MULTIPLE-MEANING WORDS

Some words have more than one meaning. Clues from the sentence tell you which meaning is being used. Read each pair of sentences below. Write the letter of the correct meaning next to each sentence.

1. __B__ The dentist said I have a <u>cavity</u>.   A A hollow space
   __A__ Does a squirrel live in that <u>cavity</u>?   B decay in a tooth

2. __A__ A hungry bear will <u>gorge</u> itself.   A to stuff with food
   __B__ Looking down into the <u>gorge</u> was scary.   B a very deep, narrow valley

3. __A__ The book weighs about a <u>pound</u>.   A measure of heaviness
   __B__ I will <u>pound</u> the nail.   B hit

4. __B__ This chocolate is <u>hollow</u>.   A a hole
   __A__ The rabbit lives in the <u>hollow</u>.   B empty inside

5. __B__ I'm a big <u>fan</u> of that singer.   A machine that blows air
   __A__ The <u>fan</u> cooled us.   B an admirer

6. __B__ The bully is really <u>mean</u>!   A a definition
   __A__ What does *aboard* <u>mean</u>?   B nasty, not nice

7. __A__ There was a traffic <u>jam</u> today.   A something blocking movement
   __B__ I like <u>jam</u> on my toast.   B a fruit spread

8. __A__ You can't <u>fool</u> me.   A trick
   __B__ Sometimes I act like a <u>fool</u>.   B silly person

30   Unit 2 • Chapter 10   Vocabulary Power

ESL

WORK WITH POSSESSIVES

Make sets of cards with these phrases:

   the cat of Tina

   the bicycles of the students

   the glasses of Chin

Give students a set of cards, and have them form possessives with the phrases on each card by removing the unnecessary words and writing an apostrophe or an apostrophe *s* in the appropriate place.

D. Write each sentence, using a possessive noun. *pages 124–125*

Example: The doctor looked at the chart belonging to Bobby.
The doctor looked at Bobby's chart.

16. He said that rest and exercise are important to the health of a body. a body's health
17. Exercise builds up the strength of the muscles. the muscles' strength
18. The sleep time of a person is also important. A person's sleep time
19. The need for rest of an individual cannot be ignored. An individual's need for rest
20. Even just the rest of an hour can give you more energy. an hour's rest

Writing Connection

Real-Life Writing: Letter Write a letter to a friend, describing the things you do during the day to take care of your body. Include several sequence words and at least three possessive nouns. For example, you could write, "First, I floss to protect my gums' health."

127

Building Oral Grammar

Tell students that in speaking and listening they sometimes must use clues in the sentence to decide whether a possessive noun is singular or plural. Put the following examples on the board: *The boy's jump rope was red. The boys' jump ropes were red.* Then read the sentences aloud. Point out that *boy's* and *boys'* are pronounced the same but that *jump rope was* and *jump ropes were* are clues to the number of boys. Have partners take turns reading aloud sentences from Part B. Have listeners identify clues that let them know whether the possessive nouns are singular or plural.

Writing Connection

Real-Life Writing: Letter When students finish writing their letters, have them participate in a class discussion about ways they take care of their bodies. Then have students list some ways they could take even better care of themselves each day.

WRAP-UP/ASSESS

Writer's Journal

SUMMARIZE Ask students to summarize in their journals what they have learned about possessive nouns.

ADDITIONAL PRACTICE An additional page of Extra Practice is provided on page 460 of the *Pupil Edition.*

PRACTICE page 34
REACHING ALL LEARNERS

Name _____

Extra Practice

A. Write the possessive form of the noun in parentheses ( ).

1. **(Estelle)** dentist looked at her teeth. — Estelle's
2. **(The dentist)** nurse helped him. — dentist's
3. Her **(mother)** car was parked outside. — mother's
4. Her **(brother)** appointment was next. — brother's
5. Mother paid for the **(day)** visits. — day's

B. Write whether the underlined possessive noun is singular or plural.

6. My friends' teeth are all pretty healthy. — plural
7. We talked in the girls' room about our teeth. — plural
8. Terri's teeth have never had cavities. — singular
9. Her brother's dentist had to put fillings into her brother's teeth. — singular
10. They both listened carefully to the nurse's advice. — singular
11. The toothpaste labels' directions also can help. — plural
12. A dentist wants to see everyone's smile. — singular

TRY THIS! Write a conversation between a dentist and someone your age. Have the dentist tell him or her about good tooth care. Circle the possessive nouns.

34 Unit 2 • Chapter 10   Practice • Possessive Nouns

CHALLENGE
REACHING ALL LEARNERS

WRITE A DESCRIPTION Have students write a description of their favorite sport or active game. They can explain whether they like to watch or play the sport or game and why they like it. Prompt students to use possessive nouns by asking that they provide information about the game's rules, the players' equipment, and so on.

TECHNOLOGY *Grammar Practice and Assessment* CD-ROM; *Writing Express* CD-ROM

INTERNET Visit *The Learning Site:* www.harcourtschool.com

Chapter Review

OBJECTIVES
• To review possessive nouns
• To use a word processing program to revise written sentences

DAILY LANGUAGE PRACTICE

TRANSPARENCY 22

1 Carla went to Dr. Novatos office
(Novato's; office.)

2 The dentist found some cavitys in
Carlas' teeth. (cavities; Carla's)

BRIDGE TO WRITING The dentist gave
Carla a new __(noun)__ .

Now __(possessive noun)__ brother will go
to the dentist.

STANDARDIZED TEST PREP

MODEL TEST-TAKING STRATEGIES Have students read the directions on page 128 silently.

Remind them to use other words in the sentences to decide on the answers. Model the thinking. Write this sentence on the board:

My school knows the importance of all
_____ health.

    1 **A** students'
       B students
       C student's
       D student

MODEL The word *all* tells me that the missing noun is plural. The noun should be possessive, since *health* is what belongs to the students. The correct answer must be **A**, the plural possessive noun *students'*.

Have students complete the Chapter Review independently.

STANDARDIZED TEST PREP

Chapter Review

Read the paragraph. Choose the correct possessive noun for each numbered space. Write the letter of your answer.

> My school wants to improve the __(1)__ physical fitness. The school is testing __(2)__ eyesight, hearing, and strength. Each class will go to the __(3)__ office. A nurse will check each __(4)__ health. All the __(5)__ results will be collected. The __(6)__ students will get any help they need. My science __(7)__ next lesson will teach us about eating right. Each __(8)__ health is important.

TIP Read all of the answer choices before deciding on your answer.

1 A student
  B students
  C students' C
  D students's

2 F everyone's F
  G everyones
  H everyones'
  J everyones's

3 A principals
  B principals'
  C principals's
  D principal's D

4 F child's F
  G child
  H childs's
  J childs

5 A tests's
  B tests
  C tests' C
  D test'

6 F schools's
  G school
  H school's H
  J schools

7 A teachers
  B teacher's B
  C teacher'
  D teachers's

8 F person's F
  G persons
  H person'
  J persons's

For additional test preparation, visit *The Learning Site*:
www.harcourtschool.com

Assessment

PORTFOLIO ASSESSMENT Have students select their best work from the Writing Connections on pages 121, 123, and 127.

ONGOING ASSESSMENT Evaluate the performance of 4–6 students using appropriate checklists and record forms from pages R74–R77.

INTERNET Activities and exercises to help students prepare for state and standardized assessments appear on *The Learning Site*:
www.harcourtschool.com

Writing on the Computer

TECHNOLOGY

Most computers have a word processing program that makes writing and revising easier. To use a word processing program, begin typing. If you make mistakes or errors, you can edit, or change, your writing easily on the computer.

To move words, groups of words, sentences, or paragraphs, highlight the words you want to move. Then, click CUT. Move the cursor to the place where you want the words. Then click PASTE.

- To add words or punctuation marks, place the cursor where you want the new parts, and just type.

- To remove words or punctuation marks, first highlight them. Then, press the DELETE key.

- You can check your spelling by clicking on the SPELL CHECK button. If a word is spelled incorrectly, the program will give you suggestions for the correct spelling.

YOUR TURN

1. **Write six to ten simple sentences by using a word processing program.**

2. **Use CUT and PASTE to combine pairs of sentences to make compound sentences.**

3. **Add commas and combining words, and use DELETE to remove any unnecessary words.**

4. **Use the SPELL CHECK to check your spelling.**

   If you do not have a computer in your school, do this activity on pieces of paper.

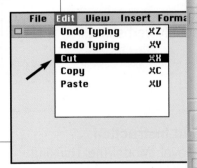

File	Edit	View	Insert	Forma
	Undo Typing	⌘Z		
	Redo Typing	⌘Y		
	Cut	⌘X		
	Copy	⌘C		
	Paste	⌘V		

129

CHALLENGE

REACHING ALL LEARNERS

CORRECT MISTAKES Have pairs of students use a word processing program to write sentences with mistakes in spelling, grammar, and punctuation. Students can then correct another pair's sentences by cutting and pasting text, inserting and deleting text, or using a spell check feature.

TECHNOLOGY

Writing On the Computer

TEACH/MODEL

Have a volunteer read aloud the first paragraph and the bulleted items. Point out to students that writing with a word processing program allows them to make changes in their work without erasing or crossing out. Explain that most word processing programs use the same commands for cutting and pasting text, inserting and deleting text, and checking spelling.

Have students complete the Your Turn activity.

WRITING APPLICATION Have students work with a partner, using a word processing program to write pairs of simple sentences about a book they like. Partners can use the editing features of the program to combine some of the simple sentences into compound sentences.

WRAP-UP/ASSESS

Writer's Journal

SUMMARIZE As a journal activity, have students reflect on and record how the editing features of a word processing program can help a writer. **REFLECTION**

TECHNOLOGY Additional writing activities are provided on the *Writing Express* CD-ROM

LESSON ORGANIZER	DAY 1	DAY 2
DAILY LANGUAGE PRACTICE TRANSPARENCIES 23, 24	1. That boys mother is a doctor. (boy's) 2. The childs' sickness made him cough. (child's) **Bridge to Writing** The <u>(possessive noun)</u> shirt was bright and clean.	1. Those doctors's clothes are white (doctors'; white.) 2. a rash appeared on the childrens's skin. (A; children's) **Bridge to Writing** We <u>(verb)</u> our vitamins every day.
ORAL WARM-UP **Listening/Speaking**	List Verbs about Health 130	Complete the Sentence 132 *Grammar Jingles*™ CD Track 8
TEACH/MODEL **GRAMMAR** **KEY** ✔ = tested skill	✔ **VERBS** 130-131 • To identify and use verbs in sentences • To identify verbs in a list	✔ **ACTION VERBS** 132-133 • To identify and use action verbs in sentences • To write and share a paragraph using strong action verbs
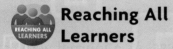 **Reaching All Learners**	**Modified Instruction** Below-Level: Model the Thinking Above-Level: Classify Verbs *ESL Manual* pp. 56, 57 **Reteach:** *Reteach Activities Copying Masters* pp. 22 and R45 **Challenge:** Activity Card 8, R65 *Practice Book* p. 36	**Modified Instruction** Below-Level: Identify Subject Above-Level: Write Original Sentences **ESL:** Sentence Frames 132 *ESL Manual* pp. 56, 58 **Reteach:** *Reteach Activities Copying Masters* pp. 23 and R45 **Challenge:** Planning for Health 133 *Practice Book* p. 37
WRITING	Writing Connection 131 Real-Life Writing: Reminder List	Writing Connection 133 Writer's Craft: Strong Verbs
CROSS-CURRICULAR/ ENRICHMENT	*Vocabulary Power* Explore Word Meaning 130 injection, medicine, remedy, treatment, **vaccine** See *Vocabulary Power* book.	*Vocabulary Power* Word Families 130 *Vocabulary Power* p. 31 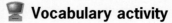 **Vocabulary activity**

DAY 3	**DAY 4**	**DAY 5**
1. The doktor sees the child. (doctor)	**1.** The doctor are a woman. (is)	**1.** I called Dr Ruiz. (Dr.)
2. what did you eat (What; eat?)	**2.** what is your doctors name (What; doctor's; ?)	**2.** My doctor am busy. (is)
Bridge to Writing Students <u>(action verb)</u> about health.	**Bridge to Writing** Doctors <u>(form of *be*)</u> helpful.	**Bridge to Writing** I <u>(action verb)</u> her how to get to the office. We <u>(form of *be*)</u> kind and caring.
Arrange Words 134 *Grammar Jingles*™ CD Track 8	Raise Hands 136	
✔ **THE VERB *BE*** 134-135 • To use the correct forms of the verb *be* in sentences • To draw a poster and write descriptive sentences using forms of the verb *be*	**EXTRA PRACTICE** 136-137 • To identify and use action verbs and the correct forms of the verb *be* • To write a paragraph that informs 🖥 **Practice and assessment**	**TEST PREP** **CHAPTER REVIEW** 138 • To review action verbs and forms of the verb *be* • To categorize words and information 🖥 **Test preparation**
Modified Instruction Below-Level: Find Simple Subject Above-Level: Explain Answers **ESL:** The *Be* Game 134 *ESL Manual* pp. 56, 59 **Reteach:** *Reteach Activities Copying Masters* pp. 24 and R45 **Challenge:** The Doctor Is In 135 *Practice Book* p. 38	**Building Oral Grammar** Read Aloud in Pairs 137 *ESL Manual* pp. 56, 60 **Challenge:** First Aid Kits 137 *Practice Book* p. 39	**Challenge:** Careers in Health 139 *Practice Book* p. 40 *ESL Manual* pp. 56, 61
Writing Connection 135 Art	Writing Connection 137 Writer's Journal: Reflections on Health	Writing Application 139 Description Tree
Vocabulary Power Classify/Categorize 130 *Vocabulary Power* p. 32 🖥 **Vocabulary activity**	**Listening and Speaking:** Public Service Announcement 136 *Vocabulary Power* Idioms 130 *Vocabulary Power* p. 33 🖥 **Vocabulary activity**	**Vocabulary:** Categorizing Words 139 *Vocabulary Power* Exemplification 130

Action Verbs and the Verb *Be*

Verbs

OBJECTIVES
- To identify and use verbs in sentences
- To identify verbs in a written list

DAILY LANGUAGE PRACTICE

TRANSPARENCY 23

1 That boys mother is a doctor. (boy's)

2 The childs' sickness made him cough. (child's)

BRIDGE TO WRITING The (possessive noun) shirt was bright and clean.

ORAL WARM-UP

USE PRIOR KNOWLEDGE What things can a person do to stay healthy? On the board, write the verbs suggested by students.

TEACH/MODEL

Read aloud the definition of a verb on page 130. Remind students that the main word in the subject is usually a noun.

Model the thinking, using the example sentences:

MODEL In the first example sentence, the subject of the sentence is *Lola and Lily*. The predicate is *sleep eight hours each night*. I know that *sleep* is the verb because it is the main word in the predicate, and it tells what Lola and Lily do.

Work through the Guided Practice orally with students.

CHAPTER 11

Action Verbs and the Verb *Be*

Vocabulary Power

vac•cine [vak•sēn′] *n*. Medicine that puts weak or dead germs into the body to prevent disease.

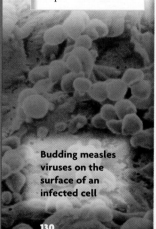

Budding measles viruses on the surface of an infected cell

130

Verbs

A **verb** is the main word in the predicate of a sentence.

You know that a sentence has a subject and a predicate. The predicate tells what the subject is or does. The verb is the main word in the predicate of a sentence.

Examples:

┌─── Predicate ───┐
Lola and Lily **sleep** eight hours each night.

┌─ Predicate ─┐
I **feel** better today.

┌─── Predicate ───┐
Everyone in my family **drinks** juice in the morning.

┌─── Predicate ───┐
We **eat** an apple every day.

┌─ Predicate ─┐
Lily **brushes** her teeth.

Guided Practice

A. Find the verb in each sentence.

Example: Lola is sick. *is*

1. My sister <u>has</u> the flu.
2. Her forehead <u>seems</u> hot.
3. Lola <u>feels</u> sleepy and weak.
4. The doctor <u>listens</u> to her heart.
5. I <u>bring</u> her medicine.
6. She <u>rests</u> in bed.
7. Dad <u>puts</u> extra blankets on her bed.
8. Mom <u>gives</u> her juice.
9. Lola's energy <u>comes</u> back.
10. She <u>is</u> better.

Vocabulary Power

DAY 1 EXPLORE WORD MEANING Introduce and define *vaccine*. **Why do you think scientists develop vaccines?**

DAY 2 WORD FAMILIES Word families are made up of words that have the same root or base word. **What are some words that are in the same word family as *vaccine*?** (See also *Vocabulary Power*, page 31.)

DAY 3 CLASSIFY/CATEGORIZE Write on the board: *bathing, brushing teeth, getting vaccinated*. **Complete this sentence: You do these things to _____.** (See also *Vocabulary Power*, page 32.)

DAY 4 IDIOMS How are vaccines given? Then discuss: **What else can "a shot in the arm" mean?** (See also *Vocabulary Power*, page 33.)

DAY 5 EXEMPLIFICATION Discuss: **What things would you create a vaccine for?**

Independent Practice

B. Write the sentences. Underline the verb in each sentence.

Example: Skin covers the whole body.
Skin <u>covers</u> the whole body.

11. Our skin <u>protects</u> us.
12. Skin <u>keeps</u> germs out of our bodies.
13. Germs <u>are</u> small and alive.
14. We all <u>carry</u> germs on our bodies.
15. Germs <u>travel</u> on our hands.

C. Choose the verb in the box that best completes each sentence. Write the sentence.

> are   fights   wins   cause   wash   make

Example: Not all germs _____ sickness.
Not all germs cause sickness.

16. Some germs _____ in your home. are
17. Sometimes germs _____ a person sick. make
18. Your body _____ them, though. fights
19. Usually the body _____ the fight. wins
20. I _____ the germs off my hands. wash

Writing Connection

Real-Life Writing: Reminder List Work with a partner. Make a list of ways to stop the spread of disease. Underline the verbs in your list. Place your list somewhere at home where family members can see it.

131

Independent Practice

Have students complete the Independent Practice, or modify it using these suggestions:

MODIFIED INSTRUCTION

BELOW-LEVEL STUDENTS Work through Parts B and C with students, modeling the thinking.

ABOVE-LEVEL STUDENTS After students have completed Parts B and C, have them write whether the verb in each sentence tells what the subject *is* or whether it tells what the subject *does*.

Writing Connection

Real-Life Writing: Reminder List Have students contribute to a class discussion on ways to avoid disease. After the discussion, students should work in pairs to write and illustrate their lists.

WRAP-UP/ASSESS

SUMMARIZE Ask students to define a verb and to give an example of a verb in a sentence.

RETEACH

INTERVENTION Lessons in **visual, auditory,** and **kinesthetic** modalities: p. R45 and *Reteach Activities Copying Masters*, p. 22.

PRACTICE page 36

Name _____

Verbs

A. Write the verb in each sentence.

1. Influenza is a disease. _____ is
2. People often call it flu. _____ call
3. People with the flu often cough hard. _____ cough
4. Their noses run. _____ run
5. Their eyes burn. _____ burn

B. Write each sentence. Underline the verb in each sentence.

6. Throats often become sore from the flu.
   Throats often <u>become</u> sore from the flu.

7. People's heads ache.
   People's heads <u>ache</u>.

8. They often have fevers.
   They often <u>have</u> fevers.

9. Fever means a high body temperature.
   Fever <u>means</u> a high body temperature.

10. Flu also gives people chills.
    Flu also <u>gives</u> people chills.

TRY THIS! Make a list of things a person with the flu should do to get well. Include in your list what someone should do to keep from spreading the flu. Underline the verbs.

36 Unit 2 • Chapter 11   Practice • Action Verbs and the Verb *Be*

CHALLENGE

A DAY IN THE LIFE OF A GERM Have students use **Challenge Activity Card 8** (page R65) to create a comic strip showing how germs can spread.

> **Challenge Activity Card 8**
>
> **A Day in the Life of a Germ**
>
> Create a comic strip about a germ. Tell what happens to the germ during one day. Follow these steps:
> - Think about different ways germs can travel from place to place.
> - Draw four to six frames for your comic strip.
> - Draw a picture for each frame. Show what the germ does in different places.
> - Write dialogue or a caption for each picture. Use strong verbs.
> - Color each picture.
> Display your comic strip in your classroom.

Verbs

Circle the verb in each sentence.

The vet (listens) to my heart.
She (checks) my ears.
She (looks) inside my mouth.
Then the vet (smiles) at my owner and me.
I (feel) much better!

Verbs

What do you do to stay healthy?

Tell a partner what you think people can do to stay healthy. Use a clear, interesting verb in each sentence you say. Then listen while your partner talks. Raise your hand each time your partner says a verb.

Verbs

What do people do to stay healthy?

Act out your ideas. Have other members of your group say a sentence about each idea you act out. Together, identify the verb in each sentence a group member says. Have one group member write down the verbs. At the end of the activity, have each group member read two verbs from the list.

Teacher: Cut apart the activities and distribute to students based on the modalities that are their strengths.
[Visual] You may want to write the sentences on the board.
[Auditory] Remind students that they will usually hear just one verb in every sentence.
[Kinesthetic] Have students work in groups of three or four.

22 Unit 2 • Chapter 11   Reteach Activities • Action Verbs and the Verb *Be*

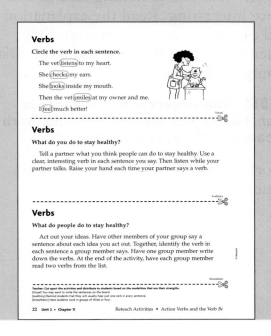

Remember that a verb is the main word in the predicate of a sentence.

CHAPTER **11** 131

Action Verbs

OBJECTIVES
- To identify and use action verbs in sentences
- To write and share a paragraph using strong action verbs

SPIRAL REVIEW

DAILY LANGUAGE PRACTICE

TRANSPARENCY 23

1 Those doctors's clothes are white *(doctors'; white.)*

2 a rash appeared on the childrens's skin. *(A; children's)*

BRIDGE TO WRITING We ___(verb)___ our vitamins every day.

ORAL WARM-UP

USE PRIOR KNOWLEDGE Write this sentence on the board: *The doctors and nurses _____ in the hospital.* Ask students to suggest a word to complete the sentence.

Grammar Jingles™ **CD, Intermediate** Use Track 8 for review and reinforcement of action verbs and the verb *be.*

TEACH/MODEL

Point out that an action verb, like all verbs, is the main word in the predicate of a sentence. Explain that using exact action verbs makes writing clearer and more interesting. Read the explanation and example sentences on page 132. Then model the thinking using the first example sentence:

MODEL **The subject of the sentence is *Juan*. I know that *opens* is the action verb because it tells what *Juan* does.**

Work with students to complete the Guided Practice items.

CHAPTER 11

Action Verbs and the Verb *Be*

Action Verbs

An **action verb** is a word that tells what the subject of a sentence does.

You know that the subject of a sentence is often a noun. An action verb tells what the subject does. To find an action verb in a sentence, look for words that tell about an action.

Examples:

Juan **opens** his eyes wide for the doctor.

The doctor **shows** him the eye chart.

Juan **sees** better with glasses.

Guided Practice

A. Find the action verb in each sentence.

Example: Anna takes a shower every day.
takes

1. Joel <u>enjoys</u> his bath.
2. They <u>use</u> mild soap and water.
3. They <u>wash</u> their hair every day, too.
4. A bath or shower <u>removes</u> germs.
5. Vaccines <u>prevent</u> disease.
6. Marta and Luis <u>play</u> outside.
7. They <u>scrub</u> their hands before lunch.
8. They <u>wear</u> clean clothes every day.
9. Thomas <u>eats</u> healthful foods.
10. Monica <u>drinks</u> eight glasses of water each day.

132

Vocabulary Power page 31

Name _____

WORD FAMILIES

▶ Word families are made up of words that have the same root or base word. Read the words below. Circle the letter of the word that does not belong.

1. A vaccine
    B vacation
    C vaccination
    D vaccinate

2. F treatment
    G treat
    H treaty
    J treasure

3. A medicine
    B medical
    C media
    D medicate

4. F light
    G flight
    H lighten
    J lightning

5. **A money**
    B harmony
    C harmonious
    D harmonica

6. F part
    G partly
    H partner
    J artistic

▶ Use a word from the Word Box to complete each sentence.

injection	remedy

7. Is chicken soup a ___remedy___ for a cold?

8. Did you get the vaccine as an ___injection___ ?

▶ Now write your own sentence using the word *vaccine.*

9. ___Possible response: Vaccines are good for us.___
   _____

Vocabulary Power   Unit 2 • Chapter 11 31

ESL

REACHING ALL LEARNERS

ACTION VERB SENTENCE FRAMES Have students practice using action verbs by completing the following sentences:

My sister _____ her hands.

The boy _____ breakfast.

Mario _____ the box of cereal.

We _____ juice.

Everybody _____ after a meal.

Independent Practice

B. Write each sentence. Underline the action verb.

Example: I visit my doctor today.
I <u>visit</u> my doctor today.

11. Dr. Ellen Brown <u>lives</u> down the street.
12. She <u>knows</u> about the human body.
13. Dr. Brown <u>works</u> at the hospital.
14. She <u>smiles</u> at her patients.
15. She <u>makes</u> me well again.

C. Choose the action verb from the box that best completes each sentence. Write the sentence.

like	listens	opens	examines	gives	looks

Example: Irma _____ her own doctor's office today.
Irma opens her own doctor's office today.

16. Now Irma _____ sick children. examines
17. She _____ to their hearts. listens
18. She _____ in their mouths and ears. looks
19. She sometimes _____ vaccines to children. gives
20. The children _____ Dr. Irma. like

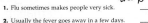
Writing Connection

Writer's Craft: Strong Verbs In a paragraph, record your ideas about what you can do to keep yourself healthy. Use strong action verbs in your sentences. Then trade paragraphs with a partner. Have your partner circle the action verbs in the paragraph.

 Remember

that an action verb tells what the subject of a sentence does.

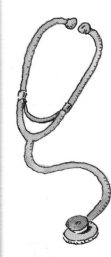

133

Independent Practice

Have students complete the Independent Practice, or modify it using these suggestions:

MODIFIED INSTRUCTION

BELOW-LEVEL STUDENTS Have students identify the subject in each sentence. Then have them find the word that tells what the subject does.

ABOVE-LEVEL STUDENTS After students complete the items in Part C, have them write original sentences for each word in the box.

Writing Connection

Writer's Craft: Strong Verbs As students write, remind them to use a thesaurus to find synonyms for verbs and to spell them correctly. Then have students work in small groups to share their paragraphs orally. Tell students to choose the appropriate volume and rate when they read their paragraphs aloud to their audience.

WRAP-UP/ASSESS

SUMMARIZE Have students give examples of sentences with strong action verbs.

RETEACH

INTERVENTION Lessons in **visual, auditory,** and **kinesthetic** modalities: p. R45 and *Reteach Activities Copying Masters,* p. 23.

PRACTICE page 37

Name _____

Action Verbs

A. Write the action verb in each sentence.

1. Flu sometimes makes people very sick. makes
2. Usually the fever goes away in a few days. goes
3. People feel well soon after. feel
4. I caught the flu from my brother. caught
5. It kept me in bed for a week. kept

B. Write each sentence. Underline the action verb.

6. Children often spread the flu at school.
   Children often <u>spread</u> the flu at school.
7. Adults give it to people at work.
   Adults <u>give</u> it to people at work.
8. Flu shots usually protect people from the flu.
   Flu shots usually <u>protect</u> people from the flu.
9. Doctors offer flu shots before flu season.
   Doctors <u>offer</u> flu shots before flu season.
10. Many patients ask their doctors for the shots.
    Many patients <u>ask</u> their doctors for the shots.

TRY THIS! Write a paragraph about activities you can do when you are healthy that you cannot do when you are sick. Circle your action verbs.

Practice • Action Verbs and the Verb *Be*   Unit 2 • Chapter 11 37

CHALLENGE

PLANNING FOR HEALTH Have students create daily schedules that include healthful activities. Have students list the things they usually do each day and tell what time they do these things. Have students make sure they include the following activities in their daily schedules:

- bathing
- brushing teeth
- sleeping
- exercising

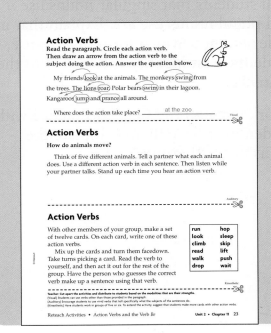

Action Verbs

Read the paragraph. Circle each action verb. Then draw an arrow from the action verb to the subject doing the action. Answer the question below.

My friends (look) at the animals. The monkeys (swing) from the trees. The lions (roar.) Polar bears (swim) in their lagoon. Kangaroos (jump) and (prance) all around.

Where does the action take place? _____ at the zoo _____

Action Verbs

How do animals move?

Think of five different animals. Tell a partner what each animal does. Use a different action verb in each sentence. Then listen while your partner talks. Stand up each time you hear an action verb.

Action Verbs

With other members of your group, make a set of twelve cards. On each card, write one of these action verbs.
Mix up the cards and turn them facedown. Take turns picking a card. Read the verb to yourself, and then act it out for the rest of the group. Have the person who guesses the correct verb make up a sentence using that verb.

run	hop
look	sleep
climb	skip
read	lift
walk	push
drop	wait

Reteach Activities • Action Verbs and the Verb *Be*   Unit 2 • Chapter 11 23

The Verb *Be*

OBJECTIVES

- To use the correct forms of the verb *be* in sentences
- To draw a poster and write descriptive sentences using forms of the verb *be*

TRANSPARENCY 23

1 The docktor sees the child. (doctor)

2 what did you eat (What; eat?)

BRIDGE TO WRITING Students (action verb) about health.

ORAL WARM-UP

USE PRIOR KNOWLEDGE Write these words on the board: *are everywhere germs.* Have students rearrange the words to form a sentence.

Grammar Jingles™ **CD, Intermediate** Use Track 8 for review and reinforcement of action verbs and the verb *be*.

TEACH/MODEL

Read aloud the explanation and the example sentences. Point out the different forms of the verb *be* in the chart. Tell students that singular nouns use *is* and plural nouns use *are*. Explain that in order to know which form of *be* to use, students must identify the subject of the sentence.

Work through the Guided Practice with students, or have them complete the items in small groups.

Subject	Form of *Be*
Singular	
I	am
you	are
he, she, it	is
Plural	
we	are
you	are
they	are

The Verb *Be*

Forms of the verb *be* link the subject to a word or words in the predicate.

You know that an action verb names what the subject of a sentence does. The verb *be* does not show action.

Examples:

Julia **is** strong.

You **are** better now.

I **am** at the nurse's office.

The verb *be* has several different forms. The subject of the sentence and the form of the verb *be* must agree. The chart shows how the forms of *be* agree with singular and plural subjects.

Guided Practice

A. For each sentence, choose the correct form of the verb *be* in parentheses ().

Example: The clinic (is|are) now ready for an emergency. *is*

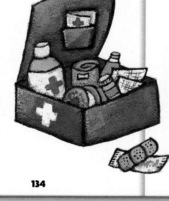

1. Sean's knee (is|are) hurt.
2. A first-aid kit (are|is) in my bathroom.
3. First-aid kits (are|is) important.
4. Bandages (am|are) good for small cuts.
5. Cleaning the cut (am|is) a type of first aid.
6. Sean's knee (is|are) dirty.
7. My hands (is|are) clean.
8. I (am|is) gentle with his knee.
9. He (is|are) better now.
10. We (am|are) both happy again.

134

Vocabulary Power page 32

Name _____

CLASSIFY/CATEGORIZE

Read each group of words. Each group has special words that are all about one topic. Circle the letter next to the correct topic. Then add a word to each group of words. Additional words will vary. Possible responses are given.

1. vaccines, healthy food, washing hands, _____ exercise
   - A things that make us sick
   - B things to do on weekends
   - C birthday gifts
   - (D) things that keep us healthy

2. crayons, paper, glue, _____ scissors
   - F things for a pet
   - (G) art and craft supplies
   - H homework
   - J things with which to clean the house

3. tag, kickball, catch, _____ softball
   - (A) games to play outside
   - B favorite books
   - C games to play inside
   - D favorite videos

4. sneezing, sore throat, fever, _____ coughing
   - F signs of health
   - G things to get vaccinated against
   - (H) signs of sickness
   - J things on a shopping list

5. remedy, treatment, injection, _____ rest
   - A favorite foods
   - B games to play outside
   - C sports teams
   - (D) things that help us when we're sick

32 Unit 2 • Chapter 11   Vocabulary Power

 ESL

THE *BE* GAME Make a game path with twelve spaces. Write *am*, *is*, and *are* in alternating spaces. Also make or use a spinner with six divisions. Have students take turns using the spinner. As they move their markers the number of spaces shown on the spinner, they will use the verb they land on in a sentence.

Independent Practice

B. Complete each sentence, using the correct form of the verb *be*. Write the sentence.

Example: Vaccines _____ available to us.
Vaccines are available to us.

11. Vaccines _____ tools for fighting disease. are
12. I _____ now vaccinated against illness. am
13. Today, the doctor _____ in charge of the vaccines. is
14. They _____ over there in his cabinet. are
15. This vaccine _____ in pill form. is

C. For each sentence, choose the correct form of the verb *be* in parentheses ( ). Write each sentence.

Example: Most vaccines (is, are) shots.
Most vaccines are shots.

16. You (am, <u>are</u>) the first in line.
17. I (are, <u>am</u>) scared of vaccines.
18. However, I (<u>am</u>, is) thankful for them.
19. My sister (are, <u>is</u>) afraid of getting a shot.
20. Now we both (is, <u>are</u>) brave.

Remember that forms of the verb *be* link the subject to a word or words in the predicate.

Writing Connection

Art Make a poster showing what you know about being healthy. Draw some things a person might do to stay well. Then write three or four sentences that describe your drawings.

135

Independent Practice

Have students complete the Independent Practice, or modify it using these suggestions:

MODIFIED INSTRUCTION

BELOW-LEVEL STUDENTS Remind students to find the simple subject and determine whether it is singular or plural before deciding which form of *be* to use.

ABOVE-LEVEL STUDENTS Have students tell how they decided which form of *be* to use in each sentence.

Writing Connection

Art Tell students to use forms of the verb *be* in the sentences on their posters. Have students check their papers for the correct use of the verb *be*, and adjust for agreement if necessary.

WRAP-UP/ASSESS

SUMMARIZE Ask students to name the form of *be* that agrees with each of these pronouns: *I, you, he, she, it, we,* and *they.*

RETEACH

INTERVENTION Lessons in **visual, auditory,** and **kinesthetic** modalities: p. R45 and *Reteach Activities Copying Masters,* p. 24.

PRACTICE page 38

Name _____

The Verb *Be*

A. For each sentence, write the correct form of the verb *be* in parentheses ( ).

1. A cold (**is**, are) a disease. ___is___
2. Many different germs (is, **are**) causes of colds. ___are___
3. Colds (is, **are**) not as dangerous as some other diseases. ___are___
4. My cold (**is**, are) not very bad. ___is___
5. My mother (**is**, are) almost over her cold. ___is___

B. Write each sentence, using the correct form of the verb *be* in parentheses ( ).

6. Medicines (is, **are**) not cures for colds.
   Medicines are not cures for colds.
7. Bed rest (**is**, are) a good idea.
   Bed rest is a good idea.
8. Temperatures (is, **are**) usually not high with colds.
   Temperatures are usually not high with colds.
9. Students absent from school (is, **are**) often ill with colds.
   Students absent from school are often ill with colds.

TRY THIS! Write about a quiet activity a person with a cold can do. Suggest something that a student home from school can do alone. Circle the action verbs.

38 Unit 2 • Chapter 11   Practice • Action Verbs and the Verb *Be*

CHALLENGE

THE DOCTOR IS IN Have each student write and illustrate a story about a visit to a doctor's office. Ask students to imagine that they are writing the story for a preschooler. Direct students to write their stories in such a way that they would be reassuring for a child who is afraid to visit the doctor. Remind students to edit their stories for the correct use of forms of *be.*

The Verb *Be*

Read each sentence. Underline the sentence that uses the correct form of the verb *be*. Circle the verb.

I is a school nurse.   Ramona (is) unhappy.   Her friends is with her.
I (am) a school nurse.   Ramona am unhappy.   Her friends am with her.
I are a school nurse.   Ramona are unhappy.   Her friends (are) with her.

Visual

The Verb *Be*

Make up a story and tell a partner about some people who are happy and other people who are sad. Use a form of *be*—*am, is,* or *are*—in each of your sentences. Listen to your partner's sentences. Raise your hand each time you hear a form of the verb *be*.

Auditory

The Verb *Be*

With a partner, make three sets of cards as shown below. There are six cards in the first set, three cards in the second set, and two cards in the third set. Take turns using a card from each set to form a complete sentence.

Card 1:	I	You	My friends	We	That girl	They
Card 2:	am		is		are	
Card 3:	a good student		good student			

Kinesthetic

Teacher: Cut apart the activities and distribute to students based on the modalities that are their strengths.
[Visual] You may want to write the sentences on the board.
[Auditory] Suggest that partners include these subjects in their sentences: I, You, We, He, She.
[Kinesthetic] If you prefer, students can complete this activity individually or in small groups.

24 Unit 2 • Chapter 11   Reteach Activities • Action Verbs and the Verb *Be*

Extra Practice

OBJECTIVES
- To identify and use action verbs and the correct forms of the verb *be*
- To write a paragraph that informs and gives directions and to edit for correct verb use

DAILY LANGUAGE PRACTICE

TRANSPARENCY 24

1 The doctor are a woman. (is)

2 what is your doctors name (What; doctor's; ?)

BRIDGE TO WRITING Doctors <u>(form of *be*)</u> helpful.

ORAL WARM-UP

USE PRIOR KNOWLEDGE Ask volunteers to tell what they know about scientists. Tell students to raise one hand when they hear a form of the verb *be* and to raise both hands when they hear an action verb.

TEACH/MODEL

Use the Remember box to review action verbs and forms of the verb *be*. Model the thinking for the example sentence in Part A:

MODEL The subject of the sentence is *Scientists*. The word that tells me what scientists do or are is *study*. I know that *study* is the verb in the sentence.

Have students complete the Extra Practice items independently.

 Remember

that a **verb** is the main word in the predicate of a sentence. An **action verb** tells what the subject of a sentence does. Forms of the verb *be* link the subject to a word or words in the predicate.

For more activities with action verbs and *be*, visit **The Learning Site:** www.harcourtschool.com

136

Extra Practice

A. Write each sentence. Underline the verb in each sentence. *pages 130–131*

Example: Scientists study disease.
Scientists <u>study</u> disease.

1. They <u>learn</u> the causes of disease.
2. It <u>is</u> hard work.
3. Often, scientists <u>find</u> new cures.
4. Sometimes it <u>takes</u> many years.
5. I <u>am</u> interested in medicine and science.

B. Write each sentence. Underline the action verb in each sentence. *pages 132–133*

Example: Some diseases spread between people.
Some diseases <u>spread</u> between people.

6. Doctors <u>know</u> about many diseases.
7. Doctors <u>keep</u> their patients healthy.
8. Some illnesses <u>strike</u> during the summer.
9. One vaccine <u>prevents</u> flu.
10. Family members <u>give</u> each other colds.

C. Write the verb in each sentence. Tell whether it is an action verb or a form of the verb *be*. *pages 132–135*

Example: My mother is a scientist.
is; form of be

11. Some scientists collect information about disease. collect; action verb
12. You are good at science. are; form of *be*
13. Scientists give the information to the public. give; action verb
14. Sasha's father examines germs through a powerful lens. examines; action verb
15. We are careful about germs on our hands. are; form of *be*

Vocabulary Power   page 33

Name _____

IDIOMS

An idiom is a group of words. The meaning of the group of words is usually different from the meaning of each word. Read and illustrate each idiom. Then use the idioms to complete the sentences below.

1. a shot in the arm	2. catch your breath
3. got cold feet	4. get a taste of your own medicine

5. The good news was <u>a shot in the arm</u>
6. Before the dive, she <u>got cold feet</u>
7. Stop running and <u>catch your breath</u>
8. If you aren't nice to others, you might <u>get a taste of your own medicine</u>

Vocabulary Power   Unit 2 • Chapter 11 33

Listening and Speaking

PUBLIC SERVICE ANNOUNCEMENT Explain that a public service announcement is a short message broadcast to give helpful information. Have each student write a thirty-second announcement telling how to stay healthy. Have students present their announcements, using verbal and nonverbal communication effectively.

D. Rewrite each sentence, using the correct form of the verb *be* in parentheses ( ). *pages 134–135*

Example: I (are, am) out in the rain with only an umbrella. *am*

16. You (am, <u>are</u>) dry.
17. I (is, <u>am</u>) sick today.
18. Mom (<u>is</u>, am) home with me.
19. I (is, <u>am</u>) at the doctor's office this morning.
20. Maggie (<u>is</u>, are) much better now.

E. Rewrite each sentence, using the correct form of the verb *be*. *pages 134–135*

21. When they _____ sick, people need to be careful about spreading their germs to others. are
22. Here _____ some good ideas. are
23. You _____ at risk for disease if you drink from another person's glass. are
24. I _____ always careful about washing my hands before I eat. am
25. It _____ a good idea to cover your mouth when you cough. is

Writing Connection

Writer's Journal: Reflections on Health Imagine that you are showing someone ways to stay healthy. Choose one of these actions: washing hands, brushing teeth, getting enough sleep, getting vaccinations. Write a paragraph that tells how to do the action you chose. Remember to use words like *first, next,* and *then* in your paragraph.

137

Building Oral Grammar

Provide students with the opportunity to practice speaking and listening skills using forms of the verb *be* by having them work in pairs to read aloud the sentences in Parts D and E.

Writing Connection

Writer's Journal: Reflections on Health Remind students that the purpose of their paragraph is to inform their audiences. Ask: *How might you teach a younger child how to do the action? What steps would you include in your instructions?* After they finish writing, tell students to edit their writing to make sure they have included either an action verb or the correct form of the verb *be.*

WRAP-UP/ASSESS

SUMMARIZE Have students name two kinds of verbs and give examples of each in a sentence.

ADDITIONAL PRACTICE An additional page of Extra Practice is provided on page 461 of the *Pupil Edition.*

PRACTICE page 39

Name _____

Extra Practice

A. Read each sentence. Underline the verb in each sentence.

1. Janet <u>has</u> strep throat.
2. Her throat <u>feels</u> sore.
3. Strep throat <u>makes</u> you very sick.
4. Germs <u>cause</u> strep throat.
5. They <u>move</u> from person to person through the air.

B. For each sentence, choose the correct form of the verb *be* in parentheses ( ). Write the sentence.

6. My temperature (**is**, are) up.
   My temperature is up.

7. My throat and ears (**is**, are) hurting.
   My throat and ears are hurting.

8. I think my sickness (**is**, are) strep throat.
   I think my sickness is strep throat.

9. I think it (**is**, are) a mild case.
   I think it is a mild case.

10. People (**is**, are) usually given medicine by their doctors.
    People are usually given medicine by their doctors.

▶ **TRY THIS!** Write a few sentences that describe the things that make you feel better when you are ill. Underline the action verbs, and circle forms of *be.*

Practice • Action Verbs and the Verb *Be*   Unit 2 • Chapter 11   **39**

CHALLENGE

FIRST-AID KITS Have students record a list of items that might go into a first-aid kit. They may use encyclopedias, magazines, or the Internet for information. Then have each student write a paragraph explaining why it is important to have a first-aid kit available. Ask students to underline the verbs in their paragraphs.

TECHNOLOGY *Grammar Practice and Assessment* CD-ROM; *Writing Express* CD-ROM

INTERNET Visit *The Learning Site:* **www.harcourtschool.com**

Chapter Review

OBJECTIVES

- To review action verbs and forms of the verb *be*
- To categorize words and information

DAILY LANGUAGE PRACTICE

TRANSPARENCY 24

❶ I called Dr Ruiz. (Dr.)

❷ My doctor am busy. (is)

BRIDGE TO WRITING I ___(action verb)___ her how to get to the office.
We ___(form of *be*)___ kind and caring.

STANDARDIZED TEST PREP

MODEL TEST-TAKING STRATEGIES Ask a volunteer to read aloud the directions on page 138.

Remind students to reread each sentence with the answer they have chosen to make sure it sounds correct.

Model the thinking. Write this example on the board:

Dr. Clarke _____ my friend.

> 1   **A** plays
>   **B** am
>   **C** are
>   **D** is

MODEL I know that the subject of the sentence is *Dr. Clarke. Dr. Clarke* is a singular noun, so the verb *are* is not correct. The verbs *plays* and *am* do not make sense in this sentence. The verb that agrees with a singular noun is *is. Dr. Clarke is my friend* sounds correct, so I know the answer must be D.

Have students complete the Chapter Review independently.

Chapter Review

Read the paragraph and choose the word that belongs in each space. Write the letter of your answer.

> Most of my classmates __(1)__ a cold. Germs __(2)__ this sickness. No one __(3)__ outside for a while. Some students in my class __(4)__ home. Now they __(5)__ better. It __(6)__ back-to-school time for everyone. We __(7)__ all healthy again. I __(8)__ happy to go back to school.

TIP Be sure you read the directions before you answer any questions.

1   **A** plays
     B are
     C have c
     D am
	5 **A** is
	     B have
	     C are c
	     D am

2   **F** am
     G is
     H cause H
     J write
	6 **F** is F
	     G am
	     H run
	     J are

3   **A** are
     B plays B
     C am
     D becomes
	7 **A** are A
	     B have
	     C am
	     D is

4   **F** am
     G feels
     H gives
     J stay J
	8 **F** is
	     G has
	     H am H
	     J are

For more test preparation, visit *The Learning Site:* www.harcourtschool.com

138

Assessment

. . . .

PORTFOLIO ASSESSMENT Have students select their best work from the Writing Connections on pages 131, 133, and 135.

ONGOING ASSESSMENT Evaluate the performance of 4–6 students using appropriate checklists and record forms from pages R74–R77.

INTERNET Activities and exercises to help students prepare for state and standardized assessments appear on *The Learning Site:*
www.harcourtschool.com

Categorizing Words

Sorting Words into Categories

Knowing how to sort things is an important skill. Sorting helps us group things that are alike into categories. When we sort, we are able to see how things are alike and how they are different.

For example, when you think of a healthful lifestyle, you may think of diet and exercise. Notice how the words below are sorted into these two categories.

Diet	Exercise
fruits	walking
vegetables	running
low-fat foods	biking

YOUR TURN

1. **How would you describe yourself? Make a list of four categories you belong in, such as sister, friend, student, and so on.**

2. **Look at your list of categories. What words would you use to describe yourself in each category? Sort some of these words into each category.**

139

VOCABULARY

Categorizing Words

VOCABULARY

Categorizing Words

TEACH/MODEL

Write the word *doctor* on the board. Then ask students to name some categories in which a doctor might belong. Students may name *scientist*, *person*, *eye doctor*, *dentist*, *surgeon*, and *adult*. Have students decide whether each of the words they name is a more specific or a less specific description than the word *doctor*.

WRITING APPLICATION Have students draw trees and write their names at the roots. On the trunk of each tree, they should write general words to describe themselves. On the upper branches, have them write more specific words to describe themselves.

WRAP-UP/ASSESS

Writer's Journal

SUMMARIZE In their journals, have students reflect on how categorizing is a useful skill.
REFLECTION

PRACTICE page 40

Name _____

Chapter Review

Choose the word that belongs in each space in the paragraph below. Fill in the oval next to your choice.

(1) Some students in my class _____ not in school today. (2) They _____ a sickness. (3) The sickness _____ probably strep throat. (4) Students with strep throat often _____ it to other students. (5) The air _____ the germs from one person to another. (6) Strep throat sometimes _____ the body temperature. (7) It _____ the throat to swallow. (8) Strep throat usually _____ quickly with rest and the right medicine.

1 ○ stays	**5** ○ carry
● are	● carries
○ has	○ feels
○ is	○ feels
2 ○ are	**6** ○ is
○ is	○ rise
● have	● raises
○ has	○ are
3 ○ are	**7** ○ sneeze
○ makes	○ sneezes
● is	● hurts
○ make	○ hurt
4 ○ catch	**8** ○ causes
● catches	○ cause
○ gives	○ heal
● give	● heals

40 Unit 2 • Chapter 11   Practice • Action Verbs and the Verb *Be*

CHALLENGE

CAREERS IN HEALTH Have students work in groups to investigate careers in the field of health. Students may take notes from the Internet or from encyclopedias. Tell them to write the names and short descriptions of each career on index cards. Have students organize the cards into categories of their own choosing.

TECHNOLOGY Additional writing activities are provided on the *Writing Express* CD-ROM

LESSON ORGANIZER	DAY 1	DAY 2

DAILY LANGUAGE PRACTICE

TRANSPARENCY 25

DAY 1:
1. Have the childs in your class ever solved a problem together (children; together?)
2. MR franklin, our teacher, says that we is good at solving problems. (Mr. Franklin,; are)

DAY 2:
1. once we had to choose a class project but we could not make a decision (Once; project,; decision.)
2. paul and I have good ideas. (Paul)

ORAL WARM-UP
Listening/Speaking

DAY 1:
Discuss Beginning Friendships 140
Suggest Occasions for Explanations 148

DAY 2:
Discuss the Benefits of Planning 149

TEACH/MODEL
WRITING

DAY 1:
Literature Model: from *How to Be a Friend* 141-145
GUIDED WRITING
✔ **Prewriting** 148
• To learn strategies for prewriting a how-to essay
• To choose a topic and generate ideas for a how-to essay
Interactive Writing 148

DAY 2:
GUIDED WRITING
✔ **Drafting** 149
• To learn strategies for drafting a how-to essay
• To draft a how-to essay

 Transparency 26

Reaching All Learners

DAY 1:
Modified Instruction 154
Below-Level: Use Examples
Above-Level: Make a Chart
ESL Manual pp. 62, 63

DAY 2:
Modified Instruction 155
Below-Level: Count Nouns
Above-Level: List Nouns
ESL Manual p. 62

GRAMMAR

DAY 1:
Unit 2 Review:
✔ More About Nouns 154

DAY 2:
Unit 2 Review:
✔ Singular and Plural Nouns 155

CROSS-CURRICULAR/ ENRICHMENT

DAY 1:
LISTENING AND SPEAKING: 146
EVALUATION CRITERIA: Establish Criteria for Writing 147
HANDS-ON ACTIVITY: Abbreviation Memory 154

Vocabulary Power

Explore Word Meaning 142

assist, collaborate, **cooperate**, partner, teamwork
See Vocabulary Power book.

DAY 2:
TEST PREP:
Use Examples 155

Vocabulary Power

Context Clues 142
Vocabulary Power book p. 34

 Vocabulary activity

KEY
✔ = tested writing form/skill

DAY **3**	DAY **4**	DAY **5**
1. we shared ideas about the plans as mr Cook instructed (We; Mr.; instructed.)	1. We voted on the ideas friday morning (Friday morning.)	1. Pauls idea won but I was not upset. (Paul's; won,)
2. My plan sounded good but were too expensive. (was)	2. Do you know which idea we chose (chose?)	2. it was my groups' project and we all voted on the topic. (It; group's project, and)
Compare Revising Artwork to Revising Writing 150	Define Proofreading and Discuss Its Advantages 151	Model Tone of Voice to Express Feelings 152
GUIDED WRITING ✔ **Revising** 150 • To learn strategies for revising a how-to essay • To revise a how-to essay **Transparencies** 27a and 27b	**GUIDED WRITING** ✔ **Proofreading** 151 • To learn strategies for proofreading a how-to essay • To proofread a how-to essay **Transparencies** 28a and 28b 💻 **Proofreading practice**	✔ **Publishing** 152 • To learn strategies for publishing a how-to essay as an oral presentation • To publish a how-to essay as an oral presentation Handwriting 152 💻 **Practice and assessment**
Modified Instruction 156 Below-Level: Identify Nouns Above-Level: Write Sentences *ESL Manual* p. 62	**Modified Instruction** 157 Below-Level: Review Forms of *Be* Above-Level: Write Sentences **ESL:** Make a Checklist 151 *ESL Manual* p. 62	*ESL Manual* p. 62
Unit 2 Review: ✔ Possessive Nouns 156	**Unit 2 Review:** ✔ Action Verbs and the Verb *Be* 157	**HANDS-ON ACTIVITIES:** 89I–89J
HANDS-ON ACTIVITY: Plurals and Possessive 156 **PEER CONFERENCES:** Make Essays Stronger 150 *Vocabulary Power* Analogies 142 *Vocabulary Power* book p. 35 💻 **Vocabulary activity**	**TEST PREP** **TEST PREP:** Extra Practice 157 *Vocabulary Power* Compound Words 142 *Vocabulary Power* book p. 36 💻 **Vocabulary activity**	**LISTENING AND SPEAKING:** Making an Oral Presentation 153 *Vocabulary Power* Exemplification 142

Using the Literature Model

OBJECTIVE
• To read and analyze a how-to essay

DAILY LANGUAGE PRACTICE

TRANSPARENCY 25

1 Have the childs in your class ever solved a problem together (children; together?)

2 MR franklin, our teacher, says that we is good at solving problems. (Mr. Franklin,; are)

ORAL WARM-UP

USE PRIOR KNOWLEDGE Read aloud the introduction to the essay, and discuss the answers to questions such as the following:

1. How did you begin a friendship with one of your friends? (Possible responses: We helped each other with a problem; we played together.)

2. What advice would you give someone to help him or her make friends? (Possible responses: Offer to help a classmate with schoolwork; ask someone to play with you.)

PREREADING STRATEGIES

PREVIEW/SET PURPOSE Have students scan the illustrations. Ask them to suggest some tips they expect to read about in *How to Be a Friend*. Have students set their own purpose for reading, or have them read to learn some ways to be a better friend and to solve arguments.

140

School-Home Connection

Family members can help students identify activities that students do well and can clearly explain, such as making a favorite dish or doing a simple project. Family members also may teach students how to complete a new but simple task. When students have finished the task, they can write the steps they followed to complete it.

Award-Winning Author and Illustrator

You know that how-to writing tries to explain how to do something. In this helpful guide, the authors explain how to be a friend and how to solve an argument. As you read, think about how the authors organize their advice to make it clear.

HOW TO BE A FRIEND

A Guide to Making Friends and Keeping Them

by Laurie Krasny Brown and Marc Brown

Ways To Be A Friend

There are many ways to show that you like someone and want to be a friend.

Heads or tails?

You can play fair. Flip a coin with a friend to see who goes first.
You can share toys and other things.

141

Ask students to think about ways they have made friends or settled arguments. Use questions like the following to help them monitor their comprehension:

3. **Who do you think the authors' audience might be?** (Possible responses: young people who have trouble making friends; young people who want to be good friends.) **INFERENTIAL: IDENTIFY AUDIENCE**

4. **Why might the authors have written this selection?** (Possible response: to help young people who don't know how to make friends or how to be a good friend.) **INFERENTIAL: DETERMINE AUTHOR'S PURPOSE**

READING LIKE A WRITER

5. **How do the authors organize and present their ideas about making and keeping friends?** (Possible response: The authors list just one or two ideas at a time, with illustrations to show examples of ideas.) **INFERENTIAL: TEXT STRUCTURE**

6. **Based on what the authors say, what do you think it means to play fair?** (Possible responses: It means not insisting on your own way all the time; giving everyone a chance to participate in an activity; sharing; taking turns.) **INFERENTIAL: DRAW CONCLUSIONS**

7. **Why is it important to stand up for friends?** (Possible responses: They might stand up for you; it shows that you care about them.) **CRITICAL: SPECULATE**

142

Vocabulary Power

DAY ① EXPLORE WORD MEANING Introduce and define *cooperate*. **How do people act when they are cooperating?**

DAY ② CONTEXT CLUES Say: **The third and fourth grades cooperated in giving the play. What words could you use in place of *cooperated*?** (See also *Vocabulary Power*, page 34.)

DAY ③ ANALOGIES **What word completes the analogy: *Cooperate is the same as collaborate; shout is the same as* _____.** (See also *Vocabulary Power*, page 35.)

DAY ④ COMPOUND WORDS **What two words are in *teamwork*? What are some other words you could add to the word *team*?** (See also *Vocabulary Power*, page 36.)

DAY ⑤ EXEMPLIFICATION Have students draw a scene that shows people cooperating.

You can try to cheer up a friend who's feeling sad.

8. What are some ways to cheer up a friend who's feeling sad? How do you like to be cheered up?

(Responses will vary.) **CRITICAL: EXPRESS PERSONAL OPINION**

You can cooperate. Go along with *your friend's* ideas sometimes.

Okay, what do *you* want to play?

Try it this way.

This math is hard. I don't get it!

You can offer help to friends when they need it.

143

READING LIKE A WRITER

9. **What does it mean to keep your word? What happens when a person doesn't keep his or her word?** (Possible responses: Keeping your word means doing what you say you'll do; when a person doesn't keep his or her word, others might not trust that person anymore.) **INFERENTIAL: CAUSE-EFFECT**

10. **Think of a time when you had to talk out an argument. Did you use any of the ideas listed? Tell about it.** (Responses will vary.) **CRITICAL: EXPRESS PERSONAL OPINIONS**

11. **Which step in Talking Out an Argument is the hardest for you?** (Possible response: It's hard for me to calm down and take deep breaths when I'm angry.) **CRITICAL: EXPRESS PERSONAL OPINIONS**

12. **The authors use the words *You can* when they describe how to make and keep friends. They don't use *You can* when they tell how to talk out an argument. Why do they write these differently?** (Possible responses: The authors use *You can* because the things they say are suggestions, and the reader doesn't have to do them all. In *Talking Out an Argument,* all of the steps should be followed.) **CRITICAL: INTERPRET TEXT STRUCTURE**

You can keep your word. Then friends will know that they can trust you.
You can do things for friends, like making them special presents.

You can compliment your friend, even when she wins and you lose. That's being a good sport.

Good jump! You win!

144

Talking Out an Argument

Here are some steps to help you talk out an argument:

1 Stop arguing.

2 Calm down. Take deep breaths, count backwards, relax your muscles, or leave the group for a minute.

3 Agree to talk it out.

4 Everyone gets a turn to tell, not yell, their story and be listened to without interruptions.

5 Think up lots of ideas for solving the problem.

6 Try to choose the best solution, the one everyone agrees on and thinks will work.

7 Decide how to go about carrying out this plan.

8 Do it!

9 Remember, arguments are allowed, but meanness is not!

Remember:
In order to please everyone at least a little, you may not get exactly what you want.

Vocabulary Power

co·op·er·ate
[kō·op′ə·rāt′] *v.* To work with another person or persons for a common purpose.

Analyze THE Model

1. The authors describe many ways to be a friend. Name three ways.

2. How do the pictures help give information in this how-to guide?

3. Why do the authors number their advice about talking out an argument?

145

Analyze THE Model

1. The authors describe many ways to be a friend. Name three ways. (Possible responses: Share things with a friend; invite friends to play with you; keep a promise you make to a friend.) **LITERAL: NOTE DETAILS**

2. How do the pictures help give information in this how-to guide? (Possible response: They make ideas clearer by giving examples to help the reader picture the situations that the authors describe.) **CRITICAL: INTERPRET TEXT STRUCTURE**

3. Why do the authors number their advice about talking out an argument? (Possible response: They want to show that these steps should be done in order.) **INFERENTIAL: AUTHOR'S CRAFT**

SUMMARIZE THE MODEL

ONE-SENTENCE SUMMARY Ask: **If you wanted to tell a family member what this selection is about, what would you say?** Have students write one sentence to summarize the selection. (Possible response: The authors give advice about how to make friends, treat them nicely, and talk out arguments.)

RESPONSE TO LITERATURE

 WRITING PROMPT To have students respond in writing to the selection, use the following prompt:

Think about a time when you had to talk out an argument with a friend or a family member. Write about how the steps listed in the essay might have helped you.

 TECHNOLOGY Additional writing activities are provided on the *Writing Express* CD-ROM

Parts of a How-To Essay

OBJECTIVES
- To recognize and understand the parts of a how-to essay
- To analyze and summarize a how-to essay
- To establish criteria for evaluating a how-to essay
- To listen critically to a how-to essay

READING LIKE A WRITER

READ AND RESPOND TO THE MODEL Tell students that you will read aloud Mario's essay. Begin by reading aloud the title and asking students to determine a purpose for listening. (to learn how to put a puzzle together) After you have read the essay aloud, discuss whether students think that Mario explained the task well. Remind students to use examples from the essay to support their evaluations.

FOCUS ON ORGANIZATION Have students reread the essay silently. Ask: **How is this how-to essay organized differently than "Talking Out an Argument" by Laurie Krasny Brown and Marc Brown?** (Possible response: The steps must be followed in sequence.)

FOCUS ON WRITER'S CRAFT Have students identify the signal/sequence words Mario uses. Ask: **How does using words like *first, next, then,* and *finally* make a how-to essay clear and easy to understand?**

READING-WRITING CONNECTION

Parts of a How-to Essay

Laurie Krasny Brown and Marc Brown tell the reader how to be a friend and settle an argument. Read the how-to essay below, written by a student named Mario. Notice the parts of the essay.

MODEL

How to Put a Puzzle Together

Putting a puzzle together can be a challenge, but when you are done, the reward is a great picture. Here are some steps that can help you when you put a puzzle together.

materials needed — You will need to find a large table. Spread out all the puzzle pieces on the table with the color side up.

steps in order — First, find all the pieces with straight edges. Those pieces will form the outside edge of the puzzle. Then, sort the rest of the pieces by colors or images. For example, you may look for blue pieces for a blue sky or green pieces for green grass. Use the picture on the cover of the puzzle box as a guide.

sequence words

Next, begin putting the edge of the puzzle together, connecting the pieces with straight edges. It may take several

Listening and Speaking

Have pairs of students take turns explaining how to do something. Tell students to choose a simple task, such as making a favorite sandwich. First, have each student write a paragraph that lists in order the steps needed to complete the task. Next, have one student read his or her how-to paragraph while the partner listens and takes notes about the steps involved. Tell students to speak in complete sentences when they read their paragraphs. After both students have read their paragraphs, they can check each other's notes to see if they heard all the steps.

tries to find which pieces fit together, but don't give up. Soon the outer edge of the puzzle will be put together.

Finally, you can begin putting the inside of the puzzle together by matching shapes of pieces with common colors. Eventually, you will have many large sections that will fit together to make the big picture.

sequence words

details to explain the step

Analyze THE Model

1. What is the purpose of Mario's essay?

2. What step does Mario describe first? Next? Finally?

3. Why is the order of the steps important?

Summarize THE Model

Use a flowchart like this one to tell the steps Mario described in his essay. Then use your notes to write a summary of his how-to essay. Remember to include only the important points.

Writer's Craft

Paragraphing Mario used paragraphs to organize his how-to essay. List the topic sentences he used. Then, list the details he included in each paragraph. Tell how the signal/sequence words help you follow the steps in Mario's essay.

How-to Topic

Step 1

Step 2

Step 3

Step 4

147

Evaluation Criteria

ESTABLISH CRITERIA FOR WRITING Tell students that they will help to evaluate their own how-to essays. Have them turn to the rubric in their Handbooks, on page 497. Explain that if students meet the criteria in the "4" column, plus the criteria that you and the class add, they will have produced their best work. Discuss the criteria, and add additional criteria based on your students' needs and interests. Remind students to refer to the rubric as they write their essays. (A teacher version of the rubric is available on page R81. For more information about evaluating writing, see pages R78–R79 in this *Teacher's Edition*.)

Analyze THE Model

1. **What is the purpose of Mario's essay?** (Possible response: Mario's purpose is to show how to put a puzzle together.) CRITICAL: RECOGNIZE AUTHOR'S PURPOSE

2. **What step does Mario describe first? Next? Then? Finally?** (His first step is spreading the puzzle pieces on the table. Next is sorting the pieces by shape, color, or image. Then he puts the outer edge of the puzzle together. Finally he puts the inside of the puzzle together.) LITERAL: NOTE DETAILS

3. **Why is the order of the steps important?** (Possible response: The steps follow a logical order to accomplish the task.) INFERENTIAL: TEXT STRUCTURE

SUMMARIZE THE MODEL

Have students work in pairs to compare their flowcharts and discuss any differences. Then have them work independently to write a summary of Mario's essay. As students compare their summaries, ask them to reach an agreement about which details in the essay are the most important.

WRITER'S CRAFT

PARAGRAPHING Remind students that a topic sentence is the sentence in a paragraph that tells what the whole paragraph is about. It is usually the first sentence. Tell students to think about how to organize their how-to essays into paragraphs.

TAKE-HOME BOOK 2 provides an additional model of informative writing and home activities. See *Practice Book* pages 125–128.

Prewriting

OBJECTIVES
- To learn strategies for prewriting a how-to essay
- To choose a topic and generate ideas for a how-to essay

ORAL WARM-UP

USE PRIOR KNOWLEDGE Ask students to suggest occasions when a person might explain to others how to do something. (Possible responses: at recess when explaining the rules of a game; in class when starting work on a group project.)

GUIDED WRITING

Discuss the writing prompt. Have students identify the audience and the purpose for writing. (audience—classmates; purpose—explain how to do an activity) Then model finding an appropriate topic:

MODEL **My friends really like chocolate milk. I know how to make it using fresh milk and chocolate syrup.**

Have students read Mario's model and make their own prewriting flowcharts, using an activity you assign or one that they suggest.

SELF-INITIATED WRITING Have students choose their own topics for their how-to essays.

WRAP-UP/ASSESS

SUMMARIZE How does making a flowchart help you put your steps in order?

Prewriting

Purpose and Audience

In this chapter, you will write a how-to essay about something you do well.

WRITING PROMPT Write a how-to essay explaining to your classmates how to do an activity that you do well. Tell what materials are needed. Then describe each step, using sequence words. Remember that each paragraph should have a topic sentence and details.

Strategies Good Writers Use
- Decide on your purpose and audience.
- Brainstorm the steps that are needed to do something.

MODEL

Mario began by thinking of things he enjoys doing. He decided to tell how to put a puzzle together. He made this flowchart to organize his ideas:

How-to Topic: Putting a Puzzle Together

1. Find all the pieces with straight edges.

2. Sort the rest of the pieces by color.

3. Connect the pieces with straight edges.

4. Connect pieces with common colors for the inside.

YOUR TURN

Choose an activity that you do well. Use a flowchart to organize the steps needed to do the activity.

148

Vocabulary Power page 34

Name _____

CONTEXT CLUES

Read each sentence, paying attention to the underlined word. Then answer the question about that word.
Responses will vary. Accept reasonable responses.

1. John's mom asked him to assist her with the dishes. What are some things you assist your family with?

2. The coach told us teamwork would help us win the game. What are some sports or games where teamwork is used?

3. The teacher gave each student a partner to do the project with. How can having a partner be helpful?

4. Emily is going to cooperate with Anne to write a story. What does cooperate mean?

5. Our teacher said our class will collaborate with the other third grade class to put on a play. What are some other projects you could collaborate on?

34   Unit 2 • Chapter 12   Vocabulary Power

Interactive Writing

You may want to prewrite and write a first draft as a group. Draw students' attention to the Strategies Good Writers Use. Have students help you complete a prewriting flowchart including all the steps in the activity. Then use the Drafting Transparency with students, coaching them to use effective organization and elaboration.

Organization and Elaboration

Follow these steps to help you draft your essay:

STEP 1 List Materials

List all the materials needed to complete the activity.

STEP 2 Describe Each Step

Give the steps to follow in order.

STEP 3 Use Sequence Words

Use details and words such as *first*, *next*, and *last* to help your readers follow the steps.

MODEL

Read the beginning of Mario's essay. What does he think about the activity he is describing?

> Putting a puzzle together can be a challenge, but when you are done, the reward is a great picture. Here are some steps that can help you when you put a puzzle together.
>
> You will need to find a large table. Spread out all the puzzle pieces on the table with the color side up.

YOUR TURN

Follow the steps above to write your draft. Look at the ideas on your flowchart from prewriting. Use Mario's how-to essay as a model.

Strategies Good Writers Use

- List all the materials needed.
- Use a signal/sequence word with each step.
- Use details that help describe each step.

You may want to use a computer to write your draft. Then you can type over words you want to change.

149

Drafting

OBJECTIVES
- To learn strategies for drafting a how-to essay
- To draft a how-to essay

DAILY LANGUAGE PRACTICE

TRANSPARENCY 25

① once we had to choose a class project but we could not make a decision (Once; project,; decision.)

② paul and I have good ideas. (Paul)

ORAL WARM-UP

USE PRIOR KNOWLEDGE Call on volunteers to tell about times when they have helped plan a project, a family outing, or another event. Discuss how planning helped make the event a success. Then point out that writers use prewriting to help them plan their writing.

GUIDED WRITING

Discuss the points in Strategies Good Writers Use, Organization and Elaboration, and the model. Ask volunteers to answer the question that precedes the model. (Mario thinks that putting a puzzle together can be a challenging but rewarding activity.)

As students draft their essays, remind them to include information from their prewriting flowcharts. Suggest to students that they number the steps to help keep them in order.

WRAP-UP/ASSESS

SUMMARIZE How does drafting help you put your ideas on paper?

Vocabulary Power page 35

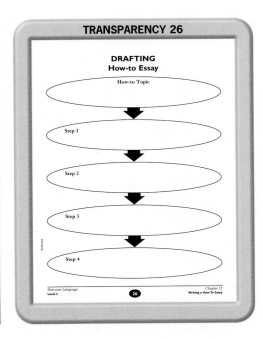

Name _____

ANALOGIES

An analogy shows how pairs of words go together.

Example:
A broom is used for sweeping; a cloth is used for dusting.
Broom is to *sweeping* as *cloth* is to *dusting*.

▶ Read each analogy below. Then choose a word from the Word Box to complete the analogy, and write it on the line.

| help | cutting | number | flies | low |

1. *Cooperate* is the opposite of *fight*; *high* is the opposite of ___low___.
2. An *instrument* is the same as a *device*; *assist* is the same as ___help___.
3. *Blue* is a color; *two* is a ___number___.
4. *Pencils* are used for *writing*; *scissors* are used for ___cutting___.
5. A *shark* swims; an *eagle* ___flies___.

▶ Now try these.

| flower | rock | drink | partner | talk |

6. *Running* is to *jogging* as *companion* is to ___partner___.
7. *Basketball* is to *game* as *daisy* is to ___flower___.
8. *Sandwich* is to *eat* as *water* is to ___drink___.
9. *Beach* is to *sand* as *mountain* is to ___rock___.
10. *Working together* is to *collaborate* as *speak* is to ___talk___.

Vocabulary Power   Unit 2 • Chapter 12 35

TRANSPARENCY 26

DRAFTING
How-to Essay

How-to Topic

↓

Step 1

↓

Step 2

↓

Step 3

↓

Step 4

Harcourt Language
Level 3
26
Chapter 12
Writing a How-To Essay

Revising

OBJECTIVES
- To learn strategies for revising a how-to essay
- To revise a how-to essay

DAILY LANGUAGE PRACTICE

TRANSPARENCY 25

1. we shared ideas about the plans as mr Cook instructed (We; Mr.; instructed.)

2. My plan sounded good but were too expensive. (was)

ORAL WARM-UP

USE PRIOR KNOWLEDGE Ask students to remember a time when they made a picture. Ask if they ever changed a picture after they thought it was done. Explain that revising an essay is similar: It is changing the original to make it better.

GUIDED WRITING

Discuss the Organization and Elaboration questions. Remind students to use these questions as they revise their drafts. Then discuss Mario's revision, pointing out the editing marks that he used to change his draft. Explain any marks that students don't understand.

Use **Transparencies 27a and 27b** to further model revising to add details and signal/sequence words. Then have students revise their drafts. They can keep their revisions in their working portfolios.

PEER CONFERENCES Have pairs of students use the **Evaluation Criteria** to evaluate their own and each other's writing, responding constructively by identifying strengths and suggesting improvements.

WRAP-UP/ASSESS

SUMMARIZE Ask: **What changes did you make to your draft? Which change improved it the most?**

CHAPTER 12
How-to Essay

Revising

Organization and Elaboration

Begin by carefully rereading your draft.

- How well have I organized the steps? Are any steps missing?
- What words did I use to make the order of the steps clear? Do I need to add a sequence word to any step?
- Have I used topic sentences and details?

Strategies Good Writers Use

- Add sequence words to make the order clear.
- Add details to make the information more interesting.
- Use topic sentences.

Save a copy of your first draft before you revise it. That way you can go back to your original if you don't like your revisions.

MODEL

Look at the changes Mario made to a part of his draft. Notice that he added sequence words to make the order of steps more clear. What other changes did he make? Were his changes helpful?

It is important to make sure none of the pieces of the puzzle are missing. First, Find all the pieces with straight edges. Those pieces will form the outside edge of the puzzle. Then, Sort the rest of the pieces by colors or images. For example, you may look for blue pieces for a blue sky or green pieces for green grass. Use the picture on the cover of the puzzle box as a guide.

YOUR TURN

Reread your how-to essay to see if the order of your steps makes sense. Check that you used signal/sequence words.

150

TRANSPARENCIES 27a and 27b

REVISING

It is important to make sure none of the pieces of the puzzle are missing. First, Find all the pieces with straight edges. Those pieces will form the outside edge of the puzzle. Then, Sort the rest of the pieces by colors or images. For example, you may look for blue pieces for a blue sky or green pieces for green grass. Use the picture on the cover of the puzzle box as a guide.

Harcourt Language
Level 3   27   Chapter 12
                                        Writing a How-To Essay

---

Vocabulary Power page 36

Name _____

COMPOUND WORDS

A compound word is two words put together to form a new word. Read the compound word in Column A. Then use the beginning word in each compound word to form a new word in Column B. Responses will vary. Possible responses are given.
Example:

Column A	Column B
teamwork	teammate
1. sunrise	sun set
2. bookcase	book shelf
3. outdoors	out side
4. everyone	every where
5. footstep	foot print
6. notepad	note book
7. campfire	camp site
8. overdone	over worked
9. fireplace	fire fighter
10. doorstep	door way
11. upstairs	up hill
12. anyone	any where
13. heartbeat	heart break
14. headline	head light

36   Unit 2 • Chapter 12   Vocabulary Power

Checking Your Language

It is important to proofread your writing for mistakes in grammar, spelling, punctuation, and capitalization. Mistakes may make it hard for your readers to understand your steps.

MODEL

Mario revised his essay. Then he proofread it. Look at another part of his essay. Notice how he corrected spelling mistakes. What grammar mistake did he correct? What other mistakes did he correct?

> ^Next^ Now, begin putting the edge of the puzzle together, (conecting) *connecting* the peices with (straite) *straight* edges. it may take several (trys) *tries* to find which pieces go together, but don't give up. Soon the outer edge of the puzzle will be put together.

YOUR TURN

Proofread your revised how-to essay. Read it three times:

- **The first time, check your spelling.**
- **Next, check for grammar mistakes.**
- **Last, check for mistakes in capitalization and punctuation.**

Strategies Good Writers Use

- Check for the correct forms of verbs.
- Use a dictionary to check the spelling of hard words.
- Check that each sentence begins with a capital letter.
- Be sure each sentence ends with a punctuation mark.

Editor's Marks

℘	delete text
∧	insert text
◯	move text
¶	new paragraph
≡	capitalize
/	lowercase
◯	correct spelling

151

MAKE A CHECKLIST Have students begin a proofreading checklist. Under the headings *Spelling, Punctuation,* and *Grammar,* have students list the corrections to errors they found in their writing. Have students use and add to this checklist throughout the year.

TRANSPARENCIES 28a and 28b

PROOFREADING

> ^Next^ Now, begin putting the edge of the puzzle together, (conecting) *connecting* the peices with (straite) *straight* edges. it may take several (trys) *tries* to find which pieces go together, but don't give up. Soon the outer edge of the puzzle will be put together.

Harcourt Language
Level 3

28a

Chapter 12
How-to Essay

Proofreading

OBJECTIVES

- To learn strategies for proofreading a how-to essay
- To proofread a how-to essay

DAILY LANGUAGE PRACTICE

TRANSPARENCY 25

1 We voted on the ideas friday morning (Friday morning.)

2 Do you know which idea we chose (chose?)

ORAL WARM-UP

USE PRIOR KNOWLEDGE Ask students to define *proofreading* in their own words. (Possible response: Proofreading is looking at a piece of writing for possible mistakes in spelling, punctuation, capitalization, and grammar.) Share with students a time when you found an error while proofreading something that you wrote. Call on volunteers to share similar experiences.

GUIDED WRITING

Read through the model, asking students to explain why Mario made each correction. Point out that Mario probably read through this draft several times, looking for a different kind of error each time. Use **Transparencies 28a and 28b** to model proofreading for spelling errors. Then have students proofread their essays. Tell them to proofread several times and to focus on a specific type of error each time.

WRAP-UP/ASSESS

SUMMARIZE What kinds of mistakes should you look for the first time you proofread? The next time? The last time?

Visit The Learning Site!
www.harcourtschool.com

Publishing

OBJECTIVES
- To learn strategies for publishing a how-to essay as an oral presentation
- To publish a how-to essay as an oral presentation

ORAL WARM-UP

USE PRIOR KNOWLEDGE Model different ways to give directions or to tell how to do something. As you speak, demonstrate the use of exaggerated tones to convey feeling angry, timid, calm, hurried, and so on. Ask students which delivery sounds most effective to them. Have students explain their answers.

GUIDED WRITING

SHARING YOUR WORK Read and discuss the questions with students. Help them decide where and how to publish their how-to essays.

If computers are available, have students make a problem-solving checklist. Ask students to use different fonts, colors, and graphics to make their checklists appealing.

REFLECTING ON YOUR WRITING Use the Portfolio Conference suggestions at right.

INTERNET Activities and exercises to help students prepare for state and standardized assessments appear on *The Learning Site:*

www.harcourtschool.com

Sharing Your Work

Now you will share your essay. Use the following questions to help you decide how to publish it:

1. Who is your audience?

2. Should you type your essay on a computer or write it by hand? Should you write in manuscript or cursive? Think about which form would be the best one for your audience.

3. Should you present your essay orally? To give an oral presentation, follow the steps on page 153.

USING YOUR
Handbook

- Use the rubric on page 497 to evaluate your paragraph.

Reflecting on Your Writing

 Using Your Portfolio Think about what you learned about writing from this chapter. Write your answer to each of these questions in your portfolio:

1. Which stage of writing did you do the best: prewriting, drafting, or revising? Explain why. Which stage was the most difficult? Why?

2. Using the rubric from your Handbook, how would you score your own writing? Explain your answer.

Add your answers and your essay to your portfolio. Then look at the writing in your portfolio. Which piece is your best writing? Tell why you think so.

152

Assessment
. . . .

PORTFOLIO CONFERENCES
Discuss the questions in the *Pupil Edition,* and direct students to write their answers and add them to their portfolios. Tell students you will meet with them individually to discuss their growth as writers. Use the Student Record Form on page R74 to record and monitor students' progress.

Handwriting
. . . .

Point out to students that using correct posture and writing grip can help them improve their penmanship. Demonstrate each tip:

- **Posture** Sit up straight with both feet on the floor.

- **Writing Grip** Hold your pencil between your thumb and pointer finger about an inch from the point.

Then ask students to use these tips as they publish their essays.

Making an Oral Presentation

Mario decided to share his how-to essay with his classmates in an oral presentation. You can also present your how-to essay orally. Follow these steps:

STEP 1 Write on note cards in big print
- the materials needed.
- the steps in order.
- the reason to do the activity.

STEP 2 When you speak, use your notes, but look at the audience some of the time. Looking at your audience will help keep them interested in your presentation.

STEP 3 Speak in a loud, clear voice so that everyone can hear and understand you.

STEP 4 After you finish, ask if anyone has questions about your how-to essay. Then answer your classmates' questions.

153

LISTENING AND SPEAKING
Making an Oral Presentation

Encourage students to practice their oral presentations several times before delivering them. Suggest that they practice before a group of friends, make the presentation in front of a mirror, or record it on videotape. Advise students that even if they do not use many gestures and facial expressions (as they might when telling a story), they will want to look interested in sharing their ideas.

Remind students that when they are listening to classmates' presentations, they should be quiet and pay attention. Explain that when the speaker finishes, they should ask questions about anything that is unclear. Use the Student Record Form on page R76 to assess students' listening and speaking skills.

WRAP-UP/ASSESS

SUMMARIZE Think about a classmate's presentation that you enjoyed. What did you like most about it?

SCORING RUBRIC

4 ADVANCED	**3 PROFICIENT**	**2 BASIC**	**1 LIMITED**
Purpose and Audience • appropriate for audience • stays focused on purpose	**Purpose and Audience** • mostly appropriate for audience • few deviations from purpose	**Purpose and Audience** • not appropriate for audience • often strays from purpose	**Purpose and Audience** • not appropriate for audience • purpose is unclear
Organization and Elaboration • clear beginning and an ending that summarizes or draws a conclusion • middle has steps in logical order • description or details • interesting words and phrases • sentence variety	**Organization and Elaboration** • clear beginning and an ending that summarizes or draws a conclusion • steps in middle not in order • some description or details • some interesting words or phrases • some sentence variety	**Organization and Elaboration** • beginning and ending not clear • directions in middle not all on same topic • few details and description • few interesting words or phrases • little sentence variety	**Organization and Elaboration** • no introduction or conclusion • directions on different topics • no description or details • no interesting words or phrases • most sentences written incorrectly
Language • uses correct grammar • uses correct spelling, usage, and mechanics	**Language** • uses mostly correct grammar • uses mostly correct spelling, usage, and mechanics	**Language** • incorrect grammar, spelling, or mechanics sometimes makes writing unclear	**Language** • incorrect grammar, spelling, or mechanics often makes writing unclear

For information on adapting this rubric to 5- or 6-point scales, see pages R78–R79.

Unit 2
Grammar Review

CHAPTER 7

More About Nouns

OBJECTIVES
- To identify nouns in sentences
- To identify proper nouns and use appropriate capitalization
- To write abbreviations correctly

Unit Review
MODIFIED INSTRUCTION

BELOW-LEVEL STUDENTS Before students begin Part B, write these sentences on the board for reference:

There is a girl named Rita.

This street is named Oak Street.

It leads to a park called Green Tree Park.

Point out that each of these sentences contains a common noun followed by a proper noun. Advise students to use these sentences as a check after they complete each item.

ABOVE-LEVEL STUDENTS After students have completed Part C, suggest that they look up a variety of measurements and make a chart of the words and their abbreviations.

Unit 2
Grammar Review
CHAPTER 7
More About Nouns
pages 92–101

Nouns   *pages 92–93*

A. Write each sentence. Then underline the nouns in each.

1. My sister made a salad.
2. My friend asked her mother to cut the vegetables.
3. Children are not supposed to use sharp knives.
4. Some dressing spilled on the floor.
5. My father cleaned up the dressing so that we would not slip.

Common and Proper Nouns   *pages 94–95*

B. Write each sentence. Capitalize each proper noun.

6. The moreno family is planning a trip to san diego.   Moreno, San Diego
7. carlos will ask his mother to help him pack.   Carlos
8. rita and carlos will ride in the back seat of the car.   Rita, Car
9. Their dog, happy, will stay home.   Happy
10. They're going to visit the san diego zoo.   San Diego Zoo

Abbreviations and Titles   *pages 96–97*

C. Write the abbreviation for the underlined word.

11. (a man) Wu believes in being careful.   Mr.
12. He has a pool behind his house on Maple Street.   St.
13. Next Wednesday he will build a fence around his pool.   Wed.
14. The fence will be six feet high.   ft.
15. It will be finished before his son's party on September 1.   Sept.

154

HANDS ON Activity

ABBREVIATION MEMORY Make two sets of index cards—one containing words that are often abbreviated and another containing the corresponding abbreviations. (The first category may include proper nouns, such as *Jackson Avenue* and *Saturday,* as well as common nouns, such as *inch.*) Mix the cards and place them face down on a table. Have students play "Memory," matching a word with its abbreviation.

Singular and Plural Nouns

pages 102–103

A. Write the common and proper nouns in each sentence. Then write whether each noun is singular or plural.

1. On some mornings Joyce wants doughnuts.
   mornings, plural; Joyce, singular; doughnuts, plural
2. Her parents say cereal is more healthful.
   parents, plural; cereal, singular
3. My brother likes eggs. brother, singular; eggs, plural
4. He eats two pieces of whole wheat toast.
   pieces, plural; toast, singular
5. He also likes fresh apples in the morning.
   apples, plural; morning, singular

Plural Nouns with *es* and *ies*

pages 104–105

B. Write the plural form of each noun in parentheses ( ).

6. Stella likes fruit in her (lunch). lunches
7. Sometimes she brings (bunch) of grapes. bunches
8. On other days she eats a handful of (cherry). cherries
9. She and Pablo ate two (box) of (berry). boxes, berries
10. She gave him some of her (peach). peaches

Nouns with Irregular Plurals

pages 106–107

C. Write the plural form of each noun in parentheses ( ).

11. Ahmed caught five (trout) for dinner. trout
12. Max cooked mutton, which comes from (sheep). sheep
13. Uncle Victor cooked three (salmon) last week. salmon
14. The two (woman) at the fish market sold us some tuna. women
15. The (child) in my family like meat and fish. children

155

Unit 2
Grammar Review

CHAPTER 8

Singular and Plural Nouns

OBJECTIVES
- To recognize and distinguish between singular and plural nouns
- To form regular and irregular plural nouns correctly

Unit Review
MODIFIED INSTRUCTION

BELOW-LEVEL STUDENTS Suggest that students check for a plural noun by trying to count. You may model this using the following examples:

Two oranges, three oranges. Oranges names things that can be counted, so it is a plural noun.

Two asks, three asks. Asks does not name things that can be counted. It is not a plural noun.

ABOVE-LEVEL STUDENTS Suggest that students list as many nouns ending in *y* as possible. Have them list in one column the ones that form plurals by changing the *y* to *i* and adding *es*. In the other column, have them list the ones that form the plural by adding *s*. Post the lists in the classroom for reference.

TEST PREP

TIP

Inform students that if the directions tell them to focus on the words in parentheses, they should look at a few examples before they start working. Sometimes (as is true in Parts B and C) you can ignore the rest of the sentence. Other times, however, the rest of the sentence is very important.

Unit 2
Grammar Review

CHAPTER 10

Possessive Nouns

OBJECTIVES
- To write singular possessive nouns correctly
- To write plural possessive nouns correctly
- To revise sentences to include possessive nouns

Unit Review
MODIFIED INSTRUCTION

BELOW-LEVEL STUDENTS As students begin Part C, advise them to ask *Who or what owns something in this sentence?* When students have identified the appropriate noun, remind them that they must determine whether it is singular or plural before they write its possessive form. You may wish to model sentence 11 as an example.

ABOVE-LEVEL STUDENTS When students have completed this page, refer them to the Unit Review for Chapter 8, Part C. Challenge them to write sentences that use the possessive forms of these irregular plural nouns.

Unit 2
Grammar Review

CHAPTER 10

Possessive Nouns
pages 120–129

Singular Possessive Nouns *pages 120–121*

A. Write the possessive form of each underlined singular noun.

1. Eric listens to his <u>mother</u> words. mother's
2. She cares about <u>Eric</u> health. Eric's
3. Eric looks at the cans on the <u>store</u> shelves. store's
4. Eric reads a soup <u>can</u> label. can's
5. All the <u>soup</u> contents are listed on the label. soup's

Plural Possessive Nouns *pages 122–123*

B. Write the possessive form of each underlined plural noun.

6. Learning to read is part of all <u>students</u> education. students'
7. It's important to read all <u>products</u> labels. products'
8. Labels tell how well a food meets our <u>bodies</u> needs. bodies'
9. It is the food <u>companies</u> job to label their products. companies'
10. Labels also warn buyers about <u>foods</u> bad effects. foods'

Revising Sentences Using Possessive Nouns *pages 124–125*

C. Rewrite each sentence, using a possessive noun.

11. Jo looked at the lunches belonging to her two friends. Jo looked at her two friends' lunches.
12. The lunch of Ali looked healthful. Ali's lunch looked healthful.
13. The lunch of another girl was full of raw vegetables. Another girl's lunch was full of raw vegetables.
14. The lunch belonging to Jo contained two packages of snacks. Jo's lunch contained two packages of snacks.
15. The labels of the two packages showed that the snacks were healthful. The two packages' labels showed that the snacks were healthful.

156

HANDS ON Activity

PLURALS AND POSSESSIVE
On twenty cards, write plural nouns such as *bears, students, women,* and *musicians.* For each plural noun, write a singular possessive form of the noun on another card (such as *bear's, student's, woman's,* and *musician's*). Mix the cards up, and have students work individually or in groups to sort the words into cans or boxes marked PLURAL NOUNS and POSSESSIVE NOUNS.

Unit 2
Grammar Review
CHAPTER 11

Action Verbs
and the Verb *Be*
pages 130–139

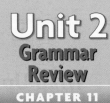

Verbs *pages 130–131*

A. Write each sentence. Underline the verb in each sentence.

1. Marta <u>stays</u> home from school.
2. She <u>protects</u> her classmates from her flu germs.
3. Sometimes she <u>catches</u> colds at school.
4. Her mother <u>warns</u> her about germs.
5. Marta's family <u>cares</u> for her.

Action Verbs *pages 132–133*

B. Write each sentence. Underline the action verb in each sentence.

6. Marta <u>eats</u> a good breakfast.
7. She <u>dresses</u> for school.
8. Her mother <u>hands</u> her warm clothes.
9. Usually Marta <u>walks</u> to school.
10. Today her father <u>drives</u> her.

The Verb *Be* *pages 134–135*

C. For each sentence, choose the correct form of the verb *be* in parentheses ( ). Write each sentence.

11. Len (is, are) nice and warm. is
12. I (is, am) taking care of him. am
13. He (is, am) almost over the flu. is
14. You (am, are) nice to bring him his homework. are
15. We (is, are) very thankful. are

Activities and exercises to help students prepare for state and standardized assessments appear on our website.

Visit
The Learning Site!
www.harcourtschool.com

Unit 2
Grammar Review
CHAPTER 11

Action Verbs
and the Verb *Be*

OBJECTIVES
- To identify verbs in sentences
- To identify action verbs in sentences
- To use correct subject-verb agreement

Unit Review
MODIFIED INSTRUCTION

BELOW-LEVEL STUDENTS As students begin Part C, you might suggest that they try each word in parentheses to decide which one sounds correct. Caution students, however, to check their answers by remembering that *am* is used only with the subject *I*, that *is* is used with other singular subjects, and that *are* is used with plural subjects.

ABOVE-LEVEL STUDENTS After students have completed Part C, have them rewrite sentences 11-15, changing plural subjects to singular and singular subjects to plural and choosing the correct form of *be* for the new subject.

Assessment

SKILLS ASSESSMENT Use the **Language Skills and Writing Assessment** to assess the grammar and writing skills taught in this unit. Model papers are included.

PORTFOLIO ASSESSMENT
Schedule portfolio conferences with individual students while others are completing the Unit Review exercises. Have students complete the Self-Assessment Checklist on page R87 and place it in their Show Portfolios. Use the Student Record Form on page R77 to monitor student progress. 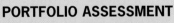 TEKS 3.19E

You Are What You Eat

OBJECTIVES

- To create a chart showing a record of foods eaten during one week, and to evaluate the healthfulness of those foods

- To write a report discussing ways to improve choice of foods

INTRODUCE THE PROJECT

USE PRIOR KNOWLEDGE Read the introduction aloud to students. Ask volunteers to tell what they know about healthful eating. Review the Food Pyramid with students. Have students consider how keeping track of what they eat may help them become more aware of their eating choices.

Writer's Journal

GENERATE QUESTIONS Have students write questions in their journals about the foods they eat. Prompt them to consider the nutritional value of various foods, as well as the importance of variety in a healthful diet.

Make a Menu Calendar

Draw a model menu calendar on the board or post one in the classroom. Show students how to record the food they eat in each of the four sections. Then provide materials to help students create their own calendars. Have students start the calendar with tomorrow's date.

Watch What You Eat

Help students research foods. Put books on reserve in the library and provide other resources in your classroom. If computers are available, visit websites that are designed for children about nutrition.

You Are What You Eat

What foods do you eat every day? Could your diet be more healthful? Here are some steps to help you decide.

Make a Menu Calendar

- Make a calendar of the next seven days. Start with tomorrow.

- Divide each day into four sections.

- Label the sections *Breakfast, Lunch, Dinner,* and *Snacks.*

Watch What You Eat

- Beginning tomorrow, notice what foods you eat.

- Write the foods in the right sections of your chart.

- Go to the school library to research the foods you ate.

Revise Your Menu Calendar

- Study your chart and circle the healthful foods. Draw a line through the foods that are not.

- List on your menu calendar healthful foods that you could have eaten. Put them next to the foods you crossed out.

- Add to your menu calendar healthful foods that you plan to eat.

158

Listening and Speaking

After three days, divide the class into groups and have students list the foods they have eaten every day so far. Group members should listen to one another's lists to find out whether there is a food that everyone in the group eats daily. Ask students to discuss why everyone eats that particular food.

Report on Your Diet

- Use your menu calendar to prepare a report. How can you make your diet more healthful?

- Decorate your menu calendar. Draw pictures of foods you want to add to your diet.

- Share your report and menu calendar with your classmates.

Revise Your Menu Calendar

To help students know what to circle, review how various foods help bodies grow strong and how others are less useful. Discuss vitamins and other nutrients that are found in different foods. Write food categories on the board and list examples of foods that belong to each category.

Report on Your Diet

Remind students that each paragraph should have a topic sentence that is supported with details. Students should use notes from their researched material to help them form conclusions about healthful foods. Have students analyze their menus and record their reflections. Students may also wish to add healthful recipes to their menu calendars.

STUDENT SELF-ASSESSMENT

Have students evaluate their own research and raise new questions for further investigation.

Books to Read Students who enjoyed researching foods might be interested in reading one or more of these books. Have them record reflections on the book or books in their journals. Then ask students to recommend to the class the book from this list that they enjoyed most.

School-Home Connection

Families can contribute to this project by working together to plan healthful menus. Have students share their calendars and reports with family members. Encourage them to work with their families to plan healthful meals and snacks. Tell students to write a brief report about any changes their families made.

ESL

SHARE HEALTHFUL FOODS
Students can describe how to prepare a simple, healthful meal that is part of their tradition or culture. Encourage students to bring props to class and act out preparing the meal. Have them explain each step. Encourage students to describe the foods and in what categories they belong in the Food Pyramid.

Sentences

OBJECTIVES
- To identify the four kinds of sentences
- To identify complete and simple subjects and predicates
- To identify simple and compound sentences

Use the Cumulative Review to assess students' continued mastery of language concepts and skills presented in Units 1–2. Refer to the pages listed after each section title to review any concepts and skills students have not mastered.

UNIT 1 REVIEW

Have students complete the exercises, or modify them using these suggestions:

MODIFIED INSTRUCTION

BELOW-LEVEL STUDENTS Before students begin exercises 11–15, point out that compound sentences will have a comma followed by the combining words *and, but,* or *or*. Sentences without commas and those joining words will be simple sentences.

ABOVE-LEVEL STUDENTS After students have completed exercises 11–15, ask whether they can figure out how to rewrite sentence 13 as a simple sentence without losing any of the meaning.

Sentences *pages 24–27*

Write each sentence. Label it *statement, command, question,* or *exclamation*.

1. The Oakwood School band has many instruments. statement
2. Have you ever heard a piccolo? question
3. How heavy the tuba is! exclamation
4. Don't drop the drum. command
5. All the students want to play in the band. statement

Subjects and Predicates

pages 34–37, 52–55

Write each sentence. Draw one line under the complete subject and two lines under the complete predicate. Circle the simple subject and the simple predicate.

6. A children's book (writer)(visited) our school.
7. The (writer)(read) her picture books to us.
8. Our (class)(looked) at all her different books.
9. The (author)(wrote) on many different subjects.
10. The (audience)(asked) the writer a lot of questions.

Simple and Compound Sentences *pages 64–65*

Write each sentence. If the sentence is a simple sentence, write *simple sentence* after it. If it is a compound sentence, write the word that joins the two simple sentences.

11. The city built a new park near our house. simple sentence
12. The park is small, but it is really beautiful. but
13. It has jogging paths, and it has a little pond. and
14. Fish and ducks swim in the pond. simple sentence
15. We can sail toy boats, or we can feed the ducks. or

160

HANDS ON Activity

SENTENCE FISH Write sentences without end marks on index cards, the correct end mark on a second card, and the type of sentence on a third card. Mix the cards and deal each player three cards. Have students take turns asking for the cards they need to create a three-card match. Players say "Go fish" if they don't have the card. The student then takes a card from the pile. The first student to show a match of sentence, type, and end mark wins.

Common and Proper Nouns

pages 92–95

Write each sentence. Underline the common nouns. Circle the proper nouns.

1. The swimmers learned about safety.
2. (Mr. Abernathy) taught the boys and girls to swim.
3. The lifeguards posted signs with rules on them.
4. (Carlos Diaz) was the lifeguard.
5. He saved a life last summer.

Possessive Nouns *pages 120–123*

Write the possessive noun or nouns in each sentence. Then write whether each possessive noun is *singular* or *plural*.

6. Clara's eyes were giving her trouble. Clara's, singular
7. She had trouble reading the teacher's writing on the board. teacher's, singular
8. Tests showed her eyes' weakness. eyes', plural
9. Her classmates' faces showed that they liked her glasses. classmates', plural
10. Tonya's glasses are smaller than Clara's glasses.
    Tonya's, singular; Clara's, singular

Action Verbs *pages 132–133*

Write the sentences. Underline the action verbs.

11. Some mosquitoes carry disease.
12. Ticks bite animals and people.
13. People get Lyme disease from ticks.
14. Lyme disease makes people tired.
15. Their muscles ache badly.

More About Nouns and Verbs

OBJECTIVES

- To identify and distinguish between common and proper nouns
- To identify and distinguish between singular and plural possessive nouns
- To identify action verbs

UNIT 2 REVIEW

Have students complete the exercises, or modify them using these suggestions:

MODIFIED INSTRUCTION

BELOW-LEVEL STUDENTS Before students begin exercises 6–10 remind them that a plural possessive noun is formed by adding an apostrophe to the end of a plural noun that ends with *s*.

ABOVE-LEVEL STUDENTS After students have completed exercises 1–5, challenge them to rewrite the sentences, substituting common nouns for proper nouns and vice versa. Then have them share and compare sentences.

HANDS ON Activity

NOUN ROUND-UP Set up four boxes and label them SINGULAR NOUNS, PLURAL NOUNS, SINGULAR POSSESSIVE NOUNS, and PLURAL POSSESSIVE NOUNS. Then make twenty-four word cards by writing six of each type of noun on a separate index card. Mix up the cards. Then have students sort the cards into the four boxes.

Cumulative Review
Units 1-2

Language Use

OBJECTIVES

- To recognize mistakes in punctuation, capitalization, and spelling
- To practice using standardized test format

STANDARDIZED TEST PREP

The format used on this page helps prepare students for standardized tests. Explain that most standardized tests have one or more sections that test language skills—grammar, usage, capitalization, and punctuation. Have students read the directions on page 162 silently and work to complete the test items independently. When students have finished, invite them to discuss these questions:

1. **How well did you understand the directions?**

2. **Which answers were you unsure of, and why?**

3. **How did you use the test-taking strategies you learned?**

Cumulative Review Units 1–2

Language Use

Read the passage, and decide which type of mistake, if any, appears in each underlined section. Mark the letter for your answer.

> Ms. hopkins, a nurse, spoke to our class about
> (1)
> nutrition. She knows a lot about childrens health. She
> (2)
> said that we should eat whole grains, drink lowfat
> (3)
> milk, and avoid sugary snacks. Even peanut butter
> (4)
> sandwichs can be good for you? She brought us some
> (5)
> whole-wheat crackers to try and they were delicious.
> (6)

1 A Spelling
   B Capitalization B
   C Punctuation
   D No mistake

2 F Spelling
   G Capitalization
   H Punctuation H
   J No mistake

3 A Spelling
   B Capitalization
   C Punctuation
   D No mistake D

4 F Spelling F
   G Capitalization
   H Punctuation
   J No mistake

5 A Spelling
   B Capitalization
   C Punctuation C
   D No mistake

6 F Spelling
   G Capitalization
   H Punctuation H
   J No mistake

162

TEST PREP

TIP

If students are taking a test on punctuating sentences, remind them that writers use punctuation to help readers better understand the meaning of their words. Suggest that students read each sentence softly to themselves to determine which answer sounds the best before making their final choices.

Written Expression

Use this paragraph to answer questions 1–4.

Before you begin to jog, you should stretch gently for several minutes. Increase your jogging speed and your time gradually. You should be able to speak while jogging. If you cannot speak, you are going too fast. Some people don't like to jog. First, be sure your shoes fit comfortably.

1 Choose the best opening sentence for this paragraph.

A You should begin a jogging program slowly. A

B Never jog alone at night.

C I used to jog, but now I walk instead.

D Joggers sometimes suffer from shin splints.

2 Which sentence should be left out of this paragraph?

F You should be able to speak while jogging.

G If you cannot speak, you are going too fast.

H Some people don't like to jog. H

J First, be sure your shoes fit comfortably.

3 Where should the last sentence in the paragraph be?

A Where it is now

B Before sentence 1 B

C Between sentences 4 and 5

D Between sentences 5 and 6

4 Choose the best closing sentence for the paragraph.

F Be careful when you are crossing streets.

G If you use caution, jogging can be good exercise. G

H You can also jog on a treadmill.

J People jog in all sorts of weather.

163

Cumulative Review
Units 1-2

Written Expression

OBJECTIVES

- To identify the purpose of a passage
- To choose the best order of sentences in a paragraph
- To practice using standardized test format

STANDARDIZED TEST PREP

Explain that some standardized tests include a section that tests written expression. The test items may not include actual errors. Many items ask for the *best or most appropriate way* to express or organize ideas.

Have students read the directions on page 163 silently and complete the test items independently. When students have finished, invite them to discuss their answer choices. If there is disagreement about an answer choice, have volunteers explain their thinking.

Assessment Strategies and Resources

FORMAL ASSESSMENT

If you want to know more about a student's mastery of the language and writing skills taught in Unit 2, **then** administer the first *Language Skills and Writing Assessment* for Unit 2. The test consists of two parts:

Language Skills: **common and proper nouns, singular and plural nouns, possessive nouns, action verbs and the verb** *be,* **and paragraphing.**

Writing Task: write a **how-to essay**. Scoring guidelines and model student papers are included.

INFORMAL ASSESSMENT TOOLS

Using Portfolio Conferences

If you want to learn more about individual students' writing and language skills development, **then** schedule **portfolio conferences** on a regular basis throughout the year.

Prepare by asking the student to select several pieces of writing that he or she especially likes. Explain that you will also select pieces that you think represent the student's best work. In addition to discussing why each of you chose the pieces you did, ask which activities the student found most and least challenging and enjoyable. Point out improvements in recent work.

Conclude the portfolio conference by writing a brief summary noting specific areas of progress and plans for further improvement. Add the summary to the student's portfolio so you can refer to it at your next conference. Use the Student Record Form on page R74 to monitor students' progress and record your notes about their portfolios.

Informal Assessment Reminder

If you used the preinstruction writing prompt suggested in Teaching Grammar from Writing, **then** remember to compare the results with the writing done by students after the grammar and writing instruction.

Vote for
José Lopez
for
Class President

Election Day
is
November 14.

	Introducing the Unit, pp. 164–165		
Chapters	**Grammar**	**Writing**	**Listening/ Speaking/Viewing**
13 **Main Verbs and Helping Verbs** pp. 166–175	**Main Verbs and Helping Verbs** **More About Helping Verbs** **Usage and Mechanics:** **Contractions with *Not*** Extra Practice, Chapter Review, Daily Language Practice, Additional Practice: p. 462	**Writing Connections** Social Studies Vivid Verbs Reflecting on Writing Make a Poster	**Activities** Building Oral Grammar Summarize
14 **Present-Tense Verbs** pp. 176–185	**Verb Tenses** **Present-Tense Verbs** **Usage and Mechanics:** **Subject-Verb Agreement** Extra Practice, Chapter Review, Daily Language Practice, Additional Practice: p. 463	**Writing Connections** Writing Idea Giving Reasons Announcement Technology	**Activities** Challenge: Collage **Listening and Speaking:** Make a Speech Make a Poster Building Oral Grammar Summarize
15 **Writer's Craft: Word Choice** pp. 186–193	**Daily Language Practice** **Hands-on Activities**	**Friendly Letter** Prewriting and Drafting Editing Sharing and Reflecting	**Activities** Analyze Persuasive Writing Read and Respond to the Model **Listening and Speaking:** Here's My Side Art Mobiles **Listening and Speaking:** Oral Invitation Summarize
16 **Past-Tense and Future-Tense Verbs** pp. 194–203	**Past-Tense and Future-Tense Verbs** **More About Past-Tense and Future-Tense Verbs** **Usage and Mechanics:** **Choosing the Correct Tense** Extra Practice, Chapter Review, Daily Language Practice, Additional Practice: p. 464	**Writing Connections** Thinking About Quotations Using Powerful Words Technology Writing a Want Ad	**Activities** ESL: Work with a Partner Branches of the Government Challenge: Discuss Issues **Listening and Speaking:** Listening for Facts and Opinions Building Oral Grammar Summarize
17 **Irregular Verbs** pp. 204–213	**Irregular Verbs** **More Irregular Verbs** **Usage and Mechanics: Commonly Misused Irregular Verbs** Extra Practice, Chapter Review, Daily Language Practice, Additional Practice: p. 465	**Writing Connections:** Art Interview Choosing a Form Social Studies	**Activities** **Writing Connections:** Interview Challenge: Verb Tag Challenge: Back Out Building Oral Grammar Summarize
18 **Writing Workshop: Persuasive Paragraph** pp. 214–225	**Unit 3 Grammar Review** **Daily Language Practice**	**Persuasive Paragraph** Prewriting Drafting Revising Proofreading Publishing Writer's Craft: Word Choice	**Activities** Reading Like a Writer Read and Respond to the Model **Listening and Speaking:** Read Aloud ESL: Practice Public Speaking **Listening and Speaking:** Making an Oral Presentation Summarize

Unit Wrap-Up   Writing Across the Curriculum: Social Studies, pp. 230–231

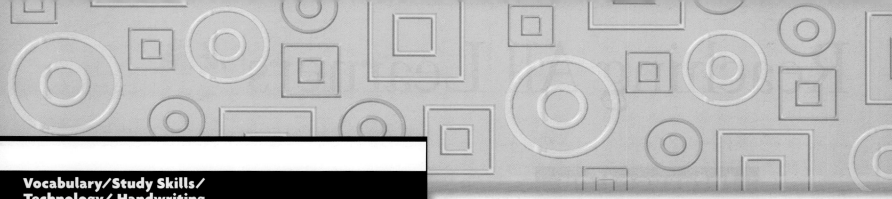

Vocabulary/Study Skills/ Technology/ Handwriting

Vocabulary Power

Words of the Week: *beliefs, ceremonies, customs, practices,* ***traditions***
Technology: Pinky Power
Challenge: Dictionary Skills
Study Skills: Using a Dictionary

Vocabulary Power

Words of the Week: *apply, enlist, enroll,* ***register,*** *request*
Challenge: Learning New Words
Writing Connection: Technology
Vocabulary: Prefixes and Suffixes

Vocabulary Power

Words of the Week: ***advertisements,*** *billboard, bulletin, logo, slogan*
Vocabulary: General and Specific Nouns
Challenge: Letters to the Editor
ESL: Sort It Out

Vocabulary Power

Words of the Week: *democracy,* ***federal,*** *government, monarchy, republic*
Writing Connections: Technology

Vocabulary Power

Words of the Week: ***community,*** *neighborhood, population, settlement, social*
ESL: Memory Joggers
Challenge: Similar Opposites
Study Skills: Using a Thesaurus

Vocabulary Power

Words of the Week: ***confidence,*** *dignity, haughty, secure, vain*
ESL: Practice Public Speaking

Language Minutes

- **Write** sentences about things that you cannot see or do at night or during a storm. Use **contractions** in your sentences. WRITING

- **Write** sentences about your favorite book or story. Use vivid **verbs** and specific **nouns** to **tell** about the characters and story events. WRITING

- **Draw** a picture of a park or building that you have visited. **Tell** a friend about what you saw and did there. Use past tense verbs in your sentences. VIEWING/SPEAKING

- **Imagine** that you will visit a zoo. **Write** sentences about what you would like to see and do there. Use future tense verbs. WRITING

- **Read** about a famous person in history in a social studies text. **List** any irregular verbs that you find. WRITING

Technology — Resources

. . . .

Grammar Jingles™ **CD**
Grammar Practice and Assessment **CD-ROM**
Writing Express **CD-ROM**
Media Literacy and Communication Skills **Package**
Visit *The Learning Site!*
  www.harcourtschool.com

Reaching All Learners

Intervention

PROVIDING ALTERNATIVES As you plan assignments, think ahead to identify students who are likely to have difficulty. Consider alternative methods that best suit those students and the particular assignment you have in mind.

- Give students additional time.

- Shorten the assignment by picking out only the most important items or pages.

- Provide an alternative assignment with a lower level of difficulty.

- Have students work with a study buddy or in a cooperative group.

- Allow for alternative responses, such as oral responses for students who have difficulty writing.

English as a Second Language

TOTAL PHYSICAL RESPONSE Activities that call for whole-body responses build both vocabulary and confidence for students who speak little or no English. You can use TPR (Total Physical Response) activities to help students become familiar with subject-verb agreement and verb tenses.

- Model and then have students follow simple commands, such as "Stand up." Use gestures to help convey the meanings of sentences such as, "I stand," "She stands," and so on.

- Tell students, "I will sit." Sit down and say "I am sitting." Call on students by name, telling them to sit and then saying, "(Name) is sitting." Follow a similar procedure to aid familiarity with common past tense verbs.

Challenge

BILLBOARD In conjunction with teaching about persuasion and persuasive writing, designate an area of the classroom where students can create an advertising billboard. Students might write and illustrate an advertisement for an imaginary product or perhaps construct a message to persuade classmates to practice certain types of behavior, such as taking care of library materials or playing team sports. Encourage students to use their imaginations and creativity to produce a striking and effective billboard. Remind them to apply grammar skills they have learned.

Inclusion

CLASSROOM ORGANIZATION When you are setting up your classroom or making changes, take time to consider the placement and organization of furniture and other items from the point of view of special-needs students in your class.

- Eliminate clutter or crowded conditions that might hamper physically disabled students from moving easily about the room.

- Make sure that learning stations are accessible to all students. Place materials on low shelves where physically disabled or visually impaired students can locate them.

- Identify containers with braille labels or tactile materials to help visually impaired students identify them. Engage students in creating labels.

- If you make any changes or move items, help visually impaired students become familiar with the new arrangement.

Teaching Grammar from Writing

PRETEST

If you wish to use students' writing to diagnose their needs, use the following prompt.

WRITING PROMPT

Imagine that you have a pen pal who has never been to the city or town where you live. What might he or she enjoy seeing or doing in your home town? Write a paragraph that you might include in a letter to persuade your pen pal to come for a visit.

EVALUATE AND PLAN

Analyze students' writing to determine how you can best meet their individual needs for instruction. Use the following chart to identify and remedy problems.

COMMON PROBLEMS	CHAPTERS TO USE
Using helping verbs incorrectly	Chapter 13: Main Verbs and Helping Verbs
Forming contractions with *not* incorrectly	Chapter 13: Main Verbs and Helping Verbs
Using verbs that do not agree with subjects	Chapter 14: Present-Tense Verbs
Not using correct verb tenses	Chapter 16: Past-Tense and Future-Tense Verbs
Using incorrect past tenses for irregular verbs	Chapter 17: Irregular Verbs
Misusing the verbs *lie, lay, rise, raise, teach,* and *learn*	Chapter 17: Irregular Verbs
Not using vivid verbs or specific nouns or not using proper form for a friendly letter	Chapter 15: Writer's Craft: Word Choice
Difficulty with persuasive writing	Chapter 18: Writing a Persuasive Paragraph

Classroom Management

DURING...	SOME STUDENTS CAN...
Grammar Reteaching	Use the Challenge Activity cards. Work on the Writing Across the Curriculum project.
Independent Practice	Do activities described in Language Arts in the Classroom. Work on the Writing Connection.
Portfolio Conferences	Complete Student Self-Assessment forms. (See pages R86–R88 in this *Teacher's Edition*.) Meet in Literature Circles.

Drama

LANGUAGE ARTS IN THE CLASSROOM

Dramatic interpretation and creation helps learners stretch their boundaries and access hidden talents. Encourage students to explore the written word through frequent formal and informal performances.

COSTUMES AND PROPS Collect clothing and prop items with student help. For creating costumes, provide boxes of supplies such as feathers, artificial flowers, ribbons, bows, costume jewelry, scarves, construction and crepe paper, newspaper, safety pins, glue, scissors, and sewing supplies.

STAGE AREA The stage can be a large rug with a screen at the rear on which butcher paper is hung. Students create backdrops for their performances on the paper. This area doubles as rehearsal space.

PUPPETRY CORNER Help students construct a puppet stage using boxes, curtains, and a frame on which to hang a blanket to hide puppeteers from the audience. Keep supplies, such as socks, paper bags, felt, and other fabric, nearby for making puppets.

THEATER MARQUEE Use a bulletin board to post a schedule of student performances and to post pictures of students at rehearsal and in performance. Add a list of stage direction terms (*wings, stage left, stage right, up and down stage*) and a list of theater terms such as *skit, monologue, dialogue,* and *pantomime.*

THEATER GAMES AREA Provide a space for students to develop their acting skills by playing "theater games." Post a list of pretend characters, animals, and forces of nature (for example, wind, thunder, and ocean waves) to imitate. Start a file box of cards with characters, settings, and situations outlined. Include everyday situations, fairy tales, and familiar and unfamiliar stories. Invite a student to pick a card and then improvise a skit with a partner or a small group. Encourage cooperation and collaboration. These games may result in a skit, play, or puppet show for presentation.

Hands-on Activities

Matching Contractions

MATERIALS: a construction paper badge for each student, masking tape

DIRECTIONS:

1. On half the paper badges, write contractions with *not.* On the rest, write the word pairs from which the contractions were formed.

2. Divide students into two groups. One group tapes contraction badges to their clothing, while the other group wears the badges with word pairs.

3. Students read each other's badges and find partners by matching contractions with the words from which they were formed.

4. Have partners write a sentence using their word pair and then rewrite the sentence using the contraction.

Digger the Dog

MATERIALS: chart paper with list of verbs, paper, pencils

DIRECTIONS:

1. Have students work in small groups. Place a list of verbs on chart paper where students can see it.

2. Tell students to write brief stories about an imaginary dog named Digger, using present-tense forms of the verbs on the chart. They may use the verbs in any order but must use them all.

3. Students can exchange stories with other groups to read for enjoyment and to see whether all the verbs were used and written correctly.

like bury dig watch find hurry crash

Word Pictures

MATERIALS: drawing paper, markers

DIRECTIONS:

1. Display word pictures of vivid verbs. For example, add petals to make both letter *o*'s in *bloom* look like flowers. Write the letters of the word *surround* so that they form a circle.

2. Then have students work in groups of three or four to experiment with ways of writing other vivid verbs to show their meanings.

3. Students can choose their best word pictures to share with classmates.

Drop In

MATERIALS: three large brown grocery bags or other containers, sentence strips, pencils or markers

DIRECTIONS:

1. On sentence strips, write simple sentences in present, past, and future tenses. Distribute sentence strips to students at random.

2. Label three bags "Present Tense," "Past Tense," and "Future Tense."

3. Students read their sentences, locate and underline the verb, and place the sentence strip in the correct bag.

4. Empty the bags one by one and have students decide whether each sentence belongs in that bag.

5. Students might also write their own sentences for classmates to sort.

Raise Your Hand

DIRECTIONS:

1. Play a variation of "Simon Says." Explain that students should do what you say only when you use the correct verb. If you use a verb incorrectly, they should not follow the command.

2. Give students a variety of commands, including some with both correct and incorrect uses of *raise, rise, lie,* and *lay.*

Examples of Commands
Raise your left hand. (correct)
Rise both hands. (incorrect)
Rise from your seat. (correct)
Raise to your feet. (incorrect)
Lie down on the rug. (correct)
Lay on the floor. (incorrect)
Lay a book on the floor. (correct)
Lie a paper on the table. (incorrect)

Verb-O

MATERIALS: cardboard squares for making bingo-type cards, markers, buttons or other tokens

DIRECTIONS:

1. Divide each card into nine squares. Write past tenses of irregular verbs in the squares so that they are in a different order on each card.

2. Give each student a card and buttons or tokens.

3. Call out the present tense of one of the verbs. Students find the past tense of that verb on their cards and cover it with a button or token.

4. Continue calling present tenses of the verbs and having students cover the past tense. The winner is the first player who covers three adjacent squares either across, down, or diagonally and then yells, "Verb-o!"

ate	write	had
said	saw	came
rode	did	gave

came	had	saw
gave	wrote	rode
did	ate	said

JACKRABBIT

FROM Desert Voices BY BYRD BAYLOR AND PETER PARNALL

THE SUDDEN LEAP,
the instant start,
the burst of speed,
knowing
when to run
and when to freeze,
how to become
a shadow
underneath
a greasewood bush . . .

these are things
I learned
almost at birth.

Now
I lie
on the shadow-side
of a clump of grass.
My long ears bring me
every far-off footstep,

every twig that snaps,
every rustle in the weeds.

I watch
Coyote move
from bush to bush.

I wait.
He's almost here.

Now . . .

Now I go
like a zig-zag
lightning flash.
With my ears laid back,
I sail.

Jumping gullies
and bushes and rocks,
doubling back,

circling,
jumping high
to see where my enemy is,
warning rabbits
along the way,
I go.

I hardly touch
the ground.

And suddenly
I disappear.

Let Coyote stand there
sniffing
old jackrabbit trails.

Where I am now
is a
jackrabbit secret.

Building Background

Discuss with students animals that live in the desert. Ask students to compare a jackrabbit and a coyote. Elicit from students that coyotes are the predators and jackrabbits are the hunted prey. Inform students that coyotes feed mainly on rabbits and rodents and are therefore the jackrabbits' enemy.

Also tell students that *jack rabbit* is usually written as two separate words and that a possible reason for spelling it as one word in the poem is to make it "sound" as fast as the animal itself.

Determine a Purpose for Listening

Tell students that these selections describe the lives of a jackrabbit and a coyote. Ask students to determine whether their purpose for listening is

- to enjoy vivid language. (to enjoy vivid language)
- to solve problems.
- to learn how to do something.

COYOTE

FROM *Desert Voices* by Byrd Baylor and Peter Parnall

I MAY LIVE
hungry.
I may live
on the run.
I may be
a wanderer
and a trickster
and one
who'll try
anything

and a lot too nosy
for my own good

and a lot
too restless, too.

But I'm going to
make it—
no matter what.

I'll eat anything,
sleep anywhere,
run any distance,
dig for water
if I have to
because
I'm going to
survive
in this dry
rocky land . . .

and while I'm
doing it,
I'm going to
sing
about it.

I sing about cold,
and traps,
and traveling on,
and new soft pups

in a sandy den,
and rabbit hunts,
and the smell of rain.

I sing
for a wandering
coyote band
over there
across the hills,
telling them
coyote things,

saying
We're here
We're here
Alive
In the moonlight.

Listening Comprehension

LISTEN FOR ACTION WORDS AND VIVID IMAGES
Explain to students that the poets use action words and vivid images to describe the animated characters in these poems. Ask students to listen for these words and images as you read the story aloud. Point out vivid word groups such as *sudden leap, burst of speed, I sail, jumping high, eat anything,* and *sleep anywhere.* Then have students draw pictures of the jackrabbit and the coyote based on the details they hear. Tell students that their illustrations will help make the vivid descriptions of the jackrabbit and the coyote more concrete.

PERSONAL RESPONSE *Would you like to live the life of the jackrabbit? Why or why not?* (Possible responses: Yes, because the jackrabbit is fast and knows how to get along in nature; no, because the jackrabbit always has to be afraid of wild animals like the coyote.) *What do you like about the coyote? Explain your answer.* (Possible responses: I like the way the coyote is determined to survive even though his life is hard. The coyote is free and wanders around singing with other coyotes.) INFERENTIAL: GENERALIZE

Unit 3

Grammar More About Verbs

Writing Persuasive Writing

Introducing the Unit

ORAL LANGUAGE/VIEWING

DISCUSS THE IMAGES Ask students to view the photograph and to name the building in the picture. (the United States Capitol Building) Tell students that this is the building where U.S. Senators and Representatives work. Explain that senators and representatives often use persuasive writing during their campaigns as well as after they are elected. Discuss other forms of persuasion, such as advertisements and newspaper editorials. Then ask these questions:

1. **What techniques might be used in written advertisements to make them more persuasive?** (Possible responses: clever slogans, eye-catching photographs or illustrations)

2. **When might a person use the spoken word to try to persuade?** (Possible responses: in an election, in an advertising campaign)

3. **Do you find print ads or television ads more persuasive? Explain.** (Possible response: television ads, because they can appeal to both the eyes and the ears)

ENCOURAGE STUDENTS' QUESTIONS Have students reflect on their knowledge of persuasive writing. Encourage students to develop questions for discussion. Have them write their questions and selected responses in their journals.

Unit 3

Grammar More About Verbs

Writing Persuasive Writing

164

Viewing and Representing

COMPARE/CONTRAST PRINT AND VISUAL MEDIA Have students find a print ad that they find very persuasive. Have them write a paragraph explaining why the ad is persuasive. Then ask students to compare the ad they have chosen to one on television or on the radio for a similar product. Have them evaluate which ad is more persuasive and explain why.

For evaluation criteria for viewing, see the Viewing Checklist, page R88.

MEDIA LITERACY AND COMMUNICATION SKILLS PACKAGE
Use the video to extend students' oral and visual literacy. See *Teacher's Guide* pages 6–7.

Tell students that Unit 3 covers verbs, including main verbs and helping verbs, verb tenses, and irregular verbs. Have students look over the list of unit contents and note which chapters cover familiar concepts and which ones introduce new concepts. Then point out the writing assignments for Chapter 15 and Chapter 18. Discuss the elements of a friendly letter with them, and ask them to share what they know about persuasive writing.

SOCIAL STUDIES CONNECTION Students will explore a variety of social studies topics in this unit:

- People from Many Places
- Citizenship
- State and National Government
- How Communities Change and Stay the Same

School-Home Connection

You may want to use School-Home Connection 3, page R94.

LESSON ORGANIZER	DAY 1	DAY 2
DAILY LANGUAGE PRACTICE TRANSPARENCIES 29, 30	1. Joes friend is from mexico. (Joe's; Mexico.) 2. Lydia's parents am from Japan. (are) **Bridge to Writing** Luis <u>(action verb)</u> baseball very well.	1. chang am celebrating the Chinese New Year (Chang; is; Year.) 2. Changs brothers are playing music at the New Year's party. (Chang's) **Bridge to Writing** Chang <u>(helping verb)</u> enjoying the party.
ORAL WARM-UP **Listening/Speaking**	Identify Main and Helping Verbs 166	Listing Verbs 168 *Grammar Jingles*™ CD Track 9
TEACH/MODEL **GRAMMAR** **KEY** ✔ = tested skill	✔ **MAIN VERBS AND HELPING VERBS** 166–167 • To identify and use main verbs and helping verbs • To write sentences using main verbs and helping verbs	✔ **MORE ABOUT HELPING VERBS** 168–169 • To recognize and use *have, do,* and forms of *be* as helping verbs • To write sentences using interesting verbs
Reaching All Learners	**Modified Instruction** Below-Level: Discuss Helping Verbs Above-Level: Use Main and Helping Verbs **Reteach:** *Reteach Activities Copying Masters* pp. 25 and R46 **Challenge:** Activity Card 9, R66 *ESL Manual* pp. 64, 65 *Practice Book* p. 41	**Modified Instruction** Below-Level: Model the Thinking Above-Level: Use Different Verbs **ESL:** Verb Match 168 *ESL Manual* pp. 64, 66 **Reteach:** *Reteach Activities Copying Masters* pp. 26 and R46 **Challenge:** Write a Story 169 *Practice Book* p. 42
WRITING	Writing Connection 167 Social Studies	Writing Connection 169 Writer's Craft: Vivid Verbs
CROSS-CURRICULAR/ ENRICHMENT	*Vocabulary Power* Explore Word Meaning 166 beliefs, ceremonies, customs, practices, **traditions** See *Vocabulary Power* book.	*Vocabulary Power* Synonyms 166 *Vocabulary Power* p. 37 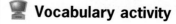 **Vocabulary activity**

DAY 3

1. Kobo am eating delicious noodles (is; noodles.)

2. he do not want any dessert. (He; does)

Bridge to Writing His brother is __(main verb)__ dessert, though.

Identify Main and Helping Verbs 170
Grammar Jingles™ CD Track 9

✔ **CONTRACTIONS WITH *NOT*** 170–171
- To identify and use contractions with *not*
- To compare the tone of sentences with contractions to the tone of sentences without contractions

---

Modified Instruction
Below-Level: Use a Chart
Above-Level: Write Sentences with Contractions
ESL: Contraction Flash Cards 170
ESL Manual pp. 64, 67
Reteach: *Reteach Activities Copying Masters* pp. 27 and R46
Challenge: Think Positively 171
Practice Book p. 43

Writing Connection 171
Writer's Journal: Reflecting on Writing

Vocabulary Power
Context Clues 166
Vocabulary Power p. 38
Vocabulary activity

DAY 4

1. they has come to this country from italy. (They; have; Italy.)

2. They dont have any relatives in America. (don't)

Bridge to Writing They __(helping verb)__ living in Dallas now.

Give Examples of Verbs and Contractions 172

EXTRA PRACTICE 172–173
- To identify and use helping verbs, main verbs, and contractions
- To make a poster, using helping verbs and contractions

Practice and assessment

Building Oral Grammar
Asking and Answering Questions with *Not* 173
Challenge: Contraction Challenge 173
ESL Manual pp. 64, 68
Practice Book p. 44

Writing Connection 173
Real-Life Writing: Make a Poster

Vocabulary Power
Word Origins 166
Vocabulary Power p. 39
Vocabulary activity
Technology: Pinky Power 172

DAY 5

1. Many people in the world are lerning English. (learning)

2. it isnt easy to learn English. (It; isn't)

Bridge to Writing __(helping verb)__ she studying tonight? I __(contraction with not)__ want to bother her.

TEST PREP **CHAPTER REVIEW** 174–175
- To review helping verbs, main verbs, and contractions with *not*
- To use a dictionary to find the meanings of words

Test preparation

Challenge: Dictionary Skills 175
Practice Book p. 45
ESL Manual pp. 64, 69

Writing Application 175
Writer's Journal: Study Skills

Vocabulary Power
Oxymoron 166
Study Skills: Using a Dictionary 175

Main Verbs and Helping Verbs

OBJECTIVES

- To identify and use main verbs and helping verbs
- To write sentences using main verbs and helping verbs

DAILY LANGUAGE PRACTICE

TRANSPARENCY 29

1 Joes friend is from mexico. (Joe's; Mexico)

2 Lydia's parents am from Japan. (are)

BRIDGE TO WRITING Luis ___(action verb)___ baseball very well.

ORAL WARM-UP

USE PRIOR KNOWLEDGE Ask: *Why might someone come to the United States from another country?* Write students' answers on the board, circling the main verbs and helping verbs.

TEACH/MODEL

Have students read the explanation of main verbs and helping verbs on page 166. Explain that helping verbs can tell when the action of a sentence happens. Note that in the Guided Practice example sentences, the action is happening in the present.

Model the thinking for the Guided Practice example:

MODEL The main verb in the sentence is *working*. The helping verb *are* comes before the main verb. The words *are working* tell me that the action is happening in the present.

Work through the Guided Practice with students.

Main Verbs and Helping Verbs

Sometimes the predicate of a sentence has two or more verb parts that work together.

> **Example:**
> Kimi **may eat** fish, black beans, and noodles.

A main verb is the most important verb in the predicate. A helping verb can work with the main verb to tell about the action.

> **Example:**
>
> helping   main
> verb   verb
> She and her family **are celebrating** the New Year.

Sometimes other words come between the helping verb and the main verb.

> **Example:**
> Her parents **have** often **talked** about life in Japan.

Guided Practice

A. For each sentence, tell which underlined verb is the main verb and which is the helping verb.

Example: Kimi's parents <u>are working</u> in the United States now.
are: helping verb; working: main verb

1. They <u>are teaching</u> Kimi Japanese ways. *are: helping; teaching: main*
2. Kimi <u>has</u> already <u>learned</u> about Japanese traditions for New Year's Day. *has: helping; learned: main*
3. "I <u>can get</u> new clothes!" Kimi announces. *can: helping; get: main*
4. <u>Did</u> the family <u>clean</u> the house yesterday? *Did: helping; clean: main*
5. Kimi's parents <u>have prepared</u> special dishes. *have: helping; prepared: main*

Vocabulary Power

tra·di·tions
[trə·dish′ənz] *n.*
Customs that are passed on from parents to children.

166

Vocabulary Power

DAY 1   EXPLORE WORD MEANING Introduce and define *traditions*. **What are some special traditions your family has?**

DAY 2   SYNONYMS Write on the board: *traditions, customers, customs.* **Which two words mean almost the same thing?** (See also *Vocabulary Power*, page 37.)

DAY 3   CONTEXT CLUES Say: *One of our family traditions is to have a picnic every year on the Fourth of July.* **Which words in the sentence help explain the meaning of traditions?** (See also *Vocabulary Power*, page 38.)

DAY 4   WORD ORIGINS Explain that *tradition* comes from a word that means "handing over." Ask: **How can knowing this help you remember the meaning of tradition?** (See also *Vocabulary Power*, page 39.)

DAY 5   OXYMORON **Do all traditions have to be old? What are some new traditions you could start?**

Independent Practice

B. For each sentence, write which underlined verb is the main verb and which is the helping verb.

Example: Chim's parents <u>are</u> no longer <u>living</u> in Vietnam.
are: helping verb; living: main verb

6. They <u>have built</u> a home in New York.
   have: helping; built: main
7. Chim's family <u>can</u> still <u>follow</u> traditions from Vietnam, too. *can: helping; follow: main*
8. His family <u>has prepared</u> special foods for New Year's Day. *has: helping; prepared: main*
9. Chim and his parents <u>are wearing</u> new clothes. *are: helping; wearing: main*
10. They <u>will give</u> Chim a red envelope. *will: helping; give: main*
11. He <u>should act</u> delighted to get an envelope. *should: helping; act: main*
12. His parents <u>have put</u> money in it! *have: helping; put: main*
13. His father <u>is</u> now <u>handing</u> him the red envelope. *is: helping; handing: main*
14. "I <u>was waiting</u> until we had eaten our rice cakes," he says. *was: helping; waiting: main*
15. "<u>May</u> I <u>count</u> my money?" asks Chim. *May: helping; count: main*

167

Remember that the main verb is the most important verb in the predicate. The helping verb works with the main verb to tell about the action.

Writing Connection

Social Studies Talk with a partner about some reasons people move from one country to another. Using a main verb and a helping verb in each sentence, write three to five sentences recording your ideas.

Independent Practice

Have students complete the Independent Practice, or modify it using these suggestions:

MODIFIED INSTRUCTION

BELOW-LEVEL STUDENTS As students complete Part B, remind them that the helping verb is the first word in the underlined verb group.

ABOVE-LEVEL STUDENTS Have students add two original sentences to the story in Part B, using main verbs and helping verbs.

Writing Connection

Social Studies Have students use a prewriting technique such as brainstorming to make a list of reasons they believe people would leave one country to live in another. Have them refine the ideas on their lists in the sentences they write.

WRAP-UP/ASSESS

SUMMARIZE Ask: **In what order do we write main verbs and helping verbs in a sentence?**

RETEACH

INTERVENTION Lessons in **visual, auditory,** and **kinesthetic** modalities: p. R46 and *Reteach Activities Copying Masters*, p. 25.

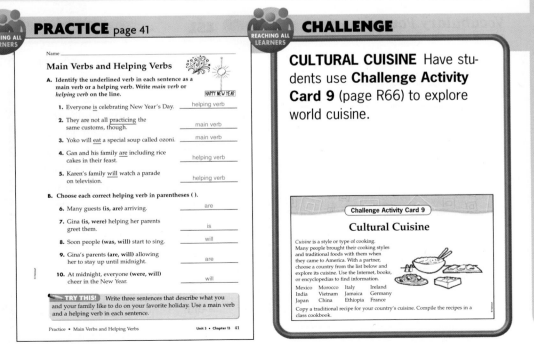

PRACTICE page 41

Name _____

Main Verbs and Helping Verbs

A. Identify the underlined verb in each sentence as a main verb or a helping verb. Write *main verb* or *helping verb* on the line.

1. Everyone <u>is</u> celebrating New Year's Day. *helping verb*
2. They are not all <u>practicing</u> the same customs, though. *main verb*
3. Yoko will <u>eat</u> a special soup called ozoni. *main verb*
4. Gan and his family <u>are</u> including rice cakes in their feast. *helping verb*
5. Karen's family <u>will</u> watch a parade on television. *helping verb*

B. Choose each correct helping verb in parentheses ( ).

6. Many guests **(is, are)** arriving. *are*
7. Gina **(is, were)** helping her parents greet them. *is*
8. Soon people **(was, will)** start to sing. *will*
9. Gina's parents **(are, will)** allowing her to stay up until midnight. *are*
10. At midnight, everyone **(were, will)** cheer in the New Year. *will*

TRY THIS! Write three sentences that describe what you and your family like to do on your favorite holiday. Use a main verb and a helping verb in each sentence.

Practice • Main Verbs and Helping Verbs   Unit 3 • Chapter 13   41

CHALLENGE

CULTURAL CUISINE Have students use **Challenge Activity Card 9** (page R66) to explore world cuisine.

Challenge Activity Card 9

Cultural Cuisine

Cuisine is a style or type of cooking. Many people brought their cooking styles and traditional foods with them when they came to America. With a partner, choose a country from the list below and explore its cuisine. Use the Internet, books, or encyclopedias to find information.

Mexico   Morocco   Italy   Ireland
India   Vietnam   Jamaica   Germany
Japan   China   Ethiopia France

Copy a traditional recipe for your country's cuisine. Compile the recipes in a class cookbook.

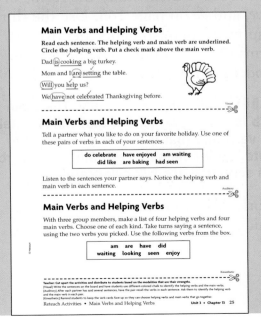

Main Verbs and Helping Verbs

Read each sentence. The helping verb and main verb are underlined. Circle the helping verb. Put a check mark above the main verb.

Dad is cooking a big turkey.
Mom and I are setting the table.
Will you help us?
We have not celebrated Thanksgiving before.

Main Verbs and Helping Verbs

Tell a partner what you like to do on your favorite holiday. Use one of these pairs of verbs in each of your sentences.

| do celebrate | have enjoyed | am waiting |
| did like | are baking | had seen |

Listen to the sentences your partner says. Notice the helping verb and main verb in each sentence.

Main Verbs and Helping Verbs

With three group members, make a list of four helping verbs and four main verbs. Choose one of each kind. Take turns saying a sentence, using the two verbs you picked. Use the following verbs from the box.

| am | are | have | did |
| waiting | looking | seen | enjoy |

Reteach Activities • Main Verbs and Helping Verbs   Unit 3 • Chapter 13   25

More About Helping Verbs

OBJECTIVES

- To recognize and use *have, do*, and forms of *be* as helping verbs
- To write sentences using interesting verbs

DAILY LANGUAGE PRACTICE

TRANSPARENCY 29

1 chang am celebrating the Chinese New Year (Chang; is; Year.)

2 Changs brothers are playing music at the New Year's party. (Chang's)

BRIDGE TO WRITING Chang __(helping verb)__ enjoying the party.

ORAL WARM-UP

USE PRIOR KNOWLEDGE Ask: **What have you done today?** Write students' responses on the board, using the form *(Name) has (main verb)*.

Grammar Jingles™ **CD, Intermediate** Use Track 9 for review and reinforcement of main verbs and helping verbs.

TEACH/MODEL

Remind students that helping verbs work with the main verb to tell about the action. Have them study the forms of *be, have,* and *do* on page 168. Use the third example to help students identify the forms of each common helping verb. Model the thinking:

MODEL The subject is *family*. The main verb is *celebrate*. I know that *will* is a helping verb and that it comes before *celebrate*. So the helping verb and main verb in this sentence are *will celebrate*.

Work with students to complete the Guided Practice.

Some Forms of Be, Have, and Do	
be	have
am	has
are	had
is	do
was	does
were	did

More About Helping Verbs

There are many verbs that can be helping verbs.

Some common helping verbs are forms of *be, have,* and *do.*

Examples:
DeShay and her family **are observing** Kwanzaa.

DeShay **does** not **want** the celebration to end.

Some other common helping verbs are *may, might, can, could, will, would,* and *should.*

Examples:
The family **will celebrate** for seven days.

They **should enjoy** their time together.

Guided Practice

A. Identify the helping verb in each sentence.

Example: Kwanzaa has always lasted seven days.
has

1. DeShay can enjoy honoring her African American traditions. can
2. Kwanzaa is ending on New Year's Day. is
3. DeShay has lit a candle on each day of Kwanzaa. has
4. She will light the last candle today. will
5. DeShay and her brother have already helped prepare the feast. have

168

Vocabulary Power page 37

Name _____

SYNONYMS

▶ Look in the Word Box for pairs of words that are synonyms. Write a pair of synonyms on each line. The first one is done for you.

| beliefs | special | pasture | jump | procedures | customs |
| traditions | ideas | ceremonies | unusual | leap | meadow |

1. _____ traditions/customs
2. _____ beliefs/ideas
3. _____ special/unusual
4. _____ ceremonies/procedures
5. _____ jump/leap
6. _____ pasture/meadow

▶ Now try these.

| nervous | sparkle | practices | twinkle | trade | plain |
| assist | habits | ordinary | worried | exchange | help |

7. _____ ordinary/plain
8. _____ worried/nervous
9. _____ twinkle/sparkle
10. _____ practices/habits
11. _____ trade/exchange
12. _____ assist/help

Vocabulary Power   Unit 3 • Chapter 13   37

REACHING ALL LEARNERS

ESL

VERB MATCH Create cards for these helping verbs: *were, does, has, am, are*. Repeat the process for these main verbs: *sung, reading, eaten, going, played*. Place the cards face down in two rows. Have students take turns selecting a card from each row. If the helping verb can be used with the action verb, have students use them orally in a sentence and keep the cards. If not, students return the cards. Play continues until all the cards have been used.

Independent Practice

B. Write each sentence. Underline the helping verb once. Underline the main verb twice.

Example: *Tom is staying up late tonight.*

6. Tom has lived in New York City all his life.
7. People in New York do love New Year's Eve!
8. Tom and his parents will go to Times Square this New Year's Eve.
9. Tom might not enjoy the long ride there.
10. They are celebrating the same way next year.
11. Tom's family have now joined the huge crowd at Times Square.
12. Moving lights on a huge sign are telling the exact time.
13. The crowd should count down the seconds to midnight.
14. Everyone will happily celebrate at midnight!
15. They can make a lot of noise!

Remember

that the helping verb works with the main verb to tell about the action. Some common helping verbs are forms of *be*, *have*, and *do*. Some other common helping verbs are *may*, *might, can, could, will, would,* and *should*.

169

Writing Connection

Writer's Craft: Vivid Verbs Think about a holiday that your family observes. List some interesting verbs that you might use to describe what your family does at this special time, such as *feast* and *celebrate*. Then choose four of these verbs and use them in sentences about the holiday. These sentences may describe what you have done in the past or what you expect to do. Use helping verbs with your main verbs in the sentences.

PRACTICE page 42

Name_____

More About Helping Verbs

A. Write the helping verb in each sentence.

1. What does Tom's family like to do? — does
2. His parents have always gone to the New Year's Day parade. — have
3. Did you ever make a New Year's resolution? — Did
4. Tom's father has resolved to get more exercise. — has
5. Sometimes New Year's resolutions can help you in the New Year. — can

B. Complete each sentence by filling in the correct helping verb. Choose from the helping verbs listed in the box.

| am | is | were | have | has | do | does |

6. Kwanzaa ___is___ becoming a tradition some African Americans celebrate.
7. Lita ___has___ made gifts for both her parents.
8. At Kwanzaa, people ___do___ appreciate handmade gifts.
9. It ___does___ take time to make gifts.
10. Lita's parents ___have___ always looked forward to the celebration.

TRY THIS! Do you like to celebrate the New Year? Write three sentences that tell about things people like to do on New Year's Day. Use a helping verb and a main verb in each sentence.

42 Unit 3 • Chapter 13   Practice • Main Verbs and Helping Verbs

---

CHALLENGE

WRITE A STORY Have students imagine what it would be like to travel from another country to live in the United States. Have students work in pairs to write a story about the new things they might see and do and how they might feel about coming to America to live. Remind students to use helping verbs in their writing. When students have finished writing their stories, have them underline the helping verbs and main verbs.

Independent Practice

Have students complete the Independent Practice, or modify it using these suggestions:

MODIFIED INSTRUCTION

BELOW-LEVEL STUDENTS Work through Part B with students, modeling the thinking.

ABOVE-LEVEL STUDENTS After completing the items, have students use different main verbs in these sentences.

Writing Connection

Writer's Craft: Vivid Verbs On the board, label two columns *Holidays* and *Feelings*. Have students name holidays for the first column. For the second column, have them name vivid verbs that tell what they do on each holiday. After students have written their sentences, tell them to make sure they have used vivid verbs, and have them make any necessary revisions.

WRAP-UP/ASSESS

SUMMARIZE Ask students to give examples of helping verbs and main verbs.

RETEACH

INTERVENTION Lessons in **visual, auditory,** and **kinesthetic** modalities: p. R46 and *Reteach Activities Copying Masters,* p. 26.

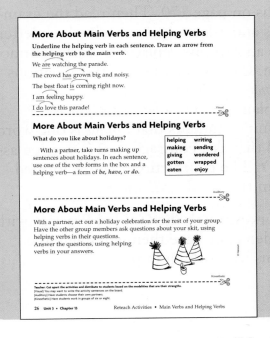

More About Main Verbs and Helping Verbs

Underline the helping verb in each sentence. Draw an arrow from the helping verb to the main verb.

We are watching the parade.
The crowd has grown big and noisy.
The best float is coming right now.
I am feeling happy.
I do love this parade!

More About Main Verbs and Helping Verbs

What do you like about holidays?

With a partner, take turns making up sentences about holidays. In each sentence, use one of the verb forms in the box and a helping verb—a form of *be, have,* or *do.*

helping	writing
making	sending
giving	wondered
gotten	wrapped
eaten	enjoy

More About Main Verbs and Helping Verbs

With a partner, act out a holiday celebration for the rest of your group. Have the other group members ask questions about your skit, using helping verbs in their questions.
Answer the questions, using helping verbs in your answers.

26 Unit 3 • Chapter 13   Reteach Activities • Main Verbs and Helping Verbs

Contractions with *Not*

OBJECTIVES
- To identify and use contractions with *not*
- To write sentences, comparing the tone of sentences with contractions to the tone of sentences without contractions

DAILY LANGUAGE PRACTICE

TRANSPARENCY 29

1 Kobo am eating delicious noodles (is; noodles.)

2 he do not want any dessert. (He; does)

BRIDGE TO WRITING His brother is (main verb) dessert, though.

ORAL WARM-UP

USE PRIOR KNOWLEDGE Write this sentence on the board: *Some Americans weren't born in the United States.* Ask students to identify the main verb and the helping verb in the sentence.

Grammar Jingles™ **CD, Intermediate** Use Track 9 for review and reinforcement of main verbs and helping verbs.

TEACH/MODEL

Read aloud the explanation of contractions on page 170. Then read the examples and ask students to tell which letter the apostrophe replaces in each contraction. On the board write the equations *cannot = can't* and *will not = won't*. Explain that these are special cases. Remind students that *cannot* is one word and that as a contraction it is written as *can't*. The contraction *won't* is formed from the words *will* and *not*.

Work through the Guided Practice with students, or have them complete the items by working in pairs.

Contractions with *Not*

A **contraction** is a shortened form of two words.

Often, the word *not* is added to a verb or a helping verb to form a contraction. An **apostrophe** (') takes the place of the *o* in *not*.

Examples:

is + not = isn't	have + not = haven't
are + not = aren't	do + not = don't
was + not = wasn't	could + not = couldn't
were + not = weren't	should + not = shouldn't

Guided Practice

A. Name the two words used to make each contraction.

Example: don't *do not*

1. isn't is not
2. wasn't was not
3. shouldn't should not
4. hasn't has not
5. doesn't does not

B. Name the contraction for each word pair.

Example: do not *don't*

6. have not haven't
7. are not aren't
8. were not weren't
9. had not hadn't
10. could not couldn't

170

Vocabulary Power page 38

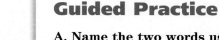

Name _____

CONTEXT CLUES

▶ Read each sentence. Then write a definition for the underlined word. Exact wording will vary. Possible responses are given.

1. One of my <u>practices</u> is to have a good breakfast every morning.
   an action done over and over

2. Blowing out candles on birthday cakes is a common <u>custom</u>.
   something that has become an accepted practice by many people

3. One of Joe's <u>beliefs</u> is that it's good to be kind to others.
   something thought to be true

4. People get married at wedding <u>ceremonies</u>.
   a formal act performed in a set manner

5. Playing games on Friday night is a <u>tradition</u> in Ellen's family.
   a custom or set of practices

▶ What is a tradition you would like to start in your family?
   Responses will vary. Accept reasonable responses.

38 Unit 3 • Chapter 13   Vocabulary Power

ESL

REACHING ALL LEARNERS

CONTRACTION FLASH CARDS Create flash cards to help students master contractions with *not*. Write each of the following contractions on a card: *isn't, hasn't, didn't, doesn't, wasn't,* and *don't*. On the other side of each card, write the verb + *not*. Show the side of the card with the verb + *not*, and ask students to say the contraction. Then ask a volunteer to use the contraction in a sentence.

Independent Practice

C. Write a contraction for the underlined words in each sentence.

Example: Some people <u>would not</u> like to travel.
wouldn't

11. However, some people <u>are not</u> happy to stay in one place. *aren't*
12. "Life <u>is not</u> fun without adventure," they say. *isn't*
13. They <u>do not</u> seem to fear new experiences. *don't*
14. Life in one country <u>does not</u> excite them. *doesn't*
15. Some people <u>would not</u> be able to follow their dreams where they live. *wouldn't*
16. My neighbor <u>could not</u> find a medical school where she lived before. *couldn't*
17. She <u>does not</u> want to give up her dream of becoming a doctor. *doesn't*
18. She <u>is not</u> a person who gives up easily. *isn't*
19. She <u>was not</u> afraid to move. *wasn't*
20. She <u>has not</u> let anything stop her. *hasn't*

> ### Remember
> that the word *not* can be added to a verb or a helping verb to form a contraction. An apostrophe (') takes the place of the *o* in *not*.

Writing Connection
Writer's Journal: Reflecting on Writing List two suggestions you might give to a newcomer in your community. Use contractions with *not* to write your suggestions. Then rewrite your sentences, spelling out the helping verb and *not*. With a partner, read both sets of sentences aloud. Which set of sentences sounds more friendly? Would you rather hear suggestions with or without contractions? Why?

Independent Practice
Have students complete the Independent Practice, or modify it using these suggestions:

MODIFIED INSTRUCTION
BELOW-LEVEL STUDENTS Have students refer to the chart on page 170 to complete the Independent Practice items.

ABOVE-LEVEL STUDENTS Have students write three original sentences, using contractions from the chart on page 170.

Writing Connection
Writer's Journal: Reflecting on Writing Tell students to punctuate their contractions correctly. Explain that writing has a tone of voice, just as speaking does. The words students use in writing may sound friendly or unfriendly. As students read their sentences aloud, remind them to listen to how contractions change the tone of a sentence.

WRAP-UP/ASSESS

SUMMARIZE Ask students to tell how a contraction is formed.

RETEACH
INTERVENTION Lessons in **visual, auditory,** and **kinesthetic** modalities: p. R46 and *Reteach Activities Copying Masters,* p. 27.

PRACTICE page 43

Name _____

Contractions with not

A. Write a contraction for the underlined words.

1. Sometimes people <u>were not</u> able to find work. *weren't*
2. During a war, some families <u>did not</u> feel safe. *didn't*
3. Some people <u>have not</u> come to the United States. *haven't*
4. It <u>is not</u> just safety they are seeking. *isn't*
5. They <u>do not</u> want to leave their homes. *don't*

B. Choose the contraction in parentheses ( ) that correctly completes the sentence.

6. She **(don't, doesn't)** know what to expect in the United States. *doesn't*
7. Fortunately, her aunt and uncle **(haven't, didn't)** forgotten to meet her plane. *haven't*
8. "**(Didn't, Don't)** worry," her aunt tells Carlita. *Don't*
9. "Your English **(aren't, isn't)** at all bad." *isn't*
10. "You **(isn't, aren't)** going to feel lonely for long." *aren't*

> **TRY THIS!** Write a few sentences about what you would miss if you had to move to another country. What wouldn't you miss? Include at least two contractions.

Practice • Main Verbs and Helping Verbs   Unit 3 • Chapter 13 43

CHALLENGE

THINK POSITIVELY Have students work in pairs to write four school rules using contractions with *not*. Then have them revise the sentences to make positive statements. For example, *Don't run in the halls* could become *Walk quietly in the halls.*

Have students share their revised rules in small groups.

Contractions with *Not*
Read each sentence. Underline the two words that can be made into a contraction. Then draw a line from the sentence to the correct contraction.

That tiger <u>was not</u> performing last year. — doesn't
It <u>is not</u> doing a good job now. — wasn't
The trainer <u>does not</u> look happy. — don't
Some people <u>do not</u> feel safe here. — isn't

Contractions with *Not*
Play a guessing game with a partner. Pick something in the classroom. Tell about things your object cannot do or be. Use one of these contractions in each clue.

| isn't | doesn't | didn't | hasn't | wasn't |

Can your partner guess what you picked? When your partner guesses your object, your partner should tell which contractions you used. Your partner should also tell which two words are used to make each contraction.

Contractions with *Not*
With a partner, make twelve cards. Write one of these words or word pairs on each card.

| is not | did not | have not | are not | were not | do not |
| isn't | didn't | haven't | aren't | weren't | don't |

Mix up the cards and turn them facedown. Then take turns picking two cards. Try to match a helping verb and *not* with its contraction.

Teacher: Cut apart the activities and distribute to students based on the modalities that are their strengths.
[Visual] You may want to have students write each word pair in parentheses on the board. Then have them erase the letters that are not included in the contraction, and use colored chalk to add the apostrophe.
[Auditory] You may want to model several clues for this guessing game.
[Kinesthetic] Have students use their cards to play Concentration.
Reteach Activities • Main Verbs and Helping Verbs   Unit 3 • Chapter 13 27

Extra Practice

OBJECTIVES
- To identify and use helping verbs, main verbs, and contractions
- To make a poster, using helping verbs and contractions

DAILY LANGUAGE PRACTICE

TRANSPARENCY 30

1 they has come to this country from italy. (They; have; Italy.)

2 They dont have any relatives in America. (don't)

BRIDGE TO WRITING They _____ living in Dallas now.
(helping verb)

ORAL WARM-UP

USE PRIOR KNOWLEDGE Ask students to give examples of oral sentences in which they use helping verbs, main verbs, and contractions with *not*.

TEACH/MODEL

Use the Remember box to review main verbs, helping verbs, and contractions with *not*. Model the thinking for the example in Extra Practice Part A:

MODEL The main verb in the sentence is *come*, which tells what the people did. *Have* is a verb that is before the verb *come*. It shows that the action happened in the past, so I know that *have* is the helping verb.

Have students work in pairs to complete the Extra Practice items.

CHAPTER 13

Main Verbs and Helping Verbs

Remember

that the helping verb works with the main verb to tell about the action. Forms of *be*, *have*, and *do* are some common helping verbs. Some other common helping verbs are *may*, *might*, *can*, *could*, *will*, *would*, and *should*.

For more activities with main verbs and helping verbs, visit *The Learning Site:* www.harcourtschool.com

172

Extra Practice

A. Write the helping verb in each sentence. *pages 166–169*

Example: People have come to America from all over the world.
have

1. The Statue of Liberty has welcomed many of them. has
2. It is still standing in New York harbor. is
3. You may see pictures of it. may
4. Many people are already planning to visit the Statue of Liberty next year. are
5. They will not forget the experience. will

B. Make a chart with two columns. Label the first column *Helping Verbs* and the second column *Main Verbs*. Write each underlined verb in the correct column. *pages 166–169*

Example: Yen <u>did</u> not <u>see</u> the Statue of Liberty.

Helping Verbs	Main Verbs
did	see

6. She <u>can remember</u> the Golden Gate Bridge, though. can|remember
7. She <u>had traveled</u> from China on a jet. had|traveled
8. "We <u>were landing</u> in San Francisco," Yen explains. were|landing
9. "I <u>was sitting</u> in a window seat." was|sitting
10. "Hundreds of cars <u>were crossing</u> the bridge." were|crossing

---

Vocabulary Power page 39

Name _____

WORD ORIGINS

Tradition comes from a Latin word that means "handing over." Families "hand over" their traditions to their children.

Look at the word web below. Fill in as many examples as you can for each kind of tradition. You could list your family's traditions or ones you have heard about, read about, or seen on television. Responses may vary. Accept reasonable responses.

Places That People Go Every Year **Example:** zoo	Holidays That People Celebrate **Example:** Kwanzaa

| Ceremonies People Go To **Example:** graduations | (Traditions) | Games That People Play **Example:** dreidel |

Food That People Eat At Special Times **Example:** cake on birthdays

Vocabulary Power   Unit 3 • Chapter 13   39

TECHNOLOGY

REACHING ALL LEARNERS

PINKY POWER Have students practice using a computer keyboard to write sentences that have contractions with *not*. Show them that the apostrophe (') key is at the right-hand side of the keyboard. Have students practice using their right pinky finger to type the apostrophe. After they practice typing words, have them write sentences using contractions. Have students print out their writing and exchange papers to proofread each other's work.

C. **Write the two words that make up each underlined contraction.** *pages 170–171*

Example: Flora thought moving to a new country <u>wasn't</u> going to be easy.
was not

11. Los Angeles <u>didn't</u> feel like home right away. *did not*
12. She <u>couldn't</u> speak much English yet. *could not*
13. Her old friends <u>weren't</u> there. *were not*
14. Flora discovered that she <u>wasn't</u> alone, though. *was not*
15. "<u>Don't</u> worry," said Maria. "I am new here, too!" *Do not*

D. **Write each sentence, using a contraction for the underlined words.** *pages 170–171*

Example: People <u>do not</u> always stay in the same place.
People don't always stay in the same place.

16. Sita <u>was not</u> born in the United States. *wasn't*
17. Her family <u>did not</u> leave India until last year. *didn't*
18. Sita <u>has not</u> stopped writing to her friends and family in India. *hasn't*
19. They <u>do not</u> forget to send e-mail to Sita. *don't*
20. Sita and her family <u>could not</u> forget their traditions and customs. *couldn't*

Writing Connection

Real-Life Writing: Make a Poster Work with a partner to list suggestions you might give to someone who has come to the United States for the first time. Use at least two helping verbs and two contractions. On notebook paper, make a poster listing these suggestions. Then illustrate your poster.

Remember
that the word *not* is often added to a verb or a helping verb to form a contraction.

DID YOU KNOW?
In 1884 the people of France gave the Statue of Liberty to the people of the United States.

173

Building Oral Grammar

Have students think of three questions that could be answered in complete sentences using the word *not,* for example, *What is one rule in physical education class?*

Have students work in pairs to ask and answer their questions. Remind them to respond in complete sentences, using a contraction with *not.* Each student should get several chances to ask and respond to questions.

Writing Connection

Real-Life Writing: Make a Poster Have students tell about signs they have seen that give instructions or help. Remind students that their posters should provide helpful information. Tell them to use helping verbs and contractions with *not* and to check the punctuation of their contractions. Display students' posters in the classroom.

WRAP-UP/ASSESS

SUMMARIZE Have students write in their journals to reflect on how using helping verbs and contractions can make their writing more effective. **REFLECTION**

ADDITIONAL PRACTICE An additional page of Extra Practice is provided on page 462 of the *Pupil Edition.*

PRACTICE page 44

Name _____

Extra Practice

A. Write the main verb in each sentence.

1. Many new vegetables are appearing in produce departments. — appearing
2. Many markets are ordering them. — ordering
3. The American population is learning new tastes. — learning
4. Yesterday, Carlita was sharing her Mexican lunch with Keiko. — sharing
5. Keiko will bring a Japanese treat for Carlita. — bring

B. Form a contraction from the two words in parentheses ( ). Write the contraction.

6. We (do not) need to travel far to meet someone from another country. — don't
7. (Does not) that make life in our country more interesting? — Doesn't
8. (Have not) some of our favorite things come from other countries? — Haven't
9. Pizza (is not) just an American food. — isn't
10. (Was not) it brought here from Italy? — Wasn't

TRY THIS! Write a few sentences about foods from other countries that you are familiar with or would like to try. Use contractions wherever possible.

44 Unit 3 • Chapter 13   Practice • Main Verbs and Helping Verbs

---

CHALLENGE

CONTRACTION CHALLENGE

Remind students that helping verbs are sometimes used as contractions with *not.* For example, *He <u>hasn't</u> lived here long.* Have students work in pairs to write two sentences using a helping verb in a contraction with *not.* If students need help, suggest that they first write sentences with a helping verb and a main verb. Then they can add *not* and revise the sentences to use contractions.

TECHNOLOGY *Grammar Practice and Assessment* CD-ROM; *Writing Express* CD-ROM

INTERNET Visit *The Learning Site:* www.harcourtschool.com

Chapter Review

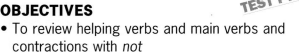

OBJECTIVES

STANDARDIZED TEST PREP

- To review helping verbs and main verbs and contractions with *not*
- To use a dictionary to find the meanings of words

STANDARDIZED TEST PREP

MODEL TEST-TAKING STRATEGIES Have students read the directions on page 174 silently.

Remind them to eliminate answers they know are wrong. Model the thinking. Write this example on the board:

The friends _____ walking to school together.

    1 A is

      B are

      C does

      D haven't

MODEL The main verb is *walking*. All the choices are helping verbs, so I must look for a helping verb that fits in the sentence. The subject of the sentence is *friends*, which is plural. I know that *is* is used with a singular subject, so A is not correct. The main verb does not make sense with answers C and D. The correct answer is B. The helping verb *are* sounds correct.

Have students complete the Chapter Review items on their own.

STANDARDIZED TEST PREP

TIP Remember to read all answer choices before making your selection.

Chapter Review

Read the passage and choose the word or group of words that belongs in each space. Write the word that best completes the sentence.

> Harry (1) "Hi" to his best friend. He always smiles at his friends. He may also (2). That is the way he lets them know he likes them. He (3) the tradition in his community. Carlita (4) people by saying "Hi!" She and her family have always (5) "Buenos Dias!" to one another. (6) it amazing how many ways there are to say "Hello"?

1 A had shouting
  B does shouting
  C can shouting
  D is shouting D

4 F isn't greet
  G haven't greet
  H doesn't greet H
  J hasn't greet

2 F wave F
  G waving
  H waved
  J will wave

5 A say
  B said B
  C says
  D sayed

3 A did following
  B has following
  C is following C
  D might following

6 F Isn't F
  G Weren't
  H Hasn't
  J Doesn't

For additional test preparation, visit *The Learning Site:* www.harcourtschool.com

174

Assessment

· ·

PORTFOLIO ASSESSMENT Have students select their best work from the Writing Connections on pages 167, 169, and 173.

ONGOING ASSESSMENT Evaluate the performance of 4–6 students using appropriate checklists and record forms from pages R74–R77.

INTERNET Activities and exercises to help students prepare for state and standardized assessments appear on *The Learning Site:*
www.harcourtschool.com

Using a Dictionary

Dictionaries are very useful study tools. A dictionary entry lets you know how to pronounce a word. It also gives the part of speech and the definitions of a word.

You know that words in a dictionary are arranged in alphabetical order. You will find **guide words** at the top of every page in the dictionary. Guide words show the first and last entry word on each page. For example, if you were looking for the word *culture*, you would know to look for it on a page with the guide words *cue* and *cumulate*, since it comes alphabetically between these words. Do you think you would find the word *custom* on the same page?

guide word   part of speech   definitions   entry word   pronunciation

cue	187	cumulate
cue [kyōō] *n., v.* **cued, cu·ing** 1 *n.* In theatrical performances, something, as an action or word, that serves as a signal or reminder to another actor: Wait for your *cue* before you start your speech. 2 *v.* To give a cue to (a performer). 3 *n.* Any signal to begin: The conductor gave the *cue* to the orchestra. 4 *n.* A helpful hint or indication, as when one is uncertain what to do. **cuff** [kuf] *n.* 1 A band or fold at the wrist of a sleeve. 2 A folded piece at the bottom of a trouser leg. 3 A handcuff. **cuff link** One of a pair of fasteners that hold together buttonless shirt cuffs. **cu ft** or **cu. ft.** 1 cubic foot. 2 cubic feet. **cui·rass** [kwi-ras'] *n.* A piece of armor worn to protect the upper part of the body. **cui·sine** [kwi-zēn'] *n.* 1 A style or type of cooking: French *cuisine.* 2 The food prepared: The *cuisine* is excellent.		**cul·tur·al** [kul'chər-əl] *adj.* Having to do with or resulting in culture: *cultural* traditions. —**cul'tur·al·ly** *adv.* **cul·ture** [kul'chər] *n., v.* **cul·tured, cul·tur·ing** 1 *n.* The entire way of life of a particular people, including its customs, religions, ideas, inventions, and tools: ancient Egyptian *culture.* 2 *n.* The training or care of the mind or body: physical *culture.* 3 *n.* The knowledge, refinement, and good taste acquired through training the mind and faculties: a person of *culture.* 4 *n.* The growing or improvement of animals or plants: the *culture* of bees. 5 *n.* A colony or growth, as of bacteria or viruses, in a prepared medium, as for study. 6 *v.* To grow and improve; cultivate: to *culture* roses. **cul·tured** [kul'chərd] *adj.* 1 Having or showing culture or refinement: a *cultured* person. 2 Produced by special methods: *cultured* bacteria.

C

YOUR TURN

Look up each word below in a dictionary. Write the page number of the page where you find each word. Then write the guide words that are on the page. Answers may vary.

1. adventure   4. observe

2. heritage   5. traditions

3. welcome   6. celebrate

TIP Before you begin looking for a word, decide whether it will most likely be in the front, the middle, or the back of the dictionary.

175

STUDY SKILLS

Using a Dictionary

TEACH/MODEL

Explain that in order to find words in a dictionary, it is important to understand how the words are alphabetized. Tell students that when words begin with the same letter, they should look at the next letter or letters to arrange them alphabetically. On the board, write *culprit, cultivate, cure,* and *culinary.* Model how to alphabetize these words.

Point out the guide words *cue* and *cumulate* on the example page. Ask: **Which of these four words would not be on this page?** Tell students that looking at the guide words is a quick way to decide if a word will be on a page without scanning the entire page.

Explain that some words have more than one definition. Note that the dictionary shows the part of speech for each usage of a word. Tell students that a dictionary will often provide examples of how to use the word correctly.

 WRITING APPLICATION Have students write in their journals why knowing how to use a dictionary is an important skill. Ask students to tell when they might need to use a dictionary.

WRAP-UP/ASSESS

SUMMARIZE Ask students to explain how to alphabetize words and how to use guide words to find an entry in the dictionary.

 TECHNOLOGY Additional writing activities are provided on the *Writing Express* CD-ROM

PRACTICE page 45

Name _____

Chapter Review

Choose the word that best completes the sentence.

1 Peter _____ said there is one thing he will never forget.
○ is
○ does
○ have
● has

2 He _____ remembering coming to the United States.
● is
○ had
○ were
○ does

3 He _____ telling the story yesterday.
○ did
● was
○ has
○ had

4 Peter and his family _____ sailed for a long time.
○ have
○ is
○ do
● had

5 They _____ seen land in weeks.
○ isn't
● hadn't
○ doesn't
○ hasn't

6 Everyone _____ wondering when they would arrive.
● was
○ were
○ are
○ don't

7 They _____ waiting to see New York City.
○ was
○ is
○ have
● were

8 At last they _____ looking at the tall buildings.
○ was
● were
○ is
○ have

Practice • Main Verbs and Helping Verbs   Unit 3 • Chapter 13   45

CHALLENGE

DICTIONARY SKILLS Have students practice their dictionary skills by using the example page to answer these questions:

• What word follows *culprit*?

• Is the word *cuisine* a noun or a verb?

• Arrange these words in alphabetical order: *cumulate, cuff, culotte,* and *cumber.*

CHAPTER 14

LESSON ORGANIZER	DAY **1**	DAY **2**
DAILY LANGUAGE PRACTICE 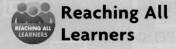 TRANSPARENCIES 31, 32	**1.** Mr Spiro hasnt missed a chance to vote. (Mr.; hasn't) **2.** voting doesnt take much Time. (Voting; doesn't; time.) **Bridge to Writing** Mr. Spiro <u>(action verb)</u> every year.	**1.** nora volunteered at the hospital (Nora; hospital.) **2.** Her work There makes the childrens feel better. (there; children) **Bridge to Writing** Nora <u>(form of the verb *be*)</u> able to help sick children.
ORAL WARM-UP **Listening/Speaking**	Use Different Tenses 176	Complete the Sentence 178 *Grammar Jingles*™ CD Track 10
TEACH/MODEL **GRAMMAR** **KEY** ✔ = tested skill	✔ **VERB TENSES** 176–177 • To recognize and use correct verb tenses • To use prewriting techniques and to write a paragraph, using the correct verb tense	✔ **PRESENT-TENSE VERBS** 178–179 • To recognize and use present-tense verbs • To write a paragraph and to respond to another's writing
Reaching All Learners	**Modified Instruction** Below-Level: Model the Thinking Above-Level: Explain Answers **Reteach:** *Reteach Activities Copying Masters* pp. 28 and R47 **Challenge:** Activity Card 10, R66 *ESL Manual* pp. 70, 71 *Practice Book* p. 46	**Modified Instruction** Below-Level: Identify Singular and Plural Subjects Above-Level: Rewrite Sentences **ESL:** Action and Movement 178 *ESL Manual* pp. 70, 72 **Reteach:** *Reteach Activities Copying Masters* pp. 29 and R47 **Challenge:** Collage 179 *Practice Book* p. 47
WRITING	Writing Connection 177 Writer's Journal: Writing Idea	Writing Connection 179 Writer's Craft: Giving Reasons
CROSS-CURRICULAR/ ENRICHMENT	*Vocabulary Power* Explore Word Meaning 176 apply, enlist, enroll, **register**, request See *Vocabulary Power* book.	*Vocabulary Power* Prefixes 176 *Vocabulary Power* p. 40 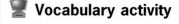 **Vocabulary activity**

DAY 3

1. andrea is a reporter for the community newspaper (Andrea; newspaper.)

2. The papers name is *The gowanville News.* (paper's; *Gowanville*)

Bridge to Writing Andrea <u>   </u> (present-tense verb) about school news.

Distinguish Between Singular and Plural
 Subjects 180
 Grammar Jingles™ CD Track 10

✔ **SUBJECT-VERB AGREEMENT**
 180–181
• To recognize and use correct subject-verb agreement
• To use correct subject-verb agreement in an announcement

Modified Instruction
Below-Level: Determine Verb
Above-Level: Rewrite Sentences
Listening and Speaking: Make a Speech 180
Reteach: *Reteach Activities Copying Masters* pp. 30 and R47
Challenge: Write to Congress 181
ESL Manual pp. 70, 73
Practice Book p. 48

Writing Connection 181
 Real-Life Writing: Announcement

Vocabulary Power
Rhyming Words 176
Vocabulary Power p. 41
Vocabulary activity

DAY 4

1. Many people helps the community. (help)

2. They dont mind giving up their time. (don't)

Bridge to Writing People <u>   </u> (helping verb) found that they get a lot of pleasure out of giving to their community.

Complete the Sentence 182

EXTRA PRACTICE 182–183
• To correct forms of present-tense verbs, and to correct subject-verb agreement
• To create an announcement and to analyze fonts
Practice and assessment

Building Oral Grammar
Play the Sounds Right Card Game 183
Challenge: Identify Subjects and Verbs 183
ESL Manual pp. 70, 74
Practice Book p. 49

Writing Connection 183
Technology

Vocabulary Power
Word Endings 176
Vocabulary Power p. 42
Vocabulary activity
 Art: Make a Poster 182

DAY 5

1. Today senator lawrence visit our school. (Senator Lawrence; visits)

2. Our teacher, mr Harris, am a friend of his. (Mr.; is)

Bridge to Writing He <u>   </u> (present-tense verb) lunch with our class. The senator <u>   </u> (contraction with *not*) stay all day.

TEST PREP CHAPTER REVIEW 184–185
• To review present-tense verb forms and subject-verb agreement
• To create new words by using prefixes and suffixes
Test preparation

Challenge: Learning New Words 185
Practice Book p. 50
ESL Manual pp. 70, 75

Writing Application 185
Prefixes and Suffixes

Vocabulary Power
Multiple–Meaning Words 176
Vocabulary Builder: Prefixes and Suffixes 185

Present-Tense Verbs

Verb Tenses

OBJECTIVES
- To recognize and use correct verb tenses
- To use prewriting techniques and to write a paragraph, using the correct verb tense

DAILY LANGUAGE PRACTICE

TRANSPARENCY 31

1 Mr Spiro hasnt missed a chance to vote. (Mr.; hasn't)

2 voting doesnt take much Time. (Voting; doesn't; time)

BRIDGE TO WRITING Mr. Spiro (action verb) every year.

ORAL WARM-UP

USE PRIOR KNOWLEDGE Ask volunteers to tell something they did yesterday, something they are doing today, and something they will do tomorrow. Write the verbs they use on the board.

TEACH/MODEL

Remind students that an action verb is a word that tells what the subject does. Read aloud the explanation and examples of verb tenses on page 176. Point out that sometimes sentences have words such as *today*, *last week*, and *tomorrow* that also tell when the action is happening. Tell students that not all sentences have these clues, so it is important to understand that the verb form changes to show that action is happening now, happened in the past, or will happen in the future.

Work through the Guided Practice orally with students.

Verb Tenses

The tense of a verb tells the time of the action.

You know that every predicate has a verb that tells what the subject is or does. The verb also tells whether the action is happening now, has happened in the past, or will happen in the future.

Examples:

Today Juan **works** at the library.

Takesha **helped** at her town's library last week.

Anna **will volunteer** there tomorrow.

Guided Practice

A. Tell whether the underlined verb shows action that is happening in the present, has happened in the past, or will happen in the future.

Example: Only citizens <u>vote</u> in United States elections.   *present*

Vocabulary Power

reg·is·ter
[rej′is·tər] *v.* To enter the name or names of in an official list.

176

1. People <u>make</u> important decisions by voting.   present
2. Every four years citizens <u>will choose</u> the President of the United States.   future
3. Congress <u>changed</u> the voting age to eighteen in 1971.   past
4. Adults <u>register</u>, or sign up, to vote.   present
5. Many people <u>will decide</u> for whom to vote.   future
6. People <u>shouted</u> out their votes in colonial times.   past
7. Later, citizens <u>recorded</u> their votes on paper.   past
8. Some people still <u>write</u> paper votes.   present
9. Most voters <u>use</u> voting machines now.   present
10. Soon people <u>will vote</u> on home computers.   future

Vocabulary Power

DAY 1 EXPLORE WORD MEANING Introduce and define *register*. Have children dictate a list of things for which people register.

DAY 2 PREFIXES **The prefix *pre-* means "before." What would *preregistered* mean?** (See also *Vocabulary Power*, page 40.)

DAY 3 RHYMING WORDS Write on the board: *enroll, register, coal, coat.* **Which of these words rhyme?** (See also *Vocabulary Power*, page 41.)

DAY 4 WORD ENDINGS Write *registered* on the board. Ask children to identify the base word and the word ending. **What other endings can we add to this word?** (See also *Vocabulary Power*, page 42.)

DAY 5 MULTIPLE-MEANING WORDS **Another meaning for *register* is a hot-air register. Make a list of words with more than one meaning.**

Independent Practice

**B. Write each sentence, and underline the verb.
Write whether the verb shows action that is
happening in the present, has happened in the
past, or will happen in the future.**

Example: Voting machines keep votes secret.
Voting machines keep votes secret.
present

11. Early voting machines <u>weighed</u> 700 pounds. past
12. Today's voting machines <u>use</u> computers. present
13. Machines <u>check</u> the votes. present
14. They <u>will read</u> 1,000 votes a minute. future
15. Voting machines <u>improve</u> over time. present
16. An election <u>allows</u> people to make choices. present
17. States <u>will make</u> voting easier next year. future
18. Some states <u>will register</u> voters on election
day. future
19. For years people away from home <u>mailed</u> their
votes. past
20. A person's vote <u>stays</u> a secret. present

Remember
that the tense of
a verb tells the
time of the
action.

DID YOU KNOW?
The famous inventor
Thomas Alva Edison
created the first
voting machine that
recorded votes in
1868. Congress
members did not like
it. They said it
moved the process
of voting along too
fast!

Writing Connection

Writer's Journal: Writing Idea
Citizens must follow many rules. Rules
help keep us safe. What is one important
rule that you follow? In a paragraph,
explain why you think it is important to follow this
rule. Since you are writing about something you do
now, remember to use present tense.

Independent Practice

Have students complete the Independent Practice, or
modify it using these suggestions:

MODIFIED INSTRUCTION

BELOW-LEVEL STUDENTS Work through the items
with students, modeling the thinking.

ABOVE-LEVEL STUDENTS Ask students to explain
their answers.

Writing Connection

Writer's Journal: Writing Idea Before
students record their reflections, have
them work in pairs to brainstorm a list
of rules that they follow. Students can
work from this list to write their paragraphs.

WRAP-UP/ASSESS

SUMMARIZE Ask students to name three
verb tenses and give a sentence using
each one.

RETEACH

INTERVENTION Lessons in **visual,
auditory,** and **kinesthetic** modalities: p. R47 and *Reteach Activities
Copying Masters,* p. 28.

Verb Tenses

Read the paragraph. Underline each verb. If the action of the verb
happens in the *present* put a *P* above it. If it happened in the *past,*
put *PA* above it. If it will happen in the *future,* put *F* above it.

Dad works in a day-care center now. I will help him tomorrow. He
takes care of small children. He worked in a school last year. I helped
him then, too because I like kids.

Verb Tenses

What do you like to do with your time?

What did you do last year? What do you do this year? What will
you do next year? With a partner, take turns telling about your ideas.
After each sentence your partner says, repeat the verb your partner
used. Then tell whether it is a present tense verb, a past tense verb, or a
future tense verb.

Verb Tenses

With the rest of your group, make a set of cards. On each of three other
cards, write one of these phrases.

| present tense | past tense | future tense |

Each member of the group should take turns choosing a card.
Say a verb in the tense shown on the card. Then say a sentence
using the verb and verb tense. Group members can write the
sentence as you say it.

Teacher: Cut apart the activities and distribute to students based on the modalities that are their strengths.
[Visual] You may wish to write the sentences on the board. Ask students to explain how they can identify the tense of the verb in each sentence.
[Auditory] You may want to have students write some of the sentences they say.
[Kinesthetic] Remind students to pick their cards without reading them first.

28 Unit 3 • Chapter 14   Reteach Activities • Present-Tense Verbs

---

PRACTICE page 46

Name _____

Verb Tenses

A. Write whether the underlined verb shows action that
happens in the present, happened in the past, or will
happen in the future.

1. People <u>needed</u> food. ___past___
2. The students sometimes <u>will help</u> people in
the city. ___future___
3. Sonya <u>talks</u> to managers of stores. ___present___
4. She <u>will ask</u> them for food. ___future___
5. The food drive <u>was</u> a success. ___past___

B. Underline the verb in each sentence. Then write whether the verb
shows action that happens in the present, happened in the past,
or will happen in the future.

6. Many people <u>needed</u> help. ___past___
7. Perhaps they <u>will need</u> it only for a short time. ___future___
8. Good citizens <u>help</u> people in need. ___present___
9. Many groups <u>do</u> things for people in trouble. ___present___
10. People <u>give</u> money to these groups for
their work. ___present___
11. Some groups <u>started</u> more than 50 years ago. ___past___

TRY THIS! People often work to help others in their
community. Write about what you and people you know do, have
done, or will do to help others. Remember to use the correct
verb tense.

46 Unit 3 • Chapter 14   Practice • Present-Tense Verbs

CHALLENGE

GET INVOLVED Have students
use **Challenge Activity Card 10**
(page R66) to write an announcement to encourage community
members to volunteer at their
school.

Challenge Activity Card 10

Get Involved

Write an announcement to encourage
community members to volunteer at
your school. To get started,

• make a list of things that volunteers
might do at your school.
• use present tense verbs to tell why
these jobs need to be done.
• describe how helping at your
school could be good for the person
who volunteers.

You may wish to illustrate your announcement to make it more effective.

Present-Tense Verbs

OBJECTIVES
- To recognize and use present-tense verbs
- To write a paragraph, using present-tense verbs, and to respond constructively to another's writing

DAILY LANGUAGE PRACTICE

TRANSPARENCY 31

1 nora volunteered at the hospital (Nora; hospital.)

2 Her work There makes the childrens feel better. (there; children)

BRIDGE TO WRITING Nora _____ (form of the verb *be*) able to help sick children.

ORAL WARM-UP

USE PRIOR KNOWLEDGE On the board, write: *Now Shelley _____ on her paper.* Ask students to suggest a word to complete the sentence.

***Grammar Jingles*™ CD, Intermediate** Use Track 10 for review and reinforcement of verb tenses.

TEACH/MODEL

Have students read the definition and rules for forming present-tense verbs on page 178. Read the examples aloud to students. Have students identify the subject in each sentence and tell whether it is singular or plural. Then model the thinking for the Guided Practice example:

MODEL **The subject of the sentence is the plural noun *Children*. The plural form of the verb should not end with *s*, so the correct answer is *work*.**

Complete the Guided Practice items orally with students, or have them work in pairs to complete the items.

Spelling Present-Tense Verbs

For most verbs, add *s*.

For verbs that end with *s*, *sh*, *ch*, or *x*, add *es*.

For verbs that end with a consonant plus *y*, change the *y* to *i* and add *es*.

178

Present-Tense Verbs

A **present-tense verb** tells about action that is happening now.

To form present-tense verbs, follow these rules:

- If the subject of the sentence is *he*, *she*, *it*, or a singular noun, add *s* or *es* to most verbs.
- If the subject of the sentence is *I*, *you*, *we*, *they*, or a plural noun, do not add *s* or *es* to most verbs.

Examples:

Mrs. Sanchez **leads** her class to the empty lot.

They **plant** a garden.

Guided Practice

A. For each sentence, choose the correct present-tense verb in parentheses ( ).

Example: Children (work, works) to improve their communities. *work*

1. Some children (join, joins) groups to help. join
2. Others (start, starts) their own groups. start
3. Some students (volunteers, volunteer). volunteer
4. They (collect, collects) toys for sick children. collect
5. They also (draw, draws) pictures. draw
6. Reka (pick, picks) up trash in the park. picks
7. Two friends (help, helps) her on Saturdays. help
8. One person (push, pushes) a cart. pushes
9. The other (toss, tosses) the trash into the cart. tosses
10. The people in the neighborhood (recognize, recognizes) the children's hard work. recognize

---

Vocabulary Power page 40

Name _____

PREFIXES

Use the prefixes from the list below to make new words. The first one is done for you.

dis- not or absence of	*mis-* wrong or wrongly
re- again	*un-* not

Beginning Word	Directions	New Word
1. registered	Add a prefix to mean "registered again."	reregistered
2. open	Add a prefix to mean "not opened."	unopened
3. apply	Add a prefix to mean "apply again."	reapply
4. easy	Add a prefix to mean "not easy."	uneasy
5. enlist	Add a prefix to mean "enlist again."	reenlist
6. understand	Add a prefix to mean "wrongly understand."	misunderstand
7. enroll	Add a prefix to mean "enroll again."	reenroll
8. encourage	Change the prefix to mean "not having courage."	discourage
9. request	Add a prefix to mean "not requested."	unrequested

40 Unit 3 • Chapter 14   Vocabulary Power

ESL

ACTION AND MOVEMENT
Make cards with a student's name and an action verb on each. For example: *Jorge walks, Chin-Lin smiles, Felix jumps.*

Have students act out the verbs. Prompt the rest of the group to guess the actions and use them in sentences.

Independent Practice

B. Choose the correct present-tense verb in parentheses ( ). Write each sentence.

Example: Community volunteers (makes, make) a
difference.
Community volunteers make a difference.

11. They (decide, decides) what they want to do. decide
12. A person (find, finds) out who needs help. finds
13. Sometimes a community group (asks, ask) for help from people. asks
14. Some children (starts, start) their own project. start
15. Adults often (help, helps) them. help
16. Shamonda and four other girls (visit, visits) a nursing home. visit
17. One of the girls (play, plays) the piano. plays
18. The girls (take, takes) gifts to their friends at the nursing home. take
19. A gift (make, makes) life more fun for the people who live there. makes
20. How can you (act, acts) to improve your community? act

Remember
that **present-tense verbs show action that is happening now.**

Writing Connection

Writer's Craft: Giving Reasons Write a paragraph about a rule you would like to make. Why is your rule important? Exchange paragraphs with a partner. Circle any present-tense verbs. Think about the reasons your partner gave for making the rule. How could the reasons be expressed more clearly? Give feedback to help your partner make his or her paragraph clearer.

179

Independent Practice

Have students complete the Independent Practice, or modify it using these suggestions:

MODIFIED INSTRUCTION

BELOW-LEVEL STUDENTS Have students underline each subject in Part B and tell whether it is singular or plural. Remind them that the verb form used with a plural subject does not end with *s*.

ABOVE-LEVEL STUDENTS Have students rewrite the sentences in Part B, using different present-tense verbs.

Writing Connection

Writer's Craft: Giving Reasons Have students work with a partner to write to develop ideas for their paragraphs. You may suggest possible areas in which rules are needed, such as school safety, community cleanup, and cafeteria manners. Remind students that they must support their opinions by telling why the new rule is needed.

WRAP-UP/ASSESS

SUMMARIZE Ask students to explain how to form present-tense verbs with singular and plural subjects. Have volunteers suggest some examples.

REACHING ALL LEARNERS

RETEACH

INTERVENTION Lessons in **visual, auditory,** and **kinesthetic** modalities: p. R47 and *Reteach Activities Copying Masters,* p. 29.

REACHING ALL LEARNERS

PRACTICE page 47

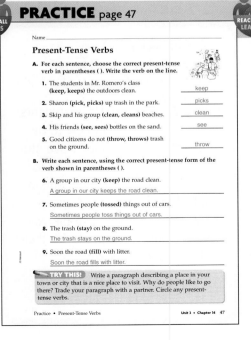

REACHING ALL LEARNERS

CHALLENGE

COLLAGE Have students draw or find pictures that show people involved in various helping jobs. Students should arrange the pictures in a collage and write captions telling what the people are doing in each picture. Remind students to use present-tense verbs in their captions.

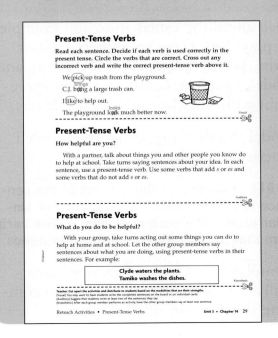

Subject-Verb Agreement

OBJECTIVES

• To recognize and use correct subject-verb agreement

• To write and present an announcement, using correct subject-verb agreement

DAILY LANGUAGE PRACTICE

TRANSPARENCY 31

① andrea is a reporter for the community newspaper (Andrea; newspaper.)

② The papers name is *The gowanville News.* (paper's; *Gowanville*)

BRIDGE TO WRITING Andrea ___(present-tense verb)___ about school news.

ORAL WARM-UP

USE PRIOR KNOWLEDGE Write on the board: *Three friends sell tickets to the basketball game.* Ask students to tell whether the subject of the sentence is singular or plural.

Grammar Jingles™ **CD, Intermediate** Use Track 10 for review and reinforcement of verb tenses.

TEACH/MODEL

Read aloud the explanation and examples on page 180. Have volunteers suggest verbs. Write the verbs on the board, and model using correct subject-verb agreement with singular and plural subjects.

Model the thinking, using the Guided Practice example:

MODEL **I know that the subject of the sentence is *citizen*, which is singular. For singular nouns, the verb ends with *s*. The verb form that agrees with the subject is *needs*.**

Complete the Guided Practice items orally with students, or have them complete the items in small groups.

180

Subject-Verb Agreement

The correct form of the verb depends on the subject of the sentence. A verb must agree with the subject.

You know that a present-tense verb has different forms for singular and plural subjects. The subject and the verb must always match, or agree. A singular subject is usually followed by a verb that ends with *s*. I, *you*, or a plural subject is usually followed by a verb that does not end with *s*.

Examples:
Each citizen **works** to improve the community.

You can **volunteer**, too.

Guided Practice

A. Tell whether the subject of each sentence is singular or plural. Choose the verb in parentheses ( ) that agrees with the subject.

Example: A citizen (need, needs) to give something to the community.   *singular, needs*

 1. Many citizens (attend, attends) government meetings. plural, attend

 2. Some citizens (interest, interests) other people in important projects. plural, interest

 3. They (put, puts) up announcements. plural, put

 4. The announcement (tell, tells) why the project is important. singular, tells

 5. I (write, writes) letters to the newspaper. singular, write

---

Vocabulary Power page 41

Name _____

RHYMING WORDS

► Use words from the Word Box to complete the sentences below. The word you write should rhyme with the underlined word in the sentence.

whale	noon	treat	test	bright	mason	enroll

 1. Stand by the <u>pole</u> if you want to _____enroll_____ for soccer.

 2. The <u>cartoon</u> comes on at _____noon_____.

 3. <u>Preheat</u> the oven before you make the _____treat_____.

 4. John will <u>request</u> to take the _____test_____.

 5. The <u>light</u> was very _____bright_____.

 6. Did you hear the <u>tale</u> about the _____whale_____?

 7. Jason plans to be a _____mason_____.

► Now try these.

enlist	show	pain	twirled	apply	event	shimmering

 8. Jennie will <u>cry</u> if you don't _____apply_____ to be in her club.

 9. Do you <u>know</u> when the _____show_____ starts?

 10. The doctor will <u>explain</u> the _____pain_____ in my foot.

 11. I <u>insist</u> that you _____enlist_____ for the project.

 12. Were you <u>sent</u> to the _____event_____?

 13. The stars were <u>glimmering</u> and _____shimmering_____ in the evening sky.

 14. The ballerina <u>swirled</u> and _____twirled_____ across the stage.

Vocabulary Power   Unit 3 • Chapter 14 41

Listening and Speaking

MAKE A SPEECH Have students write speeches about how to be good citizens at school. Have students present their speeches to small groups. Remind students to use correct subject-verb agreement. Have students use the volume and rate appropriate for their audience and purpose.

Independent Practice

B. If the verb in the sentence agrees with the subject, write *correct*. If the verb does not agree with the subject, write the sentence, using the correct verb.

Remember that a verb must agree with the subject of the sentence.

Example: Television give a lot of information about community matters.
Television gives a lot of information about community matters.

6. Interested citizens writes to Congress. write
7. Children learns about important events by reading. learn
8. A librarian shows them books about government matters. correct
9. Newspapers also tells what is happening. tell
10. A member of Congress listens to people. correct
11. Some students help people running for public office. correct
12. They addresses envelopes. address
13. An active student hand out papers. hands
14. He or she makes phone calls. correct
15. Some students decides to run for office someday. decide

Writing Connection

Real-Life Writing: Announcement With a partner, think of a group activity that could make your community a better place. Together, write an announcement telling why the project is important. You may want to ask the whole school or community to be part of the project.

181

Independent Practice

Have students complete the Independent Practice, or modify it using these suggestions:

MODIFIED INSTRUCTION

BELOW-LEVEL STUDENTS Have students write the sentences and circle the subjects. Then have them determine whether the subject is singular or plural in order to decide whether the verb form is correct.

ABOVE-LEVEL STUDENTS For Part B, have students rewrite sentences that have singular subjects by making the subjects plural and revising the verb.

Writing Connection

Real-Life Writing: Announcement Remind students to check their sentences, adjusting verbs for agreement as necessary. Have students present their announcements to the class. Have students use the appropriate rate and volume when speaking to the class.

WRAP-UP/ASSESS

SUMMARIZE Ask students how checking subject-verb agreement can make writing more effective. **REFLECTION**

RETEACH

INTERVENTION Lessons in **visual**, **auditory**, and **kinesthetic** modalities: p. R47 and *Reteach Activities Copying Masters*, p. 30.

PRACTICE page 48

Name

Subject-Verb Agreement

A. For each sentence, choose the verb in parentheses ( ) that agrees with the subject.

1. John's town (**has, have**) a large empty lot. ___has___
2. Some citizens (**want, wants**) a library in that spot. ___want___
3. A city council (**decide, decides**) about the use of land. ___decides___
4. Citizens (**write, writes**) to the city council. ___write___
5. The letters (**tell, tells**) the city council about citizens' wishes. ___tell___

B. If the verb in the sentence agrees with the subject, write **Correct**. If the verb does not agree with the subject, write the correct form of the verb.

6. Citizens need to tell their leaders about their wishes. ___Correct___
7. Some citizens speaks to the leaders at city meetings. ___speak___
8. Others writes letters. ___write___
9. Mr. Thomas meets with the mayor at times. ___Correct___
10. Mr. Thomas discuss important city business. ___discusses___

TRY THIS! Suppose you could make your city or town a better place. Write a letter to the mayor explaining your idea. Remember to make your subjects and verbs agree.

48 Unit 3 • Chapter 14   Practice • Present-Tense Verbs

CHALLENGE

WRITE TO CONGRESS Have students choose an issue in the community that is important to them. Have students work as a group to compose a letter to their congressperson to address the concern. Model the correct letter form, and prompt students to make sure the subjects and verbs agree.

Subject-Verb Agreement

Read each sentence. Circle each present-tense verb. Draw an arrow from the verb to the subject of the sentence.

Aunt Mimi (votes) in every election.
She (works) with other voters.
They (talk) about their ideas.
Uncle Oz (disagrees) with Aunt Mimi all the time.

VOTE

Subject-Verb Agreement

Why do you think people vote?

With a partner, take turns talking about voting. You may want to discuss class or school elections. In each sentence you say, use a present-tense verb. Then have your partner repeat the sentence, changing the sentence subject and using a different form of the same present-tense verb.

Subject-Verb Agreement

With the rest of your group, make at least six cards with sentence subjects and at least six cards with verbs. Use the following subjects and verbs, or make up your own.

I	talk
She	look
We	run
Our friends	stop
My brother	help
Lee	vote

Turn each group of cards facedown. Take turns picking one card from each pile. Say a sentence with the subject and verb you picked. Use the correct present-tense form of the verb.

Teacher: Cut apart the activities and distribute to students based on the modalities that are their strengths.
(Visual) You may want to have students work with partners to complete this activity.
(Auditory) Suggest that each pair of students share one pair of sentences with the rest of the class.
(Kinesthetic) Have students return their cards to the piles so they can be reused.

30 Unit 3 • Chapter 14   Reteach Activities • Present-Tense Verbs

Extra Practice

OBJECTIVES

- To recognize verb tenses, to correct forms of present-tense verbs, and to correct subject-verb agreement
- To create an announcement and to analyze fonts

DAILY LANGUAGE PRACTICE

TRANSPARENCY 32

1 Many people helps the community. (help)

2 They dont mind giving up their time. (don't)

BRIDGE TO WRITING People __(helping verb)__ found that they get a lot of pleasure out of giving to their community.

ORAL WARM-UP

USE PRIOR KNOWLEDGE Write on the board: *Now our friends _____ at the food bank.* Have students complete the sentence. Point out correct subject-verb agreement.

TEACH/MODEL

Use the Remember box to review verb tenses and subject-verb agreement. Remind students that present-tense verbs used with singular subjects end with *s*. Tell students to refer to page 178 for help with forming present-tense verbs.

Model the thinking for the example in Part A:

MODEL The verb in the sentence is *collects*. It refers to something that is happening now, so it must be a present-tense verb.

Then model the thinking for the example from Part B:

MODEL The subject of the sentence is *Chris*. I know that with a singular subject the verb ends with *s*, so *makes* is the correct answer.

Have students work in pairs to complete the Extra Practice items.

Remember

that verb tense shows when the action happens. Present-tense verbs tell about action that is happening now. A verb must agree with the subject of the sentence.

182

Extra Practice

A. Write each sentence, and underline the verb. Tell whether it shows action that is happening in the present, happened in the past, or will happen in the future. *pages 176–177*

Example: Isis collects food for hungry people. *Isis collects food for hungry people.* *present*

1. She started when she was four. past
2. Isis and her grandmother get food from neighbors. present
3. They will gather thousands of items. future
4. They helped many people with the food. past
5. Isis will help many more people. future

B. Write the correct present-tense verb in parentheses (). *pages 178–179*

Example: Chris (make, makes) his community better by helping animals. *makes*

6. He (work, works) in a shelter, a place for stray animals. works
7. The people at the shelter (takes, take) care of many cats. take
8. Chris (raise, raises) money for the shelter. raises
9. He (feed, feeds) the cats. feeds
10. The cats (play, plays) with Chris, too. play
11. Laws (protect, protects) animals. protect
12. Laws (make, makes) the community safe. make
13. Sometimes a citizen (want, wants) a new rule. wants
14. I (think, thinks) about rules. think
15. Everyone (decide, decides) whether to make rules into laws. decides

---

Vocabulary Power   page 42

Name_____

WORD ENDINGS

Words can have several endings depending on how they are used in a sentence. Read each sentence below. Then circle the letter of the word with the correct ending.

1. Have you _____ for summer camp yet?
   A register
   B registering
   C registered
   D registers

2. I will _____ tomorrow.
   F enroll
   G enrolls
   H enrolling
   J enrolled

3. I am _____ a cookie for dessert.
   A request
   B requested
   C requests
   D requesting

4. My sister is _____ for a job.
   F apply
   G applying
   H applies
   J applied

5. My uncle _____ in many activities.
   A enlist
   B enlisting
   C enlists
   D enlisted

42   Unit 3 • Chapter 14   Vocabulary Power

Art

MAKE A POSTER Have students make posters that offer suggestions for students who are new to the school. Explain that the suggestions they list should help new students be successful at school. Prompt students to state their suggestions in positive terms, such as *Walk quietly in the hall*. Tell students to use present-tense verbs and to check for subject-verb agreement.

C. For each sentence, tell whether the subject is singular or plural. Then write the sentence, using the correct verb in parentheses ( ).

pages 180–181

Example: Volunteers (help, helps) build homes for people who need them.
plural, help
Volunteers help build homes for people who need them.

16. First, they (create, creates) a plan of action. *plural, create*
17. Then the volunteers (choose, chooses) a lot on which to build. *plural, choose*
18. Each person (put, puts) effort into making the plan work. *singular, puts*
19. Another group (work, works) to place a family in the house. *singular, works*
20. Community groups (take, takes) pride in their work. *plural, take*

Writing Connection

Technology Using a computer, type an announcement of an upcoming community event. Computers have different fonts, or styles of letters. Just as subjects and verbs must agree in your writing, your message and your font should match. Try several fonts. Do some look old-fashioned? Do others look modern? If you cannot use a computer, write your announcement in different colors and types of lettering. Think about which colors and types of lettering go best with your message.

For more activities with present-tense verbs and subject-verb agreement, visit *The Learning Site:*
www.harcourtschool.com

183

Building Oral Grammar

To give students practice in recognizing subject-verb agreement, introduce a game of "Sounds Right." Have students make two cards, one that says *agrees* and one that says *does not agree*. Read aloud sentences from this chapter. Some sentences should use correct subject-verb agreement, and some sentences should be incorrect. As students listen to the sentences, have them hold up the appropriate card. For sentences in which the subject and verb do not agree, have students suggest revisions.

Writing Connection

Technology Before they begin, have students participate in small group discussions about the purpose and audience of an announcement. Then have students experiment with different fonts and discuss the differences. Students should select their favorite fonts for their announcements and be prepared to tell why they chose the particular font.

WRAP-UP/ASSESS

SUMMARIZE Have students explain how to tell if a sentence contains the correct present-tense verb form.

ADDITIONAL PRACTICE An additional page of Extra Practice is provided on page 463 of the *Pupil Edition*.

PRACTICE page 49

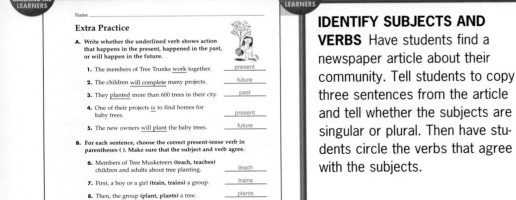

CHALLENGE

IDENTIFY SUBJECTS AND VERBS Have students find a newspaper article about their community. Tell students to copy three sentences from the article and tell whether the subjects are singular or plural. Then have students circle the verbs that agree with the subjects.

TECHNOLOGY *Grammar Practice and Assessment* CD-ROM; *Writing Express* CD-ROM

INTERNET Visit *The Learning Site:*
www.harcourtschool.com

Chapter Review

OBJECTIVES

- To review present-tense verb forms and subject-verb agreement
- To create new words by adding prefixes and suffixes to root words

DAILY LANGUAGE PRACTICE

TRANSPARENCY 32

1. Today senator lawrence visit our school. (Senator Lawrence; visits)
2. Our teacher, mr Harris, am a friend of his. (Mr.; is)

BRIDGE TO WRITING He _____(present tense verb)_____ lunch with our class. The senator _____(contraction with *not*)_____ stay all day.

STANDARDIZED TEST PREP

MODEL TEST-TAKING STRATEGIES Have students read the directions on page 184 silently. Remind them to look over all of the possible answers before choosing one.

Model the thinking. Write this sentence on the board:

Nowadays voters _____ senators.

   1   A   chooses
       B   choose
       C   did choose
       D   chose

MODEL The subject of the sentence, *voters*, is plural. Choice A is wrong because it ends with *s*. C and D are wrong because the word *Nowadays* tells me that the sentence is in the present tense, and these choices are not in the present tense. The correct answer is B.

Have students complete the Chapter Review independently.

STANDARDIZED TEST PREP

Chapter Review

Read the passage and choose the present-tense verb that belongs in each space. Mark the letter for your answer.

> Passing good laws is one way people __(1)__ the nation. Congress __(2)__ laws. Members of Congress __(3)__ to ideas for laws. They __(4)__ these ideas into bills. Members __(5)__ for or against each bill. Finally, they __(6)__ on whether to make the bill a law. The President also __(7)__ to agree or disagree with the bills. After a bill __(8)__ a law, people have to obey it.

TIP Remember to read all the answer choices before making your selection.

1 A improved
  B improve B
  C improves
  D will improve

2 F pass
  G will pass
  H passes H
  J passed

3 A listen A
  B listened
  C listens
  D will listen

4 F writed
  G wrote
  H writes
  J write J

5 A speak A
  B will speak
  C spoke
  D speaks

6 F votes
  G voted
  H vote H
  J will vote

7 A got
  B gets B
  C will get
  D get

8 F will become
  G become
  H became
  J becomes J

For additional test preparations, visit *The Learning Site*:
www.harcourtschool.com

Assessment

PORTFOLIO ASSESSMENT Have students select their best work from the Writing Connections on pages 179, 181, and 183.

ONGOING ASSESSMENT Evaluate the performance of 4–6 students using appropriate checklists and record forms from pages R74–R77.

INTERNET Activities and exercises to help students prepare for state and standardized assessments appear on *The Learning Site*:
www.harcourtschool.com

Prefixes and Suffixes

A **prefix** is a word part added to the beginning of a root word. A prefix changes the meaning of the word. A **suffix** is a word part added to the end of a root word. A suffix also changes the meaning of the word.

Combining prefixes and suffixes with root words such as *view* and *fix* creates new words with new meanings.

re- + *view* = *review* (view again)

fix + -able = *fixable* (able to be fixed)

Prefixes	
re-	again *or* back
dis-	not *or* absence of
un-	not *or* do the opposite of
mis-	bad, badly, wrong, *or* wrongly

Suffixes	
-able	can be
-less	without
-ment	result *or* condition
-ful	full of

YOUR TURN

Experiment with adding prefixes and suffixes to root words to make new words.

1. **Pick a root word from the box below.**

2. **Look at the list of prefixes. Choose a prefix to combine with the root word.**

3. **Choose another root word, and add a suffix from the list.**

4. **Continue adding prefixes and suffixes until you have used each root word in the box.**

TIP Check to make sure that your combinations are real words by looking them up in a dictionary.

Some Root Words			
honor	adjust	agree	play
comfort	do	place	

185

PRACTICE page 50

REACHING ALL LEARNERS

Name _____

Chapter Review

Choose the present-tense verb that belongs in each blank. Fill in the oval next to your choice.

Many boys and girls **(1)** _____ about the community where they live. The world **(2)** _____ also important to them. They **(3)** _____ about what is good for the neighborhood. Such children often **(4)** _____ groups. One group **(5)** _____ for animals. Another group **(6)** _____ up litter. Children's groups also **(7)** _____ trees. In letters they **(8)** _____ their leaders to protect living things.

1 ○ thinks
　● think
　○ thought
　○ will think

2 ● is
　○ are
　○ was
　○ will be

3 ● worry
　○ worries
　○ worried
　○ will worry

4 ● join
　○ joins
　○ joined
　○ will join

5 ○ care
　● cares
　○ cared
　○ will care

6 ● clean
　○ cleans
　○ cleaned
　○ will clean

7 ● plant
　○ plants
　○ planted
　○ will plant

8 ● ask
　○ asks
　○ asked
　○ will ask

50 Unit 3 • Chapter 14　　　　Practice • Present-Tense Verbs

CHALLENGE

REACHING ALL LEARNERS

LEARNING NEW WORDS Have students each use a dictionary to find three words that are new to them and that include a prefix or suffix from this lesson. Have them write each word and its definition on a separate card. Students should then read their words to a partner. Partners should guess the word's meaning. Encourage partners to make up sentences that include the new words.

VOCABULARY

Prefixes and Suffixes

TEACH/MODEL

Write these words on the board: *unfair, fairness.* Ask students what the two words have in common. Guide them to see that each root word is *fair.* Each word has a prefix or a suffix that changes its meaning.

Read aloud the explanation of prefixes and suffixes. Write these words on the board: *help, act, arrange, gentle,* and *communicate.*

Have students suggest words that combine prefixes and suffixes shown in the charts with root words on the board. Then have students complete the Your Turn activity.

WRITING APPLICATION Have students write three sentences that each include at least one word with a prefix and one word with a suffix.

WRAP-UP/ASSESS

Writer's Journal

SUMMARIZE In their journals, have students write a reflection on how knowledge of prefixes and suffixes can help them determine the meanings of unfamiliar words. **REFLECTION**

TECHNOLOGY Additional writing activities are provided on the *Writing Express* CD-ROM

Word Choice

pages 186-193

LESSON ORGANIZER	DAY 1	DAY 2
DAILY LANGUAGE PRACTICE TRANSPARENCIES 33, 34	1. i read magazine ads in scool. (I; school) 2. Ads try to persuade (persuade.)	1. some ads use slogans (Some; slogans.) 2. Slogans is catchy phrases that get peoples attention. (are; people's)
ORAL WARM-UP **Listening/Speaking**	Describe Persuasion 186	List Vivid Verbs and Specific Nouns 188
TEACH/MODEL **WRITING** 	✔ **WORD CHOICE** **Literature Model:** from *Ramona and Her Mother* 186 **Analyze the Model** 186 **Analyze Persuasive Writing** 187	**GUIDED WRITING** **Vivid Verbs** 188 **Specific Nouns** 189 Writing and Thinking: Write to Record Reflections 189
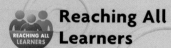 **Reaching All Learners**	**Challenge:** Letters to the Editor 187 *ESL Manual* pp. 76, 77	**ESL:** Sort It Out 189 *ESL Manual* p. 76
GRAMMAR	**HANDS-ON ACTIVITIES** 163I–163J	**HANDS-ON ACTIVITIES** 163I–163J
CROSS-CURRICULAR/ ENRICHMENT	*Vocabulary Power* Explore Word Meaning 186 **advertisements,** billboard, bulletin, logo, slogan See *Vocabulary Power* book. **Listening and Speaking:** Here's My Side 187	**ART:** Art Mobiles 189 *Vocabulary Power* Related Words 186 *Vocabulary Power* p. 43 **Vocabulary activity**

KEY
 ✔ = tested skill

DAY 3	DAY 4	DAY 5
1. Television ads sometimes uses music (use; music.) 2. a jingles is similar to a slogan. (A jingle)	1. sometimes ads can be funny (Sometimes; funny.) 2. Dont you remember any funny commercials (Don't; commercials?)	1. last night I watched an ad that showed talking sheeps! (Last; sheep) 2. The Sheep were talking to a group of childs (sheep; children.)
Discuss Friendly Letters 190	Revise a Sentence 192	Compare Nouns 193
GUIDED WRITING **Friendly Letter** 190 **Analyze the Model** 191 **Prewriting and Drafting** 191	**GUIDED WRITING** **Editing** 192 **Sharing and Reflecting** 192 **Self-Initiated Writing** 192 **Proofreading practice**	**VOCABULARY:** General and Specific Nouns 193
ESL: You've Got Mail 191 *ESL Manual* p. 76	*ESL Manual* p. 76	*ESL Manual* p. 76
HANDS-ON ACTIVITIES 163I–163J	**HANDS-ON ACTIVITIES** 163I–163J	**HANDS-ON ACTIVITIES** 163I–163J
Listening and Speaking: Oral Invitations 190 **Evaluation Criteria:** 191 *Vocabulary Power* General and Specific Nouns 186 *Vocabulary Power* p. 44 **Vocabulary activity**	*Vocabulary Power* Suffixes 186 *Vocabulary Power* p. 45 **Vocabulary activity**	*Vocabulary Power* Word Meaning 186 **Evaluation Criteria:** Self-Evaluation 193

Persuasive Writing

Writer's Craft: Word Choice

OBJECTIVES

- To understand persuasion and to analyze its use in a passage
- To analyze word choice in persuasive writing

SPIRAL REVIEW

DAILY LANGUAGE PRACTICE

TRANSPARENCY 33

1. i read magazine ads in scool. (I; school)

2. Ads try to persuade (persuade.)

ORAL WARM-UP

USE PRIOR KNOWLEDGE Ask students to describe a time when they heard one person trying to persuade another to do something.

Have students read the introduction and model, looking for the ways Beezus uses persuasion.

Analyze THE Model

1. **What does Beezus want her mother to do?** (let Beezus get her hair cut at Robert's School of Hair Design) **LITERAL: NOTE DETAILS**

2. **How does she try to persuade her mother?** (Possible responses: She tells her mother that the haircut won't cost much; she says she saved her allowance; she describes the haircut she wants.) **INFERENTIAL: IMPORTANT DETAILS**

3. **Why did Beezus describe the girl who ice skates?** (Possible responses: Her mother knows what the skater looks like and probably likes her hairstyle.) **CRITICAL: INTERPRET CHARACTERS' MOTIVATIONS**

Word Choice

Persuasion means trying to get someone to agree with your ideas. For example, you might persuade your friend to try your idea for a class project.

Read the following passage from the book *Ramona and Her Mother*. In this paragraph, Beezus persuades her mother to let her get her hair cut.

 LITERATURE MODEL

> "Some of the girls at school get their hair cut at Robert's School of Hair Design. People who are learning to cut hair do the work, but a teacher watches to see that they do it right. It doesn't cost as much as a regular beauty shop. I've saved my allowance, and there's this lady named Dawna who is really good. She can cut hair so it looks like that girl who ice skates on TV, the one with the hair that sort of floats when she twirls around and then falls in place when she stops."
>
> —from *Ramona and Her Mother* by Beverly Cleary

Analyze THE Model

1. What does Beezus want her mother to do?
2. How does she try to persuade her mother?
3. Why did Beezus describe the girl who ice skates?

Vocabulary Power

ad•ver•tise•ments [ad•vûr•tīz′mənts] *n.* Ideas that are made known to the public, especially by paid announcement.

To persuade someone, you need to choose your words carefully. Your words may change the person's feelings about your ideas. To learn more about word choice, study the chart on the next page.

Vocabulary Power

DAY 1 EXPLORE WORD MEANING Introduce and define *advertisements*. **What are some places you see and hear advertisements?**

DAY 2 RELATED WORDS **What kinds of advertisements have you seen?** (See also *Vocabulary Power*, page 43.)

DAY 3 GENERAL AND SPECIFIC NOUNS *Game* is a common noun. **What are some names of specific games?** (See also *Vocabulary Power*, page 44.)

DAY 4 SUFFIXES Write on the board: *advertisement*. **What suffix is added to the base word *advertise*? How does it change the meaning of the word?** (See also *Vocabulary Power*, page 45.)

DAY 5 WORD MEANING **Why do companies use billboards?**

186

Word Choice Strategies	How to Use Strategies	Examples
Use vivid verbs.	• Choose verbs that describe actions in an interesting way.	• A car **whizzes** by. • The puppy **tumbled** down the hill.
Use specific nouns.	• Choose nouns that name one thing instead of nouns that name a whole group. Use the most specific noun for your purpose.	• Jon loves **fruit**. • Jon loves **apples** and **peaches**.

YOUR TURN

THINK ABOUT WORD CHOICE **Work with one or two classmates. Look in your classroom for examples of writing that tries to persuade you. For example, you might look at posters, fliers, notices, and advertisements. Talk about each of the examples you find.**

Answer these questions:

1. What do the writers try to persuade you to do?
2. What vivid verbs do the writers use?
3. What specific nouns do the writers use?
4. Do the writers' words succeed in persuading you? Why or why not?

187

 CHALLENGE

Listening and Speaking

. . . .

HERE'S MY SIDE Write several topics on the board, such as *Buy New Coat* or *Make Allowance Larger*. Ask students to suggest ways they would try to persuade someone to do each thing. Have volunteers present an impromptu persuasive speech on one of the topics, using vivd verbs and specific nouns. Then ask volunteers to summarize the speech.

LETTERS TO THE EDITOR Ask students to cut out letters to the editor from recent issues of the local newspaper. Tell them to look for letters in which the writer expresses an opinion and tries to get others to take action. Have students underline examples of vivid verbs and specific nouns in the letters. Then have them write why they think the word choice makes the article more persuasive.

USING WORD CHOICE Read aloud the instruction on page 186. Guide students through the chart on page 187. Remind students that an action verb is a word that tells what the subject does. Vivid verbs are words that make the action easy to imagine, for example, *stared* instead of *looked*, or *giggled* instead of *laughed*.

Remind students that a noun names a person, an animal, a place, or a thing. Writers use specific nouns to tell their readers exactly what they mean.

Tell students that painting a clear picture with words is an important part of persuasion. Point out that using vivid verbs and specific nouns makes ideas more attractive to readers.

For the Your Turn activity, suggest that each pair or group of students choose one example, such as one poster, flier, or advertisement. Have students write answers to the questions independently and then compare their answers.

WRAP-UP/ASSESS

Writer's Journal **SUMMARIZE** Ask students to reflect in their journals on how choosing words carefully can make persuasive writing stronger. **REFLECTION**

 TECHNOLOGY Additional writing activities are provided on the *Writing Express* CD-ROM

Writer's Craft: Word Choice

OBJECTIVES
• To identify and use vivid verbs and specific nouns
• To record reflections about advertisements

DAILY LANGUAGE PRACTICE

TRANSPARENCY 33

① some ads use slogans (Some; slogans.)

② Slogans is catchy phrases that get peoples attention. (are; people's)

ORAL WARM-UP

USE PRIOR KNOWLEDGE Have students imagine that they are writing slogans to persuade people to buy lemonade at a lemonade stand. Ask: **What vivid verbs and specific nouns could you use to grab customers' attention?**

GUIDED WRITING

VIVID VERBS As students read the directions for Part A, point out that each verb will be used only once. Remind students to read through all the sentences before they make their choices. (1. skips, 2. flapped, 3. perches, 4. jingled, 5. whispered)

Point out that in Part B many different words could be correct in each blank. After students complete the activity, have students share their answers. Ask a volunteer to write on the board the vivid verbs suggested by students. Discuss why these verbs are effective. (Responses will vary; check that words students use are verbs.)

Vivid Verbs

A. Choose a vivid verb from the box to replace the underlined word in each sentence. Write the revised sentence on your paper.

flapped	perches	whispered
jingled	skips	

1. Annie <u>goes</u> down the street.
2. The bird <u>moved</u> its wings.
3. Jerry <u>sits</u> on the edge of the chair.
4. The telephone <u>rang</u>.
5. "Please be quiet," Kate <u>said</u>.

B. Read the paragraph. Think of vivid verbs you can use to fill in the blanks. Write the completed paragraph on your paper.

As the storm came closer, the children _____ across the fields. Soon, the rain began to _____ down from the sky. The wind _____ in their faces. The huge raindrops _____ their clothes. Still the children _____ outside. The thunder _____. At last the children _____ into a small shed. "Oh no," Matthew _____, "the roof _____!" The children _____.

188

Vocabulary Power page 43

Name _____

RELATED WORDS

You have just opened your own pizza place. Follow the directions to create advertisements for your new restaurant.

1. Draw a logo to put on T-shirts. Include the name of your restaurant.

2. Write a slogan to put on the cover of your menu.
   Responses will vary.

3. Create a billboard for your restaurant.

4. Write a bulletin for your restaurant that people will hear on the radio. Include rhyming words.
   Responses will vary.

Vocabulary Power   Unit 3 • Chapter 15   43

Specific Nouns

C. Choose a specific noun from the box to replace the general noun that is underlined in each sentence. Write the revised sentence on your paper.

barn	disk	table	cabin	papers

1. Put this <u>thing</u> in the slot in the computer.
2. That <u>furniture</u> is too heavy to carry.
3. Can you move that pile of <u>stuff</u>?
4. Cows live in a <u>building</u>.
5. Abraham Lincoln lived in a log <u>building</u>.

D. Look at each pair of nouns. Decide which noun is more specific. Write that noun on your paper.

1. book, textbook
2. jacket, clothing
3. machine, computer
4. checkers, game
5. instrument, piano

Writing AND Thinking

Write to Record Reflections Sometimes advertisements persuade you to buy things you really don't need. How can you decide whether or not you ought to buy what someone is trying to persuade you to buy? Write your reflections in your Writer's Journal.

Specific Nouns

Specific Nouns

Work through Part C with students, pointing out again that each answer will be used only once. (1. disk, 2. table, 3. papers, 4. barn, 5. cabin)

Have students complete Part D in pairs. Then ask them to write the general noun from each pair on their papers. Tell students to brainstorm other specific nouns that relate to each general noun. Allow approximately five minutes for this activity, and then ask volunteers to share their nouns. Discuss why the specific nouns they have brainstormed would be more effective than each general noun. (1. textbook, 2. jacket, 3. computer, 4. checkers, 5. piano)

Writing and Thinking

Write to Record Reflections Before students write, have them look at some advertisements from magazines for young people. Point out ads for products that students do not need, such as candy and collectible cards. After students write, guide them in a class discussion of wise spending habits and the influence of advertisements. Invite students to draw upon their written reflections as they contribute to the class discussion.

WRAP-UP/ASSESS

SUMMARIZE Why do advertisers use vivid verbs and specific nouns to describe their products?

Art

• • • • • • • • • • • • • • •

ART MOBILES Have students work in small groups to find an interesting picture in a magazine. Have students paste the picture to construction paper and attach it to a hanger, using string or yarn. Then have groups think of six vivid verbs and/or specific nouns that relate to the picture. Ask the groups to write each word on a colorful square of construction paper and attach the squares to the mobiles.

REACHING ALL LEARNERS

ESL

SORT IT OUT Label three boxes *Clothing*, *Toys*, and *Food*. Cut out pictures of different toys, articles of clothing, and types of foods from magazines and catalogs. Paste the pictures to cards, and label them, using specific nouns. Ask students to sort the cards into their appropriate boxes. Use the cards as a vocabulary-building tool for students. Have students make additional cards that are appropriate for these boxes. Discuss their choices.

Writer's Craft: Word Choice

OBJECTIVES
- To recognize and analyze the parts of a persuasive friendly letter
- To generate ideas and to write a persuasive friendly letter

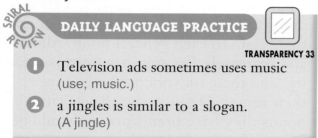

DAILY LANGUAGE PRACTICE

TRANSPARENCY 33

❶ Television ads sometimes uses music
(use; music.)

❷ a jingles is similar to a slogan.
(A jingle)

ORAL WARM-UP

USE PRIOR KNOWLEDGE Why do people write friendly letters?

GUIDED WRITING

Friendly Letter

READ AND RESPOND TO THE MODEL Tell students that you will read aloud Teresa's letter, and have them determine a purpose for listening. (to find out the reasons Teresa uses to persuade Carmen) After you have read the letter aloud, discuss whether students think Teresa does a good job of trying to persuade Carmen. Remind students to support their evaluations with examples from the letter.

FOCUS ON ORGANIZATION Have students reread the letter silently, using the side notes to find the main parts. Call on volunteers to name and explain each part. Point out the importance of Teresa's friendly and sincere final paragraph.

FOCUS ON WRITER'S CRAFT Have students find and read aloud Teresa's main point or first statement of opinion. (*I think this haircut would look great on you.*) Point out the reasons and details she gives to support her opinion. Discuss the order of her reasons, pointing out that she restates her opinion at the end.

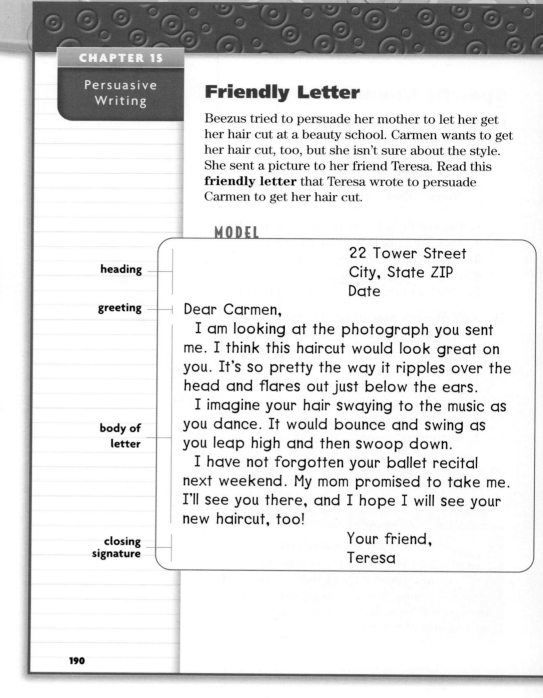

CHAPTER 15

Persuasive Writing

Friendly Letter

Beezus tried to persuade her mother to let her get her hair cut at a beauty school. Carmen wants to get her hair cut, too, but she isn't sure about the style. She sent a picture to her friend Teresa. Read this **friendly letter** that Teresa wrote to persuade Carmen to get her hair cut.

MODEL

heading
> 22 Tower Street
> City, State ZIP
> Date

greeting
> Dear Carmen,

body of letter
> I am looking at the photograph you sent me. I think this haircut would look great on you. It's so pretty the way it ripples over the head and flares out just below the ears.
>
> I imagine your hair swaying to the music as you dance. It would bounce and swing as you leap high and then swoop down.
>
> I have not forgotten your ballet recital next weekend. My mom promised to take me. I'll see you there, and I hope I will see your new haircut, too!

closing signature
> Your friend,
> Teresa

190

Vocabulary Power page 44

Name _____

GENERAL AND SPECIFIC NOUNS

Read each word. Choose a more specific noun from the Word Box and write it on the line.

General			
dictionary	circle	goose	shirt
advertisements	slogan	United States	kitchen
sandals	billboard	bulletin	logo
pancakes	ice cream		

General	Specific
1. notices	advertisements
2. bird	goose
3. saying	slogan
4. book	dictionary
5. magazine	bulletin
6. room	kitchen
7. picture	logo
8. clothing	shirt
9. food	pancakes
10. sign	billboard
11. shape	circle
12. country	United States
13. dessert	ice cream
14. shoes	sandals

44 Unit 3 • Chapter 15   Vocabulary Power

Listening and Speaking

ORAL INVITATIONS Have students work in pairs to practice giving oral invitations to one another. Have students take turns choosing an event such as a birthday party or recital. Then have them invite their partner to the event, using appropriate verbal and nonverbal communication skills. Remind students to use vivid verbs and specific nouns.

Analyze THE Model

1. What is Teresa persuading Carmen to do?
2. What vivid verbs does Teresa use?
3. Why was it a good idea for Teresa to use specific nouns instead of more general nouns like *thing*?
4. Do you think Teresa's letter will succeed in persuading Carmen? Why or why not?

YOUR TURN

WRITING PROMPT Write a friendly letter to persuade your friend who lives in the next town to come to the science fair with you. Use vivid verbs and specific nouns.

STUDY THE PROMPT Ask yourself these questions:

1. What is your purpose for writing?
2. Who is your audience?
3. What reasons will persuade your reader?

Prewriting and Drafting

Plan Your Friendly Letter Use a chart like this one to help you plan your letter.

Tell your friend about your idea.

Give reasons to persuade your friend to agree with your idea. Choose your words carefully.

End your letter in a friendly way.

USING YOUR

Handbook

• Use the Writer's Thesaurus to find vivid verbs and specific nouns to use in your letter.

191

Analyze THE Model

1. **What is Teresa persuading Carmen to do?** (to get her hair cut in a certain style) **LITERAL: NOTE DETAILS**

2. **What vivid verbs does Teresa use?** (Possible responses: *ripples, flares, bounce, swing, leap,* and *swoop.*) **LITERAL: NOTE DETAILS**

3. **Why was it a good idea for Teresa to use specific nouns instead of more general nouns like *thing*?** (Possible response: It was a good idea because specific nouns paint a clearer picture than more general nouns, and they are more persuasive.) **CRITICAL: MAKE JUDGMENTS**

4. **Do you think Teresa's letter will succeed in persuading Carmen? Why or why not?** (Possible response: It probably will because it is clear, sincere, and filled with vivid verbs and specific nouns.) **CRITICAL: SPECULATE**

Discuss the writing prompt. As students consider ways to persuade their friends, point out that they may want to focus on why the science fair will be fun and how they will have a good time together.

Prewriting and Drafting

Remind students to focus on details and reasons that are related to the topic and the purpose of the letter.

WRAP-UP/ASSESS

SUMMARIZE What are some important things to remember when writing a persuasive letter?

REACHING ALL LEARNERS

Evaluation Criteria

Review the criteria that students should apply:

• Use vivid verbs
• Use specific nouns
• Use the correct form for a friendly letter that persuades

Work with students to add other criteria.

ESL

MAIL A TOPIC Have students think of a topic for a persuasive friendly letter. Then have them e-mail their topic and a list of supporting reasons to a partner. Tell students to evaluate one another's lists of reasons, pointing out the reasons they think work best and making suggestions to strengthen less-persuasive reasons.

Writer's Craft: Word Choice

OBJECTIVES
- To revise and proofread a persuasive friendly letter, focusing on reasons, vivid verbs, and specific nouns
- To share and reflect upon a persuasive friendly letter

DAILY LANGUAGE PRACTICE

TRANSPARENCY 34

1 sometimes ads can be funny
(Sometimes; funny.)

2 Dont you remember any funny commercials (Don't; commercials?)

ORAL WARM-UP

USE PRIOR KNOWLEDGE Write on the board: *It would be nice if you came to see some special things at our school sometime.* Ask students to suggest revisions to make the sentence more specific and persuasive.

GUIDED WRITING

Editing
Discuss the editing questions with students. Have them reread Teresa's letter, using it as a model as they determine what works well in their own letters as well as how they might make improvements.

Before students proofread, review spelling strategies. Have students focus on words that follow a regular pattern, such as consonant-vowel-consonant (*hop*, *sat*) and consonant-vowel-consonant-silent *e* (*hope*, *rope*).

Sharing and Reflecting
Have students respond constructively regarding their partners' use of persuasion.

WRAP-UP/ASSESS

SUMMARIZE How did you revise and edit your letter to make it more persuasive and effective?

Editor's Marks
- ✗ take out text
- ∧ add text
- ᔆ move text
- ¶ new paragraph
- ≡ capitalize
- / lowercase
- ◯ correct spelling

Editing

Read over the draft of your friendly letter. Do you want to make any changes? Use this checklist to help you revise your letter.

- ☑ Have you made it clear what you want your reader to do?
- ☑ Have you given good reasons to persuade your reader?
- ☑ Did you use enough vivid verbs?
- ☑ Are there places where you can use more specific nouns?
- ☑ Did you use the correct form?

Use this checklist as you proofread your paragraph.

- ☑ I have begun my sentences with capital letters.
- ☑ I have used the correct end marks for my sentences.
- ☑ I have used helping verbs correctly.
- ☑ I have checked for subject-verb agreement.
- ☑ I have used a dictionary to check my spelling.

Sharing and Reflecting

Writer's Journal Exchange letters with a partner. Share ideas about how you can improve your persuasive writing by using vivid verbs and specific nouns. Write your reflections in your Writer's Journal.

192

Vocabulary Power   page 45

Name _____

SUFFIXES

Suffixes can be added to the ends of words to change their meaning.

-less	without	-ful	full of
-ment	result of condition	-en	make to be
-ness	state or condition	-er, -or	one who

Read each sentence below. Choose the word in parentheses ( ) with the correct suffix. Write it on the line. The first one is done for you.

1. Julie wanted to sell her old bike, so she wrote an <u>advertisement</u>. (advertiser, advertisement)

2. A billboard can be ___helpful___ when you're advertising. (helpful, helpless)

3. Do not be ___careless___ when you use scissors. (careful, careless)

4. Each board must be the correct ___thickness___ (thicken, thickness)

5. He works for the national ___government___ (governor, government)

6. Add color to the logo to ___brighten___ it up. (brighten, brightness)

7. Kelly considered the question for a long time. She was ___thoughtful___ (thoughtless, thoughtful)

8. This game needs another ___player___. (playful, player)

Vocabulary Power   Unit 3 • Chapter 15   45

Self-Initiated Writing

Ask students to think about recent situations in which they wanted to persuade a friend to do something, such as joining a sports team or sharing expenses for a gift. Encourage students to consider writing a persuasive friendly letter to a friend, applying the strategies they learned in the lesson.

General and Specific Nouns

General nouns, like **vehicle**, name large groups of things. More specific nouns, like **truck**, name smaller groups of things. Some nouns, like **dump truck**, are even more specific.

Vehicle (General)

Truck (More Specific)

Dump Truck (Most Specific)

YOUR TURN

Work with a partner to create your own diagram like the one on this page. You can draw the pictures or write the words. Use one of the following general nouns to begin your diagram, or think of an idea of your own.

General Nouns	
furniture	animal
plant	person
place	food

193

Evaluation Criteria

SELF-EVALUATION Revisit the Evaluation Criteria to have students informally rate their own writing on a scale of 1 to 4. You might have them use stick-on notes to label their papers.

VOCABULARY

General and Specific Nouns

OBJECTIVES
- To understand general and specific nouns
- To sequence nouns in order of specificity

DAILY LANGUAGE PRACTICE

TRANSPARENCY 34

1 last night I watched an ad that showed talking sheeps! (Last; sheep)

2 The Sheep were talking to a group of childs (sheep; children.)

ORAL WARM-UP

USE PRIOR KNOWLEDGE Write the word *bug* on the board, and ask students to think about what comes to mind. Repeat with *spider* and with *tarantula*. Ask: **How does the picture in your mind change with the different words?**

TEACH/MODEL

Guide students through the explanation and the diagram on page 193. Ask students why it might be important to know how to classify general, specific, and more specific nouns.

As students complete the Your Turn activity, have them freewrite a list of specific nouns to go with the general noun they choose. After they have generated an initial list, they can then classify the nouns as *more specific* or *most specific*.

WRAP-UP/ASSESS

Writer's Journal

SUMMARIZE Ask students to reflect in their journals on how using specific nouns and vivid verbs make writing and speaking more persuasive.

LESSON ORGANIZER	DAY 1	DAY 2
DAILY LANGUAGE PRACTICE TRANSPARENCIES 35, 36	1. each state elect a governor (Each; elects; governor.) 2. Governors is elected by Voters. (are; voters) **Bridge to Writing** The governor (present-tense verb) in the state capital.	1. Thomas jefferson wrote the Declaration of Independence. (Jefferson) 2. He worked very hardd to make it right (hard; right.) **Bridge to Writing** My class (present-tense verb) about Jefferson.
ORAL WARM-UP Listening/Speaking	Identify Verb and Tense 194	Change Verb Tense 196 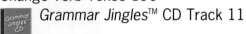 *Grammar Jingles*™ CD Track 11
TEACH/MODEL GRAMMAR **KEY** ✔ = tested skill	✔ **PAST-TENSE AND FUTURE-TENSE VERBS** 194–195 • To identify past-tense and future-tense verbs • To identify verb tense in a quotation	✔ **MORE ABOUT PAST-TENSE AND FUTURE-TENSE VERBS** 196–197 • To correctly form past-tense and future-tense verbs • To write, using past-tense and future-tense verbs
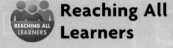 **Reaching All Learners**	**Modified Instruction** Below-Level: Determine Verb Tense Above-Level: Write Sentences **Reteach:** *Reteach Activities Copying Masters* pp. 31 and R48 **Challenge:** Activity Card 11, R67 *ESL Manual* pp. 78, 79 *Practice Book* p. 51	**Modified Instruction** Below-Level: Use a Chart Above-Level: Write New Sentences **ESL:** Sort Verbs 196 *ESL Manual* pp. 78, 80 **Reteach:** *Reteach Activities Copying Masters* pp. 32 and R48 **Challenge:** Write a Letter 197 *Practice Book* p. 52
WRITING	Writing Connection 195 Writer's Journal: Thinking About Quotations	Writing Connection 197 Writer's Craft: Using Powerful Words
CROSS-CURRICULAR/ ENRICHMENT	*Vocabulary Power* Explore Word Meaning 194 democracy, **federal**, government, monarchy, republic See *Vocabulary Power* book.	*Vocabulary Power* Compare and Contrast 194 *Vocabulary Power* p. 46 🏆 **Vocabulary activity**

WRITING ACTIVITIES
Writing Express CD-ROM

Visit *The Learning Site:*
www.harcourtschool.com

DAY 3	DAY 4	DAY 5
1. Many presidents was governors first (were; first.)	**1.** Next week we visited our state capital. (will visit)	**1.** My brother lives in washington, d.c., last year. (lived; Washington, D.C.)
2. President clinton was the governor of arkansas. (Clinton; Arkansas.)	**2.** yesterday we will watch a movie about government. (Yesterday; watched)	**2.** He workked at the Library of congress. (worked; Congress.)
Bridge to Writing He ___(past-tense verb)___ very hard to become President.	**Bridge to Writing** Many people ___(future-tense verb)___ the capital this year.	**Bridge to Writing** The Library of Congress ___(helping verb)___ founded in 1800. It ___(linking verb)___ the largest library in the world.
Use Different Tenses 198 *Grammar Jingles*™ CD Track 11	Tell Verbs in Past and Future Tense 200	
✔ **CHOOSING THE CORRECT TENSE** 198–199 • To recognize and choose the correct verb tense • To write an e-mail message, using correct verb tenses	**EXTRA PRACTICE** 200–201 • To recognize and use past-tense and future-tense verbs • To write an ad, using correct verb tenses 🖥 **Practice and assessment**	**TEST PREP** **CHAPTER REVIEW** 202–203 • To review past-tense and future-tense verbs • To practice listening for facts and opinions
Modified Instruction Below-Level: Model the Thinking Above-Level: Rewrite Sentences **ESL:** Work with a Partner 198 *ESL Manual* pp. 78, 81 **Reteach:** *Reteach Activities Copying Masters* pp. 33 and R48 **Challenge:** Find a Match 199 *Practice Book* p. 53	**Building Oral Grammar** Speak and Respond in Pairs 201 **Challenge:** Write a Story 201 *ESL Manual* pp. 78, 82 *Practice Book* p. 54	**Challenge:** Discuss Issues 203 *Practice Book* p. 55 *ESL Manual* pp. 78, 83

Writing Connection 199
   Technology
	Writing Connection 201
	   Real-Life Writing: Writing
	   a Want Ad
		Writing Application 203

Vocabulary Power
   Classify and Categorize 194
   Vocabulary Power p. 47
 🖥 **Vocabulary activity**
	Vocabulary Power
	   Explore Word Meaning 194
	   Vocabulary Power p. 48
	 🖥 **Vocabulary activity**
	 Social Studies: Branches of Government 200
		Vocabulary Power
		   Content-Area Words 194
		   Listening and Speaking: Listening for Facts and Opinions 203

CHAPTER 16 193B

Past-Tense and Future-Tense Verbs

OBJECTIVES
- To identify past-tense and future-tense verbs
- To copy a quotation, identifying past-tense and future-tense verbs

DAILY LANGUAGE PRACTICE

TRANSPARENCY 35

1 each state elect a governor (Each; elects; governor.)

2 Governors is elected by Voters. (are; voters)

BRIDGE TO WRITING The governor _(present-tense verb)_ in the state capital.

ORAL WARM-UP

USE PRIOR KNOWLEDGE Read aloud this sentence: _In 2000, voters elected a new President._ Ask students to identify the verb and tell whether the action is happening now, has happened in the past, or will happen in the future.

TEACH/MODEL

Remind students that the verb tense tells the time of the action. Read aloud the definitions, explanation, and examples on page 194.

Work through the Guided Practice with students.

Vocabulary Power

fed·er·al [fed′ər·əl] _adj._ Having to do with the central government of the United States.

194

Past-Tense and Future-Tense Verbs

A **past-tense verb** shows that an action happened earlier. A **future-tense verb** shows that an action will happen later.

You know that present-tense verbs describe action that is happening now. To tell about something that happened earlier or that will happen later, use the past tense or the future tense.

Examples:

Present tense The people **vote** for the President today.

Past tense The people **voted** for the President yesterday.

Future tense The people **will vote** for the President tomorrow.

Guided Practice

A. Find the verb in each sentence. Tell whether it is a _past-tense_ verb or _future-tense_ verb.

Example: All the states decided to elect governors. _decided; past tense_

1. Governors will discuss laws for their states. will discuss; future tense
2. The state lawmakers will vote on the laws. will vote; future tense
3. They provided money for schools last year. provided; past tense
4. They helped state parks. helped; past tense
5. They discussed state roads. discussed; past tense

Vocabulary Power

DAY 1 EXPLORE WORD MEANING Introduce and define _federal_. **Who is President of the United States? Name the governor and mayor.**

DAY 2 COMPARE AND CONTRAST **How are a monarchy and a democracy alike? How are they different?** (See also _Vocabulary Power_, page 46.)

DAY 3 CLASSIFY AND CATEGORIZE Write on the board: _federal, government, lawmakers, firefighters._ **Which word does not belong in this group? Why?** (See also _Vocabulary Power_, page 47.)

DAY 4 EXPLORE WORD MEANING Write _government_ on the board. Ask: **Why do you think we need a government?** (See also _Vocabulary Power_, page 48.)

DAY 5 CONTENT-AREA WORDS _Federal_ is a word students might read in social studies. Have students make a list of social studies words related to federal.

Independent Practice

B. Write the verb in each sentence. Tell whether the verb is *past tense* or *future tense*.

Example: Kerry presented a report.
presented; past tense

6. She explained about the President's many jobs.
   explained; past tense
7. The President will talk on television to the nation tonight. will talk; future tense
8. The President will approve new laws.
   will approve; future tense
9. Presidents visited other countries in the past.
   visited; past tense
10. Our President will greet other world leaders at the dinner next week. will greet; future tense
11. Americans elected John F. Kennedy President in 1960. elected; past tense
12. The most people voted for Richard Nixon in 1968. voted; past tense
13. They will elect a new President every four years. will elect; future tense
14. Past Presidents studied federal issues. studied; past tense
15. Our next President will listen to citizens, too.
    will listen; future tense

Remember
that a past-tense verb tells what happened in the past. A future-tense verb tells what will happen later.

**James Carter, Jr.,
39th President of the U.S.,
1977–1981.**

**Ronald Reagan,
40th President of the U.S.,
1981–1989.**

Writing Connection

Writer's Journal: Thinking About Quotations Find an interesting quotation from a speech by a President. Copy the quotation in your journal. Look for vivid verbs that the President used. Circle these words. Then underline any past-tense and future-tense verbs.

195

Independent Practice

Have students complete the Independent Practice, or modify it using these suggestions:

MODIFIED INSTRUCTION

BELOW-LEVEL STUDENTS To help students decide whether the verb is in the past tense or future tense, have them ask themselves *Did the action already happen or is it going to happen?*

ABOVE-LEVEL STUDENTS Have students write four additional sentences using past-tense and future-tense verbs.

Writing Connection

Writer's Journal: Thinking About Quotations Allow students to use several resources such as traditional and electronic encyclopedias, books of quotations, and the Internet to locate a quote from a President. Have students write a reflection on why the quote they selected appealed to them.

WRAP-UP/ASSESS

SUMMARIZE What does a past-tense verb show? What does a future-tense verb show?

RETEACH

INTERVENTION Lessons in **visual, auditory,** and **kinesthetic** modalities: p. R48 and *Reteach Activities Copying Masters,* p. 31.

PRACTICE page 51

Name _____

Past-Tense and Future-Tense Verbs

A. Underline the verb in each sentence. Write whether the verb is *past tense* or *future tense.*

1. Andy asked the librarian about the U.S. Constitution.   past tense

2. She showed him three books about the topic.   past tense

3. He finished his paper last night.   past tense

4. Tomorrow, Andy will share his report with the class.   future tense

5. He will list information about laws.   future tense

B. Write each sentence and underline the verb. Tell if the verb is *past tense* or *future tense.*

6. Andy will remind the class on Tuesday about amendments.
   Andy will remind the class on Tuesday about amendments.
   future tense

7. Lawmakers added amendments to the Constitution.
   Lawmakers added amendments to the Constitution. past tense

8. They called the first ten amendments the Bill of Rights.
   They called the first ten amendments the Bill of Rights.

TRY THIS! If you could write a law, what would it be? Why is it a good idea? Use past-tense and future-tense verbs.

Practice • Past-Tense and Future-Tense Verbs   Unit 3 • Chapter 16 51

CHALLENGE

GET ELECTED Have students use **Challenge Activity Card 11** (page R67) to plan an election campaign.

Challenge Activity Card 11

Get Elected

Imagine that you are running for public office. You must convince voters that you are the best person for the job. Create a poster and a bumper sticker to help you get elected.

• Decide what job you want. Do you want to be a senator, a governor, or the president? Make a list of reasons why you would be a good person for that office. Then make a list telling what you will do if you are elected. Be sure to use past tense and future tense.

• Design a poster that will persuade people to vote for you. Use your slogan on the poster.

• Design a bumper sticker that will remind people to vote for you.

Past-Tense and Future-Tense Verbs

Read each sentence. Underline each past-tense verb. Circle each future-tense verb.

Pablo visited the White House.

He liked the tour.

We will go to Washington soon.

I will visit the White House.

Past-Tense and Future-Tense Verbs

What do you enjoy most at school?

Talk with your partner about something you did in school last year and something you would like to do next year. Use at least three past-tense verbs and three future-tense verbs. When your partner talks, listen for the verbs he or she uses. Raise both hands when you hear a past-tense verb. Stand up when you hear a future-tense verb.

Past-Tense and Future-Tense Verbs

With a partner, make a set of six cards. On each card, write one of these verb forms.

| voted | will vote | helped | will help | asked | will ask |

Sort the cards into two groups, with past-tense verbs in one group and future-tense verbs in another group. Take turns picking a card from either group. Say a sentence using the verb you picked.

Reteach Activities • Past-Tense and Future-Tense Verbs   Unit 3 • Chapter 16 31

More About Past-Tense and Future-Tense Verbs

OBJECTIVES
- To correctly form past-tense and future-tense verbs
- To write a persuasive paragraph, using past-tense and future-tense verbs

DAILY LANGUAGE PRACTICE

TRANSPARENCY 35

1 Thomas jefferson wrote the Declaration of Independence. (Jefferson)

2 He worked very hardd to make it right (hard; right.)

BRIDGE TO WRITING My class _____ (present-tense verb) _____ about Jefferson.

ORAL WARM-UP

USE PRIOR KNOWLEDGE Write on the board: *People vote on Tuesday.* Have students first say the sentence as if *Tuesday* were in the past, and then as if it were in the future.

Grammar Jingles™ **CD, Intermediate** Use Track 11 for review and reinforcement of past-tense and future-tense verbs.

TEACH/MODEL

Read aloud the explanation and examples on page 196. Point out that students must change the spelling of some verbs ending with *y* or with one vowel followed by one consonant before they add *ed*. Model the thinking, using examples from the chart:

MODEL **To make the past tense of *cry*, I must change the *y* to *i* before I add *ed*. To make the past tense of *clap*, I have to double the *p* and add *ed*.**

Complete the Guided Practice items orally with students, or have them complete the items in pairs.

196 UNIT 3

Present Tense	Past Tense
talk	talked
save	saved
cry	cried
clap	clapped

196

More About Past-Tense and Future-Tense Verbs

To form the past tense of most verbs, add *ed* or *d* to the present-tense verbs.

The spellings of some verbs change when you add *ed*. To form the future tense of a verb, use the helping verb *will* with the main verb.

Examples:

Past tense

Last spring our class **visited** the Congress.

Another senator **stopped** by to ask a question.

Future tense

Our class **will visit** the Library of Congress.

Guided Practice

A. Give the correct form of the verb in parentheses ( ).

Example: The Constitution was (accept) in 1787. (past tense) *accepted*

1. We (want) a national capital. (past tense) wanted
2. George Washington (locate) the capital on a river. (past tense) located
3. Many people (plan) the new city. (past tense) planned
4. We (visit) our nation's capital next fall. (future tense) will visit
5. The capital (rest) in the nation's center in 1791. (past tense) rested

---

Vocabulary Power page 46

Name _____

COMPARE AND CONTRAST

The words *monarchy* and *republic* are alike in some ways and different in others. Look at the diagram below. In the center circle, write the word from the Word Box that tells about both words. In the circle with *monarchy*, write the five words that tell only about *monarchy*. In the circle with *republic*, write the five words that tell only about *republic*.

royalty	king	election
President	government	democracy
voting	queen	throne
kingdom	federal	

monarchy
royalty
kingdom
king
queen
throne

both
government

republic
President
voting
federal
election
democracy

46   Unit 3 • Chapter 16   Vocabulary Power

REACHING ALL LEARNERS

ESL

SORT VERBS Write the following verbs on cards: *carried, will grab, hopped, will play, jumped, will paint, smiled,* and *will thank*. On the board, make columns labeled *Past Tense* and *Future Tense*.

Shuffle the cards. Have each student select a card and tape it to the board in the appropriate column. Then have the student use the verb in a sentence.

Independent Practice

B. Write each sentence, using the verb in parentheses ( ). Form the tense that is given.

Example: The first Congress (form) in 1789. (past tense) *formed*

6. The first House of Representatives (include) only 59 members. (past tense) *included*
7. We (elect) new representatives next year. (future tense) *will elect*
8. The number of representatives (depend) on our state's population. (future tense) *will depend*
9. California (occupy) 52 Congressional seats in 1995. (past tense) *occupied*
10. Lois and Jill (study) the Congress. (past tense) *studied*
11. The senators (work) in the Capitol Building last month. (past tense) *worked*
12. Voters (select) a senator in the next election. (future tense) *will select*
13. Congress (pick) a leader soon. (future tense) *will pick*
14. Members of Congress (work) hard in the coming months. (future tense) *will work*
15. Congress (pass) new laws. (past tense) *passed*

Remember to add *ed* or *d* to most present-tense verbs to show past tense. Use the helping verb *will* with a main verb to show future tense.

Writing Connection

Writer's Craft: Using Powerful Words With a partner, brainstorm an idea for making an improvement in your community. Make a list of words you might use to urge people in government to act on your idea. Use your list of words to write a paragraph about your idea. Check to be sure you have used past-tense and future-tense verbs correctly.

197

Independent Practice

Have students complete the Independent Practice, or modify it using these suggestions:

MODIFIED INSTRUCTION

BELOW-LEVEL STUDENTS Have students refer to the chart on page 196 to decide how to form the past-tense and future-tense verbs.

ABOVE-LEVEL STUDENTS Have students write five new sentences, using the past-tense or future-tense forms of five of the verbs in parentheses.

Writing Connection

Writer's Craft: Using Powerful Words Have students participate in a class discussion about possible improvements in the community. When students have finished writing, have them share their paragraphs in small groups.

WRAP-UP/ASSESS

SUMMARIZE Ask students to tell how to form past-tense verbs and future-tense verbs.

RETEACH

INTERVENTION Lessons in **visual, auditory,** and **kinesthetic** modalities: p. R48 and *Reteach Activities Copying Masters,* p. 32.

PRACTICE page 52

Name

More About Past-Tense and Future-Tense Verbs

A. Give the correct form of the verb in parentheses ( ). Use the tense that is given at the end of each sentence.

1. Andy **(answer)** questions about free speech. **(past tense)** — *answered*
2. He **(describe)** the importance of privacy. **(past tense)** — *described*
3. One amendment **(include)** the right to a fair trial. **(past tense)** — *included*
4. The law **(treat)** everyone equally. **(future tense)** — *will treat*
5. A jury **(make)** the right decision. **(future tense)** — *will make*

B. Write each sentence using the verb in parentheses ( ). Form the tense that is given at the end of the sentence.

6. It said that citizens everywhere **(vote)**. **(future tense)**
   It said that citizens everywhere will vote.
7. In the United States, before 1920, only men **(vote)**. **(past tense)**
   In the United States, before 1920, only men voted.
8. A constitutional amendment **(allow)** women to vote. **(past tense)**
   A constitutional amendment allowed women to vote.

TRY THIS! Why is it important that everyone be allowed to vote? Write your answer in three sentences, using past-tense and future-tense verbs.

52 Unit 3 • Chapter 16 — Practice • Past-Tense and Future-Tense Verbs

CHALLENGE

WRITE A LETTER Ask students to choose a political leader or historical figure they find interesting or important. Have students write a letter to this person. Prompt students to tell why they think this person has been important in making the United States what it is today. Students should also tell why this person will be remembered in the years to come. Have students trade papers to check for correct verb tense.

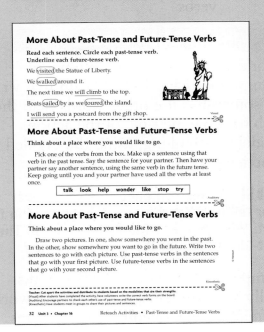

More About Past-Tense and Future-Tense Verbs

Read each sentence. Circle each past-tense verb. Underline each future-tense verb.

We visited the Statue of Liberty.
We walked around it.
The next time we will climb to the top.
Boats sailed by as we toured the island.
I will send you a postcard from the gift shop.

More About Past-Tense and Future-Tense Verbs

Think about a place where you would like to go.

Pick one of the verbs from the box. Make up a sentence using that verb in the past tense. Say the sentence for your partner. Then have your partner say another sentence, using the same verb in the future tense. Keep going until you and your partner have used all the verbs at least once.

| talk | look | help | wonder | like | stop | try |

More About Past-Tense and Future-Tense Verbs

Think about a place where you would like to go.

Draw two pictures. In one, show somewhere you went in the past. In the other, show somewhere you want to go in the future. Write two sentences to go with each picture. Use past-tense verbs in the sentences that go with your first picture. Use future-tense verbs in the sentences that go with your second picture.

32 Unit 3 • Chapter 16 — Reteach Activities • Past-Tense and Future-Tense Verbs

Choosing the Correct Tense

OBJECTIVES
- To recognize and choose the correct verb tense
- To write an e-mail message to express thoughts about an issue, using correct verb tenses

DAILY LANGUAGE PRACTICE

TRANSPARENCY 35

❶ Many presidents was governors first
(were; first.)

❷ President clinton was the governor of arkansas. (Clinton; Arkansas.)

BRIDGE TO WRITING He
(past-tense verb) very hard to become President.

ORAL WARM-UP

USE PRIOR KNOWLEDGE Ask students to tell about something that happened yesterday, something that is happening now, and something that will happen tomorrow. Write the verbs they use on the board.

Grammar Jingles™ **CD, Intermediate** Use Track 11 for review and reinforcement of past-tense and future-tense verbs.

TEACH/MODEL

Work through the explanation and examples on page 198. Explain that writers sometimes use other words than the verb to show the time of the action. Model the thinking, using the Guided Practice example:

MODEL In this sentence, the words *last year* tell me that the action happened in the past. *Will listen* is a future-tense verb. The past-tense form of the verb is *listened.*

Complete the Guided Practice items orally with students, or have them work in small groups to complete the items.

Choosing the Correct Tense

When you write a sentence, you must choose the correct tense of a verb.

If the action of a sentence takes place now, choose a present-tense verb. If the action took place in the past, choose a past-tense verb. If the action will take place later, choose a future-tense verb.

Examples:
The senator **opens** the letter.
(present tense)

The senator **opened** the letter.
(past tense)

The senator **will open** the letter.
(future tense)

Guided Practice

A. Choose the correct form of the verb in parentheses ( ) for each sentence.

Example: Senators (listened, will listen) to voters last year. *listened*

1. Senators (received, will receive) hundreds of letters last week. received
2. They (opened, will open) each letter later. will open
3. They (responded, will respond) to each writer tomorrow. will respond
4. One senator (decided, will decide) to answer all her letters last week. decided
5. She (finished, will finish) yesterday. finished

198

Vocabulary Power page 47

Name _____

CLASSIFY/CATEGORIZE

▶ Cross out the word in each group that does not belong. Then add another word to each group. The groups are based on the meanings of the words. Additional words may vary. Possible responses are given.

1. state	federal	~~New York~~	local	national
2. senator	mayor	governor	~~Teacher~~	President
3. choose	vote	~~sing~~	decide	elect
4. ~~president~~	monarchy	king	queen	kingdom
5. republic	~~prince~~	election	voting	representative
6. California	Nebraska	Alaska	~~Canada~~	Virginia
7. China	~~Utah~~	Italy	France	United States

▶ Now try these. The groups are based on the word endings. Additional words may vary. Possible responses are given.

8. listened	~~respond~~	studied	decided	responded
9. finishing	voting	serving	~~talked~~	talking
10. discussing	repairing	~~helped~~	providing	helping
11. visited	~~will invite~~	changed	increased	invited
12. talked	continued	selected	~~listen~~	listened
13. swimmer	dancer	~~running~~	jumper	runner
14. cleans	runs	elects	~~moved~~	moves

Vocabulary Power   Unit 3 • Chapter 16   47

 **ESL**

WORK WITH A PARTNER Have students work with an English-fluent partner to complete the Independent Practice items.

Encourage students to read the items aloud to develop an "ear" for the correct verb tenses.

Independent Practice

B. Write the correct form of the verb in parentheses ( ) for each sentence.

Example: Nine people now (serve, served, will serve) on the United States Supreme Court.
serve

6. The Constitution (created, create, will create) the Supreme Court many years ago. *created*
7. The Supreme Court still (will decide, decided, decides) important issues. *decides*
8. The President (select, selected, will select) a new Supreme Court judge in the future. *will select*
9. The Senate (vote, voted, will vote) on the President's choice next week. *will vote*
10. Judge Sandra Day O'Connor (lives, lived, will live) in Arizona in the 1980s. *lived*
11. The President (watched, will watch, watches) her work as a judge for many years. *watched*
12. No women (serve, serves, served) on the Supreme Court at that time. *served*
13. Next month the judges (decided, will decide, decide) many cases. *will decide*
14. Two women now (served, will serve, serve) on the Supreme Court. *serve*
15. Future Presidents (appoints, will appoint, appointed) more women. *will appoint*

Writing Connection

Technology Write an e-mail message to an official about an issue that is important to your community. Use correct verb tenses in your e-mail as you explain the importance of the issue.

Remember
that the tense of a verb tells when the action is happening.

199

Independent Practice

Have students complete the Independent Practice, or modify it using these suggestions:

MODIFIED INSTRUCTION

BELOW-LEVEL STUDENTS Work through the Independent Practice with students, modeling the thinking.

ABOVE-LEVEL STUDENTS Have students rewrite five sentences in Part B, using a different verb tense and changing other words in the sentence as needed.

Writing Connection

Technology Help students locate the names of their elected representatives by using resources such as the local library, the local newspaper, or the Internet. Have them take simple notes on what they found.

WRAP-UP/ASSESS

SUMMARIZE Ask students to tell how they know when to use the future, present, and past tenses of verbs.

RETEACH

INTERVENTION Lessons in **visual, auditory,** and **kinesthetic** modalities: p. R48 and *Reteach Activities Copying Masters,* p. 33.

PRACTICE page 53

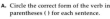 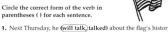

Name _____

Choosing the Correct Tense

A. Circle the correct form of the verb in parentheses ( ) for each sentence.

1. Next Thursday, he (will talk, talked) about the flag's history.
2. Later this afternoon, he (explained, will explain) why the flag has thirteen red and white stripes.
3. This first flag also (showed, will show) thirteen white stars on a blue field.
4. In 1777, the stars and stripes (matched, will match) the number of states.
5. In the 1700s, Congress (added, will add) a new star and stripe for each new state.

B. Write each sentence, using the correct form of the verb in parentheses ( ).

6. Next month, soldiers (saluted, will salute) the flag in ceremonies. Next month, soldiers will salute the flag in ceremonies.
7. This morning, Cyril (explained, will explain) how to fold the flag. Earlier this morning, Cyril explained how to fold the flag.
8. Tomorrow, we (will raise, raised) the flag if the weather is good. Tomorrow, we will raise the flag if the weather is good.

TRY THIS! Write a few sentences about the U.S. flag. Where are some places that you see the flag? Why do you think the flag is in these places? Write verbs in the correct tense.

Practice • Past-Tense and Future-Tense Verbs   Unit 3 • Chapter 16   53

CHALLENGE

FIND A MATCH On cards, write words indicating the future and the past, such as *tomorrow, next week, last year,* and *yesterday.* Make an equal number of cards with future-tense and past-tense verbs. Have each student select a card. Students with verbs should then find a partner with words that indicate future or past. Partners should then use their words to make up a sentence.

Choosing the Correct Tense

Read each sentence. Circle the verb in each one. Underline the sentences in which the verb tense is formed correctly.

Tomorrow I will wait here.
We wait for the bus here yesterday.
I waited here all day.
It probably will stop here next week.
I wish it stop near my house.

Choosing the Correct Tense

With a partner, take turns saying sentences that start with one of these sentence beginnings.

Last week we _____	Now they _____
Yesterday I _____	Next month I _____

Listen to each sentence your partner says and repeat the verb. Then tell whether it is a past-tense verb, a present-tense verb, or a future-tense verb.

Choosing the Correct Tense

With a partner, make eight cards. Write one of these verbs on each card.

walk   jump   look   follow   start   visit   wait   stay

Then make two more cards. Write *will* on one card and *ed* on the other. Take turns picking one of the verb cards. Use the other two cards to make the past-tense form and the future-tense form of the verb on the card you picked. Then say sentences using these two verb forms.

Teacher: Cut apart the activities and distribute to students based on the modalities that are their strengths.
(Visual) You may want to have students work with partners and write out the complete sentences.
(Auditory) After they have finished talking, ask each student to write one of the sentences he or she said in this activity.
(Kinesthetic) Suggest that students write each complete word in the middle of a card and *ed* at the left side of its card.

Reteach Activities • Past-Tense and Future-Tense Verbs   Unit 3 • Chapter 16   33

Extra Practice

OBJECTIVES

- To recognize and use past-tense and future-tense verbs
- To write an ad, using correct verb tenses

DAILY LANGUAGE PRACTICE

TRANSPARENCY 36

① Next week we visited our state capital. (will visit)

② yesterday we will watch a movie about government. (Yesterday; watched)

BRIDGE TO WRITING Many people (future-tense verb) the capital this year.

ORAL WARM-UP

USE PRIOR KNOWLEDGE Write these words on the board: *vote*, *act*, *stop*, *try*. Have students tell the past-tense and future-tense forms of these verbs.

TEACH/MODEL

Use the Remember box to review future-tense and past-tense verbs. Model the thinking for the example from part A in the Extra Practice:

MODEL The words in the sentence that show action are *will pass*. The helping verb *will* tells me that this is a future-tense verb.

Have students work in pairs to complete the Extra Practice exercises.

CHAPTER 16

Past-Tense and Future-Tense Verbs

Remember

that a past-tense verb tells about action that happened earlier. A future-tense verb tells about action that will happen later.

For more activities with past-tense and future-tense verbs, visit *The Learning Site:* www.harcourtschool.com

200

Extra Practice

A. Identify the verb in each sentence. Label each verb *past tense* or *future tense*.
pages 194–195

Example: Lawmakers will pass many laws this year.
will pass; future tense

1. Congress passed laws to protect workers in the early 1900s. passed; past tense
2. These laws changed workers' lives. changed; past tense
3. Workers will need more help in the future. will need; future tense
4. Workers will want new laws. will want; future tense
5. Lawmakers will help them. will help; future tense

B. Write each sentence by using the verb in parentheses ( ). Form the tense that is given at the end of the sentence. *pages 196–197*

Example: Local governments (provide) services for their citizens. (future tense)
will provide

6. Tax money (finance) the services. (future tense) will finance
7. Local governments (use) some of the taxes to buy fire trucks. (past tense) used
8. Firefighters (hurry) to fires in their new trucks. (past tense) hurried
9. We (purchase) books for the library with the money next year. (future tense) will purchase
10. Our local government also (need) money for streetlights. (past tense) needed

---

Vocabulary Power page 48

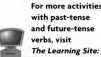

Name _____

EXPLORE WORD MEANING

Read and answer each question. Use complete sentences.
Responses will vary. Accept reasonable responses.

1. A mayor is a leader in a local government. What are some leaders in the federal government? _____

2. Which kind of government would you rather have—a monarchy or a democracy? Explain your answer. _____

3. What are some jobs the President might have to do? _____

4. Why do you think we have a government? _____

5. If you were the President, what are some things you would do? _____

6. Why do you think it is important to vote? _____

48 Unit 3 • Chapter 16   Vocabulary Power

Social Studies

. . . .

BRANCHES OF GOVERNMENT
Explain that each branch of our national government—executive, legislative, and judical—has a specific role. Divide the class into three groups, and have each group research the duties of one branch and make a poster about it. For the poster's text, students should use verbs in both the past and future tenses to tell what that branch does.

C. Write the verb from the box that best fits each sentence. *pages 198–199*

will open	changed	arrive
arrived	asked	allows	waited

Example: Yesterday's vote _____ a school rule.
changed

11. Last year, many students _____ at school early. arrived
12. They _____ outside. waited
13. The students _____ to wait inside the building. asked
14. The rule now _____ them to go inside early. allows
15. Next year, a teacher _____ the building early. will open

D. Rewrite each sentence, correcting any errors.
pages 198–199

Example: We returned our library books tomorrow.
We will return our library books tomorrow.

16. I return my books to the library tomorrow. will return
17. Then I pay a fine for my overdue book. will pay
18. Last year, my community add more books to the library. added
19. Have you decide what to read next? decided
20. I help you choose a good book later. will help

Writing Connection

Real-Life Writing: Writing a Want Ad Pretend that you need to hire someone for a government job, such as a police officer or a governor's secretary. With a partner, write a want ad for the job. Use words that will make people want the job. Be sure to use correct verb tenses.

DID YOU KNOW?
In the United States, more than 22 million people work for federal, state, and local governments.

201

Building Oral Grammar

Write these verbs on the board: *walk, move, carry, shop, give, help, offer, share, save, dry.* Ask students to work in pairs to play a game of "I will, too!" Using one of the action verbs on the board, one student makes a statement about something he or she did yesterday. The next student makes an "I will, too!" statement, telling that he or she will do the same thing tomorrow. For example, one student might say, "I walked through the mud yesterday." The next student will chime in, "I will walk through the mud tomorrow." Prompt students to come up with creative, lively sentences.

Writing Connection

Real-Life Writing: Writing a Want Ad Prompt students to begin by making lists that tell what the job involves and what skills a person would need to do the job well. Have students use ideas from their lists in their want ads. Tell them to edit their ads to make sure they have used the appropriate verb tenses.

WRAP-UP/ASSESS

Writer's Journal

SUMMARIZE Have students summarize in their journals what they have learned about past-tense and future-tense verbs.

ADDITIONAL PRACTICE An additional page of Extra Practice is provided on page 464 of the *Pupil Edition.*

PRACTICE page 54

Name _____

Extra Practice

A. On the line, write the correct form of the verb in parentheses ( ).

1. Early Spanish explorers (called, will call) the state California. _____ called
2. They (named, will name) it after an imaginary paradise. _____ named
3. Tomorrow, Geoffrey (asked, will ask) about the state of Georgia. _____ will ask
4. Long ago, this state name (honored, will honor) King George II. _____ honored

B. Write each sentence using the verb in parentheses ( ). Form the tense that is given at the end of the sentence.

5. Russians (name) Alaska after a Native American word. **(past)**
   Russians named Alaska after a Native American word.
6. The name (mean) that Alaska was "great land." **(past)**
   The name meant that Alaska was "great land."
7. Spanish speakers (know) that Colorado means red. **(future)**
   Spanish speakers will know that Colorado means red.
8. We (name) places using words from other languages. **(past)**
   We named places using words from other languages.

TRY THIS! Find out how your state was named. Look in an encyclopedia or ask your librarian to help you. Write three sentences telling what you found. Underline any verbs and name their tenses.

54 Unit 3 • Chapter 16   Practice • Past-Tense and Future-Tense Verbs

CHALLENGE

WRITE A STORY Ask students to make up a story about an imaginary person from the past who worked to improve his or her community. Prompt students to describe the character and to tell what the community needed. Ask students to describe how the character's actions improved the community. Students may illustrate their stories. Remind students to edit their work for correct use of past-tense verbs.

TECHNOLOGY *Grammar Practice and Assessment* CD-ROM; *Writing Express* CD-ROM

INTERNET Visit *The Learning Site:*
w w w . h a r c o u r t s c h o o l . c o m

Chapter Review

OBJECTIVES
- To review past-tense and future-tense verbs
- To practice listening for facts and opinions

DAILY LANGUAGE PRACTICE

TRANSPARENCY 36

1 My brother lives in washington, d.c., last year. (lived; Washington, D.C.)

2 He workked at the Library of congress. (worked; Congress.)

BRIDGE TO WRITING The Library of Congress (helping verb) founded in 1800. It (linking verb) the largest library in the world.

STANDARDIZED TEST PREP

MODEL TEST-TAKING STRATEGIES Have students silently read the directions on page 202. Remind them to look for words in the sentence that tell the time of the action.

Model the thinking. Write this example on the board:

Last night, the town council votes to repair the sidewalks.

   1 **A** will vote
      B vote
      C voted
      D No mistake

MODEL The words *Last night* tell me that the action happened in the past. *Votes* is a present-tense verb. *Will vote* shows action that will happen in the future. *Vote* is also a present-tense verb. I know that past-tense verbs end in *ed*, so *voted* is the correct answer.

TIP Read each sentence carefully to determine when the action of the sentence takes place.

For additional test preparation, visit *The Learning Site:*
www.harcourtschool.com

202

Chapter Review

Choose the correct verb form for each underlined word. If the underlined word needs no change, choose "No mistake."

> (1) In the past, people <u>construct</u> dirt roads.
> (2) Horses <u>walk</u> along the roads in those days.
> (3) Automobiles <u>create</u> big mud holes in the roads. (4) To help keep the town cleaner, people back then <u>design</u> stronger roads made of brick.
> (5) These days, our town <u>raises</u> money for new roads with taxes. (6) Next year, we <u>complete</u> a new highway.

1 A will construct
  B constructs
  C constructed C
  D No mistake

4 F will design
  G designs
  H designed H
  J No mistake

2 F walked F
  G walks
  H will walk
  J No mistake

5 A will raise
  B raised
  C raise
  D No mistake D

3 A will create
  B created B
  C creates
  D No mistake

6 F completes
  G will complete G
  H completed
  J No mistake

Assessment

PORTFOLIO ASSESSMENT Have students select their best work from the Writing Connections on pages 197, 199, and 201.

ONGOING ASSESSMENT Evaluate the performance of 4–6 students using appropriate checklists and record forms from pages R74–R77.

INTERNET Activities and exercises to help students prepare for state and standardized assessments appear on *The Learning Site:*
www.harcourtschool.com

Listening for Facts and Opinions

A fact is a statement that can be proved true. If you say, "Our nation's capital is in Washington, D.C.," you have stated a fact. You can prove that Washington, D.C., is the capital of the United States.

An opinion is a statement that cannot be proved. An opinion is a person's feeling or belief. "Dogs are better pets than cats" is an opinion. People can discuss the statement, but no one can prove it is true or false.

As you listen to a speaker, listen for judgment words such as *better*, *best*, *worst*, *always*, *never*, and *should*. These words often signal an opinion.

Examples:

Fact	Opinion
I voted for the mayor.	The mayor is a nice person.
Tomorrow is Election Day.	Elections are exciting events.

YOUR TURN

FACT AND OPINION Find three ads in magazines or newspapers. Read them to a partner. Have your partner tell which statements in the ads are facts and which are opinions. Then switch ads and tell whether the statements in your partner's ad are facts or opinions.

TIP Notice how people look and sound when they say things. Many times, people sound and look serious when they are stating facts. They often show more feeling when they are giving opinions.

203

LISTENING AND SPEAKING

Listening for Facts and Opinions

TEACH/MODEL

After reading with students the explanation and examples on page 203, select a magazine advertisement and read the text aloud. After reading each part of the advertisement, ask students to tell if the statement is a fact or an opinion. Have students identify and discuss the clues in the sentences that show whether the statement is fact or opinion. Ask students to explain why it is important to understand the difference between fact and opinion. Then have students complete the Your Turn activity.

WRITING APPLICATION Have students select a product and write four sentences telling about it. Two of the sentences should state facts, and two should state opinions.

WRAP-UP/ASSESS

SUMMARIZE Have students explain in their journals the difference between fact and opinion. Have students tell why they think it is important to recognize fact and opinion in advertisements and other writing. **REFLECTION**

PRACTICE page 55

Name _____

Chapter Review

Choose the correct verb in each underlined section. If the underlined section is correct, choose *No mistake*.

(1) Next week, Jerome will organize his report about government. **(2)** Last year, his father will serve on the city council. **(3)** Jerome learn many facts about his town. **(4)** Next Tuesday, he interview Ms. Robinson, the mayor. **(5)** The town elects her last November. **(6)** At that time, she promised to build more parks for kids.

1 ⊙ organized
⊙ organizes
⊙ organize
⊙ No mistake

2 ⊙ served
⊙ will served
⊙ serves
⊙ No mistake

3 ⊙ learns
⊙ learned
⊙ will learn
⊙ No mistake

4 ⊙ interviews
⊙ interviewed
⊙ will interview
⊙ No mistake

5 ⊙ elected
⊙ elect
⊙ will elect
⊙ No mistake

6 ⊙ promises
⊙ will promise
⊙ promise
⊙ No mistake

Practice • Past-Tense and Future-Tense Verbs   Unit 3 • Chapter 16   55

CHALLENGE

DISCUSS ISSUES Ask students to write and present speeches dealing with community issues that are important to them. Prompt them to support their opinions by using facts. Have students present their speeches to small groups. The other group members should respond, telling whether the opinions expressed were effectively supported by facts.

TECHNOLOGY Additional writing activities are provided on the *Writing Express* CD-ROM

LESSON ORGANIZER	DAY 1	DAY 2

 DAILY LANGUAGE PRACTICE

TRANSPARENCIES 37, 38

DAY 1
1. We like the trip to the mayors office last year. (liked; mayor's)
2. We go to the mayor's office again tomorrow. (will go)

Bridge to Writing I like the (plural noun) near the mayor's office.

DAY 2
1. We see the Mayor on television last week. (saw; mayor)
2. Last year I will do an interview with the cities leader. (I did; city's)

Bridge to Writing (Compound subject) would like to interview her every year.

ORAL WARM-UP
Listening/Speaking

DAY 1 Change Sentence Tense 204

DAY 2 Identify the Verb 206
 Grammar Jingles™ CD Track 12

TEACH/MODEL
GRAMMAR

> **KEY**
> ✔ = tested skill

DAY 1
✔ **IRREGULAR VERBS** 204–205
- To recognize and form the past tense of irregular verbs
- To design a poster and write captions using present-tense and past-tense verbs

DAY 2
✔ **MORE IRREGULAR VERBS** 206–207
- To recognize and use the correct form of irregular past-tense verbs
- To conduct and write about an interview using correct verb tenses and irregular verbs

---

Reaching All Learners

DAY 1
Modified Instruction
Below-Level: Use a Chart
Above-Level: Revise Sentences
Reteach: *Reteach Activities Copying Masters* pp. 34 and R49
Challenge: Activity Card 12, R67
ESL Manual pp. 84, 85
Practice Book p. 56

DAY 2
Modified Instruction
Below-Level: Use a Chart
Above-Level: Write a Sentence
ESL: Quiz Show 206
ESL Manual pp. 84, 86
Reteach: *Reteach Activities Copying Masters* pp. 35 and R49
Challenge: Verb Tag 207
Practice Book p. 57

WRITING

DAY 1
Writing Connection 205
Art

DAY 2
Writing Connection 207
Real-Life Writing: Interview

CROSS-CURRICULAR/ ENRICHMENT

DAY 1
Vocabulary Power
Synonyms 204

> **community,** neighborhood, population, settlement, social
> *See Vocabulary Power book.*

DAY 2
Vocabulary Power
Context Clues 204
Vocabulary Power p. 49

🖳 **Vocabulary activity**

DAY 3

1. We rided different busses every year. (rode; buses)

2. At noon, We eaten our lunch. (we; ate)

Bridge to Writing Maybe we __(future-tense verb)__ to a city council meeting.

Choose Correct Verb 208

Grammar Jingles™ CD Track 12

✔ **COMMONLY MISUSED IRREGULAR VERBS** 208–209
- To use *lie, lay, rise, raise, teach,* and *learn* correctly
- To write a paragraph, poem, or letter using irregular or commonly misused verbs

---

Modified Instruction
Below-Level: Refer to Chart
Above-Level: Write Sentences
ESL: Memory Joggers 208
ESL Manual pp. 84, 87
Reteach: *Reteach Activities Copying Masters* pp. 36 and R49
Challenge: Back Out 209
Practice Book p. 58

Writing Connection 209
Writer's Craft: Choosing a Form

Vocabulary Power
Word Families 204
Vocabulary Power p. 50
Vocabulary activity

DAY 4

1. You and I seed them rise the flag last year. (saw; raise)

2. Will mrs Steel learn us about it? (Mrs.; teach)

Bridge to Writing __(Complete subject)__ will write an article about the visit.

Correct the Sentence 210

EXTRA PRACTICE 210–211
- To correctly use commonly misused verbs and the past-tense forms of irregular verbs
- To write a paragraph using the correct past-tense forms of irregular verbs

Practice and assessment

Building Oral Grammar
Read Aloud Written Sentences 211
Hands-on Activity: Bingo 210
Challenge: Mime Time 211
ESL: *ESL Manual* pp. 84, 88
Practice Book p. 59

Writing Connection 211
Social Studies

Vocabulary Power
Explore Word Meaning 204
Vocabulary Power p. 51
Vocabulary activity

DAY 5

1. During the Trip, you and I growed tired. (trip; grew)

2. The mayor has gived me his idea's. (given; ideas.)

Bridge to Writing I can't wait to visit __(proper noun)__ next year.

TEST PREP **CHAPTER REVIEW** 212–213
- To review correct use of irregular verbs and commonly misused verbs
- To understand and practice strategies for using a thesaurus

Test preparation

Challenge: Similar Opposites 213
Practice Book p. 60
ESL Manual pp. 84, 89

Writing Application 213
Revise Sentences

Vocabulary Power
Word Origins 204
Study Skills: Using a Thesaurus 213

CHAPTER 17   203B

Irregular Verbs

OBJECTIVES

- To recognize and form the past tense of irregular verbs
- To design a poster and write captions using present-tense and past-tense verbs

DAILY LANGUAGE PRACTICE

TRANSPARENCY 37

1 We like the trip to the mayors office last year. (liked; mayor's)

2 We go to the mayor's office again tomorrow. (will go)

BRIDGE TO WRITING I like the (plural noun) near the mayor's office.

ORAL WARM-UP

USE PRIOR KNOWLEDGE Read aloud this sentence: *We see the city park.* Ask: **How would this sentence change if *yesterday* were added to the end of it?**

TEACH/MODEL

Explain that because there are no rules that tell how to form the past tense for all irregular verbs, students must memorize the irregular forms. Ask a volunteer to read aloud the top of page 204. Tell students that they can often tell if a verb form is correct by reading it aloud. The correct form usually sounds right. They can also use the chart on page 204 to help them.

Model the thinking for the Guided Practice example:

MODEL **When I read the sentence aloud, *saw* sounds right. I can double-check my answer by looking at the chart. Because this event happened last year, I look in the past-tense column. *Saw* is a past-tense verb, so I know I've made the correct choice.**

Complete the Guided Practice with students.

Irregular Verbs	
Verb	Past Tense
come	came
do	did
have	had
say	said
see	saw

Vocabulary Power

com·mu·ni·ty
[kə·myōō′nə·tē] *n.*
All the people living in the same place; the place, district, or area where people live.

204

Irregular Verbs

An **irregular verb** is a verb that does not end with *ed* to show past tense.

You know that past tense is the form of a verb that tells about action that happened in the past. You can make most verbs past tense by adding *ed*, but irregular verbs have different endings. Some also have different spellings.

Examples:

I **came** to this school last year. (past tense of the verb *come*)

My father **said** the school has changed since he was a student. (past tense of the verb *say*)

Guided Practice

A. Choose the verb in parentheses () that correctly completes each sentence.

Example: Last year I (see, saw) many old schools on our trip to the coast.
saw

1. Mr. Anderson (see, saw) many different schools on his trip to China last summer. saw
2. He (come, came) to our school yesterday. came
3. Mr. Anderson (have, had) pictures of different schools in China. had
4. One community (had, have) a special festival. had
5. The people (did, done) a play about their past. did

Vocabulary Power

DAY 1 SYNONYMS Introduce and define *community*. Have students complete the following: **Town is/is not a synonym for *community* because _____ .**

DAY 2 CONTEXT CLUES Say: **The social girl loved to be around other people. Which words in the sentence help explain the meaning of *social*?** (See also *Vocabulary Power*, page 49.)

DAY 3 WORD FAMILIES Word families are made up of words that have the same root or base word. **What are some words that are in the same word family as *community*?** (See also *Vocabulary Power*, page 50.)

DAY 4 EXPLORE WORD MEANING **What are some words that describe our community?** (See also *Vocabulary Power*, page 51.)

DAY 5 WORD ORIGINS ***Community*** comes from a word that means "common or shared." How does this definition relate to the meaning of *community*.** Discuss responses.

Independent Practice

B. Write each sentence. Use the past tense of the verb in parentheses ( ) to complete the sentence.

> **Example:** I _____ a new student in our school. (see)
> *I saw a new student in our school.*

6. Many new people _____ to live here last year. (come) came

7. Community leaders _____ we needed a new school. (say) said

8. They _____ a study about our community. (do) did

9. I _____ workers building our new school. (see) saw

10. The workers _____ a good job. (do) did

11. Our teacher _____ the old school was very different. (say) said

12. We _____ photographs of the old school. (see) saw

13. I _____ a drawing of our new school. (do) did

14. Mika _____ she liked my drawing. (say) said

15. Yesterday I _____ a great idea for how to decorate our school lunchroom. (have) had

Remember
that an irregular verb does not use an *ed* ending to show past tense.

Writing Connection

Art Design a poster showing what a place in your community looked like in the past and what it looks like today. Write captions for your pictures. Use present-tense verbs to tell about your community today. Use past-tense verbs to tell about your community in the past.

205

Independent Practice

Have students complete the Independent Practice, or modify it using these suggestions:

MODIFIED INSTRUCTION

BELOW-LEVEL STUDENTS Suggest that students use the chart on page 204 to help them find the past-tense forms and then read the sentences aloud to develop an ear for irregular past-tense verbs.

ABOVE-LEVEL STUDENTS After students have completed the exercises, have them rewrite three sentences, substituting the future tense for the past tense.

Writing Connection

Art Have students work in small groups to create a poster. Provide them with copies of very old photographs of familiar places. If pictures aren't available, help students imagine what their community might have looked like one hundred years ago. Help students choose vivid verbs for their captions.

WRAP-UP/ASSESS

SUMMARIZE Ask volunteers to use the past-tense verb forms from this lesson to write sentences on the board.

RETEACH

REACHING ALL LEARNERS

INTERVENTION Lessons in **visual, auditory,** and **kinesthetic** modalities: p. R49 and *Reteach Activities Copying Masters,* p. 34.

PRACTICE page 56

REACHING ALL LEARNERS

Name _____

Irregular Verbs

A. Choose the correct form of the verb in parentheses ( ) to complete each sentence.

1. Classmates **(come, came)** to visit old friends. ___ came

2. We **(seen, saw)** our former principal, Mr. Clooney. ___ saw

3. He **(did, done)** many fine things for our school. ___ did

4. We now **(have, had)** a new gym and computers. ___ have

5. He **(have, had)** a big effect on many families. ___ had

B. Write each sentence correctly. Use the correct past-tense form of the verb in parentheses ( ).

6. Bettina **(do)** well at Pioneer Elementary School.
   Bettina did well at Pioneer Elementary School.

7. She **(have)** very good grades when she was in school.
   She had very good grades when she was in school.

8. After high school she **(say)** she wanted to go to college.
   After high school she said she wanted to go to college.

9. After college, Bettina **(come)** home.
   After college, Bettina came home.

10. She **(see)** ways to help her community.
    She saw ways to help her community.

TRY THIS! Tell how your school helps the community. Use a past tense verb in each sentence.

56 Unit 3 • Chapter 17 · Practice • Irregular Verbs

CHALLENGE

REACHING ALL LEARNERS

PRINCIPAL PARTNERS Have students use **Challenge Activity Card 12** (page R67) to create a Venn diagram that compares two schools.

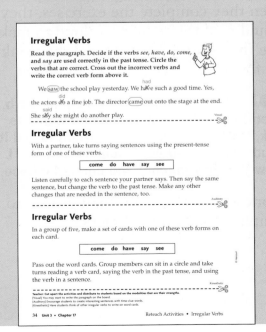

Challenge Activity Card 12

Principal Partners

Pretend your partner is the principal of another school. Your partner's school has the same number of students as your school, but everything else is different. Send an e-mail or write a letter to your partner asking about two things that are different. You may ask questions such as:

• What does your school look like?
• What grades are taught at your school?

Once you have received answers, make a Venn diagram to show how your school and your partner's school are alike and different. Then write a paragraph to tell what you have found out. Be sure that all irregular verbs are used correctly.

Irregular Verbs

Read the paragraph. Decide if the verbs *see, have, do, come,* and *say* are used correctly in the past tense. Circle the verbs that are correct. Cross out the incorrect verbs and write the correct verb form above it.

We (saw) the school play yesterday. We have such a good time. Yes, [had] the actors do a fine job. The director (came) out onto the stage at the end. [did] She say she might do another play. [said]

Irregular Verbs

With a partner, take turns saying sentences using the present-tense form of one of these verbs.

| come | do | have | say | see |

Listen carefully to each sentence your partner says. Then say the same sentence, but change the verb to the past tense. Make any other changes that are needed in the sentence, too.

Irregular Verbs

In a group of five, make a set of cards with one of these verb forms on each card.

| come | do | have | say | see |

Pass out the word cards. Group members can sit in a circle and take turns reading a verb card, saying the verb in the past tense, and using the verb in a sentence.

Teacher: Cut apart the activities and distribute to students based on the modalities that are their strengths.
[Visual] You may want to write the paragraph on the board.
[Auditory] Encourage students to create interesting sentences with time-clue words.
[Kinesthetic] Have students think of other irregular verbs to write on word cards.

34 Unit 3 • Chapter 17 · Reteach Activities • Irregular Verbs

More Irregular Verbs

OBJECTIVES
- To recognize and use the correct form of irregular past-tense verbs
- To conduct an interview and write about it using correct verb tenses and irregular verbs

DAILY LANGUAGE PRACTICE

TRANSPARENCY 37

1. We see the Mayor on television last week. (saw; mayor)
2. Last year I will do an interview with the cities leader. (I did; city's)

BRIDGE TO WRITING
(compound subject) would like to interview her every year.

ORAL WARM-UP

USE PRIOR KNOWLEDGE Read this sentence aloud: *I have grown three inches taller.* Then ask students to identify the verb.

Grammar Jingles™ **CD, Intermediate** Use Track 12 for review and reinforcement of irregular verbs.

TEACH/MODEL

Have a volunteer read the top of page 206 aloud. Point out the verbs in the example sentences. Tell students that when they complete the exercises, they should read the sentences aloud to make sure they sound right. Model the thinking for the Guided Practice example:

MODEL **I know that *has* is a helping verb. When I read the sentence aloud with *has took*, it doesn't sound right. When I read it aloud with *has taken*, it sounds correct. I know that *has taken* is the correct choice.**

Work with students in small groups to complete the Guided Practice.

More Irregular Verbs

Some **irregular verbs** end with *n* or *en* to show past tense with helping verbs.

You know that irregular verbs change spelling in the past tense. Most irregular verbs change forms again when they are used with helping verbs.

Examples:
I **took** a trip to the mayor's office.
I **have taken** many trips to the mayor's office.

More Irregular Verbs		
Verb	Past Tense	Past Tense with Have, Has, Had
eat	ate	eaten
give	gave	given
grow	grew	grown
ride	rode	ridden
write	wrote	written

Guided Practice

A. Choose the correct word or words in parentheses ( ) to complete each sentence.

Example: It (has took, has taken) years to build our new library. *has taken*

1. I (ridden, rode) over to see it on opening day. rode
2. The library (has grown, has grew) in size. has grown
3. Library helpers (given, gave) many new books to the library. gave
4. Everyone (have eaten, ate) a big dinner to celebrate. ate
5. The mayor (written, wrote) a speech. wrote

206

Vocabulary Power page 49

Name _____

CONTEXT CLUES

▶ Circle the words in each sentence that help give the meaning of the underlined word. On the line, write the word's meaning. Responses may vary slightly. Accept reasonable responses.
1. The people in our community all live near one another.
   Community means *a group of people living near one another*
2. The population of our house is five people.
   Population means *the number of a people in an area*
3. The small settlement has houses and a grocery store.
   Settlement means *a place where people live*
4. Our town is divided into six neighborhoods.
   Neighborhood means *a section of town*
5. Bees are social insects because they live in large groups.
   Social means *living together in groups*

REGIONALISMS

▶ Read each sentence and the words in parentheses. Underline the word you would use in the sentence. All of the words are used by people in different communities, so all of the words are correct. Accept all reasonable responses.
6. At home, we sit on a (sofa, couch).
7. For breakfast, some people eat (batter cakes, pancakes, flapjacks).
8. You can carry groceries in a (bag, sack, poke).
9. You can carry water in a (bucket, pail).

Vocabulary Power   Unit 3 • Chapter 17   49

ESL

QUIZ SHOW On strips of paper, write sentences using the irregular verb forms from this lesson. Put the strips in a box. Select a strip of paper from the box and read it aloud, omitting the verb. Have partners work together to make a list of all of the verbs from the chart on page 206 that make sense in the sentence. After one minute, have the pair share the verbs they've named. Partners score a point for each verb that correctly completes the sentence.

Independent Practice

B. Write each sentence, using the correct past-tense verb in parentheses ( ).

Example: Charlotte has (grew, grown) over the years.
Charlotte has grown over the years.

6. Charlotte's factories have (gave, given) many people jobs. given
7. Some people in the city have (rode, ridden) bicycles to work. ridden
8. Many people have (ate, eaten) in the city's restaurants. eaten
9. Food critics (gave, given) them good reviews. gave
10. Many cities (grew, grown) quickly in the past ten years. grew
11. I (wrote, has written) about my trip to North Carolina. wrote
12. I had (rode, ridden) the train before. ridden
13. Charlotte has (grew, grown) quite steadily. grown
14. Our class (wrote, written) a letter to the city's mayor. wrote
15. Ms. Taylor had (gave, given) us the address. given

Remember
that some irregular verbs use *n* or *en* to form the past tense with helping verbs.

Writing Connection

Real-Life Writing: Interview Talk with a person who has lived in your community for a long time. Ask him or her questions about how the community has changed over the years. Then write four sentences telling what you learned from your interview. Use present-tense and past-tense verbs in your sentences. Include at least two irregular verbs.

207

Independent Practice

Have students complete the Independent Practice, or modify it using these suggestions:

MODIFIED INSTRUCTION

BELOW-LEVEL STUDENTS Tell students to use the chart on page 206 to help them select the correct form of the verb. Suggest that students first look for a helping verb in each sentence and then refer to the appropriate column in the chart.

ABOVE-LEVEL STUDENTS After students have completed the exercises, have them use prior knowledge to write a sentence using an irregular verb that was not listed on page 206.

Writing Connection

Real-Life Writing: Interview Tell students to make eye contact, listen closely, and take clear notes during their interviews. Remind them to thank the person they interview. Tell students to refer to their notes as they write their sentences.

WRAP-UP/ASSESS

SUMMARIZE Ask: **How does memorization help when you are studying irregular verbs?**

RETEACH
INTERVENTION Lessons in **visual, auditory,** and **kinesthetic** modalities: p. R49 and *Reteach Activities Copying Masters,* p. 35.

PRACTICE page 57

Name _____

More Irregular Verbs

A. Choose the correct form of the past-tense verb in parentheses ( ) to complete each sentence.

1. We (ridden, rode) our bicycles to town. rode
2. The market has (grown, grew) very large over the past two years. grown
3. Our family has (eaten, ate) many vegetables from local farms over the years. eaten
4. We (took, have took) our favorite fruits for lunch. took
5. The farmers have (given, gave) away blueberries at the end of the season. given

B. Write each sentence correctly. Use the correct past-tense form of the verb in parentheses ( ).

6. Mrs. Kelly has (write) a thank-you note.
   Mrs. Kelly has written a thank-you note.
7. Mrs. Kelly had (grow) up on our street.
   Mrs. Kelly had grown up on our street.
8. Her grandparents had (ride) horses into town.
   Her grandparents had ridden horses into town.

> **TRY THIS!** Write three sentences about a way in which your community has changed. Use one of these verbs in the past tense: *say, do, have, ride, take, write, give, see,* and *grow.*

Practice • Irregular Verbs   Unit 3 • Chapter 17   57

CHALLENGE

VERB TAG Write the present-tense form of the verbs from this lesson on slips of paper. On the back, write *past* or *past with helping verb.* Have students sit in a circle. Give one student a ball. Draw a slip and announce the verb and the form. The student with the ball must make a sentence using the verb in the indicated form. The student then tosses the ball to another student, and you draw another slip of paper. Encourage students to answer as quickly as possible.

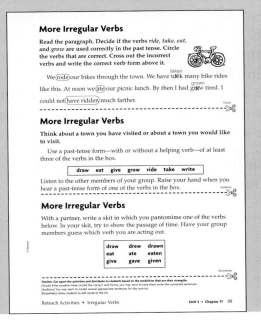

More Irregular Verbs

Read the paragraph. Decide if the verbs *ride, take, eat,* and *grow* are used correctly in the past tense. Circle the verbs that are correct. Cross out the incorrect verbs and write the correct verb form above it.

We rode our bikes through the town. We have took many bike rides like this. At noon we ate our picnic lunch. By then I had grew tired. I could not have ridden much farther.

More Irregular Verbs

Think about a town you have visited or about a town you would like to visit.

Use a past-tense form—with or without a helping verb—of at least three of the verbs in the box.

| draw | eat | give | grow | ride | take | write |

Listen to the other members of your group. Raise your hand when you hear a past-tense form of one of the verbs in the box.

More Irregular Verbs

With a partner, write a skit in which you pantomime one of the verbs below. In your skit, try to show the passage of time. Have your group members guess which verb you are acting out.

draw	drew	drawn
eat	ate	eaten
give	gave	given

Reteach Activities • Irregular Verbs   Unit 3 • Chapter 17   35

Commonly Misused Irregular Verbs

OBJECTIVES

- To use *lie*, *lay*, *rise*, *raise*, *teach*, and *learn* correctly
- To write a paragraph, poem, or letter using irregular or commonly misused verbs

DAILY LANGUAGE PRACTICE

TRANSPARENCY 37

1 We rided different busses every year. (rode; buses)

2 At noon, We eaten our lunch. (we; ate)

BRIDGE TO WRITING Maybe we ___(future-tense verb)___ to a city council meeting.

ORAL WARM-UP

USE PRIOR KNOWLEDGE Write on the board: *We often (rise/raise) our hands in class.* Ask: **Which verb is the correct choice?**

Grammar Jingles™ **CD, Intermediate** Use Track 12 for review and reinforcement of irregular verbs.

TEACH/MODEL

Read aloud the text at the top of page 208. Tell students to look back at the definitions in the chart on page 208 to help them complete the exercises. They can check their answers by substituting the definition for the word as they read the sentence aloud.

Complete the Guided Practice as a group.

Commonly Misused Irregular Verbs

Some verbs are commonly misused.

Certain verbs look or sound alike but have different meanings. Others seem to tell the same idea but are used differently.

Commonly Misused Verbs	
Verbs	**Definitions**
lie, lay	to recline; to place something
rise, raise	to go up; to lift or push something up
teach, learn	to give knowledge; to get knowledge

Examples:

Let's **lie** down on the grass.

A balloon **rises** from the crowd.

My sister **teaches** people how to play tennis.

Guided Practice

A. Identify the verb in parentheses ( ) that completes the sentence correctly.

Example: Students (teach, learn) about rules in school. *learn*

1. We (raise, rise) for "The Star-Spangled Banner." rise
2. The song (teaches, learns) us about our flag. teaches
3. (Lie, Lay) your coat on the chair. Lay
4. (Raise, Rise) your hand to salute the flag. raise
5. A plaque (lies, lays) next to the flagpole. lies

208

Vocabulary Power page 50

Name _____

WORD FAMILIES

A. Word families are made up of words that have the same root or base word. Read the words below. Circle the letter of the word that does not belong. Then replace it with a word of your own.
Additional words may vary. Possible responses are given.

1 A neighbor		5 A explain
B neighborhood		B explanation
C unneighborly		C explained
(D) unfriendly		(D) excited
neighboring		_explaining_
2 F community		6 (F) select
(G) confuse		G settlement
H communicate		H settler
J communicable		J settled
communication		_settling_
3 A populate		7 A social
B popular		B sociable
(C) popcorn		C socially
D population		(D) soccer
unpopular		_socialize_
4 (F) cavern		8 (F) prairie
G govern		G practices
H government		H practical
J governing		J practiced
governor		_practicing_

50 Unit 3 • Chapter 17   Vocabulary Power

REACHING ALL LEARNERS

ESL

MEMORY JOGGERS Have each student choose a word pair from this lesson. Work with students to write short sentences or a poem that helps him or her remember the definitions. Display the sentences and poems in the classroom.

Independent Practice

B. Write the verb in parentheses ( ) that completes each sentence correctly.

> **Example:** Some communities (teach, learn) from the changes made in other communities.
> *learn*

6. The sun (raises, rises) each morning over the buildings downtown. rises
7. I mustn't (lie, lay) in bed and miss the sunrise. lie
8. Let's (lie, lay) flowers in the community park. lay
9. I hope they let me (raise, rise) the banner at the new art gallery. raise
10. I will (teach, learn) you where to look for information about our city's history. teach
11. When the temperature (raises, rises), businesses turn on their air conditioners. rises
12. Workers (lay, lie) the bricks for the school's new sidewalk. lay
13. Leaves will soon (lay, lie) all over the ground. lie
14. (Raise, Rise) your hand if you want to rake. Raise
15. I will (teach, learn) you about the different kinds of leaves. teach

Remember

that some verbs may be easily confused. To choose the correct verb, think about the meaning of the sentence.

Writing Connection

Writer's Craft: Choosing a Form Write a paragraph, poem, or letter about how your school is different from schools of the past. Use at least three irregular or commonly misused verbs. Exchange paragraphs with a partner. Correct any sentences that have incorrect irregular or commonly misused verbs.

209

Independent Practice

Have students complete the Independent Practice, or modify it using these suggestions:

MODIFIED INSTRUCTION

BELOW-LEVEL STUDENTS Suggest that students refer to the chart on page 208 as they complete Part B.

ABOVE-LEVEL STUDENTS After students have completed the exercises, have them write three new sentences, using the verbs from this lesson.

Writing Connection

Writer's Craft: Choosing a Form Suggest that students think about the purpose of and audience for their piece and let that guide them in choosing the best form.

WRAP-UP/ASSESS

SUMMARIZE Write the following verbs in a column on the board: *lie, lay, raise, rise, teach,* and *learn*. Ask volunteers to write a sentence next to each word that uses the verb correctly.

RETEACH

INTERVENTION Lessons in **visual, auditory,** and **kinesthetic** modalities: p. R49 and *Reteach Activities Copying Masters,* p. 36.

PRACTICE page 58

Name _____

Commonly Misused Irregular Verbs

A. Choose the verb in the parentheses ( ) that correctly completes each sentence.

1. She (teaches, learns) us about immigrants who built our town. teaches
2. Mrs. Yang (lies, lays) a big book on the desk. lays
3. The photographs in it will (teach, learn) us how our town once looked. teach
4. Mrs. Yang (raises, rises) the chalk to draw a time line. raises
5. The chalk usually (lies, lays) in her desk drawer. lies

B. Write each sentence. Use the verb in parentheses ( ) that correctly completes each sentence.

6. Today, we will (teach, learn) about workers from China.
   Today, we will learn about workers from China.
7. Chunks of gold used to (lie, lay) in the streams.
   Chunks of gold used to lie in the streams.
8. Alice (raises, rises) her hand with a question.
   Alice raises her hand with a question.

TRY THIS! Write three sentences about what it was like in your community a hundred years ago. Use one verb from each of these pairs: *teach/learn, raise/rise, lie/lay.*

58 Unit 3 • Chapter 17   Practice • Irregular Verbs

CHALLENGE

BACK OUT Write on the board *lie, lay, rise, raise, teach,* and *learn*. Prepare one index card for each student. Write one commonly misused word from the board on each card. Initiate the game by having a student tape a card to another student's back. A volunteer should read the card silently and say a sentence substituting the word "blank" where the word on the card belongs. Have the other student guess the word. Have students take turns.

Commonly Misused Irregular Verbs

Proofread this list of classroom rules. Circle each verb that is used correctly. Draw a line through each verb that is misused. Write the correct verb above the crossed-out verb.

Remember that Mr. Hansen's job is to ~~learn~~ you. teach

CLASS RULES

(Raise) your hand if you want the teacher to call on you.

If you need to ~~lay~~ down, ask to go to the nurse's office. lie

~~Raise~~ from your seat when a visitor comes into the room. Rise

- -

Commonly Misused Irregular Verbs

Pick one of the verbs in the box. Ask your partner to say a sentence using that verb correctly. Listen carefully to your partner's sentence. Keep going until you and your partner have used all the words at least once.

| lie | lay | rise | raise | teach | learn |

- -

Commonly Misused Irregular Verbs

Choose one of the following word pairs.

| lie | lay | rise | raise | teach | learn |

Draw two pictures showing the difference between the two words. Write a sentence to go with each picture, and use the correct verb in each sentence.

Teacher: Cut apart the activities and distribute to students based on the modalities that are their strengths.
[Visual] You may want to write the activity sentences on the board and let volunteers use colored chalk to make corrections.
[Auditory] You may want to have partners select and write their best sentences.
[Kinesthetic] Encourage students to share their pictures and sentences.

36 Unit 3 • Chapter 17   Reteach Activities • Irregular Verbs

Extra Practice

OBJECTIVES
- To correctly use commonly misused verbs and the past-tense forms of irregular verbs
- To write a descriptive paragraph using the correct past-tense forms of irregular verbs

DAILY LANGUAGE PRACTICE

TRANSPARENCY 38

1 You and I seed them rise the flag last year. (saw; raise)

2 Will mrs Steel learn us about it? (Mrs.; teach)

BRIDGE TO WRITING (Complete subject) will write an article about the visit.

ORAL WARM-UP

USE PRIOR KNOWLEDGE Read this sentence aloud: *They had taked a field trip.* Have a volunteer name the verb and correct the sentence.

TEACH/MODEL

Read the Remember box aloud. Have volunteers list on the board examples of past-tense forms of irregular verbs from this chapter. Ask other volunteers to list the definitions of the commonly misused verbs from this chapter.

Have students complete the Extra Practice independently.

 Remember

that some commonly misused verbs include *lie/lay*, *raise/rise*, and *teach/learn*. Irregular verbs do not form the past tense by adding *ed*. They may have different forms or spellings.

For additional activities with irregular verbs, visit *The Learning Site:* www.harcourtschool.com

210

Extra Practice

A. Write each sentence. Choose the correct verb in parentheses ( ) to complete it. *pages 204–207*

Example: Our city planners (has, had) a design for our city park.
Our city planners had a design for our city park.

1. They (saw, seen) parks in other cities. saw
2. They had (wrote, written) letters to our mayor. written
3. Our city planners (gave, given) plans to the mayor, too. gave
4. They (come, came) to a town meeting last week. came
5. The people of the town (says, said) they liked the ideas. said

B. Write the correct present-tense verb in parentheses ( ) to complete each sentence. *pages 208–209*

Example: Hopes (raise, rise) among the farmers in the community as they begin to plant corn.
rise

6. They (raise, rise) their voices and sing while they work together. raise
7. Some new farmers (teach, learn) ways to grow corn. learn
8. Others (teach, learn) one another how to grow new crops. teach
9. The farmers (lie, lay) the seeds in rows. lay
10. They watch the new plants (raise, rise) from the ground. rise

---

Vocabulary Power page 51

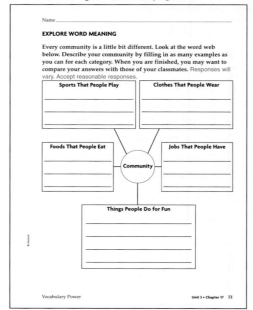

BINGO! Write the definitions of the six commonly misused verbs from page 208 on separate slips of paper. Have students create a nine-square Bingo card with the six commonly misused verbs. They will have to use some twice. Read aloud the definitions of the verbs. Tell students to cover up a word when you read its definition. The first to cover three words in a row, column, or diagonal calls Bingo!

C. Write each sentence. Choose a verb from the box and use its correct past-tense form to fill in the blank. Use each verb once. *pages 204–207*

> **give   write   come   grow   say**

11. Mr. Bergen _____ to talk to our class. *came*

12. He has _____ us a new plan for our town. *given*

13. He explained how our town has _____. *grown*

14. We _____ down his ideas as he spoke. *wrote*

15. Our teacher _____ Mr. Bergen wanted our ideas, too. *said*

D. Rewrite the sentences below, correcting each error. *pages 204–207*   Possible responses are shown.

16. Our class has gave the mayor some ideas for a new recreation center. *given*

17. We have wrote down our plan. *written*

18. We have went to Cedar City. *have gone*

19. We seen a huge recreation center there. *saw*

20. Our city has have the same playground for a long time. *has had*

Writing Connection

Social Studies Work in a small group to find out what your community was like in the past. Where did people live? What were the schools like? How did people travel to work and school? What did people in your community do for recreation? Write a paragraph that describes your community in the past. Use the past-tense forms of irregular verbs correctly.

211

Building Oral Grammar

Have students pretend that they are from another town. Ask them to write three sentences introducing themselves. Tell them to use at least two irregular verb forms from this chapter. Then have students read their sentences to the class. Ask the other students to identify the verbs and the verb forms used. Read this example aloud: **I grew up in Chicago. I am an author. I have written many books.**

Writing Connection

Social Studies Have students focus on their community as it was fifty years ago. Provide reference materials, invite a guest speaker to describe the community, or tell students what you know about that time period. Tell students to take simple notes on the sources they use for their paragraphs.

WRAP-UP/ASSESS

SUMMARIZE Make a class poster of the charts on pages 204 and 206. Have volunteers add example sentences to the poster.

ADDITIONAL PRACTICE An additional page of Extra Practice is provided on page 465 of the *Pupil Edition*.

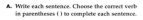
CHALLENGE

MIME TIME Write the following words on separate slips of paper: *lie, lay, raise, rise, teach,* and *learn.* Put the slips of paper in a box. Have each student choose a slip and act out the word without speaking. Tell students that they may use objects in the classroom as they act out the words. Have other students try to guess the word being acted out.

TECHNOLOGY *Grammar Practice and Assessment* CD-ROM; *Writing Express* CD-ROM

INTERNET Visit *The Learning Site:* www.harcourtschool.com

CHAPTER 17 211

Chapter Review

OBJECTIVES

- To review correct use of irregular verbs and commonly misused verbs
- To understand and practice strategies for using a thesaurus

DAILY LANGUAGE PRACTICE

TRANSPARENCY 38

1 During the Trip, you and I growed tired. (trip; grew)

2 The mayor has gived me his idea's. (given; ideas.)

BRIDGE TO WRITING I can't wait to visit (proper noun) next year.

STANDARDIZED TEST PREP

MODEL TEST-TAKING STRATEGIES Read the directions on page 212 aloud. Remind students to think about the rules and forms they have memorized from the charts on pages 204 and 206. Also remind them to double-check their answers to be sure they sound correct. Model the thinking. Write this example on the board:

The trees in the park have _____ since last year.

  1 A growed
  B grewed
  C grown
  D grow

MODEL Choices A and B must be wrong because they are incorrect verb forms. *Grow* is in the present tense. The helping verb *have* and the phrase *since last year* tell me that this action happened in the past, so *grow* cannot be correct. When I read the sentence with *grown*, it sounds right, and so I know I've made the correct choice.

Have students complete the Chapter Review independently.

Chapter Review

Read the paragraph. Choose the correct verb for each sentence.

STANDARDIZED TEST PREP

> Our class has __(1)__ a report about city planning. Our city's planner, Ms. Love, __(2)__ to our class. She has __(3)__ many drawings of plans for a new mall. We __(4)__ our hands to ask questions. We studied all of the plans. We __(5)__ her some ideas of our own. Projects like this __(6)__ us about our community.

TIP Read the entire paragraph first to get an idea of its whole meaning. Then read the sentences one at a time.

1 A wrote
  B written B
  C write
  D writed

2 F come
  G had came
  H comed
  J came J

3 A do
  B does
  C done C
  D did

4 F raised F
  G rised
  H risen
  J rose

5 A gived
  B gives
  C gave C
  D given

6 F learns
  G teach G
  H teaches
  J learn

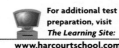
For additional test preparation, visit *The Learning Site:* www.harcourtschool.com

212

Assessment

PORTFOLIO ASSESSMENT Have students select their best work from the Writing Connections on pages 205, 207, 209, and 211.

ONGOING ASSESSMENT Evaluate the performance of 4–6 students using appropriate checklists and record forms from pages R74–R77.

INTERNET Activities and exercises to help students prepare for state and standardized assessments appear on *The Learning Site:*
www.harcourtschool.com

Using a Thesaurus

Understanding the Thesaurus

A **thesaurus** is a writer's tool. It is a book that lists words and their synonyms and antonyms. **Synonyms** are words that have similar meanings. **Antonyms** are words with opposite meanings. Entry words are listed in alphabetical order. Two guide words at the top of each page show the first and last words on that page. Some entries may also suggest another word that you can look up for more synonyms and antonyms.

Using the Thesaurus

Suppose you are writing a report. You notice that some words do not mean exactly what you want to say. You also see that you have used the same word over and over again. You can use a thesaurus to find different words to use. First, look up the entry word in the index. Use the index to find the page on which the word appears. Turn to that page, and read the synonyms. Find the synonym that most closely matches the meaning you want.

the <u>nice</u> box
the <u>colorful</u> box
the <u>pretty</u> box

YOUR TURN

Read a paragraph that you wrote for an earlier assignment. Circle any words that you have used more than once. Circle any words that do not mean exactly what you want to say. Use your thesaurus to replace these words with synonyms. Underline the new words.

TIP Make sure that your new word makes sense in the sentence. Use a dictionary to check the word's meaning.

213

TEACH/MODEL

Write *walk* and *say* on the board. Ask students to describe the picture that each of these words paints in their minds. Ask students to offer words that are more vivid. List their responses. For *walk*, elicit responses such as *march, zip, skip, twirl, plod,* and *trudge*. For *say*, elicit responses such as *shout, whisper, bellow,* and *whine*. Encourage students to note that by using a particular word they can create exactly the meaning they intend. Explain that a thesaurus can help students find just the right word.

WRITING APPLICATION After students have completed the Your Turn activity, have them use a thesaurus to rewrite three of their sentences. Their new sentences should have the opposite meaning of the originals.

WRAP-UP/ASSESS

SUMMARIZE Ask students to explain how they can use synonyms and antonyms in their writing. Ask: **Why is this skill important**?

PRACTICE page 60

Name _____

Chapter Review

Choose the best way to write each underlined verb. If the underlined verb is correct, choose *No mistake*. Fill in the oval next to your choice.

My father **(1)** <u>camed</u> to New York in 1954. He was only two years old. His family **(2)** <u>had rode</u> on a passenger ship from Italy. When they arrived, they **(3)** <u>have</u> enough money to buy a house. My father **(4)** <u>grew</u> up in our house.

Since he spoke and **(5)** <u>had wrote</u> Italian and English, my father became a translator. He worked for the United Nations. Now he sometimes **(6)** <u>teaches</u> Italian at City College. He **(7)** <u>rises</u> early every morning to go to work. He **(8)** <u>learns</u> us to become good citizens.

1 ○ come
  ● came
  ○ does come
  ○ No mistake

2 ● had ridden
  ○ have rode
  ○ ridden
  ○ No mistake

3 ○ has
  ○ have had
  ● had
  ○ No mistake

4 ○ growed
  ○ had grew
  ○ grown
  ● No mistake

5 ○ written
  ○ had writed
  ● wrote
  ○ No mistake

6 ○ learns
  ○ learned
  ○ teached
  ● No mistake

7 ● raised
  ○ raises
  ○ rised
  ○ No mistake

8 ○ learned
  ○ teach
  ● teaches
  ○ No mistake

60 Unit 3 • Chapter 17   Practice • Irregular Verbs

CHALLENGE

SIMILAR OPPOSITES Divide students into two groups. Ask each group to write down three commonly used words. One group should call out a word from its list and say, "Synonym!" or "Antonym!" The other group must look up the word in a thesaurus and say at least two sentences that contain either synonyms or antonyms as directed. Continue to play back and forth between groups.

TECHNOLOGY Additional writing activities are provided on the *Writing Express* CD-ROM

LESSON ORGANIZER	DAY 1	DAY 2
DAILY LANGUAGE PRACTICE TRANSPARENCY 39	**1.** have you ever tried to persuade someone. (Have; someone?) **2.** I are not convinced by the argument in the paragraph (am; paragraph.)	**1.** jason gived you his opinion (Jason; gave; opinion.) **2.** he told me some good reasons? (He; reasons.)
ORAL WARM-UP Listening/Speaking	Suggest Reasons to Persuade 214 Give Examples of Persuasion 220	Discuss Drafting 221
TEACH/MODEL WRITING	**Literature Model:** from *Coaching Ms. Parker* 215–217 **GUIDED WRITING** ✔ **Prewriting** 220 • To learn strategies for prewriting a persuasive paragraph • To choose a topic and generate ideas for a persuasive paragraph Interactive Writing 220	**GUIDED WRITING** ✔ **Drafting** 221 • To learn strategies for drafting a persuasive paragraph • To draft a persuasive paragraph **Transparency** 40
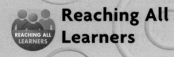 **Reaching All Learners**	**Modified Instruction** 226 Below-Level: Review Verb Order Above-Level: Revise Sentences *ESL Manual* pp. 90, 91	**Modified Instruction** 227 Below-Level: Review Verb Agreement Above-Level: Rewrite Sentences *ESL Manual* p. 90
GRAMMAR	**Unit 3 Review:** ✔ Main Verbs and Helping Verbs 226	**Unit 3 Review:** ✔ Present-Tense Verbs 227
CROSS-CURRICULAR/ ENRICHMENT **KEY** ✔ = tested writing form/skill	**LISTENING AND SPEAKING:** 218 **EVALUATION CRITERIA:** Establish Criteria for Writing 219 **TEST PREP: Say Choices Silently** 226 *Vocabulary Power* Explore Word Meaning 216 ┌─────────────────────────┐ **confidence,** dignity, haughty, secure, vain See *Vocabulary Power* book. └─────────────────────────┘	**TEST PREP:** Read Directions Carefully 227 *Vocabulary Power* Synonyms 216 *Vocabulary Power* book p. 52  **Vocabulary activity**

DAY 3

1. An opinion reasons, and details is needed in persuasive paragraphs. (opinion,; are)
2. Mrs jackson wrote a persuasive speech. (Mrs. Jackson)

Reflect on Previous Writing 222

GUIDED WRITING
✔ **Revising** 222
   • To learn strategies for revising a persuasive essay
   • To revise a persuasive essay

 Transparencies 41a and 41b

Modified Instruction 228
   Below-Level: Review Verb Endings
   Above-Level: Change Tenses
   ESL Manual p. 90

Unit 3 Review:
✔ Past-Tense and Future-Tense Verbs 228

HANDS-ON: Yesterday and Tomorrow 228

Vocabulary Power

   Homophones 216
   Vocabulary Power book p. 53

 **Vocabulary activity**

DAY 4

1. Grammar spelling and punctuation are three things she checked in her essay. (Grammar, spelling,)
2. I think a Friend helped her fix the mistake? (friend; mistakes.)

Discuss Proofreading Methods 223

GUIDED WRITING
✔ **Proofreading** 223
   • To learn strategies for proof-reading a persuasive essay
   • To proofread a persuasive essay

 Transparencies 42a and 42b
Spelling: Patterns and Blends 223

Proofreading practice

Modified Instruction 229
   Below-Level: Review Charts
   Above-Level: Write Sentences
   ESL Manual p. 90

Unit 3 Review:
✔ Irregular Verbs 229

TEST PREP **TEST PREP:** Extra Practice 229

Vocabulary Power

   Compare and Contrast 216
   Vocabulary Power book p. 54

Vocabulary activity

DAY 5

1. Mrs. Jackson gave her speech next Friday (will give; Friday.)
2. I interviewed Mr Kronski at noon tomorrow. (will interview Mr.)

Suggest Publishing Alternatives 224

GUIDED WRITING
✔ **Publishing** 224
   • To learn strategies for publishing a persuasive essay as an oral presentation
   • To publish a persuasive essay as an oral presentation

Practice and assessment

ESL: Practice Public Speaking 224
ESL Manual p. 90

HANDS-ON ACTIVITIES 163I–163J

LISTENING AND SPEAKING: Giving an Oral Presentation 225

Vocabulary Power

   Word Parts 216

Using the Literature Model

OBJECTIVE
• To read and analyze persuasion in a work of fiction

DAILY LANGUAGE PRACTICE

TRANSPARENCY 39

1 have you ever tried to persuade someone. (Have; someone?)

2 I are not convinced by the argument in the paragraph (am; paragraph.)

ORAL WARM-UP

USE PRIOR KNOWLEDGE Read aloud the introduction to the selection, and discuss questions such as the following:

1. **Why might an author show one character persuading another in a story?** (Possible response: An author might include persuasion to tell something about a character, to move the story line along, or to focus on a conflict.) **INFEREN-TIAL: AUTHOR'S CRAFT**

2. **Why is it important for a teacher to be willing to learn as well as to teach?** (Possible response: Someone who is willing to learn is a better teacher.) **CRITICAL: MAKE JUDGMENTS**

PREREADING STRATEGIES

PREVIEW/SET PURPOSE Have students read the title and the selection introduction. Ask students to predict how the story ends, and have them give reasons for their predictions. Have students set their own purpose for writing, or have them read to find out if the students persuade Ms. Parker to let them coach her.

CHAPTER 18

Writing Workshop

Persuasive Paragraph

WESTBEND

HOME

R

214

School-Home Connection

Family members can help students learn to evaluate persuasion. Advertisements and commercials are common types of persuasion. Family members can help students identify the persuasive techniques used in advertisements and commercials and evaluate whether the reasons are believable.

You know that when you try to persuade someone of something, you are trying to get that person to believe something or do something. In this story, the students in Ms. Parker's class are trying to persuade their teacher to let them coach her. As you read this story, think about the reasons the students use to support their opinions.

Coaching Ms. Parker

by Carla Heymsfeld
illustrated by Steve Royal

Ms. Parker does not want to play in Westbend Elementary's yearly baseball game between the teachers and the sixth graders. She has no confidence in her baseball skills. Her students think they should start coaching her after school to get her ready for the big game. Can they convince Ms. Parker that this is a good idea?

"Is something wrong?" Ms. Parker asked.

Several seconds passed. Mike swallowed hard. He couldn't seem to get started. Elizabeth gave him a little shove. "Mike has something to tell you," she said to Ms. Parker.

215

OPTIONS FOR READING

READ-ALOUD OPTION Read the story aloud, and have students listen to determine Ms. Parker's students' audience and purpose, and the main reasons they used.

INDEPENDENT OPTION As students read, have them take notes on the ways in which the students persuade Ms. Parker. Ask volunteers to share their notes with the rest of the class.

Ask students why they think Ms. Parker does not want to play baseball. Use questions like the following to help students monitor their comprehension:

3. **Who is Carla Heymsfeld's audience?** (Possible response: young people who read for entertainment) **INFERENTIAL: DETERMINE AUTHOR'S PURPOSE**

4. **What do the students want to persuade Ms. Parker to do? Why?** (They want to persuade her to let them coach her after school so she will be ready for the baseball game between the teachers and the sixth graders.) **LITERAL: NOTE DETAILS**

SELECTION SUMMARY

GENRE: PERSUASIVE WRITING
In this excerpt from a book by Carla Heymsfeld, students set out to persuade their teacher, Ms. Parker, to play in the annual baseball game between the teachers and the sixth graders. The students offer reasons and anticipate her objections. Ms. Parker is hesitant when her students first approach her, but with their encouragement, she agrees to let them help her learn how to play the game.

ABOUT THE AUTHOR

CARLA HEYMSFELD is an author of children's books as well as books for teachers. Heymsfeld is an elementary school reading teacher. She lives in Virginia.

5. Why might Mike feel sick as he approaches Ms. Parker with the other students? (Possible response: He is nervous about being the spokesman for the group since he does not know if Ms. Parker will like the group's idea.) **INFERENTIAL: DETERMINE CHARACTERS' EMOTIONS**

6. Do you think Mike is as persuasive as his classmates? Why or why not? (Possible responses: No. He seems nervous and doesn't know what to say to Ms. Parker; he doesn't seem to believe very strongly in their idea.) **CRITICAL: MAKING JUDGMENTS**

7. What are some examples of vivid verbs and specific nouns in the story? (Possible responses: *volunteered, enthusiasm, offered, trudged, shove, run-down, chimed, assured, demanded, sneakers, sandals, hesitated,* and *diamond.*) **LITERAL: NOTE DETAILS**

Mike wondered why Elizabeth, if she was so eager, didn't tell Ms. Parker herself. He looked at Elizabeth, who looked right back at him. It was like being trapped in a rundown. He took a deep breath. "Ms. Parker," he said, "we were wondering . . ." His voice trailed off helplessly. What *were* they wondering?

"Yes?" Ms. Parker lifted her eyebrows.

"We wondered . . . uh . . . if you'd like to come out after school and . . . er . . . play baseball with us. You know, practice a little for the . . . uh . . . game." There. He'd said it. He held his breath.

Ms. Parker nodded just a little. "That's very nice of you, Mike," she said kindly. "I understand what you are trying to do, but it won't work."

"Mike's a good teacher," Ho-Pu chimed in loyally.

Ms. Parker stared glumly at Mike. She did not seem convinced.

"All you need is a little practice," Kathy assured her.

"Wouldn't you help us if we couldn't do something?" Elizabeth demanded.

216

Vocabulary Power

DAY 1 EXPLORE WORD MEANING Introduce and define *confidence*. **Why is it good to have confidence?**

DAY 2 SYNONYMS *Cheerful* and *happy* are synonyms. **What are some synonyms for** *confidence?* (See also *Vocabulary Power*, page 52.)

DAY 3 HOMOPHONES Write the word *vein* on the board. Ask: **What is another spelling and meaning for this word?** (See also *Vocabulary Power*, page 53.)

DAY 4 COMPARE AND CONTRAST Ask: **How can you tell when people have confidence? How can you tell when people are haughty?** (See also *Vocabulary Power*, page 54.)

DAY 5 WORD PARTS Use *confide* as a base word. Make a list of new words by adding prefixes and suffixes.

"Yeees," Ms. Parker dragged the word out. Clearly, she was not an eager student. "I guess if you are willing to teach me, I ought to try to learn."

"Can you start this afternoon?" It was Elizabeth again. At least, Mike thought, she's persistent.

"I don't know. I don't have any sneakers with me." Ms. Parker looked down at her white suede sandals. "Don't you need to let your parents know if you are going to stay after school?"

"We could start tomorrow," Frank suggested. It was amazing what a little team spirit could do.

"I . . . I suppose that will be okay." Ms. Parker hesitated.

"Great!" Yussif cried. Then, before she could change her mind, they all ran back to the baseball diamond for the few minutes left of recess.

Vocabulary Power

con·fi·dence
[kon′fə·dəns] *n.* Firm belief or trust.

Analyze THE *Model*

1. Why do you think Ms. Parker's students want to coach her?
2. What reasons do the students give to convince Ms. Parker?
3. What reason do you think is the strongest?

Analyze THE *Model*

1. Why do you think Ms. Parker's students want to coach her? (Possible response: They want to help her improve her baseball skills so she can help win the game.) **INFERENTIAL: DRAW CONCLUSIONS**

2. What reasons do the students give to convince Ms. Parker? (They tell her that Mike is a good teacher, that she needs only a little practice, and that she would help them if she were in their place.) **LITERAL: NOTE DETAILS**

3. Which reason do you think is the strongest? Explain. (Possible response: The last reason because it helps Ms. Parker see the situation from the students' point of view.) **CRITICAL: MAKING JUDGMENTS**

SUMMARIZE

ONE-SENTENCE SUMMARY Ask: **If you wanted to tell a classmate what this story is about, what would you say?** Have students write one sentence to summarize the story. (Possible response: Students persuade their teacher to let them teach her to play baseball so that she can play in a teacher vs. sixth graders game.)

RESPONSE TO LITERATURE

WRITING PROMPT To have students respond in writing to the story, use the following prompt:

Why do you think the students' persuasion is effective? Write a sentence explaining your answer.

TECHNOLOGY Additional writing activities are provided on the *Writing Express* CD-ROM

Parts of a Persuasive Paragraph

OBJECTIVES

- To recognize and understand the parts of a persuasive paragraph
- To analyze and summarize a persuasive paragraph
- To establish criteria for evaluating a persuasive paragraph
- To listen critically to a persuasive paragraph

READING LIKE A WRITER

READ AND RESPOND TO THE MODEL Before you read Ben's paragraph to students, explain that they should listen to determine his purpose for writing. After you have read the paragraph, discuss his purpose. (to persuade people that practice is important for becoming a good piano player) Then ask students if they think Ben did a good job persuading his audience. Students should give reasons for their conclusions.

FOCUS ON ORGANIZATION Have students reread the paragraph independently, noting the purpose of each sentence. Then ask: **Why does Ben begin and end his paragraph with statements of opinion?** (Possible response: He wants to emphasize the topic of the paragraph and encourage his audience to take action.)

FOCUS ON WRITER'S CRAFT Ask students to identify Ben's audience. (people who are learning to play piano) Explain that choosing an audience is one of the first steps in writing a persuasive essay. Ask students how Ben's paragraph might be different if his audience were the parents of children who are learning to play the piano.

READING — WRITING CONNECTION

Parts of a Persuasive Paragraph

The students tried to persuade Ms. Parker to let them coach her so she could become a better baseball player. Read this persuasive paragraph written by a student named Ben. Notice the different parts of his paragraph. Also, watch for his use of vivid verbs and specific nouns.

MODEL

statement of opinion

first reason

second reason

supporting details

third reason

restatement of opinion/call to action

> Some people think you can play the piano without practicing, but it can't be done. There are many things you have to learn and practice. You have to figure out how to use the right fingers on the right keys. It sounds simple, but it takes a lot of work. Then you have to learn to read music. Reading music is like learning a new language, and it's a challenge! You also have to discover how to play with feeling. This is a skill that comes only with a lot of practice. If you really want to play the piano well, you have to focus on your lessons and practice playing as much as you can.

218

Listening and Speaking

Have students work in pairs, with each student writing a persuasive paragraph on the benefits of a product or an activity. Explain that the paragraph should tell why a person should either buy a product or do something. Then partners should take turns reading their paragraphs aloud to each other. As one student reads, the other should take notes, identifying statements of opinion, reasons, and supporting details. Tell students to use the appropriate vocabulary to express their ideas and feelings. Finally, have partners give each other feedback on the organization of their paragraphs and how persuasively they presented their information.

Analyze THE Model

1. What is Ben's purpose? Who do you think is his audience? Explain your answers.

2. What are Ben's reasons for practicing the piano?

3. What details does Ben give to support his reasons?

Summarize THE Model

Use a web like the one below to help you identify Ben's reasons and supporting details. Then use the web to write a summary of his persuasive paragraph. Remember that you should include the important reasons and leave out the details. Be sure to write what Ben's opinion is at the beginning of your summary.

Writer's Craft

Vivid Verbs and Specific Nouns Ben used vivid verbs and specific nouns in his persuasive paragraph. They help make his writing more persuasive. When you use vivid and specific words, your reasons will be clearer for your readers. Reread Ben's paragraph. Make a list of the words he uses that are vivid and specific. Tell why you think they make his paragraph more persuasive.

219

Analyze THE Model

1. **What is Ben's purpose? Who do you think is his audience? Explain your answers.** (Ben's purpose is to convince his audience that practice is necessary to play the piano well. His audience is his peers, or people who are learning to play the piano.) **INFERENTIAL: DETERMINE AUTHOR'S PURPOSE**

2. **What are Ben's reasons for practicing the piano?** (He practices to learn how to use the correct fingering, to learn to read music, and to learn how to play with feeling.) **LITERAL: NOTE DETAILS**

3. **What details does Ben give to support his reasons?** (Ben says that although using the correct fingering sounds easy, it's not. He says that learning to read music is like learning a new language. He also says that playing with feeling comes only with a lot of practice.) **LITERAL: NOTE DETAILS**

SUMMARIZE THE MODEL

Have students work in small groups to compare their completed webs and to discuss any differences. Ask each group to provide a summary of the paragraph, based on their completed charts.

Evaluate whether students have included all important points while omitting unnecessary details.

WRITER'S CRAFT

VIVID VERBS AND SPECIFIC NOUNS After students have listed several words, encourage them to use a thesaurus to find synonyms to expand the vocabulary that they include in their persuasive paragraphs.

TAKE-HOME BOOK 3 provides an additional model of persuasive writing and home activities. See *Practice Book* pages 129–132.

Evaluation Criteria

ESTABLISH CRITERIA FOR WRITING Tell students that they will help evaluate their own persuasive paragraphs. Have them turn to the rubric on page 498 in their Handbooks. Explain that if students meet the criteria in the "4" column, plus the criteria that you and the class add, they will have produced their best work. Discuss the criteria, and add additional criteria based on your students' needs and interests. Remind students to refer to the rubric as they write their paragraphs. (A teacher version of the rubric is available on page R82. For more information about evaluating writing, see pages R78–79 in this *Teacher's Edition*.)

Prewriting

OBJECTIVES

- To learn strategies for prewriting a persuasive paragraph
- To choose a topic and generate ideas for a persuasive paragraph

ORAL WARM-UP

USE PRIOR KNOWLEDGE Ask students to give examples of situations in which persuasion is used. (Possible responses: in advertising, in political speeches, from their peers) Ask volunteers to describe specific examples.

GUIDED WRITING

Discuss the writing prompt. Have students identify the purpose and the audience. (purpose—to persuade; audience—classmates) Then model finding an appropriate topic.

MODEL **I am now taking gymnastics classes and dance lessons. They both take a lot of practice. Practicing gymnastics helps me with my dance lessons and helps me stay fit, so I think everyone should take gymnastics and practice hard.**

Then have students reread Ben's model and make their own prewriting web, using a topic you assign or their own topics.

SELF-INITIATED WRITING Have students choose their own topics for a persuasive paragraph.

WRAP-UP/ASSESS

SUMMARIZE Why is sharing an opinion sometimes a good idea? How did making your chart help you plan your writing?

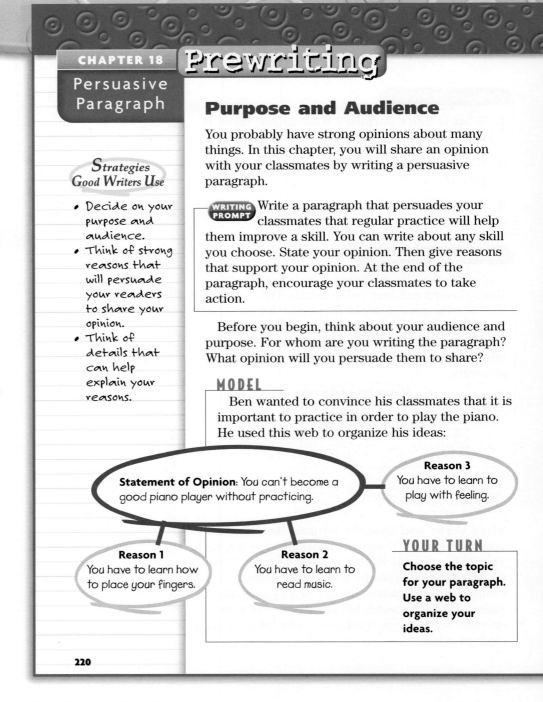

Purpose and Audience

You probably have strong opinions about many things. In this chapter, you will share an opinion with your classmates by writing a persuasive paragraph.

WRITING PROMPT Write a paragraph that persuades your classmates that regular practice will help them improve a skill. You can write about any skill you choose. State your opinion. Then give reasons that support your opinion. At the end of the paragraph, encourage your classmates to take action.

Before you begin, think about your audience and purpose. For whom are you writing the paragraph? What opinion will you persuade them to share?

MODEL

Ben wanted to convince his classmates that it is important to practice in order to play the piano. He used this web to organize his ideas:

Statement of Opinion: You can't become a good piano player without practicing.

Reason 1 You have to learn how to place your fingers.

Reason 2 You have to learn to read music.

Reason 3 You have to learn to play with feeling.

YOUR TURN

Choose the topic for your paragraph. Use a web to organize your ideas.

Strategies Good Writers Use

- Decide on your purpose and audience.
- Think of strong reasons that will persuade your readers to share your opinion.
- Think of details that can help explain your reasons.

220

Vocabulary Power page 52

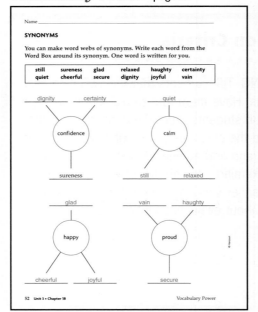

Interactive Writing

You may want to prewrite and write a first draft as a group. Draw students' attention to the Strategies Good Writers Use. Have students help you complete a prewriting web, including a statement of opinion and reasons. Then use the Drafting Transparency with students, coaching them to use effective organization and elaboration.

Drafting

Organization and Elaboration

Follow these steps to help you organize your paragraph:

STEP 1 **Get Your Audience's Attention**
Write a strong statement of opinion that will make readers want to read more.

STEP 2 **State Your Reasons**
Write at least two reasons that support your opinion.

STEP 3 **Add Details**
Think of details that will make each reason clear.

STEP 4 **Call Your Readers to Action**
Restate your opinion. Then urge your readers to take action.

MODEL

Here is the beginning of Ben's draft of his paragraph. What is his statement of opinion? How does this statement make you want to read more?

> *Some people think you can play the piano without practicing, but it can't be done. There are many things you have to learn and practice.*

YOUR TURN

Write a draft of your paragraph. Use the steps above to help you get started. You can also use your chart for ideas.

Strategies Good Writers Use

- Begin by stating your opinion.
- Include at least two reasons that support your opinion.
- Use details that tell more about your reasons.

 Use a computer to write your draft. You can use the delete feature to fix mistakes.

221

Drafting

OBJECTIVES
- To learn strategies for drafting a persuasive paragraph
- To draft a persuasive paragraph

SPIRAL REVIEW

DAILY LANGUAGE PRACTICE

TRANSPARENCY 39

1 jason gived you his opinion (Jason; gave; opinion.)

2 he told me some good reasons? (He; reasons.)

ORAL WARM-UP

USE PRIOR KNOWLEDGE Tell students about a time when a graphic organizer helped you draft a letter or essay quickly. Call on volunteers to share similar experiences in which the prewriting step helped make the drafting step easier.

GUIDED WRITING

Discuss the Organization and Elaboration steps and the model. Ask volunteers to answer the questions that precede the model. (His statement of opinion is that playing the piano without practice can't be done. This statement makes you want to read more to find out why practicing is so important.)

As students draft their paragraphs, remind them to keep their purpose and audience in mind. They should refer to Ben's paragraph as a model.

WRAP-UP/ASSESS

SUMMARIZE: How did drafting help you develop your ideas?

Vocabulary Power page 53

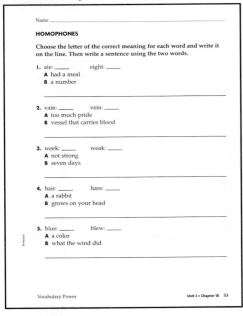

TRANSPARENCY 40

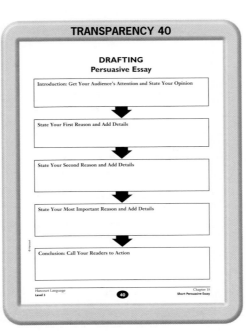

Revising

OBJECTIVES
- To learn strategies for revising a persuasive essay
- To revise a persuasive essay

DAILY LANGUAGE PRACTICE
TRANSPARENCY 39

1 An opinion reasons, and details is needed in persuasive paragraphs. (opinion,; are)

2 Mrs jackson wrote a persuasive speech. (Mrs. Jackson)

ORAL WARM-UP

USE PRIOR KNOWLEDGE Have students reflect on the writing they did in Chapters 6 and 12. Ask volunteers to recall strategies for revising a piece of writing.

GUIDED WRITING

Review with students the questions listed under Organization and Elaboration. Then ask students to add more questions to the list, such as "Are my reasons organized logically?" and "Does my essay end with a restatement of my opinion and a call to action?"

Use **Transparencies 41a and 41b** to further model organization and word choice. Then have students revise their essays. They can keep their revisions in their working portfolios.

PEER CONFERENCES Have pairs of students use the **Evaluation Criteria** to evaluate their own and each other's writing, responding constructively by identifying strengths and suggesting improvements.

WRAP-UP/ASSESS

SUMMARIZE How did the changes you made improve your essay?

Strategies Good Writers Use

- Include details to support reasons.
- Replace common verbs with vivid verbs.
- Use specific nouns.

Organization and Elaboration

Reread your draft carefully. Think about these questions as you read:

- Did I clearly state my opinion at the beginning?
- Did I use good details to help strengthen my reasons?
- Can I change any of my verbs to more vivid verbs?
- Can I make any of my nouns more specific?

MODEL

Here is part of the draft of Ben's paragraph. Notice that he changed the order of his reasons. He also changed a verb and a noun.

> You have to ~~learn~~ figure out how to use the right fingers on the right keys. It sounds simple, but it takes a lot of work. You also have to discover how to play with feeling. Then you have to learn to read music. Reading music is like learning a new language thing, and it's a challenge!

YOUR TURN

Revise your persuasive paragraph to include good details that support your reasons. What vivid verbs and specific nouns can you add to make your paragraph more interesting and persuasive?

222

TRANSPARENCIES 41a and 41b

REVISING

> You have to ~~learn~~ figure out how to use the right fingers on the right keys. It sounds simple, but it takes a lot of work. You also have to discover how to play with feeling. Then you have to learn to read music. Reading music is like learning a new language thing, and it's a challenge!

Harcourt Language
Level 3
41
Chapter 18
Short Persuasive Essay

Vocabulary Power page 54

Name _____

COMPARE AND CONTRAST

▶ Look at the diagram below. In the center circle, write the word from the Word Box that tells about both words. In the circle with *haughtiness*, write the three words that tell only about *haughtiness*. In the circle with *confidence*, write the three words that tell only about *confidence*.

vain	pride	dignity	trust
arrogant	secure	scornful	

haughtiness
scornful
vain
arrogant

both
pride

confidence
dignity
secure
trust

▶ Answer each question. You may wish to use some of the words from above to help you.

1. What are some words to describe someone who is always looking in the mirror? Possible responses: vain, arrogant, haughty

2. What are some things a person with confidence might do? Possible responses: trust other people, try new things, participate in activities

54 Unit 3 • Chapter 18
Vocabulary Power

Proofreading

Checking Your Language

When you proofread, you check for mistakes in grammar, spelling, punctuation, and capitalization. Correcting these mistakes can make your paragraph clearer and more persuasive.

MODEL

Here is the last part of Ben's paragraph. He has proofread to correct his punctuation mistakes. What other mistakes did he correct?

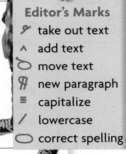

> This is a skill that comes only with a lot of ~~practise~~ practice. if you really want to play the piano well, you ~~has~~ have to focus on your lessons and practice playing as much as you can.

YOUR TURN

Proofread your revised paragraph by reading it several times. Each time you read, check for one of these kinds of mistakes:
- grammar errors
- spelling errors
- punctuation errors
- capitalization errors

Strategies Good Writers Use

- Check for subject-verb agreement.
- Check the dictionary if you are unsure how a word is spelled.
- Check sentences for correct punctuation and capitalization.

Editor's Marks

✄	take out text
∧	add text
↻	move text
¶	new paragraph
≡	capitalize
/	lowercase
◯	correct spelling

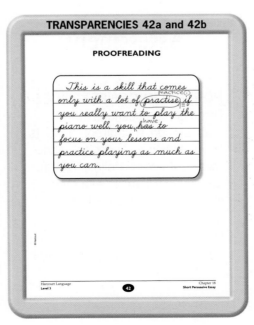

223

Proofreading

OBJECTIVES
- To learn strategies for proofreading a persuasive essay
- To proofread a persuasive essay

DAILY LANGUAGE PRACTICE

TRANSPARENCY 39

1 Grammar spelling and punctuation are three things she checked in her essay. (Grammar, spelling,)

2 I think a Friend helped her fix the mistakes? (friend; mistakes.)

ORAL WARM-UP

USE PRIOR KNOWLEDGE When you proof-read, do you look for one type of error at a time, or do you look for everything at once? Which way seems to work better for you?

GUIDED WRITING

Use **Transparencies 42a and 42b** to model the thinking. Have students explain the punctuation, grammar, and spelling errors Ben discovered when proofreading his paragraph. Review subject-verb agreement.

WRAP-UP/ASSESS

SUMMARIZE What kinds of errors did you find when you proofread your essay?

Spelling

PATTERNS AND BLENDS Have students practice spelling words with regular patterns such as *hop, hope,* and *drop.* Then, dictate lists of words with the CVC and CVCe patterns and words with blends. Have students exchange their lists with a partner for proof-reading. Remind students to proofread for words with these patterns in their persuasive para-graphs.

TRANSPARENCIES 42a and 42b

PROOFREADING

> This is a skill that comes only with a lot of ~~practise~~ practice. if you really want to play the piano well, you ~~has~~ have to focus on your lessons and practice playing as much as you can.

Harcourt Language
Level 3

42

Chapter 18
Short Persuasive Essay

Visit The Learning Site!
www.harcourtschool.com

Publishing

OBJECTIVES

- To learn strategies for publishing a persuasive essay as an oral presentation
- To publish a persuasive essay as an oral presentation

DAILY LANGUAGE PRACTICE

TRANSPARENCY 39

① Mrs. Jackson gave her speech next friday (will give; Friday.)

② I interviewed Mr Kronski at noon tomorrow. (will interview Mr.)

ORAL WARM-UP

USE PRIOR KNOWLEDGE Ask students to suggest ways people can publish or share their writing. Point out that they are now ready to publish their persuasive paragraphs.

GUIDED WRITING

SHARING YOUR WORK Read and discuss the questions with students. Help them decide where and how to publish their persuasive paragraphs.

If computers are available, have students practice keyboarding their persuasive essays after writing them by hand. Prompt students to double-space their essays. Have students select and underline their statements of opinion and their reasons. Allow students to print their essays.

REFLECTING ON YOUR WRITING Use the Portfolio Conferences suggestions at the right.

INTERNET Activities and exercises to help students prepare for state and standardized assessments appear on *The Learning Site:*

www.harcourtschool.com

Sharing Your Work

Now you can share your persuasive paragraph with an audience. Answering these questions can help you discover the best way to share your work:

1. Who is your audience? How can you share your persuasive paragraph so your audience will see or hear it?

2. Should you write your paragraph by hand or type it on the computer? Can you illustrate it with drawings or clip art?

3. Can your audience read your paragraph, or would it be better to read the paragraph to them? To give an oral presentation, use the information on page 225.

USING YOUR
Handbook

- Use the rubric on page 498 to evaluate your persuasive paragraph.

Reflecting on Your Writing

Using Your Portfolio What did you learn about your writing in this chapter? Write your answer to each question below.

1. Did your writing meet its purpose?

2. Using the rubric from your Handbook, how would you score your writing?

Add your answers and your paragraph to your portfolio. Then look through your portfolio. Find one piece of writing you like best, and write a few sentences explaining why you like it.

224

Assessment

• • • • • • • • • • • • • •

PORTFOLIO CONFERENCES

Discuss the questions in the *Pupil Edition,* and direct students to write their answers and add them to their portfolios. Tell students you will meet with them individually to discuss their growth as writers.

Use the Student Record Form on page R74 to record and monitor students' progress.

ESL

PRACTICE PUBLIC SPEAKING

As students practice their oral presentations, have them write on their note cards the pronunciation of any difficult words. Have students work with an English-fluent partner to practice pronunciation.

Giving an Oral Presentation

Ben decided the best way to share his paragraph was to present it orally. You can also give an oral presentation of your persuasive paragraph. Follow these steps:

STEP 1 Decide on your audience and purpose.

STEP 2 Use note cards to write your statement of opinion and your reasons. Number your note cards so you don't lose track of the order.

STEP 3 Use props if they will help you make your point. Charts, pictures, and objects can help you explain your reasons.

STEP 4 Speak in a loud, clear voice. Make eye contact with people in the audience, and use small hand movements to emphasize your points.

STEP 5 Take time at the end to ask for questions from your audience. Answer the questions clearly.

Strategies for Listening and Speaking

- Use details, vivid verbs, and specific nouns to describe your ideas, feelings, and experiences.
- Don't distract your listeners by moving too much or saying "um."
- If someone in the audience interrupts you, ask him or her to wait until the end of the presentation.

225

Read the instructions and Strategies for Listening and Speaking aloud. Explain that it is best not to write the presentation word for word. Instead, students should record main ideas on the note cards.

Have students refer to their typed reports as they write their note cards. Remind them to use the statements they underlined in their note cards.

Allow students time to practice their oral presentations. Suggest that students work in groups of three, with each taking a turn delivering a presentation. The two observers should give helpful comments to improve the presentation.

Review audience manners and listening strategies before students begin their presentations. Use the Student Record Form on page R76 to assess students' listening and speaking skills.

WRAP-UP/ASSESS

SUMMARIZE **What part of your persuasive presentation was the strongest? The weakest? How will you plan or present your next piece of persuasive writing differently?**

SCORING RUBRIC

4 ADVANCED

Purpose and Audience
- appropriate for audience
- stays focused on purpose

Organization and Elaboration
- clear statement of opinion at beginning
- middle gives logical reasons that support opinion
- ending restates opinion and gives call to action
- details, descriptions, and examples

Language
- uses correct grammar
- uses correct spelling, usage, and mechanics

3 PROFICIENT

Purpose and Audience
- mostly appropriate for audience
- few deviations from purpose

Organization and Elaboration
- clear statement of opinion at beginning
- reasons in middle support opinion
- ending restates opinion but gives no call to action
- some details, descriptions, and examples

Language
- mostly uses correct grammar
- mostly uses correct spelling, usage, and mechanics

2 BASIC

Purpose and Audience
- not appropriate for audience
- strays from purpose often

Organization and Elaboration
- statement of opinion at beginning
- reasons are not logical or clear
- ending does not restate opinion
- few details, descriptions, and examples

Language
- incorrect grammar, spelling, or mechanics sometimes makes writing unclear

1 LIMITED

Purpose and Audience
- not appropriate for audience
- purpose is unclear

Organization and Elaboration
- does not state opinion
- ideas not all about same topic
- no description, details, or examples

Language
- incorrect grammar, spelling, or mechanics often makes writing unclear

For information on adapting this rubric to 5- or 6-point scales, see pages R78–R79.

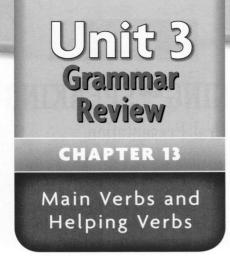

Unit 3
Grammar Review

CHAPTER 13

Main Verbs and Helping Verbs

OBJECTIVES

- To distinguish between main verbs and helping verbs
- To write contractions with *not* correctly

Unit Review

MODIFIED INSTRUCTION

BELOW-LEVEL STUDENTS Before students begin Parts A and B, point out that the helping verb usually comes before the main verb.

ABOVE-LEVEL STUDENTS After students have completed Parts A and B, suggest that they rewrite statements as questions and questions as statements. Remind them to change the order of the words. Have students compare their new sentences.

Unit 3
Grammar Review
CHAPTER 13
Main Verbs and Helping Verbs
pages 166–175

Main Verbs and Helping Verbs

pages 166–167

A. Write each sentence and underline the main verb. Then circle the helping verb.

1. Julia's ninth birthday (is) arriving tomorrow.
2. Her parents (have) secretly prepared for it.
3. Yesterday they (were) shopping for gifts.
4. The kitchen (is) smelling like chocolate cake.
5. Julia's parents (do) enjoy these birthday traditions.

More About Helping Verbs

pages 168–169

B. Write each sentence. Underline the helping verb once. Underline the main verb twice.

6. Did they create these old customs?
7. Many of their customs were learned from their parents.
8. Julia's grandmother has always served chocolate birthday cakes.
9. Some customs have come from her dad.
10. How many candles will be on Julia's cake?

Contractions with *Not*   *pages 170–171*

C. Write each sentence using a contraction to replace the underlined words.

11. We have not been to the Memorial Day parade before.   haven't
12. We do not forget the birthdays of Presidents Lincoln and Washington.   don't
13. Is not the Fourth of July a special holiday here?   Isn't
14. Does not your family have a picnic on Labor Day ?   Doesn't
15. You are not allowed to vote until you are eighteen.   aren't

TEST PREP

TIP

If students are taking a test in which a sentence has two or more variations, instruct them to try saying the sentence several times, using one of the choices each time. Because of what they know about English, the correct answer sometimes will "sound" right. Whenever possible, they should try to figure out why the answer that sounds right is correct.

Verb Tenses *pages 176–177*

A. **Write whether the underlined verb shows action that is happening in the present, happened in the past, or will happen in the future.**

  1. Tree Musketeers <u>is</u> a group run by boys and girls in El Segundo, California. present
  2. The children hope their actions <u>will keep</u> Earth clean. future
  3. They <u>started</u> their city's first recycling program. past
  4. They <u>serve</u> their city in many ways. present
  5. Their example <u>will encourage</u> other children. future

Present-Tense Verbs *pages 178–179*

B. **Choose the correct present-tense form of the verb in parentheses ( ) for each sentence.**

  6. Members of Tree Musketeers (plant, plants) trees. plant
  7. Sometimes a citizen of El Segundo (ask, asks) them to plant a special tree. asks
  8. Perhaps a family (want, wants) a tree to honor a special person. wants
  9. Tree Musketeers (dig, digs) holes for the trees. dig
  10. People (call, calls) these trees Memory Trees. call

Subject-Verb Agreement *pages 180–181*

C. **If the verb in the sentence agrees with the subject, write *correct*. If the verb does not agree with the subject, write the verb correctly.**

  11. Tree Musketeers' first tree stand near Memory Row. stands
  12. The group call it Marcie the Marvelous Tree. calls
  13. They all feel very proud of Marcie. correct
  14. Marcie grows taller every year. correct
  15. Every year Marcie have more new trees nearby. has

OBJECTIVES

• To identify present-tense, past-tense, and future-tense verbs
• To use correct subject-verb agreement
• To correct errors in subject-verb agreement

Unit Review

MODIFIED INSTRUCTION

BELOW-LEVEL STUDENTS Before students begin Parts B and C, point out that the word with which each verb must agree is not necessarily the first word in the sentence or the word closest to the verb. Remind students that each verb must agree with the word that tells who or what the sentence is about.

ABOVE-LEVEL STUDENTS Suggest to students that they rewrite each sentence from Part A in a different tense. After students have completed Parts B and C, have students identify the subject and the verb in each sentence and tell whether they are singular or plural.

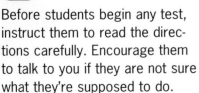

Before students begin any test, instruct them to read the directions carefully. Encourage them to talk to you if they are not sure what they're supposed to do.

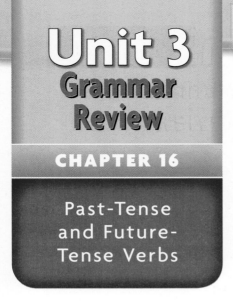

Unit 3
Grammar Review

CHAPTER 16

Past-Tense and Future-Tense Verbs

OBJECTIVES
- To recognize verb tenses past and future
- To form correctly the past tense and future tense of given verbs
- To choose the correct verb tense for a given sentence

Unit Review
MODIFIED INSTRUCTION

BELOW-LEVEL STUDENTS As students begin Part A, you might remind them that many verbs in the past tense end in *ed* and that verbs in the future tense have the helping verb *will*.

ABOVE-LEVEL STUDENTS After students have completed Parts A and B, encourage them to use the future tense to rewrite sentences in the past tense. Likewise, encourage them to use the past tense to rewrite sentences in future tense. Have students compare their new sentences.

Unit 3
Grammar Review

CHAPTER 16

Past-Tense and Future-Tense Verbs
pages 194–203

Past-Tense and Future-Tense Verbs *pages 194–195*

A. Write the verb or verb phrase in each sentence. Label each verb *past tense* or *future tense*.

1. Allison will run for class president. will run; future tense
2. She served as secretary for two years in a row. served; past tense
3. She will speak to the class on Thursday afternoon. will speak; future tense
4. She will explain her plans to the class. will explain; future tense
5. Allison planned her speech carefully. planned; past tense

More About Past-Tense and Future-Tense Verbs *pages 196–197*

B. Write the correct form of the verb, using the tense in parentheses ( ) for each sentence.

6. As president, Allison run (future) class meetings. will run
7. Last year, Carlos act (past) as president. acted
8. The class decide (past) several important issues. decided
9. They vote (past) for a field trip to the state capital. voted
10. They visit (future) the capital this spring. will visit

Choosing the Correct Tense
pages 198–199

C. Write the correct form of the verb in parentheses ( ) for each sentence.

11. Next summer, our member of Congress (traveled, will travel) to Washington, D.C. will travel
12. Two senators from this county (represented, will represent) our state next year. will represent
13. Tomorrow the voting polls (opened, will open) at seven in the morning. will open
14. My father (studied, will study) the issues last week. studied
15. He (planned, will plan) all of his choices then. planned

228

HANDS ON Activity

YESTERDAY AND TOMORROW
Have students work in groups of four. Instruct each group to make a two-column chart with the headings YESTERDAY and TOMORROW. Write four present-tense verbs (regular verbs, irregular verbs, or a mix) on the board. Have each group member use one future-tense verb in a sentence and one past-tense verb in another sentence, writing each verb in the appropriate column on the chart.

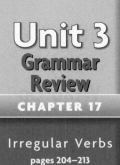

Irregular Verbs *pages 204–205*

A. Write the past tense of the verb in parentheses () to complete each sentence.

1. The City Council _____ plans for a new park. (has) had
2. Community members _____ to meetings for three months. (come) came
3. The planners _____ nothing for a long time. (do) did
4. Then we _____ the workers beside the road. (see) saw
5. People _____ they were excited. (say) said

More Irregular Verbs *pages 206–207*

B. Choose the correct past-tense verb in parentheses () to complete each sentence.

6. Mr. Rivel had (drawn, drew) plans for a bike path. drawn
7. We had (ate, eaten) at Rachel's Diner. eaten
8. Then we (rode, ridden) home safely on our bikes. rode
9. Some people had (gave, given) up on the project. given
10. Others (wrote, written) letters to the mayor. wrote
11. The support has (grew, grown) over the past year. grown
12. It has (took, taken) a big community effort. taken
13. Mrs. Shammil (took, taken) notes at the meeting. took
14. She (grew, grown) up in our town. grew
15. People (ate, eaten) cookies after the meeting. ate

Commonly Misused Irregular Verbs *pages 208–209*

C. Choose the correct verb in parentheses () to complete each sentence.

16. Mrs. Lenz (learns, teaches) gardening to me. teaches
17. She (rises, raises) corn and tomatoes. raises
18. She (lies, lays) her tools down after gardening. lays
19. She (lies, lays) down in the afternoon for an hour. lies
20. She (rises, raises) before her husband comes home. rises

Unit 3
Grammar Review
CHAPTER 17

Irregular Verbs

OBJECTIVES
- To write the correct past tense of given irregular verbs
- To choose the correct past-tense form of given irregular verbs
- To choose correctly between commonly misused irregular verbs

Unit Review
MODIFIED INSTRUCTION

BELOW-LEVEL STUDENTS You might have students review the charts of irregular verbs on pages 204 and 206 before they work through this page. As students begin Part B, you might tell them that in these sentences, verbs that end in *n* are the ones that follow *has, have,* or *had.*

ABOVE-LEVEL STUDENTS After students have completed Part C, have them write sentences using each word pair in one sentence. You might model the idea with these examples:

Mrs. Lenz teaches gardening to John, and he learns well.

She lays down her shovel, and it lies on the ground.

TEST PREP

Activities and exercises to help students prepare for state and standardized assessments appear on our website.

Visit
The Learning Site!
www.harcourtschool.com

Assessment

SKILLS ASSESSMENT Use the **Language Skills and Writing Assessment** to assess the grammar and writing skills taught in this unit. Model papers are included.

PORTFOLIO ASSESSMENT
Schedule portfolio conferences with individual students while others are completing the Unit Review exercises. Have students complete the Self-Assessment Checklist on page R87 and place it in their Show Portfolios. Use the Student Record Form on page R77 to monitor student progress. TEKS 3.19E

Make a Difference

OBJECTIVES

- To research ideas for helping the community
- To write and mail persuasive letters

INTRODUCE THE PROJECT

USE PRIOR KNOWLEDGE Read the introduction aloud to students. Ask volunteers to suggest reasons for writing different kinds of letters. Explain that persuasive letters, such as letters to newspaper editors, are a good way to express ideas and opinions about topics.

GENERATE QUESTIONS
Writer's Journal
Prompt students to generate questions about persuasive letters and to write the questions in their journals.

Pick Your Best Idea

To help students brainstorm ideas, display local newspapers, maps, or pictures of your community. Ask students to think about ideas they have to improve the community, and to get feedback from other students.

Research Your Idea

Suggest places students might look to learn more about their topic and to get support for their ideas. Provide newspapers and online resources. If appropriate, you might also suggest that students interview local or neighborhood leaders.

Make a Difference

Have you ever had a good idea about how to help your community? Why not share your idea? Write a letter to someone who can help you make a difference. Follow the steps below.

Pick Your Best Idea

- Make a list of ideas that you have for helping your community.
- Read the list to three classmates. Pick the best idea on your list.

Research Your Idea

- Learn more about your topic. Check online or in recent newspapers for information.
- Gather facts to support your idea.
- Revise your idea based on your research.

Draft a Letter

- Think about the best audience for your idea.
- Write a letter describing your idea for helping your community and why it is important.
- Explain why your audience should agree with your idea.
- Exchange letters with a classmate. Ask for suggestions on how to improve it.

Publish Your Letter

- Mail your letter.
- With classmates, photocopy all the letters and staple them together in a packet.

230

📺 Technology

SITE SKIMMING Have students locate websites about the community. Students can begin with a city website, the website of an important local organization, or a local newspaper.

Wanda's Roses
by Pat Brisson
REALISTIC FICTION
Wanda's care of a thorn bush in an abandoned lot brings her neighbors together as they work to improve their neighborhood.
Award-Winning Author

Recycle! A Handbook for Kids
by Gail Gibbons
NONFICTION
Hints and facts about the benefits of recycling and how to reduce the amount of garbage thrown away every day.
**Notable Social Studies Trade Book;
Outstanding Science Trade Book**

A Picture Book of Benjamin Franklin
by David A. Adler
BIOGRAPHY
Benjamin Franklin used his ideas to make a difference in his community and for his country.
Award-Winning Author

Draft a Letter
Remind students that vivid verbs and specific nouns will help make their letters more persuasive. Help students think about and write for the appropriate audiences for their letters. Choose one student's idea and discuss who might be the best audience for the letter about this idea. Have students discuss the reasons for their choices.

Publish Your Letter
Provide envelopes and help students locate the correct addresses. As an alternative to making a packet of students' letters, have each student make a poster that includes the letter and any research (online articles, newspaper clippings, and so on) pertaining to the topic.

STUDENT SELF-ASSESSMENT
Have students evaluate their own work and raise new questions for further investigation.

Books to Read Students who enjoyed discussing community improvements might be interested in reading one or more of these books. Have them record reflections on the book or books in their journals. Then ask students to recommend to the class the books from this list that they enjoyed most.

School-Home Connection

Have students share their ideas with their families. Family members may discuss the ideas and suggest other ways to share the ideas with community members. Families may also be able to help direct students to find how their ideas could change the community.

CHALLENGE

ARRANGE IDEAS Have students arrange the class's list of ideas according to these criteria:

- How quickly is this change needed?

- How many people will this help?

Have students explain how they arrived at their rankings.

Assessment Strategies and Resources

FORMAL ASSESSMENT

If you want to know more about a student's mastery of the language and writing skills taught in Unit 3, **then** administer the first *Language Skills and Writing Assessment* for Unit 3. The test consists of two parts:

Language Skills: **main verbs and helping verbs, present-tense verbs, past-tense verbs, future-tense verbs, irregular verbs,** and **word choice.**

Writing Task: Write a **short persuasive essay.** Scoring guidelines and model student papers are included.

INFORMAL ASSESSMENT TOOLS

Using Oral Language: Listening and Speaking

If you want to assess students' listening and speaking skills, **then** observe their use of oral language in both formal and informal settings. For example, notice whether individual students communicate thoughts, emotions, and events clearly when giving oral reports, taking part in drama activities, or participating in class or small-group discussions. Observe whether they speak expressively and modify their rate and volume appropriately.

Notice also how students listen in these situations. Do they actively enjoy and appreciate dramatic presentations? In discussions, do they interpret and evaluate what others are saying and then respond in an appropriate and relevant way?

To assess students' command of oral grammar and identify areas in which they may benefit from additional instruction, observe their listening and speaking behaviors in informal conversations as well.

Informal Assessment Reminder

If you used the preinstruction writing prompt suggested in Teaching Grammar from Writing, **then** remember to compare the results with the writing done by students after the grammar and writing instruction.

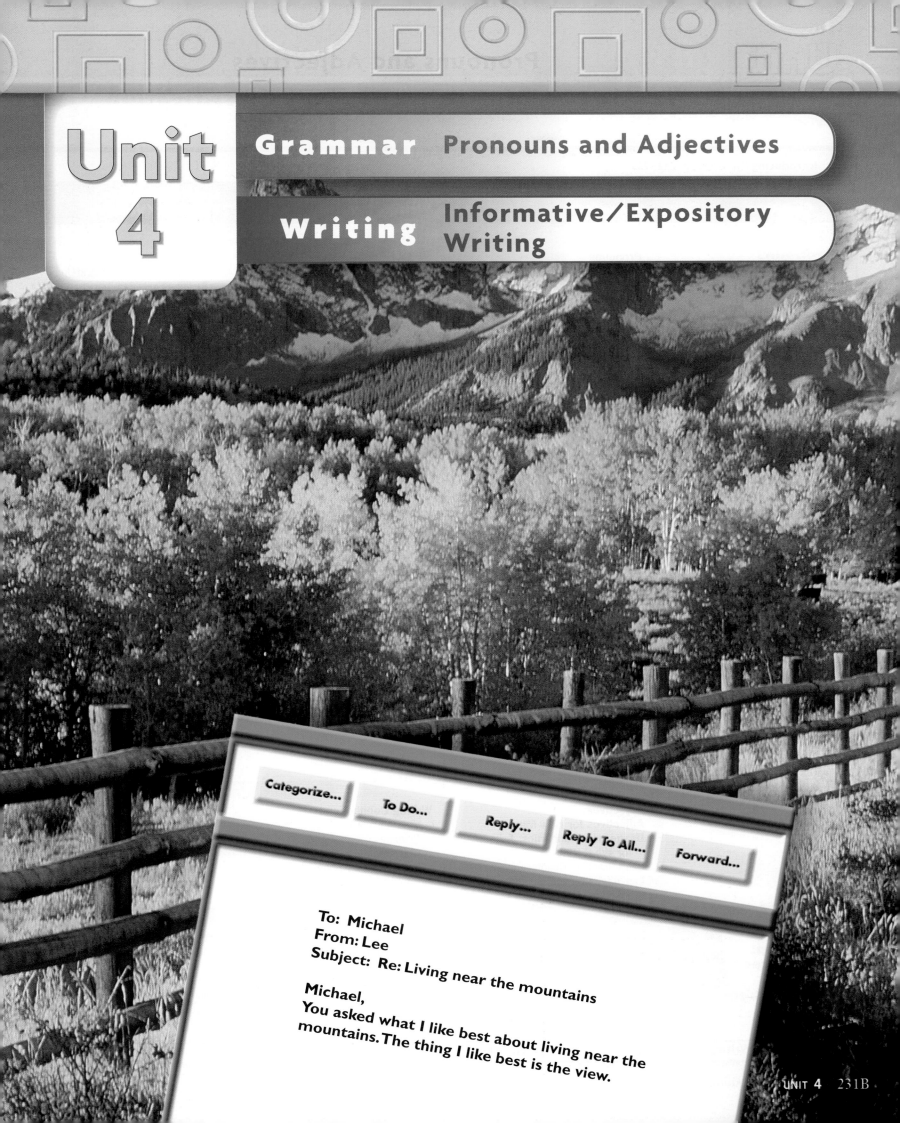

Unit 4

Grammar Pronouns and Adjectives

Writing Informative/Expository Writing

To: Michael
From: Lee
Subject: Re: Living near the mountains

Michael,
You asked what I like best about living near the mountains. The thing I like best is the view.

Unit 4

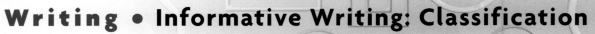

Grammar • Pronouns and Adjectives
Writing • Informative Writing: Classification

Chapters	Grammar	Writing	Listening/ Speaking/Viewing
19 **Pronouns** pp. 234–243	**Pronouns** **Singular and Plural Pronouns** **Usage and Mechanics: Pronoun-Antecedent Agreement** Extra Practice, Chapter Review, Daily Language Practice, Additional Practice: p. 466	**Writing Connections** Writing Idea Conversation Summarize Technology	**Activities** Challenge: Pronoun Stand-Up Building Oral Grammar Summarize
20 **Subject and Object Pronouns** pp. 244–253	**Subject Pronouns** **Object Pronouns** **Usage and Mechanics: Using *I* and *Me*** Extra Practice, Chapter Review, Daily Language Practice, Additional Practice: p. 467	**Writing Connections** Thinking About the Weather Clear Pronouns Art Real-Life Writing: Make a List	**Activities** ESL: Using *I* and *Me* Skits Building Oral Grammar Summarize
21 **Writer's Craft: Effective Sentences** pp. 254–261	**Daily Language Practice** **Hands-on Activities**	**Paragraph That Compares** Prewriting and Drafting Editing Sharing and Reflecting	**Activities** Comparative Talk Compound Sentences **Listening and Speaking:** Comparing Writing and Speaking Summarize
22 **More About Pronouns** pp. 262–271	**Possessive Pronouns** **More Possessive Pronouns** **Usage and Mechanics: Contractions with Pronouns** Extra Practice, Chapter Review, Daily Language Practice, Additional Practice: p. 468	**Writing Connections** Art Clear Pronouns Science Technology	**Activities** ESL: Pronoun Chart Challenge: Contraction Guessing Game Building Oral Grammar Summarize
23 **Adjectives** pp. 272–281	**Adjectives** **Adjectives for *How Many*** **Usage and Mechanics: Adjectives for *What Kind*** Extra Practice, Chapter Review, Daily Language Practice, Additional Practice: p. 469	**Writing Connections** Vivid Adjectives Science Conversation Reflecting on Writing	**Activities** Describe an Object Challenge: Animal Discovery Building Oral Grammar Summarize **Listening and Speaking:** Guest Speakers
24 **Writing Workshop: Advantages and Disadvantages Essay** pp. 282–293	**Unit 4 Grammar Review** **Daily Language Practice**	**Advantages and Disadvantages Essay** Prewriting Drafting Revising Proofreading Publishing	**Activities** Advantages and Disadvantages Lists ESL: Pronunciation Practice Summarize

Unit Wrap-Up Writing Across the Curriculum: Science, pp. 298–299

Vocabulary/Study Skills/ Technology/ Handwriting

Vocabulary Power

Words of the Week: astronomy, *galaxy, meteor, planet, solar system*
Science: Space-Related Prefixes
Writing Connection: Technology
Challenge: Use a Table of Contents and an Index
Study Skills: Parts of a Book

Vocabulary Power

Words of the Week: *Celsius, degree,* **Fahrenheit,** *mercury, temperature*
Challenge: Rating Websites
Technology: Exploring Websites

Vocabulary Power

Words of the Week: blustery, *breezy, doldrums, gusty, tranquil*
Challenge: Similes

Vocabulary Power

Words of the Week: *archaeology, biology,* **ecology,** *herpetology, technology*
Writing Connection: Technology
Challenge: Dictionary Dare
Vocabulary: Using Context Clues

Vocabulary Power

Words of the Week: *bovine,* **canine,** *equine, feline, porcine*
Writing Connection: Vivid Adjectives
Vocabulary: Synonyms and Antonyms
Challenge: Sort Adjectives

Vocabulary Power

Words of the Week: *annual, biennial, deciduous,* **evergreen,** *perennial*
Technology: Making a Video

- **Talk** with friends about people, places, and things that each of you likes. Use the **pronouns** *I, you, he, she, it, we,* and *they* in your **conversation.** SPEAKING/LISTENING

- **Write** sentences about people, places, and things that you like. Use the **pronouns** *me, him, her, it, us,* and *them* in your sentences. WRITING

- **Tell** a friend about people, places, and things in your neighborhood. Use **possessive pronouns** as much as possible. SPEAKING/LISTENING

- **Plan** a shopping trip. **List** items you will buy. Use **adjectives** to tell *what kind* and *how many* of each item. WRITING

- **Look** at an illustrated book with a friend. **Talk** about the advantages and disadvantages of using pictures to make ideas clearer in a story. VIEWING/SPEAKING/LISTENING

Technology — Resources

Grammar Jingles™ **CD**
Grammar Practice and Assessment **CD-ROM**
Writing Express **CD-ROM**
Media Literacy and Communication Skills **Package**
Writing Express **CD-ROM**
Grammar Practice and Assessment
Visit *The Learning Site!*
www.harcourtschool.com

Reaching All Learners

Intervention

ACHIEVING FOCUS Try the following ideas to help a highly-distractible student focus on a task and carry it through.

- When you introduce a task, be brief and specific in setting expectations with the student.

- Invite the student to choose a location in the classroom that will help him or her meet the expectations for that particular task.

- Make up a secret signal that you can use to remind the student of expectations you have previously established, without interrupting the flow of the classroom.

English as a Second Language

INTERACTIVE TECHNOLOGY Use TV and video interactively to enrich language experiences with second-language learners in your classroom. Here are some ideas to get you started.

- Tape or purchase instructional programs. Preview them and choose short segments to view interactively with students.

- Before viewing, engage students by giving them a purpose for viewing.

- Pause the video to allow interaction, such as checking comprehension or making predictions.

- Mute the sound, and either narrate the video or have students talk or write about it.

- Use programs with closed captioning to teach and reinforce vocabulary and reading skills.

Challenge

BULLETIN BOARD Begin a bulletin board featuring articles of interest to students. Highlight examples of the grammar concepts taught in this unit, and encourage students to identify and discuss them. Continue adding articles or other relevant print items throughout the unit. As students become more familiar with the bulletin board, they may also contribute articles or other items that they encounter in their independent reading.

Multi-age Classrooms

THINKING DEVELOPMENTALLY Teaching in a multi-age classroom allows you to stretch your thinking beyond grade-level expectations and look at students as individuals on a continuum. It challenges you to think developmentally, to weigh individual strengths and weaknesses, and to take advantage of a variety of management options.

- One way to individualize instruction is by presenting ten-minute "mini-lessons" that address specific instructional needs. After the mini-lesson, students work individually on projects according to their interests. During this time, you can circulate, observe, and conference with individual students.

- Thinking developmentally also means employing a range of options that include whole-group instruction, teacher-facilitated small groups, cooperative groups, pairs, and individual work. Use these options to allow students of different ages and ability levels to blend comfortably in your classroom.

Teaching Grammar from Writing

PRETEST

If you wish to use students' writing to diagnose their grammar instruction needs, use the following prompt.

WRITING PROMPT

Some schools are in session all year, with many short vacations. What advantages and disadvantages might there be to going to school all year? Write an essay to share your thoughts.

EVALUATE AND PLAN

Analyze students' writing to determine how you can best meet their individual needs for instruction. Use the following chart to identify and remedy problems.

COMMON PROBLEMS	CHAPTERS TO USE
Using pronouns that do not agree with antecedents	Chapter 19: Pronouns
Using *I* and *me* or other subject and object pronouns incorrectly	Chapter 20: Subject and Object Pronouns
Using possessive pronouns that do not agree with antecedents	Chapter 22: More About Pronouns
Incorrectly writing contractions with pronouns	Chapter 22: More About Pronouns
Using adjectives incorrectly	Chapter 23: Adjectives
Writing sentences that are all similar in length and type	Chapter 21: Writer's Craft: Effective Sentences
Difficulty writing an essay about advantages and disadvantages	Chapter 24: Writing an Advantages and Disadvantages Essay

Classroom Management

DURING...	SOME STUDENTS CAN...
Grammar Reteaching	Locate and begin reading the books in the Books to Read section of the Writing Across the Curriculum project. Use the Challenge Activity cards.
Independent Practice	Work on the Writing Connection. Work on *Vocabulary Power* pages.
Portfolio Conferences	Complete Student Self-Assessment forms. (See pages R86–R88 in this *Teacher's Edition*.).

Sharing Time

LANGUAGE ARTS IN THE CLASSROOM

The classroom community offers many natural opportunities for sharing—student publications, informal and formal presentations, and collaborative activities.

WRITERS' SHARING PLACE Provide a place for students to display their writing. Use a bulletin board, a peg or magnetic board, or a burlap wall covering on which students can pin their writing.

SIGN-UP SHEET Provide a sheet on which students can sign up to share their work that day. Keep track of students who have shared and those who still must be scheduled.

CHARTS Post a list of rules for sharing and for responding to others' writing in a positive and helpful way. Provide "Tips for Careful Listening" to help students focus on content and form.

AUTHOR'S CHAIR AND TABLE Keep a comfortable chair and small table in this space for students who are sharing their work. The "author" can place props or visual aids on the table next to the chair. Audience members can sit on rugs or on pillows.

WORK TABLE A center for students to publish their work requires a large table for collating pages, illustrating, and creating covers. Materials can be kept in separate labeled bins. Provide one bin for writing materials and another for supplies for making book covers. Include such materials as these:

- white and colored paper, stationery, cards, self-stick labels, blank books, and wrapping and wallpaper for book covers
- pens, pencils, markers, crayons, glue sticks, tape, stapler, rulers, yarn, brass fasteners, hole punch, pencil sharpener, date stamp, rubber stamps, and ink pads

Assign students to maintain the supplies.

Hands-on Activities

I or Me?

MATERIALS: two cards for each student, with the words *I* and *me* written on them

DIRECTIONS:

1. Give each student a card with *I* written on it, and a card with *me*.

2. Have students listen as you read aloud cloze sentences, leaving out the words *I* and *me*. Include some sentences with compounds such as *my friend and I* or *my sister and me*.

3. As you reread each sentence, students identify the missing pronoun by holding up the correct card.

Sentence Factory

MATERIALS: paper, pencils

DIRECTIONS:

1. Give students a short declarative sentence, such as *We took a trip.*

2. Have students work in pairs. Tell them to revise the sentence to make it more effective and then to add three more sentences to write a paragraph.

3. As students compare their completed paragraphs with classmates, encourage them to comment on the variety of sentences that different pairs have created.

Pronouns All Around

MATERIALS: paper, pencils, rulers

DIRECTIONS:

1. Have students work in small groups.

2. Each group must locate six sentences, each containing at least one subject or object pronoun. Students may find the sentences anywhere in the classroom, including books, magazines, newspapers, or environmental print.

3. One student in the group should be designated as Recorder, whose job it is to copy the sentences on a separate sheet of paper and number them from one to six.

4. Display a sample pronoun chart like the one shown here. Have each group make their own chart like this one. They may have to

add rows for sentences that have more than one pronoun.

5. Then students can fill in the charts with information about their sentences.

VARIATION: If you have already taught possessive pronouns, use the heading "subject, object, or possessive?" for the fourth column.

sentence number	pronoun	singular or plural?	subject or object?	antecedent
1				
2				
3				
4				
5				
6				

No Nouns

DIRECTIONS:

1. Have students work in small groups to create mini-dramas.

2. Explain that there is just one rule students must follow in developing the dialogue for their mini-dramas: No nouns. Students may use subject, object, and possessive pronouns, and may use gestures or pantomime to indicate antecedents, but they may not use any nouns.

3. When students present their mini-dramas for classmates, suggest that the audience listen for and point out any nouns that might accidentally be included.

Contraction Scramble

MATERIALS: pairs of cards with contractions and the words from which they were formed

DIRECTIONS:

1. Two to four players can play this game.

2. Mix up the cards, and spread them out face up where all players can see and reach them.

3. At a signal from you or another student, players pull out and hold matching pairs.

4. When all pairs have been matched, players take turns reading aloud the words on the cards they are holding.

5. The player with the most correct matches wins.

Guess My Flower

MATERIALS: drawing paper, crayons or markers

DIRECTIONS:

1. Distribute drawing paper, and tell students to draw any kind of real or imaginary flower.

2. When the flower drawings are completed, display about eight different drawings.

3. Call on a volunteer to secretly choose one of the flowers and give clues to help classmates guess which flower it is.

4. Each clue that the student gives must contain an adjective. You may want to give some examples, such as these: *I am thinking of a yellow flower. It has a thin stem. It has two leaves.*

5. The volunteer continues giving clues until the correct flower is identified.

6. Continue the game, having other students give clues. From time to time, replace some or all of the flower drawings.

you would

you'd

Sky Tree

BY THOMAS LOCKER

ONCE A TREE stood alone on a hill by the river. Through the long days, its leaves fluttered in the soft summer breeze.

But then the days grew shorter and the nights longer. The winds became cold, and the tree began to change.

Autumn came. The leaves of the tree turned gold, orange, and red. Squirrels hurried to store nuts and acorns.

The sun rose later each day. One morning, light glistened on a thin silver frost. By the end of the day, many leaves began to fall, first one and then another.

On a grey day, an old snapping turtle buried herself in the river mud, where she would sleep until spring. The tree's bare branches reached toward the sky. The clouds opened, and for a moment, the sky filled the branches.

On a misty morning, a flock of birds landed where the tree's leaves had been. The birds chirped, squabbled, and sang, but suddenly their wings beat the air, and they flew away.

Building Background

Brainstorm with students what they know about trees and how seasonal changes affect them. Help students understand that the description of the tree is presented not only as a part of nature and science but also as a work of art.

Students who live in "sunbelt" states may need to use reference source materials to better visualize the barrenness of the surroundings during the winter months.

Determine a Purpose for Listening

Tell students that this selection describes how the four seasons affect the world of nature. Ask students to determine whether their purpose for listening is

- to learn how to do something.
- to gain information. (to gain information)
- to solve problems.

Clouds gathered
and filled the tree's
empty branches
and then drifted
away.

Ice formed on the
river's edge. With its
roots deep in the earth,
the tree stood ready
for winter.

Snows fell.
Snug in their nest, a
family of squirrels
huddled close through
the cold winter days.

At night, millions of
stars twinkled among the
branches of the tree.
Beneath the river ice, the old
snapping turtle slept. The world
was waiting for spring.

Late one afternoon,
a golden light streamed
through the clouds and

warmed the tree.
The ice on the river
began to melt, and the
snow disappeared into
the ground.

The smell of wet earth
filled the air. Squirrels
raced through the fresh
grass and up the tree.
Sap rose to the tree's
tight buds.

The old snapper crawled
out of the mud to lay her eggs
on the warm hillside.
The tree's leaves uncurled in
the spring sunlight, and the
birds returned to build nests for
their young.

The tree stood on
the hill by the river.
Once again, its leaves
fluttered in the soft
summer breeze.

Listening Comprehension

LISTEN FOR SENTENCE VARIETY

As you read the selection aloud to the students, pause periodically and ask them to take note of the vivid descriptive sentences and the variety of sentence lengths. Explain that sentence variety makes writing interesting and helps keep the reader's attention. Then have students list some simple sentences and some compound sentences in this selection.

PERSONAL RESPONSE

How do you feel when the season changes from winter to spring? Why? (Possible responses: I feel happy because it is warmer and I can go outside; I miss the snow, but I like the sun and the birds and the new leaves on the trees.) *What is the main focus of this description of the changing seasons?* (the tree) *Name some supporting details in these nature scenes.* (Possible responses: winds are cold, turtle sleeps until spring, birds flew away, snows fell, snow disappeared, turtle lays her eggs, summer breeze) INFERENTIAL: MAIN IDEA-IMPORTANT DETAILS

Unit 4

Grammar **Pronouns and Adjectives**

Writing **Informative Writing**

Introducing the Unit

ORAL LANGUAGE/VIEWING

DISCUSS THE IMAGES Ask students to look carefully at the photograph. Then have them read the e-mail message. Have students tell how living in the mountains would be the same as living where they do now. Then have them tell some things they might like and dislike about living in the mountains. Explain that informative writing may include a comparison of two things, or it may tell the advantages and disadvantages of a situation. Information can be written, oral, or visual. Ask these questions:

1. **If you want to find out whether a new movie is good, where can you look?** (Possible responses: newspapers, entertainment news shows on television, advertisements, or the Internet)

2. **What things do you do to learn new information?** (Possible responses: take notes about the information; draw pictures to understand new information)

3. **What media could you use to compare today's weather in two different cities?** (television or the Internet)

 ENCOURAGE STUDENTS' QUESTIONS Have students reflect on ways to determine the advantages and disadvantages of a situation. Encourage students to develop questions for discussion. Have them record their questions and selected responses in their journals.

232   UNIT **4**

Unit 4

Grammar **Pronouns and Adjectives**

Writing **Informative Writing: Classification**

Viewing and Representing

COMPARE/CONTRAST PRINT AND VISUAL MEDIA Ask students to pick a city in the United States and find several weather forecasts for that city in various forms of media. They might check a newspaper, a weather station on television, and the Internet. Ask them to compare the forecasts and determine which one gives the most information.

For evaluation criteria for viewing, see the Viewing Checklist, page R88.

 MEDIA LITERACY AND COMMUNICATION SKILLS PACKAGE Use the video to extend students' oral and visual literacy. See *Teacher's Guide* pages 6–7.

To: Michael
From: Lee
Subject: Re: Living near the mountains

Michael,
You asked what I like best about living near the mountains. The thing I like best is the view.

233

Go over the list of unit contents, and tell students that Unit 4 covers pronouns and adjectives. Have them share what they already know about these topics. Point out that students will also learn about effective sentences, and will use them to write a paragraph that compares and an advantages and disadvantages essay.

SCIENCE CONNECTION Students will explore a variety of science topics in this unit:

- Earth and the Solar System
- Weather
- Ecosystems
- Plants and Animals

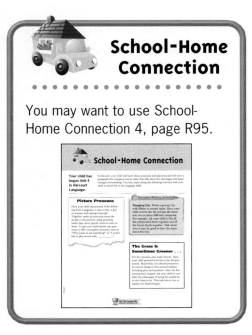

School-Home Connection

You may want to use School-Home Connection 4, page R95.

LESSON ORGANIZER	DAY 1	DAY 2
DAILY LANGUAGE PRACTICE TRANSPARENCIES 43, 44	1. Which planets am the farthest from the sun (are; sun?) 2. I thinks that neptune and pluto are the farthest. (think; Neptune; Pluto) **Bridge to Writing** Davon ___(action verb)___ on the bench and watched the stars.	1. Peter seed the moon last night. (saw) 2. He were very surprised at the moons size. (was; moon's) **Bridge to Writing** Ms. Bannon told ___(pronoun)___ about the moon.
ORAL WARM-UP Listening/Speaking	Recognize Awkward Sentences 234	Suggesting Pronouns 236 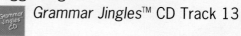 *Grammar Jingles*™ CD Track 13
TEACH/MODEL GRAMMAR **KEY** ✔ = tested skill	✔ **PRONOUNS** 234–235 • To identify and use pronouns correctly • To express thoughts in a paragraph, using pronouns	✔ **SINGULAR AND PLURAL PRONOUNS** 236–237 • To identify and use singular and plural pronouns • To write about a topic, using singular and plural pronouns
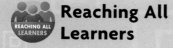 **Reaching All Learners**	**Modified Instruction** Below-Level: Model the Thinking Above-Level: Replace Noun with Pronoun **Reteach:** *Reteach Activities Copying Masters* p. 37 and R50 **Challenge:** Activity Card 13, R68 *ESL Manual* pp. 92, 93 *Practice Book* p. 61	**Modified Instruction** Below-Level: Use the Chart Above-Level: Rewrite Sentences **ESL:** Work with a Partner 236 *ESL Manual* pp. 92, 94 **Reteach:** *Reteach Activities Copying Masters* p. 38 and R50 **Challenge:** Space Journal 237 *Practice Book* p. 62
WRITING	Writing Connection 235 Writer's Journal: Writing Idea	Writing Connection 237 Real-Life Writing: Conversation
CROSS-CURRICULAR/ ENRICHMENT	*Vocabulary Power* Explore Word Meaning 234 **astronomy,** galaxy, meteor, planet, solar system See *Vocabulary Power* book.	*Vocabulary Power* Analogies 234 *Vocabulary Power* p. 55 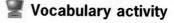 **Vocabulary activity**

DAY 3

1. we learned that the planets travels slowly around the sun. (We; travel)

2. Elizabeth and kyle has studied this in science class. (Kyle; have)

Bridge to Writing (Pronoun) want to learn more about astronomy.

Singular and Plural Pronouns 238

 Grammar Jingles™ CD Track 13

✔ **PRONOUN-ANTECEDENT AGREEMENT** 238–239
- To recognize and use pronouns that agree with their antecedents
- To write sentences using correct pronoun-antecedent agreement

---

Modified Instruction
Below-Level: Pronoun-Antecedent Agreement
Above-Level: Rewrite Sentences
ESL: Pronoun Practice 238
ESL Manual pp. 92, 95
Reteach: *Reteach Activities Copying Masters* pp. 39 and R50
Challenge: Moon Myths 239
Practice Book p. 63

Writing Connection 239
   Writer's Craft: Summarize

Vocabulary Power

   Classify and Categorize 234
   Vocabulary Power p. 56
 Vocabulary activity

DAY 4

1. Long ago, Romans know about stars, but he didnt know about planets. (knew; they; didn't)

2. the Romans called her wandering stars (The; them; stars.)

Bridge to Writing Willis told (pronoun) about the Romans.

Identify Pronoun and Antecedent 240

EXTRA PRACTICE 240–241
- To recognize and use pronouns and pronoun antecedents
- To research and write sentences, using correct pronoun-antecedent agreement

 Practice and assessment

Building Oral Grammar
Listen for Agreement 241
Challenge: Pronoun Stand-Up 241
ESL Manual pp. 92, 96
Practice Book p. 64

Writing Connection 241
Technology

Vocabulary Power

   Sequence 234
   Vocabulary Power p. 57
 Vocabulary activity
   Science: Space-Related Prefixes 240

DAY 5

1. we see a meteor shower last night. (We; saw)

2. The meteor shower was amazing and he lit up the sky. (amazing,; it)

Bridge to Writing (Noun) watched the meteor shower with me. Even people hundreds of miles away saw (pronoun) .

TEST PREP **CHAPTER REVIEW** 242
- To review pronouns and pronoun antecedents
- To locate and use the table of contents, glossary, and index of a book

Test preparation

Challenge: Use a Table of Contents and an Index 243
Practice Book p. 65
ESL Manual pp. 92, 97

Writing Application 243
Parts of a Book

Vocabulary Power

   Research 234
   Study Skills: Parts of a Book 243

Pronouns

OBJECTIVES
- To identify and use pronouns correctly
- To express thoughts in a paragraph, using pronouns

DAILY LANGUAGE PRACTICE

TRANSPARENCY 43

❶ Which planets am the farthest from the sun (are; sun?)

❷ I thinks that neptune and pluto are the farthest. (think; Neptune; Pluto)

BRIDGE TO WRITING Davon __(action verb)__ on the bench and watched the stars.

ORAL WARM-UP

USE PRIOR KNOWLEDGE Read aloud these sentences: *Jason went outside. Jason looked at the moon. Jason saw Venus.* Ask students why these sentences sound awkward when they are read together.

TEACH/MODEL

Remind students that a noun names a person, an animal, a place, or a thing. Read aloud the definition and examples of pronouns on page 234.

Model the thinking, using the Guided Practice example:

MODEL In the second example sentence, the word that takes the place of a noun is *It*. The noun in the first sentence that *It* replaces is *sun*.

Work through the Guided Practice with students, or have them complete the items in small groups.

Pronouns

A **pronoun** is a word that takes the place of one or more nouns.

Examples:
Silvia bought a telescope. *She* looked at the sky.

There are many stars and planets. Silvia saw *them* with the telescope.

Pronouns					
I	we	you	he	she	it
they	me	us	him	her	them

Guided Practice

A. Read each pair of sentences. Find the pronoun in the second sentence. Then tell which noun in the first sentence was replaced by the pronoun.

Example: The sun is important. It is the center of the solar system. *It|sun*
Pronouns are underlined once. Nouns are underlined twice.

1. Nine planets move in our sky. They move around the sun. They|planets
2. Earth is a planet. It moves around the sun. It|Earth
3. Silvia and Todd know that the planets are different sizes. They know that some planets are quite large. They|Silvia and Todd
4. Venus and Mars are the closest planets to Earth. Silvia saw them without a telescope. them|Venus and Mars
5. Silvia's brother looked for the smallest planet. He saw Mercury with Silvia's telescope. He|brother

Vocabulary Power

as·tron·o·my [ə·stro′nə·mē] *n.* The study of stars, planets, and other objects in the sky.

234

Vocabulary Power

DAY ❶ EXPLORE WORD MEANING Introduce and define *astronomy*. **What are some things you would learn about in an astronomy class?**

DAY ❷ ANALOGIES **What word completes this analogy?** *Biology is the study of life. Astronomy is the study of* _____. (See also *Vocabulary Power*, page 55.)

DAY ❸ CLASSIFY AND CATEGORIZE Write on the board: *astronomy, planets, birds, stars.* **Which word does not belong in this group? Why?** (See also *Vocabulary Power*, page 56.)

DAY ❹ SEQUENCE **Which is bigger, a planet or a solar system?** (See also *Vocabulary Power*, page 57.)

DAY ❺ RESEARCH Astronomy is the study of planets and stars. With a partner, pick a planet to research. Write a paragraph about what you find out.

Independent Practice

B. Rewrite each sentence. Use a pronoun in place of the underlined word or words.

Example: The children looked at the sky.
They

6. "<u>Anna</u> can see Mercury," said Anna. I
7. "Point out Mercury to <u>Will</u>," said Will. me
8. Anna showed <u>Will</u> where to look. him
9. Then <u>Will</u> could see the planet, too. he
10. Later <u>the children</u> saw Jupiter and Mars. they
11. Will saw <u>those planets</u> first. them
12. <u>My friends and I</u> used to think the planets were stars. We
13. <u>Jane</u> knows the difference between stars and planets. She
14. Jane told <u>my friends and me</u> that stars make light and heat. us
15. <u>A planet</u> gets light and heat from the sun. It

Remember that a pronoun is a word that takes the place of one or more nouns.

235

Writing Connection

Writer's Journal: Writing Idea Earth is the third planet from the sun, and Mars is the fourth. Someday, people may be able to travel to Mars. Suppose that you were the first person to walk on Mars. Using pronouns in place of some nouns, write a paragraph telling what you think walking on Mars would be like.

Independent Practice

Have students complete the Independent Practice, or modify it using these suggestions:

MODIFIED INSTRUCTION

BELOW-LEVEL STUDENTS Work through the Independent Practice items with students, modeling the thinking.

ABOVE-LEVEL STUDENTS For items 8, 11, and 14, have students replace the subject of the sentence, as well as the underlined words, with the appropriate pronoun.

Writing Connection

Writer's Journal: Writing Idea Remind students to use vivid descriptions as they express their thoughts about walking on Mars. Have them illustrate their paragraphs.

WRAP-UP/ASSESS

SUMMARIZE Ask students to explain what a pronoun does and to give examples of pronouns.

RETEACH

INTERVENTION Lessons in **visual, auditory,** and **kinesthetic** modalities: p. R50 and *Reteach Activities Copying Masters,* p. 37.

PRACTICE page 61

Name _____

Pronouns

A. Underline the pronoun in the second sentence. Then put two lines under the noun for which the pronoun stands in the first sentence.

1. My classmates and I will go on a field trip. We will go to Lick Observatory.
2. There is a giant telescope on top of a mountain. It is aimed at stars very far away.
3. Astronomers use the observatory for research. They watch the stars.
4. Scientists collect information about the stars and planets. They measure size, distance, and brightness.
5. David's mother works at the observatory. She invited us to visit.

B. Write each sentence below. Use a pronoun in place of the underlined word or phrase.

6. "Mark wants to look, too!" said Floyd.
"He wants to look, too!" said Floyd.

7. My classmates and I made charts of the brightest stars.
We made charts of the brightest stars.

8. Our teacher asked about a very bright star.
She/He asked about a very bright star.

TRY THIS! Suppose you have discovered a new planet. Write four sentences telling everyone about your discovery. Use pronouns in two of the sentences.

Practice • Pronouns   Unit 4 • Chapter 19   61

CHALLENGE

TAKE A TRIP Have students use **Challenge Activity Card 13** (page R68) to create a poster advertising interplanetary travel.

Challenge Activity Card 13

Take a Trip

Imagine that it's 2025 and space travel is popular. You are selling tickets for a trip to another planet. Persuade people to take the trip by making a travel poster.

Choose a planet. If you make up a planet, be sure to give it a creative name!

Draw a picture of something interesting to see or do on the planet. You may wish to brainstorm a list of possibilities before drawing your picture.

Write some sentences describing your pictures and be sure to use pronouns.

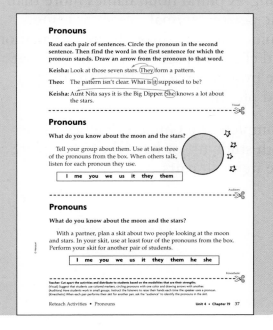

Pronouns

Read each pair of sentences. Circle the pronoun in the second sentence. Then find the word in the first sentence for which the pronoun stands. Draw an arrow from the pronoun to that word.

Keisha: Look at those seven stars. (They) form a pattern.

Theo: The pattern isn't clear. What is (it) supposed to be?

Keisha: Aunt Nita says it is the Big Dipper. (She) knows a lot about the stars.

Visual

Pronouns

What do you know about the moon and the stars?

Tell your group about them. Use at least three of the pronouns from the box. When others talk, listen for each pronoun they use.

| I | me | you | we | us | it | they | them |

Auditory

Pronouns

What do you know about the moon and the stars?

With a partner, plan a skit about two people looking at the moon and stars. In your skit, use at least four of the pronouns from the box. Perform your skit for another pair of students.

| I | me | you | we | us | it | they | them | he | she |

Teacher: Cut apart the activities and distribute to students based on the modalities that are their strengths.
[Visual] Suggest that students use colored markers, circling pronouns with one color and drawing arrows with another.
[Auditory] Have students work in small groups. Instruct the listeners to raise their hands each time the speaker uses a pronoun.
[Kinesthetic] When each pair performs their skit for another pair, ask the "audience" to identify the pronouns in the skit.

Reteach Activities • Pronouns   Unit 4 • Chapter 19   37

Singular and Plural Pronouns

OBJECTIVES
- To identify and use singular and plural pronouns
- To discuss and write about a topic, using singular and plural pronouns

DAILY LANGUAGE PRACTICE

TRANSPARENCY 43

1 Peter seed the moon last night. (saw)

2 He were very surprised at the moons size. (was; moon's)

BRIDGE TO WRITING Ms. Bannon told ___(pronoun)___ about the moon.

ORAL WARM-UP

USE PRIOR KNOWLEDGE Have students suggest pronouns to replace the nouns in the following sentence: *Monica gave the charts to Larry.*

Grammar Jingles™ **CD, Intermediate** Use Track 13 for review and reinforcement of pronouns.

TEACH/MODEL

Remind students that a singular noun names one person, animal, place, or thing. A plural noun names more than one person, animal, place, or thing. Guide students through the explanation and chart on page 236. Point out that the pronoun *you* can be both singular and plural.

Complete the Guided Practice items with students, or have them complete the items in pairs.

Pronouns	
Singular	**Plural**
I	we
me	us
you	you
he, she, it	they
him, her, it	them

Singular and Plural Pronouns

A **singular pronoun** takes the place of a singular noun. A **plural pronoun** takes the place of a plural noun.

Always capitalize the pronoun *I*.

The pronoun *you* is both singular and plural.

Examples:

I like learning about the planets.
I; singular

Earth is neither too hot nor too cold for us.
us; plural

Guided Practice

A. Find the pronoun in each sentence. Tell if it is a singular pronoun or a plural pronoun.

Example: One night I saw Mars.
I; singular

1. Emily, what do you know about astronomy? Have you ever seen Mars? you; singular
2. Mars looks like a red star, but it does not twinkle. it; singular
3. We are learning about the planets in school. We; plur
4. The class made a chart about them. them; plural
5. Uncle James gave me a telescope for looking at the planets. me; singular

236

Vocabulary Power page 55

Name _____

ANALOGIES

▶ Read each analogy below. Then choose a word from the Word Box to complete the analogy, and write it on the line.

| ground | science | stars | night | earth |

1. Biology is the study of life; astronomy is the study of ___stars___
2. The earth goes around the sun; the moon goes around the ___earth___
3. A star is in the sky; soil is on the ___ground___.
4. Addition is part of math; astronomy is part of ___science___
5. The sun can be seen during the day; stars can be seen at ___night___

▶ Now try these.

| hot | galaxy | disharmony | meteor | water |

6. *Planets* are to *solar system* as *solar system* is to ___galaxy___
7. *Forests* are to *trees* as *oceans* are to ___water___
8. *Piece* is to *whole* as *meteorite* is to ___meteor___
9. *Ice* is to *cold* as *sun* is to ___hot___.
10. *Agreement* is to *disagreement* as *harmony* is to ___disharmony___

Vocabulary Power   Unit 4 • Chapter 19   55

ESL

WORK WITH A PARTNER Have students work with an English-fluent partner to complete the Independent Practice items.

Independent Practice

B. Write a pronoun to take the place of the underlined word or words in each sentence. Then write *S* if the pronoun is singular or *P* if the pronoun is plural.

Example: <u>Mr. Hernandez</u> taught us about the planets.
He; S

6. <u>My classmates and I</u> made a model of our solar system. We; P
7. <u>The model</u> showed the sun and the planets. It; S
8. <u>Nancy</u> wanted to make the model of Jupiter. She; S
9. Jupiter is the biggest planet, so Mark helped <u>Nancy</u>. her; S
10. Ben made the model of Saturn, and I helped <u>Ben</u>. him; S
11. <u>Ben and I</u> did not know how to make Saturn's rings. We; P
12. We worked on <u>the rings</u> for a long time. them; P
13. Finally, <u>the rings</u> were finished. they; P
14. "That Saturn looks great!" Mr. Hernandez told <u>Ben and me</u>. us; P
15. "Nancy and Mark, did <u>Nancy and Mark</u> have fun?" asked the teacher. you; P

Writing Connection

Real-Life Writing: Conversation Suppose you could travel through the solar system on a space shuttle. With a partner, discuss and then write about living conditions inside the shuttle. Pay attention to each other's statements, checking to make sure that singular and plural pronouns are used correctly.

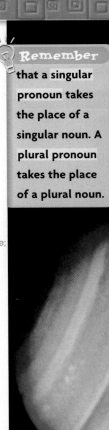

237

Independent Practice

Have students complete the Independent Practice, or modify it using these suggestions:

MODIFIED INSTRUCTION

BELOW-LEVEL STUDENTS Tell students that once they have decided whether the noun is singular or plural, they can refer to the chart on page 236 to help them find the appropriate pronoun.

ABOVE-LEVEL STUDENTS Once students have completed the items, have them select five sentences and rewrite them, changing the singular pronouns to plural pronouns and the plural pronouns to singular pronouns. Remind students to check for subject-verb agreement.

Writing Connection

Real-Life Writing: Conversation Students may use encyclopedias, the Internet, or other resources to gather information about living conditions inside actual space shuttles. Have them take simple notes on what they find.

WRAP-UP/ASSESS

SUMMARIZE Have students explain when to use singular pronouns and when to use plural pronouns.

REACHING ALL LEARNERS

RETEACH

INTERVENTION Lessons in **visual, auditory,** and **kinesthetic** modalities: p. R50 and *Reteach Activities Copying Masters*, p. 38.

REACHING ALL LEARNERS

PRACTICE page 62

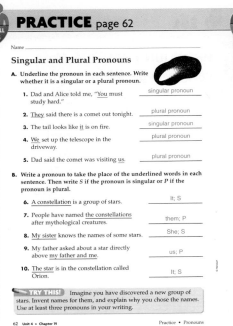

Name _____

Singular and Plural Pronouns

A. Underline the pronoun in each sentence. Write whether it is a singular or a plural pronoun.

1. Dad and Alice told me, "You must study hard." — singular pronoun
2. They said there is a comet out tonight. — plural pronoun
3. The tail looks like it is on fire. — singular pronoun
4. We set up the telescope in the driveway. — plural pronoun
5. Dad said the comet was visiting us. — plural pronoun

B. Write a pronoun to take the place of the underlined words in each sentence. Then write *S* if the pronoun is singular or *P* if the pronoun is plural.

6. A constellation is a group of stars. — It; S
7. People have named the constellations after mythological creatures. — them; P
8. My sister knows the names of some stars. — She; S
9. My father asked about a star directly above my father and me. — us; P
10. The star is in the constellation called Orion. — It; S

TRY THIS! Imagine you have discovered a new group of stars. Invent names for them, and explain why you chose the names. Use at least three pronouns in your writing.

62 Unit 4 • Chapter 19 · Practice • Pronouns

REACHING ALL LEARNERS

CHALLENGE

SPACE JOURNAL Tell students to imagine that they are scientists living on another planet. They are there to do research about living in space. Ask students to write two or three short journal entries telling what life is like on the planet. They should describe what the planet looks like, whom they are working with, and where they are living while on the planet. Remind students to use pronouns in their journal entries.

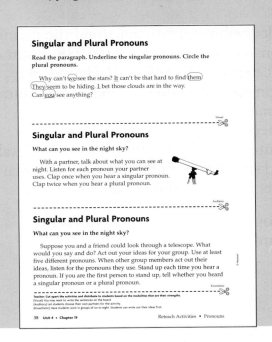

Singular and Plural Pronouns

Read the paragraph. Underline the singular pronouns. Circle the plural pronouns.

Why can't we see the stars? It can't be that hard to find them. They seem to be hiding. I bet those clouds are in the way. Can you see anything?

Visual

Singular and Plural Pronouns

What can you see in the night sky?

With a partner, talk about what you can see at night. Listen for each pronoun your partner uses. Clap once when you hear a singular pronoun. Clap twice when you hear a plural pronoun.

Auditory

Singular and Plural Pronouns

What can you see in the night sky?

Suppose you and a friend could look through a telescope. What would you say and do? Act out your ideas for your group. Use at least five different pronouns. When other group members act out their ideas, listen for the pronouns they use. Stand up each time you hear a pronoun. If you are the first person to stand up, tell whether you heard a singular pronoun or a plural pronoun.

Kinesthetic

Teacher: Cut apart the activities and distribute to students based on the modalities that are their strengths.
[Visual] You may want to write the sentences on the board.
[Auditory] Let students choose their own partners for the activity.
[Kinesthetic] Have students work in groups of six to eight. Students can write out their ideas first.

38 Unit 4 • Chapter 19 · Reteach Activities • Pronouns

USAGE AND MECHANICS
Pronoun-Antecedent Agreement

OBJECTIVES
- To recognize and use pronouns that agree with their antecedents
- To write sentences that summarize and that include correct pronoun-antecedent agreement

DAILY LANGUAGE PRACTICE

TRANSPARENCY 43

1 we learned that the planets travels slowly around the sun. (We; travel)

2 Elizabeth and kyle has studied this in science class. (Kyle; have)

BRIDGE TO WRITING (Pronoun) want to learn more about astronomy.

ORAL WARM-UP

USE PRIOR KNOWLEDGE On the board, write: *Vic and Amy looked at the sky, but they did not see the moon.* Then ask: **Does the pronoun replace a singular subject or a plural subject?**

Grammar Jingles™ **CD, Intermediate** Use Track 13 for review and reinforcement of pronouns.

TEACH/MODEL

Ask a volunteer to read aloud the definitions and examples on page 238. Point out that *number* refers to whether the pronoun antecedent is singular or plural. *Gender* refers to whether the pronoun antecedent is feminine, masculine, or neuter. Use the chart to illustrate plural and singular pronouns as well as masculine, feminine, and neuter pronouns.

Work through the Guided Practice items with students.

Antecedent	Pronoun
Kelly	she, her
Andy	he, him
star	it
stars	they, them
Kelly and Andy	they, them
children	they, them
Kelly and I	we, us

238

USAGE AND MECHANICS
Pronoun-Antecedent Agreement

The **antecedent** of a pronoun is the noun or nouns the pronoun replaces.

Example:
The **stars** were bright, and **they** were far away. (*Stars* is the antecedent of *they*.)

You have learned that a singular pronoun replaces a singular noun, and a plural pronoun replaces a plural noun. This is one part of pronoun-antecedent agreement. A pronoun must agree with its antecedent in both number and gender.

Guided Practice

A. Read each pair of sentences. Find the antecedent of each underlined pronoun.

Example: No one knows the exact number of stars. There are too many of <u>them</u> to count.
stars

1. Kelly saw lights in the sky.
<u>She</u> knew they were stars. Kelly

2. Stars look tiny in the night sky.
However, <u>they</u> are really huge. stars

3. The sun is a star.
<u>It</u> is the nearest star to Earth. sun

4. The sun warms and lights Earth.
<u>It</u> is the source of life on our planet. sun

5. Kelly and I wore special glasses to view the solar eclipse.
<u>It</u> made Earth go dark. solar eclipse

Vocabulary Power page 56

Name _____

CLASSIFY/CATEGORIZE

▶ Read the categories below. Write each word from the Word Box in the correct category. Then add five words of your own to each category. Additional words may vary. Possible responses are given.

soil	galaxies	meteors	stars	planets
trees	solar system	earthworms	rocks	roots

	Things in Space	Things In or On the Ground
1.	galaxies	soil
2.	meteors	trees
3.	planets	rocks
4.	solar system	earthworms
5.	stars	roots
6.	comets	plants
7.	asteroids	flowers
8.	moons	insects
9.	Earth	grass
10.	Mars	puddles

▶ On your own sheet of paper, draw a picture to illustrate one word from each category.

56 Unit 4 • Chapter 19   Vocabulary Power

REACHING ALL LEARNERS / **ESL**

PRONOUN PRACTICE Make cards with the following pronouns: *it, he, she, we, they, you, him, her,* and *them.*

Have students select a card and suggest a noun that could be replaced by the pronoun. Then have each student use the pronoun in a sentence.

Independent Practice

B. Read each pair of sentences. Write the antecedent of each underlined pronoun.

Example: A few stars have names. <u>They</u> are the brightest stars that we see from Earth. *stars*

6. Kelly saw what looked like a falling star. Andy told <u>her</u> it was a meteor. Kelly

7. Andy and I have seen meteors before. <u>We</u> learned about <u>them</u> in class. Andy and I; meteors

8. Meteors are pieces of rock or metal. <u>They</u> burn up as <u>they</u> travel through the air. Meteors, meteors

9. Sailors can use the North Star as a guide. <u>It</u> tells <u>them</u> which direction is north. North Star; sailors

10. Mom asked, "Do stars move?" Andy and Kelly told <u>her</u> that <u>they</u> do. Mom; stars

11. Antares and Sirius are two stars. Andy wanted to learn about <u>them</u>. Antares and Sirius

12. The librarian gave Andy and Kelly a book. <u>They</u> thanked <u>her</u> for the help. Andy and Kelly; librarian

13. Antares is a red supergiant star. <u>It</u> is more than 300 times as large as the sun. Antares

14. Kelly read about Sirius. <u>She</u> found out that <u>it</u> is really a double star. Kelly; Sirius

15. The sun is a medium-size star. <u>It</u> is part of the Milky Way. sun

239

Remember
that the antecedent of a pronoun is the noun or nouns the pronoun replaces.

Writing Connection

Writer's Craft: Summarize Write ten sentences about Earth. Use a science book to help you. Summarize the characteristics of the planet. Be sure the pronouns you use agree with their antecedents.

Independent Practice

Have students complete the Independent Practice, or modify it using these suggestions:

MODIFIED INSTRUCTION

BELOW-LEVEL STUDENTS Have students identify the nouns in each sentence before deciding on the pronoun antecedent.

ABOVE-LEVEL STUDENTS After students have completed the items, tell them to rewrite the first sentence in items 6, 10, and 12, making the subject plural. Then have students write the second sentence in each item, adjusting the pronouns correctly.

Writing Connection

Writer's Craft: Summarize Have students use a prewriting technique such as brainstorming to develop their ideas. Tell students to edit their writing for pronoun agreement.

WRAP-UP/ASSESS

Writer's Journal

SUMMARIZE Have students summarize what they learned about pronoun-antecedent agreement.

RETEACH

REACHING ALL LEARNERS

INTERVENTION Lessons in **visual, auditory,** and **kinesthetic** modalities: p. R50 and *Reteach Activities Copying Masters,* p. 39.

REACHING ALL LEARNERS

PRACTICE page 63

Name _____

Pronoun-Antecedent Agreement

A. Put two lines under the antecedent of each underlined pronoun.

1. Alice was glad the night was clear. <u>She</u> pointed at the bright star.

2. Dad and I looked over Alice's shoulder. <u>We</u> searched for the bright star.

3. My friend knows many constellations. Not everyone can recognize <u>them</u>.

4. <u>People</u> can recognize Orion easily. <u>They</u> can look for three bright stars in a row.

5. Three stars make up Orion's belt. <u>It</u> is in the center of the constellation.

B. Write the second sentence in each pair, using a pronoun in place of each noun in parentheses ( ). The pronoun and the antecedent must agree in number and gender.

6. Stars helped guide sailors long ago. The North Star never failed **(the sailors)**. The North Star never failed them.

7. Alice explained how sailors read the night sky. **(Alice)** showed us some pictures of constellations. She showed us some pictures of constellations.

8. I said clouds would cause big problems. **(Clouds)** would hide the stars. They would hide the stars.

TRY THIS! Suppose you are a sailor following the North Star. Write four sentences about what you see in the night sky. Make sure the pronouns agree with their antecedents.

Practice • Pronouns   Unit 4 • Chapter 19   63

REACHING ALL LEARNERS

CHALLENGE

MOON MYTHS Tell students that long ago, people believed that the moon was a face, which is why we sometimes refer to "the man in the moon." Have students write their own moon myths that explain why the moon is in the sky, why it is round, or why it shines. Remind students that myths can include strange and impossible details. Tell them to edit their myths for pronoun-antecedent agreement.

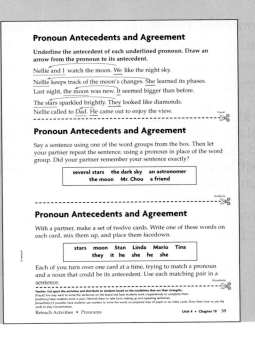

Pronoun Antecedents and Agreement

Underline the antecedent of each underlined pronoun. Draw an arrow from the pronoun to its antecedent.

Nellie and I watch the moon. <u>We</u> like the night sky.

Nellie keeps track of the moon's changes. <u>She</u> learned its phases.

Last night, the moon was new. <u>It</u> seemed bigger than before.

The stars sparkled brightly. <u>They</u> looked like diamonds.

Nellie called to Dad. <u>He</u> came out to enjoy the view.

Pronoun Antecedents and Agreement

Say a sentence using one of the word groups from the box. Then let your partner repeat the sentence, using a pronoun in place of the word group. Did your partner remember your sentence exactly?

| several stars | the dark sky | an astronomer |
| the moon | Mr. Chou | a friend |

Pronoun Antecedents and Agreement

With a partner, make a set of twelve cards. Write one of these words on each card, mix them up, and place them facedown.

| stars | moon | Stan | Linda | Mario | Tina |
| they | it | he | she | he | she |

Each of you turn over one card at a time, trying to match a pronoun and a noun that could be its antecedent. Use each matching pair in a sentence.

Reteach Activities • Pronouns   Unit 4 • Chapter 19   39

CHAPTER **19**   239

Extra Practice

OBJECTIVES
- To recognize and use pronouns and pronoun antecedents
- To conduct research and write sentences, using correct pronoun-antecedent agreement

DAILY LANGUAGE PRACTICE

TRANSPARENCY 44

1 Long ago, Romans know about stars, but he didnt know about planets.
(knew; they; didn't)

2 the Romans called her wandering stars (The; them; stars.)

BRIDGE TO WRITING Willis told ___(pronoun)___ about the Romans.

ORAL WARM-UP

USE PRIOR KNOWLEDGE Write these sentences on the board: *Mrs. Chin pointed to the sky. She told Nick to look for the moon.* Ask students to identify the pronoun and its antecedent. Have students name a pronoun to replace *Nick.*

TEACH/MODEL

Use the Remember box to review pronouns and antecedents.

Remind students to refer to the chart on page 236 for a list of pronouns.

Model the thinking. Write these sentences on the board: *DaShawn and Jasmine are in the astronomy club. They have a meeting tonight.*

MODEL In the pair of sentences, *They* replaces the compound subject *DaShawn and Jasmine*, so I know that the pronoun must be plural. The antecedent for the pronoun is *DaShawn and Jasmine.*

Have students work in pairs to complete the Extra Practice items.

Remember

that a pronoun is a word that takes the place of one or more nouns. A singular pronoun takes the place of a singular noun. A plural pronoun takes the place of a plural noun. The antecedent of a pronoun is the noun or nouns the pronoun replaces.

For more activities with pronouns, visit *The Learning Site:* www.harcourtschool.com

240

Extra Practice

A. Write the pronouns in each sentence.
pages 234–235

1. Marcie's parents gave <u>her</u> a telescope.
2. <u>It</u> was something <u>she</u> had always wanted.
3. Marcie called Angel and told <u>him</u> about <u>it</u>.
4. <u>He</u> said, "Now <u>you</u> can see Neptune and Uranus."
5. <u>She</u> said, "<u>I</u> could never see <u>them</u> before."

B. Write the pronoun that can take the place of the underlined noun or nouns. *pages 236–237*

6. <u>Mercury and Venus</u> are closest to the sun. They
7. You do not need a telescope to see <u>Venus and Mars</u>. them
8. You do not need <u>a telescope</u> to see Saturn or Jupiter either. it
9. <u>Saturn and Jupiter</u> are both very big planets. They
10. <u>Jupiter</u> is the largest planet in our solar system. It

C. Write the antecedent for each underlined pronoun. *pages 238–239*

11. Look at the moon every night and see how <u>it</u> changes. moon
12. The moon has eight phases, and you can see <u>them</u> all. phases
13. Look at a calendar. <u>It</u> tells when each phase begins. calendar
14. Marcie and Kevin looked at the moon. <u>They</u> realized <u>it</u> was a full moon. Marcie and Kevin; moon
15. Marcie saw the moon an hour later, and <u>she</u> thought <u>it</u> had moved. Marcie; moon

---

Vocabulary Power page 57

Name _____

SEQUENCE

Read each group of words and place them on the scale in the correct order.

1. From smallest to largest: solar system, universe, galaxy, planet

   | planet | solar system | galaxy | universe |

2. From smallest to largest: city, continent, state, country

   | city | state | country | continent |

3. From earliest to latest: noon, morning, night, sunset

   | morning | noon | sunset | night |

4. From youngest to oldest: teenager, adult, baby, child

   | baby | child | teenager | adult |

Vocabulary Power   Unit 4 • Chapter 19   57

Science

SPACE-RELATED PREFIXES
Remind students that they may have seen several words in their science books that begin with the prefix *astro-*. Explain that this prefix means "having to do with stars and space." Tell students to use a dictionary to find three words with this prefix. Then have students share their words in small groups, explaining how the meaning of the prefix relates to the words they found.

D. Write a pronoun in place of each noun in parentheses ( ). Use a pronoun that agrees in number and gender with the antecedent.
pages 238–239

16. Scientists who study the planets in astronomy have learned much about (the planets). them

17. The planet farthest from the sun is Pluto. People need telescopes to see (Pluto). it

18. The planet closest to the sun is Mercury. (Mercury) moves around the sun faster than any other planet. It

19. The other planets are farther from the sun. (The other planets) have farther to travel around the sun than Mercury does. They

20. Mercury goes around the sun in 88 Earth-days. Earth takes 365 Earth-days to travel around (the sun). it

Writing Connection

Technology Suppose you could live on another planet. Which planet would you choose? Use an electronic encyclopedia or another online reference work to find out about that planet. Then write several sentences supporting your choice. Check your sentences, and if possible, replace some nouns with pronouns.

DID YOU KNOW?
The planets differ greatly in distance from the sun. The Earth is nearly 100 million miles from the sun!

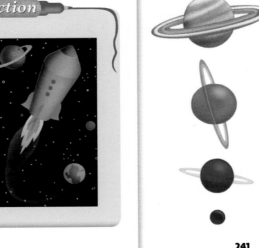

241

Building Oral Grammar

Have students work with a partner to read aloud their revised sentences from Parts B and D. Instruct students to listen for agreement between the pronoun and its antecedent. If they hear a mistake in pronoun-antecedent agreement, students should correct their partner, saying the sentence correctly.

Writing Connection

Technology Before students access the electronic encyclopedias, have them write questions to focus their research. Have students practice their keyboarding skills by typing their sentences. Remind them to edit their writing for pronoun-antecedent agreement.

WRAP-UP/ASSESS

SUMMARIZE Ask students to tell what to look for when deciding whether a pronoun agrees with its antecedent.

ADDITIONAL PRACTICE An additional page of Extra Practice is provided on page 466 of the *Pupil Edition*.

CHALLENGE

PRONOUN STAND-UP Read aloud the following sentence pairs. When students hear a pronoun that does not agree with its antecedent, they should stand up. Then ask volunteers to give the correct pronoun.

Anita wants to be a scientist. They are going to study stars.

Ali and Ralph like astronomy. They say she is interesting.

I studied the planets' names. He come from Latin and Greek words.

TECHNOLOGY *Grammar Practice and Assessment* CD-ROM; *Writing Express* CD-ROM

INTERNET Visit *The Learning Site:* www.harcourtschool.com

Chapter Review

OBJECTIVES
- To review pronouns and pronoun antecedents
- To locate and use the table of contents, glossary, and index of a book

DAILY LANGUAGE PRACTICE

TRANSPARENCY 44

① we see a meteor shower last night. (We; saw)

② The meteor shower was amazing and he lit up the sky. (amazing,; it)

BRIDGE TO WRITING (Noun) watched the meteor shower with me. Even people hundreds of miles away saw (pronoun).

STANDARDIZED TEST PREP

USE PRIOR KNOWLEDGE Write *stars*, *Ellen*, and *boys* on the board. Ask students to suggest pronouns to replace the nouns.

Have a student read aloud the directions on page 242.

Model the thinking. Write this example on the board:

Susan looked at the meteorites. (1) were so small!

   1 A It
      B Her
      C She
      D They

MODEL I know that the pronoun will take the place of either *Susan* or *meteorites* because they are the only nouns in the first sentence. The verb in the second sentence, *were*, tells me that the subject is plural, so the pronoun must take the place of *meteorites*. The correct answer is *They*.

Have the students complete the Chapter Review individually.

Chapter Review

Read the passage. Some words are missing. Choose the pronoun to fit in each blank space, and mark the letter for your answer.

STANDARDIZED TEST PREP

> Demarcus asked us to study the moon with him. (1) looked at (2) every night at the same time. Every night we drew a picture to show what (3) looked like. After a few weeks, Demarcus got all the pictures together. (4) asked his older sister to put (5) in a book. (6) made a flip book. Demarcus thanked (7) for (8).

TIP Be careful to match your answer choices to the numbers in the paragraph.

1 A She
  B They
  C We c
  D You

2 F him
  G it G
  H them
  J he

3 A they
  B it B
  C he
  D she

4 F They
  G It
  H He H
  J She

5 A she
  B he
  C them c
  D they

6 F It
  G She G
  H Her
  J Him

7 A I
  B they
  C her c
  D it

8 F he
  G I
  H they
  J it J

For additional test preparations, visit *The Learning Site:* www.harcourtschool.com

---

Assessment

PORTFOLIO ASSESSMENT Have students select their best work from the Writing Connections on pages 237, 239, and 241.

ONGOING ASSESSMENT Evaluate the performance of 4–6 students using appropriate checklists and record forms from pages R74–R77.

INTERNET Activities and exercises to help students prepare for state and standardized assessments appear on *The Learning Site:*
www.harcourtschool.com

Parts of a Book

Books have special parts that tell how to use them.

The Front of the Book

- The title page tells the name of the book.
- The copyright page tells when the book was published.
- The table of contents tells the name of each chapter or section and the page on which it begins.

The Back of the Book

- The glossary lists important words in alphabetical order and tells you their meanings.
- The index tells what page or pages in the book to find a certain topic.
- The bibliography tells the names of other books on the same subject.

STUDY SKILLS

YOUR TURN

WORK WITH A PARTNER **Choose a book that has all the features mentioned above. Then follow the numbered directions.**

1. **Find the table of contents. Tell your partner the title of the first chapter in the book.**

2. **Tell your partner the page number on which the chapter begins.**

3. **Go to the glossary. Read to your partner the first word and its definition.**

4. **Find the last topic listed in the index. Go to the page or pages cited and see what the book says about the topic.**

TIP
Nonfiction books about history or science will probably include most of these parts.

243

STUDY SKILLS

Parts of a Book

TEACH/MODEL

As students read about the features of a book, help them locate the features in this book. After students find the table of contents, for example, have them scan the chapters listed until they see Chapter 19: Pronouns. You may wish to show students that the table of contents also lists the glossary. Have students turn to the glossary. Point out that a glossary is like a dictionary but that its entries relate only to the topics in the book. Have students find *astronomy* and *pronoun* and read their definitions. Then have students find the index. Explain that an index is an alphabetical list that allows readers to search for a specific topic quickly. Ask students to look up *pronoun* and find references to that topic on the listed pages.

After completing the above activity, have students complete the Your Turn activity.

WRITING APPLICATION Have students write journal entries to tell how using a book's table of contents, glossary, and index is helpful when looking for information.

WRAP-UP/ASSESS

SUMMARIZE Ask students to tell what information is found in a table of contents, a glossary, and an index.

TECHNOLOGY Additional writing activities are provided on the *Writing Express* CD-ROM

REACHING ALL LEARNERS

PRACTICE page 65

Name _____

Chapter Review

Some words are missing in the paragraphs below. Choose the pronoun that fits in each space. Fill in the oval next to your choice.

When the moon seems to grow smaller, (1) _____ is waning. When (2) _____ seems to grow larger, the moon is waxing. The moon does not, of course, shrink or grow. It only seems like that to (3) _____. When the moon is a quarter moon, you can sometimes see a faint outline of the whole side. If you look through a telescope, you can see the whole side of the moon.

When the moon is full, it looks as if (4) _____ has a face. Alice said the dark spots are craters. (5) _____ said we could see (6) _____ through a telescope. Craters are dents in the moon's surface. I asked Alice how the craters were made. She told (7) _____ that (8) _____ were made by asteroids hitting the moon's surface.

1 ○ you ○ they ○ we ● it

2 ○ I ● it ○ them ○ he

3 ○ he ○ it ● us ○ she

4 ○ she ○ we ○ he ● it

5 ● She ○ He ○ Them ○ They

6 ○ him ○ her ○ she ● them

7 ● me ○ they ○ her ○ you

8 ○ it ● they ○ I ○ he

Practice • Pronouns

Unit 4 • Chapter 19 65

REACHING ALL LEARNERS

CHALLENGE

USE A TABLE OF CONTENTS AND AN INDEX Have students select one of the following topics: *Adjectives, Helping Verbs, Predicates, Question Marks.*

Have students

- tell which chapter in their textbook covers their topic.

- list the page numbers where the topic is found.

- write the glossary definition of the topic.

Subject and Object Pronouns

pages 244-253

LESSON ORGANIZER	DAY 1	DAY 2
DAILY LANGUAGE PRACTICE TRANSPARENCIES 45, 46	1. Sandy and i did a project about weather (I; weather.) 2. tamika learn about clouds yesterday. (Tamika; learned) **Bridge to Writing** (Pronoun) looks at the sky.	1. Him noticed dark clowds in the sky. (He; clouds) 2. us saw rain up ahead (We; ahead.) **Bridge to Writing** (Subject pronoun) uses an umbrella on rainy days.
ORAL WARM-UP **Listening/Speaking**	Choose the Pronoun Antecedent 244	Explain Pronoun Referents 246 *Grammar Jingles*™ CD Track 14
TEACH/MODEL **GRAMMAR** **KEY** ✔ = tested skill	✔ **SUBJECT PRONOUNS** 244–245 • To identify and use subject pronouns in writing • To record and express ideas using subject pronouns	✔ **OBJECT PRONOUNS** 246–247 • To identify and use object pronouns in writing • To write sentences using the correct forms of pronouns
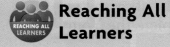 **Reaching All Learners**	**Modified Instruction** Below-Level: Ask Questions Above-Level: Rewrite Sentences **Reteach:** *Reteach Activities Copying Masters* p. 40 and R51 **Challenge:** Activity Card 14, R68 *ESL Manual* pp. 98, 99 *Practice Book* p. 66	**Modified Instruction** Below-Level: Work with Students Above-Level: Explain Answers **ESL:** Using Pronouns 246 *ESL Manual* pp. 98, 100 **Reteach:** *Reteach Activities Copying Masters* p. 41 and R51 **Challenge:** Make a Postcard 247 *Practice Book* p. 67
WRITING	Writing Connection 245 Writer's Journal: Thinking About the Weather	Writing Connection 247 Writer's Craft: Clear Pronouns
CROSS-CURRICULAR/ ENRICHMENT	*Vocabulary Power* Explore Word Meaning 244 Celsius, degree, **Fahrenheit,** mercury, temperature See *Vocabulary Power* book.	*Vocabulary Power* Analogies 244 *Vocabulary Power* p. 58 **Vocabulary activity**

DAY 3

1. Please give she that coat (her; coat.)
2. Us are shivering in the cold! (We)

Bridge to Writing Molly told <u>(object pronoun)</u> about the snow.

Identify Subject and Object Pronouns 248
Grammar Jingles™ CD Track 14

✔ **USING *I* AND *ME*** 248–249
• To identify the correct use of *I* and *me*
• To write a caption using *I* and *me* correctly

Modified Instruction
Below-Level: Read the Sentences
Above-Level: Use *Us* or *We*
ESL: Using *I* and *Me* 248
ESL Manual pp. 98, 101
Reteach: *Reteach Activities Copying Masters* p. 42 and R51
Challenge: Riddles 249
Practice Book p. 68

Writing Connection 249
Art

Vocabulary Power
Abbreviations 244
Vocabulary Power p. 59
Vocabulary activity

DAY 4

1. please tell Teri and I about the big blizzard. (Please; me)
2. We was stuck in the house for two days. (were)

Bridge to Writing Evan played games with Janet and <u>(object pronoun)</u> .

Replace Nouns with Pronouns 250

EXTRA PRACTICE 250–251
• To identify and use subject pronouns and object pronouns
• To make a list using subject and object pronouns
Practice and assessment

Building Oral Grammar
Describe a Story 251
Challenge: Poems 251
ESL Manual pp. 98, 102
Practice Book p. 69

Writing Connection 251
Real-Life Writing: Make a List

Vocabulary Power
General and Specific Nouns 244
Vocabulary Power p. 60
Vocabulary activity
Listening and Speaking: Skits 250

DAY 5

1. Me see that winter is here. (I)
2. Harry and I are going sledding with they. (them)

Bridge to Writing <u>(Subject pronoun)</u> are home now. Please tell <u>(object pronoun)</u> about the snowstorm.

TEST PREP **CHAPTER REVIEW** 252
• To review subject and object pronouns
• To understand and practice strategies for exploring websites
Test preparation

Challenge: Rating Websites 253
ESL Manual pp. 98, 103
Practice Book p. 70

Writing Application 253
Write a Review

Vocabulary Power
Content-Area Words 244
Technology: Exploring Websites 253

Subject Pronouns

OBJECTIVES
• To identify and use subject pronouns in writing
• To record and express ideas using subject pronouns

DAILY LANGUAGE PRACTICE

TRANSPARENCY 45

1 Sandy and i did a project about weather (I; weather.)

2 tamika learn about clouds yesterday. (Tamika; learned)

BRIDGE TO WRITING   (Pronoun) looks at the sky.

ORAL WARM-UP

USE PRIOR KNOWLEDGE Read aloud the following sentence: *Greg looked at the thermometer.* Ask students what word could take the place of *Greg.* Point out that *he* can take the place of *Greg,* but *him* cannot.

TEACH/MODEL

Remind students that a pronoun is a word that takes the place of one or more nouns. Explain that there are certain pronouns that take the place of subjects. Read the definition and the example sentences with students. Model the thinking for the Guided Practice example sentence:

MODEL I know that the subject is the part of the sentence that names someone or something. A subject pronoun replaces the noun or nouns in the subject. *They* must be the subject pronoun.

Have students complete the Guided Practice sentences in pairs.

Subject Pronouns

I	we
you	you
he, she, it	they

Vocabulary Power

Fahr•en•heit
[far'ən•hīt'] scale: *n.*
A temperature scale showing 32 degrees at the freezing point of water and 212 degrees at the boiling point of water.

244

Subject Pronouns

A **subject pronoun** takes the place of one or more nouns in the subject of a sentence.

Remember that the subject is the part of the sentence that names someone or something. Always capitalize the pronoun *I.*

Examples:
I love the spring.

She felt the cold air outside.

You go camping every summer.

They like to splash through the puddles.

Guided Practice

A. Name the subject pronoun in each sentence.

Example: They know what the temperature is.
They

  1. I see a thermometer on the wall.
  2. It is a tool that measures temperature.
  3. It has numbers along the side.
  4. They tell what the exact temperature is.
  5. He owns nine thermometers.
  6. They are all different sizes.
  7. We used a thermometer to measure water temperature.
  8. She was sick and needed to use a thermometer.
  9. You can borrow a thermometer.
10. It is very useful.

Vocabulary Power

DAY 1 EXPLORE WORD MEANING Introduce and define *Fahrenheit.* **Why is it important to have a way to measure temperature?**

DAY 2 ANALOGIES **Finish this analogy: Mile is to distance as _____ is to temperature.** (See also *Vocabulary Power,* page 58.)

DAY 3 ABBREVIATIONS Write *98.6°F* and *37°C* on the board. Explain that the *F* stands for Fahrenheit and the *C* stands for Celsius. **Why is it important to include an *F* or a *C* when you write a temperature?** (See also *Vocabulary Power,* page 59.)

DAY 4 GENERAL AND SPECIFIC NOUNS **What is the unit of measurement for temperature? and for weight?** (See also *Vocabulary Power,* page 60.)

DAY 5 CONTENT-AREA WORDS **The freezing point of water on the Fahrenheit scale is 32 degrees. On the Celsius scale, the freezing point is zero degrees. Which scale do you think would be easier to use?** Discuss responses.

Independent Practice

B. Write the subject pronoun in each sentence.

Example: You are learning about weather.
You

11. <u>You</u> can feel the temperature.
12. <u>It</u> can be measured in degrees Fahrenheit.
13. <u>We</u> know that winter is cold in some parts of the country.
14. <u>They</u> have warmer winters in the South.
15. <u>He</u> asked why the temperature changes.
16. <u>She</u> talked about how the sun's rays hit Earth.
17. <u>They</u> don't seem as hot in the winter.
18. <u>I</u> drew a picture of the sun and Earth.
19. <u>We</u> understand temperature better now.
20. To learn more, <u>you</u> could read a book about temperature.

Remember that a subject pronoun takes the place of one or more nouns in the subject of a sentence.

Writing Connection

Writer's Journal: Thinking About the Weather Choose a season, and write three sentences telling what you like about it. Record your ideas about why you like these things. Try to express your thoughts by using at least three subject pronouns in your sentences.

245

Independent Practice

Have students complete the Independent Practice, or modify it using these suggestions:

MODIFIED INSTRUCTION

BELOW-LEVEL STUDENTS For each sentence, have students ask themselves, *Who or what is the subject of this sentence?*

ABOVE-LEVEL STUDENTS Have students rewrite the sentences, replacing the subject pronouns with nouns. Remind students to think about the number and gender of each pronoun as they rewrite the sentences.

Writing Connection

Writer's Journal: Thinking About the Weather Before students begin, have them imagine a particular season and list key thoughts about sights or activities that they connect with that time of year. Students can refer to the list as they write.

WRAP-UP/ASSESS

SUMMARIZE Ask students to tell what a subject pronoun is and to name some subject pronouns.

RETEACH

INTERVENTION Lessons in **visual, auditory,** and **kinesthetic** modalities: p. R51 and *Reteach Activities Copying Masters,* p. 40.

PRACTICE page 66

Name _____

Subject Pronouns

A. Identify the subject pronoun in each sentence.

1. They said the moon had a halo, too. — They
2. It was glowing brightly. — It
3. He said the ring around the moon might mean rain. — He
4. She said that was an old sailor's tale. — She
5. You went outside to look at the moon. — You

B. Write each sentence. Underline the subject pronoun.

6. They need some sunlight, too.
   They need some sunlight, too.
7. We saw the sun coming out at the end of the storm.
   We saw the sun coming out at the end of the storm.
8. She looked everywhere for a rainbow.
   She looked everywhere for a rainbow.
9. He pointed to the sky.
   He pointed to the sky.
10. We found both ends of the rainbow.
    We found both ends of the rainbow.

TRY THIS! Write a poem about a rainbow or about a halo around the moon. Use at least three subject pronouns in your poem.

66 Unit 4 • Chapter 20   Practice • Subject and Object Pronouns

---

CHALLENGE

CLOTHING CATALOG Have students use **Challenge Activity Card 14** (page R68) to create a catalog of clothing for various seasons and climates.

Challenge Activity Card 14

Clothing Catalog

Create a catalog that shows clothing a person might wear during different seasons and climates. You may draw pictures or cut out examples from magazines or catalogs. Be sure to include clothes for
• hot weather
• cold weather
• rainy days
For each item, write a caption using a subject pronoun. For example,
She looks warm in this winter coat!

Subject Pronouns

Read the paragraph and circle the subject pronouns. Then write an answer to the question below the paragraph.

Jed and (I) are always happy to see snow. (We) keep two sleds on the front porch. (They) are always ready to go. Mom likes sledding, too, and sometimes (she) comes along. (It) may be cold out, but (we) don't mind!

Which season do (you) think (we) like best? ____ winter ____

Subject Pronouns

What kind of weather do you have in the winter? What do you and your friends like to do in that weather?

Tell a partner about it. As you talk, use at least three of these subject pronouns:

| I | you | he | she | it | we | they |

When your partner talks, listen for subject pronouns. Nod your head each time you hear a subject pronoun.

Subject Pronouns

What do you like to do when it snows? If you have never been in the snow, what do you wish you could do?

Pantomime your ideas for the rest of your group. Then have each member of your group say a sentence about what you did. Everyone should try to use a different subject pronoun from the list.

| I | you | he | she | it | we | they |

Teacher: Cut apart the activities and distribute to students based on the modalities that are their strengths.
[Visual] You may want to have students work with partners and complete this activity cooperatively.
[Auditory] Let students choose their own partners for this activity.
[Kinesthetic] Have students work in groups of three or four.

40 Unit 4 • Chapter 20   Reteach Activities • Subject and Object Pronouns

Object Pronouns

OBJECTIVES
- To identify and use object pronouns in writing
- To write comparative sentences using the correct forms of pronouns

DAILY LANGUAGE PRACTICE

TRANSPARENCY 45

1 Him noticed dark clowds in the sky.
(He; clouds)

2 us saw rain up ahead (We; ahead.)

BRIDGE TO WRITING (Subject pronoun) _____
uses an umbrella on rainy days.

ORAL WARM-UP

USE PRIOR KNOWLEDGE Say aloud the following sentences: *Elena carries an umbrella. The umbrella keeps her dry.* Point out to students that in the first sentence, Elena is doing the action (carrying). In the second sentence, the action (keeping dry) is done to her.

Grammar Jingles™ **CD, Intermediate** Use Track 14 for review and reinforcement of subject and object pronouns.

TEACH/MODEL

Read the definition of an object pronoun. Explain that one way to identify an object pronoun is to find the action verb in the sentence. Ask: **Who or what is receiving the action?** Model the thinking using the first example sentence:

MODEL **The action verb in the sentence is *hit*. I ask myself, *Who is being hit?* I know that the object pronoun must be *us*.**

Work through the Guided Practice sentences orally with the students.

Object Pronouns	
me	us
you	you
him, her, it	them

246

Object Pronouns

An **object pronoun** follows an action verb or a word such as *about, around, at, for, from, near, of, to,* or *with*.

Object pronouns are usually in the predicate of a sentence.

Examples:

The wind hit **us** hard.

The summer was too hot for **him**.

Nate told **her** about the Fahrenheit scale.

A fan cooled **me**.

Guided Practice

A. Name the object pronoun in each sentence.

Example: The teacher taught us about the weather.
us

1. Mr. Rivera told <u>me</u> about the air.
2. A blanket of air covers <u>us</u>.
3. The sun heats <u>it</u>.
4. The sun keeps <u>us</u> warm.
5. Wind is air that blows around <u>you</u>.
6. Wind can chill <u>you</u>.
7. The teacher told <u>her</u> about the water in air.
8. Mr. Rivera told <u>him</u> that water high up in the air forms clouds.
9. A weather forecaster watches the clouds and studies <u>them</u>.
10. Leah will tell <u>you</u> about the weather.

Vocabulary Power page 58

Name _____

ANALOGIES

► Read each analogy below. Think about how the first two italicized words go together. Then write the word from the Word Box that completes the analogy.

Fahrenheit	large	summer	den	temperature

1. *Pound* is to *weight* as *degree* is to ____temperature____
2. *Short* is to *tall* as *small* is to ____large____
3. *Winter* is to *cold* as ____summer____ is to *hot.*
4. *Volt* is to *electricity* as ____Fahrenheit____ scale is to temperature.
5. *Bird* is to *nest* as *lion* is to ____den____

► Now try these.

day	liquid	tasting	mercury	Celsius

6. *Light* is to *dark* as *night* is to ____day____
7. *Pages* are to *book* as ____mercury____ is to *thermometer.*
8. The *Richter scale* is to *earthquake strength* as the ____Celsius____ scale is to *temperature.*
9. *Ice* is to *solid* as *water* is to ____liquid____
10. *Ears* are to *hearing* as *tongue* is to ____tasting____

58 Unit 4 • Chapter 20   Vocabulary Power

ESL

USING PRONOUNS Provide students with extra practice by having them replace the underlined words in these sentences with the correct subject and object pronouns.

<u>Elena and Alice</u> were outside.

Louisa gave the jacket to <u>Adam</u>.

Lois told <u>James and me</u> about the storm.

The teacher told <u>Tina and Chin</u> to go inside.

<u>Patrick and I</u> are cold.

Independent Practice

B. Write the object pronoun in each sentence.

Example: Molly showed them a snowball.
them

11. The snowstorm caught <u>us</u> by surprise.
12. Paco and Vicki were not expecting <u>it</u>.
13. The sidewalks had a thick layer of snow on <u>them</u>.
14. Luis handed <u>him</u> a snow shovel.
15. The snow made <u>us</u> cold and wet.
16. Kim's father made <u>them</u> some hot chocolate.
17. The hills had snow on top of <u>them</u>.
18. Tom wanted to go sledding with <u>her</u>.
19. Tommeka made a snowman with <u>me</u>.
20. I hope the sun doesn't melt <u>it</u>.

Remember that object pronouns follow action verbs and words such as *about, around, at, for, from, near, of, to,* and *with.*

247

Writing Connection

Writer's Craft: Clear Pronouns Think about your favorite season. Using the correct forms of pronouns, record your thoughts about what you and your friends do during that season.

Independent Practice

Have students complete the Independent Practice, or modify it using these suggestions:

MODIFIED INSTRUCTION

BELOW-LEVEL STUDENTS Work through the Independent Practice sentences with students.

ABOVE-LEVEL STUDENTS Have students tell how they know which word is an object pronoun.

Writing Connection

Writers' Craft: Clear Pronouns Explain to students that they can choose the form that best allows them to record their ideas about the season. They may write a poem, a letter, or a journal entry to complete the assignment. Remind them to edit their writing for correct subject and object pronoun usage.

WRAP-UP/ASSESS

SUMMARIZE Have students explain how they can identify object pronouns in a sentence.

RETEACH

INTERVENTION Lessons in **visual, auditory,** and **kinesthetic** modalities: p. R51 and *Reteach Activities Copying Masters,* p. 41.

PRACTICE page 67

Name _____

Object Pronouns

A. Identify the object pronoun in each sentence.

1. Rainbows always amaze him! — *him*
2. Anna always looks for them on our walks. — *them*
3. Suri asked me how a rainbow is made. — *me*
4. I told her a rainbow is made of mist. — *her*
5. The sun shines through it and makes colors. — *it*

B. Write each sentence. Underline the object pronoun.

6. Rob asked her about the order of the colors.
   Rob asked her about the order of the colors.

7. Anna used markers to show him the colors.
   Anna used markers to show him the colors.

8. Purple, blue, and green are part of it.
   Purple, blue, and green are part of it.

9. The light always arranges them in the same way.
   The light always arranges them in the same way.

10. Our teacher will get a crystal prism for us.
    Our teacher will get a crystal prism for us.

TRY THIS! Look at the colors made by a prism. Then write three sentences describing the color patterns. Use object pronouns in your sentences.

Practice • Subject and Object Pronouns — Unit 4 • Chapter 20 67

CHALLENGE

MAKE A POSTCARD Tell students to imagine that they are on vacation in some faraway location. Using notebook paper, students will create postcards. On one side of the paper, have students draw a picture that shows what the weather is like in their vacation spot. On the other side, have students write a short note about their vacation. Tell students to use subject pronouns and object pronouns in their notes.

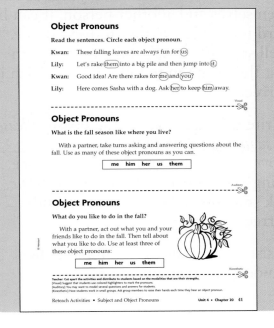

Object Pronouns

Read the sentences. Circle each object pronoun.

Kwan: These falling leaves are always fun for (us)

Lily: Let's rake (them) into a big pile and then jump into (it).

Kwan: Good idea! Are there rakes for (me) and (you)?

Lily: Here comes Sasha with a dog. Ask (her) to keep (him) away.

Object Pronouns

What is the fall season like where you live?

With a partner, take turns asking and answering questions about the fall. Use as many of these object pronouns as you can.

| me | him | her | us | them |

Object Pronouns

What do you like to do in the fall?

With a partner, act out what you and your friends like to do in the fall. Then tell about what you like to do. Use at least three of these object pronouns:

| me | him | her | us | them |

Reteach Activities • Subject and Object Pronouns — Unit 4 • Chapter 20 41

Using *I* and *Me*

OBJECTIVES
- To identify the correct use of *I* and *me* and to use them correctly in sentences
- To write a caption using *I* and *me* correctly

DAILY LANGUAGE PRACTICE

TRANSPARENCY 45

1 Please give she that coat (her; coat.)

2 Us are shivering in the cold! (We)

BRIDGE TO WRITING Molly told ___(object pronoun)___ about the snow.

ORAL WARM-UP

USE PRIOR KNOWLEDGE Write the following sentences on the board: *I looked at the pictures. Dad photographed me.* Have students identify the subject pronoun and the object pronoun.

Grammar Jingles™ **CD, Intermediate** Use Track 14 for review and reinforcement of subject and object pronouns.

TEACH/MODEL

Read through the instruction and example sentences.

Tell students that when they talk about themselves and another person, it can be hard to decide whether to use *I* or *me*. Tell students to say the sentence with just the pronoun to help decide which is correct.

Write this sentence on the board: *Please go swimming with David and _____.* Cover *David and* and say the sentence, using *I*. Repeat the sentence, using *me*. Ask students which pronoun sounds correct.

Assist students as they complete the Guided Practice sentences.

Using *I* and *Me*

The word *I* is a subject pronoun. The word *me* is an object pronoun.

Remember that *I* is used in the subject of a sentence. The word *I* is always capitalized. The word *me* is used in the predicate of a sentence.

Examples:

I am delighted by the weather.

The sun feels good to **me**.

When you talk about yourself and another person, always name the other person first.

Examples:

Tasha and **I** raked the leaves.

Dad asked Kevin and **me** to shovel the snow.

Guided Practice

A. Use *I* or *me* to complete each sentence.

Example: _____ saw a rainbow today. *I*

1. __I__ drink water to stay cool.
2. The sun shines down on Julie and __me__.
3. __I__ drink a lot of water in the summer.
4. The sun's rays can give __me__ a bad sunburn.
5. __I__ shiver with cold in the winter.
6. Wearing layers of clothing keeps __me__ warm.
7. Chad and __I__ saw the storm clouds.
8. __I__ feel chilly when I get wet.
9. Hot drinks make __me__ feel warm.
10. Pedro and __I__ use an umbrella in the rain.

248

Vocabulary Power page 59

Name _____

ABBREVIATIONS

A. Complete the chart by writing the word from the Word Box that goes with each abbreviation.

Fahrenheit	Doctor	millimeter	centimeter	Avenue	ounce

ABBREVIATION	WORD
1. oz.	ounce
2. Ave.	Avenue
3. F	Fahrenheit
4. Dr.	Doctor
5. cm	centimeter
6. mm	millimeter

B. Complete the chart by writing the abbreviation from the Word Box that goes with each word.

Wed.	C	Mr.	mi.	Oct.	Km

ABBREVIATION	WORD
7. C	Celsius
8. Wed.	Wednesday
9. Mr.	Mister
10. Oct.	October
11. mi.	mile
12. Km	Kilometer

Vocabulary Power   Unit 4 • Chapter 20   59

REACHING ALL LEARNERS

ESL

USING *I* AND *ME* Give each student a card that says *I* and a card that says *me*. Write the following sentences on the board. As you read them aloud, ask students to hold up the card that has the correct pronoun.

During the summer, _____ like to swim.

In the winter, Daniel gives _____ hats and gloves.

Gaby and _____ are sad when it rains.

Independent Practice

B. Choose the correct words in parentheses ()
to complete each sentence. Write each
completed sentence.

Example: (Sis and I, Sis and me) like rainy days.
Sis and I like rainy days.

11. The newspaper told (Ann and I, <u>Ann and me</u>)
what weather was coming.
12. (<u>Mom and I</u>, Mom and me) expected snow.
13. (<u>I</u>, Me) thought the temperature was 32
degrees Fahrenheit.
14. The fog may make (me and you, <u>you and me</u>)
late.
15. (<u>The animals and I</u>, The animals and me)
waited for the rain to stop.
16. (<u>My sister and I</u>, I and my sister) play baseball
in the summer.
17. The Smiths took (<u>me</u>, I) to the beach.
18. The heat made (I, <u>me</u>) sleepy.
19. (My friends and me, <u>My friends and I</u>) like to
swim.
20. (<u>I</u>, Me) am hungry after swimming.

> **Remember**
> that *I* is a
> subject pronoun
> and *me* is an
> object pronoun.
> When you talk
> about yourself
> and another
> person, always
> name the other
> person first.

249

Writing Connection

Art Draw a picture of yourself and a friend outside
enjoying the weather. Write a caption that describes
the weather and tells what you and your friend are
doing. Be sure to use *I* and *me* correctly in your
caption.

Independent Practice

Have students complete the Independent Practice, or
modify it using these suggestions:

MODIFIED INSTRUCTION

BELOW-LEVEL STUDENTS For sentences using *I*
or *me* and a noun, have students read the sentences
with just the pronoun.

ABOVE-LEVEL STUDENTS For each sentence with
I or *me* and a noun, have students write whether *us*
or *we* would be the correct pronoun choice.

Writing Connection

Art As students record their knowledge by drawing pictures, remind them that a caption is one or
two short sentences that describe a picture.
Explain that a caption summarizes the message
of the picture. Students should demonstrate
more proficient control of penmanship when
writing their captions.

WRAP-UP/ASSESS

SUMMARIZE Ask students to tell how they
know when to use *I* and when to use *me*.

RETEACH

INTERVENTION Lessons in **visual,
auditory,** and **kinesthetic** modalities: p. R51 and *Reteach Activities
Copying Masters*, p. 42.

REACHING ALL LEARNERS

PRACTICE page 68

Name _____

Using *I* and *Me*

A. Write *I* or *me* on the line to complete each sentence.

1. Anna wanted to show <u>me</u> how clouds are made.
2. She set down a dry glass before <u>me</u>.
3. Anna and <u>I</u> filled the glass with ice.
4. <u>I</u> saw water drops form on the outside of the glass.
5. <u>I</u> asked Anna to explain it to me.

B. Complete each sentence with the correct word in parentheses ( ).
Then write each sentence.

6. (I, Me) asked Anna, "So, when air gets cold, does it condense?"
I asked Anna, "So, when air gets cold, does it condense?"

7. Rob was watching Anna and (I, me).
Rob was watching Anna and me.

8. Anna told (I, me), "Yes, and tiny water drops form."
Anna told me, "Yes, and tiny water drops form."

9. (I, Me) felt the cold air beside the glass.
I felt the cold air beside the glass.

10. Anna taught (I, me) that the ice cooled the air.
Anna taught me that the ice cooled the air.

> **TRY THIS!** Try Anna's experiment with a friend. Then write
> a short paragraph about what you saw. Use at least three object
> pronouns in your writing.

68 Unit 4 • Chapter 20   Practice • Subject and Object Pronouns

---

REACHING ALL LEARNERS

CHALLENGE

RIDDLES Ask students to write
simple riddles using *I* and *me*.
They can follow these models
when creating their riddles:

> You can see me in the sky.
> My name rhymes with *proud*.
> What am I?

> I am cold, wet, and white.
> You see me in the winter.
> What am I?

Using *I* and *Me*

Read each sentence. Circle the sentences that use *I* and *me* correctly.

(Tell me about the weather.)
(Maybe you and I can walk the dog.)
(The cold weather isn't good for me.)
Mom and me can drive to the store.

Visual ✄

- -

Using *I* and *Me*

Which kind of weather do you like best?

Tell your group about it. Use the pronouns *I* and *me* as you talk.
When others in your group talk, listen for how often they use the
pronouns *I* and *me*. Raise your hand each time you hear one of
these pronouns.

Auditory ✄

- -

Using *I* and *Me*

How do you feel about the weather?

Have each member of your group make two cards. Write *I* on one
and *me* on the other. Put all the group's cards facedown on a table.
Take turns picking up a card. Read the pronoun on the card, and say a
sentence using it.

| I | me |

Kinesthetic ✄

Teacher: Cut apart the activities and distribute to students based on the modalities that are their strengths.
[Visual] Have students work with partners to complete the activity.
[Auditory] Remind students to listen carefully when another group member is speaking.
[Kinesthetic] Have students work in groups of four to six. Give each student a chance to draw at least twice and to say at least two different sentences.

42 Unit 4 • Chapter 20   Reteach Activities • Subject and Object Pronouns

Extra Practice

OBJECTIVES
- To identify and use subject pronouns and object pronouns
- To make a list using subject and object pronouns

DAILY LANGUAGE PRACTICE

TRANSPARENCY 46

1 please tell Teri and I about the big blizzard. (Please; me)

2 We was stuck in the house for two days. (were)

BRIDGE TO WRITING Evan played games with Janet and (object pronoun) .

ORAL WARM-UP

USE PRIOR KNOWLEDGE Ask students to replace the proper nouns with pronouns as you read aloud these sentences:

Janet and Ann waited for the sun to come out.

Give the snow shovel to Joel.

Alan told Mary about the storm.

TEACH/MODEL

Use the Remember boxes to review subject and object pronouns. Model the thinking for the example sentence in Extra Practice B:

MODEL I know that the subject of the sentence names someone or something. A subject pronoun replaces the noun or nouns in the subject. *We* must be a subject pronoun.

Have students work in pairs to complete the Extra Practice items.

CHAPTER 20
Subject and Object Pronouns

Remember

that a subject pronoun takes the place of one or more nouns in the subject of a sentence. An object pronoun follows an action verb or a word such as *about, around, at, for, from, near, of, to,* or *with.*

For more activities with subject and object pronouns, visit *The Learning Site:* www.harcourtschool.com

250

Extra Practice

A. Write each sentence, using the correct pronoun. *pages 244–247*

Example: The raindrops fell on (them, they).
The raindrops fell on them.

1. (I, Me) had never been in a big storm.
2. The storm shook (she, her) and the boat.
3. (He, Him) thinks it is safer to be indoors.
4. The rain soaked (we, us) to the skin.
5. (They, Them) cleaned up the mess from the storm.

B. Write *subject pronoun* or *object pronoun* to name the underlined word in each sentence. *pages 244–247*

Example: We shook the water from our shoes.
subject pronoun

6. He found the umbrella. subject
7. The road was too muddy for us. object
8. You ran to the house to stay dry. subject
9. She found a lost cat during the storm. subject
10. Marvin brought raincoats for them. object

C. Rewrite each sentence. Replace the underlined words with a pronoun. *pages 244–247*

Example: Terry and Jeff saw a flash in the sky.
They saw a flash in the sky.

11. The lightning scared Yoko and Pat. them
12. The car got stuck in the flood. It
13. There were extra coats for Aldo and me. us
14. Rishi and I watched the wind bend the trees. We
15. Seth helped Nia clean off the mud. He

Vocabulary Power page 60

Name _____

GENERAL AND SPECIFIC NOUNS

Read each word. Choose a more specific noun from the Word Box and write it on the line. Then add your own word.
Additional words may vary. Possible responses are given.

| Celsius scale | degree | Earth | wedding | democracy | animated film |
| mercury | astronomy | mountain | hollow | yarn | president |

	General	Specific	
1.	story	yarn	tale
2.	hole	hollow	crater
3.	temperature scale	Celsius scale	Fahrenheit scale
4.	unit of measure	degree	pound
5.	landform	mountain	hill
6.	government	democracy	monarchy
7.	leader	president	governor
8.	science	astronomy	biology
9.	planet	Earth	Mars
10.	movie	animated film	comedy
11.	ceremony	wedding	graduation
12.	element	mercury	oxygen

60 Unit 4 • Chapter 20

Vocabulary Power

Listening and Speaking

SKITS Divide the class into four groups: *Spring, Summer, Winter,* and *Fall.* Tell students to present a dramatic interpretation of activities during that season. Audience members should stand when they hear a subject pronoun or an object pronoun. Students should speak in complete sentences and use correct subject-verb agreement.

D. Write the object pronoun in each sentence.

pages 246–247

Example: Juan told us that the rain would end soon.

us

16. The teacher told <u>him</u> about fog.
17. The fog made <u>them</u> late to school.
18. Sometimes the fog scares <u>her</u>.
19. Morning fog can make <u>you</u> cold.
20. It's hard to see <u>me</u> through thick fog.

E. Rewrite each sentence to correct the errors.

pages 244–249

21. Scientists tell <u>we</u> the temperature in degrees Fahrenheit. us
22. <u>Them</u> study the weather every day. They
23. Now <u>me</u> can prepare. I
24. <u>Me and Tisha</u> wore coats today. Tisha and I
25. The boots are for <u>Rudy and I</u>, and the scarf is for Eva. Rudy and me

> **Remember**
> that *I* is a subject pronoun and *me* is an object pronoun. When you talk about yourself and another person, always name the other person first.

DID YOU KNOW?
In very powerful storms called hurricanes, winds sometimes blow at speeds of 150 miles per hour.

251

Writing Connection

Real-Life Writing: Make a List With some classmates, describe today's weather. Then make a list to record what you like or dislike about it. Include subject and object pronouns in your list.

Building Oral Grammar

In small groups, have students discuss a book or a story they read recently. Each student should describe the plot and characters, using subject and object pronouns appropriately. Then the listeners should take turns summarizing the spoken message and retelling it.

Writing Connection

Real-Life Writing: Make a List You might have students consult newspaper or online weather reports to prepare for their discussions about the day's weather. Tell students to take notes on what they find. Encourage students to be specific as they explain their responses.

WRAP-UP/ASSESS

SUMMARIZE On the board, draw a Venn diagram to show subject and object pronouns. Label one circle *Subject Pronouns* and the other circle *Object Pronouns*. Have students give examples of pronouns and tell whether they are subject or object pronouns. Words that are both subject and object pronouns should be placed in the space where the circles overlap.

ADDITIONAL PRACTICE An additional page of Extra Practice is provided on page 467 of the *Pupil Edition*.

CHALLENGE

POEMS Have students write poems about their favorite kinds of weather. Model a poetry form, such as haiku, to guide the structure of their work, or allow students to use free verse.

TECHNOLOGY *Grammar Practice and Assessment* CD-ROM; *Writing Express* CD-ROM

INTERNET Visit *The Learning Site:* w w w . h a r c o u r t s c h o o l . c o m

Chapter Review

OBJECTIVES

- To review subject and object pronouns
- To understand and practice strategies for exploring websites

DAILY LANGUAGE PRACTICE

TRANSPARENCY 46

1 Me see that winter is here. (I)

2 Harry and I are going sledding with they. (them)

BRIDGE TO WRITING ___(Subject pronoun)___ are home now. Please tell ___(object pronoun)___ about the snowstorm.

STANDARDIZED TEST PREP

MODEL TEST-TAKING STRATEGIES Have students read the directions on page 252 silently. Remind them to reread each sentence with the answer they think is correct.

Model the thinking. Write this example on the board:

_____ enjoy swimming at the beach every summer.

    1 **A** Her

         B We

         C Us

         D Them

MODEL I know that the blank in the sentence is the subject, so the pronoun must be a subject pronoun. *Her, Us,* and *Them* are all object pronouns. *We* is a subject pronoun, so that must be the answer. The sentence *We enjoy swimming at the beach every summer* is correct.

Chapter Review

Read the paragraph and choose the word that belongs in each space. Write the letter for your answer.

> __(1)__ can see the changes that autumn brings to our family. Father knows that the cool air will bring __(2)__ vegetables ready for picking. __(3)__ must gather all the crops before the winter snows. __(4)__ miss summer's hot, dry days. I am sorry to say good-bye to __(5)__ , but autumn must come. __(6)__ puts a chill in the air. Mother says the autumn winds make __(7)__ feel good. __(8)__ just make me want to play football.

TIP Choose the answer you think is correct. Then read the sentence with your answer in place to make sure it is correct.

1 A You A
  B Them
  C Her
  D Me

2 F he
  G I
  H him H
  J she

3 A Her
  B He B
  C Me
  D Them

4 F Them
  G Him
  H I H
  J Her

5 A them A
  B she
  C I
  D he

6 F It F
  G Her
  H Them
  J Me

7 A she
  B they
  C I
  D her D

8 F Me
  G They G
  H Them
  J Him

For additional test preparation, visit *The Learning Site:* www.harcourtschool.com

---

Assessment

PORTFOLIO ASSESSMENT Have students select their best work from the Writing Connections on pages 247, 249, and 251.

ONGOING ASSESSMENT Evaluate the performance of 4–6 students using appropriate checklists and record forms from pages R74–R77.

INTERNET Activities and exercises to help students prepare for state and standardized assessments appear on *The Learning Site:* **www.harcourtschool.com**

Exploring Websites

Before Going Online

• Think of a question you have about a topic.

• Choose words in your question that are important. These words will become the key words for your search.

While Online

1. Use a search engine.
2. In the search box, type your key words. You can use the words *and* or *or* between key words. Press **Enter**.
3. Look at the names of the Websites that are listed. Click on the site that seems to describe the information you want.
4. Read what is at the Website.
5. Compare the information you found on the Web with information from another source, such as an encyclopedia, to make sure it is correct.
6. Print any information that interests you or that may be useful. Then write the Web address that is in the address box. You may want to return to this Website again.

YOUR TURN

You can use the Internet to find information about weather. First, think of a question to ask about weather. Then, follow the directions above to start your Web search. When you are finished, trade Website addresses with your classmates. When you have time, visit the sites they found.

253

TECHNOLOGY

TECHNOLOGY

Exploring Websites

TEACH/MODEL

Show students how to narrow an Internet search. Explain that entering the word *weather* in the search box may produce thousands of results. Students should be specific—for example, entering words that describe particular types of weather or weather events. The results will be more focused, and students will have an easier time finding the answers they need. Remind students to take notes on the information they find in their Web searches.

WRITING APPLICATION Have students write a review of a website they selected. Students should tell what the website was about, what they liked or disliked about it, and whether they would recommend it to a friend.

WRAP-UP/ASSESS

SUMMARIZE Ask students to name the steps they would take to conduct an Internet search.

PRACTICE page 70

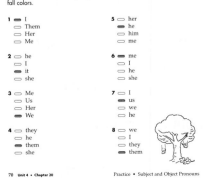

Name _____

Chapter Review

Read the passage, and choose the word that belongs in each space. Fill in the oval next to your choice.

My family and **(1)** ____ moved into a new home in April. There were pink and white blossoms on the apple trees. The maple tree had no leaves on **(2)** ____ at all. Summer was nice and hot. **(3)** ____ sat under the shady trees. The apples got ripe, and we picked **(4)** ____. Dad made applesauce. Then **(5)** ____ made an apple tart for my sister and **(6)** ____. Now it is fall. The leaves are falling every day. They fall on the lawn, and they fall on **(7)** ____. Every day we rake **(8)** ____ into a pile. I love the fall colors.

1 ⬭ I
⬭ Them
⬭ Her
⬭ Me

2 ⬭ he
⬭ I
⬭ it
⬭ she

3 ⬭ Me
⬭ Us
⬭ Her
⬛ We

4 ⬭ they
⬭ he
⬭ them
⬭ she

5 ⬭ her
⬭ he
⬭ him
⬭ me

6 ⬛ me
⬭ I
⬭ he
⬭ she

7 ⬭ I
⬭ us
⬭ we
⬭ he

8 ⬭ we
⬭ I
⬭ they
⬛ them

70 Unit 4 • Chapter 20   Practice • Subject and Object Pronouns

---

CHALLENGE

RATING WEBSITES Have students work in groups to find websites about a particular topic of interest. Have students make a list of standards by which to rate the websites, such as the following:

• useful information

• easy to understand

• pictures or drawings

Students can compile their website ratings into booklets that can be kept for other students' reference.

TECHNOLOGY Additional writing activities are provided on the *Writing Express* CD-ROM

LESSON ORGANIZER	DAY 1	DAY 2
DAILY LANGUAGE PRACTICE TRANSPARENCIES 47, 48	1. Me and my friend walked through the forest (My friend and I; forest.) 2. Us thought the trees were beautiful. (We)	1. Does the trees drop their leaves every fall! (Do; fall?) 2. I went to the forest Yesterday and seen the storm's damage. (yesterday; saw)
ORAL WARM-UP Listening/Speaking	Compare a Flower and a Tree 254	Discuss Sentence Variety 256
TEACH/MODEL WRITING 	✔ **EFFECTIVE SENTENCES** **Literature Model:** from *A Log's Life* 254 **Analyze the Model** 254 **Analyze Informative Writing** 255	**GUIDED WRITING** **Identifying Sentence Variety** 256 **Combining Sentences** 257 Writing and Thinking: Write to Record Reflections 257
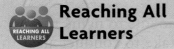 **Reaching All Learners**	**ESL:** Combine Sentences 255 *ESL Manual* pp. 104, 105	**CHALLENGE:** Similes 257 *ESL Manual* p. 104
GRAMMAR	**HANDS-ON ACTIVITIES** 231I–231J	**HANDS-ON ACTIVITIES** 231I–231J
CROSS-CURRICULAR/ ENRICHMENT	**Science:** Life on a Log 255 *Vocabulary Power* Analogies 254	**Listening and Speaking:** Comparative Talk 257 *Vocabulary Power* Synonyms 254 *Vocabulary Power* p. 61 **Vocabulary activity**

KEY
 ✔ = tested skill

 blustery, breezy, doldrums, gusty, tranquil
 See *Vocabulary Power* book.

DAY 3

1. Will the blue jays and finchs have to find new homes. (finches; homes?)
2. the storm caused they problems. (The; them)

Describe Two Similar Animals 258

GUIDED WRITING
Paragraph That Compares 258
Analyze the Model 259
Prewriting and Drafting 259

ESL: Sharing Culture 259
ESL Manual p. 104

HANDS-ON ACTIVITIES
231I–231J

Listening and Speaking:
Compound Sentences 258
Evaluation Criteria: 259

Vocabulary Power

Explore Word Meanings 254
Vocabulary Power p. 62

💻 **Vocabulary activity**

DAY 4

1. I hopes that the birds find new homes soon (hope; soon.)
2. Them will building new nests in other trees. (They; build)

Writing Effective Sentences 260

GUIDED WRITING
Editing 260
Sharing and Reflecting 260

💻 **Proofreading practice**

ESL Manual p. 104

HANDS-ON ACTIVITIES
231I–231J

Vocabulary Power

Suffixes 254
Vocabulary Power p. 63

💻 **Vocabulary activity**

DAY 5

1. Some other childs and me saw a nest of baby birds. (children; I)
2. The birds parents were gone (birds'; gone.)

Discuss Speech-Making Preparations 261

LISTENING AND SPEAKING:
Comparing Writing and Speaking 261

ESL Manual p. 104

HANDS-ON ACTIVITIES
231I–231J

Vocabulary Power

Compare and Contrast 254
Evaluation Criteria: Self-Evaluation 261

Informative Writing

Writer's Craft: Effective Sentences

OBJECTIVES

• To understand informative writing and to analyze an informative passage

• To understand and analyze the use of effective sentences in informative writing

SPIRAL REVIEW

DAILY LANGUAGE PRACTICE

TRANSPARENCY 47

① Me and my friend walked through the forest (My friend and I; forest.)

② Us thought the trees were beautiful. (We)

ORAL WARM-UP

USE PRIOR KNOWLEDGE Ask students to explain how a flower and a tree are the same. Then have them read the introduction and the model.

Analyze THE Model

1. How are the effects of lightning and wind alike? (Possible response: Both can knock down a tree.)
   INFERENTIAL: MAKE COMPARISONS

2. Why do you think the writer uses some long sentences and some short ones? (Possible response: to make the verses more interesting.)
   INFERENTIAL: AUTHOR'S CRAFT

3. Can you find a compound sentence in the first verse? How do you know it is compound? (Possible response: *Squirrels feel the trembling, and they scramble out of their hole* is a compound sentence. It is two simple sentences joined by a comma and the word *and*.) **METACOGNITIVE: TEXT STRUCTURE**

Effective Sentences

You know that you give information when you explain something or give directions. You might also compare things, or tell how they are alike.

Read these verses from the book *A Log's Life*.

LITERATURE MODEL

A thunderous crack startles the porcupine
   sleeping nearby.
The tall oak begins to topple.
   Squirrels feel the trembling,
      and they scramble out of their hole.

One strong gust of blustery wind
   tears the great oak's roots from the ground.
   The tree crashes down, shaking the forest
      floor.
   Branches break. Limbs splinter. Leaves
      scatter.

—from *A Log's Life*
by Wendy Pfeffer

Analyze THE Model

1. How are the effects of lightning and wind alike?

2. Why do you think the writer uses some long sentences and some short ones?

3. Can you find a compound sentence in the first verse? How do you know it is compound?

Vocabulary Power

blus•ter•y
[blus′tər•y] *adj.*
Noisy; forceful.

Using Effective Sentences

When you use effective sentences, you give information in a clear and interesting way. Study the chart on the next page.

254

Vocabulary Power

DAY ① ANALOGIES **What word would finish this sentence?** *Blustery* **is to wind as** *blizzard* **is to _____.**

DAY ② SYNONYMS **Synonyms are words that mean almost the same. Which of these words are synonyms:** *blustery, blurry, windy?* (See also *Vocabulary Power*, page 61.)

DAY ③ EXPLORE WORD MEANINGS **A person can be blustery, too. How do you think a blustery person acts?** (See also *Vocabulary Power*, page 62.)

DAY ④ SUFFIXES Write on the board: *blustery, blusterer.* **Which one means "a person who blusters"?** (See also *Vocabulary Power*, page 63.)

DAY ⑤ COMPARE AND CONTRAST Have students make a list of things they would do and wear on blustery days. Then have them make a similar list for sunny days. Discuss responses.

Strategies for Writing Effective Sentences

How to Use the Strategies

Write a variety of sentences.

- Don't make all your sentences alike. Use long sentences and short sentences. Use different kinds of sentences — statements, questions, exclamations.

Combine sentences.

- Look for places where you can use compound subjects and compound predicates. Combine simple sentences to write compound sentences.

YOUR TURN

ANALYZE INFORMATIVE WRITING Work with one or two classmates. Read several paragraphs from your science textbook or from a magazine article on a science topic. Look at the kinds of sentences the writer uses. Talk with your group about which sentences are most effective.

Answer these questions:

1. What is the writer's subject?
2. What is the writer's purpose?
3. What different kinds of sentences does the writer use?
4. Can you find sentences in which the writer compares things or tells how different things are alike?

Science

LIFE ON A LOG Have students use science or nature books to research what happens to a tree in a forest after the tree falls in a storm. Students should tell how plants and animals use the tree as it rots on the forest floor. Encourage students to use comparisons and a variety of sentences in their writing. Students also may find or draw pictures to illustrate what they learned.

ESL

COMBINE SENTENCES On sentence strips, write the following:

Birds live in the maple tree.

Squirrels live in the maple tree.

Moss grows on the oak tree.

Moss grows on the maple tree.

I can climb the maple tree.

I cannot climb the oak tree.

On smaller strips, write *and, and, and but.* Have students combine the sentences by cutting and taping the sentence strips.

GUIDED WRITING

USING EFFECTIVE SENTENCES Tell students that comparing things is one way to give more information about them. Point out that in informative writing, a variety of sentences is more interesting to read. It is also more fun to write different kinds of sentences.

Discuss the chart with students. Review the four sentence types: statement, command, exclamation, and question. Ask volunteers to write on the board a variety of sentences about a simple, familiar subject such as a classroom pet or the school mascot. They should write long sentences, short sentences, statements, questions, and exclamations.

Then have volunteers combine some of the sentences on the board, making compound subjects and predicates or compound sentences.

Discuss with students whether they would enjoy reading a paragraph or a report in which all the sentences were the same. Discuss why writing only in simple, short sentences is not the best way to present information.

Then have students complete the Your Turn activity in pairs or small groups. They may choose to analyze parts of a book or magazine they have already read, or they may choose to analyze a new passage.

WRAP-UP/ASSESS

SUMMARIZE **What are some different types of sentences you can use in your writing?**

TECHNOLOGY Additional writing activities are provided on the *Writing Express* CD-ROM

Writer's Craft: Effective Sentences

OBJECTIVES
- To identify and use sentence variety in informative writing
- To record reflections about sentence variety

SPIRAL REVIEW

DAILY LANGUAGE PRACTICE

TRANSPARENCY 47

1 Does the trees drop their leaves every fall! (Do; fall?)

2 I went to the forest Yesterday and seen the storm's damage. (yesterday; saw)

ORAL WARM-UP

USE PRIOR KNOWLEDGE Ask students why using a variety of sentences makes writing more interesting. Ask: **What are some ways to include sentence variety in your writing?**

GUIDED WRITING

Identifying Sentence Variety

Tell students that using sentences with different end punctuation is one way to add variety to writing. Remind them not to overuse one type of ending. Ask: **What would you think of a paragraph that was just questions?**

Work through Parts A and B with students. (Part A: 1. same, 2. different, 3. different, 4. same, 5. same; Part B: The second paragraph has more effective sentences. Responses may vary but should demonstrate an understanding of sentence variety.)

Identifying Sentence Variety

A. Read each pair of sentences. If both sentences are the same kind, write *Same* on your paper. If the sentences are a different kind, write *Different* on your paper.

1. What a big oak tree!
   It is so tall!
2. What kind of tree is this?
   It has needles instead of leaves.
3. Look at this leaf.
   On which tree did it grow?
4. I saw a chestnut, but I did not see a walnut.
   There are twigs and branches lying on the ground.
5. The trunk is thick.
   Its bark is peeling because many forest animals have used it to sharpen their claws.

B. Read the two passages. One passage has a variety of sentences. The other passage does not. On your paper, tell which passage you think has more effective sentences. Then tell why you think so.

1. Some dinosaurs ate meat. Some dinosaurs ate plants. Some dinosaurs ate both meat and plants. Some dinosaurs probably ate the eggs of other dinosaurs.
2. How big were dinosaurs? You probably know that some dinosaurs were very large. Other types of dinosaurs were small. Some of them may have been smaller than you are!

256

Vocabulary Power page 61

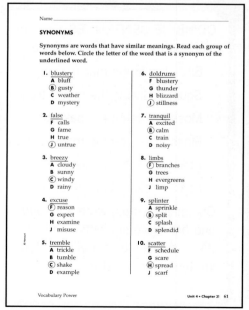

Name _____

SYNONYMS

Synonyms are words that have similar meanings. Read each group of words below. Circle the letter of the word that is a synonym of the underlined word.

1. blustery
   A bluff
   B gusty
   C weather
   D mystery

2. false
   F calls
   G fame
   H true
   J untrue

3. breezy
   A cloudy
   B sunny
   C windy
   D rainy

4. excuse
   F reason
   G expect
   H examine
   J misuse

5. tremble
   A trickle
   B tumble
   C shake
   D example

6. doldrums
   F blustery
   G thunder
   H blizzard
   J stillness

7. tranquil
   A excited
   B calm
   C train
   D noisy

8. limbs
   F branches
   G trees
   H evergreens
   J limp

9. splinter
   A sprinkle
   B split
   C splash
   D splendid

10. scatter
    F schedule
    G scare
    H spread
    J scarf

Vocabulary Power   Unit 4 • Chapter 21   61

Combining Sentences

C. **Read each pair of sentences. Combine the two sentences into one sentence. Write the new sentence on your paper.**

1. Birds make nests. Birds lay eggs.
2. Lightning flashed. Thunder boomed.
3. Fish live in this pond. Turtles live in this pond.
4. Frogs hop. Snakes slither on the ground.
5. Daffodils bloom in spring. Tulips bloom in spring.

D. **Read the paragraph. Then revise it, using a variety of sentences without changing the meaning of the paragraph. Write a final draft of the paragraph.** Responses will vary.

Winter is fun. Lakes are frozen. We ice skate. Our noses get cold. Spring is nice. It is warm. Gardens grow. We plant flowers. Summer is hot. The sun shines brightly. We swim in the lake.

Writing AND Thinking

Write to Record Reflections Reread some pages in your Writer's Journal. Think about the sentences you used. Are they mostly short, or are there longer sentences, too? How else are the sentences alike or different? Now write a paragraph in your Writer's Journal. Tell how you might write more effective sentences in the future.

257

Listening and Speaking

COMPARATIVE TALK Have partners compare pairs of classroom objects. One student names two objects. The other student must then tell ways the objects are alike. When students have finished comparing the objects, they should name two new objects for their partner to compare. Remind students to speak in complete sentences and to use correct subject-verb agreement.

CHALLENGE

SIMILES Tell students that a comparison that uses the words *like* or *as* is called a *simile*. Similes often help make descriptions more vivid. On the board, write examples of similes, such as the following:

The thunder was like a deafening drumroll.

The huge tree snapped like a twig in the storm.

Have students work in pairs to choose a subject and write three similes to describe it.

Combining Sentences

Before students begin Part C, model combining sentences. Write on the board:

Janice walked in the woods. I walked in the woods.

I picked up some leaves. Janice found pictures of them in her book.

MODEL **In the first pair of sentences, both subjects are doing the same thing. I can combine the sentences to make one sentence with a compound subject:** *Janice and I walked in the woods.* **In the second pair of sentences, different subjects are doing different but related things. I can combine the sentences to make a compound sentence:** *I picked up some leaves, and Janice found pictures of them in her book.*

Have students complete Part C in pairs. Then have them complete Part D individually.

Writing and Thinking

Write to Record Reflections Give students several minutes to review their Writer's Journals. Then have them set sentence variety goals for their writing. Encourage students to consult these goals the next time they revise a draft of their writing.

WRAP-UP/ASSESS

SUMMARIZE How does using compound sentences make your writing more interesting?

Writer's Craft: Effective Sentences

OBJECTIVES
- To recognize and analyze the parts of a paragraph that compares
- To choose a topic, generate ideas, and write a paragraph that compares

DAILY LANGUAGE PRACTICE

TRANSPARENCY 47

1 Will the blue jays and finchs have to find new homes. (finches; homes?)

2 the storm caused they problems. (The; them)

ORAL WARM-UP

USE PRIOR KNOWLEDGE Ask students to name and describe two animals that they think are similar in some way.

GUIDED WRITING

Paragraph That Compares

READ AND RESPOND TO THE MODEL Tell students you will read aloud Jake's paragraph about horses and cows, and have students determine a purpose for listening. (Possible responses: to gain information about how horses and cows are alike; to recognize sentence variety) Discuss how the variety of sentences that Jake uses helps make his writing interesting.

FOCUS ON ORGANIZATION Have students read the paragraph silently. Ask them to determine the function of the first sentence, the middle sentences, and the last sentence. Have students share their responses.

FOCUS ON WRITER'S CRAFT Discuss the variety of sentences in Jake's paragraph. Ask students why Jake includes the question. Ask students to think about how they might include questions in their own paragraphs.

Paragraph That Compares

You can compare the lightning and the wind in *A Log's Life* by telling how they are alike. They both shake the tree and make it fall down. They both are powerful forces of nature.

Jake wrote a paragraph to share with his classmates. He wanted to compare horses and cows. Read the paragraph that Jake wrote. Look at the different kinds of sentences he used.

MODEL

> **simple sentences**
>
> **compound sentence**
>
> **question**
>
> *Horses and cows are a lot alike. They are both raised on either farms or ranches. Both are quite large. Also, they both like to eat grass. Horses and cows are important to humans, too. We get milk from cows, and we can ride horses. Can you think of other ways they are alike?*

Analyze THE Model

1. What is Jake's purpose for writing this paragraph?

2. What comparisons does Jake make in the paragraph?

3. Has Jake written effective sentences? Explain your answer.

258

Vocabulary Power   page 62

Name _____

EXPLORE WORD MEANING

▶ **Read and respond to each question.** Responses will vary. Accept reasonable responses.

1. A blustery day is loud and windy. How might a blustery person act? _____

2. *Tranquil* means "calm and peaceful." What are some things that are tranquil? _____

3. How does someone who is "in the doldrums" feel?
_____

4. A sunny day is bright and warm. How do you feel when you're in a sunny mood? _____
_____

▶ **Illustrate the following kinds of people.** Drawings will vary.

a blustery person	a tranquil person

62   Unit 4 • Chapter 21   Vocabulary Power

Listening and Speaking

COMPOUND SENTENCES Have students work in groups of three to form compound sentences. One student begins by saying a simple sentence. The next student says another simple sentence on a related subject. Then the third student forms a compound sentence, using the first two sentences. Allow each student to have a turn at combining sentences.

WRITING PROMPT Think of two different things in nature that you can compare because they are alike in some ways. For example, you might compare a frog and a toad, or a butterfly and a bird. Write a paragraph for your teacher that compares the two things. Tell how they are alike. Use effective sentences to make your paragraph interesting to read.

STUDY THE PROMPT Ask yourself these questions.

1. Who is your audience?
2. What is your purpose for writing?
3. What two things will you compare?
4. What writing form will you use?

Prewriting and Drafting

Plan Your Paragraph Choose two things that you want to compare. Create a chart like this one to help you decide which common traits you will include in your paragraph.

Traits	First Subject	Second Subject
Choose traits that will be common to both subjects, such as color, feel, age, or size.	Write a describing word for each trait.	Write a describing word for each trait.

Which traits have describing words that are alike? Describe those traits in your paragraph.

259

USING YOUR Handbook

Use the Writer's Thesaurus to find words that will help you explain how the subjects are alike.

Analyze THE *Model*

1. **What is Jake's purpose for writing this paragraph?** (Possible responses: Jake's purpose is to inform the reader about how cows and horses are the same.) **INFERENTIAL: DETERMINE AUTHOR'S PURPOSE**

2. **What comparisons does Jake make in the paragraph?** (Horses and cows are raised on farms or ranches, they are large, they graze on grass, and they are important to people.) **LITERAL: NOTE DETAILS**

3. **Has Jake written effective sentences? Explain your answer.** (Possible response: Yes; the sentences are effective because they give information in a clear way and they are varied.) **CRITICAL: MAKE JUDGMENTS**

To prepare for the Your Turn activity, have students brainstorm pairs of things in nature that are alike in some way. List their suggestions on the board.

Prewriting and Drafting

Choose a pair of subjects from the list on the board. Have students tell what they know about each subject. Then model using a chart to organize comparisons.

WRAP-UP/ASSESS

SUMMARIZE In their journals, have students reflect on how using a chart helped them organize their comparisons. **REFLECTION**

REACHING ALL LEARNERS — ESL

Evaluation Criteria

Review the criteria that students should apply:

- use sentence variety
- combine sentences
- use correct paragraph of comparison form

Work with students to add other criteria.

SHARING CULTURE Allow students to select plants or animals that are native to the country of their first language as the subjects of their paragraphs that compare. Have students work with an English-fluent partner to create their charts.

Writer's Craft: Effective Sentences

OBJECTIVES

- To revise and proofread a paragraph that compares
- To share and reflect upon a paragraph that compares

1 I hopes that the birds find new homes soon (hope; soon.)

2 Them will building new nests in other trees. (They; build)

ORAL WARM-UP

USE PRIOR KNOWLEDGE Ask students to share strategies for writing effective sentences.

GUIDED WRITING

Editing

Work through the revising checklist with students. Ask students to add a question to their paragraph.

As students proofread, remind them to check the spelling of words with regular spelling patterns, such as consonant-vowel-consonant *(hop)*, and consonant-vowel-consonant-silent *e (hope)*.

Sharing and Reflecting

Have pairs of students read each other's paragraphs and tell what information they learned from them. Encourage students to offer helpful suggestions about ways in which comparisons and sentence variety might be improved.

WRAP-UP/ASSESS

SUMMARIZE Why is it important to include descriptive details in a paragraph that compares?

CHAPTER 21

Informative Writing

Editing

Reread the draft of your paragraph that compares. Use this checklist to help you revise it.

Editor's Marks

- ✄ take out text
- ∧ add text
- ꝋ move text
- ¶ new paragraph
- ≡ capitalize
- / lowercase
- ◯ correct spelling

☑ Do you give your reader enough information about the things you are comparing?

☑ Will your reader understand how the two things are alike?

☑ Are your sentences all the same, or have you used different types?

☑ Can you combine sentences to make them more effective?

Use this checklist as you proofread your paragraph.

☑ I have begun my sentences with capital letters.

☑ I have used the correct end marks for each type of sentence.

☑ I have used singular and plural pronouns correctly.

☑ I have used a dictionary to check my spelling.

Sharing and Reflecting

Writer's Journal

Make a final copy of your paragraph that compares. Then share it with a partner. Tell what you like best about your partner's paragraph. Talk about writing effective sentences. Write your reflections in your Writer's Journal.

Vocabulary Power page 63

Name _____

SUFFIXES

Below are some suffixes and their meanings.

Suffix	Meaning	Suffix	Meaning
-less	without	-y	like
-ness	state or condition	-ly	like
-ful	filled with	-en	make to be

Read each sentence. Choose the correct suffix to add to the underlined word in parentheses. The words in parentheses are clues to help you decide which suffix should be used. Write the new word on the line. The first one is done for you.

1. He is a kind and ___thoughtful___ person. (filled with **thought**)
2. Today, the wind is ___blustery___. (**gust** like)
3. Yesterday, it was ___breezy___. (**breeze** like)
4. Some sunshine would ___brighten___ up this day. (make to be **bright**)
5. Outside, it was cold and ___blustery___. (**bluster** like)
6. Would you ___kindly___ pass the salt? (**kind** like)
7. Her heart is full of ___kindness___. (condition of being **kind**)
8. I was ___thoughtless___ to forget your birthday. (without **thought**)
9. The sky began to ___darken___. (make to be **dark**)
10. There was ___darkness___ all around us. (state of being **dark**)

Vocabulary Power   Unit 4 • Chapter 21   63

Comparing Writing and Speaking

Have you ever made a speech? In some ways, making a speech is like writing. Look at the diagram to see how they are alike.

You plan what you will write or say.

You evaluate and revise before writing your final draft or giving your speech.

How Writing and Making a Speech Are Alike

You think about your purpose and your audience.

You should use effective sentences.

YOUR TURN

Work with a group of three classmates to practice making speeches. Follow these steps:

STEP 1 With your group, brainstorm a list of subjects for short speeches.

STEP 2 Choose a subject from the list. Plan a short speech to give information on that subject.

STEP 3 Practice your speeches. Help each other revise the speeches to use more effective sentences.

STEP 4 Give your speech to the group.

STEP 5 Listen to your classmates' speeches. Evaluate the speeches as well as the information.

Strategies for Listening and Speaking

- When you speak to inform, use a rate and volume that fits your audience and purpose.
- Describe ideas clearly.
- When you listen, think about and evaluate what the speaker is saying.
- When you speak to share ideas about classmates' speeches, be courteous and make comments that will be helpful.

261

LISTENING AND SPEAKING

Comparing Writing and Speaking

OBJECTIVES
- To compare written and oral presentations
- To plan and give a speech

DAILY LANGUAGE PRACTICE

TRANSPARENCY 48

❶ Some other childs and me saw a nest of baby birds. (children; I)

❷ The birds parents were gone (birds'; gone.)

ORAL WARM-UP

USE PRIOR KNOWLEDGE Ask students to suggest ways to prepare to give a speech.

TEACH/MODEL

Discuss the diagram with students. Tell them to use their tone of voice and non-verbal communication such as body language to make their presentations more effective.

Remind students that when giving a speech, they should speak in complete sentences and use the correct tense and subject-verb agreement. Encourage students to use props such as objects, charts, and pictures to help them clarify and support what they say in their speeches.

As a class, make a poster of *Tips for Making a Speech* after students have completed the Your Turn activity.

WRAP-UP/ASSESS

Writer's Journal

SUMMARIZE In their journals, have students reflect on how giving a speech is similar to writing a paragraph. **REFLECTION**

Evaluation Criteria
. . . .

SELF-EVALUATION Revisit the **Evaluation Criteria** to have students informally rate their own writing on a scale of 1 to 4. You might have them use stick-on notes to label their papers.

CHAPTER 22

More About Pronouns

pages 262–271

LESSON ORGANIZER	DAY 1	DAY 2
DAILY LANGUAGE PRACTICE TRANSPARENCIES 49, 50	1. I seed some squirrels in the yard on friday. (saw; Friday.) 2. The squirrels was hungry we fed them. (Possible response: were; hungry. We) **Bridge to Writing** A large squirrel (action verb) the corn we put out for it.	1. the squirrels quickly ate two dishs of corn (The; dishes; corn.) 2. Should i buy a bag of dried corn on the cob. (I; cob?) **Bridge to Writing** The squirrel took the corn to (possessive pronoun) nest.
ORAL WARM-UP **Listening/Speaking**	Replace Noun with Pronoun 262	Complete the Sentence 264 *Grammar Jingles*™ CD Track 15
TEACH/MODEL **GRAMMAR** **KEY** ✔ = tested skill	✔ **POSSESSIVE PRONOUNS** 262–263 • To recognize and use possessive pronouns • To write sentences using possessive pronouns	✔ **MORE POSSESSIVE PRONOUNS** 264–265 • To recognize and use the correct forms of possessive pronouns • To write a paragraph that classifies, using possessive pronouns
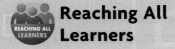 **Reaching All Learners**	**Modified Instruction** Below-Level: Consult a List Above-Level: Write Antecedent and Possessive Pronoun **Challenge:** Activity Card 15, R69 *ESL Manual* pp. 106, 107 **Reteach:** *Reteach Activities Copying Masters* p. 43 and R52 *Practice Book* p. 71	**Modified Instruction** Below-Level: Model the Thinking Above-Level: Collaborate **ESL:** Pronoun Chart 264 *ESL Manual* pp. 106, 108 **Reteach:** *Reteach Activities Copying Masters* p. 44 and R52 **Challenge:** Animal Book 265 *Practice Book* p. 72
WRITING	Writing Connection 263 Art	Writing Connection 265 Writer's Craft: Clear Pronouns
CROSS-CURRICULAR/ ENRICHMENT	*Vocabulary Power* Explore Word Meaning 262 archaeology, biology, **ecology**, herpetology, technology See *Vocabulary Power* book.	*Vocabulary Power* Classify/Categorize 262 *Vocabulary Power* p. 64 🏆 **Vocabulary activity**

261A **UNIT 4**

DAY 3

1. All the squirrel's watched my put out the corn. (squirrels; me)

2. Them rann over quickly. (They; ran)

Bridge to Writing The corn is (possessive pronoun) now!

Identify the Pronouns 266
 Grammar Jingles™ CD Track 15

✔ **CONTRACTIONS WITH PRO-NOUNS** 266–267
  • To correctly identify and form contractions with pronouns
  • To write a descriptive paragraph using contractions

Modified Instruction
Below-Level: Refer to Chart
Above-Level: Write Sentences
ESL: Mix and Match 266
ESL Manual pp. 106, 109
Reteach: *Reteach Activities Copying Masters* pp. 45 and R52
Challenge: Contraction Guessing Game 267
Practice Book p. 73

Writing Connection 267
Science

Vocabulary Power

Dictionary 262
Vocabulary Power p. 65
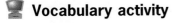 **Vocabulary activity**

DAY 4

1. Two raccoones was by the corn a few days later. (raccoons; were)

2. Did They think they're found a trea-sure (they; they'd; treasure?)

Bridge to Writing (Contraction) seen animals in the woods.

Revise a Sentence 268

EXTRA PRACTICE 268–269
  • To use possessive pronouns correctly in sentences
  • To form pronoun contractions correctly
  • To write a poem, using posses-sive pronouns and contractions
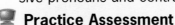 **Practice Assessment**

Building Oral Grammar
Read Aloud in Pairs 269
Challenge: Writing Clearly 269
ESL Manual pp. 106, 110
Practice Book p. 74

Writing Connection 269
Technology

Vocabulary Power

Word Parts 262
Vocabulary Power p. 66
Hands-On: Contraction Scramble 268
 Vocabulary activity

DAY 5

1. Mine friends is eager to feed the ani-mals, too. (My; are)

2. Kim and susan made birdfeeders (Susan; birdfeeders.)

Bridge to Writing (possessive pronoun) birdfeeder is beautiful! (Contraction) very proud of it.

TEST PREP **CHAPTER REVIEW** 270
  • To review possessive pronouns and contractions with pronouns
  • To use context clues to deter-mine the meanings of unfamiliar words
 Test preparation

Challenge: Dictionary Dare 271
Practice Book p. 75
ESL Manual pp. 106, 111

Writing Application 271
Using New Vocabulary

Vocabulary: Using Context Clues 271

Vocabulary Power

Usage 262

Possessive Pronouns

OBJECTIVES
- To recognize and use possessive pronouns
- To draw a picture and to write sentences using possessive pronouns

DAILY LANGUAGE PRACTICE

TRANSPARENCY 49

1 I seed some squirrels in the yard on friday. (saw; Friday)

2 The squirrels was hungry we fed them. (Possible response: were; hungry. We)

BRIDGE TO WRITING A large squirrel ___(action verb)___ the corn we put out for it.

ORAL WARM-UP

USE PRIOR KNOWLEDGE Write this sentence on the board: *The squirrel's nest is in a tree.* Ask students to suggest a word to replace *The squirrel's.*

TEACH/MODEL

Read aloud the explanation and examples of possessive pronouns. Remind students that possessive pronouns, like the other pronouns they have studied, must always agree with the nouns that they replace in both number and gender. Point out that possessive pronouns never include an apostrophe.

Work through the Guided Practice items orally with students.

Vocabulary Power

e•col•o•gy
(i•kol′ə•jē) *n.*
The relationship of plants and animals to each other and their surroundings.

Possessive Pronouns

A possessive pronoun shows ownership.

You know that a pronoun takes the place of a noun. A possessive pronoun takes the place of a possessive noun. Some possessive pronouns are *my, your, his, her, its, our,* and *their.*

The noun or pronoun that a possessive pronoun refers to is called its antecedent. The antecedents are circled in the sentences below.

Examples:

(Deer) make **their** home in the forest.

(I) clicked **my** camera and scared a deer.

A (deer) stopped eating and raised **its** head.

Guided Practice

A. Read each sentence. Name the possessive pronoun and its antecedent.

Example: I saw a deer in my backyard.

my|I Possessive pronouns are underlined twice; antecedents are underlined once.

1. If you see a male <u>deer</u>, you will probably notice <u>his</u> antlers.

2. <u>I</u> read in <u>my</u> book that antlers are horns.

3. A male <u>deer</u> uses <u>his</u> antlers for fighting.

4. A female <u>deer</u> is a doe, and <u>her</u> baby is a fawn.

5. The <u>fawns</u> I saw have white fur on <u>their</u> tails.

Vocabulary Power

DAY 1 EXPLORE WORD MEANING Introduce and define *ecology*. Write it on the board. **Are you part of the ecology of our community? In what way?**

DAY 2 CLASSIFY/CATEGORIZE **What are some things you would learn about if you studied ecology?** (See also *Vocabulary Power*, page 64.)

DAY 3 DICTIONARY **What could you learn about the word *ecology* from a dictionary?** Write suggestions on the board. Then ask students to check a dictionary and make additional suggestions. (See also *Vocabulary Power*, page 65.)

DAY 4 WORD PARTS *Eco-* means "our surroundings." *-Logy* means "the study of." Put them together and you get _____. (See also *Vocabulary Power*, page 66.)

DAY 5 USAGE Discuss: **Why is ecology important?**

Independent Practice

B. Write the possessive pronoun in each sentence.

Example: I read in my book about the ecology of the forest.

my

6. I hike in the forest during <u>my</u> vacation.
7. I see forest animals in <u>their</u> natural habitats.
8. A squirrel uses <u>its</u> sharp teeth to break a nutshell.
9. Squirrels use <u>their</u> claws to hold on to tree branches.
10. A mother squirrel makes a nest for <u>her</u> young.
11. <u>Our</u> footsteps scare the squirrel away.
12. She will probably run to one of <u>her</u> other nests.
13. For <u>their</u> safety, squirrels usually have more than one nest.
14. Jon wants a squirrel for <u>his</u> pet.
15. Keeping a squirrel as <u>your</u> pet is not a good idea.

Remember
that a possessive pronoun shows ownership and takes the place of a possessive noun.

Writing Connection

Art What kinds of animals do you see where you live? Draw a picture of these animals and their surroundings. Write several sentences about your picture that tell what the animals are doing. Use possessive pronouns in your sentences.

263

Independent Practice

Have students complete the Independent Practice, or modify it using these suggestions:

MODIFIED INSTRUCTION

BELOW-LEVEL STUDENTS Write the following possessive pronouns on the board: *my, your, his, her, its, our,* and *their.* Have students consult this list as they complete the exercises.

ABOVE-LEVEL STUDENTS For each item, have students write the antecedent as well as the possessive pronoun.

Writing Connection

Art Suggest to students that their drawings show the animals with objects, as this will make it easier to use a possessive pronoun. For example, they could write, *The squirrels ate their food,* and *A mother bird is caring for her babies,* and so on.

WRAP-UP/ASSESS

SUMMARIZE Ask students to tell what a possessive pronoun is and to explain how they know which possessive pronoun to use in a sentence.

RETEACH

INTERVENTION Lessons in **visual, auditory,** and **kinesthetic** modalities: p. R52 and *Reteach Activities Copying Masters,* p. 43.

PRACTICE page 71

Name _____

Possessive Pronouns

A. Underline the possessive pronoun once. Underline its antecedent twice.

1. Salmon are born in freshwater, and freshwater is <u>their</u> first home.
2. The female <u>salmon</u> lays <u>her</u> eggs in the stream.
3. After the babies are born, they make <u>their</u> way to the ocean.
4. That <u>salmon</u> will now make <u>its</u> home in the sea.
5. We saw one <u>salmon</u> throw <u>his</u> body up on the riverbank.

B. Read each sentence. Underline the possessive pronoun.

6. We counted fourteen salmon on <u>our</u> hike along the river.
7. Marty took a picture with <u>her</u> camera.
8. How can that salmon find <u>her</u> way home?
9. This river was <u>their</u> home for centuries.
10. Timothy said <u>his</u> uncle is a fisherman.
11. He and <u>his</u> friends have fished this river for years.
12. Fishing is <u>their</u> true favorite pastime.
13. I wanted to go with them to buy <u>my</u> fishing license.
14. <u>Our</u> teacher wants to take the entire class salmon fishing.
15. What would be <u>your</u> idea of an adventure?

> **TRY THIS!** In a book or magazine find a picture of a trout or salmon. Draw your own picture of the fish. Then write three sentences that describe the picture. Use possessive pronouns in each sentence.

Practice • More About Pronouns   Unit 4 • Chapter 22 71

CHALLENGE

INVENTORY Have students use **Challenge Activity Card 15** (page R69) to make an inventory, using possessive pronouns.

Challenge Activity Card 15

Inventory

Think of some of the things in your house, your neighborhood, and your school. Make an inventory, or a list of belongings, by following these steps:

- Make a list of three things that belong to you. Then, list three things that belong to others. Finally, list three things that belong to everyone.
- Choose six items. Write a sentence for each, using possessive pronouns. Remember to check your sentences for clear pronoun antecedents.
- You may wish to illustrate your inventory.

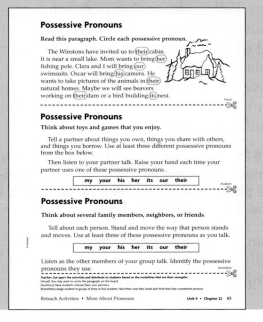

Possessive Pronouns

Read this paragraph. Circle each possessive pronoun.

The Winstons have invited us to (their) cabin. It is near a small lake. Mom wants to bring (her) fishing pole. Clara and I will bring (our) swimsuits. Oscar will bring (his) camera. He wants to take pictures of the animals in (their) natural homes. Maybe we will see beavers working on (their) dam or a bird building (its) nest.

Possessive Pronouns

Think about toys and games that you enjoy.

Tell a partner about things you own, things you share with others, and things you borrow. Use at least three different possessive pronouns from the box below.

Then listen to your partner talk. Raise your hand each time your partner uses one of these possessive pronouns.

| my | your | his | her | its | our | their |

Possessive Pronouns

Think about several family members, neighbors, or friends.

Tell about each person. Stand and move the way that person stands and moves. Use at least three of these possessive pronouns as you talk.

| my | your | his | her | its | our | their |

Listen as the other members of your group talk. Identify the possessive pronouns they use.

Reteach Activities • More About Pronouns   Unit 4 • Chapter 22 43

More Possessive Pronouns

OBJECTIVES
- To recognize and use the correct forms of possessive pronouns
- To make a chart and to write a paragraph that classifies, using possessive pronouns

DAILY LANGUAGE PRACTICE

TRANSPARENCY 49

1 the squirrels quickly ate two dishs of corn (The; dishes; corn.)

2 Should i buy a bag of dried corn on the cob. (I; cob?)

BRIDGE TO WRITING The squirrel took the corn to ___possessive pronoun___ nest.

ORAL WARM-UP

USE PRIOR KNOWLEDGE Write these sentences on the board: *Allie is packing her bags. The bags are* ____ . Ask students to complete the sentence with a word that tells who owns the bags.

Grammar Jingles™ **CD, Intermediate** Use Track 15 for review and reinforcement of pronouns.

TEACH/MODEL

Read aloud the instructions and examples. Tell students that possessive pronouns that stand alone often come at the end of the sentence. Note that they may replace a possessive noun or another possessive pronoun and the thing that is owned. Model the thinking, using the Guided Practice example:

MODEL In the sentence *The blue suitcase is mine*, the word that replaces a possessive pronoun and the thing being owned is *mine. Mine* can stand alone.

Complete the Guided Practice items orally with students, or have students complete the items in small groups.

264

More Possessive Pronouns

Some possessive pronouns can stand alone.

These possessive pronouns take the place of other possessive pronouns and the things being owned. They are *mine, yours, his, hers, ours,* and *theirs.*

Notice how the possessive pronouns *hers* and *his* stand alone in the sentences below. *His* can stand alone or be used with a noun.

Examples:
That coat is <u>her coat</u>. That coat is **hers**.

That book is <u>his book</u>. That book is **his**.

Guided Practice

A. Name the possessive pronoun in each sentence.

Example: The blue suitcase is mine.   *mine*

1. The book about South America is <u>hers</u>.
2. <u>Ours</u> is the guide who knows the most about the ecology of the rain forest.
3. The video camera is <u>his</u>.
4. Those three tickets are <u>ours</u>.
5. The eggs in the macaws' nest are <u>theirs</u>.
6. That toucan thinks the passion fruit is <u>his</u>.
7. The monkeys think the bananas are <u>theirs</u>.
8. That monkey's scream sounds a lot like <u>yours</u>.
9. That parrot looks a lot like <u>ours</u>.
10. I wish that toucan could be <u>mine</u>.

Vocabulary Power page 64

Name _____

CLASSIFY/CATEGORIZE

▶ Write each word from the Word Box under the correct category. Then write your own word for each category. Additional words will vary. Accept reasonable responses.

computers	relationships	habitat
snakes	environment	alligators
reptiles	software	microchips

herpetology	ecology	technology
reptiles	environment	computers
alligators	habitat	microchips
snakes	relationships	software

▶ Now try these.

| ancient cities | mammals | flowers |
| trees | culture | ruins |

biology	archaeology
trees	culture
flowers	ancient cities
mammals	ruins

64   Unit 4 • Chapter 22   Vocabulary Power

ESL

REACHING ALL LEARNERS

PRONOUN CHART Create a chart that students can copy and use to remember pronouns and possessive pronouns:

Subject Pronoun	Possessive Pronoun	Stand-Alone
I	my	mine
he	his	his
she	her	hers
you	your	yours
it	its	its
we	our	ours
they	their	theirs

Independent Practice

B. Read the sentence pairs. Write the possessive pronoun that belongs in each space.

Example: We took pictures of the animals in the rain forest.
Those pictures are _____. *ours*

11. A male orangutan collects some fruit.
The fruit is ____. his

12. A mother orangutan feeds a baby orangutan.
The baby is ____. hers

13. Orangutans find large leaves and use them as umbrellas.
The leaves are ____. theirs

14. I took a photograph of an orangutan that I saw in a tree.
The photograph is ____. mine

15. Maybe you will visit the rain forest someday.
I will compare my photographs with ____. yours

Remember
that some possessive pronouns can stand alone. They are *mine, yours, his, hers, ours,* and *theirs.*

DID YOU KNOW?
At least half of Earth's plants and animals live in tropical rain forests.

265

Writing Connection

Writer's Craft: Clear Pronouns Think of three different animals. Make a chart that tells where the animals live, what they look like, and what they eat. Use the information on your chart to write a paragraph that tells how the animals are alike and how they are different. Use correct possessive pronouns in your paragraph.

Independent Practice

Have students complete the Independent Practice, or modify it using these suggestions:

MODIFIED INSTRUCTION

BELOW-LEVEL STUDENTS Work through the Independent Practice items with students, modeling the thinking.

ABOVE-LEVEL STUDENTS After students have completed the Independent Practice items, have them work in pairs to write a paragraph using sentences from Part B. Tell students to revise the sentences for clarity, using possessive pronouns appropriately.

Writing Connection

Writer's Craft: Clear Pronouns Direct students to focus their paragraphs by stating, "The animals are the same because _____," and "The animals are different because _____." Have students illustrate their paragraphs and work together to create a classroom display.

WRAP-UP/ASSESS

SUMMARIZE Ask students to tell how using possessive pronouns can make their writing more effective.

RETEACH

INTERVENTION Lessons in **visual, auditory,** and **kinesthetic** modalities: p. R52 and *Reteach Activities Copying Masters,* p. 44.

PRACTICE page 72

Name _____

More Possessive Pronouns

A. Underline the possessive pronoun in each sentence.

1. Sarah does not have binoculars because she left hers at home.
2. Max brought his along to share.
3. This section of the trail is ours to keep clean.
4. I am carrying a lunch, and Max and Jerry are carrying theirs.
5. The footprints in the mud are mine.

B. From the box choose a pronoun that correctly completes the sentence.

mine	yours	his	ours	theirs

6. I have a notebook for writing nature poems. The notebook is ____ . mine
7. Your hobby is bird-watching. That hobby is ____. yours
8. Our class has "The Field Guide to Birds." The book is ____. ours
9. Philip wrote a report on migrating birds. The report is ____. his
10. The second grade made a collection of fall leaves. The collection is ____. theirs

TRY THIS! Write three new sentences using possessive pronouns from the box in Section B. Write about a class field trip to a park or a place in the country.

72 Unit 4 • Chapter 22 Practice • More About Pronouns

CHALLENGE

ANIMAL BOOK Have students work in small groups to create an animal book. Each group should choose a different animal that lives in the wild. Have students research and write a description of the animal. Remind them to include possesive pronouns in their descriptions.

Students may choose to include pictures or drawings of their animals. Compile the reports into a class book.

More Possessive Pronouns

Circle the possessive pronouns in each sentence.

This clay animal isn't mine it must be yours.
I'm sure this photo album can't be his.
Have you asked Celine what she did with hers?
These pictures are theirs, not ours.

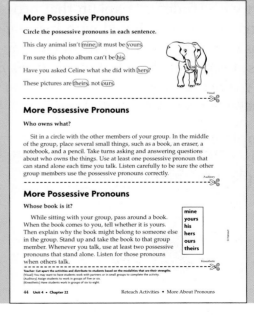

More Possessive Pronouns

Who owns what?

Sit in a circle with the other members of your group. In the middle of the group, place several small things, such as a book, an eraser, a notebook, and a pencil. Take turns asking and answering questions about who owns the things. Use at least one possessive pronoun that can stand alone each time you talk. Listen carefully to be sure the other group members use the possessive pronouns correctly.

More Possessive Pronouns

Whose book is it?

While sitting with your group, pass around a book. When the book comes to you, tell whether it is yours. Then explain why the book might belong to someone else in the group. Stand up and take the book to that group member. Whenever you talk, use at least two possessive pronouns that stand alone. Listen for those pronouns when others talk.

| mine |
| yours |
| his |
| hers |
| ours |
| theirs |

Teacher: Cut apart the activities and distribute to students based on the modalities that are their strengths.
[Visual] You may want to have students work with partners or in small groups to complete the activity.
[Auditory] Assign students to work in groups of five or six.
[Kinesthetic] Have students work in groups of six to eight.

44 Unit 4 • Chapter 22 Reteach Activities • More About Pronouns

Contractions with Pronouns

OBJECTIVES
- To correctly identify and form contractions with pronouns
- To write a descriptive paragraph, using contractions formed from pronouns and verbs

DAILY LANGUAGE PRACTICE

TRANSPARENCY 49

1 All the squirrel's watched my put out the corn. (squirrels; me)

2 Them rann over quickly. (They; ran)

BRIDGE TO WRITING The corn is _____ (possessive pronoun) now!

ORAL WARM-UP

USE PRIOR KNOWLEDGE Read the following sentences: *You've never seen my insect collection. I'm glad you asked about it.* Have students identify the pronouns they recognize.

Grammar Jingles™ CD, **Intermediate** Use Track 15 for review and reinforcement of pronouns.

TEACH/MODEL

Read through the instructions and the chart with students. Explain that pronouns may be combined with helping verbs or linking verbs to form contractions. Point out that the contractions *it's* and *you're* are often confused with the possessive pronouns *its* and *your*.

Complete the Guided Practice items orally with students, or have students complete the items in pairs.

Contractions with Pronouns

A contraction can sometimes be formed by joining a pronoun and a verb.

Remember that a contraction is a short way to write two words. Many contractions are made by joining a pronoun and a verb. In a contraction, one or more letters are left out, and an apostrophe (') takes the place of the missing letters.

Examples		
I am = I'm	I would = I'd	I have = I've
it is = it's	he would = he'd	she has = she's
you are = you're	you will = you'll	you have = you've
we are = we're	they will = they'll	they have = they've

Guided Practice

A. Name the pronoun and the verb that were used to make each contraction.

Example: you'll   *you will*

1. I'll I will
2. they're they are
3. we've we have
4. she's she is, she has
5. you're you are
6. we'd we would, we had
7. we'll we will
8. they've they have
9. she'd she would, she had
10. I'm I am

266

Vocabulary Power page 65

Name _____

DICTIONARY

Use the dictionary entry below to answer the following questions.

e·col·o·gy [ē·kol′ə·jē] *n.* 1. The study of how living things relate to their surroundings. 2. The balance between living things and their surroundings. —ecologist, *n.*

1. Which of these shows the correct syllable to stress in *ecology*? Circle the letter of the correct answer.

   A ē·kol·ə′·jē
   B ē′kol·ə·jē
   C ē·kol′ə·jē
   D ē·kol·ə·jē′

2. How many meanings does *ecology* have? _____ two

3. What part of speech is *ecology*? _____ noun

4. What word is based on *ecology* in the dictionary entry? _____ ecologist

5. If the suffix -*ist* means "a person," what do you think *ecologist* means? someone who studies how living things relate to their surroundings

6. Write a sentence using *ecology*.
   Possible response: The forest ecology is protected in this park.

7. Write a sentence using *ecologist*.
   Possible response: The ecologist studied the effects of the forest fire on the forest community.

Vocabulary Power   Unit 4 • Chapter 22   65

ESL

REACHING ALL LEARNERS

MIX AND MATCH Create two sets of index cards for students. On the cards of one set, write *am, is, are, would, will, have,* and *has*. On the cards of the other set, write *I, he, she, you, it, we,* and *they*.

Have students work in pairs, selecting one card from each set and determining whether the two words can form a contraction. If the words do form a contraction, have students say it aloud. Then have students use each contraction in a sentence.

Independent Practice

B. Find the contraction or contractions in each sentence. Write the words that were used to make each contraction.

Example: When my brother goes to the desert, he'll be searching for bugs.
he will

11. We're hoping to see beetles in the desert. We are
12. They're hard to find during the day. They are
13. My sister thinks we'll find them with her help. we will
14. She'll follow the hints she found in a book about desert insects. She will
15. If you cut open a cactus, you'll see it's full of beetles. you will, it is
16. They'll scurry away on their long legs. They will
17. When the sun goes down, you'll see beetles come out for food. you will
18. I've heard that desert insects have special ways to find water. I have
19. If they lived in the rain forest, they'd find water more easily. they would
20. I'd like to know more about desert insects and the ecology of the desert. I would

Remember that a contraction can sometimes be formed by joining a pronoun and a verb. An apostrophe takes the place of the missing letters.

Writing Connection

Science Suppose that you and your class are on a nature hike in the woods. Write a paragraph describing what you and your friends see and do. Use at least four contractions formed from pronouns and verbs in your paragraph.

267

Independent Practice

Have students complete the Independent Practice, or modify it using these suggestions:

MODIFIED INSTRUCTION

BELOW-LEVEL STUDENTS Remind students to refer to the chart on page 266 as they complete the exercises.

ABOVE-LEVEL STUDENTS Once students have completed the exercises, have them write five new sentences, using contractions they found in Part B.

Writing Connection

Science To help students develop their ideas, have them participate in a class discussion about trees, plants, and animals they may see in the woods. Tell students to edit their paragraphs for the correct use of apostrophes in contractions.

WRAP-UP/ASSESS

SUMMARIZE Ask students to explain how contractions with pronouns are formed.

RETEACH

INTERVENTION Lessons in **visual, auditory,** and **kinesthetic** modalities: p. R52 and *Reteach Activities Copying Masters*, p. 45.

PRACTICE page 73

Name _____

Contractions With Pronouns

A. Write the pronoun and the verb that were used to make each contraction.

1. they've — they have
2. you're — you are
3. he's — he is
4. we'll — we will
5. she'd — she would

B. Combine each pronoun-verb pair to make a contraction.

6. they will — they'll
7. we are — we're
8. they have — they've
9. I am — I'm
10. she has — she's

C. Write the sentence, using the correct contraction for the pronoun-verb pair shown in parentheses ( ).

11. Although animals live in the forest, **(they will)** stay out of sight.

Although animals live in the forest, they'll stay out of sight.

TRY THIS! Using contractions from this page, write three sentences about any outdoor activity you enjoy.

Practice • More About Pronouns   Unit 4 • Chapter 22 73

CHALLENGE

CONTRACTION GUESSING GAME Have students work in pairs. One student thinks of an object and gives clues about it, using contractions. For example, a student might say, *It's bigger than a bicycle* or *They'll grow leaves.*

The second student guesses what the object is, based on the clues. The second student may ask questions. Have students take turns at each role.

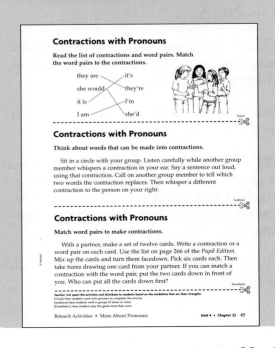

Contractions with Pronouns

Read the list of contractions and word pairs. Match the word pairs to the contractions.

they are   it's
she would   they're
it is   I'm
I am   she'd

Contractions with Pronouns

Think about words that can be made into contractions.

Sit in a circle with your group. Listen carefully while another group member whispers a contraction in your ear. Say a sentence out loud, using that contraction. Call on another group member to tell which two words the contraction replaces. Then whisper a different contraction to the person on your right.

Contractions with Pronouns

Match word pairs to make contractions.

With a partner, make a set of twelve cards. Write a contraction or a word pair on each card. Use the list on page 266 of the *Pupil Edition.* Mix up the cards and turn them facedown. Pick six cards each. Then take turns drawing one card from your partner. If you can match a contraction with the word pair, put the two cards down in front of you. Who can put all the cards down first?

Teacher: Cut apart the activities and distribute to students based on the modalities that are their strengths.
[Visual] Have students work with partners to complete the activity.
[Auditory] Have students work in groups of seven or more.
[Kinesthetic] Have students play the game more than once.

Reteach Activities • More About Pronouns   Unit 4 • Chapter 22 45

Extra Practice

OBJECTIVES
- To use possessive pronouns correctly in sentences
- To form pronoun contractions correctly
- To write a poem, using possessive pronouns and contractions, and to compare the effects of different fonts

DAILY LANGUAGE PRACTICE

TRANSPARENCY 50

1 Two raccoones was by the corn a few days later. (raccoons were)

2 Did They think they're found a treasure (they; they'd; treasure?)

BRIDGE TO WRITING _(Contraction)_ seen animals in the woods.

ORAL WARM-UP

USE PRIOR KNOWLEDGE Read aloud this sentence: _Those pictures belong to Martin and me._ Ask students to revise the sentence by using a possessive pronoun.

TEACH/MODEL

Review possessive pronouns and pronoun contractions. Remind students that possessive pronouns do not have apostrophes.

Then model the thinking for the example in Part A:

MODEL **The possessive noun in the sentence is _Maya's_. The possessive pronoun that agrees with _Maya_ is _her_.**

Model the thinking for the example in Part C:

MODEL _**I'm**_ **is the contraction. _I_ is the subject pronoun. I know that the apostrophe replaces the letter _a_ in the verb _am_. The pronoun and verb that make up this contraction are _I am_.**

Have students complete the Extra Practice independently.

CHAPTER 22

More About
Pronouns

Remember

that a possessive pronoun shows ownership and takes the place of a possessive noun. Some possessive pronouns can stand alone.

For more activities on pronouns, visit _The Learning Site:_ www.harcourtschool.com

268

Extra Practice

A. Rewrite each sentence using a possessive pronoun. _pages 262–263_

Example: Maya enjoys Maya's tropical fish tank.
Maya enjoys **her** tropical fish tank.

1. Many tropical fish make fish's homes in coral reefs. their
2. Maya loved Maya's first trip to a coral reef. her
3. She learned that the coral reef's rocks are formed by tiny animals. its
4. Maya used Maya's goggles underwater to look at the animals. her
5. Uncle Ray used Uncle Ray's underwater camera to take pictures. his

B. Read each sentence. Write the possessive pronoun that belongs in each space.

pages 264–265 Possible responses are shown.

Example: Uncle Ray bought the camera, so it is _____.
his

6. These pictures of the reef are _____ because I took them. mine
7. Maya took the pictures, so they are _____. hers
8. If we show our pictures to Maya and Uncle Ray, they will show us _____. theirs
9. Whose pictures came out better, theirs or _____? mine, yours, his, hers, ours
10. If you take pictures of a coral reef, maybe you will like _____ better than mine. yours

---

Vocabulary Power page 66

Name _____

WORD PARTS

Add the root and the suffix together to create a word. Then use the meaning of each word part to write a definition for the word.

Suffixes	Roots	
-logy the study of	archaeo ancient	
-ist a person who makes or studies	bio living things	
	chrono time	
	eco environment	
	herpeto reptiles	
	psycho mind	

1. eco + logy = _the study of the environment_

2. bio + logy = _the study of living things_

3. archaeo + logy = _the study of ancient times and cultures_

4. herpeto + logy = _the study of reptiles_

5. chrono + logy – y + ist = _a person who studies the measurement of time_

6. psycho + logy – y + ist = _a person who studies the mind and the way it works_

What are some other _-logy_ or _-ist_ words? Possible responses are given. technology, nutritionist, specialist, scientist, geology

66   Unit 4 • Chapter 22   Vocabulary Power

CONTRACTION SCRAMBLE
Have students draw on a sheet of paper five horizontal and two vertical lines, making eighteen boxes.

Write the following on the board, and have students copy them into the boxes: _I, A, M, H, E, S, Y, O, U, R, T, W, L, L, I, V, E, '_

Have students cut along the lines to separate the boxes. Tell students to rearrange the letters and the apostrophe to form as many contractions as possible in three minutes.

C. Find the contraction in each sentence. Write the two words that were used to make the contraction. *pages 266–267*

Example: I'm looking forward to our vacation. *I am*

11. We're visiting Hawaii for the second time. We are
12. We'll visit a reef in a glass-bottom boat. We will
13. I'd like to see a clown fish in the reef. I would
14. Angelfish can swim through narrow spaces because they're very thin. they are
15. A coral reef is colorful because it's full of different plants and animals. it is

D. Write a contraction for each underlined word pair. *pages 266–267*

16. <u>You would</u> be amazed to see a desert in springtime. You'd
17. Many plants are blooming, so <u>it is</u> very colorful. it's
18. Because barrel cacti have large stems to store water, <u>they will</u> survive in the desert. they'll
19. <u>I am</u> curious about some plants called living rocks. I'm
20. <u>I would</u> like to take pictures of these plants. I'd

Writing Connection

Technology Make up a rhyme about a plant or an animal. Use possessive pronouns and contractions in your rhyme. Type your rhyme on a computer. Use word-processing software to see how your rhyme looks in different type fonts. Choose the font you like best to print your rhyme.

mine their her yours its his

269

Building Oral Grammar

Some students need help distinguishing pronouns in spoken English. After they complete the Extra Practice items, have students work in pairs to read each sentence from Parts A and B aloud. Students should take turns reading the sentence and saying and spelling the pronoun or contraction they hear. They may also take turns making up sentences, with the second student repeating and spelling the pronoun or contraction.

Writing Connection

Technology Be sure students know how to create an apostrophe by using the keyboard. Show students how to copy and paste their poems so that they can look at the poems in several fonts at the same time. After students compare fonts, have a class discussion about how different fonts affect the tone of the poem. Ask: **Do some fonts look more serious or silly than others? How might using different colors change the effect of the poems?**

WRAP-UP/ASSESS

SUMMARIZE How do you know which verb to use in a contraction? Why is the contraction *you's* incorrect?

ADDITIONAL PRACTICE An additional page of Extra Practice is provided on page 468 of the *Pupil Edition*.

PRACTICE page 74

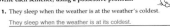

Name _____

Extra Practice

A. Write each sentence, using a possessive pronoun.

1. They sleep when the weather is at the weather's coldest.
   They sleep when the weather is at its coldest.

2. Hibernation helps an animal with an animal's survival.
   Hibernation helps an animal with its survival.

3. In springtime, the mother fox gives birth to the mother fox's kits.
   In springtime, the mother fox gives birth to her kits.

4. In warm weather, animals can find food for animals' babies.
   In the warm weather, most animals can find food for their babies.

5. The male fox comes out of the male fox's den.
   The male fox comes out of his den.

B. Write a contraction for each underlined word pair.

6. <u>You would</u> love the wildlife at our pond.   You'd
7. <u>I am</u> writing an essay on frogs.   I'm
8. The tadpoles have hatched, and <u>they have</u> started swimming around.   they've
9. <u>We will</u> watch them turn into frogs.   We'll
10. <u>They will</u> grow legs and begin to jump.   They'll

TRY THIS! Write a short paragraph about an animal. Tell about where it lives. Use these possessive pronouns in your sentences: *theirs, hers,* and *its.*

74 Unit 4 • Chapter 22   Practice • More About Pronouns

CHALLENGE

WRITING CLEARLY Read these sentences aloud: *Bob and Jim have dogs. They're very tired.* Ask: **To whom does *they're* refer?** Point out that the answer is unclear because *they're* could refer to *dogs* or to *Bob and Jim.* Have students work in pairs to write two to four sentences in which each pronoun refers clearly to only one character or thing. Have students trade papers and check the clarity of the writing and the pronouns used.

TECHNOLOGY *Grammar Practice and Assessment* CD-ROM; *Writing Express* CD-ROM

INTERNET Visit *The Learning Site:* www.harcourtschool.com

Chapter Review

OBJECTIVES

- To review possessive pronouns and contractions with pronouns
- To use context clues to determine the meanings of unfamiliar words

DAILY LANGUAGE PRACTICE

TRANSPARENCY 50

1 Mine friends is eager to feed the animals, too. (My; are)

2 Kim and susan made birdfeeders (Susan; birdfeeders.)

BRIDGE TO WRITING

(Possessive pronoun) birdfeeder is beautiful! (Contraction) very proud of it.

STANDARDIZED TEST PREP

MODEL TEST-TAKING STRATEGIES Have students silently read the directions on page 270.

Remind students that if they don't know the correct answer right away, they should eliminate answers they know are wrong. Model the thinking. Write this example on the board:

When baby frogs grow up, (1) eat insects.

    1 **A** him
       B it's
       C they'll
       D their

MODEL The subject is *frogs*, so I know that the answer must be plural. I can eliminate Choices A and B because they are singular. I can tell that *their eat* does not make sense. *They'll* is a contraction for *they will*, and *they will eat insects* does make sense. The correct answer is C.

Have students complete the Chapter Review independently.

Chapter Review

Read the passage and choose the word that belongs in each space. Write the letter for your answer.

> (1) science class studied rivers, lakes, and ponds. (2) spent two weeks finding out about animals and plants. On (3) last day, we went on a field trip to a pond.
>
> Did you know that frogs live underwater as larvae? When they become adults, (4) live out of water. Look for lily pads, and (5) probably see a frog or two! We saw something else near the lily pad. A snapping turtle raised (6) head out of the water!

TIP Remember to read all the answers before making your choice.

1 A It's	**4 F** they've
B They're	**G** they'll G
C Mine	**H** she'll
D My D	**J** it
2 F My	**5 A** they'll
G Its	**B** you'll B
H Her	**C** we're
J We J	**D** their
3 A our A	**6 F** my
B mine	**G** their
C ours	**H** its H
D yours	**J** your

For additional test preparation, visit *The Learning Site:*
www.harcourtschool.com

Assessment

. . . .

PORTFOLIO ASSESSMENT Have students choose their best work from the Writing Connections on pages 263, 265, 267, and 269.

ONGOING ASSESSMENT Evaluate the performance of 4–6 students using appropriate checklists and record forms from pages R74–R88.

INTERNET Activities and exercises to help students prepare for state and standardized assessments appear on *The Learning Site:*
www.harcourtschool.com

Using Context Clues

VOCABULARY

You may find some unfamiliar words as you read. You can use context clues to help you figure out what these new words mean. When you read the words and sentences that are near a new word, you can often find context clues.

Different Kinds of Context Clues

- synonyms and antonyms
- the way the new word is used in the sentence
- other sentences that define or explain the new word
- pictures or captions

In the example below, an unfamiliar word is circled. The context clues are underlined.

Example:

In some northern parts of the United States, there are (dense) forests. These forests are thick with spruce, pine, and other trees. There is very little room between the trees. (The word *dense* can mean "thick." A dense forest is crowded with trees.)

YOUR TURN

Find a section in your science book that tells about an animal or plant that you want to know more about. Look at one or two paragraphs. Write down any words that are unfamiliar to you. Then go back and read the paragraphs carefully, looking for context clues. List any clues you find, and write what you think the unfamiliar words mean. Then use a dictionary to check your work.

TIP When you come across an unfamiliar word, ask yourself what part this word plays in the sentence. Is it a noun? a verb? the subject? the predicate?

271

PRACTICE page 75

REACHING ALL LEARNERS

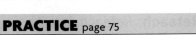

Name _____

Chapter Review

Choose the word that belongs in each space. Fill in the oval next to your choice.

A dead tree can be home to many animals. There is an old apple tree on the back of **(1)** _____ land. **(2)** _____ counted the animals and plants that make **(3)** _____ homes in the tree. Beetles crawl in and out of **(4)** _____ bark. **(5)** _____ busy carving the wood. A blackbird pokes **(6)** _____ head out of a hole in the side. Mistletoe hangs on one of the branches. **(7)** _____ leaves show it's a healthy green plant. A blackberry vine grows out of the trunk. Tree frogs sing from inside the hollow trunk. **(8)** _____ home is cool and damp there.

1 ⬭ It's
  ⬭ they're
  ⬬ our
  ⬭ I've

2 ⬬ We've
  ⬭ Our
  ⬭ Mine
  ⬭ My

3 ⬬ their
  ⬭ its
  ⬭ mine
  ⬭ they're

4 ⬭ it's
  ⬭ its
  ⬭ they're
  ⬭ mine

5 ⬭ Their
  ⬬ They're
  ⬭ Our
  ⬭ We've

6 ⬭ she'd
  ⬭ mine
  ⬭ ours
  ⬬ its

7 ⬭ It's
  ⬭ His
  ⬭ Her
  ⬬ Its

8 ⬭ She'd
  ⬭ Mine
  ⬭ It's
  ⬬ Their

Practice • More About Pronouns   Unit 4 • Chapter 22   75

CHALLENGE

REACHING ALL LEARNERS

DICTIONARY DARE Have pairs of students use a dictionary to choose one word that they do not know. Have them read the definition and then write the word in a sentence. The sentence (or two sentences, if necessary) should contain context clues that suggest the meaning of the new word. Ask pairs to trade sentences with other pairs and challenge each other to figure out the meaning of the difficult word.

VOCABULARY

Using Context Clues

TEACH/MODEL

Read aloud the explanation of context clues. Then work through the example, noting that the underlined groups of words are clues to the meaning of the highlighted word. Apply the Tip to the example, as well, pointing out that *dense* is a word that describes *forests*, making it an adjective.

In addition, offer some examples of pronouns and contractions in sentences that require context clues for understanding. For example, *It was his* requires the reader to look for clues in nearby sentences to clarify the pronouns' meanings.

Have students complete the Your Turn activity independently.

Writer's Journal

WRITING APPLICATION In their journals, have students use the vocabulary words they just learned in sentences about the plant or animal they investigated. Prompt students to include context clues to the meaning of the words.

WRAP-UP/ASSESS

SUMMARIZE What are some ways that context clues help you figure out what new words mean?

TECHNOLOGY Additional writing activities are provided on the *Writing Express* CD-ROM

LESSON ORGANIZER	DAY 1	DAY 2
DAILY LANGUAGE PRACTICE TRANSPARENCIES 51, 52	**1.** Ours ears can tell a coyote are near. (Our; is) **2.** You and me hears its sad cry. (We hear) **Bridge to Writing** (Possessive pronoun) dog wants to go for a walk.	**1.** the wind shakes the trees branches. (The; tree's) **2.** The coyote's cry sound scary and sad (sounds or sounded; sad.) **Bridge to Writing** The coyote was (adjective) .
ORAL WARM-UP **Listening/Speaking**	Brainstorm Descriptive Words 272	Describe a Number 274 *Grammar Jingles*™ CD Track 16
TEACH/MODEL **GRAMMAR** **KEY** ✔ = tested skill	✔ **ADJECTIVES** 272–273 • To identify and use adjectives in writing • To record a list and to write descriptive sentences using adjectives	✔ **ADJECTIVES FOR *HOW MANY*** 274–275 • To identify and use adjectives that tell *how many* • To write a descriptive paragraph and to respond constructively to another student's writing
Reaching All Learners	**Modified Instruction** Below-Level: Model the Thinking Above-Level: Use New Adjectives **Reteach:** *Reteach Activities Copying Masters* pp. 46 and R53 **Challenge:** Activity Card 16, R69 *ESL Manual* pp. 112, 113 *Practice Book* p. 76	**Modified Instruction** Below-Level: Underline Nouns Above-Level: Write Sentences **ESL:** Describe How Many 274 *ESL Manual* pp. 112, 114 **Reteach:** *Reteach Activities Copying Masters* pp. 47 and R53 **Challenge:** Animal Facts 275 *Practice Book* p. 77
WRITING	Writing Connection 273 Writer's Craft: Vivid Adjectives	Writing Connection 275 Science
CROSS-CURRICULAR/ ENRICHMENT	*Vocabulary Power* Explore Word Meaning 272 bovine, **canine,** equine, feline, porcine **See** *Vocabulary Power* **book.**	*Vocabulary Power* Context Clues 272 *Vocabulary Power* p. 67 🏆 **Vocabulary activity**

DAY 3

1. Both coyote parents cares for their pups. (care)
2. Most coyotes is good parents. (are)

Bridge to Writing   (Adjective) coyotes teach their pups how to hunt.

Describe Animal Behavior 276

 Grammar Jingles™ CD Track 16

✔ **ADJECTIVES FOR *WHAT KIND*** 276–277
- To identify adjectives that tell *what kind*
- To classify information and to record ideas using adjectives that tell *what kind*

Modified Instruction
Below-Level: Read Choices Before Deciding
Above-Level: Rewrite Sentences
Reteach: *Reteach Activities Copying Masters* pp. 48 and R53
Challenge: Write a Poem 277
ESL Manual pp. 112, 115
Practice Book p. 78

Writing Connection 277
Real-Life Writing: Conversation

Listening and Speaking:
Describe an Object 276
Vocabulary Power
Related Words 272
Vocabulary Power p. 68
Vocabulary activity

DAY 4

1. look at the beautiful eagle! (Look)
2. Me would like to see it up clos. (I; close.)

Bridge to Writing   (Adjective) eagles are flying above our heads.

Share and Describe 278

EXTRA PRACTICE 278–279
- To identify and use adjectives that tell *how many* and *what kind*
- To record reflections and express thoughts in a paragraph
Practice and assessment

Building Oral Grammar
Adjective Guessing Game 279
Challenge: Adjective Sort 279
ESL Manual pp. 112, 116
Practice Book p. 79

Writing Connection 279
Writer's Journal: Reflecting on Writing

Vocabulary Power
Analogies 272
Vocabulary Power p. 69
Vocabulary activity
Vocabulary: Synonyms and Antonyms 278

DAY 5

1. Coyotes is a threat to herds of sheeps. (are; sheep.)
2. last night we will hear the coyotes howl. (Last; heard)

Bridge to Writing   (Adjective) coyotes are hunting today. They are (adjective) .

TEST PREP **CHAPTER REVIEW** 280
- To review adjectives
- To practice listening for purpose and main idea
Test preparation

Challenge: Animal Discovery 281
Practice Book p. 80
ESL Manual pp. 112, 117

Writing Application 281
Writing an Advertisement

Listening and Speaking: Guest Speakers 281
Vocabulary Power
Acronyms 272

Adjectives

OBJECTIVES
- To identify and use adjectives in writing
- To record a list and to write descriptive sentences using adjectives

DAILY LANGUAGE PRACTICE

TRANSPARENCY 51

1 Ours ears can tell a coyote are near. (Our; is)

2 You and me hears its sad cry. (We hear)

BRIDGE TO WRITING

(Possessive pronoun) dog wants to go for a walk.

ORAL WARM-UP

USE PRIOR KNOWLEDGE Have children brainstorm words that describe wolves. Ask: **Which of the words would fit in this sentence? Wolves are _____.**

TEACH/MODEL

Explain that using adjectives helps writers paint clear, exact pictures with words. Adjectives provide specific information about a noun, and they make writing more interesting. Read aloud the definition and example sentences on page 272.

Work through the Guided Practice orally with students.

Adjectives

An adjective is a word that describes a noun.

Remember that a noun names a person, a place, an animal, or a thing. An adjective tells more about a noun. An adjective can come before the noun it describes. It can also follow a verb such as *is* or *seems*.

Examples:
Wolves often live in **snowy** places.

They have **thick** hair.

The leader of the pack is **smart**.

Vocabulary Power

ca•nine [kā′nīn] *adj.* Like a dog; belonging to a group of animals that includes dogs, foxes, and wolves.

Guided Practice

A. Name the adjective that describes the underlined noun in each sentence.

Example: The red <u>fox</u> is related to the wolf.
red

1. Wolves have furry <u>coats</u>.   furry
2. They can make a lot of different <u>sounds</u>.   different
3. Sometimes they make a sad <u>howl</u>.   sad
4. At times they make a quiet <u>woof</u>.   quiet
5. Sometimes <u>wolves</u> are shy.   shy
6. A wolf may have gray <u>fur</u>.   gray
7. Its <u>jaws</u> seem strong.   strong
8. Wolves sometimes eat small <u>animals</u>.   small
9. Hungry <u>wolves</u> hunt in packs.   Hungry
10. They are good <u>hunters</u>.   good

272

Vocabulary Power

DAY 1 EXPLORE WORD MEANING Introduce and define *canine*. **What are some of the different breeds of canines?**

DAY 2 CONTEXT CLUES Say: *Most of the milk we drink comes from bovines.* **Which words in the sentence help explain the meaning of *bovine*?** (See also *Vocabulary Power*, page 67.)

DAY 3 RELATED WORDS **Dogs are in the canine family. What are some other members of the canine family?** (See also *Vocabulary Power*, page 68.)

DAY 4 ANALOGIES **What word completes this analogy?** *Bovine is to cow as porcine is to* _____. (See also *Vocabulary Power*, page 69.)

DAY 5 ACRONYMS Tell students that some dogs are trained to work with police officers. These dogs are called the "K-9 Corps." Have students make a list of jobs a "police canine" might do.

Independent Practice

B. Read the sentences below. Then write the adjective in each sentence.

Example: Wolves are social animals.
social

11. A wolf is a canine animal. canine
12. Wolves have big paws. big
13. A wolf may have black fur. black
14. It may even have white fur. white
15. Sometimes wolves make a loud bark. loud
16. They have long tails. long
17. Wolves are not fierce all the time. fierce
18. Sometimes, wolves seem peaceful. peaceful
19. A wolf is a pack animal. pack
20. Young wolves follow the leader of the pack. Young

Writing Connection

Writer's Craft: Vivid Adjectives If you could be any animal, what would you be? Think about an animal you might like to be. Write a list of adjectives that describe this animal. Choose three of those adjectives, and use them in sentences that tell why you would like to be this animal.

Remember

that an adjective describes a noun. An adjective can come before the noun or after a verb such as *is* or *seems.*

273

Independent Practice

Have students complete the Independent Practice, or modify it using these suggestions:

MODIFIED INSTRUCTION

BELOW-LEVEL STUDENTS Work through the Independent Practice with students, modeling the thinking.

ABOVE-LEVEL STUDENTS After students have completed Part B, have them use a different adjective in each sentence.

Writing Connection

Writer's Craft: Vivid Adjectives Before students begin writing their lists of adjectives, tell them to imagine the animal. What does it look like? How does it sound? How does it move? Then ask students to write at least three sentences to express their thoughts. Tell students to revise their sentences to include vivid images.

WRAP-UP/ASSESS

SUMMARIZE Ask students to tell what an adjective does and where it might be found in a sentence.

RETEACH

REACHING ALL LEARNERS

INTERVENTION Lessons in **visual, auditory,** and **kinesthetic** modalities: p. R53 and *Reteach Activities Copying Masters,* p. 46.

REACHING ALL LEARNERS

PRACTICE page 76

Name _____

Adjectives

A. Underline the adjective in each sentence.

1. Frisky squirrels jump through the trees.
2. They call each other with little barks.
3. The squirrels collect brown acorns for the winter.
4. Green lizards live here, too.
5. They sun themselves on a big rock.

B. Underline the adjective and write the noun that it describes.

6. Their skin is gray. — skin
7. The quick lizard darts away. — lizard
8. Are there slow salamanders near the creek? — salamanders
9. The salamander has pink fingers! — fingers
10. He lives in cool places near the river. — places
11. Mountain streams are home to frogs. — streams
12. Their constant croaking goes on day and night. — croaking

TRY THIS! Take a walk outside or remember a walk you have taken. Then write three sentences about the animals you saw. Underline the adjectives in each of your sentences.

76 Unit 4 • Chapter 23   Practice • Adjectives

REACHING ALL LEARNERS

CHALLENGE

ADJECTIVE COLLAGE Have students use **Challenge Activity Card 16** (page R69) to create an adjective collage.

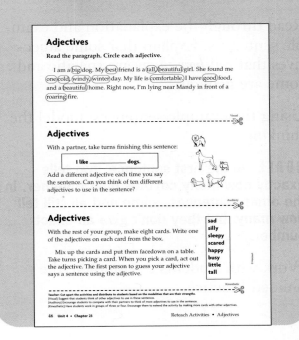

Challenge Activity Card 16

Adjective Collage

Make a collage about animals. Here are the steps to follow:

• Decide on a theme for your collage. You may choose any theme.
• Draw pictures or cut them out of old magazines.
• Use an adjective to label and describe each picture.
• Arrange the pictures and the adjectives on a large sheet of paper. Paste them in place to create your collage.

loyal, patient

perky

shaggy

Adjectives

Read the paragraph. Circle each adjective.

I am a big dog. My best friend is a tall, beautiful girl. She found me one cold, windy, winter day. My life is comfortable. I have good food, and a beautiful home. Right now, I'm lying near Mandy in front of a roaring fire.

- ✂

Adjectives

With a partner, take turns finishing this sentence:

I like _____ dogs.

Add a different adjective each time you say the sentence. Can you think of ten different adjectives to use in the sentence?

- ✂

Adjectives

With the rest of your group, make eight cards. Write one of the adjectives on each card from the box.

Mix up the cards and put them facedown on a table. Take turns picking a card. When you pick a card, act out the adjective. The first person to guess your adjective says a sentence using the adjective.

sad
silly
sleepy
scared
happy
busy
little
tall

Teacher: Cut apart the activities and distribute to students based on the modalities that use their strengths.
[Visual] Suggest that students think of other adjectives to use in these sentences.
[Auditory] Encourage students to compete with their partners to think of more adjectives to use in the sentence.
[Kinesthetic] Have students work in groups of three or four. Encourage them to extend the activity by making more cards with other adjectives.

46 Unit 4 • Chapter 23   Reteach Activities • Adjectives

Adjectives for *How Many*

OBJECTIVES
- To identify and use adjectives that tell *how many*
- To use a concept web to write a descriptive paragraph and to respond constructively to another student's writing

DAILY LANGUAGE PRACTICE
TRANSPARENCY 51

1 the wind shakes the trees branches.
(The; tree's)

2 The coyote's cry sound scary and sad (sounds or sounded; sad.)

BRIDGE TO WRITING The coyote was ___(adjective)___ .

ORAL WARM-UP

USE PRIOR KNOWLEDGE Ask students to raise their hand if their family has a dog. Then ask students to suggest words to describe the number of students in the class who have dogs.

Grammar Jingles™ **CD, Intermediate** Use Track 16 for review and reinforcement of adjectives.

TEACH/MODEL

Read through the explanation and example sentences. Explain that some adjectives that tell *how many* are specific and some are general.

Using the example sentences, model the thinking:

MODEL In the first sentence, *two* tells exactly how many coyotes hunt together. In the other sentences, *some* and *all* still tell *how many*, but they don't give an exact number.

Work with students to complete the Guided Practice.

274

Adjectives for *How Many*

Some **adjectives** tell *how many*.

You know that an adjective describes a noun. The adjectives in the following sentences tell *how many*.

Examples:

Two coyotes hunt together.

They may eat **some** berries.

All coyotes are canine animals.

Not all adjectives that tell *how many* give an exact number.

Guided Practice

A. Name the adjective in each sentence that describes the underlined noun.

Example: Most <u>coyotes</u> have bushy tails.
Most

1. Today there are coyotes in many <u>parts</u> of the United States. many
2. Most <u>coyotes</u> live in the West. Most
3. They usually live six <u>years</u>. six
4. Some <u>coyotes</u> live in the mountains. Some
5. Many <u>coyotes</u> live in the desert. Many
6. Coyotes can weigh thirty <u>pounds</u>. thirty
7. Many <u>coyotes</u> hunt alone. Many
8. Coyotes eat several <u>foods</u>. several
9. Few <u>coyotes</u> come near humans. Few
10. Coyotes can run more than twenty <u>miles</u> an hour. twenty

---

Vocabulary Power page 67

Name _____

CONTEXT CLUES

▶ Read each sentence, paying attention to the underlined word. Then complete the statements about the underlined words.

1. Susan's <u>canine</u> barks and wags its tail.
   A canine is a ___dog___.
2. John's <u>feline</u> meows when it is hungry.
   A feline is a ___cat___.
3. The <u>porcine</u> animal oinks and eats a lot.
   Porcine means ___pig-like___.
4. The <u>bovine</u> moos and produces milk.
   A bovine is a ___cow___.
5. The <u>equine</u> has a brown mane and a flowing tail.
   An equine is a ___horse___.

▶ Use each letter of the animal's name to write a word that describes it. The word can describe the way the animal looks, acts, or sounds. One example for each animal is done for you.
Responses will vary. Accept reasonable responses.

F ___furry___   C _____
E _____   A _____
L _____   N _____
I _____   I _____
N _____   N _____
E _____   E ___energetic___

Vocabulary Power   Unit 4 • Chapter 23   67

ESL

DESCRIBE HOW MANY Gather a variety of objects such as pencils, paper clips, and stickers. Have students describe the objects aloud using adjectives that tell *how many*. Tell them to use adjectives that give exact numbers as well as adjectives that give a general description. Prompt students to sort the objects into different categories as they think of ways to describe them.

Independent Practice

B. Read each sentence. Write the adjective that tells *how many* and the noun it describes.

Example: All coyotes are nocturnal.
All|coyotes

11. A coyote can have six pups. six|pups
12. A pup's eyes open after two weeks. two|weeks
13. Most female coyotes are good mothers. Most|coyotes
14. Few coyotes live in groups. Few|coyotes
15. Grown pups stay within ten miles of their parents. ten|miles
16. Coyotes have several types of barks. several|types
17. They can make many sounds. many|sounds
18. Their barks can travel three miles. three|miles
19. They howl during two seasons. two|seasons
20. There are more coyotes in America today than ever before. more|coyotes

Remember that some adjectives tell *how many*, but not all give an exact number.

Writing Connection

Science Think of an animal you like. Create a web, using adjectives that describe this animal. Be sure to include adjectives that tell *how many*. Use the web to write a paragraph about the animal. Then read the paragraph to a friend and discuss possible changes.

275

Independent Practice

Have students complete the Independent Practice, or modify it using these suggestions:

MODIFIED INSTRUCTION

BELOW-LEVEL STUDENTS Remind students that each adjective that tells *how many* describes a noun. Have students underline the nouns in each sentence before looking for the adjective that tells *how many*.

ABOVE-LEVEL STUDENTS After students have completed Part B, have them write three additional sentences with adjectives that tell *how many*.

Writing Connection

Science To help students generate their adjective webs, have pictures and books about animals available. Tell students to scan these resources for ideas. When students trade papers, ask them to suggest ways to improve their partner's adjective use and paragraph organization.

WRAP-UP/ASSESS

SUMMARIZE Ask students to name some adjectives that tell *how many* but do not give an exact number.

RETEACH

INTERVENTION Lessons in **visual, auditory,** and **kinesthetic** modalities: p. R53 and *Reteach Activities Copying Masters*, p. 47.

PRACTICE page 77

Name _____

Adjectives for How Many

A. Put two lines under the adjective that tells how many, and underline once the noun it describes.

1. Many wild deer live behind the orchard.
2. Some animals have been eating the roses.
3. All young deer are called fawns.
4. Most fawns have white spots.
5. Both babies were following their mother.
6. We saw several deer crossing the road.

B. Write the adjective in each sentence that tells how many.

7. The young buck was growing two small antlers.	two
8. Both of his little antlers were fuzzy.	Both
9. Some deer use their antlers to fight.	Some
10. All female deer are called does.	All
11. The herd had ten does.	ten
12. A herd often has many young deer.	many
13. This one is not like most herds.	most
14. There were few fawns.	few

TRY THIS! Describe a herd of wild deer. How many bucks and does are there? What are they doing? Write three sentences about the deer. Use adjectives that tell how many.

Practice • Adjectives   Unit 4 • Chapter 23 77

CHALLENGE

ANIMAL FACTS Have students select an animal and write a list of three to five facts about it. Each fact should include an adjective that tells *how many*. Then have students tell whether the adjectives give an exact number.

Adjectives for How Many

Read this paragraph. Circle each adjective that tells how many.

Fifteen dogs were entered in the local dog show. Most dogs behaved very well. However, one dog did not follow directions at all. After several problems, the dog broke away and ran toward the judges. Two judges tried to stop the dog, but one judge just turned and ran away.

Visual

Adjectives for How Many

Have you ever owned a pet? What kind of pet is your favorite?

Make up a story about lots of pets. Tell your story to a partner. Use at least five adjectives that tell how many.

When it is your turn to listen, notice each adjective that tells how many. Raise your hand each time you hear that kind of adjective.

Auditory

Adjectives for How Many

Make two cards. On each card, write a different adjective that tells how many. You might want to use some of the adjectives on page 274 of the Pupil's Edition. Pass your cards to other members of your group. Then take turns saying sentences using an adjective from one of the cards you have been given.

Kinesthetic

Teacher: Cut apart the activities and distribute to students based on the modalities that are their strengths.
[Visual] You may want to write the paragraph on the board.
[Auditory] Remind students to speak slowly and clearly while telling their stories.
[Kinesthetic] Have students work in groups of four to six. If materials are available, let students use marker to write adjectives on index cards.

Reteach Activities • Adjectives   Unit 4 • Chapter 23 47

Adjectives for *What Kind*

OBJECTIVES
- To identify adjectives that tell *what kind*
- To classify information and to record ideas using adjectives that tell *what kind*

DAILY LANGUAGE PRACTICE

TRANSPARENCY 51

❶ Both coyote parents cares for their pups. (care)

❷ Most coyotes is good parents. (are)

BRIDGE TO WRITING (Adjective) coyotes teach their pups how to hunt.

ORAL WARM-UP

USE PRIOR KNOWLEDGE Read the following sentence to students: *The coyotes started yelping.* Ask: **What kind of coyote might yelp?**

Grammar Jingles™ **CD, Intermediate** Use Track 16 for review and reinforcement of adjectives.

TEACH/MODEL

Explain that adjectives that tell *what kind* can make writing and speaking lively and vivid. Write this sentence on the board: *The dog ran up to the house.* Ask students to suggest adjectives that might make the sentence more interesting.

Tell students they can find adjectives in a sentence by asking questions that begin with *What kind.* Model the thinking, using the first example:

MODEL I ask myself *What kind of legs do frogs have?* The sentence says they have *long* legs. The adjective that tells *what kind* is *long*.

Have students complete the Guided Practice in pairs.

276

Adjectives for *What Kind*

Some **adjectives** tell *what kind.*

Remember that other adjectives tell *how many.* Adjectives for *what kind* can describe size, shape, or color. They can also tell how something looks, sounds, feels, tastes, or smells.

Examples:

Frogs have **long** legs.

Some frogs have **round** spots.

Some toads have **green** stripes.

Use adjectives for *what kind* to make sentences more interesting and more specific.

Guided Practice

A. Identify the noun that each underlined adjective describes.

Example: Frogs have <u>flat</u> heads.
heads

1. Frogs like <u>wet</u> places. places
2. Their calls are <u>loud</u>. calls
3. Some frogs have <u>yellow</u> bodies. bodies
4. Many frogs are <u>green</u>. frogs
5. Frogs have <u>smooth</u> skin. skin
6. Frogs use their <u>long</u> tongues to catch food. tongues
7. A frog has <u>webbed</u> feet. feet
8. Frogs can live in <u>cold</u> weather. weather
9. Toads like <u>rainy</u> days. days
10. Some toads are <u>brown</u>. toads

Vocabulary Power page 68

Name _____

RELATED WORDS

Many groups of animals have "family names." Dogs are part of the canine family. Cats, including pets and wild cats, are felines. Cows are bovines. Horses are in the equine family.

Write the correct family name for each animal above its picture. Then write each word from the Word Box under the correct picture. Finally, add your own example for each animal.
Examples may vary. Accept reasonable responses.

dog	lion	steer	colt	cow
wolf	horse	zebra	cattle	coyote
cat	kitten			

Canine	Feline	Bovine	Equine
dog wolf coyote	cat kitten lion	steer cow cattle	horse colt zebra

68   Unit 4 • Chapter 23   Vocabulary Power

Listening and Speaking

DESCRIBE AN OBJECT Have students work in pairs to use adjectives that tell *what kind.* Each student should silently choose an object. One student should use adjectives to describe the object while the other tries to guess what the object is. Tell students to use gestures and other nonverbal communication as they describe their objects.

Independent Practice

B. For each of the sentences below, write the adjective that tells what kind.

> **Example:** Fish can be _____ pets. (good, canine)
> *good*

11. Goldfish have _____ skin. (scaly, more)
12. Compared to adult cats, kittens are _____. (small, few)
13. Cats usually have _____ coats. (three, soft)
14. Puppies are _____ dogs. (young, some)
15. A beagle is a _____ animal. (most, canine)

C. For each of the sentences below, write the adjective and the noun that each adjective describes.

> **Example:** Dogs like to chew on rubber balls.
> *rubber|balls*

16. Saint Bernards are considered friendly dogs.   friendly|dogs
17. Poodles have curly hair.   curly|hair
18. Dalmatians have black spots.   black|spots
19. A greyhound is a tall dog.   tall|dog
20. Dogs may have pointed ears.   pointed|ears

Writing Connection

Real-Life Writing: Conversation With a partner, discuss two different animals, using adjectives that tell *what kind*. Then use the adjectives to create a chart that shows how those animals are different and alike.

Remember

that some adjectives tell *what kind*. They can describe size, shape, or color. They can tell how something looks, sounds, feels, tastes, or smells.

277

Independent Practice

Have students complete the Independent Practice, or modify it using these suggestions:

MODIFIED INSTRUCTION

BELOW-LEVEL STUDENTS For Part B, have students read the sentences using both choices before deciding which adjective is correct.

ABOVE-LEVEL STUDENTS Have students rewrite the sentences, completing each one with a different adjective that tells *what kind*.

Writing Connection

Real-Life Writing: Conversation Encourage students to keep a list of the adjectives they use in their conversations. Before they begin to record their ideas, they may want to review their lists of adjectives and choose categories in which to classify the animals.

WRAP-UP/ASSESS

SUMMARIZE Ask students to give examples of adjectives that tell how something looks, sounds, feels, tastes, and smells.

RETEACH

INTERVENTION Lessons in **visual, auditory,** and **kinesthetic** modalities: p. R53 and *Reteach Activities Copying Masters,* p. 48.

PRACTICE page 78

Name _____

Adjectives for What Kind

A. Underline the adjective that tells *what kind*. Write the noun each underlined adjective describes.

1. Their eyes are sharp, too.   eyes
2. They can see a tiny mouse from high in the sky.   mouse
3. Some hawks' eyes are yellow.   eyes
4. Speckled feathers keep them warm.   feathers
5. A falcon hunts in the high meadow.   meadow

B. Write each sentence, choosing the adjective that best describes the noun.

6. Owls hunt in the (grassy, sudden) field.
   Owls hunt in the grassy field.

7. They search for prey with their (excellent, shady) eyes.
   They search for prey with their excellent eyes.

8. They signal with a (quiet, green) hoot.
   They signal with a quiet hoot.

9. The owl sits in the (redwood, purple) tree.
   The owl sits in the redwood tree.

TRY THIS! Write three sentences describing the sounds and sights that make you think of an owl.

78   Unit 4 • Chapter 23   Practice • Adjectives

CHALLENGE

WRITE A POEM Have students use adjectives to write a poem that appeals to the five senses. Ask them to follow these steps:

1. Choose a subject that can be experienced by all five senses—sight, hearing, touch, taste, and smell.

2. Think of two or more adjectives that describe the object and appeal to each of the senses.

3. Use these adjectives in the poem to create a picture with words.

Adjectives for What Kind

Read this riddle. Circle each adjective that tells *what kind*. Then write the answer to the question.

This animal has a long neck. It has strong legs. This animal has a tan coat with brown spots. It has pointed ears and short horns. This animal eats fresh leaves from the tops of trees.
Which of these animals is it? _____ giraffe

| zebra | giraffe | elk |

Visual

Adjectives for What Kind

What type of animal can you describe?

Think of an animal. Tell a partner about the animal, but do not name it. Use at least six different adjectives that tell *what kind*. See if your partner can guess the animal.

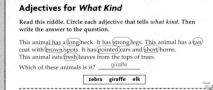

Auditory

Adjectives for What Kind

Have you seen animals in a zoo?

Act out an animal for the rest of your group. As you move, tell about the animal. Use four or more adjectives that tell *what kind*. Can the others in your group name the animal?

Kinesthetic

48   Unit 4 • Chapter 23   Reteach Activities • Adjectives

Extra Practice

OBJECTIVES

- To identify and use adjectives that tell *how many* and *what kind*
- To record reflections and to express thoughts in a paragraph using descriptive adjectives

DAILY LANGUAGE PRACTICE

TRANSPARENCY 52

1 look at the beautiful eagle! (Look)

2 Me would like to see it up clos. (I; close.)

BRIDGE TO WRITING _____(Adjective) eagles are flying above our heads.

ORAL WARM-UP

USE PRIOR KNOWLEDGE Ask students to share things they know about canines and other kinds of animals. As they offer sentences about the animals, have students identify the kinds of adjectives they use.

TEACH/MODEL

Use the Remember box to review adjectives. Remind students that an adjective can describe only a noun, not a verb or any other word.

Model the thinking by using the Extra Practice example in Part A.

MODEL I ask myself, *Which word describes a noun in this sentence? Many tells how many areas eagles live in.*

Have students complete the Extra Practice items individually or in small groups.

CHAPTER 23

Adjectives

Remember

that an adjective is a word that describes a noun. It can tell *how many* or *what kind.*

For more activities with adjectives, visit *The Learning Site:* www.harcourtschool.com

278

Extra Practice

A. Read each sentence. Then write the adjective that tells *how many*. *pages 274–275*

Example: Eagles live in many areas.
many

1. Most eagles stay away from people. Most
2. In some places, eagles nest on the ground. some
3. Their feathers have several shapes. several
4. Eagles have few enemies. few
5. They can live for fifty years. fifty

B. Write an adjective that tells *how many* to complete each sentence. The adjective may or may not be an exact number. *pages 274–275*
Responses may vary slightly.

Example: Eagles have _____ feathers.
many

6. Eagles have _____ wings. two
7. They have _____ strong beak. one
8. _____ kinds of eagles, the bald eagle and the golden eagle, live in North America. Two
9. _____ other kinds live in the tropical regions of Asia and Africa. Many, Some, Most
10. _____ eagles eat meat. All

C. Read each sentence. Write the adjective that tells *what kind*. *pages 276–277*

Example: Eagles are powerful.
powerful

11. Eagles have a large wingspan. large
12. Stiff feathers allow them to glide. Stiff
13. An eagle has good eyesight. good
14. Eagles look for small animals for food. small
15. They can eat rabbits, birds, and young deer. young

Vocabulary Power page 69

Name _____

ANALOGIES

An analogy shows how pairs of words go together.

Example:
Hot is to *cold* as *day* is to *night*.
(*Hot* is the opposite of *cold*; *day* is the opposite of *night*.)

▶ Read each analogy below. Figure out how the first two italicized words go together. Then write the word that completes the analogy.

1. *Porcine* is to *pig* as *canine* is to _____ dog
2. *Bovine* is to *cow* as *equine* is to _____ horse
3. *Canine* is to *bark* as *feline* is to _____ meow
4. *Oink* is to *porcine* as *neigh* is to _____ equine
5. *Wolf* is to *canine* as *tiger* is to _____ feline
6. *Calf* is to *cow* as *kitten* is to _____ cat
7. *Fish* are to *gills* as *people* are to _____ lungs

▶ Now try these.

8. *Pig* is to *corn* as *horse* is to _____ hay _____.
9. *Dog* is to *house* as *pig* is to _____ pen
10. *Four legs* are to *cats* as *two legs* are to _____ people or birds
11. *Fur* is to *animals* as _____ feathers _____ are to *birds*.
12. *Paws* are to *canines* as _____ hooves _____ are to *equines*.
13. *Snouts* are to *pigs* as _____ noses _____ are to *people*.
14. *Camel* is to *desert* as *stingray* is to _____ ocean

Vocabulary Power   Unit 4 • Chapter 23   69

Vocabulary

●●●●●●●●●●●●●●●●●●●●●

SYNONYMS AND ANTONYMS
Have students work in groups to explore synonyms and antonyms. One student should say a sentence that includes an adjective for *what kind*. The next student should repeat the sentence, replacing the adjective with a synonym. The third student should repeat the sentence, using an antonym. For example: I like *huge* dogs. I like *giant* dogs. I like *tiny* dogs.

D. Read each sentence and choose the adjective that best describes the noun. Then write the completed sentence. *pages 272–277*

Example: _____ eagles hunt during the day. (All, Red)
All eagles hunt during the day.

16. Eagles have _____ legs and feet. (strong, more)
17. They use their _____ claws to catch food. (purple, sharp)
18. Eagles use their _____ beaks for tearing. (some, hooked)
19. Eagles build nests in _____ trees. (tall, glass)
20. _____ eggs are cared for by the mother and the father. (Most, Happy)
21. _____ eagles are called eaglets. (Red, Young)
22. Eaglets are covered with _____ fuzz called down. (gray, any)
23. _____ feathers will grow within weeks. (Plastic, Regular)
24. Eaglets are not _____ flyers. (many, good)
25. _____ eaglets stay near their nest at first. (Many, None)

Writing Connection
Writer's Journal: Reflecting on Writing
Think about an animal book you have read. What was it about? What did you like or dislike about it? Write a paragraph about the book, and include the title of the book as well as your answers to these questions. Be sure to include at least four adjectives that tell *how many* and *what kind*.

DID YOU KNOW?
The bald eagle is the national bird of America.

279

Building Oral Grammar

Have students use adjectives to play a guessing game. They can take turns choosing an object in the room and giving adjective clues about it. Have them follow the pattern *It is _____.* Other students should use the clues to guess the object.

Writing Connection
Writer's Journal: Reflecting on Writing
Before students begin to record their reflections, remind them that it is important to give reasons when expressing their opinions about a book. Remind students to use the persuasive techniques they learned in Chapter 18 to encourage others to read or avoid the book. When students have finished writing their paragraphs, have them use a dictionary to check their spelling.

WRAP-UP/ASSESS

SUMMARIZE Have students reflect in their Writer's Journals on how adjectives improve writing and speaking. **REFLECTION**

ADDITIONAL PRACTICE An additional page of Extra Practice is provided on page 469 of the *Pupil Edition.*

PRACTICE page 79

Name _____

Extra Practice

A. Write the adjective for each sentence. Then write if that adjective tells *how many* or *what kind.*

1. The design of wings is complicated.
   complicated; what kind

2. Some dragonflies have landed on the lake.
   Some; how many

3. The blue dragonfly is hovering.
   blue; what kind

4. He reminds us of a tiny helicopter.
   tiny; what kind

5. Many dragonflies arrive in the summer.
   Many; how many

B. Choose the adjective that best describes the noun.

6. (Pink, Both) wings look exactly the same. _____ Both
7. The monarch butterflies migrate (every, tall) year. _____ every
8. They look like chains of (orange, quick) flowers. _____ orange

TRY THIS! Write six adjectives that describe a butterfly. Then use some of the adjectives to write three sentences about butterflies.

Practice • Adjectives   Unit 4 • Chapter 23   79

CHALLENGE

SORT ADJECTIVES Have students read a few paragraphs from their social studies textbook and make a list of all the adjectives they find in the text. Then have students categorize the adjectives, identifying those that tell *how many* and those that tell *what kind.*

TECHNOLOGY *Grammar Practice and Assessment* CD-ROM; *Writing Express* CD-ROM

INTERNET Visit *The Learning Site:*
www.harcourtschool.com

Chapter Review

OBJECTIVES
- To review adjectives
- To practice listening for purpose and main idea

SPIRAL REVIEW

DAILY LANGUAGE PRACTICE
TRANSPARENCY 52

1 Coyotes is a threat to herds of sheeps. (are; sheep.)

2 last night we will hear the coyotes howl. (Last; we heard)

BRIDGE TO WRITING (Adjective) coyotes are hunting today. They are (adjective) .

STANDARDIZED TEST PREP

MODEL TEST-TAKING STRATEGIES Have students read the directions on page 280 silently.

Tell students to read the test directions carefully first. Then they should read the paragraph and answer the questions.

Model the thinking. Write this example on the board:

Trees are also _____ things.

   1 **A** some
      B living
      C canine
      D one

MODEL I am looking for an adjective that describes *things. One* is not correct because it does not agree with the plural noun *things. Canine* is not correct because it describes animals, not trees. I will not choose *some* because it does not sound right in the sentence. That leaves *living*, which does sound right in the sentence: *Trees are also living things.* The correct answer is B.

Instruct students to complete the Chapter Review independently.

Chapter Review

Read the paragraph. Some words are missing. Choose the word that belongs in each space. Then write the letter of your answer.

> (1) Lemon trees are ____ trees. (2) They grow in ____ countries. (3) The flowers on a lemon tree have a ____ smell. (4) People use lemons in ____ ways. (5) ____ people use lemon juice for baking. (6) By themselves, lemons have a ____ taste. (7) Lemons are a ____ source of vitamin C. (8) Lemons are an ____ crop in the United States.

STANDARDIZED TEST PREP

TIP Read all directions carefully before you begin.

1 A sad
  B flower
  C one
  D fruit D

2 F one
  G each
  H none
  J many J

3 A seven
  B any
  C sweet C
  D several

4 F several F
  G none
  H trees
  J like

5 A None
  B Every
  C Some C
  D Tree

6 F quick
  G all
  H many
  J sour J

7 A none
  B round
  C good C
  D square

8 F few
  G eight
  H important H
  J many

For additional test preparations, visit *The Learning Site:* www.harcourtschool.com

Assessment

PORTFOLIO ASSESSMENT Have students select their best work from the Writing Connections on pages 273, 275, 277.

ONGOING ASSESSMENT Evaluate the performance of 4–6 students using appropriate checklists and record forms from pages R74–R77.

Activities and exercises to help students prepare for state and standardized assessments appear on *The Learning Site:*
www.harcourtschool.com

Guest Speakers

Have you ever had a guest speaker in your classroom? If so, you know how important it is to be a good listener. Here are some guidelines to follow before, during, and after a guest speaker's talk.

Before the Talk

- Think of what you already know about the guest speaker's topic.
- Predict what the speaker might say.

During the Talk

- Listen *carefully* to the speaker.
- Listen for ideas that the speaker *repeats*.
- Listen for *reasons* or *opinions*.
- Listen for *more information* that the speaker tells about an idea.

After the Talk

- Raise your hand to ask questions.
- Think about what you learned.
- Discuss your thoughts with someone else who heard the talk.

YOUR TURN

With a partner, take turns reading aloud the paragraphs that you wrote for the activity on page 279. After you listen to your partner's paragraph, write down the following information:

1. The title of the book that your partner read.
2. Two things your partner said about the book.
3. Whether your partner liked the book.
4. Why you want or don't want to read the book.

281

LISTENING AND SPEAKING

Guest Speakers

TEACH/MODEL

Remind students that it is very important to look at the speaker and listen carefully to what the speaker says. Tell students to think about the speaker's purpose. Does the speaker want to inform, persuade, or entertain? Point out that students should think of questions for the speaker. Have them raise their hands to ask their questions only when the speaker is finished.

Writer's Journal

WRITING APPLICATION In their journals, have students write one or two sentences that could be used in an advertisement for the animal book.

WRAP-UP/ASSESS

SUMMARIZE Ask students to tell what a good listener does before and during a talk.

PRACTICE page 80

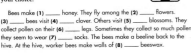

Name _____

Chapter Review

Read the passage, and choose the word that best completes each sentence. Fill in the oval next to your choice.

Bees make (1) ____ honey. They fly among the (2) ____ flowers. (3) ____ bees visit (4) ____ clover. Others visit (5) ____ blossoms. They collect pollen on their (6) ____ legs. Sometimes they collect so much pollen they seem to wear (7) ____ socks. The bees make a beeline back to the hive. At the hive, worker bees make walls of (8) ____ beeswax.

1 ⊙ old	5 ⊙ flat
⬤ delicious	⊙ honest
⊙ strange	⬤ orange
⊙ two	⊙ ugly
2 ⬤ spring	6 ⬤ tiny
⊙ sandy	⊙ lost
⊙ six	⊙ wondering
⊙ ripped	⊙ human
3 ⊙ Loud	7 ⊙ metal
⊙ One	⬤ yellow
⊙ Red	⊙ sad
⬤ Some	⊙ broken
4 ⬤ wild	8 ⊙ lonely
⊙ early	⊙ surprised
⊙ heavy	⬤ sticky
⊙ twenty	⊙ most

80 Unit 4 • Chapter 23

Practice • Adjectives

REACHING ALL LEARNERS

CHALLENGE

ANIMAL DISCOVERY Tell students to imagine that they have just discovered a new type of animal. Have them write a brief description of the animal, telling what it looks like, how it eats, and how it protects itself.

Then have students work in small groups to take turns sharing their descriptions. Remind students to listen for the speaker's purpose and main idea. They should be prepared to summarize the speaker's message.

TECHNOLOGY Additional writing activities are provided on the *Writing Express* CD-ROM

LESSON ORGANIZER	DAY 1	DAY 2
DAILY LANGUAGE PRACTICE TRANSPARENCY 53	1. Deanna enjoy looking at leaves in the woodes. (enjoys; woods) 2. She boots get muddy when she goes hiking (Her; hiking.)	1. Do you like walking in the Woods in sumer. (woods; summer?) 2. Riley Susan, and Jeff likes hiking in winter better (Riley,; like; better.)
ORAL WARM-UP **Listening/Speaking**	Suggest Information 282 Discuss Advantages and Disadvantages 288	Discuss Using Lists 289
TEACH/MODEL **WRITING** 	**Literature Model:** "Weird Leaves" 282-285 ✔ **Prewriting** 288 • To learn strategies for prewriting an advantages and disadvantages essay • To choose a topic and generate ideas for an advantages and disadvantages essay **Interactive Writing** 288	✔ **Drafting** 289 • To learn strategies for drafting an advantages and disadvantages essay • To draft an advantages and disadvantages essay **Transparency** 54
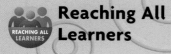 **Reaching All Learners**	**Modified Instruction** 294 Below-Level: Refer to List Above-Level: Write a Dialogue *ESL Manual* pp. 118, 119	**Modified Instruction** 295 Below-Level: Find the Subject Above-Level: Create Exercises *ESL Manual* p. 118
GRAMMAR	**Unit 4 Review:** ✔ Pronouns 294	**Unit 4 Review:** ✔ Subject and Object Pronouns 295
CROSS-CURRICULAR/ ENRICHMENT **KEY** ✔ = tested writing form/skill	**LISTENING AND SPEAKING:** 286 **EVALUATION CRITERIA:** Establish Criteria 287 **HANDS-ON ACTIVITY:** Pronoun Clipping 294 *Vocabulary Power* Explore Word Meaning 284 annual, biennial, deciduous, **evergreen**, perennnial *See Vocabulary Power book.*	**TEST PREP** **TEST PREP:** Say Choices 295 *Vocabulary Power* Compare and Contrast 284 *Vocabulary Power* book p. 70  **Vocabulary activity**

DAY 3

1. Susan storys about hiking is very funny. (Susan's stories; are)

2. Would him like to read this story (he; story?)

Add Details 290

✔ **Revising** 290
 • To learn strategies for revising an advantages and disadvantages essay
 • To revise an advantages and disadvantages essay

Transparencies 55a and 55b

Modified Instruction 296
 Below-Level: Refer to Chart
 Above-Level: Rewrite Sentences
 ESL Manual p. 118

Unit 4 Review:
✔ More About Pronouns 296

PEER CONFERENCES: Make Essays Stronger 290

TEST PREP: Eliminate Choices 296

Vocabulary Power

 Compound Words 284
 Vocabulary Power book p. 71

Vocabulary activity

DAY 4

1. jeff like writing about the woods and the ocean (Jeff; likes; ocean.)

2. Writing is hard for me but I still tries my best. (me,; try)

Share Humorous Proofreading Errors 291

✔ **Proofreading** 291
 • To learn strategies for proof-reading an advantages and disadvantages essay
 • To proofread an advantages and disadvantages essay

Transparencies 56a and 56b

Spelling: Patterns and Blends 291

Proofreading practice

Modified Instruction 297
 Below-Level: Review Adjectives
 Above-Level: Replace Adjectives
 ESL Manual p. 118

Unit 4 Review:
✔ Adjectives 297

TEST PREP: Extra Practice 297

Vocabulary Power

 Context Clues 284
 Vocabulary Power book p. 72

Vocabulary activity

DAY 5

1. Mrs. alvarez says that I would enjoy writing comic stripes (Alvarez; strips.)

2. That could be Hard work but it also might be fun (hard; work,; fun.)

Suggest Publishing Alternatives 292

✔ **Publishing** 292
 • To learn strategies for publishing an advantages and disadvantages essay as video
 • To publish an advantages and disadvantages essay as video

Practice and assessment

ESL: Pronunciation Practice 292
ESL Manual p. 118

HANDS-ON ACTIVITIES
231I–231J

TECHNOLOGY: Making a Video 293

Vocabulary Power

 Classify/Categorize 284

Using the Literature Model

OBJECTIVE
• To read and analyze an article that classifies information

DAILY LANGUAGE PRACTICE

TRANSPARENCY 53

1 Deanna enjoy looking at leaves in the woodes. (enjoys; woods.)

2 She boots get muddy when she goes hiking (Her; hiking.)

ORAL WARM-UP

USE PRIOR KNOWLEDGE Read aloud the introduction to the article, and discuss questions such as the following:

1. **List some words that describe autumn leaves.** (Possible responses: brown, red, yellow, dry, crunchy, wrinkled, flat, curly.)

2. **When writing about leaves, what kinds of information might you include?** (Possible responses: information about color, shape, smell, and texture or feel)

PREREADING STRATEGIES

PREVIEW/SET PURPOSE Ask students to look at the title, "Weird Leaves," and predict what might be weird about the leaves the author describes. Have students set their own purpose for reading, or have them read to find out what makes some leaves "weird."

poinsettia

silversword

282

School-Home Connection

Family members can help students prepare for writing an advantages and disadvantages essay by talking with them about the pros and cons of topics that interest them.

starfish plant

You know that one reason for writing is to give information. This selection is about different kinds of leaves. As you read, think about the kinds of information the author gives.

Weird Leaves

by Deborah Churchman
(from *Ranger Rick*, Oct. 1999)

When you imagine a leaf, do you see a flat, green thing that soaks up the sun in summer and then turns bright colors and flutters to the ground in the fall?

You're right. That's what many leaves are like. Some kinds of leaves are really *weird*, though.

Take the Christmasy-looking *poinsettia* in the photo, for example. Did you know that the "petals" of the flower are really special kinds of leaves called *bracts*?

Many other leaves are not what you'd imagine either. Here are just a few of the not-so-leafy, just-plain-weird leaves!

283

READING LIKE A WRITER

OPTIONS FOR READING

READ-ALOUD OPTION Read the article aloud, and have students listen to determine Churchman's audience and purpose, as well as key details.

INDEPENDENT OPTION As students read, have them take notes on the article. Ask students to name the most unusual thing they learned about one of the leaves described in the article.

Ask students to think about Churchman's writing style as they read. Use questions like the following to help students monitor their comprehension:

3. **Who do you think Churchman's audience might be?** (Possible responses: young people who are interested in nature; young people who like to learn about unusual things.) **INFERENTIAL: IDENTIFY AUDIENCE**

4. **Do you think Churchman's purpose for writing this essay is to inform, to entertain, or both? How do you know?** (Possible response: I think Churchman wants to inform and to entertain because she gives a lot of interesting information but also uses funny words like *weird* and *not-so-leafy*.) **INFERENTIAL: DETERMINE AUTHOR'S PURPOSE**

SELECTION SUMMARY

GENRE: CLASSIFICATION In this selection from *Ranger Rick*, author Deborah Churchman introduces readers to a few varieties of uncommon leaves. Churchman classifies these "weird" leaves by their color, shape, and texture. She also shares with readers a few science terms, such as *chlorophyll* and *echeveria*.

ABOUT THE AUTHOR

Deborah Churchman is the fiction editor for *Ranger Rick* magazine. She also writes scientific articles on a variety of subjects.

5. How does Churchman organize the information about leaves? (She gives an introduction and then writes about leaves in three different sections: Weird Color, Weird Shape, and Weird Feel.)

INFERENTIAL: TEXT STRUCTURE

6. Do all leaves feel smooth? What other textures do leaves have? (Not all leaves are smooth. Some leaves feel hairy, waxy, sticky, bumpy, or prickly.)

LITERAL: NOTE DETAILS

7. Do you think that people who live where these weird plants grow think that the plants are unusual? What might they think of the plants that grow in your area? (Responses will vary.) **CRITICAL: SPECULATE**

CHAPTER 24

Advantages and Disadvantages Essay

kalanchoe

Swiss cheese plant

string-of-beads plant

284

Weird Color

Most leaves are green. They get their color from a special pigment called *chlorophyll* [klôr′ə•fil]. The leaves use that pigment to make food. Leaves have red, yellow, or other pigments too. (The pigments do different jobs for the plant.) Those weird colors are easy to see in plants like the *kalanchoe* [kal′ən•kō′ē] and the *starfish plant*.

Then there's the *silversword*. Its color comes from a blanket of hairs on its leaves. The hairs help keep the plant from drying out.

Weird Shape

Some leaf shapes are real surprises. One leaf, for example, is full of holes. These holey leaves grow on a rainforest vine with a perfect name. It's called the *Swiss cheese plant*.

The *string-of-beads* plant grows in the hot, dry Namib Desert in southwestern Africa. The round leaves on this plant act just like little bottles, storing up water after a rare desert rain. They slowly supply water to the plant during the hottest, driest times.

Then there are the needles of many *evergreen trees*. Guess what? Needles are leaves too! Thin leaves like these survive better in drying winds than flat, broad leaves do.

Vocabulary Power

DAY 1 EXPLORE WORD MEANING Introduce and define *evergreen*. Write it on the board. **In the winter, how can you tell evergreens from other trees?**

DAY 2 COMPARE AND CONTRAST Ask students to complete the statement: **An evergreen is like a deciduous tree except _____.** Discuss responses. (See also *Vocabulary Power*, page 70.)

DAY 3 COMPOUND WORDS **What two words are in *evergreen*? What are some other words that can be broken down into two words?** (See also *Vocabulary Power*, page 71.)

DAY 4 CONTEXT CLUES Say: **The *annual* plant only lived for one year. What words help you understand the meaning of *annual*?** (See also *Vocabulary Power*, page 72.)

DAY 5 CLASSIFY/CATEGORIZE Ask: **What are some examples of evergreens? Of deciduous trees?**

Weird Feel

Most leaves have a waxy coating, which makes them feel smooth. (The waxy coating helps to keep moisture in.) Some other leaves feel hairy, prickly, sticky, or bumpy.

Take the leaves of one kind of *echeveria* [ech′ə•və•rē′ə]. They're lumpy and bumpy. Like the string-of-beads leaves, echeveria leaves store water for the plant to use during dry times. So those leaves are really thick.

Another kind of *echeveria* feels downright *furry!* The furry feel comes from thousands of tiny, soft hairs. As in the silversword, they help keep the plant from drying out. That's a good thing for a plant that grows in dry or windy places, such as deserts and mountains.

Now that you know about weird leaves, why not go outside and look for some?

echeveria

Vocabulary Power

ev•er•green
[ev′ər•grēn] *adj.* Having leaves that stay green throughout the year.

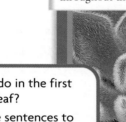

echeveria

285

Analyze THE Model

1. What does Deborah Churchman do in the first sentence to help you imagine a leaf?
2. How does she vary her first three sentences to make the beginning of her article effective?
3. Into what sections does she divide her article?
4. Why does she divide her article into sections?

RESPONSE TO LITERATURE

 WRITING PROMPT To have students respond in writing to the article, use the following prompt:

How did the section headings help you as you read the article? Why might you divide some of your writing into sections?

Analyze THE Model

1. **What does Deborah Churchman do in the first sentence to help you imagine a leaf?** (Possible response: She describes a leaf, using words that she thinks the reader might use to describe it.) **INFERENTIAL: AUTHOR'S CRAFT**

2. **How does she vary her first three sentences to make the beginning of her article effective?** (Possible responses: She gets the reader's attention in the first three sentences by starting with a question, answering it, and then making a statement. She uses both long and short sentences.) **INFERENTIAL: AUTHOR'S CRAFT**

3. **What sections does she divide the article into?** (Weird Color, Weird Shape, and Weird Feel) **LITERAL: NOTE DETAILS**

4. **Why does she divide her article into sections?** (Possible response: Each section gives a different kind of information about leaves.) **CRITICAL: INTERPRET TEXT STRUCTURE**

SUMMARIZE THE MODEL

ONE-SENTENCE SUMMARY Ask: **If you wanted to tell a classmate what this article is about, what would you say?** Have students write one sentence to summarize the article. (Possible response: The author gives information about leaves that have weird colors, weird shapes, and weird textures.)

 TECHNOLOGY Additional writing activities are provided on the *Writing Express* CD-ROM

Parts of an Advantages and Disadvantages Essay

OBJECTIVES

• To recognize and understand the parts of an advantages and disadvantages essay
• To analyze and summarize an advantages and disadvantages essay
• To establish criteria for evaluating an advantages and disadvantages essay
• To listen critically to an advantages and disadvantages essay

READING LIKE A WRITER

READ AND RESPOND TO THE MODEL Read aloud the first paragraph of Jon's essay, and ask students to determine a purpose for listening. (to learn some advantages and disadvantages of summer) Then read the essay aloud, and discuss whether Jon does a good job explaining the advantages and disadvantages of summer. Remind students to use examples from the essay to support their evaluations.

FOCUS ON ORGANIZATION Have students reread the essay silently, using the side notes to focus on the main parts. Ask: **Why do you think Jon put the disadvantages in one paragraph and the advantages in another?** (Possible response: to make it easier to tell the things he dislikes from the things he likes.)

FOCUS ON WRITER'S CRAFT Have students look through Jon's essay to find examples of sentence variety. Tell them to look for short, direct sentences and long, descriptive sentences. Ask: **How does Jon's use of sentence variety make his writing interesting?**

READING — WRITING CONNECTION

Parts of an Advantages and Disadvantages Essay

Deborah Churchman used details to describe different kinds of leaves. Study the essay, written by a student named Jon. Notice the details he uses to describe the advantages and disadvantages of summer.

MODEL

Summer
by Jon Yee

topic sentence — Sometimes, I dislike summer. Other times, I like it. How can I have both feelings? The reason is that summer has some disadvantages and some advantages.

disadvantages and details about them — There are some things I don't like about summer. One problem with summer is the hot, humid weather. If that isn't bad enough, summer insects bite my skin and make me itch. One more disadvantage of summer is that there is no school, so I do not get to see all of my friends.

advantages and details about them — There are a lot of good things about summer, though. I love the long, sunny days. I also like to go to the pool with my

286

Listening and Speaking

Have students work in small groups to create advantages and disadvantages lists. Write on slips of paper topics such as *playing sports, joining a club, watching television,* and *eating healthful foods.*

Have each group select a topic. Ask the groups to write down at least two advantages and two disadvantages for their topic. Remind students to include supporting details.

Then have each group read its lists aloud while the other groups listen to the advantages, disadvantages, and details. Tell students to choose and adapt the appropriate volume and rate for the audience, purpose, and occasion.

friends. We play water games and have races. Summer treats are great, too. Sometimes, Mom makes us glasses of icy lemonade, or Dad buys us ice cream.

Summer has many advantages and disadvantages. It seems to me that summer is wonderful and terrible at the same time!

advantages and details about them

conclusion

Analyze THE Model

1. What is the purpose of Jon's essay?

2. What audience might be interested in this essay? Why do you think so?

3. Why do you think Jon writes about the disadvantages of summer first?

Summarize THE Model

Create a web like the one shown to help you identify the advantages and disadvantages of summer in Jon's essay. Then use your graphic organizer to write a summary of Jon's essay.

Summer

Advantages

Disadvantages

Writer's Craft

Sentence Variety Jon used a variety of sentences to make his writing interesting. Find one short, direct sentence and one long, descriptive sentence. What are the different kinds of sentences that he used?

287

Analyze THE Model

1. What is the purpose of Jon's essay? (Possible response: to inform his readers about the advantages and disadvantages of summer) **INFERENTIAL: DETERMINE AUTHOR'S PURPOSE**

2. What audience might be interested in this essay? Why do you think so? (Possible responses: Other children might be interested in this essay; Jon tells about some disadvantages they may deal with in the summer, and he talks about some fun activities they may enjoy.) **INFERENTIAL: DETERMINE AUTHOR'S PURPOSE**

3. Why do you think Jon writes about the disadvantages of summer first? (Possible response: He wants to show that even though summer has some disadvantages, he really likes it after all.) **CRITICAL: INTERPRET TEXT STRUCTURE**

SUMMARIZE THE MODEL

Have students complete their graphic organizers. Then have them compare their web with a partner's web and discuss any differences. Have students write a summary of Jon's essay. Help them evaluate whether they included only the necessary details from the essay.

WRITER'S CRAFT

SENTENCE VARIETY Remind students that they should include sentence variety in all their writing, including their evaluation of Jon's writing.

TAKE-HOME BOOK 4 provides an additional model of informative writing and home activities. See *Practice Book* pages 133–136.

Evaluation Criteria

• •

ESTABLISH CRITERIA FOR WRITING Tell students that they will help evaluate their own advantages and disadvantages essays. Have them turn to the rubric in their Handbooks, on page 499. Explain that if students meet the criteria in the "4" column, plus the criteria that you and the class add, they will have produced their best work. Discuss the criteria, and add others based on your students' needs and interests. Remind students to refer to the rubric as they write their essays. (A teacher version of the rubric is available on page R83. For more information about evaluating writing, see pages R78–R79 in this *Teacher's Edition*.)

Prewriting

OBJECTIVES
- To learn strategies for prewriting an advantages and disadvantages essay
- To choose a topic and generate ideas for an advantages and disadvantages essay

ORAL WARM-UP

USE PRIOR KNOWLEDGE Tell students to imagine that they each have ten dollars to spend on anything they like. Ask: **How would you decide what to buy?** Discuss how comparing the advantages and disadvantages of something can help when making decisions.

GUIDED WRITING

Discuss the writing prompt. Have students identify the audience and the purpose for writing. (audience—classmates; purpose—to describe the advantages and disadvantages of living in a certain place) Then model finding an appropriate topic:

MODEL **I don't know much about living near the ocean or in the mountains, but I do know about living in a big city. My family moved here from Chicago two years ago. I think I'll use what I know about living in that big city for this essay.**

Then have students read Jon's model and make their own prewriting charts, using the given prompt or a prompt you assign.

SELF-INITIATED WRITING Have students choose their own topics for their advantages and disadvantages essays.

WRAP-UP/ASSESS

SUMMARIZE What topic did you choose, and why?

Prewriting

Advantages and Disadvantages Essay

Strategies Good Writers Use

- Brainstorm advantages and disadvantages.
- Think about details that support your ideas.

Purpose and Audience

There are two sides to many situations. In this chapter, you will write an advantages and disadvantages essay about living in a certain place.

WRITING PROMPT Write an essay for your classmates, telling the advantages and disadvantages of living in a certain place. Choose a place, and write about why people might like to live there and why they might not. Include details that support your ideas.

Before you begin, think about your audience and purpose. Who will your readers be? What should your essay tell them?

MODEL

Jon got ready to write his essay by listing the main disadvantages and advantages of summer. Then he thought of details to go with each idea. He used this list to organize his thoughts.

Advantages	Disadvantages
• *Long days* Detail: *sunny*	• *No School* Detail: *miss friends*
• *Treats* Details: *icy lemonade, ice cream*	• *Weather* Details: *hot and humid*
• *Pool fun* Details: *water games, races*	• *Insect bites* Detail: *make me itch*

YOUR TURN

Choose a place to write about. Think about the disadvantages and advantages of living there. Use a chart to plan your essay.

288

Vocabulary Power   page 70

Name _____

COMPARE AND CONTRAST

Complete the following statements. Responses will vary. Possible responses are given.

1. An *evergreen* is like a *deciduous tree* except that evergreens don't lose their leaves

2. An *annual* is like a *biennial* except that an annual only lives for a year

3. A *perennial* is like an *annual* because they are both types of plants

4. A *farmer* is like a *gardener* because they both grow things

5. An *orange* is like a *lemon* except that one is sweet and one is sour

6. A *year* is like a *month* except that a year is a longer period of time

7. *Flowers* are like *trees* because they both have leaves

8. A *horse* is like a *pony* except that a horse is larger than a pony

9. *Walking* is like *running* because both are ways of moving

70   Unit 4 • Chapter 24   Vocabulary Power

Interactive Writing

You may want to prewrite and write a first draft as a group. Draw students' attention to the Strategies Good Writers Use. Have students help you complete a prewriting chart, including advantages and disadvantages. Then use the Drafting Transparency with students, coaching them to use effective organization and elaboration.

Drafting

Advantages and Disadvantages Essay

Organization and Elaboration

Follow these steps to help you organize your essay:

STEP 1 **Grab Your Reader's Interest**
Make the opening interesting to your readers.

STEP 2 **Decide How to Organize Your Essay**
Look at your prewriting chart. Decide whether to start with the advantages or the disadvantages.

STEP 3 **Use Descriptive Details**
As you write, explain each idea with descriptive details.

STEP 4 **Finish with a Summary Thought**
Summarize your thoughts in an interesting way.

MODEL

Here is the beginning of Jon's essay. How does he get his readers' attention?

> Sometimes, I dislike summer. Other times, I like it. How can I have both feelings? The reason is that summer has some disadvantages and some advantages.

YOUR TURN

Now write a draft of your essay. Use your organizer and the steps above as a guide. Remember to include details that support your ideas.

Strategies Good Writers Use

- Make your beginning and ending interesting.
- Include details and examples to support your ideas.

Use a computer to draft your essay. You can use the cut and paste feature to move paragraphs.

289

Vocabulary Power page 71

TRANSPARENCY 54

DRAFTING
Advantages/Disadvantages Essay

First Paragraph

> Get Your Audience's Attention and State Your Topic:

Second Paragraph

> Introduce Advantages or Disadvantages:
>
> Supporting Descriptive Details:

Third Paragraph

> Introduce Advantages or Disadvantages:
>
> Supporting Descriptive Details:
>
> Concluding Sentence:

Harcourt Language
Level 3   54   Chapter 24
                                               Writing an Advantages and
                                               Disadvantages Essay

---

Drafting

OBJECTIVES
- To learn strategies for drafting an advantages and disadvantages essay
- To draft an advantages and disadvantages essay

DAILY LANGUAGE PRACTICE

TRANSPARENCY 53

1. Do you like walking in the Woods in sumer. (woods; summer?)
2. Riley Susan, and Jeff likes hiking in winter better (Riley,; like; better.)

ORAL WARM-UP

USE PRIOR KNOWLEDGE Ask students to tell about a time when they used a list to help them remember important ideas. Then discuss how their prewriting lists might help them draft their essays.

GUIDED WRITING

Discuss the Organization and Elaboration steps, the Strategies Good Writers Use, and the model. Ask volunteers to answer the question that precedes the model. (Possible response: He makes readers want to find out how he can both like and dislike something at the same time.)

As students draft their essays, remind them to refer to the Organization and Elaboration steps to help them remember each part their essays must include.

WRAP-UP/ASSESS

SUMMARIZE Did you use all the prewriting ideas in your draft? Why or why not?

Revising

OBJECTIVES
- To learn strategies for revising an advantages and disadvantages essay
- To revise an advantages and disadvantages essay

DAILY LANGUAGE PRACTICE

TRANSPARENCY 53

1. Susans storys about hiking is very funny. (Susan's stories; are)
2. Would him like to read this story (he; story?)

ORAL WARM-UP

USE PRIOR KNOWLEDGE Write this sentence on the board: *Living by the ocean is nice.* Ask students whether this sentence tells enough about the topic. Ask: **What details could you add to this sentence?**

GUIDED WRITING

Ask students to think of a time when they read and evaluated a classmate's writing. Point out that when revising a draft, it can be helpful to have a classmate give feedback or suggestions. Then focus on the model, and ask volunteers to discuss how Jon added and changed material. Ask students how Jon improved his essay by adding the sentence at the beginning of the paragraph.

Use **Transparencies 55a and 55b** to further model the revising process. Then have students revise their drafts.

PEER CONFERENCES Have pairs of students use the **Evaluation Criteria** to evaluate their own and each other's writing, responding constructively by identifying strengths and suggesting improvements.

WRAP-UP/ASSESS

SUMMARIZE Why did you make that revision to your draft? How does the change make the essay better?

Advantages and Disadvantages Essay

Strategies Good Writers Use

- Organize your ideas into paragraphs.
- Include enough examples and details to make ideas clear.

Use the thesaurus feature to get ideas for vivid words.

Organization and Elaboration

As you read your draft, think about these questions:
- Will my opening interest readers?
- Will readers be able to tell which ideas are advantages and which are disadvantages?
- What supporting details did I use?
- Did I end my essay with a summary thought?

MODEL

Here is a draft of the next part of Jon's essay. How did he make the topic of this paragraph clearer? What details did he add to make his writing stronger?

> ¶ There are some things I don't like about summer.
> One problem with summer is the hot, humid weather. If that isn't bad enough, summer insects bite my skin and make me itch. One more disadvantage of summer is that There is no school, so I do not get to see all of my friends. people.

YOUR TURN

Revise your essay. Make sure that you have a strong beginning and ending. Be sure that the ideas about advantages are together and the ideas about disadvantages are together.

290

TRANSPARENCIES 55a and 55b

REVISING

> ¶ There are some things I don't like about summer.
> One problem with summer is the hot, humid weather. If that isn't bad enough, summer insects bite my skin and make me itch. One more disadvantage of summer is that There is no school, so I do not get to see all of my friends. people.

Harcourt Language
Level 3
55
Chapter 24
Writing an Advantages and
Disadvantages Essay

Vocabulary Power   page 72

Name _____

CONTEXT CLUES

A. Read each sentence. Then write a definition for the underlined word. Responses may vary. Possible responses are given.

1. I have had my <u>perennial</u> plant for many years.
   a plant that lasts for many years

2. The <u>deciduous</u> tree lost its leaves when winter came.
   a tree that loses its leaves

3. The <u>annual</u> plant only lived for one year.
   a plant that only lives for one year

4. The leaves of the <u>evergreen</u> are always green.
   a tree with leaves that are always green

5. The <u>biennial</u> plant lived for two years.
   a plant that lives for two years

6. I thought the <u>everlasting</u> movie would never end.
   never ending

B. Pick two of the underlined words from above. Write one sentence for each word. Responses may vary.

7. _____
   _____

8. _____
   _____

72   Unit 4 • Chapter 24   Vocabulary Power

Making a Video

Jon presented his essay as a video. He videotaped the events in his essay and used his essay as the spoken part of the video. You can do the same. Follow these steps:

STEP 1 Think about what your audience will hear in your video. Should your essay be read as the spoken part? Should you use music in the background?

STEP 2 Think about what your audience will see. Can you videotape the subject of your essay live? If not, find photos or draw pictures to videotape.

STEP 3 Make sketches of each scene you will show in your video. Use your essay to write captions for your sketches. This step will help you decide what should be said as you film each scene.

STEP 4 Film your video. Read or have someone else read the spoken part of the video as you film the scenes.

STEP 5 Show your video to your class. Ask what they liked about it. What could you have done differently?

Strategies for Video Producers

- Hold the video camera steady.
- Stop the camera between shots.
- Speak slowly and clearly. Do not rush.

293

TECHNOLOGY
Making a Video

Work through the steps on page 293. Prompt students to read through their essays and highlight the ideas that they think are most important. Students then can focus on trying to represent these ideas visually. Discuss the role of sketching ideas in the planning of feature films, and suggest that students also make use of this planning tool.

You may wish to enlist parents' help in filming the videos.

Before students view the videos, review audience manners. Use the Student Record Form on page R76 to assess students' listening and speaking skills.

WRAP-UP/ASSESS

SUMMARIZE Would you choose making a video as the way to publish your writing again? Why or why not?

SCORING RUBRIC

4 ADVANCED	**3** PROFICIENT	**2** BASIC	**1** LIMITED
Purpose and Audience	**Purpose and Audience**	**Purpose and Audience**	**Purpose and Audience**
• appropriate for audience	• mostly appropriate for audience	• not appropriate for audience	• not appropriate for audience
• stays focused on purpose	• few deviations from purpose	• strays from purpose often	• purpose is unclear
Organization and Elaboration	**Organization and Elaboration**	**Organization and Elaboration**	**Organization and Elaboration**
• clear beginning introduces topic, and ending summarizes	• clear beginning introduces topic, and ending summarizes	• beginning does not introduce topic, and there is no clear ending	• no introduction and does not have conclusion
• middle classifies information	• information in middle not in logical order	• information in middle not about same topic	• information in middle not about same topic
• description and details	• some description and details	• little description and few details	• no description or details
• signal words and phrases	• some signal words and phrases	• few signal words and phrases	• no signal words or phrases
• sentence variety	• some sentence variety	• little sentence variety	• most sentences written incorrectly
Language	**Language**	**Language**	**Language**
• uses correct grammar	• uses mostly correct grammar	• incorrect grammar, spelling, or mechanics sometimes makes writing unclear	• incorrect grammar, spelling, or mechanics often makes writing unclear
• uses correct spelling, usage, and mechanics	• uses mostly correct spelling, usage, and mechanics		

For information on adapting this rubric to 5- or 6-point scales, see pages R78–R79.

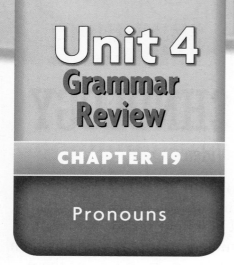

Unit 4
Grammar Review

CHAPTER 19

Pronouns

OBJECTIVES
- To use the correct form of pronouns
- To replace antecedents with correct singular or plural pronouns

Unit Review
MODIFIED INSTRUCTION

BELOW-LEVEL STUDENTS List on the board the singular and plural pronouns for students to use as a reference. Before students begin Part A, remind them to identify whether the underlined words are singular or plural and then choose the correct pronoun from the list.

ABOVE-LEVEL STUDENTS Challenge students to use the sentences from this page as the basis for dialogue about astronomy. When they share the written dialogues, have them identify various pronouns and the word or group of words for which each one stands.

Pronouns   *pages 234–235*

A. Rewrite each sentence. Use a pronoun in the place of the underlined word or words.

1. The moon lies between earth and the sun.   It
2. Mark and I watched a solar eclipse.   We
3. Elena and her dad watched it in the mountains.   They
4. People should watch the eclipse through a special lens.   You, One
5. The sun looked like it had a bite out of it.   It

Singular and Plural Pronouns

pages 236–237

B. Write a pronoun to take the place of the underlined words in each sentence. Then write *S* if the pronoun is singular or *P* if it is plural.

6. Jamie and his family watched a lunar eclipse.   They, P
7. Earth moved between the sun and the moon.   them, P
8. Sunlight could not reach the moon.   It, S
9. People everywhere saw the dim, reddish moon.   They, P
10. Elena and I could see the shadow of earth.   We, P

Pronoun-Antecedent Agreement   *pages 238–239*

C. Write the correct pronoun to replace the words in parentheses ( ).

11. Jon would like to travel in space. (Jon) says the distances are too far.   He
12. The closest star to our sun is nine light-years away. (The closest star to our sun) is named Sirius.   It
13. Venus and Mars are millions of miles away. It would take months to reach (Venus and Mars).   them
14. I told Elena that she is good at science. I told (Elena) to think about being an astronaut.   her
15. Elena said that (Elena) would like to see space.   she

294

HANDS ON Activity

PRONOUN CLIPPING On separate index cards, write the pronouns *he, him, she, her, they, them,* and *it.* Then write the names of five boys, five girls, and five plural nouns. Place the cards in a learning center, and invite students to visit the center individually or in pairs. Have students use paper clips to attach the nouns to the pronouns that could replace them.

Subject Pronouns   *pages 244–245*

A. Write the subject pronoun in each sentence.

1. He watched the news last night. He
2. They predicted our first winter storm. They
3. It will bring nearly two inches of rain. It
4. We measured the rainfall in a beaker. We
5. You can see that there is more rain than last year. You

Object Pronouns   *pages 246–247*

B. Write the object pronoun in each sentence.

6. Every day the weather affects us. us
7. Tomorrow it may snow on you. you
8. Please tell me when ski season begins. me
9. I want to go with them to Colorado. them
10. An instructor can teach her how to snowboard. her

Using *I* and *Me*   *pages 248–249*

C. Use *I* or *me* to complete each sentence. Write each sentence.

11. _____ see rain clouds gathering over the hills. I
12. The rain is pouring down on _____ . me
13. Hold the umbrella over _____ , please. me
14. _____ like to walk on a rainy day. I
15. _____ do not mind getting damp. I
16. The wind whips around Carlos and _____ . me
17. _____ wrap my raincoat tighter. I
18. Thunder and lightning scare _____ a little. me
19. _____ will run into the house to watch the rest of the storm. I
20. My sister and ____ enjoy a good storm. I

Unit 4
Grammar Review
CHAPTER 20

Subject and
Object
Pronouns
pages 244–253

295

Unit 4
Grammar Review

CHAPTER 20

Subject and
Object
Pronouns

OBJECTIVES

- To identify subject pronouns in sentences
- To identify object pronouns in sentences
- To use *I* and *me* correctly in sentences

Unit Review
MODIFIED INSTRUCTION

BELOW-LEVEL STUDENTS Before students begin Part A, remind them that to find the subject of a sentence they can ask themselves who or what the sentence is about.

ABOVE-LEVEL STUDENTS After students have completed Part C, suggest that they create similar exercises using other subject and object pronouns such as *we/us, he/him, she/her,* and *they/them.* Have them exchange papers and complete each other's exercises.

TIP

Remind students that they can often recognize mistakes in grammar when they hear them. Have them say each choice (for example, *I* or *me*) to themselves before they choose the answer.

Unit 4
Grammar Review
CHAPTER 22

More About Pronouns

OBJECTIVES
- To identify possessive pronouns in sentences
- To choose the correct possessive pronoun for an antecedent
- To form contractions from pronouns and verbs

Unit Review
MODIFIED INSTRUCTION

BELOW-LEVEL STUDENTS Before students begin this page, post a chart of possessive pronouns, or write them on the board. For each possessive pronoun, write a sentence pair such as the following:

This ball belongs to me. It is my ball.

Leave the chart and sentence pairs in a place where students can see them.

ABOVE-LEVEL STUDENTS Ask students to rewrite the sentences in Part B so that each possessive pronoun comes before a noun. Remind students to replace the possessives and rewrite other parts of the sentences accordingly.

Possessive Pronouns
pages 262–263

A. Write the possessive pronoun in each sentence.

1. Marie loves to visit the forest near her house. her
2. Marie said, "I can see the forest from my window." my
3. Many animals make their homes there. their
4. Each animal must find all its food in the forest. its
5. The male deer depends on plants for his meals. his

More Possessive Pronouns
pages 264–265

B. Write the possessive pronoun that belongs on each line.

6. Marie sometimes thinks of the forest as _____, even though it does not belong to her. hers
7. Near the stream is the perfect place for a picnic, and Marie's family thinks of it as _____. theirs
8. Marie's dad likes tuna sandwiches, so he knows that one is _____. yours
9. The fresh fruit is mom's favorite, so it is _____. hers
10. "I will eat the peanut butter sandwich, because it is _____," Marie said. mine

Contractions with Pronouns
pages 266–267

C. Write a contraction for each word pair in parentheses ( ).

11. Marie said to Manuel, "(I am) going to the park." I'm
12. "I hope (you will) come with me," she said. you'll
13. (They had) been there many times before. They'd
14. (I would) love to go to the park," said Manuel. I'd
15. "(We have) always had fun there," he added. We've

296

TEST PREP
TIP
If students are taking a test that has several answer choices, have them cross out (either on the paper or in their minds) the choices that they know are incorrect. Then they can make their choice from the answers that are left.

Adjectives *pages 272–273*

A. For each sentence below, write the adjective or adjectives that describe the underlined noun.

1. There are several <u>kinds</u> of cats near my house. several
2. The calico has orange and brown <u>spots</u>. orange, brown
3. One old tomcat has six <u>toes</u> . six
4. The Persian <u>cat</u> has long soft fur. Persian
5. A Siamese cat has blue <u>eyes</u>. blue
6. Lions and lionesses are big <u>cats</u>. big
7. They live in wild <u>places</u> in Africa. wild
8. Tigers live in the Indian <u>jungles</u>. Indian
9. Panthers can have black or spotted <u>fur</u>. black, spotted
10. Big and little <u>cats</u> like to sleep and eat. big, little

Adjectives for *How Many*

pages 274–275

B. For each sentence, write the adjective that tells *how many*.

11. A lagoon is one place birds stop for water. one
12. Many birds migrate from the north. Many
13. They stop in several places on their journey. several
14. Some birds migrate very far. Some
15. We saw twenty Canada geese flying. twenty

Adjectives for *What Kind*

pages 276–277

C. For each sentence, write the adjective that tells *what kind*.

16. The geese have wide wings. wide
17. Small birds migrate also. Small
18. You can see big flocks resting on the water. big
19. How do migrating birds know where to fly? migrating
20. They always return to their summer homes. summer

297

OBJECTIVES
- To identify adjectives in sentences
- To identify adjectives that tell *how many*
- To identify adjectives that tell *what kind*

Unit Review
MODIFIED INSTRUCTION

BELOW-LEVEL STUDENTS Remind students that an adjective is a describing word; call on volunteers to give several examples. Also, point out that most adjectives come before the words that they describe. As students begin Part A, remind them that a noun may be described by more than one adjective.

ABOVE-LEVEL STUDENTS After students have completed Part C, have them use a thesaurus to replace the adjectives in sentences 16, 17, and 18. Remind students that they can make their writing more descriptive by choosing adjectives carefully.

Activities and exercises to help students prepare for state and standardized assessments appear on our website.

Visit
The Learning Site!
www.harcourtschool.com

Assessment

SKILLS ASSESSMENT Use the **Language Skills and Writing Assessment** to assess the grammar and writing skills taught in this unit. Model papers are included.

PORTFOLIO ASSESSMENT
Schedule portfolio conferences with individual students while others are completing the Unit Review exercises. Have students complete the Self-Assessment Checklist on page R87 and place it in their Show Portfolios. Use the Student Record Form on page R77 to monitor student progress.

Friend or Foe?

OBJECTIVES

- To research the advantages of a plant or animal that people usually dislike

- To write a paragraph and create a poster to show how the plant or animal is both helpful and harmful

INTRODUCE THE PROJECT

USE PRIOR KNOWLEDGE Read the introduction aloud to students. On the board, write *Friend* and *Foe*. Ask volunteers to name some insects they think of as "pests," or foes. Then have them name animal "friends."

GENERATE QUESTIONS Ask students to generate questions about weeds and pests. Have them write in their journals questions they might ask to determine the good and bad things about a plant or animal.

Decide on a Weed or Pest

To help students with their lists, provide science or nature magazines for them to skim.

Research the Plant or Animal

Have students use library resources, research materials in your classroom, or online encyclopedias and search engines. Have students take simple notes and then compile them into their paragraphs using a word processing program.

Unit 4
Wrap-Up

Writing Across the Curriculum: Science

Friend or Foe?

Some types of plants and animals are called "weeds" or "pests." We call them this because they cause problems or are disliked. Believe it or not, many weeds and pests can be helpful to people. The steps below will help you find out how.

Decide on a Weed or Pest

- With a group of classmates, make a list of plants or animals that people dislike.

- With the help of your teacher, select one plant or animal. Choose one that you have heard several people mention.

Research the Plant or Animal

- Why do people complain about this plant or animal?

- What harm does this plant or animal cause humans?

- Can it be used in science or as medicine by doctors?

- How does it help or hurt the environment?

- Does your research show that this plant or animal is helpful to people in some way? If not, go back to your group's list and choose a different plant or animal to research.

Report Your Discoveries

- Write a paragraph that explains how your weed or pest is both helpful and harmful. Paste it onto poster board and illustrate it. Present your poster to classmates.

298

Study Skills

USING ENCYCLOPEDIAS Have students share how they use encyclopedias to gather information on their topic. Have them name the encyclopedia they used. Then ask them to explain what steps they took to locate the information they needed. Encourage them to describe how information is organized within an entry and how that helped their search.

A Desert Scrapbook
by Virginia Wright-Frierson
NONFICTION
Learn, with the help of watercolor
pictures, about the habits of the animals
that live in the Sonoran Desert.

Tiger Lilies and Other Beastly Plants
by Elizabeth Ring
NONFICTION
Many flowers and weeds look like
animals. Discover when and where these
"animals" are found in the wild.
Outstanding Science Trade Book

Cactus Hotel
by Brenda Z. Guiberson
NONFICTION
Many desert creatures find safety in the
prickly branches of a saguaro cactus.
Notable Children's Book in the Language Arts

Report Your Discoveries

Review with students the steps of the
writing process. Encourage them to follow those steps as they write their paragraphs. Display the finished posters
around the classroom.

STUDENT SELF-ASSESSMENT

Have students evaluate their own
research and raise new questions for further investigation.

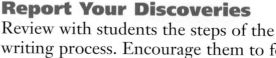 **Books to Read** Students who
enjoyed this project
might be interested in reading one or
more of these books. Have them record
reflections on the book or books in their
journals. Then ask students to recommend to the class the books from this list
that they enjoyed most.

School-Home Connection

Families can discuss the helpful
and harmful features of plants
and animals that are native to
the climate and the environment
of their areas. Students should
work with their families to make
a list of these plants and
animals.

ESL

WORD BANK Have students
make a list of five new words
they learned when they did their
research. Have them define
each word and use it in a sentence. Then have students add
the new words to their word
banks.

Cumulative Review
Unit 1

Sentences

OBJECTIVES
- To punctuate the four kinds of sentences
- To identify complete and simple subjects and predicates
- To identify complete sentences and rewrite fragments as complete sentences

Use the Cumulative Review to assess students' continued mastery of language concepts and skills presented in Units 1–4. Refer to the pages listed after each section title to review any concepts and skills students have not mastered.

UNIT 1 REVIEW

Have students complete the exercises, or modify them using these suggestions:

MODIFIED INSTRUCTION

BELOW-LEVEL STUDENTS Suggest that as students work through exercises 11–15, they identify the subject and predicate of each sentence. If they find one part of the sentence missing, they will know which part of the sentence they will need to add to make the sentence complete.

ABOVE-LEVEL STUDENTS After students have completed the exercises, have them rewrite sentence 11 as a question and sentence 15 as a statement.

Cumulative Review
Unit 1

Sentences

Sentences *pages 24–27*

Write each sentence. Add the correct end mark.

1. Mr. Montero's class visited the art museum .
2. Look at that suit of armor .
3. Isn't that stained glass window beautiful ?
4. That painting is so amazing !
5. Each student liked something different .

Subjects and Predicates
pages 34–37, 52–55

Write each sentence. Draw one line under the complete subject and two lines under the complete predicate. Then circle the simple subject and the simple predicate.

6. Our class held a photography contest.
7. Each student entered a photograph.
8. Reka's photo showed her dog asleep.
9. Tak took a picture of his twin sisters.
10. The winner received a blue ribbon.

Complete Sentences *pages 62–63*

Write *complete sentence* if the group of words is a complete sentence. If it is not a complete sentence, rewrite the group of words to make it a complete sentence. Possible responses are given.

11. A haiku is a short, simple poem. complete sentence
12. Most haiku three lines, and many of them are about nature. Most haiku have three lines, and many of them are about nature.
13. Are five, seven, and five syllables long. The lines are five, seven, and five syllables long.
14. Some haiku poets write about the seasons, but others write about animals. complete sentence
15. Would like to write a haiku? Would you like to write a haiku?

300

TIP

If students are trying to identify the different sentence types, have them look at the word order. In statements, the subject usually comes near the beginning, followed by the verb. Questions often begin with helping verbs followed by the subject. Commands begin with verbs, and the subject is often not stated. Exclamations often begin or end with a word that expresses strong feeling.

Common and Proper Nouns

pages 92–95

Write each sentence. Capitalize each proper noun.

1. mrs. garcia has taught her children safety rules. Mrs. Garcia
2. luis and carmen always cross the street at the light or in a crosswalk. Luis, Carmen
3. They wait for the crossing guard, mr. harmon. Mr. Harmon
4. They are especially careful at the corner of main street and pine street. Main Street, Pine Street
5. The children walk to patterson elementary school. Patterson Elementary School

Singular and Plural Nouns

pages 102–107

Write the plural noun or nouns in each sentence. Then write the singular form of the noun or nouns.

6. My doctor says I should eat plenty of fruits and vegetables. fruits, fruit; vegetables, vegetable
7. Sugar isn't very good for your teeth. teeth, tooth
8. It is important to get enough vitamins, minerals, and protein. vitamins, vitamin; minerals, mineral
9. Children need calcium for their bones. children, child; bones, bone
10. Vitamin A is important for eyes. eyes, eye

Verbs *pages 130–135*

Write each sentence. Underline each verb.

11. Linda is in a gymnastics class. is
12. The gymnasts perform on mats. perform
13. Some kids jump over the vaults. jump
14. Linda does cartwheels. does
15. She walks on the balance beam. walks

301

More About Nouns and Verbs

OBJECTIVES

- To identify common, proper, singular, and plural nouns and to capitalize proper nouns
- To identify verbs

UNIT 2 REVIEW

Have students complete the exercises, or modify them using these suggestions:

MODIFIED INSTRUCTION

BELOW-LEVEL STUDENTS Before students begin exercises 1–5, remind them that a common noun names any person, place, or thing. A proper noun is a name of a particular person, place, or thing. Tell students to begin by determining whether or not the noun is specific.

ABOVE-LEVEL STUDENTS After students have completed exercises 6–10, encourage them to list the singular and plural forms of as many irregular nouns as they can.

HANDS ON Activity

PLURAL AND POSSESSIVE

Write the plural forms of twenty regular nouns on separate index cards, the singular possessive forms of the same nouns on twenty more cards, and the plural possessive forms of the same nouns on twenty additional cards. Mix the cards and lay them face down. Have a pair of students take turns drawing cards and sorting them into three groups: PLURAL NOUN, SINGULAR POSSESSIVE NOUN, and PLURAL POSSESSIVE NOUN.

More About Verbs

OBJECTIVES

- To identify main verbs and helping verbs
- To use the present, past, and future tenses of regular and irregular verbs

UNIT 3 REVIEW

Have students complete the exercises, or modify them using these suggestions:

MODIFIED INSTRUCTION

BELOW-LEVEL STUDENTS Before students begin exercises 1–5, tell them that the main verb always comes after the helping verb and is often the very next word. Sometimes, a word such as *not* or *often* comes between the helping verb and main verb.

ABOVE-LEVEL STUDENTS After students have completed exercises 1–10, encourage them to rewrite each sentence in a different tense, changing, adding, or dropping as many words as necessary.

Main Verbs and Helping Verbs
pages 166–169

Write each sentence. Underline the main verb. Circle the helping verb.

1. My great-grandfather (was) born in Norway.
2. He (had) come to America at the age of eighteen.
3. He (did) not speak much English.
4. By age twenty, he (had) learned English very well.
5. Now he (is) studying Spanish.

Verb Tenses *pages 176–179, 194–199*

Choose the correct verb in parentheses ( ) to complete each sentence.

6. The first settlers (moved, will move) to my town in 1685. moved
7. Many more people (followed, will follow) them. followed
8. Over 6,000 people (live, lived) here now. live
9. The town (grew, will grow) larger in the future. will grow
10. We (will need, needed) a new school. will need

Irregular Verbs *pages 204–207*

Write the sentences. Change each underlined present-tense irregular verb to the past tense.

11. Our teacher says we should have a feast. said
12. Everyone has a dish from a different land. had
13. We eat the foods of many cultures. ate
14. My friends throw a party on Friday. threw
15. Ms. Morales comes to the party. came

302

HANDS ON Activity

PAST-TENSE PAIRS On separate index cards, write fifteen regular verbs that form the past tense by adding *ed*. Write *ed* on fifteen more index cards. On other index cards, write the irregular verbs students have learned. Mix all the cards, and place them face down. Have students play in pairs and take turns drawing cards. When a player has both a regular verb and *ed*, the cards form a pair and can be put aside. When all cards are drawn, the student with the most pairs wins.

Subject and Object Pronouns

pages 234–237, 244–247

Write each sentence. Draw one line under each subject pronoun and two lines under each object pronoun.

1. We were surprised when a snowstorm hit yesterday.
2. We were in school, and the snow started to fall.
3. When the third graders heard that school was closing early, they cheered.
4. The teacher told us to get ready to leave.
5. The children got on the buses that took them home.

Possessive Pronouns *pages 262–265*

Write each sentence. Underline the possessive pronoun.

6. My favorite animals at the zoo are the tapirs.
7. Their noses are long and thick.
8. Each tapir has his own favorite shady spot.
9. That stuffed tapir on the shelf is mine.
10. My sister left hers at Yoko's house.

Adjectives *pages 272–277*

Write each sentence. Underline each adjective.

11. Each fall the geese fly over the town.
12. Their loud honking says that winter is coming.
13. They are on their way to warm southern waters.
14. Bright cheerful chickadees stay here in winter.
15. They hop around on the icy ground.

303

Pronouns and Adjectives

OBJECTIVES
- To identify subject pronouns and object pronouns
- To identify possessive pronouns
- To identify adjectives

UNIT 4 REVIEW

Have students complete the exercises, or modify them using these suggestions:

MODIFIED INSTRUCTION

BELOW-LEVEL STUDENTS Before students begin exercises 1–10, post a chart listing subject, object, and possessive pronouns, or write the lists on the board so students can refer to them.

ABOVE-LEVEL STUDENTS After students have completed exercises 1–10, have them draw lines from the pronouns in sentences 3, 5, and 8 to the noun each pronoun replaces, or its antecedent.

TEST PREP

TIP

If students are taking a test and need to identify possessive pronouns, remind them that possessive pronouns are sometimes confused with pronoun contractions, which contain apostrophes. Although possessive nouns have apostrophes, possessive pronouns do not.

Language Use

OBJECTIVES
• To recognize correctly written sentences
• To practice using standardized test format

STANDARDIZED TEST PREP

The format used on this page helps prepare students for standardized tests. Explain that most standardized tests have one or more sections that test language skills—grammar, usage, capitalization, and punctuation. Have students read the directions on page 304 silently and work to complete the test items independently. When students have finished, invite them to discuss these questions:

1. **How well did you understand the directions?**

2. **Which answers were you unsure of, and why?**

3. **How did you use the test-taking strategy from Chapter 20?**

Language Use
Read the passage and choose the word or group of words that belongs in each space. Mark the letter for your answer.

> Rain (1) fall on the desert very often. When it (2), the whole desert (3) in flowers. The (4) colors are bright and vivid. Desert animals (5) need much water. Desert plants (6) also able to grow with little water. Some plants (7) water in (8) stems.

1   **A** doesn't   A
    B don't
    C do not
    D do

2   **F** do
    G does   G
    H will do
    J don't

3   **A** explode
    B will exploded
    C explodes   C
    D exploded

4   **F** flowers
    G flower's
    H flowers'   H
    J flowerses

5   **A** don't   A
    B doesn't
    C does not
    D didn't

6   **F** is
    G am
    H was
    J are   J

7   **A** stores
    B has stored
    C storing
    D store   D

8   **F** their   F
    G they're
    H there
    J they

Written Expression

Use this paragraph to answer questions 1–4.

> In *My Side of the Mountain*, author Jean Craighead George tells the story of Sam, a boy who runs away to the Catskill Mountains. Sam wants to live on his own for a while. He makes new friends, tames a falcon, and finds a home for himself inside a hollow tree.

1 Which of these sentences would go best after the last sentence in this paragraph?

   A Sam needs to be with his family.

   B The falcon's name is Frightful.

   C Sam learns a lot about nature and about himself. C

2 Why was this paragraph written?

   F To persuade you to do something

   G To tell about a book G

   H To tell how to do something

3 Which of these sentences would not belong in the paragraph?

   A Jean Craighead George writes many books.

   B Sam learns how to cook and eat wild plants.

   C Sam makes it through a hard winter alone. A

4 Choose the best topic sentence for this paragraph.

   F I had never read a book by Jean Craighead George.

   G Living in a tree can be fun.

   H *My Side of the Mountain* is an exciting book. H

305

Written Expression

OBJECTIVES

- To identify the purpose of a passage
- To choose the best order of sentences in a paragraph
- To practice using standardized test format

STANDARDIZED TEST PREP

Explain that some standardized tests include a section that tests written expression. The test items may not include actual errors. Many items ask for the *best* or *most appropriate way* to express or organize ideas.

Have students read the directions on page 305 silently and complete the test items independently. When students have finished, invite them to discuss their answer choices. If there is disagreement about an answer choice, have volunteers explain their thinking.

Assessment Strategies and Resources

FORMAL ASSESSMENT

If you want to know more about a student's mastery of the language and writing skills taught in Unit 4, **then** administer the first *Language Skills and Writing Assessment* for Unit 4. The test consists of two parts:

Language Skills: **pronouns, subject and object pronouns, possessive pronouns, adjectives,** and **effective sentences**

Writing Task: Write an **advantages and disadvantages essay**. Scoring guidelines and model student papers are included.

INFORMAL ASSESSMENT TOOLS

Using Student Self-Assessment
If you want to encourage students to take responsibility for their own learning, **then** provide frequent opportunities for student self-assessment. Monitor and support students in developing self-assessment strategies.

In portfolio conferences, ask questions that allow students to reflect on their own development as writers. For example, have them identify specific areas of improvement since your last conference.

Encourage students to use the questions and ideas in the Reflecting on Your Writing feature in each unit to think about their own writing. Discuss rubrics and perhaps model applying them. Guide students in developing their own self-assessment questions.

Have students use the self-assessment checklists on pages R86–R88 to assess their speaking and listening skills and writing skills.

Informal Assessment Reminder
If you used the preinstruction writing prompt suggested in Teaching Grammar from Writing, **then** remember to compare the results with the writing done by students after the grammar and writing instruction.

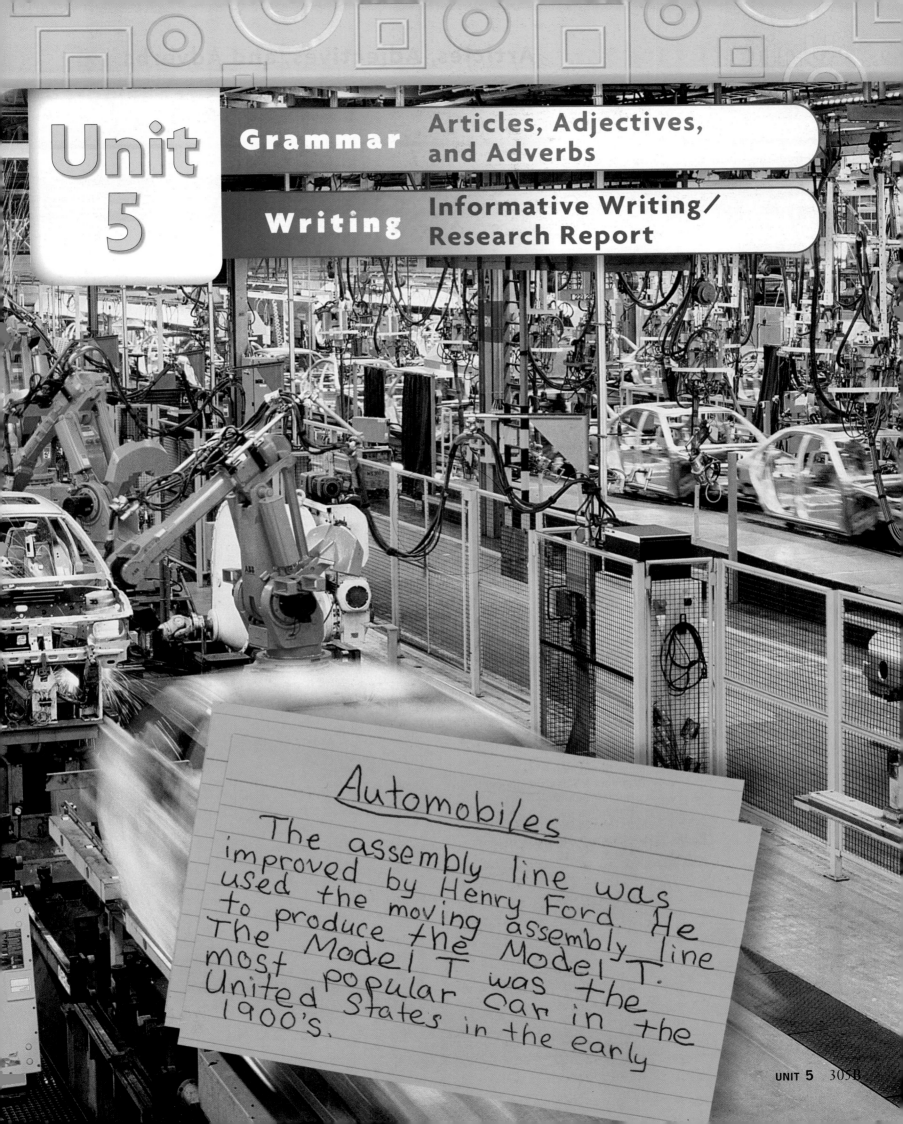

Unit 5

Grammar Articles, Adjectives, and Adverbs

Writing Informative Writing/ Research Report

Automobiles

The assembly line was improved by Henry Ford. He used the moving assembly line to produce the Model T. The Model T was the most popular car in the United States in the early 1900's.

Unit 5

Grammar • Articles, Adjectives, and Adverbs
Writing • Informative Writing/Research Report

Introducing the Unit, pp. 306–307

Chapters	Grammar	Writing	Listening/ Speaking/Viewing
25			
More About Adjectives pp. 308–317	**Articles** **Adjectives That Compare** **Usage and Mechanics: Avoiding Incorrect Comparisons** Extra Practice, Chapter Review, Daily Language Practice, Additional Practice: p. 470	**Writing Connections** Art Vivid Adjectives Comparison Postcard	**Activities** Challenge: Fair Poster Building Oral Grammar Summarize
26			
Adverbs pp. 318–327	**Adverbs** **More About Adverbs** **Grammar-Writing Connection: Comparing with Adverbs** Extra Practice, Chapter Review, Daily Language Practice, Additional Practice: p. 471	**Writing Connections** Conversation Persuasive Words Social Studies Art	**Activities** Building Oral Grammar Challenge: Write an Announcement Group Note-Taking Summarize
27			
Writer's Craft: Organizing Information pp. 328–335	**Daily Language Practice** **Hands-on Activities**	**Paragraph of Information** Prewriting and Drafting Editing Sharing and Reflecting	**Activities** A Heart for Art Analyze Informative Writing **Listening and Speaking:** Outlines for Oral Presentations Summarize
28			
More About Adverbs and Adjectives pp. 336–345	**Adjective or Adverb?** **Adverb Placement in Sentences** **Usage and Mechanics: Using Good and Well, Bad and Badly** Extra Practice, Chapter Review, Daily Language Practice, Additional Practice: p. 472	**Writing Connections** Recording Ideas Main Idea and Details Social Studies Friendly Letter	**Activities** **Listening and Speaking:** Find Examples ESL: Complete the Phrases Make a Word Picture Challenge: Mystery Visit Building Oral Grammar Summarize
29			
Easily Confused Words pp. 346–355	**Homophones** **More Homophones** **Grammar-Writing Connection: Homographs and Other Homophones** Extra Practice, Chapter Review, Daily Language Practice, Additional Practice: p. 473	**Writing Connections** Art Survey Record Responses Summarize	**Activities** Challenge: Picture Cards **Listening and Speaking:** Stand Up Building Oral Grammar Summarize
30			
Writing Workshop: Research Report pp. 356–373	**Unit 5 Grammar Review** **Daily Language Practice**	**Research Report** Prewriting Drafting Revising Proofreading Publishing Writer's Craft: Organizing Information	**Activities** Reading Like a Writer Read and Respond to the Model **Listening and Speaking:** Oral Reports Summarize

Unit Wrap-Up Writing Across the Curriculum: Social Studies, pp. 374–375

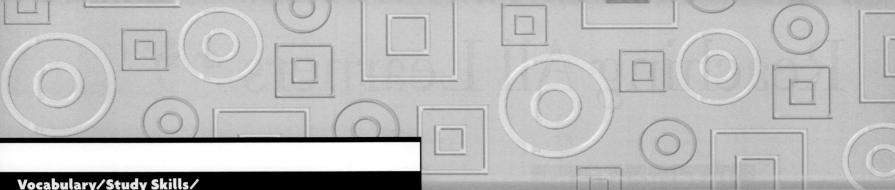

Vocabulary/Study Skills/ Technology/ Handwriting

Vocabulary Power

Words of the Week: *agricultural, natural,* **rural,** *rustic, undeveloped*
Writing Connection: Vivid Adjectives
Vocabulary: Synonyms and Antonyms

Vocabulary Power

Words of the Week: *medical,* **career,** *legal, entertainment, athletic*
Study Skills: Taking Notes and Making an Outline

Vocabulary Power

Words of the Week: *current,* **draft,** *haul, outline, recruit*
Challenge: Onward with Outlines
Study Skills: Outlines for Study

Vocabulary Power

Words of the Week: *coyote,* **fiesta,** *piñata, plaza, tortilla*
Challenge: Community Fact Sheet
ESL: Make a Word Picture
Challenge: Promotional Film
Technology: Interviewing to Learn About Your Community

Vocabulary Power

Words of the Week: *company,* **enterprise,** *project, undertaking, venture*
ESL: Matching Game
Challenge: Word Charts
      Glossary

Vocabulary Power

Words of the Week: **visible,** *vision, visor, vista, visual*
Handwriting
Technology: Giving a Multimedia Presentation

- **Brainstorm** and list adjectives with a friend. Individually try to **write** a synonym and an antonym for each adjective. Together, use the synonyms and antonyms to compare and contrast nouns. WRITING/SPEAKING/LISTENING

- **Begin** a story with a sentence that contains an adverb. Take turns with a friend **writing** sentences that add details. Use adverbs in your sentences. WRITING

- **Read** a paragraph about an interesting topic in a social studies book. **Outline** the paragraph. Use your outline to **tell** a friend about the topic. WRITING/SPEAKING/LISTENING

- **Create** silly sentences using homophones. **Share** your sentences with a friend. Ask the friend to spell each **homophone** used in your sentences. WRITING/SPEAKING/LISTENING

- **Write** sentences that compare a horse and a turtle. Use the correct comparison forms of **adjectives** and **adverbs.** WRITING

Technology — Resources

Grammar Jingles™ **CD**
Grammar Practice and Assessment **CD-ROM**
Writing Express **CD-ROM**
Media Literacy and Communication Skills **Package**
Visit *The Learning Site!*
   www.harcourtschool.com

Reaching All Learners

Intervention

INTEREST JOURNALS Interest journals invite students to exchange ideas. The journals are shared by all students in the class. Students who are otherwise reluctant to read and write are often highly motivated to participate in this activity. Because they want others to read and respond to their messages, they are motivated to develop and improve their grammar and writing skills.

- Have the class brainstorm a list of topics.

- Designate a separate notebook for each topic.

- Establish a time for journal writing and rules to prevent students from monopolizing topics.

- Encourage students to include drawings with captions, charts, and graphic organizers.

English as a Second Language

FAMILY LITERACY Family literacy programs involve family members in shared literacy activities with their children. Such programs encourage students to use literacy at home and provide a means for families to support students' literacy and academic achievements. The following Web sites provide further information.

- The Family Literacy Foundation offers information in English and Spanish. **www.read2kids.org**

- The National Clearinghouse for ESL Literacy Education provides a newsletter and other services. **www.cal.org/NCLE/**

- The National Center for Family Literacy offers information on family literacy and related topics: **www.famlit.org**

Challenge

PARAPHRASING The following activities teach students to paraphrase effectively while extending their listening and writing skills. Begin by reading aloud one or two sentences. Have students write down in their own words what they heard. As they become more proficient, increase the length of the passages. Next, have them take notes as you present facts about content area topics or subjects of interest. Students then work from their notes to paraphrase the information. As a final step, give students copies of an appropriate article to rewrite in their own words. Have them compare their versions and discuss differences in the ways different students paraphrased the same material.

Inclusion

PROMOTING LITERACY Use foresight and creativity to include students with hearing or visual impairments in literacy events. Hearing students are often eager to learn sign language. You might help them do a search for helpful Web sites, or you may purchase videos or display posters that students can refer to as needed. Encourage the use of signing to include hearing impaired students in read-alouds, literature circles, book clubs, and drama, as well as the daily life of the classroom.

In addition to braille and large-print items, think of ways to provide tactile support for visually impaired students. For example, prepare a box of dolls, toys, or other related items that students can handle to help them understand characters and important items in a story.

Teaching Grammar from Writing

PRETEST
If you wish to use students' writing to diagnose their grammar instruction needs, use the following prompt.

WRITING PROMPT
Think of an interesting topic that you have learned about in social studies. Reread the pages in your text that tell about that topic. Then write two or more paragraphs to explain the topic in your own words.

EVALUATE AND PLAN
Analyze students' writing to determine how you can best meet their individual needs for instruction. Use the following chart to identify and remedy problems.

COMMON PROBLEMS	CHAPTERS TO USE
Using incorrect comparisons with adjectives	Chapter 25: More About Adjectives
Using incorrect comparisons with adverbs	Chapter 26: Adverbs
Misusing *good* and *well*, *bad* and *badly*	Chapter 28: More About Adverbs and Adjectives
Confusing homophones	Chapter 29: Easily Confused Words
Organizing written information poorly	Chapter 27: Writer's Craft: Organizing Information
Difficulty writing a research report	Chapter 30: Writing a Research Report

Classroom Management

DURING...	SOME STUDENTS CAN...
Grammar Reteaching	Work on the Writing Across the Curriculum project. Use the Challenge Activity cards.
Independent Practice	Work at stations. Begin the Writing Connection.
Portfolio Conferences	Participate in peer conferences. Complete Student Self-Assessment forms. (See pages R86–R88 in this *Teacher's Edition*.)

Technology

LANGUAGE ARTS IN THE CLASSROOM

The possibilities for technology as a learning tool grow daily. Fortunately, you don't need the latest, most expensive equipment to take advantage of technology. Students can learn both *with* and *about* technology through relatively simple classroom routines and tools.

COMPUTER RULES At or next to the Computer Station post a set of rules for computer use and for courtesy in sharing the computer with others. Have a student volunteer make a chart telling how to turn the computer on and off, how to save work that has been done, and how to label a file. Also post a list of Internet Safety rules. (See the Handbook in the *Pupil Edition*.)

COMPUTER REFERENCES AND SUPPLIES Near the Computer Station, keep CD-ROMs, disks, and printing paper on hand. Make sure that a current manual or printed instructions for computer use are available.

REFERENCE BOOKCASE Keep a print encyclopedia and other reference books related to student research reports in this bookcase. Students can store materials they have borrowed from the school library here so that items do not get lost and are available for classroom research.

VIDEO VIEWING AREA If a television and VCR are available, set up a spot for students to use them for research. Provide earphones for private viewing. Post a schedule and time limits for using this resource. Set up chairs, rugs, or cushions in a semicircle where students can sit as they watch. A small table or a shelf can hold note-taking materials, such as paper, pencils, and pens.

MULTIMEDIA PRESENTATION SPACE Create a space for students to present multimedia reports. Provide an overhead projector and a screen or a VCR, as needed. Be sure there are adequate outlets for cassette players and other equipment. Provide extension cords if needed. A rolling cart can be used to move equipment.

Hands-on Activities

Charting Comparisons

MATERIALS: chart paper with pairs of pictures from magazines or other sources, markers

DIRECTIONS:

1. Prepare and display several sheets of chart paper, each with two pictures at the top. The pictures should show items of the same type, such as two chairs or two dogs, but with obvious differences.

2. Have students think of adjectives that compare the two items. Provide markers so that students can write the adjectives below the pictures.

Pet Show Awards

MATERIALS: construction paper, scissors, glue, markers, other art materials

DIRECTIONS:

1. Have students work in small groups. Tell them to pretend they are planning a pet show.

2. Students decide on and list six categories for prizes. Explain that the name of each category should include a comparative adjective that tells about more than two nouns.

3. Have students use art materials to create prize ribbons for each of their six categories.

Adverb Search

MATERIALS: passage from a book, chart paper, pencils or markers

DIRECTIONS:

1. Choose a passage that most students can read easily and that includes six or more adverbs.

2. Have students work in small groups. Provide a book or a copy of the passage for each group. Have each group make a chart like the one shown here. They may add as many rows as needed, according to the number of adverbs in the passage.

3. Students must locate the adverbs in the passage, record them in the chart, and make a check mark in the appropriate column to indicate whether the adverb tells how, when, or where.

Adverb	How	When	Where

Audience and Purpose

MATERIALS: chart paper, pencils or markers

DIRECTIONS:

1. Have students meet in small groups to explore the concepts of adjective and purpose in regard to their writing.

2. List several different writing forms on the board. Students discuss and identify at least one possible purpose and audience for each type of writing.

3. Have students develop a chart or other form of graphic organizer to share the results of their discussion.

letter
set of directions
report
story

All Well and Good

MATERIALS: a set of four cards (*good, well, bad, badly*) for each pair of students

DIRECTIONS:

1. Distribute *good* and *well* cards to each pair of students. Each partner holds one of the cards.

2. Have students listen as you read aloud a sentence, omitting the word *good* or *well*.

3. Reread the sentence and have students confer with their partners to decide which card to show.

4. After students have responded to four or six sentences, repeat the same sentences. This time students hold up either the *bad* or *badly* card.

Ha Ha Homophones

MATERIALS: writing paper, pencils, construction paper, markers, hole punch, yarn

DIRECTIONS:

1. Challenge students to make up tongue twisters using homophones or homographs.

2. Give some examples to get them started: **Six silly sailors set out to see the sea. Triceratops trips over trees on his trips to town.**

3. Students might choose to work individually, in pairs, or in small groups.

4. Have students copy each of their tongue twisters onto a separate sheet of construction paper. Then have them punch holes along the side of each sheet and compile the sheets into a book by looping a piece of yarn through each hole and tying a knot.

Tongue Twisters

Fernando's Gift

BY DOUGLAS KEISTER

MY NAME IS FERNANDO VANEGAS [fer• nän´dō vä• nä´gäs], and I live deep inside the rain forest in Costa Rica. My father, Jubilio [hoo• bē´lē• ō], built our house himself. The walls are wood, and the roof is made of tin. At night, the sound of the rain on the roof sings me to sleep.

Before breakfast each morning, while my mother, Cecilia [sā• sē´lē ä], gives my little sister, Evelyn, her bath, the men in my family gather on the porch and talk. Sometimes my grandfather, Raphael Dias [rä• fä• el´ dē´äs], tells us stories. Even our two dogs seem to listen! I hear that in some other places, they give dogs special names, just like people. We call our dogs Brown Dog and Black Dog.

My father says that he will spend most of the day tending our crop of achiote [ä• chē• ō´tä], a plant that's used to make red dye. Other days, my father spends his time planting trees. He also has a job teaching people about the rain forest.

When it's time for breakfast, my father milks the cow, and my mother and Evelyn chop onions to flavor our meal. This morning we're having rice and beans. If I'm not too full, I might have a banana, too. They grow right outside our house—all I have to do is pick one!

After breakfast, I go to school. It's not very far—only about three miles from our house. Often my grandfather and the dogs walk with me. Grandfather knows everything about the rain forest and what to look for along the way: fruits and nuts, insects and lizards, beautiful flowers, maybe even a bright red parrot. This morning he wants to show me a family of squirrel monkeys. They're not easy to find anymore. Grandfather says that when he was a child, there were many monkeys in the rain forest.

Grandfather spots a squirrel monkey at last. He says it's a full-grown adult, even though it's very tiny. Suddenly we hear howler monkeys barking in the treetops above us. The dogs bark right back. The rain forest can be a noisy place sometimes!

My school is in the village of Londres [lōn´drās]. Sometimes our teacher, Mr. Cordova [kôr• dō´vä], holds class outside. Today is a special day at school. It's my friend Carmina's [kär• mē´näs] eighth birthday. I want to give her a present, but I haven't decided on one yet.

Building Background

Tell students that Costa Rica is a country in Central America between Nicaragua and Panama. If possible, display a globe or a world map and have students locate Costa Rica. Explain that tropical rain forests in Central America have warm, moist climates that support plant and animal life unique to those areas. Have students tell what they know about rain forests and efforts to save them.

Determine a Purpose for Listening

Tell students that this selection describes a friendship between a boy and a girl who live in the rain forest. Ask students to determine whether their purpose for listening is

• to solve problems.

• to gain information. (to gain information)

• to be persuaded to do something.

After school, Carmina and I go fishing. We have a favorite place—a small stream that flows into the big river, Rio Naranjo [rē´ō nä•rän´hō]. On our way to the stream, we see friends from school diving into the cool river waters. We fish for a while, but there are no trout today. We'll have to have something else for supper.

Carmina wants to show me her favorite climbing tree. It's called a cristobal [krēs• tō´bäl]—and it's a very old one. Carmina's grandfather used to play in it, too, when he was our age. But when we get there, we see that someone has cut the tree down. Who would do such a thing? Maybe my grandfather knows the answer.

Grandfather explains that people have been cutting down trees in the rain forest for many years. Often they don't understand the harm they are doing. He tells us that when trees are cut down, animals no longer have a place to live. Trees also help to keep the soil from washing away. Grandfather says that this is why my father's job planting trees and teaching people about the rain forest is so important. Suddenly I know what I will give Carmina for her birthday.

My father has a plant nursery with lots of small cristobal trees in it. If I do some chores for him, he will give me one. That will be Carmina's birthday gift. I decide to let her choose the tree she wants. Then Carmina asks my father if he knows of a place in the rain forest where her tree will be safe.

My father and I know a secret spot deep in the rain forest, near a waterfall. It's a long way, even on horseback. No one else seems to know about it. Carmina's tree should be safe there.

After riding for many miles, we reach our secret spot. Carmina and I plant the little tree together. We make a wish that it will be safe and live a long, long time.

Now, my father and I go to our secret spot whenever we can. Often Carmina comes with us. We may fish or swim or play under the waterfall, but our visits always end with a picnic at Carmina's tree. On our way home, we are happy knowing that it grows tall and strong.

Listening Comprehension

LISTEN FOR ORGANIZED FACTS AND DETAILS

Have students listen for information about the rain forest as you read the selection aloud. Ask them to take notes that include facts and details from the story. Tell them that note-taking will help them learn about the plants and animals that live in this rain forest.

Start an outline on the board and show students how to organize notes for nonfiction information.

I. Rain Forest in Costa Rica
   A. Wooden houses
   B. Fruits, nuts, insects, flowers
   C. Rare monkeys

PERSONAL RESPONSE *What would your secret spot be like if you had one?* (Responses will vary. Students may talk about special rooms, places in nature, or pretend secret hide-a-ways.) *Would you like to live in the rain forest? Why or why not?* (Possible responses: Yes; I want to learn about a new way of life. No; it may be too hot and too wet.) CRITICAL: EXPRESS PERSONAL OPINIONS

Unit 5

Grammar Articles, Adjectives, and Adverbs

Writing Informative Writing

Introducing the Unit

ORAL LANGUAGE/VIEWING

DISCUSS THE IMAGES Have students look at the photograph of the factory. Then have them brainstorm some topics that relate to factories. (Possible responses: automobile factories, assembly lines) Explain that these topics could be the basis for a research report. Have students think about where they might find information for a research report. Ask them these questions:

1. **If you were writing about the history of the automobile, where might you look for information?** (Possible responses: reference books, the Internet)

2. **Where can you get the most current information on a topic?** (Possible responses: television, the Internet)

3. **Where might you look to research songs about cars?** (Possible responses: a music library, a music store)

Writer's Journal
ENCOURAGE STUDENTS' QUESTIONS Have students reflect on different sources of information. Encourage students to develop questions for discussion. Have them write their questions and selected responses in their journals.

Unit 5

Grammar Articles, Adjectives, and Adverbs

Writing Informative Writing Research Report

306

Viewing and Representing
. . . .

COMPARE/CONTRAST PRINT AND VISUAL MEDIA Ask students to pick an important news story from the newspaper that might be the basis for an interesting research report. Have them take notes on the information provided in the news article. Then ask them to watch for a story on the same topic on the nightly news and take notes on the information given in that story. Have students compare the information given in the two news sources.

For evaluation criteria for viewing, see the Viewing Checklist, page R88.

MEDIA LITERACY AND COMMUNICATION SKILLS PACKAGE Use the video to extend students' oral and visual literacy. See *Teacher's Guide* page 6–7.

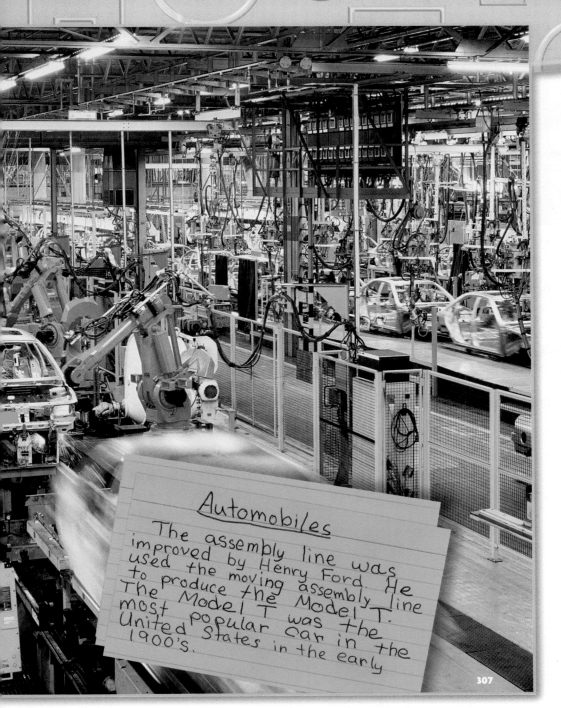

Automobiles

The assembly line was improved by Henry Ford. He used the moving assembly line to produce the Model T. The Model T was the most popular car in the United States in the early 1900's.

Have students look over the list of unit contents and note the grammar topics that are covered. Ask them to give examples of adjectives and adverbs. Discuss what students may already know about these grammar topics. Then point out that students will be writing a paragraph of information and a research report in Unit 5. Explain that they will also learn about choosing a topic, taking notes, and organizing a report.

SOCIAL STUDIES CONNECTION Students will explore a variety of social studies topics in this unit:

- Rural Communities
- Neighborhood Roles
- Community Origins
- Market and Trade

School-Home Connection

You may want to use School-Home Connection 5, page R96.

LESSON ORGANIZER	DAY 1	DAY 2
DAILY LANGUAGE PRACTICE TRANSPARENCIES 57, 58	1. Our farm is home to many goat's. (goats.) 2. goats are very sweet creatures and their milk makes good cheese. (Goats; creatures,) **Bridge to Writing** Baby goats are <u>(adjective)</u> .	1. I has farmed this land for many years. (have) 2. tomorrow we bought a new tractor. (Tomorrow; will buy) **Bridge to Writing** <u>(Article)</u> new tractor might be red.
ORAL WARM-UP **Listening/Speaking**	Describe Farms 308	Use Comparative Words 310 *Grammar Jingles™* CD Track 17
TEACH/MODEL **GRAMMAR** **KEY** ✔ = tested skill	✔ **ARTICLES** 308–309 • To identify and use articles correctly • To create a poster and to write persuasive sentences, using articles correctly	✔ **ADJECTIVES THAT COMPARE** 310–311 • To recognize and use adjectives that compare • To write sentences, using adjectives that compare
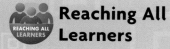 **Reaching All Learners**	**Modified Instruction** Below-Level: Identify Nouns Above-Level: Explain Choices **Reteach:** *Reteach Activities Copying Masters* pp. 49 and R54 **Challenge:** Activity Card 17, R70 *ESL Manual* pp. 120, 121 *Practice Book* p. 81	**Modified Instruction** Below-Level: Explain Comparisons Above-Level: Use Adjectives **ESL:** Using *Good* and *Bad* *ESL Manual* pp. 120, 122 **Reteach:** *Reteach Activities Copying Masters* pp. 50 and R54 **Challenge:** Choosing Animals 311 *Practice Book* p. 82
WRITING	Writing Connection 309 Art	Writing Connection 311 Writer's Craft: Vivid Adjectives
CROSS-CURRICULAR/ ENRICHMENT	*Vocabulary Power* Explore Word Meaning 308 agricultural, natural, **rural**, rustic, undeveloped *See Vocabulary Power book.*	*Vocabulary Power* Classify and Categorize 308 *Vocabulary Power* p. 73 📺 **Vocabulary activity**

WRITING ACTIVITIES
Writing Express **CD-ROM**

Visit *The Learning Site:*
www.harcourtschool.com

DAY 3	DAY 4	DAY 5
1. Him's produce was for sale at the market. (His; market.) 2. The city people am glad to buy fresh produce. (are) **Bridge to Writing** I think that apples taste <u>(adjective)</u> than pears.	1. Ginny and me is going to visit her uncle on his farm. (I are) 2. She couldnt wait until her visit begun. (couldn't; began.) **Bridge to Writing** Uncle Walter is my <u>(adjective)</u> uncle.	1. The farm have a big red Barn. (has; barn.) 2. Horses and cowes lives in the barn. (cows live) **Bridge to Writing** <u>(Article)</u> spotted cow moos loudly. She is <u>(comparative adjective)</u> than the other cows.
Discuss Comparative Adjectives 312 *Grammar Jingles*™ CD Track 17	Suggest Adjectives 314	
✔ **AVOIDING INCORRECT COMPARISONS** 312–313 • To recognize and form comparative adjectives correctly • To record a list and write sentences that compare	**EXTRA PRACTICE** 314–315 • To identify and use articles and comparative adjectives • To use adjectives that compare in a written note 💻 **Practice and assessment**	**TEST PREP** **CHAPTER REVIEW** 316 • To review articles and adjectives that compare • To demonstrate knowledge of synonyms and antonyms 💻 **Test preparation**
Modified Instruction Below-Level: Count Syllables Above-Level: Change Adjectives **Reteach:** *Reteach Activities Copying Masters* pp. 51 and R54 **Challenge:** Write a Letter 313 *ESL Manual* pp. 120, 123 *Practice Book* p. 83	**Building Oral Grammar** Listen for Adjectives 315 **Challenge:** Fair Poster 315 *ESL Manual* pp. 120, 124 *Practice Book* p. 84	**Challenge:** Using Vivid Words 317 *Practice Book* p. 85 *ESL Manual* pp. 120, 125
Writing Connection 313 Writer's Journal: Write a Comparison	Writing Connection 315 Real-Life Writing: Postcard	Writing Application 317 Create a Word Bank
Social Studies: Map 312 *Vocabulary Power* Compare and Contrast 308 *Vocabulary Power* p. 74 💻 **Vocabulary activity**	**Hands-On Activity:** Comparison Shuffle 314 *Vocabulary Power* Synonyms and Antonyms 308 *Vocabulary Power* p. 75 💻 **Vocabulary activity**	**Vocabulary:** Synonyms and Antonyms 317 *Vocabulary Power* Context Clues 308

Articles

OBJECTIVES

- To identify and use articles correctly
- To create a poster and to write persuasive sentences, using articles correctly

DAILY LANGUAGE PRACTICE

TRANSPARENCY 57

1 Our farm is home to many goat's.
(goats)

2 goats are very sweet creatures and their milk makes good cheese.
(Goats; creatures,)

BRIDGE TO WRITING Baby goats are
<u>(adjective)</u> .

ORAL WARM-UP

USE PRIOR KNOWLEDGE Ask students to name adjectives that tell *what kind* or *how many* about farms. Explain that the words *a*, *an*, and *the* also tell about nouns.

TEACH/MODEL

Have students read the explanation and examples on page 308. Point out that in the second set of example sentences, the words following the articles begin with a vowel sound. Therefore, the article used must be *an*. Stress that *a* and *an* are used to indicate "any," while *the* is used to indicate a particular noun.

Work through the rest of the Guided Practice orally with students.

Vocabulary Power

ru•ral [rŏŏr′əl] *adj.*
Belonging to or happening in the country rather than in a city.

308

Articles

The words *a*, *an*, and *the* are called **articles**.

Articles are a special group of adjectives. You know that an adjective describes a noun or pronoun. Use *a* before singular nouns and adjectives that begin with a consonant sound.

> **Examples:**
> A farmer and her family live there.   *A, farmer*
> They live in a rural area.   *a, rural*

Use *an* before singular nouns and adjectives that begin with a vowel sound.

> **Examples:**
> An orchard is near Centerville.   *An, orchard*
> It is an old apple orchard.   *an, old*

Use *the* before singular and plural nouns.

> **Examples:**
> The countryside is beautiful.   *The, countryside*
> The towns are far from each other.   *The, towns*

Guided Practice

A. Read each sentence. Choose the correct article. Be able to explain your choice.

> **Example:** (The, An) farmer raises crops.
> *The*

> **1.** Her crops are planted in (<u>the</u>, a) spring.
> **2.** (<u>The</u>, An) crops need rain to grow.
> **3.** Crops also need (an, <u>a</u>) warm temperature.
> **4.** There is (a, <u>an</u>) orchard on the farm.
> **5.** Peaches grow in (a, <u>the</u>) orchard.

Vocabulary Power

DAY 1 EXPLORE WORD MEANING Introduce and define *rural*. Write it on the board. **Do any of you live in a rural area? How do you know?**

DAY 2 CLASSIFY AND CATEGORIZE Write on the board: *rural, field, sidewalk, pasture.* **Which word does not belong?** (See also *Vocabulary Power*, page 73.)

DAY 3 COMPARE AND CONTRAST Have students name things they might see in a rural area. Then ask: **What are some things you might see in a city?** (See also *Vocabulary Power*, page 74.)

DAY 4 SYNONYMS AND ANTONYMS **The words *rural* and *country* mean almost the same, so they are synonyms. What is the opposite of *rural*? Rural and city are antonyms.** (See also *Vocabulary Power*, page 75.)

DAY 5 CONTEXT CLUES Say: **The farm was the only building in the rural area. What words in this sentence help explain the meaning of *rural*?**

Independent Practice

B. Write each sentence. Use the correct article or articles. Be ready to explain your choices.

Example: Turnips are (the, a) root crop.
Turnips are a root crop.

6. Turnips grow well in (<u>the</u>, a) winter.
7. (The, An) turnip once was used as food for animals.
8. Hay is now (<u>a</u>, an) common food for animals.
9. Some hay comes from (an, <u>a</u>) grass called alfalfa.
10. Alfalfa is left on (<u>the</u>, a) ground to dry.
11. Dried alfalfa becomes (<u>the</u>, a) hay.
12. Straw is made from (<u>the</u>, a) stems of wheat.
13. Straw is used for (a, <u>an</u>) animal's bedding.
14. Then some straw is put into (<u>the</u>, a) soil.
15. As (an, <u>a</u>) result, (<u>the</u>, an) soil becomes good for planting crops.

Remember

to use *a* before a singular noun or adjective beginning with a consonant sound and *an* before a singular noun or adjective beginning with a vowel sound. Use *the* before singular and plural nouns.

Writing Connection

Art Why might a person from a city want to visit a farm? Make a poster about a rural community. Try to get people from cities to visit that community. Trade posters with a classmate. Circle all the articles in the poster. Make sure your partner used *a, an,* and *the* correctly.

309

Independent Practice

Have students complete the Independent Practice, or modify it using these suggestions:

MODIFIED INSTRUCTION

BELOW-LEVEL STUDENTS For each sentence, have students identify the noun that the article describes and tell whether it is singular or plural.

ABOVE-LEVEL STUDENTS Ask students to explain why the article they did not choose for each example is incorrect.

Writing Connection

Art Before students begin to draw pictures, have them work with a partner to brainstorm reasons why a city person might enjoy visiting a farm. Remind students that the sentences they write should persuade their audience. Encourage students to use vivid adjectives to describe farms.

WRAP-UP/ASSESS

SUMMARIZE Ask students to explain how to decide when to use *a, an,* and *the.*

RETEACH

REACHING ALL LEARNERS

INTERVENTION Lessons in **visual, auditory,** and **kinesthetic** modalities: p. R54 and *Reteach Activities Copying Masters,* p. 49.

PRACTICE page 81

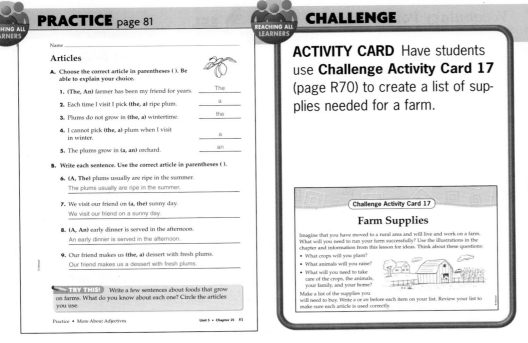

Name _____

Articles

A. Choose the correct article in parentheses ( ). Be able to explain your choice.

1. **(The, An)** farmer has been my friend for years. _The_
2. Each time I visit I pick **(the, a)** ripe plum. _a_
3. Plums do not grow in **(the, a)** wintertime. _the_
4. I cannot pick **(the, a)** plum when I visit in winter. _a_
5. The plums grow in **(a, an)** orchard. _an_

B. Write each sentence. Use the correct article in parentheses ( ).

6. **(A, The)** plums usually are ripe in the summer.
The plums usually are ripe in the summer.
7. We visit our friend on **(a, the)** sunny day.
We visit our friend on a sunny day.
8. **(A, An)** early dinner is served in the afternoon.
An early dinner is served in the afternoon.
9. Our friend makes us **(the, a)** dessert with fresh plums.
Our friend makes us a dessert with fresh plums.

TRY THIS! Write a few sentences about foods that grow on farms. What do you know about each one? Circle the articles you use.

Practice • More About Adjectives   Unit 5 • Chapter 25 **81**

CHALLENGE

ACTIVITY CARD Have students use **Challenge Activity Card 17** (page R70) to create a list of supplies needed for a farm.

Challenge Activity Card 17

Farm Supplies

Imagine that you have moved to a rural area and will live and work on a farm. What will you need to run your farm successfully? Use the illustrations in the chapter and information from this lesson for ideas. Think about these questions:
• What crops will you plant?
• What animals will you raise?
• What will you need to take care of the crops, the animals, your family, and your home?
Make a list of the supplies you will need to buy. Write *a* or *an* before each item on your list. Review your list to make sure each article is used correctly.

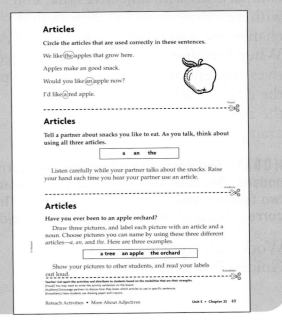

Articles

Circle the articles that are used correctly in these sentences.

We like(the)apples that grow here.

Apples make an good snack.

Would you like(an)apple now?

I'd like(a)red apple.

- ✂

Articles

Tell a partner about snacks you like to eat. As you talk, think about using all three articles.

| a | an | the |

Listen carefully while your partner talks about the snacks. Raise your hand each time you hear your partner use an article.

- ✂

Articles

Have you ever been to an apple orchard?

Draw three pictures, and label each picture with an article and a noun. Choose pictures you can name by using these three different articles—*a, an,* and *the.* Here are three examples.

| a tree | an apple | the orchard |

Show your pictures to other students, and read your labels out loud.

Reteach Activities • More About Adjectives   Unit 5 • Chapter 25 **49**

Adjectives That Compare

OBJECTIVES
- To recognize and use adjectives that compare
- To contribute to a class discussion and to write sentences, using adjectives that compare

DAILY LANGUAGE PRACTICE

TRANSPARENCY 57

1 I has farmed this land for many years. (have)

2 tomorrow we bought a new tractor. (Tomorrow; will buy)

BRIDGE TO WRITING (Article) new tractor might be red.

ORAL WARM-UP

USE PRIOR KNOWLEDGE Draw a small circle and a large circle on the board. Ask students to provide words that describe how they are alike. Point out the comparative adjectives.

Grammar Jingles™ **CD, Intermediate** Use Track 17 for review and reinforcement of adjectives.

TEACH/MODEL

Remind students that when forming comparisons with adjectives that end with a consonant and *y*, they should change the *y* to *i* before adding *er* or *est*. When forming comparisons with adjectives that end with *e*, they should drop the *e* before adding *er* or *est*. Model the thinking for the Guided Practice example:

MODEL The sentence compares two farmhouses. Because the adjective talks about two farmhouses, it should end with *er*. The correct form of the adjective must be *older*.

Work with students to complete the Guided Practice.

Some Special Forms for Comparing	
good	**bad**
better	worse
best	worst

310

Adjectives That Compare

Adjectives can be used to compare two or more people, places, or things.

Add *er* to most short adjectives to compare two people, places, or things. Add *est* to most short adjectives to compare more than two people, places, or things. If an adjective ends with a consonant and *y*, change the *y* to *i* and add *er* or *est*.

Examples:

This barn is in a **sunnier** place than the horse stable.

That dairy, though, is in the **sunniest** place of all.

Other adjectives use special forms to compare. *Good* and *bad* are two of these adjectives. Notice their special forms for comparing in the chart.

Guided Practice

A. Read each sentence. Choose the correct adjective.

Example: This farm is (older, oldest) than that one.
older

1. The (newer, newest) farmhouses of all are built with concrete.
2. Many (older, oldest) farmhouses were built with stone.
3. The stable is built in the (brighter, brightest) part of a farm.
4. Horses have (good, better) protection in their stables than out in the fields.
5. (Fewer, Fewest) oxen than tractors plow fields.

Vocabulary Power page 73

Name _____

CLASSIFY AND CATEGORIZE

Read each group of words below. Circle the letter of the word or phrase that does not belong in each group. Then name each category. Category names may vary. Possible responses are given.

1. A crops
   B rural
   C agricultural
   (D) city
   ___ farming

2. F kitchen
   G bedroom
   (H) outside
   J living room
   ___ rooms

3. A apartments
   (B) undeveloped
   C skyscrapers
   D offices
   ___ buildings

4. F green
   G blue
   (H) soft
   J purple
   ___ colors

5. (A) museum
   B rustic
   C natural
   D meadow
   ___ country

6. F lake
   G river
   (H) desert
   J ocean
   ___ water

7. A hot
   B pink
   C warm
   D cold
   ___ temperature

8. (F) computer
   G campsite
   H tent
   J hiking
   ___ camping

9. A mother
   B brother
   C sister
   (D) friend
   ___ family members

10. F dog
    (G) tiger
    H cat
    J goldfish
    ___ pets

Vocabulary Power   Unit 5 • Chapter 25 73

ESL

USING *GOOD* AND *BAD* Give students practice in using forms of *good* and *bad* by having them complete these sentences.

The Longs' harvest was ____ than ours. (good, better, best)

The Garcias had their ____ harvest ever. (good, better, best)

This was the ____ year in decades for potatoes. (bad, worse, worst)

Ask students to explain their choices.

Independent Practice

B. Rewrite each sentence, using the correct comparing form of the adjective in parentheses ( ).

Example: (Few) crops grow in winter than in spring.
Fewer crops grow in winter than in spring.

6. Apples can grow in (cool) areas than oranges. cooler
7. Peaches need (warm) climates than pears. warmer
8. Sunny places are the (good) areas to grow grapes. best
9. It is hard to farm in the (hot) regions of all. hottest
10. Growing crops is also difficult in the very (dry) regions. driest
11. Farmers do not deliver their (bad) products to market. worst
12. Farming is an (easy) job today than it was in the past. easier
13. Instead of their old equipment, farmers now use (fast) new machinery. faster
14. Before milking machines were invented, milking was a (hard) chore than it is now. harder
15. Inventions have brought rural families into (close) contact with the rest of the world. closer

Remember
that an adjective that ends with *er* compares two people, places, or things. An adjective that ends with *est* compares more than two people, places, or things. *Good* and *bad* have special forms for comparing.

Writing Connection

Writer's Craft: Vivid Adjectives Talk with a partner about the neighborhood, town, or city where each of you lives. How are these places alike? How are they different? Write several sentences comparing these places. Be sure to use adjectives that compare.

311

Independent Practice

Have students complete the Independent Practice, or modify it using these suggestions:

MODIFIED INSTRUCTION

BELOW-LEVEL STUDENTS Ask students to explain what is being compared in the example. Remind students to identify what is being compared as they complete the items.

ABOVE-LEVEL STUDENTS Ask students to use adjectives that compare to write three additional sentences about how farm life in the past might have been different from farm life today.

Writing Connection

Writer's Craft: Vivid Adjectives Before students begin, have them contribute to a class discussion about the characteristics of different kinds of communities. Have them compare their community with a small town, a large city, a suburb, or a rural area. They should choose the adjectives that make the most vivid comparisons.

WRAP-UP/ASSESS

SUMMARIZE Ask students: **How are adjectives that compare formed?**

RETEACH

INTERVENTION Lessons in **visual, auditory,** and **kinesthetic** modalities: p. R54 and *Reteach Activities Copying Masters,* p. 50.

PRACTICE page 82

Name _____

Adjectives That Compare

A. For each sentence, write the correct adjective in parentheses ( ).

1. The apple orchard is (**larger, largest**) than the plum orchard.   larger
2. In fact, it is the (**bigger, biggest**) orchard I have seen.   biggest
3. Ripe plums are (**softer, softest**) than unripe ones.   softer
4. I think plums are (**better, best**) than apples.   better
5. A peach is the (**better, best**) fruit of all.   best

B. Write each sentence using the correct form of the adjective in parentheses ( ).

6. The farmer told us to pick only the (**ripe**) plums of the bunch.
   The farmer told us to pick only the ripest plums of the bunch.

7. It was a (**hard**) job than we expected.
   It was a harder job than we expected.

8. The sun felt (**hot**) as each hour passed.
   The sun felt hotter as each hour passed.

TRY THIS! Think about a farm you have read about or seen. List some comparative adjectives that describe the farm. Then write a description that will help your readers picture it.

82 Unit 5 • Chapter 25   Practice • More About Adjectives

CHALLENGE

CHOOSING ANIMALS Ask students to suppose that they are starting their own farm where they can raise any animals they choose. Have them decide which animals they would like to raise and then use comparative words to tell why they chose each particular animal.

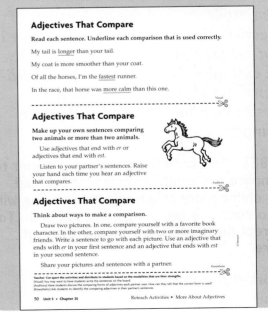

Adjectives That Compare

Read each sentence. Underline each comparison that is used correctly.

My tail is <u>longer</u> than your tail.

My coat is more smoother than your coat.

Of all the horses, I'm the <u>fastest</u> runner.

In the race, that horse was <u>more calm</u> than this one.

Visual

Adjectives That Compare

Make up your own sentences comparing two animals or more than two animals.

Use adjectives that end with *er* or adjectives that end with *est.*

Listen to your partner's sentences. Raise your hand each time you hear an adjective that compares.

Auditory

Adjectives That Compare

Think about ways to make a comparison.

Draw two pictures. In one, compare yourself with a favorite book character. In the other, compare yourself with two or more imaginary friends. Write a sentence to go with each picture. Use an adjective that ends with *er* in your first sentence and an adjective that ends with *est* in your second sentence.

Share your pictures and sentences with a partner.

Kinesthetic

Teacher: Cut apart the activities and distribute to students based on the modalities that are their strengths.
[Visual] You may want to have students write the sentences on the board.
[Auditory] Have students discuss the comparing forms of adjectives each partner uses. How can they tell that the correct form is used?
[Kinesthetic] Ask students to identify the comparing adjectives in their partner's sentences.

50 Unit 5 • Chapter 25   Reteach Activities • More About Adjectives

Avoiding Incorrect Comparisons

OBJECTIVES

- To recognize and form comparative adjectives correctly, using *more* and *most*
- To use correct adjective forms to record a list and write sentences that compare

DAILY LANGUAGE PRACTICE

TRANSPARENCY 57

1 Him's produce was for sale at the markett. (His; market.)

2 The city people am glad to buy fresh produce. (are)

BRIDGE TO WRITING I think that apples taste ___(adjective)___ than pears.

ORAL WARM-UP

USE PRIOR KNOWLEDGE Have volunteers give examples of several adjectives that compare with the use of *er* or *est*. Then tell them that there is another way to form adjectives that compare.

***Grammar Jingles*™ CD, Intermediate** Use Track 17 for review and reinforcement of adjectives.

TEACH/MODEL

Have students read the explanation of adjectives that compare by using *more* or *most* on page 312. Then ask them why the examples should not read *more deliciouser* and *most deliciousest*. Model the thinking for the Guided Practice example:

MODEL This sentence uses *more better* to compare two crops. I know that I should use either *more* or an adjective ending with *er* to compare two things, but not both. To correct the sentence, I should take out *more*.

Work through the Guided Practice items orally with students.

DID YOU KNOW?
California produces more food than any other state in the nation. Its leading products include milk, beef, grapes, tomatoes, and lettuce.

millet

312

Avoiding Incorrect Comparisons

Some **adjectives** need the word *more* or *most* for comparing.

Most adjectives with two or more syllables need the word *more* or the word *most* for comparing nouns. Use *more* when comparing two nouns. Use *most* when comparing more than two nouns.

Examples:
I think that apples are **more delicious** than grapes.

I think that kiwi is the **most delicious** fruit of all.

Never use both *er* and *more* or both *est* and *most* when you compare with adjectives.

Guided Practice

A. Read each sentence. Tell whether the adjective form is correct or incorrect.

Example: The farmer had a more better crop than his neighbor did.
incorrect; more better *should be* better

1. Rice is the most difficult crop to grow. correct
2. Rice is a plentifuler grain in California than in Texas. incorrect; more plentiful
3. Corn is a more ordinarier grain than millet. incorrect; more ordina[...]
4. Winter wheat is grown in more milder climates than other types of wheat. incorrect; milder
5. Bread wheat is the most common type of wheat. correct

Vocabulary Power page 74

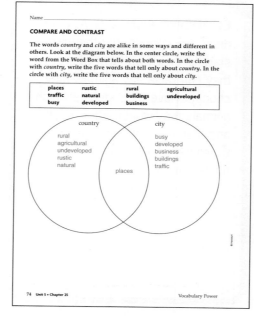

Social Studies

MAP Have students make a map of an imaginary farm. Tell them to use information from the sentences and the illustrations in the chapter for ideas about the kinds of things to include on their maps. Instruct students to invent symbols for different items on their maps and to explain their symbols in a map legend. Have students write a description of a partner's imaginary farm, based on the partner's map.

Independent Practice

B. Write each sentence, using the correct form of the comparing adjective in parentheses ().

Example: This is the (popular) farm animal at the fair.
This is the most popular farm animal at the fair.

6. A foal is (young) than a horse. younger
7. The (clumsy) horse of all is a newborn foal. clumsiest
8. Donkeys are (stubborn) than horses are. more stubborn
9. The (careful) sheepherder of all is the dog. most careful
10. Sheep are (gentle) than most animals and can't protect themselves. gentler
11. Chickens are (friendly) birds than geese are. friendlier
12. That rooster's feathers are (colorful) than this chicken's feathers. more colorful
13. Animals are the (good) helpers on a farm. best
14. That bull is the (fearless) animal on the farm. most fearless
15. Of all the animals on a farm, large animals have the (expensive) needs. most expensive

Remember
to add *er* or *est* to many short adjectives that compare. Add *more* or *most* to most adjectives with two or more syllables. Never use *er* with *more* or *est* with *most* when you compare with adjectives.

Writing Connection

Writer's Journal: Write a Comparison What do you think is the best thing about living on a farm? What is the best thing about living in a big city? Write a few sentences that compare farm life to city life. Be sure to use the correct adjective forms.

 313

Independent Practice

Have students complete the Independent Practice, or modify it using these suggestions:

MODIFIED INSTRUCTION

BELOW-LEVEL STUDENTS Have students tell whether two or more than two things are being compared. Then ask students to count the syllables in the adjective before deciding which form to use.

ABOVE-LEVEL STUDENTS For Part B, have students change the sentences in which the *er* form of the adjective is used so that the *est* form can be used, and change those in which the *est* form is used so that the *er* form can be used.

Writing Connection

Writer's Journal: Write a Comparison Before writing, have students make a chart with the headings *Farm Life* and *City Life*. Then have them record lists of positive things about each way of life. Instruct students to use correct adjective forms.

WRAP-UP/ASSESS

SUMMARIZE Ask students how to decide whether to use *er* or *est* or *more* or *most* to compare correctly with adjectives.

REACHING ALL LEARNERS

RETEACH

INTERVENTION Lessons in **visual, auditory,** and **kinesthetic** modalities: p. R54 and *Reteach Activities Copying Masters,* p. 51.

REACHING ALL LEARNERS

PRACTICE page 83

Name _____

Avoiding Incorrect Comparisons

A. Decide and write whether the comparing adjective in each sentence is correct or incorrect. If the adjective form is correct, write *correct.* If it is incorrect, write the correct form.

1. I think corn tastes better than wheat. — correct
2. Corn is a more sweeter grain than wheat. — a sweeter grain
3. The yellow corn was more riper than that white corn. — riper
4. The yellow corn is fresher. — correct
5. Do you think corn tastes more good when it is fresh? — better

B. Write each sentence, using the correct adjective that compares.

6. This has been the (wonderfulest, most wonderful) year I can remember for farming. This has been the most wonderful year I can remember for farming.
7. It was much (warmer, warmest) than last year. It was much warmer than last year.
8. Last year was also (more dry, drier) than this year. Last year was also drier than this year.

TRY THIS! Write a conversation between two farmers. Have them compare a good farming year with a poor one. Be careful to use the correct adjective forms.

Practice • More About Adjectives   Unit 5 • Chapter 25   83

CHALLENGE

REACHING ALL LEARNERS

WRITE A LETTER Have students write a letter to another third grader telling what they like about where they live. If they live in a city, they should address their letter to a student in a rural area. If they live in a rural area, they should write to a student in a large city.

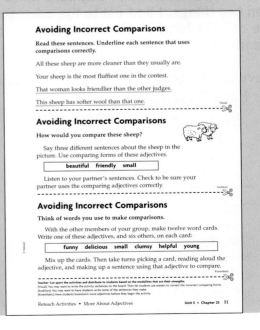

Avoiding Incorrect Comparisons

Read these sentences. Underline each sentence that uses comparisons correctly.

All these sheep are more cleaner than they usually are.

Your sheep is the most fluffiest one in the contest.

That woman looks friendlier than the other judges.

This sheep has softer wool than that one.

Avoiding Incorrect Comparisons

How would you compare these sheep?

Say three different sentences about the sheep in the picture. Use comparing forms of these adjectives.

| beautiful | friendly | small |

Listen to your partner's sentences. Check to be sure your partner uses the comparing adjectives correctly.

Avoiding Incorrect Comparisons

Think of words you use to make comparisons.

With the other members of your group, make twelve word cards. Write one of these adjectives, and six others, on each card:

| funny | delicious | small | clumsy | helpful | young |

Mix up the cards. Then take turns picking a card, reading aloud the adjective, and making up a sentence using that adjective to compare.

Teacher: Cut apart the activities and distribute to students based on the modalities that are their strengths.
[Visual] You may want to write the activity sentences on the board. Then let students use answers to correct the incorrect comparing forms.
[Auditory] You may want to have students write some of the sentences they make.
[Kinesthetic] Have students brainstorm more adjectives before they begin the activity.

Reteach Activities • More About Adjectives   Unit 5 • Chapter 25   51

Extra Practice

OBJECTIVES

- To identify and use articles and comparative adjectives
- To use adjectives that compare in a written note

DAILY LANGUAGE PRACTICE

TRANSPARENCY 58

1 Ginny and me is going to visit her uncle on his farm. (I are)

2 She couldnt wait until her visit begun. (couldn't; began.)

BRIDGE TO WRITING Uncle Walter is my _(adjective)_ uncle.

ORAL WARM-UP

USE PRIOR KNOWLEDGE Write on the board: **Dogs are _____ than cats.** Have students suggest adjectives to complete the sentence. Point out the comparative adjectives.

TEACH/MODEL

Use the Remember box to review articles and adjectives that compare.

Then model the thinking for the example sentence in Part B:

MODEL The sentence compares *places I've seen.* I know that when I compare more than two things, I add *est* to the adjective. The correct form of the adjective must be *grandest.*

Have students work in pairs to complete the Extra Practice exercises.

CHAPTER 25

More About Adjectives

Remember

that *a*, *an*, and *the* are a special group of adjectives called articles. Use *more* or *er* with adjectives that compare two nouns. Use *most* or *est* with adjectives that compare more than two nouns.

For more activities with articles and adjectives that compare, visit *The Learning Site:* www.harcourtschool.com

314

Extra Practice

A. Write each sentence. Use the correct article or articles. *pages 308–309*

Example: Farmers work hard to make (the, a) living.
Farmers work hard to make a living.

1. There are no farms in (<u>the</u>, an) city.
2. Farms are important to (<u>a</u>, an) rural area.
3. Some people who live in rural areas work on (<u>a</u>, an) farm.
4. Some farmers grow (the, <u>a</u>) single crop each year.
5. Soybeans are (an, <u>a</u>) popular crop.
6. Soybeans have (<u>a</u>, the) cover called (an, <u>a</u>) pod.
7. (<u>An</u>, A) acorn is larger than (an, <u>a</u>) soybean.
8. (<u>A</u>, An) major cooking oil is made from soybeans.
9. Soybeans are rich in (<u>a</u>, an) protein.
10. Soybean oil is used as fuel on (an, <u>the</u>) buses in some cities.

B. Write each sentence, using the correct comparing form of the adjective in parentheses ( ). *pages 310–311*

Example: This city is the (grand) place I've seen.
This city is the grandest place I've seen.

11. The (large) farms in the United States are in the Midwest. largest
12. Iowa and Texas have a (great) number of farms than other states do. greater
13. Milk cows are (tame) than some other cattle. tamer
14. The (wild) horses of all do not live on farms. wildest
15. The (strong) horse on a farm is the draft horse. strongest

---

Vocabulary Power page 75

Name _____

SYNONYMS AND ANTONYMS

Read the words below. For each word, choose a synonym and an antonym from the Word Box. Write these words on the lines. The first one is done for you.

scared small	country wrong	warm city	right cold	large brave

	Synonym	Antonym
1. rural	country	city
2. big	large	small
3. hot	warm	cold
4. afraid	scared	brave
5. correct	right	wrong

undeveloped built	lose rude	beat thoughtful	healthy aged	new sick

	Synonym	Antonym
6. polite	thoughtful	rude
7. developed	built	undeveloped
8. win	beat	lose
9. old	aged	new
10. ill	sick	healthy

Vocabulary Power   Unit 5 • Chapter 25 75

Activity

COMPARISON SHUFFLE Have students form groups of four. Give five index cards to each student. Have students write a descriptive adjective on each card. Shuffle the cards and begin the game.

The first player chooses a card. The player correctly says a comparative form of the adjective on the card and says a sentence using the comparative adjective. Continue play until all the cards are used.

C. Write each sentence. Choose the correct comparing form of the adjective in parentheses ( ). Be ready to explain your choices. *pages 310–313*

Example: I had the (most wonderful, wonderfulest) time at the county fair.
I had the most wonderful time at the county fair.

16. County fairs are (more rarer, rarer) events in cities than in small towns. rarer

17. Only the (most splendid, most splendidest) animals win prizes at a fair. most splendid

18. Prizewinners become the (most valuable, valuablest) animals. most valuable

19. The sheepdog is a (skillfuler, more skillful) dog than many other dogs. more skillful

20. A donkey is a (more powerful, more powerfuler) worker than a sheepdog. more powerful

Writing Connection

Real-Life Writing: Postcard Make a postcard about your community. On the front, draw a picture of your neighborhood or town. Write a sentence about your community that compares it to another place. Use at least one adjective that compares. On the back, write a message inviting a friend to visit.

Building Oral Grammar

Students may find that they can recognize the correct form of adjectives that compare by hearing them read aloud. Have students work in pairs to read aloud the sentences in Part C. One student can read the sentence, using the first choice in parentheses, and the other student can use the second choice. Partners can discuss which choice sounds correct.

Writing Connection

Real-Life Writing: Postcard Have students use a prewriting technique such as brainstorming to generate ideas about favorite areas of their community before they write their postcards. Encourage students to list as many comparative adjectives as possible. Remind students that they can refer to the list when writing and drawing the postcard.

WRAP-UP/ASSESS

Writer's Journal

SUMMARIZE In their journals, ask students to reflect on what they learned about adjectives.
REFLECTION

ADDITIONAL PRACTICE An additional page of Extra Practice is provided on page 470 of the *Pupil Edition*.

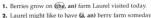

PRACTICE page 84

Name _____

Extra Practice

A. Read each sentence. Circle the correct article or articles in parentheses ( ).

1. Berries grow on (**the**, an) farm Laurel visited today.
2. Laurel might like to have (**a**, an) berry farm someday.
3. She knows (**a**, an) farm can be a lot of work.
4. (**An**, A) outdoor job is more fun for her than (**an**, a) desk job.
5. She also wants to live in (an, **the**) country.

B. Write each sentence, using the correct form of the adjective.

6. I want to grow raspberries because I think they are the (**good**) berries of all. I want to grow raspberries because I think they are the best berries of all.

7. Raspberries are usually (**red**) than strawberries.
Raspberries are usually redder than strawberries.

8. Blackberries are (**mild**) than boysenberries.
Blackberries are milder than boysenberries.

9. They are also (**small**) than strawberries.
They are also smaller than strawberries.

10. Strawberries are the (**large**) berries of all.
Strawberries are the largest berries of all.

TRY THIS! Think about the different kinds of berries you have eaten. Which ones do you like the most? Write a few sentences comparing the different berries.

84 Unit 5 • Chapter 25 — Practice • More About Adjectives

CHALLENGE

FAIR POSTER Have students work in small groups to create posters for an agricultural fair. The posters should tell what activities and exhibits the fair will host and what will be special about the fair. Remind students to include articles and adjectives that compare in their posters.

TECHNOLOGY *Grammar Practice and Assessment* CD-ROM; *Writing Express* CD-ROM

INTERNET Visit *The Learning Site:*
w w w . h a r c o u r t s c h o o l . c o m

Chapter Review

OBJECTIVES

- To review articles and adjectives that compare
- To demonstrate knowledge of synonyms and antonyms and to use them to create a word bank of vivid words

DAILY LANGUAGE PRACTICE

TRANSPARENCY 58

1 The farm have a big red Barn. (has; barn.)

2 Horses and cowes lives in the barn. (cows live)

BRIDGE TO WRITING (Article) spotted cow moos loudly. She is (comparative adjective) than the other cows.

STANDARDIZED TEST PREP

MODEL TEST-TAKING STRATEGIES Have students read the directions on page 316 silently. Remind them to read all possible answers before choosing the correct answer.

Model the thinking. Write this example on the board:

A cows have to be milked twice a day.

  1 **A** An
     B The
     C More
     D Correct as is

MODEL The article describes the plural noun *cows*. I know that *A* and *An* are not correct, because they are used only before singular nouns. The sentence does not compare, so I know that *More* is not the right choice. *The* is used before singular and plural nouns, so I know that the correct answer is *B*.

Have students complete the Chapter Review independently.

CHAPTER 2

More About Adjectives

STANDARDIZED TEST PREP

TIP Answer the questions you are sure about first. Then go back and answer the others.

For additional test preparation, visit *The Learning Site:* www.harcourtschool.com

316

Chapter Review

Read the sentences. Check the underlined words to see whether they are used correctly. If you find a mistake, choose the answer that could replace the underlined words. If there is no mistake, choose *Correct as is*.

1 <u>An</u> sheep often is raised for its wool.

  A A A
  B Most
  C More
  D Correct as is

2 In the United States, <u>most</u> sheep are raised in the west than anywhere else.

  F an
  G more G
  H a
  J Correct as is

3 Some sheep feed on the open range. Others have <u>more controlled</u> feedings in pastures.

  A controlledest
  B controlleder
  C most controlled
  D Correct as is D

4 As you may know, <u>a</u> wool we use for clothing comes from a sheep's coat.

  F an
  G the G
  H more
  J Correct as is

5 Many people like <u>the</u> comfort of wool.

  A more
  B the
  C an
  D Correct as is D

6 A wool sweater is <u>warmest</u> than a cotton sweater.

  F warmer F
  G warm
  H an
  J Correct as is

Assessment

PORTFOLIO ASSESSMENT Have students select their best work from the Writing Connections on pages 309, 311, and 315.

ONGOING ASSESSMENT Evaluate the performance of 4–6 students using appropriate checklists and record forms from pages R74–R77.

INTERNET Activities and exercises to help students prepare for state and standardized assessments appear on *The Learning Site:*
www.harcourtschool.com

Synonyms and Antonyms

VOCABULARY

You have learned about many kinds of adjectives. You may have noticed that some adjectives mean almost the same thing. Other pairs of adjectives are opposites.

Words that mean almost the same thing are called **synonyms**. Look at this sentence:

A barn is a **bigger** building than a stable.

You could replace the word *bigger* with *larger* or *more enormous*. These words are synonyms. Look for other synonyms for *bigger* in a thesaurus.

Antonyms are words with opposite meanings. The adjectives in these sentences are antonyms:

The barn is **older** than the stable.

The stable is **newer** than the barn.

Can you think of other adjectives that are antonyms?

YOUR TURN

Write a mystery story. Use words from the list below in your story. Then trade stories with a partner. In your partner's story, underline the adjectives. Rewrite your partner's story, using synonyms and antonyms for the underlined words. Talk about how word choice changes the meaning of the story.

TIP You can make your writing more interesting by using more vivid synonyms and antonyms for ordinary words.

awful	bright	fast	many
beautiful	clean	happy	noisy
brave	empty	heavy	old

317

VOCABULARY

Synonyms and Antonyms

TEACH/MODEL

Ask volunteers to name words that mean almost the same thing as these words: *cold*, *strong*, *wild*, and *dangerous*. Then have them name words that have the opposite meaning. Explain that the words that mean almost the same are synonyms, and the words that mean the opposite are antonyms. Show students how to use a thesaurus to find synonyms and antonyms.

WRITING APPLICATION Have students create a word bank of vivid words. Have them use a thesaurus to find and write as many synonyms and antonyms as they can find for these words: *nice, many, old, happy, bad, children, picture, town, work,* and *play*. Encourage students to use their word banks to help them make their writing more vivid.

WRAP-UP/ASSESS

Writer's Journal

SUMMARIZE In their journals, have students reflect on how using synonyms and antonyms can make their writing more effective. **REFLECTION**

PRACTICE page 85

Name _____

Chapter Review

Check each underlined word in the sentences for a mistake in word usage. Choose the word or words that should replace the underlined word. Fill in the oval next to your choice. If there is no mistake, choose *No mistake*.

1 An farmer does important work.
  - A
  ○ Many
  ○ Some
  ○ No mistake

2 In this country there are few people raising food than buying it.
  - fewer
  ○ fewest
  ○ more few
  ○ No mistake

3 A farmer often grows enough food for many families.
  ○ An
  ○ Fewer
  ○ More
  - No mistake

4 Farming can be hard work than many other jobs.
  ○ hardest
  - harder
  ○ more hard
  ○ No mistake

5 Vegetables bought directly from the farmer may be freshest than the ones in stores.
  ○ fresh
  - fresher
  ○ more fresh
  ○ No mistake

6 Smart shoppers know how to pick the best fruits and vegetables.
  ○ most good
  ○ better
  ○ goodest
  ○ No mistake

Practice • More About Adjectives   Unit 5 • Chapter 25 85

CHALLENGE

USING VIVID WORDS Have students rewrite this advertisement, using vivid synonyms for the underlined words.

Have a <u>nice</u> vacation on a farm! For a <u>good</u> week this summer, you can live with a <u>great</u> family on a farm in the country. Milk <u>brown</u> cows, ride on a <u>big</u> tractor, and swim in a <u>cold</u> swimming hole! A <u>fun</u> country experience can be yours!

TECHNOLOGY Additional writing activities are provided on the *Writing Express* CD-ROM

LESSON ORGANIZER	DAY 1	DAY 2
DAILY LANGUAGE PRACTICE TRANSPARENCIES 59, 60	1. A librarians job are to help people find books. (librarian's; is) 2. Our librarian, mrs. rush, is always happy to help. (Mrs. Rush) **Bridge to Writing** My book is (adjective) than the other book.	1. The fire chief comed to our school yesterday. (came) 2. Him told us about fire safety (He; safety.) **Bridge to Writing** We listened (adverb that tells *how*) .
ORAL WARM-UP **Listening/Speaking**	Suggest Verbs 318	Use Adverbs That Tell When or Where 320 *Grammar Jingles*™ CD Track 18
TEACH/MODEL **GRAMMAR** **KEY** ✔ = tested skill	✔ **ADVERBS** 318–319 • To identify and use adverbs that tell *how* • To brainstorm a topic and to write sentences, using adverbs that tell *how*	✔ **MORE ABOUT ADVERBS** 320–321 • To identify and use adverbs that tell *when* and *where* • To write sentences, using adverbs that tell *when* and *where*
Reaching All Learners	**Modified Instruction** Below-Level: Review Adverbs Above-Level: Brainstorm Adverbs **Reteach:** *Reteach Activities Copying Masters* pp. 52 and R55 **Challenge:** Activity Card 18, R70 *ESL Manual* pp. 126, 127 *Practice Book* p. 86	**Modified Instruction** Below-Level: Identify Adverbs Above-Level: Change the Adverb **ESL:** Adverb Cards 320 *ESL Manual* pp. 126, 128 **Reteach:** *Reteach Activities Copying Masters* pp. 53 and R55 **Challenge:** Thank-You Note 321 *Practice Book* p. 87
WRITING	Writing Connection 319 Real-Life Writing: Conversation	Writing Connection 321 Writer's Craft: Persuasive Words
CROSS-CURRICULAR/ ENRICHMENT	*Vocabulary Power* Context Clues 318 medical, **career**, legal, entertainment, athletic See *Vocabulary Power* book.	*Vocabulary Power* Related Words 318 *Vocabulary Power* p. 76 🏆 **Vocabulary activity**

DAY 3

1. A campfire can be fun but you must always put it out completely. (fun,)

2. Careless campers have cause terrible fires. (caused)

Bridge to Writing There was a fire (adverb that tells *when* or *where*) .

Compare with Adverbs 322
Grammar Jingles™ CD Track 18

✔ **COMPARING WITH ADVERBS** 322–323
• To form and use comparative and superlative adverbs
• To write a paragraph, using adverbs that compare correctly

Modified Instruction
Below-Level: Count Syllables
Above-Level: Rewrite Sentences
ESL: Counting Syllables 322
ESL Manual pp. 126, 129
Reteach: *Reteach Activities Copying Masters* pp. 54 and R55
Challenge: Negative Comparisons 323
Practice Book p. 88

Writing Connection 323
Social Studies

Vocabulary Power

Explore Word Meaning 318
Vocabulary Power p. 77

💻 **Vocabulary activity**

DAY 4

1. Some police officers rides on horses. (ride)

2. the brown horse ran the most fastest of all. (The; the fastest)

Bridge to Writing David walks (adverb that compares) than his little sister.

Use Adverbs to Explain Emergency Situations 324

EXTRA PRACTICE 324–325
• To correctly identify and use adverbs and adverb forms
• To design a poster that includes adverbs

💻 **Practice and assessment**

Building Oral Grammar
Listen for Correct Adverbs 325
Challenge: Write an Announcement 325
ESL Manual pp. 126, 130
Practice Book p. 89

Writing Connection 325
Art

Hands-On Activity: 911 Information 324

Vocabulary Power

Word Families 318
Vocabulary Power p. 78

💻 **Vocabulary activity**

DAY 5

1. Once I need help from an police officer. (needed; a)

2. I were lost, and he helped I. (was; me.)

Bridge to Writing I got home (adverb) with his help. I live (adverb) .

TEST PREP **CHAPTER REVIEW** 326
• To review adverbs
• To take simple notes from relevant sources and make an outline

💻 **Test preparation**

Challenge: Group Note-Taking 327
Practice Book p. 90
ESL Manual pp. 126, 131

Writing Application 327
Create an Outline

Study Skills: Taking Notes and Making an Outline 327

Vocabulary Power

Graphics 318

Adverbs

OBJECTIVES

- To identify adverbs that tell *how* and use them correctly in sentences
- To brainstorm a topic and to write sentences, using adverbs that tell *how*

DAILY LANGUAGE PRACTICE

TRANSPARENCY 59

1 A librarians job are to help people find books. (librarian's; is)

2 Our librarian, mrs. rush, is always happy to help. (Mrs. Rush,)

BRIDGE TO WRITING My book is (adjective) than the other book.

ORAL WARM-UP

USE PRIOR KNOWLEDGE Ask students what their school and public librarians do on a typical day. Write on the board the verbs students suggest. Then ask them to suggest any words that describe or tell about those verbs.

TEACH/MODEL

Read aloud the definition and examples on page 318. Write on the board: *People read quietly in the library.* Ask students which word is the verb in the sentence. Then ask which word tells how people read. Tell students that this word is an adverb that tells *how*. Explain that using adverbs makes speaking and writing more descriptive. Then model the thinking for the Guided Practice example:

MODEL The verb in the sentence is *closed.* The word that tells how the storyteller closed the book is *gently. Gently* is the adverb that tells *how*.

Work through the Guided Practice sentences orally with students.

Vocabulary Power

ca•reer [kə•rir'] *n.* A person's lifework or profession.

318

Adverbs

An **adverb** is a word that describes, or tells about, a verb.

Some adverbs tell *how* an action happens.

Examples:
Firefighters and police officers work **hard** for you.

The librarian asked us to work **quietly** in the library.

The gym teacher said I ran **fast**.

Juan **carefully** crossed the street.

Guided Practice

A. Name the adverb that tells *how*. Then name the verb it describes.

Example: The storyteller closed the book gently.
gently, closed

1. Librarians search the Internet quickly. quickly, search
2. They happily help people do research. happily, help
3. Children listen quietly as librarians read them stories. quietly, listen
4. Librarians carefully replace books on shelves. carefully, replace
5. They work hard to keep the library in order. hard, wo
6. We must talk softly in the library. softly, talk
7. Our class easily won the reading contest. easily, won
8. People from our neighborhood use the public library regularly. regularly, use
9. My group finished the book quickly. quickly, finished
10. We must treat the books gently. gently, treat

Vocabulary Power

DAY 1 CONTEXT CLUES Say: **"I have a career."** What words could you add to this sentence to make the meaning of *career* clearer?

DAY 2 RELATED WORDS **The word *paramedic* is related to *medical*.** What are some words that are related to *athletic*? (See also *Vocabulary Power*, page 76.)

DAY 3 EXPLORE WORD MEANING **Name some careers you have heard of or read about.** (See also *Vocabulary Power*, page 77.)

DAY 4 WORD FAMILIES **The words *career* and *car* are both based on a word that means "car."** What other words might be related to *career*? (See also *Vocabulary Power*, page 78.)

DAY 5 GRAPHICS Have students draw and label pictures of at least two careers they are interested in. Provide time for them to share their pictures.

Independent Practice

B. Write the adverb that tells *how*. Then write the verb it describes.

Example: The librarian searched the shelves calmly.
calmly, searched

11. She quickly found the book she wanted. quickly, found
12. The librarian cheerfully offered to show Jeff a good website. cheerfully, offered
13. Jeff easily found the website. easily, found
14. He went to a table and sat quietly. quietly, sat
15. Two girls spoke softly at the next table. softly, spoke
16. Please ask nicely if you need more help. nicely, ask
17. Nikki happily searched the shelves for books on kittens. happily, searched
18. We watched the librarian's helper put the books back on the shelf correctly. correctly, put
19. Nikki carefully put her books on the counter. carefully, put
20. Jeff eagerly searched the website for facts. eagerly, searched

> **Remember**
> that some adverbs tell how an action happens.

Writing Connection

Real-Life Writing: Conversation Brainstorm with a partner a list of people who are helpful in your community. Then discuss with your partner the jobs these people have. After your discussion, write three sentences that describe what one person on your list does. Use adverbs that tell *how* in your description.

Independent Practice

Have students complete the Independent Practice, or modify it using these suggestions:

MODIFIED INSTRUCTION

BELOW-LEVEL STUDENTS Remind students that the verb is the word that tells what the subject of a sentence is or does. Tell them that adverbs describe the verb and often end in *ly*.

ABOVE-LEVEL STUDENTS After students have completed Part B, ask them to think of another adverb that tells *how*.

Writing Connection

Real-Life Writing: Conversation To get students started, suggest that they think about people in the community who help them when they need something. For example, doctors and nurses *quickly* help them when they are sick. Remind students to include adverbs that tell *how* in their sentences.

WRAP-UP/ASSESS

SUMMARIZE Ask students to explain how to find the adverb that tells *how* in a sentence.

REACHING ALL LEARNERS

RETEACH

INTERVENTION Lessons in **visual, auditory,** and **kinesthetic** modalities: p. R55 and *Reteach Activities Copying Masters*, p. 52.

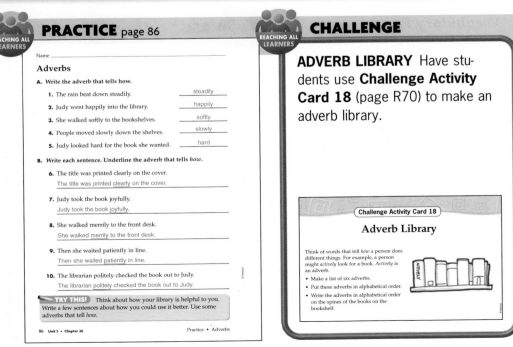

PRACTICE page 86

Name _____

Adverbs

A. Write the adverb that tells how.

1. The rain beat down steadily. — steadily
2. Judy went happily into the library. — happily
3. She walked softly to the bookshelves. — softly
4. People moved slowly down the shelves. — slowly
5. Judy looked hard for the book she wanted. — hard

B. Write each sentence. Underline the adverb that tells *how*.

6. The title was printed clearly on the cover.
   The title was printed clearly on the cover.
7. Judy took the book joyfully.
   Judy took the book joyfully.
8. She walked merrily to the front desk.
   She walked merrily to the front desk.
9. Then she waited patiently in line.
   Then she waited patiently in line.
10. The librarian politely checked the book out to Judy.
    The librarian politely checked the book out to Judy.

TRY THIS! Think about how your library is helpful to you. Write a few sentences about how you could use it better. Use some adverbs that tell *how*.

86 Unit 5 • Chapter 26   Practice • Adverbs

CHALLENGE

ADVERB LIBRARY Have students use **Challenge Activity Card 18** (page R70) to make an adverb library.

Challenge Activity Card 18

Adverb Library

Think of words that tell *how* a person does different things. For example, a person might *actively* look for a book. *Actively* is an adverb.

• Make a list of six adverbs.
• Put these adverbs in alphabetical order.
• Write the adverbs in alphabetical order on the spines of the books on the bookshelf.

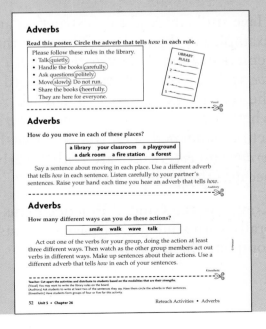

Adverbs

Read this poster. Circle the adverb that tells *how* in each rule.

Please follow these rules in the library.
• Talk (quietly.)
• Handle the books (carefully.)
• Ask questions (politely.)
• Move (slowly.) Do not run.
• Share the books (cheerfully.)
  They are here for everyone.

LIBRARY RULES

Adverbs

How do you move in each of these places?

a library   your classroom   a playground
a dark room   a fire station   a forest

Say a sentence about moving in each place. Use a different adverb that tells *how* in each sentence. Listen carefully to your partner's sentences. Raise your hand each time you hear an adverb that tells *how*.

Adverbs

How many different ways can you do these actions?

smile   walk   wave   talk

Act out one of the verbs for your group, doing the action at least three different ways. Then watch as the other group members act out verbs in different ways. Make up sentences about their actions. Use a different adverb that tells *how* in each of your sentences.

Teacher: Cut apart the activities and distribute to students based on the modalities that are their strengths.
[Visual] You may want to write the library rules on the board.
[Auditory] Ask students to write at least two of the sentences they say. Have them circle the adverbs in their sentences.
[Kinesthetic] Have students form groups of four or five for this activity.

52 Unit 5 • Chapter 26   Reteach Activities • Adverbs

More About Adverbs

OBJECTIVES
- To identify adverbs that tell *when* and *where* and use them correctly in sentences
- To brainstorm a list and write descriptive sentences, using adverbs that tell *when* and *where*

DAILY LANGUAGE PRACTICE

TRANSPARENCY 59

1 The fire chief comed to our school yesterday. (came)

2 Him told us about fire safety (He; safety.)

BRIDGE TO WRITING We listened __(adverb that tells *how*)__ .

ORAL WARM-UP

USE PRIOR KNOWLEDGE Write these sentences on the board:

_____ *the firefighters got a call.*

The fire trucks are parked _____.

Ask students to complete the sentences with one word that tells *when* or *where.*

***Grammar Jingles*™ CD, Intermediate** Use Track 18 for review and reinforcement of adverbs.

TEACH/MODEL

Have students read the instruction and examples to themselves. Then say this sentence aloud: *Yesterday the rain fell everywhere.* Ask students which word is the verb in the sentence. Then ask whether any word tells *when* or *where* the action happened. Tell students that *Yesterday* and *everywhere* are both adverbs because they tell about the verb.

Complete the Guided Practice items orally with students, or have students complete the items in pairs.

More About Adverbs

An **adverb** is a word that describes, or tells about, a verb.

Some adverbs tell *when* or *where* an action happens.

> **Examples:**
>
> I **always** like talking with firefighters about their work. *tells when*
>
> I just saw a firefighter **outside**. *tells where*

Guided Practice

A. Identify the adverb and whether it tells *when* or *where*.

> **Example:** May we visit the police station soon?
> *soon, when*

1. Police officers work there. there, where
2. Heidi often reads books about police officers. often, when
3. May we visit the fire station tomorrow? tomorrow, when
4. We sometimes ask the police for information. sometimes, when
5. The police always help people. always, when
6. You can find community helpers everywhere. everywhere, where
7. The firefighters will go anywhere someone needs help. anywhere, where
8. We should stand here until the light changes. here, where
9. The light is green, so let's cross now. now, when
10. Cho is waiting outside for the crossing guard. outside, where

320

Vocabulary Power page 76

ESL
REACHING ALL LEARNERS

Name _____

RELATED WORDS

Every career has jobs that are related to it. Underneath each career, draw a picture that represents it. Then write each job from the Word Box underneath the career it is related to. Finally, add your own job to each list.

paramedic	paralegal	referee	coach	doctor
singer	trainer	lawyer	legal secretary	actress
director	nurse	actor	surgeon	basketball player

Athletic	Medical	Legal	Entertainment
coach	doctor	lawyer	actor
trainer	nurse	paralegal	actress
referee	surgeon	legal secretary	singer
basketball player	paramedic		director

76 Unit 5 • Chapter 26 — Vocabulary Power

ADVERB CARDS Tell students that some adverbs are formed by adding *ly* to an adjective. Write *ly* on one index card, and list the following adjectives on other index cards: *sad, quick, slow, soft, careful,* and *quiet.* Then have students take turns drawing cards. Each student should match the adjective card with the *ly* card, say the adverb, and say a sentence using the adverb.

Independent Practice

B. Write each sentence. Underline the adverb that tells *where* or *when*.

Example: *Eliott left his house early* .

11. <u>Soon</u> he was at the community center.
12. He opened the door and went <u>inside</u>.
13. Children were playing <u>everywhere</u>.
14. He and his friends are playing basketball <u>today</u>.
15. They practice <u>often</u>.
16. Eliott <u>sometimes</u> helps clean the gym.
17. He swept the floor <u>yesterday</u>.
18. His friends will help out <u>tomorrow</u>.
19. The broom they use is <u>here</u>.
20. I think we should start practicing <u>now</u>.
21. We cannot go <u>outside</u> in the rain.
22. Let's go to the library <u>later</u>.
23. Will you go <u>there</u> with me?
24. I <u>always</u> look for books about basketball.
25. I <u>usually</u> find magazines, too.

Writing Connection

Writer's Craft: Persuasive Words Firefighters help others by keeping people, land, and communities safe. Write four sentences that describe another "helping" career in your community. Use adverbs to help explain *when* and *where* the helping takes place.

Remember that some adverbs tell *when* or *where* an action happens.

Independent Practice

Have students complete the Independent Practice, or modify it using these suggestions:

MODIFIED INSTRUCTION

BELOW-LEVEL STUDENTS Have students write the sentences and circle the verb. Then ask them to decide which word in the sentence tells *when* or *where* about the verb.

ABOVE-LEVEL STUDENTS Have students decide whether each adverb tells *when* or *where* about each verb. In the sentences with adverbs that tell *when*, have students change the adverb to a different *when* adverb and revise the sentence as needed.

Writing Connection

Writer's Craft: Persuasive Words Before students begin to write, have them work in pairs to brainstorm a list of helping careers in the community. Ask them to think about ways people in these careers have helped their families.

WRAP-UP/ASSESS

SUMMARIZE Ask students to tell how to find an adverb that tells *when* or *where* in a sentence.

RETEACH

INTERVENTION Lessons in **visual**, **auditory**, and **kinesthetic** modalities: p. R55 and *Reteach Activities Copying Masters*, p. 53.

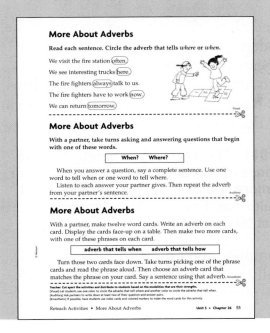

PRACTICE page 87

Name _____

More About Adverbs   LIBRARY

A. Write the adverb that tells *when* or *where*.

1. Roger goes to the library daily.   daily
2. Sometimes he checks out books.   Sometimes
3. He reads them outside on the lawn.   outside
4. Later we read books at home.   Later
5. We often discuss the books.   often

B. Write the sentence. Underline the adverb. Then write whether the adverb tells *where* or *when*.

6. Roger wants to work at a library someday.
   Roger wants to work at a library someday.   when

7. He is always in the library.
   He is always in the library.   when

8. He reads all his books there.
   He reads all his books there.   where

9. The librarian often asks him to help.
   The librarian often asks him to help.   when

10. He reaches up to put books on the shelves.
    He reaches up to put books on the shelves.   where

TRY THIS! Write three sentences about things librarians do in your school or city library. Circle the adverbs you use.

Practice • Adverbs   Unit 5 • Chapter 26 87

CHALLENGE

THANK-YOU NOTE Ask students to write a thank-you note to someone who has helped them or their family. Have students describe the help that was given and tell why it was needed. Students should also tell how the help made something different or better. Prompt them to include adverbs that tell *when* or *where* in their notes. Have students follow the model for writing a thank-you note on page 492.

More About Adverbs

Read each sentence. Circle the adverb that tells *where* or *when*.

We visit the fire station often.
We see interesting trucks here.
The fire fighters always talk to us.
The fire fighters have to work now.
We can return tomorrow.

More About Adverbs

With a partner, take turns asking and answering questions that begin with one of these words.

        When?   Where?

When you answer a question, say a complete sentence. Use one word to tell when or one word to tell where.
Listen to each answer your partner gives. Then repeat the adverb from your partner's sentence.

More About Adverbs

With a partner, make twelve word cards. Write an adverb on each card. Display the cards face-up on a table. Then make two more cards, with one of these phrases on each card.

    adverb that tells when   adverb that tells how

Turn those two cards face down. Take turns picking one of the phrase cards and read the phrase aloud. Then choose an adverb card that matches the phrase on your card. Say a sentence using that adverb.

Reteach Activities • More About Adverbs   Unit 5 • Chapter 26 53

Comparing with Adverbs

OBJECTIVES

- To form comparative and superlative adverbs and use them correctly in sentences
- To develop ideas and express thoughts in a paragraph, using adverbs that compare correctly

SPIRAL REVIEW

DAILY LANGUAGE PRACTICE

TRANSPARENCY 59

1 A campfire can be fun but you must always put it out completely. (fun,)

2 Careless campers have cause terrible fires. (caused)

BRIDGE TO WRITING There was a fire (adverb that tells *when* or *where*) .

ORAL WARM-UP

USE PRIOR KNOWLEDGE Ask students to tell how the way they walk is different from the way they run, using adverbs.

Grammar Jingles™ **CD, Intermediate** Use Track 18 for review and reinforcement of adverbs.

TEACH/MODEL

Read aloud the rules and examples. Tell students to choose whether to use *er/more* or *est/most* by first deciding whether two or more than two actions are being compared. Model the thinking for the Guided Practice example:

MODEL The sentence is comparing the actions of two animals, so I use either *er* or *more*. *Quickly* has two syllables, so I wouldn't add *er* to it. The right answer must be *more quickly*.

Complete the Guided Practice items orally with students, or have students complete the items in small groups.

322

Comparing with Adverbs

Adverbs can compare two or more actions.

When comparing two actions, add *er* to most short adverbs. Use *more* before adverbs with two or more syllables. When comparing more than two actions, add *est* to most short adverbs. Use *most* before adverbs with two or more syllables.

Examples:

This fire spread **faster** than last week's fire.

This fire spread the **fastest** of all the fires.

The firefighters came **more rapidly** than the police.

They came the **most rapidly** of all the workers.

Do not use both *er* and *more* or *est* and *most* when you compare with adverbs.

Guided Practice

A. Tell how you would change the underlined adverb to make the sentence correct.

Example: The deer ran <u>quickly</u> from the fire than the turtles did. *more quickly*

1. Some campers act <u>carefully</u> than others. more carefully

2. Some fires spread <u>fast</u> than others. faster

3. We will follow our fire safety plan <u>closely</u> next time. more closely

4. The fire burned <u>long</u> than the firefighters thought it would. longer

5. The water sprays <u>quickly</u> when it's first turned on than it does later. more quickly

---

Vocabulary Power page 77

Name

EXPLORE WORD MEANING

▶ Read and respond to each question. Use complete sentences.
Responses will vary. Accept reasonable responses.

1. What are some special skills that people with careers in athletics need to have?

2. What kind of personality do you think you would need if you wanted a legal career?

3. When might you need to see someone who has a medical career?

4. There are many different entertainment careers. In what type of entertainment career would you be most interested? Why?

▶ Rank the types of careers from one to four. Your number-one career should be the one in which you are most interested. Your number-four career should be the one in which you are least interested. Then explain the reason for your order.

_____ athletic   _____ legal

_____ entertainment   _____ medical

Vocabulary Power   Unit 5 • Chapter 26 77

 ESL
REACHING ALL LEARNERS

COUNTING SYLLABLES Tell students to count the syllables in the adverb. Remind them that most one-syllable adverbs take *er/est*, while most longer adverbs take *more/most*. Ask students to count the syllables in these adverbs and choose how to form adverbs with them.

soon	quickly	often	happily
loud	fast	slowly	easily
carefully	gently		

Independent Practice

B. Write each sentence using the correct form of the underlined adverb.

Example: The forest fire raced <u>fast</u> than the wind.
The forest fire raced faster than the wind.

6. The flames jumped <u>high</u> than the trees. higher
7. The top of the fire burned the <u>hot</u>. hottest
8. Of all the grasses, the dry brush burned the <u>rapidly</u>. most rapidly
9. The wind changed, and the fire burned <u>wildly</u> than ever. more wildly
10. As the fire spread, firefighters had to work <u>quickly</u> than before. more quickly
11. They dug <u>rapidly</u> than they had in the morning. more rapidly
12. The fire spread <u>slowly</u> than before. more slowly
13. Water from the hoses sprayed <u>hard</u> than a rainstorm. harder
14. When the fire was out, firefighters stayed <u>long</u> to make sure new fires did not start. longer
15. No one cheered <u>loudly</u> than the chief after the fire was out. more loudly

> **Remember**
> to add *er* to adverbs to compare two actions. Add *est* when you compare more than two actions. Use *more* or *most* before adverbs that have two or more syllables.

Writing Connection

Social Studies Think of things you can do to help others in your community or at your school. Talk about these ideas with a partner. Together, list your four favorite ideas. Then write a paragraph that compares your ideas. Be sure to use adverbs that compare correctly.

Independent Practice

Have students complete the Independent Practice, or modify it using these suggestions:

MODIFIED INSTRUCTION

BELOW-LEVEL STUDENTS Before students write the sentences, have them count the syllables in each underlined adverb to help them decide how to form the comparison.

ABOVE-LEVEL STUDENTS After students have completed Part B, have them rewrite five of the items, using a different adverb that compares.

Writing Connection

Social Studies As students compare their ideas, remind them to include their thoughts about whether the actions they suggest can be done easily by anyone and whether they are activities people would be willing to do on a regular basis.

WRAP-UP/ASSESS

SUMMARIZE Ask students how they know whether to use *er/more* or *est/most* in adverb forms.

RETEACH

INTERVENTION Lessons in **visual, auditory,** and **kinesthetic** modalities: p. R55 and *Reteach Activities Copying Masters*, p. 54.

PRACTICE page 88

Name _____

Comparing with Adverbs

A. Change the underlined adverb to make the sentence correct. Write the corrected adverb.

1. I dressed <u>fast</u> than usual this morning. _____ faster
2. My brother dressed <u>slowly</u> than I. _____ more slowly
3. I could reach <u>high</u> than he could. _____ higher
4. I got my shirt off the shelf <u>easily</u> than he did. _____ more easily
5. My sister dressed the <u>carefully</u>. _____ most carefully

B. Write each sentence using the correct form of the underlined adverb.

6. We walked to school <u>quickly</u> than usual.
   We walked to school more quickly than usual.
7. A police officer warned us to cross the street <u>carefully</u> than we did.
   A police officer warned us to cross the street more carefully than we did.
8. We had crossed <u>carelessly</u> than usual.
   We had crossed more carelessly than usual.

▶ **TRY THIS!** What can you do to help others at home or at school? List your best ideas. Write a sentence for each idea. Use adverbs in your explanations.

88 Unit 5 • Chapter 26   Practice • Adverbs

CHALLENGE

NEGATIVE COMPARISONS

Point out to students that they also can make negative comparisons. Explain that they should use *less* when comparing two actions and *least* when comparing more than two actions. Read aloud Independent Practice sentence 8, using *least* in place of *most:* Point out that using *least* instead of *most* gives the sentence the opposite meaning.

Have students collaborate to rewrite sentences 9–12, using *less* or *least.*

Comparing with Adverbs

Circle the adverb phrases that are used correctly in these sentences.

The ranger explained the rules (more carefully) than our teacher did.

A campfire can get out of control most fast in the summer than in the winter.

Of all the people in the forest, rangers can spot problems (most quickly).

A forest animal can sense danger from a fire (more clearly) than a person can.

Comparing with Adverbs

Think about five things you can do well.

Then, tell them to a partner. In each sentence, use a comparing form of one of these adverbs.

| fast | high | slowly | carefully | quickly |

Listen carefully to each sentence your partner says. Be sure your partner uses the correct form of the adverb that compares.

Comparing with Adverbs

Pick one of these adverbs.

| fast | high | slowly | carefully | quickly |

Make up a sentence using the adverb you chose to compare something you can do well to something one or two students can do well. Say your sentence for your group. Then have one or two other group members help you act out your sentence.

Teacher: Cut apart the activities and distribute to students based on the modalities that are their strengths.
(Visual) You may want to have students work with partners to complete this activity.
(Auditory) Suggest that students write two of the sentences they say to their partners.
(Kinesthetic) Ask the students in each group to choose adverbs that other group members have not yet used.

54 Unit 5 • Chapter 26   Reteach Activities • Adverbs

Extra Practice

OBJECTIVES
- To correctly identify and use adverbs and adverb forms
- To design a poster that illustrates an idea and includes adverbs

DAILY LANGUAGE PRACTICE

TRANSPARENCY 60

1 Some police officers rides on horses. (ride)

2 the brown horse ran the most fastest of all. (The; the fastest)

BRIDGE TO WRITING David walks __(adverb that compares)__ than his little sister.

ORAL WARM-UP

USE PRIOR KNOWLEDGE Ask students to explain how to contact the police or fire department in the event of an emergency. Prompt them to use adverbs in their explanations.

TEACH/MODEL

Use the Remember boxes to review adverbs. Model the thinking for the first example sentence:

MODEL I know that *fight* is the verb in the sentence. I need to identify the word that tells *how, when,* or *where* the officers fight crime. *Often* tells *when* they fight crime, so I know that *often* is the adverb.

Remind students to count the syllables in the adverb and to think about how many actions are being compared before they decide which comparing form of an adverb to use.

Have students complete the Extra Practice items independently.

Adverbs

Remember

that an adverb describes a verb. Adverbs can tell *how, when,* or *where* an action happens.

For more activities with adverbs, visit *The Learning Site:* www.harcourtschool.com

Extra Practice

A. Write the adverb in each sentence.
pages 318–321

Example: Police officers often fight crime.   *often*

1. Officers must behave <u>bravely</u>.
2. They act <u>swiftly</u> to protect people.
3. Police officers <u>sometimes</u> call for extra help.
4. The officers visited our school <u>again</u>.
5. Traffic officers drive <u>quickly</u> to catch speeding cars.
6. Their sirens blare <u>loudly</u>.
7. Officers riding horses work <u>outside</u>.
8. Police officers <u>often</u> talk to students.
9. A police captain questions the driver <u>closely</u>.
10. The officers <u>carefully</u> climb the tower.

B. Write the word or words in parentheses ( ) that make the sentence correct. *pages 322–323*

Example: The police officer moved _____ than the criminal.   (more fast, faster)
faster

11. Police officers use cars _____ than bicycles. (more often, most often) more often
12. In bad weather, people should drive _____ than they do in good weather. (more slowly, slowlier) more slowly
13. Police helicopters fly _____ than skyscrapers. (more high, higher) higher
14. Police officers have to work _____ than we imagined. (more carefully, carefuller) more carefully
15. The police got to the accident _____ than the firefighters did. (quick, more quickly) more quickly

---

Vocabulary Power page 78

Name _____

WORD FAMILIES

A. The word *career* is based on a word which means "car." All the words below are in the same family because they come from this word. Read the words and their meanings. Then use each word to complete the sentences.

car	an automobile that takes you places
career	work that takes you through life
carriage	a fancy kind of wagon pulled by a horse
carry	to move something from one place to another
chariots	carts with two wheels, pulled by horses; used long ago in races

1. My uncle plans a _____career_____ as a farmer.
2. We drove to Florida in our _____car_____.
3. The ancient Romans raced each other in their _____chariots_____.
4. A horse pulled our _____carriage_____ in a ride around the park.
5. You are too heavy for me to _____carry_____.
6. My sister has a _____career_____ as a doctor.

B. Use two of the words in the list above in sentences of your own.
Responses may vary. Accept reasonable responses.
7. _____
8. _____

78   Unit 5 • Chapter 26   Vocabulary Power

Activity

911 INFORMATION Have students make cards to keep near the telephone for help in an emergency. Have them include the following information:

- name, address, and phone number
- the local emergency number
- how to speak when reporting an emergency

Prompt students to use adverbs when writing their instructions.

C. Write the adverb in each sentence. Then write whether it tells *how, when,* or *where*.
pages 318–321

Example: Police dogs work well with their police partners.
well, how

16. Officers choose dogs that can be trained easily. easily, how
17. The dogs always obey commands. always, when
18. They work hard. hard, how
19. Police dogs sometimes guard buildings. sometimes, when
20. The fire station dog may ride somewhere on the fire engine. somewhere, where

D. Write the adverb in each sentence. Then write the verb it describes. *pages 318–323*

Example: Officer Jackson drove carefully down the street.
carefully, drove

21. Suddenly a car passed him. Suddenly, passed
22. It was going faster than his police car. faster, was going
23. Officer Jackson quickly started his flashing lights. quickly, started
24. The siren on his car blared loudly. loudly, blared
25. Finally, the car stopped. Finally, stopped

Writing Connection

Art Think about something you could do to improve your community. Talk about your idea with a partner. Work with your partner to design a poster that illustrates your idea. Use adverbs to explain *how, when,* and *where* your idea could be used.

Remember
that adverbs can be used to compare actions. Add *er* or use *more* to compare two actions. Add *est* or use *most* to compare more than two actions.

325

Building Oral Grammar
Students will find that they can recognize correct adverb use by listening for it. After they complete Part B, have partners take turns reading the completed sentences to each other. They should listen for errors and point out any they hear.

Writing Connection

Art Tell students that the most important part of a poster is the center because most people look there first. Tell students to put their main illustration and words in the center and put details around the edges.

WRAP-UP/ASSESS

SUMMARIZE Have students select a piece of writing from their journals or portfolios. Ask them to trade papers with a partner. Have students look for examples of adverbs in their partner's writing sample. Tell them to identify whether the adverbs tell *how, when,* or *where*.

ADDITIONAL PRACTICE An additional page of Extra Practice is provided on page 471 of the *Pupil Edition.*

TECHNOLOGY *Grammar Practice and Assessment* CD-ROM; *Writing Express* CD-ROM

INTERNET Visit *The Learning Site:*
www.harcourtschool.com

PRACTICE page 89

Name _____

Extra Practice

A. Write the adverb in each sentence.

1. The woman spoke tearfully into the telephone. _tearfully_
2. Her child had disappeared outside. _outside_
3. The police responded fast. _fast_
4. The police cars raced quickly to the house. _quickly_
5. An officer found the boy and carried him gently home. _gently_

B. Write each sentence. Choose the word or words in parentheses ( ) that makes the sentence correct.

6. The students entered the room (more excitedly, more excited) than yesterday. The students entered the room more excitedly than yesterday.

7. The teacher came in (cheerfullest, most cheerfully) of all. The teacher came in most cheerfully of all.

8. He listened even (more closely, most closely) than the students did to the speaker. He listened even more closely than the the students did to the speaker.

TRY THIS! Write three sentences about how the police help people in your community. Circle the adverbs in your sentences.

Practice • Adverbs   Unit 5 • Chapter 26   89

CHALLENGE

WRITE AN ANNOUNCEMENT
Tell students to imagine that their class is planning a career fair at which people will talk about their jobs. Have students work in small groups to write an announcement about the career fair that tells which careers might be represented, who should attend, and when and where the career fair will be held.

Students should make the announcement as vivid as possible by using adverbs to describe the event.

Chapter Review

OBJECTIVES

- To review adverbs
- To take simple notes from relevant sources and make an outline

SPIRAL REVIEW

DAILY LANGUAGE PRACTICE

TRANSPARENCY 60

1 Once I need help from an police officer. (needed; a)

2 I were lost, and he helped I. (was; me.)

BRIDGE TO WRITING I got home ___(adverb)___ with his help. I live ___(adverb)___ .

STANDARDIZED TEST PREP

MODEL TEST-TAKING STRATEGIES Read aloud the directions on page 326. Remind students to find the verb and decide what the adverb tells about the verb. Model the thinking. Write this example on the board:

(1) The street-cleaning crew works <u>hard</u> to keep our neighborhood clean.

  1 **A** tells *where*

      B tells *when*

      C tells *how*

MODEL The underlined adverb tells about the verb *works*. The adverb *hard* does not tell *when* or *where* the crew works, but it does tell *how* the crew works. The answer must be C.

STANDARDIZED TEST PREP

TIP Don't spend too much time on one question. Make sure to save some time to check your answers.

For additional test preparation, visit *The Learning Site:* www.harcourtschool.com

326

Chapter Review

Read each sentence and look at the underlined words. There may be a mistake in word usage. If you find a mistake, choose the answer that shows the correct usage. If there is not a mistake, choose *Correct as is.*

1 Think about the community workers <u>who cheerful help you</u>.

  A who most cheerful help you

  B who cheerfully help you B

  C who more cheerful help you

  D Correct as is

2 Police and firefighters <u>work more harder</u> to keep you safe.

  F work most hardest   **H** work hard H

  G work better hard   **J** Correct as is

3 Volunteers in the school office or library are <u>the most friendly</u>.

  A the more friendly   **C** the more friendlier

  B the most friendliest   **D** Correct as is D

4 Construction crews <u>work inside</u> on roads and bridges.

  F work behind   **H** work over

  G work outside G   **J** Correct as is

5 Doctors and nurses always <u>take goodest care</u> of you.

  A take best care   **C** take good care C

  B take more gooder care   **D** Correct as is

6 Many people <u>usual work</u> together to make a neighborhood nice.

  F more usual work   **H** most usually

  G usually work G   **J** Correct as is

Assessment

PORTFOLIO ASSESSMENT Have students select their best work from the Writing Connections on pages 319, 321, 323, and 325.

ONGOING ASSESSMENT Evaluate the performance of 4–6 students using appropriate checklists and record forms from pages R74–R77.

INTERNET Activities and exercises to help students prepare for state and standardized assessments appear on *The Learning Site:* www.harcourtschool.com

Taking Notes and Making an Outline

Gathering Information

Reading for information is different from reading for fun. When you are reading for information, you should take notes. Write information you find about a subject on separate cards. Include the name of the source where you find the information.

School crossing guards help children safely cross the street. — from newspaper story in the Daily News

Making an Outline

Use your note cards to prepare an outline. Start by listing the main idea in each group of cards. You do not need to use complete sentences in an outline. Number the main ideas. Under each main idea, include some facts or details. Use capital letters to list the facts and details. Here is an outline that organizes information about volunteers.

Volunteers Needed!

I. At schools
   A. Crossing guards
   B. Recess monitors
   C. After-school tutors
II. At hospitals
   A. Flower deliverers
   B. Gift shop helpers
   C. Patient visitors

YOUR TURN

Find a magazine article or newspaper story about something that interests you. As you read, take notes on separate cards. Before you write about the subject, use your notes to make an outline. Use your outline to write four sentences about this subject.

327

PRACTICE page 90

Name _____

Chapter Review

Read the passage. Choose the answer that describes each underlined word. Fill in the oval next to your choice.

Do you (1) ever see trash on the street? Some city workers do nothing but clean the (2) streets. They work (3) hard to keep them clean. They sweep a street (4) weekly. Brooms spin (5) rapidly around on a truck. Workers sit (6) high on the truck and drive it down the street. (7) Afterward, leaves fall, and people drop trash. (8) Soon the street needs cleaning again.

1. ⚪ an adverb that tells where
   ⚫ an adverb that tells when
   ⚪ an adverb that tells how
   ⚪ not an adverb

2. ⚪ an adverb that tells where
   ⚪ an adverb that tells when
   ⚪ an adverb that tells how
   ⚪ not an adverb

3. ⚪ an adverb that tells where
   ⚪ an adverb that tells when
   ⚪ an adverb that tells how
   ⚪ not an adverb

4. ⚪ an adverb that tells where
   ⚪ an adverb that tells when
   ⚪ an adverb that tells how
   ⚪ not an adverb

5. ⚪ an adverb that tells where
   ⚪ an adverb that tells when
   ⚪ an adverb that tells how
   ⚪ not an adverb

6. ⚫ an adverb that tells where
   ⚪ an adverb that tells when
   ⚪ an adverb that tells how
   ⚪ not an adverb

7. ⚪ an adverb that tells where
   ⚪ an adverb that tells when
   ⚪ an adverb that tells how
   ⚪ not an adverb

8. ⚪ an adverb that tells where
   ⚪ an adverb that tells when
   ⚪ an adverb that tells how
   ⚪ not an adverb

90 Unit 5 • Chapter 26   Practice • Adverbs

CHALLENGE

GROUP NOTE-TAKING Have students work in small groups. One member of each group can read aloud a newspaper article. The other members will use note cards to take notes. When they are finished, group members can compare notes to see whether they included all the important information from the article. Then have the group members use their notes to make a group outline of the important information in the article.

STUDY SKILLS
Taking Notes and Making an Outline

TEACH/MODEL

After students have read page 327, ask them to name times when they may need to take notes or make an outline. Tell students that they should use a separate note card for each source and limit each card to notes about one idea. Remind them to use their own words when taking notes.

Have students begin the Your Turn activity. After students have taken notes on cards, tell them that they can easily use their notes to make an outline. Have them sort their cards by main idea and then number them to write an outline.

WRITING APPLICATION Ask students to choose a newspaper article about a community event. They should take notes on the article and then use their notes to create an outline with at least two main headings. Have students use available technology to write sentences from their outlines.

WRAP-UP/ASSESS

SUMMARIZE Have students write in their journals to reflect on what they have learned about taking notes and making an outline. **REFLECTION**

TECHNOLOGY Additional writing activities are provided on the *Writing Express* CD-ROM

LESSON ORGANIZER	DAY 1	DAY 2
DAILY LANGUAGE PRACTICE TRANSPARENCIES 61, 62	1. me did an report on panda bears. (I; a) 2. They am called giant pandas. (are)	1. pandas climbs trees. (Pandas; climb) 2. some pandas weigh more than two hundred poundes. (Some; pounds.)
ORAL WARM-UP Listening/Speaking	Informative Writing Examples 328	Discuss Outlining 330
TEACH/MODEL **WRITING** 	✔ **ORGANIZING INFORMATION** **Literature Model:** from *Horsepower: The Wonder of Draft Horses* 328 **Analyze the Model** 328	**GUIDED WRITING** *Making an Outline* 330 *Audience and Purpose* 331 Writing and Thinking: Write to Record Reflections
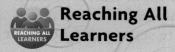 **Reaching All Learners**	**Challenge:** Onward with Outlines 329 *ESL Manual* pp. 132, 133	**Challenge:** Weather Report 331 *ESL Manual* p. 132
GRAMMAR	**HANDS-ON ACTIVITIES** 305I–305J	**HANDS-ON ACTIVITIES** 305I–305J
CROSS-CURRICULAR/ ENRICHMENT	**Art:** A Heart for Art 329 *Vocabulary Power* Explore Word Meaning 328 current, **draft**, haul, outline, recruit *See Vocabulary Power book.*	**Study Skills:** Outlines for Study 331 *Vocabulary Power* Multiple-Meaning Words 328 *Vocabulary Power* book p. 79 **Vocabulary activity**

KEY
✔ = tested skill

DAY 3

1. Bamboo is a pandas favorite food (panda's; food.)
2. Them eats up to seventy pounds of bamboo a day! (They eat)

Compare Outlines, Webs, and Flow Charts 332

GUIDED WRITING
Paragraph of Information 332
Analyze the Model 333
Prewriting and Drafting 333

ESL: Planning the Paragraph 333
ESL Manual p. 132

HANDS-ON ACTIVITIES
305I–305J

Listening and Speaking: Outlines for Oral Presentations 332
Evaluation Criteria 333

Vocabulary Power

Rhyming Words 328
Vocabulary Power p. 80

Vocabulary activity

DAY 4

1. about one hundred pandas am kept in different zoos (About; are; zoos.)
2. Last summer us see pandas at the zoo. (we; saw)

Discuss Revising 334

GUIDED WRITING
Editing 334
Sharing and Reflecting 334

Proofreading Practice

ESL Manual p. 132

HANDS-ON ACTIVITIES
305I–305J

Vocabulary Power

Word Families 328
Vocabulary Power p. 81

Vocabulary activity

DAY 5

1. The panda's At the zoo were cute and funny (pandas at; funny.)
2. My sister and me waited a longg time to see them. (I; long)

Describe Information Gathering 335

STUDY SKILLS:
Taking Notes 335

ESL Manual p. 132

HANDS-ON ACTIVITIES
305I–305J

Vocabulary Power

Graphics 328
Evaluation Criteria: Self-Evaluation 335

Informative Writing

Writer's Craft: Organizing Information

OBJECTIVES
- To understand informative writing and analyze its use in a passage
- To analyze organization in informative writing

DAILY LANGUAGE PRACTICE

TRANSPARENCY 61

1 me did an report on panda bears. (I; a)

2 They am called giant pandas. (are)

ORAL WARM-UP

USE PRIOR KNOWLEDGE Ask volunteers to give examples of informative writing. Then have students read the introduction and the model.

Analyze THE Model

1. What is the writer's main subject? (draft horses) **INFERENTIAL: MAIN IDEA**

2. What facts does the writer give about the size of draft horses? (Their hooves are as big as dinner plates, they are as tall as a basketball player, and they weigh as much as a whole class of third graders.) **LITERAL: NOTE DETAILS**

3. What information does the writer give about the work done by draft horses? (Draft horses pulled carriages, wagons, plows, and corn pickers.) **LITERAL: NOTE DETAILS**

CHAPTER 27

Informative Writing

Writer's Craft

Organizing Information

Before you write to inform, you can find out facts about a subject and organize them.

Read the following passage. Look at the different kinds of facts the writer tells about draft horses.

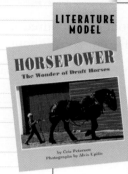

LITERATURE MODEL

> A most remarkable horse named Kate has huge black hooves the size of dinner plates. She is as tall as a basketball player and weighs as much as a classroom of third-graders. Kate is a Percheron draft horse.
>
> One hundred years ago, draft horses like Kate pulled carriages full of people and wagons full of milk. Before there were tractors or combines, horses pulled plows through spring sod and corn pickers through fall fields.
>
> —from *Horsepower: The Wonder of Draft Horses* by Cris Peterson

Analyze THE Model

1. What is the writer's main subject?

2. What facts does the writer give about the size of draft horses?

3. What information does the writer give about the work done by draft horses?

Vocabulary Power

draft [draft] *adj.* Used for pulling heavy loads.

Using an Outline

Before you write to inform, you must consider your audience and purpose. It is also a good idea to use an outline to help you plan what you will write. An **outline** is like a map for writing and organizing information. Study the examples on the next page.

328

Vocabulary Power

DAY 1 EXPLORE WORD MEANING Introduce and define *draft*. **Draft can mean "used for pulling loads." What might you use a draft horse for?**

DAY 2 MULTIPLE-MEANING WORDS Draft has more than one meaning. **What are some of the other meanings of *draft*?** (See also *Vocabulary Power*, page 79.)

DAY 3 RHYMING WORDS Write on the board: *draft, drain, laughed.* **Which of these words rhyme?** (See also *Vocabulary Power*, page 80.)

DAY 4 WORD FAMILIES **Sometimes the spelling in the same word family changes over time. *Draw* and *draft* come from the same word. What are some other words in this family?** (See also *Vocabulary Power*, page 81.)

DAY 5 GRAPHICS **Draft also refers to a gentle breeze. Write the word *draft* in a way that illustrates this meaning.**

Strategies for Organizing Information

Audience and Purpose

How old is the reader?

How hard is the information?

Write so that the audience will understand the new information.

After you think about your audience and purpose, use an outline to plan the best way to present your information to them.

Percheron Draft Horses

I. Size
   A. Hooves as big as dinner plates
   B. As tall as a basketball player
   C. Weigh as much as a classroom of third-graders
II. Work done by draft horses
   A. Pulled carriages full of people
   B. Pulled wagons full of milk
   C. Pulled plows and corn pickers

YOUR TURN

THINK ABOUT HOW INFORMATION IS ORGANIZED Work with a partner. Choose a chapter in your social studies textbook. Look through the chapter to find heads and subheads. Then use the heads and subheads to make an outline of the chapter.

329

CHALLENGE

Art
. . . .

A HEART FOR ART Have students locate articles about or biographies of artists such as Mary Cassatt, Pablo Picasso, or Auguste Renoir. They may use encyclopedias or the Internet. Have students outline the article or biography, using the headings or topic sentences.

Then have students illustrate their outlines by drawing a picture of the artist or by reproducing one of his or her works.

ONWARD WITH OUTLINES
Show students how to outline a passage in greater detail by using Arabic numerals and lowercase letters. Point out that the information is organized from general to more specific with each level.

Then have students outline a section from the chapter they selected for the Your Turn activity.

ORGANIZING INFORMATION Explain that writers use outlines to organize information. Discuss the structure of outlines, using the example on page 329. Point out that the items beside the Roman numerals are the main heads, or topics. The items beside the capital letters are subheads, or details about the main heads. Note that the subtopics are indented. Tell students that an outline does not have to be written in complete sentences.

When discussing audience and purpose, point out that students' audiences often will be their classmates. Ask students why it is important to think about the audience when writing. Ask them to describe how their writing might be different for other audiences, such as younger readers or adults.

Have students complete the Your Turn activity. Some students may have more success with the activity if they choose a chapter they have already read. Others may wish to choose an upcoming chapter.

WRAP-UP/ASSESS

SUMMARIZE Why is it important to know your audience and purpose before you begin writing?

TECHNOLOGY Additional writing activities are provided on the *Writing Express* CD-ROM

Writer's Craft: Organizing Information

OBJECTIVES
- To outline information and to identify the purpose and audience for a given kind of writing
- To record reflections about the nature of a writer's audience

DAILY LANGUAGE PRACTICE

TRANSPARENCY 61

1 pandas climbs trees. (Pandas; climb)

2 some pandas weigh more than two hundred poundes. (Some; pounds.)

ORAL WARM-UP

USE PRIOR KNOWLEDGE Ask students to explain the purpose of outlining. Ask: **How do you decide what kind of information to put in an outline?**

GUIDED WRITING

MAKING AN OUTLINE Review the structure of outlines. Remind students that the main heads are indicated by Roman numerals. Subheads, or facts about the main topics, belong beside the capital letters. Tell students that outlines do not have to have complete sentences.

Have students complete Part A in pairs.
(I. Wheat
   A. Used to make bread
   B. Used to make pastry
   C. Used to make cereal
   D. Used to make pasta
II. Corn
   A. Eaten as a vegetable
   B. Made into cereal
   C. Used to feed cattle and other livestock)

Making an Outline

A. Read the paragraph. On your paper, make an outline like the one shown below. Write facts from the paragraph to complete the outline.

> Wheat and corn are important crops. Wheat is used mainly to make bread, pastries, cereal, and pasta. Corn is eaten as a vegetable, made into cereal, or used to feed cattle and other livestock.

Important Crops

I. (name of crop)

    A. _____

    B. _____

    C. _____

    D. _____

II. (name of crop)

    A. _____

    B. _____

    C. _____

Vocabulary Power page 79

Name _____

MULTIPLE-MEANING WORDS

Many words have more than one meaning. Clues from the sentence will tell you which meaning is being used.

A. Read each sentence below. Circle the letter of the meaning of the underlined word. Then write a sentence using the other meaning.

1. Have you finished with the first <u>draft</u> of your letter?
   A used for pulling loads
   (B) a beginning sketch or outline
   _____

2. The math club will <u>recruit</u> for new members.
   A a new member of a club
   (B) to enlist
   _____

3. Make an <u>outline</u> before you start your report.
   (A) written notes
   B a line drawing
   _____

4. We needed a wagon to <u>haul</u> the bricks home.
   A a large or heavy load
   (B) to pull
   _____

5. The river's <u>current</u> was strong.
   (A) a swift part of a stream
   B part of the present time
   _____

Vocabulary Power   Unit 5 • Chapter 27 79

Matching Audience and Purpose

B. On your paper, write the number for each kind of writing. Next to the number, write the letter of the purpose and audience that matches that kind of writing.

Kind of Writing

1. a letter to a magazine asking for more science articles to be printed

2. a science report about frogs

3. an article for your school newspaper about your class trip to the museum

4. a friendly letter to share some facts you learned in social studies

Purpose and Audience

a. to inform classmates about a topic

b. to persuade a magazine editor to do something

c. to inform a friend about a topic

d. to describe something for all the other students in your school

 Writing AND Thinking

Write to Record Reflections If you put on a show, your audience is the people who watch the show. Why do you think the people who read something you write are also called an audience? How is an audience of readers like an audience who watches you dance, sing, give a speech, or put on a play? Write your reflections in your Writer's Journal.

331

AUDIENCE AND PURPOSE Before students begin Part B, lead a discussion about audience and purpose. Ask questions such as: **Who has read your writing, and what did they learn from it? Do you think people write informative writing mostly for other people or mostly for themselves? Why?**

Have students complete Part B independently. Then discuss the answers and students' reasons for choosing them. (1. b, 2. a, 3. d, 4. c)

 Writing and Thinking

Write to Record Reflections Ask students to think about what they like about having someone else read their writing. Have a class discussion about how the audience at a play, a concert, or a recital lets the performers know that they enjoyed the show. Ask students to suggest ways that readers can let writers know they appreciate their work.

WRAP-UP/ASSESS

SUMMARIZE Why is outlining helpful for writers?

Study Skills

• • • • • • • • • • •

OUTLINES FOR STUDY Have students prepare for a science, history, or geography mini-quiz by outlining a textbook page. Check their work by drawing an outline on the board and having students complete it with details from their own outlines. Then cover the outline and ask questions about the material. Afterward, ask students how outlining helped them remember the information.

CHALLENGE

WEATHER REPORT On the board, write *Audience* and *Purpose.* Under *Audience,* write *a friend, readers of a magazine, a pen pal in China,* and so on. Under *Purpose,* write *to express, to inform,* and *to persuade.* Ask students to write two paragraphs about the weather, using different audiences and purposes.

When students finish writing, ask them to describe how their writing changed with each audience and purpose.

Writer's Craft: Organizing Information

OBJECTIVES

- To recognize and analyze the parts of an outline and a paragraph of information
- To choose a topic
- To generate and outline ideas for a paragraph of information

DAILY LANGUAGE PRACTICE

TRANSPARENCY 61

1 Bamboo is a pandas favorite food (panda's; food.)

2 Them eats up to seventy pounds of bamboo a day! (They eat)

ORAL WARM-UP

USE PRIOR KNOWLEDGE Ask students how making an outline is similar to making a web or a flow chart.

GUIDED WRITING

Paragraph of Information

READ AND RESPOND TO THE MODEL Before reading aloud Becky's outline and paragraph, have students determine a purpose for listening. (Possible responses: to gain information; to see how one writer used an outline to write a paragraph)

Discuss whether Becky effectively makes her outline into a paragraph. Remind students to support their evaluations with examples from the models.

FOCUS ON ORGANIZATION Have students reread the outline silently, using the sidenotes to find the main parts. Discuss how Becky follows the same order of information in both the outline and the paragraph of information.

FOCUS ON WRITER'S CRAFT Have students find the title and two main heads. Discuss why Becky separates the details under two headings. (The details tell information about two different main ideas.)

CHAPTER 27
Informative Writing

Paragraph of Information

The purpose of the book *Horsepower: The Wonder of Draft Horses* is to inform readers about draft horses. The audience is readers like you. Becky, a third grader, researched the subject of zebras. She made an outline to organize her facts. Then she used the outline to help her write a paragraph of information to share with her classmates. Read the outline and paragraph that Becky wrote.

MODEL

title
main idea
detail
detail
main idea
detail

detail
detail

Zebras

I. Size
  A. Smaller than a horse
  B. 4–5 feet high at shoulders
II. Appearance
  A. White or pale yellow with black stripes
  B. Short mane
  C. Large ears

Zebras are smaller than horses. Most are four to five feet high at the shoulders. They have white or pale yellow coats with black stripes. Zebras' manes are short, but their ears are large.

332

Vocabulary Power page 80

Name _____

RHYMING WORDS

▶ Use words from the Word Box to complete the sentences below. The word you write should rhyme with the underlined word in the sentence.

fed	tent	fine	rice	mall	sketch	draft

1. I almost <u>laughed</u> when I read my first ___ draft ___
2. I'll ask Rover to <u>fetch</u> my ___ sketch ___
3. We need a truck to <u>haul</u> what we bought at the ___ mall ___
4. The teacher said my <u>outline</u> was ___ fine ___
5. Wheat is made into <u>bread</u> so that people can be ___ fed ___
6. The main <u>event</u> is in the ___ tent ___
7. She has a special <u>device</u> for cooking ___ rice ___

▶ Now try these.

moth	horse	draw	types	boot	toast	time

8. Everyone <u>saw</u> that he could ___ draw ___
9. Did the <u>recruit</u> find his ___ boot ___?
10. Fabrics have <u>stripes</u> of many ___ types ___
11. The zebra, of <u>course</u>, looks like a ___ horse ___
12. It's not hard to <u>rhyme</u> if you take your ___ time ___
13. The holes in the <u>cloth</u> are from the ___ moth ___
14. Who ate the <u>most</u> ___ toast ___?

80   Unit 5 • Chapter 27   Vocabulary Power

Listening and Speaking

OUTLINES FOR ORAL PRESENTATIONS Have students work in pairs. Each student chooses a different outline from the chapter and uses it as the basis for a brief oral presentation.

Allow students a few minutes to prepare, and then have them take turns giving an oral presentation for their partner. Remind them to speak in complete sentences.

---

1. What two main heads did Becky use in her outline?
2. Did Becky follow her outline? How can you tell?
3. Does Becky's paragraph explain the information clearly? Why or why not?

YOUR TURN

WRITING PROMPT Write a paragraph for your classmates about a topic you have learned about in Social Studies. Use your textbook to help you put the facts about your topic in an outline. Then use your outline to write your paragraph.

STUDY THE PROMPT Ask yourself these questions:

1. What is your purpose for writing the paragraph?
2. Who is your audience for the paragraph?
3. What will you do before you begin writing?

Prewriting and Drafting

Organizing Your Information Write down facts that you want to include in your paragraph. Then organize the facts by making an outline.

Title of Outline (your topic)

I. An important idea
   A. Detail about the idea
   B. Another detail

II. Another important idea
   A. Detail about this idea
   B. Another detail

Add more main heads and subheads if you need them. When your outline is complete, use it to write a draft of your paragraph.

USING YOUR
Handbook

- Use the Writer's Thesaurus to help you restate information in your own words.

333

Evaluation Criteria
. . . .

Review the criteria that students should apply:

- Use an outline.
- Focus on audience and purpose.
- Use correct paragraph form.

Work with students to add additional criteria.

ESL
REACHING ALL LEARNERS

PLANNING THE PARAGRAPH
Have students work with English-fluent partners to create their outlines and draft their paragraphs. Students should focus on:

- organizing information
- eliminating details that do not directly relate to their topics
- using word order that makes sense.

Analyze THE *Model*

1. **What two main heads did Becky use in her outline?** (*Size* and *Appearance*) LITERAL: NOTE DETAILS
2. **Did Becky follow her outline? How can you tell?** (Possible response: Yes; the same details are there, and they are in the same order.) CRITICAL: INTERPRET TEXT STRUCTURE
3. **Does Becky's paragraph explain the information clearly? Why or why not?** (Possible response: Yes; the ideas are organized and they all relate to one another.) CRITICAL: MAKE JUDGMENTS

After students read the writing prompt and the Study the Prompt questions, have them brainstorm a list of social studies topics. Remind them that their information should come from only one source.

Prewriting and Drafting

Monitor students as they work on their outlines. Have them draft their informative paragraphs on a separate sheet of paper or on the computer. As they draft, have students check that their paragraphs include all the information from their outlines.

WRAP-UP/ASSESS

Writer's Journal

SUMMARIZE Ask students to reflect in their journals about what is the most difficult part of creating an outline.

Writer's Craft: Organizing Information

OBJECTIVES
- To revise and proofread a paragraph of information, focusing on purpose, audience, and organization
- To share and reflect on a paragraph of information

DAILY LANGUAGE PRACTICE

TRANSPARENCY 62

1 about one hundred pandas am kept in different zoos (About; are; zoos.)

2 Last summer us see pandas at the zoo. (we; saw)

ORAL WARM-UP

USE PRIOR KNOWLEDGE Ask: **Why are revising and proofreading important steps in informative writing?** Call on volunteers to explain how revising has improved their writing in the past.

GUIDED WRITING

Editing
Remind students to check that each item on their outline has been included. Have students trade papers with a partner. Ask students to respond constructively to their partner's writing by suggesting ways to improve the paragraphs.

Sharing and Reflecting
Remind students to respond to their classmates' work with positive, supportive statements. Remind them that feelings and ideas recorded in their Writer's Journals may help them with future writing projects. Students should write reflections about their partner's work as well as their own.

WRAP-UP/ASSESS

SUMMARIZE How did organizing your information into an outline make writing your paragraph easier?

Editor's Marks
- ✗ take out text
- ∧ add text
- ◯ move text
- ¶ new paragraph
- ≡ capitalize
- / lowercase
- ◯ correct spelling

Editing

Read over the draft of your paragraph of information. Is there anything you would like to change or add? Use this checklist to help you revise your paragraph.

- ☑ Does your writing fulfill your purpose?
- ☑ Is the information well organized?
- ☑ Will your audience understand the information in your paragraph?

Use this checklist as you proofread your paragraph.

- ☑ I have begun my sentences with capital letters.
- ☑ I have used the correct end marks.
- ☑ I have used adjectives and adverbs correctly.
- ☑ I have used subject and object pronouns correctly.
- ☑ I have used a dictionary to check my spelling.

Sharing and Reflecting

Make a final copy of your paragraph, and share it with a partner. Is there any information you don't understand? If there is, talk about how to explain it better. Discuss how organizing information helps you carry out your purpose for writing. Write your reflections in your Writer's Journal.

Vocabulary Power page 81

Name _____

WORD FAMILIES

▶ Two words in each group belong in the same word family. Circle the word that does not belong in that word family. Then replace it with another word. The first one is tricky, so it is done for you. (Did you know that *draft* and *draw* both come from the same word family?) Additional words may vary. Possible responses are given.

1. draft	(drama)	draw	drawing
2. discover	(discourage)	uncover	recover
3. replace	place	(play)	placement
4. value	valueless	(valve)	valuable
5. (us)	useful	use	useless
6. handy	handkerchief	(hamburger)	handful
7. seashore	(search)	seaweed	seaside
8. current	currency	(rent)	occurrence
9. (ant)	army	armor	armful
10. enjoyment	(engine)	enjoy	enjoyable
11. football	footstep	(food)	footprint
12. (friendship)	fruit	fruitcake	fruity
13. gentle	gentleman	(gemstone)	gently
14. grandfather	(children)	grandmother	grandson
15. (cheerful)	colorful	coloring	color

Vocabulary Power   Unit 5 • Chapter 27 81

Taking Notes

STUDY SKILLS

You need to write down the facts you find in your research to remember them. You don't need to copy all the words, though. Instead, you can take notes.

Read the encyclopedia article below. Then look at the notes Tammy took when she read the article. Later she used her notes to make an outline.

Encyclopedia Article

Corn Oil
Corn oil is used for cooking and as salad oil. It is also used in the manufacture of products ranging from margarine to paint, soap, and linoleum.

Tammy's Notes
uses for corn oil – cooking, salad oil
also margarine, paint, soap, linoleum

Notice that Tammy's notes are much shorter than the article. Tammy wrote only the words she needed to remember.

YOUR TURN

Now you can practice taking notes. Follow these steps:

STEP 1 Work with a partner. Look up an interesting subject in an encyclopedia.

STEP 2 Choose an article or part of an article. Take notes on the information. You and your partner should each take your own notes.

STEP 3 Now compare your notes with your partner's notes. Talk about why each of you wrote down certain words and left out other words.

STEP 4 Then talk about what you and your partner have learned that will help both of you take better notes next time.

TIP When taking notes from different sources, use a separate note card for each detail. Write the title of the source on the note card.

335

Evaluation Criteria

SELF-EVALUATION Revisit the Evaluation Criteria to have students informally rate their own writing on a scale of 1 to 4. You might have them use stick-on notes to label their papers.

STUDY SKILLS

Taking Notes

OBJECTIVES
- To take notes from an encyclopedia entry
- To work with a partner to compare notes

 **DAILY LANGUAGE PRACTICE**

TRANSPARENCY 62

1 The panda's At the zoo were cute and funny (pandas at; funny.)

2 My sister and me waited a longg time to see them. (I; long)

ORAL WARM-UP

USE PRIOR KNOWLEDGE Ask students to describe a time when they gathered information for a report or a presentation.

TEACH/MODEL

Have students read the instructions and compare the article and Tammy's notes. Explain that another student might take different notes on the article, depending upon what he or she wanted to remember. Point out Tammy's neat handwriting; discuss how writing notes neatly will save time.

After students complete the Your Turn activity, ask them to share what they learned. As a class, make a poster listing Tips for Taking Notes.

WRAP-UP/ASSESS

Writer's Journal

SUMMARIZE In their journals, have students reflect on how the notes they took were different from their partner's notes.

For information on adapting this rubric to 5- or 6-point scales, see pages R78–R79.

CHAPTER 28
More About Adverbs and Adjectives
pages 336–345

LESSON ORGANIZER	DAY 1	DAY 2
DAILY LANGUAGE PRACTICE TRANSPARENCIES 63, 64	1. ours is the most smallest school in the state. (Ours; the smallest) 2. Next year the school got bigger. (will get) **Bridge to Writing** Many towns are growing (adverb).	1. Many peeple settled peacefully in our state (people; state.) 2. The hills reminded them of they homeland. (their) **Bridge to Writing** The (adjective) settlers brought their customs with them.
ORAL WARM-UP Listening/Speaking	Add an Adjective and an Adverb 336	Revise Using Adverbs 338 *Grammar Jingles*™ CD Track 19
TEACH/MODEL GRAMMAR **KEY** ✔ = tested skill	✔ **ADJECTIVE OR ADVERB?** 336–337 • To recognize and use adjectives and adverbs in writing • To write a list using adverbs and adjectives	✔ **ADVERB PLACEMENT IN SENTENCES** 338–339 • To identify and place adverbs in sentences • To use correct adverb placement in a list
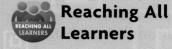 **Reaching All Learners**	**Modified Instruction** Below-Level: Model the Thinking Above-Level: Replace Adverbs and Adjectives **Reteach:** *Reteach Activities Copying Masters* pp. 55 and R56 **Challenge:** Activity Card 19, R71 *ESL Manual* pp. 134, 135 *Practice Book* p. 91	**Modified Instruction** Below-Level: Hear the Adverbs Above-Level: Rewrite Sentences **Reteach:** *Reteach Activities Copying Masters* pp. 56 and R56 **Challenge:** Where Would You Like to Go? 339 *ESL Manual* pp. 134, 136 *Practice Book* p. 92
WRITING	Writing Connection 337 Writer's Journal: Recording Ideas	Writing Connection 339 Writer's Craft: Main Idea and Details
CROSS-CURRICULAR/ ENRICHMENT	*Vocabulary Power* Explore Word Meaning 336 coyote, **fiesta,** piñata, plaza, tortilla **See *Vocabulary Power* book.**	**Listening and Speaking:** Find Examples 338 *Vocabulary Power* Word Origins 336 *Vocabulary Power* p. 82 **Vocabulary activity**

335A UNIT 5

DAY 3

1. san antonio are a nice plase to live.
   (San Antonio is; place)

2. My house is more older than him
   house. (is older; his)

Bridge to Writing San Antonio has
changed _(adverb)_ in the last century.

Complete the Sentences 340
Grammar Jingles™ CD Track 19

✔ **USING *GOOD* AND *WELL*, *BAD*
   AND *BADLY*** 340–341
   • To use *good, well, bad,* and
     badly correctly in sentences
   • To make a poster, using adjec-
     tives and adverbs

Modified Instruction
Below-Level: Identify Words
Above-Level: Rewrite Sentences
ESL: Complete the Phrases 340
ESL Manual pp. 134, 137
Reteach: *Reteach Activities
   Copying Masters* pp. 57 and
   R56
Challenge: Plan a Tour 341
Practice Book p. 93

Writing Connection 341
   Social Studies

Vocabulary Power
   Figurative Language 336
   Vocabulary Power p. 83
Vocabulary activity

DAY 4

1. Celebrations in San Antonio have well
   parades (good parades.)

2. My sister rode she horse in the parade
   (her; parade.)

Bridge to Writing I could see
(adverb) from the street.

Move Adverbs 342

EXTRA PRACTICE 342–343
   • To identify adjectives and
     adverbs and use *good, well,
     bad,* and *badly* correctly
   • To place adverbs and adjectives
     correctly in a letter
Practice and assessment

Building Oral Grammar
Work in Pairs and Read Aloud 343
ESL: Make a Word Picture 342
ESL Manual pp. 134, 138
Challenge: Mystery Visit 343
Practice Book p. 94

Writing Connection 343
   Real-Life Writing: Friendly Letter

Vocabulary Power
   Analogies 336
   Vocabulary Power p. 84
Vocabulary activity

DAY 5

1. tomorrow the parade went down the
   street. (Tomorrow; will go)

2. Will There be clownz, fire trucks, and
   floats in the parade (there; clowns;
   parade?)

Bridge to Writing _(Adjective)_ bands
play. The bands play _(adverb)_ .

TEST PREP **CHAPTER REVIEW** 344
   • To review correct use of adjec-
     tives and adverbs
   • To conduct an interview and to
     make a multimedia presentation
Test preparation

Challenge: Promotional Film 345
Practice Book p. 95
ESL Manual pp. 134, 139

Writing Application 345
   Interview

Technology: Interviewing to
   Learn About Your Community
   345

Vocabulary Power
   Exemplification 336

More About Adverbs and Adjectives

Adjective or Adverb?

OBJECTIVES
- To recognize and use adjectives and adverbs in writing
- To write a list using adverbs and adjectives

DAILY LANGUAGE PRACTICE

TRANSPARENCY 63

1 ours is the most smallest school in the state. (Ours; the smallest)

2 Next year the school got bigger. (will get)

BRIDGE TO WRITING Many towns are growing ___(adverb)___ .

ORAL WARM-UP

USE PRIOR KNOWLEDGE Read aloud this sentence: *People live in our town.* Ask students to add an adjective and an adverb to the sentence.

TEACH/MODEL

Remind students that adjectives tell *how many* or *what kind*. Adjectives often come before the noun they describe or after a linking verb such as *is* or *seems*. Adverbs tell *when*, *where*, or *how* about an action. Adverbs that tell *how* often end in *ly*.

Model the thinking, using the example sentences:

MODEL In the example sentences, the word *peaceful* tells what kind of city. The word *peacefully* tells how people live. I know that it is an adverb because it describes a verb.

Work with students to complete the Guided Practice.

Adjective or Adverb?

You can tell whether a word is an **adjective** or an **adverb** by looking at the word it describes.

Remember that an adjective describes a noun. It tells *what kind* or *how many*. An adverb describes a verb. It tells *where*, *when*, or *how*.

> **Examples:**
> San Antonio is a **peaceful** city. (adjective; tells *what kind*)
> People can live **peacefully** in San Antonio. (adverb; tells *how*)

Often, words that end in *ly* are adverbs. Several of these adverbs are in the chart. However, you should always check if a word ending in *ly* describes a noun or a verb.

Adjective	Adverb
soft	softly
slow	slowly
clear	clearly

Vocabulary Power

fi•es•ta [fē•es′tə] *n.* A festival; a time of celebration marked by special events such as a parade and dancing.

Guided Practice

A. Tell whether each underlined word is an adjective or an adverb.

Example: We listened <u>quietly</u> to the tour guide.
adverb

1. She told us about the <u>beautiful</u> city of San Antonio. adjective
2. She spoke <u>calmly</u> to our group. adverb
3. I listened <u>carefully</u> for facts about the city. adverb
4. She used a <u>quiet</u> voice when she spoke of the Alamo. adjective
5. The Alamo is the location of a <u>famous</u> battle. adjective

---

Vocabulary Power

DAY 1 EXPLORE WORD MEANING Introduce and define *fiesta*. **What are some things that people do during a fiesta?**

DAY 2 WORD ORIGINS *Fiesta* **is a Spanish word. What are some other Spanish words that we use?** (See also *Vocabulary Power*, page 82.)

DAY 3 FIGURATIVE LANGUAGE **You might hear someone say, "It was a feast for my eyes." What do you think this means?** (See also *Vocabulary Power*, page 83.)

DAY 4 ANALOGIES **Finish this analogy:** *Fiesta is to dance as race is to* ___. (See also *Vocabulary Power*, page 84.)

DAY 5 EXEMPLIFICATION Have students plan a fiesta. **List all the things you want your fiesta to include.**

Independent Practice

B. Write whether each underlined word is an adjective or an adverb. Then write the noun or verb it describes.

Example: The birds outside our hotel chirped <u>cheerfully</u>.
adverb; chirped

6. I awoke <u>early</u>. *adverb; awoke*
7. We rode on a <u>new</u> bus to *La Villita*, or Little Village. *adjective; bus*
8. "Exit <u>carefully</u>!" said the bus driver. *adverb; Exit*
9. *La Villita* takes up a <u>square</u> block. *adjective; block*
10. It has beautiful <u>old</u> houses. *adjective; houses*
11. "Good afternoon!" the tour guide said <u>cheerfully</u>. *adverb; said*
12. "<u>Two</u> people are missing from our group today," she said. *adjective; people*
13. She gave <u>some</u> directions to the group. *adjective; directions*
14. We walked <u>rapidly</u> to the riverfront. *adverb; walked*
15. <u>Soon</u> we were eating lunch <u>happily</u>. *adverb; eating*

Remember that an adjective describes a noun. An adverb describes a verb.

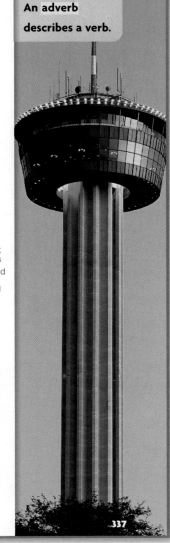

.337

Writing Connection

Writer's Journal: Recording Ideas
Think about your community. What are some places that visitors might enjoy? Record your favorite ideas in a list. Then write several sentences about what you can see and do at the places on your list. Use adjectives and adverbs in your sentences.

Independent Practice

Have students complete the Independent Practice, or modify it using these suggestions:

MODIFIED INSTRUCTION

BELOW-LEVEL STUDENTS Work through the Independent Practice with students, modeling the thinking.

ABOVE-LEVEL STUDENTS Have students rewrite the items, replacing the adverbs and adjectives with their antonyms, as appropriate.

Writing Connection

Writer's Journal: Recording Ideas
Allow students to look for the websites of the local government or office of tourism. Have students write and illustrate a pamphlet to inform others about their community. Tell students to check and revise their pamphlets to make sure they use vivid adjectives and adverbs.

WRAP-UP/ASSESS

SUMMARIZE Ask: **What does an adjective do? What does an adverb do?**

RETEACH

INTERVENTION Lessons in **visual, auditory,** and **kinesthetic** modalities: p. R56 and *Reteach Activities Copying Masters,* p. 55.

PRACTICE page 91

Name _____

Adjective or Adverb?

A. Write whether each underlined word is an *adjective* or an *adverb*.

1. Ellen was <u>happy</u> about moving to San Antonio. — adjective
2. She talked <u>excitedly</u> as they drove from Dallas. — adverb
3. She read the signs <u>carefully</u> along the way. — adverb
4. She was a <u>good</u> reader. — adjective
5. The letters on the signs were <u>large</u> enough for her to see. — adjective

B. Write whether each underlined word is an adjective or an adverb. Then write the noun or verb it describes.

6. Ellen wanted the car to go <u>fast</u>. — adverb; go
7. She knew her parents were <u>safe</u> drivers. — adjective; drivers
8. Ellen wanted them to reach San Antonio <u>quickly</u>. — adverb; reach
9. They <u>finally</u> arrived in the city. — adverb; arrived
10. Ellen was <u>impatient</u> to see her new home. — adjective; Ellen

TRY THIS! Suppose you wanted to get people to move to your community. Write a letter that tells a person about your community. Use adjectives and adverbs to describe it.

Practice • More About Adverbs and Adjectives   Unit 5 • Chapter 28   91

CHALLENGE

COMMUNITY FACT SHEET
Have students use **Challenge Activity Card 19** (page R71) to create a community fact sheet.

Challenge Activity Card 19

Community Fact Sheet

Choose a community, a city, or a town that interests you. Use an encyclopedia, the Internet, or other resources to make a fact sheet about the community you chose. Your fact sheet should:

• tell when and how the community was founded or settled.
• describe what the community is like today.
• list the population and major businesses of the community.
• tell why the community interests you.

You may also wish to illustrate your fact sheet with pictures or drawings that represent the community you chose.

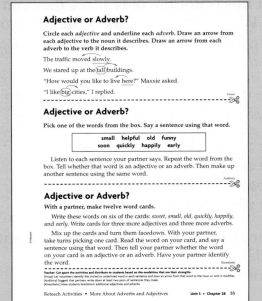

Adjective or Adverb?

Circle each *adjective* and underline each *adverb*. Draw an arrow from each adjective to the noun it describes. Draw an arrow from each adverb to the verb it describes.

The traffic moved slowly.
We stared up at the tall buildings.
"How would you like to live here?" Maxxie asked.
"I like big cities," I replied.

Adjective or Adverb?

Pick one of the words from the box. Say a sentence using that word.

| small | helpful | old | funny |
| soon | quickly | happily | early |

Listen to each sentence your partner says. Repeat the word from the box. Tell whether that word is an adjective or an adverb. Then make up another sentence using the same word.

Adjective or Adverb?

With a partner, make twelve word cards.

Write these words on six of the cards: *sweet, small, old, quickly, happily,* and *early.* Write cards for three more adjectives and three more adverbs.

Mix up the cards and turn them facedown. With your partner, take turns picking one card. Read the word on your card, and say a sentence using that word. Then tell your partner whether the word on your card is an adjective or an adverb. Have your partner identify the word.

Reteach Activities • More About Adverbs and Adjectives   Unit 5 • Chapter 28   55

Adverb Placement in Sentences

OBJECTIVES

- To identify adverbs in sentences and to place them properly in sentences
- To use correct adverb placement in a written list to record information

DAILY LANGUAGE PRACTICE

TRANSPARENCY 63

1 Many peeple settled peacefully in our state (people; state.)

2 The hills reminded them of they homeland. (their)

BRIDGE TO WRITING The ___(adjective)___ settlers brought their customs with them.

ORAL WARM-UP

USE PRIOR KNOWLEDGE Read the following sentence to students: *My friend speaks.* Have students take turns revising the sentence by adding an adverb.

Grammar Jingles™ **CD, Intermediate** Use Track 19 for review and reinforcement of adverbs and adjectives.

TEACH/MODEL

Explain that adverbs often come after the verbs they modify in sentences but that this is not the only place they can be. Write each word in this sentence on a separate card: *The visitors chatted happily together.*

Use the cards to show how the adverb *happily* can appear in different places:

The visitors chatted happily together.
The visitors chatted together happily.
Happily the visitors chatted together.
The visitors happily chatted together.

Work through the Guided Practice with students, or have them complete the items in small groups.

Adverb Placement in Sentences

Adverbs can be in different places in a sentence.

You know that adverbs describe verbs. Sometimes, an adverb may come directly before or after the verb in a sentence. Other times, an adverb may be at the beginning or the end of a sentence. Notice that the adverb *eagerly* is in a different place in each sentence below.

Examples:

People **eagerly** travel to Texas.

People travel **eagerly** to Texas.

Eagerly, people travel to Texas.

People travel to Texas **eagerly**.

To vary your writing, try putting the adverbs in different places in your sentences.

Guided Practice

A. Identify the adverb in each sentence.

Example: Early settlers in Texas depended mostly on the land.
mostly

1. Many people farmed <u>successfully</u>.
2. Some people depended <u>mainly</u> on animals.
3. Farmers and ranchers <u>carefully</u> caught wild horses.
4. They tamed the wild horses <u>quickly</u>.
5. <u>Finally</u>, people could ride the horses.

338

Vocabulary Power page 82

Name _____

WORD ORIGINS

See how many words from Spanish you already know. Read each pair of words below. Then write the word next to the correct definition.

1. coyote, mustang	a small wild horse	mustang
	a small wolf	coyote
2. avocado, vanilla	a pear-shaped fruit with dark skin	avocado
	a flavoring	vanilla
3. Colorado, Florida	a state known for its red rocks	Colorado
	a state known for its oranges	Florida
4. mosquito, alligator	a kind of reptile	alligator
	a small insect that bites	mosquito
5. fiesta, guitar	a festival	fiesta
	a musical instrument with strings	guitar
6. tortilla, taco	a kind of sandwich	taco
	a flat bread	tortilla
7. piñata, plaza	a marketplace	plaza
	a candy-filled container hung from the ceiling	piñata
8. patio, burro	the courtyard of a Spanish building	patio
	a donkey	burro

82   Unit 5 • Chapter 28   Vocabulary Power

Listening and Speaking

FIND EXAMPLES Have students work in pairs. One student should skim a book or a magazine article for a sentence that contains an adverb and read aloud that sentence. Have partners listen and identify where the adverb is placed in the sentence. Have partners switch roles. At the conclusion of the activity, each pair can share one example they found.

Independent Practice

B. Write each sentence. Put the underlined adverb in a different place.

Example: Once, Texas was the largest state in the United States.

Texas was once the largest state in the United States.

Answers may vary.

6. Texans <u>proudly</u> show visitors their capital city, Austin.
7. There are parks in Austin <u>everywhere</u>.
8. There are <u>also</u> seven beautiful lakes.
9. Austin's population has increased <u>rapidly</u>.
10. <u>Now</u>, almost a half million people live in the city.
11. Texas was a part of Mexico <u>once</u>.
12. It is <u>now</u> the second largest state in the United States.
13. Some people <u>still</u> wear cowboy boots in Texas.
14. Texas is <u>widely</u> known for its open spaces.
15. However, people <u>usually</u> live in cities.

Remember
that you can put adverbs in different places in a sentence. This is one way to make your writing more interesting.

Writing Connection

Writer's Craft: Main Idea and Details Do some research to find out about a special event from your community's past. Work in a small group, and write a paragraph about the event. Be sure your paragraph includes details about when, how, and where this event took place. Place adverbs in different positions in your sentences.

Independent Practice

Have students complete the Independent Practice, or modify it using these suggestions:

MODIFIED INSTRUCTION

BELOW-LEVEL STUDENTS Have students softly read each sentence aloud to hear how the adverbs sound in different places before writing the sentences.

ABOVE-LEVEL STUDENTS Have students rewrite three sentences using different adverbs.

Writing Connection

Writer's Craft: Main Idea and Details Have students participate in a class discussion on an event in the community. Discuss what the event celebrates, when it takes place, and what kinds of activities are part of the event. Have students record their information in a list.

WRAP-UP/ASSESS

SUMMARIZE Ask students to explain how using adverbs in different places in a sentence can improve their writing.

RETEACH

INTERVENTION Lessons in **visual, auditory,** and **kinesthetic** modalities: p. R56 and *Reteach Activities Copying Masters,* p. 56.

PRACTICE page 92

Name _____

Adverb Placement in Sentences

A. Write the adverb in each sentence.

1. Ellen's family read the street signs carefully. — carefully
2. Ellen's mother spoke Spanish well. — well
3. She easily read the street names. — easily
4. She could tell Ellen exactly what the street names meant. — exactly
5. Proudly, Ellen listened to her mother speaking Spanish. — Proudly

B. Add the adverb from the parentheses ( ) to each sentence. Place the adverb where it goes best.
Responses will vary. Possible responses are shown.

6. (finally) The trip was over.
   The trip was finally over.
7. (often) Ellen had pictured her new home.
   Ellen had often pictured her new home.
8. (now) She would see it.
   She would see it now.

TRY THIS! Write three sentences about the world around you. What are some things that you see often? What are some things that you have never seen? Use adjectives and adverbs in your sentences.

92 Unit 5 • Chapter 28   Practice • More About Adverbs and Adjectives

---

CHALLENGE

WHERE WOULD YOU LIKE TO GO? Have students write a paragraph describing a place they would like to visit.

Students should give reasons for choosing a particular place and tell what they would like to do there.

Remind students to use adjectives and adverbs to make their descriptions more vivid.

Adverb Placement in Sentences

Read each sentence, and circle the adverb. Then write the sentence again. Move the adverb to another place in the sentence.

The camp bus (finally) arrived.
Finally, the camp bus arrived.

(Cheerfully) our driver greeted us.
Our driver greeted us cheerfully.

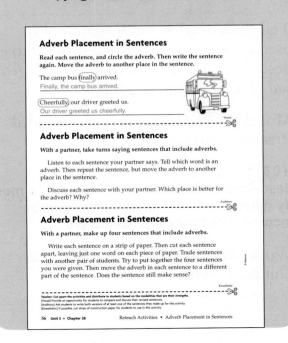

Adverb Placement in Sentences

With a partner, take turns saying sentences that include adverbs.

Listen to each sentence your partner says. Tell which word is an adverb. Then repeat the sentence, but move the adverb to another place in the sentence.

Discuss each sentence with your partner. Which place is better for the adverb? Why?

Adverb Placement in Sentences

With a partner, make up four sentences that include adverbs.

Write each sentence on a strip of paper. Then cut each sentence apart, leaving just one word on each piece of paper. Trade sentences with another pair of students. Try to put together the four sentences you were given. Then move the adverb in each sentence to a different part of the sentence. Does the sentence still make sense?

Teacher: Cut apart the activities and distribute to students based on the modalities that are their strength.
(Visual) Provide an opportunity for students to compare and discuss their revised sentences.
(Auditory) Ask students to write both versions of at least one of the sentences they make up for this activity.
(Kinesthetic) If possible, cut strips of construction paper for students to use in this activity.

56 Unit 5 • Chapter 28   Reteach Activities • Adverb Placement in Sentences

Using *Good* and *Well*, *Bad* and *Badly*

OBJECTIVES
- To use *good*, *well*, *bad*, and *badly* correctly in sentences
- To use adjectives and adverbs correctly in written sentences on a poster

DAILY LANGUAGE PRACTICE

TRANSPARENCY 63

1 san antonio are a nice plase to live.
(San Antonio is; place)

2 My house is more older than him house. (is older; his)

BRIDGE TO WRITING San Antonio has changed ___(adverb)___ in the last century.

ORAL WARM-UP

USE PRIOR KNOWLEDGE Write these sentences on the board: *Juanita is a good ____. Juanita can ____ well.* Ask students to suggest words to complete the sentences.

Grammar Jingles™ **CD, Intermediate** Use Track 19 for review and reinforcement of adverbs and adjectives.

TEACH/MODEL

Tell students that *bad* is sometimes used after verbs such as *feel* or *smell* to describe a subject. For example, *She feels bad* or *The garbage smells bad.*

Model the thinking, using the Guided Practice example:

MODEL **I know that the word being described is the noun *start*. Adjectives modify nouns, so I know that *badly* must be incorrect because it is an adverb.**

Work with students to complete the Guided Practice items.

340

Using *Good* and *Well*, *Bad* and *Badly*

Remember that an **adjective** describes a noun. An **adverb** describes a verb.

Good is always an adjective that tells *what kind*. It describes a noun. *Well* is usually an adverb that tells *how*. It describes a verb.

Examples:

Adjective: Texas is a **good** place to live.

Adverb: You can live **well** there.

Bad is an adjective. It is used to describe a noun. It is sometimes used after the word *feel* to describe the subject. *Badly* is an adverb. It is used to describe a verb.

Examples:

Adjective: San Antonio has **bad** dry spells.

Adverb: Crops grow **badly** in dry spells.

Guided Practice

A. Tell whether each sentence is correct or incorrect.

Example: The Battle of Flowers, an event during Fiesta San Antonio, had a badly start. *incorrect*

1. A battle sounds like a bad thing. correct
2. The Battle of Flowers is a well event. incorrect
3. It rained badly the first year of the event. correct
4. People felt bad that they had to wait four days to start it. correct
5. The event was held later and went good. incorrect

Vocabulary Power page 83

Name _____

FIGURATIVE LANGUAGE

Figurative language is using words in a colorful way. Often, the words take on a meaning that is different from the one they usually have.

Example:
Go nuts really means "to get very excited."

▶ Read each sentence. Then write the meaning of the underlined phrases on the lines. Definitions may vary slightly. Possible responses are given.
1. The colorful flowers were a <u>feast for my eyes</u>.
_____ beautiful to look at
2. When our team won, we <u>went bananas</u>.
_____ got very excited
3. The hungry baby <u>howled like a coyote</u>.
_____ cried loudly
4. The land was as <u>flat as a tortilla</u>.
_____ very flat
5. The cookies were like a <u>fiesta for my mouth</u>.
_____ delicious; tasty

▶ Pick two of the underlined phrases and illustrate them. Label your illustrations on the lines provided.

Vocabulary Power   Unit 5 • Chapter 28 83

REACHING ALL LEARNERS **ESL**

COMPLETE THE PHRASES

Write the following on the board:

good _____

bad _____

_____ well

_____ badly

Have students brainstorm several words to complete each phrase. Then have students select four phrases and use them in oral sentences.

Independent Practice

B. Write *good* or *well* to complete each sentence.

Example: How _____ do you know your community?
     well

6. Name three _____ places to visit in your community. *good*
7. Where can you get more _____ information? *good*
8. What kinds of businesses do _____ in your community? *well*
9. Do any crops grow _____ in your area? *well*
10. Are there any _____ parks where you live? *good*

C. Write *bad* or *badly* to complete each sentence.

Example: Usually San Antonio does not have _____ weather.
     bad

11. However, people can feel _____ when the temperature is over 100 degrees. *bad*
12. In the heat, people's bodies need water _____. *badly*
13. Some people sleep _____ on hot nights. *badly*
14. The heat can be _____ during the day. *bad*
15. It is not so _____ at night. *bad*

> **Remember**
> that *good* and *bad* are adjectives, and *well* and *badly* are adverbs.

TEXAS

San Antonio ★

Writing Connection

Social Studies What do you like about your community? Are there some things your community should improve? Write several sentences telling what you like and dislike about your community. Use *good, well, bad,* and *badly* in the sentences.

341

Independent Practice

Have students complete the Independent Practice, or modify it using these suggestions:

MODIFIED INSTRUCTION

BELOW-LEVEL STUDENTS Tell students to decide whether the word being modified is a noun or a verb before choosing *good* or *well* and *bad* or *badly*.

ABOVE-LEVEL STUDENTS Have students rewrite each sentence in Part C so that it makes sense using either *good* or *well*.

Writing Connection

Social Studies After students record their ideas, have them work in pairs to make a poster advertising the community. Students should choose two sentences to use as slogans for their posters. Tell students that the purpose of the poster is to persuade others to visit the community. Tell students to edit their posters for appropriate spelling and punctuation.

WRAP-UP/ASSESS

SUMMARIZE Ask students to explain when to use *good* and *bad* and when to use *well* and *badly*.

RETEACH

INTERVENTION Lessons in **visual, auditory,** and **kinesthetic** modalities: p. R56 and *Reteach Activities Copying Masters,* p. 57.

PRACTICE page 93

Name _____

Using *Good* and *Well*, *Bad* and *Badly*

A. Write *good* or *well* in each sentence.

1. The house was in _____good_____ condition.
2. The former owners had taken _____good_____ care of it.
3. The family planned to decorate it _____well_____.
4. The park down the street was a _____good_____ place to run.
5. Ellen could run very _____well_____.
6. She thought she would do _____well_____ in her new home.

B. Write *bad* or *badly* in each sentence.

7. The weather was _____bad_____ for the first few days.
8. Ellen wanted so _____badly_____ to visit the park near her house.
9. She spent the time helping her mother, who had a _____bad_____ headache.
10. Things were not too _____bad_____.
11. The first few days in San Antonio went _____badly_____, but then things got better.
12. Ellen discovered that sometimes you have to take the _____bad_____ with the good.

TRY THIS! Write a paragraph telling about some of the things you like to do in your community. Use *good, well, bad,* and *badly* in some of your sentences.

Practice • More About Adverbs and Adjectives   Unit 5 • Chapter 28   93

CHALLENGE

PLAN A TOUR Have students work in small groups to plan a tour of their school. Students should create a written guide such as a pamphlet, brochure, or map for their tour. Students should:

• write an introduction for visitors.
• tell things that students at their school do well
• list three things a visitor should see when touring the school.
• write a description for each stop on the tour.

Using *Good* and *Well*, *Bad* and *Badly*

Circle *good, well, bad,* and *badly* where they are used correctly.

Hi Lil!
  We are having a (good) time. Mom was sick last week, but she feels good now. On a trail ride yesterday, I rode (well) Irv didn't do too (badly) either. I feel (bad) that you couldn't come with us.
          Your friend,
          Kiki

Using *Good* and *Well*, *Bad* and *Badly*

Tell a partner about things you do well and things you wish you could do better. Make a point of using all four of these words: *good, well, bad,* and *badly.*

  Listen carefully during your partner's turn. Raise your hand each time you hear one of the words. When your partner has finished, tell which words your partner used as an adjective and which ones he or she used as an adverb.

Using *Good* and *Well*, *Bad* and *Badly*

With a partner, make four word cards.

  Write *good, well, bad,* and *badly* on the cards. Use the word cards to complete each sentence.

I feel _____.	It runs _____.
It tastes _____.	It squeaks _____.

How many different words can you use to finish each sentence?

Teacher: Cut apart the activities and distribute to students based on the modalities that are their strengths.
[Visual] You may want to have students write out the complete postcard message.
[Auditory] You may want to have students write paragraphs to read aloud to their partners.
[Kinesthetic] Encourage students to print the same-size letters in the incomplete sentences and on their word cards.

Reteach Activities • More About Adverbs and Adjectives   Unit 5 • Chapter 28   57

Extra Practice

OBJECTIVES
- To identify adjectives and adverbs and use *good*, *well*, *bad*, and *badly* correctly
- To place adverbs and adjectives correctly in a letter

DAILY LANGUAGE PRACTICE

TRANSPARENCY 64

1 Celebrations in San Antonio have well parades (good parades.)

2 My sister rode she horse in the parade (her; parade.)

BRIDGE TO WRITING I could see ___(adverb)___ from the street.

ORAL WARM-UP

USE PRIOR KNOWLEDGE Read aloud these sentences to students: *The boy rode happily down the street. The boy happily rode down the street.* Ask students whether the meaning of the sentence changed when the adverb was moved in the second sentence.

TEACH/MODEL

Review adjectives and adverbs and the correct use of *good*, *well*, *bad*, and *badly*. Model the thinking for the example in Part A:

MODEL The underlined word tells *when* Native Americans settled in Texas. Adverbs tell *when*, so I know that *first* must be an adverb.

Then model the thinking using the example in Part C:

MODEL The word that I choose needs to describe the verb *grow*. *Well* is an adverb, so it must be the correct choice.

Have students work in pairs to complete the Extra Practice items.

CHAPTER 28

More About Adverbs and Adjectives

Remember

that an adjective describes a noun. An adverb describes a verb. You can put adverbs in different places in a sentence.

For more activities with adjectives and adverbs, visit *The Learning Site:* www.harcourtschool.com

342

Extra Practice

A. Write whether the underlined word is an adjective or an adverb. *pages 336–337*

Example: Native Americans settled in Texas <u>first</u>.
adverb

1. Other settlers came more <u>recently</u>. *adverb*
2. Some <u>brave</u> pioneers came from Mexico. *adjective*
3. Mexican Texans brought along <u>many</u> customs and traditions. *adjective*
4. <u>Today</u>, Mexican traditions are common. *adverb*
5. Traditional Mexican foods are <u>popular</u> dishes in Texas. *adjective*

B. Add the adverb from the parentheses ( ) to each sentence. Put it in the best place. *pages 338–339*

Example: (today) We learned about the cowhands in early Texas.
Today, we learned about the cowhands in early Texas.
Answers may vary.

6. (often) They wore hats like the big Mexican hats.
7. (skillfully) They rode their horses.
8. (sometimes) The cattle were frightened by noises.
9. (softly) Cowhands sang to them at night.
10. (usually) Cowhands slept outdoors.

Vocabulary Power page 84

Name _____

ANALOGIES

An analogy shows how pairs of words go together.

Example:
Dog is to *bark* as *cat* is to *meow*.
(A dog barks; a cat meows.)

Read each analogy below. Figure out how the first two italicized words go together. Then write the word that completes the analogy.

tortilla warms	leg enormous	asleep sleeping	piñata year	fire plaza	late coyote

1. *Fiesta* is to *holiday* as *blaze* is to ___fire___
2. *Elbow* is to *arm* as *knee* is to ___leg___
3. *Medicine* is to *cures* as *coat* is to ___warms___
4. *Merry* is to *miserable* as *small* is to ___enormous___
5. *Cookie* is to *jar* as *candy* is to ___piñata___
6. *Tiger* is to *feline* as ___coyote___ is to *canine*.
7. *Bread* is to *sandwich* as ___tortilla___ is to *taco*.
8. *Restaurant* is to *eating* as ___plaza___ is to *shopping*.
9. *Boiling* is to *freezing* as *early* is to ___late___
10. *Standing* is to *sitting* as *awake* is to ___asleep___
11. *Day* is to *week* as *month* is to ___year___
12. *Kitchen* is to *cooking* as *bedroom* is to ___sleeping___

84 Unit 5 • Chapter 28   Vocabulary Power

ESL

REACHING ALL LEARNERS

MAKE A WORD PICTURE Ask students to find a picture that appeals to them and to paste the picture on a sheet of paper.

Have students write around the picture adjectives that describe the people and things shown. Have them include adverbs that relate to actions or feelings they see.

C. Rewrite the sentences below, using the correct word in parentheses ( ). *pages 340–341*

Example: Crops grow (well, good) in San Antonio.
Crops grow well in San Antonio.

11. Our tour guide said we would like the (<u>good</u>, well) climate in San Antonio.
12. Every community has (badly, <u>bad</u>) weather sometimes, though.
13. The San Antonio Symphony plays (<u>well</u>, good).
14. There are many (well, <u>good</u>) parks in San Antonio.
15. We visited *La Villita*, or Little Village, for a (<u>good</u>, well) look at old San Antonio buildings.
16. Many people in San Antonio speak both English and Spanish (good, <u>well</u>).
17. Unfortunately, our field trip to San Antonio went (bad, <u>badly</u>).
18. The weather was not (<u>good</u>, well).
19. The museum's roof was leaking (<u>badly</u>, bad).
20. Our teacher hopes our next trip will not be so (<u>badly</u>, bad).

Remember
that *good* and *bad* are adjectives. *Well* and *badly* are adverbs.

DID YOU KNOW?
Fiesta San Antonio is held every April. It celebrates the creation of the Texas Republic in 1836. The festival lasts one week.

Fiesta San Antonio
343

Writing Connection

Real-Life Writing: Friendly Letter Think about a fair, festival, or other event in your community or at your school. Write a letter to a friend or family member telling about the special event. Use adjectives and adverbs in your letter. Put the adverbs in different places in your sentences.

Building Oral Grammar

For students with an ear for conventionally correct English usage, using an adjective when an adverb is called for sounds wrong. To help students develop an ear for correct usage, have them work with partners and take turns reading the sentences they completed or corrected in the Extra Practice activities.

Writing Connection

Real-Life Writing: Friendly Letter If possible, have students use a word-processing program to type and print their letters. Before students send or deliver their letters, have them trade papers and respond constructively to each other's writing, focusing on clear adverb use.

WRAP-UP/ASSESS

Writer's Journal

SUMMARIZE Have students reflect in their journals on how using adjectives and adverbs correctly can make their writing more effective. **REFLECTION**

ADDITIONAL PRACTICE An additional page of Extra Practice is provided on page 472 of the *Pupil Edition*.

PRACTICE page 94

REACHING ALL LEARNERS

Name _____

Extra Practice

A. Write whether the underlined word is an *adjective* or an *adverb*.

1. Ellen's family decided <u>together</u> what places to visit first. — adverb
2. San Antonio has many <u>famous</u> places. — adjective
3. They decided to take a <u>slow</u> drive through the city first. — adjective
4. On this drive, they would take a <u>quick</u> look at many places. — adjective
5. <u>Later</u>, they would spend a long time in one place of interest. — adverb

B. Write *good, well, bad,* or *badly* to complete each sentence.

6. The family wanted to eat in one of San Antonio's (**good, well**) restaurants. — good
7. It was a (**bad, badly**) time to try to get a table. — bad
8. They found a restaurant where the cook prepared Chinese food (**good, well**). — well
9. Ellen used chopsticks (**bad, badly**), but she improved. — badly
10. They agreed it was a very (**good, well**) meal. — good

TRY THIS! Think about people who are new to your community. Write a few sentences that tell them what to see or do on their first day there. Underline the adverbs and adjectives you use.

94 Unit 5 • Chapter 28   Practice • More About Adverbs and Adjectives

CHALLENGE

REACHING ALL LEARNERS

MYSTERY VISIT Have students write a description of a familiar place in their community. Tell them not to give the name of the place in their writing. Remind students to use adjectives and adverbs to describe aspects of the place and how people feel when visiting it.

Have students read their finished description aloud. Listeners should try to guess the place that is described.

TECHNOLOGY *Grammar Practice and Assessment* CD-ROM; *Writing Express* CD-ROM

INTERNET Visit *The Learning Site:* www.harcourtschool.com

Chapter Review

OBJECTIVES

STANDARDIZED TEST PREP

- To review correct use of adjectives and adverbs
- To conduct an effective interview, and to report results through written, audio, and visual presentation

DAILY LANGUAGE PRACTICE

TRANSPARENCY 64

1 tomorrow the parade went down the street. (Tomorrow; will go)

2 Will There be clownz, fire trucks, and floats in the parade (there; clowns; parade?)

BRIDGE TO WRITING (Adjective) bands play. The bands play (adverb) .

STANDARDIZED TEST PREP

MODEL TEST-TAKING STRATEGIES Have students read the directions on page 342 silently.

Encourage them to think about where the blank is placed in each sentence and to decide if the missing word should describe a noun or a verb.

Model the thinking. Write this example on the board:

We went on a _____ trip.

  1 **A** well
     B badly
     C long
     D eagerly

MODEL **The blank in the sentence comes right before the noun *trip.* That tells me that the missing word is probably an adjective. *Well, badly,* and *eagerly* are adverbs. The only adjective is *long,* so answer C is correct: *We went on a long trip.***

CHAPTER 28 More About Adverbs and Adjectives

STANDARDIZED TEST PREP

For additional test preparation, visit *The Learning Site:* www.harcourtschool.com

Chapter Review

Read the paragraph. Choose the word that belongs in each numbered blank. Mark the letter for your answer.

> My grandmother moved to San Antonio, and I miss her (1) _____. Yesterday I felt (2) _____ when I got a letter from her. She wrote that San Antonio has lots of (3) _____ parks and museums. People can eat (4) _____ at many restaurants. She said she likes to shop in the *Paseo del Rio.* There's not a (5) _____ store there. She told me she fell and hurt her arm (6) _____. The doctor at the hospital treated her (7) _____. Sometimes the heat gets pretty (8) _____ in San Antonio. There's lots of sunshine, though, and the climate is (9) _____. I hope the sun is shining (10) _____ when I visit Grandma next month.

1 **A** good   **C** bad
    B terrible   **D** terribly D

2 **F** happily   **H** happy H
    G madly   **J** badly

3 **A** good A   **C** funnest
    B well   **D** badly

4 **F** good   **H** bad
    G well G   **J** happy

5 **A** swiftly   **C** bad C
    B well   **D** badly

6 **F** good   **H** bad
    G well   **J** badly J

7 **A** good   **C** bad
    B gently B   **D** gentle

8 **F** brightly   **H** bad H
    G well   **J** badly

9 **A** pleasant A   **C** nicest
    B well   **D** pleasantly

10 **F** healthy   **H** badly
    G brightly G   **J** healthier

Assessment

. . . .

PORTFOLIO ASSESSMENT Have students select their best work from the Writing Connections on pages 339, 341, and 343.

ONGOING ASSESSMENT Evaluate the performance of 4–6 students using appropriate checklists and record forms from pages R74–R77.

INTERNET Activities and exercises to help students prepare for state and standardized assessments appear on *The Learning Site:*

www.harcourtschool.com

Interviewing to Learn About Your Community

Preparing for an Interview

You will need:
- a videocamera or an audiocassette recorder
- videotape or audiotape

Planning an Interview
- If you will be recording the interview on videotape, think about how you want your interview to look. Where can you conduct your interview? What kind of background do you want to see in the picture?
- Learn something about the subject.
- Make up interesting questions. They should be the kind that need more than *yes* or *no* answers.

After an Interview
- Add music or other interesting sound effects to the videotape or audiotape before and after the interview.
- Write what you will say to introduce your tape to the class.

YOUR TURN

Interview someone in your community who knows about a community event, or ask a partner to act the part of such a person. Record the interview on videotape or audiotape. Be sure you know some facts about the event before you tape the interview. After you have finished the interview, present it to your class.

345

TECHNOLOGY

Interviewing to Learn About Your Community

To help students plan their own interviews, you may wish to show them video recordings of interviews that have appeared on TV. Students may also tell about interviews they have seen. Discuss with students the importance of the setting for the interview, including how it will appear on videotape or sound on audiotape. Remind students that they must always prepare in advance for an interview. Tell students to speak in complete sentences and to use the correct subject-verb agreement in their interviews.

WRITING APPLICATION Tell students to imagine that they have the opportunity to interview anyone they choose. Have them select one person and prepare for the interview. They should describe the setting and any music or sound effects they would use, write a short introduction of the person, and make a list of questions to ask during the interview.

WRAP-UP/ASSESS

Writer's Journal

SUMMARIZE Have students write in their journals to reflect upon their experiences of planning and conducting interviews.
REFLECTION

PRACTICE page 95

Name _____

Chapter Review

Read the passage below. Choose the word that belongs in each numbered space. Fill in the oval next to your choice.

Ellen loved San Antonio, but she wanted (1) _____ to talk to her best friend in Dallas. He (2) _____ called her. Her friend Leo said he had scored (3) _____ on his last test. Ellen said she was off to a (4) _____ start in school. Leo was (5) _____ to hear it. He knew Ellen worked (6) _____ at her studies. They said good-bye, promising to write (7) _____.

1	○ good ○ well ○ bad ● badly	5	○ happily ○ good ● happy ○ well
2	○ early ○ late ● finally ○ proud	6	○ good ● hard ○ hardly ○ badly
3	○ good ● well ○ bad ○ finally	7	● often ○ oftenly ○ good ○ fine
4	● good ○ well ○ finely ○ badly		

Practice • More About Adverbs and Adjectives   Unit 5 • Chapter 28   95

CHALLENGE

PROMOTIONAL FILM Have students work in small groups to create a promotional videotape about their school. Students may prepare and record interviews with school personnel, students, and parents. Remind students that the purpose of the videotape is to inform others about positive aspects of their school.

TECHNOLOGY Additional writing activities are provided on the *Writing Express* CD-ROM

LESSON ORGANIZER	DAY 1	DAY 2
DAILY LANGUAGE PRACTICE TRANSPARENCIES 65, 66	1. We had a well time shopping. (good) 2. The mall on market street was the most closer one of all. (Market Street; closest) **Bridge to Writing** This mall was (adjective) than the other one.	1. kyle goed two work this morning. (Kyle went to) 2. He will right a report on him job. (write; his) **Bridge to Writing** After work, Kyle will (action verb) with his friends.
ORAL WARM-UP **Listening/Speaking**	Give Examples of Same-Sounding Words 346	Identify Homophones 348 *Grammar Jingles*™ CD Track 20
TEACH/MODEL **GRAMMAR** **KEY** ✔ = tested skill	✔ **HOMOPHONES** 346–347 • To use the homophones *write/right* and *to/too/two* correctly • To make a poster using homophones	✔ **MORE HOMOPHONES** 348–349 • To correctly use the homophones *their/there/they're, your/you're,* and *its/it's* • To write survey questions using homophones
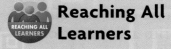 **Reaching All Learners**	**Modified Instruction** Below-Level: Choose Homophones Above-Level: Write Sentences **Reteach:** *Reteach Activities Copying Masters* pp. 58 and R57 **Challenge:** Activity Card 20 R71 *ESL Manual* pp. 140, 141 *Practice Book* p. 96	**Modified Instruction** Below-Level: Identify Homophones Above-Level: Rewrite Sentences **ESL:** Sentence Frames 348 *ESL Manual* pp. 140, 142 **Reteach:** *Reteach Activities Copying Masters* pp. 59 and R57 **Challenge:** Write a Commercial 349 *Practice Book* p. 97
WRITING	Writing Connection 347 Art	Writing Connection 349 Real-Life Writing: Survey
CROSS-CURRICULAR/ ENRICHMENT	*Vocabulary Power* Explore Word Meaning 346 company, **enterprise,** project, undertaking, venture See *Vocabulary Power* book.	*Vocabulary Power* Connotation–Denotation 346 *Vocabulary Power* p. 85 **Vocabulary activity**

DAY 3

1. where is you're money (Where; your money?)
2. There money is over their. (Their; there.)

Bridge to Writing ___(Subject pronoun)___ earned five dollars.

Distinguish Between Homographs 350
Grammar Jingles™ CD Track 20

✔ **HOMOGRAPHS AND OTHER HOMOPHONES** 350–351
- To correctly use *see/sea, know/no, trip* (n.)/*trip* (v.), and *bow* (n.)/*bow* (v.) in sentences
- To record responses to survey questions

Modified Instruction
Below-Level: Check Definitions
Above-Level: Write Sentences
ESL: Matching Game 350
ESL Manual pp. 140, 143
Reteach: *Reteach Activities Copying Masters* pp. 60 and R57
Challenge: Word Charts 351
Practice Book p. 98

Writing Connection 351
 Writer's Journal: Record Responses

Vocabulary Power
 Multiple-Meaning Words 346
 Vocabulary Power p. 86
 Vocabulary activity

DAY 4

1. From my storre window, I sea the shoppers (store; see; shoppers.)
2. I no how to get they're business. (know; their)

Bridge to Writing
___(Compound subject)___ bought their umbrellas at my store.

Choose the Right Words 352

EXTRA PRACTICE 352–353
- To correctly use homophones and homographs
- To write a paragraph summarizing information

Practice and assessment

Building Oral Grammar
Group Story with Homophones and Homographs 353
Challenge: Tall Tale 353
ESL Manual pp. 140, 144
Practice Book p. 99

Writing Connection 353
 Writer's Craft: Summarize

Listening and Speaking: Stand Up 352

Vocabulary Power
 Synonyms 346
 Vocabulary Power p. 87
 Vocabulary activity

DAY 5

1. we brought banana bread two the bake sale. (We; to)
2. Its a sale to raise money for us soccer team. *(It's; our)*

Bridge to Writing The oatmeal cookies were ___(adjective)___ . They sold ___(adverb)___ than the cupcakes.

TEST PREP **CHAPTER REVIEW** 354–355
- To review homophones and homographs
- To use *sit, set, picture,* and *pitcher* correctly in writing

Test preparation

Challenge: Glossary 355
Practice Book p. 100
ESL Manual pp. 140, 145

Writing Application 355
 Write and Illustrate

Vocabulary: Troublesome Words 355

Vocabulary Power

 Related Words 346

Homophones

OBJECTIVES

• To use the homophones *write/right* and
to/too/two correctly
• To make a poster using homophones

DAILY LANGUAGE PRACTICE

TRANSPARENCY 65

❶ We had a well time shopping. (good)
❷ The mall on market street was the
most closer one of all. (Market Street;
the closest)

BRIDGE TO WRITING This mall was
(adjective) than the other one.

ORAL WARM-UP

USE PRIOR KNOWLEDGE Ask students to
give examples of words that sound the
same but have different spellings. Write
students suggestions on the board.

TEACH/MODEL

Read aloud the explanation and examples
of homophones on page 346. Explain
that *write* is a verb and *right* can be an
adjective or an adverb. Remind students
that *right* can also be a direction word.
Model the thinking for the Guided Practice example, spelling the homophones:

MODEL **This sentence is missing the main
verb. *Right* is not a verb. I know that *write*
is a verb meaning "to put pen or pencil to
paper." *Write* is the correct answer.**

Work through the Guided Practice with
students.

Homophones

Homophones are words that sound alike but
have different meanings and different
spellings.

> **Examples:**
> **Write** a letter. *(to put pen or pencil to paper)*
> He did not charge me the **right** amount. *(correct)*

> **Examples:**
> Take this road **to** the mall. *(toward)*
> Those pants are **too** long for me. *(more than needed)*
> This shirt is large, **too**. *(also)*
> I will buy **two** new sweaters. *(a number)*

Vocabulary Power

en•ter•prise
[en′tər•prīz′] *n.* An
activity set up to
earn money.

346

Guided Practice

**A. Choose the homophone in parentheses ( ) to
complete each sentence.**

Example: (write|right) They will _____ the store's
address on a card. *write*

1. (write|right) The clerk will _____ the price on
tags. write
2. (write|right) The owner will make sure the
prices are _____. right
3. (to|too|two) These _____ items are the same
price. two
4. (to|too|two) This item is _____ expensive. too
5. (to|too|two) Take it _____ the back room. to

Vocabulary Power

DAY ❶ EXPLORE WORD MEANING Introduce and define *enterprise*. **A store is one kind
of enterprise. What are some other enterprises in our community?**

DAY ❷ CONNOTATION AND DENOTATION **Which word sounds more formal, *enterprise*
or *business*?** (See also *Vocabulary Power*, page 85.)

DAY ❸ HOMOGRAPHS AND MULTIPLE-MEANING WORDS **One meaning of company is "a
business." What is another meaning?** (See also *Vocabulary Power*, page
86.)

DAY ❹ SYNONYMS Have students complete the following: **Undertaking is/is not a
synonym for *enterprise*.** Discuss responses. (See also *Vocabulary Power*,
page 87.)

DAY ❺ RELATED WORDS Have students make a word web of words and phrases related
to *enterprise*. Then have them write a sentence about an enterprise they
would like to try.

Independent Practice

B. Complete each sentence with the correct homophone in parentheses ( ). Write each sentence.

Remember
that homophones are words that sound alike but have different meanings and different spellings.

Example: (to|too|two) I want _____ make money. *to*

6. (write|right) We should _____ down our ideas for a new business. *write*
7. (to|too|two) The _____ of us can buy what we need to make candy. *two*
8. (to|too|two) We can take the candy _____ a store. *to*
9. (write|right) If I am _____, we can sell lots of candy. *right*
10. (to|too|two) Someone should take the money we make _____ the bank. *to*
11. (to|too|two) I will put my savings in the bank, _____. *too*
12. (to|too|two) There are _____ banks in our town. *two*
13. (write|right) I will _____ to them both. *write*
14. (to|too|two) Let's go _____ the candy sale. *to*
15. (to|too|two) This costs _____ much! *too*

Writing Connection

Art Connection What is your favorite store? Make a poster advertising the store. Show the products it sells and what is on sale. Write a sentence across the bottom of the poster to tell what makes the store special and why people should shop there. Try to use these words in your poster: *write, right, to, too, two.*

347

Independent Practice

Have students complete the Independent Practice, or modify it using these suggestions:

MODIFIED INSTRUCTION

BELOW-LEVEL STUDENTS For sentences with *write/right,* have students determine what part of speech is missing in the sentence before deciding which choice is correct.

ABOVE-LEVEL STUDENTS After students complete Part B, have them write two original sentences using the words *write* and *right* correctly.

Writing Connection

Art As a prewriting technique, have students write the answers to these questions: *Who usually shops at this store? What kinds of things does the store sell?* Have students trade their completed posters with a partner to edit them for correct usage of homophones.

WRAP-UP/ASSESS

SUMMARIZE Ask students to tell what a homophone is and to give examples of homophones in sentences.

RETEACH

INTERVENTION Lessons in **visual, auditory,** and **kinesthetic** modalities: p. R57 and *Reteach Activities Copying Masters,* p. 58.

PRACTICE page 96

Name _____

Homophones

A. Choose the correct word in parentheses ( ) that completes each sentence. Write the word.

1. The shopper will (write|right) a check for the groceries. *write*
2. First she will check the math to be sure the total price is (write|right). *right*
3. The clerk will check it, (to/too/two). *too*
4. It seemed she might be paying (to/too/two) much. *too*
5. She spoke (to/too/two) the clerk about it. *to*

B. Choose the correct word in parentheses ( ) that completes each sentence. Write the sentence.

6. The clerk had accidentally charged for (to/too/two) frozen dinners instead of one. *The clerk had accidentally charged for two frozen dinners instead of one.*
7. She gave the shopper the (write/right) total. *She gave the shopper the right total.*
8. Then the shopper could (write/right) the check. *Then the shopper could write the check.*

TRY THIS! Write a few sentences about a store where you shop. Tell why you like to shop there. Use some of these words in your sentences: *write, right, to, too,* and *two.*

96 Unit 5 • Chapter 29   Practice • Easily Confused Words

CHALLENGE

PICTURE CARDS Have students use **Challenge Activity Card 20** (page R71) to create picture cards for easily confused words.

Challenge Activity Card 20

Picture Cards

Work with a partner to create picture cards for homophones. You may use these words, or think of other homophones:

mail/male   see/sea   son/sun

- Make rectangles using construction paper.
- On one side of the paper, write the homophone.
- On the other side, paste or draw a picture that shows the meaning of the word.
- Underneath the picture, write a sentence that uses the homophone. Draw a blank where the homophone would be.
- Trade cards with other classmates. See if they can fill in the blank.

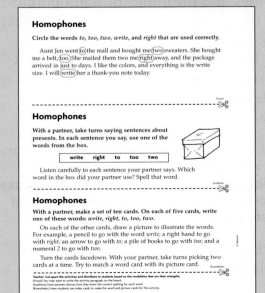

Homophones

Circle the words *to, too, two, write,* and *right* that are used correctly.

Aunt Jen went (to) the mall and bought me (two) sweaters. She bought me a belt, (too). She mailed them two me (right) away, and the package arrived in just days. I like the colors, and everything is the write size. I will (write) her a thank-you note today.

Visual

Homophones

With a partner, take turns saying sentences about presents. In each sentence you say, use one of the words from the box.

| write | right | to | too | two |

Listen carefully to each sentence your partner says. Which word in the box did your partner use? Spell that word.

Auditory

Homophones

With a partner, make a set of ten cards. On each of five cards, write one of these words: *write, right, to, too, two.*

On each of the other cards, draw a picture to illustrate the words. For example, a pencil to go with the word *write;* a right hand to go with *right;* an arrow to go with *to;* a pile of books to go with *too;* and a numeral 2 to go with *two.*

Turn the cards facedown. With your partner, take turns picking two cards at a time. Try to match a word card with its picture card.

Kinesthetic

Teacher: Cut apart the activities and distribute to students based on the modalities that are their strengths.
(Visual) You may want to write the activity paragraph on the board.
(Auditory) Have partners discuss how they knew the correct spelling for each word.
(Kinesthetic) Have students use index cards to make the word and picture cards for this activity.

58 Unit 5 • Chapter 29   Reteach Activities • Easily Confused Words

More Homophones

OBJECTIVES
- To correctly use the homophones *their/there/they're, your/you're,* and *its/it's*
- To write survey questions using homophones

TRANSPARENCY 65

1 kyle goed two work this morning.
(Kyle went to)

2 He will right a report on him job.
(write; his)

BRIDGE TO WRITING After work, Kyle will ___(action verb)___ with his friends.

ORAL WARM-UP

USE PRIOR KNOWLEDGE Write on the board these two sentences: *Your jacket is blue. I heard that you're on the basketball team.* Ask a volunteer to name the homophones.

***Grammar Jingles*™ CD, Intermediate** Use Track 20 for review and reinforcement of easily confused words.

TEACH/MODEL

Work through the explanation and examples on page 348. Explain to students that they must memorize the spellings and meanings of homophones. Tell them that one way to decide which choice is correct is to say the sentence with both of the words that make up a contraction: *you are, they are,* and *it is.* Model the thinking, using the Guided Practice example:

MODEL **I will say the sentence with the pronoun and the verb: *Is you are business making money? You're* doesn't make sense. The pronoun *your* is the correct choice in this sentence.**

Work with students to complete the Guided Practice.

More Homophones

You know that **homophones** are words that sound alike but have different meanings and different spellings.

Here are some more homophones. Look at their different meanings and spellings.

Examples:
The children sold **their** toys.   *(belonging to them)*
You will find the prices listed **there**.   *(tells where)*
They're looking for the new shop.   *(they are)*
You can start **your** own enterprise.   *(belonging to you)*
You're old enough to have a paper route.   *(you are)*
The store opens **its** doors early.   *(belonging to it)*
It's good to use a shopping list.   *(it is)*

Guided Practice

A. Choose one of the homophones in parentheses () to complete the sentence.

Example: (your|you're) Is ___ business making money?   *your*

1. (their|there|they're) Hank wants to open a store over ___.   there
2. (its|it's) He has some money, but ___ not enough.   it's
3. (your|you're) He wants to borrow some of ___ money.   your
4. (its|it's) Then you can share in ___ profits.   its
5. (Your|You're) ___ going to be glad you helped.   You're

348

Vocabulary Power   page 85

Name ___

CONNOTATION/DENOTATION

Many words have similar meanings, but similar words can give you different feelings. Would you rather hear someone *sing* or *screech*?

A. Rate each word in the pair as more formal or less formal. Write each word next to the correct category.

	more formal	less formal
1. company, enterprise	enterprise	company
2. dined, ate	dine	ate
3. job, project	project	job
4. undertaking, duty	undertaking	duty
5. dare, venture	venture	dare
6. car, automobile	automobile	car

B. Rate each word in the pair as more positive or less positive. Write each word next to the correct category.

	more positive	less positive
7. slimy, slippery	slippery	slimy
8. wet, soggy	wet	soggy
9. unusual, weird	unusual	weird
10. scrawny, thin	thin	scrawny
11. tangy, sour	tangy	sour
12. house, shack	house	shack

When would you use formal language instead of informal language?
Responses may vary; accept reasonable responses.

Vocabulary Power   Unit 5 • Chapter 29   85

 **ESL**

SENTENCE FRAMES Write on cards: *it's, your, there, its, their.* Then, write these sentence frames on the board. Have students take turns selecting the appropriate card and taping it to the board to fill in the blank.

Doris, ___ raining today.

Did you bring ___ umbrella?

I left it over ___.

Mario and Rhonda let me use ___ game.

The game is still in ___ box.

Independent Practice

B. Complete each sentence with the correct word in parentheses ( ). Write each sentence.

Example: (Your|You're) _____ going to have a job this summer.   *You're*

6. (their|there|they're) Mr. and Mrs. Harker invited us to help on _____ farm. *their*

7. (their|there|they're) The Harkers have an office _____. *there*

8. (Their|There|They're) _____ going to show us the business side of farming. *They're*

9. (their|there|they're) The farmers send _____ crops to stores far away. *their*

10. (their|there|they're) We can help with _____ business. *their*

11. (Your|You're) _____ going to help send bills to the stores. *You're*

12. (its|it's) Check each bill to make sure _____ correct. *it's*

13. (its|it's) A business should keep _____ records in a file. *its*

14. (your|you're) Mr. Harker will mail _____ pay for the work. *your*

15. (your|you're) How will you spend _____ money? *your*

> **Remember**
> that these words are homophones:
> their, there, they're; your, you're; its, it's

349

Writing Connection

Real-Life Writing: Survey With a partner, write three survey questions to ask classmates about their favorite stores. Try to use some of these words in your questions: *their, there, they're, its, it's, your, you're.*

Independent Practice

Have students complete the Independent Practice, or modify it using these suggestions:

MODIFIED INSTRUCTION

BELOW-LEVEL STUDENTS For sentences with *their/there/they're*, help students decide whether the sentence calls for an adverb or a pronoun.

ABOVE-LEVEL STUDENTS For Part B, have students rewrite the sentences, using the other choice.

Writing Connection

Real-Life Writing: Survey Have students participate in a class discussion about the functions of surveys. Explain that surveys are used to find out different kinds of information for various purposes. Have students discuss what kinds of responses they hope to get to their questions.

WRAP-UP/ASSESS

SUMMARIZE Ask: **How do you decide which homophone to use in a sentence?**

RETEACH

INTERVENTION Lessons in **visual, auditory,** and **kinesthetic** modalities: p. R57 and *Reteach Activities Copying Masters,* p. 59.

PRACTICE page 97

Name _____

More Homophones

A. Circle the correct word in parentheses ( ) that completes each sentence.

1. My parents' bookstore is over (their/there/they're).
2. They spend a lot of time (their/there/they're).
3. (Its/It's) the best bookstore in town.
4. Often, other bookstores do not have the book of (your/you're) choice.
5. The owners want the bookstore to keep (its/it's) customers happy.

B. Choose the correct word in parentheses ( ) that completes each sentence. Write the sentence.

6. People want to buy books by (their/there/they're) favorite authors. People want to buy books by their favorite authors.
7. (Their/There/They're) happy customers if the store carries what they want. They're happy customers if the store carries what they want.
8. (Your/You're) going to be satisfied shopping at this store. You're going to be satisfied shopping at this store.

TRY THIS! Work with a partner to write a conversation between a clerk in a bookstore and a customer. Try to use some of these words: *their, there, they're, your, you're, its,* and *it's.*

Practice • Easily Confused Words   Unit 5 • Chapter 29   97

CHALLENGE

WRITE A COMMERCIAL Have students work in small groups to write a television commercial for an imaginary product that helps students succeed in school. Ask students to tell whether the product helps with homework, with taking tests, or with answering questions in class.

Have students write a short script for the commercial using homophones. Students should present their commercials to the class.

More Homophones

Circle the words from the box that are used correctly.

| their   their   they're   your   you're   its   it's |

Why are Jo and Bo standing their?
(They're) waiting for (their) bus.
(It's) not going to stop at that corner.
The bus company has changed (its) route.
Are you sure you're facts are right?

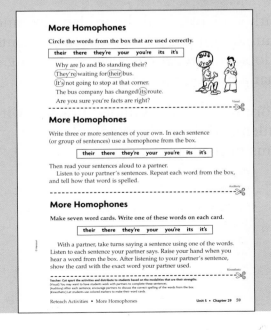

More Homophones

Write three or more sentences of your own. In each sentence (or group of sentences) use a homophone from the box.

| their   there   they're   your   you're   its   it's |

Then read your sentences aloud to a partner.
Listen to your partner's sentences. Repeat each word from the box, and tell how that word is spelled.

More Homophones

Make seven word cards. Write one of these words on each card.

| their   there   they're   your   you're   its   it's |

With a partner, take turns saying a sentence using one of the words. Listen to each sentence your partner says. Raise your hand when you hear a word from the box. After listening to your partner's sentence, show the card with the exact word your partner used.

Reteach Activities • More Homophones   Unit 5 • Chapter 29   59

Homographs and Other Homophones

OBJECTIVES
- To correctly use *see/sea, know/no, trip* (n.)/*trip* (v.), and *bow* (n.)/*bow* (v.) in sentences
- To record responses to survey questions

DAILY LANGUAGE PRACTICE

TRANSPARENCY 65

1 where is you're money (Where; your money?)

2 There money is over their. (Their; there.)

BRIDGE TO WRITING (subject pronoun) earned five dollars.

ORAL WARM-UP

USE PRIOR KNOWLEDGE Read aloud these sentences: *I will fly in a small plane. A fly landed on my desk.* Ask students to tell how the word *fly* has a different meaning in each sentence.

Grammar Jingles™ **CD, Intermediate** Use Track 20 for review and reinforcement of easily confused words.

TEACH/MODEL

With students, read the explanation and examples on page 350. Remind students to look at context clues when deciding what a homograph means.

Work through the Guided Practice with students, or have them complete the items in small groups.

Homographs and Other Homophones

Homographs are spelled the same but have different meanings. Notice that some homographs do not sound the same.

Examples:

Our class is taking a **trip**. *(a journey)*
Be careful not to **trip**. *(to stumble)*

It is in the **bow** of the ship. *(front of a boat)*
The singers **bow** at the end of the show. *(to bend at the waist)*
I have a **bow** and arrow. *(tool used in archery)*

You know that homophones sound alike but have different meanings and spellings.

Examples:

Did you **see** the sign? *(take in with the eyes)*
It shows a picture of the **sea**. *(body of water)*

Do you **know** her name? *(to understand)*
No, I do not. *(opposite of yes)*

Guided Practice

A. Tell the meaning of each underlined homograph.

Example: Gentlemen sometimes bow to one another. *to bend at the waist*

1. Dad is going on a hunting <u>trip</u>. *a journey*
2. On the ship, he will <u>bow</u> to the captain. *to bend at the waist*
3. His luggage will be stored in the <u>bow</u>. *front part of a boat*
4. No one will <u>trip</u> over his archery equipment. *to stumble*
5. He is taking his <u>bow</u> and arrows. *tool used in archery*

350

Vocabulary Power page 86

Name _____

HOMOGRAPHS AND MULTIPLE-MEANING WORDS

Some words have more than one meaning. Clues from the sentence tell you which meaning is being used. Read each pair of sentences below. Write the letter of the correct meaning next to each sentence.

1. _B_ Use the machine to <u>project</u> the slide onto the screen.
   _A_ What are you doing for your science <u>project</u>?
   A a piece of work
   B to cause to be seen on a surface

2. _A_ Don't lean against the sign <u>post</u>.
   _B_ Did you remember to <u>post</u> the letter?
   A a support
   B to mail

3. _B_ We started a dog-walking <u>company</u>.
   _A_ She enjoyed her friend's <u>company</u>.
   A companionship
   B a business

4. _A_ She shed a <u>tear</u> when she fell off her bike.
   _B_ Will Mom be able to fix the <u>tear</u> in my shirt?
   A a drop of water from the eye
   B a rip

5. _B_ <u>Close</u> the door after yourself.
   _A_ We stood <u>close</u> to the fire to stay warm.
   A near
   B to shut

6. _A_ I wouldn't <u>venture</u> my life by riding in a car without a seat belt.
   _B_ John hopes his business <u>venture</u> will be a success.
   A to risk
   B an investment

7. _A_ Sue will <u>wind</u> the thread around the spool.
   _B_ Is there enough <u>wind</u> to fly the kite?
   A to wrap around
   B blowing air

86 **Unit 5 • Chapter 29**   Vocabulary Power

 ESL

REACHING ALL LEARNERS

MATCHING GAME Write each of these words on a card: *see, sea, know, no, trip* (n.), *trip* (v.), *bow* (n.), and *bow* (v.). Write the definitions on separate cards. Mix the cards and arrange them face up on the table. Have students take turns rearranging the cards to match the words with their definitions. As each student matches a pair, ask him or her to use the word in a sentence.

Independent Practice

B. Write each sentence, using the correct word from the box.

see	sea	trip	know	no	bow

Example: I _____ that fishing is an important enterprise.   *know*

6. People catch fish from the _____.   sea
7. We _____ them go out each day.   see
8. The ship's _____ holds the equipment.   bow
9. Usually the fishing _____ is very short.   trip
10. It is important to _____ about changes in the weather.   know
11. The workers on the boat _____ their heads when the wind blows.   bow
12. A storm may come with _____ warning.   no
13. Sometimes they _____ storm clouds.   see
14. Workers keep the deck clear so no one will _____.   trip
15. _____, there will not be any fishing today.   No

Remember
that homophones sound alike but have different spellings. Homographs are spelled alike but have different meanings.

Writing Connection

Writer's Journal: Record Responses
Ask some classmates the questions that you wrote about favorite stores in your community. Record their answers on a chart. Check all the responses for homographs and homophones. Be sure you wrote them correctly in your chart.

ONE SISTER

351

Independent Practice

Have students complete the Independent Practice, or modify it using these suggestions:

MODIFIED INSTRUCTION

BELOW-LEVEL STUDENTS Remind students to check page 350 for the definitions of these homographs and homophones as they complete Part B.

ABOVE-LEVEL STUDENTS Ask students to write an original sentence for each word in the box.

Writing Connection

Writer's Journal: Record Responses
Ask students to record reflections in their journals about the similarities and differences in their classmates' answers. Have students show connections among ideas by predicting how this information could be useful to a store owner.

WRAP-UP/ASSESS

SUMMARIZE Ask students to reflect on why it is important to be careful when using homophones in writing.   **REFLECTION**

RETEACH

INTERVENTION Lessons in **visual, auditory,** and **kinesthetic** modalities: p. R57 and *Reteach Activities Copying Masters,* p. 60.

PRACTICE page 98

Name _____

Homographs and Other Homophones

A. Choose the correct word from the box to complete each sentence. Write the word.

see/sea	know/no	trip (n.)/trip (v.)	bow (n.)/bow (v.)

1. We order goods from across the _____ sea _____.
2. The goods travel inside the _____ bow (n.) _____ of a ship.
3. The crew to protects the goods on the _____ trip (n.) _____.
4. We _____ know _____ when the goods will arrive.
5. We lose _____ no _____ time in unloading them.

B. Write each sentence. Complete each sentence with the correct word from the box above.

6. There are lights below the deck so workers can _____ their way.
   There are lights below the deck so workers can see their way.
7. After being at _____, they are ready for some time on land.
   After being at sea, they are ready for some time on land.
8. The crew has a few days before the _____ home.
   The crew has a few days before the trip (n.) home.

TRY THIS! Read the labels on some of the objects in your classroom. Choose six of these things to write about, and tell where they came from. Use some of these words: *see/sea, know/no, trip (n.)/trip (v.),* and *bow (n.)/bow (v.).*

98   Unit 5 • Chapter 29   Practice • Easily Confused Words

CHALLENGE

WORD CHARTS Have students work in pairs to make charts of three pairs of easily confused words. They may use words from this chapter or find other homophones and homographs. The charts should show the words, their definitions, and example sentences. Display the charts in the classroom.

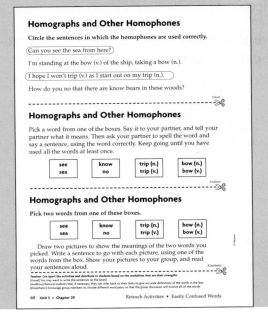

Homographs and Other Homophones

Circle the sentences in which the homophones are used correctly.

(Can you see the sea from here?)

I'm standing at the bow (v.) of the ship, taking a bow (n.).

(I hope I won't trip (v.) as I start out on my trip (n.).)

How do you no that there are know bears in these woods?

Homographs and Other Homophones

Pick a word from one of the boxes. Say it to your partner, and tell your partner what it means. Then ask your partner to spell the word and say a sentence, using the word correctly. Keep going until you have used all the words at least once.

see	know	trip (n.)	bow (n.)
sea	no	trip (v.)	bow (v.)

Homographs and Other Homophones

Pick two words from one of these boxes.

see	know	trip (n.)	bow (n.)
sea	no	trip (v.)	bow (v.)

Draw two pictures to show the meanings of the two words you picked. Write a sentence to go with each picture, using one of the words from the box. Show your pictures to your group, and read your sentences aloud.

60   Unit 5 • Chapter 29   Reteach Activities • Easily Confused Words

Extra Practice

OBJECTIVES
- To correctly use homophones and homographs
- To write a paragraph summarizing information

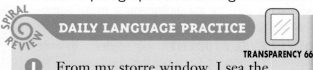

DAILY LANGUAGE PRACTICE

TRANSPARENCY 66

1 From my storre window, I sea the shoppers (store; see; shoppers.)

2 I no how to get they're business. (know; their)

BRIDGE TO WRITING

(Compound subject) _____ bought their umbrellas at my store.

ORAL WARM-UP

USE PRIOR KNOWLEDGE Write on the board this sentence: *I took _____ dogs _____ the park, _____.* Ask students to explain how to determine which of these words to use in the blanks: *to, too, two.*

TEACH/MODEL

Use the Remember box to review easily confused words. Model the thinking for the example in Extra Practice Part A:

MODEL The word *write* is a verb meaning "to put pen or pencil to paper," and the word *right* is an adjective meaning "correct." This sentence is missing the main verb, so I know that *write* is the correct choice.

Have students complete the Extra Practice exercises in small groups.

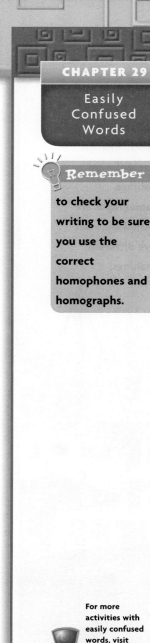

CHAPTER 29
Easily Confused Words

Remember

to check your writing to be sure you use the correct homophones and homographs.

For more activities with easily confused words, visit *The Learning Site:* www.harcourtschool.com

352

Extra Practice

A. Complete each sentence with the correct word in parentheses ( ). Write each sentence. *pages 346-347*

Example: We can (write|right) a list of ways to earn money. *write*

1. Yolanda has a list, (to|too|two). *too*
2. She came up with (to|too|two) different enterprises. *two*
3. A dog-walking service seems like the (write|right) idea. *right*
4. She won't charge (to|too|two) much. *too*
5. She will (write|right) an ad. *write*

B. Complete each sentence with the correct word in parentheses ( ). Write each sentence. *pages 348-349*

Example: What is (your|you're) idea for a new product? *your*

6. (Their|There|They're) thinking of ideas. *They're*
7. (Its|It's) not easy to create a new product. *It's*
8. Think about what things are already out (their|there|they're). *there*
9. (Your|You're) going to think about buyers. *You're*
10. What are (their|there|they're) interests? *their*
11. Talk about (your|you're) idea with others. *your*
12. (Their|There|They're) thoughts are important. *Their*
13. Build your product over (their|there|they're). *there*
14. What is (its|it's) name? *its*
15. Be proud of (your|you're) idea! *your*

Vocabulary Power page 87

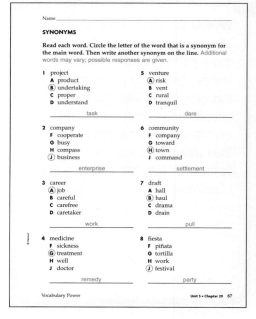

Name _____

SYNONYMS

Read each word. Circle the letter of the word that is a synonym for the main word. Then write another synonym on the line. Additional words may vary; possible responses are given.

1 project
 A product
 B undertaking
 C proper
 D understand
 _____ task

2 company
 F cooperate
 G busy
 H compass
 J business
 _____ enterprise

3 career
 A job
 B careful
 C carefree
 D caretaker
 _____ work

4 medicine
 F sickness
 G treatment
 H well
 J doctor
 _____ remedy

5 venture
 A risk
 B vent
 C rural
 D tranquil
 _____ dare

6 community
 F company
 G toward
 H town
 J command
 _____ settlement

7 draft
 A hall
 B haul
 C drama
 D drain
 _____ pull

8 fiesta
 F piñata
 G tortilla
 H work
 J festival
 _____ party

Vocabulary Power   Unit 5 • Chapter 29 87

Listening and Speaking

STAND UP Make cards with these words: *to, too, two, write, right, its, it's, your, you're, their, there,* and *they're.* Make enough of the cards so that each student has one. Read aloud the sentences from Extra Practice Parts A and B. As they listen to the sentences, students with the correct word should stand up. Then they should say a new sentence using the word.

C. Complete each sentence with the correct word from the box. Write each sentence. *pages 350-351*

> **see, sea   know, no   trip   bow**

Example: Do you —— what kind of job you want to do? *know*

16. My mom is going on a business _____. *trip*
17. She is going across the _____. *sea*
18. She will sleep in a cabin in the _____ of the ship. *bow*
19. There is _____ other place to sleep. *no*
20. I will _____ her when she gets home. *see*
21. Don't _____ over her suitcase! *trip*
22. I _____ that I will have a job like hers someday. *know*
23. I will _____ different parts of the world. *see*
24. People _____ when they say "Hello" in some countries. *bow*
25. I _____ my mom works hard. *know*

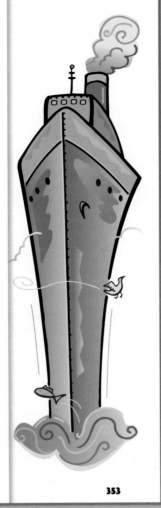

353

Writing Connection

Writer's Craft: Summarize Look at the chart you made about your classmates' favorite stores. With a partner, write a paragraph summarizing what you learned from your classmates' answers. Then trade papers with another group and check the paragraph for easily confused words.

Building Oral Grammar

Write these words on the board: *write, right, to, too, two, their, there, they're, your, you're, its, it's, trip, bow, see, sea, know* and *no.* Ask students to work in small groups to compose a silly story. Have students take turns adding a sentence to the story, using one of the easily confused words on the board. Groups should use each word at least once, and they may repeat turns. As they add to the story, students should demonstrate increasing control of grammar when speaking, such as using subject-verb agreement, complete sentences, and correct tense.

Writing Connection

Writer's Craft: Summarize Have students select the most important piece of information from their charts and use it as the topic of their paragraphs. Have students respond constructively to one another's writing by checking any easily confused words and providing feedback on how to improve the summary.

WRAP-UP/ASSESS

Writer's Journal

SUMMARIZE Have students write in their journals to reflect on what they have learned about homophones and homographs.
REFLECTION

ADDITIONAL PRACTICE An additional page of Extra Practice is provided on page 473 of the *Pupil Edition.*

PRACTICE page 99

REACHING ALL LEARNERS

Name _____

Extra Practice

A. Choose the correct word in parentheses ( ) that completes each sentence. Write the word.

1. I ordered books by mail and was charged **(to/too/two)** much. *too*
2. I only ordered **(to/too/two)** books. *two*
3. The price on the bill would have been **(write/right)** for four books. *right*
4. I will send the bill **(to/too/two)** the manager. *to*
5. I will **(write/right)** the company today. *write*

B. Complete each sentence with the correct word from the box.

| your, you're | its, it's | their, there, they're |
| sea, see | know, no | trip (n.), trip (v.)   bow (n.), bow (v.) |

6. I heard _____ *you're* going to have an exciting job.
7. You will take a _____ *trip (n.)* as part of your job.
8. In fact, you will go to a factory across the _____ *sea*.
9. Once you get _____ *there*, you will have exciting work.
10. I _____ *know* you are just right for the job.

TRY THIS! Write a paragraph about a place you would like to visit. How would you get there? Use some of the easily confused words from this chapter correctly.

Practice • Easily Confused Words   Unit 5 • Chapter 29   99

CHALLENGE

REACHING ALL LEARNERS

TALL TALE Have students work in pairs to write a tall tale using some of the easily confused words they learned. Remind students that tall tales contain colorful characters and fantastic events. The tall tales should be fun and exciting to read. Have students check their stories to make sure they used the homophones and homographs correctly.

TECHNOLOGY *Grammar Practice and Assessment* CD-ROM; *Writing Express* CD-ROM

INTERNET Visit *The Learning Site:* www.harcourtschool.com

Chapter Review

OBJECTIVES
- To review homophones and homographs
- To use *sit, set, picture,* and *pitcher* correctly in writing

DAILY LANGUAGE PRACTICE

TRANSPARENCY 66

1 we brought banana bread two the bake sale. (We; to)

2 Its a sale to raise money for us soccer team. (It's; our)

BRIDGE TO WRITING The oatmeal cookies were __(adjective)__ . They sold __(adverb)__ than the cupcakes.

STANDARDIZED TEST PREP

MODEL TEST-TAKING STRATEGIES Have students read the directions on page 354 silently. Remind them that trying each choice in the blank can help them decide which answer is correct. Model the thinking. Write this example on the board:

I have never been near the (1) _____.

    1 A see
       B there
       C trip
       D sea

MODEL I know that choice A, *see*, is a verb meaning "to take in with the eyes." That doesn't make sense in this sentence. Choice B is the adverb *there*. *I have never been near the there* doesn't make sense either. Choice C, t*rip* can be a noun or a verb. *I have never been near the trip* doesn't sound correct. Choice D is *sea*, a noun meaning "a body of water." *I have never been near the sea* makes sense. The correct answer is D.

Have students complete the Chapter Review independently.

CHAPTER 29

Easily Confused Words

STANDARDIZED TEST PREP

TIP When you cannot answer a question right away, skip it and go on. Then come back to it after you have finished answering the other questions.

For additional test preparation, visit *The Learning Site:* www.harcourtschool.com

354

Chapter Review

Choose the word that belongs in each space in the paragraph below. Write the letter for your answer.

> Do you want to go on a (1) _____? Do you (2) _____ how to plan a vacation? Many people (3) _____ to me for advice on where to visit. I might say they should go (4) _____ another country. I tell them what they should (5) _____. I have had (6) _____ unhappy customers. (7) _____ all planning to travel with me again. I can help you plan (8) _____ vacation.

1 A trip A
  B sea
  C see
  D right

2 F trip
  G bow
  H know H
  J no

3 A write A
  B right
  C see
  D you're

4 F your
  G to G
  H too
  J two

5 A no
  B trip
  C see C
  D sea

6 F its
  G it's
  H know
  J no J

7 A Their
  B There
  C They're C
  D see

8 F your F
  G you're
  H know
  J no

Assessment

PORTFOLIO ASSESSMENT Have students select their best work from the Writing Connections on pages 347, 349, and 353.

ONGOING ASSESSMENT Evaluate the performance of 4–6 students using appropriate checklists and record forms from pages R74–R77.

INTERNET Activities and exercises to help students prepare for state and standardized assessments appear on *The Learning Site:*

www.harcourtschool.com

Troublesome Words

Not all easily confused words are homophones or homographs. Some words sound so much like each other that they are often misused.

Examples:

Isabela **set** her book on the table. *(to place)*

She will **sit** down to do her homework. *(to rest)*

set   **sit**

Her assignment is to draw a **picture**. *(an image)*

This **pitcher** of water is a good subject. *(a container)*

picture   **pitcher**

YOUR TURN

What are some word pairs that you find confusing? These words can be homophones, homographs, or words that sound like each other.

1. **Make a list of at least four words.**
2. **Use a dictionary or a grammar book to find the definition of each one.**
3. **Use each word in a sentence.**

 TIP When using words that are easily confused, be sure to speak clearly so that others can understand you.

355

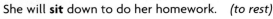 REACHING ALL LEARNERS

PRACTICE page 100

Name _____

Chapter Review

Choose the word that belongs in each space in the paragraph below. Fill in the oval next to your choice.

I **(1)** _____ where I would like to go. I would like to go **(2)** _____ France. I hope **(3)** _____ able to come with me. We could take a **(4)** _____ by **(5)** _____. Can you **(6)** _____ us standing on the **(7)** _____ of the ship? When we get **(8)** _____, we will see some beautiful art. France has many famous museums.

1 ◯ trip (n.)
◯ trip (v.)
⬛ know
◯ no

2 ⬛ to
◯ too
◯ two
◯ them

3 ◯ too
◯ to
◯ your
⬛ you're

4 ⬛ trip (n.)
◯ trip (v.)
◯ too
◯ two

5 ◯ you're
◯ to
◯ see
⬛ sea

6 ⬛ see
◯ sea
◯ know
◯ no

7 ◯ their
◯ there
⬛ bow (n.)
◯ they're

8 ◯ they're
◯ you're
⬛ there
◯ their

100   Unit 5 • Chapter 29   Practice • Easily Confused Words

REACHING ALL LEARNERS

CHALLENGE

GLOSSARY Ask students to make a glossary of easily confused words.

Have students follow these steps:

- Make a list of six easily confused words.
- Alphabetize the list.
- Write the definition for each word.
- Write an example sentence for each word.

Have students keep their glossaries in their portfolios.

VOCABULARY

Troublesome Words

TEACH/MODEL

Work through the explanation and examples of troublesome words on page 355. Ask students to explain why they think people confuse these words. Have volunteers use the words *set*, *sit*, *picture*, and *pitcher* in sentences. Point out that *picture* can be used as a verb, as in *Picture a scene with birds and trees*. Ask students to think of another definition for *pitcher*.

With students, brainstorm a list of troublesome words. Write the list on the board. The list may include: *pear/pair*, *leave/let*, *flower/flour*, *past/passed*, and *than/then*. Have students work in small groups to find out the definitions of these words.

WRITING APPLICATION Have students write and illustrate a story that uses some of the troublesome words on the board. Remind students to check their stories to make sure they used the words correctly. Tell students to revise their stories to achieve precise word choices.

WRAP-UP/ASSESS

 Writer's Journal

SUMMARIZE In their Writer's Journals, have students write their own guidelines for using troublesome words such as *set/sit* and *picture/pitcher*.

 TECHNOLOGY Additional writing activities are provided on the *Writing Express* CD-ROM

CHAPTER 30

Writing Workshop

Research Report
pages 356–369

LESSON ORGANIZER	DAY 1	DAY 2
DAILY LANGUAGE PRACTICE TRANSPARENCY 67	1. lighthouse keepers have a important job. (Lighthouse; an) 2. Does lighthouses still play a part in seaside communitys (Do; communities?)	1. My uncl is a volunteer at the Boys & Girls Club in hims town. (uncle; his) 2. When they're is a fire, firefighters must go quick to put it out. (there; quickly)
ORAL WARM-UP Listening/Speaking	Discuss Lighthouses and Purposes of Research 356 Discuss Methods of Research 364	Suggest Organizational Strategies 365
TEACH/MODEL **WRITING** 	**Literature Model:** from *Beacons of Light: Lighthouses* 357-361 ✔ **Prewriting** 364 • To learn strategies for pre-writing a research report • To choose a topic and generate ideas for a research report Interactive Writing 364	✔ **Drafting** 365 • To learn strategies for drafting a research report • To draft a research report **Transparency** 67
Reaching All Learners	**Modified Instruction** 370 Below-Level: Say Sentences Above-Level: Rewrite Sentences *ESL Manual* pp. 146, 147	**Modified Instruction** 371 Below-Level: Suggest Adverbs Above-Level: Rewrite Sentences *ESL Manual* p. 146
GRAMMAR	**Unit 5 Review:** ✔ More About Adjectives 370	**Unit 5 Review:** ✔ Adverbs 371
CROSS-CURRICULAR/ ENRICHMENT **KEY** ✔ = tested writing form/skill	**LISTENING AND SPEAKING:** Oral Report 362 **EVALUATION CRITERIA:** Establish Criteria 363 **HANDS-ON:** What's That Form? 370 *Vocabulary Power* Related Words 358 ⎯⎯⎯⎯⎯⎯⎯⎯⎯ **visible**, vision, visor, vista, visual See *Vocabulary Power* book.	**TEST PREP:** Eliminate Choices 371 *Vocabulary Power* Greek and Latin Roots 358 *Vocabulary Power* book p. 88 Vocabulary activity

DAY 3

1. Last week at the club, he does an craft project. (did, a)
2. they made pitcher frames. (They; picture)

Suggest Synonyms 366

✔ **Revising** 366
  • To learn strategies for revising a research report
  • To revise a research report

 Transparencies 69a and 69b

Modified Instruction 372
  Below-Level: Review Adjectives and Adverbs
  Above-Level: Write Sentences
ESL Manual p. 146

Unit 5 Review:
✔ More About Adjectives and Adverbs 372

PEER CONFERENCES: Make Essays Stronger 366

HANDS-ON ACTIVITY: Prop Presentation 372

Vocabulary Power

  Explore Word Meaning 358
  Vocabulary Power book p. 89

 Vocabulary activity

DAY 4

1. my freinds belong to the club in our city (My friends; city.)
2. they play basketball their after skool. (They; there; school.)

Suggest Problems Caused by Proofreading Errors 367

✔ **Proofreading** 367
  • To learn strategies for proofreading a research report
  • To proofread a research report

Transparencies 70a and 70b

Proofreading practice

Modified Instruction 373
  Below-Level: Review Apostrophes
  Above-Level: Use Homophones
ESL: Peer Editing 367
ESL Manual p. 146

Unit 5 Review:
✔ Easily Confused Words 373

TEST PREP: Extra Practice 373

Vocabulary Power

  Suffixes 358
  Vocabulary Power book p. 90

Vocabulary activity

DAY 5

1. My sister, and me might join two. (sister and I; join, too.)
2. it could be fun (It; fun!)

Suggest Enhancements for Oral Reports 368

✔ **Publishing** 368
  • To learn strategies for publishing a research report as a multimedia presentation
  • To publish a research report as a multimedia presentation
Handwriting 368

Proofreading practice

ESL Manual p. 146

HANDS-ON ACTIVITIES
  305I–305J

TECHNOLOGY: Giving a Multimedia Presentation 369

Vocabulary Power

  Compare/Contrast 358
  ASSESSMENT: Portfolio Conferences 368

CHAPTER 30 355B

Using the Literature Model

OBJECTIVE

• To read and analyze a research report

 DAILY LANGUAGE PRACTICE

TRANSPARENCY 67

❶ lighthouse keepers have a important job. (Lighthouse; an)

❷ Does lighthouses still play a part in seaside communitys (Do; communities?)

ORAL WARM-UP

USE PRIOR KNOWLEDGE Read aloud the introduction to the research report, and discuss questions such as the following:

1. What is a lighthouse? (Possible response: A lighthouse is a tall building that stands on a shore and that has a light at its top.)

2. What is the purpose of a research report? (Possible response: to inform an audience about a topic)

PREREADING STRATEGIES

PREVIEW/SET PURPOSE Ask students to think about what the research report might tell about lighthouses. List their suggestions on the board. Then have students set their own purpose for reading, or have them read to learn how lighthouses have changed over the years.

356

 School-Home Connection

Family members can help students prepare for their research reports by helping them think of careers that are important in a community. Suggest that together students and family members look in a newspaper or a community newsletter for ideas and discuss how these careers are important.

Award-
Winning
Author

You know that a research report gives facts about a subject. The writer uses different sources to find facts. In this research report, Gail Gibbons writes about lighthouses. As you read, notice the facts she gives about the history of lighthouses.

Beacons of Light
LIGHTHOUSES
by Gail Gibbons

Lighthouses help guide ships and boats safely from one place to another. They warn of dangerous rocks and ledges, hidden points of land, sandbars, and narrow entrances to harbors.

The first guiding lights were huge bonfires that burned brightly from the tops of hills. In some places, sailors watched for landmarks, such as volcanoes, glowing in the night. For thousands of years, light signals didn't change very much. When lighthouses were built, they were often stone towers with fires burning at the top.

357

OPTIONS FOR READING

READ-ALOUD OPTION Read the selection aloud, and have students listen to determine Gibbons's audience, purpose, and key facts.

INDEPENDENT OPTION As students read the selection silently, have them take notes on the facts presented in the report.

Use questions like the following to help students monitor their comprehension:

3. **What is the purpose of Gibbons's research report?** (Possible response: to inform readers about lighthouses) **INFERENTIAL: DETERMINE AUTHOR'S PURPOSE**

4. **What is the function of a lighthouse?** (to guide ships safely by warning them of rocks and other dangers) **LITERAL: NOTE DETAILS**

SELECTION SUMMARY

GENRE: RESEARCH REPORT
This research report gives a brief history of lighthouses. It describes the structure, function, and operation of lighthouses, and tells how these elements have changed over time. Gail Gibbons provides an example of how to organize facts sequentially and how to use descriptions and details in a research report.

ABOUT THE AUTHOR

Gail Gibbons specializes in nonfiction books for children. Her fact-filled books are interesting and fun to read. Gibbons has written more than 80 nonfiction books and has won many awards, including the Washington Post Children's Book Guild Award for her contribution to children's nonfiction.

5. **How do you know whether Gibbons is giving facts or stating opinions?** (Possible response: I know that Gibbons is giving facts when the details she uses can be proved true.) **METACOGNITIVE: DISTINGUISH FACT FROM OPINION**

6. **Why do lighthouses have a round, narrow shape?** (to resist wind and waves during a storm) **LITERAL: NOTE DETAILS**

7. **Gibbons describes the ways lighthouses have changed. How does she organize her information?** (Possible response: The report is organized in time order, from the past to the present.) **CRITICAL: INTERPRET TEXT STRUCTURE**

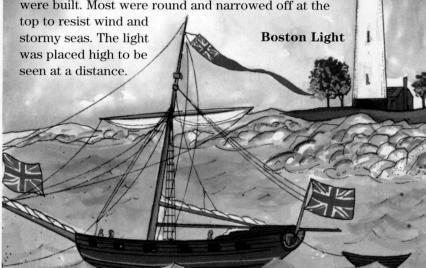

The first lighthouse in North America was the Boston Light, built in 1716. From Little Brewster Island, it guided sailing vessels in and out of Boston harbor. Over the next hundred years, many more lighthouses were built. Most were round and narrowed off at the top to resist wind and stormy seas. The light was placed high to be seen at a distance.

Boston Light

These early lighthouses used wick lamps as a source of light, burning whale oil or fish oil for fuel. The lighthouse keepers learned to increase the lamps' brightness by placing reflectors behind them.

In 1782, a Swiss scientist, Aimé Argand, developed a brighter lamp. It had a circular wick. When whale oil became scarce, colza (a form of vegetable oil), lard (from animal fat), and, later, kerosene were used. At that time, signals from lighthouses were visible only a few miles, even on a clear night.

358

Vocabulary Power

DAY 1 RELATED WORDS Introduce and define *visible*. **What are some words related to *visible*?**

DAY 2 GREEK AND LATIN ROOTS Write *vis* on the board. **This root means "see." How does knowing this help you understand the meaning of the word *visible*?** (See also *Vocabulary Power*, page 88.)

DAY 3 EXPLORE WORD MEANING **What are some things that are visible in this classroom?** (See also *Vocabulary Power*, page 89.)

DAY 4 SUFFIXES Write *visible* on the board. **What is the suffix in this word?** (See also *Vocabulary Power*, page 90.)

DAY 5 COMPARE AND CONTRAST ***Visible* means "able to be seen." *Audible* means "able to be heard." Can something be both visible and audible?** Discuss responses.

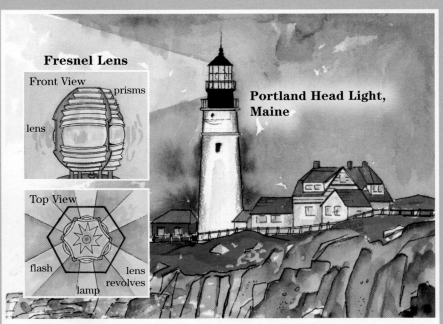

Fresnel Lens

Front View

prisms

lens

Top View

flash

lens revolves

lamp

Portland Head Light, Maine

Then, in 1822, the first modern lighthouse lens was invented by a Frenchman named Augustin Fresnel, who found a way to increase the light by using prisms. The prisms of the lens bent the light beam and concentrated it, making the light visible for many miles. In 1841, the Fresnel lens was installed for the first time in a lighthouse in the United States. Its beam could be seen twenty miles away at night.

The top of a lighthouse is like a giant lantern. Usually, a winding staircase goes to the top. Years ago, the lighthouse keeper made many trips up and down the stairs, doing chores. The burned lamp wick had to be *trimmed*—or adjusted and cut off—to keep the lamp from smoking. Lighthouse keepers were sometimes called *wick trimmers* or *wickies*.

359

8. **Why was trimming the wick an important job for a lighthouse keeper?** (Possible responses: The light was brighter when the wick burned cleanly. The flame got smoky and harder to see when the wick was dirty.) **INFERENTIAL: CAUSE-EFFECT**

9. **Most of the improvements Gibbons describes involve making the light brighter. Why was it important to make the light brighter?** (Possible responses: to make the light easier to see from a distance or in a storm; to give sailors more time to steer their ships in the right direction) **INFERENTIAL: DRAW CONCLUSIONS**

10. **Why are few lighthouse keepers needed today?** (Possible responses: Because the lights run on electricity, lighthouse keepers have less work to do; electricity turns the light on and off automatically.) **INFERENTIAL: DRAW CONCLUSIONS**

11. **Why are lighthouses still needed today?** (Possible responses: Ships still need to be guided at night; they still can hit rocks that cannot be seen at night.) **INFERENTIAL: SYNTHESIZE**

12. **How does Gibbons use details and descriptions to make her report interesting and informative?** (Possible responses: She talks about the dangers ships face, the different fuels used in lamps, and the duties of the lighthouse keepers and their families.) **INFERENTIAL: AUTHOR'S CRAFT**

barn · house · lighthouse · kerosene · fog bell · fuel house

Lighthouse keepers and their families were kept busy cleaning and polishing the lenses, shining all the brass in the lighthouse, and cleaning soot off the tower windows. The keeper's house stood near or was attached to the base of the lighthouse. Sometimes, the keeper lived right inside the lighthouse. Often, there were a number of other structures around the lighthouse, called outbuildings. Everything in and around the lighthouse was kept tidy. All of these buildings had to be maintained and frequently painted. It was hard work.

360

electric lamp

Today, lighthouses are powered by electricity. There are very few lighthouse keepers needed. Some lights stay on all the time. Others go on and off automatically.

boat house

They are maintained by the Coast Guard. Although they have changed over the years, lighthouses are still beacons of light to guide and warn of danger and to remind us of the past.

Vocabulary Power

vis•i•ble [vi′zə•bəl] *adj.* Able to be seen.

Analyze THE Model

1. What is the topic of this research report? How far do you have to read to find out?
2. What facts does Gail Gibbons give about the first lighthouse in North America?
3. What facts does she give about today's lighthouses?
4. Why do you think Gail Gibbons included facts about the history of lighthouses in this piece of writing?

361

Analyze THE Model

1. **What is the topic of this research report? How far do you have to read to find out?** (The topic, lighthouses, is introduced immediately, in the title and in the first sentence.)
   LITERAL: NOTE DETAILS

2. **What facts does Gail Gibbons give about the first lighthouse in North America?** (It was built on Little Brewster Island in 1716, and it guided ships in and out of Boston harbor.)
   LITERAL: NOTE DETAILS

3. **What facts does she give about today's lighthouses?** (Possible responses: They are powered by electricity; the lights are automatic; the U.S. Coast Guard is in charge of lighthouses; they still serve the same purpose as lighthouses in the past.)
   LITERAL: NOTE DETAILS

4. **Why do you think Gail Gibbons included facts about the history of lighthouses in this piece of writing?** (Possible response: to show how lighthouses have changed over the years.)
   CRITICAL: INTERPRET TEXT STRUCTURE

SUMMARIZE THE MODEL

ONE-SENTENCE SUMMARY If you wanted to tell a classmate what this research report is about, what would you say? Have students write one sentence to summarize the report. (Possible response: Gibbons explains that although lighthouses have changed over the years, their purpose has remained the same.)

RESPONSE TO LITERATURE

WRITING PROMPT To have students respond in writing to the selection, use the following prompt:

What facts included in this report made it interesting to read? What other kinds of information would you have added?

TECHNOLOGY Additional writing activities are provided on the *Writing Express* CD-ROM

Parts of a Research Report

OBJECTIVES

- To recognize and understand the parts of a research report
- To analyze and summarize a research report
- To establish criteria for evaluating a research report
- To listen critically to a research report

READING LIKE A WRITER

READ AND RESPOND TO THE MODEL Tell students that you will read aloud Lita's research report. Have them determine a purpose for listening. (to understand the topic of the report; to gain information about the topic) Then read the research report aloud, and discuss whether Lita does a good job of presenting the topic and providing interesting facts about it. Remind students to support their evaluations with examples from the report.

FOCUS ON ORGANIZATION Have students reread the research report silently, using the side notes to find the main parts. Call on students to name and explain each part. Point out that Lita first discusses clubs in general and then gives more details about what the Boys & Girls Clubs do.

FOCUS ON WRITER'S CRAFT Have students find and read aloud examples of the facts that Lita provides. (There are more than 1,200 Boys & Girls Clubs; clubs offer activities after school; the first clubs were started in the 1860's.) Note that Lita uses the first sentence in each paragraph to give a general introduction and then supports it with facts in the body of each paragraph.

READING — WRITING CONNECTION

Parts of a Research Report

Gail Gibbons researched lighthouses and told the facts she learned about them. Read this research report that a student named Lita wrote. Pay attention to the parts of a research report.

MODEL

Helping Boys and Girls

introduction | main topic — There are over 1,200 Boys & Girls Clubs in the United States, Puerto Rico, and the Virgin Islands. Communities organize the clubs to provide safe, caring places for young people to go. It does not cost much to belong to these clubs, so almost any boy or girl can join.

subtopic — The clubs offer activities after school for students whose parents work. Boys and girls

supporting facts | details — can play sports and make crafts at the clubs. They can also learn about finding careers and helping their communities. The skills boys and girls learn at the clubs can help them lead successful lives.

subtopic — The clubs have grown over the years. The

supporting facts | details — first clubs were started in the 1860's and were for boys only. Later, girls were allowed to join. Today, the clubs help about 1 1/2 million young people.

Listening and Speaking

ORAL REPORTS Have students work in small groups to brainstorm topics about which they know simple facts. Have them use notecards to organize their information.

Tell each student to choose a topic and write it at the top of a notecard. Have students take turns reading their topic aloud to the group. Then, as group members share facts they know about that topic, have the student record the facts on the notecard. After each student has had a turn, have students give informal oral reports about their topics.

Though they have changed in some ways, Boys & Girls Clubs continue to help young people to be ready for the future. These clubs are in many communities, from big cities to small towns. Maybe there is one near you!

conclusion

Analyze THE Model

1. Who do you think is Lita's audience? What is her writing purpose?

2. What facts does Lita mention to introduce her topic?

3. What facts about the history of Boys & Girls Clubs did Lita find in her research?

Summarize THE Model

Use an outline to list the important facts that Lita included in her report. Look back at Chapter 27 if you need to review outline format. Include a main point on your outline for each paragraph in Lita's report. Then, list the facts in each paragraph under the correct main point. When your outline is complete, use it to write a summary of Lita's report.

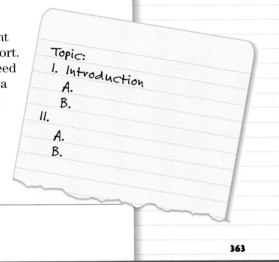

Topic:
I. Introduction
   A.
   B.
II.
   A.
   B.

363

Evaluation Criteria

· ·

ESTABLISH CRITERIA FOR WRITING Tell students that they will help to evaluate their own research reports. Have them turn to the rubric on page 500 in their Handbooks. Explain that if students meet the criteria in the "4" column, plus the criteria that you and the class add, they will have produced their best work. Discuss the criteria, and add additional criteria based on your students' needs and interests. Remind students to refer to the rubric as they write their research reports. (A teacher version of the rubric is available on page R84. For more information about evaluating writing, see pages R78–R79 in this *Teacher's Edition*.)

Analyze THE Model

1. **Who do you think is Lita's audience? What is her writing purpose?** (Possible response: Lita's audience is her classmates. Her purpose is to inform them about Boys & Girls Clubs.) **INFERENTIAL: DETERMINE AUTHOR'S PURPOSE**

2. **What facts does Lita mention to introduce her topic?** (She tells her audience how many clubs there are, why the clubs are formed, and who can join.) **LITERAL: NOTE DETAILS**

3. **What facts about the history of Boys & Girls Clubs did Lita find in her research?** (The first clubs were for boys and were started in 1860. Girls were allowed to join later.) **LITERAL: NOTE DETAILS**

SUMMARIZE THE MODEL

Have students work in pairs to write one introductory sentence that includes the main idea for a paragraph about Boys & Girls Clubs. Then have them work individually to write a summary of Lita's research report.

WRITER'S CRAFT

AUDIENCE AND PURPOSE Remind students to note how the facts and details Lita includes in her report support her writing purpose.

TAKE-HOME BOOK 5 provides an additional model of informative writing and home activities. See *Practice Book* pages 137–140.

Prewriting

OBJECTIVES
- To learn strategies for prewriting a research report
- To choose a topic and generate ideas for a research report

ORAL WARM-UP

USE PRIOR KNOWLEDGE Have a volunteer describe a time when he or she wanted to know more about something. Ask: **What did you do to get more information?**

GUIDED WRITING

Discuss the writing prompt. Have students identify the purpose and the audience. (purpose—to inform; audience—classmates) Then model finding an appropriate topic.

MODEL **Firefighters are important to the community, and their career is interesting. My readers might like to learn how firefighters used to fight fires and how they fight fires today.**

Then have students read Lita's model and make their own prewriting outlines, using a topic you assign or their own topics.

SELF-INITIATED WRITING Have students choose their own topics for research reports.

WRAP-UP/ASSESS

SUMMARIZE How does making an outline help you organize a research report?

Strategies Good Writers Use

- Decide on your audience.
- Decide on the purpose of your report.
- Include facts that will inform your audience.

Purpose and Audience

You can learn more about a topic by doing research. In this chapter, you will share what you learn about a career by writing a research report.

WRITING PROMPT Write a research report to share with your classmates about a career that is important to the community. Begin with a paragraph that introduces your topic. Your report should include at least two subtopics with supporting details. Make sure your report also has a concluding paragraph.

Before you begin, think about your purpose and audience. What parts should your report include? Who will your readers be?

MODEL

Lita chose the Boys & Girls Clubs for her topic. Then she did research. She put the facts she found into an outline to organize her ideas. Here is the first part of her outline:

Topic: Boys & Girls Clubs
I. Introduction
  A. 1,200 clubs
  B. Communities organize
  C. Safe places
  D. Low cost of membership
II. Activities

YOUR TURN

Choose the job that you will write about. Research the job in one or more books. Take notes on important information. Then use an outline to organize your notes.

364

Vocabulary Power page 88

Name _____

GREEK AND LATIN ROOTS

A. The Latin root *-vis-*, meaning "see," appears in many English words. Study the chart below. Then choose a word to complete each sentence.

Root Word	English Word	Meaning
vis	vision	the sense of sight
vis	visible	able to be seen
vis	visual	having to do with sight
vis	visit	to go or come to see
vis	visor	a brim on the front of a cap
vis	vista	a distant view

1. The lighthouse's beacon was _____visible_____ for miles.
2. As a part of our vacation, we planned to _____visit_____ a lighthouse.
3. A cap's _____visor_____ shades your eyes from the sun.
4. The _____vista_____ of the sunset over the ocean spread out before us.
5. A picture is an example of a _____visual_____ aid.
6. When you go to the eye doctor, you get your _____vision_____ checked.

B. Now complete the chart with two of your own *-vis-* words.
Responses may vary. Accept reasonable responses.

Root Word	English Word	Meaning
vis		
vis		

88   Unit 6 • Chapter 30   Vocabulary Power

Interactive Writing

You may want to prewrite and write a first draft as a group. Draw students' attention to the Strategies Good Writers Use. Have students help you complete a prewriting outline, including main ideas and details. Then use the Drafting Transparency with students, coaching them to use effective organization and elaboration.

Drafting

Organization and Elaboration

Follow these steps to help you organize your report:

STEP 1 Introduce the Topic
Introduce your main topic in the first paragraph.

STEP 2 Organize the Subtopics
Decide how to order the subtopics you researched.

STEP 3 Add Supporting Facts and Details
Add facts and details that support your subtopics.

STEP 4 End with a Summary
Summarize your main points in the last paragraph.

MODEL

Here is the first paragraph of Lita's research report. What interesting facts does she include?

> There are over 1,200 Boys & Girls Clubs in the United States, Puerto Rico, and the Virgin Islands. Communities organize the clubs to provide safe, caring places for young people to go. It does not cost much to belong to these clubs, so almost any boy or girl can join.

YOUR TURN

Now draft your research report. Follow the steps above. Use the outline you made.

Strategies Good Writers Use

- Introduce your topic with interesting facts.
- Use other facts to support your subtopics.
- End with a strong concluding paragraph.

 Use a computer to write your draft. You can use the delete key to take out sentences that you decide to rewrite.

365

Drafting

OBJECTIVES

- To learn strategies for drafting a research report
- To draft a research report

DAILY LANGUAGE PRACTICE

TRANSPARENCY 67

1. My uncl is a volunteer at the Boys & Girls Club in hims town. (uncle; his)

2. When they're is a fire, firefighters must go quick to put it out. (there; quickly)

ORAL WARM-UP

USE PRIOR KNOWLEDGE Ask students to suggest ways to organize the facts in their research reports.

GUIDED WRITING

Discuss the steps and model. Ask volunteers to answer the questions that precede the model. (Lita explains that almost anyone can belong to a Boys & Girls Club. She also talks about the number of clubs, their locations, and their general purpose.)

Point out to students that when they explain why a career is important to the community, they must use facts to support their opinions. Ask students to give examples of opinions and statements using facts.

As students draft their research reports, remind them to keep their purpose and audience in mind. Students may refer back to both Gail Gibbons's and Lita's essays as models.

WRAP-UP/ASSESS

SUMMARIZE Why is it a good idea to start your research report with an interesting fact or statement?

Vocabulary Power page 89

Name _____

EXPLORE WORD MEANINGS

Read and respond to each of the following questions or statements.

1. What are some activities you do where you use your sense of vision? _____

2. If your vision isn't perfect, what might you wear or do to make it better? _____

3. What are some visual aids your teacher uses in your classroom? _____

4. Draw a picture of a cap with a visor.

5. Draw a vista you might see from a window.

Vocabulary Power   Unit 6 • Chapter 30 89

TRANSPARENCY 68

**DRAFTING
Research Report**

Step 1: Introduction

Step 2: Subtopic with Supporting Facts and Details

Step 3: Subtopic with Supporting Facts and Details

Step 4: Summary

Harcourt Language   68   Chapter 30
Level 3   Writing a Research Report

Revising

OBJECTIVES
- To learn strategies for revising a research report
- To revise a research report

DAILY LANGUAGE PRACTICE

TRANSPARENCY 67

1 Last week at the club, he does an craft project. (did a)

2 they made pitcher frames. (They; picture)

ORAL WARM-UP

USE PRIOR KNOWLEDGE Write the word *person* on the board. Ask students to suggest synonyms for *person*. Discuss how using exact words makes writing more effective.

GUIDED WRITING

Guide students through the Organization and Elaboration questions. Have students compare their drafts with their outlines, checking to ensure that the first sentence in each paragraph conveys the main idea and that the other sentences present facts that support it. Tell students that they may add examples to make their writing more clear.

Use **Transparencies 69a and 69b** to model adding examples. Then have students revise their research reports to achieve a sense of audience. They can keep their revisions in their working portfolios.

PEER CONFERENCES Have pairs of students use the **Evaluation Criteria** to evaluate their own and each other's writing, responding constructively by identifying strengths and suggesting improvements.

WRAP-UP/ASSESS

SUMMARIZE How can you tell whether a fact truly belongs in a report?

Revising

Strategies Good Writers Use

- Include facts that will interest your audience.
- Replace weak words with exact ones.

Use the cut and paste feature to reorganize your facts.

Organization and Elaboration

Reread your draft and think about these questions:

- How could I make my beginning more interesting?
- Does the order of my subtopics make sense?
- What facts could I add to better support my subtopics?
- How might I make my ending stronger?

MODEL

Here is another part of Lita's research report. Notice that she used some more precise words. She also added a sentence with more examples to support her subtopic.

> The clubs offer activities after school for students whose parents work. Boys and girls can play sports and make ~~things~~ crafts at the clubs. They can also learn about finding careers and helping their communities. The skills boys and girls learn at the clubs can help them lead ~~good~~ successful lives.

YOUR TURN

Now revise your research report. Think about facts you might add to tell more about your subtopics.

366

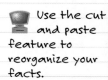

TRANSPARENCIES 69a and 69b

REVISING

> The clubs offer activities after school for students whose parents work. Boys and girls can play sports and make ~~things~~ crafts at the clubs. They can also learn about finding careers and helping their communities. The skills boys and girls learn at the clubs can help them lead ~~good~~ successful lives.

Harcourt Language
Level 3 · **69** · Chapter 30 Writing a Research Report

Vocabulary Power page 90

Name _____

SUFFIXES

The suffix *-ible*, also spelled *-able*, means "capable of being."

Example:
audi, meaning "hear," + *-ible* = *audible*, a word that means "capable of being heard"

Add the suffix *-ible*, *-able*, to the base words in the chart below to form new words. Write a definition for each new word. The first one is done for you.

Root Word or Base Word	Suffix	New Word	Definition
1. vis	-ible	visible	capable of being seen
2. read	-able	readable	capable of being read
3. enjoy	-able	enjoyable	capable of being enjoyed
4. break	-able	breakable	capable of being broken
5. use	-able	usable	capable of being used
6. change	-able	changeable	capable of being changed
7. love	-able	lovable	capable of being loved

90 Unit 5 • Chapter 30   Vocabulary Power

Checking Your Language

Proofreading helps you find and correct mistakes in grammar, spelling, punctuation, and capitalization. It will be easier for your readers to understand your report if it has no mistakes.

MODEL

After Lita revised her research report, she proofread it. Here is another part of her report. What spelling mistakes did she correct? What other kinds of mistakes did she correct?

> The clubs have ~~grone~~ *grown* over the yaers. The first clubs ~~are~~ *were* started in the 1860's and ~~are~~ *were* for boys only. Later, girls were ~~allowd~~ *allowed* to join. today, the clubs help about 1 1/2 million young people.

YOUR TURN

Now proofread your revised research report. You may want to ask another writer to proofread it, too. Look for

- grammar mistakes.
- spelling mistakes.
- mistakes in capitalization and punctuation.

Strategies Good Writers Use

- Look up words if you are not sure how to spell them.
- Watch out for easily confused words, such as *to, two,* and *too.*

Editor's Marks

℘	take out text
∧	add text
⌒	move text
¶	new paragraph
≡	capitalize
/	lowercase
◯	correct spelling

367

Proofreading

OBJECTIVES

- To learn strategies for proofreading a research report
- To proofread a research report

DAILY LANGUAGE PRACTICE

TRANSPARENCY 67

1 my freinds belong to the club in our city (My friends; city.)

2 they play basketball their after skool. (They; there; school.)

ORAL WARM-UP

USE PRIOR KNOWLEDGE What might happen if a help-wanted ad for a job contained errors?

GUIDED WRITING

Use **Transparencies 70a and 70b** to further model spelling and capitalization changes. Have students explain Lita's corrections.

Review the spellings of some regular and irregular plural nouns, such as *sheep, deer,* and nouns ending with *ch, sh, x, s,* or a consonant and *y*. Write on the board: *sheep, deer, match, brush, fox, cross,* and *diary*. Have students write the correct plural form of these nouns on the board. Tell students to refer to these examples as they proofread their research reports.

WRAP-UP/ASSESS

SUMMARIZE Why is it a good idea to proofread your research report several times?

ESL

PEER EDITING Have students proofread their reports once on their own. Then have them exchange papers with another English-language learner to double-check spelling, punctuation, and capitalization. Have students underline words that they think may be misspelled and then locate those words in a dictionary.

TRANSPARENCIES 70a and 70b

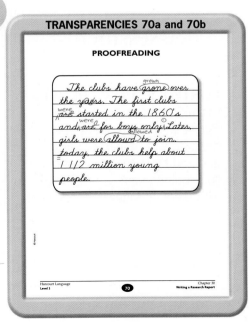

PROOFREADING

> The clubs have ~~grone~~ *grown* over the yaers. The first clubs ~~are~~ *were* started in the 1860's and ~~are~~ *were* for boys only. Later, girls were ~~allowd~~ *allowed* to join. today, the clubs help about 1 1/2 million young people.

Harcourt Language
Level 3

70

Chapter 30
Writing a Research Report

Visit The Learning Site!
www.harcourtschool.com

Publishing

OBJECTIVES
- To learn strategies for publishing a research report as a multimedia presentation
- To publish a research report as a multimedia presentation

DAILY LANGUAGE PRACTICE

SPIRAL REVIEW

TRANSPARENCY 67

1 My sister, and me might join two.
(sister and I; join, too.)

2 it could be fun (It; fun!)

ORAL WARM-UP

USE PRIOR KNOWLEDGE Ask volunteers to suggest ways to make an oral report more interesting and informative.
(Possible responses: by using props, music, pictures)

GUIDED WRITING

SHARING YOUR WORK Read and discuss the questions with students. Help them decide where and how to publish their research reports.

 If computers are available, have students search the Internet for pictures and images to use with their presentations. Students may look for websites that have clip art available, or they may wish to search by using key words from their reports.

REFLECTING ON YOUR WRITING Use the Portfolio Conference suggestions at the right.

 TECHNOLOGY *Grammar Practice* and *Assessment* **CD-ROM**
INTERNET *Visit The Learning Site:*
www.harcourtschool.com

USING YOUR
Handbook

- Use the rubric on page 500 to evaluate your research report.

368

Sharing Your Work

Now you will share your research report with your audience. Use the following questions to help you decide how to publish your work:

1. Who is your audience? How can you present your research report so your audience will enjoy it and learn from it?

2. Should you type your report on a computer or write it by hand? Should you use manuscript or cursive writing?

3. Would a multimedia presentation be an interesting way to present your research report? To give a multimedia presentation, follow the steps on page 369.

Reflecting on Your Writing

 Using Your Portfolio What did you learn about your writing in this chapter? Write your answer to each question below.

1. How did prewriting help you write a better research report?

2. What kinds of mistakes did you correct after proofreading your writing?

Place your answers and your research report in your portfolio. Take time to look through your portfolio and read your work. Write one or two sentences telling how your writing has improved.

Assessment

PORTFOLIO CONFERENCES
Discuss the questions in the *Pupil Edition,* and direct students to write their answers and add them to their portfolios. Tell students you will meet with them individually to discuss their growth as writers.

Use the Student Record Form on page R74 to record and monitor students' progress.

Handwriting

Point out the importance of correct letter size and of spacing between letters, words, and sentences.

- **Size** Use the words *dog* and *got* to show the relative size of ascenders and descenders.
- **Spacing** Letters should be equally spaced. The space between words should be as wide as a pencil.

Ask students to use the tips as they publish their essays.

Technology: Giving a Multimedia Presentation

A *multimedia* presentation involves several different means of communication, such as pictures, videos, music, or drama. After thinking about it, Lita decided to share her report with the class as a multimedia presentation. You can do the same. Use these steps:

STEP 1 Decide which multimedia aids might help your audience better understand your report. Can you use photos, drawings, videos, or music? Can you act out part of the information in your report?

STEP 2 Get permission to use any equipment you need, such as an audiotape or videotape player. If you need "actors," ask classmates to help.

STEP 3 Plan when you will use multimedia aids in your presentation. Prepare them ahead of time.

STEP 4 Organize your presentation. Write notes of what you will say. Practice your presentation.

STEP 5 At the end of your presentation, answer any questions your classmates ask.

Strategies for Multi-Media Presentations

- Choose multimedia aids that your whole audience can see and hear.
- Learn how to operate any equipment you need ahead of time. Practice using the equipment.
- Make sure that the equipment you plan to use works properly.

369

TECHNOLOGY
Giving a Multimedia Presentation

Read aloud the steps for creating a multimedia presentation. Ask students to suggest examples of multimedia aids that might help them present their research reports.

Provide time for students to plan and create their multimedia presentations. Remind students to use pictures to clarify and support their descriptions and details.

Before students begin their presentations, review how to be a good listener and speaker. Use the Student Record Form on page R76 to assess students' listening and speaking skills.

WRAP-UP/ASSESS

SUMMARIZE Would you use multimedia to present other writing in your portfolio? Why or why not?

SCORING RUBRIC

4 ADVANCED
Purpose and Audience
- appropriate for audience
- stays focused on purpose

Organization and Elaboration
- has a clear introduction
- the information is organized logically, and the ending summarizes or draws a conclusion
- has description and details that add information
- uses signal words to show how ideas are related

Language
- uses correct grammar, spelling, usage, and mechanics

3 PROFICIENT
Purpose and Audience
- mostly appropriate for audience
- few deviations from purpose

Organization and Elaboration
- has a clear introduction
- the information is not all in logical order, but the ending summarizes or draws a conclusion
- has some description and details
- has some signal words and phrases

Language
- uses mostly correct grammar, spelling, usage, and mechanics

2 BASIC
Purpose and Audience
- not appropriate for audience
- often strays from purpose

Organization and Elaboration
- introduction is unclear
- the information is not all about the same topic, and the ending is not clear
- doesn't have many details or much description
- has very few signal words or phrases

Language
- incorrect grammar, spelling, or mechanics sometimes makes writing unclear

1 LIMITED
Purpose and Audience
- not appropriate for audience
- purpose is unclear

Organization and Elaboration
- does not have an introduction
- does not organize ideas about one topic and does not give a summary or conclusion
- has no signal words or phrases

Language
- incorrect grammar, spelling, or mechanics often makes writing unclear

For information on adapting this rubric to 5- or 6-point scales, see pages R78–R79.

OBJECTIVES
- To choose the correct article to describe a given noun
- To choose the correct form of an adjective that compares
- To write the correct forms of adjectives

Unit Review

MODIFIED INSTRUCTION

BELOW-LEVEL STUDENTS As students begin Part A, point out that the word *a* never comes before a plural noun. As students begin Parts A and B, advise them to say the sentence both ways in a whisper. The one that sounds right is likely to be correct.

ABOVE-LEVEL STUDENTS After students have completed Part B, have them rewrite sentences 6, 8, and 9 so that a superlative is the correct choice.

Articles   *pages 308–309*

A. Write the correct article in parentheses ( ) for each sentence.

1. Calves are born in (the, an) spring. the
2. (A, An) veterinarian comes to check the newborns. A
3. The doctor brings (a, an) helper. a
4. (The, A) new calves are healthy. The
5. The birth was quite (a, an) adventure. an

Adjectives That Compare
pages 310–311

B. Write the correct adjective that compares in parentheses ( ) for each sentence.

6. The farm down the road is (larger, largest) than our farm. larger
7. This is the (better, best) crop we have ever had. best
8. Our machine works (faster, fastest) than theirs. faster
9. The rainy season was (heavier, heaviest) this year than last year. heavier
10. It was the (baddest, worst) rainy season of all. worst

Avoiding Incorrect Comparisons   *pages 312–313*

C. Write the correct form of the adjective in parentheses ( ) for each sentence.

11. (Few) sheep were born this year than last year. Fewer
12. Our sheep produce the (beautiful) wool in the county. most beautiful
13. Their fleece is (soft) than anything else. softer
14. These lambs seem (active) than those lambs. more active
15. They are (playful) than the other lambs. more playful

HANDS ON Activity

WHAT'S THAT FORM? Write fifteen one-syllable and fifteen two-syllable adjectives on index cards, for a total of thirty cards. Write *more/most* on one large envelope and *er/est* on another. Give the cards and envelopes to a group of students. See how quickly they can sort the adjectives into the correct envelopes.

Adverbs   *pages 318–319*

A. Write the adverb that tells *how* in each sentence.

1. My kitten quickly raced out the door.   *quickly*
2. It easily climbed up on the roof.   *easily*
3. It meowed loudly for help.   *loudly*
4. My neighbor, Mr. Kwan, softly called for the kitten.   *softly*
5. It eagerly jumped into his arms.   *eagerly*

More About Adverbs   *pages 320–321*

B. Write the adverb that tells *when* or *where* in each sentence.

6. Lindsay often visits the library.   *often*
7. She enjoys going there with her best friend.   *there*
8. They look everywhere for good books.   *everywhere*
9. Soon they find three interesting stories.   *Soon*
10. Lindsay is now ready to go.   *now*

Comparing with Adverbs

pages 322–323

C. Write the correct form of the underlined adverb.

11. The car was traveling <u>fast</u> than the others.   *faster*
12. The patrol officer went after the speeding car <u>quickly</u> than the other officers.   *more quickly*
13. His siren sounded <u>loudly</u> than the patrol car behind him.   *louder*
14. He drove the <u>carefully</u> of all.   *most carefully*
15. He was the <u>more</u> praised officer of the year.   *most*

Unit 5
Grammar Review
CHAPTER 26

Adverbs
pages 318–327

371

Unit 5
Grammar Review
CHAPTER 26

Adverbs

OBJECTIVES
- To identify adverbs that tell *how* in sentences
- To identify adverbs that tell *when* or *where* in sentences
- To write the correct forms of adverbs

Unit Review
MODIFIED INSTRUCTION

BELOW-LEVEL STUDENTS Before students begin the page, refresh their memories by calling on volunteers to suggest adverbs that answer the questions *how*, *when*, and *where*.

ABOVE-LEVEL STUDENTS After students have completed Part C, have them rewrite sentences 11–13 so that a superlative is the correct choice. You also might have students select sentences from Parts A and B and suggest other adverbs that make sense in each sentence.

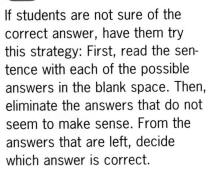

TEST PREP

TIP

If students are not sure of the correct answer, have them try this strategy: First, read the sentence with each of the possible answers in the blank space. Then, eliminate the answers that do not seem to make sense. From the answers that are left, decide which answer is correct.

Unit 5
Grammar Review
CHAPTER 28

More About
Adverbs and
Adjectives

OBJECTIVES

- To identify and distinguish between adjectives and adverbs in sentences
- To identify the words that adjectives and adverbs describe
- To choose the correct placement of adverbs in sentences
- To use *good, well, bad,* and *badly* correctly

Unit Review
MODIFIED INSTRUCTION

BELOW-LEVEL STUDENTS Before students begin Part A, remind them that only adjectives describe nouns and that only adverbs describe verbs. You may wish to point out that *ly* comes at the end of many adverbs but that it is not a reliable rule for identifying adverbs.

ABOVE-LEVEL STUDENTS After students have completed Part B, encourage them to write similar sentences of their own. Tell them to write each sentence twice, each time with the adverb in a different place. Call on volunteers to share and discuss the differences in the resulting sentences.

Unit 5
Grammar Review
CHAPTER 28

More About
Adjectives and
Adverbs
pages 336–345

Adjective or Adverb? pages 336–337

A. Write whether each underlined word is an adjective or an adverb. Then write the noun or verb it describes.

1. I went to the new museum <u>early</u>. adverb; went
2. The paintings were shown <u>beautifully</u>. adverb; were shown
3. I chose <u>some</u> gifts from the gift shop. adjective; gifts
4. The <u>old</u> museum was much smaller. adjective; museum
5. "Come back again," the tour guide said <u>cheerfully</u>. adverb; said

Adverb Placement in Sentences pages 338–339

B. Add the adverb in parentheses ( ) to each sentence. Try to put the adverb in a different place in each sentence. Possible responses are shown.

6. (regularly) Visitors come to our city. Visitors come regularly to our city
7. (especially) They like the new science museum. They especially like the new science museum.
8. (everywhere) There are interesting sites in our city. There are interesting sites everywhere in our city.
9. (now) The new museum is open. The new museum is now open.
10. (soon) More visitors will come. Soon more visitors will come.

Using *Good* and *Well, Bad* and *Badly* pages 340–341

C. Write *good, well, bad,* or *badly* to complete each sentence.

11. There is a _____ park near my home. good or bad
12. The park _____ needs cleaning. badly
13. I will do a _____ deed and help clean up the park. good
14. We _____ need other volunteers. badly
15. We will clean the park _____. well

HANDS ON Activity

PROP PRESENTATION Have students clarify and support the use of *good, well, bad,* and *badly* in oral sentences by using props like these:

What a good drawing that is! *(point to drawing)*

I did well on the spelling test. *(display an A+ paper)*

That messy window looks bad. *(point to window)*

I wrote my name badly. *(display sloppily written signature)*

Homophones *pages 346–347*

A. Complete each sentence with the correct word in parentheses ().

1. (write/right) Mom was _____ about the many kinds of stores in the mall. *right*
2. (to/too/two) I want _____ look in that hobby shop. *to*
3. (write/right) I like to _____ letters decorated with rubber stamps. *write*
4. (to/too/two) The hobby shop has _____ different rubber stamps for sale. *two*
5. (to/too/two) We plan to visit the pet store, _____. *too*

More Homophones *pages 348–349*

B. Complete each sentence with the correct word in parentheses ().

6. (Your/You're) _____ coming with us to the grocery. *You're*
7. (its/it's) I think _____ the store down on the corner. *it's*
8. (your/you're) Is this where _____ family shops? *your*
9. (its/it's) This store has _____ own fresh vegetable section. *its*
10. (their/there/they're) They have fresh fish _____. *there*

Homographs and Other Homophones *pages 350–351*

C. Complete each sentence with the correct word from the box.

see	know	trip (n.)	bow (n.)
sea	no	trip (v.)	bow (v.)

11. We traveled to a village on our _____. *trip (n.)*
12. I wanted to _____ all the fishing boats. *see*
13. I _____ a lot about fishing. *know*
14. I got to stand on the _____ of a fishing boat. *bow (n.)*
15. _____ two boats were alike. *No*

Unit 5
Grammar Review
CHAPTER 29

Easily Confused Words
pages 346–355

373

Unit 5
Grammar Review

CHAPTER 29

Easily Confused Words

OBJECTIVES
- To choose the correct homophone to complete a given sentence
- To choose the correct homograph to complete a given sentence

Unit Review
MODIFIED INSTRUCTION

BELOW-LEVEL STUDENTS Before students begin Part B, remind them that contractions always have apostrophes. Possessive nouns have apostrophes, but possessive pronouns do not. You may wish to point out that all the answer choices with apostrophes in Part B are contractions.

ABOVE-LEVEL STUDENTS Ask students to choose three homophone pairs from this page. Then challenge students to write three original sentences, using both homophones from a pair in the same sentence, as in this example:

I will <u>write</u> a thank-you note to my aunt <u>right</u> now.

TEST PREP

Activities and exercises to help students prepare for state and standardized assessments appear on our website.

Visit
The Learning Site!
www.harcourtschool.com

Assessment

SKILLS ASSESSMENT Use the **Language Skills and Writing Assessment** to assess the grammar and writing skills taught in this unit. Model papers are included.

PORTFOLIO ASSESSMENT
Schedule portfolio conferences with individual students while others are completing the Unit Review exercises. Have students complete the Self-Assessment Checklist on page R78 and place it in their Show Portfolios. Use the Student Record Form on page R77 to monitor student progress.

Oral History

OBJECTIVES

- To interview a neighbor to learn about changes and history of a neighborhood

- To write and publish a report based on the interview

INTRODUCE THE PROJECT

USE PRIOR KNOWLEDGE Read the introduction aloud to students. Ask volunteers to tell about some of the people who have lived in their neighborhoods for a long time. Ask them to consider what kinds of changes their neighborhoods may have undergone.

GENERATE QUESTIONS Prompt students to make a list of questions they want to know about their neighborhoods. Have them write their questions in their journals.

Writer's Journal

Find a Neighbor to Interview

Prompt students to tell a neighbor about the project. Suggest to students that they arrange the interview with the neighbor at least a week in advance. Tell them to write down the date, time, and place of the interview.

Ask Your Neighbor Questions About Your Neighborhood

Review the list of questions on page 374, and ask students to add other questions. Have students write the questions on notebook paper and leave plenty of space between the questions for taking notes. Also, remind students to use correct tense and subject-verb agreement when speaking with their neighbors.

Unit 5
Wrap-Up

Writing Across the Curriculum:
Social Studies

Oral History

What is your neighborhood like? What was it like many years ago? How has it changed? Find a neighbor who has lived in your neighborhood a very long time. With the permission of your parent or guardian, interview your neighbor. You could learn many things about your neighborhood's history. The steps below will help you.

Find a Neighbor to Interview

- Ask family members to help you decide on someone to interview.

- Arrange an interview with your neighbor. Set a date and time.

- Plan to take notes during the interview. Ask permission if you want to tape the interview.

Ask Your Neighbor Questions About Your Neighborhood

- What did our neighborhood look like when you first lived here?

- Who used to live in our neighborhood? What jobs did they have?

- What types of businesses and houses used to be here?

- What big changes have happened in our neighborhood?

- How has our neighborhood stayed the same?

374

Listening and Speaking

Have students work in pairs to practice their interviewing skills. Remind students to use appropriate rate and volume when asking and answering questions. While one student answers the questions, the other should try to write down the main points of the responses. If necessary, interviewers can ask speakers to slow down or repeat parts of their answers.

Make a Report About Your Neighborhood

- Use notes from your interview to write a report. Tell something about the neighbor you interviewed. Explain what he or she said.

- Publish your report in a class newsletter or on your class website. E-mail it to people from your neighborhood.

Books to Read

Back Home
by Gloria Jean Pinkney
HISTORICAL FICTION
Ernestine visits the country town where her mother grew up. Although everything seems different from the city she knows, Ernestine still hopes to become friends with her cousin Jack.
ALA Notable Book; Notable Social Studies Trade Book

The Hundred Penny Box
by Sharon Bell Mathis
REALISTIC FICTION
Michael's great-great-aunt Dew has one penny for every year of her life and a story for every penny.
Newbery Honor; ALA Notable Book; Notable Social Studies Trade Book

375

Make a Report About Your Neighborhood

Review what students have learned about writing a report based on research. Students may want to distribute their reports as neighborhood newsletters.

Make time in class for students to write thank-you letters to the people they interviewed. They may even wish to send the neighbors copies of their finished reports.

STUDENT SELF-ASSESSMENT

Have students evaluate their own research and raise new questions for further investigation.

 **Books to Read** Students who enjoyed this project might be interested in reading one or more of these books. Have them record reflections on the book or books in their journals. Then ask students to recommend to the class the book from this list that they enjoyed most.

School-Home Connection

Families can add to students' reports. Have students interview family members about their own history in the neighborhood. They might focus on why they moved to the neighborhood, why they stayed, or what important events have happened while they lived there. Students should summarize the interviews in brief essays and add them to the class collection.

CHALLENGE

REACHING ALL LEARNERS

PULLING IT ALL TOGETHER
Students can create an introduction for the neighborhood reports. Have them use library materials to research the history of their town, city, or community. They can include the date it was founded, the industries that helped build it, and the people who have run it. Also encourage them to include photographs and current facts and statistics about the area.

Assessment Strategies and Resources

FORMAL ASSESSMENT

If you want to know more about a student's mastery of the language and writing skills taught in Unit 5, **then** administer the first *Language Skills and Writing Assessment* for Unit 5. The test consists of two parts:

Language Skills: **articles, adjectives that compare, adverbs, more about adverbs and adjectives, easily confused words,** and **organizing information**

Writing Task: Write a **research report**. Scoring guidelines and model student papers are included.

INFORMAL ASSESSMENT TOOLS

Using Reading and Writing Assessment

If you want to know how well students integrate reading and writing skills, **then** look for opportunities to assess how they apply concepts gained from one area of concentration to the other.

After completing the Reading Like a Writer feature, discuss with students the connections between reading and writing and how they might apply what they learned. In a portfolio conference or other informal conversation, ask students to show you an example of how they may have applied a particular concept to their own writing.

Observe the types of self-selected reading a student is doing and whether the reading serves as a motivator for self-initiated writing. How does the student's writing reflect the kind of reading he or she is doing? Similarly, notice how students integrate their reading from the Books to Read section into Writing Across the Curriculum.

Informal Assessment Reminder

If you used the preinstruction writing prompt suggested in Teaching Grammar from Writing, **then** remember to compare the results with the writing done by students after the grammar and writing instruction.

Space Ride
by Tonya Jackson

The day of Rosa's first ride into space was foggy and cold. She was worried that the engines on the spaceship would

Unit 6

Grammar • Usage and Mechanics
Writing • Expressive Writing

Chapters	Grammar	Writing	Listening/ Speaking/Viewing
31 **Negatives** pp. 378–387	**Negatives with *No* and *Not* Other Negatives Usage and Mechanics: Avoiding Double Negatives** Extra Practice, Chapter Review, Daily Language Practice, Additional Practice: p. 474	**Writing Connections** Story Ideas Point of View Advertisement Science	**Activities** Challenge: Comic Strip Challenge: Create a Poster ESL: Make the Sign Building Oral Grammar Challenge: Compare Illustrations Summarize **Viewing:** Comparing Images
32 **Commas** pp. 388–397	**Commas More About Commas Usage and Mechanics: Combining Sentences with Commas** Extra Practice, Chapter Review, Daily Language Practice, Additional Practice: p. 475	**Writing Connections** Taking Notes Art Personal Voice Sentence Variety	**Activities** Challenge: Draw a Webpage ESL: Comma Placement Building Oral Grammar Summarize **Listening and Speaking:** Listening Outside the Classroom
33 **Writer's Craft: Elaboration** pp. 398–405	**Daily Language Practice Hands-on Activities**	**Character Study** Prewriting and Drafting Editing Sharing and Reflecting Self-Initiated Writing	**Activities** Analyze a Character Study Poetry Reading Nature Poster Role-Play Summarize **Viewing:** Looking at Fine Art
34 **Quotation Marks** pp. 406–415	**Direct Quotations More About Quotation Marks Usage and Mechanics: Punctuating Dialogue** Extra Practice, Chapter Review, Daily Language Practice, Additional Practice: p. 476	**Writing Connections** Comic Strip Recording Ideas Technology Time-Order Words	**Activities** Challenge: Clear Science ESL: Whispered Laughs Stellar Answers Challenge: Drama Quotes Building Oral Grammar Summarize
35 **Titles** pp. 416–425	**Underlining Titles Quotation Marks with Titles Usage and Mechanics: Capitalizing Words in Titles** Extra Practice, Chapter Review, Daily Language Practice, Additional Practice: p. 477	**Writing Connections** Science Story Titles Advertisement Choosing a Form	**Activities** Building Oral Grammar Challenge: Happy Art Summarize **Viewing:** Interpreting a Picture
36 **Writing Workshop: Story** pp. 426–439	**Unit 6 Grammar Review Daily Language Practice**	**Story** Prewriting Drafting Revising Proofreading Publishing Writer's Craft: Elaboration	**Activities** Reading Like a Writer Read and Respond to the Model Speaking with Feeling Summarize **Listening and Speaking:** Teamwork

Unit Wrap-Up Writing Across the Curriculum: Science, pp. 444–445

Vocabulary Power

Words of the Week: detect, discover, examine, **investigate**, research
ESL: Double Negatives

Vocabulary Power

Words of the Week: geode, lode, miner, **mineral**, mineralogist
Challenge: Draw a Webpage
Challenge: Give Directions

Vocabulary Power

Words of the Week: addition, description, **elaboration**, embellishment, expansion
ESL: Character Study Sentence Starters
ESL: Mix and Match

Vocabulary Power

Words of the Week: calorie, **energy**, zeal, fatigue, watt
ESL: Whispered Laughs
Writing Connection: Technology

Vocabulary Power

Words of the Week: impossible, **invisible**, irregular, possible, regular
ESL: Title Trade
Challenge: Card Catalog

Vocabulary Power

Words of the week: deputy, governor, ruler, vice president, **viceroy**
Handwriting

Language Minutes

- **Write** two sentences about your favorite TV show. Use **commas** to combine the sentences. WRITING

- **Tell** a friend about a character in your favorite story. Use exact words to **explain** why you like this character. **Answer** any questions that your friend may have. SPEAKING/LISTENING

- **Look** at a picture or painting in your science text book. **Write** sentences that describe what you see. Use figurative language. VIEWING/WRITING

- **Write** one sentence about each of the following: a favorite book, movie, song, and poem. Remember to use correct **capitalization** and **punctuation**, especially when writing the titles. WRITING

- **Ask** a friend to tell you an interesting fact about an animal. **Write** the friend's name and what he or she said in a complete sentence. Place **quotation marks** around your friend's exact words. SPEAKING/LISTENING/WRITING

Technology Resources

Grammar Jingles™ **CD**
Grammar Practice and Assessment **CD-ROM**
Writing Express **CD-ROM**
Media Literacy and Communication Skills **Package**
Visit *The Learning Site!*
   www.harcourtschool.com

Reaching All Learners

REACHING ALL LEARNERS

Intervention

CHARACTER INTERVIEWS When small groups of students read a book together and then role-play interviews with story characters, they are motivated to engage in reading, writing, speaking, and listening behaviors.

- Select a book on the appropriate reading level with well-developed characters.

- After reading the book, each student writes at least five questions that he or she would like to ask characters in the book. Writing these questions on colored paper strips often provides additional motivation for reluctant writers.

- The group then sorts the questions by character and eliminates duplicates. They may think of additional questions, as well.

- Students take turns interviewing and portraying characters of their choice. Provide simple props such as articles of clothing, eyeglass frames, and other items appropriate to characters in the story.

English as a Second Language

LANGUAGE EXPERIENCE As students develop oral language skills in English, use language experience strategies to help them develop reading and writing skills. Create reading materials for students by writing down their exact words as they describe a situation or experience. Have them use their dictated stories to frame and match words and to build sentences with word cards. Encourage them to share their stories with classmates in cooperative learning groups. Answering questions about their stories helps students expand oral language skills.

Challenge

CREATING WEB SITES Students can work in pairs or small groups to create a Web site that features student work for this unit. Depending on the technology available in your classroom and the level of students' expertise, they might develop the Web site on the computer or design "virtual" Web pages on separate sheets of drawing paper that can be displayed in the classroom. Encourage students to seek contributions to the Web site from classmates. They can update or add to the Web site throughout the course of the unit.

Multi-age Classrooms

COLLABORATIVE LEARNING Flexible grouping in the multi-age classroom creates numerous opportunities for collaborative learning. Consider how you might use the following possibilities to enrich your students' learning. All of these groups may include students on different grade levels, depending on their needs and interests.

- **Co-operative Task Groups** are created to allow students to collaborate in completing a task.

- **Reader Response Groups** are based on ability or interest. Their purpose is to examine concerns, situations, or questions, or to clarify and share information and viewpoints on various texts.

- **Instructional Groups** are needs or ability groups formed to teach, clarify, reinforce, or review lessons and minilessons.

- **Problem-Solving Groups** are informal ability or interest groups whose purpose is to seek solutions to a meaningful problem or issue.

Teaching Grammar from Writing

PRETEST

If you wish to use students' writing to diagnose their grammar instruction needs, use the following prompt.

WRITING PROMPT

Write a short story about a student your age who invents a wonderful new product and becomes famous. Your story can be realistic or fantastic, silly or serious.

EVALUATE AND PLAN

Analyze students' writing to determine how you can best meet their individual needs for instruction. Use the following chart to identify and remedy problems.

COMMON PROBLEMS	CHAPTERS TO USE
Using negatives incorrectly; using double negatives	Chapter 31: Negatives
Misplacing commas or failing to use them	Chapter 32: Commas
Punctuating or capitalizing direct quotations incorrectly	Chapter 34: Quotation Marks
Punctuating or capitalizing titles incorrectly (books, magazines, newspapers, stories, poems, articles, songs)	Chapter 35: Titles
Not able to elaborate on a topic	Chapter 33: Writer's Craft: Elaboration
Difficulty writing a story	Chapter 36: Writing a Story

Classroom Management

DURING...	SOME STUDENTS CAN...
Grammar Reteaching	Locate and begin reading the books in the Books to Read section of the Writing Across the Curriculum project.
Independent Practice	Practice keyboarding and editing skills on the classroom computer or in the computer lab. Work on *Vocabulary Power* pages.
Portfolio Conferences	Complete Student Self-Assessment forms. (See pages R86–R88 in this *Teacher's Edition*.)

Across the Curriculum

LANGUAGE ARTS IN THE CLASSROOM

Writing, of course, should not be restricted to a language arts "block." Students need to become proficient writers in every subject area. Writing in science, social studies, and other content areas helps students learn not only the content but also important research and organizational skills.

REFERENCE CORNER Provide a bookcase that contains reference books such as an encyclopedia, an atlas, and an almanac. Include works on specific cross-curricular topics featured in the units. For example, for Unit 1 include books on Native American and Mexican decorative arts; a children's biography of Mozart; and books about music, musicians, and musical instruments. Provide similar material for other topics such as nutrition, the solar system, weather, ecosystems, communities, and government. Also include children's magazines devoted to these or related topics. Plan a reading area nearby where students can consult references and take notes.

PICTURE BOX Pictures cut from magazines, newspapers, and brochures can be organized in folders by specific cross-curricular topics and subtopics. Students can use the pictures to generate writing ideas or to illustrate their writing. Add to the box regularly.

"TO DO" LIST Encourage students working in groups to keep an up-to-date list of things to do to complete their projects. Provide a model of a "To Do" list with names, tasks, and dates when tasks should be completed.

CLASSROOM MUSEUM Have students create an exhibit about a relevant cross-curricular topic. For social studies, for example, they can make an exhibit of their community in the past or in the future, and for science, they can exhibit rocks, minerals, or seashells. Create a committee of tour guides and have them collaborate to compose a recorded tour of the museum. Provide earphones for student visitors to listen to the recorded tour.

Hands-on Activities

Combinations

MATERIALS: sentence strips with compound sentences, blank sentence strips, pencils or markers

DIRECTIONS:

1. Give pairs of students a set of sentence strips with compound sentences and a set of blank strips.

2. One partner reads aloud one of the sentences, while the other copies it on a blank sentence strip. Students then compare it to the original sentence. Have them correct any errors.

3. Partners alternate reading and writing until they have used all of the sentence strips.

Who Is It?

DIRECTIONS:

1. Prepare a list of characters from stories that students have read.

2. Whisper the name of one of the characters to a volunteer who then gives an oral description of the character.

3. The other students must guess the name of the character from the description.

4. Continue asking for volunteers until all of the characters have been described. You may want to choose the same character for different students to describe and then point out that there is more than one way to give a good description of the same person.

Commas, Commas, Commas

MATERIALS: a set of cards with directions on them for writing sentences and other items with commas

DIRECTIONS:

1. Mix up the cards and place them face down in a pile.

2. Students take turns picking the top card, reading the directions aloud, and following them on the chalkboard. The other students check to see whether the student has written the item correctly.

3. Discard each card after it is used. Continue until no cards remain.

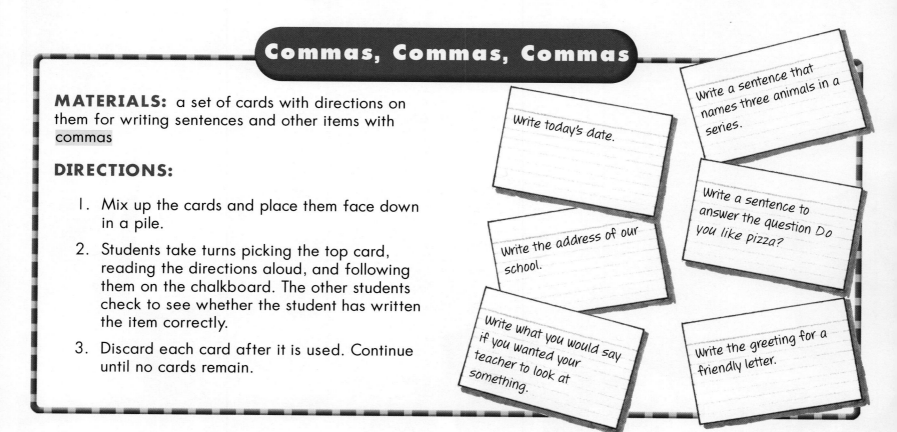

Write a sentence that names three animals in a series.

Write today's date.

Write a sentence to answer the question Do you like pizza?

Write the address of our school.

Write what you would say if you wanted your teacher to look at something.

Write the greeting for a friendly letter.

Figuratively Speaking

MATERIALS: drawing paper, markers

DIRECTIONS:

1. Tell students that they are going to make drawings and then write captions that use figurative language to describe the picture or something in the picture.

2. Provide an area where students can display their drawings.

Her kite is a red bird in the sky.

Story Relay

MATERIALS: rulers

DIRECTIONS:

1. Have groups of six to eight students sit in storytelling circles.

2. Give one student in each group a ruler. Tell groups that the person holding the ruler is the first storyteller for the group. Explain that each storyteller will speak briefly and then pass the ruler along to another person in the group, who picks up the story where the previous storyteller left off. The story continues from person to person, with each storyteller adding a little bit to it, until someone comes up with a good ending.

3. You may want to start the story and give help as needed through the storytelling process.

Turtle Titles

MATERIALS: chart paper; markers; eight slips of paper with the words (1) **book**, (2) **magazine**, (3) **newspaper**, (4) **story**, (5) **song**, (6) **article**, (7) **poem**, and (8) **your choice**; bag or box

DIRECTIONS:

1. Place the eight slips of paper in a bag or box. Have a student draw one of the slips and read it aloud.

2. Students think of a title for a work of that type about turtles. The student who drew the slip must write the title on the board.

3. The other students decide whether or not the title is written correctly.

4. Continue until students have written at least one title of each type on the board.

The Turtle Times

"Turtles on the Move"

Listening to Literature

Read aloud to students.

In the Children's Garden

BY CAROLE LEXA SCHAEFER

ON AN OPEN LOT between Old City Park
and Maestro [mīs′trō] Finelli's Music School,
there's a garden patch grown by children
who live in the neighborhood.

A sign on the garden's gate says
        Children's Garden
            WELCOME!
That means: Come in, please. Listen, see, smell, touch—
even taste.

In the Children's Garden, deep, dark dirt,
rich with rotted grass, apple peels, and onionskins,
is tunneled through by worms
who wriggle it loose, and give it air—
ah-h-h.

In the Children's Garden, well-worn tools,
rows of spades, rakes, and hoes
are used—*sca-ritch, sca-rutch*—
to turn, to pile, to dig the dirt,
making mounds and holes.

In the Children's Garden, all sorts of seeds—
round brown, plump white, flat black—
are scattered, or dropped one by one,
then covered with dirt by hands that
pat, pat, pat.

In the Children's Garden, boxes, pots, and plots
full of dirt and seeds get soaked by showers
from clouds or hoses, buckets or cans,
so everything stays drip-drop damp—
even under the sizzling sun.

In the Children's Garden, tender sprouts
pop out of soft dirt beds,
slim-stemmed with leaves in twos
—all small—
yet strong enough to stretch their green tops up,
and reach their root toes down.

In the Children's Garden, corn rows, strawberry clumps,
pumpkin tangles, lettuce groups, tomato clusters,
sunflower stands, zucchini tumbles, and green bean tents

Building Background

Have students discuss community gardens. Ask a volunteer
to explain how an area of land is divided and what type
of crop or flower may grow well there. Then introduce the
concept that this community garden is just for children.

Determine a Purpose for Listening

Tell students that this selection describes a fruit and vegetable garden planted by children. Ask students to determine whether their purpose for listening is

• to solve problems.

• to be persuaded to do something.

• to enjoy and appreciate. (to enjoy and appreciate)

grow, forming patterns that fill the spaces
with leaves and flowers, vegetables and fruit.

In the Children's Garden, children call:
"Listen to those crows caw and cackle."
"Well, talk back. Tell them to stay out
of our corn."

"Look at the shape of this funny tomato."
"Ha! It's a clown's head with a big red nose."
"Smell the spearmint I grew. Rub it with
your fingers."
"Mmm, I like to chew it."

"Whew, pulling weeds is hot, hard work!"
"It's cool in the bean tent. Let's take a rest."

In the Children's Garden, near the gate,
dust-brown children carrying
brimful baskets home
stop a moment to watch
while a sunflower does an evening dance,

nodding its shaggy head,
and rustling its leafy dress.

On the gate, the sign still says
        Children's Garden
            WELCOME!

That means: Come back to visit anytime,
with one friend or ten. And, if you like,
in your own dirt spot—a yard, a lot,
or even a giant-size flowerpot—
plant another children's garden.

Listening Comprehension

LISTEN FOR EXACT WORDS AND FIGURATIVE LANGUAGE Have students listen for exact words and figurative language that help describe the children's garden as you read the story to them. When you've finished the story, ask students to list as many examples of exact words and figurative language as they can, for example, *zucchini tumbles*. Have them share their ideas with a neighbor, and encourage them to add new information to their lists. Then ask them to return to the story to check the answers they have given.

PERSONAL RESPONSE *What would you plant in your garden if you had one?* (Possible responses: The garden would be full of corn and tomato plants because those are my favorite vegetables; I would fill my garden with colorful flowers and dig a pond in the center.) *How would you organize a community garden?* (Possible response: I may ask family members to help and inform my neighbors. I may talk to community leaders.) INFERENTIAL: SPECULATE

Unit 6

| Grammar | Usage and Mechanics |
| Writing | Expressive Writing |

Introducing the Unit

ORAL LANGUAGE/VIEWING

DISCUSS THE IMAGES Have students look closely at the photograph. Ask volunteers to describe the sights and sounds a person might experience while traveling in space. Explain that expressive details such as these help make stories interesting and fun to read. Point out that stories may be written, spoken, or presented visually, as on television or in films. Ask questions such as these:

1. **How can a film reveal a character's personality?** (Possible response: A film shows a character's words and actions.)

2. **How can a written story tell about a setting?** (Possible response: A written story tells the setting through description.)

3. **Would you rather listen to an audiotape of a story or read the story? Why?** (Responses may vary.)

Writer's Journal

ENCOURAGE STUDENTS' QUESTIONS Have students reflect on things that make a story fun to read. Encourage students to develop questions for discussion. Have them write their questions and selected responses in their journals.

Unit 6

| Grammar | Usage and Mechanics |
| Writing | Expressive Writing |

376

Viewing and Representing

COMPARE/CONTRAST PRINT AND VISUAL MEDIA Have students read a story and then view a videotape of the same story. Ask them to write a paragraph telling how their mental images of the story's characters and setting differed from or were similar to the characters and setting in the videotape.

For evaluation criteria for viewing, see the Viewing Checklist, page R88.

MEDIA LITERACY AND COMMUNICATION SKILLS PACKAGE
Use the video to extend students' oral and visual literacy. See *Teacher's Guide* pages 6–7.

Space Ride

by Tonya Jackson

The day of Rosa's first ride into space was foggy and cold. She was worried that the engines on the space...

377

Have students look over the list of unit contents. Tell them that the unit focuses on punctuation and the use of negatives. Have volunteers give examples of correct comma use, and discuss with the class what they would like to learn about punctuation. Point out to students that the unit's writing chapters focus on a character study and a story. Discuss with them the importance of character development in a story. Have volunteers give examples of strong, well-developed story characters from familiar stories, and talk about what makes these figures memorable.

SCIENCE CONNECTION Students will explore a variety of science topics in this unit:

- Scientists and Inventions
- Earth's Land
- Heat and Light
- Forces and Motion

School-Home Connection

You may want to use School-Home Connection 6, page R97.

LESSON ORGANIZER	DAY **1**	DAY **2**
DAILY LANGUAGE PRACTICE TRANSPARENCIES 71, 72	1. I'm reddy to write about my idea for a new Invention. (ready; invention.) 2. I have a well idea, to. (good; too.) **Bridge to Writing** Let's talk about our <u>(adjective)</u> ideas.	1. Your going to be surprised when I tell you about my invention (You're; invention.) 2. its a talking refrigerator for you and I. (It's; me.) **Bridge to Writing** It can tell <u>(object pronoun)</u> what we need to do!
ORAL WARM-UP **Listening/Speaking**	Discuss Change in Meaning 378	Revise a Sentence with Negatives 380 *Grammar Jingles™* CD Track 21
TEACH/MODEL **GRAMMAR** **KEY** ✔ = tested skill	✔ **NEGATIVES WITH *NO* AND *NOT*** 378–379 • To identify and use negatives • To create a web and write a description using negatives	✔ **OTHER NEGATIVES** 380–381 • To identify and use negatives • To write a descriptive paragraph by using negatives
Reaching All Learners	**Modified Instruction** Below-Level: Look for Negatives Above-Level: Revise Sentences **Reteach:** *Reteach Activities Copying Masters* pp. 61 and R58 **Challenge:** Activity Card 21, R72 *ESL Manual* pp. 148, 149 *Practice Book* p. 101	**Modified Instruction** Below-Level: Refer to Chart Above-Level: Write Sentences **ESL:** Using Negatives 380 *ESL Manual* pp. 148, 150 **Reteach:** *Reteach Activities Copying Masters* pp. 62 and R58 **Challenge:** Write a Riddle 381 *Practice Book* p. 102
WRITING	Writing Connection 379 Writer's Journal: Story Ideas	Writing Connection 381 Writer's Craft: Point of View
CROSS-CURRICULAR/ ENRICHMENT	*Vocabulary Power* Explore Word Meaning 378 detect, discover, examine, **investigate**, research *See Vocabulary Power book.*	*Vocabulary Power* Prefixes 378 *Vocabulary Power* p. 91 **Vocabulary activity**

DAY 3

1. You think of new Ideas more quicklier than I do. (ideas more quickly)
2. Come set by I so we can plan together. (sit; me)

Bridge to Writing Our friends (future-tense verb) when they hear the idea!

Revise a Sentence 382
Grammar Jingles™ CD Track 21

✔ **AVOIDING DOUBLE NEGATIVES** 382–383
- To recognize and correct double negatives
- To write an advertisement, correcting double negatives

Modified Instruction
Below-Level: Use a Chart
Above-Level: Correct Sentences
ESL: Double Negatives 382
ESL Manual pp. 148, 151
Reteach: *Reteach Activities Copying Masters* pp. 63 and R58
Challenge: Create a Poster 383
Practice Book p. 103

Writing Connection 383
Real-Life Writing: Advertisement

Vocabulary Power
Words in Context 378
Vocabulary Power p. 92
🖥 **Vocabulary activity**

DAY 4

1. Their are many ways two plan an invention. (There; to)
2. Sean will help James and I. (me.)

Bridge to Writing Maybe we will be a (adjective) team.

Identify and Express Negatives 384

EXTRA PRACTICE 384–385
- To identify and use negative words correctly
- To write a descriptive paragraph, using negative words
🖥 **Practice and assessment**

Building Oral Grammar
Correct the Double Negative 385
Challenge: Warning Label 385
ESL: Make the Sign 384
ESL Manual pp. 148, 152
Practice Book p. 104

Writing Connection 385
Science

Vocabulary Power
Classify/Categorize 378
Vocabulary Power p. 93
🖥 **Vocabulary activity**

DAY 5

1. Them could become famous (They; famous.)
2. I dont know any famous peeple! (don't; people.)

Bridge to Writing (Compound subject) will become part of history.

TEST PREP **CHAPTER REVIEW** 386
- To review negatives
- To understand and practice strategies for comparing images
🖥 **Test preparation**

Challenge: Compare Illustrations 387
Practice Book p. 105
ESL Manual pp. 148, 153

Writing Application 387
Compare and Contrast

Viewing: Comparing Images 387

Vocabulary Power
Word Endings 378

Negatives with *No* and *Not*

OBJECTIVES
- To identify and use negatives
- To create a web and write a description by using negatives

DAILY LANGUAGE PRACTICE

TRANSPARENCY 71

1 I'm reddy to write about my idea for a new Invention. (ready; invention.)

2 I have a well idea, to. (good; too.)

BRIDGE TO WRITING Let's talk about our ___(adjective)___ ideas.

ORAL WARM-UP

USE PRIOR KNOWLEDGE Write on the board: *Science is _____ difficult. I have _____ homework today.* Read aloud the sentences, and then reread them inserting *not* and *no*, respectively. Discuss how the meaning changes when *not* and *no* are used.

TEACH/MODEL

Read aloud the explanation and examples on page 378. Hold up an empty hand and ask: **Do I have pencils in my hand?** Ask students to answer in complete sentences. Elicit responses such as *You do not have pencils in your hand. You don't have pencils in your hand. You have no pencils in your hand.*

Point out that some negatives are contractions that join a verb and the word *not*. Explain that the apostrophe in contractions like *don't* replaces the letter *o* in the word *not*.

Work through the Guided Practice orally with students.

Some Negative Contractions	
do not	don't
can not	can't
will not	won't
have not	haven't
was not	wasn't
is not	isn't

Vocabulary Power

in•ves•ti•gate [in•ves′tə•gāt′] *v.* To study thoroughly in order to learn facts or details.

378

Negatives with *No* and *Not*

The words *no* and *not* are negative words.

Negative words such as *no* and *not* change the meaning of a sentence. *No* is often used as an adjective.

Example:
I think **no** subject is more important than science.

Not is an adverb. It makes the meaning of a verb negative.

Example:
We would **not** have electricity without science.

Remember that a contraction can sometimes be formed by joining a verb and the word *not*. A verb becomes a negative word when it is made into a contraction with *not*.

Example:
Scientific facts **aren't** opinions.

Guided Practice

A. Tell the negative word in each sentence.

Example: Some people do not know what science involves.
not

1. Science is <u>not</u> about just one thing.
2. <u>No</u> book could tell everything about science.
3. Science gives us answers we <u>didn't</u> have before.
4. Science <u>hasn't</u> explained everything.
5. Some things are <u>not</u> easy to understand.

Vocabulary Power

DAY 1 EXPLORE WORD MEANING Introduce and define *investigate*. **How would you investigate a problem or a question?**

DAY 2 PREFIXES **What prefix could you add to *investigate* to make it mean "investigate again"?** (See also *Vocabulary Power*, page 91.)

DAY 3 WORDS IN CONTEXT **What kind of story might include words like *investigate* and *detect*?** (See also *Vocabulary Power*, page 92.)

DAY 4 CLASSIFY AND CATEGORIZE **What are some books you could use if you wanted to investigate a topic?** (See also *Vocabulary Power*, page 93.)

DAY 5 WORD ENDINGS Write on the board: *investigate, investigated*. **What do you notice about the endings of each word? What other endings can you add to *investigate*?**

Independent Practice

B. Write the negative word in each sentence.

Example: Wasn't Thomas Edison a great inventor?
Wasn't

6. Thomas Edison did <u>not</u> do well in school.
7. His mother <u>wasn't</u> concerned, and she taught him everything she knew.
8. As a child, Edison <u>couldn't</u> stop reading science books.
9. Experimenting did <u>not</u> frighten him.
10. Even hearing problems <u>didn't</u> discourage young Edison.
11. One of his first inventions was <u>not</u> used.
12. However, Edison <u>didn't</u> give up.
13. Most homes had <u>no</u> electricity when Edison first invented the electric light.
14. I <u>can't</u> imagine life without electric power!
15. Edison's favorite invention was the phonograph, <u>not</u> the electric light.

Remember
that negative words such as *no* and *not* change the meaning of a sentence. A verb becomes a negative word when it is made into a contraction with *not*.

Writing Connection

Writer's Journal: Story Ideas Think of a character for a story about a scientist. Write the name of your character in the center of a web. Then think of six sentences that describe the character, using negatives such as "She does not make wild guesses." Write these sentences on branches of the web. Use the ideas on your web to write a description of your character. Include at least three contractions made from a verb and the word *not* in your description.

Independent Practice

Have students complete the Independent Practice, or modify it using these suggestions:

MODIFIED INSTRUCTION

BELOW-LEVEL STUDENTS *Write no, not,* and *n't* on the board. Tell students to look for one of these to find the negative word in each sentence.

ABOVE-LEVEL STUDENTS Have students rewrite the sentences to make them positive statements.

Writing Connection

Writer's Journal: Story Ideas Have students work in small groups to discuss different types of scientists, such as doctors, chemists, and paleontologists. Students should write a list of qualities that make a scientist successful, such as curiosity and an interest in reading. Prompt students to use these lists as they create their webs.

WRAP-UP/ASSESS

SUMMARIZE Ask students to revise this sentence, making it negative: *The students read about science.*

RETEACH

INTERVENTION Lessons in **visual, auditory,** and **kinesthetic** modalities: p. R58 and *Reteach Activities Copying Masters,* p. 61.

PRACTICE page 101

Name _____

Negatives

A. Write the negative word in each sentence.

1. Sylvia hadn't any ice cubes in her drink. — hadn't
2. She isn't able to see them. — isn't
3. They didn't leave the glass. — didn't
4. They just weren't solid anymore. — weren't
5. We don't call water *ice* except when it is solid. — don't

B. Write each sentence. Underline the negative word in each sentence.

6. Sylvia didn't have any ice cubes in the freezer.
   Sylvia didn't have any ice cubes in the freezer.

7. There was no ice in the ice maker.
   There was no ice in the ice maker.

8. Sylvia wasn't in a hurry to go out to play.
   Sylvia wasn't in a hurry to go out to play.

9. It wouldn't take long to make some more ice.
   It wouldn't take long to make some more ice.

10. Soon the trays were full, not of water, but of ice.
    Soon the trays were full, not of water, but of ice.

TRY THIS! Write a few sentences about some of the things you cannot do at home without electricity.

Practice • Negatives   Unit 6 • Chapter 31   101

CHALLENGE

COMIC STRIP Have students use **Challenge Activity Card 21** (page R72) to create a comic strip about a character who gets a new attitude.

Challenge Activity Card 21

Comic Strip

Work with a partner to create a comic strip about a character who is negative about everything and everyone. As the ending to your comic strip, show an event that makes the character positive.

• Think of some negative things this character might say.
• Imagine a surprising event that will give the character a better attitude.
• Draw your comic strip and display it in your classroom.

Negatives

Read this paragraph. Circle each negative word.

Boris looked all over for his science book, but he couldn't find it. Still, Boris wasn't discouraged. He was sure the book was not lost. No book matters more to me than that science book," he said. "I can't stop looking until I find it."

Negatives

Think about the things in your classroom.

With a partner, take turns saying sentences about things in your classroom. Listen carefully to each sentence your partner says. Then repeat the sentence but change its meaning. Add a negative word—*no* or *not*—to the sentence.

Negatives

With a partner, think of two opposite sentences. The sentences should be just alike—except one should include a negative word. Here are some example sentences:

| I am angry. | The book is in my desk. |
| I am not angry. | The book is not in my desk. |

With your partner, act out your two sentences for the group. See if group members can guess your two sentences.

Reteach Activities • Negatives   Unit 6 • Chapter 31 61

Other Negatives

OBJECTIVES
• To identify and use negatives
• To write a descriptive paragraph by using negatives

DAILY LANGUAGE PRACTICE

TRANSPARENCY 71

1 Your going to be surprised when I tell you about my invention (You're; invention.)

2 its a talking refrigerator for you and I. (It's; me.)

BRIDGE TO WRITING It can tell (object pronoun) what we need to do!

ORAL WARM-UP

USE PRIOR KNOWLEDGE Read aloud this sentence: *Everyone is curious about the new space hotels.* Ask students to revise the sentence by using negatives to give it the opposite meaning.

Grammar Jingles™ **CD, Intermediate** Use Track 21 for review and reinforcement of negatives.

TEACH/MODEL

Work through the explanation and examples on page 380. Write on the board: *no one, nobody, nothing, none, nowhere, never,* and *hardly*. Ask a volunteer to circle *no* each time it appears in these words. Have another volunteer draw a box around the words *never* and *hardly*. Explain that most negative words contain the letters *no*, but the word *never* is an exception. It is an adverb that tells *when*.

Complete the Guided Practice items orally with students, or have students work in small groups to complete the items.

Other Negatives

No one, nobody, nothing, none, nowhere, never, **and** *hardly* **are also negative words.**

Like *no* and *not*, each of these negative words changes the meaning of a sentence. Notice how the meaning of the sentence below changes when a negative word is used instead of a positive word.

Example:
(positive) We **always** do experiments.
(negative) We **never** do experiments.

Here are more negative and positive word pairs.

Negative Words	Positive Words
no one	everyone, someone
nothing	everything, something
none	one, all, some
hardly	almost

Guided Practice

A. Tell the negative word or words in each sentence.

Example: Before the Wright brothers, nobody could travel by plane.   *nobody*

1. Nothing could stop the inventors from their dream of learning how to fly.
2. Orville and Wilbur Wright never grew tired of experimenting.
3. At first, nobody paid much attention to their work.
4. No one believed that a machine could fly.
5. Never before in history had anyone been able to fly in a machine.

380

Vocabulary Power page 91

Name _____

PREFIXES

Prefixes are added to the beginning of words. They change the meaning of the words. Here are some prefixes and their meanings.

re- again	over- too much	un- not

A. Read each word and the directions. Then choose the correct prefix and add it to the word. Write the new word. The first one is done for you.

Word	Directions	New Word
1. happy	Change to mean "not happy."	unhappy
2. investigate	Change to mean "to investigate again."	reinvestigate
3. researched	Change to mean "not researched."	unresearched
4. examine	Change to mean "to examine again."	reexamine
5. build	Change to mean "to build again."	rebuild
6. flow	Change to mean "to flow too much"	overflow
7. detected	Change to mean "not detected."	undetected
8. discover	Change to mean "to discover again."	rediscover

B. Use one of the new words in a sentence.

_____

_____

Vocabulary Power   Unit 6 • Chapter 31 91

ESL

REACHING ALL LEARNERS

USING NEGATIVES Write the following words on cards: *not, no one, nobody, nowhere,* and *never*. Then write these sentences on the board:

_____ wants to miss recess!

We have _____ to go this afternoon.

I have _____ played that game.

Distribute the cards to students. Have them work together to complete the sentences with the words on their cards.

Independent Practice

B. Make each sentence a true statement by replacing the underlined positive word with a negative word. Write the new sentence.

Accept reasonable responses.

Example: <u>Always</u> work alone in the science lab.
Never work alone in the science lab.

6. Wait if <u>someone</u> can help you.
7. Sometimes, you need <u>something</u> but your eyes to study science.
8. You <u>always</u> know what you will find to study.
9. <u>Many</u> tools are needed to observe a plant.
10. You may notice something <u>everyone</u> else has observed.
11. <u>Always</u> pass up a chance to investigate nature.
12. <u>Somebody</u> has to tell you that science is fun.
13. You can use a book on experiments if <u>everyone</u> can help you.
14. You can <u>always</u> tell what interesting science facts you will find in a science book.
15. <u>Something</u> is more fun than learning.

Remember
that *no one*, *nobody*, *nothing*, *none*, *nowhere*, *never*, and *hardly* are negative words. These words change the meaning of a sentence.

Writing Connection

Writer's Craft: Point of View Choose an object to observe as a scientist might. Describe it using the following sentence starters:

Everybody would say this object is _____.
Nobody would say this object is _____.
This object is always _____.
This object is never _____.

Then write a descriptive paragraph about the object.

381

Independent Practice

Have students complete the Independent Practice, or modify it using these suggestions:

MODIFIED INSTRUCTION

BELOW-LEVEL STUDENTS Have students refer to the chart on page 380 to find the corresponding negative word for each positive word in Part B.

ABOVE-LEVEL STUDENTS After students complete Part B, have them write three statements about science, using negative words from the chart on page 380.

Writing Connection

Writer's Craft: Point of View Before students begin to write, have them look around the room and brainstorm a list of adjectives to describe items they see. Remind them that they can use the adjectives to complete negative as well as positive sentences.

WRAP-UP/ASSESS

SUMMARIZE Write on the board: *She always discovers dinosaur bones on her trips.* Invite volunteers to write at least two sentences that make this statement negative.

REACHING ALL LEARNERS

RETEACH

INTERVENTION Lessons in **visual, auditory,** and **kinesthetic** modalities: p. R58 and *Reteach Activities Copying Masters,* p. 62.

REACHING ALL LEARNERS

PRACTICE page 102

Name _____

Other Negatives

A. Circle the correct word in parentheses ( ) to complete each sentence.

1. Skip likes (no one, **nothing**) better than science experiments.
2. I have (nobody, **never**) met a student as interested in science as Skip.
3. In fact, I think there may be (**no one**, nothing) like Skip.
4. (**None**, Nothing) of the students in his class are as interested as he is.
5. He studies his facts like (**no one**, nowhere) else.

B. Write each sentence. Use a word from the box to fill the blank.

| no one | nobody | nowhere | never |

6. Often Skip is _____ to be found.
   Often Skip is nowhere to be found.
7. _____ knows where he is.
   Nobody (or no one) knows where he is.
8. However, _____ worries.
   However, no one (or nobody) worries.
9. We know he is curled up with a science book he has _____ read before. We know he is curled up with a science book he has never read before.

TRY THIS! Write some sentences about the world around you. What are some things that you see regularly? What are some things that you have never seen?

102 Unit 6 • Chapter 31   Practice • Negatives

REACHING ALL LEARNERS

CHALLENGE

WRITE A RIDDLE Have students work in pairs to write riddles about common objects. Have them use the following format:

It is _____.
It has _____.
It isn't _____.
It doesn't _____.

After students write their riddles, they can read them to other students and have them guess the answers.

More Negatives

Read each sentence. Circle each negative word.

(None) of these planes can fly.
I'm afraid (no one) can get them into the air.
My plane has (never) been off the ground.
This little plane is going (nowhere).
I guess (nobody) can make them fly.

Visual

More Negatives

With the other members of your group, take turns saying sentences about things you like to do. Use a positive word from the box.

| someone | somebody | something | no one | nobody | nothing |

Listen to each sentence the other group members say. Take turns repeating the sentences, using a negative word instead of the positive word.

Auditory

More Negatives

With the other members of your group, make six word cards. Write one of these negative words on each card.

| no one | nobody | nothing | none | nowhere | never |

Turn the cards face down and mix them up. Take turns picking a card. Say a sentence using the word on your card. Then return the card to the pile.

Kinesthetic

Teacher: Cut apart the activities and distribute to students based on the modalities that are their strengths.
[Visual] You may want to write the activity sentences on the board.
[Auditory] Have students work in groups of three or four.
[Kinesthetic] You may want to have students at least one of the sentences they say.

62 Unit 6 • Chapter 31   Reteach Activities • More Negatives

Avoiding Double Negatives

OBJECTIVES
- To recognize and correct double negatives
- To write an advertisement, correcting double negatives

DAILY LANGUAGE PRACTICE

TRANSPARENCY 71

1 You think of new Ideas more quick-lier than I do. (ideas more quickly)

2 Come set by I so we can plan together. (sit; me)

BRIDGE TO WRITING Our friends ___(future-tense verb)___ when they hear the idea!

ORAL WARM-UP

USE PRIOR KNOWLEDGE Write on the board: *We tried to do it.* Ask students to revise the sentence to make it negative.

***Grammar Jingles*™ CD, Intermediate** Use Track 21 for review and reinforcement of negatives.

TEACH/MODEL

Read aloud the instructions and examples on page 382. Tell students that they may refer to the chart on page 380 to help them replace a negative word with the correct positive word.

Write on the board: *We do not have no science kits.* Model the thinking.

MODEL In this sentence, there are two negative words, *not* and *no*. I know I should have only one negative word, so I could delete the words *do not* or replace *no* with *any*. The correct versions of the sentence are *We have no science kits* and *We do not have any science kits.*

Complete the Guided Practice items orally with students.

382

Avoiding Double Negatives

When you use two negative words in one sentence, you are using a double negative.

Never use double negatives. They make the meaning of a sentence positive instead of negative and confuse readers. To correct a sentence with a double negative, delete one negative word or change one of the negative words to a positive word.

Examples:

Incorrect: I have <u>not</u> <u>never</u> studied chemistry.

Correct: I have <u>never</u> studied chemistry.

Correct: I have <u>not</u> <u>ever</u> studied chemistry.

Guided Practice

A. The sentences below are incorrect because they have double negatives. Name the double negative in each sentence.

Example: We had not never learned about George Washington Carver. *not never*

1. There was <u>hardly no</u> reason to believe Carver would become a famous scientist.
2. He <u>didn't</u> have <u>no</u> easy childhood.
3. There was <u>not nothing</u> he could do except investigate plants and animals.
4. He <u>didn't</u> have <u>no one</u> to help him study.
5. He <u>hardly never</u> had any free time to go to school.

Vocabulary Power page 92

Name _____

WORDS IN CONTEXT

▶ Detective Sharpnose is about to write a mystery novel about his first case. Help him fill in his notes about the case. Responses will vary. Accept reasonable responses.
1. Today I'm going to begin to **investigate** a case about _____
2. Before I started, I decided to do some **research** about _____
3. The **research** really helped! I found out _____
4. When I got to the scene, I began to **examine** _____
5. I was excited to **discover** _____ This discovery would help me solve the case!
6. Then I thought I could **detect** a _____ coming from the _____
7. I finally solved the case when _____

▶ Now write a title for Detective Sharpnose's story.
_____

92 Unit 6 • Chapter 31   Vocabulary Power

ESL

DOUBLE NEGATIVES Many English language learners have difficulty avoiding double negatives because they are used in many languages. Encourage students to compare the English usage of negatives with that of their first language. Provide additional support by working through the Independent Practice items with students.

Independent Practice

B. Each sentence has a double negative. Rewrite each sentence to correct the double negative.

Accept reasonable responses.

Example: Hardly no colleges would admit Carver.
Almost no colleges would admit Carver.

6. Carver didn't never give up.
7. He wouldn't let nothing keep him from earning his science degree in 1896.
8. He couldn't never have become a famous inventor without studying hard in school.
9. Carver knew farmers wouldn't grow nothing because of poor soil.
10. Carver found there wasn't nothing better than peanuts and sweet potatoes for Alabama's soil.
11. Farmers didn't know nothing about these.
12. George Washington Carver wasn't never afraid to work hard to help people.
13. Because of him, Southern farmers wouldn't never grow only cotton in their fields.
14. George couldn't never stop there.
15. If it wasn't never for Carver, it would be much harder to be a farmer.

Remember
that you should never use two negative words in one sentence.

383

Writing Connection

Real Life Writing: Advertisement Write an advertisement for a product that a scientist might find useful. Include three incorrect sentences that include double negatives. Then trade papers with a partner and correct the double negatives in each other's advertisements. Read your corrected advertisement to your class.

Independent Practice

Have students complete the Independent Practice, or modify it using these suggestions:

MODIFIED INSTRUCTION

BELOW-LEVEL STUDENTS For help in revising the sentences, have students refer to the chart on page 380.

ABOVE-LEVEL STUDENTS For three sentences in Part B, have students correct the sentence in two ways: first by eliminating one of the negative words and then by substituting a positive word.

Writing Connection

Real-Life Writing: Advertisement Allow students to review science books, encyclopedias, or the Internet to take simple notes on information about different science-related objects. Remind students to purposefully include double negatives in the first draft of their advertisement for their partner to correct.

WRAP-UP/ASSESS

SUMMARIZE Ask students to explain how to identify and correct a double negative.

RETEACH

INTERVENTION Lessons in **visual, auditory,** and **kinesthetic** modalities: p. R58 and *Reteach Activities Copying Masters,* p. 63.

PRACTICE page 103

Name _____

Avoiding Double Negatives

A. Some of the sentences below are incorrect because they have double negatives. Tell whether each sentence is correct or incorrect.

1. Mother didn't have no tea made. — incorrect
2. She said, "Why don't I make some mint tea?" — correct
3. It wasn't no trouble. — incorrect
4. It wouldn't take long for water to boil. — correct
5. Nobody stayed in the kitchen to watch the pot. — correct

B. Each sentence has a double negative. Write each sentence to correct the double negative.

6. Nobody didn't see the steam rising from the kettle.
   Nobody saw the steam rising from the kettle.

7. There wasn't nobody in the kitchen.
   There was nobody in the kitchen. *or* There wasn't anybody in the kitchen.

8. Soon there wasn't no water left in the kettle.
   Soon there was no water left in the kettle. *or* Soon there wasn't any water left in the kettle.

9. We knew water isn't never just gone.
   We knew water is never just gone. *or* We knew water isn't ever just gone.

TRY THIS! Write a few sentences about what you would like to study if you were a scientist. Exchange papers with a partner. Proofread each other's sentences. Check for double negatives.

Practice • Negatives   Unit 6 • Chapter 31   103

CHALLENGE

CREATE A POSTER Have students cut out or draw pictures of scientists at work. Have each student glue his or her picture to a large sheet of paper. Tell students to write three *Do statements* and three *Don't statements* to go with each picture. Example:

Do
Scientists do use lab equipment carefully.

Don't
Scientists don't use lab equipment carelessly.

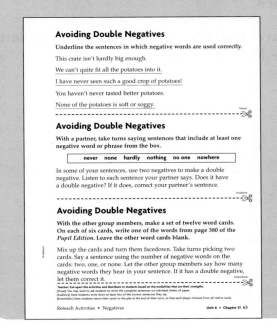

Avoiding Double Negatives

Underline the sentences in which negative words are used correctly.

This crate isn't hardly big enough.

We can't quite fit all the potatoes into it.

I have never seen such a good crop of potatoes!

You haven't never tasted better potatoes.

None of the potatoes is soft or soggy.

Avoiding Double Negatives

With a partner, take turns saying sentences that include at least one negative word or phrase from the box.

| never | none | hardly | nothing | no one | nowhere |

In some of your sentences, use two negatives to make a double negative. Listen to each sentence your partner says. Does it have a double negative? If it does, correct your partner's sentence.

Avoiding Double Negatives

With the other group members, make a set of twelve word cards. On each of six cards, write one of the words from page 380 of the *Pupil Edition.* Leave the other word cards blank.

Mix up the cards and turn them facedown. Take turns picking two cards. Say a sentence using the number of negative words on the cards: two, one, or none. Let the other group members say how many negative words they hear in your sentence. If it has a double negative, let them correct it.

Reteach Activities • Negatives   Unit 6 • Chapter 31   63

Extra Practice

OBJECTIVES

- To identify and use negative words correctly
- To write a descriptive paragraph, using negative words

DAILY LANGUAGE PRACTICE

TRANSPARENCY 72

1 Their are many ways two plan an invention. (There; to)

2 Sean will help James and I. (me)

BRIDGE TO WRITING Maybe we will be a ___(adjective)___ team.

ORAL WARM-UP

USE PRIOR KNOWLEDGE Write this sentence on the board: *He hasn't ever had experience with inventors.* Ask students to identify the negative word in the sentence. Then ask students to express the same idea in a different way.

TEACH/MODEL

Use the Remember box to review negative words. Model the thinking for the example in Part A:

MODEL I don't see words like *no* or *never* in this sentence, but I do see the word *Don't*. I know that the *n't* in *don't* stands for *not*. *Don't* is the negative word in the sentence.

Have students work in pairs to complete the Extra Practice items.

Remember

that negative words change the meaning of a sentence. *No, not, no one, nobody, nothing, none, nowhere, never,* and *hardly* are all negative words. A verb becomes a negative word when it is made into a contraction with *not.*

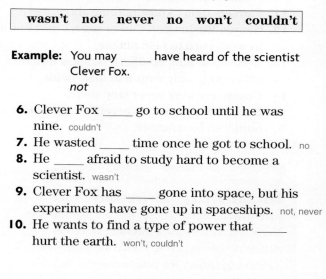

For more activities with negatives, visit *The Learning Site:* www.harcourtschool.com

384

Extra Practice

A. Write the negative word or words in each sentence. *pages 378–381*

Example: Don't you know about the scientist Eloy Rodriguez?   *Don't*

1. Eloy Rodriguez <u>wasn't</u> from a rich family.
2. <u>Nothing</u> could stop him from becoming a scientist.
3. He <u>never</u> stopped studying hard.
4. He learned from his family that medicines <u>aren't</u> the only things that cure people.
5. Dr. Rodriguez knows that plants called chiles can help people who are <u>not</u> well.

B. Write the negative word from the box that best completes each sentence. *pages 378–381*

wasn't   not   never   no   won't   couldn't

Example: You may _____ have heard of the scientist Clever Fox.
not

6. Clever Fox _____ go to school until he was nine. couldn't
7. He wasted _____ time once he got to school. no
8. He _____ afraid to study hard to become a scientist. wasn't
9. Clever Fox has _____ gone into space, but his experiments have gone up in spaceships. not, never
10. He wants to find a type of power that _____ hurt the earth. won't, couldn't

---

Vocabulary Power   page 93

Name _____

CLASSIFY/CATEGORIZE

A. Write each word from the Word Box under the correct category. Then add your own word to each category. Additional words may vary. Accept reasonable responses.

| atlas | fairy tale | comic book |
| encyclopedia | dictionary | mystery story |

Books You Use for Research	Books You Read for Fun
encyclopedia	mystery story
dictionary	comic book
atlas	fairy tale

B. Now try these.

| mixer | microscope | fork |
| binoculars | spoon | magnifying glass |

Tools You Use to Investigate	Tools You Use in Cooking
microscope	fork
magnifying glass	spoon
binoculars	mixer

Vocabulary Power   Unit 6 • Chapter 31   93

ESL

MAKE THE SIGN Look up the sign for *not* in an American Sign Language dictionary, and teach it to students. Have students say sentences using contractions with *not*. To reinforce the meaning of these contractions, have students make the sign for *not* as they say the contraction in the sentence.

C. Rewrite each sentence to correct the double negative. *pages 382–383*

Example: Robert Jones couldn't not stop asking questions when he was a boy.
Robert Jones couldn't stop asking questions when he was a boy.

Accept reasonable responses.

11. He didn't hardly mind making his own science experiments.
12. However, he invented things that no one else had never imagined.
13. He didn't never quit in college.
14. Jones never doubted that he would not become a scientist.
15. Nothing has never interested Jones as much as investigating better ways to grow crops.
16. Inventors aren't hardly very different from scientists.
17. Many inventions couldn't hardly have been made without scientific thinking.
18. Inventors can't never forget about science facts.
19. They can't not settle for the way things are.
20. They don't never quit looking for new ideas.

Remember never to use a double negative in a sentence. To correct a double negative, drop one negative or replace one with a positive word.

Writing Connection

Science Imagine that you are a scientist and you've just invented a new kind of shoe that helps people go places faster. Describe what worked and didn't work as you did your experiments. Use several negative words in your description. When you proofread, make sure there are no double negatives to confuse your readers.

385

Building Oral Grammar

Tell students that it is helpful to be able to tell whether a sentence that uses negative words sounds correct.

Select from pages 382, 383, and 385 sentences that have double negatives. Read them aloud, correcting some sentences but keeping the double negatives in others. Tell students that when they hear a double negative, they are to hold up their hands. Then ask volunteers to revise the sentence to correct the double negative.

Writing Connection

Science Before they write, have students work in small groups to brainstorm some ways they might test an idea for a new type of shoe. Prompt them to discuss some methods that might not be very effective. Then have them write to refine their ideas.

WRAP-UP/ASSESS

SUMMARIZE Have students write in their journals, to reflect on what they have learned about negatives. Ask them to comment on how using negatives correctly makes their writing more effective.
REFLECTION

ADDITIONAL PRACTICE An additional page of Extra Practice is provided on page 474 of the *Pupil Edition*.

CHALLENGE

REACHING ALL LEARNERS

WARNING LABEL Tell students to think of a tool that is used in cooking, building, science, or some other field. Have students create a "warning label" that tells people how to use the item safely. The label should have at least three sentences and include negative statements such as these: *Never leave a hammer where a small child can reach it. Don't use a hammer without wearing safety goggles. Don't use a hammer unless an adult is helping.*

TECHNOLOGY *Grammar Practice and Assessment* CD-ROM; *Writing Express* CD-ROM

INTERNET Visit *The Learning Site:*
www.harcourtschool.com

Chapter Review

OBJECTIVES

- To review negatives
- To understand and practice strategies for comparing images

DAILY LANGUAGE PRACTICE

TRANSPARENCY 72

1 Them could become famous (They; famous.)

2 I dont know any famous peeple! (don't; people.)

BRIDGE TO WRITING (Compound subject) will become part of history.

STANDARDIZED TEST PREP

MODEL TEST-TAKING STRATEGIES Have students read the directions on page 386 silently. Remind them to eliminate choices that include double negatives. Model the thinking. Write this example on the board:

(1) Didn't you never think about a new invention?

    1 **A** Did you not never
          B Didn't you ever
          C Did you never not
          D No mistake

MODEL The underlined word group uses two negatives, *didn't* and *never*. This means that D is not the correct choice. Answers A and C also contain double negatives. Answer B does not contain a double negative, and the sentence *Didn't you ever think about a new invention?* sounds correct.

Have students complete the Chapter Review independently.

Chapter Review

Read the paragraph. Choose the best way to rewrite each underlined section, and mark the letter for your answer. If the underlined section needs no change, mark the choice *No mistake*.

> (1) Haven't you never thought about all the inventions around you? An invention starts with an idea, but it (2) doesn't never end there. Lots of hard work goes into inventing new things. (3) Not all inventors work in fancy labs. Some work on kitchen tables or in their basements. A few inventions make lots of money right away. Others (4) do not.
>
> There have been some inventions, like cars, that (5) aren't hardly popular right away. Later, people accept the idea. There are other inventions that (6) no one never wants. One example is glasses for chickens, invented in 1903.

TIP Read the directions carefully. Be sure you know exactly what you are supposed to do.

For additional test preparations, visit *The Learning Site:* www.harcourtschool.com

386

1 **A** Have you not never
    B Haven't you ever B
    C Have you never not
    D No mistake

2 **F** doesn't never ever
    G doesn't G
    H doesn't not
    J No mistake

3 **A** Not no
    B Hardly no
    C Not hardly no
    D No mistake D

4 **F** hardly never
    G don't never
    H never don't
    J No mistake J

5 **A** are not hardly
    B are hardly not
    C aren't C
    D No mistake

6 **F** no one ever F
    G not nobody
    H no one don't
    J No mistake

Assessment

PORTFOLIO ASSESSMENT Have students select their best work from the Writing Connections on pages 381, 383, and 385.

ONGOING ASSESSMENT Evaluate the performance of 4–6 students using appropriate checklists and record forms from pages R74–R77.

INTERNET Activities and exercises to help students prepare for state and standardized assessments appear on *The Learning Site:*
www.harcourtschool.com

Comparing Images

Sometimes artists draw pictures to help show what a writer's words mean. When choosing pictures for a story, it's important to select ones that best fit the story or the characters.

Imagine that a writer has created a funny story about a scientist. The scientist loves his work, but he is always making mistakes. The reason he makes mistakes is that he does everything backward.

If you were the writer, you might want to compare the pictures below and then decide which one fits your story best. Follow these three steps to compare the drawings:

1. List what is the same about the drawings.
2. List what is different about each drawing.
3. Look at the completed lists. Decide which picture best fits the way the character is described in the story.

TIP
Remember that readers need to know how the characters act and feel, not just how they look. Be sure to look for these things when you read and when you compare drawings of characters.

YOUR TURN

Write a short paragraph about a scientist. Create three quick drawings of the person you have imagined. Then exchange with a partner your pictures and the paragraphs you wrote. Use the steps above to compare the pictures your partner has drawn. Then choose the picture that best fits your partner's paragraph. Tell your partner why you made this choice.

387

PRACTICE page 105

Name _____

Chapter Review

Choose the correct way to write each underlined section in the paragraph below. Fill in the oval next to your choice. If the underlined section needs no change, choose *No mistake*.

(1) Don't you never think about what science has made possible? Without science, we **(2)** wouldn't have no CD-ROMs at school. **(3)** You couldn't call nobody on the telephone. The school bus **(4)** wouldn't bring no students to school. There **(5)** isn't hardly anything we do that doesn't use scientific knowledge. **(6)** No one ever guessed how many uses we would find for computers. Scientists **(7)** don't always know how people will use scientific discoveries. I **(8)** wouldn't never try to guess all the uses computers will have in the future. The list would be too long!

1. ⬭ Do you not never
   ⬭ Don't you ever
   ⬭ Do you never not
   ⬭ No mistake

2. ⬭ wouldn't have none
   ⬭ would have no
   ⬭ would not have no
   ⬭ No mistake

3. ⬭ could not call nobody
   ⬭ couldn't call anybody
   ⬭ couldn't hardly call anybody
   ⬭ No mistake

4. ⬭ would not bring no
   ⬭ wouldn't bring none
   ⬭ wouldn't bring any
   ⬭ No mistake

5. ⬭ is not hardly
   ⬭ is hardly not
   ⬭ is hardly
   ⬭ No mistake

6. ⬭ No one never
   ⬭ No one not ever
   ⬭ Nobody never
   ⬭ No mistake

7. ⬭ do not hardly
   ⬭ don't never
   ⬭ hardly never
   ⬭ No mistake

8. ⬭ would not never
   ⬭ wouldn't ever
   ⬭ won't never
   ⬭ No mistake

Practice • Negatives   Unit 6 • Chapter 31   105

CHALLENGE

COMPARE ILLUSTRATIONS

Have students work in groups to compare illustrations. Students should select a well-known fable or fairy tale and look for versions with illustrations by different artists. Have students write paragraphs that compare the different versions. Suggest that students consider the use of color and the details included in the drawings and how well they match the story.

VIEWING

Comparing Images

TEACH/MODEL

Read the explanation and strategies aloud. Explain that the illustrations in a book or story can add to the writer's words by helping readers better understand the story's events, the characters' feelings, and the consequences of the characters' actions.

Point out that often the person who illustrates a story is not the writer. The artist must think about the writer's words and create illustrations that show how he or she pictures the story. Sometimes the same story is illustrated in different ways by different artists.

Have students work in pairs to complete the Your Turn activity. As they analyze their partner's illustrations, have students look for the way the character expresses different feelings through body language as well as facial expressions.

Ask students to share the illustrations they chose and to explain how they decided what each character is feeling. Guide students in observing differences among the ways emotions are depicted.

WRITING APPLICATION Have students write paragraphs comparing and contrasting two images of similar emotions or situations.

WRAP-UP/ASSESS

Writer's Journal

SUMMARIZE Have students write in their journals to explain why understanding how to compare images is useful to them as readers and as illustrators of their own writings.

TECHNOLOGY Additional writing activities are provided on the *Writing Express* CD-ROM

CHAPTER 32

Commas
pages 388–397

LESSON ORGANIZER	DAY 1	DAY 2
DAILY LANGUAGE PRACTICE TRANSPARENCIES 73, 74	**1.** i didnt see any gemstones at the muse-um (I; didn't; museum.) **2.** Its the most beautifulest ruby of all! (It's; most beautiful) **Bridge to Writing** I will ___(negative)___ want to leave this museum.	**1.** are all gems minerals (Are; minerals?) **2.** Yes minerals comes in many colors and shapes. (Yes,; come) **Bridge to Writing** I ___(adverb)___ picked up the gemstone.
ORAL WARM-UP **Listening/Speaking**	Listen for Pauses 388	Explain Differences in Letters 390 *Grammar Jingles*™ CD Track 22
TEACH/MODEL **GRAMMAR** **KEY** ✔ = tested skill	✔ **COMMAS** 388–389 • To use commas correctly in sentences • To take notes and to write sentences, using commas correctly	✔ **MORE ABOUT COMMAS** 390–391 • To use commas correctly in letters, dates, and addresses • To draw a map and to write a paragraph, using commas correctly
Reaching All Learners	**Modified Instruction** Below-Level: Listen for Pauses Above-Level: Explain Comma Placement **Reteach:** *Reteach Activities Copying Masters* pp. 64 and R59 **Challenge:** Activity Card 22, R72 *ESL Manual* pp. 154, 155 *Practice Book* p. 106	**Modified Instruction** Below-Level: Model the Thinking Above-Level: Write a Reply **ESL:** Working with Peers 390 *ESL Manual* pp. 154, 156 **Reteach:** *Reteach Activities Copying Masters* pp. 65 and R59 **Challenge:** Write a Letter 391 *Practice Book* p. 107
WRITING	Writing Connection 389 Writer's Journal: Taking Notes	Writing Connection 391 Art
CROSS-CURRICULAR/ ENRICHMENT	*Vocabulary Power* Explore Word Meaning 388 geode, lode, miner, **mineral**, mineralogist See *Vocabulary Power* book.	*Vocabulary Power* Related Words 388 *Vocabulary Power* p. 94 **Vocabulary activity**

DAY 3

1. An topaz is blu or gold. (A; blue)

2. the diamond had been cut, polished and displayed. (The; polished,)

Bridge to Writing Will your class (action verb) a report on the gem exhibit?

Combine Sentences 392

Grammar Jingles™ CD Track 22

✔ **COMBINING SENTENCES WITH COMMAS** 392–393
- To use commas correctly in compound sentences
- To write a narrative paragraph, using commas to combine sentences

---

Modified Instruction
Below-Level: Insert Words
Above-Level: Add New Sentences
Reteach: *Reteach Activities Copying Masters* pp. 66 and R59
Challenge: Sentence Stems 393
ESL Manual pp. 154, 157
Practice Book p. 108

Writing Connection 393
  Writer's Craft: Personal Voice

Vocabulary Power
Word Families 388
Vocabulary Power p. 95
🖥 **Vocabulary activity**

DAY 4

1. Therese and me found fossils in ours yard (I; our yard.)

2. Yesterday we will show them to Thomas Patrick and Sheila. (we showed; Thomas, Patrick,)

Bridge to Writing The museum guide (linking verb) well-informed about minerals.

Place Commas in Sentences 394

EXTRA PRACTICE 394–395
- To use commas in sentences and letters
- To write an informative paragraph, using commas correctly

🖥 **Practice and assessment**

Building Oral Grammar
Listen for Pauses 395
ESL: Comma Placement 394
ESL Manual pp. 154, 158
Challenge: Cave Painting 395
Practice Book p. 109

Writing Connection 395
  Writer's Craft: Sentence Variety

Vocabulary Power
Homophones 388
Vocabulary Power p. 96
🖥 **Vocabulary activity**

DAY 5

1. my grandfather workked in a coal Mine. (My; worked; mine.)

2. He went deep underground and he dug up coal. (underground,)

Bridge to Writing There are (adjective) coal mines in West Virginia. Coal is (adverb) used for fuel.

TEST PREP **CHAPTER REVIEW** 396–397
- To review comma usage in sentences and parts of letters
- To practice giving and following directions

🖥 **Test preparation**

Challenge: Give Directions 397
Practice Book p. 110
ESL Manual pp. 154, 159

Writing Application 397
  Reflect on Directions

Listening and Speaking:
  Listening Outside the Classroom 397

Vocabulary Power
Research 388

Commas

OBJECTIVES
- To use commas correctly in sentences
- To take notes and to write sentences, using commas correctly

SPIRAL REVIEW

DAILY LANGUAGE PRACTICE

TRANSPARENCY 73

1. i didnt see any gemstones at the museum (I didn't; museum.)

2. Its the most beautifulest ruby of all! (It's; most beautiful)

BRIDGE TO WRITING I will ___(negative)___ want to leave this museum.

ORAL WARM-UP

USE PRIOR KNOWLEDGE Read aloud a short passage from a trade book, exaggerating the pauses indicated by commas. Ask: **In writing, how do you show the reader where to pause?**

TEACH/MODEL

Read aloud the instructions and examples on page 388. Remind students that other kinds of punctuation, such as end marks, make writers' meanings clear to readers.

Model the thinking for the Guided Practice example:

MODEL For items in a series, I need to have a comma after each item except the last one. In the example sentence, I know that I need to place a comma after *Sue* and after *Paul*.

Work through the Guided Practice with students, or have them complete the items in small groups.

Commas

A **comma** (,) separates parts of a sentence and helps make the meaning clear.

Three or more similar words listed together are called a **series**. In a series of three or more similar words, put a comma after each item except the last one. The last comma should be before *and* or *or*.

> **Example:**
> **Mountains, valleys, and islands** are three natural landforms on Earth's surface.

When a sentence is addressed to someone directly, put a comma after the person's name. Also use commas after the words *yes*, *no*, and *well* at the beginning of a sentence.

> **Examples:**
> Lilly, will you pack my lunch for the hike?
> Yes, a diamond is a mineral.

Guided Practice

A. Tell where commas are needed in each sentence. Be ready to explain why.

> **Example:** I am meeting Sue Paul and Emily.
> *I am meeting Sue, Paul, and Emily.*

1. Yes I have been to the museum before.
   Yes, I have been to the museum before.
2. The museum has information about plants animals and Earth.
   The museum has information about plants, animals, and Earth.
3. Rickie let's make sure we take notes.
   Rickie, let's make sure we take notes.
4. Well we should see the movie about minerals.
   Well, we should see the movie about minerals.
5. It will show uses for minerals like diamonds quartz and iron.
   It will show uses for minerals like diamonds, quartz, and iron.

Vocabulary Power

min•er•al
[min′ər •əl] *n.* A natural material that does not come from a plant or an animal.

388

Vocabulary Power

DAY 1 EXPLORE WORD MEANING Introduce and define *mineral*. **What types of minerals might be included in a mineral or rock collection?**

DAY 2 RELATED WORDS Write on the board: *mineral, rocks, grass, gemstone*. **Three of these words are related to each other by meaning. Which one is not related to the others?** (See also *Vocabulary Power*, page 94.)

DAY 3 WORD FAMILIES ***Mine*** and ***mineral*** are in the same word family. What other words might be in this family?** (See also *Vocabulary Power*, page 95.)

DAY 4 HOMOPHONES **Homophones sound the same but have different spellings and meanings. What is a homophone for *miner*?** (See also *Vocabulary Power*, page 96.)

DAY 5 RESEARCH **Different parts of the country have different minerals. With a partner, find out what kinds of minerals can be found in our state and list them on a sheet of paper.**

Independent Practice

B. Write the sentence. Add a comma or commas where they are needed.

> **Example:** I rowed toward the island with Dad Mr. Omerjee and Elena.
> *I rowed toward the island with Dad, Mr. Omerjee, and Elena.*

6. We sang whistled and hummed as we rowed.
   sang, whistled, and hummed
7. Yes the sandy island seemed far away. Yes, the
8. Dad how is the sand formed? Dad, how
9. It is made of minerals and rocks that are sharp round and very small. sharp, round, and very small.
10. Well we passed a beach with lots of sand. Well, we
11. Mr. Omerjee how did the sand get there? Mr. Omerjee, how
12. Wind sun and rain can change rocks into sand. Wind, sun, and rain
13. We could see sand wood and shells on the shore. sand, wood, and shells
14. Dad I think the sand will feel hot on my toes. Dad, I
15. Sand can be found on the shores of islands rivers lakes and oceans. islands, rivers, lakes, and oceans.

Remember
to use commas with a series of three or more similar words. Also, use a comma after the name of a person being spoken to in a sentence and after the words *yes, no,* and *well* at the beginning of a sentence.

389

Writing Connection

Writer's Journal: Taking Notes Talk with a classmate about the kinds of rocks you have seen in your neighborhood. Then make a list of these different rocks. Choose two rocks on your list, and write a sentence about each one. In your sentences, use exact words to give three details about each rock's look and feel. Make sure to use commas correctly.

Independent Practice

Have students complete the Independent Practice, or modify it using these suggestions:

MODIFIED INSTRUCTION

BELOW-LEVEL STUDENTS Before students complete each item, have them read each sentence aloud, listening for places where they must pause to understand the sentence.

ABOVE-LEVEL STUDENTS Have students tell how they know where to place the commas in each sentence.

Writing Connection

Writer's Journal: Taking Notes Have students participate in a class discussion about where rocks are found and how they are used. For example, many people use rocks as decorations in yards and gardens. Students should take simple notes from various references to identify different kinds of rocks.

WRAP-UP/ASSESS

SUMMARIZE Ask students to tell where commas are used in sentences.

RETEACH

INTERVENTION Lessons in **visual, auditory,** and **kinesthetic** modalities: p. R59 and *Reteach Activities Copying Masters,* p. 64.

Commas

Add commas where they belong in each sentence.

Will: Jill, what do you think of this rock?

Jill: Well, it's smooth and shiny. It has pink, black, and gray spots.

Will: Yes, but do you like it?

Jill: Oh, I think it's beautiful!

Will: I think Les, Maya, and Tam will like it, too.

- ✂

Commas

With a partner, take turns asking and answering questions. When it's your turn to answer, begin your sentence with your partner's name or with one of these words—*Yes, No,* or *Well.*

When your partner answers a question, listen carefully. Tell where a comma belongs in your partner's sentence.

- ✂

Commas

With a partner, write a skit about a favorite place.

In your skit, talk to each other in complete sentences. Begin some of your sentences with your partner's name or with the word *Yes, No,* or *Well.* Also use a series of words in at least one sentence. Practice your skit. Then act it out for the rest of your group.

Watch and listen while other group members perform their skits. Raise your hand each time you hear a word that should be followed by a comma.

Teacher: Cut apart the activities and distribute to students based on the modalities that are their strengths.
[Visual] You may want to write the activity sentences on the board.
[Auditory] Have students in each pair discuss how they know where a comma is needed.
[Kinesthetic] Have students form groups of six or more for this activity.

64 Unit 6 • Chapter 32   Reteach Activities • Commas

PRACTICE page 106

Name _____

Commas

A. Read each sentence. Add commas where they are needed.

1. Ms. Nims's class hiked through mountains, valleys, and fields.
2. They were looking for samples of rocks, minerals, and fossils.
3. Ms. Madison, Mr. White, and Ms. Short came along to help.
4. Students carried their samples in bags, boxes, and backpacks.
5. Joan, Hakeem, and Joe found the most rocks.

B. Write each sentence, adding commas where they are needed.

6. The rocks were white gray and brown.
   The rocks were white, gray, and brown.
7. They stopped rested and ate beside the stream.
   They stopped, rested, and ate beside the stream.
8. Did anyone find the hammer shovel and bucket?
   Did anyone find the hammer, shovel, and bucket?
9. Ms. Nims is this a fossil in my rock?
   Ms. Nims, is this a fossil in my rock?
10. Phil I think that might be a fossil.
    Phil, I think that might be a fossil.

TRY THIS! Write a few sentences about fossils. Where might you find them? What kind of fossils would you like to find? Use commas correctly.

106 Unit 6 • Chapter 32   Practice • Commas

CHALLENGE

DRAW A WEBPAGE Have students use **Challenge Activity Card 22** (page R72) to sketch a web page about a mineral discovery.

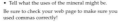

Challenge Activity Card 22

Draw a Web Page

Imagine that you are a scientist and that you have just discovered a new type of mineral. It's very valuable, and you've decided that a web page would be the best way to share your discovery. Make a sketch of your web page.

- Draw a picture of your mineral. Show the color, shape, and size.
- Write a description of the mineral. Tell where and how you found it.
- Tell what the uses of the mineral might be.

Be sure to check your web page to make sure you used commas correctly!

More About Commas

OBJECTIVES
- To use commas correctly in letters, dates, and addresses
- To draw a map and to write a paragraph, using commas correctly

DAILY LANGUAGE PRACTICE

TRANSPARENCY 73

1. are all gems minerals (Are; minerals?)
2. Yes minerals comes in many colors and shapes. (Yes,; come)

BRIDGE TO WRITING I __(adverb)__ picked up the gemstone.

ORAL WARM-UP

USE PRIOR KNOWLEDGE Ask students to explain some differences between sending a letter by mail or sending an e-mail message.

Grammar Jingles™ **CD, Intermediate** Use Track 22 for review and reinforcement of commas.

TEACH/MODEL

Guide students through the instructions and examples on page 390. Point out that placing commas correctly in addresses and dates helps avoid confusion. Write the following letter parts on the board without commas:

2324 Geswein Blvd.

Austin TX 78722

May 26 2001

Dear Clara

Ask students to tell where to place commas in the letter parts.

Then complete the Guided Practice items orally with students, or have students complete the items with partners.

More About Commas

Commas are used in letters, dates, and addresses.

Commas follow both the greeting and the closing of a letter. Use a comma after greetings such as *Dear Grandmother* in a letter and after the closing words such as *Thank you*, *Love*, and *Good-bye*.

Examples:

Greeting

> *Dear Grandmother,*
> *I had a wonderful vacation.*
> *Love,*
> *Sean*

Closing

A comma belongs between the name of the city and the state. A comma is also placed between the day and the year.

Examples:
Heading in a Letter

> 27 North 4th Street
> Olean, New York 14760
> June 16, 2000

Guided Practice

A. Tell where a comma is needed in each sentence or letter part.

Example: Sincerely Mom   *Sincerely, Mom*

1. Your friend Ahmad   Your friend, Ahmad
2. My baby brother was born on March 24 1999.   My baby brother was born on March 24, 1999.
3. Many cars are made in Detroit Michigan.   Many cars are made in Detroit, Michigan.
4. Dear Aunt Rita   Dear Aunt Rita,
5. Love Mama and Dad   Love, Mama and Dad

390

> Dear Rom
> I'm having fun panning for gold with Aunt Kim.
> Love,
> Alice

> Rom Chen
> 3 Harbor Dr.
> San Diego, CA
> 92015

Vocabulary Power   page 94

Name _____

RELATED WORDS

The words in the Word Box are related by meaning. Use the Word Box to help you complete the word web about minerals. Fill in the remaining lines with your own words or phrases.

mines	lodes	geodes	mineralogist	coins

People Who Work with Minerals
mineralogists

Places Where Minerals Can Be Found
mines

Mineral

Things a Miner Hopes to Find
geodes
lodes

Uses for Minerals
coins

94   Unit 6 • Chapter 32   Vocabulary Power

ESL

REACHING ALL LEARNERS

WORKING WITH PEERS Have each student work with an English-fluent partner to complete the Independent Practice items.

Independent Practice

B. Write the letter in the box. Add commas where they are needed.

Example:

> 28 Rockford Street
> Los Angeles, California 91107
> August 9, 2001
>
> Dear Grandpa,
>
>   I miss you and wish you were here in Los Angeles, California. You could see my great fossil collection. I will show it to you when you visit.
>
>   Love,
>   Susan

6. 253 Lee Street
   Alexandria Virginia 22206 *Alexandria, Virginia 22206*
7. December 25 2001 *December 25, 2001*
8. Dear Aunt Annie *Dear Aunt Annie,*
9. Thank you very much for the great book on rocks. My science class took a field trip to Charlottesville Virginia. I hope you are having a happy winter! I'll see you on January 1 2001!
   Charlottesville, Virginia; January 1, 2001
10. Miss you *Miss you,*
    Leah *Leah*

> *Remember*
> that commas are used in letters, dates, and addresses.

Writing Connection

Art Pretend that you know where a hidden mine can be found. Draw a map to show the mine's location. Then write a paragraph that tells how to find the mine and what is in it. Remember to use commas in the paragraph as you mention locations and dates.

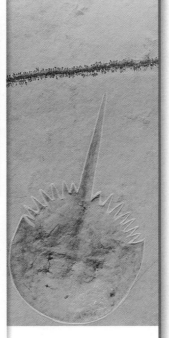

391

Independent Practice

Have students complete the Independent Practice, or modify it using these suggestions:

MODIFIED INSTRUCTION

BELOW-LEVEL STUDENTS Work through the Independent Practice with students, modeling the thinking.

ABOVE-LEVEL STUDENTS Have students write a reply to the letter in Part B, using commas correctly.

Writing Connection

Art As an alternative, students may choose to write letters to go with the map. Their letters should tell what the mine contains and give directions to the mine. Their letters should also include commas as needed in the address, greeting, and closing.

WRAP-UP/ASSESS

SUMMARIZE Ask students to explain why it is important to use correct punctuation when addressing letters.

RETEACH

INTERVENTION Lessons in **visual**, **auditory**, and **kinesthetic** modalities: p. R59 and *Reteach Activities Copying Masters*, p. 65.

PRACTICE page 107

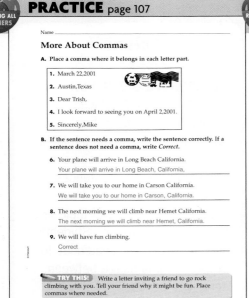

More About Commas

A. Place a comma where it belongs in each letter part.

1. March 22, 2001
2. Austin, Texas
3. Dear Trish,
4. I look forward to seeing you on April 2, 2001.
5. Sincerely, Mike

B. If the sentence needs a comma, write the sentence correctly. If a sentence does not need a comma, write *Correct*.

6. Your plane will arrive in Long Beach California.
   Your plane will arrive in Long Beach, California.
7. We will take you to our home in Carson California.
   We will take you to our home in Carson, California.
8. The next morning we will climb near Hemet California.
   The next morning we will climb near Hemet, California.
9. We will have fun climbing.
   Correct

TRY THIS! Write a letter inviting a friend to go rock climbing with you. Tell your friend why it might be fun. Place commas where needed.

Practice • Commas   Unit 6 • Chapter 32   107

CHALLENGE

WRITE A LETTER Have students write letters to a national park requesting information about the park. Tell students to choose a park that is famous for its natural rock formations, such as Yosemite National Park or the Grand Canyon. Remind students to punctuate their letters correctly.

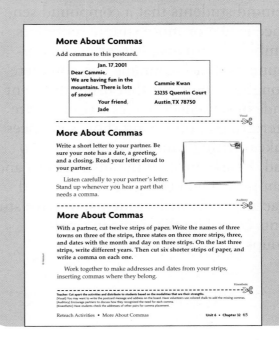

More About Commas

Add commas to this postcard.

> Jan. 17, 2001
> Dear Cammie,
> We are having fun in the mountains. There is lots of snow!
>
> Your friend,
> Jade
>
> Cammie Kwan
> 23235 Quentin Court
> Austin, TX 78750

More About Commas

Write a short letter to your partner. Be sure your note has a date, a greeting, and a closing. Read your letter aloud to your partner.

Listen carefully to your partner's letter. Stand up whenever you hear a part that needs a comma.

More About Commas

With a partner, cut twelve strips of paper. Write the names of three towns on three of the strips, three states on three more strips, three dates with the month and day on three strips. On the last three strips, write different years. Then cut six shorter strips of paper, and write a comma on each one.

Work together to make addresses and dates from your strips, inserting commas where they belong.

Reteach Activities • More About Commas   Unit 6 • Chapter 32   65

Combining Sentences with Commas

OBJECTIVES
- To use commas correctly in compound sentences
- To write a narrative paragraph, using commas to combine sentences

DAILY LANGUAGE PRACTICE

TRANSPARENCY 73

1. An topaz is blu or gold. (A; blue)

2. the diamond had been cut, polished and displayed. (The; polished,)

BRIDGE TO WRITING Will your class ___(action verb)___ a report on the gem exhibit?

ORAL WARM-UP

USE PRIOR KNOWLEDGE Ask students to combine the following sentences: *We found pretty rocks in the creek bed. They were smooth and shiny.*

Grammar Jingles™ **CD, Intermediate** Use Track 22 for review and reinforcement of commas.

TEACH/MODEL

Remind students that a compound sentence is two or more simple sentences combined with *and*, *but*, or *or*. A compound sentence contains two complete thoughts. Point out that using different kinds of sentences makes writing more interesting. Combining short sentences makes writing smoother and easier to read. Work through the instructions and examples. Then complete the Guided Practice items with students, or have students complete the items in small groups.

Combining Sentences with Commas

Commas are used to help separate parts of a sentence.

When you join two simple sentences with the word *and*, *or*, or *but*, the new sentence is called a compound sentence. Use a comma before the word *and*, *or*, or *but* in compound sentences.

Examples:

I like emeralds. Ruth likes diamonds.

I like emeralds, but Ruth likes diamonds.

My mom likes opals. My dad gave her one.

My mom likes opals, and my dad gave her one.

Guided Practice

A. Tell where a comma is needed in each sentence.

Example: Our class likes hiking and we go on nature walks together. *hiking, and*

1. Marisol climbed Mount Red and she hiked in River Park. Red, and
2. She looks for new kinds of birds and once she saw a blue heron. birds, and
3. I like birds but I hope to find some neat insects on my hike. birds, but
4. Joshua looks for striped rocks but they are hard to find. rocks, but
5. Sasha walked along a mountain path and he found animal tracks in the snow. path, and

392

Vocabulary Power page 95

Name _____

WORD FAMILIES

Word families are made up of words that have the same root or base word. Read the words below. Circle the letter of the word that does not belong. Then replace it with a word of your own. Additional words may vary. Possible responses are given.

1	A miner	5	A write
	B mineral		B writer
	C mineralogist		C wren
	(D) minute		D wrote
	mine		*writing*

2	F explore	6	(F) discontent
	(G) examine		G discover
	H explorer		H discovery
	J exploration		J discovered
	exploring		*discovering*

3	A secure	7	A geode
	B security		B geography
	(C) second		C geographic
	D secured		(D) gentle
	securing		*geographer*

4	F vision	8	F cover
	(G) violin		G uncover
	H visor		(H) unusual
	J vista		J covered
	revise		*recover*

Vocabulary Power   Unit 6 • Chapter 32 95

Science

DESCRIBING GEMS Have students look up several kinds of gems in their science books, in an encyclopedia, or on the Internet and take notes. Then have them write several sentences describing these gems. Have them combine some of their sentences using commas. Students should check their sentences for proper comma usage between items in a series.

Independent Practice

B. Combine the sentences to form a compound sentence using *and* or *but*. Add commas where they are needed. Possible responses are given.

Example: We've been to Crater Lake. We loved it
We've been to Crater Lake, and we loved it.

6. Crater Lake is in Oregon. It is at the top of a mountain. Crater Lake is in Oregon, and it is at the top of a mountain.
7. The mountain is a volcano. It has not erupted for a long time. The mountain is a volcano, but it has not erupted for a long time.
8. The lake is in the crater of the volcano. There is an island in the lake. The lake is in the crater of the volcano, and there is an island in the lake.
9. Crater Lake is beautiful. I want to swim in it. Crater Lake is beautiful, and I want to swim in it.
10. I plan to go back next year. I don't know who will come with me. I plan to go back next year, but I don't know who will come with me.

Remember to use a comma before *and, or,* or *but* when joining two sentences in a compound sentence.

DID YOU KNOW
Crater Lake used to be called Deep Blue Lake because of its dark blue color. No streams flow into or out of the lake. It gets all its water from rain and snow.

Writing Connection

Writer's Craft: Personal Voice Pretend that you and a partner are fossils. Decide what plant or animal you used to be. Write a paragraph about the changes you have gone through. For example, are you a dinosaur's footprints? Did some rocks cover you? Using commas correctly, combine some of your sentences into compound sentences.

393

Independent Practice

Have students complete the Independent Practice, or modify it using these suggestions:

MODIFIED INSTRUCTION

BELOW-LEVEL STUDENTS Before students write a compound sentence for each item, have them read each sentence pair aloud, inserting *and, but,* or *or* before the second sentence.

ABOVE-LEVEL STUDENTS For three items, have students write a different second sentence and then combine it with the first sentence given.

Writing Connection

Writer's Craft: Personal Voice Have students illustrate their narratives and display them in the classroom. Have students present dramatic interpretations of their narratives.

WRAP-UP/ASSESS

SUMMARIZE What is a compound sentence? Where does the comma belong in a compound sentence?

RETEACH

REACHING ALL LEARNERS

INTERVENTION Lessons in **visual, auditory,** and **kinesthetic** modalities: p. R59 and *Reteach Activities Copying Masters,* p. 66.

REACHING ALL LEARNERS

PRACTICE page 108

Name _____

Combining Sentences Using Commas

A. Write each sentence, adding a comma where needed.

1. I went to a mineral show and I saw some beautiful geodes.
   I went to a mineral show, and I saw some beautiful geodes.

2. A geode is a few inches in size and it is round.
   A geode is a few inches in size, and it is round.

3. This rock looks plain outside but it has crystals inside.
   This rock looks plain outside, but it has crystals inside.

4. They cut them open and the crystals look beautiful.
   They cut them open, and the crystals look beautiful.

5. The clerk wrapped up the bookends and I took them home.
   The clerk wrapped up the bookends, and I took them home.

B. A sentence may contain a comma mistake. If the sentence is correct, write *Correct*. If it is incorrect, write the sentence correctly.

6. I handed them to my mother, and she was so surprised.
   Correct

7. Well did she like them?
   Well, did she like them?

8. Yes she loved them. Yes, she loved them.

TRY THIS! Write a few sentences about rocks and minerals. Be sure to use commas correctly.

108 Unit 6 • Chapter 32   Practice • Present-Tense Verbs

REACHING ALL LEARNERS

CHALLENGE

SENTENCE STEMS Write the following sentence stems on the board:

The fossil was _____.

I found it _____.

The scientist told me _____.

It looks like _____.

Have students work in pairs to complete the sentence stems. Then have students combine the sentences using *and* or *but*. Remind them to use commas correctly.

Combining Sentences with Commas

Read each sentence. Add a comma where it is needed.

Our hike was long but we had a good time.

Kip found some interesting rocks and we all some pretty wildflowers.

We wanted to hike to Deer Lake but it was too far away.

Mom wants to fish there and I want to swim in it.

Visual

Combining Sentences with Commas

Look through books and magazines to find at least four compound sentences. Read the sentences aloud to a partner.

Listen to each compound sentence your partner reads to you. Then tell your partner where a comma belongs in that sentence.

Auditory

Combining Sentences with Commas

With a partner, make up four compound sentences. Write each compound sentence on a strip of paper. Then cut each paper strip into three parts. Leave the first sentence on one part. Leave the comma on a part. Leave the part with *and* or *but* and the second sentence on the third part.

Trade sentence parts with another pair of students. With your partner, put together the sentence strips. Be sure to put the comma where it belongs in the compound sentence.

Kinesthetic

Teacher: Cut apart the activities and distribute to students based on the modalities that are their strengths.
(Visual) You may want to write the activity sentences on the board or on an overhead transparency.
(Auditory) Have students refer to the written sentences they have selected to check their partners' responses.
(Kinesthetic) If possible, cut long pieces of construction paper into strips for this activity.

66 Unit 6 • Chapter 32   Reteach Activities • Combining Sentences with Commas

Extra Practice

OBJECTIVES
- To use commas correctly in sentences and parts of letters
- To write an informative paragraph, using commas correctly

DAILY LANGUAGE PRACTICE

TRANSPARENCY 74

1 Therese and me found fossils in ours yard (I; our yard.)

2 Yesterday we will show them to Thomas Patrick and Sheila. (we showed; Thomas, Patrick,)

BRIDGE TO WRITING The museum guide (linking verb) well-informed about minerals.

ORAL WARM-UP

USE PRIOR KNOWLEDGE Write these sentences on the board: *Well we saw rocks covered with moss but I forgot to take a picture. Angie did Karen Mary and Antonia see the rocks?* Ask volunteers to tell where to insert commas in the sentences.

TEACH/MODEL

Use the Remember boxes to review the use of commas. Model the thinking for the example sentence in Part A:

MODEL I know that a comma belongs between the names of a city and a state, so I must write *Denver, Colorado.*

Have students work in small groups to complete the Extra Practice items.

CHAPTER 32

Commas

Remember

to use commas with a series of three or more words. Use a comma after the name of the person being spoken to in a sentence. Also use commas after *yes, no,* and *well* at the beginning of a sentence.

For more activities with commas, visit *The Learning Site:* www.harcourtschool.com

394

Extra Practice

A. Write the sentence. Add commas where they are needed. *pages 388–389*

Example: It took two days to drive from St. Louis to Denver Colorado. **Denver, Colorado**

1. We went on a vacation to Death Valley California. Valley, California
2. It was 100 degrees at midnight and that's hot! midnight, and
3. Well if it's that hot at midnight, I would not want to be outside in the afternoon! Well, if
4. Tina did you know that Death Valley is a desert? Tina, did
5. It is hot dry and rocky in many places. hot, dry, and

B. Combine the sentences to form a compound sentence using *and* or *but*. Add commas where they are needed. *pages 392–393*

Example: We will go to the large caves. We will look for pictures on the walls.
We will go to the large caves, and we will look for pictures on the walls.

6. Some cave paintings are handprints. Some are pictures of animals. handprints, and (or but) some
7. I read about cave paintings in France. They are pictures of horses and bulls. France, and they
8. Many cave paintings show lions. Only one painting is a panther. lions, but only
9. Some caves form on the sides of hills. They are all sizes and shapes. hills, and they
10. Caves by the sea are called sea caves. They are formed by waves hitting cliffs on the shore. caves, and they

---

Vocabulary Power page 96

Name _____

HOMOPHONES

The words in each homophone pair below are pronounced the same but have different spellings and different meanings. Write the word that matches each clue below.

load–lode	flour–flower	new–knew	sew–sow

1. recently made — new
2. had knowledge of — knew
3. to scatter seeds — sow
4. to make using needle and thread — sew
5. a blossom — flower
6. a soft powder used to make bread — flour
7. what a person is carrying — load
8. a streak of ore of a metal — new

right–write	minor–miner	herd–heard

9. the opposite of left — right
10. to make letters or numbers with a pen or pencil — write
11. a group of animals — herd
12. listened to — heard
13. a person who digs minerals — miner
14. not important — minor

96   Unit 6 • Chapter 32   Vocabulary Power

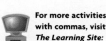

ESL

REACHING ALL LEARNERS

COMMA PLACEMENT Write the following sentences on the board:

Antonia did you see the mountains?

Yes I saw them.

I saw snow ice and plants on the mountain.

Have students come to the board and insert commas where needed as they read each sentence aloud.

C. Read the parts of the letter. Then write the letter and add commas where they are needed. *pages 390–391*

11. 131 Winthrop Road
    Topeka Kansas 66616   131 Winthrop Road
    Topeka, Kansas 66616

12. April 19 2001   April 19, 2001
    Dear Uncle Jasper,   Dear Uncle Jasper,

13. Will you be able to come to our school farm picnic on May 1 2001?   May 1, 2001

14. It will be held in Kansas City Kansas.   Kansas City, Kansas.

15. Your nephew,
    Sidney   Your nephew,
    Sidney

D. Write each sentence, adding a comma or commas where they are needed. *pages 388–391*

16. My family visited the Luray Caverns on June 19 2000.   June 19, 2000

17. They are near Luray Virginia.   Luray, Virginia

18. We arrived at about 9:30 A.M. and then we went through the caves.   9:30 A.M., and

19. My favorite places were Giant's Hall Dream Lake and the Stalacpipe Organ.   Giant's Hall, Dream Lake, and the Stalacpipe Organ

20. I had a wonderful time at the cavern and I hope to go back.   cavern, and

Remember
to use commas in the heading, greeting, and closing of a letter. Also use a comma before *and* or *but* when joining two sentences in a compound sentence.

Writing Connection

Writer's Craft: Sentence Variety Write a paragraph about different kinds of rocks you have seen. Vary the kinds of sentences that you use. Make some sentences short and some compound. Write at least one sentence that has a series of items. Be sure to use commas correctly in your paragraph.

Building Oral Grammar

To reinforce correct speaking patterns, have students work in pairs to read aloud the sentences from Parts A, B, and D. Ask them to note the brief pause that occurs between two sentences in a compound sentence, as well as the pauses between items in a series. Listening to everyday speech can help students understand the uses and placement of commas.

Writing Connection

Writer's Craft: Sentence Variety Students may use resources such as encyclopedias or the Internet to take simple notes to write their informative paragraphs. When students have finished their paragraphs, have them trade papers with a partner and respond constructively to each other's writing, concentrating on comma use and sentence variety.

WRAP-UP/ASSESS

SUMMARIZE Ask students to reflect in their journals on how using commas correctly can make their writing easier to understand. **REFLECTION**

ADDITIONAL PRACTICE An additional page of Extra Practice is provided on page 475 of the *Pupil Edition*.

PRACTICE page 109

Name _____

Extra Practice

A. Write the sentence. Add a comma or commas where they are needed.

1. July 17 1999 was a day to remember.
   July 17, 1999, was a day to remember.

2. My whole family left for San Francisco California.
   My whole family left for San Francisco, California.

3. Well guess where we stopped on the way?
   Well, guess where we stopped on the way?

4. Yes we went to see the Grand Canyon.
   Yes, we went to see the Grand Canyon.

5. Grandma Grandpa and Uncle Roger met us there.
   Grandma, Grandpa, and Uncle Roger met us there.

B. Combine each pair of sentences to form a compound sentence using *and* or *but*. Add a comma to make the compound sentence correct.

6. Quartz is a rock. There are many different kinds.
   Quartz is a rock, and there are many different kinds.

7. You said you liked agate. I do not know what it is.
   You said you liked agate, but I do not know what it is.

TRY THIS! What can be made from rocks? Write a paragraph about how rocks are used every day. Use commas correctly in your paragraph.

Practice • Commas   Unit 6 • Chapter 32   109

CHALLENGE

CAVE PAINTING Tell students to imagine that they have just discovered ancient paintings on a cave wall. Have them write a letter to a family member describing the paintings. They should tell where the paintings are located and use at least one compound sentence to describe how they look. Students may also choose to draw what the paintings look like. Remind students to use commas correctly in their letters.

TECHNOLOGY *Grammar Practice and Assessment* CD-ROM; *Writing Express* CD-ROM

INTERNET Visit *The Learning Site:*
www.harcourtschool.com

Chapter Review

OBJECTIVES

• To review comma usage in sentences and parts of letters
• To practice giving and following directions

DAILY LANGUAGE PRACTICE

TRANSPARENCY 74

1 my grandfather workked in a coal Mine. (My; worked; mine.)

2 He went deep underground and he dug up coal. (underground,)

BRIDGE TO WRITING There are (adjective) coal mines in West Virginia. Coal is (adverb) used for fuel.

STANDARDIZED TEST PREP

MODEL TEST-TAKING STRATEGIES Have students read the directions on page 396 silently.

Remind them to read all of the answer choices carefully before choosing one. Then model the thinking. Write this example on the board:

(1) <u>Yes I will write</u> a letter to Latrell.

> **1** **A** Yes I, will write
> **B** Yes, I will write
> **C** Yes I will write,
> **D** No mistake

MODEL I know that a comma can tell readers where to pause in a sentence. I don't want my readers to pause after *I* or *write*, so answers A and C are not correct. I know that I need a comma after a word such as *yes* at the beginning of a sentence, so answer *B* is correct.

Have students complete the Chapter Review independently.

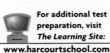

Chapter Review

Read the letter. Some sections are underlined. Choose the best way to write each section and mark the letter for your answer. If the underlined section needs no change, mark the choice "No mistake."

For additional test preparation, visit *The Learning Site:* www.harcourtschool.com

TIP Read the whole sentence before deciding how to punctuate it correctly.

> 89 Cherry Lane
>
> (1) <u>Menlo Park. CA 94025</u>
> (2) <u>May 26 2002</u>
>
> Dear Latrell,
>
>   We just got back. (3) <u>Latrell we had fun</u> in (4) <u>Boston, but im glad</u> to be home. I saw (5) <u>fish birds and shells</u> at the beach.
>
> (5) <u>Your cousin</u>
> Andrea

1 A Menlo Park! CA
  B Menlo Park, CA B
  C Menlo Park CA
  D No mistake

2 F May 26, 2002 F
  G May, 26, 2002
  H May 26. 2002
  J No mistake

3 A Latrell, we had fun A
  B Latrell. we had fun
  C Latrell we had fun,
  D No mistake

4 F Boston, but I'm glad
  G Boston? but I'm glad
  H Boston but, I'm glad
  J No mistake J

5 A fish birds and shells,
  B fish, birds, and shells B
  C fish, birds and shells
  D No mistake

6 F Your, cousin
  G Your cousin, G
  H Your cousin.
  J No mistake

396

Assessment

PORTFOLIO ASSESSMENT Have students select their best work from the Writing Connections on pages 391, 393, and 395.

ONGOING ASSESSMENT Evaluate the performance of 4–6 students using appropriate checklists and record forms from pages R74–R77.

INTERNET Activities and exercises to help students prepare for state and standardized assessments appear on *The Learning Site:*
www.harcourtschool.com

Listening Outside the Classroom

LISTENING AND SPEAKING

People who give directions use special words. They name directions, distance, and landmarks. A landmark is a place, like a big building, a river, or a hill. Notice these kinds of words as you listen to directions.

Directions	Distance	Landmarks
left, right east straight ahead	block, mile near, far	Go beyond the bridge . . . When you see the big white house . . .

Here are some ways to help you follow directions:

- Picture in your mind what you are supposed to do.
- Ask the person giving the directions to repeat them.
- Say the directions back to the person who gave them.
- On a map, follow any instructions you are given.
- Write down the directions.

YOUR TURN

With a partner, choose a place in your classroom where you want your classmates to go. Then draw a map of the route.

- **Label landmarks in the room, such as windows, cabinets, or desks.**
- **Make an *X* on the starting point and an *X* at the ending point.**
- **Draw a line that shows the path people should take from the starting point to the ending point.**

Exchange directions with another team, and see if your classmates can follow your directions.

TIP Try out one or two of the ideas listed as you do YOUR TURN. Find out which one works best for you.

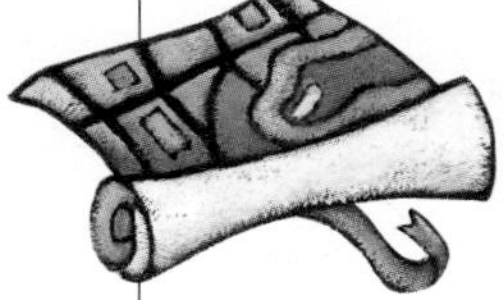

397

LISTENING AND SPEAKING

Listening Outside the Classroom

TEACH/MODEL

Read the explanation and strategies to students. Tell them that giving directions can mean more than telling someone how to get someplace. Have students participate in a class discussion about times when they have either given or followed directions. Point out that when they learned how to play a game or sport, they were following directions.

Explain that one way to remember directions is to visualize doing the actions as they are being explained. Then have students complete the Your Turn activity.

Writer's Journal

WRITING APPLICATION In their journals, have students reflect on why it is important to be able to give and follow directions. **REFLECTION**

WRAP-UP/ASSESS

SUMMARIZE Have students write a list of tips for listening to directions.

REACHING ALL LEARNERS — PRACTICE page 110

Name ______________________

Chapter Review

Choose the letter of the correct way to write the underlined words. Fill in the oval next to your choice. If the underlined words are correctly written, choose *Correct*.

1048 East I Street
(1) Ontario. California
(2) May 26 2002

(3) Dear Larissa

We saw the most beautiful rock shapes on our trip. Larissa, I wished so much you were there. It was (4) fun. but I am glad to get home. I can hardly wait to see (5) Betty Fred and Al.

(6) Your friend
Alice

1. ○ Ontario: California
   ● Ontario, California
   ○ Ontario California,
   ○ Correct
2. ● May 26, 2002
   ○ May, 26, 2002
   ○ May, 26 2002
   ○ Correct
3. ● Larissa,
   ○ Larissa.
   ○ Larissa;
   ○ Correct
4. ○ fun:
   ● fun,
   ○ fun;
   ○ Correct
5. ● Betty, Fred, and Al
   ○ Betty Fred, and Al
   ○ Betty, Fred, and, Al
   ○ Correct
6. ○ Your friend:
   ● Your friend,
   ○ Your friend.
   ○ Correct

110 Unit 6 • Chapter 32 Practice • Commas

REACHING ALL LEARNERS — CHALLENGE

GIVE DIRECTIONS Have each student write a note to invite a friend to play, telling the friend where and when to meet. Have students write directions for their friend's parent or guardian telling how to get from their school to the places where they are to meet. Remind students to name directions, distance, and landmarks in telling how to get to the meeting place. Also, tell students to check their notes for correct punctuation.

TECHNOLOGY Additional writing activities are provided on the *Writing Express* CD-ROM

LESSON ORGANIZER	DAY 1	DAY 2
DAILY LANGUAGE PRACTICE TRANSPARENCIES 75, 76	1. My Aunt martha is a interesting person (Martha; an; person.) 2. She love to travel and she has many hobbys. (loves; travel,; hobbies.)	1. Aunt Martha took I to the Rocky mountains last August. (me; Rocky Mountains) 2. We hiked many Mountain trails and took some beautiful picturs. (mountain; pictures.)
ORAL WARM-UP Listening/Speaking	Discuss Characterization 398	Use Figurative Language 400
TEACH/MODEL **WRITING** 	✔ **ELABORATION** **Literature Model:** from *Back Home* 398 **Analyze the Model** 398 **Using Elaboration** 399	**GUIDED WRITING** **Using Figurative Language** 400 **Using Exact Words** 401 Writing and Thinking: Writing to Record Reflections 401
Reaching All Learners	**Challenge:** Using Figurative Language 399 *ESL Manual* pp. 160, 161	**ESL:** Mix and Match 401 *ESL Manual* p. 160
GRAMMAR	**HANDS-ON ACTIVITIES** 375I–375J	**HANDS-ON ACTIVITIES** 375I–375J
CROSS-CURRICULAR/ ENRICHMENT	**Listening and Speaking:** Poetry Reading 399 *Vocabulary Power* Synonyms 398	**Art:** Nature Poster 401 *Vocabulary Power* Explore Word Meaning 398 *Vocabulary Power* book p. 97 **Vocabulary activity**

KEY
✔ = tested skill

addition, description, **elaboration**, embellishment, expansion

See *Vocabulary Power* book.

DAY **3**	DAY **4**	DAY **5**
1. Me, Mom, and Aunt Martha dont have to travel to have fun. (Mom, Aunt Martha, and I don't) 2. We goed to the movies on sunday (went; Sunday.)	1. I showed Aunt Martha my cactus garden and she was very surprised. (garden,) 2. She gave me two more plant. (gave; plants.)	1. My aunt also enjoys painting drawing and working with clay. (painting, drawing,) 2. she give me a art lesson last saturday (She gave; an; Saturday.)
Using Exact Words 402	Discuss Character Study Revisions 404	Artists' Character Studies 405
GUIDED WRITING **Character Study** 402 **Analyze the Model** 403 **Prewriting and Drafting** 403	**GUIDED WRITING** **Editing** 404 **Sharing and Reflecting** 404 **Self Initiated Writing** 404 **Proofreading practice**	**Viewing:** Looking at Fine Art 405
ESL: Character Study Sentence Starters 403 *ESL Manual* p. 160	*ESL Manual* p. 160	*ESL Manual* p. 160
HANDS-ON ACTIVITIES 375I–375J	**HANDS-ON ACTIVITIES** 375I–375J	**HANDS-ON ACTIVITIES** 375I–375J
Listening and Speaking: Role-Play 402 **Evaluation Criteria** 403 *Vocabulary Power* Analogies 398 *Vocabulary Power* book p. 98 **Vocabulary activity**	*Vocabulary Power* Context Clues 398 *Vocabulary Power* book p. 99 **Vocabulary activity**	*Vocabulary Power* Compare and Contrast 398 **Evaluation Criteria:** Self-Evaluation 405

Writer's Craft: Elaboration

OBJECTIVES

- To understand expressive writing and analyze its use in a passage
- To understand and analyze the use of elaboration in expressive writing

SPIRAL REVIEW

DAILY LANGUAGE PRACTICE

TRANSPARENCY 75

1 My Aunt martha is a interesting person (Martha; an; person.)

2 She love to travel and she has many hobbys. (loves; travel,; hobbies.)

ORAL WARM-UP

USE PRIOR KNOWLEDGE Ask: **How does a writer create a vivid character?**

As students read the model, have them try to picture Uncle June Avery.

Analyze THE *Model*

1. Who is the author describing? (June Avery, Ernestine's uncle) **LITERAL: NOTE DETAILS**

2. How did Ernestine recognize him? (He has flowers and looks like Grandmama Zulah.) **LITERAL: IDENTIFY CHARACTERS' TRAITS**

3. What kind of person do you think he is? Why do you think so? (Possible response: He is friendly. His eyes sparkle, and he smiles a lot.) **INFERENTIAL: DETERMINE CHARACTERS' TRAITS**

Elaboration

Suppose you want to write to express an idea or a feeling. This kind of writing is called expressive writing. A character study is a special form of expressive writing that describes a person.

Read the following passage from the book *Back Home*. Look at how the writer describes a character in the story.

LITERATURE MODEL

> Ernestine recognized Uncle June Avery right away. She remembered Mama saying, "He'll probably bring you flowers." He also had the same sparkling eyes and apple-dumpling cheeks as Grandmama Zulah in Mama's old photograph.
>
> He was waiting on the platform as the Silver Star slowly pulled into Robeson County Depot. When he caught a glimpse of Ernestine peering through the window, his face lit up in a broad smile.
>
> —from *Back Home*
> by Gloria Jean Pinkney

Analyze THE *Model*

1. What character is the author describing?
2. How did Ernestine recognize him?
3. What kind of person do you think he is? Why do you think so?

Vocabulary Power

e·lab·o·ra·tion
[i·lab′ə·rā′shən] *n.*
Developing and expanding a topic by adding details and reasons.

Using Elaboration

Using elaboration means using ideas and words that help your readers picture in their minds the person you are describing. Study the chart on the next page.

398

Vocabulary Power

DAY 1 SYNONYMS Introduce and define *elaboration*. **What are some synonyms for elaboration?**

DAY 2 EXPLORE WORD MEANING **How could you add elaboration to this sentence?** *The meal was delicious.* (See also *Vocabulary Power*, page 97.)

DAY 3 ANALOGIES: *Elaboration* is to *details* as *cold* is to *freezing*. **How are these pairs of words related?** (See also *Vocabulary Power*, page 98.)

DAY 4 CONTEXT CLUES **What words are clues to the meaning of *elaboration* in this sentence?** *Writers use elaboration to describe characters in detail.* (See also *Vocabulary Power*, page 99.)

DAY 5 COMPARE AND CONTRAST **Complete this statement:** *Elaboration is like expansion except _____.*

Strategies to Use for Elaboration | How to Use Strategies | Examples

Strategies to Use for Elaboration	How to Use Strategies	Examples
Use figurative language.	• Figurative language describes something by comparing it to something else.	• apple-dumpling cheeks • hair as white as snow
Use exact words.	• Choose words that say exactly what you mean.	• "he **caught a glimpse** of Ernestine **peering** through the window."

YOUR TURN

THINK ABOUT ELABORATION **Work with two or three classmates. Look at some stories and find examples of how writers describe different characters. Discuss the examples with your group.**

Answer these questions:

1. What character is the writer describing?
2. How does the writer help you see in your mind a picture of the character?
3. Does the writer make comparisons to describe the character? If so, explain the comparisons.
4. How does the writer use exact words to describe?

399

Listening and Speaking

POETRY READING Provide students with expressive poems that include vivid descriptions. Have volunteers choose poems to read aloud. Remind students to adapt voice volume and rate appropriate to their purpose. Allow students to practice before they present their poems. Tell listeners to visualize the people and the scenes in the poems.

REACHING ALL LEARNERS

CHALLENGE

USING FIGURATIVE LANGUAGE
Have students write their own descriptive poems. Suggest a place, such as a forest or a circus, or a season of the year as the subject for a poem. Prompt students to visualize the subject and to write phrases or sentences that create a vivid picture. Then they can choose the most interesting descriptions to work into a poem. Display students' poetry in the classroom.

USING ELABORATION Discuss figurative language with students, using examples in the chart. Ask: **Are Uncle June Avery's cheeks really apple dumplings? Why is *hair as white as snow* more interesting than *white hair*?** Explain that both expressions are comparisons that create pictures in readers' minds.

Expand the concept of exact words by reading the example in the chart and then offering others. For example, ask: **Which word is more exact—*walk* or *stroll*? *Move* or *gallop*? *Colorful* or *fiery yellow*?** Urge students to think about exact words as they continue this chapter.

Guide students through the Your Turn activity. As an alternative to having students choose stories on their own, you might assign a character in a particular story that the class has enjoyed together. Write the character's name on the board. As students suggest words and phrases that describe the character, use their responses to create a word web around the character's name. Then have students answer the questions.

WRAP-UP/ASSESS

SUMMARIZE **How can elaboration help you write a good description? What are some strategies writers can use to bring characters to life?**

TECHNOLOGY Additional writing activities are provided on the *Writing Express* CD-ROM

Writer's Craft: Elaboration

OBJECTIVES

- To identify and use figurative language and exact words
- To record reflections about the effect of figurative language

DAILY LANGUAGE PRACTICE

TRANSPARENCY 75

1 Aunt Martha took I to the Rocky mountains last August. (me; Rocky Mountains)

2 We hiked many Mountain trails and took some beautiful picturs. (mountain; pictures.)

ORAL WARM-UP

USE PRIOR KNOWLEDGE Write on the board: **There are clouds in the sky.** Ask students to suggest ways to make this sentence more interesting by using figurative language.

GUIDED WRITING

Using Figurative Language

Remind students that figurative language is powerful because it makes new, interesting comparisons for readers.

Work through Part A as a class, discussing the comparisons made in each sentence. (1. eyes, diamonds; 2. arms, steel; 3. hair, banner; 4. Willie, spider; 5. voices, bells; 6. blanket, kitten; 7. excitement, wildfire; 8. he, apple; 9. pleasure, moonbeam; 10. scent, flowers)

Have students complete Part B independently. Remind them to say the sentences quietly to themselves, trying each of the words from the box to see which word makes sense. Then have volunteers share their answers. (11. roses; 12. thundercloud; 13. garden; 14. sunshine; 15. birds)

Using Figurative Language

A. Read each sentence. On your paper, name the items that the writer compares in each sentence.

1. Jody's eyes sparkled like diamonds.
2. Dad's arms were as strong as steel.
3. Her long hair was a banner flying in the wind.
4. Willie runs like a spider on his long, thin legs.
5. The children's voices were little bells jingling with laughter.
6. The blanket was as soft as a kitten.
7. Excitement spread like wildfire.
8. He was the apple of his father's eye.
9. Mom's pleasure shone through her eyes like a moonbeam.
10. This scent smells like fresh flowers.

B. Choose a word from the box to complete each comparison. Write the completed sentences on your paper.

> birds   garden   roses
> sunshine   thundercloud

11. The baby's cheeks were as red as _____.
12. Grandfather's frown was a _____.
13. Mrs. Henderson's colorful hat looks like a _____ on her head.
14. His smile is as warm as_____.
15. Her hands are fluttering _____ looking for a place to land.

400

Vocabulary Power page 97

Name_____

EXPLORE WORD MEANING

Read and respond to each question or statement. Responses will vary. Accept reasonable responses.

1. Add **elaboration** to the following statement: It was a very hot day.
_____
_____

2. Write a **description** of your favorite animal, but don't tell what animal you are describing. Have a partner try to guess what animal you described.
_____
_____

3. What kind of **addition** would you like to make to the school playground?
_____
_____

4. Here is a plain cake. Add **embellishment** to it.
_____

5. The local mall is thinking about getting bigger. What stores should be part of the **expansion**?
_____
_____

Vocabulary Power   Unit 6 • Chapter 33   97

Using Exact Words

C. Choose a more exact word from the box to replace the underlined word in each sentence. Write the revised sentence on your paper.

wade	basket	friendly	switch
hammer	hike	enjoyable	bounced

1. Peter has a <u>nice</u> smile.
2. We had a very <u>nice</u> time at the party.
3. They had to <u>walk</u> a long way up the mountain.
4. Kelly likes to <u>walk</u> in the shallow water at the beach.
5. Put the trash in that green <u>thing</u>.
6. Where is the <u>thing</u> to turn on the light?
7. Dad used a <u>tool</u> to pound in these nails.
8. I need <u>something</u> to hold these picnic supplies.
9. Skating is a very <u>good</u> form of exercise.
10. The ball <u>went</u> down the steps.

Writing AND Thinking

Writer's Journal

Write to Record Reflections We use figurative language every day. For instance, you may say that something is as blue as the sky or that someone runs like the wind. Why do people enjoy using, hearing, and reading figurative language? Write your reflections in your Writer's Journal.

Using Exact Words

Point out to students that the underlined words do not create a vivid picture. The words in the box will make the sentences clearer and more interesting. If necessary, suggest that students use dictionaries to check the meanings of the words in the box. (1. friendly; 2. enjoyable; 3. hike; 4. wade; 5. basket; 6. switch; 7. hammer; 8. basket; 9. enjoyabe; 10. bounced)

Writing and Thinking

Writer's Journal

Write to Record Reflections Allow students to work in pairs or small groups to reflect on figurative language. To prompt students' thinking, you might read aloud some story passages or poems that use figurative language for humor or for striking effect. Ask students what the figurative language makes them think about and how it makes them feel. Have students write their reflections in their journals.

WRAP-UP/ASSESS

SUMMARIZE What is figurative language? Why do writers use figurative language?

Art

NATURE POSTER Have students make a poster describing an unusual animal or plant. Allow them to use the Internet or an encyclopedia to find information.

On a sheet of paper, have students draw or paste a picture of the plant or animal. Then have them write descriptions around the picture, using figurative language and exact words. Prompt students to use a thesaurus.

REACHING ALL LEARNERS — ESL

MIX AND MATCH Write the following on sentence strips:

Manuel is / as smart as a fox.

Julia's hair is / shiny and soft.

Ishiro jumps / like a frog.

Sita has / a bright orange dress.

Cut the strips as indicated, mix them up, and place them face up on a table. Have students match the sentence parts, and explain how figurative language or exact words are used in each sentence.

Writer's Craft: Elaboration

OBJECTIVES
- To recognize the parts of a character study
- To analyze a character study
- To choose a topic and generate ideas for a character study

1 Me, Mom, and Aunt Martha dont have to travel to have fun. (Mom, Aunt Martha, and I don't)

2 We goed to the movies on sunday (went; Sunday.)

ORAL WARM-UP

USE PRIOR KNOWLEDGE Ask students to give some examples of exact words to replace these words: *talk*, *look at*, and *try*.

GUIDED WRITING

Character Study

READ AND RESPOND TO THE MODEL Before reading aloud Paul's character study, have students determine a purpose for listening. (to find out what Aunt Jessie is like; to find out how Paul uses elaboration) Discuss whether Paul does a good job of using elaboration to describe Aunt Jessie. Remind students to support their evaluations with examples.

FOCUS ON ORGANIZATION Have students reread the character study silently, using the side notes to find the main parts. Discuss how Paul begins his character study by setting up a scene for the reader.

FOCUS ON WRITER'S CRAFT Have students find examples of effective language in Paul's character study. Ask: **Why is Paul's writing more interesting than this statement?** *Aunt Jessie is thin. I thought that she was stern, but she is friendly.*

402   UNIT **6**

Character Study

Gloria Jean Pinkney wrote a description of Uncle June Avery. Paul decided to write a character study of his mother's Aunt Jessie. As you read what Paul wrote, look at how he used elaboration in his description.

MODEL

figurative language

exact words

figurative language

> The first time I met my mother's Aunt Jessie, I didn't know what to think of her. Aunt Jessie is as thin as a stick. She frowned at me and muttered, "So you're Paul, are you?"
>
> "Yes, Aunt Jessie," I replied politely. Suddenly she let out a lion's roar of a laugh. "We're going to be great friends, Paul," she declared.
>
> I didn't know it then, but Aunt Jessie was right.

Analyze THE Model

1. Does Paul's description give you a clear picture of Aunt Jessie? Why or why not?
2. How does Paul use figurative language to elaborate his description?
3. How does Paul use exact words to elaborate his description?
4. What kind of person do you think Aunt Jessie is? Why do you think so?

402

Vocabulary Power page 98

Name _____

ANALOGIES

An analogy is made up of two pairs of words. Each pair of words is related in the same way.
- For example, the two words in each part of the analogy may be opposites, such as:
  Hot is to cold as tall is to __short__.
- Or, the two words in each part of the analogy may be synonyms, such as:
  Beautiful is to pretty as jump is to __leap__.

Look at each pair of words below. Decide how words are related. Then complete the analogy. The first one is done for you. Possible responses are given.

1. (Elaboration, description)
   Elaboration is to description as hot is to ___warm___.
2. (Sharp, dull)
   Sharp is to dull as wet is to ___dry___
3. (Embellishment, decoration)
   Embellishment is to decoration as photograph is to ___picture___
4. (Diary, journal)
   Diary is to journal as bake is to ___cook___
5. (Child, adult)
   Child is to adult as small is to ___big___
6. (Addition, expansion)
   Addition is to expansion as describe is to ___tell___
7. (Famous, unknown)
   Famous is to unknown as dark is to ___light___
8. (Smile, grin)
   Smile is to grin as laugh is to ___giggle___

98 Unit 6 • Chapter 33   Vocabulary Power

Listening and Speaking

ROLE-PLAY Have students work in pairs to role-play Paul's character study. Have them take turns playing Paul and Aunt Jessie.

As students finish, ask them to tell what parts of Paul's character study give them clues about how Aunt Jessie and Paul act.

Ask students to think about how to use clues in their own writing.

WRITING PROMPT Choose an interesting character that you have seen in a movie or a video. Write a character study to describe the character to your classmates. Use elaboration to make your description interesting and exact.

STUDY THE PROMPT Ask yourself these questions:

1. What is your purpose for writing?
2. Who is your audience?
3. What is your subject?
4. What writing form will you use?

Prewriting and Drafting

Plan Your Character Study Choose a character whom you would like to describe. Think of details you can tell your readers to help them imagine the character. Use a web like this one to organize your ideas.

what the character looks like

personality traits

character's name

actions that show what kind of person the character is

USING YOUR
Handbook

• Use the Writer's Thesaurus to find interesting and exact words to use in your character study.

403

Analyze THE Model

1. Does Paul's description give you a clear picture of Aunt Jessie? Why or why not? (Possible response: Yes; Paul describes how she looks and acts.) **CRITICAL: MAKE JUDGMENTS**

2. How does Paul use figurative language to elaborate his description? (Possible response: He writes *thin as a stick* to help the reader picture her.) **INFERENTIAL: AUTHOR'S CRAFT/DETERMINE IMAGERY**

3. How does Paul use exact words to elaborate his description? (Possible response: He uses words like *frowned, muttered,* and *politely.*) **CRITICAL: AUTHOR'S CRAFT/APPRECIATE LANGUAGE**

4. What kind of person do you think Aunt Jessie is? Why do you think so? (Possible response: She is friendly and fun. She laughs and smiles, and Paul says that they are great friends.) **METACOGNITIVE: DETERMINE CHARACTERS' TRAITS**

Have students work in pairs to brainstorm possible subjects for their character studies.

Prewriting and Drafting

Discuss the web on page 403. Explain to students that when they write, they should include the most important details from their webs.

WRAP-UP/ASSESS

SUMMARIZE How might your character study be similar to Paul's? How might it be different from Paul's?

Evaluation Criteria

Review the criteria that students should apply:

• Use figurative language.
• Use exact words.
• Use the correct form for writing a character study.

Work with students to add other criteria.

ESL

CHARACTER STUDY SENTENCE STARTERS To help students draft their character studies, have them complete the following sentence frames:

The character's name is _____.

_____ looks like _____.

_____ acts like _____.

_____ is _____.

Then have students work in pairs to write their character studies. Tell students to focus on elaboration as they work together.

Writer's Craft: Elaboration

OBJECTIVES

- To revise a character study, focusing on figurative language and exact words
- To proofread a character study
- To share and reflect upon a character study

DAILY LANGUAGE PRACTICE

TRANSPARENCY 76

1 I showed Aunt Martha my cactus garden and she was very surprised. (garden,)

2 She gave me two more plant. (gave; plants.)

ORAL WARM-UP

USE PRIOR KNOWLEDGE What kinds of things will you look for as you revise your character study?

GUIDED WRITING

Editing

Work through the revising questions with students. Ask volunteers to explain each item. Then have students revise and proofread their character studies. After they finish proofreading, have them trade papers with a partner. Have students look at the revising questions again and respond constructively to their partner's writing.

Sharing and Reflecting

Have students display their character studies in a "Character Hall of Fame." After students make final copies of their work, they should make pictures or models of their characters. Conduct "opening ceremonies," and have students introduce their characters.

WRAP-UP/ASSESS

SUMMARIZE Ask students to reflect on what they have learned about elaboration. **REFLECTION**

CHAPTER 33

Expressive Writing

Editing

Reread the draft of your character study. Do you want to add or change anything? Use this checklist to help you revise your work.

Editor's Marks

- ✐ take out text
- ∧ add text
- ↶ move text
- ¶ new paragraph
- ≡ capitalize
- / lowercase
- ◯ correct spelling

- ☑ Do you give your reader a clear picture of the character?
- ☑ Are there details you can add to describe the character better?
- ☑ Can you add figurative language to help the reader understand your description?
- ☑ Have you used exact words?

Use this checklist as you proofread your paragraph.

- ☑ I have begun my sentences with capital letters.
- ☑ I have used the correct end marks for my sentences.
- ☑ I have used negatives correctly and avoided double negatives.
- ☑ I have used commas and colons correctly.
- ☑ I have used a dictionary to check my spelling.

Sharing and Reflecting

Writer's Journal

Make a final copy of your character study. Share it with a partner. Discuss how each of you can use elaboration to make your writing better. Write your reflections in your Writer's Journal.

404

Vocabulary Power page 99

Name _____

CONTEXT CLUES

You can often figure out the meaning of an unfamiliar word by looking at the words around it. Read each of the following sentences. Then write a definition of the underlined word. Look at the other words in the sentence for clues. Possible responses are given.

1. Elaboration, or using descriptive words, paints a mental picture for readers. ____using descriptive words____

2. Her funny, lop-sided grin was higher on one side than the other. ____uneven____

3. The new bedroom was an addition to our house. ____something added____

4. The cake had yellow stars and pink flowers as embellishments. ____decorations____

5. His aged hat was worn and faded. ____old____

6. The amicable shopkeeper was friendly to every customer. ____friendly____

7. The circus clown wore a ridiculous rubber nose that made all the children laugh. ____funny____

8. The cowardly lion was afraid of everything. ____full of fear____

9. After rolling in the dirt, the puppy was grubby. ____dirty____

10. Her gracious greeting made me feel welcome. ____nice____

Vocabulary Power   Unit 6 • Chapter 33   99

Self-Initiated Writing

Provide students with the opportunity for self-initiated writing by asking them to think about how their earlier work might be improved by additional elaboration. Students may wish to revise a piece of writing from their portfolio, adding figurative language and exact words to improve the clarity and to add interest to their descriptions.

Looking at Fine Art

VIEWING

In a character study, a writer uses words to describe someone. An artist may draw or paint a picture to show what a person looks like. Details in the drawing or painting can help you understand the subject's personality, too.

Look at this painting. It is called *Woman with a Cat.* It was painted by a famous artist named Pierre-Auguste Renoir.

YOUR TURN

Discuss *Woman with a Cat* in a group with two or three classmates. Talk about these questions:

- Why do you think the artist decided to include the cat in this picture?
- What can you tell about the woman from the way she holds the cat?
- What other details do you notice in this painting?
- How can you describe the woman in words? Use exact words and examples of figurative language.
- How else could the artist have shown you the kind of person this woman was?

Detail, National Gallery of Art, Washington, Gift of Mr. and Mrs. Benjamin E. Levy

405

Evaluation Criteria

. . . .

SELF-EVALUATION Revisit the Evaluation Criteria to have students informally rate their own writing on a scale of 1 to 4. You might have them use stick-on notes to label their papers. Have students review a collection of their written work to monitor their growth as writers.

VIEWING

Looking at Fine Art

OBJECTIVES

- To understand how pieces of fine art can include descriptive details
- To discuss a work of art with classmates, focusing on artistic details

DAILY LANGUAGE PRACTICE

TRANSPARENCY 76

1 My aunt also enjoys painting drawing and working with clay. (painting, drawing,)

2 she give me a art lesson last saturday (She gave; an; Saturday.)

ORAL WARM-UP

USE PRIOR KNOWLEDGE How do painters create character studies? How does an artist show a subject's personality?

TEACH/MODEL

Remind students that people often have different feelings about a piece of art and that when evaluating a painting, it is important to use details to support opinions.

Have students work in small groups to complete the Your Turn questions. Ask them to use details to support their opinions. Then have students share their answers in a class discussion. To expand the lesson, have students choose a subject and draw a portrait. They may use the subject of their character study, or they may draw a different person, including themselves. Remind students to try to show what the person in the portrait is like.

WRAP-UP/ASSESS

SUMMARIZE How are writers and artists similar? How are they different?

LESSON ORGANIZER	DAY 1	DAY 2
DAILY LANGUAGE PRACTICE TRANSPARENCIES 77, 78	**1.** Yes I am visiting the science museum with she. (Yes,; her) **2.** We will learn about energy gravity and the solar system. (energy, gravity,) **Bridge to Writing** The museum (verb) many displays.	**1.** Anne asked, Isn't it hot today? ("Isn't; today?") **2.** "I don't think it's to hot," replied her sister. (too) **Bridge to Writing** Anne learned about the sun from (proper noun).
ORAL WARM-UP Listening/Speaking	Identify Sentence Differences 406	Form a Quotation 408 *Grammar Jingles*™ CD Track 23
TEACH/MODEL GRAMMAR **KEY** ✔ = tested skill	✔ **DIRECT QUOTATIONS** 406–407 • To identify direct quotations and to correctly use quotation marks • To create a comic strip and to write dialogue using quotation marks	✔ **MORE ABOUT QUOTATION MARKS** 408–409 • To recognize and use correct punctuation and capitalization in direct quotations • To discuss stories and write direct quotes
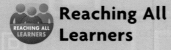 **Reaching All Learners**	**Modified Instruction** Below-Level: Identify Speaker and Quotation Above-Level: Write Sentences **Reteach:** *Reteach Activities Copying Masters* pp. 67 and R60 **Challenge:** Activity Card 23, R73 *ESL Manual* pp. 162, 163 *Practice Book* p. 111	**Modified Instruction** Below-Level: Punctuate Quotes Above-Level: Write Original Sentences **ESL:** Whispered Laughs 408 *ESL Manual* pp. 162, 164 **Reteach:** *Reteach Activities Copying Masters* pp. 68 and R60 **Challenge:** Character Chatter 409 *Practice Book* p. 112
WRITING	Writing Connection 407 Real-Life Writing: Comic Strip	Writing Connection 409 Writer's Journal: Recording Ideas
CROSS-CURRICULAR/ ENRICHMENT	*Vocabulary Power* Explore Word Meaning 406 calorie, **energy**, zeal, fatigue, watt See *Vocabulary Power* book.	*Vocabulary Power* Analogies 406 *Vocabulary Power* p. 100 🏆 **Vocabulary activity**

DAY 3

1. "Is that they're shadow," Fred asked. (their shadow?")

2. Emily answered "no its our shadow." (answered, "No, it's)

Bridge to Writing Shadows
<u>(complete predicate)</u> .

Add Correct Punctuation 410
 Grammar Jingles™ CD Track 23

✔ **PUNCTUATING DIALOGUE**
   410–411
   • To identify the speaker and to correct capitalization and punctuation errors in dialogue
   • To write and correctly punctuate a dialogue between two people

Modified Instruction
Below-Level: Recognize Quotations
Above-Level: Add Dialogue
            Sentences
Reteach: *Reteach Activities Copying Masters* pp. 69 and R60
Challenge: Drama quotes 411
ESL Manual pp. 162, 165
Practice Book p. 113

Writing Connection 411
   Technology

Listening and Speaking: Stellar
   Answers 410

Vocabulary Power
   Classify and Categorize 406
   Vocabulary Power p. 101
💻 **Vocabulary activity**

DAY 4

1. Did your mother study astronomy Mohmar asked? ("Did; astronomy?" asked.)

2. "Yes," Sue replied, "She did." ("she)

Bridge to Writing Mom
<u>(past-tense verb)</u> about stars, planets, and asteroids.

Write a Quotation 412

EXTRA PRACTICE 412–413
   • To recognize and use correct punctuation and capitalization in direct quotations
   • To write using time-order words correctly in a dialogue
💻 **Practice and assessment**

Building Oral Grammar
Read and Listen to Dialogue 413
ESL: Space Stumpers 412
ESL Manual pp. 162, 166
Challenge: Quotation Jumble 413
Practice Book p. 114

Writing Connection 413
   Writer's Craft: Time-Order Words

Vocabulary Power
   Antonyms and Synonyms 406
   Vocabulary Power p. 102
 Vocabulary activity

DAY 5

1. Jupiter is the largest planet, Ellen reported. ("Jupiter; planet,")

2. She added that It has a big red spot on it." (it; it.)

Bridge to Writing Though it looks like a spot to <u>(object pronoun)</u> , it is actually a <u>(adjective)</u> storm.

TEST PREP **CHAPTER REVIEW** 414
   • To review proper usage of punctuation in dialogue
   • To use effective test-taking strategies
💻 **Test preparation**

Challenge: Posters of Advice
   415
Practice Book p. 115
ESL Manual p. 162, 167

Writer's Journal Writing Application 415
   Explain Test-Taking Strategy

Study Skills: Test-Taking
   Strategies 415

Vocabulary Power
   Exemplification 406

Direct Quotations

OBJECTIVES
• To identify direct quotations and to correctly use quotation marks in direct quotations
• To create a comic strip and to write dialogue using quotation marks

DAILY LANGUAGE PRACTICE

TRANSPARENCY 77

1 Yes I am visiting the science museum with she. (Yes,; her.)

2 We will learn about energy gravity and the solar system. (energy, gravity,)

BRIDGE TO WRITING The museum (verb) many displays.

ORAL WARM-UP

USE PRIOR KNOWLEDGE Write these two sentences on the board: *Gabriela said that we will study about energy in science class. Gabriela said, "We will study about energy in science class."* Ask students to identify the differences between these two sentences.

TEACH/MODEL

Have a volunteer read aloud the text at the top of page 406. Tell students that quotation marks represent a frame. The exact words a person says go inside the frame to make the sentence complete. When the word *that* is used in the sentence, it is probably not a direct quotation. Model the first example:

MODEL I see the words *Maria said,* so I know that the rest of the sentence tells her exact words. Also, I see quotation marks, so I know that the sentence is a direct quotation.

Complete the Guided Practice with students.

Direct Quotations

Someone's exact words are called a **direct quotation.**

Use quotation marks (" ") to show the exact words of a speaker. Quotation marks should be placed around all of the speaker's words.

Examples:

Maria said, "I found out what causes heat."

"It has to do with energy," she explained.

"Everything is made of matter," she added.

Guided Practice

A. Tell whether or not each sentence has a direct quotation.

Example: "Matter is made of particles," Maria told us.
   direct quotation

1. She added that it takes energy for the particles to move. no direct quotation
2. Kareem stated, "The particles move all the time." direct quotation
3. "When something is hot, it has a lot of energy," Marsha said. direct quotation
4. She explained that the hotter something is, the faster its particles are moving. no direct quotation
5. "Do particles in my soup move faster than particles in my sandwich?" Robert asked. direct quotation

---

Vocabulary Power

en•er•gy
[en′ər•jē] *n.* The ability to do work or give power; usable electric or heat power.

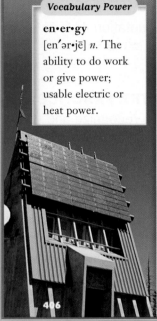

406

Vocabulary Power

DAY 1 EXPLORE WORD MEANING Introduce and define *energy.* **How can you tell if something has heat *energy?***

DAY 2 ANALOGIES **Write a word to complete the following: *Energy* is to *fatigue* as *active* is to _____ .** (See also *Vocabulary Power,* page 100.)

DAY 3 CLASSIFY AND CATEGORIZE Write on the board: *thermometer, heat, chair, energy.* **Which of these words does not belong in this group? Why?** (See also *Vocabulary Power,* page 101.)

DAY 4 ANTONYMS AND SYNONYMS **What is an antonym for *energy?*** (See also *Vocabulary Power,* page 102.)

DAY 5 EXEMPLIFICATION **Make a list of things in your house that use *energy.***

Independent Practice

B. Write the sentences. Put quotation marks where they are needed.

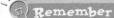

Remember to put quotation marks around direct quotations.

Example: Today we are going to learn about thermometers, Ms. Jefferson said.

"Today we are going to learn about thermometers," Ms. Jefferson said.

6. She said, A thermometer measures heat.
   She said, "A thermometer measures heat."

7. Most thermometers are tubes with special liquid, she explained.
   "Most thermometers are tubes with special liquid," she explained.

8. What do thermometers do? Joseph asked.
   "What do thermometers do?" Joseph asked.

9. The teacher told him, A thermometer can tell us what the temperature is outside.
   The teacher told him, "A thermometer can tell us what the temperature is outside."

10. She added, It can also tell us how warm it is inside.
    She added, "It can also tell us how warm it is inside."

11. Thermometers have numbers printed on them, Ms. Jefferson explained.
    "Thermometers have numbers printed on them," Ms. Jefferson explained.

12. She told us, The numbers show the temperature.
    She told us, "The numbers show the temperature."

13. Lydia said, Water boils at 100° Celsius.
    Lydia said, "Water boils at 100° Celsius."

14. That is right! Ms. Jefferson exclaimed.
    "That is right!" Ms. Jefferson exclaimed.

15. She asked, Did you know that paper burns at 184° Celsius?
    She asked, "Did you know that paper burns at 184° Celsius?"

Writing Connection

Real-Life Writing: Comic Strip With a partner, create a comic strip that shows how people are affected by hot and cold temperatures. Put your characters' words in quotation marks to show exactly what they are saying.

407

Independent Practice

Have students complete the Independent Practice, or modify it using these suggestions:

MODIFIED INSTRUCTION

BELOW-LEVEL STUDENTS For Part B, have students find the word group that identifies the speaker and how the quote is said. Then have them place quotation marks at the beginning and end of the speaker's exact words. Advise students to read the quote aloud to double-check that they've placed the quotation marks correctly.

ABOVE-LEVEL STUDENTS Have students rewrite items 6 and 7 so that they are no longer direct quotations.

Writing Connection

Real-Life Writing: Comic Strip Tell students to use the correct capitalization when using quotation marks.

WRAP-UP/ASSESS

SUMMARIZE Ask students to explain how they can identify a direct quotation while reading.

RETEACH

INTERVENTION Lessons in **visual, auditory,** and **kinesthetic** modalities: p. R60 and *Reteach Activities Copying Masters,* p. 67.

PRACTICE page 111

Name _____

Using Quotation Marks in Direct Quotations

A. Add quotation marks to each direct quotation.

1. "Are you ready for school?" asked Cara.
2. "I'm almost ready," answered her sister Lila.
3. "Will you drive us to school?" Lila asked her mother.
4. "I think we should walk," said Cara.
5. She explained, "We will get some exercise and save fuel."

B. Write each sentence. Place quotation marks where they are needed.

6. Let us talk about some ways to save energy, Mr. Woods said to the class. "Let us talk about some ways to save energy," Mr. Woods said to the class.

7. He went on, What can you do at your age? He went on, "What can you do at your age?"

8. I walk instead of having my mother drive me, said Liz. "I walk instead of having my mother drive me," said Liz.

9. Ken said, I hope you walk in safe places. Ken said, "I hope you walk in safe places."

10. I am always careful about that, said Liz. "I am always careful about that," said Liz.

TRY THIS! Suppose you could interview an energy expert. Write three direct questions you would ask.

Practice • Quotation Marks   Unit 6 • Chapter 34   111

CHALLENGE

CLEAR SCIENCE Have students use **Challenge Activity Card 23** (page R73) to illustrate a science concept from this lesson.

Challenge Activity Card 23

Clear Science

Think about the science discussed in this lesson's exercises. Make up a poster using a character of your choice to clearly illustrate the concept. Follow these steps:

• Choose a direct quotation from the Guided Practice or Independent Practice Exercises.
• Make up a character.
• Draw a picture of your character.
• The direct quotation should be the caption for your picture. Change the speaker's name to your character's name.
• Share your poster with the class.

Using Quotation Marks in Direct Quotations

Read each sentence. Add quotation marks if they are needed. Put a check mark after each sentence that does not have a direct quotation.

Gillian asked, "Doesn't it ever snow here?"

She explained that it snowed every winter in her hometown. ✓

"I'm used to long, cold winters," she told us.

"Do you get to ski and ice skate?" Tamara asked.

Using Quotation Marks in Direct Quotations

In a book you are reading, find three sentences that have direct quotations. Read each sentence out loud to the rest of your group. Listen to the sentences read by other group members. After each sentence, answer these questions:

> Which words tell who is talking?
> Which words tell the words that person is saying?
> Where should quotation marks be used?

Using Quotation Marks in Direct Quotations

With a partner, choose a short section of a story you have read. Pick a section that has two or more direct quotations.

First, read that story section aloud to the rest of your group. Then act that story section out. As you act, say only the words that are direct quotations in your story.

Teacher: Cut apart the activities and distribute to students based on the modalities that are their strengths.
(Visual) Write the activity sentences on the board and have volunteers use colored chalk to add the missing quotation marks.
(Auditory) Encourage students to select short sentences, preferably from their free-reading books.
(Kinesthetic) Have the "audience" members of each group check to be sure students speak only the words that are direct quotations.

Reteach Activities • Using Quotation Marks in Direct Quotations   Unit 6 • Chapter 34 67

More About
Quotation Marks

OBJECTIVES

- To recognize and use correct punctuation and capitalization in direct quotations
- To discuss stories with a partner and write direct quotes from the conversation

DAILY LANGUAGE PRACTICE

TRANSPARENCY 77

❶ Anne asked, Isn't it hot today? ("Isn't; today?")

❷ "I don't think it's to hot," replied her sister. (too)

BRIDGE TO WRITING Anne learned about the sun from ___(proper noun)___ .

ORAL WARM-UP

USE PRIOR KNOWLEDGE Read aloud: **Our teacher said that we will visit the science museum.** Have students reword the sentence to form a direct quotation.

Grammar Jingles™ **CD, Intermediate** Use Track 23 for review and reinforcement of quotation marks.

TEACH/MODEL

Have a volunteer read aloud the top of page 408. Tell students that the first word in a quotation begins with a capital letter. Model the Guided Practice example:

MODEL The sentence ends with the word group *Mr. Nadal said,* which means he made a statement. So, I know that the words inside the quotation marks are a direct quotation. There should be a comma right before the closing quotation marks. To fix the error, I need to add a comma between the word *energy* and the closing quotation marks.

Work with students to complete the Guided Practice.

More About
Quotation Marks

When using quotation marks, you must be sure to use correct punctuation and capitalization.

Use a comma (,) to separate a speaker's words from the other words in a sentence. Capitalize the first word of a quotation.

Examples:

"The sun provides much of Earth's energy," our teacher said.

She explained, "Earth has lots of energy."

Put the end mark inside the second set of quotation marks. Do not use a comma when there is an exclamation point or a question mark.

Examples:

"The sun provides heat," she added.

"The sun is stronger than a heater!" exclaimed Todd.

Guided Practice

A. Tell how you would fix the punctuation or capitalization mistake in each sentence.

Example: "Light is a kind of energy" Mr. Nadal said.
"Light is a kind of energy," Mr. Nadal said.

1. "Light gives things their colors" he said.
   things their colors," he said.
2. "Wow, that's neat" Thomas shouted loudly.
   neat!" Thomas shouted
3. "what do you see in a mirror?" Mr. Nadal asked. "What
4. Jesse answered "I see myself." answered, "I see
5. "Your reflection is light bouncing off the mirror, he said. mirror," he said.

408

Vocabulary Power page 100

ANALOGIES

In an analogy, two pairs of words are related in the same way.

Example:
Eyes are to *see* as *ears* are to *hear.*

Complete each analogy. The first one is done for you. Responses may vary slightly. Possible responses are given.

1. *Tranquil* is to *blustery* as *fatigue* is to ___zeal___
2. *Active* is to *inactive* as *lost* is to ___found___
3. *Visor* is to *cap* as *collar* is to ___shirt___
4. *Plate* is to *food* as *cup* is to ___beverage___
5. *Shimmer* is to *star* as *glimmer* is to ___candle___
6. *Calorie* is to *food* as *watt* is to ___electricity___
7. *Running* is to *track* as *swimming* is to ___pool___
8. *Mineralogist* is to *minerals* as *herpetologist* is to ___reptiles___
9. *Nose* is to *smell* as *eyes* are to ___see___
10. *Mittens* are to *hands* as *socks* are to ___feet___
11. *Fork* is to *eating* as *pencil* is to ___writing___
12. *Fur* is to *cat* as *scale* is to ___fish___
13. *Food* is to *a person* as *gasoline* is to a ___car___
14. An *instrument* is to *a musician* as *a saw* is to a ___carpenter___
15. The *President* is to *the country* as *the mayor* is to the ___city___

100 Unit 6 • Chapter 34   Vocabulary Power

ESL

WHISPERED LAUGHS Work with students to brainstorm a list of action verbs that describe how a quote is said. The list should include verbs that can be used with statements, questions, exclamations, and commands. Have students write direct quotations using the verbs from the list. Then have them read aloud their quotations, using the correct inflection for each sentence type.

Independent Practice

B. Each sentence has one or more mistakes in capitalization or punctuation. Write the sentence, correcting the mistake.

Example: Callie said, "Earth spins around like a top.
Callie said, "Earth spins around like a top."

6. "Earth's movement is called rotation" she said.
   rotation," she said.
7. Jerome added, "Earth rotates once each day"
   each day."
8. "do you know why we have light in the daytime?" Callie asked. *"Do*
9. "I do! I do" Francesca shouted. *I do!" Francesca*
10. She explained, It is daytime when our part of Earth faces the sun." *She explained, "It is*
11. He asked, "how can it be day here and night somewhere else" *He asked, "How; somewhere else?"*
12. Callie explained As Earth rotates, one part of Earth is facing the sun and one isn't" *explained, "As; one isn't."*
13. "it's daytime on the part of Earth that is facing the sun, she noted. *"It's daytime; the sun," she noted.*
14. She added "It is night on the side of Earth that is facing away from the sun. *She added, "It is; the sun."*
15. I get it! Warren cried. *"I get it!" Warren cried.*

409

Writing Connection

Writer's Journal: Recording Ideas
Talk to a partner about why stories that take place at night can be scary. Are stories that are set during the day always happy stories? Write three sentences about what you and your partner discuss. Use quotation marks to include the exact words you and your partner say.

Independent Practice

Have students complete the Independent Practice, or modify it using these suggestions:

MODIFIED INSTRUCTION

BELOW-LEVEL STUDENTS Tell students to treat the direct quote as a separate sentence with a capital letter and end punctuation. Remind them that if the quote comes at the beginning of a sentence and ends in a period, the period becomes a comma. If the quote comes at the end of a sentence, then a comma is placed after the last word before the quote.

ABOVE-LEVEL STUDENTS Have students write three sentences with direct quotes that might follow the sentences in Part B.

Writing Connection

Writer's Journal: Recording Ideas
Suggest that students take notes during their conversation and ask their partner to pause so that they can write down his or her exact words.

WRAP-UP/ASSESS

SUMMARIZE Ask: **Where do you place the punctuation in a sentence containing a quotation?**

REACHING ALL LEARNERS — RETEACH

INTERVENTION Lessons in **visual, auditory,** and **kinesthetic** modalities: p. R60 and *Reteach Activities Copying Masters,* p. 68.

REACHING ALL LEARNERS — PRACTICE page 112

Name _____

More About Quotation Marks

A. Each sentence has one or more mistakes in punctuation or capitalization. Edit each sentence, using the correct punctuation and capitalization.

1. "Do we use much energy heating the house" asked Bruce. *?*
2. Ms. Pats answered, "yes, and we use quite a bit cooling it."
3. "What can we do about it?" Asked Amy.
4. Bruce said, "I keep the doors closed when the heat is on."
5. He went on, "keep them closed when the air conditioner is on, too."

B. Write each sentence. Correct punctuation or capitalization mistakes. If a sentence has no mistake, write *Correct.*

6. "Where should I park the car," asked Mr. Villa.
   "Where should I park the car?" asked Mr. Villa.
7. Park it in the shade, said Jaime.
   "Park it in the shade," said Jaime.
8. Jaime explained, "That way the car will not heat up in the sun.
   Jaime explained, "That way the car will not heat up in the sun."
9. He finished, "Then we will not need to turn on the air conditioner." Correct
10. "Wow, what a great idea" exclaimed his father.
    "Wow, what a great idea!" exclaimed his father.

TRY THIS! Write a conversation between you and your friends about saving energy. Use quotation marks, where necessary.

112 Unit 6 • Chapter 34   Practice • Quotation Marks

REACHING ALL LEARNERS — CHALLENGE

CHARACTER CHATTER Have each student choose a character from a popular book or TV show. Then have students work in pairs to write a conversation between the two characters. One partner should begin by writing a direct quotation. The other partner should then write a response. The written conversation should continue in this way until each partner has had a chance to write at least three direct quotes for his or her character.

More About Quotation Marks

Read each sentence. Add quotation marks and commas. Underline words that should begin with a capital letter.

"Look at the moon," said Gabe.

"isn't it beautiful" said Nolani.

Brad asked, "why is it so bright tonight?"

"the moon reflects light from the sun," added Nolani.

Visual

More About Quotation Marks

Write three sentences that have direct quotations. Read your sentences out loud to the other members of your group.

Listen to each sentence the other members of your group read. Stand up when you hear a word that begins with a capital letter. Clap when there should be a comma in the sentence. Raise both hands when a direct quotation begins. Put both hands down again when a direct quotation ends.

Auditory

More About Quotation Marks

On separate strips of paper, write four sentences with direct quotations. Leave out commas, quotation marks, and end marks.

Then make six small punctuation cards. Write quotation marks on two cards. On each of the other cards, write a comma, a period, a question mark, and an exclamation point.

Mix the group's strips together. Take turns picking a sentence. Use your small cards to add the correct punctuation to the sentence.

Kinesthetic

Teacher: Cut apart the activities and distribute to students based on the modalities that are their strengths.
(Visual) Write the activity sentences on the board and let students use colored chalk to make corrections.
(Auditory) Have students work in groups of four or five.
(Kinesthetic) Have group members check each other's sentences.

68 Unit 6 • Chapter 34   Reteach Activities • Quotation Marks

USAGE AND MECHANICS
Punctuating Dialogue

OBJECTIVES
- To identify the speaker and to correct capitalization and punctuation errors in dialogue
- To write and correctly punctuate a dialogue between two people

DAILY LANGUAGE PRACTICE
TRANSPARENCY 77

1 "Is that they're shadow," Fred asked.
(their shadow?")

2 Emily answered "no its our shadow."
(answered, "No, it's)

BRIDGE TO WRITING Shadows
(complete predicate) .

ORAL WARM-UP

USE PRIOR KNOWLEDGE Write these sentences on the board: *Murray said I want to make shadows. We can use my mom's flashlight I replied.* Have volunteers add correct punctuation marks.

Grammar Jingles™ **CD, Intermediate** Use Track 23 for review and reinforcement of quotation marks.

TEACH/MODEL

Have a volunteer read aloud the top of page 410. For each example, point out the speaker, the verb that tells how the speaker says the words, and the capitalization and punctuation. Model the Guided Practice example:

MODEL I see two word groups set off by quotation marks. These are the exact words the speaker says. The words *Marc told us* name the speaker and tell how he said the words.

Complete the Guided Practice with students. Have them explain the punctuation marks.

410

USAGE AND MECHANICS
Punctuating Dialogue

Dialogue is conversation between two or more speakers.

Dialogue uses direct quotations to show a person's exact words. Dialogue also uses a noun or a pronoun with words such as *said, replied, asked, added,* and *shouted* to tell who the speaker is.

Example:
"I love early mornings!" exclaimed Ellen.

When the part of the dialogue that identifies the speaker divides a direct quotation, you need two commas.

Examples:
"I know," explained Marc, "that Earth circles the sun."

"I love learning about science," he said, "because you can see it all around you."

Guided Practice

A. In each sentence, identify the words that tell who is speaking and how you know.

Example: "Each circle around the sun," Marc told us, "is called a revolution." *Marc told us*

1. "How does that relate to the seasons?" asked Paula. *asked Paula*
2. "It's very interesting!" Marc exclaimed. *Marc exclaimed*
3. He continued, "Each revolution around the sun takes one year." *He continued*
4. Sam added, "Earth also tilts." *Sam added*
5. "You are right," Marc said with a smile. *Marc said with a smile*

Vocabulary Power page 101

Name _____

CLASSIFY/CATEGORIZE

Read each group of words below. Circle the letter of the word that does not belong in each group. Then add a category name for each group. Possible responses are given.

1. A rotating
   B talking
   C spinning
   D revolving
   circular motions

2. F morning
   G night
   H afternoon
   J winter
   times of day

3. A calorie
   B watt
   C volt
   D thermometer
   units for measuring energy

4. F spring
   G summer
   H noon
   J fall
   seasons

5. **A** sleeping
   B swimming
   C jogging
   D dancing
   kinds of exercise

6. **F** diamond
   G gold
   H silver
   J bracelet
   kinds of minerals

7. **A** ice
   B sun
   C oven
   D fire
   things that are hot

8. F Washington
   G China
   H Idaho
   J Virginia
   states

9. A pony
   B donkey
   C wolf
   D horse
   equines

10. **F** flame
    G icicle
    H snow
    J glacier
    things that are cold

Vocabulary Power
Unit 6 • Chapter 34 101

Listening and Speaking

STELLAR ANSWERS Have each student write three questions about the solar system. Then have students work in small groups. Tell students to ask group members the questions they have written. Then have each student write sentences using direct quotations from group members' answers. Tell students to use the correct capitalization in their direct quotations.

Independent Practice

B. Identify the speaker in each sentence.

Example: "What causes shadows?" asked Melanie.
Melanie

6. "Yes," said Paul, "sunlight causes shadows." Paul

7. He added, "In the morning, trees cast long shadows." Paul

8. "As Earth rotates, the shadows grow shorter," Juanita said. Juanita

9. Kim replied, "At noon, the shadows are short." Kim

10. "Later in the day," he went on, "the shadows grow longer again." Kim

C. Each sentence contains errors in capitalization or punctuation. Write each sentence, correcting the errors.

Example: How many seasons are there?" Jon asked.
"How many seasons are there?" Jon asked.

11. There are four seasons," Claire answered. "There are

12. "My favorite season" Joy shouted, "is spring" season,"; "is spring!"

13. "How do the seasons change" asked Pierre. change?"

14. "The seasons change, explained Tim, "because Earth spins and tilts on an axis." change,"

15. I said, "It is warm when Earth tilts toward the sun. sun."

411

Writing Connection

Technology Work with a partner to write a dialogue between two people discussing the seasons. Write your sentences on a computer or on paper. Use correct capitalization and punctuation in your quotations.

Remember to use quotation marks when you are writing dialogue. Use a comma to separate a direct quotation from the words that tell who is speaking.

Independent Practice

Have students complete the Independent Practice, or modify it using these suggestions:

MODIFIED INSTRUCTION

BELOW-LEVEL STUDENTS Tell students that when a quote is broken into two parts, they can treat the second part of the quote as a continuation of the first. Unless the second part is the start of a new sentence, it doesn't need to be capitalized. Also, both parts of the quote must be set off by quotation marks.

ABOVE-LEVEL STUDENTS Have students add three sentences to continue the dialogue in Part C.

Writing Connection

Technology As students are working with their partners, have them read their dialogues aloud. Tell students that hearing the conversations will help them create more interesting, realistic dialogues.

WRAP-UP/ASSESS

SUMMARIZE Ask students how to punctuate a sentence in which the direct quote is interrupted by a word group identifying the speaker.

REACHING ALL LEARNERS

RETEACH

INTERVENTION Lessons in **visual, auditory,** and **kinesthetic** modalities: p. R60 and *Reteach Activities Copying Masters*, p. 69.

REACHING ALL LEARNERS

PRACTICE page 113

Name _____

Punctuating Dialogue

~ = add text
≡ = capitalize
/ = lowercase

A. Each sentence has a mistake in punctuation. Correct the punctuation, using editing marks from the chart.

1. "Dad," said Todd, "how can we save more energy at home?"

2. "Well," said his father, "we use a lot of energy heating water."

3. "How can we help," asked Jess.

4. "turn off the water when you soap your hands," said Todd.

5. Amy said, "What a good idea?"

B. Each sentence may have a mistake in punctuation. Rewrite each sentence, and correct each mistake. If a sentence has no mistake, write *Correct.*

6. It will be hot on the hike," Marge warned.
"It will be hot on the hike," Marge warned.

7. "How will we keep our cans of juice cold," she asked.
"How will we keep our cans of juice cold?" she asked.

8. "Well, Charles said, we can freeze the cans."
"Well," Charles said, "we can freeze the cans."

9. "Then," he added, "we can wrap them in two layers of foil."
Correct

10. "You are so smart"! cried Marge.
"You are so smart!" cried Marge.

TRY THIS! Write a conversation between two people who want to stay cool on a summer hike. Use quotation marks.

Practice • Quotation Marks   Unit 6 • Chapter 34   113

REACHING ALL LEARNERS

CHALLENGE

DRAMA QUOTES Provide small groups of students with copies of a page from a short play. The groups should have the same number of members as there are characters speaking on the page you provide. Have group members rewrite their page as a conversation with quotation marks. Have each group read its rewritten dialogue aloud.

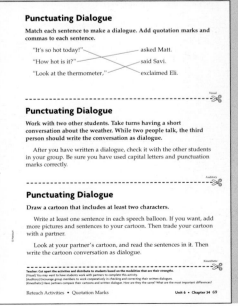

Punctuating Dialogue

Match each sentence to make a dialogue. Add quotation marks and commas to each sentence.

"It's so hot today!"   asked Matt.
"How hot is it?"   said Savi.
"Look at the thermometer,"   exclaimed Eli.

Visual

Punctuating Dialogue

Work with two other students. Take turns having a short conversation about the weather. While two people talk, the third person should write the conversation as dialogue.

After you have written a dialogue, check it with the other students in your group. Be sure you have used capital letters and punctuation marks correctly.

Auditory

Punctuating Dialogue

Draw a cartoon that includes at least two characters.

Write at least one sentence in each speech balloon. If you want, add more pictures and sentences to your cartoon. Then trade your cartoon with a partner.

Look at your partner's cartoon, and read the sentences in it. Then write the cartoon conversation as dialogue.

Kinesthetic

Teacher: Cut apart the activities and distribute to students based on the modalities that are their strengths.
(Visual) You may want to have students work with partners to complete this activity.
(Auditory) Encourage group members to work cooperatively in checking and correcting their written dialogues.
(Kinesthetic) Have partners compare their cartoons and written dialogue. How are they the same? What are the most important differences?

Reteach Activities • Quotation Marks   Unit 6 • Chapter 34 69

Extra Practice

OBJECTIVES
- To recognize and use correct punctuation and capitalization in direct quotations
- To write a dialogue using time-order words correctly

DAILY LANGUAGE PRACTICE

TRANSPARENCY 78

❶ Did your mother study astronomy Mohmar asked? ("Did; astronomy?"; asked.)

❷ "Yes," Sue replied, "She did." ("she)

BRIDGE TO WRITING Mom ___(past-tense verb)___ about stars, planets, and asteroids.

ORAL WARM-UP

USE PRIOR KNOWLEDGE Ask a volunteer to correctly write on the board a quotation which is interrupted by a word group that identifies the speaker.

TEACH/MODEL

Use the Remember box to review the use of quotation marks. Have students complete the Extra Practice independently.

Remember to use quotation marks to show a speaker's exact words. Be careful to use correct capitalization and punctuation with quotation marks.

For more activities about quotation marks and punctuation, visit *The Learning Site:* www.harcourtschool.com

412

Extra Practice

A. Write each sentence. Add quotation marks where they are needed. *pages 406–407*

Example: Eliza told us, The sun's energy can change the air pressure on Earth.
Eliza told us, "The sun's energy can change the air pressure on Earth."

1. That change in air pressure causes storms, she went on. "That; storms,"
2. Do you mean storms can be caused by the sun? Alex asked. "Do; sun?"
3. Yes, and so was last month's snow, Eliza told him. "Yes,; snow,"
4. She explained, Some of the sun's energy isn't good for us. explained, "Some; us."
5. The sun's rays can give you a sunburn, she said. "The; sunburn,"

B. Each sentence contains mistakes in punctuation or capitalization. Write each sentence, correcting the errors. *pages 406–411*

Example: Channa said "The center of the sun is called the core.
Channa said , "The center of the sun is called the core."

6. "The core is small compared with the size of the sun, she told us. the sun," she told us.
7. Do you know how hot it is" she asked. "Do; it is?"
8. She said it is about 27 million degrees!" said, "It is
9. "that's hot Frank shouted. "That's hot!" Frank shouted.
10. Channa said, it is the hottest part of the sun" "It is; sun."

Vocabulary Power page 102

Name _____

ANTONYMS AND SYNONYMS

A. Read each word. Find its antonym in the Word Box and write it on the line. Then think of a synonym for the word and write it on the line. Synonyms may vary. Possible responses are given.

fatigue	boring	subtraction	lose	real-life	slow

	ANTONYM	SYNONYM
1. zeal	fatigue	enthusiasm
2. addition	subtraction	expansion
3. exciting	boring	interesting
4. discover	lose	find
5. fantasy	real-life	make-believe
6. rapid	slow	quick

B. Now try these.

lower	confuse	rough	cry	dislike	impolite

	ANTONYM	SYNONYM
7. laugh	cry	giggle
8. like	dislike	enjoy
9. raise	lower	elevate
10. smooth	rough	sleek
11. clarify	confuse	explain
12. considerate	impolite	polite

102 Unit 6 • Chapter 34   Vocabulary Power

REACHING ALL LEARNERS

ESL

SPACE STUMPERS Have students write a dialogue with three sentences in which the speakers describe something in our solar system without naming it. Then have them read the dialogue aloud to the class, and ask the class to guess what the student wrote about.

C. For each sentence, identify the words that tell who is speaking and how. *pages 410–411*

Example: Ishiro explained, "A sunspot is a cool spot on the sun."
Ishiro explained

11. "Because it is cooler, it looks darker," he said.
he said
12. Tony said, "There are many sunspots." *Tony said*
13. "Sometimes," Ishiro added, "a sunspot can cause a burst of energy." *Ishiro added*
14. "What is that energy called?" asked the teacher.
asked the teacher
15. "It is called a flare," the two boys said together.
the two boys said together

D. Write each sentence, correcting the errors.
pages 406–411

Example: "Many sunspots are larger than Earth" stated Ms. Smith.
"Many sunspots are larger than Earth," stated Ms. Smith.

16. "Did you know that a solar flare can cause wind on the sun" asked the teacher. *sun?" asked*
17. "The wind is a stream of particles, she said.
particles," she said.
18. "what happens then" asked Daniel. *"What; then?"*
19. "Then" the teacher told him, "the wind can reach Earth." *"Then," the teacher told him,*
20. She added, "This wind makes our radios sound funny" *sound funny."*

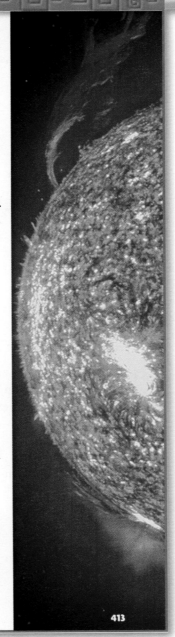
413

Writing Connection
Writer's Craft: Time-Order Words Write a dialogue between two students who are describing Earth's movement around the sun. Use time-order words such as *first, next, then,* and *finally.*

Building Oral Grammar
Have two volunteers read aloud the sentences from Extra Practice Part A. Have one volunteer read the part of Eliza and one read the part of Alex as if having a conversation. Tell them to follow the action verbs that tell how the sentences should be said. Discuss how this is different from quoting people during a conversation. Ask how speakers can let listeners know when they are using direct quotes in their speech. How can they let listeners know when the quote begins and ends?

Writing Connection
Writer's Craft: Time-Order Words Have students read their dialogues aloud. Ask them to use their voices to let listeners know when quotes begin and end and when the speaker changes.

WRAP-UP/ASSESS

SUMMARIZE Ask: **How can you identify direct quotations in speech?**

ADDITIONAL PRACTICE An additional page of Extra Practice is provided on page 476 of the *Pupil Edition.*

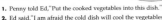
CHALLENGE

QUOTATION JUMBLE Have students write sentences containing quotations on strips, leaving space between each word and punctuation mark. Then have them cut their sentences apart, separating the words and the punctuation marks. Have students exchange their jumbled quotations and reconstruct the sentences correctly.

TECHNOLOGY *Grammar Practice and Assessment* CD-ROM; *Writing Express* CD-ROM

INTERNET Visit *The Learning Site:*
w w w . h a r c o u r t s c h o o l . c o m

Chapter Review

OBJECTIVES
- To review proper usage of punctuation in dialogue
- To use effective test-taking strategies

DAILY LANGUAGE PRACTICE

TRANSPARENCY 78

1 Jupiter is the largest planet, Ellen reported. ("Jupiter; planet,")

2 She added that It has a big red spot on it." (it; it.)

BRIDGE TO WRITING Though it looks like a spot to __(object pronoun)__ , it is actually a __(adjective)__ storm.

STANDARDIZED TEST PREP

MODEL TEST-TAKING STRATEGIES Have a volunteer read the directions on page 414 aloud. Write this example on the board and model the thinking:

(1) "You'll enjoy learning about energy" said Ms. Masterson.

    1   **A**   quotation mark

        B   comma

        C   question mark

        D   Correct as is

MODEL The word group, *said Ms. Masterson,* at the end of the sentence tells me that the words in the quotation marks are her exact words. There are already quotation marks at the beginning and at the end of what she says, so Choice A is not correct. Since she is not asking a question, Choice C is not correct. That leaves Choice B and Choice D. There should be a comma separating the exact words of the speaker from the rest of the sentence. So, the correct answer is B.

Have students complete the Chapter Review independently.

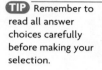

For additional test preparation, visit *The Learning Site:* www.harcourtschool.com

Chapter Review

Read the dialogue and decide which type of mistake, if any, appears in each line. Choose the letter that best describes the type of mistake, or choose *No mistake.*

> (1) "There are many ways to produce energy, said Ms. Masterson.
> (2) My sister, Kammy, sead, "One way is by burning fuel."
> (3) "that is right," said Ms. Masterson.
> (4) "But how do people use energy" I asked.
> (5) "Well" she answered, "we use energy to cook food."
> (6) "we also use energy to keep us warm," added Shirley.
> (7) "I think," she added, "that energy heats the water we use to wash our faces
> (8) "Wow!" exclaimed Ms. Masterson. "You reely do understand how energy works."

TIP Remember to read all answer choices carefully before making your selection.

1   **A** Spelling
    B Capitalization
    C Punctuation C
    D No mistake

2   **F** Spelling F
    G Capitalization
    H Punctuation
    J No mistake

3   **A** Spelling
    B Capitalization B
    C Punctuation
    D No mistake

4   **F** Spelling
    G Capitalization
    H Punctuation H
    J No mistake

5   **A** Spelling
    B Capitalization
    C Punctuation C
    D No mistake

6   **F** Spelling
    G Capitalization G
    H Punctuation
    J No mistake

7   **A** Spelling
    B Capitalization
    C Punctuation C
    D No mistake

8   **F** Spelling F
    G Capitalization
    H Punctuation
    J No mistake

414

Assessment

• •

PORTFOLIO ASSESSMENT Have students choose their best work from the Writing Connections on pages 407, 411, and 413.

ONGOING ASSESSMENT Evaluate the performance of 4–6 students using appropriate checklists and record forms from pages R74–R77.

INTERNET Activities and exercises to help students prepare for state and standardized assessments appear on *The Learning Site:*
www.harcourtschool.com

Test-Taking Strategies

You know that you must study before a test in order to do your best on it. There are also strategies you can use during a test that will help you. The chart below lists several test-taking strategies and how they can help you when taking a test. Have you used any of these strategies before?

Strategy	What It Does
Read directions and questions carefully.	It helps you understand exactly what to do on the test.
Look for key words in the directions.	It helps you quickly identify the type of question you must answer.
Budget your time.	It helps you finish the test on time.
Read all of the choices before you choose your answer.	It helps you choose the right answer.
Eliminate choices you know are wrong.	It helps you focus on the most likely choices.
Go back to make sure all questions are answered.	It keeps you from losing points for skipped questions.

YOUR TURN

Go back to the Chapter Review test on page 414. Using the test-taking strategies you've just learned, take the test again. Did the strategies help?

415

TEACH/MODEL

Ask volunteers to read on the chart each strategy and what it does. Discuss each strategy and its purpose. Tell students that test-taking can be simplified if they follow these steps each time they take a test. Not only will they perform better on their tests, but they will also be less nervous during the test. Ask students to suggest other test-taking strategies that they use.

WRITING APPLICATION Have each student pretend that he or she has a friend who is having difficulty taking tests. Have students use their journals to write a short letter to their friend explaining a test-taking strategy and the benefits of using it. Have volunteers read their letters aloud.

WRAP-UP/ASSESS

SUMMARIZE Ask: **What are some test-taking strategies not listed on page 415? What are the benefits of these strategies?**

PRACTICE page 115

Name _____

Chapter Review

Read the paragraph. Each sentence includes dialogue. Some sentences need punctuation marks. Choose the oval next to the correct punctuation mark that needs to be added, or choose *Correct as is*.

(1) "What we should do, said Joy, "is try some experiments." (2) "What experiments should we do," asked Miles. (3) "Well" said Joy, "we could put a can of juice in the stream." (4) "What do you think will happen?" asked Miles. (5) "I think, said Joy, "that the juice will get really cold." (6) "Let us put a can of juice in the hot sand," said Miles. (7) "We can leave the cans for an hour" said Joy. (8) She went on "Then we will use a thermometer to take the temperature of the juice in each can."

1. ◖ Quotation mark
   ○ Period
   ○ Comma
   ○ Correct as is

2. ○ Quotation mark
   ○ Period
   ◖ Question mark
   ○ Correct as is

3. ◖ Comma
   ○ Quotation mark
   ○ Period
   ○ Correct as is

4. ◖ Period
   ○ Quotation mark
   ○ Comma
   ◖ Correct as is

5. ○ Question mark
   ◖ Quotation mark
   ○ Period
   ○ Correct as is

6. ○ Quotation mark
   ○ Question mark
   ○ Period
   ◖ Correct as is

7. ○ Period
   ○ Quotation mark
   ◖ Comma
   ○ Correct as is

8. ◖ Comma
   ○ Period
   ○ Quotation mark
   ○ Correct as is

Practice • Quotation Marks   Unit 6 • Chapter 34   115

CHALLENGE

POSTERS OF ADVICE Have students record quotes on test-taking strategies from the discussion. Then have them create posters. The poster should include the quote and use color for emphasis. Display the posters in the classroom.

TECHNOLOGY Additional writing activities are provided on the *Writing Express* CD-ROM

LESSON ORGANIZER	DAY 1	DAY 2
DAILY LANGUAGE PRACTICE TRANSPARENCIES 79, 80	1. "I know," she said "that Isaac Newton discovered gravity. (said,; gravity.") 2. People buildings and the air itself are pulled by Earth's gravity. (People, buildings,) **Bridge to Writing** Have you ever <u>(main verb)</u> much about gravity?	1. A report in the Daily News told how wind water and ice wear away rock. (<u>Daily News</u>; wind, water,) 2. The <u>article</u> in the <u>Times</u> was about gravity on mars. (article; Mars) **Bridge to Writing** Our local newspaper, <u>(title of newspaper)</u>, reports new science discoveries.
ORAL WARM-UP **Listening/Speaking**	List Magazine Titles 416	Name Favorite Songs 418 *Grammar Jingles*™ CD Track 24
TEACH/MODEL **GRAMMAR** ┌─────────────┐ │ **KEY** │ │ ✔ = tested skill │ └─────────────┘	✔ **UNDERLINING TITLES** 416–417 • To correctly identify titles and underline them • To make a list and to write a paragraph, underlining titles	✔ **QUOTATION MARKS WITH TITLES** 418–419 • To identify and punctuate titles • To write titles
Reaching All Learners	**Modified Instruction** Below-Level: Look for Clue Words Above-Level: Write New Sentences **Reteach:** *Reteach Activities Copying Masters* pp. 70 and R61 **Challenge:** Activity Card 24, R73 *ESL Manual* pp. 168, 169 *Practice Book* p. 116	**Modified Instruction** Below-Level: Find Capitalized Words Above-Level: Move Titles **ESL:** Title Teams 418 *ESL Manual* pp. 168, 170 **Reteach:** *Reteach Activities Copying Masters* pp. 71 and R61 **Challenge:** More Than a Title 419 *Practice Book* p. 117
WRITING	Writing Connection 417 Science	Writing Connection 419 Writer's Journal: Story Titles
CROSS-CURRICULAR/ ENRICHMENT	*Vocabulary Power* Explore Word Meaning 416 ┌──────────────────────────────┐ │ impossible, **invisible**, irregular, possible, regular │ │ See *Vocabulary Power* book. │ └──────────────────────────────┘	*Vocabulary Power* Prefixes 416 *Vocabulary Power* p. 103 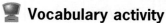 **Vocabulary activity**

WRITING ACTIVITIES
Writing Express CD-ROM

Visit *The Learning Site:*
www.harcourtschool.com

DAY 3

1. No I didn't know about the article (No,; article.)

2. The Big Pull is an article in Science Today magazine. ("The Big Pull"; Science Today)

Bridge to Writing The last (noun) I read, "Heavy Talk About Gravity," was very interesting.

Suggest Book Titles 420

Grammar Jingles™ CD Track 24

✔ **CAPITALIZING WORDS IN TITLES** 420–421
  • To capitalize titles correctly
  • To create an advertisement and to list magazines where it might appear

---

Modified Instruction
Below-Level: List Title Words
Above-Level: Write New Titles
ESL: Title Trade 420
ESL Manual pp. 168, 171
Reteach: *Reteach Activities Copying Masters* pp. 72 and R61
Challenge: Card Catalog 421
Practice Book p. 118

Writing Connection 421
  Real-Life Writing: Advertisement

Vocabulary Power

Antonyms and Synonyms 416
Vocabulary Power p. 104

 Vocabulary activity

DAY 4

1. Sir Isaac Newton discovered gravity more than 300 year's ago. (years)

2. The book "newtons discovery" tells about his work. (Newton's Discovery)

Bridge to Writing (Title) sounds like another interesting book about science.

Compare Titles 422

EXTRA PRACTICE 422–423
  • To identify, punctuate, and capitalize titles correctly
  • To adapt an idea and write a title

Practice and assessment

Building Oral Grammar
Guess the Titles 423
Challenge: Title Types 423
ESL Manual pp. 168, 172
Practice Book p. 119

Writing Connection 423
  Writer's Craft: Choosing a Form

Hands-On: Title Scramble 422

Vocabulary Power

Word Families 416
Vocabulary Power p. 105

Vocabulary activity

DAY 5

1. Our teacher said "The strength of gravity is different on other planets." (said,)

2. The World encyclopedia of Science includes the article Gravity on Other planets. (The World Encyclopedia of Science; "Gravity on Other Planets.")

Bridge to Writing The planet Mars (predicate) . What a (adjective) time I would have if I (verb) there!

TEST PREP CHAPTER REVIEW 424–425
  • To review punctuation and capitalization in titles
  • To interpret the main idea and supporting details of a picture

Test preparation

Challenge: Happy Art 425
Practice Book p. 120
ESL Manual pp. 168, 173

Writer's Journal Writing Application 425
  Group Reactions

Viewing: Interpreting a Picture 425

Vocabulary Power

Explore Word Meaning 416

Underlining Titles

OBJECTIVES
• To correctly identify titles and underline them
• To make a list and to write a paragraph, underlining titles

DAILY LANGUAGE PRACTICE

TRANSPARENCY 79

① "I know," she said "that Isaac Newton discovered gravity. (said,; gravity.")

② People buildings and the air itself are pulled by Earth's gravity. (People, buildings,)

BRIDGE TO WRITING Have you ever __(main verb)__ much about gravity?

ORAL WARM-UP

USE PRIOR KNOWLEDGE Have students brainstorm a list of magazine titles as a group.

TEACH/MODEL

Read aloud the instructions at the top of page 416. Write on the board:

I lost Kim's recipes.

I lost Kim's Recipes.

Explain to students the differences between these two sentences. Use the examples to show students that the names of books, magazines, and newspapers are underlined in sentences. Point out that titles are capitalized. Model the thinking for the Guided Practice example:

MODEL The important words in *The Science Book of Forces* are capitalized. I see the word *Book*. So, *The Science Book of Forces* is the title of a book and needs to be underlined.

Complete the Guided Practice orally with students.

Vocabulary Power

in•vis•i•ble
[in•viz′ə•bəl] *adj.*
Not able to be seen.

416

Underlining Titles

A title is the name of something.

Underline the titles of books, magazines, and newspapers. Proper punctuation of titles keeps your readers from being confused.

Examples:

The book **Forces Around Us** says that a force is what pushes and pulls objects.

An article in **Science for Kids** magazine says force makes things speed up or slow down.

A report in **Science Times** newspaper describes gravity as an invisible force.

Guided Practice

A. Identify the title in each sentence. Name the words that should be underlined.

Example: The Science Book of Forces has a picture of someone hammering to show force.
The Science Book of Forces

1. Isabel Carillo wrote an article for Science Works magazine.
2. I read about muscle power in the book Forces, Forces, Forces.
3. An article in The Journal says that some forces can pull and push at the same time.
4. The book Moving talks about pushing and pulling in the game tug-of-war.
5. An article in Science Fun magazine says that force can stretch things into different shapes.

Vocabulary Power

DAY ① EXPLORE WORD MEANING Introduce and define *invisible*. **If something is invisible, which of your five senses can you use to figure out what it is?**

DAY ② PREFIXES **The prefix *in-* can mean "into" or "not." Which meaning do you think *in-* has in the word *invisible*?** (See also *Vocabulary Power*, page 103.)

DAY ③ ANTONYMS AND SYNONYMS **Antonyms are words with opposite meanings, such as *up* and *down*. What is an antonym for *invisible*?** (See also *Vocabulary Power*, page 104.)

DAY ④ WORD FAMILIES *Invisible* and many other words are based on the Latin root word *vis* or *vid*, which means "see." For example, a *visitor* comes to see you. (See also *Vocabulary Power*, page 105.)

DAY ⑤ EXPLORE WORD MEANING Write: **Is it always impossible to "see" something that is invisible?**

Independent Practice

B. Write each sentence. Underline the title of the book, magazine, or newspaper.

Example: Motion and Force discusses friction.

Motion and Force

Remember to underline the titles of books, magazines, and newspapers.

6. An article in <u>Science and Nature</u> explains that friction makes things slow down.

7. The newspaper <u>Elementary Science for Kids</u> says sports shoes create lots of friction.

8. The book <u>Motion Everywhere</u> shows how skates glide on ice.

9. The book <u>Push and Pull</u> says that air can also slow down objects.

10. <u>Young Scientist's Book of Motion</u> defines *drag* as the "force that slows things down."

11. The magazine <u>Experiment</u> shows you how to measure the force of your muscles.

12. <u>Pushing and Pulling</u> tells how to measure friction.

13. I read an article in <u>Bird Watcher</u> magazine.

14. An experiment in the book <u>Kitchen Science</u> shows that oil is more slippery than water.

15. A drawing in <u>Force and Motion</u> shows how force changes the shape of things.

Writing Connection

Science Think about how some of the machines in your house came to be invented. Choose three machines and write a letter to a friend including titles of imaginary books about each one.

Independent Practice

Have students complete the Independent Practice, or modify it using these suggestions:

MODIFIED INSTRUCTION

BELOW-LEVEL STUDENTS Have students look for clue words such as *book* or *magazine* that may be part of a title or indicate that a title follows. Remind them that titles are capitalized.

ABOVE-LEVEL STUDENTS After students have completed Part B, have them write new sentences using three of the titles.

Writing Connection

Science Ask a volunteer to name a chore that he or she doesn't like to do. Ask why he or she dislikes doing it. Tell students that their machines should make a task that they dislike easier or more enjoyable.

WRAP-UP/ASSESS

SUMMARIZE How do you write the name of a book, magazine, or newspaper in a sentence?

REACHING ALL LEARNERS — RETEACH

INTERVENTION Lessons in **visual, auditory,** and **kinesthetic** modalities: p. R61 and *Reteach Activities Copying Masters,* p. 70.

REACHING ALL LEARNERS — PRACTICE page 116

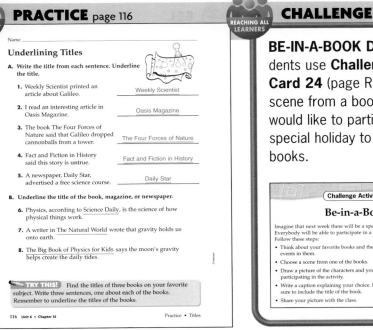

Name _____

Underlining Titles

A. Write the title from each sentence. Underline the title.

1. Weekly Scientist printed an article about Galileo. — *Weekly Scientist*

2. I read an interesting article in Oasis Magazine. — *Oasis Magazine*

3. The book The Four Forces of Nature said that Galileo dropped cannonballs from a tower. — *The Four Forces of Nature*

4. Fact and Fiction in History said this story is untrue. — *Fact and Fiction in History*

5. A newspaper, Daily Star, advertised a free science course. — *Daily Star*

B. Underline the title of the book, magazine, or newspaper.

6. Physics, according to Science Daily, is the science of how physical things work.

7. A writer in The Natural World wrote that gravity holds us onto earth.

8. The Big Book of Physics for Kids says the moon's gravity helps create the daily tides.

TRY THIS! Find the titles of three books on your favorite subject. Write three sentences, one about each of the books. Remember to underline the titles of the books.

116 Unit 6 • Chapter 35 — Practice • Titles

REACHING ALL LEARNERS — CHALLENGE

BE-IN-A-BOOK DAY Have students use **Challenge Activity Card 24** (page R73) to choose a scene from a book that each would like to participate in for a special holiday to celebrate books.

Challenge Activity Card 24

Be-in-a-Book Day

Imagine that next week there will be a special holiday to celebrate books. Everybody will be able to participate in a scene from their favorite book. Follow these steps:

• Think about your favorite books and the events in them.

• Choose a scene from one of the books.

• Draw a picture of the characters and you participating in the activity.

• Write a caption explaining your choice. Be sure to include the title of the book.

• Share your picture with the class.

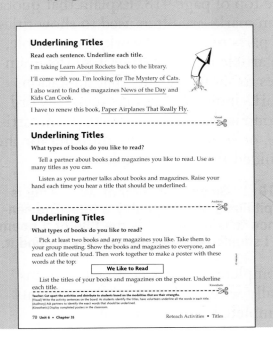

Underlining Titles

Read each sentence. Underline each title.

I'm taking Learn About Rockets back to the library.

I'll come with you. I'm looking for The Mystery of Cats.

I also want to find the magazines News of the Day and Kids Can Cook.

I have to renew this book, Paper Airplanes That Really Fly.

Underlining Titles

What types of books do you like to read?

Tell a partner about books and magazines you like to read. Use as many titles as you can.

Listen as your partner talks about books and magazines. Raise your hand each time you hear a title that should be underlined.

Underlining Titles

What types of books do you like to read?

Pick at least two books and any magazines you like. Take them to your group meeting. Show the books and magazines to everyone, and read each title out loud. Then work together to make a poster with these words at the top:

We Like to Read

List the titles of your books and magazines on the poster. Underline each title.

70 Unit 6 • Chapter 35 — Reteach Activities • Titles

417

Quotation Marks with Titles

OBJECTIVES
- To identify titles correctly and set them off with quotation marks
- To brainstorm and correctly write titles for stories or poems

DAILY LANGUAGE PRACTICE

TRANSPARENCY 79

1 A report in the Daily News told how wind water and ice wear away rock. (Daily News; wind, water,)

2 The article in the Times was about gravity on mars. (article; Mars.)

BRIDGE TO WRITING Our local newspaper, (title of newspaper) , reports new science discoveries.

ORAL WARM-UP

USE PRIOR KNOWLEDGE Call on volunteers to name favorite songs.

Grammar Jingles™ **CD, Intermediate** Use Track 24 for review and reinforcement of titles.

TEACH/MODEL

Have a volunteer read aloud the text at the top of page 418. Explain that quotation marks are often used to show titles of parts of a longer work, for example, an article in a magazine. Use the examples to show students that quotation marks indicate that a capitalized word group is the title of a story, poem, article, or song. Model the thinking for the Guided Practice example:

MODEL Since *The Thrill of Sky Diving* is capitalized, it is probably a title. The sentence tells me that it is the title of a poem, so I should put quotation marks around it.

Complete the Guided Practice items orally with students, or have students complete the items in pairs.

Quotation Marks with Titles

Place **quotation marks** around the titles of stories, poems, magazine articles, newspaper articles, and songs.

Examples:

Rishi created a clever song about gravity called **"Gravity Rap."**

The story **"The Talented Seal"** is about a seal that uses gravity to balance a ball.

Tonya's poem is titled **"Moon Path."**

Guided Practice

A. Identify the title in each sentence. Tell where quotation marks need to be added.

Example: The Thrill of Sky Diving is a poem about the feeling a diver gets when gravity pulls her into the pool.
"The Thrill of Sky Diving"

1. Because you can't see gravity, Tom called his story about an invisible man Gravity Man. "Gravity Man"
2. Drifting is a song about falling leaves. "Drifting"
3. Hold on Tight is a true story about a roller coaster. "Hold on Tight"
4. The Life of Newton is an article about the discoveries of Isaac Newton. "The Life of Newton"
5. Same Speed is a funny poem about how all things fall to Earth at the same speed. "Same Speed"

Vocabulary Power page 103

Name _____

PREFIXES

Prefixes are added to the beginning of words. They change the meaning of the words. Here are some prefixes and their meanings.

over- too much	re- again	pre- before	in-, im-, il-, ir- not

When you are adding a prefix that means "not," use *il-* before base words that start with *l*, *ir-* before base words that start with "r", and *im-* before base words that start with *b, m,* or *p*. Use *in-* for base words starting with any other letter.

Read each word and the directions. Then choose the correct prefix and add it to the word. Write the new word.

Word	Directions	New Word
1. visible	Change to mean "not visible"	invisible
2. pay	Change to mean "pay too much"	overpay
3. arrange	Change to mean "arrange before"	prearrange
4. possible	Change to mean "not possible"	impossible
5. enter	Change to mean "enter again"	reenter
6. perfect	Change to mean "not perfect"	imperfect
7. regular	Change to mean "not regular"	irregular
8. active	Change to mean "not active"	inactive
9. register	Change to mean "register again"	reregister

Vocabulary Power   Unit 6 • Chapter 35   103

ESL

REACHING ALL LEARNERS

TITLE TEAMS Ask each student to write on a sheet of paper an original title for a book of stories or poems. Have them underline the title. Then have students choose a partner and trade papers with him or her. Ask students to write the titles of three stories or poems that might appear in their partner's book. Remind students to place quotation marks around story or poem titles.

Independent Practice

B. Write the sentences. Put quotation marks around the titles of stories, songs, articles, and poems.

Example: Greater Force is a Greek myth.
"Greater Force" is a Greek myth.

6. The poem Mighty Machine says that machines increase people's power to do work. "Mighty Machine"

7. People use ramps to build pyramids in the story The Age of the Pyramids. "The Age of the Pyramids."

8. The sound of the wheel is repeated in the poem Potter's Wheel. "Potter's Wheel."

9. The magazine article Pedal Power explains how bicycles work. "Pedal Power"

10. The story An Apple a Day tells how a falling apple helped Isaac Newton figure out gravity. "An Apple a Day"

11. Fighting Friction is an exciting story about a man who works with race cars. "Fighting Friction"

12. The poem Forces of Nature is about a woman fighting the forces of wind and water. "Forces of Nature"

13. World in Motion is an article about movement. "World in Motion"

14. The Push and Pull is a song about machines. "The Push and Pull"

15. Waterwheel is a song about a water-powered machine used long ago. "Waterwheel"

Remember to use quotation marks around the titles of stories, poems, magazine articles, newspaper articles, and songs.

419

Writing Connection

Writer's Journal: Story Titles You probably have ideas for a story or a poem, but what about a title? A title should grab the reader's attention. Brainstorm titles for a story or a poem. Be sure to write them correctly.

Writer's Journal

Independent Practice

Have students complete the Independent Practice, or modify it using these suggestions:

MODIFIED INSTRUCTION

BELOW-LEVEL STUDENTS Remind students to look for a capitalized word group in each sentence.

ABOVE-LEVEL STUDENTS Have students rewrite sentences 9, 10, and 11, moving the titles from the subject to the predicate.

Writing Connection

Writer's Journal: Story Titles Explain that a catchy title makes people want to read a story, article, or poem. Tell students to use the correct capitalization and punctuation in their titles.

Writer's Journal

WRAP-UP/ASSESS

SUMMARIZE What kinds of works have titles that are set off by quotation marks?

RETEACH

REACHING ALL LEARNERS

INTERVENTION Lessons in **visual, auditory,** and **kinesthetic** modalities: p. R61 and *Reteach Activities Copying Masters,* p. 71.

REACHING ALL LEARNERS

PRACTICE page 117

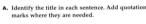
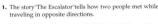

Name _____

Quotation Marks with Titles

A. Identify the title in each sentence. Add quotation marks where are needed.

1. The story The Escalator tells how two people met while traveling in opposite directions.

2. Before Ralph read a poem called The Ballet Dancer, he told the class how dancers defy gravity.

3. The story If I Had Known Willie Mays showed a picture of Mays slugging a baseball.

4. An article called How Baseball Uses Physics said that the baseball bat is used like a lever.

5. The song Take Me Out to the Ball Game is everyone's favorite.

B. Write each sentence, placing quotation marks around the title of stories, songs, magazine and newspaper articles, and poems.

6. The article Baseball Facts tells you how to hit a home run.

The article "Baseball Facts" tells you how to hit a home run.

7. Allison wrote Faster Than the Wind, a poem about sledding.

Allison wrote "Faster Than the Wind," a poem about sledding.

8. The band played Winter Holiday Waltz while we ice skated.

The band played "Winter Holiday Waltz" while we ice skated.

TRY THIS! Write a short story, article, poem, or song about a sport. Give your work a title. Be sure to use quotation marks around the title.

Practice • Titles
Unit 6 • Chapter 35 117

REACHING ALL LEARNERS

CHALLENGE

MORE THAN A TITLE Ask each student to write a paragraph or a poem for one of the titles he or she brainstormed in the Writing Connection activity above. Tell students to revise their titles, if needed, to better fit what they have written.

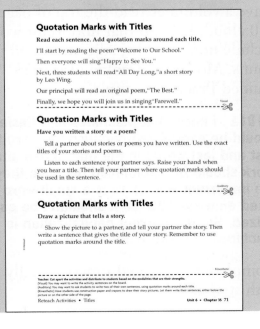

Quotation Marks with Titles

Read each sentence. Add quotation marks around each title.

I'll start by reading the poem "Welcome to Our School."

Then everyone will sing "Happy to See You."

Next, three students will read "All Day Long," a short story by Leo Wing.

Our principal will read an original poem, "The Best."

Finally, we hope you will join us in singing "Farewell."

Visual

Quotation Marks with Titles

Have you written a story or a poem?

Tell a partner about stories or poems you have written. Use the exact titles of your stories and poems.

Listen to each sentence your partner says. Raise your hand when you hear a title. Then tell your partner where quotation marks should be used in the sentence.

Auditory

Quotation Marks with Titles

Draw a picture that tells a story.

Show the picture to a partner, and tell your partner the story. Then write a sentence that gives the title of your story. Remember to use quotation marks around the title.

Kinesthetic

Teacher: Cut apart the activities and distribute to students based on the modalities that are their strengths.
[Visual] You may want to write the activity sentences on the board.
[Auditory] You may want to ask students to write two of their own sentences, using quotation marks around each title.
[Kinesthetic] Have students use construction paper and crayons to draw their story pictures. Let them write their sentences, either below the picture or on the other side of the page.

Reteach Activities • Titles
Unit 6 • Chapter 35 71

Capitalizing Words in Titles

OBJECTIVES
- To capitalize titles correctly
- To create an advertisement and to list magazines where it might appear

DAILY LANGUAGE PRACTICE

TRANSPARENCY 79

1 No I didn't know about the article
(No,; article.)

2 The Big Pull is an article in Science Today magazine. ("The Big Pull"; Science Today)

BRIDGE TO WRITING The last (noun) I read, "Heavy Talk About Gravity," was very interesting.

ORAL WARM-UP

USE PRIOR KNOWLEDGE Ask volunteers to suggest book titles. Ask other students to identify the important words in the titles that were named.

Grammar Jingles™ **CD, Intermediate** Use Track 24 for review and reinforcement of titles.

TEACH/MODEL

Have a volunteer read the top of page 420 aloud. Explain that important words include nouns, verbs, adjectives, and pronouns. Model the thinking for the Guided Practice example:

MODEL I know that *Machines* and *Easier* should be capitalized because they are the first and last words in the title. *Make* and *Work* should be capitalized because they are important words. *To* is a small word listed on page 420, so it shouldn't be capitalized. So, the correct capitalization is *Machines to Make Work Easier.*

Complete the Guided Practice orally with students.

Capitalizing Words in Titles

Capitalize the first word, last word, and every important word in a title.

Capital letters are used to let readers know a group of words is a title. Be sure to capitalize all verbs, including all forms of the verb *be*, such as *is* and *are*. Also capitalize all pronouns, including *he*, *she*, and *it*. Small words, such as *and*, *or*, *but*, *the*, *a*, *of*, *to*, *for*, and *with* are not capitalized unless they are the first or last word in a title.

Examples:
Building with Machines

"The World of Machines"

"Machines at Work"

Guided Practice

A. Tell how you would capitalize each title correctly.

Example: Machines to make Work Easier
            Machines to Make Work Easier

1. "simple tools" "Simple Tools"
2. the lever   The Lever
3. "Using a pulley" "Using a Pulley"
4. the invention of the wheel   The Invention of the Wheel
5. "hammering without hitting your thumb"
            "Hammering Without Hitting Your Thumb"

Vocabulary Power   page 104

Name _____

ANTONYMS AND SYNONYMS

▶ Read each word. Write its antonym on the line. Then think of a synonym for the word and write it on the next line. Antonyms and synonyms will vary. Possible responses are given.

	Antonym	Synonym
1. visible	invisible	apparent
2. strength	weakness	power
3. easy	difficult	simple
4. push	pull	shove
5. floating	sinking	drifting
6. scamper	plod	run
7. wonderful	awful	terrific

▶ Now try these.

	Antonym	Synonym
8. heavy	light	weighty
9. regular	irregular	normal
10. tear	mend	rip
11. noisy	silent	loud
12. pleased	displeased	happy
13. ragged	smooth	frayed
14. blustery	tranquil	gusty

104   Unit 6 • Chapter 35   Vocabulary Power

ESL
REACHING ALL LEARNERS

TITLE TRADE Have each student write three nouns and three verbs on a sheet of paper. Then have students trade papers with a partner. Have each partner write three titles. Each title should include one of the nouns, one of the verbs, and at least one of the small words mentioned on page 420.

Independent Practice

B. Write each title, using correct capitalization.

Example: "Machine force"
"Machine Force"

6. ramps and planes   Ramps and Planes
7. "what is a drill?"   "What Is a Drill?"
8. The story of scissors   The Story of Scissors
9. "the uses of axles"   "The Uses of Axles"
10. Ropes Plus Wheels equal Pulleys   Ropes Plus Wheels Equal Pulleys

C. Read each title. If it is capitalized correctly, write *correct*. If it is capitalized incorrectly, write it correctly.

Example: "How the wheel changed The world"
"How the Wheel Changed the World"

11. "Playground Machines"   correct
12. Gentle and Steep Slopes   correct
13. Lighten The Load   Lighten the Load
14. "Tools for less Friction"   "Tools for Less Friction"
15. Invisible Forces   correct

Remember to capitalize the first, last, and all other important words in a title.

Writing Connection

Real-Life Writing: Advertisement Create an advertisement for a product. You may use the machine you invented, or you may choose a different product. Your ad can tell what the product does and where to buy it. Make a list of real or imaginary magazines where your ad might appear. Make sure to underline the magazine titles and to use correct capitalization.

421

Independent Practice

Have students complete the Independent Practice, or modify it using these suggestions:

MODIFIED INSTRUCTION

BELOW-LEVEL STUDENTS Help students make a list of some words that should be capitalized in a title (first word, last word, nouns, verbs, adjectives, and pronouns). Advise students to use this list as they work through the exercises.

ABOVE-LEVEL STUDENTS Have students write three new titles that begin with "Tools for… ." Ask students to trade papers with a partner and check each other's capitalization.

Writing Connection

Real-Life Writing: Advertisement Have students give their products catchy names. Discuss how the name of the product is meant to make people want to buy it. Have students work in a small group to brainstorm a list of names for their invented product before they create an advertisement for it. The ad should have both words and pictures.

WRAP-UP/ASSESS

SUMMARIZE What kinds of words are capitalized in titles?

REACHING ALL LEARNERS

RETEACH

INTERVENTION Lessons in **visual, auditory,** and **kinesthetic** modalities: p. R61 and *Reteach Activities Copying Masters*, p. 72.

REACHING ALL LEARNERS

PRACTICE page 118

Name _____

Capitalizing Words in Titles

A. Proofread each title. Use editing marks to show which words should be capitalized.

1. the invisible forces of nature   (book)
2. "where would we be without the wheel?"   (article)
3. twenty experiments for young scientists   (book)
4. "simple machines that work"   (article)
5. "a student's guide to gravity"   (article)

B. Read each title. If it is correct, write *Correct*. If it is incorrect, write it correctly. Underline or use quotation marks for each title.

6. "The physics of Skateboarding"   (article)
   "The Physics of Skateboarding"
7. Surfing and science   (book)
   Surfing and Science
8. "Using Levers in Everyday Life"   (article)
   Correct
9. the History of Men and Machines   (book)
   The History of Men and Machines
10. "sails and steam: the history of boatbuilding"   (book)
    Sails and Steam: The History of Boatbuilding

TRY THIS! Write a title for a book, article, poem, story, or song on a new way to fly kites. Punctuate the title correctly.

118   Unit 6 • Chapter 35   Practice • Titles

REACHING ALL LEARNERS

CHALLENGE

CARD CATALOG Have each student choose from the class library up to three books or magazines that interest them. For each publication, ask them to write on an index card the title and author, and whether it is a book or magazine. Remind students to capitalize titles correctly and to underline them. Arrange the index cards in alphabetical order, and put them in a shoe box for students to use as a resource for interesting reading materials.

Capitalizing Words in Titles

On the lines, write these book titles. Use correct capitalization.

| fun with kites | a rising wind |
| listen to the wind | poems for a windy day |

Fun with Kites   A Rising Wind

Listen to the Wind   Poems for a Windy Day

Capitalizing Words in Titles

Tell a partner about some poems and stories you would like to write. Listen to your partner's ideas for poems and stories.

Together, think of the best title for each idea. Say the title and tell which words should begin with capital letters.

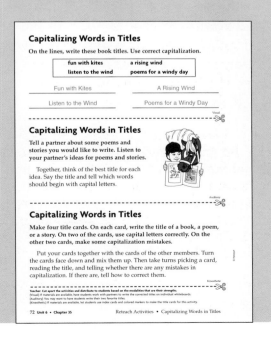

Capitalizing Words in Titles

Make four title cards. On each card, write the title of a book, a poem, or a story. On two of the cards, use capital letters correctly. On the other two cards, make some capitalization mistakes.

Put your cards together with the cards of the other members. Turn the cards face down and mix them up. Then take turns picking a card, reading the title, and telling whether there are any mistakes in capitalization. If there are, tell how to correct them.

Teacher: Cut apart the activities and distribute to students based on the modalities that are their strengths.
[Visual] If materials are available, have students work with partners to write the corrected titles on individual whiteboards.
[Auditory] You may want to have students write their two favorite titles.
[Kinesthetic] If materials are available, let students use index cards and colored markers to make the title cards for this activity.

72   Unit 6 • Chapter 35   Reteach Activities • Capitalizing Words in Titles

Extra Practice

OBJECTIVES
- To identify, punctuate, and capitalize titles correctly
- To adapt an idea from an earlier assignment into a story and to correctly capitalize a title for it

DAILY LANGUAGE PRACTICE

TRANSPARENCY 80

1 Sir Isaac Newton discovered gravity more than 300 year's ago. (years)

2 The book "newtons discovery" tells about his work. (Newton's Discovery)

BRIDGE TO WRITING (Title) sounds like another interesting book about science.

ORAL WARM-UP

USE PRIOR KNOWLEDGE Ask a volunteer to write the title of a book and the title of a song on the board. Ask: **What is different about how you write these two titles?**

TEACH/MODEL

Use the Remember box to review punctuation and capitalization of titles. Have students complete the Extra Practice independently.

 Remember

to underline the titles of books, magazines, and newspapers. Place quotation marks around the titles of stories, songs, magazine articles, and newspaper articles, and poems. Capitalize the first, last and all other important words in a title.

For more activities with titles, visit
The Learning Site:
www.harcourtschool.com

422

Extra Practice

A. Write the sentences. Underline each book, magazine, and newspaper title. Place quotation marks around the titles of stories, poems, articles, and songs. *pages 416–419*

Example: The book Doing Work explains that work is the force that moves objects.
The book <u>Doing Work</u> *explains that work is the force that moves objects.*

1. The book Work and You tells about machines that move things. <u>Work and You</u>
2. We sang the song Climbing Higher. "Climbing Higher."
3. A Science Kids article says that some wheels have teeth called cogs. <u>Science Kids</u>
4. An article in Atlanta Weekly says that there are levers in people's bodies. <u>Atlanta Weekly</u>
5. The poem Easy Walk is about a hike. "Easy Walk"
6. My song Stepping Stairs is about how steps make it easier to climb slopes. "Stepping Stairs"
7. The book Force and Work explains how wheels were invented. <u>Force and Work</u>
8. An article titled What Is Physics? says that physics is the study of force and motion. "What Is Physics?"
9. The story Free of Gravity is about space. "Free of Gravity"
10. Kevin wrote a poem called No Up or Down. "No Up or Down"

B. Write the titles, using correct capitalization. *pages 420–421*

Example: skiers and gravity
Skiers and Gravity

11. <u>What a Slope Means To A Skier</u> What a Slope Means to a Skier
12. "Heavy Object, big force" "Heavy Object, Big Force"
13. <u>Friction And Fire</u> Friction and Fire
14. "rolling and sliding" "Rolling and Sliding"
15. <u>machines with muscles</u> Machines with Muscles

Vocabulary Power page 105

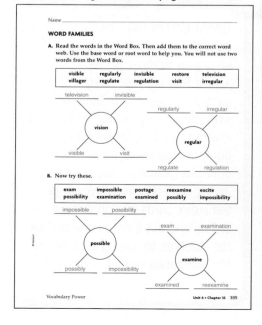

TITLE SCRAMBLE Have students write on note cards four different book, story, or song titles, writing each word of the titles on a separate card without any punctuation or capitalization. Then have students mix up their note cards and rearrange them to make new titles. Tell them to write down the titles they make, indicating whether each would be the title of a book, a story, a song, etc. Students must then capitalize and punctuate the titles correctly.

C. Read the titles below. If the title is correct, write *correct*. If the title is incorrect, write it correctly. *pages 420–421*

Example: <u>Smoothing Forces</u>
　　　　　correct

16. "No one Falls up" "No One Falls Up"
17. force and everyday objects Force and Everyday Objects
18. "Bicycle Experiments with Motion" correct
19. Skateboarding ramps Skateboarding Ramps
20. Rollers To Wheels Rollers to Wheels

D. The following sentences contain titles with punctuation and capitalization errors. Write each sentence, correcting the errors.
pages 416–421

Example: My teacher read the story Push, Push, Push.
　　　　　My teacher read the story "Push, Push, Push."

21. Super Force is the title of my story. "Super Force"
22. My science book, Our World, says that force is what pushes and pulls objects. Our World
23. I also decided to include some ideas from an article in Science World. Science World
24. There was a picture of a man lifting weights to show force in The Book Of Forces. The Book of Forces
25. My next poem will be called Favorite forces. "Favorite Forces."

Writing Connection

Writer's Craft: Choosing a Form Look in your Writer's Journal for an idea you wrote about in an earlier chapter. Then, rewrite the idea as a story or in another form. Create a title for the story, and use correct capitalization.

423

Building Oral Grammar

Have each student describe in one or two sentences a familiar book, song, story, or movie. Tell students not to include the title in their descriptions. Ask audience members to guess the titles.

Writing Connection

Writer's Craft: Choosing a Form Tell students that instead of writing a story, they can rewrite the piece in any form, so long as it is different from the original. Have students trade papers with a partner. Tell them to respond constructively to their partner's writing.

WRAP-UP/ASSESS

SUMMARIZE Ask students to list those words that are not generally capitalized in titles. Ask: **What is the exception to this rule?**

ADDITIONAL PRACTICE An additional page of Extra Practice is provided on page 477 of the *Pupil Edition*.

CHALLENGE

TITLE TYPES Cut out and supply newspaper articles to small groups of students. Give each group twice as many articles as group members. Then have the groups list the titles of their articles on a sheet of paper and decide whether each title is primarily informative (clearly tells about the content) or attention-getting (tries to grab the reader's attention without saying much about the content). Have groups share their findings.

TECHNOLOGY *Grammar Practice and Assessment* CD-ROM; *Writing Express* CD-ROM

INTERNET Visit *The Learning Site:* w w w . h a r c o u r t s c h o o l . c o m

Chapter Review

OBJECTIVES
- To review punctuation and capitalization of titles
- To interpret the main idea and supporting details of a picture

DAILY LANGUAGE PRACTICE

TRANSPARENCY 80

1 Our teacher said "The strength of gravity is different on other planets." (said,)

2 The World encyclopedia of Science includes the article Gravity on Other planets. (The World Encyclopedia of Science; "Gravity on Other Planets.")

BRIDGE TO WRITING The planet Mars ___(predicate)___. What a ___(adjective)___ time I would have if I ___(verb)___ there!

STANDARDIZED TEST PREP

MODEL TEST-TAKING STRATEGIES Have a volunteer read aloud the directions on page 424. Remind students to answer each question by first eliminating answers that they know are wrong. Model the thinking. Write this example on the board:

1 The first chapter in The wheels of Time tells about ancient Egypt.

- **A** the "wheels of time"
- **B** "The wheels Of Time"
- **C** The Wheels of Time
- **D** The Wheels Of Time

MODEL I notice the word *chapter* in the sentence. A chapter is part of a book, so I know that *The Wheels of Time* is the title of a book. Since book titles are underlined, I can eliminate choices A and B. I know that the word *of* should not be capitalized unless it is the first or last word of a title, so choice D is incorrect. Choice C must be the correct answer.

Have students complete the Chapter Review independently.

TIP Be sure to read all the choices carefully before selecting an answer.

Chapter Review

The underlined words in each sentence contain mistakes in punctuation and capitalization. Choose the answer that is the correct way to write the underlined section of the sentence.

1 The song Work With Wheels tells how wheels make it easier to do work.
- **A** The song "Work with wheels"
- **B** The song Work with Wheels
- **C** The song "Work with Wheels" c

2 An article in the Magazine Fun with History says wheels were invented more than 6,000 years ago.
- **F** the magazine Fun with History F
- **G** the magazine "Fun With History"
- **H** the magazine Fun With History

3 The book "Inventors of the Past" says no one knows who invented wheels.
- **A** The book Inventors of the Past A
- **B** The book Inventors Of The Past
- **C** The book "Inventors Of The Past"

4 The article Ball Bearings explains how ball bearings are used in bicycles.
- **F** Ball Bearings
- **G** "Ball Bearings" G
- **H** "Ball bearings"

5 In the book Mystery at the Ranch, a pulley is a clue to figuring out the mystery.
- **A** In the book "Mystery At The Ranch"
- **B** In the book Mystery at The Ranch
- **C** In the book Mystery at the Ranch c

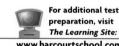 For additional test preparation, visit *The Learning Site:* www.harcourtschool.com

424

Assessment

PORTFOLIO ASSESSMENT Have students choose their best work from the Writing Connections on pages 417, 421, and 423.

ONGOING ASSESSMENT Evaluate the performance of 4–6 students using appropriate checklists and record forms from pages R74–R77.

 INTERNET Activities and exercises to help students prepare for state and standardized assessments appear on *The Learning Site:* **www.harcourtschool.com**

Interpreting a Picture

When you look at a picture, you should ask yourself the following questions:

1. **What is the artist trying to say?** Sometimes pictures can inform or explain. Often, artists want to say something in their work. What is the main idea of the picture? How does he or she say it?
2. **What details do you notice?** Look at the details and think about how they communicate the main idea.
3. **What do the details mean?** Sometimes the details in a picture can have more than one meaning. For example, besides being a bird, a dove can mean peace.

TIP Look for the elements of art in a picture. These include line, shape, color, and space. Notice how the artist uses these elements to tell a story or express a mood.

YOUR TURN

Look carefully at this painting. Answer the three questions above. Then tell what you think about the painting. Explain your reaction to it.

VIEWING

Interpreting a Picture

TEACH/MODEL

Have volunteers read aloud the interpretation techniques and Tip on page 425. Help students complete the Your Turn activity. Begin by making three columns on the board, and writing the headings *Main Idea*, *Details*, and *Meaning of Details*. Have students look carefully at the painting on page 425. Help them decide what it is about; list responses under *Main Idea*. Then help students see the details the artist included to reinforce that main idea; list these responses under *Details*. Finally, help students determine what the details mean and what is the overall feeling of the picture; list these responses under *Meaning of Details*. Have students discuss their thoughts about the painting and their reaction to it in small groups.

WRITING APPLICATION Have students write a paragraph in their journals describing the different ways their group's members reacted to the painting on page 425.

WRAP-UP/ASSESS

SUMMARIZE Besides paintings, what other kinds of pictures are there? How can viewing pictures change a person's mood? REFLECTION

CHALLENGE

HAPPY ART Have a class discussion about things or experiences that make a person happy. Discuss how people show that they are happy. Then have each student draw a picture of something that makes him or her happy. Tell students to title their pictures. Then display the pictures in the classroom.

TECHNOLOGY Additional writing activities are provided on the *Writing Express* CD-ROM

LESSON ORGANIZER	DAY 1	DAY 2
DAILY LANGUAGE PRACTICE TRANSPARENCY 81	1. Chandra writes good, but her friend write gooder. (well; writes; better.) 2. Robin Steve and Yoshi has read their stories. (Robin, Steve,; have)	1. i think that my main character will flew to a new City. (I; fly; city.) 2. Her will meet a new friend their. (She; there.)
ORAL WARM-UP **Listening/Speaking**	Discuss Setting and Character 426 Examine How Audience Determines Language and Content 434	Discuss Graphic Organizers 435
TEACH/MODEL **WRITING** 	**Literature Model:** *Half-Chicken* 427–431 ✔ **Prewriting** 434 • To learn strategies for prewriting a story • To choose a topic and generate ideas for a story Interactive Writing 434	✔ **Drafting** 435 • To learn strategies for drafting a story • To draft a story **Transparency** 82
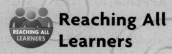 **Reaching All Learners**	**Modified Instruction** 440 Below-Level: Discuss Contractions Above-Level: Rewrite Sentences *ESL Manual* pp. 174, 175	**Modified Instruction** 441 Below-Level: Use a Chart Above-Level: Rewrite a Letter *ESL Manual* p. 174
GRAMMAR	**Unit 6 Review:** ✔ Negatives 440	**Unit 6 Review:** ✔ Commas 441
CROSS-CURRICULAR/ ENRICHMENT	**Listening and Speaking:** 432 **Evaluation Criteria:** Establish Criteria 433 **TEST PREP: TEST PREP:** Following Hunches 440 *Vocabulary Power* Explore Word Meaning 428	**HANDS-ON ACTIVITY:** Place That Comma! 441 *Vocabulary Power* Context Clues 428 *Vocabulary Power* book p. 106 🏆 **Vocabulary activity**

KEY
 ✔ = tested writing form/skill

deputy, governor, ruler, vice president, **viceroy**

See *Vocabulary Power* book.

DAY 3

1. All storys should include setting plot, and characters (stories; setting,; characters.)

2. Do you think Jamie and me should have dogs in their story (I; our story?)

Discuss Speaking and Revising 436

✔ **Revising** 436
  • To learn strategies for revising a story
  • To revise a story

Transparencies 83a and 83b

Modified Instruction 442
  Below-Level: Say Sentences
  Above-Level: Revise Sentences
  ESL Manual p. 174

Unit 6 Review:
✔ Quotation Marks 442

PEER CONFERENCES: Make Essays Stronger 436
HANDS-ON ACTIVITY: Partner Punctuation 442

Vocabulary Power

Compare and Contrast 428
Vocabulary Power book p. 107

DAY 4

1. Proofreading alows an writer to avoid simple errors (allows; a; errors.)

2. She caught mistaks in me story. (mistakes; my)

Suggest Problems Caused by Proofreading Errors 437

✔ **Proofreading** 437
  • To learn strategies for proof-reading a story
  • To proofread a story

Transparencies 84a and 84b

🖥 **Vocabulary activity**

Modified Instruction 443
  Below-Level: Finding Titles
  Above-Level: Punctuate Titles Correctly
ESL: Proofreading Techniques 437
  ESL Manual p. 174

Unit 6 Review:
✔ Titles 443

TEST PREP: Extra Practice 443

Vocabulary Power

Multiple-Meaning Words 428
Vocabulary Power book p. 108

🖥 **Vocabulary activity**

DAY 5

1. what the exciting story this is (What an; is!)

2. A boy his family, and his best friend is characters in it. (boy,; are)

Share Experiences of Listening to Stories 438

✔ **Publishing** 438
  • To learn strategies for publishing a story orally
  • To publish a story orally
  Handwriting 438

🖥 **Vocabulary activity**

ESL Manual p. 174

HANDS-ON ACTIVITIES
  375I-375J

LISTENING AND SPEAKING:
  Teamwork 439

Vocabulary Power

Exemplification 428

Using the Literature Model

OBJECTIVE
• To read and analyze a story

DAILY LANGUAGE PRACTICE

TRANSPARENCY 81

1 Chandra writes good, but her friend write gooder. (well; writes; better.)

2 Robin Steve and Yoshi has read their stories. (Robin, Steve,; have)

ORAL WARM-UP

USE PRIOR KNOWLEDGE Read aloud the introduction to the story, and discuss questions such as the following:

1. **What is the setting of a story?** (The setting tells when and where a story takes place.)

2. **Why might an author write a story that has animals as characters?** (Possible responses: Animals are fun to read about; they can be cute and easy to like.)

PREREADING STRATEGIES

PREVIEW/PREDICT Have students read the story introduction and the first paragraph of the story. Ask them to predict where Half-Chicken will go. Have students set their own purpose for reading, or have them read to find out where Half-Chicken goes and what happens when he gets there.

CHAPTER

36

Story

Writing Workshop

426

School-Home Connection

Family members can help students prepare to write their stories by discussing the settings, characters, and plots of classic stories such as "Little Red Riding Hood" and "The Three Little Pigs."

Award-Winning Author

Stories can be fun to read and write because they involve characters, settings, and plots. Remember that characters can be real or imaginary. When reading this story by Alma Flor Ada, follow the events that happen to the characters, and notice where the author uses elaboration to help tell the story.

Half-Chicken

by Alma Flor Ada
illustrated by Kim Howard

One day on a Mexican ranch, a chick is born that has only one eye, one leg, one wing, and only half as many feathers as the other chicks. The ranch animals decide to call him "Half-Chicken," and they give this special chick lots of attention!

ne day he overheard the swallows, who traveled a great deal, talking about him: "Not even at the court of the viceroy in Mexico City is there anyone so unique."

427

OPTIONS FOR READING

READ-ALOUD OPTION Read the story aloud, and have students listen to determine Alma Flor Ada's audience and purpose. They should also listen to determine the characters, the setting, and the plot.

INDEPENDENT OPTION As students read, have them list the important plot events as they occur.

Ask students to think about the setting of the story. Use questions like the following to help students monitor their comprehension:

3. **What does the word *unique* mean?**
   (Possible responses: "special," "unusual," "different," "original.") **INFERENTIAL: IMPORTANT DETAILS**

4. **Who is Alma Flor Ada's audience?**
   (Possible responses: young people who read for entertainment; anyone who enjoys folktales or animal stories.) **INFERENTIAL: IDENTIFY AUDIENCE**

SELECTION SUMMARY

GENRE: STORY In this story by Alma Flor Ada, a unique chicken sets off to see the court of the viceroy in Mexico City. On his way, he encounters and helps three characters: water, fire, and wind. When the chicken finds himself in trouble in Mexico City, those same three characters come to his rescue.

ABOUT THE AUTHOR

An accomplished translator of children's books from English to Spanish, **Alma Flor Ada** was born in Cuba and has lived in Spain, Peru, and the United States. Her works often introduce children to Central and South American landscapes and cultures.

5. **What does Half-Chicken want to do in Mexico City?** (He wants to visit the viceroy's court.) **LITERAL: NOTE DETAILS**

6. **Is Half-Chicken kind? How do you know?** (Possible response: Half-Chicken is kind. He stops to help the stream, the fire, and the wind even though he is in a hurry.) **METACOGNITIVE: DETERMINE CHARACTERS' TRAITS**

7. **Why do you think the stream, the fire, and the wind ask Half-Chicken to stay with them for a time?** (Possible response: They are grateful for Half-Chicken's help and want to play with him or do something for him.) **CRITICAL: INTERPRET CHARACTERS' MOTIVATIONS**

Story

Then Half-Chicken decided that it was time for him to leave the ranch. Early one morning he said his farewells. Then *hip hop hip hop*, off he went, hippety-hopping along on his only foot.

Half-Chicken had not walked very far when he found a stream whose waters were blocked by some branches.

"Good morning, Half-Chicken. Would you please move the branches that are blocking my way?" asked the stream.

Half-Chicken moved the branches aside, but when the stream suggested that he stay awhile and take a swim, he answered:

"I have no time to lose.
I'm off to Mexico City
to see the court of the viceroy!"

Then *hip hop hip hop*, off he went, hippety-hopping along on his only foot.

A little while later, Half-Chicken found a small fire burning between some rocks. The fire was almost out.

"Good morning, Half-Chicken. Please, fan me a little with your wing, for I am about to go out," asked the fire.

428

Vocabulary Power

DAY ① EXPLORE WORD MEANING Introduce and define *viceroy*. Write it on the board. **Do we have viceroys in the United States? Why or why not?**

DAY ② CONTEXT CLUES Write on the board: **The *viceroy* made laws in place of the king. What words help you understand the meaning of *viceroy*?** (See also *Vocabulary Power*, page 106.)

DAY ③ COMPARE AND CONTRAST **Which ruler is more powerful, a *viceroy* or a *king*? Why?** (See also *Vocabulary Power*, page 107.)

DAY ④ MULTIPLE-MEANING WORDS ***Viceroy* can mean a ruler or a specific kind of butterfly. Why would a butterfly that looks like the monarch be called a *viceroy*?** (See also *Vocabulary Power*, page 108.)

DAY ⑤ EXEMPLIFICATION **How would our country be different if we had a viceroy as a leader instead of a president?** Discuss responses.

Half-Chicken fanned the fire with his wing. It blazed up again, but when the fire suggested that he stay awhile and warm up, he answered:

"I have no time to lose.
I'm off to Mexico City
to see the court of the viceroy!"

Then *hip hop hip hop*, off he went, hippety-hopping along on his only foot.

After he had walked a little farther, Half-Chicken found the wind tangled in some bushes.

"Good Morning, Half-Chicken. Would you please untangle me, so that I can go on my way?" asked the wind.

Half-Chicken untangled the branches. When the wind suggested that he stay and play, and offered to help him fly here and there like a dry leaf, he answered:

"I have no time to lose.
I'm off to Mexico City
to see the court of the viceroy!"

Then *hip hop hip hop*, off he went, hippety-hopping along on his only foot. At last he reached Mexico City.

429

8. **What situations or descriptions are repeated in the story?** (Possible response: Half-Chicken helps characters he meets; he recites the same stanza over and over; the description of how he hops away is repeated; when the fire, water, and wind help Half-Chicken, they each say the same sentences.) **INFERENTIAL: TEXT STRUCTURE**

9. **How do you think Half-Chicken feels as he reaches the palace?** (Possible response: Half-Chicken probably feels nervous, excited, or happy.) **CRITICAL: IDENTIFY WITH CHARACTERS**

10. Why do the guards laugh at Half-Chicken? (Possible response: They think the idea of a chicken visiting the viceroy is ridiculous.) **CRITICAL: DETERMINE CHARACTERS' MOTIVATIONS**

11. How does the author use elaboration to tell what happens to Half-Chicken at the palace? (Possible response: The author uses vivid descriptions such as *fancy uniforms*, and dialog such as *"I've come to see the viceroy."*) **INFERENTIAL: AUTHOR'S CRAFT**

12. What do you think is the lesson of this story? (Possible response: Help others and they will help you.) **INFERENTIAL: DETERMINE THEME**

CHAPTER 36

Story

"Good afternoon," said Half-Chicken to the guards in fancy uniforms who stood in front of the palace. "I've come to see the viceroy."

One of the guards began to laugh. The other one said, "You'd better go in around the back and through the kitchen."

So Half-Chicken went, *hip hop hip hop*, around the palace and to the kitchen door.

The cook who saw him said, "What luck! This chicken is just what I need to make a soup for the vicereine." He threw Half-Chicken into a kettle of water that was sitting on the fire.

When Half-Chicken felt how hot the water was, he said, "Oh, fire, help me! Please, don't burn me!"

The fire answered, "You helped me when I needed help. Now it's my turn to help you. Ask the water to jump on me and put me out."

Then Half-Chicken asked the water, "Oh, water, help me! Please jump on the fire and put him out, so he won't burn me."

The water answered, "You helped me when I needed help. Now it's my turn to help you." He jumped on the fire and put him out.

When the cook returned, he saw that the water had spilled and the fire was out.

430

"This chicken has been more trouble than he's worth!" exclaimed the cook.

He picked Half-Chicken up by his only leg and flung him out the window.

When Half-Chicken was tumbling through the air, he called out: "Oh, wind, help me, please!"

The wind answered, "You helped me when I needed help. Now it's my turn to help you."

The wind blew fiercely. He lifted Half-Chicken higher and higher, until the little rooster landed on one of the towers of the palace.

"From there you can see everything you want, Half-Chicken, with no danger of ending up in the cooking pot."

From that day on, weathercocks have stood on their only leg, seeing everything that happens below, and pointing whichever way their friend the wind blows.

Vocabulary Power

vice·roy [vīs´roy] *n.* A person who helps rule a country, colony, or province.

Analyze THE Model

1. How does Alma Flor Ada use elaboration in the first paragraph to give the reader more details about the swallows?

2. Give at least two examples of figurative language or exact words that the author uses to describe a character, the setting, or the plot.

3. What characters did Half-Chicken help on his way to Mexico City?

4. How does Half-Chicken rely on these characters to solve his own problem?

431

Analyze THE Model

1. **How does Alma Flor Ada use elaboration in the first paragraph to give the reader more details about the swallows?** (Possible response: She says that the swallows traveled a great deal.) **INFERENTIAL: AUTHOR'S CRAFT**

2. **Give at least two examples of figurative language or exact words that the author uses to describe a character, the setting, or the plot.** (Possible responses: She describes the time that Half-Chicken leaves as "early one morning." She uses figurative language by writing that the wind "offered to help him fly here and there like a dry leaf.") **INFERENTIAL: UNDERSTAND FIGURATIVE LANGUAGE**

3. **What characters did Half-Chicken help on his way to Mexico City?** (He helped the water, the fire, and the wind.) **LITERAL: NOTE DETAILS**

4. **How does Half-Chicken rely on these characters to solve his own problems?** (Possible response: He asks the fire not to burn him after he is thrown into the kettle; he asks the water to put out the fire under the kettle; and he asks the wind to help him when he is thrown out the window.) **INFERENTIAL: SUMMARIZE**

RESPONSE TO LITERATURE

 To have students respond in writing to the story, use the following prompt:

Reflect on whether most readers would enjoy this story. Record your reflections, supporting your opinion with examples from the story. REFLECTION

SUMMARIZE THE MODEL

ONE-SENTENCE SUMMARY Have students write one sentence to summarize the story. (Possible response: A unique chicken on a journey to Mexico City helps others who later help him.)

 TECHNOLOGY Additional writing activities are provided on the *Writing Express* CD-ROM

Parts of a Story

OBJECTIVES

- To recognize and understand the parts of a story
- To analyze and summarize a story
- To establish criteria for evaluating a story
- To listen critically to a story

READING LIKE A WRITER

READ AND RESPOND TO THE MODEL Before you read "Lost and Found" aloud to students, ask them to listen to determine Ruth's purpose and audience. (purpose— to entertain; audience—classmates) Discuss whether students think Ruth does a good job describing the setting and the characters. Students should give reasons for their conclusions. Tell students to speak in complete sentences and use correct tense.

FOCUS ON ORGANIZATION Have students reread the story independently, noting the sequence of events. Then ask them why the order of events is so important. (Possible response: Each event builds up to the ending. Without any one of the events, the ending would not be as effective.)

FOCUS ON WRITER'S CRAFT Ask students to point out an example of elaboration in the story. (A tall man with gray hair) Ask: **How does Ruth use elaboration to help us "see" the setting and the characters?** (Possible response: Ruth uses elaboration to add interest and specific details to the setting and to the characters.)

READING — WRITING CONNECTION

Parts of a Story

Alma Flor Ada told her readers a story that showed characters helping each other. Study the story below, written by a student named Ruth. Pay attention to how she uses elaboration.

MODEL

setting/characters

figurative wording

character/event

event

event

dialogue/problem

event/dialogue/solve problem

Lost and Found

The ticket agent explained, "Go to Gate 48 for Flight 233 to Houston." Dad, Mom, and Tasha carried their bags to the security machine to be x-rayed. Then they walked to Gate 48.

Time dragged on in the gate area. A tall man with gray hair used the pay phone nearby. Later, the gate agent announced, "Flight 233 will be two hours late."

Mom and Tasha went to the pay phone to tell Grandpa. As Mom returned to her seat, Tasha yelled, "Mom, you forgot your keys!"

"Those aren't mine," Mom answered.

Tasha thought of the tall man with the gray hair. Tasha walked over to him and asked, "Are these your keys?" The man felt in his left pocket.

"Yes, thank you." The man introduced himself as Mr. Fellows.

Listening and Speaking

FEELINGS Have students brainstorm and write a list of ten feelings on slips of paper. Then write these sentences on the board:

> I have a long way to go!
> Who is there?
> Thank you for helping me!

Have students take turns choosing a slip of paper and saying one of the sentences in a way that demonstrates the feeling they chose.

At last the gate agent called Flight 233. Tasha reached for her backpack, but it wasn't there. Then she remembered she had put it on the floor at the security gate. Mr. Fellows heard Tasha telling her parents. He said, "I can go look. You helped me when I needed help."

Soon Tasha saw Mr. Fellows returning with the backpack. Her roller skates were safe!

— elaboration
— problem
— event
— dialogue
— event
— solve problem

Analyze THE Model

1. What is Ruth's purpose? Explain your answer.

2. What does Ruth tell about the setting?

3. How does dialogue make the story seem real?

Summarize THE Model

Use a flowchart like the one shown to help summarize Ruth's story. Name the setting, main characters, and important events in the story.

Writer's Craft

Elaboration Ruth used elaboration to help tell her story. Tell what exact or figurative words she used to help you understand what happened in the story. Then, rewrite three sentences from Ruth's story that give more detail about a character.

433

Title of Story → Characters / Setting / Events

Evaluation Criteria

ESTABLISH CRITERIA FOR WRITING Tell students that they will help evaluate their own stories. Have them turn to the rubric in their Handbooks, on page 501. Explain that if students meet the criteria in the "4" column, plus the criteria that you and the class add, they will have produced their best work. Discuss the criteria, and add others based on your students' needs and interests. Remind students to refer to the rubric as they write their essays. (A teacher version of the rubric is available on R85. For more information about evaluating writing, see pages R78–79 in this *Teacher's Edition*.)

Analyze THE Model

1. **What is Ruth's purpose? Explain your answer.** (Possible responses: Ruth's purpose is to entertain; to show how people can help each other solve problems.) **INFERENTIAL: DETERMINE AUTHOR'S PURPOSE**

2. **What does Ruth tell about the setting?** (The setting is an airport with a security machine and a pay phone.) **LITERAL: NOTE DETAILS**

3. **How does dialogue make the story seem real?** (Possible response: Ruth's characters talk the way people really talk.) **CRITICAL: AUTHOR'S CRAFT**

SUMMARIZE THE MODEL

Tell students to work in pairs to compare their flowcharts and discuss any differences. Have them work independently to write brief summaries of Ruth's story. Evaluate whether students have included all important points while omitting unnecessary details.

WRITER'S CRAFT

ELABORATION Have students share their changes. Ask them to explain how they improved the sentences by adding more details.

TAKE-HOME BOOK 6 provides an additional model of expressive writing and home activities. See *Practice Book* pages 141–143.

Prewriting

OBJECTIVES
- To learn strategies for prewriting a story
- To choose a topic and generate ideas for a story

ORAL WARM-UP

USE PRIOR KNOWLEDGE Ask: **How are stories for younger readers different from stories for older readers?**

GUIDED WRITING

Discuss the writing prompt with students. Have students identify the purpose and the audience for the story. (purpose—to entertain; audience—younger students) As a class, brainstorm story ideas. Write on the board the headings *Places*, *Characters*, and *Problems*. Write students' suggestions under the appropriate headings. Prompt students to consider real and imaginary places, human and animal characters, and different kinds of problems a traveler may face on a journey.

Have students read Ruth's model and make their own prewriting web for the story that they have in mind. They may select ideas from the brainstorming session or use their own ideas.

SELF-INITIATED WRITING Have students choose their own topics for their stories.

WRAP-UP/ASSESS

SUMMARIZE How does brainstorming help you with prewriting?

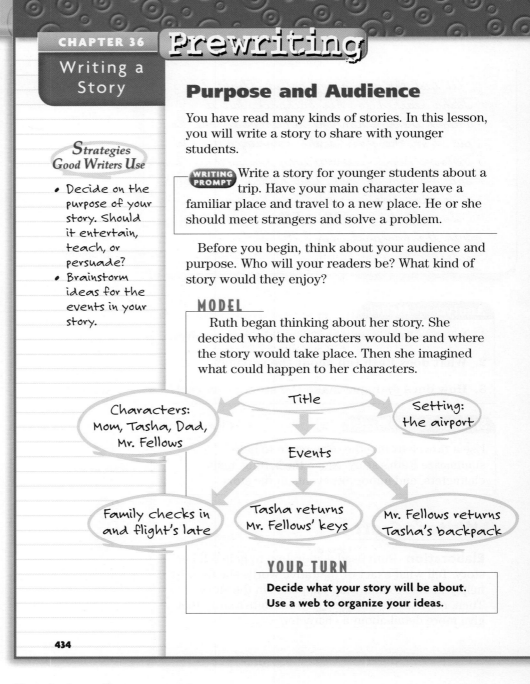

Prewriting

Purpose and Audience

You have read many kinds of stories. In this lesson, you will write a story to share with younger students.

WRITING PROMPT Write a story for younger students about a trip. Have your main character leave a familiar place and travel to a new place. He or she should meet strangers and solve a problem.

Before you begin, think about your audience and purpose. Who will your readers be? What kind of story would they enjoy?

MODEL

Ruth began thinking about her story. She decided who the characters would be and where the story would take place. Then she imagined what could happen to her characters.

Strategies Good Writers Use
- Decide on the purpose of your story. Should it entertain, teach, or persuade?
- Brainstorm ideas for the events in your story.

Title

Characters: Mom, Tasha, Dad, Mr. Fellows

Setting: the airport

Events

Family checks in and flight's late

Tasha returns Mr. Fellows' keys

Mr. Fellows returns Tasha's backpack

YOUR TURN

Decide what your story will be about. Use a web to organize your ideas.

434

Vocabulary Power   page 106

Name _____

CONTEXT CLUES

A. Read each sentence, paying attention to the underlined words. Then write a definition for each underlined word. Responses may vary slightly. Possible responses are given.
1. The king sent <u>viceroys</u> to the country to rule in his place.
   A viceroy is *a leader who rules in place of a king*
2. The <u>ruler</u> governs her country with fairness and kindness.
   A ruler is *a person who governs*
3. When the president of the club was sick, the <u>vice president</u> led the meetings.
   A vice president is *a person who leads in the president's place*
4. Every state elects a <u>governor</u> to lead it.
   A governor is *an elected leader of a state*
5. When the sheriff was off duty, the <u>deputy</u> took his place.
   A deputy is *a person who acts in place of another*

B. Now answer these questions.
6. What kind of leader does the United States have?
   a president
7. List qualities of a good leader.
   Responses will vary.

106   Unit 6 • Chapter 36   Vocabulary Power

Interactive Writing

You may want to prewrite and write a first draft as a group. Draw students' attention to the Strategies Good Writers Use. Have students help you complete a prewriting flowchart, including the title, the characters, the events, and the setting. Then use the Drafting Transparency with students, coaching them to use effective organization and elaboration.

Drafting

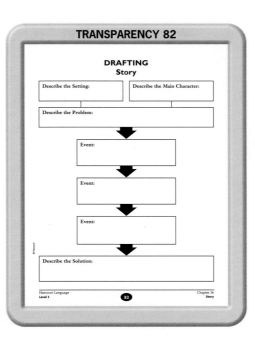

Organization and Elaboration

Follow these steps to help you organize your story.

STEP 1 Get Your Audience's Attention
Write about an event or use dialogue that will interest your reader.

STEP 2 Give the Events in Time Order
Tell the events in the order that they happen.

STEP 3 Solve the Problem
Have your main character figure out a way to solve the problem.

MODEL

Read the first paragraph of Ruth's story. How does she get the reader's attention? What words does she use to help you see the setting?

> The ticket agent explained, "Go to Gate 48 for Flight 233 to Houston." Dad, Mom, and Tasha carried their bags to the security machine to be x-rayed. Then, they walked to Gate 48.

YOUR TURN

Now draft your story. Look back at your prewriting web for ideas. Reread the stories by Alma Flor Ada and Ruth to see how they used elaboration.

CHAPTER 36

Writing a Story

Strategies Good Writers Use

- Use elaboration to give details about the characters.
- Use exact words to tell about the problem or problems that the main character has to solve.

Use a computer to draft your story. You can use the Delete key to erase parts that you want to change.

435

Drafting

OBJECTIVES
- To learn strategies for drafting a story
- To draft a story

DAILY LANGUAGE PRACTICE

TRANSPARENCY 81

1 i think that my main character will flew to a new City. (I; fly; city.)

2 Her will meet a new friend their. (She; there.)

ORAL WARM-UP

USE PRIOR KNOWLEDGE Ask volunteers to reflect on their writing experiences. Prompt students to comment on how the graphic organizers they created in the prewriting step may help them in the drafting process.

GUIDED WRITING

Discuss the Strategies Good Writers Use and the Organization and Elaboration steps. Ask volunteers to answer the questions that precede the model. (Possible responses: Ruth grabs the reader's attention by beginning with dialogue. She uses words such as *bags, security machine,* and *x-ray.* The story probably is about Tasha's family and something that happens as they travel.)

As students draft their stories, remind them to keep their purpose and audience in mind. Encourage students to use "Half-Chicken" and Ruth's story as models for their writing.

WRAP-UP/ASSESS

SUMMARIZE **How would you explain drafting to someone who did not know anything about it?**

Vocabulary Power page 107

Name _____

COMPARE AND CONTRAST

Read and respond to each question. Then explain your answer.

1. In the United States, who has more responsibility, the vice president or the president?
   president; explanations will vary.

2. Who would report to a sheriff, a king or a deputy?
   a deputy; explanations will vary.

3. Who has more responsibility, a king or a viceroy?
   a king; explanations will vary.

4. Who has more responsibility, the mayor of a city or the governor of a state?
   governor; explanations will vary.

5. Who has more responsibility, the governor of a state or the vice president of a country?
   vice president; explanations will vary.

6. Are a president of a country and a ruler of a country alike?
   Responses will vary.

7. Which would you rather be, a president or a vice president?
   Responses will vary.

8. Are a vice president and a viceroy alike?
   Responses will vary.

Vocabulary Power   Unit 6 • Chapter 36   107

TRANSPARENCY 82

DRAFTING
Story

Describe the Setting: | Describe the Main Character:

Describe the Problem:

Event:

Event:

Event:

Describe the Solution:

Harcourt Language
Level 3   82   Chapter 36
                                                 Story

Revising

OBJECTIVES
- To learn strategies for revising a story
- To revise a story

DAILY LANGUAGE PRACTICE

TRANSPARENCY 81

1. All storys should include setting plot, and characters (stories; setting,; characters.)

2. Do you think Jamie and me should have dogs in their story (I; our story?)

ORAL WARM-UP

USE PRIOR KNOWLEDGE Ask students to think about a time when they wished they could change something they'd said. Explain that revising gives writers a chance to change their writing.

GUIDED WRITING

Review the questions with students. Then ask them to give ideas for interesting beginnings and for checking the order of events, as in this model:

MODEL As I revise my story, I try to "see" the events, as I would at a movie. This helps me decide whether the events are in order and whether I'm missing any important events or details.

Use **Transparencies 83a and 83b** to further model the thinking. Then have students revise their drafts. They can keep their revisions in their working portfolios.

PEER CONFERENCES Have pairs of students use the **Evaluation Criteria** to evaluate their own and each other's writing, responding constructively by identifying strengths and suggesting improvements.

WRAP-UP/ASSESS

SUMMARIZE What changes did you make to improve your story?

Writing a Story

Strategies Good Writers Use

- Include details about the characters, setting, and events.
- Vary the kinds of sentences you use, and include dialogue.

Use the mouse to click and drag words and sentences to move them in your story.

436

Organization and Elaboration

Reread your draft. Think about these questions.
- Is my beginning interesting?
- Are the events in an order that makes sense?
- How well do details show the setting?
- Does the character solve the problem?

MODEL

Here is part of Ruth's story. Notice the exact words and dialogue she uses to make the action seem like real life.

> Time dragged on
> They sat in the gate area. A tall man with gray hair used the pay phone nearby. Later, the gate agent announced, the woman who worked for the airlines said that "Flight 233 will be two hours was late."
> Mom and Tasha went to the pay phone to tell Grandpa. As Mom returned to her seat, Tasha yelled, "Mom, told her she had forgotten her keys," but she You forgot your said they weren't hers. "Those aren't mine," Mom answered.

YOUR TURN

Revise your story. Look for places where you can use exact or figurative words to help the reader better "see" the setting, characters, and events.

TRANSPARENCIES 83a and 83b

REVISING

> Time dragged on
> They sat in the gate area. tall with gray hair A man used the pay phone nearby. Later, the the gate agent announced, woman who worked for the airlines said that, "Flight 233 will be two hours was late."
> Mom and Tasha went to the pay phone to tell Grandpa. As Mom returned yelled, "Mom, You forgot your to her seat. Tasha told her she had forgotten her keys," but she said they weren't hers? "Those aren't mine," Mom answered.

Harcourt Language
Level 3
83
Chapter 36
Story

Vocabulary Power page 108

Name _____

MULTIPLE-MEANING WORDS

Many words have more than one meaning. Clues from the sentence will tell you which meaning is being used.

A. Read each sentence below. Circle the letter of the meaning of the underlined word. Then write a sentence using the other meaning. Sentences may vary. Accept reasonable responses.

1. The viceroy made laws for the country.
   - A a butterfly
   - **B** a person who rules in place of a king

2. We measured the string with a ruler.
   - **A** a measuring stick
   - B a leader

3. The balloon rose into the air.
   - A a flower
   - **B** to go up

4. The board is one foot long.
   - **A** a unit of length equal to twelve inches
   - B the end of the leg

5. The doctor gave me medicine to treat my poison ivy.
   - **A** to cure or make better
   - B something that gives pleasure

B. Read the following sentence. Then write at least two other meanings for the underlined word.

6. The governor of our state is going to run for office.

_____
_____

108 Unit 6 • Chapter 36   Vocabulary Power

Proofreading

Checking Your Language

You look for mistakes in grammar and spelling when you proofread. You also check for errors in punctuation and capitalization. Readers may not understand your story if you do not correct mistakes.

MODEL

Below is another part of Ruth's story. Look at how Ruth corrected mistakes in punctuation. What else did she fix?

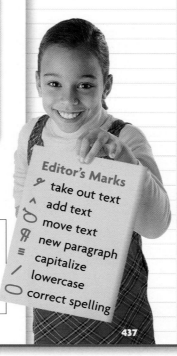

> At last the gate ~~agint~~ *agent* called Flight 233. Tasha reached for her backpack, but it wasn't there. Then she ~~remembred~~ *remembered* she had put it on the floor at the ~~securty~~ *security* gate. Mr. Fellows hear Tasha telling her parents. He said, "I can go look, you helped me when I needed help."

YOUR TURN

Proofread your revised story. Reread it several times to
- **check grammar and spelling**
- **check punctuation**
- **check capitalization**

Strategies Good Writers Use

- Make sure you have not left out any words.
- Check for correct spelling of similar words.
- Use quotation marks in your dialogue.

Editor's Marks

- ✄ take out text
- ∧ add text
- ∽ move text
- ¶ new paragraph
- ≡ capitalize
- / lowercase
- ○ correct spelling

437

ESL

REACHING ALL LEARNERS

PROOFREADING TECHNIQUES

Remind students that they do not have to catch all errors the first time they proofread. Have students work in pairs to proofread their stories for punctuation by taking turns reading their partner's story aloud as the writer listens.

Have the writer note places where the reader pauses or is confused and double-check those sections for spelling and punctuation errors.

TRANSPARENCIES 84a and 84b

PROOFREADING

> At last the gate ~~agint~~ *agent* called Flight 233. Tasha reached for her backpack, but it wasn't there. Then she ~~remembred~~ *remembered* she had put it on the floor at the ~~securty~~ *security* gate. Mr. Fellows hear Tasha telling her parents. He said, "I can go look, you helped me when I needed help."

Harcourt Language
Level 3

84

Chapter 36
Story

Proofreading

OBJECTIVES
- To learn strategies for proofreading a story
- To proofread a story

SPIRAL REVIEW

DAILY LANGUAGE PRACTICE

TRANSPARENCY 81

① Proofreading alows an writer to avoid simple errors (allows a; errors.)

② She caught mistaks in me story. (mistakes; my)

ORAL WARM-UP

USE PRIOR KNOWLEDGE What might happen if a story for younger children were published with spelling, punctuation, capitalization, and grammar errors?

GUIDED WRITING

Ask a volunteer to explain why Ruth added a comma after the word *backpack*. Use **Transparencies 84a and 84b** to further model the thinking for punctuating dialogue. Remind students that a compound sentence is two simple sentences combined with the word *and* or *but*. Remind them to use a comma before the combining word. Have students proofread their stories on their own, then have them trade papers with a partner and proofread their partner's story.

WRAP-UP/ASSESS

SUMMARIZE What errors did your partner find that you missed when you proofread your story? How does having another person proofread your work help you?

Visit The Learning Site!
www.harcourtschool.com

Publishing

OBJECTIVES
• To learn strategies for publishing a story orally
• To publish a story orally

DAILY LANGUAGE PRACTICE

TRANSPARENCY 81

1 what the exciting story this is
(What an; is!)

2 A boy his family, and his best friend
is characters in it. (boy,; are)

ORAL WARM-UP

USE PRIOR KNOWLEDGE Ask students to
name different ways people share their
stories. (Possible responses: in books and
magazines; through storytelling.) Invite students to recall times when they have
enjoyed hearing someone tell or read
aloud a story.

GUIDED WRITING

SHARING YOUR WORK Read and discuss the
questions with students. Help them
decide where and how to publish their
stories.

If computers are available, work with
students to enhance their stories with
pictures, graphics, or clip art. Students
should choose illustrations that work
with the plots and characters of their
stories.

REFLECTING ON YOUR WRITING Use the
Portfolio Conference suggestions at the
right.

**INTERNET Activities and exercises to help students
prepare for state and standardized assessments
appear on *The Learning Site:***

www.harcourtschool.com

Sharing Your Work

It is now time to publish your story. Think about the
audience you chose. Answer these questions to help
you choose the best way to share your story.

1. Who is your audience?

2. Would pictures help your audience understand
the story?

3. Can your audience read your story? Will you have
to read the story to them? Use the information on
page 439 for a read-aloud story.

> USING YOUR
> **Handbook**
>
> • Use the rubric
> on page 501 to
> evaluate your
> story.

Reflecting on Your Writing

Using Your Portfolio What did you learn
about your writing from this chapter? Write
your answer to each of these questions:

1. Would a reader be able to correctly describe your
main character? Why or why not?

2. Was the problem in your story clear? Why or why
not?

3. Look at the rubric in your Handbook. How would
you score your writing? Explain your answer.

Add your answers and your story to your portfolio.
Compare this story to your writing for Chapters 6,
21, and 33. Write a few sentences to explain how
well you met your goals and how you can do better.

438

Assessment

. . . .

PORTFOLIO CONFERENCES

Discuss the questions in the
Pupil Edition, and direct students to write their answers
and add them to their portfolios. Tell students you will meet
with them individually to discuss
their growth as writers. Use the
Student Record Form on page
R74 to record and monitor students' progress.

Handwriting

. . . .

Tell students that as they write,
they should pay special attention
to shape and stroke. On the board,
demonstrate these techniques.

• **Shape** Write the words *apple*
and *cut* on the board. Point out
the importance of closing the letters *a* and *e* so they won't be confused with the letters *u* and *c*.

• **Stroke** Write using a smooth,
even stroke that is not too light
or too dark.

Teamwork

You have been reading stories about people helping others. Now you have an opportunity to work with a classmate and help him or her make a presentation. Ruth and a friend decided to read Ruth's story to a first-grade class. You and a partner can present a story in the same way. Follow these steps:

STEP 1 Print your story on poster board. Write in large letters. Then first graders can follow along as you read. Leave space for pictures.

STEP 2 Have your partner help proofread the story.

STEP 3 With the help of your partner, add pictures to the story.

STEP 4 Practice reading your story aloud to your partner. Decide if you will point to the pictures.

STEP 5 Have your partner help you set up the poster board. Read the story to the children. Each of you can read the words of different characters.

Strategies for Listening and Speaking

These strategies will help you become a better storyteller:

• Learn your story well so you don't have to read every word as you present it. Then you will be less likely to lose your place.

• Vary the sound of your voice to match what is happening in the story. For example, you might want to sound excited, scared, or happy.

• Say the dialogue as if you are the character.

LISTENING AND SPEAKING
Teamwork

Remind students to use their voices, facial expressions, and gestures while speaking to hold the audience's attention instead of depending solely upon visual aids. Have students clarify and support their stories with pictures and objects.

Tell students to choose and adapt the appropriate volume and rate for the audience, purpose, and occasion.

Allow partners time to work on their storytelling. Have students take turns practicing their stories.

Review Acting Out a Story on page 83 before students present their stories. Use the Student Record Form on page R76 to assess students' listening and speaking skills.

WRAP-UP/ASSESS

SUMMARIZE Which did you like better, writing your story or telling it? Why?

SCORING RUBRIC

4 ADVANCED
Purpose and Audience
• appropriate for audience
• stays focused on purpose

Organization and Elaboration
• developed characters and a setting
• characters solve a problem
• description and details
• interesting words and phrases
• sentence variety

Language
• uses correct grammar
• uses correct spelling, usage, and mechanics

3 PROFICIENT
Purpose and Audience
• mostly appropriate for audience
• few deviations from purpose

Organization and Elaboration
• developed characters and a setting
• the problem not always clear
• some description and details
• some interesting words and phrases
• some sentence variety

Language
• uses mostly correct grammar
• uses mostly correct spelling, usage, and mechanics

2 BASIC
Purpose and Audience
• not appropriate for audience
• strays from purpose often

Organization and Elaboration
• does not have clear characters and a setting
• the problem is difficult to follow
• little description and few details
• few interesting words and phrases
• little sentence variety

Language
• incorrect grammar, spelling, or mechanics sometimes makes writing unclear

1 LIMITED
Purpose and Audience
• not appropriate to audience
• purpose is unclear

Organization and Elaboration
• does not have characters or setting
• does not have a problem to solve
• no description or details
• no interesting words or phrases
• no sentence variety

Language
• incorrect grammar, spelling, or mechanics often makes writing unclear

For information on adapting this rubric to 5- or 6-point scales, see pages R78–R79.

Unit 6
Grammar Review

CHAPTER 31

Negatives

OBJECTIVES
- To identify negative words in sentences
- To use appropriate negative words in sentences
- To correct double negatives in sentences

Unit Review
MODIFIED INSTRUCTION

BELOW-LEVEL STUDENTS As students begin Part A, remind them that the *n't* in contractions stands for *not*, making any word that includes *n't* a negative. Before students begin Part C, point out that there is more than one way to correct a sentence that contains a double negative.

ABOVE-LEVEL STUDENTS After students have completed Part C, have them rewrite each sentence in a different way to avoid a double negative.

Unit 6
Grammar Review

CHAPTER 31

Negatives
pages 378–387

440

Negatives   *pages 378–379*

A. Write the negative word in each sentence.

1. I couldn't stop reading a book about Thomas Edison, the inventor. couldn't
2. I didn't know he had invented the light bulb. didn't
3. Homes hadn't any electricity until then. hadn't
4. That did not stop him from inventing other things. not
5. Edison's inventions will not be forgotten. not

No, Not, and Other Negatives   *pages 380–381*

B. Use the correct word from the box to fill in the blank in each sentence.

no	none	no one	nowhere
not	never	nobody	nothing

6. It seems there is ____ left to learn about Earth. nothing
7. Yet scientists ____ stop learning about it. never
8. There is almost ____ new for scientists to go. nowhere
9. Yet we always find life forms that were ____ known about before. not
10. ____ knows everything about the world. No one or Nobody

Avoiding Double Negatives
pages 382–383

C. Each sentence has a double negative. Write each sentence with only one negative word. Possible responses are shown.

11. I don't like no subject as much as science.
    I don't like any subject as much as science.
12. I can't never get enough of it.
    I can't ever get enough of it.
13. There isn't nothing I like as much as learning about nature. There is nothing I like as much as learning about nature.
14. I can't hardly wait for science class each day.
    I can hardly wait for science class each day.
15. I won't never stop studying science.
    I will never stop studying science.

TEST PREP

TIP

Ask students if they have ever looked at a test item and felt that they knew the correct answer right away. That feeling might be more than a guess. Sometimes it is called a gut reaction or a hunch. Experts say that often our hunches prove to be right. Encourage students to check their work but to remember that their hunch might be right.

Commas *pages 388–389*

A. Write each sentence. Add commas where they are needed.

1. Miguel did you know that people used flint to make tools many thousands of years ago?
   Miguel, did you know that people used flint to make tools many thousands of years ago?
2. Well they needed tools to prepare animal hides.
   Well, they needed tools to prepare animal hides.
3. The adze was a tool made from flint wood and leather.
   The adze was a tool made from flint, wood, and leather.
4. Flint tools could cut scrape and chop.
   Flint tools could cut, scrape, and chop.
5. Yes flint was a very useful kind of rock.
   Yes, flint was a very useful kind of rock.

More About Commas *pages 390–391*

B. Add a comma to each letter part where it is needed.

6. Manchester New Hampshire   Manchester, New Hampshire
7. December 14 2001   December 14, 2001
8. Dear Uncle Hideo   Uncle Hideo,
9. I found the best rocks near Portland Maine.   Portland, Maine
10. Your nephew Deepak   Your nephew, Deepak

Combining Sentences Using Commas *pages 392–393*

C. Combine each pair of sentences with the word *and* or *but*. Write the new sentence, adding a comma where it is needed.

11. The coal we burn is rock now. It began many years ago as plants in wet forests.
    The coal we burn is rock now, but it began many years ago as plants in wet forests.
12. The plants rotted. They became buried over time.
    The plants rotted, and they became buried over time.
13. More plants rotted. They became heavy.
    More plants rotted, and they became heavy.
14. The weight of the plants pressed out the water. The bottom layers became hard.
    The weight of the plants pressed out the water, and the bottom layers became hard.
15. These layers turned into coal. People mine the coal for fuel.
    These layers turned into coal, and people mine the coal for fuel.

441

Unit 6
Grammar Review
CHAPTER 32
Commas

OBJECTIVES

- To add commas where needed in sentences
- To add commas where needed in parts of a letter
- To use commas in sentences that are combined to form compound sentences

Unit Review
MODIFIED INSTRUCTION

BELOW-LEVEL STUDENTS Before students begin Part A, write a chart of examples on the board. In one column, list examples of two similar items joined by *and;* in another column, examples of three similar items using commas. Leave the list on the board for reference.

ABOVE-LEVEL STUDENTS Challenge students to rewrite and expand upon Part B. The new letter should follow the form of a friendly letter but should also include new sentences that illustrate the other comma rules tested on this page (serial commas, commas in direct address and/or with introductory words, and commas in compound sentences).

PLACE THAT COMMA! Divide the class into two teams. Have each team, in turn, write a sentence that should have a comma in it. A speaker for that team should read the sentence twice, pausing between readings so that the other team can confer and agree upon its answer. At the second reading, members of the other team should clap when they hear the place that a comma should appear.

Unit 6
Grammar Review

CHAPTER 34

Quotation Marks

OBJECTIVES
- To place quotation marks where needed in direct quotations
- To use appropriate capitalization and punctuation with quotation marks
- To correct errors in a passage of dialogue

Unit Review

MODIFIED INSTRUCTION

BELOW-LEVEL STUDENTS Before students begin Part A, review the use of a speaker "tag," pointing out that "tags" are not included within quotation marks. Advise students to say the sentences to themselves to get a feel for which words are actually spoken.

ABOVE-LEVEL STUDENTS Challenge students to rewrite the sentences in Parts B and C, placing the speaker tags in different positions and adjusting the punctuation as necessary.

Unit 6
Grammar Review

CHAPTER 34

Quotation Marks
pages 406–415

Quotation Marks in Direct Quotations   pages 406–407

A. Rewrite each sentence. Put quotation marks where they are needed.

1. Carol said, We do not heat our pool. Carol said, "We do not heat our pool."
2. Pedro asked, Why not? Pedro asked, "Why not?"
3. Carol explained, We want to save energy. Carol explained, "We want to save energy."
4. Baker asked, Is it really cold? Baker asked, "Is it really cold?"
5. Carol answered, The sun warms it up. Carol answered, "The sun warms it up."

More About Quotation Marks

pages 408–409

B. Write each sentence, using the correct capitalization and punctuation with the quotation marks. If the sentence is correct as is, write *Correct*.

6. "Can you swim in your pool all year" asked Pedro. "Can you swim in your pool all year?" asked Pedro.
7. "it is not warm enough in the winter," said Carol. "It is not warm enough in the winter," said Carol.
8. Carol explained "The trees shade the pool when the sun is low in the sky. Carol explained, "The trees shade the pool when the sun is low in the sky."
9. "The sun is low in winter," Carol added. Correct
10. "may I swim in the pool?" asked Pedro. "May I swim in the pool?" asked Pedro.

Punctuating Dialogue   pages 410–411

C. If a sentence has mistakes in punctuation, write it correctly. If a sentence has no mistakes, write *Correct*.

11. Derek, I saw a rainbow yesterday, said Jameela. "Derek, I saw a rainbow yesterday," said Jameela.
12. "Was the rainbow colorful?" asked Derek. Correct
13. "It was made up of many colors said Jameela. "It was made up of many colors," said Jameela.
14. Rainbows seem high when the sun is low" added Derek. "Rainbows seem high when the sun is low," added Derek.
15. He said "Sometimes the rainbow goes across the whole sky. He said, "Sometimes the rainbow goes across the whole sky."

442

PARTNER PUNCTUATION Have students work in pairs. Tell them to take turns writing sentences with quotations. Each time one partner writes a sentence, the other partner should check the quotations and other punctuation for accuracy. Call on volunteers to share examples for the class to discuss.

Underlining Titles   *pages 416–417*

A. **Underline the book, magazine, or newspaper title in each sentence.**

1. Robin read <u>Gravity</u>, by Tess Gerrit, for her report.
2. Just for fun, she read <u>Bowled Over: The Case of the Gravity Goof-Up</u>.
3. She gave Andy a copy of <u>Balloons in the Pool</u>.
4. In the <u>Brereton Daily News</u>, José read about being without gravity in space.
5. He also learned some interesting facts in a magazine called <u>Highlights on the Sky</u>.

Quotation Marks with Titles   *pages 418–419*

B. **Place quotation marks around the titles of stories, articles, or songs in each sentence.**

6. Danielle taught her little brothers the song The Wheels on the Bus. "The Wheels on the Bus."
7. She made up another song and called it Gravity Gets Me Down. "Gravity Gets Me Down."
8. Rob wrote a song called Set Me Free, Oh Gravity. "Set Me Free, Oh Gravity."
9. He wrote an article called The Force of Gravity for the school paper. "The Force of Gravity"
10. Danielle and Rob want to write a story called The Day Gravity Stopped Working. "The Day Gravity Stopped Working"

Capitalizing Words in Titles   *pages 420–421*

C. **Write each title, using correct capitalization.**

11. "Gravity: simple experiments for Young Scientists" "Gravity: Simple Experiments for Young Scientists"
12. <u>newton and gravity</u>   Newton and Gravity
13. <u>The laws of gravity</u>   The Laws of Gravity
14. "The Lighter Side Of Gravity"   "The Lighter Side of Gravity"
15. <u>Motion And Gravity</u>   Motion and Gravity

443

Unit 6
Grammar Review
CHAPTER 35

Titles

OBJECTIVES
- To underline book, magazine, and newspaper titles in sentences
- To place quotation marks around the titles of stories, poems, articles, and songs in sentences
- To use appropriate capitalization in titles

Unit Review
MODIFIED INSTRUCTION

BELOW-LEVEL STUDENTS Before students begin Parts A and B, point out that they can find the titles by looking for capitalized words within the sentence. Suggest that as they complete Part C, they use the titles in Parts A and B as models.

ABOVE-LEVEL STUDENTS Write several sentences on the board, with each sentence containing both the title of a story or an article and the title of the book or magazine in which it appears. Have students punctuate the titles correctly.

TEST PREP

Activities and exercises to help students prepare for state and standardized assessments appear on our website.

Visit
The Learning Site!

www.harcourtschool.com

Assessment

SKILLS ASSESSMENT Use the **Language Skills and Writing Assessment** to assess the grammar and writing skills taught in this unit. Model papers are included.

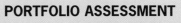
PORTFOLIO ASSESSMENT
Schedule portfolio conferences with individual students while others are completing the Unit Review exercises. Have students complete the Self-Assessment Checklist on page R87 and place it in their Show Portfolios. Use the Student Record Form on page R77 to monitor student progress.

An Inventor's Story

OBJECTIVES

- To research a famous inventor
- To write a story about the history of an invention and its intention to solve a problem

INTRODUCE THE PROJECT

USE PRIOR KNOWLEDGE Read the introduction aloud to the class. Have students make a list of famous inventions and tell how those inventions are useful today.

GENERATE QUESTIONS Have students generate and write in their journals questions about inventors. Encourage them to share their responses to one another's questions.

Research the Inventor's Story

Brainstorm with students famous inventors, and write their names on the board. Divide the class into groups, and ask each group to choose an inventor to research. Help students narrow their focus. If they choose someone who created many inventions, make sure they research the story behind just one invention. Direct them to encyclopedias, science textbooks, and other resources that will help them answer questions about the inventor and the invention.

Write the Story

Have students draft their stories. Remind them to include dialogue. Review the rules for correctly punctuating dialogue. Provide crayons, colored pencils, and other materials to help students illustrate their stories.

An Inventor's Story

Most inventions are created to solve problems. With a group of classmates, research a famous inventor from the past. Write a story that shows how he or she tried to solve a problem by inventing something. Follow the steps below.

Research the Inventor's Story

- What did the inventor do? When and where did he or she live? Did others help him or her?
- What problem did the inventor want to solve?
- How did the invention work? Did it solve the problem?
- What happened to the inventor later?

Write the Story

- Use the facts you found in your research to create your story.
- Make sure your story has a beginning, a middle, and an ending.
- Part of the story can be told by a narrator, but make sure to include dialogue between the characters.
- Illustrate your story. Draw pictures or use computer drawing software.

Publish Your Story

- Display your story on the bulletin board in your classroom.

444

Listening and Speaking

READER'S THEATER Explain that reader's theater is like a play, but the actors read from scripts. Have students work in groups to perform their stories. Have them assign parts and practice their readings. Remind students to use verbal and non-verbal communication effectively as they read. Have groups perform their stories for the class.

The Gadget War
by Betsy Duffey
REALISTIC FICTION
Kelly, a third-grade inventor, faces
competition as the class inventor when
a new student joins her class.
Award-Winning Author

Five Notable Inventors
by Wade Hudson
BIOGRAPHY
This book tells the stories of five
important African American inventors. It
also describes what they invented and
how their inventions improved society.
Award-Winning Author

A Picture Book of Thomas Alva Edison
by David A. Adler
BIOGRAPHY
Thomas Edison loved to solve problems
and invented many items, such as the
light bulb, that are still used today.
Award-Winning Author

445

Publish Your Story
Display the finished stories on a bulletin
board in the classroom. Arrange for the
school librarian to display certain stories
on inventors' birthdays or on the
anniversaries of particular inventions.

STUDENT SELF-ASSESSMENT
Have students evaluate their own
research and raise new questions for further investigation.

Books to Read Students who
enjoyed this project
might be interested in reading one or
more of these books. Have them record
reflections on the book or books in their
journals. Then ask students to recommend to the class the books from this list
that they enjoyed most.

School-Home Connection

Families can extend this project
by discussing with students
ways they have found to solve
household problems. As part of
the discussion, make a list of
"Helpful Hints" that students can
share with their classmates.

ESL

INVENTED STORIES Students
can write their stories on an
inventor from their country of
origin. Encourage them to have
the narrator explain cultural references that may be unfamiliar
to some listeners. Allow them
to use some technical words
from their first language, but
ask that students provide
translations.

Sentences

OBJECTIVES

• To identify four kinds of sentences

• To identify complete and simple subjects and predicates

• To recognize complete sentences and to rewrite fragments as complete sentences

Use the Cumulative Review to assess students' continued mastery of language concepts and skills presented in Units 1–6. Refer to the pages listed after each section title to review any concepts and skills students have not mastered.

UNIT 1 REVIEW

Have students complete the exercises, or modify them using these suggestions:

MODIFIED INSTRUCTION

BELOW-LEVEL STUDENTS Before students begin exercises 11–15, remind them that a complete sentence must have a subject and a predicate and it must express a complete thought. Write this reminder on the board as a checklist, and leave it there as a reference for students.

ABOVE-LEVEL STUDENTS After students have completed exercises 1–5, have them rewrite sentences 1 and 2 as questions and sentence 3 as a statement.

Cumulative Review
Unit 1
Sentences

Sentences *pages 24–27*

Write each sentence. Label it _statement_, _command_, _question_, or _exclamation_.

1. The piano recital was held on Wednesday. statement
2. Kate played a piece by Beethoven. statement
3. Did you like her performance? question
4. She was so great! exclamation
5. Listen carefully to the next piece. command

Subjects and Predicates

pages 34–37, 52–55

Write each sentence. Draw one line under the complete subject and two lines under the complete predicate. Then circle the simple subject and the simple predicate.

6. Naomi's father is an architect.
7. Her father designed the family's new home.
8. Naomi's friends watched with interest.
9. Naomi's family moved in last month.
10. The family is very happy with the new house.

Complete Sentences *pages 62–65*

Rewrite each group of words to make it a complete sentence. If the group of words is already a complete sentence, write _complete sentence_.

Possible responses are given.

11. I went to an opera called *Hansel and Gretel.*
    complete sentence
12. It is a fairy tale set in modern times.
    It was a fairy tale, but it was set in modern times.
13. The singers' words appeared above the stage.
    complete sentence
14. Was beautiful, and the costumes were great.
    The music was beautiful, and the costumes were great.
15. Some of the scenes scary, but I knew it would end
    happily. Some of the scenes were scary, but I knew it would end happily.

HANDS ON Activity

SENTENCE MATCH Write ten statements on index cards. On other index cards, rewrite the statements as questions, commands, and exclamations. Place the cards face down in one mixed stack. Have a pair of students take turns drawing cards. Students try to form four-card sets of sentences with similar content and words, each of a different type. Before laying down a set, the student must identify each sentence type. The student with the most sets wins.

Common and Proper Nouns

pages 92–95

Replace the underlined words with proper nouns. You may make up names of people, places, and things for this activity. Possible responses are shown.

1. This girl sleeps eight hours a day. Janine
2. That boy needs nine hours of sleep. Juan
3. Our local college did a study on sleep. Monroe Community College
4. Some professors were in charge of the study. Dr. Werner and Professor Diaz
5. The professors found that some people need ten hours of sleep each day. Dr. Werner and Professor Diaz

Singular and Plural Nouns

pages 102–107

Write the plural form of each noun in parentheses ( ).

6. Lisa eats many healthful (food). foods
7. She likes to eat (vegetable) and (fruit) at The Sprout, a local restaurant. vegetables, fruits
8. Her favorite foods are (cherry), (radish), and (orange). cherries, radishes, oranges
9. She also eats (bean) and (nut) to stay healthy. beans, nuts
10. She eats different (cheese), (bread), (cracker), and (fish), too. cheeses, breads, crackers, fish

Possessive Nouns pages 120–123

Write the possessive form of each underlined noun.

11. Charlie father works at a construction site. Charlie's
12. He is in charge of the workers safety. workers'
13. Construction workers hard hats protect them. workers'
14. Charlie father job is very important. Charlie's father's
15. Each person life is in his hands. person's

Cumulative Review
Unit 2

More About Nouns and Verbs

OBJECTIVES

- To replace common nouns with proper nouns
- To write plural forms of regular and irregular nouns
- To write singular and plural possessive nouns

UNIT 2 REVIEW

Have students complete the exercises, or modify them using these suggestions:

MODIFIED INSTRUCTION

BELOW-LEVEL STUDENTS Before students begin exercises 6–10, review the spelling rules for forming plural nouns, and write the rules on the board. If necessary, remind students of the rule for adding *es* to a noun: Add *es* to form plurals of nouns ending with *s*, *x*, *ch*, or *sh*. To form the plural of a noun ending with a consonant and *y*, change the *y* to *i* before adding *es*. Allow students to refer to the rules as they complete the exercises.

ABOVE-LEVEL STUDENTS After students have completed exercises 11–15, encourage them to rewrite sentence 15, using the plural possessive form of *person*.

Activity

VERB SEARCH Have students work in pairs. Tell each student to use a textbook. One partner should find and copy sentences with action verbs, circling the action verbs. The other partner should find and copy sentences with forms of the verb *be*, circling each form he or she finds. Partners should share their sentences, and then switch roles.

Cumulative Review
Unit 3

More About Verbs

OBJECTIVES
- To identify and use helping verbs and main verbs
- To identify present-tense, past-tense, and future-tense verbs
- To use the past tense of irregular verbs

UNIT 3 REVIEW

Have students complete the exercises, or modify them using these suggestions:

MODIFIED INSTRUCTION

BELOW-LEVEL STUDENTS Before students begin exercises 6–10, remind them that most past-tense verbs are formed by adding an *ed* ending and that future-tense verbs include the helping verb *will*.

ABOVE-LEVEL STUDENTS After students have completed the exercises, encourage them to write three original sentences using past-tense forms of different irregular verbs.

Cumulative Review
Unit 3

More About Verbs

Main Verbs and Helping Verbs
pages 166–169

Choose the correct helping verb in parentheses ( ) to complete each sentence. Then underline the main verb.

1. Yolanda's class (is, are) <u>worried</u> about the garbage in Decatur Park. is
2. They (has, have) <u>planned</u> to clean up the park. have
3. Yes, the class (do, does) <u>use</u> donated garbage bags. does
4. The Civic Association (is, are) <u>helping</u> them. is
5. The park (has, have) never <u>looked</u> better. has

Verb Tenses *pages 176–179, 194–197*

Write each sentence. Write whether the verb is *present tense*, *past tense*, or *future tense*.

6. Lina's family lived in Russia years ago. past tense
7. Her great-grandfather traveled to New York City. past tense
8. From there he moved to a town in Wisconsin. past tense
9. Now Lina's whole family lives in Wisconsin. present tense
10. They will visit Russia again one day. future tense

Irregular Verbs *pages 204–207*

Choose the correct word in parentheses ( ) to complete each sentence.

11. Our senator (came, comed) to our school. came
12. He (rided, rode) from his office in a taxi. rode
13. The senator (gived, gave) a speech about how important it is to vote. gave
14. He (said, sayed) that every citizen should vote. said
15. We (writed, wrote) him a letter thanking him for coming. wrote

448

TIP

If students are taking a test and must decide which present-tense verb agrees with a subject, remind them that most plural nouns end in *s*. However, most verbs that end in *s* agree with singular nouns. If both the subject and the verb in an answer choice end in *s*, or if neither ends in *s*, the answer is likely to be incorrect.

Subject and Object Pronouns

pages 234–237, 242–245

Write a pronoun to take the place of the underlined words in each sentence.

1. The oceans are important to my friends and me.
2. You and I get food of all kinds from the sea. They, us
3. The sea gives us fish and seaweed to eat. We It
4. These foods are important parts of many people's diets. They
5. Scientists study the oceans and ocean life. They

Possessive Pronouns *pages 262–265*

Write each sentence. Draw one line under the possessive pronoun. Then draw two lines under the antecedent.

6. We watched a shower of shooting stars from our backyard.
7. I looked through my telescope.
8. Pablo's sister tried to take a picture of one with her camera.
9. Pablo took a picture with his camera.
10. Pablo and Maria are proud of their pictures.

Adjectives *pages 272–277*

Write each sentence. Underline each adjective.

11. The penguins at the aquarium are funny.
12. They waddle around on their short, unsteady legs.
13. In the water, they are graceful and quick.
14. They can pop out of the water like little corks.
15. They make loud honking noises.

Pronouns and Adjectives

OBJECTIVES

- To use the correct forms of pronouns
- To identify possessive pronouns and their antecedents
- To recognize adjectives

UNIT 4 REVIEW

Have students complete the exercises, or modify them using these suggestions:

MODIFIED INSTRUCTION

BELOW-LEVEL STUDENTS Before students begin exercises 11–15, tell them that adjectives come before the nouns they describe or after a form of the verb *be*. Remind them that in some sentences, two adjectives can describe one noun.

ABOVE-LEVEL STUDENTS After students have completed exercises 1–5, have them label each pronoun as a subject or object pronoun.

HANDS ON Activity

ADJECTIVE CIRCLE Have students work in groups. Each student should write five nouns on separate index cards, and five adjectives on five more cards. Tell them to put all noun cards face down in one pile, and place the adjective cards face up. Students take turns drawing noun cards, then choosing all the adjectives that could reasonably describe the noun. Have each student in the group use the noun and at least one of the adjectives in a sentence.

Articles, Adjectives, and Adverbs

OBJECTIVES
- To use articles and adjectives that compare correctly
- To identify adverbs
- To use *good/well*, *bad/badly*, and other easily confused words correctly

UNIT 5 REVIEW

Have students complete the exercises, or modify them using these suggestions:

MODIFIED INSTRUCTION

BELOW-LEVEL STUDENTS Before students begin exercises 1–5, point out that the article *a* is not usually used before *most* or an adjective ending in *est*.

ABOVE-LEVEL STUDENTS After students have completed exercises 6–10, suggest that they rewrite sentences 6, 7, and 10 by moving the adverb to a different place in each sentence.

Articles and Adjectives That Compare *pages 308–313*

Rewrite each sentence. Use the correct article and adjective that compares in parentheses ().

1. (A, The) Potters have the (bigger, biggest) goat farm in the area. The, biggest
2. They have a (larger, largest) selection of goats than (an, the) others do. larger, the
3. (The, An) goat cheese they make is (popularer, more popular) than anyone else's. The, more popular
4. Our (favorite, favoritist) goat cheese is sold at (a, an) local market. favorite, a
5. It is (a, the) (tastier, tastiest) cheese of all. the, tastiest

Adverbs *pages 318–321*

Write the sentence. Underline each adverb.

6. The Gardiners <u>recently</u> moved from the city.
7. They <u>quickly</u> bought a house in the country.
8. Their son <u>now</u> goes to our school.
9. He runs <u>faster</u> than anyone else in school.
10. He <u>easily</u> won the race last week.

Using *Good* and *Well*, *Bad* and *Badly* *pages 340–341*

Write each sentence using the correct word in parentheses ().

11. Our town (bad, badly) needed a new supermarket. badly
12. Everyone thought it was a (good, well) idea. good
13. The store did very (good, well). well
14. The produce was (better, best) than anywhere else. better
15. This was the (goodest, best) thing to happen to our town in years. best

450

TEST PREP

TIP

If students are taking a test in which they must decide which words are adjectives and which are adverbs, remind them that most words ending in *ly* are adverbs. However, a few adjectives, such as *lovely*, also end in *ly*. Encourage them to read all the answer choices carefully before they decide.

Negatives *pages 378–381*

Write the sentence. Use a word from the box to fill in the blank.

| nobody | never | no | not | nothing |

1. I _____ saw a rainbow until recently. *never*
2. I did _____ know that they had so many colors. *not*
3. There was _____ warning before it came. *no*
4. _____ could believe how clear the colors were. *Nobody*
5. In a few minutes, there was _____ left to see. *nothing*

Commas *pages 388–391*

Write each sentence, placing commas where they are needed.

6. An earthquake shook California Arizona and Nevada. *An earthquake shook California, Arizona, and Nevada.*
7. Manuel the earthquake hit in the morning. *Manuel, the earthquake hit in the morning.*
8. It woke people up and they felt the ground shaking. *It woke people up, and they felt the ground shaking.*
9. No there weren't any injuries. *No, there weren't any injuries.*
10. Highway 113 Main Street and Cramer Avenue were closed. *Highway 113, Main Street, and Cramer Avenue were closed.*

Quotation Marks *pages 406–409*

Write each sentence, placing quotation marks and punctuation marks where they are needed.

11. How cold is it?" asked Jane. *"How cold is it?" asked Jane.*
12. Mrs. Fenice said "It is ten degrees above zero. *Mrs. Fenice replied, "It is only ten degrees above zero."*
13. "Wow! Jane cried We'd better dress warmly." *"Wow!" Jane cried. "We'd better dress warmly."*
14. Wear your boots," Mrs. Fenice said. *"Wear your boots," Mrs. Fenice said.*
15. "Don't stay outside too long Mrs Fenice warned, "or you might get frostbite." *"Don't stay outside too long," Mrs. Fenice warned, "or you might get frostbite."*

Cumulative Review
Unit 6

Usage and Mechanics

OBJECTIVES
- To use negative words correctly
- To use the fundamentals of punctuation

UNIT 6 REVIEW

Have students complete the exercises, or modify them using these suggestions:

MODIFIED INSTRUCTION

BELOW-LEVEL STUDENTS Before students begin exercises 11–15, tell them to look for speaker tags. Remind them that they need to begin a quotation with a capital letter, even when the speaker tags come before the quoted words.

ABOVE-LEVEL STUDENTS After students have completed the exercises, suggest that they rewrite sentences 11–15, changing the placement of the speaker tags and making the necessary adjustments in capitalization and punctuation.

HANDS ON Activity

NEGATIVE SENTENCES Write simple sentences on separate index cards. Have students work in groups and take turns drawing cards. The student who draws the card makes the sentence into a negative statement by adding a negative word or contraction.

Cumulative Review
Units 1-6

Language Use

OBJECTIVES
- To recognize mistakes in punctuation, capitalization, and spelling
- To practice using standardized test format

STANDARDIZED TEST PREP

The format used on this page helps prepare students for standardized tests. Explain that most standardized tests have one or more sections that test language skills—grammar, usage, capitalization, and punctuation. Have students read the directions on page 452 silently and work independently to complete the test items. When students have finished, invite them to discuss these questions:

1. **How well did you understand the directions?**

2. **Which answers were you unsure of, and why?**

3. **Did you pay attention to punctuation? How did it help you choose the correct answer?**

Language Use

Read the passage and decide which type of mistake, if any, appears in each underlined section. Mark the letter for your answer.

> "How does a thermometer <u>work," asked James?</u> Ms.
>   (1)
> Perry gave him an article <u>called "Measuring heat."</u> It
>   (2)
> said <u>"that a thermometer contains a thin glass tube."</u>
>   (3)
> The tube is partly filled with liquid. The liquid may be
> <u>alcohol colored red, or it may be mercury.</u> When the
>   (4)
> liquid gets warmer, it <u>expands and risses</u> up the tube.
>   (5)
> <u>"Thats simple,"</u> James said.
>   (6)

1   **A** Spelling
     B Capitalization
     C Punctuation   C
     D No mistake

4   **F** Spelling
     G Capitalization
     H Punctuation
     J No mistake   J

2   **F** Spelling
     G Capitalization   G
     H Punctuation
     J No mistake

5   **A** Spelling   A
     B Capitalization
     C Punctuation
     D No mistake

3   **A** Spelling
     B Capitalization
     C Punctuation   C
     D No mistake

6   **F** Spelling
     G Capitalization
     H Punctuation   H
     J No mistake

452

Written Expression

Use this paragraph to answer questions 1–4.

> Dutch settlers settled my town in the 1600s. They traveled up the Hudson River in ships. They built houses. They built churches. Many of their houses are still standing. My town is called Mount Kill. Next year I'm moving to a different town. Many people think "Kill" is a strange name for a town, but it really means "stream."

1 Choose the best opening sentence to add to this paragraph.

  A My town is one of the oldest in the area. A

  B Some towns were settled by the English.

  C My town is on the Hudson River.

2 Which sentences can best be combined?

  F 2 and 3

  G 5 and 6

  H 3 and 4 H

3 Choose the best concluding sentence to add to this paragraph.

  A Some of the settlers returned to Holland.

  B The old buildings are still standing.

  C Mount Kill is very proud of its Dutch heritage. C

4 Which of these sentences does not belong in the paragraph?

  F Dutch settlers settled my town in the 1600s.

  G They built houses.

  H Next year I'm moving to a different town. H

453

Cumulative Review
Units 1–6

Written Expression

OBJECTIVES

- To identify the purpose of a passage
- To choose the best order of sentences in a paragraph
- To practice using standardized test format

STANDARDIZED TEST PREP

Explain that some standardized tests include a section that tests written expression. The test items may not include actual errors. Many items ask for the *best* or *most appropriate way* to express or organize ideas.

Have students read the directions on page 453 silently and complete the test items independently. When students have finished, invite them to discuss their answer choices. If there is disagreement about an answer choice, have volunteers explain their thinking.

Assessment Strategies and Resources

FORMAL ASSESSMENT

If you want to know more about a student's mastery of the language and writing skills taught in Unit 6, **then** administer the first *Language Skills and Writing Assessment* for Unit 6. The test consists of two parts:

Language Skills: **negatives, commas, quotation marks, titles,** and **elaboration**

Writing Task: Write a **story**. Scoring guidelines and model student papers are included.

INFORMAL ASSESSMENT TOOLS

Using Interactive Writing
If you want to assess individual students' participation in interactive writing groups, **then** observe and record their responses. You may want to use an evaluation form with columns for the student's name, what the student knows, what he or she needs to learn, and what you plan to teach. You can quickly jot notes on cards or stick-on notes and later transfer them to the evaluation form, which becomes an ongoing assessment tool as you continue to add new notes.

This information will help you group students for instruction focused on particular areas or concepts and will aid in identifying students who need more individual support. Supplement your observational notes by examining samples of a student's writing, such as journal entries, and noting areas of progress and individual needs. Add that information to the evaluation form.

Informal Assessment Reminder
If you used the preinstruction writing prompt suggested in Teaching Grammar from Writing, **then** remember to compare the results with the writing done by students after the grammar and writing instruction.

Resources

Extra Practice

A. Write whether each sentence is a statement, a question, a command, or an exclamation. *pages 26–27*

1. Dave likes vacation time.
2. What does he enjoy most?
3. He likes to go fishing with his Uncle Freddie.
4. He also rides his bicycle along the river.
5. Wow, he saw some cranes!

B. Write each sentence. Add the correct end mark. *pages 28–29*

6. Once he saw a big fish along the river bank
7. Did he try to catch it by hand
8. Guess what happened
9. Wow, he got wet
10. What happened on your vacation

C. Read each group of words. Put the words in an order that makes sense. Make the kind of sentence shown. Use correct end marks. *pages 24–29*

11. Command—your line cast water into the
12. Exclamation—fish huge wow a what
13. Question—you do what do now
14. Command—tight line the keep
15. Command—fish the bring land to
16. Statement—eat fish the we'll later
17. Statement—to I don't cook like
18. Question—campfire you do how start a
19. Exclamation—hungry I'm wow really
20. Command—soon eat let's

454

Extra Practice

A. Write each sentence. Underline the complete subject. Then circle the simple subject. *pages 34–35*

1. The class is planning a school event.
2. Many students offered ideas.
3. One idea was to collect pennies.
4. The pennies will buy school equipment.
5. One student is in charge of the project.

B. Write the noun in each subject. *pages 36–37*

6. Many students brought in pennies.
7. The teacher made a big yardstick to show the number of pennies collected.
8. The yardstick was placed in the hall.
9. The principal contributed pennies.
10. This school project was a big success.

C. Combine each group of sentences into one sentence that has a compound subject. Write the new sentence. *pages 38–39*

11. Parents brought in pennies. Children brought in pennies. Teachers brought in pennies.
12. The principal counted the pennies. Her student helper counted the pennies.
13. The students received small ice cream cones. Their teachers received small ice cream cones.
14. Basketballs were bought with the money. Tumbling mats were bought with the money.
15. Davon hoped we'd have another school event soon. I hoped we'd have another school event soon.

Chapter 1

A.
1. statement
2. question
3. statement
4. statement
5. exclamation

B.
6. .
7. ?
8. .
9. !
10. ?

C.
11. Cast your line into the water.
12. Wow, what a huge fish!
13. What do you do now?
14. Keep the line tight.
15. Bring the fish to land.
16. We'll eat the fish later.
17. I don't like to cook.
18. How do you start a campfire?
19. Wow, I'm really hungry!
20. Let's eat soon.

Chapter 2

A.
1. The (class)
2. Many (students)
3. One (idea)
4. The (pennies)
5. One (student)

B.
6. Students
7. teacher
8. yardstick
9. principal
10. project

C.
11. Parents, children, and teachers brought in pennies.
12. The principal and her student helper counted the pennies.
13. The students and their teachers received small ice cream cones.
14. Basketballs and tumbling mats were bought with the money.
15. Davon and I hoped we'd have another school event soon.

Extra Practice

A. Write each sentence. Underline the complete predicate once. Underline the simple predicate twice. *pages 52–53*

1. Weather changes often in many places around the world.
2. Hawaii has nice weather all the time.
3. I plan vacations to warm islands.
4. Some places have cold weather outdoors and swimming pools inside.
5. Some people like skiing and sledding.

B. Write the verb in each sentence. *pages 54–55*

6. People talk about the weather every day.
7. Children fly kites in windy spring weather.
8. Children and adults swim in the summer.
9. The breeze becomes cooler in the fall.
10. The sky is often gray in winter.

C. Read the sentences in each group. Then write one sentence with a compound predicate. *pages 56–57*

11. The sky is blue. The sky has many fluffy white clouds.
12. A weather station watches for weather changes. A weather station warns about storms.
13. Some people plan for big storms. Some people have flashlights. Some people store bottled water.
14. Some bad storms roar like a train. Some bad storms pass quickly.
15. Farmers plant their seeds in good weather. Farmers hope rain will water their seeds.

456

Extra Practice

A. Write *complete sentence* if the group of words is a complete sentence. If it is not, make a complete sentence. *pages 62–63*

1. Bob and Ishiro play baseball after school.
2. Meet at the park near their home.
3. All their friends on the diamond.
4. Three players are pitchers.
5. During the game.

B. Write whether each sentence is a simple sentence or a compound sentence. *pages 64–65*

6. The batter swung at a bad pitch.
7. Bob hit a home run, and his team won the game.
8. A teacher helps coach the team.
9. Darkness ends most games.
10. Pablo is a good batter, and Jessica likes to pitch.

C. Use the word shown to combine each pair of sentences into a compound sentence. *pages 66–67*

11. Marta plays first base. Sometimes she plays right field. *and*
12. Johnny is a great pitcher. He's a fast runner, too. *and*
13. Rishi is a good hitter. He's an even better fielder. *but*
14. Our team made it to the play-offs. We didn't win. *but*
15. Next year we'll practice harder. Maybe we'll win the championship. *and*

457

Chapter 4

A.

1. <u>changes</u> often in many places around the world.
2. <u>has</u> nice weather all the time.
3. <u>plan</u> vacations to warm islands.
4. <u>have</u> cold weather outdoors and swimming pools inside.
5. <u>like</u> skiing and sledding.

B.

6. talk
7. fly
8. swim
9. becomes
10. is

C.

11. The sky is blue and has many fluffy white clouds.
12. A weather station watches for weather changes and warms about storms.
13. Some people plan for big storms, have flashlights, and store bottled water.
14. Some bad storms roar like a train and pass quickly.
15. Farmers plant their seeds in good weather and hope rain will water their seeds.

Chapter 5

A.

1. complete sentence
2. Possible response: They meet at the park near their home.
3. Possible response: All their friends meet on the diamond.
4. complete sentence
5. Possible response: The fans cheer during the game.

B.

6. simple sentence
7. compound sentence
8. simple sentence
9. simple sentence
10. compound sentence

C.

11. Marta plays first base, and sometimes she plays right field.
12. Johnny is a great pitcher, and he's a fast runner, too.
13. Rishi is a good hitter, but he's an even better fielder.
14. Our team made it to the play-offs, but we didn't win.
15. Next year we'll practice harder, and maybe we'll win the championship.

Extra Practice

A. Write each noun in the sentence.
pages 92–93

1. Good readers enjoy books that are written well.
2. The class listed exciting stories on the board.
3. A good story does not have to be long.
4. Will the knight rescue the queen from the beast?
5. My teacher reads the class a mystery.

B. Rewrite each sentence. Capitalize each proper noun. *pages 94–95*

6. Mr. johnson says that books are full of facts.
7. Dr. yoon says there are astonishing ideas in books.
8. Are you a visitor to discovery park library?
9. My friend roberto is eager to learn and chooses lots of books.
10. Some people buy books at the blue butterfly book market.

C. Write the abbreviation for each underlined word or words. *pages 96–97*

11. We completed the book by 11:30 (<u>before noon</u>).
12. At 1:00 (<u>after noon</u>) we recorded ideas on tape.
13. We each had three <u>minutes</u> for our message.
14. In <u>November</u> our classes shared these tapes.
15. At Copper <u>Road</u> School, everybody discovers new books.

458

Extra Practice

A. Write each plural noun in the sentence. Then write the singular form of each.
pages 102–103

1. Many boys and girls like animals.
2. Tom's hamsters have several food bowls.
3. Wet dogs make their fur shake after baths.
4. Cats like to explore holes and chase toys.
5. Snakes and lizards make interesting pets.

B. Form a plural noun from the underlined singular noun. *pages 104–105*

6. There are special combs and <u>brush</u> for horses.
7. The farmer keeps horse harnesses in <u>box</u>.
8. One of the farm animals ate some <u>berry</u>.
9. The rooster made <u>scratch</u> in the dirt.
10. The farmer has two <u>pony</u>.

C. Write the plural noun in each sentence. Then write the singular form.
pages 106–107

11. Do sheep have wool that is soft and curly?
12. Thirsty deer drink at the farm's water tank.
13. Geese are swimming in the lake.
14. Did you hear mice in the barn?
15. There are three trout in that pond.
16. My feet got wet near the pond.
17. Those women gave me a blanket.
18. Later, I'll try to catch some fish.
19. I won't catch any salmon, though.
20. My teeth start to chatter when it gets cold.

Chapter 7

A.
1. readers, books
2. class, stories, board
3. story
4. knight, queen, beast
5. teacher, class, mystery

B.
6. Johnson
7. Yoon
8. Discovery Park Library
9. Roberto
10. Blue Butterfly Book Market

C.
11. A.M.
12. P.M.
13. min.
14. Nov.
15. Rd.

Chapter 8

A.
1. boys, girls, animals / boy, girl, animal
2. hamsters, bowls / hamster, bowl
3. dogs, fur, baths / dog, fur, bath
4. cats, holes, toys / cat, hole, toy
5. Snakes, lizards, pets / snake, lizard, pet

B.
6. brushes
7. boxes
8. berries
9. scratches
10. ponies

C.
11. sheep, sheep
12. deer, deer
13. Geese, Goose
14. mice, mouse
15. trout, trout
16. feet, foot
17. women, woman
18. fish, fish
19. salmon, salmon
20. teeth, tooth

Extra Practice

A. Write the possessive form of each singular or plural noun. *pages 120–123*

1. teacher
2. seasons
3. Todd
4. sister
5. presidents

B. Write whether the underlined possessive noun is singular or plural. *pages 120–123*

6. The <u>company's</u> picnic includes children.
7. Each <u>guest's</u> child will receive a prize.
8. All the <u>pumpkins'</u> seeds are roasted.
9. The <u>winners'</u> prizes will be announced.
10. The <u>storyteller's</u> story was funny.

C. Complete each sentence. Choose the correct word in parentheses ( ). *pages 120–123*

11. We celebrate our (countrys', country's) birthday on the Fourth of July.
12. We always have fun at our (neighborhoods, neighborhood's) Fourth of July picnic.
13. My (dad's, dads') tie has white stars on it.
14. My (sisters, sister's) dress is red, white, and blue.
15. Everyone loves my (mom's, moms) cookies.

D. Rewrite each sentence using a possessive noun. *pages 124–125*

16. The lights of the city are beautiful.
17. Some people like the flame of a candle.
18. Others like the sparkle of fireworks.
19. The hug of a grandparent is special.
20. The rules of the games are fair.

Extra Practice

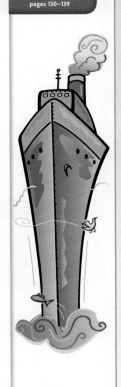

A. Write each sentence. Underline the verb in each sentence. *pages 130–131*

1. The automobile is one way of traveling.
2. The Model T took early drivers many places.
3. Those early motor cars were all black.
4. Now automobiles are many colors.
5. What color is your car?

B. Write each sentence. Underline the action verb in each sentence. *pages 132–133*

6. Today pilots jet around the world easily.
7. Airplanes fly overhead day and night.
8. Some carry cargo only.
9. Airports handle a lot of luggage.
10. Children visit grandparents by plane.

C. Write the verb in each sentence. Tell whether it is an action verb or a form of the verb *be*. *pages 132–135*

11. Some people go places by train or boat.
12. Trains plow slowly through snow.
13. They climb up steep hills.
14. Some people travel aboard a passenger ship.
15. It is fun on the deck of a ship.

D. Write each sentence, using the correct form of the verb *be* in parentheses ( ). *pages 134–135*

16. Some people (is, are) happy to exercise.
17. I (am, are) in a tennis tournament.
18. My dad (is, are) always in his car.
19. My mom and dad (is, are) walking more.
20. My friends (am, are) on the soccer team.

Chapter 10

A.
1. teacher's
2. seasons'
3. Todd's
4. sister's
5. presidents'

B.
6. singular
7. singular
8. plural
9. plural
10. singular

C.
11. country's
12. neighborhood's
13. dad's
14. sister's
15. Mom's

D.
16. The city's lights
17. a candle's flame
18. the fireworks' sparkle
19. A grandparent's hug
20. The games' rules

Chapter 11

A.
1. is
2. took
3. were
4. are
5. is

B.
6. jet
7. fly
8. carry
9. handle
10. visit

C.
11. go; action
12. plow; action
13. climb; action
14. travel; action
15. is; form of *be*

D.
16. are
17. am
18. is
19. are
20. are

Extra Practice

A. Write each sentence. Circle the helping verb and underline the main verb. *pages 166–169*

1. The new girl in school is smiling at everyone.
2. We are welcoming her to our class.
3. Have you made new friends before?
4. Are you sitting next to her at lunch?
5. Do not forget her name.

B. Make a chart with two columns. Label the first column *Helping Verbs* and the second column *Main Verbs*. Write each underlined verb in the correct column. *pages 166–169*

6. The new girl <u>does</u> not <u>know</u> anyone at our school.
7. She <u>has</u> <u>moved</u> here from New Jersey.
8. We <u>were</u> <u>talking</u> about her old school.
9. She <u>is</u> <u>hoping</u> other children will talk to her.
10. She <u>was</u> <u>smiling</u> so that the class would know she is friendly.

C. Write each sentence, using a contraction for the underlined words. *pages 170–171*

11. <u>Do not</u> worry if it takes a few days for children to talk to you.
12. You <u>are not</u> someone they know well yet.
13. It <u>is not</u> unusual for new students to be shy at first.
14. I <u>should not</u> forget that it takes time to make friends.
15. I <u>have not</u> forgotten how exciting it is to go to a new school.

462

Extra Practice

A. Write each sentence, and underline the verb. Write whether the verb shows action that is happening in the present, happened in the past, or will happen in the future. *pages 176–177*

1. Jeff likes history.
2. He learned a lot from older people.
3. They told him about the difference between their early years and now.
4. Jeff will study ancient Rome soon.
5. He will use books from the library.

B. Choose the correct present-tense verb in parentheses ( ). *pages 178–179*

6. The class (study, studies) American history.
7. Each student (dress, dresses) in clothing from colonial days.
8. Jeff (wear, wears) an army uniform.
9. Some of the girls' skirts (touch, touches) the floor.
10. Jeff's friends Jake and Alberto (own, owns) costumes of famous men.

C. For each sentence, tell whether the subject is singular or plural. Then write the sentence, using the correct verb in parentheses ( ). *pages 180–181*

11. Jeff (learn, learns) a lot from a history channel on television.
12. The channel (has, have) old news stories.
13. Paintings (show, shows) the days before cameras.
14. Internet searches (find, finds) some interesting facts.
15. These books (explain, explains) the history of the Civil War.

Chapter 13

A.
1. (is), smiling
2. (are), welcoming
3. (Have), made
4. (Are), sitting
5. (Do), forget

B.

Helping Verbs	Main Verbs
6. does	know
7. has	moved
8. were	talking
9. is	hoping
10. was	smiling

C.
11. Don't
12. aren't
13. isn't
14. shouldn't
15. haven't

Chapter 14

A.
1. likes; present
2. learned; past
3. told; past
4. will study; future
5. will use; future

B.
6. studies
7. dresses
8. wears
9. touch
10. own

C.
11. singular, learns
12. singular, has
13. plural, show
14. plural, find
15. plural, explain

Extra Practice

A. Write the verb in each sentence. Label each verb *past tense* or *future tense*.
pages 194–195

1. A famous writer will visit our school.
2. The writer will bring his books.
3. Jim and Maki wrote him a letter.
4. The writer sent us a poster for the school library.
5. We will invite a different author to our school next year.

B. Write each sentence, using the verb in parentheses ( ). Form the tense that is given at the end of the sentence. *pages 196–197*

6. We (promise) our teacher to give the author a warm welcome. (past)
7. The mayor (honor) the author with a special visitor's ribbon. (future)
8. His fan club (meet) him at the airport. (future)
9. The teachers (plan) a class activity. (past)
10. We (purchase) his books for the library so everyone could read his stories. (past)

C. Write the correct form of the verb in parentheses ( ) for each sentence. *pages 198–199*

11. On the day of the program, we (hurries, hurried) to school.
12. After greeting the writer, our teacher (disappears, disappeared) behind the curtain.
13. The crowd (cheers, cheered) for him when he arrived.
14. All the rest of the year we (remembers, will remember) his visit.
15. I (will decide, decided) he is my new hero.

464

Extra Practice

A. Write the sentence. Choose the correct verb in parentheses ( ) to complete each sentence. *pages 204–207*

1. He (saw, seen) the beautiful meadow.
2. He (say, said) it was filled with flowers.
3. He (drew, drawn) a picture of a beehive.
4. The sound of the bees (growed, grew) louder.
5. He (rode, rided) home with no stings at all and a beautiful picture.

B. Write the past-tense form of the verb in parentheses ( ) to complete the sentence. *pages 204–207*

6. Long ago, children from this village _____ beans, peas, and carrots. (grow)
7. They _____ the packages of seeds outside. (take)
8. They _____ lines in the dirt. (draw)
9. The leaky hose _____ enough water for the garden. (give)
10. Helpers, parents, and friends _____ the ripe vegetables. (eat)

C. Write the verb in parentheses ( ) that completes each sentence correctly. *pages 208–209*

11. The flower garden (lies, lays) between the house and the river.
12. Gardeners (teach, learn) others about plants.
13. Spring flowers start to bloom when the temperature (raises, rises).
14. Gardeners (teach, learn) from nature, too.
15. Elena (lies, lays) her garden tools on a shelf in the shed.

465

Chapter 16

A.
1. will visit; future tense
2. will bring; future tense
3. wrote; past tense
4. sent; past tense
5. will invite; future tense

B.
6. promised
7. will honor
8. will meet
9. planned
10. purchased

C.
11. hurried
12. disappeared
13. cheered
14. will remember
15. decided

Chapter 17

A.
1. saw
2. said
3. drew
4. grew
5. rode

B.
6. grew
7. took
8. drew
9. gave
10. ate

C.
11. lies
12. teach
13. rises
14. learn
15. lays

Extra Practice

A. **Write each pronoun in the sentence. Write *S* if the pronoun is singular or *P* if the pronoun is plural.** *pages 234–235*

1. Brian smiled as he fed the turtles.
2. Maki was silent and just looked at him.
3. She didn't want to touch the turtles.
4. Maki doesn't like them as much as she likes hamsters.
5. Brian thinks you should have lots of different pets.

B. **Write the pronoun that can take the place of the underlined noun or nouns.** *pages 236–237*

6. <u>Maki and Brian</u> both have dogs.
7. They like to walk <u>the dogs</u> in the park.
8. <u>Maki</u> has a beagle.
9. <u>Maki's dog</u> is white, brown, and black.
10. <u>Brian</u> has a spaniel that plays catch with <u>Brian</u>.

C. **Write the antecedent from the first sentence for each underlined pronoun.** *pages 238–239*

11. My hamsters run fast. <u>They</u> could be track stars.
12. Their wheel turns a lot. <u>It</u> lets me know they want to race.
13. Brian looked at the hamsters. <u>He</u> thought <u>they</u> were cute, soft, and furry.
14. Maki and Brian talked about the animals. <u>They</u> decided to have a pet show.
15. Isabel could bring her pets, too. <u>She</u> has many of <u>them</u>.

466

Extra Practice

A. **Write each sentence, using the correct pronoun in parentheses ( ).** *pages 244–249*

1. (I, Me) like Nidia's parents' store.
2. (She, Her) thinks it is wonderful, too.
3. The customers often call (she, her) by name.
4. Her parents give (we, us) treats.
5. (They, Them) know we like to help, too.

B. **Write *subject pronoun* or *object pronoun* to name the underlined word in each sentence.** *pages 244–247*

6. <u>She</u> enjoys Saturdays best.
7. The empty shelves make a lot of work for <u>us</u>.
8. <u>You</u> came in last Saturday with your husband.
9. <u>He</u> found some tires in back that were just right.
10. Mr. Ramos put them on for <u>you</u>.

C. **Rewrite each sentence. Replace the underlined words with a pronoun.** *pages 244–247*

11. <u>My friend and I</u> built a tool display.
12. <u>The tool display</u> is popular.
13. People smiled at <u>my friend and me</u>.
14. <u>A man</u> took a picture of it.
15. The story in the newspaper surprised <u>her parents</u>.

467

Chapter 19

A.
1. he, S
2. him, S
3. She, S
4. them, P; she, S
5. you, S

B.
6. They
7. them
8. She
9. It
10. He, him

C.
11. hamsters
12. wheel
13. Brian; hamsters
14. Maki and Brian
15. Isabel, pets

Chapter 20

A.
1. I
2. She
3. her
4. us
5. They

B.
6. subject pronoun
7. object pronoun
8. subject pronoun
9. subject pronoun
10. object pronoun

C.
11. We built a tool display.
12. It is popular.
13. People smiled at us.
14. He took a picture of it.
15. The story in the newspaper surprised them.

Extra Practice

A. Write each possessive pronoun in the sentence. *pages 262–263*

 1. I think Missy has taken her baggage to the airport by now.
 2. Its handles are silver.
 3. My suitcase has wheels on it.
 4. Put your suitcase next to my backpack.
 5. At least our bags will start the trip next to each other.

B. Write the possessive pronoun that belongs in each space. *pages 264–265*

 6. Since Missy likes pink bags, the pink bag is _____.
 7. The blue one is _____.
 8. They are renting a cabin, and _____ windows look over a lake.
 9. When are you taking _____ vacation?
 10. _____ vacation next year will be at my grandmother's house.

C. Underline the contraction in each sentence. Write the two words that were used to make the contraction. *pages 266–267*

 11. We're not going anywhere this year.
 12. I'm helping my dad repair a house in my neighborhood.
 13. We'll volunteer every year to help out a family in need.
 14. They've always helped other people in our community.
 15. You get a special feeling when you've helped someone else.

Extra Practice

A. For each sentence, write the adjective that tells *how many*. *pages 274–275*

 1. Most people enjoy birthdays.
 2. Do you have a party each year?
 3. Some people have birthdays on the same day.
 4. Several people are twins.
 5. Two cousins in my family were born on the same day.

B. Complete each sentence with an adjective that tells *how many*. The answer may or may not be an exact number. *pages 274–275*

 6. I know _____ thing about getting older.
 7. _____ people have birthdays.
 8. Triplets celebrate _____ birthdays at the same time.
 9. _____ birthdays are in the summer.
 10. This year I will be _____ years old.

C. Read each sentence. Write each adjective that tells *what kind*. *pages 276–277*

 11. Birthday cakes usually have candles.
 12. Cakes can be round or flat.
 13. There are red roses on the cake for my mother.
 14. Is that a tiny nibble on the corner of the cake?
 15. This chocolate cake is delicious!

Chapter 22

A.
 1. her
 2. Its
 3. My
 4. your; my
 5. our

B.
 6. Possible response: hers
 7. Possible responses: mine, ours, theirs
 8. Possible responses: its, their
 9. Possible response: your
 10. possible responses: Our, My

C.
 11. We're; We are
 12. I'm; I am
 13. We'll ; We will
 14. They've; They have
 15. you've; you have

Chapter 23

A.
 1. Most
 2. each
 3. Some
 4. Several
 5. Two

B.
 6. Possible response: one
 7. Possible response: All
 8. Possible response: three
 9. Possible responses: Some, Many
 10. Possible response: nine

C.
 11. Birthday
 12. round, flat
 13. red
 14. tiny
 15. chocolate, delicious

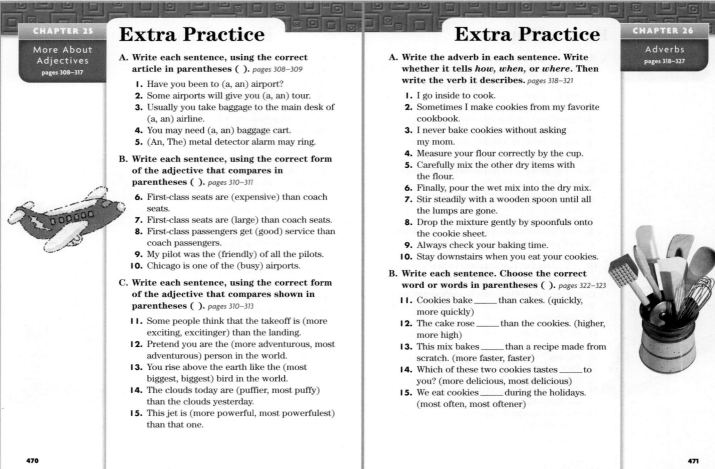

Extra Practice

A. Write each sentence, using the correct article in parentheses ( ). *pages 308–309*

1. Have you been to (a, an) airport?
2. Some airports will give you (a, an) tour.
3. Usually you take baggage to the main desk of (a, an) airline.
4. You may need (a, an) baggage cart.
5. (An, The) metal detector alarm may ring.

B. Write each sentence, using the correct form of the adjective that compares in parentheses ( ). *pages 310–311*

6. First-class seats are (expensive) than coach seats.
7. First-class seats are (large) than coach seats.
8. First-class passengers get (good) service than coach passengers.
9. My pilot was the (friendly) of all the pilots.
10. Chicago is one of the (busy) airports.

C. Write each sentence, using the correct form of the adjective that compares shown in parentheses ( ). *pages 310–313*

11. Some people think that the takeoff is (more exciting, excitinger) than the landing.
12. Pretend you are the (more adventurous, most adventurous) person in the world.
13. You rise above the earth like the (most biggest, biggest) bird in the world.
14. The clouds today are (puffier, most puffy) than the clouds yesterday.
15. This jet is (more powerful, most powerfulest) than that one.

470

Extra Practice

A. Write the adverb in each sentence. Write whether it tells *how*, *when*, or *where*. Then write the verb it describes. *pages 318–321*

1. I go inside to cook.
2. Sometimes I make cookies from my favorite cookbook.
3. I never bake cookies without asking my mom.
4. Measure your flour correctly by the cup.
5. Carefully mix the other dry items with the flour.
6. Finally, pour the wet mix into the dry mix.
7. Stir steadily with a wooden spoon until all the lumps are gone.
8. Drop the mixture gently by spoonfuls onto the cookie sheet.
9. Always check your baking time.
10. Stay downstairs when you eat your cookies.

B. Write each sentence. Choose the correct word or words in parentheses ( ). *pages 322–323*

11. Cookies bake _____ than cakes. (quickly, more quickly)
12. The cake rose _____ than the cookies. (higher, more high)
13. This mix bakes _____ than a recipe made from scratch. (more faster, faster)
14. Which of these two cookies tastes _____ to you? (more delicious, most delicious)
15. We eat cookies _____ during the holidays. (most often, most oftener)

471

Chapter 25

A.
1. an
2. a
3. an
4. a
5. The

B.
6. more expensive
7. larger
8. better
9. friendliest
10. busiest

C.
11. more exciting
12. most adventurous
13. biggest
14. puffier
15. more powerful

Chapter 26

A.
1. inside, where, go
2. Sometimes, when, make
3. never, when, bake
4. correctly, how, measure
5. Carefully, how, mix
6. Finally, when, pour
7. steadily, how, stir
8. gently, how, drop
9. Always, when, check
10. downstairs, where, Stay

B.
11. more quickly
12. higher
13. faster
14. more delicious
15. most often

Extra Practice

A. Write whether the underlined word is an adjective or an adverb. *pages 336–337*

1. <u>Regular</u> exercise helps keep your body healthy.
2. Running <u>fast</u> expands your lungs.
3. Your <u>many</u> leg muscles also get a workout.
4. A <u>mountain</u> bicycle is fun to ride.
5. Ride <u>carefully</u> along the trail.

B. Write each sentence. Include the adverb in parentheses ( ). Put it in the best place. *pages 338–339*

6. (skillfully) The children played soccer at the picnic.
7. (often) The score was tied.
8. (later) They shot baskets.
9. (peacefully) Some people canoed on the river.
10. (rapidly) Others hiked through the woods.

C. Rewrite each sentence, using the correct word in parentheses ( ). *pages 340–341*

11. Your class did (good, well) in the school fitness test.
12. Most of the students had a (good, well) heart rate.
13. The teachers felt (bad, badly) for the children who never exercise.
14. The weather was (good, well) on the day of the test.
15. My friend was ill, so he thought he would do (bad, badly) on the test.

472

Extra Practice

A. Write each sentence, using the correct word in parentheses ( ). *pages 346–347*

1. Sally plans a trip (to, too, two) Japan.
2. She will stay for (to, too, two) weeks.
3. She will (write, right) postcards each day.
4. She would not feel (write, right) if she did not keep in touch.
5. Do you feel that way, (to, too, two)?

B. Write each sentence, using the correct word in parentheses ( ). *pages 348–349*

6. (Their, There, They're) thinking of places to go.
7. (Its, It's) exciting to plan trips for other people.
8. You have to know (their, there, they're) likes and dislikes.
9. (Your, You're) the one who presents the ideas.
10. Make certain they want to go (their, there, they're).

C. Write each sentence, using the correct words from the box. *pages 350–351*

sea	know	trip (v.)	bow (n.)
see	no	trip (n.)	bow (v.)

11. If you don't _____ well, you might _____ .
12. Be especially careful if you are taking a _____ across the _____ to Japan.
13. I _____ how to _____ to my Japanese host.
14. I _____ where a gift with a _____ is hidden.
15. He will _____ that I am polite.

473

Chapter 28

A.
1. adjective
2. adverb
3. adjective
4. adjective
5. adverb

B.
6. Possible response: The children played soccer skillfully at the picnic.
7. Possible response: Often the score was tied.
8. Possible response: Later they shot baskets.
9. Possible response: Some people canoed peacefully on the river.
10. Possible response: Others hiked rapidly through the woods.

C.
11. well
12. good
13. bad
14. good
15. badly

Chapter 29

A.
1. to
2. two
3. write
4. right
5. too

B.
6. They're
7. It's
8. their
9. You're
10. there

C.
11. see, trip (v.)
12. trip (n.), sea
13. know, bow (v.)
14. know, bow (n.)
15. see or know

Extra Practice

A. Write each sentence, and underline the negative word or words. *pages 378–381*

1. Sonja told her sister she wouldn't get lost.
2. No one could change her mind about going.
3. She never stopped planning the adventure.
4. Friends didn't believe she would go.
5. Nobody wanted to go with her.

B. Choose a negative word from the box to best complete each sentence. *pages 378–381*

nowhere	never	nothing	not	none

6. _____ of this bothered Sonja.
7. _____ was standing in her way.
8. She knew there was _____ else for her to go.
9. _____ a person came to say good-bye.
10. She is going to a place I _____ heard of.

C. Rewrite each sentence to correct the double negative. *pages 382–383*

11. I couldn't not be as brave as Sonja.
12. I don't have no plans for a big adventure.
13. She wasn't never worried to leave her family behind.
14. I will never not go alone when I take a trip.
15. It won't be no fun to travel without you.
16. Tom didn't never think about the farm.
17. Lucy wasn't going not far to visit him.
18. Her mother knew nobody not in the city.
19. She couldn't write not one letter.
20. She didn't have no pens or pencils.

474

Extra Practice

A. Write the sentence. Add commas where they are needed. *pages 388–389*

1. Manuel took his camera and went hunting for people birds and wild animals.
2. What can you find in Santa Rosa California?
3. He found lizards hamsters and friends.
4. Manuel will your friends at school smile when you take their picture?
5. Yes they love to have their pictures taken!

B. Rewrite the letter. Add commas where they are needed. *pages 390–391*

6. Chicago Illinois
7. April 19 2002
   Dear Mr. Fuentes
8. I have some wonderful pictures of wildlife in Santa Rosa California.
9. They will be in the show on May 2 2002.
10. Sincerely
    Manuel

C. Combine each group of sentences to form a compound sentence, using *and* or *but*. Add commas where they are needed. *pages 392–393*

11. Manuel took his camera to school. His teacher let him take pictures of the class pet.
12. Crows flew into the schoolyard at recess. Manuel had his camera ready.
13. He wanted to get several pictures of lizards. They rushed away.
14. Some friends brought their pet lizards to school. Manuel got great shots of them.
15. Manuel took his film to the store. The pictures were great.

475

Chapter 31

A.
1. Wouldn't
2. No one
3. never
4. didn't
5. Nobody

B.
6. None
7. Nothing
8. nowhere
9. not
10. never

C.
11. I couldn't be as brave as Sonja.
12. I don't have plans for a big adventure.
13. She wasn't worried to leave her family behind.
14. I will never go alone when I take a trip.
15. It won't be fun to travel without you.
16. Tom didn't think about the farm.
17. Lucy wasn't going far to visit him.
18. Her mother knew nobody in the city.
19. She couldn't write one letter.
20. She didn't have pens or pencils.

Chapter 32

A.
1. people, birds, and
2. Rosa, California
3. lizards, hamsters, and
4. Manuel, will
5. yes, they

B.
6. Chicago, Illinois
7. April 19, 2002; Dear Mr. Fuentes,
8. I have some wonderful pictures of wildlife in Santa Rosa, California.
9. May 2, 2002.
10. Sincerely, Manuel

C.
11. school, and his
12. recess, and Manuel
13. lizards, but they
14. school, and Manuel
15. store, and the

Extra Practice

A. Write each sentence, adding quotation marks where they are needed. *pages 406–407*

1. We expect everybody to be part of our community volunteer program, said the mayor.
2. Do you mean even us? Ryan asked.
3. Yes, and even the rest of your family, the mayor told him.
4. She explained, Some of the families who live here will make a great difference in our community.
5. The helpers will meet next week to get started, she said.

B. Write the sentence, correcting each error in punctuation and capitalization. *pages 406–409*

6. "The group is small, she told us.
7. Do you know how large the neighborhood is" she asked.
8. Betsy shouted Farther than I can walk
9. "That's so big exclaimed Frank.
10. The mayor said, It is a key part of the city.

C. Write each sentence and underline the words that tell who is speaking and how. *pages 410–411*

11. "That's why it is important for us to clean it up as an example for others," she continued.
12. Ryan exclaimed, "It will be so much work!"
13. "Yes," Betsy said, "but we can do it."
14. "What questions do you have?" asked the mayor.
15. "When do we start?" Betsy and Ryan asked together.

476

Extra Practice

A. Write the sentence. Underline each book, magazine, or newspaper title. *pages 416–417*

1. The main characters in the book Charlotte's Web are a pig and a spider.
2. Ranger Rick magazine had a story with facts about spiders.
3. The Evening Tribune told about a pet pig named Wilbur.
4. Have you read the book Mr. Popper's Penguins?
5. My sister wrote a review of that book for the Woodland Middle School News.

B. Write each sentence. Place quotation marks around the titles of stories, poems, articles, and songs. *pages 418–419*

6. Where the Sidewalk Ends is a famous poem in a book with the same name.
7. I read an article about poetry called Other Dangers of Poetry Writing.
8. An unusual song is Grandma Wore Her Nightcap to Work in the Garden.
9. Peter Rabbit is a great children's story.
10. I wrote a poem called The End.

C. Rewrite each title, using correct capitalization. *pages 420–421*

11. "Going on a bear hunt"
12. A child's garden of verses
13. "Jack and the beanstalk"
14. "singing in the rain"
15. folktales of Texas

477

Chapter 34

A.
1. "We ... volunteer program," said the mayor.
2. "Do ... <u>us</u>?" Ryan asked.
3. "Yes, and ... family," the mayor told him.
4. She explained, "Some of ... community."
5. "The helpers ... started," she said.

B.
6. "The group is small," she told us.
7. "Do you know how large the neighborhood is?" she asked.
8. Betsy shouted, "Farther than I can walk!"
9. "That's so big!" exclaimed Frank.
10. The mayor said, "It is a key part of the city."

C.
11. she continued
12. Ryan exclaimed
13. Betsy said
14. asked the mayor
15. Betsy and Ryan asked together

Chapter 35

A.
1. <u>Charlotte's Web</u>
2. <u>Ranger Rick</u>
3. <u>The Evening Tribune</u>
4. <u>Mr. Popper's Penguins</u>
5. <u>Woodland Middle School News</u>

B.
6. "Where the Sidewalk Ends"
7. "Other Dangers of Poetry Writing."
8. "Grandma Wore Her Nightcap to Work in the Garden."
9. "Peter Rabbit"
10. "The End."

C.
11. "Going on a Bear Hunt"
12. <u>A Child's Garden of Verses</u>
13. "Jack and the Beanstalk"
14. "Singing in the Rain"
15. <u>Folktales of Texas</u>

Handbook

Contents

Writing Models

Personal Narrative

A **narrative** is a story. A **personal narrative** is a story about a writer's own experiences.

How to Write a Personal Narrative

- Write from your **point of view**. Use the pronouns *I*, *me*, and *my*.
- Tell about an **event** that happened to you.
- Include **details** to help your readers picture the event.
- Express how you felt about the event.

writer's viewpoint using *I* and *my*

beginning/ details

middle/ details

end/details

writer's viewpoint

The One That Didn't Get Away

I am just crazy about my cat, Creamy. My mom and dad gave her to me on my sixth birthday. She sleeps on my bed every night and wakes me up every morning.

Last summer, though, I thought I'd lost her forever. My family moved to a new house about a mile away. Creamy got scared by the noise of the furniture being moved, and she ran off. We could not find her anywhere. I didn't want to leave, but we had to go to our new house without her.

Every day, I got sadder and sadder. Then one morning, about ten days after we moved, I heard scratching and meowing at the door. It was Creamy! She had found us on her own. I always knew cats were smart. I'll never let Creamy get lost again!

How-to Essay

A **how-to essay** gives directions that tell how to do something. These directions are given in order.

How to Write a How-to Essay

- Write an opening paragraph that tells what you will explain how to do.
- List all the materials needed.
- Write sentences that tell the steps in order.
- Use sequence words such as *first*, *next*, *then*, and *last* to show the correct order.

opening paragraph

materials the reader will need

steps in order/ sequence words

It can be fun to decorate the table for a party. One way is to make animals from vegetables and fruits. Suppose you want to make a horse. Here are some steps that can help you. You will need the following items:

- fruit (berries, bananas, or other colorful fruits)
- vegetables (green and red peppers, cucumbers, carrots, and lettuce)
- toothpicks

First, choose a large fruit or vegetable to use for the body, such as a banana or a cucumber. Next, cut long pieces of carrot for the legs. Then, choose a small pepper for the head. Use berries for the eyes and pieces of red pepper for the ears. Attach them to the head with toothpicks. Next, slice lettuce for the mane and tail. Finally, attach the legs, head, mane, and tail to the body with toothpicks.

Persuasive Essay

A **persuasive essay** tells how a writer feels about a topic. The writer tries to persuade the reader to agree.

How to Write a Persuasive Essay

- Write a topic sentence that tells how you feel about the topic.
- Give reasons that support how you feel. Add details to make your reasons clearer.
- List your strongest reason last.
- At the end of your essay, tell how you feel about the topic again. Ask your audience to take action.

topic sentence that gives opinion

reasons and details

call to action

Many people like to play and watch different sports. I think that baseball is the best sport of all. Everyone who likes to play sports should learn how to play baseball.

Baseball is a great sport to play. When you play baseball a lot, you make the muscles in your arms and legs strong. You also learn how to run fast. Baseball teaches you how to work with other team players. It's really fun when your team wins. The best part is that your teammates make good friends!

Baseball is my favorite sport. It provides exercise and helps players work together and make friends. Find out about baseball leagues in your neighborhood and join up.

Advantages and Disadvantages Essay

An essay that tells **advantages and disadvantages** explains the good and bad things about a topic.

How to Write an Advantages and Disadvantages Essay

- Get your readers' interest with your introduction.
- Write one paragraph about the disadvantages and one about the advantages of the topic.
- Use detail sentences and clear examples.
- Summarize your thoughts in a concluding paragraph.

title

introduction

disadvantages and details about them

advantages and details about them

conclusion

Summer Visitors

My cousins come to visit every summer. I always look forward to their visits because I like them very much. There are also some things I do not like about their visits.

There are some disadvantages to my cousins coming to visit. For example, one of my cousins gets to sleep in my bed at night, so I sleep on the floor. I also have to share my things with my cousins. Sometimes, one cousin leaves dirty fingerprints on my books.

We always have a lot of fun during their visits, though. That is the biggest advantage. For example, we get to go to special places, like the water park and a baseball game. My cousins are also really fun friends for me to play with.

When my cousins go home, I miss them a lot. So, even though there are some bad things about my cousins' visits, I'm always excited to see them again the next year.

Research Report

A **research report** gives information about a topic. Writers gather facts from different sources, such as books or magazines. They take notes to remember the facts, and they make outlines to organize the facts. Then they write their reports.

How to Write a Research Report

- Write an interesting paragraph to introduce your topic.
- Use your notes to write detailed paragraphs about each main topic in your outline. Remember to use your own words when you write.
- Write a concluding paragraph to end your report.

title

introduction/ main topic

subtopic and details

Tiny Helpers

Ants are not just tiny insects. They are very interesting creatures. They make their own homes, work together, and are helpful to nature and humans.

Ants live everywhere on Earth except in very cold areas. They live together in communities called colonies. Each colony may have as few as a dozen or as many as a million ant members. Most ants make homes in underground tunnels. Some ants, however, live inside trees or other plants.

An ant colony is very organized. Each ant has a special purpose in the colony. Most of the ants are female worker ants. These ants build and protect the nest. They also find food for the colony and care for the young ants. Each colony has at least one queen ant whose main job is to lay eggs. Male ants live in the colony part-time.

Ants are very important in nature. They help keep things in balance on Earth. By eating other insects, ants help keep the insect population from getting too big. Ants are also helpful to humans. When they dig tunnels, ants help farmers by breaking up hard-packed soil. What helps farmers is good for all of us, since farmers produce much of our food.

Many people think ants are just pests because they get into buildings where people do not want them. Ants are actually very hard workers that are very important to the world. Maybe you will think of ants differently next time you see one of these tiny helpers!

subtopic and details

subtopic and details

concluding paragraph

Short Story

A **short story** tells about characters solving a problem. A short story has a beginning, a middle, and an end.

How to Write a Short Story

- Write a beginning. Name the story characters, and tell where the story takes place. Give the characters a problem to solve.
- Write the middle of the story. Tell what the characters do to try to solve the problem.
- Write the end. Tell how the problem is solved.
- Write a title for the story.

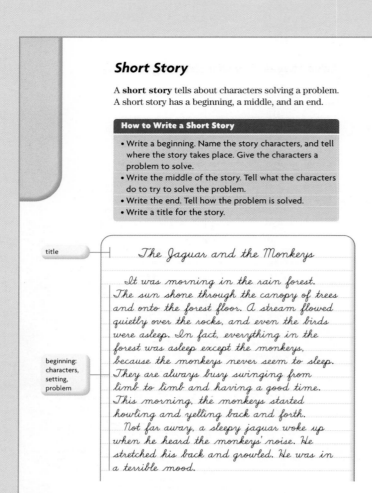

title →

The Jaguar and the Monkeys

beginning: characters, setting, problem →

It was morning in the rain forest. The sun shone through the canopy of trees and onto the forest floor. A stream flowed quietly over the rocks, and even the birds were asleep. In fact, everything in the forest was asleep except the monkeys, because the monkeys never seem to sleep. They are always busy swinging from limb to limb and having a good time. This morning, the monkeys started howling and yelling back and forth.

Not far away, a sleepy jaguar woke up when he heard the monkeys' noise. He stretched his back and growled. He was in a terrible mood.

486

"I have to make those monkeys be quiet," said the jaguar. "I need my sleep." So the jaguar went to the banana trees. He picked bunches and bunches of bananas. Then he went to the mango trees. He picked buckets and buckets of mangoes. The giant cat took the bananas and mangoes to the other side of the forest.

← middle

When the jaguar returned home, he spoke to the monkeys. "There is a surprise for you on the other side of the forest," he said. "Go there soon before someone else finds it!"

The monkeys ran off as fast as they could. The tired jaguar then climbed back into bed. Finally, he would be able to sleep for as long as he wanted.

← end

487

Descriptive Paragraph

A **descriptive paragraph** is writing that describes an object, a feeling, an event, or anything else a person is writing about.

How to Write a Descriptive Paragraph

- Use vivid words to describe how things look, sound, taste, or feel.
- You may express your personal viewpoint, telling the reader how you feel about the subject.

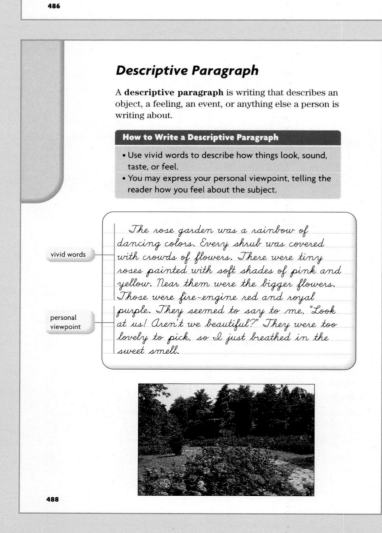

vivid words →

The rose garden was a rainbow of dancing colors. Every shrub was covered with crowds of flowers. There were tiny roses painted with soft shades of pink and yellow. Near them were the bigger flowers.

personal viewpoint →

Those were fire-engine red and royal purple. They seemed to say to me, "Look at us! Aren't we beautiful?" They were too lovely to pick, so I just breathed in the sweet smell.

488

Book Review

A **book review** tells what a book is about. It tells what the writer thinks about the book.

How to Write a Book Review

- Write the title of the book and the author's name in the first sentence.
- Tell about the most important characters and the main idea.
- Then tell about the important events.
- Include interesting details, but do not tell the ending.
- Give your opinion of the book and tell why someone might or might not like to read it.

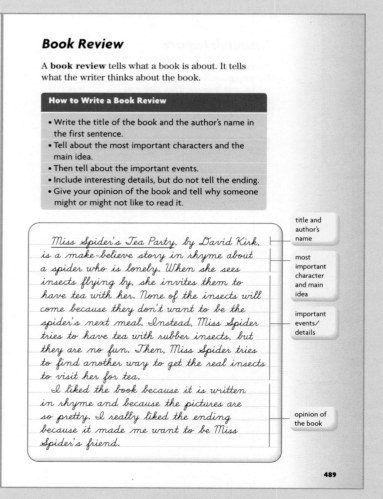

title and author's name →

Miss Spider's Tea Party, by David Kirk, is a make-believe story in rhyme about a spider who is lonely.

most important character and main idea →

When she sees insects flying by, she invites them to have tea with her. None of the insects will come because they don't want to be the spider's next meal.

important events/ details →

Instead, Miss Spider tries to have tea with rubber insects, but they are no fun. Then, Miss Spider tries to find another way to get the real insects to visit her for tea.

opinion of the book →

I liked the book because it is written in rhyme and because the pictures are so pretty. I really liked the ending because it made me want to be Miss Spider's friend.

489

Paragraph That Compares

A **paragraph that compares** tells how two or more people, places, or things are alike.

How to Write a Paragraph That Compares

- Write a topic sentence. Name the subjects and tell how they are alike.
- Write detail sentences that give clear examples.
- In the detail sentences, list the two subjects in the same order you used in the topic sentence.

topic sentence → Parakeets and macaws are alike because they are the same colors, they live in pairs, and they eat the same things. Both birds' feathers can be blue, red, yellow, and green. Parakeets and macaws like to live in pairs, and you can see them gather in larger groups at night. Parakeets and macaws eat nuts, berries, and seeds. One interesting thing that both parakeets and macaws eat is clay. Each morning you can see up to 500 parakeets and macaws eating lumps of clay near the riverbank!

← **detail sentences**

Paragraph That Contrasts

A **paragraph that contrasts** tells how two or more people, places, or things are different.

How to Write a Paragraph That Contrasts

- Write a topic sentence. Name the subjects and tell how they are different.
- Write detail sentences that give clear examples.
- List the two subjects in the same order you used in the topic sentence.

parakeets   macaw

Parakeets and macaws are different sizes and make different noises. Parakeets are small, slender birds. They are seven to eleven inches long. Macaws are very large birds and can be thirty to forty inches long. Parakeets can chirp loudly, but not as loudly as macaws. Macaws can make a loud screeching noise that would scare any animal that might want to eat them. ← **topic sentence** / **detail sentences**

Friendly Letter with Envelope

A **friendly letter** is a letter you write to someone you know well. Friendly letters include a heading, greeting, body, closing, and signature.

A **thank-you note** is one kind of friendly letter. A thank-you note thanks someone for giving a gift or for doing something.

How to Write a Friendly Letter

- Include a heading that gives your address and the date.
- In the greeting, include the name of the person to whom you are writing.
- In the body, tell why you are writing to the person.
- Include an appropriate closing before your signature.
- Write your signature at the bottom.

Thank-You Note

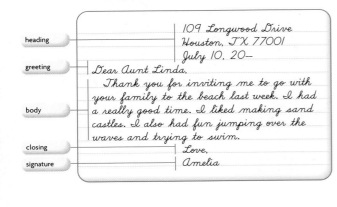

heading → 109 Longwood Drive / Houston, TX 77001 / July 10, 20—

greeting → Dear Aunt Linda,

body → Thank you for inviting me to go with your family to the beach last week. I had a really good time. I liked making sand castles. I also had fun jumping over the waves and trying to swim.

closing → Love,

signature → Amelia

Envelope

After you have written your friendly letter, you can mail it. Be sure to write the correct information on the envelope.

Amelia Donnell
109 Longwood Drive
Houston, TX 77001

Ms. Linda Donnell
23 Corn Hill Road
Galveston, TX 77550

— stamp
— return address
— mailing address

The mailing address is the address of the person who receives the letter. It is written in the center. The return address is the address of the person who writes the letter. It is written in the upper left corner.

Both the mailing address and the return address will include a postal abbreviation, or a shorter form of the state name. They will also include a ZIP code, a special number that helps the post office deliver the letter.

Your envelope must have a stamp as payment for sending the letter. The stamp is placed in the upper right corner of the envelope.

Postal Abbreviations

Alabama AL	Idaho ID	Missouri MO	Pennsylvania PA
Alaska AK	Illinois IL	Montana MT	Rhode Island RI
Arizona AZ	Indiana IN	Nebraska NE	S. Carolina SC
Arkansas AR	Iowa IA	Nevada NV	S. Dakota SD
California CA	Kansas KS	New Hampshire NH	Tennessee TN
Colorado CO	Kentucky KY	New Jersey NJ	Texas TX
Connecticut CT	Louisiana LA	New Mexico NM	Utah UT
Delaware DE	Maine ME	New York NY	Vermont VT
District of Columbia DC	Maryland MD	North Carolina NC	Virginia VA
	Massachusetts MA	North Dakota ND	Washington WA
Florida FL	Michigan MI	Ohio OH	W. Virginia WV
Georgia GA	Minnesota MN	Oklahoma OK	Wisconsin WI
Hawaii HI	Mississippi MS	Oregon OR	Wyoming WY

Poems: Rhymed and Unrhymed

A **poem** is one way for a writer to describe something or to express feelings about a subject. Poets use vivid words to help readers picture what they are describing.

A **rhyming poem** is a poem in which some or all of the lines end with a rhyming word. When two words rhyme, their final sounds are the same.

How to Write a Rhyming Poem

- Choose a subject.
- Use vivid words.
- Include rhyming words at the ends of some or all lines.
- Read your poem aloud a few times. Pay attention to the rhyme.

Here are two rhyming poems about a pet:

My Dog

rhyming words → He sniffles and snuffles and snoozes all day.
He's old and he's tired, but he likes to play.

A Good Friend

My dog is my buddy.
My dog is my friend.
rhyming words → Now that I've said it,
My poem will <u>END</u>!

Writing Unrhymed Poems

Poems do not always rhyme. **Unrhymed poems** are not like stories, though. They look and sound different, and they use special language.

How to Write an Unrhymed Poem

- Choose a subject.
- Use vivid words.
- Use repetition of words and sounds.

One kind of poem that does not use a regular rhythm or rhyme is a **free-verse poem**. Notice the vivid words in the poem below. Also notice the repetition of the "b" sound and of the phrase "But Bo doesn't yell."

My Basketball Buddy

Dribbling the ball down the court,
I feel so good that I forget to pass,
But Bo doesn't yell, "BALL HOG!"

I put up a shot from the 3-point line,
It slams BAM! hard off the backboard . . .
But Bo doesn't yell, "BRICK!"

Because he's my basketball buddy.

Writing Rubrics

Expressive Writing: *Personal Narrative*

The best personal narratives show all the points on the checklist below. Here is how you can use it:

Before writing Look at the checklist to remind yourself of how to make your personal narrative the best it can be.

During writing Check your drafts against the list to see how you can make your personal narrative better.

After writing Check your work against the list to see if it has all the points of the best personal narratives.

SCORE OF 4 ★★★★

- The story fits the purpose for writing. The audience it was written for would enjoy it. The ideas are interesting.
- The story has a clear beginning that tells the problem, a middle that tells events in order, and an ending that gives the solution to the problem.
- The story has description and rich details that help the reader visualize the events.
- The story has interesting words and phrases, such as specific nouns, vivid verbs, sensory words, and comparisons. It shows the writer's feelings.
- The sentences are written in a variety of ways to make the writing interesting to read.
- The story has few errors in spelling, grammar, and punctuation.

What else is important in a personal narrative?

Informative Writing: *How-to Essay*

The best how-to essays show all the points on the checklist below. Here is how you can use it:

Before writing Look at the checklist to remind yourself of how to make your how-to essay the best it can be.

During writing Check your drafts against the list to see how you can make your how-to essay better.

After writing Check your finished work against the list to see if it shows all the points of the best how-to essays.

SCORE OF 4 ★★★★

- The essay fits the purpose for writing well. The audience it was written for would understand it.
- The essay has a clear beginning that introduces the topic, a middle that gives facts or directions about the topic in a logical order, and an ending that summarizes or draws a conclusion. The topic is interesting.
- The essay has description and rich details that add information about the facts or directions.
- The essay has interesting words and phrases, especially specific nouns. It shows the writer's style.
- The sentences are written in a variety of ways to make the writing interesting to read.
- The essay has few errors in spelling, grammar, and punctuation.

What other points are important in a how-to essay?

Persuasive Writing: *Persuasive Paragraph*

The best persuasive essays show all the points on the checklist below. Here is how you can use it:

Before writing Look at the checklist to remind yourself of how to make your persuasive essay the best it can be.

During writing Check your drafts against the list to see how you can make your persuasive essay better.

After writing Check your finished work against the list to see if it shows all the points of the best persuasive essays.

SCORE OF 4 ★★★★

★ The essay was well written to persuade a particular audience.

★ The essay has a clear statement of opinion at the beginning, a middle that gives good reasons that support the opinion, and an ending that restates the opinion and calls for action. The writer cares about the topic.

★ The essay has details, description, or examples that give more information about the reasons.

★ The essay has interesting words and phrases, such as specific nouns, vivid verbs, emotional language, and comparisons.

★ The sentences are written in a variety of ways to make the writing interesting.

★ The essay has few errors in spelling, grammar, and punctuation.

What else is important in a persuasive essay?

498

Informative Writing: *Advantages and Disadvantages Essay*

The best advantages and disadvantages essays show all the points on the checklist below. Here is how you can use it:

Before writing Look at the checklist to remind yourself of how to make your advantages and disadvantages essay the best it can be.

During writing Check your drafts against the list to see how you can make your essay better.

After writing Check your finished work against the list to see if it shows all the points of the best essays.

SCORE OF 4 ★★★★

★ The essay fits the purpose for writing well. The audience it was written for would understand it. The writer cares about the topic.

★ The essay has a clear beginning that introduces the topic, a middle that explains information and ideas about the topic, and an ending that summarizes or draws a conclusion.

★ The essay has description and rich details that add information about the topic.

★ The essay has signal words and phrases that help the reader understand how the ideas are related.

★ The essay has few errors in spelling, grammar, and punctuation.

What else is important in this kind of essay?

499

Informative Writing: *Research Report*

The best research reports show all the points on the checklist below. Here is how you can use it:

Before writing Look at the checklist to remind yourself of how to make your research report the best it can be.

During writing Check your drafts against the list to see how you can make your research report better.

After writing Check your finished work against the list to see if it shows all the points of the best research reports.

SCORE OF 4 ★★★★

★ The research report fits the purpose for writing well. The audience it was written for would understand it.

★ The report has a clear beginning that introduces the topic. The middle sections explain information and interesting ideas about the topic. The ending summarizes or draws a conclusion.

★ The report presents ideas and information from a variety of sources in the writer's own words.

★ The report has description, rich details, or narrative parts that add information about the topic.

★ The report has signal words and phrases that help the reader understand how the ideas are related.

★ The sentences are written in a variety of ways.

★ The report has few errors in spelling, grammar, and punctuation.

500

Expressive Writing: *Story*

The best stories show all the points on the checklist below. Here is how you can use it:

Before writing Look at the checklist to remind yourself of how to make your story the best it can be.

During writing Check your drafts against the list to see how you can make your story better.

After writing Check your finished work against the list to see if it shows all the points of the best stories.

SCORE OF 4 ★★★★

★ The story fits the purpose for writing well. The audience it was written for would enjoy it.

★ The story has developed characters and a setting. The characters solve a problem by the end of the story.

★ The story has description and rich details that help the reader visualize the events. The ideas are interesting.

★ The story has interesting words and phrases, such as specific nouns, vivid verbs, sensory words, and comparisons. It shows the writer's feelings.

★ The sentences are written in a variety of ways to make the writing interesting to read.

★ The story has few errors in spelling, grammar, and punctuation.

What other points do you think are important in a story?

501

Study Skills and Strategies

Skimming and Scanning

Skimming is a way to look at a book or story quickly. Skimming helps you learn the main ideas that are in a book or in a story. It can also help you decide whether you want to read the book or story.

Scanning is a way to read quickly to find information about a subject. When you are scanning a book or story, look for key words about your subject. Key words may be in titles, headings, or the text of the book or story itself.

Here are some tips for skimming:

How to Skim a Book

1. Read the **chapter titles** in the **table of contents** at the beginning.
2. Look at the **index** to find main topics.
3. Read the **beginning** to decide whether you want to read the whole book or chapter.

Suppose you want to know more about taking photos. Scan the selection below to learn what one person who takes photos does and where he works. Before you begin, think about what kinds of words might be key words for this topic.

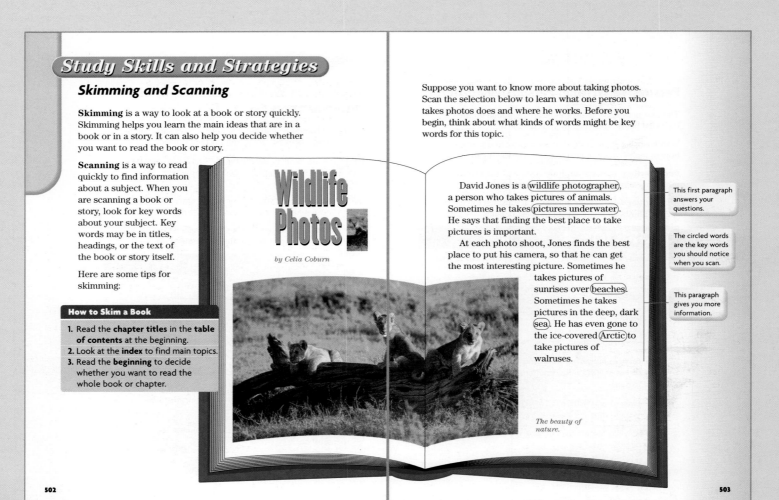

Wildlife Photos

by Celia Coburn

David Jones is a (wildlife photographer), a person who takes pictures of animals. Sometimes he takes (pictures underwater). He says that finding the best place to take pictures is important.

At each photo shoot, Jones finds the best place to put his camera, so that he can get the most interesting picture. Sometimes he takes pictures of sunrises over (beaches). Sometimes he takes pictures in the deep, dark (sea). He has even gone to the ice-covered (Arctic) to take pictures of walruses.

The beauty of nature.

> This first paragraph answers your questions.

> The circled words are the key words you should notice when you scan.

> This paragraph gives you more information.

502   503

Using Book Parts

Books have special parts that help you find information.

Front of the Book

The **title page** tells you
- the title of the book.
- the name of the author.
- the name of the company that made, or published, the book.
- the city or cities where the company is located.

The **copyright page** tells you
- what year the book was made.

The **table of contents** lists
- the different parts, or chapters, in the book.
- the title of each chapter.
- the page on which each chapter begins.

Back of the Book

The **glossary**
- gives the meanings of important words in the book.
- is arranged in alphabetical order.

The **index** shows what topics are in a book.
- An **entry** is a main topic in the book.
- Page numbers tell where in the book you can find information on the entry.
- A **cross-reference** tells you about another entry that has more information.

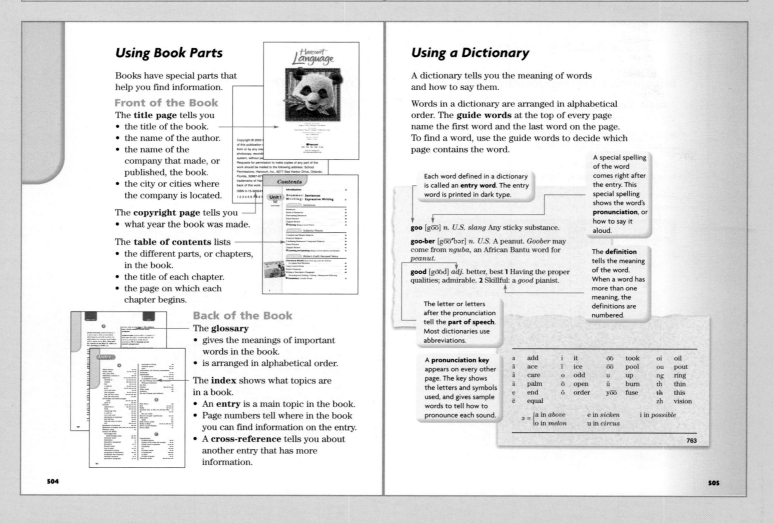

Using a Dictionary

A dictionary tells you the meaning of words and how to say them.

Words in a dictionary are arranged in alphabetical order. The **guide words** at the top of every page name the first word and the last word on the page. To find a word, use the guide words to decide which page contains the word.

> Each word defined in a dictionary is called an **entry word**. The entry word is printed in dark type.

goo [gōo] *n. U.S. slang* Any sticky substance.

goo-ber [gōo′bər] *n. U.S.* A peanut. *Goober* may come from *nguba*, an African Bantu word for *peanut.*

good [gŏod] *adj.* better, best **1** Having the proper qualities; admirable. **2** Skillful: a *good* pianist.

> A special spelling of the word comes right after the entry. This special spelling shows the word's **pronunciation**, or how to say it aloud.

> The **definition** tells the meaning of the word. When a word has more than one meaning, the definitions are numbered.

> The letter or letters after the pronunciation tell the **part of speech**. Most dictionaries use abbreviations.

> A **pronunciation key** appears on every other page. The key shows the letters and symbols used, and gives sample words to tell how to pronounce each sound.

a	add	i	it	oŏ	took	oi	oil
ā	ace	ī	ice	ōō	pool	ou	pout
â	care	o	odd	u	up	ng	ring
ä	palm	ō	open	û	burn	th	thin
e	end	ô	order	yōō	fuse	th	this
ē	equal					zh	vision

ə =	{ a in *above*	e in *sicken*	i in *possible*
	o in *melon*	u in *circus*	

763

504   505

Using the Internet

Most computers can be connected to the **Internet**. The Internet can be used to get information, to do work, or to have fun.

When you connect your computer to the Internet, you are **online**. This means your computer can communicate with other computers on the Internet.

Information on the Net is found at **websites**. Every website has its own **address**. The ending of the address tells you what kind of site it is.

.gov means this is a government site.
.org means this is an organization's site.
.com means this is a person's or a business's site.

Sometimes you may not know what website you want. You can use a **search engine** to help you. You can type in keywords, and the search engine will find websites that have information about those words.

You can also communicate with people you know. One common way of communicating is through **e-mail**. E-mail is a lot like regular mail, but much faster. You can send someone a note, a picture, or even a song. All you need is the e-mail address. An e-mail address works like a home address.

An e-mail address.

Using an Encyclopedia

An **encyclopedia** is a set of books with information on many different topics. Each **volume**, or book, has one or more letters on its spine. The letters go from A to Z. Sometimes there is also a number for each book.

Encyclopedia topics are arranged in alphabetical order. If you wanted to learn about stagecoaches, you would look in Volume 10, *S-T.*

These **guide words** tell you the last topic on this page.

Articles give information about the topics in the encyclopedia.

Cross-references tell you where to look for information on a related topic.

Stagecoach was a horse-drawn coach used to carry passengers and mail on a regular route. Sometimes it also carried freight. The first long stage line was established about 1670 between London and Edinburgh, Scotland, a distance of 392 miles (631 kilometers).
See also **Western frontier life in America** (Transportation).

Using Periodicals and Newspapers

Newspapers and other **periodicals**, such as magazines, can be sources of information for all sorts of topics. A newspaper tells about current events in your neighborhood and around the world. Magazines have reports and photos about special topics. Knowing the parts of a periodical will help you find information.

Big Bend Gets Thousands of Visitors — headline

Park Draws Record Number of Visitors — subhead

Big Bend National Park got a record number of visitors this week. More than 10,000 people came to see its famous landmarks.
Many of the visitors were from Europe and (*see A 12*) — reference

A 12
Asia, though most of the visitors were from Texas.
Some people who came to the park played games and hiked there.

The table of contents lists the articles in a periodical. You will find the table of contents near the front, usually on the first or second page. The table of contents tells you

- the title of each article or feature.
- the page number where it begins.

JUNE 20   **Vol. 8 No. 6**

page number — **4** (Sea Mammals) — title

Using an Atlas

An **atlas** is a book of maps. A world atlas has maps of every country in the world. Some atlases have maps of only one country. Different kinds of maps show different facts about places.

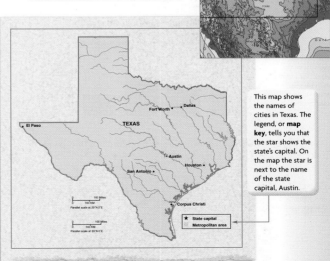

Map colors are used to show how high the land is. The **legend** tells you what the colors mean. On this map the color brown shows high mountain areas. The color blue shows water.

This map shows the names of cities in Texas. The legend, or **map key**, tells you that the star shows the state's capital. On the map the star is next to the name of the state capital, Austin.

★ State capital
Metropolitan area

Using an Almanac

An **almanac** is a book of facts. It has information about people, places, weather, sports, history, and important events. Most almanacs also have facts about different countries. A new almanac is published every year.

Every almanac has an **index**, which lists all of the subjects in the almanac. The index tells you the page on which you can find the facts you want.

United States of America
Farm Products from Texas

TYPE	AMOUNT PRODUCED
Corn	201,600,000 bushels
Cotton	4,345,000 bushels
Hay	7,815,000 tons
Oats	3,400,000 bushels
Soybeans	7,020,000 bushels
Wheat	75,400,000 bushels

Spain

Area: 195,364 square miles **Number of People:** 39,167,744 (1999) **Language:** Spanish **Capital:** Madrid **Major Crops:** olives, wine grapes, grain **Major Factories and Businesses:** clothes, shoes, steel, cars, ships

An almanac may show facts in maps, tables, or charts.

Using a Map

A **map** is a drawing that shows what a place would look like from above. A map can show a large part of the world, an entire country, a city, or a smaller place like a shopping mall. Maps can also help people find their way from one place to another.

This is a map of Grand Canyon National Park. It has some features found on many maps.

The **compass rose** tells you which way is north (*N*), south (*S*), east (*E*), or west (*W*).

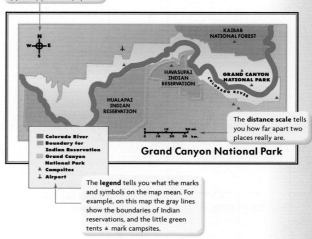

The **distance scale** tells you how far apart two places really are.

Grand Canyon National Park

The **legend** tells you what the marks and symbols on the map mean. For example, on this map the gray lines show the boundaries of Indian reservations, and the little green tents ▲ mark campsites.

Using Graphs

Graphs are used to show information in a way that is easy to understand. Graphs compare information that is measured with numbers.

Suppose a student counted the number of her classmates who wore sneakers to school. She did this every day for a week and recorded this information.

This information can be shown in a **bar graph**.

There is a bar for each day of the week. The height of each bar tells how many students wore sneakers that day.

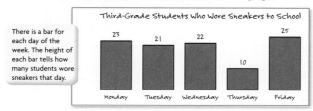

The information could also be shown in a **line graph**.

A line graph shows how something changes over time.

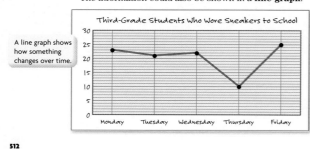

Using Tables

A **table** is a way to present a lot of facts in a form that is easy to use.

To use the table below, you must first find where you live on this map. The colors on the map tell you which column to look at on the table. If you lived in Texas, you would look in the green rectangles.

This table tells the best time to plant certain plants in different parts of the country.

Gardeners in Texas should plant cucumbers between March 7 and April 15.

Cucumbers	May 7 to June 20	April 7 to May 15	March 7 to April 15
Lettuce	May 15 to June 30	March 1 to March 31	February 15 to March 7
Squash	May 15 to June 15	April 15 to April 30	March 15 to April 15
Sweet Potatoes	May 15 to June 15	April 21 to May 2	March 23 to April 6
Watermelon	May 15 to June 30	April 15 to May 7	March 15 to March 28

→ row

Find what you want to plant at the left. Then move to the right until you get to the column that matches your area on the map.

column

Using Charts

A **chart** is a picture that shows information. Some charts are arranged in columns. This one tells you how much food to give a dog. To use this chart, find your dog's weight in the left column. The right column tells how much to feed him or her each day.

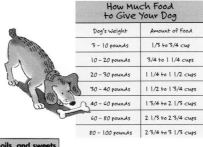

How Much Food to Give Your Dog	
Dog's Weight	Amount of Food
3 – 10 pounds	1/3 to 3/4 cup
10 – 20 pounds	3/4 to 1 1/4 cups
20 – 30 pounds	1 1/4 to 1 1/2 cups
30 – 40 pounds	1 1/2 to 1 3/4 cups
40 – 60 pounds	1 3/4 to 2 1/3 cups
60 – 80 pounds	2 1/3 to 2 3/4 cups
80 – 100 pounds	2 3/4 to 3 1/3 cups

The **food pyramid** is also a kind of chart. It defines the different food groups.

514

Pie Charts

A **pie chart** is a good way to show parts of a whole. By looking at the size of the pieces of this pie, you can tell what a typical third grader does in a day.

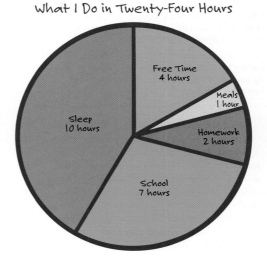

What I Do in Twenty-Four Hours

Free Time 4 hours
Meals 1 hour
Sleep 10 hours
Homework 2 hours
School 7 hours

515

Note-Taking

Taking notes helps you remember what you read. You can look at your notes, whenever you need to, to check your facts when writing a report or studying for a test.

A good way to take notes is on cards. Make a separate card for each main idea. This lets you put the cards in order in different ways. This can be helpful if you are writing a report.

Write on the card the title and author of the book where you found the information. If your source has numbered pages, include the page number.

Gail Gibbons, Weather Words and What They Mean

What kinds of clouds are there?
1. *cumulus clouds (puffy clouds)—fair weather*
2. *cirrus clouds (streaky clouds high in the sky)—fair weather*
3. *stratus clouds (low, gray clouds)—rain or snow*

Write the main idea of the information on the card. Sometimes it helps to write the main idea as a question.

Write the most important facts and details. Put the information in your own words. Write in phrases instead of sentences.

Note-Taking with Graphic Organizers

Sometimes it helps to use a **graphic organizer** when you are taking notes. A **K-W-L chart** is a good chart for taking notes. The chart has three columns.

- Before you read, write what you already **know** about the subject in the **K** column.
- Think about what you **want** to find out. Write those questions in the **W** column.
- As you are reading, write what you **learn** in the **L** column.

516

Clouds		
K	W	L
Moisture in the air causes clouds.	What kinds of clouds are there? What makes clouds release their moisture?	cumulus (puffy clouds) cirrus (streaky clouds) stratus (low, gray clouds)
Rain comes from clouds.		

A **web** can also be helpful when you are taking notes. A web is a good way to show how facts or ideas are connected.

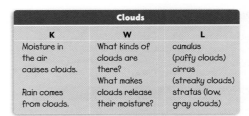

cirrocumulus— changing weather
cumulus— fair weather
cirrus— fair weather
Clouds
stratocumulus— winter clouds
cirrostratus— rain or snow, often
stratus—rain or snow, sometimes

A **Venn diagram** helps you compare two things. This Venn diagram shows what is alike and what is different about rain and snow.

Where the two circles overlap, write facts that are true about both rain and snow.

In this space, write facts that are true only about snow.

In this space, write facts that are true only about rain.

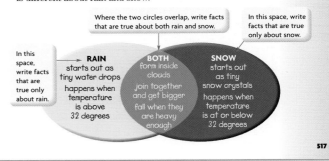

RAIN
starts out as tiny water drops
happens when temperature is above 32 degrees

BOTH
form inside clouds
join together and get bigger
fall when they are heavy enough

SNOW
starts out as tiny snow crystals
happens when temperature is at or below 32 degrees

517

Summarizing

A **summary** is a brief explanation in your own words that includes

- the main idea of the work.
- the most important details that support the main idea.

Writing a summary is a good way of making sure you understand what you have read. A summary can also help you remember something later.

Read the paragraphs below. Look for the main idea and the most important supporting details. Then read the summary. Notice that it tells only the most important details.

> Giant pandas and red pandas look very different. Giant pandas are huge black-and-white animals. They are shaped like bears. Giant pandas have round heads and chubby bodies. They measure between five and six feet long. They also have short tails and can stand on their hind legs. Adult giant pandas may look cuddly, but they are not lightweights! They usually weigh between 200 and 300 pounds. Bai-yun, a panda at the San Diego Zoo, weighed 600 pounds after she had her cub (a baby panda). Giant pandas eat up to eighty-five pounds of bamboo a day!

> The red panda, on the other hand, is much smaller. Weighing about eleven pounds, red pandas are usually about two feet long (tails not included). They have long reddish-brown fur and pale faces with red markings under each eye. Red pandas are not active most of the day. However, they are great climbers. Like raccoons, they use their front paws for grasping. They sleep away most of the day in trees. They do not go looking for food except at dawn and dusk. Also, unlike the giant pandas, red pandas will eat something besides bamboo. They sometimes will eat fruit and berries.

Summary

Giant pandas and red pandas are different. Giant pandas are much bigger than red pandas. Red pandas climb a lot and eat more different kinds of foods than do giant pandas.

How would you summarize the paragraphs in one sentence?

Outlining

Outlining is a way to understand information. It will help you see the main ideas and the details of an article or book you read. You can also use an outline to help plan your own writing.

Tips for Outlining

- Make an outline before you write.
- Write the topic of your outline at the top as your title.
- The most important ideas are called main ideas.
- Write main ideas after Roman numerals and periods.
- Supporting details follow each main idea.
- Write each detail after a capital letter and a period.

This outline uses words and phrases for main ideas and supporting details. You can also create a **sentence outline**, in which all the items are complete sentences.

```
                    Woodchucks
    I. Name
        A. Where the name came from
        B. Other name for woodchuck (groundhog)
    II. Where Woodchucks Live
        A. Northeastern United States and Canada
        B. In woods and on farms
        C. In backyards
    III. The Woodchuck's Habits
        A. Active during the day
        B. Sleeps underground
        C. Sleeps all winter long
        D. Wakes up on Groundhog Day
        E. If sees shadow, goes back to sleep
        F. Sleeps for another six weeks until spring comes
```

Here is the report about woodchucks that was written using the outline. Compare the outline and the report.

Woodchuck

The name woodchuck looks like a compound word, but it isn't. Woodchuck comes from the Native American word *otchek* or *otchig*. Woodchucks are also called groundhogs, because they are round like hogs and they dig holes in the ground.

*The first paragraph tells about the woodchuck's **name**.*

Woodchucks can be found all over the northeastern United States and Canada. They live in the woods and on farms. They are happy in backyards, too.

*The second paragraph tells about **where woodchucks live**.*

Woodchucks move around during the day. At night, they sleep underground. They sleep all winter long. They usually wake up on, or around, February 2. This is called Groundhog Day. According to legend, if the woodchuck sees its shadow, it goes back to sleep. It sleeps for another six weeks, which is when spring comes.

*The third paragraph tells about the woodchuck's **habits**.*

Test-Taking Strategies

Follow these test-taking tips for all kinds of tests.

> **In class:**
> • Listen carefully. Write down important facts.
> • Ask questions.
> **The night before the test:**
> • Study in a quiet place with good light.
> • Skim your textbook and reread your notes.

Multiple-Choice Tests

A multiple-choice test asks you to choose the correct answer from several possible answers.

Here are some tips for taking multiple-choice tests:
• Answer the easy questions first.
• Read each choice and cross out the ones you know are wrong.
• Double-check your answers.

Here is a sample test question:

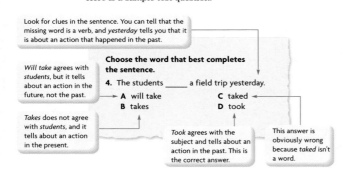

Look for clues in the sentence. You can tell that the missing word is a verb, and *yesterday* tells you that it is about an action that happened in the past.

Will take agrees with *students*, but it tells about an action in the future, not the past.

Takes does not agree with *students*, and it tells about an action in the present.

Choose the word that best completes the sentence.

4. The students _____ a field trip yesterday.
   A will take   C taked
   B takes   D took

Took agrees with the subject and tells about an action in the past. This is the correct answer.

This answer is obviously wrong because *taked* isn't a word.

Essay Tests

An **essay test** asks you to write answers in the form of sentences or paragraphs.

Understanding Essay Test Questions
As in all writing, think about your purpose and audience when taking an essay test. Are you being asked to inform or persuade your audience? Are you being asked to compare or contrast something?

> Here are some tips to help you do well on essay tests:
> 1. Read the questions carefully.
> 2. Develop a plan.
> 3. Answer all parts of the question.
> 4. Check your writing.

Tell the main point clearly at the beginning. Use many details to tell about the main ideas. Use the writing steps you learned in the writing chapters—prewrite, draft, revise, proofread, and publish.

Here are several kinds of essay questions:

Explain When you explain something, you tell more details about it.

Compare When you compare two or more things, you write about how the things are like each other.

Contrast When you contrast two or more things, you write about how the things are different from each other.

Describe When you describe something, you give details about it. You might tell how it looks or sounds or what it does.

Solve a Problem Some questions give information and then ask you to solve a problem. Think about the problem, and read the information several times. Underline important words in the question. Then explain your solution in your answer.

Spelling Strategies

Use these five steps to learn a new word.

STEP 1 **Say** the word. Remember times you have heard it used. Think about what it means.

STEP 2 **Look** at the word. Find prefixes and suffixes that you know. Think about words that are spelled like the new word. Think of words that have the same meaning.

STEP 3 **Spell** the word to yourself. Think about the letter sounds. Try to picture the word in your mind.

STEP 4 **Write** the word while you are looking at it. Look at the way you have formed your letters. Write the word again if you did not write it clearly or correctly.

STEP 5 **Check** your learning. Cover the word and write it again. If you did not spell the word correctly, repeat these steps.

Vowel Sounds

Short Vowel Sounds

• The **short vowel sounds** are usually spelled with one letter but not always.

/a/ is spelled **a**, as in *tap*
/e/ is spelled **e**, as in *ten*
/e/ is spelled **ea**, as in *bread*
/i/ is spelled **i**, as in *pit*
/o/ is spelled **o**, as in *lot*
/u/ is spelled **u**, as in *run*

Long Vowel Sounds

• Here are five ways to spell the /ā/ sound.
a-consonant-e, as in *date*
ai, as in *maid*
ay, as in *say*
ey, as in *obey*
eigh, as in *sleigh*

• Here are four ways to spell the /ē/ sound.
ea, as in *bean*
ee, as in *feel*
e, as in *me*
y, as in *happy*

• Here are five ways to spell the /ī/ sound.
i-consonant-e, as in *time*
i, as in *climb*
igh, as in *night*
y, as in *my*
uy, as in *buy*

• Here are four ways to spell the /ō/ sound.
o-consonant-e, as in *rope*
oa, as in *loaf*
o, as in *colt*
ow, as in *show*

• Here are two ways to spell the /ōō/ or /yōō/ sound.
u-consonant-e, as in *tube*
u, as in *music*

Letter Combinations

• The letter *i* usually comes before *e* when these two letters are written together in a word. If the letters follow *c*, or if they make the /ā/ sound, they are written *ei*.

piece
receive
weigh

• Here are two ways to spell the /ər/ sound.

er, as in *cover*
ar, as in *sugar*

• Here are two ways to spell the /əl/ sound.

le, as in *middle*
el, as in *barrel*

Commonly Misspelled Words

again	it's	through
another	kept	tomorrow
anything	knew	too
before	let's	trouble
bought	maybe	trying
boy's	missed	until
brought	outside	upon
caught	practice	we're
decided	really	what's
everybody	scared	where
everyone	sometimes	whole
everything	stopped	won't
field	suddenly	
finally	surprise	
getting	than	
girl's	that's	
guess	their	
happened	thought	
heard	threw	

Handwriting Models

Cursive Alphabet

D'Nealian Cursive Alphabet

Thesaurus

Using a Thesaurus

A **synonym** is a word that has almost the same meaning as another word.
An **antonym** is a word that means the opposite of another word.

A thesaurus is an important tool because it can help you find just the right word to use. If you were writing about the weather in this picture, you might say it is cold. If you wanted a word that means *very, very cold,* you could check a thesaurus for synonyms for the word *cold.* One synonym you could choose is *frosty.* *Frosty* may be a much better word to describe the weather in this picture. *Frosty* may be better because it is a vivid and exact word. An *exact* word is one that has just the right meaning. A *vivid* word is one that helps bring the scene to life.

| The weather is *cold.* |
| The weather is *frosty.* |

530

Entry Word In the Writer's Thesaurus, the word **cold** is an entry word. Entry words are listed in alphabetical order in the thesaurus. Entry words are in color and in bold letters.

cold *adj.* Having a low temperature: We braved the *cold* weather to go sledding. — Adjective

chilly Too cool or cold: I put on a coat because the air was becoming *chilly.*

cool Slightly cold; not warm: Swimming on a hot day will keep you *cool.*

freezing Very cold: I asked Dad to get my jacket, because I was *freezing.*

frosty Cold enough to make frost: I knew it was a *frosty* day outside because the window was covered in ice.

icy As cold as ice: The *icy* water was too cold for swimming.
ANTONYMS: hot, warm, steaming, thawed

Synonyms Synonyms for entry words look like this: *icy.* Read each definition to find the word that has the meaning you want.

Antonyms Antonyms for entry words look like this: hot.

You can also look in the index of a thesaurus to find antonyms and synonyms for entry words.

Entry Word
smile *v.* — Verb
Synonym — *grin*

The index shows that *grin* is listed as a synonym for smile. If you wanted another word for *grin,* you would look up *smile* in the thesaurus.

531

Thesaurus

break **broken** **cold**

A

afraid *adj.* Filled with fear; feeling frightened: My dog is *afraid* of thunder and lightning.
anxious Worried: Andrea was *anxious* about her first day at school.
fearful Expecting danger or a bad outcome: My little sister is *fearful* of spiders.
frightened Suddenly scared; startled: The *frightened* birds scattered when the car drove by them.
terrified Having great fear; filled with terror: The *terrified* cat ran away from the barking dog.
ANTONYMS: bold, unafraid, confident

angry *adj.* Feeling or showing rage or annoyance: The *angry* little girl stamped her feet.
furious Very angry: Chin was *furious* when her dog ate her homework.
mad Feeling hurt or unhappy: I was *mad* at my brother for messing up my room.
upset To feel bothered by someone or something: I was *upset* at first when we moved to our new home.
ANTONYMS: calm, pleased

ask *v.* To request; to invite: I can *ask* the teacher if I don't understand.
explore To think about; to examine: The students *explore* the causes of fog.
inquire To seek information: My mother *inquired* about the tickets for tonight's concert.
question To ask in a challenging way: The news reporters *question* the mayor about the new law.
ANTONYMS: answer, explain, reply, respond

B

bad *adj.* Not good; unkind or unsafe: It is a *bad* idea to lie to a friend.
harmful Causing damage: Eating too many sweets can be *harmful* to your health.
mean Selfish or nasty: The *mean* person said awful things about Jo.
poor Not good: The air is *poor* today because of the smog.
severe Causing damage or hardship: There is a *severe* storm forming over the ocean.
unpleasant Not pleasing; not fun: Being sick with the flu is an *unpleasant* experience.
ANTONYMS: good, pleasant, all right

big *adj.* Of great size: The box was too *big* for me to carry.
enormous Much larger in size than usual: The circus elephant was *enormous.*
giant Huge or great: The *giant* basketball player towered over the little boy.
grand Large and wonderful: Everyone admired the *grand* library building.
great Large; important: The *great* oak tree was the tallest and oldest tree in the town.
huge Of very great size: *Huge* machines called cranes are used to build skyscrapers.
ANTONYMS: little, ordinary, small, tiny

break *n.* A short rest from an activity: Fasal took a *break* from studying and ate a snack.
holiday A day when many offices and schools are closed; a national or religious festival: Independence Day is my favorite *holiday.*

532

---

recess A break from work for rest or play: The students will have *recess* outside after lunch.
vacation A longer break from work or school; a pleasure trip: We visited my grandparents on our *vacation.*

broken *adj.* Not in good condition; not working; damaged: The *broken* cup lay in many pieces.
cracked Broken but not completely falling apart: The *cracked* mirror still hung on the wall.
crushed Broken completely by being pressed between two things: A *crushed* tomato was at the bottom of the grocery bag.
ANTONYMS: fixed, mended, repaired

C

call *v.* To speak in a loud voice: The teacher will *call* us in from the playground.
bellow To say something in a very loud voice: Sergeants *bellow* orders to their troops as they march across the field.
greet To welcome someone, using friendly words: The teachers *greet* the students at the door on the first day of school.
roar To make a very loud and deep sound in pain, excitement, or anger: The fans *roar* every time their favorite team scores a point.
scream To make a loud, sharp sound because of fright: Viewers *scream* during the scary parts of the movie.
shout To say loudly: The conductor had to *shout* to be heard over the noise of the train.

telephone To call by telephone: I will *telephone* my friend.
yell To shout, scream, or roar: The outfielder had to *yell* to the catcher.

carry *v.* To take from one place to another: Many students *carry* their homework in a backpack.
cart To carry a weight or burden: Every week I have to *cart* the trash cans out to the curb.
haul To carry a heavy load: A moving truck will *haul* the furniture to our new home.
move To carry from one place to another: When it gets cold, I will *move* some of the plants inside the house.
remove To carry or take away: Please *remove* your dirty boots from the kitchen.
ANTONYMS: drop, leave behind

catch *v.* To take hold of a moving object: The children *catch* butterflies with a net.
capture To catch by force, with skill, or by surprise: The cat tried to *capture* the mouse.
clutch To hold tightly: The little girl will *clutch* her mother's hand when crossing the street.
grasp To take hold of firmly: Grandmother must *grasp* the handrail as she walks down the stairs.
trap To catch by using a trick: Spiders *trap* insects in their webs.
ANTONYMS: drop, let go, miss, release, throw

cold *adj.* Having a low temperature: We braved the *cold* weather to go sledding.
chilly Quite cool or cold: I put on a coat because the air was becoming *chilly.*

533

cool Slightly cold; not warm: Swimming on a hot day will keep you *cool*.

freezing Very cold: I asked Dad to get my jacket, because I was *freezing*.

frosty Cold enough to make frost: I knew it was a *frosty* day outside because the window was covered in ice.

icy As cold as ice: The *icy* water was too cold for swimming.

ANTONYMS: hot, warm, steaming, thawed

cook *v.* To heat food: We had to *cook* the oatmeal before we could eat it.

bake To cook in an oven: *Bake* the cake for twenty-five minutes.

boil To heat until it is hot and bubbling: My mother will *boil* water to fix rice for dinner.

fry To cook in hot oil: Restaurants *fry* potato sticks in hot oil to make french fries.

prepare To put together or make ready: After we *prepare* dinner, we will sit down and eat it.

steam To cook in the hot mist that rises from boiling water: We *steam* carrots until they are soft.

cut *v.* To divide or break into parts: *Cut* the cake into ten pieces.

carve To cut up or slice: My uncle will *carve* the turkey.

chop To cut with a sharp tool: I asked him to *chop* some tomatoes for my salad.

clip To cut short; to cut out with scissors: I asked the barber to *clip* my hair.

crack To split apart: To eat the nut, you will have to *crack* open its shell.

slice To cut into thin pieces: Dad asked Alex to *slice* cucumbers for the salad.

split To cut from end to end: A lightning bolt *split* the tree down the middle.

trim To cut just a little: I hope she will only *trim* my hair and not cut it too short.

ANTONYMS: repair, combine, join

draw *v.* To make pictures with a marker or pencil: I like to *draw* horses.

design To draw plans for something that can be made: Judy will *design* our tree house before we build it.

sketch To draw quickly to give a general idea: He will first *sketch* his idea for the poster.

ANTONYM: erase

eat *v.* To take in food: You must *eat* a variety of food to stay healthy.

chew To bite up and down many times: You should *chew* your food carefully before you swallow it.

dine To eat a meal: We will *dine* at a Chinese restaurant on my mother's birthday.

feast To eat a large and special meal: Every Thanksgiving we *feast* on turkey and other foods.

gobble To eat quickly and greedily: The dog will *gobble* down the food as soon as you put it in the dish.

gulp To drink in large swallows: The thirsty basketball players *gulp* water after each game.

munch To eat happily and with a crunching sound: I like to *munch* on popcorn during a movie.

nibble To take small bites: The small birds *nibble* on bits of crackers.

swallow To pass something from one's mouth to one's stomach: Be sure to *swallow* your cold medicine.

fast *adj.* Moving with speed: The team needs *fast* runners to win races.

quick Taking little time: The goalkeeper's *quick* movement prevented a goal.

swift Moving easily and with speed: He picked up the ball and threw it to first base in one *swift* move.

ANTONYMS: slow, sluggish

find *v.* To come upon by surprise; to look for and discover: I cannot go outside until I *find* my jacket.

discover To find out; to come upon before anyone else; to know about: Students *discover* new words by looking in a thesaurus.

locate To find the place where something is: When I saw a flag on the building, I was able to *locate* the post office.

search To look for someone or something: I will *search* until I find my sneakers.

uncover To take the cover or covering off; to make known: They move the pile of newspapers and *uncover* a litter of kittens.

ANTONYMS: bury, cover, hide, lose

funny *adj.* Causing people to laugh or smile: Everyone laughed at the *funny* joke.

amusing Funny in a quiet way: The *amusing* story made the reader smile.

entertaining Funny in an interesting way: He always has *entertaining* stories to tell.

silly Funny in a foolish way: In the cartoon a *silly* bear bumps into a tree.

witty Funny in a clever way: A *witty* comic makes us laugh and think about things in a new way.

ANTONYMS: serious, sad

good *adj.* Not bad; helpful: Giving toys to a sick child is a *good* idea.

excellent Very good: He gave an *excellent* review of the movie.

kind Good-hearted: A *kind* student made friends with the new third grader.

right Behaving by the rules: Both runners started at the same time, which was the *right* thing to do.

worthy Having worth, value, or honor: A *worthy* person can be trusted with a secret.

ANTONYMS: bad, evil, mean, unfair, unworthy

grow *v.* To get larger in size, older in age, or greater in amount: If you water the seed, it will *grow*.

develop To grow in stages: You must exercise to *develop* strong muscles.

gain To increase in size or amount; to grow better, stronger, or more skillful:

534   535

Basketball practice will help you *gain* skills in passing and shooting.

raise To bring up or to help grow: Parents work hard to *raise* their children.

sprout To begin to grow: In spring the park is filled with new plants just starting to *sprout*.

ANTONYMS: decrease, die, shrink, wither

happy *adj.* Full of joy: The *happy* little girl clapped and giggled as she ran under the sprinkler.

cheerful Happy; joyous; bright and pleasant: Party balloons and colored streamers make our classroom look *cheerful*.

excited Having strong, lively feelings about something: The *excited* camper jumped up and down when he caught his first fish.

jolly Full of fun; merry: The *jolly* singers sang holiday songs on our doorstep.

joyful Showing much happiness: The friends felt *joyful* when they saw each other again on the first day of school.

merry Full of fun and laughter; joyous: My family had a *merry* time together during the holidays.

pleased Having good feelings about something: The teacher was *pleased* that everyone passed the test.

ANTONYMS: gloomy, sad, depressed, upset

healthy *adj.* Feeling and being well; free from disease: Exercise helps us feel *healthy*.

fit In good physical shape: The soccer player is *fit*.

hearty Healthy and strong: The mountain climber is a *hearty* person.

normal Not ill: The doctor said that my skin looks *normal*.

well In good health: When you are *well* again, you may play outside.

ANTONYMS: ailing, ill, sick, unhealthy, unwell

hot *adj.* Having a high temperature: It was 100 degrees on that *hot* summer day.

boiling Having such a high temperature that liquid bubbles: The *boiling* water in the pot bubbled.

burning Being covered by fire: We could smell the *burning* hot dogs all over the camp.

sizzling Having such a high temperature that a crackling sound is made: We heard the *sizzling* bacon cooking on the stove.

steaming Having such a high temperature that a gas is created: When I saw the *steaming* cup, I knew the hot chocolate would warm me.

warm Comfortably hot: The heavy blanket kept her *warm* on cold nights.

ANTONYMS: cold, freezing, chilly, nippy

interesting *adj.* Holding the attention: We learned about the weather by watching an *interesting* video.

entertaining Holding the attention by being enjoyable: The book was so *entertaining* that I kept reading until late at night.

exciting Causing strong, lively feelings: Their first ride in an airplane was very *exciting*.

fascinating Causing amazement: In her report, Leah told us many *fascinating* facts about pyramids.

ANTONYMS: uninteresting, boring, dull

jump *v.* To move up quickly from the ground to the air: My dog can *jump* over that fence.

bounce To jump or leap suddenly: If a player falls, he needs to *bounce* right up again.

hop To make short jumps or leaps: The birds *hop* around picking up seeds.

leap To make a big jump; to rise free of the ground: I had to run and then *leap* to get over the large puddle in the street.

skip To move by stepping, hopping, and sliding on each foot in turn: It is more fun to *skip* to school than to walk.

spring To make a quick jump from one spot to another: If a deer is scared, it may *spring* away from the danger.

land *n.* Solid surface of the earth: We could see the ocean and the *land* from our airplane.

earth The dry surface of our planet; dirt or soil: We planted flower seeds in the *earth* in our backyard.

ground The part of the Earth's surface that is solid: The *ground* looked very far away when we flew in an airplane.

ANTONYMS: air, water, sky

little *adj.* Not big in size, amount, or importance: I was not hungry, so I ate only a *little* slice of pizza.

puny Small and feeble: The *puny* kitten fit inside a teacup.

short Small in height: Compared to a giraffe, a human being is *short*.

small Not large in size or amount: We paid a *small* price for that jigsaw puzzle at the garage sale.

skinny Thin: Because the dog was so *skinny*, we named him Stringbean.

teeny Very, very small: I have *teeny* pots and pans in my dollhouse.

tiny Very small: I saw a *tiny* bug crawling on a leaf.

ANTONYMS: big, great, huge, large, mighty, giant

make *v.* To put together; to bring into being: We will *make* a castle out of sand.

build To make by putting parts or materials together: They *build* computers by fitting together many small parts.

complete To make whole with no parts missing: She will *complete* her story as soon as she thinks of an ending.

536   537

create To make, using imagination or skill: Because he draws so well, he can *create* wonderful pictures.

form To make something by shaping it: The artist will *form* a clay pot with her hands.

produce To grow or manufacture: These farmers *produce* the best corn I ever tasted.

put together To connect two or more parts: To make a model airplane, you must *put together* many small parts.

ANTONYMS: destroy, smash, take apart, undo

mix v. To put together or combine different things: The directions say to *mix* the ingredients well.

add To put one thing with another: The artist will *add* red paint to white and make pink.

beat To mix something by stirring it hard: *Beat* the cake batter until it is smooth.

blend To mix two or more things together: To make chili, the cook will *blend* meat, beans, and spices.

combine To put or mix two or more things together: *Combine* water, flour, and salt to make paste.

mingle To bring or come together: We wanted to *mingle* with the guests at the party.

stir To mix, using a spoon or stick: The chef must *stir* the soup.

ANTONYMS: divide, separate, unravel

new adj. Just made, started, or arrived: The *new* teacher introduced himself to the class.

current Taking place now: The *current* school year is half over.

fresh Unused; clean; not spoiled: Ginny turned to a *fresh* page in her notebook.

latest Most recent: The *latest* space mission took place a month ago.

modern In the present time; up-to-date: Computers are a *modern* invention.

original Not copied: The song is based on an *original* poem.

ANTONYMS: old, used, worn

nice adj. Pleasant; enjoyable: It's a *nice* day for a walk in the park.

attractive Likable; pleasing to the eye: The new gymnastics uniforms are very *attractive*.

friendly Showing kindness: Our *friendly* neighbors visited us when we moved in.

good Admired; well-behaved or helpful; of high quality: Angelo is a *good* athlete.

kind Helpful; gentle; generous: The *kind* student stayed to help.

pleasant Likable, enjoyable: We had a *pleasant* time at the party.

pleasing Giving pleasure: Taking a long walk outdoors is a *pleasing* way to spend a fall afternoon.

ANTONYMS: mean, nasty, rude, unpleasant

538

O

old adj. Having lived or existed for a long time: The stone tools in the museum are very *old*.

ancient From times long past: *Ancient* tribes hunted animals with bows and arrows.

used Made use of already; not new: Gary bought a *used* bike for twenty dollars.

worn Damaged by use: Her favorite jeans were badly *worn*.

ANTONYMS: current, modern, new, young, fresh, unused

P

part n. A portion of a whole: He saved *part* of the melon for me.

fraction A part of a whole; a small amount: The dog ate only a *fraction* of its food.

piece A section of something; a part taken from a whole: A *piece* of the broken plate is still missing.

scrap A small or unwanted piece, as of paper, food, or metal: Oscar wrote the information on a *scrap* of paper.

section A division of something; a part of an area: The downtown *section* of my city is beautiful.

ANTONYMS: whole, all

person n. A man, woman, or child; a single human being: A bicycle is made for one *person*.

child A young girl or boy; a son or daughter: The *child* enjoyed playing on the swings.

human A human being: That footprint was made by a *human*.

man An adult male human being: The *man* and his son sat together.

woman An adult female human being: The *woman* in the red coat is my sister.

pretty adj. Nice to look at: The shiny blue and silver fish was *pretty*.

beautiful Especially pleasant to look at or listen to: The singer had a *beautiful* voice.

handsome Having pleasing looks, especially in a noble or dignified way: My grandfather was a *handsome* man.

lovely Having a pleasing appearance or effect: A *lovely* breeze cooled us on the hot afternoon.

ANTONYMS: plain, unattractive

pull v. To move something toward you: *Pull* the chain to turn on the light.

draw To pull forward: Two horses *draw* the cart along the road.

haul To carry by pulling; to pull with difficulty: Lucia agreed to *haul* her little brother up the hill in her wagon.

tow To pull something behind a vehicle: We used our car to *tow* the boat to the dock.

tug To pull hard: If you *tug* the loose thread, you may make a hole in your sweater.

ANTONYMS: push, shove, thrust

put v. To set or lay something: *Put* your dirty shoes outside.

lay To place in a certain order or position: Please *lay* that blanket on the bed.

place To move a thing carefully or on purpose: Let's *place* the flowerpot on the kitchen table.

539

spread To stretch out; to cover with something: Jake likes to *spread* peanut butter on his toast.

sprinkle To scatter something over a surface: Many people *sprinkle* sugar on cereal.

quiet adj. With little or no noise; calm: The classroom was *quiet* during the test.

calm Quiet; peaceful; still; not upset: You can see your face in the *calm* water of the lake.

peaceful Pleasantly calm and quiet: After the boys went outside to play, the house was *peaceful*.

silent With no noise at all: *Silent* movies have pictures but no sound.

still Without noise or movement: Please keep *still* during the concert.

ANTONYMS: loud, noisy, upset

rest v. To take a break from activity: Josie will *rest* after playing tennis.

nap To sleep for a short time, usually during the day: I like to *nap* in the car when we go on long trips.

relax To become less tense; to rest: Nell likes to *relax* by reading.

sleep To rest the body and mind with the eyes closed: Most people dream when they *sleep*.

snooze To sleep lightly for a short time: Cats like to *snooze* in sunny places.

ANTONYM: wake

540

road n. A wide path made for traveling: The *road* to our house is bumpy.

avenue An especially wide road in a town or city: The parade will take place on the main *avenue*.

highway A main road: The *highway* is busy at rush hour.

lane A narrow road or street: The swimmers walked down the *lane* to the lake.

path A narrow way, especially for walking or bicycling: Teresa rides to school on the bike *path*.

route A road or course leading from one place to another: We always take the shortest *route* to the beach.

street A road in a town or city, usually lined with buildings: All my friends live on the same *street*.

run v. To move by using steps that are faster than walking: Hideo can *run* farther than I can.

dash To run a short distance quickly: Naomi must *dash* to her locker between classes.

race To move quickly, as in a contest to see who is fastest: The sisters *race* each other home.

scramble To rush or struggle to reach a goal: We sometimes *scramble* to get the best seats.

ANTONYMS: walk, crawl, creep

sad adj. Feeling unhappy or low: Rainy days make some people *sad*.

sorry Feeling sadness for someone; feeling regret for something you have

done: Tony was *sorry* he had hurt his friend's feelings.

unhappy Without joy: The team was *unhappy* when they lost the game.

ANTONYMS: glad, happy, pleased, joyful

say v. To put something into words: Rebecca is shy and does not *say* much.

describe To tell about: Can you *describe* the picture to me?

mention To say something in passing: Did she *mention* what time we will leave?

recount To tell in great detail: He is eager to *recount* his adventure.

whisper To speak in a soft tone: We should *whisper* so we don't wake up the baby.

see v. To use your eyes; to notice something: Did you *see* the sunset?

glimpse To see something for a short time: I hope we get to *glimpse* the baby eagles.

observe To look at something carefully: Dana likes to *observe* insects.

view To look at something: They will *view* the fireworks tonight.

smart adj. Fast in thinking or learning: The *smart* math student subtracted the numbers in his head.

bright Having a quick, clever mind: The *bright* girl was the first one to raise her hand for every question.

clever Good at learning and solving problems; skillful: The *clever* boy fixed the broken computer.

quick Swift to learn or understand: The *quick* boy figured out the answer right away.

sharp Fast in thinking; lively and alert; quick to notice: Denny is *sharp* when dealing with an emergency.

wise Showing good judgment: He made a *wise* decision to tell the truth.

ANTONYMS: foolish, senseless, stupid

smile v. To express joy or pleasure by curving the corners of your mouth upward: It is friendly to *smile* at others.

grin To give a large smile: Sometimes people *grin* when they do something silly.

laugh To show pleasure by making sounds: Cartoons can make children *laugh*.

ANTONYMS: frown, scowl

stop v. To come to an end; to prevent something from going or moving: The new traffic light will *stop* the cars at this busy corner.

end To be over or done: The meeting will *end* at 9:30.

finish To complete something; to come to an end: You must *finish* the assignment by tomorrow.

halt To stop: The guard at the gate asked the driver to *halt*.

quit To stop doing something: Carlos plans to *quit* the team at the end of the season.

ANTONYMS: begin, continue, go, start

strong adj. Having great force or power: Running every day will help make your legs *strong*.

mighty Having great force: The *mighty* storm brought heavy winds.

541

powerful Having great physical strength or force: The soccer player has *powerful* legs.

sturdy Solid or well built: The chair was *sturdy* and not easily broken.

ANTONYMS: fragile, weak, delicate, frail, sickly

talk v. To put ideas into words: She likes to *talk* about horses.

chatter To talk a lot; to talk about silly things: The teacher does not allow students to *chatter* during class.

discuss To talk about a topic: We will *discuss* our homework after dinner.

gossip To talk about other people's business: It is not polite to *gossip*.

think v. To form ideas in your mind; to have an opinion: *Think* carefully before you mark your answer.

consider To think about something: *Consider* your choices carefully.

imagine To picture something in one's mind: Can you *imagine* living under the ocean?

ponder To think about carefully: He wanted to *ponder* his decision calmly for a while.

reflect To think about something carefully: I sometimes *reflect* on things that happened in the past.

throw v. To send something through the air: *Throw* the ball to Francis.

hurl To throw with great force: Peter tried to *hurl* the heavy rock into the water.

pitch To throw: Some baseball players can *pitch* a ball at ninety miles an hour.

toss To throw lightly: Please *toss* me that magazine.

town n. A small city: Camille lives in a small *town* in West Texas.

city A large town: The *city* has many tall office buildings.

community A group of people who live in the same area or share an interest: Our *community* has a parade every Fourth of July.

village A small town: The *village* has only one traffic light.

trouble n. A bad or dangerous situation; something that causes worry: Stormy weather can cause *trouble* for farmers.

bother Something that is annoying: Driving you home will be no *bother*.

difficulty Something that causes worry and must be figured out: The math question gave Sam *difficulty*.

problem A difficulty: Barry was stumped by the *problem* with his computer.

worry Nervousness; something that causes nervousness: Her tooth decay was a *worry* to her dentist.

ANTONYMS: comfort, joy, pleasure

very adv. To a great degree; much or most: My family is *very* proud of me.

awfully Very much: I'm *awfully* glad it did not rain on my birthday.

extremely Much more than usual: Be *extremely* careful when you cross the street.

greatly In a big way; importantly or wonderfully: The students were *greatly* moved by the soldier's story.

terribly Extremely: They were all *terribly* happy about winning the spelling bee.

ANTONYMS: barely, hardly, merely

wait v. To stay idle until something happens; to look forward to something: We had to *wait* all afternoon for our guest to come.

delay To put something off until later; to cause someone or something to be late: We will *delay* the start of school because of the snow.

pause To stop for a short while: The crowd will *pause* for a moment of silence.

remain To stay in one place; to continue to be: The Steins will *remain* in their old house until the new one is built.

ANTONYM: hurry

walk v. To move, using the legs: Some of the children are able to *walk* to school.

hike To walk a long distance, especially in the country: Sharon likes to *hike* in the hills.

march To walk together in formation; to walk in a determined way: The school band will *march* in the parade.

stroll To walk slowly and casually: Visitors often *stroll* through the garden.

win v. To finish first in a race or contest: Who will *win* the soccer game tonight?

succeed To reach a goal; to do well: Jason will surely *succeed* in his new job.

triumph To win a victory: The team hopes to *triumph* in the finals.

ANTONYMS: fail, lose

Thesaurus Index

mean nice *adj.*
mended broken *adj.*
mention say *v.*
merely very *adv.*
merry happy *adj.*
mighty little *adj.*
mighty strong *adj.*
mingle mix *v.*
miss catch *v.*
mix *v.*
modern new *adj.*
modern old *adj.*
move carry *v.*
munch eat *v.*

N
nap rest *v.*
nasty nice *adj.*
new *adj.*
new old *adj.*
nibble eat *v.*
nice *adj.*
nippy hot *adj.*
noisy quiet *adj.*
normal healthy *adj.*

O
observe see *v.*
old *adj.*
old new *adj.*
ordinary big *adj.*
original new *adj.*

P
part *n.*
path road *n.*
pause wait *v.*
peaceful quiet *adj.*
person *n.*
piece part *n.*
pitch throw *v.*
place put *v.*

plain pretty *adj.*
pleasant bad *adj.*
pleasant nice *adj.*
pleased angry *adj.*
pleased happy *adj.*
pleased sad *adj.*
pleasing nice *adj.*
pleasure trouble *n.*
ponder think *v.*
poor bad *adj.*
powerful strong *adj.*
prepare cook *v.*
pretty *adj.*
problem trouble *n.*
produce make *v.*
pull *v.*
puny little *adj.*
push pull *v.*
put *v.*
put together make *v.*

Q
question ask *v.*
quick smart *adj.*
quick fast *adj.*
quiet *adj.*
quit stop *v.*

R
race run *v.*
raise grow *v.*
recess break *n.*
recount say *v.*
reflect think *v.*
relax rest *v.*
release catch *v.*
remain wait *v.*
remove carry *v.*
repair cut *v.*
repaired broken *adj.*
reply ask *v.*
respond ask *v.*

rest *v.*
right good *adj.*
road *n.*
roar call *v.*
route road *n.*
rude nice *adj.*
run *v.*

S
sad *adj.*
sad funny *adj.*
sad happy *adj.*
say *v.*
scowl smile *v.*
scramble run *v.*
scrap part *n.*
scream call *v.*
search find *v.*
section part *n.*
see *v.*
senseless smart *adj.*
separate mix *v.*
severe bad *adj.*
serious funny *adj.*
sharp smart *adj.*
short little *adj.*
shout call *v.*
shove pull *v.*
shrink grow *v.*
sick healthy *adj.*
sickly strong *adj.*
silent quiet *adj.*
silly funny *adj.*
sizzling hot *adj.*
sketch draw *v.*
skinny little *adj.*
skip jump *v.*
sky land *n.*
sleep rest *v.*
slice cut *v.*
slow fast *adj.*

sluggish fast *adj.*
small big *adj.*
small little *adj.*
smart *adj.*
smash make *v.*
smile *v.*
snooze rest *v.*
sorry sad *adj.*
split cut *v.*
spread put *v.*
spring jump *v.*
sprinkle put *v.*
sprout grow *v.*
start stop *v.*
steam cook *v.*
steaming cold *adj.*
steaming hot *adj.*
still quiet *adj.*
stir mix *v.*
stop *v.*
street road *n.*
stroll walk *v.*
strong *adj.*
stupid smart *adj.*
sturdy strong *adj.*
succeed win *v.*
swallow eat *v.*
swift fast *adj.*

T
take apart make *v.*
talk *v.*
teeny little *adj.*
telephone call *v.*
terribly very *adv.*
terrified afraid *adj.*
thawed cold *adj.*
think *v.*
throw *v.*
throw catch *v.*
thrust pull *v.*
tiny big *adj.*

tiny little *adj.*
toss throw *v.*
tow pull *v.*
town *n.*
trap catch *v.*
trim cut *v.*
triumph win *v.*
trouble *n.*
tug pull *v.*

U
unafraid afraid *adj.*
unattractive pretty *adj.*
uncover find *v.*
undo make *v.*
unfair good *adj.*
unhappy sad *adj.*
unhealthy healthy *adj.*
uninteresting interesting *adj.*
unpleasant bad *adj.*
unpleasant nice *adj.*
unravel mix *v.*
unused old *adj.*
unwell healthy *adj.*
unworthy good *adj.*
upset angry *adj.*
upset happy *adj.*
upset quiet *adj.*
used new *adj.*
used old *adj.*

V
vacation break *n.*
very *adv.*
view see *v.*
village town *n.*

W
wait *v.*
wake rest *v.*
walk *v.*
walk run *v.*

warm cold *adj.*
warm hot *adj.*
water land *n.*
weak strong *adj.*
well healthy *adj.*
whisper say *v.*
whole part *n.*
win *v.*
wise smart *adj.*
wither grow *v.*
witty funny *adj.*
woman person *n.*
worn new *adj.*
worn old *adj.*
worry trouble *n.*
worthy good *adj.*

Y
yell call *v.*
young old *adj.*

Glossary

Using the Glossary

Like a dictionary, this glossary lists words in alphabetical order. It contains the Vocabulary Power words, grammar terms, and writing forms covered in this book. To find a word, grammar term, or writing form, look it up by the first letter of the word.

To save time, use the **guide words** at the top of each page. These show you the first and last entry words on the page. Look at the guide words to see if your entry word falls between them alphabetically.

Here is an example of a glossary entry:

This is the entry word. It's the word you look up.

Look here to find out how to pronounce the entry word.

The letter *n.* means the entry word is a noun.

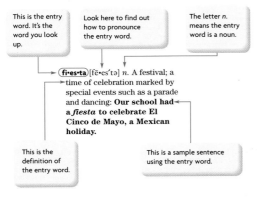

fi·es·ta [fĕ•es´tə] *n.* A festival; a time of celebration marked by special events such as a parade and dancing: **Our school had a *fiesta* to celebrate El Cinco de Mayo, a Mexican holiday.**

This is the definition of the entry word.

This is a sample sentence using the entry word.

Pronunciation

The pronunciation in brackets [ ] is a respelling that shows how the word is pronounced.

The **pronunciation key** explains what the symbols in a respelling mean. A shortened pronunciation key appears on every other page of the glossary.

Pronunciation Key*

a	add, map	m	move, seem	u	up, done
ā	ace, rate	n	nice, tin	û(r)	burn, turn
â(r)	care, air	ng	ring, song	yōō	fuse, few
ä	palm, father	o	odd, hot	v	vain, eve
b	bat, rub	ō	open, so	w	win, away
ch	check, catch	ô	order, jaw	y	yet, yearn
d	dog, rod	oi	oil, boy	z	zest, muse
e	end, pet	ou	pout, now	zh	vision, pleasure
ē	equal, tree	ŏŏ	took, full	ə	the schwa, an
f	fit, half	ōō	pool, food		unstressed vowel
g	go, log	p	pit, step		representing the
h	hope, hate	r	run, poor		sound spelled
i	it, give	s	see, pass		*a* in *above*
ī	ice, write	sh	sure, rush		*e* in *sicken*
j	joy, ledge	t	talk, sit		*i* in *possible*
k	cool, take	th	thin, both		*o* in *melon*
l	look, rule	ŧh	this, bathe		*u* in *citrus*

Other symbols
• separates words into syllables
´ indicates heavier stress on a syllable
` indicates lighter stress on a syllable

Abbreviations: *adj.* adjective, *adv.* adverb, *conj.* conjunction, *interj.* interjection, *n.* noun, *prep.* preposition, *pron.* pronoun, *syn.* synonym, *v.* verb

* This Pronunciation Key, adapted entries, and the Short Key that appear on the following pages are reprinted from *HBJ School Dictionary*. Copyright © 1990 by Harcourt, Inc. Reprinted by permission of Harcourt, Inc.

A

ab•bre•vi•a•tion [ə•brē•vē•ā′shən] *n.* A short way to write a word. Most abbreviations end with a period. An abbreviation for a proper noun begins with a capital letter: ***Mrs.* Chen met *Dr.* Garcia at his Main *St.* office on *Fri.* morning at 10:00 *A.M.***

ac•tion verb [ak′shən vûrb] *n.* A verb that tells what the subject of a sentence does: **The girl *ran* on the playground.**

ad•jec•tive [aj′ik•tiv] A word that describes a noun. Some adjectives tell *how many.* Other adjectives tell *what kind:* **Ms. Ling buys *five* bags of soil for her garden. I jog *several* times a week. The *large, brown* dog is playful.**

ad•van•tag•es and dis•ad•van•tag•es es•say [ad•van′tij•iz and dis′əd•van•tij•iz es′ā] *n.* An essay that explains the good and bad points about a topic: **Roberto wrote about the good and bad parts of winter in his *advantages and disadvantages essay.***

ad•verb [ad′vûrb] *n.* A word that describes a verb. An adverb may tell *how, when,* or *where* an action happens: **We walk *quickly* to the theater. The movie begins *soon.* The theater is *near* our home.**

ad•ver•tise•ments [ad•vûr•tīz′mənts] *n.* Things that are made known to the public, especially by paid announcement: **The TV *advertisement* said that your teeth would be whiter if you used the new toothpaste.**

an•i•ma•ted film [an′ə•mā•tid film] *n.* A series of drawings shown as a motion picture with moving figures: **The children saw a lively *animated film* about penguins.**

a•pos•tro•phe [ə•pos′trə•fē] *n.* A symbol (′) that takes the place of letters that are left out in a contraction or that shows possession: ***We're* cleaning up the *school's* playground.**

ar•ti•cle [är′ti•kəl] *n.* A word in a special group of adjectives that includes *a, an,* and *the*: **We saw *a* gorilla, *an* elephant, and many other animals at *the* zoo.**

as•tron•omy [ə•stron′ə•mē] *n.* The study of stars, planets, and other objects in the sky: **We learned a lot about Earth and Mars in our *astronomy* class.**

au•di•ence [ô′dē•əns] *n.* The people who are reached by books, programs, and so on: **A writer's *audience* is made up of his or her readers.**

B

blus•ter•y [blus′tər•ē] *adj.* Stormy and noisy; very windy: **The leaves fly through the air on a *blustery* autumn day.**

book re•view [bŏŏk ri•vyōō′] *n.* An article that tells what a book is about. It also tells what the writer thinks about the book: **Pablo's *book review* on *Wolves* said that he enjoyed the book.**

C

ca•nine [kā′nīn] *adj.* Like a dog; belonging to a group of animals that includes dogs,

foxes, and wolves: **The wolf is a *canine* animal.**

ca•reer [kə•rir′] *n.* A person's lifework or profession: **E.B. White, the author of *Charlotte's Web,* made writing his *career.***

car•pen•ter [kär′pən•tər] *n.* A person who uses wood to make, build, or repair things: **The *carpenter* built a table and some chairs.**

cav•i•ty [kav′i•tē] *n.* A small hole, caused by decay in a tooth: **Tommy went to the dentist to get his *cavity* filled.**

col•or•ful words [kul′ər•fəl wûrdz] *n.* Interesting words that help the reader picture what the writer is describing: ***Enormous* and *scurry* are examples of *colorful words.***

com•bin•ing sen•ten•ces [kəm•bīn′ing sen′tən•səz] *n.* Putting related ideas and information together in one sentence instead of in two or three: *(separated)* **The day is snowy. The day is windy.** *(combined)* ***The day is snowy and windy.***

com•ma [kom′ə] *n.* A punctuation mark (,) that separates parts of a sentence, tells readers where to pause, and helps make the meaning clear: **Yes, I like carrots, broccoli, and celery. I like cucumbers, but I like tomatoes better. We're having a health fair on August 5, 2001, in Denver, Colorado.**

com•mand [kə•mand′] *n.* A kind of sentence that gives an order or a direction. Use a period (.) at the end of a command: **Help me feed the ducks.**

com•mon noun [kom′ən noun] *n.* A noun that names any person, animal, place, or thing. A common noun begins with a lowercase letter: **The *farmer* fed *hay* to the *horses.***

com•mu•ni•ty [kə•myōō′nə•tē] *n.* All the people living in a place; the place, district, or area where people live: **The people in my *community* organized a neighborhood watch group.**

com•plete pred•i•cate [kəm•plēt′ pred′i•kit] *n.* All the words that tell what the subject of the sentence is or does: **The student *finished his homework at 8 P.M.***

com•plete sen•tence [kəm•plēt′ sen′təns] *n.* A group of words that has a subject and a predicate and expresses a complete thought: ***Elena missed the school bus today.***

com•plete sub•ject [kəm•plēt′ sub′jikt] *n.* The simple subject and all the other words in the subject that describe it: ***My younger sister* takes ballet lessons.**

com•pound pred•i•cate [kom′pound pred′i•kit] *n.* Two or more predicates that have the same subject. The word *and* or *or* is usually used to join the predicates: **Her brother *dances and sings.* Before bed, we *watch TV or play checkers.***

a add	e end	o odd	ōō pool	oi oil	th this		ə = a in *above*
ā ace	ē equal	ō open	u up	ou pout	zh vision		e in *sicken*
â care	i it	ô order	û burn	ng ring			i in *possible*
ä palm	ī ice	ŏŏ took	yōō fuse	th thin			o in *melon*
							u in *circus*

com•pound sen•tence [kom′pound sen′təns] *n.* A sentence made up of two or more simple sentences. The sentences are connected with a comma (,) and the word *and, or,* or *but:* **Sarah met her friends, *and* they played jump rope together.**

com•pound sub•ject [kom′pound sub′jikt] *n.* Two or more subjects that have the same predicate. The word *and* or *or* is usually used to join the subjects: ***Janet and Davon* went to the store. *My mother, my brother, or I* cook breakfast.**

con•fi•dence [kon′fə•dəns] *n.* Firm belief or trust: **Because Yoko studied hard for the test, she has *confidence* that she will do well on it.**

con•trac•tion [kən•trak′shən] *n.* A short way to write two words. When a contraction is made, one or more letters are left out. An apostrophe (′) takes the place of the missing letters: ***I'm* happy that *you're* in my class this year. *We'll* be able to work together.**

co•op•er•ate [kō•op′ər•āt] *v.* To work with one person or others for a common purpose: **Diego and Sam were able to finish their project together after they learned how to *cooperate.***

D

de•scrip•tive par•a•graph [di•skrip′tiv par′ə•graf] *n.* Writing that gives details about something. A descriptive paragraph may describe an object, a feeling, an event, or any other subject: **In my *descriptive paragraph,* I gave lots of details about the weather.**

de•tail [dē′tāl] *n.* A fact or an example that helps explain a topic: **Rishi gave many *details* about the foods farm animals eat in his story about growing up on a farm.**

dou•ble neg•a•tive [dub′əl neg′ə•tiv] *n.* Two negative words in one sentence. Double negatives make the meaning of a sentence unclear and should never be used: *(Incorrect)* **You *shouldn't never* do that.** *(Correct)* **You *should never* do that.**

draft [draft] *adj.* Used or adapted for pulling loads: **The *draft* horses pulled the heavy cart.**

E

e•col•o•gy [i•kol′ə•jē] *n.* The relationship of plants and animals to their surroundings and to one another: **We are studying the *ecology* of the rain forest in our science class.**

ef•fec•tive sen•ten•ces [i•fek′tiv sen′tən•siz] *n.* Sentences that give information in a clear and interesting way: **John's paragraph had *effective sentences* that were filled with vivid verbs and adjectives.**

e•lab•o•ra•tion [i•lab′ə•rā′shən] *n.* Developing and expanding a topic by adding details and reasons: **The author's use of *elaboration* in describing Alaska showed us how weather, transportation, animal life, and the fishing industry affect the people who live there.**

end marks [end märks] *n.* Punctuation marks that come at the end of a sentence:

Did you see my new dog? Yes, she's really cute! I wish I had a dog.

en•er•gy [en′ər•jē] *n.* The ability to do work or give power; electric or heat power: **After eating a healthful snack, LaToya had the *energy* to finish her chores.**

en•ter•prise [en′tər•prīz] *n.* An activity set up to earn money: **Manny's newest *enterprise* is a lemonade stand.**

ev•er•green [ev′ər•grēn] *adj.* Trees or shrubs that have green leaves throughout the year: **The *evergreen* tree looks pretty when its needles are covered with snow.**

ex•act words [ig•zakt′ wûrdz] *n.* Words that are very specific instead of general: **The teacher asked us to use *exact words,* such as *panther* instead of *animal.***

ex•cla•ma•tion [eks•klə•mā′shən] *n.* A kind of sentence that shows strong feeling. Use an exclamation point (!) at the end of an exclamation: ***What a great electric light show!***

ex•cla•ma•tion point [eks•klə•mā′shən point] *n.* An end mark (!) that follows an exclamation: **Wow, what a great idea!**

ex•pe•ri•ence [ik•spir′ē•əns] *n.* Something one has gone through; knowledge or skill gained by doing something: **Paco got a lot of job *experience* by working during the summer in his dad's shop.**

F

Fahr•en•heit scale [far′ən•hīt skāl] *n.* A temperature scale showing 32 degrees as the freezing point of water and 212 degrees as the boiling point: **The average temperature last summer was 75 degrees on the *Fahrenheit scale.***

fan•ta•sy [fan′tə•sē] *n.* Imagination; a creation, as a story, that is different from reality: **The story about Babe the talking pig is a *fantasy.***

fed•er•al [fed′ər•əl] *adj.* Having to do with the central government of the United States: **When Gina's family visited Washington, D.C., they toured several of the *federal* buildings and learned a lot about the U.S. government.**

fi•es•ta [fē•es′tə] *n.* A festival; a time of celebration marked by special events such as parades and dancing: **Our class had a *fiesta* to celebrate El Cinco de Mayo, a Mexican holiday.**

fig•ur•a•tive lan•guage [fig′yər•ə•tiv lang′gwij] *n.* Words that are used in an unusual way to create a vivid description: **Mitchell used *figurative language* to compare a firefly to a blinking flashlight.**

friend•ly let•ter [frend′lē let′ər] *n.* A letter written in a conversational style to someone the letter writer knows well. Its purpose is to exchange news or send greetings: **Josh sent a *friendly letter* about his vacation to his best friend, José.**

a add	e end	o odd	ōō pool	oi oil	th this		ə = a in *above*
ā ace	ē equal	ō open	u up	ou pout	zh vision		e in *sicken*
â care	i it	ô order	û burn	ng ring			i in *possible*
ä palm	ī ice	ŏŏ took	yōō fuse	th thin			o in *melon*
							u in *circus*

fu•ture-tense verb [fyōō′chər tens vûrb] *n.* A verb that shows action that will happen at a later time. To form the future tense of a verb, use the helping verb *will* with the main verb: **Bryan *will buy* some grapes at the supermarket.**

H

help•ing verb [help′ing vûrb] *n.* A verb that works with the main verb to tell about an action. The helping verb always comes before the main verb: **Jennifer *has* written an answer to her friend Sue's letter. She *did* enjoy the jokes Sue sent!**

hom•o•graph [hom′ə•graf] *n.* A word that sounds like another word and is spelled the same but has a different meaning: **Did you see Miguel *trip* over the hose? Mary took a *trip* to San Diego.**

hom•o•phone [hom′ə•fōn] *n.* A word that sounds like another word but has a different meaning and a different spelling: **Please *write* me a letter while you're on vacation. Tara was proud that she knew the *right* answer.**

how-to es•say [hou tōō es′ā] *n.* An essay that gives step-by-step directions that explain how to do or make something: **Marina's *how-to essay* gave steps for making a hot-fudge sundae.**

I

il•lu•mi•nate [i•lōō′mə•nāt] *v.* To brighten with light: **After dark they *illuminate* the playing field so that players can see.**

in•stru•ment [in′strə•mənt] *n.* A tool for making music: **My favorite musical *instrument* is the guitar.**

in•ves•ti•gate [in•ves′tə•gāt] *v.* To study thoroughly in order to learn facts or details: **The police officer had to *investigate* the crime scene in order to solve the crime.**

in•vis•i•ble [in•viz′ə•bəl] *adj.* Not able to be seen: **You can't see the oxygen in the air because it is *invisible*.**

in•vi•ta•tion [in′və•tā′shən] *n.* A form of writing used to invite someone to a party or other event: **Marty sent out *invitations* to his ninth birthday party.**

ir•reg•u•lar noun [i•reg′yə•lər noun] *n.* A noun that has a special plural form or that stays the same in the plural form: **The *women* and *children* saw some *sheep* at the petting zoo.**

ir•reg•u•lar verb [i•reg′yə•lər vûrb] *n.* A verb that does not end with *ed* to show past tense: **A child *ran* down the aisle at the movie theater. Mom has *written* a check for the groceries.**

M

main verb [mān vûrb] *n.* The most important verb in the predicate. It comes after the helping verb: **Jennifer is *reading* a letter from a friend. The letter was *sent* last Tuesday.**

min•er•al [min′ər•əl] *n.* A natural material that does not come from a plant or an animal: **Rocks, metals, jewels, and oil are all *minerals* that come from the earth.**

N

neg•a•tive [neg′ə•tiv] *n.* A word that means "no." Some negatives are *never, no, nobody, not, nothing,* and *nowhere.* Contractions with *not* are also negatives: ***No* other nation was larger than the Soviet Union. The United States is *not* larger than Canada. India *doesn't* have as many people as China.**

noun [noun] *n.* A word that names a person, an animal, a place, or a thing: **That *woman* is cheerful. The *horse* runs and jumps over a high, white *fence*.**

nu•tri•ent [nōō′trē•ənt] *n.* A substance in food that helps people, animals, and plants stay healthy: **Vegetables and fruits are good for you because they're rich in *nutrients*.**

O

ob•ject pro•noun [ob′jikt prō′noun] *n.* A pronoun that follows either an action verb or a word such as *about, at, for, from, near, of, to,* or *with.* The words *me, you, him, her, it, us,* and *them* are object pronouns: **Our teacher tells *us* about volcanoes. We are very interested in *them*.**

out•line [out′līn] *n.* A way of organizing information into main parts and details: **We made an *outline* to plan our writing.**

P

par•a•graph•ing [par′ə•graf•ing] *n.* The division of information or ideas into paragraphs, or groups of sentences about one main idea: ***Paragraphing* is important in organizing information for a research report.**

par•a•graph that com•pares [par′ə•graf ~~that~~ kəm•pârz′] *n.* A paragraph that tells how two or more people, places, or things are alike: **Nancy's *paragraph that compares* was about the similarities between frogs and toads.**

par•a•graph that con•trasts [par′ə•graf ~~that~~ kən•trasts′] A paragraph that tells how two or more people, places, or things are different: **Chin wrote a *paragraph that contrasts* about the differences between butterflies and moths.**

past-tense verb [past tens vûrb] *n.* A verb that shows action that happened in the past. Add *ed* or *d* to most present-tense verbs to make them show past tense: **Josh *walked* to the park. Then he *hiked* up the hill.**

pe•ri•od [pir′ē•əd] *n.* A punctuation mark (.) used with an abbreviation and at the end of a statement or command: ***Tues.* is the abbreviation for *Tuesday*. Please take turns.**

per•son•al nar•ra•tive [pûr′sən•əl nar′ə•tiv] *n.* A true story about a writer's own experiences: **I wrote about my summer vacation when we were asked to write a *personal narrative*.**

a add	e end	o odd	ōō pool	oi oil	th this	ə =	a in *above*	
ā ace	ē equal	ō open	u up	ou pout	zh vision		e in *sicken*	
â care	i it	ô order	û burn	ng ring			i in *possible*	
ä palm	ī ice	ŏŏ took	yōō fuse	th thin			o in *melon*	
							u in *circus*	

per•son•al voice [pûr′sən•əl vois] *n.* A person's own special way of expressing himself or herself through words and ideas: **Renaldo found his *personal voice* when he began writing poetry.**

per•sua•sive es•say [pər•swā′siv es′ā] *n.* A type of writing that shows how a writer feels about a topic. The writer tries to persuade the reader to agree: **Angela's *persuasive essay* encouraged readers to exercise at least three times a week.**

plu•ral noun [plŏŏr′əl noun] *n.* A noun that names more than one person, animal, place, or thing. Add *s* to most singular nouns to form the plural: **The *students* took their *books* to the library.**

plu•ral pos•ses•sive noun [plŏŏr′əl pə•zes′iv noun] *n.* A noun that shows ownership by more than one person or thing: **The *players'* uniforms are red and blue. All of the *books'* covers are new.**

plu•ral pro•noun [plŏŏr′əl prō′noun] *n.* A pronoun that takes the place of a plural noun or of two or more nouns. The words *we, you, they, us,* and *them* are plural pronouns: **The children put stamps in a book. *They* put *them* in a book. Carlos gave stamps to Brandon and me. Carlos gave stamps to *us*.**

po•em [pō′əm] *n.* A form of writing in which a writer uses vivid or unusual words to describe something or to express feelings about a subject. A poem often has rhyme or rhythm: **Our class wrote a *poem* about how we felt on the first day of school.**

pos•ses•sive noun [pə•zes′iv noun] *n.* A noun that shows ownership. An apostrophe (') is used to form a possessive noun: **The *girl's* soccer ball is new. The *tractor's* wheels are huge.**

pos•ses•sive pro•noun [pə•zes′iv prō′noun] *n.* A pronoun that shows ownership, taking the place of a possessive noun. One type of possessive pronoun is used before a noun. The other type of possessive pronoun stands alone: ***My* dog is bigger than *yours*.**

pre•cau•tion [pri•kô′shən] *n.* A measure taken to avoid possible harm or danger; care taken ahead of time: **As a *precaution* against sunburn, we used sunscreen lotion at the beach.**

pred•i•cate [pred′i•kit] *n.* The part of a sentence that tells what the subject of the sentence is or does. The predicate usually comes after the subject: **My family *went to the festival on Saturday*.**

pre•sent-tense verb [prez′ənt tens vûrb] *n.* A verb that tells about action that is happening now: **He *brings* a towel to the pool. She *swims* in the pool. Water *splashes* on the lifeguard.**

pro•noun [prō′noun] *n.* A word that takes the place of one or more nouns: **Luis collects stamps. *He* collects stamps. Michael and Chan trade stamps. *They* trade stamps.**

pro•noun an•te•ce•dent [prō′noun an•tə•sēd′ənt] *n.* The noun or nouns to which a pronoun refers. A pronoun must agree with its antecedent in number and gender: ***Laurie* practices *her* jump shot every day. *Laurie and Ron* play basketball in *their* backyard.**

prop•er noun [prop′ər noun] *n.* A noun that names a particular person, animal, place, or thing. People's titles and the names of holidays, days of the week, and months are also proper nouns: ***Jason* visited the *Statue of Liberty* last *Tuesday*.**

pur•pose [pûr′pəs] *n.* A reason for doing something, such as writing: **The *purpose* of my research report is to inform my readers about working dogs.**

Q

ques•tion [kwes′chən] *n.* A sentence that asks something. Use a question mark (?) at the end of a question: ***How many ducks are in the pond?***

ques•tion mark [kwes′chən märk] *n.* An end mark (?) used after a sentence that asks a question: **Did you water the plants?**

quo•ta•tion marks [kwō•tā′shən märks] *n.* Punctuation marks (" ") used to show the exact words a speaker says or to identify the title of a story, poem, or song: **"*I love to read poetry*," said Emma. Emma's favorite poem is Robert Frost's "*Birches*."**

R

reg•is•ter [rej′is•tər] *v.* To enter one's name in an official record, such as a list of voters: **When Maria turned eighteen, she *registered* to vote in the presidential election.**

reg•u•lar verb [reg′yə•lər vûrb] *n.* A verb that ends with *ed* in the past tense: **We *walked* to the library and picked out our books.**

re•search re•port [rē′sûrch ri•pôrt′] *n.* A type of writing that gives information about a topic. Writers gather facts from several sources, such as books or magazines: **Helen went to the library to get information for her *research report* about dolphins.**

rur•al [rŏŏr′əl] *adj.* A person or thing belonging to or happening in the country: **Photographs of country churches and other *rural* scenes are very popular in calendars.**

S

sen•tence [sen′təns] *n.* A group of words that tells a complete thought. A sentence begins with a capital letter, ends with an end mark, and has a subject and a predicate: ***The ducks live near the pond. Is the water cold? Yes, it's freezing!***

sen•tence va•ri•e•ty [sen′təns və•rī′ə•tē] *n.* A way of making writing interesting by combining different types of sentences: **This story is fun to read because it has *sentence variety*.**

se•quence words [sē′kwəns wûrdz] *n.* Words that tell the reader the order of steps or ideas: **The writer's *sequence words* included *first, then, next,* and *last*.**

a add	e end	o odd	ōō pool	oi oil	th this	ə =	a in *above*	
ā ace	ē equal	ō open	u up	ou pout	zh vision		e in *sicken*	
â care	i it	ô order	û burn	ng ring			i in *possible*	
ä palm	ī ice	ŏŏ took	yōō fuse	th thin			o in *melon*	
							u in *circus*	

shim·mer·ing [shim′ər·ing] *adj.* Shining with a reflected light; glimmering: **The metal beads had a *shimmering* glow in the sun.**

sim·ple pred·i·cate [sim′pəl pred′i·kit] *n.* The main word or words in the complete predicate. The simple predicate is always a verb: **Amy *ran* around the track. Misha *has played* the piano all morning.**

sim·ple sen·tence [sim′pəl sen′təns] *n.* A sentence that has a subject and a predicate and expresses one complete thought: **Sarah walked to school. Maki found a quarter.**

sim·ple sub·ject [sim′pəl sub′jikt] *n.* The main word in the complete subject of the sentence: **My *father* works in the garden.**

sin·gu·lar noun [sing′gyə·lər noun] *n.* A noun that names one person, animal, place, or thing: **The *girl* lives near me. The *lake* is deep. That *boat* is fast.**

sin·gu·lar pos·ses·sive noun [sing′gyə·lər pə·zes′iv noun] *n.* A noun that shows ownership by one person or thing. Add an apostrophe (′) and *s* to a singular noun to form the possessive: **A *firefighter′s* helmet is heavy. The *sun′s* rays are hot.**

sin·gu·lar pro·noun [sing′gyə·lər prō′noun] *n.* A word that takes the place of a singular noun. The words *I, me, you, he, she, him, her,* and *it* are singular pronouns: **Ashley gives Hideo a stamp from Mexico. *She* gives *him* a stamp from Mexico. The stamp shows an eagle and a sun. *It* shows an eagle and a sun.**

spe·cif·ic noun [spi·sif′ik noun] *n.* A noun that names a particular thing instead of a whole group of things: ***Pear* is a *specific noun*, but *fruit* is not.**

state·ment [stāt′mənt] *n.* A sentence that tells something. Use a period (.) at the end of a statement: **Ducks lay eggs in the spring.**

sto·ry [stôr′ē] *n.* A type of writing that has a setting, a plot, and characters. A story is made up and has a beginning, a middle, and an ending: **The *story* we read in class today is about a pig that wants to win a prize at the county fair.**

sub·ject [sub′jikt] *n.* The part of a sentence that names the person or thing the sentence is about. The subject is usually at the beginning of a sentence: ***Rocco* went to the grocery store. The *cats* ran outside.**

sub·ject pro·noun [sub′jikt prō′noun] *n.* A word that takes the place of one or more nouns in the subject of a sentence. The words *I, you, he, she, it, we,* and *they* are subject pronouns: ***I* will be nine years old in October. *You* are older than my sister is.**

sub·ject-verb a·gree·ment [sub′jikt vûrb ə·grē′mənt] *n.* The form of the verb in a sentence must match, or agree with, the subject of the sentence: **She *drinks* orange juice for breakfast. Oranges *grow* in warm places.**

tense [tens] *n.* The verb form that tells the time of the action. It tells whether the action is happening now, has happened in the past, or will happen in the future: **Sandy *sends* an e-mail to Pepe. Pepe *spoke* to Sandy yesterday. Tomorrow they *will see* each other at school.**

thank-you note [thangk yōō nōt] *n.* A form of writing used to thank someone for a gift or for doing something: **You should always write a *thank-you note* after you receive a gift.**

ti·tle [tīt′əl] *n.* The name of something such as a book, magazine, or newspaper. Titles of long works such as books and newspapers are underlined or italicized. Titles of shorter works such as poems and stories are placed in quotation marks: **Did you read The Story of Little Tree? I′m reading a poem called "The Owl and the Pussycat."**

tra·di·tions [trə·dish′·ənz] *n.* Customs that are passed on from parents to children: **Ricardo and his family celebrate many Spanish *traditions.***

vac·cine [vak·sēn′] *n.* Medicine that puts germs of a certain kind into the body to prevent illness: **Children can be given a *vaccine* to protect them against mumps.**

verb [vûrb] *n.* The main word in the predicate of a sentence. It tells what the subject of the sentence is or does: **The boy *rides* a bike. His bike *is* new.**

vice·roy [vīs′roy] *n.* A person who helps a king rule a country, colony, or province: **The *viceroy* told the king that the people in the kingdom wished him well.**

vis·i·ble [viz′zə·bəl] *adj.* Able to be seen: **On sunny days, the mountains are *visible* from my window.**

viv·id verb [viv′id vûrb] *n.* A strong verb that describes action in an interesting way: **Instead of the verb *hurry*, use a *vivid verb* such as *bolt*, *speed*, or *zoom*.**

word choice [wûrd chois] *n.* Choice of words and phrases to give the effect that the writer intends: **The writer′s *word choice* makes it clear that she loves dogs.**

writ·er′s view·point [rī′tərz vyōō′point] *n.* The way a writer expresses himself or herself to let the reader know how he or she feels about the subject: **The writer′s *viewpoint* is that summer is her least-liked season.**

a	add	e	end	o	odd	ōō	pool	oi	oil	th	this	ə =	a in *above*
ā	ace	ē	equal	ō	open	u	up	ou	pout	zh	vision		e in *sicken*
â	care	i	it	ô	order	ū	burn	ng	ring				i in *possible*
ä	palm	ī	ice	ōō	took	yōō	fuse	th	thin				o in *melon*
													u in *circus*

Vocabulary Power

advertisements If the **advertisements** are true, this shampoo will make your hair shiny and beautiful.

animated film Do you like **animated films** such as *The Lion King* and *Toy Story*?

astronomy My brother is studying **astronomy** and learning about Mars.

blustery The trees were bending in the wind on the cold, **blustery** day.

canine Dogs and wolves are members of the **canine** family.

career Marta wants to play on a pro soccer team so she can have a **career** in sports.

carpenter The **carpenter** hammered nails into the desk he was building.

cavity Jimmy had a **cavity** in his tooth filled by the dentist.

community People in my **community** decided to have a neighborhood picnic.

confidence Our coach has **confidence** in our team because we practice very hard.

cooperate If you and your sister **cooperate**, you will work well together.

draft Farms in the past used **draft** horses to pull heavy loads.

ecology Rishi is learning about animals and their environment in his study of **ecology**.

elaboration Mrs. Diaz said that using **elaboration** in our stories would explain more about our characters.

energy If you eat healthful foods, you will have the **energy** to run the race.

enterprise Elena set up a baby-sitting **enterprise** to earn money for camp.

evergreen An **evergreen** tree is green even in winter.

experience Yoko has a lot of **experience** with animals because she lives on a farm.

Fahrenheit scale Water boils at 212 degrees on the **Fahrenheit scale**.

fantasy Jen wrote a story that is a **fantasy** about a trip to Pluto.

federal Paul′s father is a **federal** worker who works for the government.

fiesta We enjoyed a parade, music, and dancing during a **fiesta** to celebrate Mexican independence.

illuminate Lights **illuminate** the tennis courts so that people can play after dark.

instrument Mary′s favorite musical **instrument** is the piano.

investigate The detective **investigated** the area where the burglar was last seen.

invisible Carlos couldn′t read the message because it was written in **invisible** ink.

mineral Coal is a **mineral** used as a fuel.

nutrient Vitamin C is a **nutrient** you get when you eat oranges.

precaution Check the battery in your home fire alarm as a safety **precaution**.

register All students **register** for class on the same day.

rural There is not as much traffic in **rural** areas as there is in a city.

shimmering The sun shines on the icicles, giving them a **shimmering** glow.

traditions One of our **traditions** is to break a piñata filled with candy at a birthday party.

vaccine A **vaccine** helps protect children against disease.

viceroy The **viceroy** told the people in the kingdom that taxes would be cut.

visible The stars are not **visible** in the sky tonight because it is too cloudy.

Index

Acknowledgments

For permission to reprint copyrighted material, grateful acknowledgment is made to the following sources:

Boyds Mills Press, Inc.: Cover illustration by Maryann Cocca-Leffler from *Wanda's Roses* by Pat Brisson. Illustration copyright © 1994 by Maryann Cocca-Leffler. From *Horsepower: The Wonder of Draft Horses* by Cris Peterson, cover photograph by Alvis Upitis. Text copyright © 1997 by Cris Peterson; photograph copyright © 1997 by Alvis Upitis.

Delacorte Press, a division of Random House, Inc.: From *Half-Chicken* by Alma Flor Ada, illustrated by Kim Howard. Text copyright © 1995 by Alma Flor Ada; illustrations copyright © 1995 by Kim Howard.

Dial Books for Young Readers, a division of Penguin Putnam Inc.: From *Back Home* by Gloria Jean Pinkney, cover illustration by Jerry Pinkney. Text copyright © 1992 by Gloria Jean Pinkney; cover illustration copyright © 1992 by Jerry Pinkney.

HarperCollins Publishers: From *Ramona and Her Mother* by Beverly Cleary, cover illustration by Alan Tiegreen. Text and cover illustration copyright © 1979 by Beverly Cleary. From *Beacons of Light: Lighthouses* by Gail Gibbons. Copyright © 1990 by Gail Gibbons.

Holiday House, Inc.: Cover illustration by John and Alexandra Wallner from *A Picture Book of Benjamin Franklin* by David A. Adler. Illustration copyright © 1990 by John and Alexandra Wallner. Cover illustration by John and Alexandra Wallner from *A Picture Book of Thomas Alva Edison* by David A. Adler. Illustration copyright © 1996 by John and Alexandra Wallner. From *Dancing With the Indians* by Angela Shelf Medearis, cover illustration by Samuel Byrd. Text copyright © 1991 by Angela Shelf Medearis; illustration copyright © 1991 by Samuel Byrd.

Henry Holt and Company, Inc.: Cover illustration by Megan Lloyd from *Cactus Hotel* by Brenda Z. Guiberson. Illustration copyright © 1991 by Megan Lloyd.

Little, Brown and Company (Inc.): From *How to Be a Friend* by Laurie Krasny Brown and Marc Brown. Copyright © 1998 by Laurene Krasny Brown and Marc Brown. Cover illustration from *Dinosaurs Alive and Well!* by Laurie Krasny Brown and Marc Brown. Copyright © 1990 by Laurene Krasny Brown and Marc Brown. Cover illustration from *Arthur Writes a Story* by Marc Brown. Copyright © 1996 by Marc Brown. Cover illustration from *Recycle!* by Gail Gibbons. Copyright © 1992 by Gail Gibbons. Cover illustration from *Click! A Book about Cameras and Taking Pictures* by Gail Gibbons. Copyright © 1997 by Gail Gibbons.

National Wildlife Federation: "Weird Leaves" by Deborah Churchman from *Ranger Rick Magazine*, October 1999. Text copyright 1999 by the National Wildlife Federation.

Puffin Books, a division of Penguin Putnam Inc.: Cover illustration by Janet Wilson from *The Gadget War* by Betsy Duffey. Illustration copyright © 1991 by Janet Wilson.

Scholastic Inc.: Cover photograph from *What Food Is This?* by Rosmarie Hausherr. Copyright © 1994 by Rosmarie Hausherr. Cover illustration by Ron Garnett from *Great Black Heroes: Five Notable Inventors* by Wade Hudson. Illustration copyright © 1995 by Ron Garnett. HELLO READER! and CARTWHEEL BOOKS are registered trademarks of Scholastic Inc.

Simon & Schuster Books for Young Readers, an imprint of Simon & Schuster Children's Publishing Division: From *Coaching Ms. Parker* by Carla Heymsfeld, cover illustration by Jane O'Conor. Text copyright © 1992 by Carla Heymsfeld; illustration copyright © 1992 by Jane O'Conor. From *A Log's Life* by Wendy Pfeffer, cover illustration by Robin Brickman. Text copyright © 1997 by Wendy Pfeffer; illustration copyright © 1997 by Robin Brickman. Cover illustration from *A Desert Scrapbook: Dawn to Dusk in the Sonoran Desert* by Virginia Wright-Frierson. Copyright © 1996 by Virginia Wright-Frierson.

Steck-Vaughn Company: From *My First American Friend* by Sarunna Jin, cover illustration by Shirley Y. Beckes. Text and cover illustration copyright © 1992 by Steck-Vaughn Company; text and cover illustration copyright © 1991 by Rainbow Publishers Limited Partnership. From *Baseball: How to Play the All-Star Way* by Mark Alan Teirstein, cover photograph by Frank Becerra, Jr. Text and cover photograph © copyright 1994 by Steck-Vaughn Company.

Viking Penguin, a division of Penguin Putnam Inc.: Cover illustration by Leo and Diane Dillon from *The Hundred Penny Box* by Sharon Bell Mathis. Illustration copyright © 1975 by Leo and Diane Dillon.

Walker Publishing Company: Cover illustration by Barbara Bash from *Tiger Lilies and Other Beastly Plants* by Elizabeth Ring. Illustration copyright © 1984 by Barbara Bash.

Photo Credits

Page Placement Key: (t)-top (c)-center (b)-bottom (l)-left (r)-right (fg)-foreground (bg)-background

Photos by Richard Hutchings/Harcourt: Page 47, 50, 64, 81, 83, 131, 109, 180, 189, 222, 223, 225, 280, 293, 367, 368, 415, 437.

Other:

Abbreviations for frequently used stock photo agencies:

PR– Photo Researchers, NY; SM –The Stock Market NY, TSI -Stone.

Unit One:

22-23 Bernard Boutrit/Woodfin Camp & Associates; 24 Duudier/Jerrican/PR; 25 Index Stock Photography; 28 The Granger Collection; 33 Harcourt; 34 Harcourt; 35 Prof. J.H. Nkatia, University of California, Los Angeles Ethnomusicology Dept.; 37 PhotoDisc; 39 Joe Sohm/SM; 52 Walter Hodges/TSI; 53 Mark Joseph/TSI; 55 Phil Jude/Science Photo Library/PR; 62 Joseph Nettis/TSI; 67 Sean Ellis/TSI; 69 The Granger Collection, New York; 84 Cathlyn Melloan/TSI; 85 Howard Kingsworth/TSI; 86 Jay S. Simon/TSI; 87 The Granger Collection; 88-89 J. Burgum/P. Boorman/TSI.

Unit Two:

90-91 Susan Leavines/PR; 92 Lori Adamski Peek/TSI; 93 Bob Downey/Harcourt; 95 Carl Scofield/Index Stock Photography; 102 Tom Martin/SM; 103 Bo Zaunders/SM; 105 Index Stock Photography; 109 Harcourt; 120 Chip Henderson/TSI; 121 Barmana/PR; 123 Harcourt; 125 Pete Saloutos/SM; 130 NIBSC/Science Photo Library/PR; 154 Harcourt; 155 Laurence Monneret/TSI; 156 Weronica Ankerorn/Harcourt; 158-159 Charles Krebs/SM.

Unit Three:

164-165 Chris McLaughlin/SM; 166 Cameramann International; 167 Index Stock Photography; 171 Kevin Horan/Stock, Boston; 176 Bachmann/PR; 177 Bob Daemmrich/Stock, Boston; 179 Ed Young/Science Photo Library/PR; 181 Dana White/PhotoEdit; 194 Ed Pritchard/TSI; 195 (t) D. B. Owen/Black Star; 195 (b) Karl Schumacher/The White House; 196 Peggy and Ronald Barnett/SM; 197 AFP/Corbis; 199 Ross Ressmeyer/Corbis; 201 David Phillips/Harcourt; 204 Randy Wells/TSI; 205 Index Stock Photography; 207 J. Faircloth/Transparencies; 230-231 Harcourt.

Unit Four:

232-233 Lois Moulton/TSI; 234 David Parker/Science Photo Library/PR; 235 NASA; 237 NASA; 239 Jerry Schad/PR; 245 H.A. Miller/PR; 246 Bob Daemmrich/Stock, Boston; 247 (t) Harcourt; 247 (r) Hans Strand/TSI; 249 Steve Terrill/SM; 251 John Callahan/TSI; 262 Art Wolfe/TSI; 264 Francois Gohier/PR; 265 Renee Lynn/PR; 267 F. Gohier/PR; 272 Tom Brakefield/SM; 273 Renee Lynn/TSI; 274 Gerard Laca/Peter Arnold, Inc.; 275 Tim Davis/PR; 279 Daniel J. Cox/TSI; 282 (t) Robert & Linda Mitchell; 282 (b) Uniphoto; 283, 284 (t), (c), (b) J. H. (Pete) Carmichael/Nature Photographics; 285 (b) Lori Franzen; 285 (t) Derek Fell; 294 Kevin Kelley/TSI; 296 Charles Krebs/TSI; 298-299 Sonny Senser/Harcourt; 306-307 Benelux Press/Index Stock Photography.

Unit Five:

308 Larry Lefever from Grant Heilman Photography; 309 Adam Jones/PR; 311 B. Seitz/PR; 313 Renee Lynn/PR; 319 James Strachan/TSI; 321 David Madison/TSI; 325 Grantpix/PR; 336 Bob Daemmrich Photography; 337 David L. Brown/The Picture Cube/Index Stock Photography; 339 Myron Taplin/TSI; 340 David Stoecklein/SM; 343 Robert E. Daemmrich/TSI; 346 Rich Franco/Harcourt; 347 Harcourt; 349 Zane Williams/TSI; 351 Richard Pasley/Stock, Boston; 370 Larry Lefever from Grant Heilman Photography; 371 Weronica Ankerorn/Harcourt; 373 Murray & Associates/Picturesque Stock Photo; 374-375 Tom Sobolik/Black Star/Harcourt.

Unit Six:

376-377 Kevin Kelley/TSI; 378 Michal Heron/Woodfin Camp & Associates; 379 National Park Service, Edison National Historic Site; 381 Photo, (1995 Wright Bros. Flyer)/04/05 Simms Station Huffman Prairie) Wright State University, Special Collections & Archives (Dayton, OH), The Wright Bros. TradeMark, Licensed by The Wright Family Fund, Represented by The Roger Richman Agency, Inc.; Beverly Hills, CA 90212 (www.wrightbrothers2003.com); 382 Harcourt Photo Library; 383 Bonnie Sue/PR; 388 Roberto De Gugliermo/Science Photo Library/PR; 389 David N. Davis/PR; 390 Art Wolfe/TSI; 391 James Martin/TSI; 393 John M. Roberts/SM; 395 Vanessa Vick/PR; 405 (detail) Gift of Mr. and Mrs. Benjamin E. Levy © 2000 Board of Trustees, National Gallery of Art, Washington, DC; 406 Richard E. Hansen/PR; 410 Paul Souders/TSI; 411 Index Stock Photography; 413 Stocktrek/SM; 416 Jim Corwin/TSI; 417 World Perspectives/TSI; 419 Wolfgang Kaehler; 421 Tony Freeman/PhotoEdit; 423 L.L.T. Rhodes/TSI; 440 I. Burgum/P. Boorman/TSI; 441 Art Wolfe/TSI; 442 Michael Giannechini/PR; 443 NASA; 444-445 L. P. Winfrey/Woodfin Camp & Associates.

Extra Practice:

454 Paul Souders/TSI; 455 Harcourt; 456 Michael Giannechini/PR; 459 Renee Lynn/PR; 462 Harcourt; 463 Sean Ellis/TSI; 464 Joseph Nettis/TSI; 465 Index Stock Photography; 467 Zane Williams/TSI; 471 Don Mason/SM; 474 Jose Fuste Raga/SM.

Handbook:

488 Lee Snider/The Image Works; 494 (1) Chris Warbey/TSI; 494 (r) Francois Gohier/PR; 502-503 Michele Burgess/SM; 530 Tom Benoit/TSI.

Art List

Harcourt, 23, Elizabeth Wolf, 27; Nathan Young Jarvis, 29; Claude Martinot, 31; Myron Grossman, 36; Harcourt, 37 (Left); Myron Grossman, 38; Elizabeth Wolf, 40; Nathan Young Jarvis, 41; Harcourt, 43; Jane Winsor, 54; Claude Martinot, 73; Nathan Young Jarvis, 65-66; Harcourt, 69 (bottom); Ilya Bereznickas, 71; Stacey Schuett, 72-75; Karen Pritchett, 77-78, 80; Harcourt, 85, 91; Andy Levine, 94; Ilya Bereznickas, 96; Andy Levine, 99; Harcourt, 101; Donna Turner, 103 (bottom), 104 (left), 104 (right), 106; Alexi Natchev, 107; Ken Batkman, 111; Claude Martinot, 122; Ilya Bereznickas, 124; George Ulrich, 127; Andy Levine, 129, 132; Myron Grossman, 133; Christine Mau, 134; Andy Levine, 137; Christine Mau, 139; Karen Pritchett, 153; Elizabeth Wolf, 157; Harcourt, 163; Elizabeth Wolf, 168; Andy Levine, 170; Myron Grossman, 173; Tamara Petrosino, 176; Alexi Natchev, 183; Andy Levine, 193 (ALL); Claude Martinot, 196, 198; Elizabeth Wolf, 203; Tamara Petrosino, 206; Myron Grossman, 208, 211; Ilene Robinette, 214-217; Nathan Young Jarvis, 218; Tammara Petrosino, 226-227; Christine Mau, 228; Tamara Petrosino, 229; Harcourt, 230-231, 233; Myron Grossman, 236; Nathan Young Jarvis, 241(right); Harcourt, 241 (bottom); Christine Mau, 243; Nathan Young Jarvis, 244; Harcourt, 247 (Snowflake); 248; Andy Levine, 253; Claude Martinot, 263, 266, 268; Jane Wilson, 269; Andy Levine, 271; Donna Turner, 273 (bottom); Karen Pritchett, 276; Donna Turner, 277; Harcourt, 281, 307; Myron Grossman, 310; Karen Pritchett, 312; Patricia Pila, 315; Myron Grossman, 317 (Top), 317 (Bottom); Nathan Young Jarvis, 319; Elizabeth Wolf, 320, 323- 323; Ezra Tucker, 338; Alexi Natchev, 341; Myron Grossman, 342; Nathan Young Jarvis, 345; Ilya Bereznicka, 348; Harcourt, 350; Andy Levine, 353; Tamara Petrosino, 355 (All); Harcourt, 369; Myron Grossman, 372, 377; Karen Pritchett, 385; Tamara Petrosino, 387; Elizabeth Wolf, 392; Christine Mau, 397; Myron Grossman, 407; Nathan Jarvis, 408-409; Christine Mau, 418; Andy Levine, 420; Alexi Natchev, 425; Karen Pritchett, 439; LP. Winfrey/Woodfin Camp And Associates, 444-445; Janet Wilson, 445 (top book); John and Alexander Wallner, 445 (bottom book); L.P Winfrey/Woodfin Camp And Associates, 445; Janet Wilson, 445 (top book); Ron Garnett, 445 (middle book).

Reteach

	Sentences	Kinds of Sentences	Punctuating Sentences
	Objective: to identify and use complete sentences; to use correct capitalization and end punctuation	**Objective**: to identify questions, commands, and exclamations	**Objective**: to identify and use correct end punctuation
Visual	On the board, write several word groups, including some complete sentences; for example: *my mom likes quilts, the drawing is colorful, Susan's cat, and the red bicycle.* Have volunteers add capitalization and punctuation to the complete sentences.	Write six or more sentences on the board, including questions, commands, and exclamations. Have students read each sentence aloud and identify its type. Then write more sentences leaving off the end punctuation. Have students use colored chalk to add the correct end marks.	Write several sentences on the board. Have students read the sentences and add the correct end punctuation. Suggest that students color-code their punctuation, using a different color for each type of sentence.
Auditory	One at a time, say word groups, only some of which are complete sentences. Ask students to identify those that are sentences and to use the other word groups to make complete sentences. Then ask students how they would capitalize and punctuate each complete sentence.	Using an expressive voice, say several questions, commands, and exclamations, such as: *Do you like our mural? Add water to the paint. Wow, that's terrific!* Have students identify which kind each sentence is and tell which punctuation mark should be used at the end of it. Allow students to take turns making up their own questions, commands, and exclamations.	Say a sentence. Call on a student and ask: *What punctuation mark appears at the end of the sentence? How do you know?* Then have the student say another sentence ending with the same punctuation mark.
Kinesthetic	Write several complete sentences on individual sentence strips. Then cut each sentence into pieces, with one word on each piece. Let students work with partners to put the words from each sentence in order, using the initial capital letter and the final period as clues.	Write several questions, commands, and exclamations on the board, omitting end punctuation. Have a student act out a sentence. Ask the other students to identify the sentence. Once students have guessed correctly, have the actor add the correct end punctuation.	Prepare three large flashcards: one for a period, a question mark, and an exclamation point. Put the cards face down on a table. Let students take turns choosing a flashcard, identifying the mark on their card, telling the kind of sentence that ends with that mark, and saying a sentence of that kind.

Reteach

	Complete and Simple Subjects **Objective:** To identify simple and complete subjects	Nouns in Subjects **Objective:** To identify nouns in subjects	Combining Sentences: Compound Subjects **Objective:** To identify and use sentences with compound subjects
Visual	On the board, write a series of short sentences. Underline the simple subject in one color and the complete subject in another color. Have students identify the simple subjects and complete subjects. Write more sentences and have students color-code them the same way.	Write several sentences with complete subjects on the board. Have students use one color to underline the complete subject of each sentence. Then have students use a second color to circle the noun that is the simple subject of each sentence.	On the board, write several pairs of sentences with related subjects and identical predicates. Have volunteers use colored chalk to circle the parts of the sentences that can be joined. Then have all students write the new sentences with compound subjects.
Auditory	Say short, simple statements, one at a time. Ask students to identify the simple subject and the complete subject of the sentence. Then have them make up new sentences, with different simple subjects and complete subjects.	Say short, simple statements, one at a time. After each statement, ask: *What is the complete subject of that sentence? Which noun names the person, place, or thing the sentence is about?* Then ask students to say sentences with a complete subject. Call on a volunteer to name the noun in the sentence.	Say several sentences, one at a time, such as: *Maya played the drums. Terrell played the drums. Maya and Terrell played the drums.* Use sentences that have compound subjects, as well as some that do not. After each sentence, ask: *Does this sentence have a compound subject? How can you tell?* Have students recite the two sentences that were joined to make the new sentence with a compound subject.
Kinesthetic	Prepare a set of sentence cards. On one fourth, write simple subjects; on another fourth, write complete subjects; and on the rest write sentence predicates. Have students use the cards to make sentences. Ask them to identify the simple subjects and complete subjects in their sentences.	Prepare several word cards with a different noun on each card. Hand one card to each student. Have students read aloud their nouns and then make up sentences about that person, place, or thing. For each sentence, ask: *What is the simple subject? What is the complete subject?*	Using paired sentences that have the same predicate and related subjects, prepare individual sentence strips, one for each student. Pass out the strips. Have each student find a student who has a sentence with the same predicate. Ask pairs of students to read their sentences aloud and then combine them to form a sentence with a compound subject.

Reteach

	Complete and Simple Predicates **Objective:** To identify and use complete and simple predicates	Verbs in Predicates **Objective:** To identify verbs in sentence predicates	Combining Sentences: Compound Predicates **Objective:** To identify compound predicates
Visual	Write several sentence subjects on the board. Ask students to add a predicate to each subject to create a complete sentence. Then write some of the students' sentences on the board, and ask volunteers to underline the predicates.	Write a series of simple sentences on the board, such as: *Uncle José drew this plan. It is a blueprint.* Write the sentence subjects in one color and the predicates in another color. Have students read aloud each sentence, its predicate, and the verb in that predicate, and let a volunteer point to the verb.	Prepare worksheets with pairs of sentences that have identical subjects and can be combined to form sentences with compound predicates. Let students use markers to color code the sentences. Then have them write the new sentences with compound predicates.
Auditory	Say a sentence subject. Ask a volunteer to add a predicate to that subject and to say the complete sentence. Have the other students repeat the added predicate. Repeat to provide practice.	Read the following sentence aloud: *We read at school.* Have students identify the predicate and the verb. Then challenge students to make as many different sentences as they can that follow that pattern, changing only the verb.	Say aloud a variety of sentences. Include mostly sentences that have compound predicates, as well as some sentences that do not. After saying each sentence, ask: *Does this sentence have a compound predicate?* If the sentence does have a compound predicate, also ask: *What two sentences were combined to make this sentence?*
Kinesthetic	Remind students that a predicate tells what the subject of a sentence does or is. Have each student write a sentence with the subject *I*, telling what he or she likes to do. Then let students act out their sentences and see whether the others can guess each predicate.	Write several short sentences on the board. Have students take turns acting out a sentence without reading it aloud. Ask the other students to guess which sentence is being acted out. Then have the actor point to the verb in the sentence he or she acted out.	On strips of paper, write groups of sentences: two with identical subjects; and a third that combines the first two, using a compound predicate. Display the strips on a bulletin board. Have students take down a sentence with a compound predicate and the two that were joined to make it.

Reteach

	Complete Sentences **Objective:** To identify and write complete sentences	Simple and Compound Sentences **Objective:** To identify and use simple and compound sentences	Combining Sentences **Objective:** To combine simple sentences to form compound sentences
Visual	On the board, write a list of word groups, only some of which are complete sentences. Have students read each group aloud and identify it as *a sentence* or *not a sentence*. Ask volunteers to add one or more words to each sentence fragment to make a complete sentence.	On the board, write a paragraph made up of simple and compound sentences. Have volunteers color-code the sentences with chalk, using one color to circle simple sentences and another to circle compound sentences.	On the board, write pairs of simple sentences that can be combined into compound sentences. Mix the sentences up. Have students decide which ones make meaningful pairs. Have students write one compound sentence from the simple sentences on the board.
Auditory	Read aloud a list of word groups, one at a time, only some of which should be complete sentences. After each word group, ask: *Is that a complete sentence? How can you tell? If it is not, ask: What words can you add to make this a complete sentence?*	Say simple and compound sentences, one at a time. After each sentence ask: *Is this a simple sentence or a compound sentence? How can you tell?* If it is a compound sentence, ask: *What two simple sentences are joined in that compound sentence?*	Say pairs of simple sentences. In most cases, say two sentences that can be combined to make a compound sentence; for example, *Michael pulled on the rope. I helped him.* In a few cases, say completely unrelated sentences. After each sentence pair, ask: *Can you combine these two sentences to make a compound sentence?* If the sentences are related, have a volunteer say the compound sentence.
Kinesthetic	Prepare a set of sentence strips. Write complete sentences on half of the strips; on the other half, write word groups that are not complete sentences. Have students sort the strips into two groups: complete sentences and word groups that are not complete sentences.	Divide a bulletin board into two parts: *Simple Sentences* and *Compound Sentences*. Write a mix of simple and compound sentences on strips of paper. Have students pick sentence strips, identify the sentence as simple or compound, and pin the strip to the correct part of the bulletin board.	Write simple sentences on individual strips that can be combined into a compound sentence. Make a word card for *and*, *but*, *or*, and a comma. Give each student a sentence strip, and have them find a partner with whom they will form a compound sentence, using their sentence strips, the comma card and a combining word.

Reteach

	Nouns	Common and Proper Nouns	Abbreviations and Titles
	Objective: To identify and use nouns in sentences	**Objective:** To identify and use common nouns and proper nouns	**Objective:** To identify and use abbreviations and titles
Visual	Write several sentences on the board. Include common nouns in each sentence; avoid proper nouns. Have students read the sentences and circle each noun, using different colors for people, animals, places, and things.	On worksheets, write sentences that each contain one common noun and one proper noun. Include the names of students, the school, and other familiar proper nouns. Have students underline each common noun and circle each proper noun.	Prepare a two-column worksheet with a list of words that can be abbreviated in the left column. In the right column, write the abbreviations of those words in random order. Have students match the words and their abbreviations, using a different color marker to circle each pair.
Auditory	Ask students to listen to identify the noun. Say a sentence that has just one noun. Then have them repeat the sentence, substituting a different noun. Repeat this activity with different sentences until all students have had an opportunity to contribute.	Say a sentence that has just one common noun. Choose a noun for which students can readily substitute a proper noun—for example, *boy*, *girl*, *teacher*, or *street*. Have students identify the common noun and then repeat your sentence, substituting a proper noun for the common noun. Repeat to provide practice for all students.	Say sentences, one at a time, that include words that can be abbreviated. Have students identify each word that can be abbreviated and then spell the abbreviation aloud, including capital letters (if needed) and periods.
Kinesthetic	Hand each student a common classroom object, such as a book or an eraser. Ask students to say nouns naming these things. Then have each student go around the classroom touching objects and using nouns to name them.	Prepare a set of flashcards, writing a different common or proper noun on each card. Put the cards into a box. Have each student pull a card, read the word aloud, identify it as a common noun or a proper noun, and then use it in a sentence.	Provide a set of upper- and lowercase letter cards as well as period cards. Have each student use the cards to make words that can be abbreviated. For each word, call on a student to remove the appropriate letters and add a period to make the abbreviation of that word.

Reteach

	Singular and Plural Nouns **Objective:** To identify singular nouns and plural nouns	Plural Nouns with -es and -ies **Objective:** To write and use plural noun forms that end with -es or -ies	Irregular Plural Nouns **Objective:** To identify and use irregular plural noun forms
Visual	Write a short paragraph on the board. Include singular nouns as well as plural nouns, formed by adding *s*. Have students use one color to circle all the singular nouns and another color to circle all the plural nouns.	Prepare a worksheet of singular nouns, which have plural forms ending with *-es* or *-ies*. Have students circle all the nouns that end with *s*, *x*, *ch*, or *sh* and all the nouns that end with a consonant and *y*. Then have them write the plural form of each noun.	On the board, write a series of sentences using irregular plural nouns. Have students circle each of these nouns and then write their singular forms.
Auditory	Using a sentence frame such as *I see (a) _____ .* Say a series of sentences, one at a time. Include one singular noun or one plural noun in each sentence. After each sentence, ask: *What is the noun in that sentence? Is it a singular noun or a plural noun?* If it is a singular noun, have students spell the plural form. If it is a plural noun, have them spell the singular form.	Prepare a list of singular nouns ending with *s*, *x*, *ch*, *sh*, or a consonant and *y*. Read the nouns aloud, one at a time. After each noun, ask students to identify the ending of the word and to explain how to make the plural form. Then have them spell aloud the plural form of the word.	Say a sentence using either a singular or a plural form of an irregular noun. Ask students to identify the noun and tell whether it is singular or plural. Then let a volunteer revise your sentence, using the other form of the same noun. Continue to provide practice with a number of irregular nouns.
Kinesthetic	Prepare a set of word cards. Write a singular noun on one card and its plural on another. Only use words whose plural form ends in *s*. Have students play Concentration, turning over two cards at a time and trying to match the singular and plural forms of the same noun.	On a set of word cards, write singular nouns that end with *s*, *x*, *ch*, *sh*, or a consonant and *y*. Turn the cards face down on a table and mix them up. Let each student pick a card, read the singular noun aloud, and then write the plural form of that noun on the board.	Prepare a set of word cards. On half the cards, write various irregular plural noun forms. On the other half, write the singular form of the same nouns. Give one card to each student. Then have each student find the student who has a card with a form of the same noun. Ask each pair of students to read their noun forms aloud and to use them in sentences.

Reteach

	Singular Possessive Nouns	Plural Possessive Nouns	Revising Sentences Using Possessive Nouns
	Objective: To identify and use singular possessive nouns	**Objective:** To identify and use plural possessive nouns	**Objective:** To revise sentences by using possessive nouns
Visual	On the board, write a series of sentences. Instead of the possessive form, write the singular noun form in each sentence. Have students read each sentence aloud, saying the possessive form of the noun. Then have a volunteer write the possessive form on the board.	On the board, write several short sentences that include plural possessive nouns. Leave the apostrophe off each one. Have students read each sentence aloud and identify the word that should be possessive. Have a volunteer use colored chalk to add the apostrophe.	On the board, write several sentences that contain phrases that can be replaced by possessive nouns. First have volunteers underline the phrases that can be replaced using colored chalk. Then have other volunteers erase the phrases and substitute the correct possessive nouns.
Auditory	One at a time, say sentences that include singular possessive nouns. After each sentence, ask: *What possessive noun did you hear?* Have a volunteer write that possessive noun on the board.	Read aloud a series of sentences that include possessive nouns, some singular and some plural. After each sentence, ask: *What is the possessive noun in that sentence? Is it a singular possessive noun or a plural possessive noun? How does that possessive form end—with 's or with s'?*	Say a sentence with a phrase that can be replaced by a possessive noun. For example, *Is this the comb that belongs to Carol?* Have students identify the phrase and then repeat the sentence, substituting the correct possessive noun. For example, *Yes, it is Carol's comb.* Repeat to provide additional practice.
Kinesthetic	Hand a book to a student (for example, Hank) and say: *I'm giving this book to Hank. Now it is Hank's book.* Write the possessive noun on the board. Have students pass the book, say the sentence, use a possessive noun, and write the possessive noun on the board.	Prepare a set of word cards, each with a singular noun whose plural is formed by adding just *s*. Also prepare a card with just the letter *s* and a card with just an apostrophe. Have students take turns putting the cards together to form the plural possessive form of each noun.	Have partners make pairs of cards: one with a phrase beginning with *belonging to* or *of* and the other with a possessive noun that can replace that phrase. Place the phrase cards down and the possessive noun cards up. Each student picks and reads a phrase card aloud and then finds and reads the card with a matching possessive noun.

Reteach

	Verbs **Objective:** To identify and use verbs	Action Verbs **Objective:** To identify and use action verbs	The Verb *Be* **Objective:** To identify and use present-tense forms of *be*
Visual	On the board, write a list of short sentences, each with a one-word verb; for example, *The puppy looks healthy.* Have students use one color to underline the predicate of each sentence and a different color to circle the verb.	On the board, write a series of short sentences, each with an action verb. Have students read each sentence aloud. Ask: *What did (the subject) do?* When students have answered correctly, ask: *What is the action verb in the sentence?* Circle the verb.	On the board, write a list of sentence frames students can complete by adding a present-tense form of *be.* Have students read each sentence aloud, adding *am, is,* or *are.* Then have a volunteer write the correct verb form in the blank.
Auditory	Say a series of short sentences, one at a time. After each sentence, ask: *What is the predicate in the sentence? What is the most important word—the verb—in the predicate?* Then have a volunteer repeat your sentence, substituting a different verb for the one you said.	Say a short sentence such as this: *I clapped my hands.* Ask students to identify the action verb. Then challenge them to substitute as many other action verbs as they can. When students run out of action verbs for that sentence, present a different sentence and repeat the activity.	Say sentences that include present-tense forms of the main verb *be.* Clap your hands instead of saying *am, is,* or *are.* Ask: *What word is missing from the sentence?* After students have identified the correct form of *be,* have them repeat the whole sentence using the verb form.
Kinesthetic	Write the following sentence frame on the board. *My friends _____ with me.* Have students write one word on a card and insert it in the blank. Have students read their completed sentences aloud. Ask: *What is the verb in your sentence?*	Prepare a set of word cards with a different action verb on each one. Let each student pick a card. Have students act out the action verbs on their cards. Ask students to guess which verb is being acted out. Then have the student who acted the verb out say a sentence using that verb.	On the board, write sentence frames that can be completed by adding a present-tense form of *be.* Make word cards with *am, is,* or *are,* and give one to each student. Point to a sentence and ask: *Who has a verb that can be used in this sentence?* Let that student hold up his or her card and read the completed sentence aloud.

Reteach

	Main Verbs and Helping Verbs	More About Helping Verbs	Contractions with *Not*
	Objective: To identify helping verbs and main verbs	**Objective:** To identify and use forms of *be*, *have*, and *do* as helping verbs	**Objective:** To identify and use contractions with *not*
Visual	On the board, write several short sentences, each with a helping verb and a main verb. Let students underline the predicate of each sentence. Then have them use one color to circle the helping verb and a second color to circle the main verb.	On the board, write several sentence frames that can be completed with a missing form of *be*, *have*, or *do*. Have students read the sentences aloud, adding the correct helping verb. Then ask volunteers to write the helping verbs in the blanks.	On the board, write a list of sentences, each with a helping verb and *not*. Have students read each sentence and identify the two words that can be replaced by a contraction. Ask a volunteer to circle those two words. Have another volunteer write the contraction.
Auditory	Write a list of short sentences, some with a helping verb and a main verb, others with just an action verb. Have students read each sentence aloud. Ask: *What is the predicate of that sentence? Did you hear both a helping verb and a main verb in that predicate?* Have students repeat the sentences and identify each helping verb and main verb.	Prepare a list of sentences, each of which includes a helping verb (a form of *be*, *have*, or *do*) and a main verb. Read the sentences aloud, one at a time. After you have read each sentence, have students identify the helping verb and the main verb in the sentence. Then ask students whether the helping verb is a form of *be*, *have*, or *do*.	Say a helping verb and *not*. Ask students to say the contraction that can be made from the two words. Let a volunteer spell the contraction aloud, being careful to include the apostrophe, or write that contraction on the board. Then have several students say sentences using the contraction. Continue with other verbs and *not*.
Kinesthetic	Print on different colored paper strips main verbs and helping verbs. Hand students the strips. Have them form two rows with main verbs on one side and helping verbs on the other. Have students read their verbs aloud and change places to make main and helping verb partnerships.	Plan several verb phrases, each with a helping verb that is a form of *be*, *have*, or *do*. For each phrase, prepare two word cards: a helping verb and a main verb. Give one card to each student, and have them find a partner with whom to make a helping verb–main verb pair.	Have several groups choose a verb and *not* that can be made into a contraction. Have them make letter cards, with one card for each student. Choose one student to be an apostrophe. Have each group stand up and spell out their verb and *not*. Then have the student "apostrophe" replace the letter *o* in *not*.

Reteach

	Verb Tenses **Objective:** To identify and use verb tenses	Present-Tense Verbs **Objective:** To identify and use present-tense verbs that agree with sentence subjects	Subject-Verb Agreement **Objective:** To use verb forms that agree with sentence subjects
Visual	On the board, write sentences with action verbs. *I walk my dog Cuddles.* *I walked Cuddles yesterday.* *I will walk Cuddles tomorrow.* Have volunteers identify a present-tense verb, past-tense verb, and a future-tense verb.	On the board, write sentences with present-tense action verbs. Include sentences in which the verb forms agree with the subjects and disagree. Have students read each sentence aloud, identify the verb, and identify the form as correct or incorrect.	On the board, write sentences that use present-tense verbs, leaving a blank for each verb. Have students suggest a present-tense verb that agrees with the subject to complete each one. Then have a volunteer write one of the verb forms in the blank.
Auditory	Say a short sentence, and have students identify the verb. Then ask: *Is that a present-tense verb, a past-tense verb, or a future-tense verb? How can you tell?* Continue with other sentences to provide plenty of practice.	Say three sentences, each with a present-tense action verb. In two of the sentences, use verb forms that agree with the subjects. In one of the sentences, use a verb form that does not agree. Ask: *Which sentence is not correct? How can you tell? How can you correct that sentence?* Continue with other sets of sentences to provide practice for all students.	Say a short sentence with a present-tense action verb: *Monroe cooks every day.* Have students name the subject and the verb in the sentence. Then have them revise the sentence, changing the subject and the verb form to make a new sentence: *They cook every day.* Continue with other sentences to provide practice with a variety of present-tense verbs.
Kinesthetic	Prepare a set of cards with one verb form on each card. For each verb, make three cards: present tense, past tense, and future tense. Have students play *Go Fish*, asking players for each card; for example, Do you have the past-tense form of *walk*?	On individual cards, write several subjects and several action verbs. Also write *Add* s, *Add* es, and *No ending* on cards. Place subject and verb cards on the chalk tray. Call on students to choose and place the correct verb ending cards next to the verbs and read the sentences aloud.	Make a set of subject cards. Also make a set of present-tense verb cards, each with an action verb, some that end with s and others that do not. Pass out the cards. Have students find partners with cards that go together—a subject and a verb that agree. Have them make up a sentence, using their subject and verb.

Reteach

	Past-Tense and Future-Tense Verbs	More About Past-Tense and Future-Tense Verbs	Choosing the Correct Tense
	Objective: To identify and use past-tense verbs and future-tense verbs	**Objective:** To use regular verbs in the past tense and the future tense	**Objective:** To identify and use the correct verb tense
Visual	On the board or on a worksheet to hand out, write a list of short sentences, each with a past-tense or future-tense verb. Have students circle the verb in each sentence, using one color for past-tense verbs and another for future-tense verbs.	On the board, write pairs of sentence frames that can be completed with past-tense and future-tense forms of the same verb. Ask students to choose a verb that, in different forms, can be added to complete both sentences. Have a volunteer write those verb forms in the blanks.	Write a list of sentence frames on the board, leaving the verb blank. Include a time-clue word or phrase, such as *now*, *last week*, or *tomorrow*. Have students write *present*, *past* or *future* next to the appropriate sentences. Then have students suggest verbs to complete the sentences.
Auditory	Say a sentence, using either a past-tense or a future-tense verb. Have students identify the verb. Then ask: *Is that a past-tense verb or a future-tense verb? How can you tell?* Repeat with other sentences to provide practice with a variety of verbs.	Say a sentence with a present-tense verb form. Ask students to change the sentence, first using the past-tense form of the verb and then using the future-tense form of the verb. Repeat with different verbs, being careful to choose regular verbs with past-tense forms that end with *ed* or *d*.	Say a sentence that includes a time-clue word or phrase, such as *now*, *yesterday*, or *next week*. Instead of saying the verb, clap your hands. Ask: *What is missing from that sentence—a present-tense verb, a past-tense verb, or a future-tense verb? How can you tell?* Then let students suggest verbs to complete your sentence. Repeat the procedure with other sentences.
Kinesthetic	Use a brad to attach a paper arrow to the center of a piece of paper. Divide the paper into wedges radiating from the center, and write a past-tense verb or a future-tense verb in each area. Let students spin the arrow, read aloud the verb to which the arrow points, and use that verb form in a sentence.	Give each student several cards. Write a list of verbs on the board. Have students write the past-tense form on one side of a card and the future-tense form on the other. Have students make up sentences using one of their cards. Have them hold up the card as they repeat the sentence.	Prepare a set of seven time-clue words and seven verbs. Write any verb and one of the following on each: *now, yesterday, last week, two years ago, tomorrow, next month, next year*. Mix the cards up. Have students pick two cards and use the time-clue and a verb in a sentence.

Reteach

	Irregular Verbs **Objective:** To identify and use irregular past-tense verb forms	More Irregular Verbs **Objective:** To identify and use irregular verbs with forms of the helping verb *have*	Commonly Misused Irregular Verbs **Objective:** To use the verbs *lie, lay, rise, raise, teach,* and *learn* correctly
Visual	On the board, write a variety of sentences, using both present-tense and past-tense forms of these verbs: *come, do, have, say, see.* Have students circle the verb in each sentence, using one color for present-tense forms and another for past-tense forms.	Prepare a worksheet with sentences that include a form of the helping verb *have* and one of these verbs: *draw, eat, give, grow, ride, take, write.* Leave a blank where the main verb should go. Have students complete the sentences with the correct verb forms.	On the board, write a series of sentences with the main verbs *lie, lay, rise, raise, teach,* and *learn.* Instead of writing the verb in each sentence, write its definition in parentheses. Have students decide which verb should be used.
Auditory	Ask questions that will prompt students to answer with sentences using past-tense forms of the verbs *come, do, have, say,* and *see.* For example, ask: *Did the train come into the station on time?* Model an answer: *Yes, the train came in on time.* Ask a variety of questions, using the same verb in different contexts, to provide practice for all students.	Prepare a list of sentences using a form of the helping verb *have* and one of these verbs: *draw, eat, give, grow, ride, take, write.* In some sentences, use the correct main verb form; in others, use an incorrect form. Read each sentence aloud and ask: *Is the verb form in that sentence correct?* If the verb form is incorrect, have students say the entire sentence, substituting the correct form of the main verb.	Write a list of sentences using the verbs *lie, lay, rise, raise, teach,* and *learn.* Use the verbs correctly in some sentences and incorrectly in others. Read each sentence aloud and ask: *Does that sentence have the correct verb? How can you tell?* If the verb is incorrect, have students repeat the sentence, substituting the correct verb.
Kinesthetic	Prepare several sets of ten word cards. Write one of these verb forms on each card: *come, came, do, did, have, had, say, said, see, saw.* Give a set of cards to groups of three to play Concentration. After finding each match, the student should create sentences using the pair of verbs correctly.	Make a set of eight word cards: *drew, drawn, ate, eaten, gave, given, grew, grown.* Let students sort the verbs into two groups: past-tense verbs and verb forms that take the helping verb *has, have,* or *had.* Have students use the verbs and verb phrases in their own sentences.	Have students choose partners, and assign each pair of students one of these three verb pairs: *lie* and *lay, rise* and *raise,* or *teach* and *learn.* Have the partners plan and perform a very brief skit that illustrates the meanings of their assigned verbs.

Reteach

	Pronouns **Objective:** To identify and use pronouns in sentences	Singular and Plural Pronouns **Objective:** To distinguish between singular and plural pronouns	Pronoun-Antecedent Agreement **Objective:** To identify and use pronouns and antecedents
Visual	On the board, write several sentences that include at least one pronoun. Have students circle each pronoun that can be used as a subject and each pronoun that often follows a verb. Help students recognize when *you* and *it* are used as subjects.	On the board, write sentences that include nouns. Write the nouns (and articles) in a different color. Have students decide whether a singular or a plural pronoun can replace the noun. Then have a volunteer use pronouns in the revised sentence and write it on the board.	On the board, write sentence pairs; include an antecedent in the first sentence and its pronoun in the second sentence. Have students read each sentence pair. Let volunteers circle the pronoun in the second sentence and then draw an arrow to the antecedent.
Auditory	On the board, write a list of sentences that include pronouns, and read them aloud to students, one at a time. Ask students to raise their hands each time they hear a pronoun. After you read each sentence, have a volunteer repeat the pronoun or pronouns.	Say several sentences that include a single pronoun. Have students stand up as soon as they hear a pronoun. When you have finished saying each sentence, ask the student who stood first to identify the pronoun and tell whether it is singular or plural.	Pose a question that includes an antecedent and model an answer that includes a pronoun. For example: *Where were the boxes? They were on the top shelf.* Ask: *What is the pronoun in the answer? What noun in the question is the antecedent?* Then pose other questions and have students answer in complete sentences that include pronouns.
Kinesthetic	On the board or a large sheet of paper, write sentences that include common or proper nouns. Prepare twelve word cards with a different pronoun on each. Let students use the pronoun cards to replace nouns in the sentences, holding a card over each appropriate word.	Make a set of word cards, with a different pronoun on each card. Put the cards face down on a table and mix them up. Let students take turns picking a card, reading the pronoun aloud, identifying it as singular or plural, and using it in an original sentence.	Use construction paper to make a game board. Divide the paper into boxes and write a noun or pair of nouns in each box. Have students use an eraser as a marker and read the noun or nouns where the eraser lands. Have students say a pronoun that agrees with that antecedent.

Reteach

	Subject Pronouns **Objective:** To identify subject pronouns in sentences	Object Pronouns **Objective:** To identify object pronouns in sentences	Using *I* and *Me* **Objective:** To use the pronouns *I* and *me* in sentences
Visual	Write a paragraph on the board. Include some sentences with subject pronouns, avoiding object pronouns. Have students read the paragraph and identify the subject pronouns. Let volunteers use colored chalk or markers to circle them.	Prepare a worksheet with sentences that include at least one object pronoun. Do not use subject pronouns in these sentences. Have students circle all the object pronouns, using colored pencils or markers.	On the board, write sentences that include *I* and *me*. Use subject and object pronouns correctly and incorrectly. Have students read each sentence, circle the pronouns that are used correctly, and replace pronouns that are used incorrectly.
Auditory	Say several sentences, one at a time. Begin some of the sentences with subject pronouns, avoid using object pronouns in these sentences. Have students raise their hands when they hear a subject pronoun. After each sentence, let one of the students whose hand is raised identify the subject pronoun.	Say a short sentence that includes an object pronoun. Ask a student to repeat the pronoun and then say a different sentence using the same object pronoun. Repeat to provide practice for all students.	Ask students a series of questions about their hobbies, interests, and activities. Model answering your first question, using the pronoun *I* or *me*. For example, *I like to bike ride, but rollerblading is not for me.* Then have students take turns answering your questions. Remind them to include *I* or *me* in each answer.
Kinesthetic	Have students work in small groups. Allow each student to make up a sentence, using a classmate as the subject; for example, *Enrique likes music.* Ask another student to change the sentence, using a pronoun. Continue until everyone has made up sentences.	Have each student write a sentence using one object pronoun and illustrate the sentence. Give students an opportunity to read their sentences aloud and share their drawings with classmates.	Have each student prepare two flashcards, one with *I* and one with *me*. Say a series of sentences, one at a time, that include either *I* or *me*. Instead of saying the pronoun, clap your hands. Have students hold up the flashcard that tells which pronoun belongs in the sentence.

Reteach

	Possessive Pronouns **Objective:** To identify possessive pronouns in sentences	More Possessive Pronouns **Objective:** To identify and use possessive pronouns that stand alone	Contractions with Pronouns **Objective:** To identify and write contractions with pronouns
Visual	On the board, write several sentences that include at least one possessive pronoun. Have students read the sentences and identify the possessive pronouns. Ask volunteers to use colored chalk or markers to circle the pronouns.	On the board, write a list of sentences, most of which include a possessive pronoun that stands alone. Have students read each sentence; then ask: *Does that sentence include a possessive pronoun? If it does, what is the pronoun? How can you tell it is a possessive pronoun that stands alone?* If the sentence includes a possessive pronoun, ask a volunteer to circle it.	Write pairs of words on the board, most of them being pronouns and verbs that can form contractions. Have students read each pair to decide whether it can form a contraction. Ask volunteers to circle the two words in these pairs. Then have each student choose five word pairs and write their contractions.
Auditory	Say a sentence that includes one or more possessive pronouns. Have students raise one hand when they hear a possessive pronoun and the other hand if they hear a second possessive pronoun. When you have finished the sentence, ask a student whose hand is raised to identify the possessive pronoun(s). Continue to provide practice with all the possessive pronouns.	Say a sentence that includes a possessive pronoun followed by a noun; for example: *Our puppy is the puppy with the red collar.* Have students identify the possessive pronoun and the noun. Then have them say the sentence again, using a possessive pronoun that stands alone; for example: *Ours is the puppy with the red collar.* Repeat to provide practice with all the possessive pronouns.	Say a sentence that includes a pronoun-verb contraction. Ask students to raise their hands as soon as they hear the contraction. When you finish the sentence, let students identify the contraction as well as the two words that make up the contraction. Write the contraction on the board, emphasizing the placement of the apostrophe. Repeat with a variety of pronoun-verb contractions.
Kinesthetic	Make a set of seven flashcards; print a possessive pronoun on each card. Then print sentences on the board which include a possessive noun in each one. Have students read each sentence, identify the possessive noun, find the card with a possessive pronoun that replaces the noun, and hold the card in place in the sentence.	Have students work with partners to plan short skits about two friends who must decide who owns an item or is responsible for a task. Ask students to include at least three different possessive pronouns that stand alone in their dialogue. After planning and practicing, have each pair perform their skit for classmates.	Place a set of letter cards, including capital *I* and an apostrophe, face up on a table. Have one student use the letters to make a pronoun and a verb that can form a contraction. Have another student use those letters to make the contraction, substituting an apostrophe for the correct letter or letters. Continue to provide practice for all students.

Reteach

	Adjectives **Objective:** To identify adjectives	Adjectives for *How Many* **Objective:** To identify and use adjectives that tell *how many*	Adjectives for *What Kind* **Objective:** To identify and use adjectives that tell *what kind*
Visual	On the board, write sentences, each with a single adjective. In each sentence, write the noun that the adjective modifies in color. Have students read each sentence and name the adjective. Have a volunteer use the same color to circle it.	Show students pictures of groups of people, animals, or things. Ask questions about the pictures, such as *How many horses do you see?* Let students answer in complete sentences, using an adjective that tells *how many*. Record their sentences and underline each adjective.	On the chalk tray, display a picture and write on the board several sentences about that picture. In each sentence, leave at least one blank for an adjective that tells *what kind*. Have students refer to the picture as they suggest adjectives to add to the sentences.
Auditory	Say sentences that include adjectives; for example, *We saw the huge horses. They looked gentle.* Have students raise their hands as soon as they hear an adjective. When you finish a sentence, ask a student whose hand is raised to repeat the adjective and to name the noun it modifies.	Say a sentence that includes one adjective that tells *how many*; for example, *Our school has ten computers. Our school has several computers.* Ask students to repeat that adjective. Then have a volunteer repeat your sentence, substituting a different adjective that tells *how many*. Continue with other sentences until all students have participated.	Using the sentence frame *I see a [adjective] [noun]*, say sentences about specific objects in the classroom. In most of the sentences, use an adjective that accurately describes the object. Have students identify the adjective and tell whether your statement is true. If it is untrue, have students repeat your sentence, substituting an accurate adjective.
Kinesthetic	Have students use building blocks to play a guessing game. Display the blocks. Let students use one adjective to identify a specific block. Students can use a sentence frame with one adjective: *I am looking at a _____ block.* Have students find the block the speaker is looking at.	Provide a collection of books. Call on students to display a certain number of books and then to add an adjective that tells *how many* to this sentence frame: *Now I see _____ books.* Tell students to add an adjective that tells *how many*, either a specific number (*three*) or one that is general (*several*).	Have students draw self-portraits and then label them with a sentence that follows this sentence frame: *I am a _____ person.* Instruct students to add an adjective that tells *what kind*. Allow students to show their drawings and read their sentences aloud to classmates.

Reteach

	Articles	Adjectives That Compare	Avoiding Incorrect Comparisons
	Objective: To identify and use articles in sentences	**Objective:** To identify and use adjectives in comparisons	**Objective:** To identify and use adjectives in comparisons
Visual	Prepare a worksheet for students. Write a list of sentences that include articles; in some of the sentences, use articles incorrectly. Let students work with partners to read the sentences, circling the correctly used articles and correcting the errors.	On the board, write sentences that compare. Don't write the comparing form, write just the adjective. Have students identify each adjective that needs to be changed, and tell whether *er* or *est* should be added. Then have a volunteer add the correct letters to the word on the board.	On the board, write sentences that include adjective comparisons. Use correct and incorrect comparing forms. Have students identify each adjective that compares. Ask: *Is this the correct form? How can you tell?* If it is correct, have a volunteer circle it in color. If it is incorrect, have students correct it on the board.
Auditory	Read aloud sentences that include articles, using them correctly and incorrectly. Pause after each sentence and ask: *What article (or Which articles) did you hear in that sentence? Was that the correct article? How do you know?* If an article was used incorrectly, have students correct the sentence.	Ask students questions about comparisons between familiar people or objects. In each question, use a short adjective ending with *er* or *est*. Have students answer in complete sentences, using the correct comparing forms.	Say sentences, one at a time, using comparing forms of adjectives. In some cases, form the comparing adjective correctly; in others, incorrectly. After each sentence, ask: *Which adjective in that sentence makes a comparison? Is that the correct comparing form? How can you tell?* If the form is incorrect, have students say the sentence again, using the correct form.
Kinesthetic	Prepare flashcards with plural nouns, singular nouns beginning with a consonant sound, and singular nouns beginning with a vowel sound. Have each student pick a card, read the noun aloud, identify an article to be used before that noun, and say a sentence with the article and noun.	Have students form groups of three in which to demonstrate comparisons. Group members may compare objects or may use themselves to make comparisons. Have each one say one comparing sentence, using an adjective ending with *er* or *est*. *I am shorter than Clay. I am the shortest person in this group.*	Prepare a set of flashcards; print an adjective on each. Print *er*, *est*, *more*, and *most* on individual cards. Hold up an adjective card and call on students to choose a comparison form card. The student is to use the adjective with the comparison form in a sentence.

Reteach

	Adverbs	More About Adverbs	Comparing with Adverbs
	Objective: To identify and use adverbs that tell *how* an action happens	**Objective:** To identify and use adverbs that tell *when* or *where* an action happens	**Objective:** To identify and use adverbs in comparisons
Visual	On the board, write sentences that include an adverb telling *how*. For example: *The dog wagged its tail excitedly* and *The dog wagged its tail slowly*. Have students identify and circle the adverbs. Then have them revise the sentences, substituting different adverbs that *tell how*.	On the board, write sentences with adverbs that tell *when* or *where*, with a blank for each adverb. Let students suggest adverbs to add to each sentence. Remind students to use just one word to tell *where* or *when*. Then have them write three of the sentences.	On the board, write sentences with adverbs that compare. Include some incorrect comparisons. Have students identify each comparing adverb and tell whether the form is correct. Mark sentences that need to be revised, and have students write them correctly.
Auditory	Ask students questions that begin with *How*, and have them answer your questions with complete statements that include adverbs that tell *how*. After each student's response, ask: *Which word in that sentence is an adverb that tells* how?	Ask students questions that begin with *Where* or *When*, and have them answer your questions with complete statements that include adverbs. If necessary, remind students to use a word to tell *where* or *when*. After each student's response, ask: *Which word in that sentence is an adverb? Does the adverb tell* where *or* when?	Say sentences with adverbs that compare. Include some sentences with incorrect comparing forms. After each sentence, ask: *What is the comparing adverb in that sentence? Is the comparing form correct? How can you tell?* If the form is not correct, have students repeat the sentence, using the correct adverb form in the comparison.
Kinesthetic	Prepare word cards, each with a different adverb that tells *how*. Hand each student a card, and ask students to keep their adverbs a secret. Then have each student move in the way described by the adverb on the card. Ask the others to guess the adverb on the actor's card.	Ask students to suggest adverbs that tell *when* and *where*; list their suggestions on the board. Then have students write and illustrate sentences that include at least one adverb from the board. Allow students to share their sentences and drawings with classmates.	Have two or three students work together to plan and perform an action that can be compared. Ask the other students to make up sentences about what the actors are doing, using correct comparing forms of adverbs.

Reteach

	Adjective or Adverb? **Objective:** To distinguish between adjectives and adverbs in sentences	Adverb Placement in Sentences **Objective:** To revise sentences by using adverbs in different places	Using *Good* and *Well, Bad* and *Badly* **Objective:** To use *good, well, bad,* and *badly* correctly in sentences
Visual	On the board, write sentences that include adjectives and add adverbs. In each sentence, add an adjective or an adverb. Have students read each sentence; then ask: *What kind of word is added? How can you tell?* Then have students revise the sentence, adding another adjective or adverb.	On the board, write several sentences with an adverb. Have students identify the adverbs and use colored chalk to circle them. Ask: *Where else could the adverb go?* Have volunteers put check marks in the suggested locations, say the revised sentence, and try out the adverb in all positions.	On the board, write sentences like the following with missing adjectives or adverbs. *You did a _____ job.* *You skate _____.* *The game started _____.* Have students use *good, bad, badly,* or *well* to complete the sentences.
Auditory	Say a sentence, and focus students' attention on an adjective or an adverb by raising your hand as you say that word. After saying the sentence, ask: *What kind of word is _____? How can you tell?* Repeat with other sentences to provide practice identifying various adjectives and adverbs.	Say a simple sentence that includes an adverb; for example, *Max quietly opened the door.* Let students identify the adverb and then repeat the sentence, moving the adverb to another place in the sentence. Encourage students to try all the possible places in the sentence. Then continue the activity with other sentences.	Say sentences in which you use *good, well, bad,* and *badly.* In some cases, use the words correctly; in others, incorrectly. After each sentence, ask: *Did I use the correct word? How can you tell?* If the word was incorrect, have students repeat the sentence, substituting the correct adjective or adverb.
Kinesthetic	Prepare word cards with an adjective or adverb on each card. Divide students into two groups. Give the cards to one group. Have the second group write sentences, leaving room for an adverb or adjective. Call on the students with cards to fill in the sentences. All of the students can determine if each adverb or adjective is used correctly.	Write several sentences, with adverbs, on individual strips. Give a sentence strip to each group of students. Have them read their sentences, identify the adverbs, and cut their sentences into one-word pieces. Tell students to rearrange the sentence, putting the adverb in different places.	Make four small beanbags; write *good, well, bad,* or *badly* on each. Toss one of the beanbags to a student. The student should read the word on it and use it in a sentence. When the student has used the word correctly, he or she should toss the beanbag back to you.

Reteach

	Homophones	More Homophones	Homographs and Other Homophones
	Objective: To use the homophones *write* and *right* and *to, too,* and *two* correctly	**Objective:** To use the homophones *their, they're,* and *there; your, you're; its* and *it's* correctly	**Objective:** To use more homographs and homophones correctly
Visual	On the board, write sentences that can be completed by adding *write* or *right* and sentences that can be completed by adding *to, too,* or *two.* Have students identify the word that correctly completes each sentence. Have students explain how they know which word is correct and write the correct word in each sentence.	With students, assign a color to each of the homophones in this lesson. Then have each student write a sentence for each homophone, using the color assigned to that word.	On the board, write sentences students can complete with the homophones and homographs from this lesson. Have students read and discuss each sentence, identifying the word that belongs in it. Then have students write the complete sentences.
Auditory	Say sentences using the words *write, right, to, too,* and *two.* For example: *I* write *with my* right *hand. Are you going* to *leave at* two *o'clock,* too? After each sentence, ask: *Which meaning of the word fits that sentence? How should that word be spelled?*	Say sentences that include these words: *their, there, they're, your, you're, its, it's.* At the end of each sentence, ask students about the homophone you used: *How is the word spelled? How can you tell?*	Say sentences students can complete with the homophones and homographs in this lesson. As you say each sentence, clap your hands instead of saying the lesson word. Then ask students which word completes the sentence. Have students spell the correct word. Then ask students to repeat the complete sentence, using the word.
Kinesthetic	Have each student choose a homophone, write a sentence using the word correctly, and illustrate the sentence. Ask students to show their pictures while reading their sentences aloud. Have the other students identify and spell the homophone each student used.	Prepare flashcards with these words: *their, there, they're, your, you're, its, it's.* Make sure every student has one. Say sentences, one at a time, that include one of the homophones. After each sentence, ask students with the correct spelling of the homophone to hold up that card.	Make two sets of flashcards. Write the words from the lessons on one set and their word meanings on the other. Hand out the cards. Call on students to hold up a card. Have the student with the appropriate word or meaning card stand up and match it. Let each student form a sentence, using a word correctly.

Reteach

	Negatives **Objective:** To identify *no, not,* and *contractions with not* as negative words in sentences	More Negatives **Objective:** To identify *no one, nobody, nothing, none, nowhere,* and *never* as negatives	Avoiding Double Negatives **Objective:** To avoid and correct double negatives in sentences
Visual	Write sentences on the board. Include *no, not,* or a *contraction with not* in most of the sentences. Have students choose the sentences that include a negative word. Ask: *What is the negative word?* Let volunteers circle the negative words the group identifies.	Make a simple word search puzzle, using the negative words in this lesson as well as *no, not,* and *contractions with not.* Distribute copies of the puzzle to students. Let them work independently or with partners to circle the negative words.	On the board, write sentences that include single and double negatives. Have students read each sentence and identify the negatives. Let volunteers underline these words. If the sentence has a double negative, have students correct it.
Auditory	Say sentences that include *no, not,* or a *contraction with not.* Ask students to stand up when they hear a negative word. When you finish a sentence, ask students who are standing to identify the negative word.	Say sentences, most of which include the negative words in this lesson. After each sentence, ask: *Did you hear a negative word? What was it?* Then have students make up sentences using that negative word.	One at a time, say sentences with negative words; include sentences with double negatives. Tell students to raise one hand each time they hear a negative word. When you complete a sentence that has a double negative, ask students with both hands raised to identify both negative words. Call on volunteers to correct the sentence.
Kinesthetic	Let students work with partners to write pairs of sentences—one with *no* or *not,* and the other exactly the same but without the negative word. Have partners act out their sentences, and let others try to guess the sentences.	Write the negative words in this lesson on individual word cards. Have students take turns picking a card, reading aloud the negative word, using the word in a sentence, and then writing the sentence on the board.	On individual strips, write sentences that include double negatives. Distribute the strips to students. For each double negative, have the student revise the sentence by cutting the strip apart, taking a negative out, and taping the strip back together. Then have students show and read their sentence strips.

Reteach

	Commas **Objective:** To use commas correctly	More About Commas **Objective:** To use commas correctly in letters, dates, and addresses	Combining Sentences with Commas **Objective:** To identify and use commas in compound sentences
Visual	On the board, write sentences that include a series, nouns of direct address, and the introductory words *yes*, *no*, and *well*. Do not include commas. Have students decide where commas should be placed and explain their reasons for adding each one. Then have volunteers add commas to the sentences.	Draw the message side of a picture postcard on the board. Write *Dear Minnie* at the top and *Sincerely Donna* at the bottom. On the address side, put two blank lines and *Austin TX*. Have students tell where commas should be placed.	Write these sentences on the board. *Marcus wanted to surprise me. I had been warned. Marcus wanted to surprise me but I had been warned.* Ask: *Is this a sentence that needs a comma?* If the sentence is compound, have students explain where the comma should be added and add it.
Auditory	Say sentences that include series, introductory nouns of direct address, and the introductory words *yes*, *no*, and *well*. Ask students to raise their hands when they hear a part of a sentence to which a comma should be added. After saying each sentence, let students add commas and explain the reason for using each one.	Read aloud a short letter and the address on an envelope. Have students raise their hands each time they think a comma should be added. Pause and ask students to explain their ideas. When you have finished reading the letter and address and students have noted the commas, you may want to display a correct, complete copy.	Say several compound sentences, one at a time. Let students identify where the comma should be added to each sentence. Then say more sentences, some simple and some compound. After each sentence, ask: *Do we need to add a comma to this sentence? Why or why not?*
Kinesthetic	Have students work with partners to write short skits. Instruct them to include nouns of address; *yes*, *no*, and *well* at the beginning of their sentences; and at least one series comma in their dialogue. Let partners practice and then present their skits to classmates.	On a sheet of paper, print a short letter, including a date, greeting, and closing. On another sheet, print an address. Leave out the commas. Make comma cards. Pin up the letter and address. Let volunteers pin a comma card to the letter or address and explain the reason for adding that comma.	Write compound sentences on sentence strips of various colors. Cut each sentence strip into pieces, with one word on each piece. Leave the period with the last word, but cut a separate piece for the comma. Have partners put the words in order, adding the comma in the correct place.

Reteach

	Direct Quotations **Objective:** To identify direct quotations and to use quotation marks	More About Quotation Marks **Objective:** To use capital letters, commas, and end punctuation	Punctuating Dialogue **Objective:** To use correct punctuation in direct quotations
Visual	On the board, write this sentence: *"Why didn't it work?" asked Abdul.* Let a volunteer underline the words of the direct quotation. Have students identify the quotation marks at the beginning and at the end of the direct quotation, and let a volunteer circle them.	On the board, write sentences with direct quotations. In each sentence, leave out a comma, end punctuation mark, or fail to capitalize a word. Have students read and discuss each sentence, identifying and correcting the mistakes.	Write the following on the board, leaving out some punctuation. *"Did you like our play?" asked Kev. "It was terrific!" his dad said. "In fact," added his mother, "it was the best school play we've ever seen."* Have students read the sentences aloud, noting the corrections. Then have them write the dialogue correctly.
Auditory	Read aloud sentences that include direct quotations. After each sentence, ask: *What are the exact words the person said? Where are quotation marks used in this sentence?* You may want to reinforce students' responses by writing some of the sentences on the board.	Say a sentence that includes a direct quotation. Then repeat the sentence slowly, asking students to say where to place capital letters, commas, end marks, and quotation marks. When students have identified the correct capitalization and punctuation, write the sentence on the board. Repeat with other sentences.	Ask two volunteers to read aloud from a short, simple script. Have the other students listen carefully during the first reading. Then have the volunteers slowly read the script again, pausing after each sentence. Have students write the conversation as dialogue, using correct capitalization and punctuation.
Kinesthetic	On the board, write sentences with direct quotations but without quotation marks. Have each student make cards with opening and closing quotation marks. Have students take turns reading a sentence and holding up their cards to show where the marks belong in the sentence.	Write short sentences with direct quotations on different-colored sentence strips. Use correct capitalization and punctuation. Cut each strip into pieces, with a word or punctuation mark on each card. Have partners put the cards together to make complete, correctly punctuated sentences.	Prepare flashcards with words that identify speakers; for example, *said Marty* or *Cora asked.* Let students take turns picking a card. Have a student read aloud the phrase and use it in a direct quotation. Then, have the student write the quotation in a complete sentence on the board, using correct capitalization and punctuation.

Reteach

	Underlining Titles **Objective:** To underline the titles of books, magazines, and newspapers	Quotation Marks with Titles **Objective:** To use quotation marks in titles	Capitalizing Words in Titles **Objective:** To capitalize the first word and every important word in a title
Visual	On the board, write sentences that include the titles of books, magazines, and newspapers; do not underline the titles. Ask: *What title(s) do you see in this sentence? Which words should be underlined? Why?* Have a volunteer underline the title(s).	On the board, write sentences that include the titles of stories, poems, magazine articles, newspaper articles, and songs; do not include quotation marks. Have students identify each title and explain where they would add quotation marks. Call on students to correctly write the sentences.	Ask students to suggest sentences about books, stories, poems, and songs they enjoy. Write their sentences on the board, making intentional mistakes in capitalization. Have students identify the mistakes and explain how they should be corrected.
Auditory	Say sentences that include the titles of books, magazines, and newspapers. After each sentence, ask: *Which words in the sentence should be underlined? Why?* Then call on volunteers to say similar sentences, and have the others identify the words that should be underlined.	Say sentences that include the titles of stories, poems, magazine articles, newspaper articles, and songs. After each sentence, ask: *What title did you hear in that sentence? Where would you place quotation marks? How would those marks help a reader understand the sentence?*	Say various titles of familiar books, stories, poems, and magazines. After saying each title, ask: *Which words in that title should begin with capital letters?* Ask volunteers to suggest other titles. Write those titles on the board, asking students to identify which words should be capitalized.
Kinesthetic	Hand each student a different book or magazine. Then have students take turns displaying the book or magazine, saying a sentence that includes the book or magazine title, and explaining which words in that sentence should be underlined.	On individual strips, write sentences that include the titles of stories, poems, magazine articles, newspaper articles, and songs. Place quotation marks correctly and incorrectly. Have students sort them into two groups: those with correct punctuation and those without. Then have students correct each sentence in the second pile.	Ask students to draw book-cover designs for their favorite books. Have students include the book title in the cover design, using capital letters correctly. Display these designs on a classroom bulletin board.

Design a Quilt

Some quilts have pretty patterns and colors, and some tell a story. Think about a quilt you might create. Answer each question below about the quilt you would like to design.

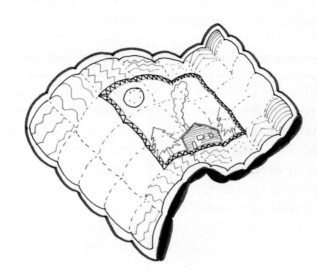

- What shapes or objects will you show or what story will you tell?

- What kind of border will you use?

- What colors will you use?

After you have answered the questions, sketch a design. Color your sketch. Write three sentences to tell about your design.

© Harcourt

Make a Fact Sheet

Create a fact sheet about the musical instrument of your choice. Use an encyclopedia or the Internet to find information about your instrument. You may wish to include facts such as:

- countries where the instrument is played

- how the instrument is played

- musicians who are well-known for playing that instrument

As you write your fact sheet, be sure that your sentences contain both a subject and a predicate.

© Harcourt

Design a School

Imagine that you have been chosen to design a school of the future. Many people want to see your plans. To share your ideas, follow these steps:

- Draw a floor plan of your school.

- Include special features that today's schools do not have.

- Write a paragraph about your school and how it will be better than schools today.

Share your plan with classmates.

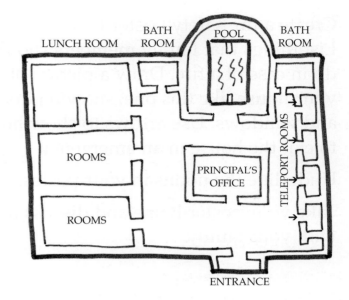

Challenge Activity Card 4

Sentences in Poetry

Sentences in poems and rhymes sometimes look different from sentences in stories. Sentences in poems do have subjects and predicates, though. See if you can find the sentences in a poem. Follow these steps:

- Copy a nursery rhyme from a book.

- Read the rhyme. Underline the first sentence you find.

- Circle the simple subject and the simple predicate of the sentence.

- Continue with the next sentence, and so on.

Make a list of the ways sentences in poems are the same as and different from sentences in stories.

Fire Safety

Create a fire safety poster for your home. List things that family members should do in case of a fire. Draw a picture of your house like this one, showing doors and windows. Use arrows to show how to exit the house in an emergency.

Underline the nouns in your poster.

Take your poster home and discuss it with your family.

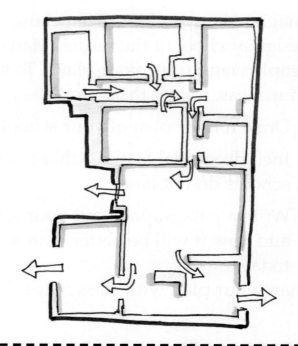

Plan a Picnic

Imagine that you and your friends are having a picnic. What foods would you serve? Answer the questions below to help you plan the picnic.

• List the names of your friends at the picnic.

• What kinds of sandwiches do they like?

• How many sandwiches should you bring?

• What other foods or drinks will you have?

Look at your answers and make a shopping list for the picnic. Notice the singular and plural nouns on your list.

Healthy Smiles

What do you need to do to keep your teeth healthy and your smile bright? Make a poster with tips for good dental health. Use possessive nouns in your poster.

- Use resources such as encyclopedias, a health book, or the Internet to find information.

- Use your best handwriting to write your tips.

- Illustrate your poster to make it stand out.

- Hang up your poster at school or at home.

✂ --

A Day in the Life of a Germ

Create a comic strip about a germ. Tell what happens to the germ during one day. Follow these steps:

- Think about different ways germs can travel from place to place.

- Draw four to six frames for your comic strip.

- Draw a picture for each frame. Show what the germ does in different places.

- Write dialogue or a caption for each picture. Use strong verbs.

- Color each picture.

Display your comic strip in your classroom.

© Harcourt

Cultural Cuisine

Cuisine is a style or type of cooking. Many people brought their cooking styles and traditional foods with them when they came to America. With a partner, choose a country from the list below and explore its cuisine. Use the Internet, books, or encyclopedias to find information.

Mexico	Morocco	Italy	Ireland
India	Vietnam	Jamaica	Germany
Japan	China	Ethiopia	France

Copy a traditional recipe for your country's cuisine. Compile the recipes in a class cookbook.

© Harcourt

Get Involved

Write an announcement to encourage community members to volunteer at your school. To get started,

- make a list of things that volunteers might do at your school.

- use present tense verbs to tell why these jobs need to be done.

- describe how helping at your school could be good for the person who volunteers.

You may wish to illustrate your announcement to make it more effective.

© Harcourt

Get Elected

Imagine that you are running for public office. You must convince voters that you are the best person for the job. Create a poster and a bumper sticker to help you get elected.

- Decide what job you want. Do you want to be a senator, a governor, or the president? Make a list of reasons why you would be a good person for that office. Then make a list telling what you will do if you are elected. Be sure to use past tense and future tense.

- Design a poster that will persuade people to vote for you. Use your slogan on the poster.

- Design a bumper sticker that will remind people to vote for you.

© Harcourt

Principal Partners

Pretend your partner is the principal of another school. Your partner's school has the same number of students as your school, but everything else is different. Send an e-mail or write a letter to your partner asking about two things that are different. You may ask questions such as:

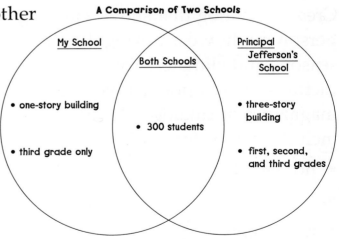

A Comparison of Two Schools

- What does your school look like?

- What grades are taught at your school?

Once you have received answers, make a Venn diagram to show how your school and your partner's school are alike and different. Then write a paragraph to tell what you have found out. Be sure that all irregular verbs are used correctly.

© Harcourt

Take a Trip

Imagine that it's 2025 and space travel is popular. You are selling tickets for a trip to another planet. Persuade people to take the trip by making a travel poster.

Choose a planet. If you make up a planet, be sure to give it a creative name!

Draw a picture of something interesting to see or do on the planet. You may wish to brainstorm a list of possibilities before drawing your picture.

Write some sentences describing your pictures and be sure to use pronouns.

Clothing Catalog

Create a catalog that shows clothing a person might wear during different seasons and climates. You may draw pictures or cut out examples from magazines or catalogs. Be sure to include clothes for

• hot weather

• cold weather

• rainy days

For each item, write a caption using a subject pronoun. For example, *She looks warm in this winter coat!*

Inventory

Think of some of the things in your house, your neighborhood, and your school. Make an inventory, or a list of belongings, by following these steps:

- Make a list of three things that belong to you. Then, list three things that belong to others. Finally, list three things that belong to everyone.

- Choose six items. Write a sentence for each, using possessive pronouns. Remember to check your sentences for clear pronoun antecedents.

- You may wish to illustrate your inventory.

Adjective Collage

Make a collage about animals. Here are the steps to follow:

- Decide on a theme for your collage. You may choose any theme.

- Draw pictures or cut them out of old magazines.

- Use an adjective to label and describe each picture.

- Arrange the pictures and the adjectives on a large sheet of paper. Paste them in place to create your collage.

loyal, patient

perky

shaggy

Challenge Activity Card 17

Farm Supplies

Imagine that you have moved to a rural area and will live and work on a farm. What will you need to run your farm successfully? Use the illustrations in the chapter and information from this lesson for ideas. Think about these questions:

- What crops will you plant?

- What animals will you raise?

- What will you need to take care of the crops, the animals, your family, and your home?

Make a list of the supplies you will need to buy. Write *a* or *an* before each item on your list. Review your list to make sure each article is used correctly.

Challenge Activity Card 18

Adverb Library

Think of words that tell *how* a person does different things. For example, a person might *actively* look for a book. *Actively* is an adverb.

- Make a list of six adverbs.

- Put these adverbs in alphabetical order.

- Write the adverbs in alphabetical order on the spines of the books on the bookshelf.

Community Fact Sheet

Choose a community, a city, or a town that interests you. Use an encyclopedia, the Internet, or other resources to make a fact sheet about the community you chose. Your fact sheet should:

- tell when and how the community was founded or settled.
- describe what the community is like today.
- list the population and major businesses of the community.
- tell why the community interests you.

You may also wish to illustrate your fact sheet with pictures or drawings that represent the community you chose.

Picture Cards

Work with a partner to create picture cards for homophones. You may use these words, or think of other homophones:

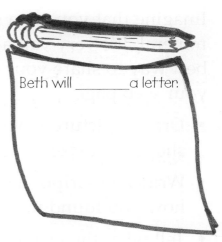

Beth will _____ a letter.

mail/male   see/sea   son/sun

- Make rectangles using construction paper.
- On one side of the paper, write the homophone.
- On the other side, paste or draw a picture that shows the meaning of the word.
- Underneath the picture, write a sentence that uses the homophone. Draw a blank where the homophone would be.
- Trade cards with other classmates. See if they can fill in the blank.

Challenge Activity Card 21

Comic Strip

Work with a partner to create a comic strip about a character who is negative about everything and everyone. As the ending to your comic strip, show an event that makes the character positive.

- Think of some negative things this character might say.

- Imagine a surprising event that will give the character a better attitude.

- Draw your comic strip and display it in your classroom.

Challenge Activity Card 22

Draw a Web Page

Imagine that you are a scientist and that you have just discovered a new type of mineral. It's very valuable, and you've decided that a web page would be the best way to share your discovery. Make a sketch of your web page.

- Draw a picture of your mineral. Show the color, shape, and size.

- Write a description of the mineral. Tell where and how you found it.

- Tell what the uses of the mineral might be.

Be sure to check your web page to make sure you used commas correctly!

Clear Science

Think about the science discussed in this lesson's exercises. Make a poster using a character of your choice to clearly illustrate the concept. Follow these steps:

- Choose a direct quotation from the Guided Practice or Independent Practice Exercises.

- Make up a character.

- Draw a picture of your character.

- The direct quotation should be the caption for your picture. Change the speaker's name to your character's name.

- Share your poster with the class.

Be-in-a-Book Day

Imagine that next week there will be a special holiday to celebrate books. Everybody will be able to participate in a scene from their favorite book. Follow these steps:

- Think about your favorite books and the events in them.

- Choose a scene from one of the books.

- Draw a picture of the characters and you participating in the activity.

- Write a caption explaining your choice. Be sure to include the title of the book.

- Share your picture with the class.

Student Record Form: Writing Conference

Student _____ Teacher _____ Grade _____

	Date ___	Date ___	Date ___	Date ___	Date ___	Date ___
CONTENT AND ORGANIZATION						
Writes to record, reflect on, discover, develop, and refine ideas						
Writes in different forms including lists, letters, stories, and poems						
Generates ideas for writing by using prewriting techniques						
Develops drafts by organizing information and ideas						
Stays on topic and sequences ideas						
Revises selected drafts to achieve a sense of audience, precise word choices, and vivid images						
Edits for appropriate grammar, spelling, punctuation, and for features of polished writing						
Uses available technology for aspects of writing						
Demonstrates understanding of language use and spelling by publishing selected pieces for audiences						
Evaluates writing by using criteria, and using published pieces as models for writing determining how writing achieves its purposes						
Responds constructively to others' writing						
Records knowledge of a topic in a variety of ways						
SPELLING						
Writes with more proficient spelling of regularly spelled patterns such as (CVC), (CVCe), and one-syllable words with blends						
Uses resources to find correct spellings, synonyms, and replacement words						

Comments:

Key:

N = Not Observed

O = Observed Occasionally

R = Observed Regularly

© Harcourt

Student Record Form: Handwriting and Technology

Student _____ Teacher _____ Grade _____

	Date ____	Date ____	Date ____	Date ____	Date ____	Date ____
HANDWRITING						
Gains more proficient control of all aspects of penmanship						
Uses correct letter and word spacing						
Indents paragraphs correctly						
Uses capital and lowercase letters appropriately						
Uses correct posture						
Positions paper and pencil effectively						
TECHNOLOGY						
Uses available technology for aspects of writing such as word processing, spell checking, and printing						
Compiles notes into outlines, reports, summaries, or other written efforts using available technology						
Chooses appropriately between handwriting and word processing						
Presents information in various forms using technology						

Comments:

Key:

N = Not Observed

O = Observed Occasionally

R = Observed Regularly

Student Record Form: Listening and Speaking

Student _____ Teacher _____ Grade _____

	Date ____	Date ____	Date ____	Date ____	Date ____	Date ____
LISTENING						
Determines purpose for listening						
Listens attentively and responds appropriately to a variety of literature and texts						
Participates effectively in groups						
Monitors understanding of spoken messages; seeks clarification as needed						
Understands the major ideas and supporting evidence of spoken messages and presentations						
Interprets speaker's verbal and nonverbal messages, purposes, and perspectives						
Eliminates barriers to effective listening						
Distinguishes between a speaker's opinion and verifiable fact						
SPEAKING						
Discusses a variety of texts						
Chooses and adapts spoken language appropriate to audience, purpose, and occasion including use of appropriate volume and rate						
Clarifies and supports spoken messages using appropriate props including objects, pictures, and charts; supports ideas with evidence and props						
Uses vocabulary to describe clearly ideas, feelings, and experiences						
Presents dramatic interpretations of experiences, stories, poems, or plays						
Uses verbal and nonverbal communication in effective ways						
Retells spoken messages by summarizing or clarifying						
Makes contributions asks and answers relevant questions in small or large group discussions						
Gains increasing control of grammar when speaking						
Speaks confidently and effectively to reflect the demands of a variety of situations						
Reads aloud with accuracy, comprehension, expression						

Comments:

Key:

N = Not Observed

O = Observed Occasionally

R = Observed Regularly

© Harcourt

Student Record Form: Grammar in Writing

Student _____ Teacher _____ Grade _____

	Date ___	Date ___	Date ___	Date ___	Date ___	Date ___
GRAMMAR AND USAGE						
Uses singular and plural forms of regular nouns correctly						
Uses correct irregular plural nouns						
Adjusts verbs for agreement						
Edits writing toward standard grammar and usage for subject-verb agreement						
Edits writing toward standard grammar and usage for appropriate verb tenses						
Uses irregular verbs correctly						
Edits writing toward standard grammar and usage for pronoun agreement						
Uses correct form of adjectives						
Uses correct form of adverbs						
Composes elaborated sentences in written texts						
Composes sentences with interesting, elaborated subjects						
MECHANICS						
Uses punctuation with increasing accuracy						
Uses capitalization with increasing accuracy						
ORAL LANGUAGE						
Gains increasing control of grammar when speaking						

Comments:

Key:

N = Not Observed

O = Observed Occasionally

R = Observed Regularly

© Harcourt

How to Score Writing

Teachers may use a variety of strategies to monitor students' growth as writers. You can adapt the strategies on these pages to your own teaching methods and the requirements of your school or district. Other assessment ideas are provided at point of use in the chapters, on the Assessment Strategies and Resources page at the end of each unit of this *Teacher's Edition,* and in the *Language Skills and Writing Assessment Teacher's Edition.*

USING RUBRICS

Rubrics for the teacher are provided at point of use in the Writing Workshop. Simplified rubrics for the students are provided in the Handbook in the *Pupil Edition.* You can also make photocopies of the student rubrics on pages R80–R85. Work with students to add additional criteria to the rubrics. Students should refer to the rubrics before, during, and after writing. If your school or district uses a 5- or 6-point rating scale, you can use strategies like these to adapt the rubrics.

USING A 5-POINT SCALE

1	2	3	4	5
limited	basic	basic+	proficient	advanced

Use the rubric criteria for a score of 4 to evaluate the papers. Follow these steps to rank them on a 5-point scale.

1. Read through all the papers and sort them into two piles: a score of 2 (basic) and 4 (proficient).

2. Reread the 2 papers, and reconsider them. You may move some into a 3 (basic+) pile. Some papers may be below basic. Move these to a 1 pile.

3. Reread the 4 papers, and reconsider them. You may move some to the 3 pile or make a new pile with a score of 5.

After completing the steps, you should have five piles of papers to be rated 1-5.

USING A 6-POINT SCALE

1	2	3	4	5	6
limited	basic	basic+	proficient	proficient+	advanced

Use the criteria for a score of "4" to evaluate each paper. Then follow these steps to rank them on a 6-point scale: Divide the papers into three piles: below-level, on-level, above-level. Then reread the papers in each pile and divide those into two piles. You now have six piles of papers to be rated 1-6.

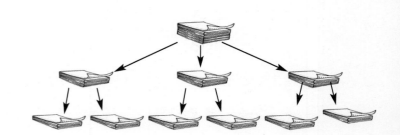

SELF-INITIATED WRITING/ONGOING ASSESSMENT

In addition to assigned writing tasks, establish expectations for self-initiated writing. Tell students that you expect them to write independently on a regular basis, choosing the topic and the form of writing themselves. Meet with individuals and small groups periodically to review their progress. Make one copy of the Student Record Form (page R74) for each student at each evaluation point, and use it to record your observations and plans for instruction.

The rubrics in *Harcourt Language* can be used to analyze students' work for the traits of good writing.

The Traits of Good Writing

Conventions
Correct punctuation, grammar, spelling

Organization
Logical and clear structure

Word Choice
Vivid verbs, strong adjectives, specific nouns

Ideas
Interesting, focused content

Voice
Original, personal mood and tone

Sentence Fluency
Flow, rhythm, variety

Based on your assessment, target your instruction to emphasize the **Strategies Good Writers Use.**

Strategies Good Writers Use

- Set a purpose for your writing.
- Focus on your audience.
- List or draw your main ideas.
- Use an organization that makes sense.
- Use your own personal voice.
- Choose exact, vivid words.
- Use a variety of effective sentences.
- Elaborate with facts and details.
- Group your ideas in paragraphs.
- Proofread to check for errors.

Look for:

- Writer's Craft chapters for direct instruction in strategies.
- Writing Workshop chapters for application.

Score of 4

The story fits the purpose for writing very well. The audience it was written for would enjoy it. The ideas are very interesting.

The story has a clear beginning that tells the problem, a middle that tells events in order, and an ending that gives the solution to the problem.

The story has description and rich details that help the reader visualize the events. The writer shows his or her own feelings.

The story has interesting words and phrases, such as specific nouns, vivid verbs, sensory words, and comparisons.

The sentences are written in a variety of ways to make the writing interesting to read.

The story has very few errors in spelling, grammar, and punctuation.

Other:

Score of 3

The story fits the purpose for writing. The audience it was written for would probably like it. The ideas are interesting.

The story has a beginning that tells the problem. The order of the events in the middle is not always clear. The ending tells how the problem was solved.

The story has some description and a few good details.

The story has some interesting words and phrases.

Some of the sentences show variety, but many are the same type.

There are a few errors in spelling, grammar, and punctuation.

Other:

Score of 2

The purpose of the story is not very clear. It is hard to tell what audience it was written for.

The story does not have a clear beginning, middle, or ending. There is a problem, but the story does not give a good solution. The events are not told in order.

The story has only a few details and just a little description.

The story has very few words or phrases that are colorful or interesting.

Almost all of the sentences are written in the same way.

There are many errors in spelling, grammar, and punctuation.

Other:

Score of 1

The story does not have a clear purpose. There is no way to tell what audience it was written for.

The story does not have a beginning, a middle, and an ending. The events are hard to follow. There is no problem to solve.

The story has no description or details.

The story has no interesting words or phrases.

Most sentences are not written correctly.

There are so many errors that the writing is hard to understand.

Other:

© Harcourt

INFORMATIVE WRITING: HOW-TO ESSAY

Score of 4

The essay fits the purpose for writing very well. The audience it was written for would understand it. The ideas are very interesting.

The essay has a clear beginning that introduces the topic, a middle that gives facts or directions about the topic in a logical order, and an ending that summarizes or draws a conclusion. The writer is writing about a topic he or she finds interesting.

The essay has description and rich details that add information about the facts or directions. The writer is writing about a topic he or she finds interesting.

The essay has interesting words and phrases, especially specific nouns.

The sentences are written in a variety of ways to make the writing interesting to read.

The essay has very few errors in spelling, grammar, and punctuation.

Other:

Score of 3

The essay fits the purpose for writing. The audience it was written for would probably understand it. The ideas are interesting.

The essay has a beginning that introduces the topic. The facts or directions about the topic in the middle are not in logical order. The ending does not have a clear ending.

The essay has some description and a few good details about the facts or directions.

The essay has some interesting words or phrases, but most of the writing is not very specific.

Some of the sentences show variety, but many are the same type.

There are a few errors in spelling, grammar, and punctuation.

Other:

Score of 2

The purpose of the essay is not very clear. It is hard to tell what audience it was written for.

The essay does not clearly introduce the topic at the beginning. The facts or directions in the middle are not all about the same topic. The essay does not have a clear ending.

The essay has only a few details and not enough description to help the reader understand the facts or directions.

The essay has very few words or phrases that are interesting or specific.

Almost all of the sentences are written in the same way.

There are many errors in spelling, grammar, and punctuation.

Other:

Score of 1

The essay does not have a clear purpose. There is no way to tell what audience it was written for.

The essay does not have an introduction. It does not contain facts or directions about one topic. The essay has no summary or conclusion.

The essay has no description or details about the facts or directions.

The essay has no interesting or specific words or phrases.

Most sentences are not written correctly.

There are so many errors that the writing is hard to understand.

Other:

Score of 4

The essay fits the purpose for writing very well. It was well-written to persuade a particular audience. The ideas are very interesting.

The essay has a clear statement of opinion at the beginning, a middle that gives logical reasons that support the opinion, and an ending that restates the opinion and calls for action.

The essay has details, description, and/or examples that give more information about the reasons. The writer has strong feelings about this topic.

The essay has interesting words and phrases, such as specific nouns, vivid verbs, emotional language, and comparisons.

The sentences are written in a variety of ways to make the writing interesting.

The essay has very few errors in spelling, grammar, and punctuation.

Other:

Score of 3

The essay fits the purpose for writing. It might persuade the audience it was written for. The ideas are interesting.

The essay has a statement of opinion at the beginning. Most of the reasons in the middle support the opinion. The ending restates the opinion but does not call for action.

The essay has some description, examples, and/or a few good details that give information about the reasons. The writer has some feelings about this topic.

The essay has some interesting and/or emotional words and phrases, but most of the writing is not very vivid or colorful.

Some of the sentences show variety, but many are the same type.

There are a few errors in spelling, grammar, and punctuation.

Other:

Score of 2

The purpose of the essay is not very clear. It is hard to tell what audience it was written for.

The essay has a statement of opinion at the beginning, but the reasons for the opinion are not logical or clear. The ending does not restate the opinion.

The essay has only a few or no details that add information.

The essay has very few words or phrases that are interesting or emotional.

Almost all of the sentences are written in the same way.

There are many errors in spelling, grammar, and punctuation.

Other:

Score of 1

The essay does not have a clear purpose. There is no way to tell what audience it was written for.

The essay does not state an opinion at the beginning. The ideas are not all about the same topic.

The essay has no description or details.

The essay has no interesting or emotional words or phrases.

Most sentences are not written correctly.

There are so many errors that the writing is hard to understand.

Other:

© Harcourt

INFORMATIVE WRITING: ADVANTAGES AND DISADVANTAGES ESSAY

Score of 4

The essay fits the purpose for writing very well. The audience it was written for would understand it. The ideas are very interesting.

The essay has a clear beginning that introduces the topic, a middle that logically classifies information and ideas about the topic, and an ending that summarizes or draws a conclusion.

The essay has description and rich details that add information about the topic. The writer's feelings toward the advantages and disadvantages are very clear.

The essay has signal words and phrases that help the reader understand how the ideas are related.

The sentences are written in a variety of ways to make the writing interesting to read.

The essay has very few errors in spelling, grammar, and punctuation.

Other:

Score of 3

The essay fits the purpose for writing. The audience it was written for would probably understand it. The ideas are interesting.

The essay has a beginning that introduces the topic. The ideas and information about the topic in the middle are not all in logical order. The ending summarizes or draws a conclusion.

The essay has some description and a few good details about the topic. The writer's feelings toward the advantages and disadvantages are somewhat clear.

The essay has some signal words and phrases, but they do not always help the reader understand how the ideas are related.

Some of the sentences show variety, but most are the same type.

There are a few errors in spelling, grammar, and punctuation.

Other:

Score of 2

The purpose of the essay is not very clear. It is hard to tell what audience it was written for.

The essay does not clearly introduce the topic at the beginning. The information and ideas in the middle are not all about the same topic. The essay does not have a clear ending.

The essay has only a few details and not enough description to help the reader to understand the topic.

The essay has very few signal words or phrases that help the reader understand how the ideas are related.

Almost all of the sentences are written in the same way.

There are many errors in spelling, grammar, and punctuation.

Other:

Score of 1

The essay does not have a clear purpose. There is no way to tell what audience it was written for.

The essay does not have an introduction. It does not classify ideas about one topic. The essay has no summary or conclusion.

The essay has no description or details about the topic.

The essay has no signal words or phrases.

Most sentences are not written correctly.

There are so many errors that the writing is hard to understand.

Other:

Score of 4	Score of 3	Score of 2 	Score of 1 
The research report fits the purpose for writing very well. The ideas are very interesting. The audience it was written for would understand it.	The research report fits the purpose for writing. The audience it was written for would probably understand it. The ideas are interesting.	The purpose of the research report is not very clear. It is hard to tell what audience it was written for.	The research report does not have a clear purpose. There is no way to tell what audience it was written for.
The report has a clear beginning that introduces the topic. The middle sections give logically organized information and ideas about the topic. The ending summarizes or draws a conclusion.	The report has a beginning that introduces the topic. The ideas and information about the topic in the middle are not all in logical order. The ending summarizes or draws a conclusion.	The report does not clearly introduce the topic at the beginning. The information and ideas in the middle are not all about the same topic. The report does not have a clear ending.	The report does not have an introduction. It does not organize ideas about one topic. The report has no summary or conclusion.
The report presents ideas and information from a variety of sources.	The report presents information from a few sources.	The report presents information from only one source.	The report does not present information from any sources.
The report has description, rich details, and/or narrative parts that add information about the topic. The writer chose a topic that he or she finds interesting.	The report has some description and a few good details about the topic. Some of the details are about a different topic.	The report doesn't have many details or much description. Some of the details are not about the topic.	The report has no description or details about a topic.
The report has signal words and phrases that help the reader understand how the ideas are related.	The report has some signal words and phrases, but they do not always help the reader understand how the ideas are related.	The report has very few signal words or phrases that help the reader understand how the ideas are related.	The report has no signal words or phrases.
The sentences are written in a variety of ways to make the writing interesting to read.	Some of the sentences show variety, but many are the same type.	Almost all of the sentences are written in the same way.	Most sentences are not written correctly.
The report has very few errors in spelling, grammar, and punctuation.	There are a few errors in spelling, grammar, and punctuation.	There are many errors in spelling, grammar, and punctuation.	There are so many errors that the writing is hard to understand.
Other:	Other:	Other:	Other:

EXPRESSIVE WRITING: STORY

Score of 4

The story fits the purpose for writing it. The audience it was written for would enjoy it. The ideas and story line are very interesting.

The story has developed characters and a setting. The characters solve a problem by the end of the story.

The story has description and rich details that help the reader visualize the events. The writer uses language that shows his or her voice.

The story has interesting words and phrases, such as specific nouns, vivid verbs, sensory words, and comparisons.

The sentences are written in a variety of ways to make the writing interesting to read.

The story has very few errors in spelling, grammar, and punctuation.

Other:

Score of 3

The story fits the purpose for writing. The audience it was written for would probably like it. The ideas and story line are interesting.

The story has characters and a setting. The problem is not always clear and may not be solved by the end of the story.

The story has some description and a few good details.

The story has some interesting words and phrases.

Some of the sentences show variety, but many are the same type.

There are a few errors in spelling, grammar, and punctuation.

Other:

Score of 2

The purpose of the story is not very clear. It is hard to tell what audience it was written for.

The story does not have clear characters and a setting. The problem is difficult to follow and is not solved by the end of the story.

The story has only a few details and just a little description.

The story has very few words or phrases that are colorful or interesting.

Almost all of the sentences are written in the same way.

There are many errors in spelling, grammar, and punctuation.

Other:

Score of 1

The story does not have a clear purpose. There is no way to tell what audience it was written for.

The story does not have characters or a setting. There is no problem to solve.

The story has no description or details.

The story has no interesting words or phrases.

Most sentences are not written correctly.

There are so many errors that the writing is hard to understand.

Other:

Thinking About My Grammar

Student:_____   Date:_____   Grade:_____

Teacher:_____   School:_____

When I write or speak,

I use correct forms of singular and plural nouns.

I make sure my subjects and verbs agree.

I use complete sentences.

I use correct punctuation.

I use the right verb tenses.

I combine short sentences into longer ones.

I avoid sentence fragments and run-ons.

When I edit something I've written, I look for _____

_____

The hardest grammar rule for me is _____

_____

When I give an oral report, I _____

_____

I am becoming better at grammar because _____

_____

Thinking About My Writing

Student:_____ Date:_____ Grade:_____

Teacher:_____ School:_____

When I write,

I think about my purpose and my reader.

I list or draw my main ideas.

I use an organization that makes sense.

I use my own words and ideas.

I choose exact, vivid words.

I use a variety of sentences.

My writing sounds smooth when I read it aloud.

I add facts and details when they are needed.

I group my ideas in paragraphs.

I proofread to check for errors.

Thinking About My Listening, Speaking, and Viewing

Student:_____   Date:_____   Grade:_____

Teacher:_____   School:_____

When I speak,

I use words that my audience will understand.

I speak loudly, clearly, and slowly to a large group.

I think about why I'm speaking.

I use gestures and movements to help show my meaning.

I use words that describe my ideas and feelings.

I answer questions from my audience.

When I listen,

I pay close attention.

I ask questions if I don't understand.

I summarize the speaker's ideas in my mind.

I picture in my mind what a speaker is saying.

I listen for facts and opinions.

When I view,

I think about the ways an artist shows meaning.

I think about the artist's message.

I describe what I see clearly.

I share my thoughts and feelings.

I think about how pictures add to a story.

© Harcourt

Handwriting

Individual students come to third grade with various levels of handwriting skills, but they all have the desire to communicate effectively. To write correctly, they must be familiar with concepts of

- **size (tall, short).**
- **open and closed.**
- **capital and lowercase letters.**
- **manuscript vs. cursive letters.**
- **letter and word spacing.**
- **punctuation.**

The lessons in *Harcourt Language* build on these concepts in both formal and informal handwriting instruction so that students develop the skills they need to become independent writers. To assess students' handwriting skills, review samples of their written work. Note whether they use correct letter formation and appropriate size and spacing. Note whether students follow the conventions of print such as correct capitalization and punctuation. Encourage students to edit and proofread their work and to use editing marks. When writing messages, notes, and letters, or when publishing their writing, students should leave adequate margins and indent new paragraphs to help make their work more readable for their audience. Keep a record of students' increasing proficiency on the Student Record Form on page R75.

STROKE AND LETTER FORMATION

The shape and formation of letters taught in *Harcourt Language* are based on the way experienced writers write their letters. Most manuscript letters are formed with a continuous stroke, so students do not often pick up their pencils when writing a single letter. When students begin to use cursive handwriting, they will have to lift their pencils from the paper less frequently and will be able to write more fluently. Models for Harcourt and D'Nealian handwriting are provided in the *Pupil Edition* Handbook.

POSITION FOR WRITING

Establishing the correct posture, pen or pencil grip, and paper position for writing will help prevent handwriting problems.

POSTURE Students should sit with both feet on the floor and with hips to the back of the chair. They can lean forward slightly but should not slouch. The writing surface should be smooth and flat and at a height that allows the upper arms to be perpendicular to the surface and the elbows to be under the shoulders.

WRITING INSTRUMENT An adult-sized number-two lead pencil is a satisfactory writing tool for most students. As students become proficient in the use of cursive handwriting, have them use pens for writing final drafts. Use your judgment in determining what type of instrument is most suitable.

PAPER POSITION AND PENCIL GRIP   The paper is slanted along the line of the student's writing arm, and the student uses his or her nonwriting hand to hold the paper in place. The student holds the pencil or pen slightly above the paint line—about one inch from the lead tip.

REACHING ALL LEARNERS

The best instruction builds on what students already know and can do. Given the wide range in students' handwriting abilities, a variety of approaches may be needed.

EXTRA SUPPORT   For students who need more practice keeping their handwriting legible, one of the most important under-standings is that legible writing is impor-tant for clear communication. Provide many opportunities for writing that communicates among students. For example, students can

- make a class directory listing names and phone numbers of their classmates.
- record observations in science.

- draw and label maps, pictures, graphs, and picture dictionaries.
- write and post messages about class assignments or group activities.

ESL   Students learning English as a second language can participate in meaningful print experiences. They can

- write signs, labels for centers, and messages.
- label drawings.
- contribute in group writing activities.
- write independently in journals.

You may also want to have students practice handwriting skills in their first language.

CHALLENGE   To ensure continued rapid advancement of students who come to third grade writing fluently, provide

- a wide range of writing assignments.
- opportunities for independent writing on self-selected and assigned topics.

School-Home Connection

Your child has begun Unit 1 in *Harcourt Language*.

In this unit, your child will learn about sentences and will write a descriptive paragraph and a personal narrative. You may enjoy doing the following activities with your child to enrich his or her language skills.

Punctuate Properly!

Find a paragraph in a children's book or magazine. Cover the punctuation marks with sticky notes or tiny slips of paper. Have your child read the paragraph to you. Then ask what punctuation mark belongs after each sentence.

Everyday Writing Activity

Personal Notes Start a routine of writing short notes back and forth with your child. Use the notes to give encouragement and to share happy thoughts. For example, you might put a note in your child's backpack saying, "Have a great day at school!"

As Far As I Can See . . .

With your child, stand in a room of your house and examine it closely. Then each of you should write notes about how the room looks and how you feel there. After five minutes, compare notes. How are your perceptions of the room different? Ask your child, "What did you see that I didn't?" Together, talk about how you thought the same or differently about the room.

Story of the Day

Tell your child about your day. Include your thoughts and feelings about different things that happened or different people you met. Then ask your child to tell about his or her day. To help him or her share thoughts and feelings, ask questions such as, "How did you feel when that happened?" or "What did you think of that person's decision?"

© Harcourt

Visit *The Learning Site!* www.harcourtschool.com

School-Home Connection

Your child has begun Unit 2 in _Harcourt Language_.

In this unit, your child will learn more about nouns and verbs and will write directions and a how-to essay. You may enjoy doing the following activities with your child to enrich his or her language skills.

A Noun Hunt

Show your child a bill or letter that you have recently received. Ask him or her to identify all the nouns. Then ask, "Which nouns are singular? Which are plural?" Finish by helping your child make the plural forms of the singular nouns.

Rescue the Recipe

Copy a simple recipe onto a piece of paper. Leave out sequence words, such as _first, second, third, then_, and _afterwards_. Then cut the paper into pieces so each step is on a separate slip of paper. Give the slips to your child, and help him or her arrange the steps in the right order. Then ask him or her to write appropriate sequence words on the slips of paper.

Everyday Writing Activity

Directions for Living In your home, find some product assembly instructions or materials that explain how to use or repair household appliances. Share these with your child, and ask him or her to think about when these how-to instructions would be useful.

All Around the Town

Show your child a map of your town or community, and explain how to use it. Pick several destinations, and then go for a walk or a drive together. Have your child use the map to give directions to each destination.

© Harcourt

Visit _The Learning Site!_
www.harcourtschool.com

# School-Home Connection

Your child has begun Unit 3 in *Harcourt Language*.

In this unit, your child will learn more about verbs and will write a friendly letter and a short persuasive essay. You may enjoy doing the following activities with your child to enrich his or her language skills.

Help with Helping Verbs

Make two columns on a sheet of paper. In column one, write the name of each member of your family. In column two, write simple verbs that describe activities people do every day. Then make nine index cards: three with the word *is*, three with the word *are*, and three with the word *will*. Flash the cards at your child one at a time, and ask him or her to use the word on the card and the words in the columns to create sentences.

Proving a Point

Name two movies or television shows your child likes, and ask him or her to decide which one is better. Then ask your child to explain why he or she thinks so. Encourage him or her to provide at least three reasons to support his or her answer.

 Everyday Writing Activity

Friendly Letter With your child, think of a family member or a friend who might like to receive a friendly letter. Begin the letter yourself and write about something interesting that you'd like to share. Then ask your child to continue the letter by telling about something he or she has learned at school recently.

Verbs with Verve!

Have your child circle all the verbs in the first paragraph of a newspaper story or magazine article. Ask him or her to tell you which verbs seem general and which ones are more specific. For each general verb, have him or her think of a more vivid verb that has a similar meaning. Your child may need your help or the help of a thesaurus for this activity. Substitute the vivid verbs for the general ones as you take turns reading the sentences out loud.

© Harcourt

Visit *The Learning Site!*
www.harcourtschool.com

School-Home Connection

Your child has begun Unit 4 in *Harcourt Language*.

In this unit, your child will learn about pronouns and adjectives and will write a paragraph that compares and an essay that tells about the advantages and disadvantages of something. You may enjoy doing the following activities with your child to enrich his or her language skills.

Picture Pronouns

Have your child clip pictures of the following from a magazine: a man or boy, a girl or woman, and a group of people. Together, make up sentences about the people in the pictures, using pronouns rather than more specific terms to refer to them. To get your child started, ask questions or offer incomplete sentences, such as "Who wants to eat something?" or "I would like to play soccer with _____."

Everyday Writing Activity

Shopping List Write a grocery list with fifteen to twenty items. Have your child rewrite the list and put the items into two or three different categories. For example, ask your child to list all the refrigerated items together and all the frozen foods together. Talk about why it may be good to have the items listed this way.

The Grass Is Sometimes Greener . . .

For five minutes, play make-believe. Have your child pretend to be his or her favorite animal. Meanwhile, you should pretend to be various things in that animal's habitat, including prey and predators. After the five minutes have elapsed, ask your child to consider the advantages of being the animal he or she chose to be. Then ask him or her to explain the disadvantages.

Visit *The Learning Site!*
www.harcourtschool.com

© Harcourt

School-Home Connection

Your child has begun Unit 5 in *Harcourt Language*.

In this unit, your child will learn more about articles, adjectives, and adverbs and will write a paragraph of information and a research report. You may enjoy doing the following activities with your child to enrich his or her language skills.

All in the Family

Ask your child to write ten adjectives that can be used to describe people. Then help him or her use forms of each adjective to make comparisons between members of your family. Make sure that the comparisons are true and that your child uses the correct form of the adjective to make them.

Fact Finding

Ask your child to identify an interesting building or monument near your home. Together, create a list of questions about it that he or she would like to have answered. Your questions may include, "Who built it and why?" "What is it used for?" "When was it built?" Discuss the best ways to find answers to your child's questions.

Everyday Writing Activity

Family Pictures Have your child imagine that you will soon be attending a family reunion together. His or her job will be to report on what your family has been doing in the last year. Ask your child to write some notes about important things that have happened to your family. If there are family photos available, have your child write about what's happening in several of the photos and put together a simple photo album.

Television As Teacher?

Television can be a great tool for helping children learn to take notes. Watch ten minutes of an educational show with your child. During the commercial, ask him or her to write down the most important things he or she learned from those ten minutes. Review the notes together, and point out any important details your child might have missed.

© Harcourt

Visit *The Learning Site!*
www.harcourtschool.com

School-Home Connection

Your child has begun Unit 6 in *Harcourt Language*.

In this unit, your child will learn more about usage and mechanics and will write a character study and a story. You may enjoy doing the following activities with your child to enrich his or her language skills.

Just the Opposite

Read one page of a favorite story with your child. Ask him or her to point out the words *no* and *not* when they appear. When you finish reading, look at the remaining sentences. Have your child make them negative by adding *no* or *not* in the proper place.

Tale Tellers

On a sheet of paper, write the opening line of a story. Give the sheet to your child, and ask him or her to write the next sentence. Between turns, discuss things that your story needs, such as a problem and a solution. Take turns writing until you have a complete story.

Everyday Writing Activity

Letter Ask your child to write a letter describing you to someone who doesn't know you. Have your child describe you and tell what he or she thinks are your best qualities.

Be Art Experts

Take your child to a museum, or check out an art book from the local library. Find a painting he or she likes. Ask him or her what is interesting about the painting. You might ask some questions such as, "What colors are important here?" "Are they dark or light?" "Do objects in the painting look like they have texture?" "How does the painting make you feel?" "How do you suppose the artist felt when he or she painted it?"

© Harcourt

Visit *The Learning Site!*
www.harcourtschool.com

Drafting a Personal Narrative Flowchart

Describe the activity. Tell why you like it.

Use details and words people say to bring your personal narrative to life.

Use personal voice.

Tell readers what you learned while doing this activity.

© Harcourt

Drafting a How-to Essay
Cluster Map

State the Problem

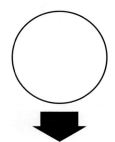

Describe How to Solve the Problem

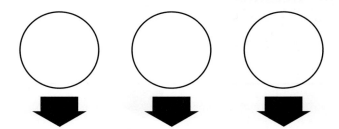

Include Details

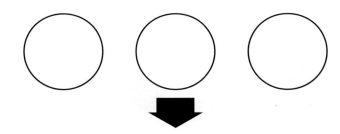

End with the Solution

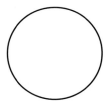

Drafting a Persuasive Essay Flowchart

Step 1: Get Your Audience's Attention

Step 2: State Your Reasons

Step 3: Add Details

Step 4: Call Your Readers to Action

Drafting an Advantages and Disadvantages Essay Outline

First Paragraph

Topic Sentence:

Second Paragraph

Introduce Advantages/Disadvantages:

Supporting Descriptive Details:

Third Paragraph

Introduce Advantages/Disadvantages:

Supporting Descriptive Details:

Concluding Sentence:

© Harcourt

Drafting a Research Report
Flowchart

Step 1: INTRODUCTION

Step 2: FACTS

Step 3: FACTS

Step 4: ENDING

Drafting a Story
Story Map

Describe the Setting:	Describe the Main Character:

Describe the Problem:

Event:

Event:

Event:

Describe the Solution:

© Harcourt

Sentence Strips

Photocopy the page, cut apart the strips, and distribute them to students. One or more sentences can be distributed at a time. You may also need to distribute blanks and punctuation marks. Students can cut the strips apart into cards and can write replacement words on the backs of cards for some activities. Depending on the needs of your students, have them use the cards to practice and reinforce word order and other grammatical concepts with activities such as the following:

SENTENCES

- rearrange words to change a statement to a question
- change the sentence type by adding, replacing, or rearranging words
- identify the correct end mark
- combine sentences using conjunctions

SUBJECTS/NOUNS

- replace common nouns with proper nouns, and vice versa
- identify the simple and complete subject
- combine sentences using compound subjects
- replace general nouns with specific nouns

PREDICATES/VERBS

- identify complete and simple predicates
- combine sentences using compound predicates
- replace common verbs with more interesting verbs
- change the subject and then change the verb to agree
- change present-tense verbs to past-tense verbs

PRONOUNS

- replace nouns with pronouns
- replace possessive nouns with possessive pronouns
- change the pronoun and then change the verb to agree

ADJECTIVES AND ADVERBS

- add or remove adjectives or adverbs
- replace common adjectives or adverbs with more vivid ones
- experiment with changing the order of two adjectives

School is closed every Sunday .

Is her dog ' s name Pogo ?

Jody plays the piano , sings , and

dances .

One kitten ' s face is white .

There are many different apples .

First , you must read the directions .

Popcorn is a good snack .

Ranchers help sick cows get better .

.   ?   !   ,   "   "   ,   .

Monica washes the dishes , and I dry them .

Did the mayor read your letter ?

My watch is broken again .

The family prepares to celebrate .

A train engine puffs smoke and steam .

We have eaten ripe berries .

George took my ball .

What lovely eyes she has !

| . | ? | ! | , | " | " | ' | . |

A soft breeze was blowing .

She is a talented artist .

The magazine printed an interesting article .

Juan runs faster than Pete .

A marathon is the longest race of all .

A few people watched silently .

There was no school that day .

. ? ! , " " , .

Mr . Hart will mow the lawn .

My parents bought theater tickets .

Some mammals have very sharp teeth .

They chase butterflies outdoors .

The girls ' masks are colorful .

Uncle Ryan is an astronomer .

Sue and Lakeesha rode the bus .

They watch my mother water the flowers .

| . | ? | ! | , | " | " | , | . |

Betty forgot her lunch money .

It is a small , furry , gentle animal .

Kari ' s address is 2832 W . Fairbanks St

Which was the better speech ?

This rain is never going to stop .

The tall , gray stalk looks like a bird ' s

neck .

Lisa is a good pitcher .

Houston , Texas is a busy city .

| . | ? | ! | , | " | " | , | . |

© Harcourt

Vocabulary Power Cumulative List

addition
advertisements
agricultural
animated film
annual
apply
archaeology
assist
astronomy
athletic

beliefs
biennial
billboard
biology
blustery
bovine
breezy
brighten
bulletin

calorie
canine
carbohydrate
career
carpenter
cartoon
cavity
Celsius
ceremonies
chasm
cinema
clarify
collaborate
community

company
confidence
cooperate
coyote
crater
current
customs

deciduous
degree
democracy
deputy
description
detect
device
dignity
discover
doldrums
draft

ecology
elaboration
electrician
embellishment
energy
enlist
enroll
enterprise
entertainment
episode
equine
event
evergreen
examine
expansion

experience
explain

Fahrenheit
fantasy
fatigue
federal
feline
fiesta

galaxy
geode
glimmering
glistening
gorge
government
governor
gusty

haughty
haul
herpetology
hollow

illuminate
imaginary
impossible
incident
injection
instrument
investigate
invisible
irregular

Vocabulary Power Cumulative List

legal
lighten
lode
logo

machinist
mason
medical
medicine
mercury
meteor
miner
mineral
mineralogist
monarchy
motion picture
movie

natural
neighborhood
nutrient
nutritionist
nutritious

outline

partner
percussion
perennial
piñata
planet
plaza
plumber
population
porcine

possible
practices
precaution
preheat
prehistoric
prejudge
prepay
pretend
project
protein

recruit
registered
regular
remedy
republic
request
research
ruler
rural
rustic

secure
settlement
shimmering
situation
slogan
social
solar system
sparkling

tale
teamwork
technology
temperature

tortilla
traditions
tranquil
treatment
twinkling

undertaking
undeveloped
utensil

vaccine
vain
venture
vice president
viceroy
visible
vision
visor
vista
visual

watt
woodwind

yarn

zeal

Cross-Curricular Connections

Chapter	Arts and Creativity					Health				Science						Social Studies						
	Artful Objects	Literature	Music	Performing Arts	Architecture	Disease Prevention	Nutrition	Physical Fitness	Safety and First Aid	Earth and the Solar System	Ecosystems	Exploring Matter	Forces and Motion	Heat and Light	Weather	Citizenship	Communities Grow and Change	Community Histories	How Government Works	Kinds of Communities	Market and Trade	People from Many Places
1	•																					
2			•																			
3				•																		
4					•																	
5		•																				
6			•																			
7									•													
8							•															
9								•														
10								•														
11						•																
12																			•			
13																						•
14																•						
15																			•			
16																			•			
17																	•					
18																•						
19										•												
20													•									
21													•									
22											•											
23											•											
24											•											
25																					•	
26																•						
27																	•					
28																		•				
29																					•	
30																•						
31												•										
32										•												
33		•																				
34														•								
35													•									
36											•											

Theme Connections

Chapter	Communities	Connections	Creativity	Experience	Explorations	Growth and Change	Inquiry	Journeys in Time and Space	Learning and Working	Managing Information	Myself and Others	Personal Voice	Problem-Solving	Self-Discovery	Traditions	Working Together
1		•	•	•								•		•	•	
2		•	•		•						•	•		•	•	
3	•	•	•		•		•				•	•			•	
4	•		•						•			•		•		•
5		•	•				•			•	•	•				
6	•	•	•	•	•		•	•			•	•	•	•		•
7				•		•		•	•	•		•	•	•		•
8	•						•									
9		•		•			•		•				•			•
10				•		•	•	•								
11				•		•	•	•								•
12	•	•		•							•		•			•
13	•	•		•	•						•		•		•	•
14	•	•							•		•		•			
15			•	•							•	•	•	•		
16	•				•		•	•	•	•						•
17	•	•	•			•		•	•							•
18		•	•						•			•	•			
19					•	•		•	•	•						
20					•		•	•								
21		•	•		•											
22	•				•	•					•					
23		•				•										
24		•	•		•	•	•	•								
25	•	•			•	•		•							•	•
26	•	•							•		•		•			•
27	•							•	•						•	•
28	•	•				•		•							•	
29	•								•	•						•
30	•				•	•	•		•	•			•		•	•
31					•	•	•		•	•			•			
32	•				•	•	•	•								•
33	•	•	•	•		•	•				•	•		•		
34					•	•	•	•	•				•			
35			•			•	•	•	•							
36	•	•		•	•	•	•	•			•	•	•	•	•	•

Scope and Sequence

Grammar	GR K	GR 1	GR 2	GR 3	GR 4	GR 5
Sentences		•	•	•	•	•
Declarative Sentence		•	•	•	•	•
Interrogative Sentence		•	•	•	•	•
Exclamatory Sentence			•	•	•	•
Imperative Sentence			•	•	•	•
End Punctuation			•	•	•	•
Sentence Structure		•	•	•	•	•
Simple Sentence		•	•	•	•	•
Compound Sentence				•	•	•
Complex Sentence					•	•
Word Order in Sentences		•	•			
Sentence Parts		•	•	•	•	•
Complete Subject				•	•	•
Simple Subject			•	•	•	•
You (understood)				•	•	•
Compound Subject				•	•	•
Complete Predicate				•	•	•
Simple Predicate			•	•	•	•
Compound Predicate			•	•	•	•
Independent Clauses					•	•
Dependent Clauses					•	•
Phrases					•	•
Direct Object						•
Nouns		•	•	•	•	•
Singular Nouns		•	•	•	•	•
Plural Nouns		•	•	•	•	•
Irregular Plural Nouns			•	•	•	•
Possessive Nouns			•	•	•	•
Common and Proper Nouns		•	•	•	•	•
Verbs		•	•	•	•	•
Action Verbs		•	•	•	•	•
Helping Verbs		•	•	•	•	•
Linking Verbs				•	•	•
Regular Verbs		•	•	•	•	•
Irregular Verbs			•	•	•	•
Verb Contractions			•	•	•	•
Verb Tenses		•	•	•	•	•
Present Tense		•	•	•	•	•
Past Tense		•	•	•	•	•
Future Tense				•	•	•
Present Perfect Tense						•
Past Perfect Tense						•
Future Perfect Tense						•

Shaded Area Explicit Instruction/Modeling/Application   • Tested

	GR K	GR 1	GR 2	GR 3	GR 4	GR 5
Adjectives		•	•	•	•	•
Common Adjectives		•	•	•	•	•
Proper Adjectives				•	•	•
Articles			•	•	•	•
Comparison with Adjectives			•	•	•	•
Adverbs			•	•	•	•
Adverbs of Place			•	•	•	•
Adverbs of Time			•	•	•	•
Adverbs of Manner			•	•	•	•
Adverbs of Degree			•	•	•	•
Comparison with Adverbs				•	•	•
Pronouns		•	•	•	•	•
Subject Pronouns		•	•	•	•	•
Object Pronouns			•	•	•	•
Possessive Pronouns			•	•	•	•
Reflexive Pronouns						•
Pronouns and Antecedents			•	•	•	•
Prepositions					•	•
Prepositional Phrases					•	•
Negatives				•	•	•
Avoiding Double Negatives				•	•	•
Conjunctions				•	•	•
Coordinating Conjunctions				•	•	•
Subordinating Conjunctions					•	•
Usage and Mechanics						
Sentences						
Avoid Sentence Fragments and Run-on Sentences				•	•	•
Punctuation and Capitalization	•	•	•	•	•	•
Avoid Run-ons, Fragments			•	•	•	•
Nouns						
Abbreviations			•	•	•	•
Plural Forms			•	•	•	•
Appositives					•	•
Verbs						
Subject-Verb Agreement			•	•	•	•
Forms of *Be*		•	•	•	•	•
Commonly Misused Verbs			•	•	•	•
Contractions with *Not*			•	•	•	•
Forms of Irregular Verbs			•	•	•	•
Choosing Correct Tense			•	•	•	•
Adjectives						
Articles			•	•	•	•
Comparative and Superlative Adjectives		•	•	•	•	•
Adverbs						
Comparative and Superlative Adverbs				•	•	•
Distinguish Between Adverbs and Adjectives				•	•	•
Avoiding Double Negatives				•	•	•
Pronouns						
Subject Pronouns			•	•	•	•
Object Pronouns			•	•	•	•
Possessive Pronouns			•	•	•	•
Reflexive Pronouns						•
Pronoun-Antecedent Agreement			•	•	•	•

	GR K	GR 1	GR 2	GR 3	GR 4	GR 5
Troublesome Words and Commonly Confused Words			•	•	•	•
Capitalization						
Sentence Beginning		•	•	•	•	•
Pronoun *I*			•	•	•	•
Proper Nouns (Names, Days, Months, Holidays, Titles, Initials)		•	•	•	•	•
Proper Adjectives				•	•	•
Direct Quotations and Dialogue			•	•	•	•
Greetings and Closings of Letters, Addresses			•	•	•	•
Punctuation						
Indentation				•	•	•
Period		•	•	•	•	•
To End Sentences		•	•	•	•	•
In Titles and Abbreviations			•	•	•	•
Question Mark		•	•	•	•	•
Exclamation Point		•	•	•	•	•
Comma			•	•	•	•
In a Series			•	•	•	•
In Letter Parts			•	•	•	•
In Dates and Addresses			•	•	•	•
Compound Sentences				•	•	•
After Introductory Words or Phrases				•	•	•
In Direct Quotations				•	•	•
In Direct Address				•	•	•
With Appositives						•
With Dependent Clauses					•	•
Underlining				•	•	•
Apostrophe			•	•	•	•
In Contractions			•	•	•	•
In Possessive Nouns			•	•	•	•
Quotation Marks			•	•	•	•
Colon				•	•	•
Hyphen					•	•
Writing						
Composition/Writing Process						
Approaches to Writing (Shared, Interactive, Guided; Timed; Writing to Prompts)						
Analyze published models						
Prewriting						
Brainstorming						
Gathering Information; Taking Notes						
Lists						
Graphic Organizers						
Logs and Journals						
Consider Audience and Purpose						
Drafting						
Use Graphic Organizers						
Organize and Categorize Ideas; Elaboration						
Editing/Revising						
Add, Delete, Combine, and Rearrange Text						
Elaboration						
Coherence; Progression; Logical Support						

Shaded Area Explicit Instruction/Modeling/Application • Tested

	GR K	GR 1	GR 2	GR 3	GR 4	GR 5
Editing/Proofreading						
Spelling						
Grammar						
Punctuation						
Usage						
Features of Polished Writing						
Correct Sentence Fragments; Run-ons; Comma Splices						
Publishing						
Refine Selected Pieces						
Oral Presentation						
Printed						
Multimedia						
Performance/Dramatic Interpretation						
Select and Use Reference Materials for Writing, Revising, and Editing						
Use Technology to Create, Revise, Edit, and Publish Texts						

Writer's Craft/Strategies

	GR K	GR 1	GR 2	GR 3	GR 4	GR 5
Identify Audience and Purpose						
Personal Voice, Writer's Viewpoint				•	•	•
Organizing Information				•	•	•
Effective Sentences: Opening Sentences, Combining Sentences, Sentence Variety			•	•	•	•
Elaboration; Reasons and Details; Developing Ideas; Staying on the Topic			•	•	•	•
Paragraphing; Topic Sentence and Details				•	•	•
Word Choice: Vivid Words, Sensory Details, Description, Figurative Language			•	•	•	•
Appropriate Language; Tone						
Capture Reader's Interest						
Sequence; Transitions						

Writing Purposes

	GR K	GR 1	GR 2	GR 3	GR 4	GR 5
Informative/Expository Writing		•	•	•	•	•
Expressive/Narrative Writing		•	•	•	•	•
Persuasive Writing				•	•	•
Cross-Curricular Writing (Art/Creativity, Health, Science, Social Studies)						

Forms of Writing

	GR K	GR 1	GR 2	GR 3	GR 4	GR 5
Informative/Expository			•	•	•	•
Paragraph that Compares						
Paragraph that Contrasts						
Compare/Contrast Essay; Advantages/Disadvantages Essay				•	•	•
Paragraph of Information						
Directions						
How-to Essay, How-to Paragraph		•	•	•	•	•
Business Letters						
News Story						
Research Report			•	•	•	•
Summaries						
Morning Message						
Expressive/Narrative Writing			•	•	•	•
Story, Folktale		•	•	•	•	•
Descriptive Paragraph		•	•			
Personal Narrative, Self-Portrait			•	•	•	•
Personal Journal						
Play						
Poetry						
Character Study						

	GR K	GR 1	GR 2	GR 3	GR 4	GR 5
Persuasive Writing				•	•	•
Friendly Letter		•	•			
Business Letter						
Letter to the Editor						
Persuasive Essay				•	•	•
Everyday Writing						
Advertisements, Pamphlets, Posters						
Captions, Labels, Titles						
E-mail, Messages						
Forms						
Invitations, Thank-you Notes						
Journals						
Name						
Note Taking						
Recipes						
Surveys						

Reading Comprehension/Strategies

	GR K	GR 1	GR 2	GR 3	GR 4	GR 5
Apply Prior Knowledge; Predict/Preview						
Author's Purpose						
Cause-Effect						
Main Idea and Details: Descriptive, Important, Supporting						
Draw Conclusions						
Evaluating/Making Judgments						
Making Inferences						
Sequencing Events/Summarize						
Use Text Structure and Format						

Vocabulary

	GR K	GR 1	GR 2	GR 3	GR 4	GR 5
Language of School (colors, numbers, position words)						
Synonyms/Antonyms; Connotation/Denotation						
Multiple-Meaning Words; Homophones/Homographs						
Context Clues						
Glossary/Dictionary (for Word Meaning)						
Word or Phrase Origins (Acronyms, Brand Names, Clipped and Coined Words, Regionalisms, Etymology, Jargon and Slang, Euphemisms)						
Classifying/Categorizing; Comparing/Contrasting						
Analogies						
Prefixes, Suffixes, Derivatives						
Greek and Latin Roots						

Listening and Speaking

	GR K	GR 1	GR 2	GR 3	GR 4	GR 5
Respond/React to a Variety of Literature and Spoken Messages						
Listen for Purpose (enjoyment, information, vocabulary development, directions, problem solve, main idea and details, fact and opinion, recognize persuasion techniques/bias, plan an activity, take notes)						
Interpret Speakers' Verbal and Nonverbal Messages, Purposes, and Perspectives						
Eliminate Barriers to Effective Listening						
Participate in Conversations, Discussions, Small Groups, Cooperative Groups; Ask and Answer Questions						
Listen Critically to Interpret and Evaluate						
Develop/Acquire Vocabulary						
Identify Rhyme, Repetition, Patterns, Musical Elements of Language						
Ask for Repetition, Restatement, or Explanation to Clarify Meaning						
Participate in Storytelling, Drama, Music, Poems, Stories						
Discuss and Compare/Contrast a Variety of Texts						

Shaded Area   Explicit Instruction/Modeling/Application   • Tested

	GR K	GR 1	GR 2	GR 3	GR 4	GR 5
Reenact, Retell, Dramatize, Role Play Literature Read or Heard	■	■	■	■	■	■
Communicate Experiences, Ideas, Opinions with Others; Clarify or Support Ideas with Evidence	■	■	■	■	■	■
Use Appropriate Rate, Volume, Pitch, Tone	■	■	■	■	■	■
Adapt Spoken Vocabulary to the Purpose, Audience, and Occasion to Describe, Inform, Communicate, Persuade	■	■	■	■	■	■
Read or Retell Stories Orally with Expression, Phrasing, Intonation, Comprehension	■	■	■	■	■	■
Present Oral Reports or Speeches, Conduct Interview or Surveys		■	■	■	■	■
Clarify/Support Spoken Messages with Props		■	■	■	■	■
Give and Follow Oral Directions	■	■	■	■	■	■

Viewing and Representing

	GR K	GR 1	GR 2	GR 3	GR 4	GR 5
Enjoy and Discuss a Variety of Illustrations and Illustrators	■	■	■	■	■	■
Analyze the Purposes and Effects of Illustrations, Visuals, Media	■	■	■	■	■	■
Discuss Illustrator's Choices of Techniques and Media	■	■	■	■	■	■
Analyze the Way Visual Images, Graphics, and Media Represent, Contribute to, and Support Meaning	■	■	■	■	■	■
Interpret Information from Maps, Charts, Tables, Diagrams, Graphs, Timelines, Media, Illustrations	■	■	■	■	■	■
Select, Organize, Produce Visuals to Complement and Extend Meaning	■	■	■	■	■	■
Use Available Technology or Appropriate Media to Communicate Information and Ideas; to Compare Ideas, Information, Viewpoints	■	■	■	■	■	■
Compare and Contrast Print and Electronic Media			■	■	■	■

Research/Study Skills/Inquiry

	GR K	GR 1	GR 2	GR 3	GR 4	GR 5
Use Study Strategies to Learn and Recall Important Ideas from Text (KWL, SQ3R, Note Taking, Reading Rate, Skim/Scan, Outline)		■	■	■	■	■
Follow and Give Directions	■	■	■	■	■	■
Test-Taking Strategies	■	■	■	■	■	■
Frame, Identify, Revise Questions for Inquiry	■	■	■	■	■	■
Select and Use Pictures, Print, People, Media, Multiple Sources, Alphabetical Order to Gather Information and Answer Questions	■	■	■	■	■	■
Library, Media Center, Card Catalog, Databases, Search Engines, Media	■	■	■	■	■	■
Almanac, Atlas, Dictionary, Electronic Text, Encyclopedia, Globe, Telephone Directory, Thesaurus, Synonym Finder, Books in Print	■	■	■	■	■	■
Maps, Charts, Graphs, Diagrams, Timelines, Tables, Schedules, Calendars	■	■	■	■	■	■
Book Parts and Text Organizers (Title Page, Table of Contents, Indices, Chapter Titles, Headings, Graphic Features, Guide Words, Entry Words, Bibliography, Glossary, Footnotes, Marginal Notes)	■	■	■	■	■	■
Summarize and Organize Information to Present Findings			■	■	■	■
Outline, Map, Web, Cluster, Venn Diagram, Chart, Table, Time Line	■	■	■	■	■	■
Displays, Murals, Dramatizations, Oral Reports, Written Reports, Projects, Posters, Speeches	■	■	■	■	■	■
Evaluate and Document Information and Research	■	■	■	■	■	■

Handwriting and Spelling

	GR K	GR 1	GR 2	GR 3	GR 4	GR 5
Apply Spelling Generalizations and Spelling Strategies	■	■	■	■	■	■
Letter Forms (Manuscript, Cursive)	■	■	■	■	■	■
Elements	■	■	■	■	■	■
Posture, Paper Position	■	■	■	■	■	■
Writing Utensils/Pencil Grip	■	■	■	■	■	■
Directionality/Stroke	■	■	■	■	■	■

Reviewers

Joan Y. Ashley
Teacher
Salisbury, NC

Pamela J. Beaver
Teacher
Dana, NC

Carolyn Warren Bennett
Lead Teacher
Newton Grove, NC

Pearle B. Collins
Success For All Facilitator
Houston, TX

Barbara Cummings
Teacher
Arlington, TX

Andrea Currier
Teacher
Towson, MD

Brenda D. Ford
Writing Resource Teacher
Chicago, IL

Barbara Haack
Teacher
Des Moines, IA

Deborah S. Hardesty
Teacher
Evansville, IN

Valerie Johse
Teacher
Pearland, TX

Mary Beth Kreml
Instructional Technology Teacher
Klein, TX

Ms. Esther Lauderman
Teacher
Williamstown, WV

Anita Layton
Teacher
Houston, TX

Katherine V. Lee
Teacher
Indianapolis, IN

Frances Martinez
Teacher
El Paso, TX

Majestra McFadden
Language Arts Supervisor
East St. Louis, IL

Gwendolyn D. Mills
Lead Teacher
Houston, TX

Barbara Minnich
Teacher
New Albany, IN

Thelma Muñoz
Teacher
Corpus Christi, TX

Dorothy W. Nolan
Curriculum Specialist
Omaha, NE

Valerie J. Reeves
Teacher
Katy, TX

Betty B. Rickman
Teacher
Horse Shoe, NC

Maureen McLaughlin Scott, Ph.D.
Language Arts Coordinator
Monroe, CT

Cecile Smith
Teacher
Camden, NJ

Linda Smolen
Director of Reading
Buffalo, NY

Amy Tapp
Teacher
Ft. Wayne, IN

Ms. Dominga A. Vela
Principal
Edinburg, TX

Index

Index

portfolio conferences, 82, 152, 224, 292, 368, 438

possessive nouns, 121, 123, 125, 127

possessive pronouns, 263, 265, 267, 269

predicates, 53, 55, 57, 59, 61

prefixes, 185

prewriting, 78, 79, 148, 288, 289, 329, 331, 333, 334, 335, 364, 403, 434

pronouns, 235, 237, 239, 241, 245, 247, 249, 251

proofreading, 81, 151, 291, 367, 437

quotation marks, 407, 409, 411, 413

reflecting, 83

research, 71

revising, 80, 150, 290, 366, 436

self-evaluation, 261, 335

sentences, 25, 27, 29, 31

singular and plural nouns, 103, 105, 107, 109

stories, 439

student self-assessment checklists, R86–R88

study skills, 71

subjects and nouns, 35, 37, 39, 41

suffixes, 185

synonyms, 213, 317

test taking strategies, 415

titles of written works, 417, 419, 421, 423

verbs, 131, 133, 135, 137, 167, 169, 171, 173

verb tenses, 177, 179, 181, 183, 195, 197, 199, 201

videos, 293

websites, 253

word choice, 187, 189, 191, 193

word processing, 129

ongoing, 32, 42, 60, 70, 100, 110, 128, 138, 174, 184, 202, 212, 242, 252, 270, 280, 316, 326, 344, 354, 386, 396, 414, 424

portfolio, 32, 42, 60, 70, 100, 110, 128, 138, 174, 184, 202, 212, 242, 252, 270, 280, 316, 326, 344, 354, 386, 396, 414, 424

Assessment Strategies and Resources, 89A, 163A, 231A, 305A, 375A, 453A

Atlas, using, R21

Audience

how-to essay, 148

identifying, 218, 329, 331, 363

personal narrative, 78

persuasive paragraph, 220

research report, 364

stories, 434

Auditory learners.

See **Reteach lessons**

Back Home, 398

✓*Bad and badly,* 310–311, 340–341, 343

Baseball: How to Play the All-Star Way, 112

Baylor, Byrd, 163K–163L

✓*Be,* 134–135, 136–139, R45.

See also **Verbs**

Beacons of Light: Lighthouses, 356–361

Below-level students.

See **Reaching All Learners**

Book parts, 243, R20

Book report, oral, 68

Book review, R16

Books, Read to Enjoy, 89, 159, 231, 299, 375, 445

Brown, Laurie Krasny, 141

Brown, Marc, 141

✓**Capitalization**

of abbreviations, 96–97, 98–101

of days of the week and months, 94–95

of direct quotations, 408–409

of first word in sentence, 24–25, 30

of holidays, 94–95

of I, 245, 249–251

in outlines, 329, 330

of personal titles, 94–95, 96–97

in proofreading, 81

of proper nouns, 94–95, 98, 101

in quotations, 408–409, 410–413

in titles of written works, 420–425, R61

Card catalog, 421

Challenge Activities.

See **Reaching All Learners**

Chapter Reviews, 32–33, 42–43, 60–61, 70–71, 100–101, 110–111, 128–129, 138–139, 174–175, 184–185, 202–203, 212–213, 242–243, 252–253, 270–271, 280–281, 316–317, 326–327, 344–345, 354–355, 386–387, 396–397, 414–415, 424–425

Character study, 398–405

Charts, 101, 104, 264, 288, 313, 351

K-W-L, 516

understanding, 101

Checklists, 151, 152

student self-assessment, R86–R88

Churchman, Deborah, 283

Classroom Management

See also **Oral Warm-up**

groups, 33, 36, 38, 41, 64, 66, 76, 94, 95, 96, 98, 101, 106, 108, 111, 124, 127, 133, 134, 168, 171, 180, 181, 197, 198, 203, 205, 213, 219, 234, 253, 255, 258, 264, 278, 281, 286, 310, 314, 319, 322, 338, 345, 349, 350, 352, 379, 380, 387, 388, 392, 394, 401, 408, 411, 423

independent practice

above-level and below-level students, 25, 27, 29, 35, 37, 39, 53, 55, 57, 63, 65, 67, 93, 95, 97, 103, 105, 107, 121, 123, 125, 131, 133, 135, 167, 169, 171, 177, 179, 181, 195, 197, 199, 205, 207, 209, 235, 237, 239, 245, 247, 249, 263, 265, 267, 273, 275, 277, 309, 311, 313, 319, 321, 323, 337, 339, 341, 347, 349, 351, 379, 381, 383, 389, 391, 393, 407, 409, 411, 417, 419, 421

pairs, 27, 28, 40, 45, 48, 50, 56, 61, 98, 99, 107, 113, 120, 129, 131, 146, 170, 171, 172, 173, 177, 178, 182, 187, 196, 198, 199, 200, 206, 218, 236, 240, 244, 250, 257, 266, 267, 269, 275, 276, 291, 314, 315, 320, 338, 341, 342, 348, 353, 381, 384, 390, 393, 401, 403, 409, 411, 418, 433, 437, 439

read aloud, 24, 34, 36, 41, 44, 48, 66, 72, 82, 92, 104, 112, 116, 122, 124,

Index

KEY
✔ = Tested

Index

Index

KEY
✔ = Tested

Index

Me.
 See **Pronouns**
Mechanics
 abbreviations, 96–100
 capitalization, 94–100, 408–412, 420–424
 combining sentences, 38–42, 66–70, 392–396
 contractions, 170–174, 266–270, 378–379
 punctuating dialogue, 410–414
 punctuating sentences, 28–32
 revising sentences using possessive nouns, 124–125
 titles, 96–97, 416–425
Medearis, Angela Shelf, 44
Modified Instruction.
 See **Reaching All Learners**
Months, capitalization of, 94–95
More and most, 312–316, 322–325
Multimedia presentation, 369
Music Connection, 35, 37
My First American Friend, 72–75

Names.
 See **Nouns; Proper nouns**
Negative words, 378–381, 384–387, R12, R58
 double, 382–383
Newspapers, using, R21
No.
 See **Negatives**
Not, contractions with, 170–171, 174–175, 378–379, 384, R46
Notetaking, 327, 335, 516–517
 with graphic organizers, 516–517
Nouns, 36–37, 92–100, R2, R4–R5, R39, R42
 adjectives with, 272–273
 common, 94–95, 98–100, R42
 irregular plural, 106–110
 plural, 102–110, 367, R43
 possessive, 120–128, R44
 proper, 94–100
 singular, 102–103, 108–110, R43

specific, 93, 187, 189, 193, 219
in subjects, 34–37

Object pronouns, 246–252, R51
Ongoing assessment.
 See **Assessment**
Opinions, 203
Options for Reading, independent and read aloud, 73, 141, 215, 283, 357, 427
Oral book report, 68
Oral directions, 113, 119
Oral invitations, 190
Oral Language Development.
 See also **Listening and Speaking; Oral Warm-up**
 building oral grammar, 31, 41, 59, 69, 99, 109, 127, 137, 173, 183, 201, 211, 241, 251, 269, 279, 315, 325, 343, 353, 385, 395, 413, 423
 pronunciation, 82, 292
Oral presentations, 83, 99, 119 153, 225, 332
Oral Warm-up, 24, 26, 28, 30, 34, 36, 38, 40, 44, 46, 48, 50, 51, 52, 54, 56, 58, 62, 64, 72, 78, 79, 80, 81, 82, 92, 94, 96, 98, 102, 104, 106, 108, 112, 114, 116, 118, 119, 120, 122, 124, 126, 130, 132, 134, 136, 140, 148, 149, 150, 151, 152, 166, 168, 170, 172, 176, 180, 182, 186, 188, 190, 192, 194, 196, 198, 200, 204, 206, 208, 210, 214, 220, 222, 224, 234, 236, 238, 240, 244, 246, 248, 250, 254, 256, 258, 260, 262, 264, 266, 268, 272, 274, 276, 278, 282, 288, 290, 292, 308, 310, 312, 314, 318, 320, 322, 324, 328, 330, 332, 334–336, 338, 340, 346, 348, 350, 352, 356, 364–366, 368, 378, 380, 382, 384, 388, 390, 392, 394, 398, 400, 402, 404–406, 408, 410, 412, 416, 418, 420, 422, 426, 434, 435, 436, 437, 438
Organization
 advantages and disadvantages essay, 289–290
 how-to essay, 149–150
 informative writing, 328–331

personal narrative, 79–80
persuasive paragraph, 221–222
research report, 365–366
story, 435–436
Outlines, 327, 329–330, 332, 333, 334, R24

Paragraphing, 112–118, 147
Paragraphs, 112, 147
 descriptive, 48–50, R16
 of information, 332–334
 persuasive, 214–224
 that compare, 258–260, R17
 that contrast, R17
Parnall, Peter, 163K–163L
Past-tense verbs, 194–202, 204–207, 210–211, R48
Periodicals, using, R21
Periods, 29–32
 with abbreviations, 96–100
 with quotations, 408–414
Personal narrative, 72–83, R14, R18
 acting out, 83
 graphic organizer, R98
 parts of, 76–77
 writing rubric, R80
Personal titles.
 See **Titles, personal**
Personal voice
 in descriptive writing, 44–51
 in narrative writing, 65, 76, 77, 393
Persuasive writing, 186–192, 214–224, 279, 309, 321, R19
 letters, 181, 190–192, 197, 415, R17
 letters to the editor, 69, 187
 paragraph, 214–225, R15, R19
  graphic organizer, R100
  parts of, 218–219
  writing rubric, R82
 speeches, 187, 203, 224
Peterson, Cris, 328

Index

KEY

✔ = Tested

Index

Index

KEY

✔ = Tested

Index

Index

KEY
✔ = Tested

Index

Acknowledgments

For permission to reprint copyrighted material, grateful acknowledgment is made to the following sources:

Atheneum Books for Young Readers, an imprint of Simon & Schuster Children's Publishing Division: "Jackrabbit" and "Coyote" from *Desert Voices* by Byrd Baylor. Text copyright © 1981 by Byrd Baylor.

Black Butterfly Children's Books: "Making Friends" from *Nathaniel Talking* by Eloise Greenfield. Text copyright © 1988 Eloise Greenfield.

HarperCollins Publishers: Sky Tree by Thomas Locker. Text copyright © 1995 by Thomas Locker, Inc. From *Through Grandpa's Eyes* by Patricia MacLachlan. Text copyright © 1980 by Patricia MacLachlan.

Henry Holt and Company, Inc.: In the Children's Garden by Carole Lexa Shaefer. Text copyright © 1994 by Carole Lexa Shaefer.

Mike Makley: "The New Kid" by Mike Makley.

Sierra Club Books for Children: Fernando's Gift by Douglas Keister. Text copyright © 1995 by Douglas Keister.

Patrick Walsh: "The New Boy" from *The Truants* by John Walsh.

The following is the credit list for all photos used in Teacher's Edition Grade 3 Language Arts 2002:

Harcourt Photos by:

21G-H, Ken Kinzie

89G-H, Ron Kunzman

305G-H, Richard Hutchings

375G-H, Eric Camden

Stock Photos:

163G-H, Lawrence Migdale/Photo Researchers

231G-H, Tony Freeman/PhotoEdit

The following is the credit for cover illustrations used in Teacher's Edition Grade 3 Language Arts 2002:

Richard Cowdrey